Memories and Glimpses

A. L. Rowse is well known as an authority on the Elizabethan age and as the author of the Churchill family history.
He has contributed equally to literature, with seven volumes of poetry, literary biographies of Shakespeare,
Marlowe, Milton, Swift and Matthew Arnold, and four
volumes of autobiography, of which the first, *A Cornish
Childhood*, has become a classic. Rowse has also written
several standard books about Cornwall, including *Tudor
Cornwall*, *The Cornish in America*, and several volumes of
short stories, of which the latest are *Night at the Corn*, and
the forthcoming *Stories from Trenarren*. He is a Fellow of
the British Academy, Emeritus Fellow of All Souls
College, Oxford, and Benson Medallist of the Royal
Society of Literature.

Some Books by A. L. Rowse

Autobiography
A Cornish Childhood
A Cornishman at Oxford
A Cornishman Abroad
A Man of the Thirties

Shakespeare
Shakespeare's Characters: A Complete Guide
Shakespeare the Man
Prefaces to Shakespeare's Plays
Shakespeare's Sonnets, *ed.*
The Contemporary Shakespeare, *ed.*
The Poems of Shakespeare's Dark Lady, *ed.*

Poetry
A Life: Collected Poems

A. L. ROWSE

Memories and Glimpses

METHUEN

A METHUEN PAPERBACK

First published in 1986
by Methuen London Ltd
11 New Fetter Lane, London EC4P 4EE

Memories of Men and Women first published in 1980
Glimpses of the Great first published in 1985
by Methuen London Ltd
Copyright © 1980, 1985, 1986 by A. L. Rowse

Printed in Great Britain by
Richard Clay (The Chaucer Press) Ltd, Bungay, Suffolk

British Library Cataloguing in Publication Data

Rowse, A.L.
    Memories and glimpses.
    1. Biography – 20th century   2. Europe –
    Biography
    I. Title   II. Rowse, A.L. Memories of men and
    women   III. Rowse, A.L. Glimpses of the great
    920'.04   CT759

ISBN 0-413-40870-1

Contents

Memories of
Men and Women

Preface

It has been suggested to me that a word of preface might be in order, threading these ten studies together along the line of what they had in common. What indeed had they in common? Some of them knew each other quite well, for all of them were public figures who had made notable contributions to the life of their time.

Looking back over them all, I note that all of them were writers, even the politicians (except for Nancy Astor, who was rather more than a politician). I note too that they represent the two sides of my own interests, public and private: history and politics, literature, in particular poetry.

The earliest friendship here recorded is that with the poet Auden, going back to his undergraduate days, when I was hardly more than an undergraduate myself. My acquaintance with Maurois went back to those early days, when he devoted a couple of pages to my first essay, *On History*, in his *Aspects of Biography*. For the rest, I came to know them in the years after those recorded in my own autobiography, years beyond which I do not intend to go. Hence these portraits of others – I feel signally honoured to have had their friendship, and how much poorer the world since they have gone. And how much I miss them from it!

A.L.R.

I

My Acquaintance with Churchill

My acquaintance with Churchill was brief, but not without significance. Hundreds of people knew him politically, and scores of people have written about him as such; my acquaintance with him was something different – over history, the family history of the Churchills which I was writing and in which he took a close interest, and his own *History of the English-Speaking Peoples*, of which he asked me to vet the Tudor volume.

Plenty of jackals have rushed in to attack the dead lion, in the usual way; my acquaintance with him was wholly pleasurable – I was interested in him as an historical phenomenon. Even all that he told me about himself and the war was a contribution to history – and I wrote down everything. He was generosity itself – not like a cagey politician, as it might be with Clem Attlee or John Simon, all shut up and unwilling to divulge anything, or Harold Wilson, bent on putting something across (understandable enough in a politician, but whom does he think he is taking in?).

Churchill was not like a politician – as a matter of fact, he was not a good politician, but he graduated – in his sixties and seventies! – into a statesman. He was completely open and honest, not shut up like a clam; I remembered in talking to him that he had started as a soldier and war correspondent, that he had earned his living, as he said, by his pen and his tongue, and that in addition he was an artist, with the temperament of an artist, the ups and downs – like the ups and downs of his career. A combination of soldier plus artist – that

was what struck me in facing him and in my dealings with
him.

Though he had the courage of a lion and a rock-like endurance – I don't think he ever knew what fear was – he had a
rather feminine temperament. This may surprise people, but
his close and early friend, Birkenhead, knew it. The disasters
of war, like the sinking of the *Hood*, plunged his spirits into
depression. This is where Beaverbrook came in – people have
wondered what their relationship was and why the Beaver
should have had such a hold. Beaverbrook would arrive, give
Winston an injection of his primitive vitality and rattling
spirits, they would spend an evening together, and next day
Winston would feel better, able to take up the intolerable
burden, the inhuman task. (Winston to me: 'When the war
was over, I couldn't walk upstairs.')

Historically I owe him a great debt. In deciding to write
the family history of the Churchills, who were West Country
in origin (instead of the Cecils, which my pupil, Dicky Cecil
– killed in the war – wanted me to write), I took a risk. The
first volume, *The Early Churchills*, was plain sailing: all the
materials were in printed sources or otherwise accessible. But
the second volume, *The Later Churchills*, could not be written
without access to the archives at Blenheim Palace – and those
had been closed to G. M. Trevelyan when writing his *England in the Age of Queen Anne*. I decided to make Winston's
acquaintance, the only man I have ever gone out of my way
to know. Goodness, how it paid! He was extremely interested
in his family history, the generous side came uppermost: the
Blenheim archives were opened to me, and I could complete
the book. How lucky this was – and, as a bonus, he was ready
and willing to tell me everything else I wanted to know.

I recall with pleasure those daily excursions out from
Oxford to delightful Woodstock, the pass I had in at the grand
gate Duchess Sarah built to the Duke's memory, and where
Winston's father, Lord Randolph, had paused to impress his
bride, Jenny Jerome of New York. It is indeed spectacular –
the splendid park, the monumental bridge over an arm of the
lake, the outspread wings of the Palace on the skyline – I have
always thought that not for nothing was the architect Van-

brugh also a dramatist: it all presents itself like a grand stage-set.

Thence I would make my way, skirting the lake, to the military-looking gate, pillars resting on stone cannon-balls, into the side-court where the archives were kept. 'This Way to the Tomb' I used to think, after Ronald Duncan's play, as I settled down to the dank inspissated gloom within. I have never known gloomier surroundings for historical research, not even the prison of the Public Record Office. However, I was grateful to be there, alone with the letters and missives of Marlborough and his Duchess, and their great friend Godolphin.

Even so, the archives came to an end in 1815 – I can well understand why, from the family doings in Regency days. The Duke (Consuelo's son) to me one day at dinner: 'You didn't spare us in your book.' I said, 'Look, I was careful there to say what was already in print, though I knew a good deal more!' I believe that, since his death, with death-duties and what not, the archives have now been moved from Blenheim to the British Library.

When my first volume was written and Winston wanted to see it, it was to Chartwell down in Kent that I was bidden.

He was then eighty-three, still at work on his own *History of the English-Speaking Peoples*. I have often been asked, especially in America, whether he wrote his own books, or whether they were written for him. I can assure people that he wrote, or dictated, his own books, as he painted his own paintings (disconsidered by the critics, simply because painted by him). He did employ research assistants to gather materials for him, like my friend Maurice Ashley who did a lot of work for the big biography of Marlborough. But Churchill shaped up the masses of material and wrote every word of his books himself. (Unlike his friend Lord Birkenhead, or his rival, Lord Baldwin.) Churchill was a conscientious artist as a writer – if, naturally, somewhat too rhetorical, for, like Henry James, he dictated his later works. I had experience of the thought he put into the choice of words, the artist seeking for the right expression, his strong likes and dislikes (which I did not always agree with). It was fascinating to observe him at work, the intensity of concentration, the irritability, the bursts of naughty humour.

Other people have thought that I did some of his research for him. Not so: each volume of his *History* he conscientiously submitted to a recognized authority in the field to be vetted, and I was honoured by his submitting the sixteenth-century volume to me. His galleys had exceptionally wide margins, for corrections and comments; it was rather fun getting some of my own back, after his comments on the typescript of *The Early Churchills*. I found few corrections to be made, but was amused to see that where I had commented, 'Sentence much too long: please divide', it was conscientiously divided in the published work.

What fun co-operating with so idiosyncratic, outsize a man, who knew his own mind – as I knew mine! The day at Chartwell which we spent in part over my book was quite the most wonderful day I have ever known; perhaps the immediacy of it may best be recovered by resorting to my Journals.

'11 July 1955. While waiting for Churchill's car to pick me up at the English-Speaking Union, I spent half an hour at Lancaster House looking at the portraits of Churchill women, Henrietta and her sisters. Henrietta was the eldest, second Duke in her own right, married to Godolphin's son and heir; so that, if their boy hadn't died, the Churchill family would have been Godolphins, instead of Spencers. When the car appeared, it turned out a very grand affair flying Churchill's standard as Lord Warden of the Cinque Ports. Evidently everything was to be done in style.

'As we sped down into Kent I reflected that I had never seen him in private. I had missed my opportunity of a whole weekend when he came down to stay at All Souls in the thirties. I was away, but heard some echoes of the talk, of his onslaught on Baldwin as a "corpse", who would not wake up and take notice. (When foreign affairs came up in Cabinet, he would say, "Wake me up when that's over.") I had had an unforgettable glimpse of Churchill on VE day 1945, when I saw him stepping out with Attlee, chin up, leading the members of the House of Commons across Parliament Square to give thanks for victory (survival rather) in St Margaret's, Westminster. Now, at last, I was to meet the man of that hour, of those heroic years.

'Arriving at Chartwell I was surprised by the beauty of the place. I should have reflected that he was an artist, and this was his creation. He had added on to a small Elizabethan redbrick house to make it pretty considerable, walled terraces defining the situation: confronting an open valley which he had improved with a lake in the hollow, a sickle-shaped ridge of wood down the opposite side, looking sideways away to the South Downs in the distance.

'Within, I was struck by the hum of activity – evidently there was a dynamo at work somewhere in the house. First, turned up a waxed-moustached ex-Guardsman of a valet, a Scot of ferocious aspect and whisky complexion: I suppose the famous Sawyers of the story of Winston, squeezing himself into a tight bunk on a plane somewhere in the war, right on top of his hotwater bottle. Sawyers remonstrated: "Do you think that a good idea?" Winston already half-asleep: "It's not an idea, Sawyers, it's just a coincidence." Then appeared the private detective, with fine eyes that took in everything, Sergeant Pride, who accompanied us in the garden most of the afternoon, to see that the visiting professor was not tempted to win fame by bumping off the most celebrated man in the world – at that moment. Next came the housekeeper, devoted to Clementina's exquisite Siamese cat, Gabriel, and a pretty young secretary. Workmen were changing rooms about, moving books to and fro, those upstairs being brought down, others from downstairs being carried up. Evidently at the behest of the unseen genie of the house.

'The downstairs library, into which I was shown, gave a fair indication – as libraries do – of the Man. Above the chimneypiece a vivid Frank Salisbury portrait of the war-time Prime Minister, in familiar zip-suit of RAF blue-grey. Opposite, a big diagram of Port Arromanches – the floating harbour that so surprised the Germans, with all the ships, tracks, quays, etc. marked. On a table, a new biography of Anthony Eden uppermost. The books revealed the man: modern political history, biography, memoirs dominant. In one corner the original Correspondence of Lord Randolph Spencer-Churchill, two shelves of folios, upon which Winston based his biography. (The copy of the published work in two volumes which he had presented to the Kaiser, at the German Military Manoeuvres of 1909, I had seen in the Kaiser's study in the Berlin Schloss before its utter destruction in the second German war.) There were some eight or ten volumes of Marlborough's Letters, I suppose from Blenheim. In addition, shelves of English classics and historians, complete sets of Scott, Johnson, Macaulay, etc.

'Before lunch I was summoned up to his bedroom, and there, at last, was the so familiar face, much aged: that of an old man who had gone back to his baby looks. The eyes a cloudy blue, a little bloodshot, spectacles on snub nose, a large cigar rolled round in his mouth. He had been at work – "I like work" (unlike ordinary workpeople today, who have no other *raison d'être*. What else are they for?) Beside the bed a small aluminium pail for cigar-ash; before him, stretching right across the bed, a tray-desk (*that* was a good idea!), on which were the long galleys of his *History of the English-Speaking Peoples*.

'He welcomed me with a touch of old-fashioned exaggerated courtesy, as if the honour were his that the professional historian had come to see him. I returned the compliment, sincerely meant, that he had beaten the professionals at their own game, that his *Marlborough* was an historical masterpiece along with Trevelyan's *Age of Queen Anne*. He said that, now that he had some time, he was rereading the *History* he had written before the war, but he wasn't satisfied with it. However, there were people who would read it on account of his "notoriety". Pause. I was evidently expected to say *something*; so I said, "Just as in the emotion of love there is an element of volition, so in great fame there is an element of merit."

'He was pleased at this sally – something was called for, and I had passed the test. I was relieved, for I knew that he was apt to be bored at meeting a stranger. After this we were on easy terms, and shortly he sent me off to read his chapters about Henry VII and Henry VIII, while he got up and was dressed.

'This process took some half an hour, before I was alerted to the dining-room, with its Orpen portrait of the young Parliamentarian. The corridors, I noticed, were filled with his own paintings, in themselves a revelation of the hidden side of his character – the gentler and more feminine: I do not underestimate them, but they gave no evidence of power (unlike his speeches and writing), they were impressionistic and descriptive, expressions of his delight in the appearances of things (like his pleasure in costume) and of his joy in life.

'The figure all the world knew then entered: striped blue zip-suit, blue velvet slippers with WSC worked in gold braid, outwards, in case anybody didn't know who was approaching. He led me to the window to look at his beautiful mare cropping with her foal below – I think, Hyperion, out of whom by someone I didn't take in. He soon saw that I hadn't come to talk horses, even if I could; we looked away down the valley, "up which the planes came", he said. The memory of 1940, when the Germans had everything their own way, was still vivid.

'I knew his dislike of making the acquaintance of somebody new at his age, so I shifted the conversation away from history, which was beginning to stick, on to the war. There were so many things I wanted to know. He was at once all interest, told me everything I asked for, uninhibited and generously.

'The first thing I wanted to know was what he thought Hitler thought of him. He considered that Hitler thought him representative of a minority in Britain, and that if Hitler pushed hard enough he could topple him over. I said that Hitler understood evil to his fingertips, but had no understanding of the power of the good in men. I reflected, but did not say, that perhaps all those idiotic Appeasers who had gone to the footstool at Berlin or Munich – Philip Lothian, Tom Jones, Clifford Allen, Arnold Wilson, etc. – had served a useful purpose after all: they had served to mislead the autodidact of genius as to the real character of Britain. But suppose if he had been an educated man, and knew what the

situation really was and the latent forces he was up against –
how even more dangerous that would have been! (Of course,
if he had been really educated – particularly, morally educated, he wouldn't have tried it all over again as in 1914–1918.
The Kaiser on the subject: "I hope the machine won't run
away with him, as it did with me!" – i.e. the German military
machine, responsible for it all.)

'Stalin had a revealing exchange with Eden on his last visit
to Moscow. He said to Eden, "You know Hitler was a
remarkable man – only he had no sense of moderation." He
caught Eden's expression, and said: "I see that you think I
have no sense of moderation. That's where you are wrong."
And, for all his enormities and mass-murders, Stalin did
know where to draw the line – when he came up against
superior force. He was not a Hitler, but a Bismarck, an utter
realist, with not a spark of idealism in him – and, of course,
immeasurably more brutal, for Bismarck belonged to a civilized world; where Stalin was in keeping with the emergent
people, with their lack of civilized standards or any cultiva-
tion. Where now are the idealist illusions of 1917, of our
fellow-travellers, the parlour Communists of the thirties? *Où
sont les neiges d'antan?*

'Churchill added that, since Britain was anti-Communist,
Hitler thought she should go along with him. I said that he
had behaved too criminally for that ever to be possible (quite
apart from the question of power: we should have been at his
mercy). What a providence it was that he didn't really know
England!

'The next thing I asked was even more crucial: did he think
that this country could have been invaded and overthrown in
1940?

'No, he said firmly. We should have put everything into it:
the whole of the Navy and Air Force. They couldn't have got
across – and he made the gesture familiar to us at the time, of
their swimming in the Channel in vain.

'This was a piece of information of the first historical
importance; for it meant that Churchill's resistance in 1940
had not been mere bravado, but rested on a firm estimation
of Britain's capacity to resist. This was what he was able to

assure President Roosevelt of, and convince him with; and upon this Roosevelt made his decision to back Britain.

'At this point Churchill added subsidiary bits of information. If any of the Germans had got across, he had a slogan ready: "You Can Always Take One With You". I think that would have appealed in the circumstances of 1940, after Dunkirk and what we had had to put up with for so long. If the Germans *had* invaded the country and government had to scatter, he had it in mind to form a triumvirate with Ernest Bevin and Beaverbrook. But the Germans weren't prepared with ways and means of crossing the water.

'(They would have been by 1943, with all Europe under their heel – by which time Hitler meant his show-down with Britain: not in 1939, which was inconveniently early for him. The Foreign Office stole a march on him there, with the assurance to Poland, which could not be waved away, like his own assurances to so many others. The liar was caught in the net at last – not by Chamberlain, but by the Foreign Office, which knew better.)

'I drew him on the subject of Chamberlain. He wouldn't say anything unkind, but didn't approve. It wasn't straight, that interview with his own Foreign Secretary (Eden) in the presence of Grandi; and saying one thing to one, another to another. And he knew another thing. At the end of Mr Baldwin's premiership, when he wanted to go and various people said he couldn't, there was a test by-election in a safe Tory seat in Westminster, completely blue. Moore-Brabazon said he wouldn't fight it so long as Baldwin remained PM. "That settles me," said Baldwin. Duff Cooper was prepared to fight it, and went to Chamberlain, who was head of the Party Office. [Duff Cooper was with Churchill and Eden against Appeasement.] Chamberlain told Duff Cooper that there would be no funds for him to fight the seat. "Not straight. Take your chance" – said the old sportsman.

'That was just like Neville Chamberlain, with his small-minded personal resentments. His main motive for returning to politics was his detestation of Lloyd George, whom he succeeded in keeping out at the height of LG's powers, a man of genius – to the country's loss. And Chamberlain kept him out on Churchill's formation of his government in 1940 – made it a choice even at that moment of crisis between himself and Lloyd George, whose name would have been a legion in itself.

'Winston spoke with gallantry of Mrs Chamberlain – "wonderful woman: twenty years, and she's quite unchanged". I responded that I was glad he had asked her to his Farewell Dinner at 10 Downing Street, and delighted that he had asked the Attlees and Morrisons. "That was not much after five years of comradeship in war," he said feelingly. He added that the new Mrs Herbert Morrison was a strong Tory, though they were not advertising the fact.

'A third thing I much wanted to know was how it came about that Attlee made Bevin Foreign Secretary at the last moment, when he expected and wanted the Exchequer, to which Hugh Dalton was appointed – who had expected to go to the Foreign Office, for which he was well qualified. It seems now that Churchill was not informed about this, for he told me that it was the King who did not want Dalton at the Foreign Office. It does not now appear that the King had any part in it – that Attlee, above all shrewd, realized that it would not do to have Bevin and Morrison, who detested each other, both dealing with Home Affairs. Attlee effectively divided them by sending Bevin to the Foreign Office – where he made a great Foreign Secretary – and making Morrison Leader of the House of Commons, where he did equally well, for he was an efficient Parliamentarian.

'The change of government was a great surprise to Stalin, who could not make out what the British were up to. When Churchill had warned him in Moscow that in Britain there were two parties and he might be defeated at the election of 1945, Uncle Joe was able to assure him that "One Party is much better". As for Molotov, he obviously preferred dealing with Churchill – Bevin knew only too intimately, from a life-time's experience, the nefarious ways of Communists and how to deal with them.

'Winston spoke kindly of Dalton, and said that of all the letters he had received on leaving office in 1945, his was the nicest. I told him of Dalton's admiration for the weekly talks he used to give the Cabinet, to strengthen morale in the worst days of 1940, and that Dalton used to go away and write them down. Winston didn't know that. Of Eden he said that he and "Anthony saw very much eye to eye: if you presented us both with a set of papers we should take very much the same line." I said politely (I was still paying my subscription to the Labour Party up to Suez, though not subscribing intellectually) that the handover had taken place in the right way at the right time. He replied, with *politesse*, that he had been very lucky: he hadn't done anything, it was the people – he but gave the *Roar* – and he emitted the roar for my benefit.

'(He was indeed lucky to be out before Suez, which would never have occurred if shrewd Clem Attlee had been there. Almost the last thing, he went into 10 Downing Street and said: "Now, Anthony, no getting caught out on a limb with the French." Which was exactly what happened.)

'Winston told me quite candidly of the severe stroke he had, said that he couldn't feed himself – and yet managed to hold on to office (for Eden too was ill at the time. They had all of them been exhausted by the war – hence, in part, Britain's poor showing after it). He talked about the Labour Party, with no animus or opposition: all that had drossed away with the years. He did not speak like a party-man, indeed he never had been a mere party-politician, had sat loosely to party-ties. I noticed that he referred to the Tories, not as "we" but as "they" – as if he sat on some Olympus above the party struggle, as indeed he did. He had made that most difficult walk in life, crossing the floor of the House of Commons, not once but twice – "I have never had any objection to the rat, as such". When Jowett awkwardly left the Liberal Party to become Labour's Lord Chancellor, Winston with a twinkle: "He has disgraced the name of rat." He asked me what would happen to Labour now that they were finding out that nationalization wasn't a solution. I suggested that it should mean that Labour would take the place of the old Liberal Party. He agreed, and went on to say that you don't create wealth by just taking it away from other people.

There should be minimum standards beyond which people should not be allowed to fall – and beyond that, *Free Run*!

'There was the old sportsman again, but I did not forget that earlier he had had a great part in creating those minimum standards, laying the foundations of the Welfare State. Of course, he was quite right in maintaining the crucial importance of incentive: when that is damaged, as it is under the social revolution, whether in Soviet Russia or Britain, it eats like a cancer at the vitals of society. Witness Britain, twenty years later: not a democracy so much as a trade-union bureaucracy, a squalid kind of society, a second-rate country. He was indeed lucky not to live to see it. I was in California when he died, and had to give an obituary address at a memorial service at Occidental College. A friend at All Souls went out into the High as Churchill's funeral train passed through Oxford on the way to his resting-place at Bladon – the western sky filled with the lurid glow of winter sunset, the sun setting upon the British Empire.'

We went back to the war; I told him how much I admired his chapter on the sinking of the *Bismarck* (as I had years before that on the battle of Jutland in his First War memoirs). He said how bad it was to wake up in the morning to receive the news of the sinking of some great ship. He asked what was the name – he couldn't remember. The *Hood*, I supplied, she was manned from Devonport; we were all miserable in the West Country at her sinking. 'Yes, the *Hood*,' he said, tears in his eyes, remembering. Then, perking up, 'We *had* to get the *Bismarck*: the nation expected it.' One admiral said his ship hadn't enough oil to get to the spot and back again. 'I sent the telegram: "You get there and we'll tow you back."'

His mind went back to the First World War and combined operations, on which he obviously felt that he had made a contribution to the art (or science) of war. While Lloyd George was working to reduce Tory prejudice against him, before his return to office in 1917, he had written a private paper for LG advocating our seizure of the island of Borkum, as a base to bring the blockade nearer to Germany, to alleviate the strain of maintaining it hundreds of miles out at sea.

In this he had put forward in embryo form the idea of landing tanks, and the later developments of landing-craft. By the mercy of Providence he hadn't published this paper in *The World Crisis*, when he might well have done so – nothing against it; and the German General Staff scrutinized everything he wrote. When the second war came, the Germans had nothing of the sort: they hadn't thought of it. He himself gave orders for building landing-craft immediately after Dunkirk. Yet it was three years before we had enough to invade.

Unqualified to assess that, I leave the pros and cons to the military historian. One knows, however, as a non-military historian how anxious Churchill was to shine in the expertise of war, worthy of his ancestor Marlborough.

I recall now a most significant remark he dropped, almost casually, without following it up. 'If only I had had more time . . . to make peace . . .' I saw at once what he meant. He was very self-conscious about the accusation that had been cast at him all through his life that he was a 'war-monger'. (After all, he was a soldier by origin and training, and he *understood* war, as pacific politicians like Asquith and Neville Chamberlain did not.)

Now, enormously ambitious as he was about his place in history, having won the war, he had longed to be the man to end the Cold War with Russia. I believe that he hung on and on to office in the hope of outliving Stalin, or at least of a change of mind in Moscow. Harold Macmillan told me that in the end the old man was more friendly disposed to Soviet Russia than Anthony Eden, with his more rigid mind, was.

Lunch was coming to an end, but well after three o'clock! It had been a good one: fried fish, then lamb cutlets and peas, ice-cream and fruit. I am really a teetotaller: I did not dare to confess that with Winston: he would not have been able to support so dire a confession. I had had some Bristol Milk in the library, as ordered, while waiting for him; an excellent hock accompanied the meal. When it came to cheese, I wasn't going to have any – let alone port with it. Port in the middle of the day! or indeed at any time. I was forced to compromise with a bit of cheese. Then – 'Some brandy?' A lifelong member of the Duodenal Club, I drew the line at brandy. 'Then have some Cointreau with your coffee! It's very soothing.' It was very soothing.

He tottered out on his stick; I tottered out, wondering whether I was not a little sozzled. 'Like to go round the corner? Or are you like those people coming to lunch who, asked if they would like to wash, said, "Thank you, we did that at the gate."'

Upstairs we went, to the big study next his bedroom – over the fireplace a large eighteenth-century landscape of Blenheim – for our work-session at my typescript.

It was like taking one's essay up to the headmaster. Making after-lunch noises, he is going to fall asleep over my book, I thought. Not a bit of it: he was all attention, to points of detail and style – here was the conscientious artist – as well as content. *A propos* of Charles I, he made an impressive point. I had written him down as an inept politician, in the usual academic manner (the 'Whig Interpretation of History'). Churchill didn't agree: he said that we did not sufficiently consider how much more difficult things were for these people in the past, that they had far less efficient instruments and had to cope with everything themselves. Things were so much easier for us, with specialists to advise, a machine upon which things move and are handed up to us for decision.

Even at the time I registered how generous a judgment this was, and salutary coming from a man of action who knew how things are done and the difficulties in getting them done. Actually I did not agree about Charles I, and I kept to my own opinion of him, though I did not say so. Now I am inclined to think that I was wrong and Churchill more nearly right: Charles I had a well-nigh impossible situation to cope with, a revolution on his hands, the fatal Puritan Revolution. Either Stalin or Hitler would have known better how to cope with such people.

Winston was particularly attentive to words. He did not like my describing the days of the Restoration – when everybody claimed to have been descended from the Conqueror, including the Churchills (who had no such Norman descent)

– as 'snobbish'. 'Why do you say "snobbish"?' I explained why. 'But I don't like the word "snobbish".' So, in deference to the great man, the printed text reads, 'in the grand days of the Restoration' (however, they were snobbish). He took exception to a phrase about the Civil War 'degenerating' at the end, and asked what it meant. I explained about the low-ering of standards, the increasing inhumanity of it. 'But I don't like the word. Now [engagingly] – why don't you say "spiteful"? I like the word "spiteful".' Well, I didn't, so I kept to my own text. When I used the phrase 'pooh-poohed' in conversation, 'I hope you don't say that,' he said mocking. We both laughed. And so it went on.

He sat in an armchair, back to his bedroom; a chair had been placed for me opposite him. A photograph of Roosevelt faced me, and high up on the wall behind, the black-and-white caricature of the Bull-dog Winston. Before going down, he showed me everything with old-fashioned cour-tesy. Everything had been laid on for me – I suspect that he knew I would record it all. A fine George I card-table had been given him by some section of Conservatives; a curious upright desk by his children – upon it the proofs of his *His-tory*, some of which I was to work at later, were laid out.

Somewhat recovered, we went down into the broiling rose-garden, to go on with our task – he was clearly inter-ested – sitting in a deep seat together. The detective walked round behind the rose-bushes unobtrusively, never leaving him out of eyesight, unless sent off for something – to get the gardener to put up a sunshade, or the secretary to send out *Marlborough* vol. I, or to fetch the stuff for feeding the gold-fish. Drinks were sent for – whisky and soda for him, oran-geade for me, though this was the tea-hour and I would have given anything for a pot of tea.

I could not believe that he would be so interested, until, partly out of self-deprecation, I chipped in to explain some-thing. And was at once ticked off. 'I can't read, if you inter-rupt,' he said firmly. I laughed at myself – just the way I am with people, I registered; and kept quiet, while *he* com-mented. 'Very good,' or 'Quite right,' he would say. 'Quite right about James I's execution of Ralegh: I have always thought that one of the worst blots against that' – he paused for a word, or for effect – 'that extravagant . . . sodomite'. Actually, I have changed my mind since then, and now think that there was more to be said for James I than for Ralegh. Then, the old gentleman rippled over with amusement at my description of handsome young John Churchill returning from service of arms in the Mediterranean to those other arms awaiting him at Court of – who but the beautiful Lady Castlemaine? 'Very good,' he twinkled, 'to have been seduced by the King's mistress at sixteen [actually rather older] must have been interesting – and valuable experience.'

Reading my typescript reawakened his interest in his own *Marlborough*, which he sent in for. It was Lord Rosebery who suggested that he should write it. Winston objected that he had never liked the Camaret Bay affair, in which Marlborough had been charged with giving treasonable information to the enemy (apparently he told them only what they knew already). Rosebery said, 'But you have never read Paget's *New Examen*' – which cleared the matter up and exonerated Marlborough. Winston had never heard of the book; Rosebery lent it to him and that settled it. He called Macaulay, roundly, a liar.

I don't think that was quite right, but Macaulay certainly saw only one side of a case at the time; he had the boring 'either-or' mentality of the Parliamentary orator. Often 'both' is better, the subtlety of ambivalence; there was no subtlety in Macaulay.

Once Winston's own book was fetched he became immersed in it, read some of it with approbation and tears of appreciation as he turned over the pages. It was a little the mood of Swift's 'What a genius had I then!'; or the stricken Marlborough catching sight of an earlier Kneller portrait of himself and saying, 'There was a man.' He had been to see all his ancestor's great battlefields: Blenheim, Ramillies, Oudenarde, Malplaquet. Down there on the terrace was the Marlborough pavilion his nephew had decorated for him with a frieze in relief, roundels of Queen Anne, John and Sarah.

The afternoon wore on, the time had come to feed the

goldfish. On the way he showed me round his creation: the little ponds, the stream and cascade, looking down to the swimming pool, inviting in the heat. The hay was all cut and lying in bundles pretty thick along the upper valley. The Churchill flag was flying from the flagstaff over all. Up the slope we went, where I remarked on a sickle-shaped swathe of blue anchusa and white foxgloves – splendid. 'Yes. That's Clemmie – now with regard to the battle of Blenheim . . .' I saw something of what Clemmie had had to put up with. She was in London, much preferring London life; surprisingly, Winston preferred the country. And, after all, this place was his creation – he had even done brick-laying on the walls himself.

I had at various times made motions of taking my leave. No notice was taken: he had evidently allotted the whole day to me. When we at last went in, he took me into yet another study, plainer and simpler, full of mementoes of the first German war, signed photographs of Foch, Pétain, Pershing and so on. Above them better photographs from the Second War – Eisenhower, Montgomery, Tedder, and the rest. At the end he drew my attention to the Notice from the South African war, advertising in Afrikaans £25 reward for the escaped Prisioner [sic] Churchill, dead or alive. What a space in history he covered! 'Twenty-Five Pounds,' he said with emphasis; 'that is all I am worth.' He sank into a chair dejectedly, acting the part for me – I thought, more like a weary Titan.

We went out into the entrance hall, a big wooden bust of Roosevelt beside the door. Winston was now taking off his shoes, having some difficulty in putting on a slipper. I dared to help – but he would not be helped: the same self-willed, self-reliant, self-centred spirit from childhood, as his mother had written of him then.

Sun poured from the west into the front door, upon the flowers, the Roosevelt bust, the aged bulky figure waving goodbye in so friendly fashion. He would go off to bed for a couple of hours, for Beaverbrook was coming to dine, and no doubt they would make a night of it.

I was utterly tired out, by the fullest and richest day's

experience I had ever had. My Journal ends: 'It was infinitely sad and touching. One may never see or hear him again. At any moment the last stroke may come.'

But it did not, for – unbelievably – another ten years; I did see him again and spent an evening with him at Blenheim where he was born.

Thousands of people now will know the ground-floor room inside the entrance hall, which was as far as his mother, Lady Randolph Churchill, could get that November day in 1874 when she had been outside prancing about with the guns, and baby Winston arrived prematurely, he was so anxious to start on his public career. He was said to have been a seven-months child.

Blenheim meant much to him all through his life – clearly a formative influence in the career he shaped for himself, history as inspiration for the life of politics, as was characteristic in the aristocratic days now over, but with exceptional force in his case. He was an historian of eminence as well as a politician; history shaped his mind and gave him his understanding of Britain and the United States, of Europe and the world. From his aristocratic side he drew his political courage, his sense of and care for the well-being of the state, no matter what anybody else thought, popular or unpopular. From his American side he got his boyishness and zest, his optimism and generosity, his bounce.

In the intervening time we exchanged books: the two volumes of family history, *The Early Churchills* and *The Later Churchills*; and he sent me each volume of his four-volume *History of the English-Speaking Peoples* as it came out. I received several friendly, brief missives. Here are a couple relating to his *History*, from 28 Hyde Park Gate, 12 April 1956:

My dear Rowse,
　　I am indeed obliged to you for your letter of April 7 and for all the trouble you have taken. Your comments are most valuable, and it is very good of you to have devoted so much time to my affairs.

Thank you also so much for sending me a copy of your review of Volume I. I am much complimented by what you say.

Yours vy sincerely,
Winston S. Churchill

Shortly after, on 4 May, he wrote: 'I am grateful to you for reading my chapters on the Tudors and for commenting on them. I hope you will also read my chapter on *The May-flower*, which is now being re-proofed. Your observations on it would be most valuable to me.'

I think he was pleased with my history of the family. He was taken by my account of his namesake, the original Sir Winston of the Civil War, the Cavalier Colonel, whom the Restoration Parliament always called the 'Colonel'. 'Oh, so they called him that, did they? I didn't know that.' There was a fine phrase in the old Colonel's *Divi Britannici*, forerunner of his descendant's *History*, referring to 'those far-distant regions, now become a part of us and growing apace to be the bigger part, in the sun-burnt America'. Winston was much taken with this: 'Would you mind if I made use of it?' 'Goodness, it's *your* ancestor's phrase, isn't it?'

Like other people, I did not expect him to survive yet more years. On the occasion of the launching of the *History*, St George's Day 1956, I was invited to the luncheon given by his publishers at the Royal College of Surgeons in Lincoln's Inn Fields. The Hall was packed with a curious company – none of his political associates but his connexions with the world of journalism and publishing and those who had helped him with the book.

The old journalist and war correspondent beamed with pleasure at the company, and made a short speech. I sat at the top table not far from him, but there was no chance of speaking with him there.

But I spent an evening in his company on Saturday, 28 June 1958, when he and Clemmie were stopping at Blenheim for the weekend, to celebrate some anniversary of their engagement; for it was there in the garden that they had got engaged so many years ago. It was a sentimental family occasion – I was rather touched to be included. Winston as a guest was as special a case as ever, as troublesome as a child, everything arranged to suit his convenience. The Duchess, Mary Marlborough, was wonderful at coping with him – not for nothing was she descended from the great Duke's Quartermaster-general, Cadogan. A good trooper, she would both humour Winston and give him his orders.

Much more successful with him than the high-minded Eleanor Roosevelt, hopelessly gone to the good: 'How anybody can *drink* so much – how anybody can *eat* so much – how anybody can *smoke* so much – and remain healthy! . . .' It is indeed astonishing that he survived, in spite of all Lord Moran's gloomy prognostications, to be over ninety. I did not expect him to live for much longer after that evening at Blenheim. Like so many great men in history – like Napoleon or, for that matter, Stalin – he was rather a small man, an advantage for longevity.

When staying at the White House he always upset Eleanor's domestic arrangements. The President liked to go to bed early – Winston kept him up late; he was the only person for whom Roosevelt would stay up at night. At their last meeting the survivors of those fateful encounters made it up; Winston, with his boyish smile: 'You never did like me, Eleanor, did you?' Rather irresistible.

I resort to my Journal for the occasion. I had dined out at Blenheim the previous Saturday, but was now 'bidden again specially to sit beside Winston. He could hear me, but could take no part in general conversation. It was two years since he had been at the so familiar place – he had spent some time there off and on during the war – and this fairly certainly would be his last. I arrived early, again the little girls, the Russell granddaughters, absorbed in television – one of them the image of her great-grandmother, Consuelo Vanderbilt, with that exquisite swan-neck.'

I had owed my introduction to her in New York to Winston; in her apartment in Sutton Place – Marie Antoinette's console-tables, Pissaros, Segonzacs ('a friend of ours') – we had a good deal of talk about Churchills, not wholly favourable on her part. She had a complex about her former husband, the ninth Duke, Winston's cousin, as being a sad, unhappy man: *'fin de race'*, she described him. I did my best to *rapprocher les deux*, said what an historic job they had done together for Blenheim; without either of them it would not have been possible.

This reflection rather reconciled her. She was ready to admit to a mistake – that in the redecoration of the rooms they should have adhered to Vanbrugh, instead of the French taste. But 'Eve*rr*ything *Fr*rench is best,' she said with her French accent, expecting a patriotic protest from me. 'But of course,' I agreed – and that took her aback, for a moment she didn't know how to go on. Mary Marlborough had told me that Consuelo was doing up the Grand Cabinet at Blenheim, which had been all rather overpowering red and gold; she had called in the best decorator from Paris, who had covered the walls with silvery grey silk. On a night when the Queen Mother was dining, I noticed how this background brought out the colour of the women's hair, particularly the Duchess's auburn.

I couldn't but think of the irony of things, Consuelo's breach with her husband, 'Sunny', as they called him, long dead, and she herself still going on, regularly back at Blenheim, her son in possession. 'But what about Winston?' said she; 'Where does he get his looks from?' All sorts of things used to be said of Winston's paternity in gay Edwardian days, that he had Gambetta's red hair, for example. I was able to tell her: he was exactly like his respectable old grandfather, the seventh Duke, the same pug-face and extraordinary eyes, with the red hair of the Spencers. (They are all Spencers; they resumed the Churchill name in 1815.)[1]

Winston remembered his grandfather, a curious outcrop of religiosity in their divagatory nineteenth-century story. He told me that, when a boy at Blenheim, he had the impression that things were distinctly 'tight' – this was after the great agricultural depression of the late 1870s; the Duchess used to collect left-overs and scraps from the meals, pack them into panniers to be carried round to the tenantry on the estate.

Here I was at Blenheim again. 'At last the circle assembled,

1. v. my *The Later Churchills*.

and Winston and Clemmie appeared, Clemmie all billowing gown and broadened out with age. I was shocked to see how much he had aged, much more feeble, another illness will puff him away – or possibly without. Unsteady on his feet he took a low seat, beaming happily, contentedly around, saying nothing, kissing the children goodnight. It was sad to see him: still the centre of all our attention, the embers of a great fire, all the force gone. Very deaf now and rather impenetrable, apparently he had asked for me to sit beside him at dinner, the ladies' talk being like "the twittering of birds" to him.

'We went into dinner, he on the Duchess's right, I next to him. She was very good at managing him, but we were reduced, as with the very old, to treating him like a child. He spent much of the time holding her miniature dachshund in his arms, at one point offering it some of the delicious lobster *mousse* on a fork: the expression of disgust was charming to see, little velvet paws hanging limply down, head drawn back, nose averted. "Darling," said the old man, always sentimental about animals.

'Not that he has become senile: he is still capable of a good phrase, an echo of his former power. Someone asked whether he would be attending church tomorrow. "At my age," he replied, "I think my devotions may be attended in private." I did not worry him any more about the past, though I should have liked to know more about the St George's by-election in 1923, which he said he had enjoyed more than any other, and when the Duchess had canvassed for him. If he had won it, might he have won the lead of all the anti-socialist forces, instead of everything falling into Baldwin's lap? I did not like to put the point too clearly, and he did not catch the drift of it. He commented vaguely, "it all seemed to work out very harmoniously", the kind of Parliamentary formula he must often have employed.

'He still could make single comments, rather than command an argument. He thought the failure of the new French constitution to provide for an interim dissolution of the Chamber a mistake. Similarly of the statutory limitation upon American Presidents to two terms of office. (He would!

Never say die, his motto.) This led to a long disquisition in
the American manner by the Duke's son-in-law, the Duke
obviously impatient, Winston all bland courtesy. (He
couldn't hear it.)

'Indeed it was the most touching thing to observe – all
force gone after these strokes, now all contentment and old-
world courtesy. He was still *compos mentis*: he had won £21
off the Duchess at bezique that evening, and during the weekend had cleaned her out of £50 altogether. He takes his own
cards, case and spectacles around with him, laid out cer-
emoniously upon a red velvet cloth. Upstairs in his bedroom
he had brought his love-bird in a cage – boyish, troublesome,
lovable as ever. To everyone's surprise he demanded water:
"Oh, I drink a lot of water – the doctor tells me to – along
with everything else."

'I took my leave fairly early, after a few words with the
Duke, who had been helpful in letting me have the run of his
archives. Once before, at dessert, he had asked *à propos* of my
history of the family a blunt, direct question: "What did Lord
Randolph [Winston's father] die of?" I felt that he knew that
I knew, but wasn't going to say; I gave a noncommittal
answer, from which he could be certain that I knew.

'Scaffolding was up all around the great hall under repair;
I went down through those Vanbrugh corridors into the basement to the private entrance, a moon appearing above the
forest of spars, shedding a strange unreal glimmer about that
place of ghosts, the park, the bridge, the Victory column: the
place where Winston was born, to which he was for a time
the heir-presumptive (until Consuelo's son was born), the
inspiration of so much of his life and work.'

It was historically appropriate that I should last see him there.
Though my contact with him was cursory, in a way sketchy,
it was different from anybody else's, and significant for both,
since we cared for history more than anything – to him politics was history. This was why he spoke to me more than all
the Baldwins and Chamberlains, or even the men of my own
party whom I knew better, Attlee, Bevin, Morrison.

To me as an historian, my contacts with Churchill were contacts with history, direct and live.

2

Nancy Astor

Now that Nancy Astor – dear, gallant, golden-hearted woman – has vanished from the scene and is forgotten in the House of Commons, where she was a unique figure, and even at Plymouth, which she loved and for which she did so much, what was her importance in history? Most people would find it hard to say, but an historian should be able to define it.

She was an idiosyncratic character, a public figure, scintillating like a star, perhaps a meteor across a sombre firmament. More than that, she was a symbol of two historic themes: first, of the emancipation of women and their political rights; second, of the *rapprochement* between Britain and America, indispensable to Britain's survival in the two German wars of our century, and of Anglo-American friendship, a stabilizing factor in the upheaval of our time.

Besides that, she did a mass of good work, public and private, countless good deeds, for individuals even more than for institutions. In one way her life could be summed up quite simply – *doing good*; in another, it is not easy to get her quite right, for hers was a complex character, mercurial and contradictory, and few have been able to grasp it, let alone render it in words, do her justice. For she was at once overbearing and modest, censorious yet kind, fierce and direct yet sympathetic, tactless at the same time as sensitive, didactic and even minatory yet remarkably intuitive and willing to learn. Her general ideas were apt to be wrong and largely emotional prejudice. She hardly ever read a book, except the

Bible – in that so like a Southern Puritan, which she was, for all her Christian Science; but she was well read in the book of life: she was rarely mistaken in her judgment of people. For all her natural gifts, Nancy wasn't educated; but that is no disadvantage in a democracy.

She had the courage of a lion and a heart of gold – which may sound a little equivocal, for of course she had the gold of the Astors to work on and with.

Oddly enough, for all that I knew her intimately – and it was hardly possible to know her, if at all, *un*intimately – I cannot remember when I first met her. My first memory of Waldorf, her husband – whom I also came to know better than most – goes right back to when as a schoolboy I attended a Sunday evening meeting at my home town, St Austell. It was a Temperance affair, and I didn't take in anything of what was said – just like any other member of an audience. Later on, as a Labour man and (mistakenly) a political candidate for my home constituency, I did not hold with the Astors' grip on Plymouth, notwithstanding the good works they did there. After all, I belonged to the perpetual Opposition and thought that my working people should stand on their own feet. Caught in a dilemma as I was, a cleft stick of my own making, I would not allow, as a Marxist, that concrete good deeds were worth all the politicizing in the world.

So my acquaintance with the Astors did not come from the West Country, where we were politically on opposite sides, but from the All Souls end. They were very close to All Souls (their son and heir, Bill, even made the College his residuary legatee, he told me). They were close friends of Lionel Curtis, Geoffrey Dawson and most of the Round Table group. Lord Brand, married to Nancy's sister, was their brother-in-law. Waldorf was Chairman of Curtis's Royal Institution of International Affairs, one of Lionel's many brain-children. (I do not suppose that the Institution, Chatham House, served much purpose, except to provide jobs for several excellent people, Arnold Toynbee chief among them.) Philip Kerr, to become Lord Lothian, closest of all to Nancy, was constantly in and out of All Souls as of

Cliveden – he had, like a lot of other eminent persons, tried for the Fellowship but not been elected. It gave him, unlike some others, a friendly feeling for the place.

Hence, when I became a guest at Cliveden, for all its somewhat daunting grandeur – an Italianate palazzo with terrace and fountains from the Borghese villa ('loot,' I once remarked within hearing of some of the family) – I was not on wholly unfamiliar territory. The books in the library had been selected by a posse from All Souls, headed by Craster and Curtis. Arthur Salter had also been a *habitué* before his marriage to a rival American, not much liked by Nancy, for Ethel was a New England Bagge, a 'dam' Yankee', and Nancy was an unreconstructed Southerner, a Virginian first and last. For all her life lived in England, she never ceased to be a Virginian. When I told her of my visit to the National Cemetery at Arlington (where now the two Kennedys lie), she exclaimed, 'National Cemetery? – dam' Yankees – it's *Lee's* place, Arlington.'

In the entrance-hall at Cliveden was Sargent's portrait of her, slim, radiant, beautiful; he had intended to portray her carrying baby Bill pickaback, but it hadn't worked out, hence the original pose, back half-turned. Improbably in this strict household was a portrait of the wicked Countess of Shrewsbury, a previous owner, who was said to have held her lover's horse while he killed her husband. But that was an acquisition of Waldorf's father, the first Lord, a collector on the grand scale.

William, the first Lord, was a strange and fascinating character, creator of it all – dead, he loomed in the background, both here and at Hever Castle, the second son's, J.J.'s, place. But he is not my subject; I must confine myself to what Nancy told me – and, the soul of indiscretion, she told me a lot. The most placid and least quarrelsome of men, Waldorf had quarrelled with his father for taking a peerage. Waldorf considered that, already a member of the House of Commons, this ruined the prospects of a political career for him. He was thereupon excommunicated by unforgiving father. Things work out ironically in people's lives, which form the stuff of history; I doubt if Waldorf would have had much of a political career anyway. Paradoxically, and unexpectedly, Nancy had the political career; Waldorf took second place to her, was her chief of staff, content to remain in the background – though in the family, he had the last word: the gentlest and most considerate of men, he carried authority.

The older Astor background was strangely withdrawn and reserved, Waldorf's father shy to the point of incommunicativeness. This gay, unrepressed Virginian girl brought gales of laughter and fun into the conventional stuffiness of Cliveden under the first Lord: she was the light of Waldorf's eyes, she released his spirit and made the happiness of his life. She gave him five children, though herself as sexually cold as Elizabeth I, whom she resembled in some ways, looked a bit like her – though better looking. She told me that she had experienced sexual desire only once in her life – so I supposed that the children were conceived, like the British Empire, in a fit of absence of mind. The fabulous structure of their lives was based on Waldorf's consuming love for her. This corroborated her telling Curtis – though not all Nancy's *dicta* were to be taken literally – that he had pestered her to marry him; eventually she capitulated and – 'his possessions were magnificent'.

She held out some time before consenting, for she had had a disillusioning experience in her first marriage – to Robert Gould Shaw, who turned out an alcoholic. Unacquainted with the facts of life and a Puritan *enragée*, on her wedding night she had fought him like a wildcat. Once, when I remarked on the beauty of the turquoise bracelets she was wearing – the colour of her eyes – she said, 'Yes, I put them on the hotel bill, in Vienna, on our honeymoon; Waldorf wouldn't notice.' Then, sadly, 'I couldn't do that now.'

True or not, it was in keeping with her account of her one experience of desire. Everyone accepted that her relations with Philip Lothian were entirely platonic. Only once, in a bedroom, was she overcome by desire. Acknowledging this weakness of the flesh – though to Nancy and Philip as Christian Scientists matter wasn't real – they knelt on opposite sides of the bed until this cup passed away. Thereupon Philip said, 'Now, Nancy, you know what men have to put up with.' (I rather think that she gave him his Christian Science, of which he died, in the Embassy at Washington, without calling a doctor. Lionel Curtis on his friend's death, arch-advocate of Appeasement of Hitler: 'Philip died in the know-ledge that he had been wrong.') I dare say Waldorf was rather bored with Philip perpetually on a pedestal.

This lends point to the celebrated exchange with Lloyd George, whom Nancy admired most of public men – nor was she wrong: he was a man of genius. Because she was so censorious she was the last person in their circle to know that L.G. lived with his secretary, Frances Stevenson. The moment Nancy heard the rumour she went straight to the great little man: 'L.G., what is this I hear about you and Frances?' Lloyd George, not the least perturbed, retorted, 'And what about you and Philip?' Nancy replied hotly: 'Everybody knows that my relations with Philip are com-pletely innocent.' L.G., spectacles gleaming with mischief: 'Then you should be ashamed of yourself.' End of the inter-view.

Nancy exposed herself to being scored off like that by her interfering, head on, in other people's affairs. She really was innocent and never learned in this regard – perhaps because she almost always had the ace of trumps up her sleeve and got the last word. Only a Lloyd George or a Churchill could trump her: nobody else could. One of the well-known exchanges with Winston (whom she didn't like) was undoubtedly true: 'If I were your wife I would put poison in your coffee.' To which Winston replied, 'And if I were your husband I would drink it.' The imagination boggles at the thought of those two married: bull-dog confronting wildcat.

Her wit made her superb at dealing with hecklers: she always scored. A countryman in her constituency thought to floor her with 'Missus, how many toes have a pig got?' I'm sure Nancy wouldn't know, but what he got was: 'Take off your boot, man, and count them for yourself.' One thinks of her sudden inspirations – at a solemn Temperance meeting to raise funds in dreary Glasgow, when things weren't going well: 'It's hard enough to be a Christian when sober; it's impossible when drunk.' The meeting raised £7,000. She was

a natural wit, to whom droll ideas came bubbling over: like
'those rich houses where the sheets are so fine that the blankets tickle the guests all night so that they wake up in the
morning exhausted with laughing' – such an odd idea. 'Did
I say that?' she said to me.

And to such a spontaneous natural comic odd happenings
attached themselves, as to Bernard Shaw, a great friend.
They had some things in common, as teetotallers, non-
smokers, Puritans; to this Shaw added vegetarianism, so that
at ninety-two or so he just couldn't die. Nancy sat with him
at his death-bed. The old boy woke up suddenly from a coma
and said, 'Nancy, did you ever hear the story of Patti's husband?' No, she did not go back so far as Adela Patti. It
appears that the *prima donna* and her (foreign) husband
arranged a country-house party after what they supposed to
be the English fashion. The guests were assembled, the music
struck up, when the husband appeared running down the
staircase: 'You must all go away: I have found a man in bed
with my wife.' Consternated, the guests hardly knew what
to do and were preparing to leave when the husband appeared
again: 'You must all come back. It is quite all right: he has
apologized.' Apparently this was Shaw's last communication
to the world: he thereupon relapsed into coma.

Sexually cold, Nancy could exploit her sex appeal shame-
lessly, like Elizabeth I, though more appealingly: both tremendous exhibitionists, for ever playing to the gallery. A
Queen hardly enjoyed such opportunities as Nancy, who,
accosting a young American sailor in the second German war
outside the House of Commons, asked him if he would like
to come in with her. He replied that she was just the sort of
woman his mother had warned him against. That night she
was able to tell Admiral Sims that he had one perfectly
upright sailor under his command in the American Navy.
And I have heard her tell similar salty yarns about her marine
constituency at Plymouth, and the misunderstandings with
which respectable couples were apt to be greeted at lodging
house doors, with rates of prices for the night.

But there was a serious side to Nancy's capers and jests,
her fishwife's haranguing and teasing, scolding and cheering

people up, in Barbican style at Plymouth as everywhere she appeared. At Cliveden the Astors supported a hospital for wounded soldiers in the two German wars. In the first, 1914–18, 24,000 men passed through the hospital, 'so, if I have a sergeant-major's manners, no wonder'. During the second war Nancy took me along with her as she went through the ward, doing her turn – like her niece, Joyce Grenfell. Nancy's mother was Irish-American, so the Irish strain – the wit and warm-heartedness – accounted for something in her make-up. The ward woke up at once on her appearance, everybody galvanized to attention, jokes and answering her back. She carried a basket and marched up through like a fishwife on the Barbican. Then her demeanour completely changed, beside a bed where a young RAF officer was too ill to take part in the fun. His face had been fearfully smashed, and she got no reaction from him lying there passive and inert. Quietly and gently she coaxed him along, until he took a bite at the peach she held out to him. Coming back to me, she said, 'He'll recover.' I was reduced to tears by the spectacle.

Here was the splendid side of Nancy. I would forgive her anything she said – though she never came within a millimetre of infringing any of my too-exposed sensibilities – for the sake of the things she did. Only once did she indicate disapproval with a shrug – when she found that, after all I had had to put up with as a Labour candidate in Cornwall throughout the thirties, I had turned my back and wouldn't raise a finger for the place, or even speak there. *They* had had it all their own way for the whole decade – they could now get on with it, and without me.

During the Plymouth Blitz – it lasted the best part of a week, until the centre of the city was completely shattered – Nancy and Waldorf were there through it all in their house on the Hoe, damaged as it was, Nancy's maid, Rose, picking the glass out of her hair from the blown-in windows. From thirty miles away at St Austell we could see Plymouth burning; the little local fire-brigades went up from Cornwall and stood there in St Andrew's Square fighting the flames, until half of them were obliterated where they stood. Plymouth was stunned and demoralized after five nights of it, and the population streamed out into the countryside.

Waldorf told me that it was Nancy's own idea that helped to recover morale: she thought of public dancing on the Hoe, and led off with Menzies, Prime Minister of Australia, who was staying with them, RAF men and WAAFs, soldiers and sailors and WRENs, British and Americans, all joined in – and people began to come back to the city and recover their nerve. Nancy never said a word to me of what she had done – and that was like her, for underneath the public turns and playing to the gallery was a woman who was not just modest (modesty is an overrated quality) but one who was humble of heart, who lived to do good.

Her religious belief – however one might rate it intellectually – sustained her and enabled her to console and help simple people in the way no rationalist could. I remember her coming back dejected from an afternoon in Devonport, visiting homes where women had lost husband or son at sea. 'It's nothing but misery, isn't it?', looking into some poor woman's face and holding her hand – I suppose, praying with her. Consolation that we high and mighty intellectuals could never give, I reflected, as Nancy told me how her afternoon had gone. She could give people something of her spirit – she was always giving out. Looking out on Plymouth burning, 'There goes thirty years of our lives,' she said; and immediately added, 'But we'll build it up again.'

The Astors had done so much for Plymouth – I don't know the full tale of their good deeds. They created a social centre and built a children's *crêche*; at Exeter a hostel was given to the university. From the Hoe one looks down upon a rather nondescript tail-end of the town, in a prominent position fronting the bay, looking towards Drake's Island. Before the 1914–18 war, when Waldorf was rich indeed, they hoped to clear that area and make a fine public park of it. What might not have been achieved, if it had not been for the two wars the Germans let loose upon Europe!

There was always fun where Nancy was about; taking me under her wing, she let me in for a number of amusing occasions, meeting the local worthies, some of them bearers of historic names – all grist to the mill for a budding histor-ian. One year I had to make the speech at the annual Feast to celebrate Sir Francis Drake's bringing water to the town – a considerable feat, cutting a channel for miles to bring a leat down from the highlands of Burrator. Up there we gathered, civic dignitaries in fur and feather, plumed and robed alder-men, Commander-in-chief from Devonport and other naval and military grandees, clerics to sanctify the proceedings. Assembled on the sacred spot, the silver loving-cup was passed round. When it came to me I wondered whatever the liquid tasted of – until I realized that it was Sir Francis Drake's water, nothing more nor less. At that the heavens descended; we were deluged. It was fun to see the dignitaries picking up their skirts and skedaddling for the marquee, where, slightly sodden, I had to make my speech.

Among the naval personnel I met with her was an heroic submarine-man, Dunbar-Naesmith, then in command at Devonport. When he was a young officer, his submarine went to the bottom and failed to come up for some appalling number of hours – while Dunbar-Naesmith coolly kept all under control until their rescue. Admiral Lord Chatfield, First Sea Lord, I remember – but wasn't he a Chamberlainite? – I've no idea how good he was at his job. Rumbustious Cork and Orrery turned up, a red-headed fire-eater; what a title, however historic! One of Nancy's introductions led to a firm friendship with the dear Mount Edgcumbes – only son killed in the war, so that the title passed to a remote cousin in New Zealand. Something romantic as well as historic about that: back this representative of an ancient Cornish family came, from more congenial farming, to take up the burden of Mount Edgcumbe across the water from the Hoe. In the Blitz the house was gutted, historic contents – pictures, books, archives – all destroyed. West Country folklore liked to think – when people still had that penumbra of interest to their minds – that the Duke of Medina Sidonia in '88 fancied Mount Edgcumbe for himself. 1588 – those were the days!

One thing Nancy could not make me do, that was to visit her children's crêche. She found this incomprehensible: 'Just like Bobby', the son of her first marriage. And indeed it was

just like Bobby – though whether he had the excuse of preferring to look into St Budeaux church of the Budocksides,
cousins of Sir Richard Grenville, with its Elizabethan tomb
of a Gorges, I doubt. Anyway, it provided an alibi from
philanthropy for me.

The house on the Hoe, 3 Elliot Terrace – the 'lodging-
house' the Astors called it – became very familiar, with its
first-floor drawing-room looking out to sea; over the chimney-piece a contemporary picture of Winstanley's baroque
Eddystone light-house. (He boasted that it was so staunch
that he would not mind being in it in the worst of storms –
and was. And that was it: it totally disappeared.) The house
was ultimately given to the city as an official residence for the
Lord Mayor.

I remember, at my first lunch there, wondering who the
glamorous young RAF officer was who gaily contradicted
me from the bottom of the table. This was Bobby, whom I
was not to meet until after the war at Cliveden. Talented, but
a problem for his mother. She had her own private griefs. It
was over this that she eventually became friends with T. E.
Lawrence, who, a misogynist, had refused to meet her,
though a friend of Curtis and a Fellow of All Souls. When
Nancy was in trouble, he came to her rescue: sailed her down
and up the coast of Cornwall in his speed-boat one night of
crisis, until day came and she had to go through the hoop of
meeting the Prince of Wales on an official visit to Plymouth.

She had indeed done her bit to try to help the Prince in the
duties that attended upon him – these he regarded as 'chores'
(his own word), and so in the fullness of time, aided by
another American woman of spirit, he demoted himself to
Duke of Windsor. One of Nancy's leading ideas – since she
was totally without snobbery herself – was to bring people of
different sorts together. She had helped to arrange for stiff
King George V and Queen Mary to meet the Labour leaders,
improbably clad in knee-breeches and silk stockings, at a
dinner-party at 4 St James's Square. It was a great success –
the formality of the occasion lightened by Nancy telling J.
H. Thomas to pull his stockings up. Jimmy became a favourite with George V – they talked much the same language,

though I doubt the exchange: 'I've got such a 'orrible 'eadache, your Majesty.' 'Take a couple of aspirates, Mr Thomas.'

An anthropologist well understands the aura that surrounds royal personages – or used to; so I will say no more than that Nancy, bless her heart, was anxious that I should write the official biography of George VI. I suspect that it was no advantage to be pushed in those quarters by her, and anyhow I rather fancied a career (in writing) for myself. I had already turned down the more enticing offer – pressed upon me by both sides of the Lloyd George family – of writing his official biography. And I had already rejected proposals to write the history of the RAF in the war, and that of the DCLI, our own Cornish regiment. I recall the colonel of the regiment, a general in fact, coming down to All Souls to persuade me to undertake it, and his inability to understand that I really couldn't do it – I knew some of my limitations. A conventional royal biography was certainly not my idea of bliss – I was bent on the more exciting Elizabethans. Jack Wheeler-Bennett was their choice, and an appropriate one: George VI had little historic importance to speak of, such as even his father had had. Wheeler-Bennett turned out a dull, over-long volume – to be rewarded suitably with a knighthood, along with such luminaries as Sir Stanley Rouse, Chairman of the Football Association in his day.

Far more important historically than this kind of thing was the whole issue of Appeasement; for, though I became a friend of the Astors and knew well their friends, leading Appeasers – Geoffrey Dawson, Halifax, Simon, Lothian, Tom Jones – I was militantly opposed to them and their policy. I agreed with Vansittart, who was 100 per cent right about Germany, and with the Foreign Office view on the matter. The Foreign Office was well informed about it all – it was its business. The Appeasers were prejudiced against the Foreign Office: they did not know what they were dealing with.

I will not go into the historic issue here – merely record that I had a controversy on it in *The Times* in 1937 with Nancy's mentor, Philip Lothian. Anyone who wants to read it can look it up in my book, *The End of an Epoch*, and see who was right – the noble Marquis (Vansittart used to call him a Mr Know-all, but it was worse) or the young historian who knew Germany and her record in the past century.

So, since I was a friend of the family and a familiar at Cliveden – though after Appeasement was over, and it had brought its consequences down upon us – when I wrote my little *aide-mémoire, All Souls and Appeasement* (C. P. Snow wrote, 'This is exactly as it was'), I sent the first copy of the book in honesty to Bill Astor, who had then succeeded his father. He wrote me a reasoned letter, which in itself made clear why they had been so wrong.

> As to the misapprehension of the German character, Halifax, Lothian, Dawson, my father and others were very sincere Christians, who could not believe that people could be basically evil. This was, of course, all the worse with those who were Christian Scientists (Lothian and Papa) who did not believe in the reality of evil at all.

[One sees how silly they were to believe any such thing. Lord Hugh Cecil knew better, and said that the trouble with Halifax was that 'Edward did not believe in Original Sin'. Naturally such types had no idea what they were dealing with in Hitler, Göring, Goebbels, Streicher, Heydrich etc.]

Bill went on to explain why they had been anti-French – though that had proved equally mistaken and disastrous – and hostile to the Foreign Office, which was better informed. 'The Foreign Office was not helped by their very bad public relations and by Vansittart's way of expressing himself, which seemed to be hysterical and exaggerated and offering no hope.' But it was precisely these people who gave the Foreign Office and Vansittart a bad press; and Vansittart was driven to distraction by the evil emanating from Nazi Germany, the increasing threat, and the refusal of the politicians to recognize it for what it was.

Lord Brand, who knew Germany from the City's dealings

with Schacht – who made Hitler's rearmament possible – knew better. He wrote me about my Appeasement book:

> Philip [Lothian], Geoffrey Dawson, and Halifax were among my closest friends and I feel, if I reviewed your book, I would have to say how wrong I thought they had been in their judgment of Germany, and I do not want publicly to criticize them . . . You have been very fair to me and I make no criticism.

Brand wrote again:

> The Baldwin and Neville Chamberlain period is a very curious one. We so happened to have two Prime Ministers who knew nothing whatever about the Continent of Europe. Baldwin was a more able man in my opinion than Chamberlain. Chamberlain was a courageous man in many ways, but extremely limited and extremely sure of himself.

I quote his opinion, since he knew both of them; I did not – and did not want to.

There were plenty of people who remained mum, and many more who had been Appeasers to the last and resented my little book. So it made no impression and had no success in Britain (though it had in America). Nevertheless, the book stands for what it was intended to be – an *aide-mémoire pour servir à l'histoire*.

Interestingly enough, young David Astor was right about all this, since he had the advantage of knowing the German situation intimately through his friendship with Adam von Trott, as I had. No attention was paid to him or me: we were too young and unimportant. Bill's brother, Michael, tells us that Geoffrey Dawson and Barrington Ward on *The Times* went further than Waldorf thought wise in pushing Appeasement; while John Walter, of the historic *Times* family, raised an official objection to the fatal policy *The Times* was pushing. Michael tells us, 'I thought at the time, and I still believe, that Geoffrey Dawson was blinded by a form of self-conceit'

– and that was true enough; a powerful man, he was totally ignorant of Europe. As for Barrington-Ward, Foreign Office people thought him a 'wet', and that was about right. As for Philip Lothian, he wrote to Lionel Curtis, 'I am increasingly convinced that Christian Science is the real key to all our problems, political and economic, no less than personal.' He should have told that to Hitler. Isn't it extraordinary what fools intelligent people can be? When H. A. L. Fisher's brilliant book came out, *Our New Religion*, Philip wrote a review in *The Observer*, which was always at his disposal, to answer Fisher and advocate this profound nostrum for our troubles.

As for Nancy, an American observed that, though the Astors owned two of the most influential papers in Britain, she had a wider circulation than both put together. Surrounded by such men – actually I never met Dawson at Cliveden, but regularly at All Souls, where he was impermeable to argument – how could Nancy be blamed for the nonsense she thought about Germany? It fitted in with her emotional prejudices: the French were immoral, and Catholic when they weren't atheists, the Germans were moral and largely Protestant. After all, this was the dominant point of view in nineteenth-century Britain, of such asses as Carlyle.

How did I get along with such nonsense? Really, quite easily: I never took seriously anything Nancy thought, about politics or religion. I was fond of the essential woman, the wonderful creature she was, and her intuition told her never to argue with me on any of these subjects. On Sunday mornings at Cliveden, when she and Waldorf went off to their Christian Science meeting, she would place a Bible on the arm of my chair stuffed with markers to places indicated, I suppose, by the sainted Mary Baker Eddy. I never took the slightest notice. And I was already sufficiently sceptical to know that human beings can often be helped by nonsense, when rational sense can do little for them.

I am sure that Nancy's faith helped to keep Waldorf going, who was not strong, as indeed it had recovered her from serious illness and breakdown earlier. It was no use to her daughter, Wissie, when she had a fall from her horse and injured her back, indeed it did positive harm; as, ironically, it did to Philip Lothian. Ironically again, Philip, who was such a fool about Germany, was very successful as ambassador to the United States. *You never can tell*, Shaw says; or as William Shakespeare puts it better: 'The web of our life is of a mingled yarn, good and ill together; our virtues would be proud if our faults whipped them not, and our crimes would despair if they were not cherished by our virtues.' I expect Nancy would have agreed with that, if she had ever come across it – it would have done her good to read more Shakespeare and less Bible. The nugget of sense in her faith was just that the state of one's mind is related to one's physical well-being, and affects it: that is all.

I was surprised when Nancy told me that Belloc had for a time been one of her literary lions. With her anti-Catholic nonsense, her 'doxy could not have got on for long with his 'doxy. Though he was an educated man, a man of genius, his 'doxy had no more to be said for it than hers – rationally. Historically, of course, and from the point of view of civilization and culture, it had almost everything to be said for it. She would not have appreciated that; but she had been kind to him and his family in a time of trouble, and put them all up for weeks – I don't know whether in one of the cottages on the place. There was a delightful one down beside the Thames, where usually some lame dog or other was being put up. Their generosity of spirit and kindness were boundless, and sometimes taken for granted. She told me that her Labour MPs hardly ever said 'thank you' after a meal.

Bernard Shaw worked in with her pattern of things very well, where a Belloc could not possibly. Shaw became a friend, and they all went off on a historic mission to Moscow in the thirties together. As usual stories were told against Nancy, about her innocently quaffing a glass of vodka thinking it was water, etc. Actually, there was an exchange with Stalin the significance of which escaped her. Winston Churchill was out of power and out of favour; he never was in much favour with her, and not more than a handful of Tories were with him in the House – that deplorable assembly that led the country bound and gagged (willingly, it must be admitted) into the war. Stalin pressed her for information about political leaders in Britain, and their prospects. 'Chamberlain is the coming man,' she said. 'What about Churchill?' said Stalin. 'Oh, he's finished,' said she – which was what most people thought at the time. But Stalin, who had a first-class political brain, replied, 'If ever your country is in trouble, he will come back.' The sense of power – which is what politics is about – recognized itself in another.

Nancy had no success with T. S. Eliot. One day she rang him up out of the blue to come and meet Shaw. What she got was that quiet, precise voice at the end of the telephone: 'Lady Astor, I am sorry to say that I do not have the pleasure of your acquaintance.' She did not resent it: too good a sport to resent snubs. Eliot would have been no more her cup of tea than Belloc was. I can't think how I was, for my whole outlook, Oxford and the rest of it, was much more in keeping with those two Oxford men.

She had a real feeling for Oxford, a kind of respect and deference that was rather endearing in one with little deference in her composition – it was partly, I think, a touching respect for learning. She came over to All Souls for Encaenia fairly often – I recall her once in a costume of rarest blue, which went with her eyes; upon which my friend, Arthur Bryant, always an appeaser, not only of the ladies, complimented her with enthusiasm. Sometimes she came to cheer fellow Americans receiving honorary degrees. The university should certainly have given her one, if only as the first woman Member of Parliament, who had thus made history. And, if Oxford could confer degrees on those entertainers, P. G. Wodehouse and Charlie Chaplin (rightly), it should have extended itself to include her, peerless (if that is the word) among women entertainers. The authorities simply hadn't the imagination.

One little success I had with her was once when she came to my rooms before making a speech. She was tired and out of sorts, and I actually got her to drink half a glass of sherry, against her principles. I achieved it by telling her that it was against my principles too, as a 95 per cent teetotaller; but for a good purpose we were to give ourselves a dispensation. She obeyed – I can see her now, sitting on a stool, a good little girl doing as she was told. She went off and made a rousing speech.

To understand her, one had to know something of, and allow for, her American background – she was far more American than Waldorf, an Etonian and Oxonian. As an historian I have always been surprised by the way Americans remain, indefeasibly and irreducibly, American after a lifetime in England. It is remarkable evidence of the strength of American characteristics; that there is such a thing as an American national character is again a remarkable achievement after only two or three hundred years of national history. Perhaps that is long enough – it is certainly an answer to Leftist illusionists who cannot see that national (or racial) characteristics even exist.

Nancy was born in 1879, a Virginia Langhorne. ('I was born a Virginian, so naturally I am a politician.') This meant that she had no inferiority complex about Astor wealth and grandeur; though the first Lord Astor regarded himself as a Renaissance prince and Nancy once remarked that at that time the Astors were treated in the US as semi-royal. (There had been a grand progress earlier in the United States with Waldorf and the Pierpont Morgans. Pierpont Morgan had a proboscis of a nose which grew and grew, for all the operations he had upon it to reduce the offending feature. Nancy said that when he kissed her, it stuck to her.) Even Waldorf, an unsnobbish man, once told me with innocent pleasure the number of 'royals' Cliveden had collected for the weekend, as against none at the Kemsleys, his rival newspaper proprietor across the way at Dropmore.

Naturally I didn't know Nancy in those early days of her first glory, when as the first woman MP she was world news, and when the world regarded what took place in Britain as important. The Americans were proud of her; no public woman competed with her at the time – those were the days before the rise of Eleanor Roosevelt. And I never knew until quite recently that the Langhornes originally came from Cornwall.

Not long ago on a visit to the Library of Reading University, to which the Astor papers were bequeathed, I was surprised to find that Nancy had kept my letters to her. I had naturally kept hers to me, for, a regular magpie, I keep everything. The Library very kindly gave me a Xerox, so now I have both sides of the correspondence. Mine begins by being properly deferential, goes on to become flirtatious and occasionally teasing, and ends up with genuine affection. The trouble with her letters is that they are largely illegible: after a lifetime of Elizabethan handwritings I can make out only half of what she is saying – her friends would say that this was to disguise her shaky spelling. It certainly succeeded.

My first letter was to try to persuade her to buy and save lovely Elizabethan Trerice (near Newquay), when it was empty and in danger. I suggested it might make a base for one of her sons setting up for a nearby constituency. I got a characteristic reply: 'It was funny you should write and ask me to have a corner in my heart for Cornwall, because I have fallen completely in love with it, having spent several weeks at Rock and played on the St Enodoc Golf Course quite alone . . .' Then, 'being Cornish there is a hitch in your mentality which I long to talk to you about! There are a lot of hitches in mine – or shall we call them stitches?'

She regarded Bertie Abdy's fabulous Newton Ferrers with disapproval, because he had given its Queen Anne interior the *décor* of a Louis Philippe house in Paris. It certainly was a bit exotic with its Winterhalters and Hubert Roberts, books with precious bindings from French royal libraries, its Houdon bust of Marie Antoinette, etc. – exquisite creation, I suspect Nancy thought it the least bit wicked because French.

An undated letter refers to the death of Adam von Trott, who had been David Astor's friend as well as mine, and an intimate at Cliveden. Adam had been in the generals' plot against Hitler and was hanged on a butcher's hook in Plötzensee Prison. Nancy:

> Oh dear. David feared this some time ago. Are you certain that it was Adam? I can't feel that death is anything save an open door. The real suffering is for those who are left and who believe it's the end . . . I've had

four weeks with my Bible and Books in a horrid house at Trebetherick. I wondered where you were as we truly want to see you. You are not a very sociable friend. Would you come to us at Cliveden any time? . . . Adam had a full life and great faith, but still how ghastly it is. A world that Hates and Kills and Envies. There are good Germans but no good Nazis, I agree. Do come soon and see us.

In October 1954 it was:

You know perfectly well that you have entirely forgotten me – I suppose for some dumb duchess! I have waited anxiously and never a line! You always win me back again with a book, and it looks very interesting. If I can tear myself away from the Book of Samuel I will read it.

Next, from Sandwich, where there was a quiet bay and golf at hand – a kind of millionaires' *enclave*:

I am bothered on all sides about my Life. I think you will have to write it – would you like to? If so you better go to Virginia and pick up what you can, *or* are you too busy for that? [As usual, I was.] I wrote you and had no reply before you left . . . General Slim wants me to come to Australia. I am torn. I'm no traveller . . . I know you will love my native land, tho' alas there are no Duchesses there. How you could fall for Duchess — — has rather shaken me. But then you are Cornish! *Not* Devon. God help and keep you in the strait and narrow way. Nancy, Her Grace of Sandwich, Kent.

In September 1955,

I wrote you before you left and never got an answer. I have now had your letter from the *Britannic*. I see you have fallen for Winston. I haven't yet. He is paying his usual visit to Lord Beaverbrook. The Bible says 'he is known by his friends.' I see you will be in the East [of

U.S.] from Dec. 1st. I hope to come over about January 1st. This is to know if you can wait so long.

I was so much enjoying myself in America that I wrote to her: 'Shall I stay over here for good? People are so good to me – so much more so than Cornwall has ever been, or Oxford, or the intellectuals.' To this she replied from Plymouth: 'Please don't go to Charlottesville or anywhere in Virginia until I get there. If possible change your programme, because I could ask you to stop with me near Charlottesville, and you would love it.' Of course, I couldn't change my programme of lectures, and didn't. 'I certainly don't advise you to leave your native land, though I admit you'll want to if you go to Virginia. Naturally a prophet is never with honour in his own country: have you forgotten your Bible? If you are returning for Duchesses it isn't worth while,' etc. More banter.

In October 1955,

> Your book has come [this was *The Expansion of Elizabethan England*] and I am looking forward to reading it – particularly the part about Virginia. I am off to Cumberland to unveil a tablet to the memory of G. Washington's Grandmother. I ask you, your Duchess has asked me to dine tonight!

There follows more banter about falling for duchesses . . . In February 1956, from Hill Street: 'I went to Cliveden, but no word of you. I sent you a wire. I sail for USA Sat 25 as ever is – I wish you could go with me. Ring me up here. I go aboard *Queen Elizabeth* Friday night.' [I don't suppose I did, I so much hate telephoning.]

Virginia regarded her as a favourite daughter, and had her portrait painted for the Capitol in Richmond. I have seen Mirador, where she was born, standing up on its bluff above the road from Richmond going up to the beautiful Blue Ridge country, which Nancy cantered all over as a girl on her horse, a fearless rider to hounds. It was as a hunting-woman that her father sent her and her sister to England –

for a change after the disillusioning experience of her first marriage. Propositions, as well as proposals, came from the Edwardian gallants of the hunting field to a beautiful, unattached young woman, full of spirit and daring. They got precious little change out of her, except some pretty smart repartees, and she took time before making up her mind even to Waldorf, as virtuous as she. She disapproved of the 'fast set' of the Edwardian age, and gave no encouragement to Edward VII himself: he was not welcome at Cliveden. Once he turned up, she told me, with his escort of dubious ladies, and commented that he had not had the pleasure of a visit from her. He had a mania for cards, among other things; she wouldn't play, and is said to have said to the old *roué* that she couldn't even tell the difference between a king and a knave. I don't know whether that was authentic, but certainly no Virginian ever felt inferior to anybody.

She made Cliveden a great centre of Anglo-American *camaraderie*, and what a contribution that was to good fellowship. One met any number of people in public life from both sides of the Atlantic, ambassadors and admirals, cabinet ministers, politicians, writers. I cannot remember them all: charming and cultivated Frances Perkins, close friend of Franklin Roosevelt, the one woman member of his Cabinet; Governor Darden, with all that Virginian charm, who on ceasing to be governor, became President of Jefferson's University of Virginia; Herbert Agar and Leonard Brockington, Canadian publicist; Vincent Massey, to become Governor General of Canada; Mrs Vincent Astor, rather distant and grand, in pearls; genial and friendly Field-Marshal Slim. And always a wide spectrum of the British aristocracy, along with a sampling from politics; hardly any writers, publicists rather, such as Alan Moorhead; and even one artist, Stanley Spencer, diminutive as a cock robin, up from neighbouring Cookham.

The young historian watched it all as so much history unfolding, for the benefit of his education, from the sidelines or, rather, from a front seat in the stalls. For, as Nancy once said in her wobbly French, I was *'bien placé'*, usually next to her on her left-hand side. One certainly observed some funny scenes. She was a marvellous mimic, and could do Margot Oxford so convincingly, that one was reduced to helpless laughter – Lady Oxford with Nancy's boys at the theatre, wondering what they found so much to laugh at, unconscious that it was herself with a nose more like a limb than a feature and baring her teeth for the extraordinary things she would say, describing someone: 'She hasn't got a roof or a rafter to her mouth.'

If the table lagged for a moment, or things became too solemn, politics or whatnot, one looked round and there was Nancy, the anarchist, at the head of it with a false red nose, mimicking somebody else's way of talking. She could do the nasal accent, as if with a cold in the head, of the German 'royals' of the Edwardian royal family to perfection. No superfluous reverence, or conventional English flunkeyism, in that quarter.

Awkward moments occasionally occurred. She was giving a large tea-party for Paul Hoffman, the Administrator of European Relief, a key post after all the devastation of the war. It is a pity that, now that we know blacks are better than whites, only whites may be regarded as a subject of amusement, blacks not; while *Huckleberry Finn*, a work of genius, may be withdrawn from schools and libraries for its use of the term 'niggers' (not very nice) or even, affectionately, 'darkies'. Nancy adored the darkies she had been brought up with, loved them as they loved her, and she had a mass of good stories about them, could speak their lingo to perfection and sing their songs. Paul Hoffman was sitting beside her when she began on some of these imitations; Mrs Hoffman was sitting beside me, a do-gooder who, like many who have gone to the good, was without a sense of humour. I sensed her gorge rising, and felt her beginning to rise from her seat to do battle; I managed to restrain her with, 'Wait, you'll see he'll deal with her.' And, of course, he did. The golden rule was not to take too seriously whatever she said, at least place a large pair of inverted commas around it.

It was on that occasion that I took the opportunity to suggest to Paul Hoffman the desirability of an Anglo-American literary magazine to draw us together – out of which I rather think *Encounter* ultimately took shape. I may be wrong, but they wouldn't know about this *éminence grise*.

Sometimes things were more awkward – as with Nancy's broadside against Mrs Admiral Nimitz: 'Why did you allow your daughter to become a Roman Catholic nun?' That was not funny, and none of her business anyway. But Nancy was a past master at the quip direct, not sparing her own children, and that embarrassed them dreadfully. Once she attacked Bobby at table, in my presence, drawing the contrast with 'Look at what *he* has done,' meaning me. I wasn't going to have that. After lunch I took her aside – I can see her now standing above me on the stairs, holding her tiny wrists jangling with Astor jewelry – and said, 'Nancy, I won't hear a word against Bobby. All you can say is that he's a bit idle, and everybody ought to do a job of work. Bobby did his duty in the war, and you should be thankful they all survived,' etc. She took it like a lamb and, I think, was pleased at my standing up for him; for the trouble with Bobby was that he loved her and she him, perhaps too much.

She never once put her nose into my affairs, except to say innocently, 'What do you want to get married for? You don't want to get married – you are best off as you are.' Since I knew that already, and had no intention of getting married, it made me laugh; for it was just the line Elizabeth I used to take with *her* ladies-in-waiting.

Nancy had confidence in me, deserved or no – she certainly had in my taste. Once down in the Barbican at Plymouth we were looking into the window of an antique shop, in those days when they had antiques worth looking at – before they had been burgled or sold out of a run-down country, a dispiriting society. My eye was taken by a pair of pretty Victorian stools with seed-pearl decoration; while I hesitated Nancy was in like a shot, and beat me to the post. I thought that rather naughty of her; but it wasn't the only time that a gamesome lady has made up her mind by noticing what caught my eye. I shouldn't have hesitated.

I made it a principle with these grand ladies not to dine out at each other's expense. Plenty of them were malicious about Nancy – she wasn't malicious herself, though she could give as good as she got. I always stood up for her with others, and for the others too when their turn came. After all, I didn't need to dine out at anybody's expense; it was more fun standing up for people, carrying the game into the opponent's camp. Any fool can criticize – it is far more worth-while analysing a person's good qualities, and exposing those. More difficult too! – goodness, if I devoted my brains to criticizing, what could I not do, with my view of human beings (Swift's)?

I think this ultimately paid off: it won their confidence, and the historian who was a complete outsider learned a lot of things, without giving them his, or giving himself away. He knew all about them; they knew little about him. Nor did it matter: he was not one of them, for ever outside. The man on the margins of life sees most, and this was the right thing for a writer, at any rate for the kind of writer I was – never to be involved. Henry James said of the human aquarium that a writer should be half outside life, so as to be able to see what was going on, and half inside, enough to know what it was like. Most humans don't ever glimpse the aquarium, or realize that they are inside it. I sometimes vary the image and, as I watch their antics, think of them as my menagerie.

When poor George VI's reign was over and it came to Elizabeth II's coronation (I was rather sorry that that sacred name was to have a second innings), I had the job of reporting it for the *Western Morning News*. This paper had treated me outrageously as a candidate during the appalling election of 1931, which led to a disastrous decade under the 'National' Government. (Pure humbug, of course: a frame-up against Labour. They have paid for it since.) However, it was my one way of seeing a coronation – I should not have been invited otherwise, unlike the Sitwells and Willie Walton whom I was enskied amongst, up in the north transept of Westminster Abbey. London was full up – nowhere to stay so as to get up at 5.30 a.m. and present myself in my best fettle, doctoral scarlet and all. Nancy came to the rescue and got Bill to put me up; with whom, resplendent in his peer's robes, I duly sallied forth and all was well.

What ever could I do for her to show my appreciation of

her – no possibility of return for her constant kindness? Well, I could at least dedicate a book to her – not even Shaw had done that, though he wrote *The Apple Cart* mostly at Cliveden. I thought my Trevelyan Lectures on *The Elizabethans and America* a suitable offering, with its theme that English-speaking America went back beyond the dreary Pilgrim Fathers (G. K. Chesterton: 'The Pilgrim Fathers landed on Plymouth Rock: would that Plymouth Rock had landed on the Pilgrim Fathers!') to Virginia, beyond Jamestown to Ralegh's colonial enterprise, backed by Elizabeth I. In fact, English-speaking America, along with the Shakepearean drama, was the greatest creation of the Elizabethan Age. I don't know whether Nancy appreciated the dedication to her two chief loves, Virginia and Plymouth; I'm pretty sure she didn't read the book.

What was a weekend at Cliveden like? Of several accounts in my Journals I choose one of the most interesting for readers next century – in case no one else has taken the trouble to write them up.

Mid December 1952. 'I missed Nuffield lunching there, though Nancy insisted I should come over in time; for I had already promised dear Geoffrey Hudson and didn't want to let him down . . . Arrived late at Cliveden, I was flung into the middle of the large round tea-table – Nancy Mitford's image occurred to me, the flock of starlings all rising up to settle on the newcomer. Menzies, Prime Minister of Australia, and his pretty daughter were there, and Field-Marshal Slim just going out as Governor General; Bob Brand, Bill Astor and Nancy herself, looking like a girl, elegant in black, jangling the jewelry on tiny wrists. Another very noticeable woman whom I couldn't make out had been a close former friend of the Duke of Windsor, now disguised as an Italian Marchesa, flashing brilliant green ear-rings.

'Slim turned out a largish, square-shouldered, pleasant, very masculine type – and full of himself: in the manner of these strong silent soldiers, very loquacious. Not a public-school man, but from King Edward's Birmingham: he talked across the wide space of that table mostly at, or to, me.

Conversation pitched on me at once. Did I know A. J. P. Taylor, whom they had seen and heard on TV? (Indeed, only too well, from his undergraduate days.) From that to the Leftist intellectuals and their influence. I said that business magnates paid no attention to literature and writing; for example, their next door neighbour at Dropmore, Kemsley, had the literary pages of his *Sunday Times* written by *New Statesman* types, and was probably unaware of it. They thought these things didn't matter, and were surprised when the young people at the universities turned out Leftists. From that to the intellectuals in general and the BBC. Brand is on its advisory council, but couldn't find out who appointed people to give the talks – it was done much lower down, invisibly from the heights of high policy.

'Slim, pleased with himself but equally impressive and likeable, thought Western propaganda misconceived in always attacking Communism as such – particularly American propaganda, for reasons of internal American politics. This had the effect of aligning the Iron Curtain countries, and China, with Soviet Russia – stressing their one common bond. Our line should be directed against Russia as such, attacking Russia's interference with their internal affairs, running *their* countries.

'I said that this was not only right in itself but in line with the profoundest force we had with us – the desire of peoples to run their own affairs their own way. If this could be elicited and canalized, it would eventually win. But we mustn't neglect to frame Communism for the malign thing it is – witness the Prague Trials and the sickening effect they had on some English Communists, e.g. the composer Arthur Benjamin leaving them. The wonder was that anybody stuck.[1]

'Towards dinner the party filled out. Mary, Duchess of Devonshire came down looking infinitely distinguished in black dress, rather short, but with long Spanish-looking fringes. Everybody says that she is the most modest of people, simple and good and kind; but I find such sensibility

---

[1] It was not until Hungary and Krushchev's revelations of Stalin's crimes that many became unstuck.

and distinction rather paralysing, so I never attempt to talk
to her. Besides, she has been through a great deal in late years
– I remember *how* she looked last time at Cliveden after her
husband's death. This time she said to me she was much
better, with that impulsive Cecilian girlishness: I saw how
irresistible she was, and observed her at night go up the staircase alone, a wonderful, rather sad, figure.

'Menzies made a friendly, cheerful impression, also well
pleased with himself in the manner of the ordinary male animal. Much more at ease in Zion than fifteen years or so ago
when he came to All Souls with Dick Latham. Ambition
now satisfied, he was more relaxed, fatter, eupeptic, complexion positively blooming. "The trouble with me," he said
to the observant young historian, "is that I'm a very bad
butcher. Gladstone said that, to be any good as a Prime Minister, you have to be a good butcher. I just can't do it: I
haven't the heart. The result is that I let a lot of chaps go on
when they are past it." The historian registered the way of
commending oneself by running oneself down, commented
on by La Rochefoucauld, Swift, and other cynical observers
of mankind.

'He realizes, rather pathetically, that it is his obvious ability that has always stood in the way of his being popular with
Australians. Similarly, Smuts's trouble in South Africa –
"Slim Janny" – a great man. So Menzies has to bring up his
heart for the benefit of the dear people. Now I should say
that, in spite of his ability, he probably has a good heart. He
is touchingly proud of his daughter – like her father, very
good-looking. The girl fell asleep and didn't come down in
time for dinner. Nancy was in favour of letting her sleep.
"No, let her get up," said her stern parent; and when she
appeared in pretty frock and I remarked on her charm –
"No," said father fondly, "I rather like looking at her
myself."

'They had naturally been at the Buckingham Palace party,
and the PM had to tell me the latest Winston story. The
Prime Minister of Pakistan is a teetotaller, as a Muslim; when
drinks came round after dinner and he rejected them all,
Winston said, "What, Mr Prime Minister, you don't drink?"

On his affirming no, Winston said, "Christ! – I mean God! – I mean Allah!" Tommy Lascelles thought the footman would have dropped the tray.

'At dinner I was placed beside Joan Hammond – Nancy never told me who she was. When I tumbled to it, we got on like anything, and we spent most of the evening together: luscious, glittering look of an Italian *prima donna*, black wave of hair, collusive smile, pretty mole on cheek. After dinner we chummed up in the library with Bill Astor and Leonard Brockington – asthmatic, hunch-backed, ginger-grizzled hair, close-fitting gold-rimmed spectacles, endlessly cigar-smoking; clever, humorous, benevolent, full of stories – too many. Canadian friend of Lionel Curtis and all the Round Table group. Like all such lonely men who can't sleep, he wanted me to stay up talking with him. But I had arrived fagged out, almost faint with fatigue over proofs, several nights up to 1 a.m. at them; never have I arrived at Cliveden so flagging.

'We had a pleasant evening in our little group, jokes, stories, giggles – the *prima donna* beaming down from behind the glittering armour of her Brunhilde corsage. I didn't know Bill was so interested in music or moves in these circles, and goes to Aldeburgh (on B.B., "Oh, he's a happy little fairy"). He had had a chamber orchestra giving a concert in his house to celebrate his baby's christening. I was happy to see him so cheerful and gay – after the melancholy appearance he has been making since his wife walked out on him . . . He is a good host, with kind, affable manners. Joan Hammond is a *dévote* of Beecham, to her no conductor like him. Bill told us about "Rule, Britannia" having been first sung in the little open-air theatre in the grounds here, at the end of the first act of Thomson's *Masque of Liberty*. (I suppose that a piece of Frederick, Prince of Wales's nonsense directed against his father, George II.)

'At the end of the evening when Joan was leaving, Nancy said to the assembled group, "This girl can fill the Albert Hall any time: that's more than you can do!" Menzies was taken aback, quite nettled by this *boutade*; and instead of tak-ing it in good part stumbled rather clumsily with, "Oh, well

– we can do other things perhaps." Nobody seemed to notice the comedy; I was rather amused.

'One elderly dame appeared in what looked like a bath-robe plus a solitary rose at her waist. Little did I realize that she was to be my buddy through the weekend. But she was a Cornish Vivian from Glyn; beneath white hair, dark, coal-glowing eyes, full of intelligence and vivacity. She had married into the Yarborough family, grand Brocklesby, which I visited a year or two ago to see a portrait of the Elizabethan soldier, Sir William Pelham. The usual story – two lots of death-duties had reduced that vast estate to something quite small. Now the case of someone just managing to hang on by cheese-paring and prudent land-management, the house much reduced.

'So unlike the state of things at Glyn, where her nephew, the dance-band leader, made no effort. Result – that beautiful estate in the most romantic of valleys is in the hands of the estate-breaker. [This man lived on the opposite side of the road to me at home, in a hideous villa called Soulsbyville – I thought of calling my place All Soulsbyville. He recouped the price of the place simply by cutting trees – couldn't the dance-band peer have done as much? I would have done, if only it had come to me.]

'After breakfast we walked out, December mildness in the air, peacock-blue sky, sun up. Down the glen we went to the river, church bells ringing across the suburbanized Thames countryside. We got on easily like two Cornish folk in a foreign land. She had spent much of her childhood abroad, though refusing to learn languages out of exaggerated patriotism. I saw something masculine in this descendant of dashing Hussey Vivian, Wellington's cavalry leader, Waterloo and all, who made a fortune out of soldiering and bought Glyn from the Glyns, who had gambled their patrimony away. Now – the Vivians in turn make way – what will become of the lovely place?

'Her life-story simple, husband killed in the first German war, no children. We talked about the responsibilities of governments and parties before the second war. These people of the governing class are uneasy on the subject – as well they might be. One and all, they defend themselves; some of them, like Nancy, blame the Labour Party. (Of course, they were idiots to oppose rearmament, when the Germans were working all hours to rearm; but Labour was kept in a small minority, theirs a secondary responsibility.) These people realize that their record in the twenties and thirties – when they had everything their own way – needs defending. She had rushed to the defence of Edward Halifax, when someone called him a collaborator. (He was not that, but he was in favour of compromise with Hitler.)

'She made a sensible claim for her own line: "I had neither husband nor son, nobody to lose, but I should feel all the more blameworthy if I didn't do all I could to support peace." I recognized the Chamberlain line, and said – unfortunately we learn from history and experience that to make concessions to thugs and criminals is the very way to bring war down upon us. And I did not fail to make the point on behalf of my own people that Labour, when in power, had done better in standing up to Communist Russia than the Conservatives had to Nazi Germany. A sensible, honest woman, she at once admitted it, and spoke with real appreciation of Attlee and Bevin. A lady-in-waiting to the Queen Mother, she is above the humbug of party allegiances.

'Coming back along the river, we paused on that delicious eighteenth-century Italian bridge with steps down to the water's edge, a stream made for it to arch over. Michael Astor told me a lot about his grandfather, my picture of him as a buccaneer coming over from the jungle of American politics evidently quite wrong. A much stranger and more complex, unhappy, solitary man, thwarted in his ambition to become a US Senator, left New York for Europe, was Minister in Rome for a bit. Whence he picked up the terrace of the Borghese Villa and placed it admirably at Cliveden, with the Giovanni da Bologna fountain to terminate the vista. A connoisseur – hence too the French Renaissance chimney piece in the hall, the dining-room panelling from the Pompadour's Château d'Asnières, the Louis XV portraits of the French royal family in the small drawing-room. Michael told me a great deal about the strange personality of this remarkable man, walled up in himself after the early death of his wife.[2]

'Sunday afternoon a shorter walk around the grounds with Bill, Miss Menzies and the American Rear-Admiral (who spoke so long at the Berger Lunch that I had to cut my speech down to five minutes). We did a round of the temples – the Leoni temple has been made a family mausoleum, where Waldorf is buried. Another was built by Lord Orkney, Marlborough's cavalry-general; his clever screw-eyed wife was William III's mistress and Swift's friend. After them came Frederick Prince of Wales –

> Here lies poor Fred,
> Who was alive and is dead . . .
> Since it's only Fred,
> There's no more to be said.

Next came the Sutherlands, who called in Barry to build the present house, 1851; then the Westminsters from whom the first Lord Astor bought it. I suggested to Bill that he write up the history of Cliveden; it could make an interesting book, based on proper research, going into all the associations, and embellishments. Bill was unenthusiastic: "I am much too idle," he said; and unfortunately I believe him.

'Before dinner the household was keyed up and unusual preparations were evidently being made: the Queen Mother and Princess Margaret were coming to dinner. "I have given you a very good place," said Nancy to me – only two away, between the Marchesa and charming Pam Ruthven, whom I had met several times with the Gowries. Last time I read the poignant book about her husband, their only child, killed in the war, based on his letters from childhood up. How touching – simple and courageous and loving, heart-breaking for the old couple; gallant old war-horses, both of them.

'When we joined the ladies in the library after dinner, Princess Margaret was ensconced in the sofa by the fire. I made no effort to talk to her, considering myself much too old to

[2] Since he has written all this up in his admirable *Tribal Feeling*, I omit the account in my Journals.

interest a young girl: I left her to Bill, then to Michael, then to A. P. Jones's brother, a Korda young man. I devoted myself to the Marchesa, an interesting study. Twice she said, "If you had a wonderful time when you were young – what is called a mis-spent youth . . . when you get older you find life disappointing, things pall." I said, if you had had a great deal of illness all the years of your youth, you would be grateful for life when you got older: I have never been so happy as since I was forty: I enjoy being middle-aged.

'She was obviously *mécontente*, perhaps I should say *malcontenta* . . . She was still somebody to be looked at – not to talk to, but to study. I studied her. She carped at the party, at the royal family. She thought they should do without all this formality (her own contact had been on a less formal level) – why can't they be more matey? I said that the People would be disappointed: since they paid out all the money to keep the thing up, they expected something different for their money. Mrs Jones of the Surbiton Conservative Ladies adored going down on her creaking old knees and would feel cheated not to be able to do it. Besides life was so monochrome and boring for ordinary people, wasn't it a good thing to have something *different* in the plum pudding of society?

'The Marchesa, herself a Conservative, couldn't deal with this one, and fell back on – "But need it be so stiff and silly? Look at it!" I looked: the Queen Mother was seated at the other end of the library, across an acre of parquet flooring – which Bill means to cover with a savonnerie rug. I turned round: there she was sitting upright in her regal chair, talking one by one to the person presented to her. "But *they* insist on keeping it up: they shouldn't insist on it: they should give it up." (I suppose this was the Duke of Windsor's line, and he had certainly given up.) I conceded that it did make people shy and nervous. "Well, of course: look how ridiculously they are all behaving, just because *they* are here."

'I looked: a charade was going on – not very successfully – Nancy and most of the others were seated in a ring on the floor, she and her nephew, Reggie Wynne, making fantastic noises. "How ridiculous of them," said the Marchesa, "all sitting on the floor, because *they* are here. Nancy is a nervous hostess. What is the point of it? It's ridiculous." It was a bit absurd; but why take against it? I was amused – and I never thought Nancy a nervous hostess: quite the contrary.

'The charade broke up and I was next to be summoned to the Presence. I gave the Marchesa an incriminating glance – not too obvious a one: even so it was intercepted by the Princess Margaret, on whom nothing is lost, sharp little girl. Reggie Wynne was hanging over the QM's chair: I waited till he had gone, I wasn't going to have a conversation *à trois* with him. The QM, looking more beautiful than I have ever seen her, was resplendent in an enormous crinoline, black velvet, black silk (I thought of Queen Elizabeth I's dresses in her Account Book in the British Museum – black velvet, puffed sleeves slashed with ivory satin – in the 1570s); three rows of huge pearls, a diamond ornament in (Balzac's) *place la plus mignonne*, diamond ear-rings dangling. All like something out of the Victorian Age, Queen Victoria again.

'We took up the conversation where we had dropped it at the tea-table at Lambeth – as the QM said to Nancy we always did. Nancy disappeared. I asked about the Castle o' Mey she had recently acquired at the furthermost tip of Scotland, and said that if she moved any further away from her loving subjects she would find herself right off the island. She laughed, "Perhaps it was all a mistake." I said, "Yes, if they ran Sunday buses from neighbouring towns to have a look." "They won't see much," she said; it was the nearest thing to going abroad, now that it was so difficult to go abroad. Very like Norway. I said she ought to be able to go abroad more – she said that it meant about eleven persons going, all told. Couldn't she go incognita? She said that once when the King was Duke of York they had gone to Belgium as Earl and Countess of Inverness. But it wasn't any good: everybody behaved very well, but they looked . . . She made a pretty *mou*, from which it was clear that she rather enjoyed recognition.

'I talked about Spain, and that she would enjoy the Escorial: her security would be looked after now, or Alba would look after her and show her everything. (I forgot that that would be impossible for political reasons.) We talked a little

about the King. I said that history would record how much
he owed to her and all she had done for him. "Oh, no. I did
nothing – except that I was his loving wife. It was he that had
the character. He made the decisions – I think he made the
right decisions." I said I hoped that he knew the great feeling
his people had for him – though people can't express it very
well to a man: they can more easily to a woman. She said that
there wasn't time for that (as there had been for George V;
so the son died without realizing how much people felt for
him). First, there was the Abdication, and all the trouble that
gave rise to. (The historian reflected to himself on the ironies
of history, with the Marchesa in the offing – but she had not
been responsible for it.) Then came the war, and after that
there was never any time . . .

'We talked of the social revolution that had taken place –
she said that it had been led from the top. Certainly those
two had worked hard enough . . . "I am rather a revolutionary," she said, eyes smiling, those most expressive eyes,
sometimes the suggestion of tears in them. "Ah, *la belle révo-
lutionnaire*," I thought, but did not dare to say. What I said
was, "I thought you were a Jacobite, not a Jacobin." "Oh,
yes, a Jacobite and a Jacobin too," she said gaily; "it doesn't
prevent me from being a revolutionary." I said that the English social revolution meant that a Prime Minister who was
an Old Harrovian (Winston) was succeeded by a Prime
Minister who was an Old Haileyburian (Clem Attlee).

'We were certainly having fun, Nancy now hovering to
give someone else a chance, quite rightly. The Queen said,
with more than *politesse*, "Oh, but we were *just* beginning to
have a real talk." "I'll go away," said Nancy, "don't let me
interrupt." But I had had more than my fair share, and was
going to make way. Nancy whispered, "I'll get him to come
to a party in London." Will it, I wonder, eventuate? Bob
Brand took my place; I saw the elderly peer, with the frosty,
rimless-spectacled banker's appearance, settle shyly into my
chair.

'Was the Marchesa right after all? For, not long after, the
Queen Mother gave the signal: the formal circle gathered
once more, as on her entry, and we all bowed and scraped, or

curtsied. Arrived at the other end of the circle, she stopped specially to have a few words with the Marchesa, David's former friend, not forgotten. That was nice of her, considerate and thoughtful as always. Did the Marchesa appreciate it? The irony of the encounter was not lost upon the observant historian nor how prettily the *convenances* were kept. What memories, it flashed across my mind, those two women could exchange!'

Nancy was as good as her word: I take from my Journals the account of the party she gave in London for various literary people to be presented to the Queen Mother.

'Nancy had asked me to recommend some, and I sent her a list with John Betjeman, Arthur Bryant, Carola Oman and Veronica Wedgwood, among others. Very few writers had she asked, it was more like a journalists' party, with editors of *The Times*, *Observer*, *Sunday Times*, *Literary Supplement*, etc. I arrived early in case she wanted help with writers like Veronica and Carola whom she didn't know; but she had not asked them.

'All the Astors were there in force, though they must have plenty of opportunity of meeting the QM – Bill (without wife), David (with new wife), Jakey, Michael (no doubt *with* wife), Bob Brand, Nancy Lancaster without either husband but wonderfully dressed: her vibrant sexy figure appearing out of a sea-foam of white-pearl-grey tulle, another Venus with resplendent pearls and rubies. Nancy A. herself equally impressive in black velvet with long train and a superb jewel looking like a three-tiered Boadicea's buckler. (What it is to be an Astor!)

'The house was looking lovely – never such flowers in the depth of December, cyclamen, African violets, orchids; pictures rich against the background of a savonnerie carpet, honey colour, dark browns, rose-red flower-festoons. Nancy however, complained that this [Hill Street] wasn't the same thing as at St James's Square, where all you had to do was to give orders and the whole thing was done.

'We were not a large party for dinner. The QM was rather late as usual, I suppose *pour faire impression*, so we were caught in some disarray. We had been standing up waiting; then we sat down; *then* she appeared, with Nancy at the door saying, in her serjeant-major's voice, "Get up, all of you." Curious that with all her looks and experience, she doesn't bother about dignity – perhaps the American allergy to dignity, as in their public life. [I have seen Nancy at a garden-party on the lawn at Cliveden doing her Barbican fish-wife's turn to the crowd, the QM only a few paces away trying to appear oblivious of the indignity.]

'The QM looked girlish as ever, fresh as a flower. The presentations began the other end of the half-circle and finished with me; she seemed pleased, but stopped, not thinking of anything to say. So I stepped in with some gallant nonsense about how fine it was, driving through gloomy December London, to see her flag flying over Clarence House – she was "keeping the flag flying", the only one to be seen. This closed the gap – it must be so boring for the royal family that people are so petrified on meeting them that there is nothing to say. She responded at once with the girlish enthusiasm that is so effective, "Oh, everybody ought to have a flag: there should be flags all over London."

'Arthur Bryant's wife, Anne, in a terrible state of nerves, was agog to know what I had found to talk about. Nothing much.

'The dinner, as always with Nancy, was first-rate, though the QM declined soup, with an eye to her figure, I registered. None but the Astors can have such a chef – I don't suppose the royal family has, though I don't know, for I haven't eaten their food. After dinner in came the party, among the first Harry Hodson (my first election when examining for the Fellowship at All Souls) – evidently embarrassed and excusing himself for the nasty photograph of me and malicious comment the *Sunday Times* had published – the usual literary animus. I took the opportunity to make the point that what Arthur Bryant and I have to say was far more in keeping with the readers of the *Sunday Times* than anything their recruits from the *New Statesman*, Mortimer and Connolly, have to say. "I dare say," he stammered, "but that is – that is a matter of policy" – which gave the game away.

'Next tripped in David Cecil and bright-eyed Rachel, followed by Harold Nicolson. I don't speak to him, after his shocking review of *The English Past* in *The Observer*. This is what humans are like – I have always been nothing but kind to his son and his nephew at Oxford. I know as well as the next man that one is supposed to take no notice, but I wrote in to protest; I always do react. After all, I don't want to know people – I am here only as an observer, watching the fish in the aquarium gawping and gaping. Just like Henry James, a *voyeur*, uncommitted, an outsider, inassimilable.

'Then came the dear Betjemans, much more congenial, whom I had suggested to Nancy: Penelope bringing her air of a country farmyard into this metropolitan atmosphere, John in the usual disarray, looking like a clergyman who had lost his way. I propelled him forward to the little formal circle in the inner drawing room where the QM was holding her levee – it was more like the doctor's waiting-room where we awaited our turn in the outer room.

'Nancy called me up along with A. P. Jones of the *Lit. Sup*. There couldn't have been a worse choice: he so sophisticated, so "cultivated", as John said, it made me shy and awkward. He was very much at his ease; I would have done better by myself. It was frightfully hot, with Nancy's American standards of central heating; the QM was occasionally reduced to lifting one of the enormous emeralds sticking to her. We talked away about Disraeli, and Harold Macmillan's having something of his forward-looking quality. (I did not mention other things.) I uttered some nonsense about too many houses being put up everywhere, spoiling the countryside; the QM protested, with an understanding smile, "O, *not enough* houses!" She had evidently learnt her lesson well: no mistakes in that quarter.

'Mrs A. P. Jones chipped in dexterously about her daughter's tour in the South Seas. Had I read Herman Melville? No, I had not. This gave the QM an opportunity to score, and she promised to send me *Omoo* and *Typee*. Fancy her remembering! Shortly after Christmas there arrived a little parcel, addressed in her own clear hand, along with a grand coloured photograph of herself and Margaret in their coronation robes. Autographed too – all very well conceived: she had done her bit for the monarchy.'

And what of Waldorf?

Quiet and reserved, shy and content to sit back while Nancy performed, his rôle was far more important than people suspected. He was the real ruler, not Nancy. At times she behaved like a naughty girl, and pestered and bounced him into things. He was doubtful about some philanthropic project of hers – I forget what – and dragging his feet, when she said, 'If he doesn't do it, I'll sell all my pearls.' I don't know how often she used that threat, but it is not impossible that she might have carried it out.

It happens that she has occasionally asked me to stay on when the large weekend party had gone, and then one could see the terms of mutual understanding between them, the long dining-room table contracted for the three of us, a simple teetotal meal that suited this perpetual member of the Duodenal Club. Waldorf adored her good qualities, realized all that he owed to her for releasing him from the shadow of his father's presence, the endemic family shyness that held up communication with the outside world. Her dynamism was indispensable to him, a precious element in his own life; they had created a wonderful life together, and accomplished what neither of them could have done without the other. A selfless man, a good deal of a saint, Waldorf put up with a lot; but, in the last resort, he had the last word, the withdrawn presence ruled. It wasn't only that he held the reins of this very flighty mare, but he provided the steady element in her life that prevented her from going too far – to mix the metaphor, and frankly, from going off the rails. An educated man, of an achieved spirit, he set the standards, and she knew it.

Nancy was a democrat – I was not; Waldorf had a pathetic belief in the principles of democracy – I had not. No aesthete can be a democrat; I was about as much of a democrat as Proust was – or, for that matter, Karl Marx or Lenin (perhaps a bit more than the latter). If anyone wonders then why I was a Labour man – it was that I was desperately anti-Baldwin and Chamberlain; I may add that they had the great heart of the democracy with them. (And how I hated the fatuous people for that, allowing themselves to be so bamboozled. I suppose now I was in revolt simply against *la condition humaine*.)

Waldorf and Nancy were too independent and liberal-minded to be hardened partisans: reliable enough members of the Conservative Party, they were certainly not Tories. I think that, during the second war, Waldorf was glad to escape party controversy and operate as a genuine Independent, as Lord Mayor of Plymouth. He held that office all through the war, something like a German burgomaster – such as Adenauer was in Cologne; he worked night and day for the city, trying to find housing for the people whose homes were shattered, and planning to build up again, as Nancy had promised with the city in flames before her eyes. This exceptional span of office enabled Waldorf to plan well for Plymouth: it was owing to him that Plymouth was first in the field with Abercrombie's scheme for replanning and rebuilding the city as we see it today. For all Waldorf's good work, the Conservative caucus hoofed him out before the job was finished, and installed an old war-horse of the caucus as Lord Mayor in his place.

I never heard a word of resentment from Waldorf – but judge if he was just a party-man.

The election of 1945 was to visit upon the Conservatives retribution for their record over the past twenty years. As Lord Boothby admits in his memoirs, they were governed throughout by their own economic and class interest. So, when the election of 1945 initiated a social revolution, they had only themselves to blame. Waldorf plainly had no such narrow views, though he had more to lose than almost anyone. He saw, however, that it was time to withdraw Nancy from Parliament; her day, her contribution, was really over.

Waldorf was right, but Nancy was both furious and miserable. She fought hard against the decision; she argued that, if she had been allowed to fight her seat again, it would not have been lost to Labour. That may have been so; but Waldorf did not want to expose her to defeat, or indeed allow her to expose herself any more. She had fought seven elections, and never once been defeated. (I found it intolerable that the Conservatives were in power virtually in permanence between the wars: they alone bear the responsibility for what happened to the country.)

Nancy's fighting spirit took the form of a line against the Astors – this was unreasonable of her, but reason was never her strong point. If only she could have taken to reading, developing the inner resources of the mind – with that, one is no longer dependent on outer circumstances or other people. She was like other women of natural ability but uneducated – she had not the resources to fall back upon. 'Oh dear, I should never have believed that I should miss the House of Commons so much.' The limelight had become a drug she could not do without.

Waldorf was happy to retire and withdraw from the conflicts and bitternesses of politics. He had had a heart-attack, and lived quietly to himself in a ground-floor suite giving on to the terrace, whence he could propel himself about the grounds in his electric chair. They took all the care he could give them. One post-war weekend when the house was full of guests, the place was visited by expert lead-thieves who rolled all the lead off the roof of a garden-temple: portent of the Brave New World, the society we enjoy with the people, on every hand, out of hand. The last time I saw the dear good man, frail in his chair, we were alone with Frances Perkins; he turned to each of us, with tears in his eyes, 'What am I to do with Nancy?' There was nothing either of us could suggest.

She went on grieving for the House of Commons. Almost the last time I saw her she told me that, sitting beside Winston at dinner the night before, he had said, 'Nancy, we very much miss you in the House.' The old couple who had sparred there so often – Winston could not bear being interrupted – had at length made it up, in view of the end, having experienced so much, been in so many fights.

Sometimes Nancy regretted Bill having taken her place at Cliveden. 'The Astors have no taste.' This was not true of the younger generation: Bill much improved Cliveden with exquisite French eighteenth-century furniture, savonnerie carpets laid upon the creaking parquet floor of the library, his own collection of water-colours upstairs, and resurrecting the rare books his grandfather had collected from a closet where they had been put away out of view. Sometimes she wished she had taken over beautiful Bletchingdon when he left it, within easy distance from Oxford, whence she could have drawn a salon. In the end she spent a good deal of time not far away, with her niece, Nancy Lancaster, in the exquisite house with topiary garden she brought to perfection, out at Great Haseley.

'It was here that I saw her the last time. There was smart company, and I much wanted to see what her niece had done to make the house so ravishing, since I first saw it with her when derelict from the war. Actually I spent the greater part of the time with dear Nancy – worth all of them. It was nice to talk to her in a quiet mood, no public turn at all – come back to the country girl she had once been. She was sad, worried about the country and what is going to happen to us (as we all are), and about Bill's matrimonial troubles. [We need not go into those, as she did, the intolerable joys of family life.] Nancy wanted to talk to me so much that I hadn't much opportunity to see the house. It tantalized my imagination the more. *Such* taste, such flair as Nancy Lancaster has got . . . I have never seen such candelabra and girandoles, Italian coloured glass, the whole place winking in pale misty winter sun across level fields, glittering in the coloured glass like raindrops.

'Nancy A. took me into the high saloon occupying two storeys of the east front looking out on the topiary chessmen. Her niece had decorated it herself, pale blues and pearl greys, ovals and garlanded Adam wreaths in the high coved ceiling, long slim Chippendale mirrors and Chinese silk curtains from Ditchley. The house has possessed my mind.' Nancy came to occupy the most splendid room upstairs, the Chapel room, with fine canopied bed in the middle.

She was very much lost, withdrawn from her world of politics, Westminster and Plymouth. 'Why don't you marry her?' said Nancy L. 'It could be a *marriage blanche*.' 'I don't see why it should be a *marriage blanche*,' I said, to her amusement. She knew very well that, like Arthur Balfour when someone thought he might marry Margot (who ruined Asquith, or at any rate weakened his fibre), I rather fancied a career for myself.

And now they have both gone, Waldorf and Nancy, from Cliveden, the great days over. I have never been there since, the place too full of ghosts: Nancy coming out from her boudoir to galvanize a party of inert menfolk in their capacious red seats in the hall; or appearing on the terrace, a bunch of grapes in hand for breakfast; or suddenly boasting, 'I haven't a hair on my body.' (She didn't invite me to inspect – if I were to lay a hand on her, 'I'd kick you in the belly.' I'll bet she was as beautiful and chaste a figure as a marble Diana.) She could still turn cartwheels at seventy. Or Nancy in London, going to the theatre with her and her friends, the King and Queen of Sweden; or meeting at Cliveden, Queen Margarethe of Denmark with the beautiful eyes.

Or I see her on the rounds we did at Plymouth, over to Mount Edgcumbe, to Admiralty House at Devonport, or out to Buckland Abbey, which Drake bought with the money he made from the Voyage round the World – which was then being refitted as a museum after the fire – with Nancy wondering why her car wouldn't start up the hill, having forgotten about the gears.

Frequently as I go to Plymouth, I never go there without thinking of her. The centre of the new city – Armada Way and the rest of it – we owe to Waldorf. Still, without her, somehow the spirit is missing from the place; the vivacity, the magic of her presence gone.

One Sunday after the war, I went into St Andrew's, roofless and gutted, the church-bells ringing, a garden growing in the empty interior. I was reduced to tears by the scene, the destruction, to think of all we had been through, church-bells ringing to empty space. Since then St Andrew's has been restored, more beautiful than before, a splendid west window in the tower, to Waldorf's memory: designed by John Piper, a work of art.

Today I still sometimes take shelter from the noise of traffic in the new Plymouth, in St Andrew's, and there in the quiet of the church remember Nancy and Waldorf and all the good they did, there by myself, alone.

3

Agatha Christie

So much has been written about Agatha Christie, besides what she wrote herself − getting on for a hundred books when one includes her plays and half-a-dozen straight novels under the name of 'Mary Westmacott' − that I must concentrate on my friendship with her and Max Mallowan, her husband. In any case I am not a detective story addict: I knew Agatha as a person before I ever read one of her detective stories. She knew that I was not a reader of hers − which put our friendship on a different footing from the beginning. Most people thought of her only in relation to her detective stories − 'Queen of Crime', 'First Lady of Crime', etc.; quite a number of her friends were professionals, publishers or theatre people. It was only slowly and gradually that I came to read any of her books.

So I am not going to write about them, but about her and Max. All the same − Agatha wrote me a warm and encouraging letter about my Shakespeare discoveries. 'From the mistress of low-brow detection to the master of high-brow detection' − so the discoverer of Shakespeare's Dark Lady could, if called upon, sleuth the trail of Agatha and her own story in her work. Max is quite right in saying that, for all her personal reserve, an impenetrable armour, she reveals herself fully in her books. All writers do, after all; but it is rather fun following up the clues to herself strewn across her work.

But I had another clue to the crux in her life, the near-tragedy of the breakdown of her first marriage, which was so important, abnormally so – to so sensitive and vulnerable a nature, with old-fashioned religious standards. It may be said to have shaped her subsequent life; it was always there in the background. Nothing was ever said about it, it had wounded her so deeply, and well nigh cost her her life. I never knew if she knew that I knew; in their last years Max realized that I was aware of it, though of how much he did not know. I had learned the story from an old friend of Agatha's – married to a Cornishman – who had known them before ever Max came on the scene.

In the end it worked out happily, though it might so easily not have done – and very narrowly did not.

All that the world knew was that Agatha Christie disappeared, and was lost for a matter of ten or twelve days. This was in the twenties, when it was possible to disappear – not so easy today. I remember the papers being full of the hue and cry – 'Disappearance of Agatha Christie', her abandoned car found, a shoe and scarf found on the Downs; an organized search for her, photographs of how she might have disguised herself, how she was to be recognized, age thirty-five, etc. Hundreds and thousands of people joined in the search. She was eventually recognized staying in a quiet hotel in Harrogate, suffering from complete loss of memory. When brought back to London by her husband, crowds gathered at King's Cross to greet the train.

After that, as a detective story writer, she never looked back. She jumped to first place, and held it for the rest of her life.

Most people thought that it had been a stunt, and she was acting out one of her own mysteries. But it was far more serious than that. As an historian, and the discoverer of Shakespeare's secret, I know that the truth about people, if only one can find it, is far more interesting than third-rate conjectures about it; and an experience such as she had undergone is far more powerful for being authentic and true, than any put-up job.

It was Max who reconciled her to life, their marriage and mutual love that readjusted her and gave her happiness. But the mark remained; such a wound never heals.

I never knew them until Max was elected a Research Fellow, in archaeology, at All Souls and for some time took little note of them. They were away a good deal in Mesopotamia, Max making his wonderful finds of ivories at Nimrud, about which he produced a superb book a few years later. Each winter I was away in California researching and writing, with a couple of months in Cornwall.

Coming back to All Souls for summer term I used to have a large lunch-party, occasionally filling the long table in the Hall, to mingle Anglo-American friends. To one of these I invited Max and Agatha, along with her West Country publisher, Allen Lane, creator of Penguins. I remember the extraordinary hat she had bought for the occasion, a large, floppy black shiny affair that looked like an eighteenth-century parson's shovel hat. I had no chance of talking to her, with so many guests on my hands, devotees of hers like Christobel Aberconway, Geoffrey Harmsworth, Jack Simmons, all anxious to meet her.

But I remember Max later on telling me something of her publishing experience. A Devon girl herself, she had gone to a Devonian publisher, canny John Lane, who gave her £25 for her first book! (One remembers his extraordinary meanness with poor Corvo, and Corvo's curses.) The nephew Allen Lane became a friend as well as publisher, with a castle in Spain, having made a million. All the same . . . said Max.

From Agatha I received my first letter in her own hand, large and clear – she had old-fashioned courtesy and good manners, very much a lady; for all her being the world's bestseller, nothing vulgar about her – retiring and modest. What a contrast to best-sellers today! She actually avoided publicity all she could, never gave an interview or made a speech, let alone appeared on TV. She was an old-world lady – and, for the rest, her fearful experience in the twenties, hounded by the press, made her keep it at arm's length ever after. 'We did enjoy your luncheon party so much,' she wrote. 'Too bad Max had to forgo the very pleasant coffee drinking and sitting about in chairs, which really was delightful, and how glorious to be able to sit.' We used to sit out on the terrace between the twin towers, the most splendid scene in Oxford, like a stage-set before us, the majesty of Gibbs's dome of the Radcliffe Camera, St Mary's spire, with the eighteenth-century spire of All Saints behind – all framed by our own chapel, cloisters and Codrington Library.

Max and Agatha had an eighteenth-century house right on the road at the end of the town at Wallingford, Winterbrook House, very convenient for Oxford. I used to wonder at first how they could put up with traffic right on the road. But the house had a heavy cushion of shrubbery in front, and for the most part went back in depth to a garden and meadow going down to the river. The rooms they occupied were mostly in the back, a spacious drawing-room giving on to the garden, a long wing projecting where, upstairs, each had a study for their so different work.

In Devon they had a finer Georgian house, Greenway, in a splendid situation on a bend of the river Dart with a view right down it, steamers passing, and a magnificent garden, full of the rare shrubs the West Country can grow. This had been created by the Cornish family of Bolitho, from whom Agatha's growing earnings – after parting from Christie – had enabled her to buy it. Here I was invited to stay for a wedding anniversary – I remember that Max had had his classic work on Nimrud, with its astonishing illustrations, specially bound in two large morocco-and-gold volumes for Agatha. At that time I had not realized how closely associated with the work there she had been: it was there that she had met Max on the job, who insisted on her marrying him, and she had gone out year after year with him. How well it had turned out – the experience of the Near East, the expertise and personnel of archaeology, new fields and subjects for her prolific pen!

Greenway was of interest to the West Country historian because it had been the home of the Gilberts, half-brothers of the Raleghs. Hardly anything of their time remained, but not far away – nearer Agatha's home-town of Torquay – was the medieval home of the Gilberts, rose-red Compton Castle, rehabilitated by Commander Walter Raleigh Gilbert, who came over with his wife. His saving Compton was a romantic story. As a young Dartmouth cadet he used occasionally to have a farm-tea with the farmer who owned the Castle, then more than half a ruin. Gilbert determined that one day he would restore the home of his ancestors – and lived to do it.

He began by reroofing and restoring the ruined wing. There remained the gap between the two, where the great hall had been – you could see the line of gable upon the walls. The Castle was complete once more; we went over to see it – the Commander chaffing me that it was I who had pointed out the gable-ends aching for a roof years before and he had carried out my command! He always intended to do it; Agatha said – let him have his way about Greenway and he'd rebuild it too: suspiciously he sniffed around the old foundations at the back. I don't recall much more, except looking into the church at Churston Ferrers and over the wall at the old manor-house – and the good fare Agatha provided wherever she was (she was a good trencherman): a fine Devon turkey and Devonshire cream.

That same summer I was able to take them over to Hawksmoor's grandiose *palazzo*, Easton Neston, under the aegis of my friend, Kisty Hesketh, who much appreciated the architecture of Hawksmoor's All Souls, similar idiom and idiosyncrasies. Later on, I took them over the hills and up the valley to medieval and Elizabethan Stonor, fascinating house with its Catholic associations, where they made friends with the Stonors and became regular visitors.

From the first Agatha was interested in my work on Shakespeare, herself a life-long devotee, very familiar with the plays on the stage and very well read in and about them. When I eventually found the Dark Lady, contrary to my expectations – right there across the way from All Souls, in the Bodleian – she gave me public support with a letter to *The Times*, and came to my lecture about the Simon Forman finds at the Royal Society of Literature.

It was consoling to have her support, for though she was not a so-called 'expert' in the field, she had a first-class brain, an extraordinary combination of perception and common sense such as few of the experts possessed. And, after all, she had the kindness, as well as the sense, to see that the findings of the leading authority on the Elizabethan Age, Shakespeare's lifetime, were probably right. They have proved unanswerable, for they are the answer. The problems have been solved.

She herself was extraordinarily good at setting and solving problems, as all the world knows. What the world does not know is, what Max knew, that this came from her exceptional combination of 'inner sensitivity with an intuitive understanding of situations hidden from mere normal mortals'. To a degree that made her rather formidable, until one found out how kind and good she was. But it made her a personality that I was rather wary of, to begin with – those silences in which one was aware that she took in everything about one and saw right through one. (I was rather intuitive myself.) No taking any liberties with her; one had to be rather careful what one said – nothing off-beat, even one's jokes had to be proper, for she was very much a Victorian lady. She once said to me, 'There is nothing immoral in my books – only murder.'

Max thought of her books as moralities as much as thrillers, and that she was much concerned with the struggle between good and evil. Naturally I didn't appreciate that side, but he was emphatic that she was a good *novelist*, not merely a detective story writer. That I did come to appreciate: her gifts for creating character, her wide understanding of human beings, especially of children (sympathy too), her natural and convincing dialogue, her firm construction and setting of the scene.

In one of her straight novels written as Mary Westmacott, *The Burden*, there is wonderful dialogue between a crusty old don, Mr Baldock, and a little girl, Laura.

> Mr Baldock, grinding his teeth and snorting with venom, was penning a really vitriolic review for a learned journal of a fellow historian's life work.
>
> He turned a ferocious face to the door, as Mrs Rouse, giving a perfunctory knock and pushing it open, announced:
>
> 'Here's little Miss Laura for you.'

There follows a virtuoso performance in dialogue, if it were not so utterly natural and funny. Agatha knew all about children and the way they talk. (In one of her detective stories she actually says that children's evidence is best and most to be trusted.)

In the earlier days of our friendship I used to think of her as a geometrician, and she did say to me that in writing a detective story you begin at the end. As a girl she had been good at mathematics – I don't wonder at that. Max corroborates that she had a mathematical brain, and that this appears in 'the neat solution of the most complex tangles, an ability in analysis as well as synthesis'.

Though she was not communicative, one way and another she came to tell me a good bit about her writing. People were for ever sending her plots of stories which they fancied for her to write up. Courteous and patient, she always replied that thinking up her plots was the one great pleasure she took in writing: all the rest was hard work. That this was so one sees from the revealing preface she wrote – a rare thing – to *The Crooked House*, a favourite of hers. 'I saved it up for years, thinking about it, working it out, saying to myself: "One day, when I've plenty of time, and want to really enjoy myself – I'll begin it!" I should say that of one's output, five books are work to one that is pure pleasure.' There is a rare glimpse into the workings of that mind, naturally secretive. Max speaks of her horror of the invasion of her privacy (redoubled by its exposure to the world in the twenties, a veil drawn over it ever afterwards) and her refusal to talk about 'the esoteric world of her invention'. This was the fantasy world in which she lived her imaginative life, to outward appearance the most conventional of middle-class old ladies.

Considering that, I am touched by how much she did tell me about her work – never about her life. She would give people her autograph generously – she was naturally generous; never a photograph. She was very careful and cagey about her public relations. One can see that in a significant respect in regard to the handling of her straight novels, by 'Mary Westmacott'. Her publisher would never allow her to deviate from what her enormous public expected of her as

Agatha Christie – she had to be as cautious as a pope or prime minister. Whatever the reason, her straight novels had no success whatever – ludicrous, from the most widely read woman in the world: it shows how stupid people are, for, in my opinion, they are excellent – and more to my taste than detective stories.

In the course of my campaign for common sense about Shakespeare I sent her my biography of Marlowe, which was a strategic move though people hadn't the sense to spot it. As the result of the hopeless confusion perpetuated by the Shakespeare establishment, the gates have been needlessly left open for all the crackpots to canter through. Many innocent folk can't feel sure whether Shakespeare ever existed, or whether his plays weren't written by Bacon or Marlowe – both 100 per cent homosexual, by the way; while Shakespeare, the author of his own work, was 100 per cent heterosexual, all for women in love. Some of these crackpots actually make a living out of confusing the poor public – for ordinary people cannot tell a good egg from a bad egg intellectually. So my *Marlowe* was intended to close one gate to the crackpots – though the third-rate academics never saw the point, for they perceive nothing.

I sent the book to Agatha down in Devon, who replied courteously as always, for all her burden of work. (Lesser people, even in the peerage, are apt not to acknowledge the gift of a book: Agatha was very old-fashioned, better brought up.) She had been away from Greenway much of that summer: 'I've been judging at a rose show in Holland. What do I know of the finer technical points of roses? *Nothing!* It's a great world!' Evidently she had enjoyed it. But just like her modesty – I'll bet she knew a good deal. There were always roses in the garden at Wallingford, and I have been struck by the extraordinary number of things she did know, the sheer range of her experience – apart from archaeology, the Middle East, the law and police, medicines, poisons and all that. She was knowledgeable about china, and at Wallingford had a special collection of slagware. I have noticed in just one of her books the mention of things I have never heard of. What is a 'tantalus'? I don't know. What's a 'shebunkin'? I don't know – quite apart from innias from Baghdad. It may be a truism, though it will be news to some people: Agatha was a *writer*.

What was she like at home?

Here I have my Journals to fall back upon: 'Sunday, 23 November 1969, a crisp golden day, out to Wallingford to lunch with Max and Agatha: a cosy, warm, hospitable, upper middle-class interior, with all the comforts and amenities, the pretty china and good furniture that Agatha's prosperity has brought. Better still the warm, generous, kindly atmosphere both radiate. Max has (Austrian) charm and kindness; Agatha large-chested, full-bosomed English comfortableness, plus the American strain of generosity. Wine-coloured autumn sun came flooding into the blowsy, cosy room – the too-large billowing chairs (like Agatha), the lavender colour of the slagware on the chimneypiece. She brought out piece after piece of old china for me – nothing spectacular, like Jack Plumb's Sèvres, just pleasant Victorian pieces (again like Agatha herself).

'I have always been curious to know the truth of *her* detective story – that of her first marriage, her background, whether the episode of her losing her memory and being identified (at Harrogate) was true. Last week, lunching in London with a Cornish fan of mine, I learned the truth from his wife, an old friend of Agatha's . . .

'It must be remembered that at this time nothing was known except the external facts of the famous disappearance. Before they died Agatha and Max each wrote an autobiography, in which they told as much of the story as they felt they could. They corroborate what I was told – and kept to myself (and my Journals) as long as they lived. Agatha said that during that appalling experience she had lived in a dream; but there was more to it than that . . .

'I knew that Agatha's father was an American expatriate, who lived at Torquay and married a Devon girl. Agatha is very patriotic about Devon and, when the thousands began to roll in, bought Mary Bolitho's Greenway on the Dart. She married Christie, had one girl, and lived in London, not well off. She went back to Torquay for some time to look after her sick mother, leaving her best friend [according to Mrs X] to look after her husband while away.'

What happened was just like the Windsor story, when Lady Furness left David (then Prince of Wales) to her friend, Wallis, to look after him and 'keep him out of mischief' while away in America. When she got back, she found that the friend had *got* him, and for keeps. The same thing happened to Agatha. Plenty of people have broken marriages nowadays; what made the experience shattering to her was that she had never dreamed of it. She had had a peculiarly happy and sheltered childhood, loving and beloved by her parents; she was more than conventionally religious, but had old-fashioned conventional standards, believing in the sanctity of marriage and horrified by the idea of divorce. She knew that the dashing army officer, who had had a brave record in the first German war, had a ruthless streak, but had no idea that he would behave brutally to her throughout this ghastly period of strain. Psychotic elements entered into it on both sides: he was brutal and abrupt *because* he had loved her; she continued to love him throughout it all, but it shattered the world of fantasy in which her spirit – her genius – lived. This is what led to her breakdown.

I have never felt at liberty to say what Agatha's former friend told me, until Max gave a hint in his *Memoirs*. He told me that he had only once set eyes on Christie, in later life, greying hair, but still an upstanding 'good-looking fellow'. Agatha, when young, had been beautiful: he had swept her off her feet. With her abnormally sensitive nature – the delicate balance of genius – and her exceptional fabric of security, the shock was terrible, and pushed her over the edge. Mrs X told me that Agatha had been prevented from throwing herself over the balcony; this is now corroborated by Max's 'acts which came near to *felo de se*'.[1] This is why the wound was

---

[1] In Max's *Memoirs* by a slip of the pen he said *auto da fe* for *felo de se*. The fool who saw his book through the press passed this obvious mistake, as well as getting my well-known initials wrong. It is a duty to describe a fool as such; I deliberately do all through my work – how else are they to learn?

so deep and, though she made a marvellous recovery – largely through Max – it had left its traces all through her work. It also made her the great woman she became.

I continue from my Journals.

'I just remember the furore in the newspapers, the nation-wide hunt; and her being identified in the hotel: "You are Agatha Christie," someone said, and received the monetary reward. "Am I?" she said, and it all came back. Everybody thought it a publicity stunt; but it was genuine – so much better than the best of jobs. After that every book was a best-seller, everything fell into her hands.

'Agatha's woman friend thought that the original Mr Christie had reason to regret his conduct since. She was very much in love with him, a perfectly contented wife, geared to domestic happiness. Max has achieved this with and for her – and has had the reward of his goodness and niceness. Everything genuine about the old couple. Actually Max is my age, but he has had a slight stroke, left hand and arm dragging – which brings him up more to her age in appearance.'

Mrs X had told me about Agatha's innate modesty. She hadn't thought highly of her play *The Mousetrap* – it surprised her that it had gone on year after year, now for nearly twenty years, bringing in £4,000 a year to her grandson. No wonder he can afford to collect pictures. Max had placed this (to me unknown) youth beside me when dining in Hall. We talked about painting. He said he had bought a Sidney Nolan. 'That must have cost a lot,' I said. 'It did,' he replied. 'How did you manage that?' I said in wonderment. 'I have a rich grand-mother.'

'Max told me, "Money means nothing to her." It pours in, in hundreds of thousands – and nearly all is lost in taxes. She is trustified, trusts in every direction for her family, very much a family woman. Poor Mr Christie – what a story he would make, looking at it from his point of view! What a mistake he made! Latterly she has had to join some corporation to deal with tax getting beyond her – and has to turn out a detective story a year, like some bank-manager turning in his annual account.'

Actually, what a waste this was – going into the maw of

the trivial consumption of a consumptive society, the shopping bags of the people bulging with rubbish. Think what it could have done in preserving historic houses in Devon falling to ruin; or saving historic treasures from dispersal abroad, or simply burgled, like Lord Clifford's at neighbouring Ugbrooke. A contemptible society. Max said to me that, if they were younger, they wouldn't stay here five minutes. I agree. With his long acquaintance with the Middle East, he said that, much as we used to laugh at the Arabs for their unreliability and slatternliness, the general squalor of their society, ours was now just like it. (Look at the filth and dirt of railway platforms – and the men striking for the heavy responsibility they carry in checking tickets.)

I agree with him, but I do not subscribe to the word 'ours'. I have no part nor lot in it, nor obligations to it. I am Cornish, not English – if I were, I should be ashamed, after the record they achieved in history, under the direction of their governing class. But only *under direction*, for of course ordinary people are incapable of operating without direction. As on one of Max's archaeological sites in the Near East, so in any industry in Britain.

I had an independent link with Max, besides All Souls, for we were of the same seniority at Oxford. He was at New College, and was criticized for saying in his *Memoirs* that Warden H. A. L. Fisher, though a great man, was pompous. Fisher *was* pompous; and it was more than generous to call him a 'great man' – he was just a distinguished, an eminent, man. At Lancing Max had been one of a group with Evelyn Waugh and Hugh Molson, an undergraduate acquaintance of mine. Hugh was known to them as 'Preters', from his addiction to the word 'preternaturally'. Waugh has a description of his extraordinary affectation of pomposity, which Evelyn says he adopted out of mockery. It used to mesmerize me as an undergraduate, it became second nature to him: he carried it through life and indeed into the House of Lords.

Max used to tell me how unpopular Evelyn was, a distinct streak of mischief, getting other people into trouble and himself out of it, a vein of cruelty. What an extraordinary character his was! With him too there was a strong element of affectation which entered into his character and formed his personality. Why ever? Why not be oneself? But his was not a very nice self. Max's was. I think life was straightforward for him. He was always simply heterosexual; the homo side to public school life seems to have meant nothing to him. I used to chaff him about this – not in front of Agatha, of course. Like Christie before him, Max made the running and carried off Agatha captive, several years his senior. Only once did I gather a hint. After my stimulating lecture to the Royal Society of Literature about Simon Forman and the Sex Life of the Elizabethans, Agatha did say, 'I hope it won't start up Max again.' Though love normally appears in her books, there is nothing about sex as such. I wonder if that wasn't an element in the failure with the dashing, perhaps demanding, army officer?

Agatha's friend may have been wrong about his missing the millions. Max rather contradicts this; he says that Christie did quite well for himself in the City, but was not much interested in money. I suspect that sex, raising its ugly head, was responsible for more.

Agatha showed what a dear, good, Christian soul she was, after all she had suffered, the irreparable wound he had inflicted upon her spirit. When, some fifteen years after, the woman for whom Christie had left her and whom he had married, died of cancer, Agatha wrote him a kind, consoling letter. I regard his reply as rather unfeeling: perhaps it is difficult for a proud man to accept forgiveness. Agatha knew all about the defects of men henceforth, how inconsiderate they are compared with women: in one place she has a tell-tale phrase about someone who was 'rather considerate for a man'; in another, that where men are concerned there is no end to the flattery that may be applied; for a third, that 'women can put up with a lot – when they have got what they want'.

I did not realize the religious side to Agatha until I read her *Poems*, and her beautiful little book of Christmas fables, *Star over Bethlehem*, both of which she gave me. I did not know that she always kept Thomas à Kempis' *Imitation of Christ* by her bedside. I should have noticed from her books how familiar she was with the Bible, the phrases continually coming up, especially those about loving kindness which truly guided her life. This comes out more openly in the 'Mary Westmacott' novels, along with other clues. 'How often he had heard and said those words: *Thy loving kindness to us and to all men*. Man himself could have that feeling, although he could not hold it long.' And then: 'Those are the magical moments – the moments of belonging – of everlasting sweetness – not sex. And yet if sex goes wrong, a marriage is completely ruined.' And again, 'We all have fantasies that help us to bear the lives we live.'

And here is a penetrating historical reflection – life with Max gave her a good historical sense, such as life with Christie could never have done:

> People were burned at the stake, not by sadists or brutes but by earnest and high-minded men, who believed that what they did was right. Read some of the law cases in ancient Greece [that came from Max, a classical scholar], of a man who refused to let his slaves be tortured so as to get at the truth, as was the prevalent custom. He was looked upon as a man who deliberately obscured justice. There was an earnest God-fearing clergyman in the States who beat his three-year-old son, whom he loved, to death, because the child refused to say his prayers.

I see that my gloss on that passage is: 'They *were* brutes. Right and wrong are absolutes – not relative.' And then the Swiftian condemnation, appropriate for an historian: 'They were idiots.'

There were other clues. In *The Crooked House* – 'Never explain': a maxim I adhere to myself. In *Five Little Pigs* a woman thinks of taking poison – Agatha knew about poisons from her nursing days as a VAD in the first German war: 'I had received a bad shock. My husband was proposing to leave me for another woman. If that was so, I didn't want to live.' The husband had said, 'Do try and be reasonable about this, Caroline. I'm fond of you and will always wish you well – you and the children. But I'm going to marry Elsa.' That was exactly it. I don't suppose that anyone has noticed that the husband's initials, Amyas Crale – A.C. – were the same as those of Archie Christie. Then comes in Agatha herself:

> She had that enormous mental and moral advantage of a strict Victorian upbringing denied to us in these days – she had done her duty in that station of life to which it had pleased God to call her, and that assurance encased her in an armour impregnable to the slings and darts [Shakespeare's image] of envy, discontent and regret.

As for the absurd suggestion of her disappearance being a publicity stunt (Henry James: 'Nobody ever understands *any*-thing'), Agatha herself gives a pointer, in the voice of Hercule Poirot, no less:

> But consider two points. First, that the lady had by that time not the slightest need for publicity. She had a full measure of it already. Secondly, a more important point . . . the known character of the suspect. Can you really visualize a lady of genuine modesty, with a retiring disposition and an extreme dislike of public intervention in her affairs deliberately making herself the centre of a *cause célèbre* and bringing down on herself the countrywide attention of the sensational press?

Murder in Mesopotamia has several corroborative clues. A woman says: 'Lots of people wanted to marry me, but I always refused. I'd had too bad a shock. I didn't feel I could ever *trust* anyone again . . . Of course, I thought at first I was mad or dreaming.' Later on after various sensational happenings, 'another idea flashed across my mind. Perhaps soon, in the natural course of things . . . a new and happy state of things might come about.' We recall that it was Mesopotamia that brought Agatha and Max together, where he proposed marriage, to be held off for quite a time, for like the woman in *The Curtain* who had suffered too deeply, she was mistrustful of life – and, anyway, 'a good brain, yes, but women seldom fall for brains alone'.

I was getting to know both of them better: a real feeling of affection grew up, barriers lowered. From 'Dear Mr Rowse', or 'Dear Dr Rowse', Agatha's letters began 'Dear Leslie' – my name in family and College – though she never dated them by the year. One November day in the late sixties she is writing:

> What fun your party was! I enjoyed it immensely – and liked talking to both of my neighbouring guests at lunch. I also enjoyed eating what was certainly one of All Souls' best lunches. Delicious trout. Thank you very much for the book you have bestowed on Max and myself. There is lots of Devon I don't really know – and this will, I see, fill in interesting gaps. Time to begin to be industrious again – How hard one has to drive oneself to begin a new book. Only disgusting weather outside really drives one on.

So much for those who think writing is easy for even natural and gifted writers. As she said, planning and thinking about the book beforehand is all the fun – the rest is hard work.

When the Dark Lady was discovered, Agatha was fascinated and wrote in her own contribution to the discussion in *The Times*. She was, as I have said, well versed in Shakespeare and had thought a lot about him. So she said that she had always thought that in the character of Cleopatra Shakespeare was remembering his own experience – and someone he had experienced and suffered from: a dark, bewitching, foreign beauty, gypsy-like in her moods and tantrums, temperamental, mercurial and not to be trusted; yet whose spell was so irresistible her man could not break free from it. This was certainly Shakespeare's situation in the Sonnets, and I dare say Agatha was right, with her abnormal intuition about human beings. It is a brilliant conjecture – and Agatha's sheer cleverness has often been commented on. One never saw that in life, she was so modest; her essential self so subdued and withdrawn in society; her persona as a writer was something quite different, almost as if there were two personalities. Her intuition was really rather alarming – one felt one had to pass the test to be admitted to confidence. But though she may well have been right that in Cleopatra Shakespeare was remembering Emilia Lanier (born a Bassano), the historian could not use even the most penetrating of conjectures.

On the other hand, we *know* that Rosaline, Berowne's lady in *Love's Labour's Lost*, was the Dark Lady of the Sonnets, for both are described in practically the same words. I always realized that, if ever the Dark Lady were discovered, she would be found to be someone known to the circle of South-ampton, Shakespeare's patron. And this turned out to be so: she had been the mistress of the Lord Chamberlain, patron of Shakespeare's Company – one could hardly get closer – while Southampton's stepfather, Sir Thomas Heneage, was Vice-Chamberlain.

Agatha, with her first-rate detective brain, could see the bearing of all that; the third-rate, of course, couldn't. No point in discussing it with them: they had nothing to discuss with: a first-rate authority was telling them.

Here's for another of those happy visits out to Wallingford.

'Sunday, 17 January 1971, I drove out to lunch alone with Max and Agatha – always a pleasant homey atmosphere, largely due to his Austrian charm – in that sunny house where the living rooms at the back look over their flat water-meadows to the river. They have been there since 1930, per-haps immediately after her marrying Max. She has been cele-brating her eightieth birthday, with lots of public notice and hundreds of letters to answer – one of the most famous women in the world, and just been made a Dame by the Queen, one of her constant readers. Max knighted. But, thir-teen years younger, he is less well preserved than Agatha, a powerful big woman with prominent features.

'It is impossible to penetrate her reserve – that mixture of shyness and formidable resources of power, of outer diffid-ence with a massive inner confidence, as Max puts it – and no wonder, with that story in the background. We talked about money, as all best-sellers will, Agatha complaining at the amount of tax lifted off her – on top of all the trusts she must have made for the family. She told me one couldn't even donate a story to a cause now; years ago she gave to the Westminster Abbey Appeal, a short story which fetched £1500. I told her what I was doing for Charlestown Church bells, no tax relief. And was rather surprised to learn that they had bought a plot to be buried in neighbouring Cholsey churchyard. I should have expected Torquay, where she was born. She said that it was so spoiled, one of those ghastly great town cemeteries.

'She is not one to encourage questions, said that she had always hated being questioned from a girl on, and never gives interviews. But a little boy from the local school had come to interview her for his school paper; she took a fancy to him and asked him in. On her birthday came a sheaf of flowers from his parents. All Wallingford must know the world celebrity living in their midst, in the Georgian house right on the road, if invisible behind thick shrubbery growing up to the top windows.

'She has a secretary to deal with her correspondence; says firmly when asked for large donations for this or that, "It's no use asking authors for £30,000 or whatever – they're far too heavily taxed: you must ask a tycoon." She has had jacket trouble with her American paperbacks, when the publishers, without consulting her, would come out with a naked girl recumbent in a park – nothing about sex in the book. Or in any of her respectable books, "which deal only in murder" (this a little apologetically). Two years ago she had had a showdown with the Americans and insisted on seeing the jacket designs. I told her that I had suffered similarly with two American paperbacks: one, by some ill-attuned Slav, had given Shakespeare the hairless head of a surprised egg; the other made him a doddering old man with straggling beard, in imminent decay. Idiots!

'About five years ago she had accepted an interesting and very lucrative assignment from Hollywood to do a TV script of *Bleak House*. She became very much interested, had never done one before – only plays of her own (this with modesty). Hollywood interfered so much and it involved so much discussion, so many changes, etc. that she gave it up. She had done two parts, and received the money, but was not going to do the third part. She said that she had never got headaches from worry over her work before, as with this. She was never going to finish it. A pity, for she had found it fascinating. [The fools – fancy frustrating a famous writer with their constant interference. I know what 'editors' in American publishing houses are like from experience – most of their authors can't write, so their books have to be rewritten in the office. Not good enough for Agatha, or for me.]

'At the moment she has stopped after writing two chapters of a new story – the energy, at eighty! What characteristic has all genius in common? C. E. M. Joad was asked, and replied unhesitatingly – Energy. I should qualify that only by – energy *of mind*. Since all the letters came pouring in and the book wasn't going very well, she has stopped work on it for the time to attend to the letters. "You know how it is – you have to give yourself to a book, you can't do anything else." So that is how she works – in spells, with concentration. I told her that I don't waste time answering most of my letters: Napoleon's secretary Bourrienne said that, if you leave them a fortnight, most of them will have answered themselves. And of course I never answer dotty letters about Shakespeare's plays having been written by Queen Elizabeth, or Richard III having been as innocent as a new-born babe.

'She talked a good deal, without vanity – she has no vanity, remarkable in an author, especially a world-famous author (contrast – , or – ,) and about the nuisance people will make of themselves. Never at Wallingford, but sometimes in Devon. Once a woman invaded her summerhouse, where she was sunbathing – just to show her to her young hopeful of a youth, who was covered with embarrassment at his mother. Then a party of Finnish journalists got through the barriers and pursued her into the house, where her brother-in-law backed her up in refusing an interview. She was thereupon described in the Finnish press most unfavourably and as protected by an armed guard – her harmless elderly brother-in-law.

'Worst of all was Spain, where they couldn't get any peace for themselves on holiday at all. It ended with a woman getting into her bathroom when she was changing for dinner:

"I thought you wouldn't mind – anyway you've got to see me now", etc. Agatha put on her dress, and went straight down to the management.

'The house is always warm and cosy, with a nice wood fire, sun coming cheerfully into the back drawing-room from the side. There's always good food, they both like their food and have second helpings – today a favourite of Agatha's, boiled silverside with dumplings. Max likes his wine, face a bit flushed. She's an apple-juice drinker, like me. The dining-room, on the road side of the house, is small, with rather low Victorian French tapestry chairs, good silver not scarce, and a *very* good cook-housekeeper. She tells me that Wallingford is far better than Greenway for milk, cream, butter, poultry, provisions – in Devon the best is skimmed off to London.

'Max and she must have had good times together in his diggings in Iraq, when the going was good – and several of her books came out of it. He's had an interesting life and friendships, with Mortimer Wheeler (what a character!), Leonard Woolley, archaeologists all. We talked a bit about Preters, a nice man under the extraordinary mannerism, and Evelyn's Anglo-Catholic religiosity at school – Rome let him down in the end, dropping the Latin Mass and going demotic, all that he hated. Unlike Tom Eliot, he didn't die in time; he saw his world crumble.'

I find that on a golden day that autumn, 3 October 1971, Max and Agatha came over the hill to lunch at Stonor, 'Agatha having recovered marvellously from breaking her hip that summer . . . Agatha was warm in praise of my 'Chalky Jenkins' story [about the half-grown cat that used to come up from down in the valley at Trenarren, liked visiting at the big house, and then was lost]. She said it made her cry – as it did me to write it . . .

'After this friendly lunch, a wine-coloured light came out over the pastures.' Max, who as an archaeologist was vir-tually professional as a photographer, took pictures of us all standing in front of that historic house. 'Max and Agatha took off across country to Wallingford, I up and up the Wat-lington road into the hanging beechwoods of the Chilterns, where the Britons survived into Saxon England.'

A prominent and troublesome character in those last years was Bingo. Agatha had always had a dog, and this was a present of a very idiosyncratic kind. He was a Manchester terrier, black and tan, so overbred as to be positively neurotic. Noisy, he would snap and bite for tuppence, or less – he bit the cook: he didn't know which side his bread was buttered. She couldn't bear him, neither could I – though I became intrigued by him, he was so odd; as he was by me. At tea-time he would come sniffing around me, curiosity aroused, one dared not move, he might bite. If the telephone rang Max had to shut him out or he would snap at his heels. Agatha had a fantasy that Bingo believed there was a devil who lived in the telephone, and he meant to warn Max and pull him back by biting his heels.

Both Agatha and Max loved him; I couldn't understand it, and would say, 'You know, Agatha, your dog's dotty.' She rather agreed, loved him all the same, and would recount his endearing ways. The source of his trouble was nerves: overbred, he was frightened of everything, terrified of getting up the stairs; but once having overcome it, new every morning was the love with which he snuggled under Agatha's eiderdown while she had her morning tea. I think that Max gave me the answer why they put up with him, always having to put him on a lead if anybody came into the house, etc. – it was that they would have found an easy conventional dog uninteresting. He had his uses: he gave the alarm when a burglar set a ladder up against Agatha's bedroom window, and made off with only a couple of old fur coats, interrupted in his intentions. It was a drawn battle between Bingo and me: no love, but mutual curiosity: I never met so odd a dog. As for Max, Bingo provided him with a tease for me: he pretended that Bingo had a special devotion to me, held me in high regard, etc. and regaled me with the latest news of him and his dear little ways, how he had bitten the postman, etc.

When I wrote a little book about my beloved cat, *Peter the White Cat of Trenarren* – of an angelic disposition, never once bit or scratched anyone, no horrid Bingo – Agatha wrote to me: 'I enjoyed your book about the White Cat so much that

I really must ponder seriously about your suggestion of a little book about my cats and dogs, possibly in the Christmas Season, though I rather doubt whether my publisher would care for the idea!' There you are, the old lady was the prisoner of her world *réclame*. Max wrote me a characteristically charming and intuitive letter – that the book showed my need to give, as well as receive, affection. I knew that well enough, but it was very sweet of him to say it. There must be other letters from both of them, that have not yet come to the surface in my enormous *Archiv*.

Agatha said that she was not ambitious, and everyone who knew her accepts that that was true. You could see her innate modesty in her bearing. She never put herself forward, but held back. I have seen her at a lecture of Max's in a crowded room at Cal. Tec. (the California Institute of Technology) in Pasadena, the whole audience keyed up that the most famous woman in the world was present. For her part she might not have been, sitting away close to the wall in the third or fourth row, in an anonymous position. She was given an ovation, to which she responded with a brief curtsey politely, never turning round – and that was that.

But we must not underrate her literary ambition and accomplishment, as her publishers did, simply because she was the first of detective story writers – any more than we should write off Churchill's paintings because he was Churchill. I have said that Agatha was a *real* writer – I mean by that that she was a compulsive writer: writing was her life. Or one of her two lives – for outwardly she had a full and normal social life, family, two marriages, friends, hospitality, entertainment, housekeeping (which she was very good at), shopping (which she much enjoyed); she had even, through Max, something of an academic circle, more in London than at Oxford, to which they came late. All ministered to Agatha's inner life of the imagination.

I remember an odd story of the old witch Margaret Murray, an authority on witchcraft, who dabbled in it, and lived to be a hundred. One of Max's London colleagues crossed the beldame in some departmental matter. She proceeded to boil up some witch's brew, with appropriate curses – and, sure enough, the offending man's face came out covered in pustules. I couldn't make out whether both Agatha and Max believed this – certainly Max did: one of Koestler's unexplained 'coincidences' perhaps.

I had never read a detective story until Agatha gave me her *4.50 From Paddington* and, no professional thriller reader, tended to take the story *au sérieux*, if not *au grand sérieux*. So I was able to tell Agatha that I was now rather alarmed at taking the regular 4.45 from Paddington to Oxford, which we relied on to get back in time for dinner. Similarly with *Passenger to Frankfurt*: now I was frightened to take a plane to Germany. I find from my Journals that I did not much care for *Hallowe'en Party*. which she also gave me – nor is it one of her best. I must say, however, that her gift extended to titles: she was a dab hand at them. Nor did her American publishers improve on them, though they had, of course, to change *Ten Little Niggers*.

I am not competent to estimate her form in this (to me) esoteric field; though another Fellow of All Souls, Geoffrey Faber, who was a good judge, always put her first. Oddly enough, another Fellow, G. D. H. Cole – socialist writer on dreary politics – made a regular income for some years from his detective stories. I read only one, which he gave me, because the scene was placed in Cornwall. Nor had I read Agatha's real Oxford rival, Dorothy Sayers – quite unlike Douglas Cole's undistinguished prose, and a contrast with Agatha. Dorothy Sayers was a first-class academic scholar, witness her work on Dante; but when I read her *Nine Tailors* I was bowled over by her sheer virtuosity, her knowledge of campanology.

I remain convinced, with Max, that Agatha was a better novelist than people realize – her creation of Miss Marple, for example, is a lasting one, a character added to literature. Poirot is, of course, a caricature, of whom Agatha tired: she never tired of Miss Marple, into whom she put something of herself. Other characters, too, are authentic personalities, some of them recognizably drawn from life. So, she was a novelist, and that will keep her best books alive, not mere thrillers.

A real writer, she had been writing all her life, from girl-hood, stories, fables, verse. She wrote, I believe, something like a score of plays, some of them eminently successful, like *Witness for the Prosecution*. Max thought *Akhnaton* the finest. I am not qualified to judge: I must be the only person in Britain who has never seen *The Mousetrap* (suggested to Agatha by Queen Mary, of all people!).

Agatha was a devoted reader of poetry, and a fairly constant writer of verse at times throughout her life. Here was a field where we could meet – and, of course, her poetry gives clues. I am surprised that there are not more Devon poems, or perhaps I have not found them; there is one on Dartmoor but, as Agatha said to me, large parts of Devon she did not know – only South Devon around Torquay and the Dart. Here is a clue, however, to that earlier suffering:

> Love passes! On the hearth dead embers lie
> Where once there burned a living fire of flame . . .
> Love passes out into the silent night,
> We may not hold him who has served our will
> And, for a while, made magic common
>   things . . .

And a witness to the later happiness she found with Max, written in his absence:

> Now is the winter past, but for my part
> Still winter stays until we meet again.
> Dear love, I have your promise and your heart
> But lacking touch and sight, spring birds bring pain.
> *Friendship* is ours, and still in absence grows.
> No dearer friend I own, so close, so kind.

I wonder whether there wasn't a further bond they may have been unconscious of, but which means something to the historian. Everybody thought of them as a very English couple. But Max was Austrian by blood, and Agatha's mother was a Clara Boehmer. Agatha had been when young a beautiful Teutonic blonde, with a fine singing voice. In old age she looked like a large cushiony German *frau*. Both were, however, witness to the English genius for *Verschmelzung*, for the peculiar power of environment and tradition – and no one could have made more distinguished contributions to it.

Latterly, we exchanged poems and, as Agatha grew old, Max took over letter-writing.

> 1 June 1979. What a charming appreciative letter you wrote to Agatha [I don't know whether they kept letters, they must have received thousands] on receiving her Poems, and what pleasure it gave us both to have these words from one so sensitive and artistic. Yes, we have been lucky in our companionship and in the enjoyment of things shared together. May you not feel lonely too often, for you must know that you have many good friends who are sensitive to your affection – among them the two of us, however much guarded by a black dragon who holds you in high esteem. I have no doubt that we should very much enjoy *Strange Encounter* if you can find a copy . . . I shall hope to see you at Gaudy [compare Dorothy Sayers' *Gaudy Night*], if not before.

So I sent them *Strange Encounter*. Max wrote,

> We have enjoyed your poems very much indeed, and I particularly love 'Strange Encounter' [the title piece], dramatic and the reflection of you. It is strange that you, a poet, would believe and cannot and that I, who am not a poet, can believe and would not. We admire your variety and range: the 'Portrait of a German Woman', and 'Before Cortés', a frightening glimpse of what art means. Agatha liked 'Dover Pier' and I enclose the list of her favourites. Perhaps one day you will write a poem about Bingo, an inscrutable character who has his own particular and private regard for you. Love from us both.

The acquaintance that began so casually ended then with affection on both sides. Agatha appended and autographed a list in her own hand of her favourites in this volume, no less than nine, beginning with 'Dover Pier' and 'Strange Encounter', both elegiac poems (Dover Pier a Civil War bastion in Magdalen walks overlooking the Cherwell). The old couple had evidently taken trouble: they took literature seriously – unlike the third-rate 'critics' of literary journalism.

I saw them together only once more, when they crossed the Tamar and came over the border into Cornwall to lunch at Ince, a paradise almost wholly surrounded by water. Agatha was visibly failing, memory going, this time for good. I went out to say a word to Bingo, on guard inside the big black car: fatter and more quiescent now, he didn't even growl – did he recognize me after all, since I addressed him by his name, extraordinary little character?

Max I saw yet once more, in the Athenaeum, pressing me to look him up at Wallingford. But we had both retired from Oxford, and shortly he too was dead.

Away in America, or marooned on my headland in Cornwall, I did not attend either of the crowded memorial services for them in London. But when, very infrequently now, I pass Cholsey Church on the railway line from Oxford to Paddington, the fine tower standing planted on its dead, I do not fail to send a thought of those dear good souls, among all the souls of the faithful departed, in that direction.

4

G. M. Trevelyan

A whole book could be written about Trevelyan as an historian. He was the leading English historian of his time, admired and read more widely than any other, in Britain as also in America; and we looked up to him as the head of our profession, its *doyen*. He should have had the Nobel Prize, rather than his contemporary, Bertrand Russell; as his *compère* in America, Samuel Eliot Morison, should have had instead of a second-rate writer like John Steinbeck. But Steinbeck appealed to popular Leftist sentimentality, and the half-educated of today do not realize that history is a department of literature. Think of English literature without Clarendon, Gibbon and Hume, or without Macaulay, Carlyle or Froude! Or Latin literature without Tacitus and Livy; Greek without Thucydides and Herodotus!

Trevelyan stood staunchly throughout his life, and exemplified it by his practice, for history as an art, and the writing of it as a literary art. As a young man at Cambridge he had been admonished by Seeley, with his Germanic standards, 'Remember always that history is a science, no more and no less.' As he went away, Trevelyan told me, he said to himself, 'Nevertheless, history *is* an art.' That was his *eppur se muove*, from which he did not depart for the rest of his long and fruitful life.

I am not going here to estimate his qualities as an historian, except to say that they were very much part of the man. In his case the man and the writer were singularly homogeneous – as they are not with many men of genius, with whom there is often a split in the personality, some conflict within producing tension. Trevelyan was all of a piece, monolithic, presenting to the spectator who did not know him a rather bleak surface. He had indeed no small talk, and no time for it, or for little human foibles – unlike that endearing side to Gibbon, which mitigates the pomposity of the manner.

Trevelyan was, in some ways, not easy to know. I knew him better than most, and over a considerable number of years in his later life, when he had by all accounts mellowed. Indeed, I saw only a warm and generous side, as his letters will show; true, he was a formidable, no-nonsense man, direct and crashing, liable to knock down any piece of silliness. I think that people found that alarming. Trevelyan was never one who stood fools gladly, or wasted any time on them. He was an uncompromising man, rudely direct, who could be crushing. I never found him anything but kind, and encouraging as only the first-rate themselves are. I could take knocks – and answer them back; Trevelyan enjoyed sparring and a good argument with someone who knew what he was talking about.

He was consistently encouraging to young people and their work – though he had singularly little influence on the generation after him at Cambridge. That may need explanation; but the explanation is clear. Genius is inimitable; literary art cannot well be imitated. Academic methods and preferences, 'lines' of investigation and fashions in subjects taken up can easily be imitated, like the populist school among the younger historians today, complete with graphs and statistics. Anybody can compile statistics, and computerized history is on the way. A work of art stands by itself, in its own right, and cannot be repeated. Nobody else could write my books, any more than they could Trevelyan's.

One further point, the bigness of the man and his achievement. Quite good academics are content to have accomplished one or two good books; Trevelyan did it a dozen or more times over, a shelf of substantial works which go on being read today, while his critics are forgotten. (One Montague, for example, who wrote a nasty review of *England under the Stuarts* in the *English Historical Review*, and is now forgotten, wrote nothing himself. That is the way it is with them. Why don't they have the sense of humour to see it?)

I don't think Trevelyan bothered his head much with critics, or perhaps even noticed them. For he had the advantage of being born on Olympus – all those generations of Trevelyans, his father, Sir George Otto Trevelyan, an eminent historian in his own right; his great-uncle Macaulay, of whom the family had a cult and for whom he was named, to whom he might be said to have been dedicated at the font. Indeed, observing the family over a long period of time I sometimes suspect that they think there are Trevelyans, and then the rest of the human race. They are certainly rather a race apart. I once heard G.M.T. refer to the Regius Professor at Oxford, H. W. C. Davis (who first introduced me as a young Fellow of All Souls to the great man) as 'the excellent Davis': I saw at once what that particular professor's place was in the scheme of things. Regius professors recur; there was only one G. M. Trevelyan.

The scale and quality of the achievement went with the greatness of the man. Those few men I have encountered who could be called 'great' all had something in common: an indefeasible integrity, something rock-like in their character. Churchill obviously had it, and so had Ernest Bevin. One saw it in Vaughan Williams, as in Robert Bridges, for all that it is the fashion of lesser people to depreciate him now. Nimitz had it, for all his charm; Eliot, for all his diffidence. Samuel Eliot Morison had it, that rock-like quality. It may be that Lloyd George had something of it, in spite of his obvious defects of character. Genius does not necessarily go along with character – Dylan Thomas had no character to speak of, any more than Edgar Allan Poe or Baudelaire.

I saw little of Trevelyan during the years when he was at work as Regius Professor at Cambridge (how he disliked the chore of lecturing – and how bad he was at it, just reading from a typescript!). Then Churchill appointed him Master of Trinity. He did not want to take on this chore either, but Winston said, 'If you don't take it, I will appoint somebody

you don't like.' Apparently a scientist – and it did stand
out that the grandest of English colleges, so far as science was
concerned, came to be presided over by someone with no
feeling for science at all. (No more had Winston: he
depended on 'The Prof', Lindemann.)

Early in our acquaintance, in June 1942, I had a long letter
from him à propos of A Cornish Childhood, which he found

> an extraordinarily fascinating story, made up of the two
> threads of Cornwall and yourself. I have, as you rightly
> suppose, a very strong Cornish feeling. As you know
> the Trevelyan papers in the Camden Society you realize
> the origin of that feeling on my part. I have walked
> round the whole coast of Cornwall twice and many parts
> very often, in my younger days, and I should be quite a
> good guide to all the old Trevelyan places near Fowey.
> In the eighteenth century the Trevelyans were settled in
> the beautiful old country house of Nettlecombe in
> Somerset, where they had been for two hundred years,
> but they still kept their smaller Cornish estates and con-
> nexions. Then in 1777 my branch of the family inherited
> the Wallington estate in Northumberland by marriage
> with the Blacketts, and moved up there at one step . . .
> I think in some ways the part of your book that inter-
> ested me most is the part about the Church and its effect
> upon you. I was, by the way, delighted to find how
> much you admire Frere [Bishop of Truro]. I always
> thought from his history books that he must have been
> a delightful person.

He was more than that: not only scholar and musician, but a
gentleman, a saint. Joe Hunkin who followed him was a poor
come-down.[1]

Trevelyan went on to a slashing attack on the Labour
Party's record, and charged me with letting them off lightly,
which I had done.

I do not at all disagree with your attack on the Conserv-

[1] See my A Man of the Thirties.

ative statesmen, but . . . the Left Wing parties were violently opposed to rearmament . . . and this was utterly
incompatible with the other part of their policy, which
was to oppose and check the Nazis and Fascists in
Europe.

Trevelyan was right – it was.

I am in a great many matters a Socialist, and I am certain
that after the war we shall become Socialist even more
than we have already done. *But Socialism means duties as
well as rights for the working classes*. One of those duties is
military preparedness and readiness not only to fight in
time of war, but in peace time to *prepare* to fight. This
the working class and its leaders have hitherto steadfastly
refused to believe, and it seems to be a matter which you
also have not taken into account.

Alas, I was only too well aware of it, and what we had to put
up with from the illusory pacifism of the lunatic fringe.
Even Attlee admitted afterwards that he had been wrong – in
the endeavour to keep party unity – for he must have *known*.
    Trevelyan himself had come a long way from the extreme
radicalism of his youth – while his brother, Sir Charles, had
taken the pacifist line in 1914. G.M. was writing from the
Master's Lodge at Trinity: 'If ever you get to Cambridge, be
sure you let me know beforehand, so that we can see you
here. We can have good talk.' Busy as he was, he was ever
hospitable, though I have always been chary of imposing
myself upon people with such burdens, and only once called
on him while he was installed in that historic Lodge, about
which he wrote so well in his little book on Trinity.
    When Trevelyan appeared in London to give some
National Book League lecture, at a private dinner party afterwards I was suddenly called upon to make a speech in his
honour. Somewhat at a loss, I could not think of anything to
lighten the occasion except to twit him on so Cornish a name
– the Trevelyans go back to the early Middle Ages at Trevelyan in St Veep parish – getting annexed to Northumberland.

What were they doing there? And how ironical that so radical a family, almost republican, should have got its first leg-up through a royal favourite, John Trevelyan, favourite of Henry VI. It did not appear that G.M. was amused.

We were to have many better opportunities of getting closer together – especially, as it happened, in Northumberland, where I stayed with him several summers running, though at Cambridge also. I could not get him back to Cornwall. In Northumberland an attractive small estate fell to him from a remote cousin, just as the money coming in from his *History of England* enabled him to live there. It was only a dozen miles or so from the family home at Wallington, the splendid William and Mary house where his brother, the radical baronet, lived.

G.M. loved Hallington. Northumberland was in his blood; from the garden one could almost see Housesteads on the Roman Wall. The house was a small Georgian country house, improved and made more roomy by the Victorians, with a high-walled kitchen garden to shelter from those northern blasts. In front was a remarkable deep 'dene', a ravine with a pond at the bottom, and luxuriant vegetation, rhododendrons and such as one might find in Cornwall. It was a striking contrast with the bare uplands of the home-farm which he loved to stride across, the squire on his own place.

For all his attachment to Northumberland he had never seen the most dramatic of the fine houses within it – Vanbrugh's Seaton Delaval – until I persuaded him to. He did not appreciate it: his taste was Victorian, he was one of those people who could not appreciate the imaginative nobility of Blenheim. He was a moralist, not an aesthete.

This leads to the philosophic difference of opinion between us. I do not think he understood any form of scepticism, any more than Macaulay could: he was too downright. He would take me to task for my dislike of the Puritans: if it had not been for them, he would say, the Elizabethans would not have fought the Spaniards. If it had not been for the Counter-Reformation and the Jesuits, I would reply, perhaps we should not have had to. He did not seem to appreciate that it was the extremes on *both* sides, who make life intolerable for sensible people in the middle, that I detested. He did not like Laodiceanism.

Trevelyan never grasped how sceptical I was – but an aggressive sceptic, detesting extremists on *both* sides. I think he assumed that I was just on the other side – a simple point of view. There was a grand simplicity about him: there was right, and there was wrong.

He was also liberal-minded. When we talked about the French Revolution and Pitt's repressive measures against the Corresponding Societies and fellow-travellers, nuisances like Horne Tooke, G.M. talked like a Foxite Whig. 'Billy Pitt – damn his eyes,' he said with indignation; it was all contemporary to him. All my sympathies were the other way: I should have had no compunction in shutting up the trouble-makers, only bringing suffering down on people's heads. The paradox was that I was a man of the people, standing for order, authority – as it might be Bevin or, for that matter, Stalin who well knew what to do with trouble-makers. Trevelyan was an aristocrat; he could afford to be liberal-minded.

This is not to say that I was not prepared to learn from him. I was out to learn all I could. About John Bright, for example. So, on one of my visits to Hallington, I read his biography of Bright, the only one of his books I had not read and – allergic to the subject – I remember nothing of it. Disraeli was much more my cup of tea (not Trevelyan's): genius, romantic imagination, humour, a cynical turn about humans, no humbug, no illusions, fun. I remembered his summing up of Quaker John Bright: 'He was a self-made man, and adored his creator.'

Then, too, G.M. had been a Baldwinian, not a Churchillian. He knew that I was strongly anti-Baldwin and Chamberlain; nor did I regard with much sympathy his own progress from the radicalism of his early days to the inert complacency of Baldwin, the reign of humbug which led us to 1939 and war. Trevelyan had the honesty – the most transparently honest of men – to admit that he may have been wrong in supporting Baldwin. He then made the best defence of him he could. He said that it was very rare for a man to be good at both home affairs and foreign affairs. Take the case of Sir Robert Walpole, first-class at home, a failure in his foreign policy. Baldwin had been good about home affairs, a failure on the foreign front. (Myself, I do not think that Baldwin's home record is much good either: the settlement of the war debt to the USA on extremely harsh terms; the return to the gold standard when he was Prime Minister and First Lord of the Treasury; his behaviour over the coal-industry, taking the line of least resistance. He always took the line of least resistance, instead of giving leadership; for all his humbug about helping Labour to take responsibility, the artful party-politician kept them in a perpetual minority position, fatally so in the elections of 1931 and 1935.)

However, we did not talk politics much – G.M. was as much disillusioned by the contemporary scene as I was, though he did not take so badly the loss of the Empire: he had always been anti-Imperialist, a little Englander. *Ich nicht!* I agreed with Canning: 'England is either great, or she is nothing at all.' It was curious that he was not more interested in the British Empire, for he several times repeated that 'the best of us' was Sir Charles Trevelyan, the Indian administrator, who shaped that historic institution, the Indian Civil Service, by the introduction of entry by examination. Trevelyan's disenchantment reached further back: I was amused one day to discover that he disliked practically everything since the Industrial Revolution. Even I thought that that was going a bit far – eliminating the Age of Steam, of the Railway, the Victorian Age, the apogee of our history!

It was consistent with his country gentleman's view of landscape and history. Then the country was at its most beautiful, all was still on the human scale and yet at its most creative – the age of Walter Scott, Wordsworth and Byron; of Gainsborough, Reynolds, Lawrence, Constable; of Robert Adam, the Wyatts and Soane, of Georgian architecture in town and country; the country-house life which presented the best and most balanced way of life the world has ever seen.

His conversation was not very personal – rather a defect, I think – no gossip, nothing mean or malicious. But he did express disapproval of Bertrand Russell, and in reasonable

terms. 'He may be a genius at mathematics – as to that I am
no judge; but he is a perfect goose about politics.' Russell was
incapable of seeing that: he had little human perception. We
now know about the struggle within the Cambridge Apostles
between the conventional heteros led by Trevelyan, and the
homos led by Lytton Strachey. The latter won – to G.M.'s
disgust; for he was not only conventional but positively pru-
dish. Though he kept the formal *convenances* with Strachey
over their books, he deeply disapproved of Bloomsbury: 'A
dreadful lot!'

He was a late Victorian, his chief admiration Meredith:
G.M. had met his wife, Janet Penrose Ward – Matthew
Arnold's great-niece – over and through Meredith. All very
high-minded. And, since both were rationalists, they had a
Unitarian marriage service put together for them and celebrated at Oxford. G.M.: 'If anybody had told me when
young that I should be sitting in the Master's seat in Trinity
Chapel, I should have been *scandalized*!' Well, he matured and
mellowed, and sat there all right. His daughter Mary married
a High Church cleric; his Cornish nurse-attendant was also
High Church. G.M. would say, 'You and I seem the only
rationalists left'; and once: 'I am a flying buttress of the
Church; I support it, but from the outside.'

We did not talk literature much, though poetry was a great
love in his life. Here we might not have been *en rapport*: his
taste was late Victorian, couldn't see anything in Eliot, and
was geared to Browning and Meredith, to neither of whom
do I respond. In any case he has told us all about his love of
literature in his delightful *A Layman's Love of Letters*, which
he sent me with a p.c. 'It is a real issue how literature should
be approached – for love or by some rule. P.S. So glad the
great Eliza is getting on full steam ahead.'

It is a personal book, its message clear.

> It is the love of great poetry and good prose that we want
> to instil into the young. It is our greatest national inher-
> itance, and how little use we make of it . . . It has been
> to me a great part of the value of life . . . Poetry in
> particular but good prose only to a less degree appeals

through the ear to the heart; by sound and melody and the happy use of words it touches the inmost soul in each of us. That is how great poetry works if it works at all. It is not a set of intellectual conundrums, to be solved by certain rules. It is joy, joy in our inmost heart. It is a passion like love or it is nothing. One's passion for a poem often lasts all one's life.

That this was true he knew from his own experience. Poetry often moved him to tears, 'tears of pleasure in the sound of words, tears of gratitude for the beauty of the world in which we live' – and he quoted, for example, Dante's *Dolce color d'oriental zaffiro*. He speaks of 'the unbearable pathos' of Keats' sonnet on the presentiment of his early death, 'in view of what actually happened to Keats'. The truth was that, under the granite of G.M.'s exterior, the formidability of manner, there was intense pressure of feeling liable to burst out, as I found. In his last years, with eyesight failing, so that he could not read, and he would not listen to wireless or music, almost his only solace was to repeat reams of poetry he knew by heart. It is rather paradoxical that he criticizes Housman's pessimism about 'nature, heartless, witless nature': 'I have not this feeling. The Wordsworthian joy in nature is not dimmed for me by the knowledge that I shall not possess it for ever. We come and pass and are not, but nature remains, the friend of each of us in turn.' He was desperately sad towards the end himself – he had not Housman's stoicism: he was a romantic at heart.

He shared Housman's judgment, characteristically stated in prosaic terms, that there were passages in Blake and Shakespeare that give us 'poetry neat or unadulterated with so little meaning that nothing except poetic emotion is perceived and matters'. In other words, the touchstone was *'la poésie pure'* – so much for the cult of Meaning and the Word in the Cambridge school of Richards and Leavis. Though he did not mention their names the whole gravamen of the Lectures was, salutarily, against their dogmatism, or dogmatic criticism in general. 'Above all I object to excommunication ("debunking") of great writers of the past on some modern theory, or to suit some phase of thought or feeling, which like all phases of thought and feeling will itself pass away.'

No one knows that better than an historian. He scored two bull's-eyes in his demonstration of the silliness of E. M. Forster's depreciation of Scott, and of Raymond Mortimer's denunciation of Kipling. From his own long experience he had observed two deplorable examples of the temporary effect of critical prejudice upon great writers. Victorian moralists so objected to the theme of Meredith's *Modern Love* that they excluded him for a whole generation: the second was the absurd decline in Trollope's stock upon the publication of his *Autobiography*. Trevelyan proposed a positive formula: 'Any author who was for a number of years together, considered to be a great writer by a large number of the elect spirits of any former age must have some great merit.' Note the significance of the definitive word 'elect', left unemphasized.

Trevelyan was able to sum up:

> So you see these wholesale condemnations of writers who have for many years been admired by competent literary opinion are not always right, or even final. The fashion of the hour, even of the latest hour, will change some day, and is moreover quite as likely to be wrong as the fashion of earlier times.

This is not merely true, but a commonplace with historians. Trevelyan was always looking for the positive, even in criticism: 'the positive side of criticism is more important than the negative'.

He did detect in 'the English language as we have developed it in our own time' a deficiency in poetic quality. He was at one with Housman in diagnosing the highest levels in literature as poetic – 'that grip of the vitals, that disturbance of the whole being, which the *sound* of very great poetry alone can give'. There are literary people to whom that means nothing. Trevelyan was happy in his generation – and his position in that elect society: for him they did not exist. We are not so lucky.

Trevelyan understood quite well the way things were going.

> It is possible that the country may become even poorer than it is now, and it is probable that what wealth it has will be yet more evenly distributed. In that case the more expensive newspapers, weekly and daily, who still do serious reviewing are likely to disappear, and we shall be left with nothing but the cheap Press.

Not a good prospect for literature, as writers today find; but in a social revolution Quality is the first thing that goes.

> Now that economic and political circumstances are rapidly finishing off what is left of the independence of the English middle and professional classes, posterity will perhaps soon be able to judge for itself how much literature has gained by the disappearance of the hated bourgeois.

Meredith had written that, if England fell, 'mankind would breathe a harsher air'. Trevelyan commented on that: 'Well, she has not fallen, but she has relatively declined, and the air is already more harsh.' When one thinks of what the England of the past stood for, and what it achieved! Trevelyan had not much opinion of the present or hope of the future.

He said to me once, 'When you were young, we thought you were never going to start. But, my goodness, once you started . . .' I told him of the years when illness held me up: I was working all right, researching hard enough, but hadn't the strength to write my books. When I had recovered and was getting forward with published work, G. N. Clark appeared in my rooms one morning with *empressement* and instructed me that I must be sure to be in – for the Master of Trinity was over in Oxford and wanted to see me specially. The Master's visit was characteristically brief and to the point. 'I want you to give everything to accomplishing your big work on the Elizabethan Age. I don't know anybody else who is writing a book on that scale: nothing must come in the way of it.' That made me sit up. I thought, if that is what he thinks and has taken the trouble to come and tell me so, I really must stick to my last and grapple with it. While still at work as Master, he took the trouble to send me a useful reference for the state of the Borders in mid-Tudor times, and followed this up with a letter, having sent me a book as 'a reminder and a stimulus for the great work you have got on hand, throwing aside lesser things. I have "great expectations".'

I didn't know then that the two volumes would grow into three, and the third volume bifurcate, so that my 'trilogy' on the Elizabethan Age is really a quartet. He later gave me some practical advice: nowadays one can't publish a book in two volumes. Take a continuous title to cover the whole, as he did with *England in the Age of Queen Anne*, and publish each volume under a separate title but with that connecting thread.

Of the technique of historical writing he was a master. He told me that one reason why Macaulay was irresistibly readable was because of his mastery of the paragraph: each firm as a shaped block in the building, so that you have to go on to the next. Macaulay, like his great-nephew, was suffused with the sense of the poetry of the past (and was a good poet – a rare thing for an historian). He thought Acton over-estimated, but was grateful to him for one thing; he remembered the exact spot in the Madingley Road where Acton said, 'Never believe these people who run down Macaulay: with all his faults he is the greatest of our historians.' Trevelyan had a very high opinion of Lecky, while I prefer Froude.

Paradoxically, though I was so much closer personally to Trevelyan, intellectually I was more in sympathy with Namier's tragic vision of history, his disillusioned view of human idiocy, violence, brutality, his clear understanding of what modern Europe owed specially to the Germans; and his scepticism and penetrating insight into political humbug – he was a Churchillian, with little respect for Baldwin, and a Tory with not much respect for democracy. Namier had a cutting, ruthless, sardonic mind, like an Old Testament prophet. I am not with him in his analytical technique of writing; in the writing of history I am with Trevelyan, the constructive builder, who was also an artist and saw the poetry and pathos of history.

He very much wanted me to be Regius professor at Oxford. When I said that I could not even consider it – the only person to whom I gave my confidence in the matter – he said, with his usual brusque directness: 'Why not?' I said that the only thing I cared for was writing my books. He replied: 'I wrote my books while I was Regius professor.' I replied, 'There are two things to remember: you were much stronger than I – I have always had to be careful of my health. Secondly, the whole conditions of the job have changed: there are now so many research people to be directed, so many more committees to waste one's time.' At once: 'Then you mustn't have it. What about —— ——?' I said, after some thought, 'That would be all right.' Actually, the whole succession at Oxford went agley: the two most eminent Oxford historians were Namier and G. N. Clark, whom Richard Pares might then have followed, if not stricken with fatal illness.

At Cambridge Trevelyan was curiously followed by Dom David Knowles, a Roman Catholic monk. But that was much to Trevelyan's broadminded satisfaction: 'He is so polite, you can say anything to that man.' Strangely enough, Knowles wrote one of the most perceptive pieces ever written about Macaulay. He saw that under Macaulay's front was an extraordinarily emotional temperament, passionate feelings pent up – and, as I have said, there was something of this in G.M. Few knew it.

There was the extraordinary intensity of his and his wife's cult of their dead child, Theo, a boy of brilliant promise, who died at five, I think. Never spoken of, but always there in the background – yearly pilgrimages to his grave in the Lake District, uncontrolled grief and lamentations one must not go into, it was so strange. And his wife's death actually broke G.M. – no less strange: 'I am finished,' he said to me. His elder brother, Sir Charles, tougher and more resilient, less sensitive, spoke to me with disapproval of G.M.'s giving up. But here was the difference: the brother had genius, and something about that is inexplicable.

G.M. had his reservations, on the other hand, about his elder brother, head of the family, which we will also not go into. Suffice it to say that, where G.M. was a complete Victorian, his handsome brother was more of an eighteenth-century type, proper companion for Charles James Fox whom he adored – tutelary deity of the family. Once, when Sir Charles was showing me a box of counters which had belonged to Fox, the compulsive gambler, I said, knowing that Sir Charles was careful about money: 'Do you remember when Charles Fox as a lad at Eton, with another fellow, gambled away £32,000 one weekend? Really, he should have been horsewhipped!' The baronet was taken aback, then recovered with, 'Well, if he hadn't afterwards horsewhipped George III, then he *should* have been horsewhipped.'

I laughed to see the religion of Charles Fox still going on in the family – my own sympathies, of course, being entirely with poor George III. Fancy having a compulsive gambler, however gifted, at the head of the Treasury! Still, Sir Charles went on to make a good point against the great man, his younger brother. The baronet was way out on the Left, a sympathizer with the Russian Revolution. He said to me, wasn't it strange that G.M. who had made name and fame with his sympathy for the Italian Risorgimento should have no understanding whatever of the Russian Revolution? It was a debating point, possibly no more. For perhaps G.M. had had second thoughts about his early enthusiasm for the Risorgimento when he saw what it had led to in Mussolini.

When eventually, rather deferentially, I called at the Lodge of the grandest of English colleges, Trevelyan took me upstairs to see the portraits assembled in the drawing-room overlooking the Great Court. I remember his leading me up to pay my respects to Newton, and the Master telling me that such was the intensity of Newton's mental concentration that his friends were afraid of his going off his head, and conspired to get him made Master of the Mint, to remove him to London and society. He certainly looked mad enough in that portrait.

By my next visit Trevelyan had retired, to the house in West Road which became familiar. The visit is described in my Journal. 'Sexagesima Sunday, 13 February 1955. The taxi slushed across snowy Cambridge to a road behind the Library and an Edwardian neo-Georgian house. G.M.T. came to the door, looking an old man at last, after so many years of healthy walking and tramping. (One of the original Tramps, under the lead of Leslie Stephen.) He was quite white and hadn't shaved well for days – a Victorian outcrop of white hair on jaw and neck adding to the distinction of his appearance. He was warm and welcoming, lithe and energetic as ever.'

I had never met his wife, Janet (descended from the Cornish Penroses), now stricken with paralysis, but gay and lively, ready to giggle and chaff G.M.T. We had plenty to talk about, Cornwall and the Penroses, Oxford and the Arnolds. Over the chimneypiece was Will Arnold-Forster's engaging portrait of her – 'the woman you married, George' – sunlight filtering through the sunshade under which she was seated. One saw the cultivated circle, Cambridge of the early 1900s, superior and secure, refined, given to high thoughts and good causes: Trevelyans, Darwins, Sidgwicks, Keyneses, Butlers.

'Lunch was very gay, Janet T. prepared to be amused and ready to be flirted with. I don't suppose she gets much of that; I liked her enormously, and apparently excited her too much, for after lunch G.M. took me sharply away, for fear of exhausting her. "As brilliant as ever," said G.M. – and I remembered that, with the older Cambridge, "brilliant" has a questionable note. No one could accuse G.M.T. of being "brilliant", nor would he welcome it; absolutely solid, big-minded common sense, plumb right judgement, plus imagination and poetry, rather than brilliance or subtlety.'

His attitude to his wife's illness was strange – it made him ill. His Cornish nurse told me that no Trevelyan was allowed to be ill. He could not accept the fact of illness. Two nurses were in attendance, Janet practically helpless. She didn't look it at the table, rather flushed with excitement; I had amused her, given her a change. What pathos in the phrase, 'the woman you married, George', all now coming to an end.

'He took me away into his study. It was some time after Winston's H-bomb speech. Trevelyan hates the modern world, more completely and consistently than any of us – and no wonder, after the hopes of that late Victorian circle with their radical belief in progress. He hates modern science and the world it has made – rather piquant for one who was Master of the most distinguished scientific college in the world. I said that all these horrors sprang out of the Cavendish Laboratory, where they had split the atom. "Yes," said G.M., "there are Rutherford and J.J. [Thomson] buried in Westminster Abbey; when the atomic ash rains down on London, they will be well and truly buried under it."

'I said a word for science as the most important development of rational thought in the past three centuries. "But I don't like the world it has made – the Industrial Revolution, with industrial development all over the country and all that has come with it." I suddenly saw that G.M.T. is really an eighteenth-century figure; I had always thought of him as nineteenth and early twentieth century. He would like to go back beyond the whole development of modern industry to a world of coaches and carriages, farms, villages and estates, of squires, farmers, labourers. He saw himself as a squire in a stable country society. (Even I don't go back as far as that – I see 1914 as the terminus of the civilization I care for, smaller, on a mere human scale.)

'Thence to history. What he has to say about Elizabethan Ireland was old-fashioned to me, coloured by the sentimental pro-Irishry of the Gladstonian Liberals (right enough as they were about Home Rule). *There* his views hadn't kept pace with the rest. His attitude to history springs from the proximity of the old governing class to government, rather than the specialist outlook of the historian. Therein lies its advantage. When I asked if he was writing anything, he said sadly, "No, I'm too old to write any more." He had what will be, I suppose, his last book lying out before him, *A Layman's Love of Letters*.

'Something touching about the scene – as I walked away over the Cambridge snow I registered: "Work while it is yet day, for the night cometh in which no man can work".' However, they were pleased by my visit, for he wrote to say, 'let us see you whenever you come to Cambridge'.

In the autumn of 1955 I was able to send him my second volume, *The Expansion of Elizabethan England*, which he considered 'extremely well planned'. Next autumn,

> Your jolly letter about the ultra-Whig pleased me well, for I saw clearly you had not heard of Janet's death. She has suffered so much mentally and physically, for so long a time, that it is a mercy which she hoped for. It leaves me indeed the shadow of a shade. I am glad to stay here alone [at Hallington] till Christmas. I am sure I shall love your *Early Churchills* when I see it.

A week later he was pleased to think 'I had had a share in pushing off the happy voyage of so remarkable an historian as you'.

In October, 'I have now read all your *Early Churchills* very carefully and with great pleasure and great admiration. Though only a parergon, it will certainly add to your rapidly rising historical reputation.' In January 1957 he wrote:

> I cannot imagine a nicer letter than the one you have written me and I thank you most sincerely. It touches me closely. I am also greatly touched by your kind suggestion about a possible visit to you in Cornwall for April. It is an extraordinarily attractive suggestion, but I am afraid I am too old to carry it out. The journey back from Northumberland was really too much for me and as I shall need to go to Northumberland again in May, for the greater part of the year, I do not think I could manage another long expedition like that which you suggest, however pleasant it should be. My gratitude for the suggestion is none the less.

That March he had learned that I was to give the first Trevelyan Lectures: 'I want to tell you at once that you are the person I should most of all wish to be so chosen to open that show.'

In June of that year, I was bidden up to stay with him at Hallington, and duly scooted up via Nottingham in my large Humber along A1 to Scotch Corner, Corbridge, and thence on. Next morning we drove out to see over Housesteads, the camp on the Roman Wall – which he bought out of his royalties and gave the farm there as an endowment to the National Trust, to which he had also given many years of work as Chairman. How public-spirited of him, with all the other work on his hands – no wonder he had always been a man of no small talk and no waste of time. He told me a curious story of Kipling, who had the Highland 'second sight' and certainly was psychic. In one of his Roman Wall stories he had placed a certain legionary detachment somewhere along the Wall, purely out of his head; later, a coin came up from the soil, which showed that it had in fact been stationed just there. (One of Koestler's 'coincidences'?) G.M. wrote to Kipling, who was thrilled, and immensely pleased at Trevelyan's appreciation of his historic sense.

Trevelyan's books had made him a comparatively rich man, though earlier old Sir George Otto had kept him rather short. At the end of the war his *English Social History* had made in its first year £42,000 – of which, with double British and American income tax plus supertax – he paid out £39,500. I said, why ever didn't you hand the book over to the National Trust? He said he would have done, if he had thought of it. Instead of that money going on some historic or cultural object, of significance to the heritage if not to the people, it was swallowed up in the maw of the trivial consumption of a mass society (one should see the rubbish they buy in their bulging shopping-bags); the earnings of those who work confiscated for the benefit of those who do not, eternally striking over nothing, like a lot of stupid kids. (What could I not have done for Cornwall, if I had not had my hard-earned savings confiscated so wastefully, purposelessly! I suppose society today was always intended for the benefit of the third-rate, so naturally the third-rate like it. The elect despise it.)

Next morning we took another turn out around upper Tyne country, passing by Errington, I suppose the Catholic house whence the redoubtable Anne Lucy, Lady Arundell of Wardour, came (whom I had put into a short story, 'All Souls Night'). We saw also Brunton, best preserved of the Roman towers along the Wall, and stopped to look at splendid four-teenth-century and Jacobean Chipchase Castle, tawny in the sun. Doubt was expressed as to its future. I remember think-ing dejectedly how uncertain was the future of these splendid houses from the historic past – hundreds of them destroyed every year. What historian of any taste could care tuppence about the rubbish proliferating in their place?

Next morning we walked in the plantations G.M. had himself been able to make, from his own earnings, before taxation got such a stranglehold on the cultured classes and the cultural life of the country. He was a fundamentally con-structive man, a positive not a negative type – the antithesis of the destroyer, the estate-breaker, on top in the squalid society of today. Though we came from opposite ends of society – he from the top, I from the bottom – G.M. and I were at one in our fundamental values.

One thing surprised me: he had no such disapprobation as I had of the Jacobite Rising of 1715, which led to the ruin of Derwentwater and his family. He thought that anyone was justified in taking a sporting chance. I was surprised at the old sporting instinct coming out, myself not being ever in favour of taking such chances. There never was a chance of the '15 succeeding.

On my return he wrote: 'Yes, what a lovely and memor-able time we had.' I had sent a volume of my poems for his daughter, Mary Moorman, who wrote the finest biography of Wordsworth – of which he was very proud. 'I have been reading the poems with great pleasure myself' – I had not intended them for him, doubtful as I was of his liking mod-ern verse.

Of my next summer's visit to Hallington, in June 1958, I

have a full record in my Journal, a close-up of the great man, which tells one what his conversation was like.

'This year he looks better, in better colour, was even a little pink and obviously delighted to see me. Talked animatedly with vigorous gestures, argued with conviction and even passion – the old G.M.T. one used to see before his wife's long illness got him down and discouraged him. Why this should have done so, I don't understand. (Like Elgar.) On our first walk down in the dene: "I am finished."

'I had urged him several times to devote himself to a history of the Trevelyan family – such a remarkable story. But he wouldn't – said that it broke into two distinct parts, the West Country – Cornwall and Somerset – and the Northumberland branch. We must hope that a junior member of the family will undertake it. He had written charmingly of its origins in his memoir of his father, and he certainly knew the Cornish background: he had twice walked the whole coast. He was a terrific walker in his prime, could do sixty miles a day; and had once walked from Cambridge to Oxford, a matter of eighty-three miles, within twenty-four hours.

'Apparently G.M.T. and Janet were not all that close together: in earlier years they were a good deal apart, leading their separate lives – Janet doing public work, children's playgrounds and other good causes (the Foundling Hospital, as I remember from my Bloomsbury days); he in Italy, or absorbed in writing. Only in later years were they so much thrown together, not wholly good for them. Amusing their upper-class domestic unhandiness: neither of them could make a cup of tea. G.M.'s only contribution is, when tea has gone on long enough (he is naturally impatient) to carry the tea-pot and hot-water jug out into the kitchen. Similarly with coffee after lunch. Not, apparently, a saving measure, just an odd habit, like so many things about him. (cf. Barrès' brilliantly observant *Huit Jours chez M. Renan*.)

'Conversation with him was much more rewarding this year, more vivacity and fire. Just as T. E. Lawrence noticed how Hardy talked of Scott naturally as an equal and of *Marmion* as if it were contemporary, so G.M. talks of Johnny Russell and Melbourne, Bright and Pam [Palmerston], judging the good and the bad about them as if he had known them. It is partly due to the immense span of life lengthened by his father's, so much of whose knowledge he absorbed: a double advantage – in addition to that of having been born into the old governing class, a fairly small circle of people who knew the circumstances and facts, the political lives and personal situations of those Victorians. What immense advantages! He has made the most of them by his inherited qualities of mind – absolute integrity, a devastating candour, no nonsense, genuine high-mindedness amounting to nobility, rare justice of mind. He knew Edward Grey, about whom he wrote, as a personal friend. (I observed him only as a guest at All Souls, dear, sad, good man – what utter rubbish the Germans and those pro-Germans, the Cambridge pacifists, wrote about that transparent character!)

'In consequence, he comes out with surprising things, no waffle, no havering or hovering. That is why we get on so well. He obviously enjoys our talk, always about history, sometimes literature – and was glum when the family threatened to descend. This evening we talked about Marlborough, Sarah and Sunderland. He admired Sarah: "For one thing, she was never up for sale. Now Marlborough was." I defended him as far as I could. G.M. allowed that he would not have sold the pass where the Protestant establishment was concerned or constitutional monarchy; however, "there were large parts of him, large parts of the time, that were for sale". With my sceptical view of human beings, I expect that.

'I told him about a new biography of Sunderland, where I had been able to help with a few bits from the archives at Blenheim. I said that Sunderland was now more intelligible to me. G.M. kept pressing me to condemn him. I wouldn't go any further than to say that I didn't approve. He then teased me about not being a moral man; which I improved on with an account of my scepticism, which people didn't understand. [Nor did he – too direct and simple, black or white.] He gave a vivacious sketch of Sunderland's reptilian career, and what it amounted to – to which I had to assent – and ended triumphantly: "There's a rogue." There was no denying that G.M. had won.

'We greatly enjoyed this banter. I stuck to my point of disliking James II much more for his (sincere) stupidity than Sunderland for his insincerity. I hate fools like James more than rogues like Sunderland: they do more harm.

'I have learned something I value: a better appreciation of John Bright. I have been reading G.M.'s biography, the only one of his books I had not read. He insisted how important the cause of the North was for us and for the world. The victory of the South would have meant an extension of slavery in the Tropics – witness the Congo – and a revival of the slave trade. The division of North America might have meant that, in the twentieth century, she would not be strong enough to see us through to safety against Germany. That was an argument to appeal to me.

'Only on one point do I differ, and G.M. himself has learnt since his early days, with its semi-pacifist radicalism. (His brother, the baronet, even opposed resisting the Kaiser's Germany, along with Bertrand Russell and other such asses.) Bright was too ignorant – and conceited – to learn the real meaning of the Balance of Power: that maintaining the liberties of Europe against the great aggressors – Philip II, Louis XIV and Napoleon, Germany in the twentieth century – has depended on it, really a Grand Alliance against the aggressor. Departing from this sheet-anchor of our security in the thirties had brought down the second war upon us in the worst possible circumstances. G.M. was forced to agree.

'I had not realized the significance of the Manchester Philips element in the family – no doubt it accounted partly for his feeling for Bright. (By Sir George Otto's marriage came in a lot of money – G.M. was born in a second large country-house, Welcombe near Stratford-upon-Avon. Did there come in a foreign streak with this, the dark glittering look they all have, the marked intellectualism?) He told me of some Manchester meeting to protest against the Crimean War, at which uncle Mark Phillips was presiding and took too long before opening. His brother shouted from the back of the hall, "Damn it, Mark! Ask a blessing."

'Saturday afternoon: a fire lit in the Library, a shelf or two of Macaulay's books marked M. on the wall, a late photograph of him with close-set puffy eyes and high stiff collar, while I sit in his slippery Victorian armchair on castors. (At Wallington the naughty baronet, whom G.M. never mentions, had made me place both hands flat on the table upon which Macaulay wrote his *History*, that some influence might accrue to me – more power to my elbow!) What a presence he still is in the family, what a cult! And yet there is the authentic story of Sir George Otto on his death-bed, having difficulty in communicating something on his mind: "Uncle Tom – Uncle Tom [what was it so important he had to leave as his last message?] – Uncle Tom was a common man."

'When G.M. was writing his *Lord Grey of the Reform Bill*, Halifax's ancient father was helpful with information, but G.M. guessed it would not be without its price. Nor was it. When old Halifax read the book before publication, he was scandalized to find that G.M. had mentioned Grey's illegitimate daughter, born before marriage, brought up along with the other fifteen children. He added that, after marrying, Grey was completely faithful; nothing sexual in his relations with the Princess de Lieven. In deference to old Lord Halifax, he had cut this bit out of the book. "I knew what would happen: several reviewers got on to it and said that I was too favourable to Grey."

'Old prig, Lord Halifax. What *does* it matter? Lord Brand at All Souls told me that he was similarly descended from the great Lord Grey of the Reform Bill. His great-grandfather was supposed to be a younger son of the Duke of Devonshire, but in Regency days almost everybody who was anybody was somebody else's child. At Eydon Hall Bob Brand took me to look at a portrait of Lord Frederick Cavendish and then at one of the famous Lord Grey: Bob was the image of Grey, with that splendid high forehead and noble cranium. Who wouldn't prefer to be descended from a great man, rather than from some 'tenth transmitter of a foolish face'?

'Of Gladstone, a number of the Liberal Unionists, men of exceptional ability – like the men G.M. used to meet when he came to All Souls, Anson, Dicey, W. P. Ker – used to think that there was a good deal of an ass in Mr G.: witness his views on Homer, and on the Church.

'G.M. owed the original suggestion of his Garibaldi book to Bernard Pares. About 1905–6 some Italian Memoirs about Garibaldi had come out – Pares had given them to him as a wedding present. By then he could read Italian and saw that here was a subject. Never did he work so hard or so fast as in the year in which he wrote his first Garibaldi book. [The first three became best-sellers. I remember the appearance of the fourth, on Daniele Manin and Venice, after the 1914–18 war. At All Souls Keith Hancock wrote his *Ricasoli* largely in reaction to Trevelyan's Garibaldi books. No hero of mine anyway: I prefer the political type of Cavour.]

'Passing by a battered funerary figure in the loggia, of a lady from the Roman Wall: "She doesn't look much now, but I expect she was called the Rose of Procolitia in her day."

'He used to see a good deal of John Simon (of All Souls) in their radical days. Once, when the young Simon had been staying at Welcombe, Sir George Otto said afterwards that he wasn't really any good for politics. Then, with his usual fairness, G.M. added, "Of course, one must remember the blow that the death of his wife was to him. It shut him up like a flower in the evening. It was defect of character to allow that to happen – but that was the reason." [There were others.]

'He didn't ask me to like John Knox (I detest him); all he asked was to do him this justice: before Knox the Scotch peasantry were under the foot of the nobles, mere feudal vassals. Knox taught them to look the nobles in the face. Scotland didn't have a monarchy strong enough to carry through the Reformation: Knox was the best they could do. As for Henry VIII, he settled the Welsh problem, he extruded the Pope, was the real founder of the Navy and resuscitated Parliament: a big achievement for one man. A bad man, but a good King.

'One sees how personal his view of history is, and how moral: last of the Victorians.

'About his grandfather, Sir Charles Trevelyan – "the best of us all" – Trollope, who was much opposed to his introduction of the examination system into the Civil Service, put him into his novel, *The Three Clerks*, as Sir Gregory Hardlines. Afterwards the two became friends, without ever giving up their opposed convictions.

'How paradoxical it was that all three men – Palmerston, Lord John Russell, Gladstone – who were so sympathetic to Italian freedom and did so much to advance it, were all pro-South in the American Civil War. The aristocrats were more ignorant and out of touch with America; but they were always going to Italy and knew what was going on there. They hadn't yet begun to make American marriages; the working people were more in touch; through emigration and correspondence they knew the North, as the aristocrats did not.

'He was much interested by what I had to tell him about the historian Sir Charles Firth's background, and repeated to me his remark *à propos* of the Queen Anne material out of his splendid collection of tracts and pamphlets (Firth was always generous in lending him stuff): "You like writing about these old fellows?" "Yes, don't you?" "No, I only like reading about them."

'One day, walking in the Parks at Oxford with A. L. Smith, G.M. was astonished by his violent outburst against Firth. I explained that this came from the history tutors' inveterate feud against Firth: they never forgave him for his Inaugural Lecture, with its aggressive claims for research as against their teaching. Firth was a Yorkshireman, direct and forthright; the result was that they excommunicated him, and kept the most eminent Oxford historian of his day insulated and never sent their pupils to his lectures. His *protégé*, Godfrey Davis, good scholar, could never get a job in Oxford, and ultimately found a refuge in the Huntington Library in California. How small-minded academics are! G.M. thought the outburst all the more extraordinary coming from so fine a man as A. L. Smith. (He wrote nothing, gave all to Balliol.)

'Sir George Otto, after his First at Cambridge, missed a Fellowship at Trinity, so he decided to go out to India as private secretary to his father, the great Sir Charles, then Finance Member of Council, a terrific Reformer. As a result, Sir George wrote the book in my bedroom, *Cawnpore*, and *The Competition Wallah*, which Kipling admired.

'G.M. has just been into the Library, making up the fire and showing me books along the shelves: of Kennaway's *On Sherman's Track* – "he was in the House of Commons with my father in the sixties". An early edition of Purchas' *Pilgrims* had belonged to Holland House and was given to Macaulay by the Hollands. [That wonderful house with its splendid library was destroyed by the Germans in the Blitz. A friend of mine saw Lord Ilchester next morning, picking his way among the smoking ruins and saving here and there a rare book from his burned treasures.]

'G.M. wished that Macaulay had finished the reign of William III. He was imperceptive as to character; his great strength lay in his understanding of political situations, of mass-forces at work, and the movement of opinion. So that he wondered what he would have made of the reign of Queen Anne, where so much depended on the personalities of Marlborough, the Queen, and Sarah. He specified the three persons over whom Macaulay went badly wrong: Claverhouse, William Penn and Marlborough. He appreciated my point as to the defect of Macaulay's rhetorical method and the application of antithesis to character. Macaulay had blackened the portrait of the early Marlborough in order to make him appear the more shining as the hero of Queen Anne's reign – then Macaulay died before he got there. Unfair on Marlborough, unsubtle of Macaulay. He agreed as to this.

'This put in perspective a letter I had had from him about my own work, which had greatly elated me. I took it as the greatest compliment I had ever received: "You have a far subtler sense of character than Macaulay, but you do not have his tall measure of events." It took the compliment down a peg or two, when I reflected that Macaulay's sense of character was not very subtle after all.

'He was most interesting about Carlyle – most of whom I had read when young, and today cannot stand. One cannot understand anything of Carlyle, he said, unless one recognizes that there were *two* Carlyles. The Carlyle of *The French Revolution* had pity for men – this he said with great feeling and quoted a passage that moved him deeply, though not me; and then the Carlyle of *Frederick* – better not to read that.

How it could have happened, why the change, he could not conceive. At that I took over – he thought there was a good deal in what I said. Disillusionment above all – with people's folly, with democratic and Parliamentary cant, with the rationalist assumption, the idiotic liberal assumption that people are rational. Disillusionment too with his private life, the emptiness of it with no sex. He felt strongly against the later Carlyle, and evidently regarded what he wrote as immoral. I remembered how shocked the middle-class Quaker, W. E. Forster, was on tour with Carlyle in Ireland at Carlyle's views on the Irish peasantry: Forster thought him a moral scoundrel, and never held him in regard after. But, of course, one peasant would know better as to other peasants than a high-minded middle-class type like Forster, hopelessly gone to the good. He clearly thought Carlyle had gone to the bad. So too thought the high-minded G.M.

'Naturally, I feel this less strongly, and held forth on what made for Carlyle's originality: a peasant of genius who knew instinctively, as well as from experience, what nonsense the superficial rationalism of the *Edinburgh Review*, and of John Stuart Mill, was. Again, a lower-class man, an outsider, in their upper-class world, who was yet better educated and far more widely read than they were – not only in their classics, not only in French and Italian, like some of them, but also in Spanish, above all in German, which none of them knew. No wonder he was a phenomenon, who burst upon them from the north like a smouldering meteor. Actually, I preferred his earlier writings in conventional English, the *Scottish Essays* for instance, before he developed his appalling personal style.

'G.M. listened to all this, much impressed.

'Next morning occurred a *contretemps*. An ugly morning, would I walk with him? I had only my oldest shoes, most comfortable for driving, with a crack in the right sole. He led me up the road and straight across a hideously wet field, my shoes squelching, feet, socks, trouser-bottoms drenched (himself equipped with hobnailed boots, thick woollen stockings, breeches). All the while talking about the Reform Bills of 1832 and 1867, and why the Whigs chose Melbourne for Prime Minister; the paradoxes of the nineteenth century, that the Liberals should have been so good at Army Reform with Cardwell and Haldane, while the Conservatives should have brought in Free Trade and the Reform Bill of 1867. To this I added the Education Act of 1902, the most significant measure of social progress in this century.

'All the while I was in misery, squelch, squelch, squelch – inwardly amused at my predicament. I might have known it would happen, so I lost no equanimity. When I got back, I had a complete change, the nice woman who looks after me washed my socks and dried everything out. In earlier days G.M.'s capacity for walking was terrific, and when he came to a stream he walked right through it.

'This evening he was very lively – more conversation about the contrast between the conduct of our policy before 1914 – when we entered the war with Russia and France as allies, and shortly Italy – and that before 1939, which left us alone without an ally in 1940. The last time G.M. had seen Grey was at Fallodon in 1933, after Hitler had come in. Grey said that this was the end for Europe. All that G.M. could say was that it wasn't his fault. (Of course it was the end of their Europe – the old civilized Europe.)

'After supper G.M. was quite cheerful on the sofa, putting little bits into the conversation. Once to the effect that there couldn't be a better composer than Vaughan Williams, he was by far the nicest man! (G.M. has no ear for music.) On going to bed he scored joyfully off me. All the rest are going to early service and breakfast at Wallington; so he said, 'Since you and I are breakfasting alone tomorrow, *you*'ll be able to get a word in edgeways.' Everybody roared at this sally, for I have been talking nineteen to the dozen.

How much he appreciated it I overheard next morning, for he dresses in the room next to mine and I heard him talking to himself, 'Good friend. Good jaw.'

Writing the family history of the Churchills broke into the sequence of volumes on the Elizabethan Age; but Trevelyan evidently ceased to think of the book with which I hoped to set a new model of readable family history as a mere parergon. For he wrote in August 1958 that he thought *The Later Churchills* very good.

Indeed I think it is your best written and most readable book of all. Old Sarah and young Lord Randolph and, above all, Winston are A1, and all the figures are good. You have, what Macaulay had not, the power of drawing individual people rightly. His other qualities you have not, in his tall measure, nor has anyone had since his death.

> But thou Cornwall's and fortune's son
> March indefatigably on
> And for the best effect
> Still keep the pen erect.

When he had finished the book he wrote again: 'A very great book indeed – the Winston part of course the best of it all. How deeply moving. So grateful to you for doing it.'

In September he was very pleased by my telling him that I had learned from Macaulay my habit of noting down places and things just as and when I had them under my eye, to get them right and vivid when transcribing them into my books.

He was looking forward to attending the first of my Trevelyan Lectures on *The Elizabethans and America*. I much enjoyed those autumn jaunts along the roads between Oxford and Cambridge, picnicking in country lanes and looking in on the churches – as also the chance to explore Cambridge further, always a pleasure. Those two university towns, with their colleges and churches, so similar in character to a foreign eye, are two wholly different worlds with different luminaries, different tutelary deities to an inhabitant of one or the other.

'3 October 1959: afternoon at Hallington. I have brought my chair out to a favourite spot on the lawn, at the edge of the deep dene, the still water of the dammed burn spattered with fallen leaves, the noise of the water going through the weir coming up with the breeze that just stirs the beeches not yet turning. Some colour about: lemon yellow of chestnut, crimson blush of dogwood, striped scarlet of sumach.'

It was his remote cousin, the Taormina widow, who had re-created the place, Victorianizing the house rather well, 'considering it was done in the 1860s – nothing Gothic about it'. The essential thing was that she had bought the bank on the other side of the burn, pretty well impassable jungle and planted the dene as a whole; blocked the stream to fill the bottom with water, laid out paths on either side. The dene makes the whole charm of the place, purple and gold in summer, lemon, russet, scarlet in autumn. I have never seen it in spring.

'The Master's talk was as incisive as ever. I read to him from a new book about the Anglo-Florentines; he proceeded to quote forty or fifty lines from Browning's "Old Pictures in Florence". His memory for verse is astonishing. He said merely a good natural memory, nothing out of the ordinary; Macaulay could recite the whole of *Paradise Lost*. All the more remarkable with blank verse; G.M. remembered verse by the aid of the rhymes. I said that Edgeworth of All Souls, overcome by sea-sickness crossing the Atlantic, had lain in his bunk reconstructing the *Odyssey*, and found that he could do two-thirds of it. The older generation at All Souls, Malcolm and Oman, had hundreds of lines by heart.

'G.M. said that a great mistake had been made when they ceased to learn poetry by heart: it meant that the younger generation didn't care for poetry. Except Shakespeare – for they liked plays. "Shakespeare and Eliot," I said to tease him. "Oomph," he said with contempt. (However, he had been pleased when Eliot wrote him a nice letter about *A Layman's Love of Letters*, saying politely that he had no reason to regard him as a layman.)

'In truth he knows masses of poetry by heart, which he recites over and over, Milton, Wordsworth, Browning, Meredith. Walking in the dene he recited several stanzas of "Love in the Valley" – "the most beautiful poem of them all" – with more feeling than he usually puts into it. (Was he thinking of Janet? But only once had he fallen in love, at nineteen, for a girl who refused him. A second time he met a girl whom he thought he would like to marry. He studied her mother, and saw the kind of woman she would become – as I do the front

photographs in *Country Life* – and decided against. The third
time he met Janet – over Meredith. Was it a love-match? Janet
was a personality, not content just to be the wife of a great
man: she made a career for herself.) He was loud in praise of
Browning for the courage with which he took Elizabeth Barrett away from her possessive father to the climate of Italy,
which cured her illness. (Was it only the climate? Perhaps it
was greensickness which Browning cured in her.)

'Henry Jackson was one day out at Madingley, about 1860,
with some friends, well-read and educated. They were talking of Mrs Browning. One of them said, "Hasn't she got a
husband who writes poetry too?" Mrs Browning was much
the better known then. All Browning's best poems were
written in the forties and fifties; his *reputation* was the work
of the sixties.

'The lady who had created this place was the widow of
Edward Spencer Trevelyan, younger brother of Sir Walter.
Neither of them had a son, or Wallington would not have
come to his grandfather, Sir Charles. This lady's daughter
"had not much of what you and I call resources and was
utterly bored at Hallington. She asked Sir Charles's advice,
who suggested a six-month tour in Italy. She never came
back, but lived in a large *palazzo* in the centre of Taormina.
When I was there I called on her, and had tea with her;
touched by this attention, she left me the estate. For the last
twenty years it had been let: that came to an end in 1927, I
came here in 1928."

'All very luckily for him – for, the most eminent member
of the family, he was the youngest son: Wallington went to
the eldest, Welcombe to the second son, Robert, poet and
translator (whom I never met). Nothing for G.M., until out
of the blue came this, and he made it his very own. "I had
enough money then to look after it properly." Hence the
loving care lavished on it: planting those belts of woodland,
the coppices and spinneys he delighted to walk in, putting in
the engine that brings water from the never-failing spring –
"Hallington water is very good"; thinning and planting up
the dene with flowering shrubs – like a patch of Cornwall in
its luxuriance amid the bare uplands. He had filled the house

with furniture from the antique shops at Hexham, books from Steedman's at Newcastle (with whom I had long dealt). He had some Edward Lear water-colours, Georgian prints of Cambridge colleges on the walls, good old wardrobes, chests, and clocks.

'In the dressing-room next my bedroom are family photographs: Sir George Otto and wife, remote and withdrawn, with family grouped on the steps at Welcombe. The eldest son, Charles, handsome, sexy, looking rather slyly out of key with all that high-mindedness; R.C., the poet; and the youthful G.M. looking abstracted, *mécontent*. (Thomas Hodgkin's daughter, who knew them all, said that G.M. was decidedly a prig then. Big brother Charles used to complain that out shooting he would break the line and wander away on his own. They would shout at him, and he would come back sulky. It is only in the second half of his life that he has broadened out, in his last years positively mellowed and developed a charm of his own.)

'I see that in his copy of "Bishop Blougram" he has marked the lines:

> Myself – by no immoderate exercise
> Of intellect and learning, but the tact
> To let external forces work for me.

(They worked for him all right: Baldwin, a Trinity man, gave him an O.M. in his fifties. And this was how he thought of himself.) This morning we walked along the terrace, he admiring the colour of the dahlias against the stone, for there is little that he can see – though this morning in the walled garden he could see a brilliant Red Admiral feeding on a chrysanthemum. He was modest about himself: in his will he had enjoined that there was to be no biography of him. He had written his *Autobiographical Essay* to forestall anyone else writing it.

'Why ever? He would not be able to prevent people writing about him. Consider the case of Thackeray, who insisted that no biography be written – and behold Gordon Ray's two, immensely detailed volumes. He rejoined that Thackeray was in a totally different class – a man of genius, where he himself was only a man of talents who had done his best with them. I said he was underestimating the value of the historian's work compared with the novelist's. And overestimating Thackeray – not in the same class with Dickens. He agreed with that. Historians like Gibbon, Macaulay, Carlyle were quite as important as novelists. He agreed about them, but did not compare himself with them.

'At one point in the discussion he paid me a grand compliment. I said that I did not count. "Oh, yes," with conviction, "you *count* – very much so."

'Today, I know that that is wrong. In a society where all contours have gone, all landmarks removed, nobody *can* count. So nobody counts, where all are alike: and what matter?

'I said that we historians had different things to contribute. Though Gibbon had a generalized interest in geography, he had not G.M.'s sense of the bone-structure of England and her landscape, which I loved in his work, and which he owed to his life-long habit of walking. For another, Gibbon had been essentially unjust to Christianity.

'I can admire his liberalism, though I do not share it. His income had come down now to £6000 a year: to pay tax on that, keep the place going with all its dependents, and the Cambridge house, with nurse-housekeeper – he must live on capital. He said, "I agree with death-duties and supertax. I think it is right. I pay my taxes gladly." I do not. What? – those who work hard pay for those who don't? We are sick to death with too much of all that – and many of the country's best writers and artists have left it on account of it. I think they are right to leave it to those who like it.

'G.M. has very strict and upright Victorian principles, irrelevant in a shiftless society like this. At tea he was approving of Dismal – the saturnine Earl of Nottingham – for holding no correspondence with Saint-Germain. (I forgot to score the point that this Right-wing Tory made an unprincipled deal with the Left-wing Whigs, over Occasional Conformity, to do in the men of the centre, Marlborough and Godolphin, who were carrying the burden of the war. Politicians are much of a muchness at all times.) To tease G.M. I praised Marlborough's subtlety. "Subtlety is another word for treachery," he said.

'I was admiring the subtlest intellect of them all, Halifax, the Trimmer. "But he would not sign the invitation to William," G.M. said. I replied that that was very understandable, with his point of view. "You mean to say that you wouldn't have signed the invitation?" (i.e. to come over and save the country from James II). I said, "No." "I think the less of you for that," he said. "You mean, you wouldn't?" I said that, with my scepticism, I should not have approved of signing it; I hope that I should not have been carried away emotionally.

'He was very disapproving. He said that Halifax was not disinterested. I replied that the Whigs who signed were even less so: they had every interest in bringing William in. Halifax's position was a consistent one: he had saved the principle of monarchy and James II's accession by defeating the Exclusion Bill. He may have thought that the best thing would be to retain James as titular King, with William, his son-in-law, exercising power as Regent. G.M. said that though Halifax knew James was a fool, he had not realized how great a fool, nor that he would bunk from the country. Precisely, I said, if James hadn't fled, Halifax's view would have been perfectly applicable. G.M. replied that William would not have accepted this subordinate position; and at the critical moment, as with a lot of distinguished men, Halifax was NO USE.

'That was that – just like G.M. to cut through all the cackle, all the complexities, to the core of the matter. But I do not share his view. When I was young, and a fanatic, I would have signed the party manifesto all right, and gone to the stake for my convictions. Not so today. I have seen too much of human foolery.

' "Why not?" said G.M., visibly moved.

' "Because I despair of the futility of so much of human action." (I did not quote an old-time Liberal friend of his: 'The longer I live the more I see that things really are as silly as they seem.' But that's what I meant.)

' "Go away with you," said he. "Take the tea things away, and come back again."

'I came back for another set-to, significantly on the issue of the Civil War. He was vehement that it was not avoidable. "For two reasons. One was that you could not trust Charles I. The other was that neither side had the idea of religious toleration. Bad as the Whigs were at the end of the seventeenth century, in many ways, they had the idea of religious toleration. I'm a great believer in liberty. I'm glad I live in a country where everybody can express his own opinion."

'He is a man of absolutely firm and simple principles, which he applies consistently to history, and this gives him a grasp of the essentials of a situation. I am left as a Laodicean to deplore the obstinacy of both sides that led to war, the destruction of beautiful buildings, irreplaceable works of art, which I value more than I do people's "principles" or their silly convictions. As against the inestimable losses – some irreplaceable lives of men of genius too – what gain?

'I did not tell him that I would have left the country with the philosopher Hobbes – to return when it had gained its sanity. That would have shocked him. No point in arguing that point: his mind was made up. So was mine.

'Sunday morning we went for a walk up through one of the plantations he made thirty years ago, giving protection to the fields from north-east and south-west winds. "I hope I die before I go stone-blind," he said, in one of those explosions of melancholy that afflict him. This made him think of Leslie Stephen, who made such an impression speaking for blind Henry Fawcett that the constituency asked him to stand for the second seat. "Damn you, don't you know that I'm a clergyman?" said he. The militant rationalist was in deacon's orders, and clergymen couldn't stand for Parliament. J. A. Froude was in the same case.

'He had no liking for Stephen's daughter, Virginia Woolf – a "horrid woman"; but, then, she had no liking for her father and gave a very unflattering portrait of him in *To the Lighthouse*. He detested Bloomsbury and all its works, making an exception for Keynes, who didn't really belong. "For one thing, he was infinitely public-spirited, and one of the things they discouraged was public spirit. Then, they were all very angry with him for getting married. One of the things they had no use for was marriage. He married one of the nicest women possible" [Lydia Lopokova].

'When I said of Bloomsbury that they wrote well, he replied that that made their influence all the more deplorable. A whole generation was ruined by them – gave them a debunking attitude towards great writers. He once listened to a paper of Lytton Strachey's and registered, "This is the end of all I care for. And it was."

'That night I had an acute attack of sciatica, excruciating pain all down my leg and had to stay in bed, under a drug administered by G.M.'s nurse. Now we were both invalid-ish, and G.M.'s real kindness came out, shuffling along the corridor to see how I was. When I got down he kept me by the warm fireside in the drawing room, charming with the colours of dahlias and Michaelmas daisies along the terrace, the room filled with October sunshine. He was lying on the sofa, silvery and frail in full sun, half dozing, almost blind, nothing to do but wait for death.

'Resuming our talk, he said: "The nineteenth century was better than the twentieth in a great many ways, and one of them was that it wasn't possessed with a passion for debunk-ing. Roger Fry, for instance, thought that Greek art wasn't any good! Pshaw!" When I reflected how Roger Fry pontifi-cated about art in those years, and was held up to us for mentor, his own painting lifeless and uninspired – King's is filled with his pictures, academic and dead – it is obvious enough that G.M. with his historical sense was right. *One* of Fry's portraits has life and was indeed inspired; an American friend owns his portrait of Bertrand Russell, which uncovers a real strain of evil in his face. Eliot, on Russell's playing round with his wife, upsetting her mental balance, already rocky: "Bertie has wrought Evil." He made up for it by unburdening himself of his armaments shares on Eliot, to ease his conscience as a pacifist. Michael Foot on Russell: "He is my man of the century." I share Trevelyan's view what asses these people were.

'What a contrast to them Henry James was – more genius

and a great gentleman. G.M. knew him well, and I have never heard him speak of anyone with more warmth and enthusiasm: a "lovable man", and then in a low voice, as if to himself, "adorable". It is the only time I have heard from him such a strong expression of that kind, though he spoke affectionately – who wouldn't? – of Gilbert Murray, "dear Gilbert". Of Henry James, "underneath the complicated and subtle machine there were simple and direct feelings. No action was more characteristic of him than his taking British nationality, out of anger that the Americans were keeping out of the war. He knew that the world wouldn't be a better place if the German militarists won. President Wilson couldn't see it".

'Well, by 1917 he did see it. Russell never did – until Hitler and the second German war, when his *volte face* showed up his attitude to the first for the nonsense it was.

'G.M. doesn't discuss people much: he sums them up incisively in a brief mention. Of Rupert Brooke: "he was a charming fellow". Of Belloc: "he was a liar" (he was; also a man of genius). Namier: "He's a good historical researcher, but I don't think he's a good historian. He has no sense of the past". Or, grandly, "You and I know that Veronica is a historian of the second rank".

'Next day I was well enough to risk driving. He came out on the terrace to see me off, and I took a photograph of him, looking sad and disconsolate, with that well known grumpy expression. There was the place he had re-created around him, hall-door open to the beds of snapdragons and dahlias, the curve of the drive with beeches as good as at Wallington; up on the horizon the Romans watching us from their Wall.'

In December he was thanking me for my

most interesting article on that extraordinary person, Hawker of Morwenstow. His love of the poor and understanding of their case, his selflessness and his poetry appeal to me very much. But his superstition repels me. Therefore on the whole I prefer a man who in general work and character was very like him – "wonderful Walker" of Duddon, whose memory interested

Wordsworth so much. He did on the Duddon very much the works that Hawker did in Morwenstow. I remember the wonderful region of Morwenstow, and its terrible coast, from walking there some sixty years ago. It is all very vivid to me still.

Next year my birthday message gave him 'special pleasure because it hailed me as a Cornishman'.

In July 1962 his faithful Cornish nurse wrote to me a touching account of the Master's death, and that she would be accompanying the body from Cambridge up to Langdale. There, I suppose he was buried with Janet, beside their little Theo, of so many years before.

It was sad that none of the family loved Hallington as he did. Janet, with her South Country background, never liked it, and in her last illness would not admit that she was there – she would be at Welcombe, or Stocks (her mother's place, Mrs Humphrey Ward, Matthew Arnold's redoubtable niece). Taken into the walled garden, where G.M. had set up her initials with his, along with Edward Spencer Trevelyan and his wife's, Janet would say, 'This *is* Stocks.'

This wounded G.M., to whom Hallington meant so much, and which he hoped would go on in the family, of which he had such an historic sense. When he died, his son at once took the opportunity to sell Hallington, and shortly died himself.

As with so much in our time of decline, decay and destruction, it made an end.

5

Samuel Eliot Morison

Samuel Eliot Morison was the opposite number to George Macaulay Trevelyan in England: each stood at the head of the historical profession, one in England, the other in the United States; each born in the purple, with a distinguished line and family tradition behind him; each the most widely read in his respective country. Morison was, like Trevelyan, not only a great historian but a great man. He had that quality of crashing integrity which I have singled out as possessed by all such men: his integrity, like Churchill's or Trevelyan's, crashed through all barriers, every kind of nonsense or humbug. I used, privately to myself, to call him a piece of Plymouth Rock – though he doubted whether the Pilgrim Fathers ever landed on that exposed piece of New England folklore.

On mature reflection I am inclined to think that Morison was the greatest of all American historians, when one considers the sheer range that he encompassed, the variety of his historical work, the amount of original research that he accomplished, and the quality of his writing, the honesty, justice of mind, his gift for words, the touches of poetry. Putting all this together, one must place him ahead of Parkman and Prescott, and even that more original and brilliant intellect, Henry Adams. Invidious as it is for a Cornishman to say so, in the end he beats Trevelyan – larger in scope, and he had the tremendous advantage of his knowledge of the sea, as well as the inspiration of it.

Curiously enough, Morison and Trevelyan had very little contact, for all that one was Cambridge *pur sang* (US) and the other Cambridge (Eng.). All Morison's English contacts were with Oxford, and he was a loyal Oxford man. His period as the first professor of American History at Oxford, where he was a student of Christ Church, exactly coincided with my undergraduate years at the same college, 1922–5, though I never set eyes on him. My history tutors, Feiling and Masterman, did not encourage an interest in American history, and Feiling thought the young Morison 'brash' – he would, reserved and not very forthcoming as he was. I dare say Morison was brash; but he was quite right, as the first holder of the chair, to be aggressive about American history, which was disconsidered at Oxford.

As if the story of the greatest of the English-speaking peoples were not immeasurably more important – with all the lessons it had to convey, and just after Britain had survived Germany's onslaught only by the intervention of the United States – than the intimacies of the Wardrobe or Privy Seal under Edward II! I came to sympathize with Raymond Asquith's unpublished Epitaph on a Tired Statesman (his father?):

> He loathed affairs and hated the state:
>   He wrapped his lunch in Livy;
> He threw the Great Seal into the grate,
>   And the Privy Seal into the privy.

Medieval administrative history was the fashion then, in the dreary volumes of Tout (to know Tout was *not*, as somebody said, *tout pardonner*); just as today populist history is fashionable with Leftist historians, though it cannot be denied that interesting people are more interesting than uninteresting ones.

In his Inaugural Lecture at Oxford Morison made a reasoned and unanswerable statement for the study of American history, very wise and mature for so young a man. He always thought that 'the story of mankind, with all his nobility and baseness, wisdom and folly, is the most interesting and fascinating of stories; that history is to the community what memory is to the individual'. Where should we be without memory? And he was not afraid to say that the vast majority of people read or studied history for pleasure – very unacademic of him. He did not fail to make a salutary point against pedants: 'the study of roots is doubtless profitable, and pleasant for those who do not like the colour of leaves or the taste of fruit; but to learn something about a plant, you must give your main attention to what is above ground'.

Still more to the point is what he had to say about the upshot of the American Revolution, and the contentiousness that followed. 'This was not entirely the fault of one side, but it was unnecessary. Although the feeling of the American people was not friendly to Britain in 1783, the antipathy was recent and could easily have been allayed – it was allayed in New England, where the anti-British feeling had been strongest . . . But the British governments of the late eighteenth century refused to carry out the treaty of peace in good faith, refused to conclude a commercial treaty with the United States . . . No British minister was sent to the United States for almost ten years after the war, and the first one appointed almost brought on another war. But for Washington's resolute insistence on keeping the peace, war would have come in 1793 . . . Not that the British government during these years was hostile to the United States; its attitude may rather be characterized as one of contemptuous indifference; which is the very worst attitude to adopt toward a new or weak nation which, like the America of 1790, is suffering from what the current jargon calls an "inferiority complex".' Wise words.

Sam Morison was indeed a patriot. He tells us in his admirable recollections of boyhood, *One Boy's Boston*, that so far from Boston being snobbishly pro-British, 'the traditions of the American Revolution were central to my upbringing; memorials and landmarks of it were all about us . . . It was only after growing up that I began to entertain feelings of kindness and admiration toward our mother country.' This balanced judgment – justice of mind, rarest of qualities – is evident in the three big American histories he wrote: the *Oxford History of the United States*, which he wrote as a textbook for students while at Oxford, the first book of his I read; *The Growth of the American Republic*, in which he co-operated with Henry Steele Commager; and his final *Oxford History of the American People*, the book of which he was proudest. It might be said that that Inaugural, more than any that I can think of, provided a blue-print for what the young professor would eventually accomplish.

I am not going to deal with his historical work as such, but, as with Trevelyan, to present the man as I knew him: I count myself honoured to have had his friendship for some thirty years.

There is a clue to Sam Morison in *One Boy's Boston* which he does not make much of and which most people miss. They think of him as the essential Bostonian, descended from Otises (of revolutionary fame) and Eliots, kinsman of the celebrated Charles Eliot Norton and almost everybody who was anybody in Boston, formed and shaped by Harvard, to the service of which he gave his life, and ended up as its chief landmark. He said in his Inaugural that 'the average American today is living in a different spot from his birthplace. A house that has sheltered the same family for a century is a curiosity'. His was one of the curiosities: he lived all his life in the house that had been built by his Eliot grandfather, 44 Brimmer Street, Boston, an address that became very familiar to me.

But all that, the Boston purple, was on his mother's side; his father came of Irish stock from Baltimore. One would never think of Sam as a Southerner, and yet this element was important in his make-up. Temperament is something deeper than one's intellectual formation; and Sam had an ebullience, an outspokenness, an enjoyable concern with himself and his own doings, which made him unpopular with the faceless tribe of his own profession. Trevelyan, a strong personality, was yet rather withdrawn and impersonal in his contacts; he thus avoided hostilities with lesser people who envied him. Sam was very personal, apt to be contentious, rather liked a fight and, I suspect, was out to provoke a fool and shoot him down. He was a gentleman, all done in good sport without rancour; all the same, he couldn't stand nonsense, and this made enemies. In fact, there was some Irish blood on both sides of his family.

Sam had a normal, extrovert boyhood, with all a boy's interest in horses – in those days of horse-drawn traffic, stables all round Brimmer Street – skating, camping, an igloo in the woods in those ferocious winters; above all, the summers on Mount Desert Island, swimming, sailing, everything to do with the sea, which generated his passion for the ocean and equipped him to be the greatest naval historian in our language. He admits at one point that his passion is almost indescribable: 'My feeling for the sea is such that writing about it is almost as embarrassing as making a confession of religious faith.' He then goes on to make a good shot at it. 'To ply, unhurried, the blue deeps, or skirt the shining margents of the land, communing with the element whence life sprang, hearing no other sound but the splash of the oar, the flap of sail, the whistling of wind in the rigging, and the swish and gurgle of cloven waves, revives one's strength and refreshes one's spirit.'

He then betrays himself: 'Once in a while some incident, view, or scrap of poetry strikes a bell that reverberates through the deeps . . . when that happens I feel impelled to write something immediately.' All his life, from early on, he was like that, keeping diary, journal or notes; and what it reveals is that he was *a born writer*.

For all that the Eliots knew that they were 'top drawer', there was a democratic quality in their life, which Sam carried still further in his, all the more for rubbing shoulders with everybody, especially the sea-folk along the coast. Boston itself was an open society. 'Once you were "in", more or less wealth made no difference.' How different from old Philadelphia, the most closed society in the States: unless you belonged to one of the old families there, you were nobody at all. No despising trade in Boston; nobody was too proud to earn his living; while the public spirit, which led to all those philanthropic foundations, was beyond praise – the best legacy of Puritanism. Hence it was that Bostonians bought Washington's original library, such an index to the man; it reposes in the Boston Athenaeum, to which Sam directed me. He was the heir to all this and improved on it.

All this is evident in his beautiful little book *The Story of Mount Desert Island*, which originated in a lecture he gave for the benefit of the public libraries there. Anyone who has written local history knows that in some ways it is more difficult than history on a larger scale, the evidence is often so minute and hard to get. Sam extracted the evidence from a vast quantity of sources for so small a space, and added to it his lifelong acquaintance with its local lore, people, folkways and language, its seacraft. All written in the idiomatic style of a master; Sam had such a command of language that he could afford to take risks which lesser people couldn't. He used the whole spectrum of the language from good, vivid, direct slang to the poetic and moving; his usage was as concrete as sea-objects themselves, instead of the nerveless abstractions of academics. He had a nose for rare words, his books are full of them, as for eloquence and poetry. And, of course, he was so much better educated than they, properly grounded in the classics – so that he could cite, along with St Jean Perse and Hérédia – Virgil's hexameters giving the very rumble of the sea:

> *et gemitum ingentem pelagi pulsataque saxa* . . .[1]

Or

> *Di, maris et terrae tempestatumque potentes*
> *ferte viam vento facilem et spirate secundi* . . .[2]

Or the trumpet call of

> *dat clarum e puppi signum; nos castra movemus.*[3]

From such a hand we accept 'Asticou's savvy salesmanship

[1] And the huge roar of the sea and battered rocks.
[2] Ye gods of sea and land, with power over storms, give us easy passage with following wind and breezes.
[3] He gives clear signal from the poop; we break camp.

succeeded'; 'Captain Argall ordered "Boarders Away", and
in a jiffy his merry men were swarming over the French
bulwarks . . . Argall gave Saussaye the longboat and told him
to shove off'. So much more vivid, and in keeping with the
genius of the language, than dreary Germanic academese.
Since Sam kindly corrected a book of mine on a few nautical
points, perhaps I may correct him, if only as a joke: this
Captain Argall was not an Englishman but a Cornishman
(the name means 'the shelter'), though I didn't know about
his doings on Mount Desert.[4] Look at all those rare words –
quahang, the 'long since departed porgy or menhaden' and
the 'fry-houses' for extracting oil; beside the sea-terms, 'the
fore gaff doubled as derrick', which Sam loved and by which
inferiors thought, I suspect, he liked to take the mickey out
of us. A serious point is involved: somewhere he points out
that naval history written by landsmen is apt to be riddled
with errors. Nor would this good stylist confuse the proper
use of 'shall' and 'will', 'should' and 'would' any more than
on the island: 'The speech of the Mount Deserters was
remarkably correct as well as muscular and virile – instinctively they used "shall" and "will", "should" and "would"
correctly.'

That is more than even an educated novelist like Louis
Auchincloss can do today; to anyone who knows the correct
usage, this is a perpetual irritation. But he has the excuse of
his Scotch descent, for with Scots and Irish the distinction
did not exist – it does not in Yeats, for instance; Oscar Wilde
got his friends to look out for these solecisms in his work, for
he at least knew that his usage was wobbly. Today, in the
obliteration of all standards in demotic society, there is complete confusion; myself, I should be ashamed not to adhere to
the correct usage: it is quite easy to learn.

Sam loved the Island people and their lore.

> Your true Mount Deserter disproved the old adage, 'Jack
> of all trades, master of none'. He could be fisherman,
> sailor, farmer, lumberman, shipwright and quarryman
> rolled into one, and master of all . . . I have watched

[4] It is a Truro name, cf. my *The Cornish in America*, 184.

Wilbur Herrick select a straight hickory tree in the woods, square off a balk about three feet long, split it longitudinally into four sticks of equal size and fashion each into a beautifully fashioned axe-handle. All done with no other tools but an axe and a drawknife.

How much better than third-rate writers of theses!

Sam had the soul of a poet; he appreciated music, but his aesthetic sense was essentially directed towards seascape and landscape. 'It was one of those perfect June days that you often experience in these waters: a light offshore breeze, fleecy clouds rolling up over the land; sky, island and ocean in three deepening shades of blue, and the air filled with the spicy fragrance of early summer in Maine.' He loved the land almost as much.

These rocky shore pastures had a beauty, to my way of thinking, far surpassing the massed groves of spruce and hardwood that the summer people allowed to grow up, after they bought these properties. The close-cropped grass, the purple rhodora and blueberry blossoms in June, the pink sheep-laurel in July, the asters and golden rod in August, had a peculiar charm. Songbirds loved these clearings; one of my earliest recollections is hearing a flock of white-throated sparrows singing their 'Old Sam Peabody! Peabody! Peabody!'

His mastery of all the technical terms of sea-craft, every kind of sailing ship, is still more in evidence. We recall his lyrical description of the most beautiful ships ever made by the hand of man, the New England clippers. All this went into his bigger books from the early *Maritime History of Massachusetts* through his four Columbus volumes, his *History of the United States Naval Operations in World War Two*, in fifteen; to his final works on *The European Discovery of America*, besides naval biographies by the way of Commodore Perry, Champlain and Paul Jones.

It is along this field or, rather, coast that he has our Trevelyan beaten, along with a more popular contact with people, all sorts and conditions of men. Both men were aristocrats, but democrats by conviction; they had the liberalism of the true aristocrat, and supported liberal causes. Sam, when young, actually wanted a woman as President of Harvard, and supported Ada Comstock, head of rival Radcliffe – sporting, but rather provocative. One can't imagine Trevelyan rubbing shoulders with people; he would never describe South Bunkers Ledge, in Mount Desert language, as 'Bunker's Whore', or translate such a bawdy ditty as the Greek one on the brothel-keeper who built a ship out of his profits, and makes the little vessel invite company, ending:

Come, all ye hearty mariners, come mount me by the
    stern;
So long as you can ply an oar, free passage you may earn!

But what a full life Sam had! Responsive to women: he parallels 'a well-built hull with a fair woman's body', and 'the sweet chuckling of water like the laughter of young girls, that you hear outside the hull while lying in a small yacht's bunk'. He read Greek and Latin for pleasure, as well as those other languages, Portuguese and Spanish, French and Italian; he was an excellent connoisseur of food and wine. Some of the menus of those old Boston dinners, and meals on board his yacht, make the mouth water. But one mustn't think of him in terms only of those New England waters; he sailed Columbus' ocean-course in a ship of the same design and specification; he knew the Caribbean and the Pacific; he had sailed the Aegean. One of the best pieces in *Spring Tides* is his account of a summer cruise long ago in the Aegean, and another is his evocative and scholarly essay on 'The Ancients and the Sea'.

What advantages he had! – no wonder people were jealous of him. And if he boasted a bit, isn't that true to an old salt? He would certainly regard it as a greater term of honour to be hailed as an 'old salt' than a professor, and he properly earned his rank of Rear-Admiral. I know academics who refused it to him, friends who would never address him as such – small-minded of them. Sam had been involved in several of the actions in the Pacific with the Japanese, and was proud of having been dive-bombed by *Kamikazi*, Japanese suicide planes. He was a man of spirit and courage, as well as all the rest; a very masculine type for one who was also an intellectual – and rather better at it than the intellectuals.

Oddly enough with someone who became such a good friend, I cannot remember when I first met him – probably in Oxford, for Sam was devoted to Oxford and came over nearly every year. He would give a dinner-party at Christ Church, while I gave a large lunch-party for him at All Souls. On one of these latter occasions I got him to meet Boies Penrose, head of the Philadelphia Penroses – a distinguished clan, most eminent of Cornish-American families[5] – who was scholar and bibliographer, and had written good books on historical geography and Renaissance travellers. On such social occasions one could not have much talk, but we were already exchanging books and letters.

In October 1946 he was acknowledging my little book on *The Use of History*, which he found 'most interesting and stimulating'. He had also been reading my *Poems of a Decade, 1931–1941*; 'I liked particularly "The Stricken Grove". It appeals to me personally because I had the misfortune to lose my beloved wife last year, and the next to the last stanza seems to apply particularly to the house and garden that she built . . . I am back at work at Harvard now, but continuing the Naval History until it is done.' His next letter, 1 March 1947, from the Navy Department in Washington was rather dispirited. He had read my *Poems of Deliverance*,

> which I like *very* much. Especially 'All that was most passionate' which might have been written for me! The death of my wife last year has left me rather played out and discouraged, and I find it difficult to pump up the necessary energy and enthusiasm to carry this Naval History through, but fortunately have some young men working with me; and of course the material conditions

---

[5] cf. *The Cornish in America*, 97–101.

here, though difficult, are infinitely better than with you, so I really shouldn't complain.

No one would ever think of Morison being discouraged, his achievement was so monumental; but he had his ups and downs. He did not give up – as Trevelyan did; but was given a new lease of life by his marriage, three years later, to a Baltimore cousin, Priscilla Barton. I did not know Sam's first wife, the mother of his children; but I knew Priscilla, who made Sam blissfully happy, and no wonder. She was twenty years younger, a beautiful woman, talented as well as spirited – she had a good voice, and sang, up to almost professional standard. Sam adored her – she appears in many of his later books, in dedications and prefaces, he owed so much to her. The finest thing about her – considering that she was entirely a land-girl, brought up to ride horses, like a good Southern girl – was the way she took to the sea so courageously, making an ideal companion for Sam.

Sam has an exciting account of how, once while she was only a learner, the cable he was throwing out to the yacht under sail just missed, and there was Priscilla in the fairway having to deal with the crisis, the sails taking her out into the ocean. 'But she showed her breeding,' says Sam proudly, 'by keeping her head and using it, just as her grandfather Major Barton, on Stonewall Jackson's staff, had done at Chancellorsville.' (Here's Southern spirit again!) Priscilla, only a novice, was headed straight for Lisbon; she said that, although she loved Lisbon she didn't care to go there right then. Sam was inordinately proud of her, and they were the closest of companions. At 44 Brimmer Street I was amused by the close companionship Priscilla's nightie and Sam's pyjamas kept in their bedroom closet.

I was about the last of my friends to get to America – what with long illness, the war and a relapse in the middle of it, then the currency restrictions: we had no money. At last, in 1951, the Rockefeller Foundation laid on a visit for me to the Huntington Library, so that my acquaintance with the United States came that way round. In the arid, deserty Spanish south-west – New Mexico, Arizona, California – I felt how right that the Spaniards should have colonized country just like Old Spain; while, when I got to New England, the English colonization made sense – just like Old England.

In New England my one contact was Morison, and he very kindly took me under his wing. He invited me to Brimmer Street, gave a lunch party for me to meet academic colleagues. Unfortunately I didn't keep a Journal on this visit, and I remember nothing of it, except one significant episode. For coffee we adjourned upstairs to his grandfather's library, classical busts on top of the crowded bookshelves – all very unchanged, as one can see from the photographs juxtaposed in *One Boy's Boston*. In a moment of silence Sam dropped the remark that he had been down to Washington to see the Great White Chief. There followed an awkward pause; his colleagues affected not to know whom he meant. It was embarrassing for Sam to have to explain that he meant the President – I think President Truman at the time; and they meant to embarrass him.[6] They clearly thought that this was a piece of Sam's hubris – they would, and they were taking him down a peg.

The scene was not lost on the observant young visitor, used to the ways of academics, but whose sympathies were entirely with Sam. Of course, an historian ought to want to meet the President, and it would have been interesting to know what had passed. We never learned, for they stopped Sam dead in his tracks, and shortly the party broke up. Somewhere Sam says that he was glad to have seen every one of the Presidents since his boyhood in the 1890s. Quite right: just the sort of thing an historian should value: Presidents are a part of history.

Sam arranged for me to spend the afternoon with Perry Miller, the guru or high priest of the Puritan Mind, on which he had written several unreadable, coagulated books. I didn't find him at all inspiring or the conversation profitable; I should have been more amused if I had known at the time that his life – in contrast to his life's work – was rather un-

[6] Morison's acquaintance with President Truman paid a further historical dividend: he was able to tell him that the early accounts of pre-Civil War doings in Missouri were all lies. Truman knew.

Puritan. Good for him! That evening I was dined at the Society of Fellows, an attempt to recapitulate the Senior Common Room of an Oxford college, silver candlesticks and all. It was very agreeable, and there I was amused to meet the Bishop of Massachusetts – enough to make the Puritans turn in their graves! Especially when one thinks what rot they uttered, even an educated man like Elbridge Gerry, as late as 1772: 'To plunder America is the plan, and the Bishops will be entitled to their share by the ungodly mode of Tithes.' Before ever the Boston Tea Party he was writing, 'I understand that [British] soldiers are attended to their graves with Mass, and expect that Popery will be soon not only tolerated but established in Boston.' As the result of the American Revolution it is today the dominant religion in Boston.

As with Trevelyan, so with Morison, Puritanism was the one subject on which we disagreed: they found me a heretic from what had been nineteenth century orthodoxy. Sam sent me most of his books; his fascinating essays, *By Land and By Sea*, he inscribed 'for A. L. Rowse – still hoping to educate him about the Puritans!' He certainly made the New England Puritans as attractive as ever they could be made; I still could not like a society without Anglican or Catholic ritual, without the music of the Church, without church-bells, or much secular music; no opera, no theatre; not much in the way of visual arts, no sculpture, nor any real painting – nor even literature, until their dreary addiction to sermonizing broke down. No – Santayana is my cup of tea in these matters, and he detested the Puritan ethos – about which Morison wrote, by the way: *The Intellectual Life of Colonial New England*. We must not forget, when people regard him patronizingly as merely a narrative historian (like Thucydides or Tacitus, Gibbon or Macaulay!) that he made a hefty contribution to intellectual history with four or five volumes on Harvard.

In January 1956 he wrote from the Office of Naval Records and History, of the Department of the Navy: 'I had hoped to see you at Washington, where I hear you gave a very witty speech'. I had been asked by Allan Nevins to speak to a society of historians he had gathered in the hope of improving the academic writing of history – in vain, I fear. This was at the huge American Historical Association – I had never attended such a concourse, such *Kuh-handel* in my life. Morison rarely attended these gatherings, though the profession could not but make him its President one year. To it he gave his address, 'Faith of an Historian', which he summed up in one word: '*Quaero*, I seek to learn'. He did not usually waste time on such gatherings: he once replied when asked what he did when he did attend: 'I raised the glad hand' – not calculated to make him popular with his *chers collègues*. Matey with sea-folk, not with them.

I remember once, when he came to lecture at Oxford, some woman had mugged up a book of his to tell the great man how much she admired his work. On such occasions I let such people off lightly with some rigmarole or other, 'How kind of you'. Not so Sam: he said loudly, 'Which one?', leaving the poor lady stumped, for of course she couldn't remember.

He had read *The Expansion of Elizabethan England* and, a conscientious scholar, sent me a few errata.

> The chapter Oceanic Voyages is very well done indeed. You are right to stress the fact that exploration and colonization were a national enterprise, and the contrast with France, or even with Spain. It has always puzzled me why Spanish painters and sculptors in the sixteenth century never chose an American subject. The Portuguese, however, did to some extent . . . I don't think there is any evidence that Drake raised a monument at Drake's Bay; wasn't it merely an inscription on a brass plate nailed to a tree? I'm glad you do not by implication accept the plate now displayed at Berkeley as genuine. The Capes of the Chesapeake named by Captain Newport are Henry and Charles. Point (not Cape) Comfort is inside the Bay . . . I'm glad you wrote plenty of 'After' to 'The Armada', as most Americans assume that Gloriana captured the trident, definitely, in 1588. The bare-legged portrait of Captain Lee is probably the one I saw

thirty years ago at Ditchley,[7] and always hoped to see reproduced. Too bad Lord Dillon didn't leave it to the National Portrait Gallery.

In November 1956 he wrote from Brimmer Street that, after a long summer, he had now found time to read *The Early Churchills*.

> The idea and execution seem to me to be most admirable. I like your modern, almost staccato, style. The books on distinguished ancestors are few indeed; the only one I know of in this country is one on the Adamses; I do, however, notice a few American Jerome traits in Sir Winston . . . We are going abroad again in mid-April for the Radio Free Europe meeting in Lisbon, but I don't know whether or not we shall be going to England after that . . . it depends on the turn of events. I shall not comment on these now except to say that Priscilla and I see eye to eye with Eden rather than Ike [over Suez] and are seriously contemplating voting for Stevenson tomorrow.

A postscript added, 'Well, we held our noses and voted for Ike; the determining factors being that (1) Dulles can't muck about any more and (2) repudiation of Ike would be used by Russia.'

One would very much like a forthright account by Sam of the insufferable Dulles, who ruined Britain's position in the Middle East, with what consequences for the United States can now be appreciated.

In January 1958 he wrote,

> Priscilla was delighted to get the book and I am equally so to hear that you are to give the Trevelyan Lectures at Cambridge. I see that you are treading in the footsteps of Doyle, and I am sure that you will write more inter-

---

[7] Now emptied of its historic contents, monument to the disgrace of our time.

estingly than that worthy Fellow of All Souls.[8] C. M.
Andrews' *Colonial History* is much the best in covering
the Elizabethan attempts at colonization that failed.
There is also a good recent book, I think in the Home
University Library, by Quinn about the Ralegh colony.

Actually, I had recruited him to write it for my *Teach Yourself
History* series – he did not respond to my *Ralegh and the
Throckmortons*.

Morison, of course, was in marked contrast.

One more fine book of yours to add to my Elizabethan
shelf! As I hate to receive acknowledgements of books I
send to people along the line 'I know I shall enjoy reading it', I have waited until reading your *Ralegh* to thank
you for it. A fascinating book, and the weaving in of the
new Throckmorton material is skillfully done. It will
hardly please the Americans – especially the Virginians
– who have a romantic conception of Ralegh as the pink
of chivalry etc, or the New Englanders to whom he was
one of the martyrs to Stuart tyranny . . . By a curious
chain of circumstances, there is a Raleigh Street in Boston. Although there is a despairing pathos about Ralegh's Guiana adventure which will always appeal to me,
Humphry Gilbert was indisputably the better man on
every count.

As independent-minded as Morison, I do not think he gets
that quite right. Ralegh, though not a nice man, was a man
of genius, which puts him into a different class. But it is like
Sam's chivalrous nature to have a sentimental feeling for Ralegh's forlorn hope in Guiana; I have none, it was a dubious
gamble from the beginning – James I was quite right about
it.

Sam wished me to send him a suggested route for a tour of
Cornwall; 'having been frustrated last visit for want of time

---

[8] This was J. A. Doyle, whose books on the Colonial period of American history were authoritative for his time. Morison is a little hard on
them. Several Fellows of All Souls made contributions to American history, in action as well as in writing.

we saw nothing of the Duchy. By the way, did you observe that in Birkenhead's *Life of Cherwell* he confesses what I told you (*à propos* Appeasers) that Henlein pulled Lindemann's leg – and Churchill's too'.

On the subject of the second war into which the Germans plunged the world, and the folly of Appeasement – Morison and I were at one. About my *All Souls and Appeasement* he had written to me:

> Thanks ever so much for sending me your little book. Beautifully done![9] Terrifying example for our people now – all the more honour to F.D.R. and Churchill. I spent a few days in Oxford in the fall of 1938, after the Anschluss [annexation of Austria] but before Munich, and found only one don who did not support Chamberlain – he was a Labour man in Exeter College. Even Lindemann, who had just seen Henlein for Chamberlain, was soothing – assured Common Room at Christ Church that Henlein did not want to be annexed because he would lose his importance. I wish the conversations at Cliveden had been 'bugged'.

One sees that Sam was under the impression that conversations at Cliveden were more important than they were.

When I was in Boston in the autumn of 1960 Sam arranged for his friends of the Massachusetts Historical Society to show me some historic treasures. I was conducted down steep Chestnut Street to see No. 50, Parkman's house, with his study in the attic at the top. Then up to the big Otis house – of Sam's family – which has been largely furnished with things Walter Whitehill has collected. A complete room of William Ellery Channing (Unitarian deity of Victorian Boston), furniture, portraits intense and soulful. More moving was Parkman's study; his desk with noctograph – which Prescott used too – when sight was failing, leather sofa behind; a bundle of Indian relics from the Oregon Trail, prints of Blind

---

[9] A Junior Fellow of All Souls, no more than a journalist, wrote that 'if the story was to be told at all, this was not the way it should be done'. He evidently knew better than a great historian, cf p. 30.

Homer and Blind Belisarius, a fine engraving of Walter Scott in *his* study. Out of the desk came the originals of Parkman's Journals only a few years ago: they had lain there undisturbed during the long reign of his granddaughter, who died a centenarian. There was a print of the lily which Parkman developed after his sight had failed – I never knew he wrote a book about roses.

At the Athenaeum I noticed replicas of three hands: Lincoln's scrawny hand of a rail-splitter; Whitman's, a big longshoreman's; Thackeray's, small and delicate, quite feminine. At the Historical Society more treasures: I had John Winthrop's Journal in my hand, the small vellum-covered volume he started on board the *Arbella*. The second was taken home by an Officer of the Society to work at, and got burned! (Some fool, I suppose, like John Stuart Mill's servant-girl burning the manuscript of Carlyle's *French Revolution* so that he had to write it again.) Volumes of early letters, Winthrop evidently brought his family papers with him: a uniform, small, scholarly hand. Upstairs were the Adams papers, planned to be edited in some forty or sixty volumes. Absurd – like the American giantism in everything; another forty for Jefferson! Ten or a dozen volumes would be ample for each, selecting the best and most important with due sense of proportion, instead of cluttering the things up with the irrelevant and trivial.

Sam corrected my impression that he had been awarded the Nobel Prize – which he certainly should have had.

> My award was not Nobel, but Balzan for history only – G.M.T. would certainly have got it if he had lived. The Balzan was founded to award areas of culture not covered by Nobel. As for the American Academy, it was my fault I wasn't elected earlier. To be elected to Nicholas Miraculous's [the very self-important Nicholas Murray Butler, President of Columbia] Fifty Immortals, one has first to join the National Institute of Arts and Letters. I was elected to it some twenty-five years ago, but as I didn't like the other historians then in it – James Truslow Adams and Beard, I declined. Last year they awarded me

their gold medal, so I *had* to join – and the Academy followed. The only other historian in it is Nevins.

Sam certainly mopped up a whole binful of medals and prizes, Pulitzer Prizes and what not – the more opulent culture of America has wads of these things to dispose of. Again his mopping them up didn't exactly endear him to colleagues.

He next wrote *à propos* of my *William Shakespeare: A Biography*, and the rumpus it caused among the Shakespeare establishment – anyone would have expected them to be grateful for having their problems solved for them and to feed on it in their heart with thanksgiving. Sam wrote now, as Rear-Admiral, USNR (Ret.): 'You certainly have become a famous man, what with being an authority on Shakespeare, Cornwall, pre-war English politics, etc, etc. I don't know whether I acknowledged your Memoir of Richard Pares which appeared in the British Academy, but I greatly appreciated it.' He had previously written to me that he found Pares's work 'disappointing'. I saw what he meant by this, though the question is a more subtle one. Pares had a brilliant mind, and could have written brilliantly, had he chosen to. But he was dogged by the idea that historical writing ought not to be interesting, but academic; it was only in his last two books that he got away from this nonsense. It was then too late, for he died when only in his fifties.

Sam's next letter dealt with some of the troubles he himself had to put up with from the inferior – naturally on the increase in a demotic society where people no longer know their place, and do not even have the sense of humour to realize their rating. I had had an example of this from some miserable instructor at an obscure college in the Mid-West. He couldn't see that Morison was a great historian. I tried patiently to explain to him the elements of greatness, the combination of quantity with quality, the size of the achievement, the original research, the justice and bigness of mind, all expressed in vivid, direct, eloquent writing. The poor young man replied: 'You mean that he is just a good writer.'

At the end of my patience, I said, 'If you were not so third-rate, you'd understand why Samuel Eliot Morison is a first-rate historian.'

And that is the kernel of the matter: I suppose that, if they did understand, it would mean that they were not so third-rate. I know as well as the next man that in a gentle-manly society that had standards, it would not be necessary to say these things. But in a levelling society one may as well tell these people what *we* think of them and it – so far it is still possible to express our opinion of it, as it is not in Soviet Russia. Morison and Trevelyan were alike disquieted at the way things were going, with the people having their way. Even Sam's paradise of Mount Desert suffered from 'rowdy motor tourists who throw trash about, and the ruth-less ambition of the Maine Highway Commission to make speedways out of beautiful winding roads'. 'The final era is that of the motel and the Acadia National Park Camp and trailer grounds, which has had the effect of sprinkling many of our beauty spots with empty beer cans, broken bottles and other trash.' Morison and Trevelyan were liberal-minded men. A product of the working people, I have never been a liberal: I know the people too well from the inside to entertain illusions. Morison and Trevelyan were very much concerned for liberty. One can have too much of a good thing: with the people out of control in democratic society, liberty means anarchy. Communists know that: they have no illusions about the people. Said Lenin, when a fellow-traveller thought there was insufficient liberty in Soviet Russia: 'Liberty? What for?'

The situation is not dissimilar in the over-crowded and in-ferior universities of democracy, where the professors can't write and the students can hardly read – at least they haven't read anything, in my experience of some two hundred American campuses – and modern British education is fol-lowing in their tracks, when it is only a small proportion of people who are educable up to real university standards. Morison devoted a salutary paper to his seminar at Harvard, some of whom would become professors, 'History as a Lit-erary Art'. 'In the period between the two world wars,' he wrote, 'I became exercised over the bad English used by students of history, especially graduate students, and over the dull, pedantic manner in which many historical monographs were presented.'

The paper contains many valuable reflections impossible to go into in detail here, and useful hints as to how to write. The dominant fact is really a sociological one: there is a complete breach between the productions of the academic history profession and the reading public, which 'for the most part is blissfully ignorant of this vast output'. No wonder, for it is unreadable. Morison points out that the Americans had a good historical tradition of their own: 'Prescott and Motley, Irving and Bancroft, Parkman and Fiske, were great literary craftsmen.' They knew how to write, and in consequence were widely read. As, indeed, with Morison himself. 'There has been a chain reaction of dullness. Professors who have risen to eminence by writing dull, solid, valuable [?] monographs that nobody reads outside the profession, teach graduate students to write dull, solid, valuable [?] monographs like theirs; the road to academic security is that of writing dull, solid, valuable [?] monographs.'

This is the case: I remember a clever graduate student in California who came to me for advice about her thesis on Graham Wallas. She was intelligent and grasped very well how it should be written; she said to me, 'I know you are right; but, if I wrote it like that, I should never get my Ph.D.' I regard this as shocking, but recognize the situation. Morison, himself a master, gives valuable advice as to historical standards, aims and methods. It is all waste of time – I waste none of my time on it: one might as well save one's breath to cool one's porridge, and march ahead alone.

The writing in American historical journals is like the clicking of a thousand typewriters: no music in it, no tone, no rhythm; no rise or fall of inflexion in the prose; no directness or vividness, no concreteness, all lifeless abstractions; no humour, no jokes; all chaff, tasteless, colourless, savourless – so unlike Morison's own writing. These people – like the Shakespeare industry – write for each other, not the intelligent public. Edmund Wilson had a quarrel with the Modern

Languages Association of America as to their over-editing of literary texts, weighing them down with irrelevant footnotes, etc. The issue here was mainly textual, but that of writing was also involved: Edmund Wilson knew how to write, they very largely do not. I happened to say to Garrett Mattingly one day – he was an exception, who wrote well: 'The trouble with these people is that they do not know how to write.' Mattingly answered: 'No: they *do* know how to write; *but they know it all wrong.*'

In 1965 Morison put the coping-stone on his work with a great book, his *History of the American People*, the work of which he was most proud. It is indeed a magnificent book in scope and scale, in justice of mind, understanding of politics and people, feeling for landscape and scene, power of evocation. Look at the setting of the Lincoln-Douglas debates through the summer and autumn of 1858.

> Imagine a parched little prairie town of central Illinois, set in fields of rustling corn; a dusty courthouse square, surrounded by low wooden houses and shops blistering in the August sunshine, decked with flags and party emblems; shirtsleeved farmers and their families in waggons and buggies and on foot, brass bands blaring out 'Hail! Columbia' and 'Oh! Susanna';[10] wooden platform with railing, a perspiring semicircle of local dignitaries in black frockcoats and immense beaver hats.

How it calls up the scene, and how true it is to those little prairie townships – as good as Willa Cather: the historian writes as well.

It is not my purpose to delve into the historian, except for personal traits. But I cannot forbear a professional tribute to the Master. When younger, I did not take to American history, what with the Puritans, the Boston mob and rabble-rousers like Sam Adams, and all. Morison cured me of this:

[10] Cornish folk were close to America and American folklore through constant emigration: my father would sing this song to me as a child, cf. *A Cornish Childhood.*

he made it so fascinating one wanted to read on and on, as with Macaulay. When I read this book I was most impressed by the political judgment – the way he could do justice to both Lincoln and Jefferson Davis, Grant and Robert E. Lee (Churchill's favourite American); perhaps, above all, by the way in which, though a patriot, he was just to the British stand as well as to the American Revolution. My sentiments were Tory: Morison brought me round; no one else could – certainly not Sir George Otto Trevelyan with his partisan Whig and naively pro-American view of it all. Perhaps I might tease Sam, as over the odious John Brown, who brought on the Civil War. Sam describes him, the 'perpetrator of the Potawatomi massacre in Kansas, a belated Puritan who would have found congenial work in Cromwell's invasion of Ireland'. QED.

But we are looking for personal clues, and they are many; for Sam knew instinctively, as real writers do, that the element of personality is what gives a man's work life and keeps it alive. He has a give-away phrase about Senator Charles Sumner, who was friendly with the British ambassador, Sir Charles Vaughan, with whom he stayed at All Souls. (Morison was, characteristically, the one person who researched into Vaughan's voluminous papers there – English historians hadn't bothered to do so, except for Oman, our librarian.) Sam says of Sumner: 'He was one of those fortunately rare and rarely fortunate persons who are not only thick-skinned themselves but assume that everyone else is.'

Sam was not thin-skinned, but he was not thick-skinned either. He was more sensitive than G. M. Trevelyan, who – aristocratic and Olympian – simply didn't notice the yelping of jackals. When Sam's masterly work came out, it was given a disgraceful review in the *Manchester Guardian* – too much regarded in the United States – by the son of a well-known professor of politics who was more of a political journalist than political thinker. I was enraged by it, and when I caught the young offender gave him a piece of my mind. Nothing daunted, he repeated that it was 'a bad book', and was without the sense of humour to see how foolish this was coming from him, who had accomplished nothing and was not likely to. Such are demotic standards all too prevalent.

Sam wrote from his cubicle in the Widener Library, no. 417, where he did so much research:

> I wasn't really put out by — — 's review: it was so typically Left-wing Labour. But I have been somewhat grieved by the reviews here by my academic colleagues, either making picayune faults or praising with faint damns. Reviews by professional critics in the newspapers, etc, have been uniformly favourable and I can't expect anything better.

The book had the nation-wide respect and success it deserved.

Some years before, Sam had written a biography of Paul Jones, the dashing Scotch privateer during the American Revolution, who became a folk-hero to the new nation and entered into their myth. In his usual way Morison had done a lot of original research on this rather elusive subject, had come up with a lot of new facts, and was able to interpret it all with his sailing expertise: he called it *A Sailor's Biography*. In England an article appeared by one Oliver Warner, a writer of no importance, who repeated all the old stuff about Paul Jones without any reference to the new information assembled by the master in the field.

Sam, who had come up with much new information from original research, minded about this, and protested to the historical journal which featured the offending article. He wrote to me, enclosing his protest, 'Why is it that when English historians write on American subjects, they constantly ignore everything written by American historians on those subjects?' I think he was more vexed, and rightly, by the general point than by the off-hand treatment by a third-rater. But, when he got no satisfactory reply, he did drop his subscription to the journal.

He enclosed with this a charming article he had written about his kinsman T. S. Eliot's poem, 'The Dry Salvages and the Thacher Shipwreck'. Sam had discovered that 'he and I are really only seventh cousins, the same relation as Franklin D. and Theodore Roosevelt, but I was very devoted to him'. (Who wasn't that knew him?) 'Cousin Tom' thought that the name the 'Dry Selvages' came from the French *Les Trois Sauvages*. Sam was able to show that 'selvage' meant a strand or edge (cf. OED), in this case, of rock; and that 'dry' meant that it was exposed at low water. Cousin Tom 'came to believe that his first American ancestor was in Anthony Thacher's shipwreck in 1635'. Tom wrote to Sam, 'Did you know that the Reverend Andrew Eliot was in the company with the Reverend Mr Thacher, when they went ashore on Thacher's Island?' The historian had to disillusion the poet: there was no relationship.

But he paid tribute to the poet's knowledge of the coast.

> Tom was not only steeped in the lore of Cape Ann; he became familiar with the encompassing ocean. Cruising in college days with his friend Harold Peters, the Dry Salvages was the last seamark they passed outward bound, and the first they picked up homeward bound. Approaching or departing in a fog, they listened for the mournful moans of the 'groaner', the whistling buoy east of Thacher Island, and the 'wailing warning' of the diaphone on Thacher's itself.

Morison, we have seen, had a fine appreciation of poetry, and was a prose-poet himself.

> Tom remembered the music of Cape Ann – 'the sea howl and the sea yelp':
>
> . . . the whine in the rigging . . .
> The distant rote in the granite teeth,
> And the wailing warning from the approaching headland.

These lines, and indeed all that follow, ring a bell in any sailor's heart. Notice 'the distant rote'. *Rote* or *Rut* is an old English word now seldom heard outside New England. It means a distant, continuous roar made by waves dashing on a long rocky coast. Often have I heard a Maine man say, 'Sea's making up. Hear that rote!' T. S. Eliot doubtless listened to the rote from his parents' house, during the windless calm after a storm, or on a 'weather-breeder' day when swells from the eastward begin crashing on the 'granite teeth' of Cape Ann before a storm breaks. These youthful impressions stayed with Eliot for almost twoscore years, producing at last the setting and background of his great poem.

Not even yet was Morison's work complete. In his later seventies he embarked on his vast conclusive work, *The European Discovery of America*. Here also was a culmination of a lifetime's work in research, sailing, exploration. In accordance with his regular habit he travelled to see the places he was writing about: this involved innumerable flights by plane, voyages by sea, as well as research in libraries. He had by now a cohort of helpers, friends all round the world – however he managed to keep in touch with them all, or even remember them, I cannot conceive.

It was a prodigious effort conducted into his eighties; the photographs and maps alone illuminate the enterprise, the ships' courses of his precursors, contemporary views of where they came from – the centre of the Cabots' Bristol, for example – the landfalls, the bays and straits, all round North and South America. There is Sam in cockpit of plane, or at the helm of launch, himself an Admiral of the Ocean Sea, like Columbus whose voyages he had definitively settled in history.

Again, I must restrict myself to the personal. In the first volume, *The Northern Voyages, A.D. 500–1600*, we have a photograph of him, sturdy and upstanding, with his two comrades by their plane 'setting forth to check on Lief Ericsson and John Cabot'. Vast quantities of nonsense have been written about the discovery of America, as about Shakespeare, and Sam had no hesitation in laying about him. For academics –

having been deprived of a classical education, they find the learning of a foreign language very difficult, and they dislike getting their feet wet. One cannot do much about their want of basic Latin; but if only they would take a cruise in a sailing vessel they might learn something about the facts of life at sea and not write the nonsense they do about voyages. The late Eva G. R. Taylor, professor of geography in the University of London, once laughingly admitted, 'I am absolutely terrified of the water and would not go on it for anything!' Yet for years she pontificated about the great navigators of history in a highly disparaging fashion.

Disparagement of their betters seems to be an occupational disease of academics; he wrote to me about several of this professor's navigational errors.

Then for the crackpots – 'the sheer weight of literature on St Brendan is enormous and most of it is worthless'. (The same might be said for Shakespeare.) 'The late William B. Goodwin, an insurance executive of Hartford, Connecticut, spent a fortune following various archaeological will o' the wisps, including an alleged pre-Vinland or at least pre-Columbian "Irish stone" village in North Salem, New Hampshire.' The Harvard archaeologist, Hencken, an authority on Ireland and Cornwall, investigated and found it to be rubbish – like the old fool in Philadelphia who spent $2 million trying to prove that Bacon was Shakespeare. They may spend as much on trying to disprove that Emilia Lanier was not Shakespeare's Dark Lady, and get no further; for the answer is unanswerable.

When Morison came to the southern voyages of discovery, he found that he had not to deal with so much nonsense as in the northern voyages; though 'crackpot theories about Columbus continue to proliferate, and Portuguese historians still claim that their compatriots were first everywhere . . . Nobody has yet claimed that Vikings sailed through the great Strait before Magellan', though one professor insisted that Africans were in Mexico before Cortés, and a Brandeis pro-

fessor 'has Phoenicians swarming over Brazil even before
that', etc.

The first of these final volumes was dedicated to Priscilla,
'who has followed all these Voyages with me in spirit, and
some of them in person'; the second 'To the memory of my
beloved wife, Priscilla Barton Morison, 1906–1973', with a
quotation from Tennyson:

> And o'er the hills, and far away
>   Beyond their utmost purple rim,
> Beyond the night, across the day,
>   Through all the world she followed him.

She was indeed a gallant spirit, a worthy comrade for him. It
was a great sorrow to him that, twenty years younger, she
died before him. He had written to me of his intended trip to
Japan – with her, for his book on Commodore Perry – 'but
all such things are now very uncertain'. Priscilla suffered
from cancer for some years, putting up the fight one would
expect of her. Sam's last book was written

> under the shadow of a great grief, the loss of my beloved
> Priscilla, still sharing my life as we approached the end
> of a long literary voyage. She accompanied me almost
> everywhere by land, sea, and air . . . almost every page
> of this volume prior to the chapters on Drake I read
> aloud to her before grievous pain made it impossible for
> her to pay attention. Her favourite criticism, born of her
> early experience on charitable boards, was, 'Sam, that
> sounds like the secretary reading the minutes of the last
> meeting!'

Any such passage was cast out – little of that remains in
Morison's published work.

All things considered and, counting the claims of many
British and American historians, I think that Morison was
probably the foremost historian in our language in this century. One can think of some who may have had more original minds: Maitland, for example, had genius; Namier had a

deeper tragic sense of history – no wonder, with his Jewish background and the wicked suffering inflicted on his seminal people all through history. Morison's was a sane and balanced view of it all, big-minded like the good sailing fellow he was. As a writer, when one considers all that he accomplished and the excellence of his craftsmanship, one must also place him among the great American writers.

6

André Maurois

When I was young, only just ceased to be an undergraduate and become a Fellow of All Souls, I wrote a little book, no more than an essay, *On History*. C. K. Ogden recruited it for his well known *Psyche Miniatures* series, along with celebrities like Bertrand Russell, J. B. S. Haldane, Malinowski, I. A. Richards – and I received all of £15 down.

But André Maurois, in his Clark Lectures at Cambridge, *Aspects de la Biographie*, gave the little book the whole of two pages. This was more than encouraging to a young man commencing author, and I remained always grateful to Maurois for his generous notice. A Celt never forgets kindnesses – or unkindnesses either.

No matter what Maurois said about my essay, which was in effect a summing up of my strenuous experience of reading the History School at Oxford, when I had expected the softer option of reading English Literature. The little book was to be a blue-print of my life's work in history; when I have read it years later, I have had the welcome experience of finding that I still agreed with it (as not with a subsequent book about politics, *Politics and the Younger Generation*. Young people's views on politics are of no value: the subject needs, of all things, experience.) As an undergraduate I was obsessed by the discovery of Marxism and the light it threw on the conflicts, the clashes and movements, of history. But I was determined, in my Marxist enthusiasm, not to go a millimetre beyond what I really thought myself; to subscribe in empirical fashion to what we familiarly called the MCH (the materialist conception of history), without swallowing Marxism whole, certainly not Lenin's Dialectical Materialism – though I struggled through his dogmatic *Dialectical Materialism and Empiriocriticism* and other rebarbative works.

I was quite well read in Marxism, for those days, but retained my own judgment. Paradoxically, when so many of the faithful have regurgitated everything of the Marxism they too uncritically swallowed, I have retained about as much of it as is useful or suggestive for the understanding and writing of history; for example, the decisive importance of classes, class-interest and class-conflict. It is unnecessary to throw out the baby with the bath-water. I had never given my adhesion to Marxism as a complete system of economics and politics, let alone philosophy. The bonus I received from this stubborn working-class independence of mind – as against middle-class parlour Communists (some of them friends, like Ralph Fox and Maurice Dobb) – was that I had nothing to retract. And I can still agree with my little manifesto, *On History*.

Not so much of a novel-reader, I doubt if I read *Les Silences du Colonel Bramble*, with which André Maurois first won attention and some fame. A liaison officer with the British Army in the 1914–18 war, this gave him the insight into the British character upon which he based much of his early work. It provided the foundation of his literary and speaking career – for he was an assiduous lecturer; he became the leading French authority on, and interpreter of, the English, not only to Europe, but to the British themselves and in the United States. It won him a wide public throughout the English-speaking world, honorary degrees and what all.

To tell the truth he had a very good understanding of the British. Half-Jewish himself – his real name was Herzog – this gave him the advantage of a certain ambivalence: his was fundamentally a *sympathetic* mind, I don't think he had any particular bias, as Paul Valéry had towards the Mediterranean, Mauriac towards the South, Montherlant towards Spain and North Africa. Maurois was a marked contrast with André Siegfried, for example, who – for all his being regarded as an authority on the British Empire and his periods of residence at All Souls – was too inflexible a mind to understand the English. I remember how baffled he was when I told him that George Lansbury, socialist Parliamentary leader in the thirties, was an Anglo-Catholic. Anglo-Catholic socialist – impossible! Siegfried, erect as a ramrod, was a Lorrainer – I liked him, dogmatic and rather *raide* as he was; but Maurois and Elie Halévy had a more sympathetic and subtle understanding of the English.

Maurois' earlier books, on which he built up his reputation on the subject, were slighter. Though I do not remember his novels – *Le Discours du Docteur O'Grady*, *Climats* and so on – I read his *Ariel, ou la Vie de Shelley*, his admiring *La Vie de Disraeli*, and *Edouard VII et son Temps*. His little book, *La Conversation*, was deft and perceptive as always, though it did not have the power of François Mauriac's *La Vie de Province*, which I gave to Edward VII's old mistress, Lady Warwick, a fellow socialist.

As a novelist, Mauriac was much more powerful, obsessive, fundamentally creative, and I did read his novels, every one of them as they came out.

Maurois was much more of a biographer, skilful in attuning himself to his subjects, and he gradually deepened his treatment of them; they became less literary and – dare one say? – superficial, and more historical. His approach became fundamentally historical, and that brought its rewards, in depth, breadth and command. I learned from his *Lyautey*, that great colonial administrator from whom French North Africa, in particular Morocco, gained so much – as Algeria did from the remarkable Cardinal Lavigerie. The civilizing benefit of their work mostly lost today, I suspect.

I recall too a charming *livre de circonstance* that Maurois wrote about Rouen, which he described as a *ville-musée*, which it was, though it had its literary associations too, particularly with Flaubert and Maupassant. Normandy was also Maurois' background, where the family business, a textile firm, was. And, of course, I read his life of Châteaubriand – one of the greatest and most recognizable of Celts – if only, though not only, for its Breton interest.

The second German war and the fall of France made an
appalling breach between Britain and France, in which Maurois was caught, much to his detriment. I have always
excused it on the grounds of hysteria, near to panic, for what
Maurois did was so superfluous – he had only to keep his
mouth shut and there would have been no trouble.

The fall of France in 1940 was agonizing for any Frenchman, and many of them – perhaps most – were rendered anti-
British by the disaster to their country. I remember four
ranking sea officers who, opting for Pétain, passed through
All Souls, being rerouted for France. They were all sullen
and anti-British. The French Fleet had been brought up to its
highest level of strength and efficiency by 1939 – if only the
French had continued the struggle with Hitler and Mussolini
from North Africa, it would have shortened the war by a
couple of years.

When the war was over and France liberated, I happened
to call on the chancellor of the Legion of Honour on the Quai
d'Orsay. Descended on one side from a family of the *ancien
régime* and on the other from a family in Napoleonic service,
he virtually broke down and said that he was *ashamed* of
France for 1940 and after. I assured him that the catastrophe
was more Britain's fault than France's; that British pro-Ger-
manism had been fatal, had gravely weakened France, that
Appeasement of Hitler had confused French policy and led
straight to 1940.

Maurois fled to England and thence to the United States;
but arrived there, he made an attack on Britain. It was so
unnecessary and, at that moment dangerous, that I think he
must have panicked, and lost not only his nerve but his sen-
ses. It was, of course, intensely resented. A fellow Jew publicly assaulted him in the foyer of his New York hotel and
struck him twice in the face: '*Un comme juif, et un comme
français.*' I will not repeat what Maurois' wife is reported to
have said about it, but it occasioned one of Churchill's memorable *mots*: 'We thought we had a friend, but found we had
only a client.'

It was years before Maurois recovered respect and something of his old position; there remained always this shadow.

After the liberation of France, he was for years excluded by the British Embassy from its functions; it was not until Queen Elizabeth II's visit to Paris that he was once more received, and peace was restored.

He must have known that I knew what had happened, though it was never mentioned between us. I had never forgotten his early kindness to an unknown young man, and I put down his break in New York simply to sudden nerves – after all, it was unintelligent for a very intelligent man: he had only to keep silent.

In Maurois' later years he wrote a series of splendid literary biographies – research deeper still (aided by his second wife), uncovering new, original material, sympathy lively as ever, judgment mature. This period began, after the war, with his *A la Recherche de Marcel Proust*. It was the first book to reveal the sources of Proust's genius, and may be said to have initiated the subsequent enormous growth of Proust studies. (We now know enough.)

I have always regarded Proust as the most symptomatic, and probably greatest, writer of the twentieth century; in his vast novel he wrote its Paradiso, Purgatorio, and at length Inferno. So I was both grateful for, and immensely impressed by, Maurois' revelation of the Master, and the mystery. Maurois shared with Proust (and Montaigne) the inestimable advantage of being half-Jewish, so that he had the key to both worlds, with the insight and the *souplesse* to render it.

I had written to congratulate Maurois on this most revealing work – he was the first, too, to have permission to draw on the Proust family papers. He replied, 5 April 1951:

> First I must say your letter filled me with joy. Praise from you is praise indeed and what you say is exactly what an author dreams of, but cannot believe he deserves. Your *England of Elizabeth* has arrived and I read it with delight. I always admired those 'spacious times', but never realized so well how much present England owes to them. I could return to you the compliment about the themes delicately woven into the texture of the

book. I always thought that every book – history, biography, novel – should be built as a symphony with recurrent themes. But very few historians realized that. You mention Neale and Trevelyan and they are certainly among the best. Yet from an artistic point of view I prefer your book. Your plan is perfect and the richness of information makes Elizabethan times come alive again.

I had always been clear that a living historical work must be an organic whole, and have beginning, middle and end. It was the trouble with my friend Pares's immensely learned books that they were not – until he learned eventually with *A West India Fortune*; while Namier's books were a succession of brilliant chapters. But the symphonic conception was subtler: I had deliberately interwoven themes to knit together this and the following volumes on the Elizabethan Age as I had observed Proust doing in his great work. There were internal rhythms also, up and down, rise and fall. A writer should learn from all his reading, literary as well as historical, music too; for history includes the whole of life.

Maurois' next book, *Lélia ou la Vie de George Sand*, gave me pure pleasure – or possibly impure, for there are comic episodes like the fiasco when Mérimée failed to come up to scratch with the insatiable woman who had exhausted Chopin. What a woman she was, and what zest for life! What fun they had in the France of Louis Philippe, without the modern shadow upon life – plenty of money and all the entertaining that went on at Nohant. I recall her entertaining Matthew Arnold, when young, athletic and handsome, and the liberating effect she had on his generation, after Rugby and the Oxford of the Tractarians.

Maurois sent me his next biography, *Olympio ou la Vie de Victor Hugo*, with a kind *dédicace* – to me the most valuable of the whole series, for it makes the monster intelligible. Olympio is Hugo's name for himself ('*Tristesse d'Olympio*'): colossal egoist that he was, out of it came his colossal output.

As a part of working his passage back to Britain Maurois was invited to lecture once more at Oxford. Jean Seznec, professor of French Literature, as a Breton a fellow-Celt, was a little nervous of Maurois' reception and asked me to look after him at dinner. He need not have worried on either score. The young men had no knowledge of what had happened during the war, and Maurois received a positive ovation at the end of his lecture. I told him how exceptional this was at Oxford; he was immensely pleased, but it was thoroughly deserved. I couldn't attend the lecture, but he gave me a copy. It was quite extraordinary in its sympathy and understanding for the writing of the generation much younger than his own, with which he could not be expected to be in accord. No wonder the young men had cheered him.

Our next meeting was in New York in November 1960, for which I resort to my American Journals. 'The PEN Club in Washington Square was entertaining André Maurois to dinner. I was very glad to see him again, as he was to see me. I have never held against him his bad break against Britain in 1940 – he must have been unnerved, it was so superfluous . . . When he was at last invited back to Oxford, I did my best, and Maurois was happy and pleased. Isaiah Berlin wouldn't meet him, and Ava Waverley took the trouble to write me a letter of protest, saying that she had heard that I had been very kind to Maurois, that the Paris Embassy did not receive him and people ought not to welcome him, etc. As if I would take my line from her, or anybody else!

'Anyhow, Maurois was visibly pleased to see me at the PEN Club, among all those people he didn't know. I refrained from taking up his time, since I was lunching with him next day; I introduced Leon Edel to him, who had never met him. His speech after dinner was adroit, amusing, perceptive, not at all profound, a wonderful performance for a man of seventy-five. At sixty-five he had declined an American lecture tour on the ground that he was too old. But now it happened to work in with the book he was writing: the American half to a parallel history with Russia – an interesting idea – including interviews with leading Americans in various fields of science, etc.

'In the questions afterwards it was noticeable how doggedly he refused to enter a single note of criticism, and

kept consistently to the optimistic line he finds so profitable
– and which may genuinely reflect his temperament. (Not
mine.) He found cause for a favourable view of the prospects
of American culture in the multiplication of paperbacks, the
fact that one can buy Plato's *Dialogues* or *Phèdre* at the airport.
What does this amount to? I could have put the point to him
whether the multiplication of mass-media did not put a premium on all the third-rate purveyors of it. What do popular
standards matter where culture is concerned? Is there any
increase in first-class achievement? I should have thought a
great diminution. [Seznec tells me that the present state of
literature in France is appalling compared with before the
war. Same in Britain.]

'Maurois was determined to look on the bright side, and
of course this pays – though everything is in the balances.
Some sense of this was at the back of some people's minds:
Robert Halsband said afterwards that the address 'lacked
teeth'. But they wouldn't have liked it if Maurois *had* criticized. I understood well enough what the astute old boy was
up to. He made one point that appealed to me – the necessity
for justice of mind in one people's interpretation of another,
the importance of responsible judgments, instead of easy
scoring off each other. This should be the historian's attitude.'

Next day, 24 November, Thanksgiving day: 'I went down
to Cass Canfield's pretty house on East Side for lunch. Of all
the houses in New York this is the one I should like to
inhabit: a small, narrow early nineteenth-century house of
three storeys, back from the street, with patio, wall and iron
gates before it, opened only from the house on ringing. I
went early for a business chat with Cass in that downstairs
drawing-room, old furniture, flowers, sculpture by Cass's
wife. (By contrast with me, I gather that Maurois is an
extremely hard bargainer over his books, actually getting
'more than the traffic can afford' . . .)

'The Maurois now arrived. I had never met Madame
before, daughter of Anatole France's Egeria, Mme Caillavet,
who used to keep his nose to the grindstone and prevent him
from falling into indolence. I presented myself with a com-

pliment about her husband's devoting a couple of pages to
my first little book – "as if that were not like having one's
name inscribed on the dome of St Paul's". After that, no
awkwardness, everything went swimmingly. We got on to
the subject of Princess Bibesco, and this was not displeasing
to Mme Maurois. She made a point of telling us how pleased
she was at being remembered, after fifteen years, by the
woman at the shop whence she had sent so many food parcels
to Europe during the war. This was a useful line, I registered,
in case I knew about the awkwardness.

'What made that still more inexplicable was something that
Maurois proceeded to tell us, that he had written the text of
the Queen's [now Queen Mother's] speech to the women of
France in 1940, and for that she had given him a pair of
diamond cuff-links, so valuable that they kept them in the
safe at home. In going through the speech with her they came
to a phrase like 'tels hommes", which the Queen pronounced
without the "s", said that her tutor had taught her that way
(he must have been English!), and why was "s" to be pronounced there, in other instances not? etc.

'Maurois had often had his work confused with Mauriac's.
The old King of the Belgians said he thought *Le Désert de
L'Amour* a good book, wasn't it? When Maurois said, yes, it
was a good book, the King looked surprised: he evidently
had taken it to be by Maurois.

'I didn't know that they had a country place in the Dor-
dogne, and almost made the mistake of saying "the Mauriac
country", through whose books it was familiar to me – but
saved myself by saying that they were very near. "Yes, he is
in the Gironde – two principalities," Maurois added.
Actually he does not *belong*, as Mauriac does. When he was
asked at the PEN Club which of his books he most enjoyed
writing, two of them were about Jews, Disraeli and Proust,
the third about George Sand.

'Cecil Roberts had written me of a visit to the Maurois'
house at Neuilly, and the impression of luxury it gave. He
must have made a pile of money by his books, and looked
after it well. It is obvious that he is a hard worker, and says
that he has the best secretary in the world – his wife. She does

much of the research for his books, and all the typing. I liked her: clever and perceptive, and not in the least overpowering. She asked me to be sure to let them know when coming to Paris.

'Their house is next door to the Windsors', whom they know; they regard him as pathetic, a fish out of water. Wallis has recently written an article for the Paris press on how the English people treated her husband – they make a lot of money by such stuff. She has a terrific anti-English complex.

'Talk was easy and agreeable, mainly historical and literary – Maurois well informed about American history, upon which he has written, as upon English. I could not but admire the vitality of this old couple, who seemed not aged at all. The lunch was the most delicious, and elegant, I have had in the States. Cass's beautiful wife runs the house like clockwork, in addition to being quite a good sculptor. I drew Madame Maurois' attention to the sculpted pieces about and, on Cass's behalf, prevailed on his wife to do a head of him.'

In May 1961 I was to be in Paris to give a lecture for the British Institute at the Sorbonne, and I let Maurois know. He, however, had to leave for Bordeaux, 'where Chaban-Delmas, the Mayor of the town, asked us a long time ago'. Would I still be in Paris for the eleventh or twelfth? – 'Thursday being a holiday we would have to take you to a restaurant, whereas Friday we would have the pleasure to receive you here.'

That summer he was gravely ill with sclerosis of the lungs; we did not know whether he would recover and I wrote to his wife for news of him. In September he wrote back himself in French, his handwriting more minute than ever. '*Mon cher ami*,' but I will translate into English, 'I reply myself, first because since my illness my poor wife has been overwhelmed with work, and further to prove that I am getting much better. My lungs remain somewhat affected, but I can begin to work a little. I shall try not to work too much.'

He renewed his invitation to come and see him, 'if M.K. [Khrushchev] does not intervene: which I don't think, for his régime would die of it and perhaps himself also. It is a game of poker, very disagreeable.' I suppose this refers to the Cuban crisis, and the showdown.

Maurois made a marvellous recovery, went on with his work and continued to be productive. I had not cared so much for his book on the Dumas – there were three of them, and this distracted from unity and dissipated the impact. But the life of Balzac which he went on to stands at the summit of his biographical work, not inferior to the *Victor Hugo* and again with fresh material which he brought to light.

In Shakespeare Quatercentenary Year I was again in Paris, to lecture at the Sorbonne for the British Institute, stopping at the Hotel Lutétia. I did not know that under the German Occupation it had been a Gestapo headquarters: I found it highly respectable, '*bon-bourgeois, très familial* and crawling with priests – just the place for me.' I was very busy with lectures and parties, mainly under the wing of Princess Bibesco; but before I left I spent an hour with Maurois, completely recovered and in good spirits, anxious to talk. I resort to my Journal:

'29 April 1964, at 5.30 I duly presented myself at 86 Boulevard Maurice Barrès, the Maurois' opulent but somewhat characterless apartment, looking out on the greenery of the Bois de Boulogne just beginning. A most interesting hour together: he really is a superior man, no nonsense from him about D. H. Lawrence being in the same class with Shakespeare [Leavis nonsense]. He made it clear, without denigrating Anatole France, that he did not regard him as on a level with Kipling.[1] He regarded Saint Exupéry as a kind of minor Kipling. When he had published *Colonel Bramble* he sent a copy to Kipling, who responded generously and asked him to stay with him in Sussex. Which he did – I suppose the book may have been influenced by Kipling's stories of army life.

'When younger Maurois had grown up with the expectation of a large inheritance from the family business; but textiles went down and down, until some years ago the business had closed down – and he had only the money he earned from his books. (He has done immensely well with *them* – no

[1] I do not myself underrate Anatole France.

evidence of want in the luxurious apartment.) He has not left his country place at Essendiéras (near Saint Médard d'Excideuil – how medieval it all sounds), which belongs to his wife; merely parted with the farm, on which he did nothing but lose money on cows. Everybody told him to buy Friesians, since they gave the best yield of milk: with him they ceased to give any milk at all. (I thought how like my literary friends who had put their money into farming, and how much of my savings had gone to the bottom of the sea.)

'We talked for a moment about de Gaulle, who had written me a grand, magistral letter about my Shakespeare biography (Harold Macmillan was even more enthusiastic and warm in its praise, but he was also its publisher). It had been suggested to me that de Gaulle would welcome this attention in Shakespeare Quatercentenary Year, but that the book should be sent to him in both the English and French editions. I was very proud that the great statesman, whom I chiefly admired along with Churchill, should take notice of it: "*C'est avec l'interêt le plus vif que j'ai lu votre oeuvre magistral sur le grand dramaturge élizabethain,*" etc.

'Maurois told me something illuminating about de Gaulle's way of conducting business. He would ask each Minister separately to come and place his views before him, thank him courteously – and that was that. Not waste time in futile Cabinet talky-talky, as revealed in the Crossman Diaries. De Gaulle didn't go in for discussion, he listened to the other's point of view, then made up his own mind. I find this temperamentally, and intellectually, very sympathetic. Never discuss anything with anybody: *il n'y a pas de quoi.* There is nothing to discuss with. The process of decision is a more subtle one than that of mere ratiocination, even if other people are rational – as they rarely are; intuitive choices enter in, subtler than the rationalist accounting of economists, philosophers, theorists in general. Churchill and de Gaulle are my "men of the century", not Bertie Russell.

'The best part of our talk was devoted to Shakespeare and Proust. I explained to him again that the Dedication of the Sonnets to Mr W.H. was the publisher, Thorp's, not Shakespeare's at all; hence the young lord in the Sonnets is *not* Mr

W.H., but the obvious person, Shakespeare's patron, Southampton. But Maurois had already grasped it all, at once – so unlike the bulk of human fools. Veronica, for example, has made an ass of herself falling for Hotson's crackpot William Hatcliffe! The only reputable person to do so, and my old pupil: very poor.'

Maurois, with his perception and literary experience, had grasped that the problems of the Sonnets, except for the identity of the Dark Lady, were now solved, and had allowed my publishers to quote his opinion. Of course, he was not an Elizabethan expert, but he had a great deal more common sense than those who were supposed to be so.

'I said that Proust was perhaps the most Shakespearean writer of the twentieth century – allowing for the immense difference that the twentieth was a prose century. The whole atmosphere of *A la Recherche du Temps Perdu* was poetic – moreover, a musical atmosphere, like Shakespeare's. Maurois at once saw that here was a theme, and that I should write it up. He added that the Baron de Charlus was a Shakespearean creation. (I did not think of comparing him, *ceteris paribus*, with Falstaff: a decadent, outsize twentieth century Falstaff, both comic and tragic.)

'He had no very high opinion of Gide as a writer, even less than mine. He told me of an amusing essay of Rebecca West, starting on a journey to Paris with a high opinion of Gide as a writer, and a batch of his books to read. The first she did not much care for – but still she had a high opinion of Gide as a writer. The second and third did not come up to expectation either; by the time she arrived in Paris and had tried all of them, she found that she had not much opinion of Gide as a writer at all.'

A naughty story. I have given my opinion of Gide in *Homosexuals in History*. In earlier years I was very well read in Gide, and read most of his books as they came out. I regularly subscribed to the *Nouvelle revue française* which he had founded and made into some sort of propaganda vehicle for his literary circle. When he turned up at Oxford he looked, as David Cecil said, a *maître d'école*: he was obviously used to being treated with deference as the Master. His creative inspiration was small – one sees it at its best in *La porte étroite* or *Isabelle* – everything in him turned to autobiography. But his curiosity was insatiable, and he had, in those years, the adventitious attraction of his scandalous interest in homosexuality. Today, nobody would turn a (pubic) hair. Then, he was at his apogee with his Nobel Prize – for his stance was liberal; but Maurois was right about him. He was altogether too literary, in the pejorative sense of the French phrase, 'C'est de la littérature.'

I was more anxious to learn about Montherlant, who intrigued me greatly: he was the French writer with whom I felt most temperamental affinity – pride, disenchantment, no illusions; realism plus poetry; self-reliance, reliance upon no-one outside oneself; the uttermost exploration of one's own ego, one's own world of the imagination; the sense of history and the drama of human lives; seared by contempt for human folly; hedonist and stoic, a solitary spirit: a dug-out from which to confront the disgrace of the time we live in.

I longed to know more about Montherlant: I was a fool never to have written to him to tell him that here was a kindred spirit. He would have responded, I now know. Maurois could tell me very little about him. He saw him at sessions of the French Academy, where he made his laconic contributions. But he had an iron reserve, and no-one knew him. He had some affection of the throat, and did not go out into society.

'When I made a motion to go, Maurois bade me stay on: he was enjoying the conversation and twice said how pleased he was at my coming to see him. (He has natural courtesy.) He repeated his invitation to stay at Essendiéras. Shall I? – I always forego these chances in the interest of work. But the chance will not come often again – he is nearing eighty, though recovered from his severe illness of two years ago.'

In the event, I did not go – fool that I was, with my genius for missing chances in life, I can hardly explain why: natural deference, not wanting to impose myself on people, not wanting people to impose themselves on me, or even to be in close proximity with them, preferring my own company: a solitary spirit, like Montherlant, not normal and gregarious like Maurois. Now I am sorry: I might have gathered material for something like Barrès' naughty and amusing *Huit Jours chez M. Renan*. But I doubt it – Maurois would have been too aware.

'It was good of *him* to allow me to take up his time, for he was obviously working. *Balzac* would be ready in time in October, he told me to tell Cass Canfield in New York. His admiration for Balzac as a writer was immense, but now that he had made researches into his life he found a number of things that were not admirable. (Was this an unspoken apology for himself?) When I get back to Oxford I will send him a Shakespeare epigraph for his book: "The web of our life is of a mingled yarn, good and ill together." How will he take the textile reference – apply it to himself?

'On my leaving we went up together to the de Laszlo portrait of him, large as life in his Oxford D. Litt. gown, both of us Oxford Doctors of Letters.'

7

Princess Marthe Bibesco

I first met Princess Bibesco with the Abdys at their exotic house of Newton Ferrers in East Cornwall. At least they had made it exotic, with their French taste. The exterior is a rather *gauche* Queen Anne manor-house, but with one spectacular feature: a series of semi-circular granite *perrons*, descending to a forecourt, with a heavy balustrade, big balusters with balls on top. Sir Robert Abdy told me that, in the moonlight under snow, they looked like a regiment of grenadiers. The formal forecourt ended at a gate, which looked down a gorge to the River Lynher (Cornish for long pool).

It was the interior that was exotic, filled with French furniture and rugs, a striking Boldini in sharp perspective, a lovely shadowed Winterhalter of Princess Troubetskaya, an enviable Hubert Robert on the staircase. The library, looking like a Paris *salon* of the time of Louis Philippe, filled with sumptuous bindings, red and gold from his queen's collection, a Houdon bust of Marie Antoinette from St Petersburg (now Leningrad, as if Lenin built it!).

Bertie had got to work on the surroundings: at the back a pool with a big Rodin in the centre; the hillside along the cherried drive he had torn up to install a series of descending fountains and pools, *les Grandes Eaux de* Newton Ferrers. At vast expense: when Diane pointed this out, Bertie replied simply, 'Well, Louis XIV did it at Versailles.' During the war the house was damaged by fire; all the panelling was lost, except for the library wing; the other wing remained a shell, adding to the haunted look of the place.

The place indeed had its ghost, a story only I knew from the documents: of the Coryton son and heir who had killed his father, sometime in the late Elizabethan age – and the Corytons left it in the eighteenth century for Pentillie on the Tamar.

It was, and is, a strangely lost place, a *pays du grand Meaulnes*. One can see the house, lost in its trees and woods, from hardly anywhere. Often as I visited it at intervals I had difficulty in finding it among the long winding lanes; my best bet was to make for the known beauty-spot of Clapper Bridge, two bridges and an island in the stream, and up the valley which Bertie had planted with cherries.

There I met the Princess, with the Abdys whom she had known from their Paris days – if not before; for she was well acquainted with English life. Asquith's daughter, Elizabeth, had married a cousin, Antoine Bibesco; Marthe was a friend of the MacDonalds, through her friend from Roumanian days, Lord Thomson. She was indeed a European figure, with her Roumanian and Greek, French and Italian descents; she had known the Russian Imperial Court in the days of its glory before 1914, and was a friend of the Hohenzollerns. Her literary friendships were even more interesting, for she had known Anatole France and Proust. She was a distinguished writer herself, a member of various academies, and had written several good books.

It was through her friendship with the Abdys that she fell for Cornwall – it reminded her of the Bosphorus – and bought a pretty Regency villa at Perran-ar-worthal (Perran-the-wharf), above the river going down to Restronguet, across from the woods of Carclew, about which I had written my poem, 'How Many Miles to Mylor?' This charming property had already appeared in literature in Kilvert's Diary – Tullimaar, home of young Mrs Hockin, with whom the inflammable curate was enamoured.

The Princess in turn loved Tullimaar – I hear her French pronunciation of it as I write – and set about refashioning and planting with her extraordinary zest and vigour. The dining-room there she repapered to look like a tent, after the room at Malmaison (for she enjoyed an illegitimate descent from Napoleon). Not much money can have been left from the confiscation of the Bibesco fortune, but the shelves of the little library she had gold-leafed, to go with the few fine eighteenth-century bindings the Communists kindly allowed her from her palace, which they had taken over.

She had been one of the richest, as well as most beautiful, women of Europe – and the family had suffered terribly. She had restored the splendid sixteenth-century palace, designed by a Venetian architect. When Hitler's hordes invaded Roumania, she managed to get away with the family emeralds, first to South Africa, I think. She once told me the adventures of her escape, but unfortunately I did not write it into my Journals, and have forgotten them. She never once complained of what she had lost, or what they had all suffered – this was one of the things I most admired about her: courage, magnanimity, zest for life: she was a *great* woman, besides being a great lady. Instead of repining and regretting lost wealth and grandeur, when now she had to earn her living by her writings, she one day said to me: 'I like this better.' I thought it wonderful of her.

Her only child, a daughter, Princess Ghika, and her husband had been caught and held by the Nazis in internment camp for five years. When liberated, they were held by the Russians for another seven years! No word of complaint from the daughter either, with a charm and gentleness all her own – though it had wrecked her and her husband's health and made invalids of them both. Cornwall was chosen partly to get away from it all, in the depths of the countryside, to recuperate physically and mentally, cultivating their garden at Tullimaar.

It was an honour for Cornwall that she should have chosen it. It amused me, as well as irritated me, that small-minded Cornish gentry in their crevices did not appreciate their acquisition – too ignorant of Europe (they had all been Appeasers), let alone of European literature. I made the most of this stroke of fortune in the summers, when we were both down in the county. She spent most winters in her apartment in the Bibesco house on the Île St Louis, the old heart of Paris – is it the house that appears in perhaps the best of her books,

Catherine-Paris? We became playmates, with all Cornwall to explore, with me – her 'Professor' – as guide. She became very patriotic about Cornwall; I promised that when Cornwall was happily cut off at the Tamar from insanely tax-ridden England, she should become *Madame la Présidente de la République Cornouaillaise*.

The first of many letters to me mentions her pleasure at my introducing her to Kilvert and his enchantment with Tullimaar. The house had more recent associations: General Eisenhower had occupied it during the fortnight before D-Day, 1944, making final preparations with Montgomery nearby. I had met Montgomery at lunch at Trenarren before I came to live there, and had an argument with him about the place of war in history. The Princess wanted to know all about that; fortunately I had recorded it in an article for some magazine at Oxford – it led to a marginal acquaintance with him. Someone here saw the two generals upon whom so much depended – the liberation of Europe – walking out along our headland to the Black Head, in those unforgettable historic days.

The first of our expeditions was to the beautiful sequestered church of Landulph by the Tamar, where a descendant of the Greek Emperors from Constantinople lies buried – of interest to her, since she was one herself. I can see her now sitting in the aisle, my obedient pupil taking down the inscription which I dictated to her:

> Here lieth the body of Theodore Palaeologus,
> of Pesaro in Italy, descended from the
> Imperial line of the last Christian Emperors
> of Greece; being the son of Camillo, the son
> of Prospero, the son of Theodore, the son of
> John, the son of Thomas, second brother to
> Constantine, Palaeologus, the 8th of that name
> and last of that line that reigned in
> Constantinople, until subdued by the Turks;
> who married with Mary, the daughter of William
> Balls of Hadleigh in Suffolk, gent., and had
> issue five children, Theodore, John,

Ferdinando, Mary, and Dorothy, and departed
this life at Clifton the 21 of January, 1636.[1]

The Princess was always game for an expedition with
something to see at the end of it; nothing deterred her –
certainly not the weather. As at the Rector's Lodgings at
Lincoln College, Oxford, in the days of Mark Pattison and
his highbrow wife, the weather was not to be mentioned; I
was more easily deterrable, the Princess not. I remember a
somewhat damp expedition to Roche, the most extraordinary
natural feature in our vicinity at St Austell: an exciting
upthrust of rocks high up on the moor, on top of which a
hermitage had been built for an anchorite about 1400. Two
storeys of huge shaped stones, living room on the living
rock, with chapel above – he must have had great charisma
to have had that built for him and supplied with food by the
folk around – resident confessor and psychiatrist for all mid-
Cornwall (or, perhaps in still more demotic terms, TV star).

All round, prehistoric country: Hensbarrow (i.e. old barrow), the tumulus of some prehistoric chieftain; in the distance, the ridged encampment of Helman (i.e. rocks on the
moor) Tor. In one of the recumbent rocks at Roche, like an
Irish bawn, there was a suggestive deep hole, filled with
water, into which one cast a copper and made one's wish –
such was the folklore. I had often enacted the ritual, and been
televized doing it; the Princess was game, and followed suit.

More frequently we drove round to friendly, more intelligent country-houses, to lunch – most often at Newton Ferrers – with me as chauffeur, the Princess anxious not to go
too fast along Cornish roads and lanes. One trip abroad I
regret that I had not confidence enough in my driving to
undertake – to the grandest of medieval *châteaux* in Brittany,
Josselin, where she was a kinswoman of the La Rochefou-
caulds. Once again my lack of social enterprise meant that I
have never seen Josselin.

However, we met outside Cornwall – at Oxford, where
she came down to lunch with me at All Souls, or in London
at the Ritz where she regularly stayed. On one occasion I

[1] i.e. 1637. I have modernized the spelling.

took her up to the American Embassy to meet the most beautiful ambassadress in London, Evangeline Bruce. There Marthe told us a sensational story of the Comtesse de Noailles, which appalled me. The best woman poet of her time, a self-absorbed egoist, she was the mistress of Maurice Barrès, who ultimately tired of her (I don't wonder). By way of revenge, Anna de Noailles got Barrès' adolescent son to fall in love with her and gave him an assignation at an hotel, I think by the Rhine. When the youth got there, he found no beautiful woman awaiting him; having been made a fool of, he committed suicide. (I have no sympathy for the young ass – typical French fixation on women.) Naturally, a complete breach followed between the father (a writer of genius, underrated today)[2] and his mistress. They did not meet again for years; when they did eventually, by accident, she said precisely how long it had been since: — — years, — — months, — — minutes. She was a fine poet. I thought the story a pretty example of French bitchery.

Marthe had been a close friend of the Crown Prince William, the Kaiser's son and heir. She never told me, but that it was so I judge from the intimate piece of information she once gave me about the Kaiser. His notorious *Daily Telegraph* interview caused a first-class political crisis in Germany; the Kaiser was left exposed by his Chancellor, the treacherous Bülow (what a lot they were!). The Princess told me that during one whole night of despair, the Kaiser thought of abdicating (others have seen a comparison between him and his young cousin, the Herzog von Windsor). He would have been succeeded by the Crown Prince, of whom the Princess had a more favourable view, as a 'normal' man, not unpopular in England before 1914, as his father was. Was the implication that the Kaiser was not 'normal'? He certainly was psychotic, with his schizophrenia about England, his complex about his uncle, Edward VII; his entourage liberally sprinkled with homosexuals, it was probable enough that William was not operative – though that would not have made him any more normal. We did not go any further into the matter, but I drew my own conclusions.

[2] Barrès' *La Sainte Colline* is a classic that will endure.

Once more, at the time of the suicide of the Kaiser's grandson, who drowned himself in the Rhine, it was evident that the Princess was closely concerned. She knew the young man, the most Anglophile of the family, married to a Guinness, ambivalent between Germany and England, torn in two. Marthe said nothing, except – she had a rhetorical way of speaking and writing – that he had heard the 'call of the Rhine-maidens'. She evidently knew the family well, if not too well.

She was a piece of history herself, with a living sense of history: this was a main part of her charm for me and what doubled the fun of going about with her. Her publishers, Plon (who published the French translation of my *William Shakespeare: A Biography*) occupied the house where Talleyrand lived 'when he became *"Ce coquin, le Prince de Bénévent,"* as Louis XVIII used to put it, mildly.' She was able to tell me that the proper family pronunciation of the name omitted the 'y' – Tallerand, but that Napoleon couldn't manage it: he pronounced it 'ey'. The family pronunciation of Montesquieu – of the poet, Robert de Montesquieu – was Montesquiou. Comte Robert, a baroque comic character – the chief original of the Baron de Charlus – was mad with family pride, descended from Charlemagne; at the nadir of depression one day, he sighed, *'Je ne m'intéresse même dans mon propre nom.'* Once in Paris, the Princess pointed out the large mansion that Napoleon's mother had occupied, Madame Mère, and her strong Corsican accent, *'Pourvou que ça doure' (pourvu que ça dure)*. I often think of Marthe when looking at the tiny little wildflower so common upon our walls here in Cornwall, ivy-leaved crowfoot – she told me its romantic French name, *'les ruines de Rome'*.

In return for my tutoring her in Cornish matters, she was my tutor in regard to France – and how much I learnt from her. Under the *ancien régime*, for example, people at Court didn't say 'le roi', they said 'le rey'. Her own taste in literature turned to the rhetorical and romantic: her literary hero was Châteaubriand, of whom she could recite whole paragraphs. This was not an English taste – the English have never liked French rhetoric – but Châteaubriand as a Breton had his appeal for me. I once was reading his description of primeval American forest in the *Mémoires d'Outre Tombe* and of the Ohio, as the train was headed for the Mid-West alongside a great river – and found that it was the Ohio. Marthe could tell me of Châteaubriand's Egeria, Madame Récamier, and her close friendship with Madame de Staël – at Coppet are many mementoes of the friendship. We both appreciated the psychological subtlety and ethical refinement of Mme de la Fayette's *La Princesse de Clèves* – that the crux of it was not the renunciation of love, common enough, but the avowal of renunciation, which brought not satisfaction but further unhappiness to both wife and husband.

Marthe and I had plenty to talk about – her first glimpse of young Marcel Proust, for instance, arriving at a country house of her relations who had invited him: all informally dressed in weekend country clothes, for tennis and sport, and the young Proust uncomfortable in black suit and stiff collar. Oddly enough, I do not recall her *Au Bal avec Marcel Proust*. And it was disappointing that she did not know my chief admiration among women writers, Colette. She told me of her strong Bourguignon accent, and thought there was something '*couvie*' about her – surely quite wrong: was that a touch of feminine jealousy for a woman of transcendent gifts as a writer?

The Princess knew de Gaulle – as she knew Churchill, Asquith and Ramsay Macdonald. When de Gaulle was opposed by the intellectuals, she said, he has 40,000 against him, but 40 million French people with him. I remember a well-known academic saying to me, '*Il parle comme ma grand'mère.*' In France the intellectuals had counted for much more than in other countries; they, and what they thought, were taken seriously. De Gaulle, an intellectual himself, but a far better one, showed how little they really mattered and could be disregarded.

What wonder, when so many of them took their cue from a muddle-headed Franco-German like Sartre, who urged that Soviet Russia was the incarnation of human freedom?! And in another outburst of wisdom argued that, to understand a person, one need know nothing of his origins, upbringing, or early development! Completely contrary to all the findings of modern psychology, of history, or even of common sense. No wonder that de Gaulle was able to manoeuvre these Leftists into the Cave of Adullam where they belonged.

Mauriac was worthy of respect – with a record of resistance to the German Occupation, yet anxious that there should be as little revenge as possible against the collaborators, and, with sympathies liberal and humane, doing his best to serve as interpreter between de Gaulle and the people. All the same, it was rather comic to meet Mauriac at Oxford, on his one visit to England and not knowing a word of English, to note his surprise that there were cultivated people in the island who were well read in his books. He gave the impression of thinking that civilization ended at the Channel. I remember his description, in talk with Graham Greene, of Evelyn Waugh: '*Ce n'est pas un romancier: c'est un fantaisiste.*'

Marthe's letter of May 1960 is full of the fuss of launching the first volume of her autobiography, *La Nymphe Europe* – curious title (on the back of what bull did she think she was being carried off? What Zeus?). 'Childbirth is nothing (Valentine my only experience) compared to publishing a book in Paris: 300 inscriptions to invent straight off, *Radio-diffusion* in one's private home, a snake coming through the window and a little group of passers-by in the street busy talking about you with your own *concierge*, swelling with pride.' Then TV, etc. – those were early days, and of course Marthe enjoyed all the fuss and fume around her: she had a way of creating it (I found it the least bit troublesome), and always had been used to it. Sometimes, the most impatient man in the world, I showed my impatience; she never once resented it – it proved her own magnanimity, 'greatness of mind' – as a lesser person would have done. Perhaps it witnessed to an inner sympathy for, like all intelligent persons, she was highly impatient too, never once with me.

On her way to Cornwall in December 1960 she was meeting our Cornish friends at Burlington House 'in the presence of Charles II. How very Continental the King of England looks! No wonder the Restoration did not last' – a very pertinent remark, for the Stuarts had hardly any English blood at all, and Charles II took after his French grandfather Henri IV and the swarthy Medicis. In Paris she had been at some reception to celebrate St Jean Perse's getting the Nobel Prize: there were the Academicians in a row, Mauriac, Lacretelle, Émile Henriot – that old worthy left over from the Third Republic. 'The secret about St Jean Perse getting the prize is that his poems have been translated into Swedish by no less a person than Mr Hammarskjöld.' Perhaps this was a sufficient explanation, when more important writers – Montherlant or Robert Frost, Trevelyan or S. E. Morison – went unrecognized; the liberal Hammarskjöld was always anxious to be in the van with the intellectuals. The state of Africa, for which he sacrificed his life uselessly, might dispel his illusions today. Not Marthe, who sped on to me the *mot* circulating in Paris: a cable from the Congo government to the United Nations – '*Envoyez troupes fraîches – les dernières étaient délicieuses.*'

The oysters at Prunier's made her suggest an expedition to the Duchy oyster-fishery on the Helford. This was not for me: an Oyster Feast there had been one of the least agreeable chores of my candidature for the Penryn and Falmouth constituency. But Marthe had an appetite corresponding to her zest for life. I once faced a lunch at Tullimaar which provided a feast of fresh lobster from Falmouth, and on top of that, out of Cornish patriotism, a proper Cornish pasty. Professor Simmons, when I took him there to lunch, was fascinated by the spectacle of the little parrot – who had had a book written about him, *Le Perroquet vert* – perched on the Princess's head and horrified to see him descend on the table to be fed from her plate.

Invitations to Paris were regular. 'If I wanted to know the situation there, "Come and see" – as Lytton Strachey answered Margot Oxford, when she inquired if he slept at night with his beard outside or inside the blanket.'

On her way to lunch in my vicinity she had brought Prince Charles Murat (with all that history in the name). I was away a great deal in America or at Oxford, so Marthe and the Prince peeped in at my gate to see 'the enchanted view down the valley to blue sea, framed by *walls* of rhododendron in

full bloom'. When she came to Trenarren she indulged a
fantasy: from the terrace the sea looked as if enclosed in a
chalice, with the optical illusion that it was above the level of
the terrace. Now she was bringing to Cornwall the holo-
graph letters Proust had written to the Abbé Mugnier, her
confessor and the spiritual guide, if not director, of a large
circle in Paris. Much of his literary correspondence he left to
her, and she made a book out of it.

Her letters of 1962 and 1963 complain increasingly of my
absence and her sense of desertion – I was more and more
committed to California, where my Shakespeare campaign
was unfolding. Not only his biography with the solution of
the problems of the Sonnets (except for the Dark Lady – that
was an unexpected bonus for getting the answers right: if
they had not been correct, I should never have been able to
pinpoint her by dating and corroborative circumstances), but
following it up with biographies of Southampton and Marlowe. I was up to my eyes with work, and occasionally sent
a close friend as messenger to keep touch. From 45 Quai de
Bourbon, 24 May 1962: 'Your friend you made mine by one
of your magical tricks, Robert Halsband, was *here* – where
you ought to be at least from time to time – yesterday.' He
would bring me her news – of her election to the Belgian
Royal Academy and festivities beginning with a dinner with
Proust's niece. Meanwhile, the French translation of my
Shakespeare biography was coming out with her publishers,
Plon, and the British Institute had arranged a lecture at the
Sorbonne to celebrate the Quatercentenary. At last I was
going to pay one of my rare visits to Paris.

'28 April 1964. Here I am at the Hotel Lutétia where I have
stayed twice before (in earlier years at the Hotel du Quai
Voltaire, where Wilde and the poets of the '90s used to stay).
My old friend Princess Bibesco has been as good as her word
and drummed up a good deal of interest. Last evening I at
last penetrated into her apartment, a couple of floors up in
the seventeenth-century house on the Île St Louis, right at the
prow of the stone ship islanded in the Seine.

'What a situation! Plenty of windows, the room full of

white light: on one side the church of St Gervais, and further
up the Tour St Jacques; on the left the towers and *flèche* of
Notre Dame, and the spire of the Sainte Chapelle. The heart
of ancient French civilization, still beating: the Seine barges
going up and down, the greenery along the quays just coming out. She told me that at the angle of the island just
beneath, Baudelaire wrote the famous poem beginning:

> *Sois sage, O ma douleur,*
> *Et tiens-toi plus tranquille.*

'Looking out on the scene from the Princess's apartment,
my mind flashed back to the impoverished student circling
the Île St Louis and looking up eagerly at those historic
houses, the Hotel de Lauzun and the rest, with never a hope
of penetrating into them.

'I was enchanted by what she had made of the little apartment, the windows banked with flowers from Tullimaar,
camellias, rhododendrons, viburnum scenting the room with
its subtle incense. On a glass table in front of the sybaritic,
invitatory divan was an arrangement of flowers bespeaking
her originality: an array of large scent-bottles, an ox-eyed
daffodil in each one, a procession of white nuns bowing their
heads to Notre Dame. Charming myth, perhaps in the end,
it doesn't have to be true.

'Inside the door was a large portrait of the Abbé Mugnier,
confidant of many years, with penetrating grey eyes, seeing
through everything. A Boldini pencil sketch for the portrait
of the Princess, some sketches by Renoir, a large Boucher
overdoor in each room – such were relics put together from
the palaces she has inhabited before the rape and destruction
of our time. The *perroquet vert* was very much at home,
crouching in and out of the stalks of vegetation with a nut-
shell in beak, playing with Blanche (the *femme de chambre*)
and talking to her with almost the affability of a kitten: for
the first time I saw his charm.

'On our way out to dinner she told me of her early morning walk along the quays with Ramsay Macdonald back from

the Stresa Conference.[3] Macdonald always liked early walks
– and she was young then. She looked back to see that they
were followed by four detectives, two French, two English.
"They must have thought, What are those two doing so early
in the morning?" Ramsay had a *tendresse* for *grandes dames* –
who can blame him? – but was very proper; while power is
incense to *their* nostrils.

'We arrived at the Hotel Vendôme – the square looking
so different from the shabby, squalid days of the Third
Republic – all cleaned, rich cream stone, balconies properly
gilded. Under the German Occupation a guard every night,
au clair de lune, marched up and solemnly saluted the column,
all on his own. (Rather nice, but all the same, so like the
Germans, a goose-stepping ass.)

'Napoleon III in his youth had stayed in this pleasant old-
fashioned hotel, and we dined in a Second Empire apartment
occupied by an American, more French than the French,
widow of a gifted scientist, Le Comte du Nöuy, who wrote
books on science and religion. A woman of strong prejudices, which jangled throughout the evening as her Middle
Eastern turquoises jangled and jarred. She was very argumentative, in the manner of American women, her arguments all
prejudice, though she didn't recognize it: violently anti-
American, pro-French, Gaullist. When in the United States,
I always put the case for the French and for de Gaulle; and it
is true that Roosevelt and the State Department treated them
with appalling arrogance and ignorance. It was bound to
bank up fires of resentment; all the same I am appalled by the
depth of anti-Americanism everywhere in Paris. So I set
myself to try and put the American case – anyway, to explain
it reasonably. Of course, one is always sustained by contempt
for human fools' incapacity to *think*: their thinking is merely
reacting, usually emotional. They can't think (*pace* A. E.
Housman), and that is all there is to it.'

The Princess remained silent while the argument, if that is
the word for it, raged. I hope I did not disgrace her, for I kept
my temper and plodded patiently on. A fourth at table was a

[3] In 1935, at which neither Macdonald nor Simon warned Mussolini of the
consequences of an attack on Abyssinia.

delightful old boy, Raymond Eschollier, author of a book on Delacroix. He was just as enraged with the Americans as the American expatriate, our hostess: they treated us *'comme des singes, comme des singes,'* he repeated – and the Americans had treated the French tactlessly, after all the most distinguished people in Europe, the heart of European civilization.

In the end we came down to the monopoly of nuclear power which the Americans possessed at the time, and were withholding from others. Of course they would, chimed the two anti-Americans: it is in their own interest to do so, they are just looking after themselves. I allowed that this was so – people have to look after themselves; but *all the same* the extension of nuclear power was contrary to the interest of the human race. I went half way to meet them for, after all, I had not approved of the American frustration of the Anglo-French stand over Suez, nor of the Americans' anti-imperialism directed against the French in Algeria. Was it any improvement to civilization when they went?

My statement of an in-between position, sympathetic to both French and Americans, had its effect; for, at the end of it all, I won an accolade from the American expatriate lady, who thanked me for defending her country. I was relieved not to have disgraced Marthe, for they were friends – and I had given them a good run for their dinner. I was more taken with the distinguished old boy, with his *cordon* of the *Légion d'Honneur.*

'He had had an interesting public career, secretary to Briand, of whom he gave a close-up account. A Gaullist, Eschollier was contemptuous of democracy (that was all right with me): on a tour of the South of France, the European statesman had to put up with being told his business by café proprietors, commercial travellers, small town business men: "If I were in your place I should have done this" – knowing nothing whatever of what they were talking about. (Like ordinary folk about Shakespeare: they don't qualify to hold an opinion.) That had finished democracy for him. How right de Gaulle is to cut the cackle, *discuss* nothing: they haven't anything to discuss with.

'And yet – the opinions of superior people, like those at

that dinner-table at the Hotel Vendôme, are not much better than those of the café proprietors or commercial travellers. The only difference is that, in the end, superior people are amenable to reason, or can at least follow it. Inferior people, i.e. the vast majority, not. What then is best? When a great man like de Gaulle, or Churchill, arises let him lead, but with proper constitutional checks on him, not such as to impede or obstruct the process of government itself. Mass-democracies, in large countries, are apt to be ungovernable, even in their own best interest.

'28 April: I went along to collect the Princess early. While I waited I observed the pretty picture of Louis XIV as a child, seated on cushions, holding a large Madonna-lily as a sceptre, order of the Saint Esprit round his neck, a little crown on head, rosy naked feet exposed. The picture had belonged to SAR the Duc de Berry. I looked again at the dark, cinder-coloured sketch done by Carpeaux at the Château de Ménars in 1870, of Valentin de Riquet, Comtesse de Caraman Chimay, Princess Bibesco. Immensely aristocratic, perfect oval of a face, looking downwards, slightly slanted large eyes, aquiline, ribbed nose, controlled lips – all of a Chinese perfection. The ash colour of it accentuated the sense of that disastrous year. Was it painted in the country while the Germans were invading? Had the family left Paris to take refuge in the country? What was her story? When did she die? It is difficult to think of this perfect creature, in such control of herself and life, as dead – the whole thing radiated the sadness of mortal perfection under the threat of time.

' – Like the Princess, my old friend – and Ramsay Macdonald's, Charlie Londonderry's, Mr Asquith's, Lord Thomson's friend – gallant, courageous, in decay. What fun simply going through the streets of Paris with one who has been part of it all her life! Going along the *quais* we passed one fine eighteenth-century *hôtel*, which had been her mother-in-law's, very grand with entrance court, grille, and screen of one-storey buildings looking on the Seine. She knew the seventeenth-century *hôtel* at the bottom of the Boulevard St Germain, of which I possess an attractive painting at home – now, I gathered, the Roumanian (Communist) Embassy.

'In former days, what wealth power meant! – it must have
been a chief incentive, almost as important as power in itself.
It is obvious *how* it accrued as an accompaniment of acquaintance with the holders of power – the families of kings' mistresses, their descendants, the favourites of Valois and
Bourbons, as of Tudors and Stuarts.' But – until the social
revolution of today – power and culture went together: the
cultivated minority had the power. Today, no longer:
whether it is Soviet Russia, or Britain, or the United States,
it is the uncultivated who have the power, whether philistine
trade union bosses, or lower-middle-class types like Brezhnev
or Carter, Harold Wilson or Callaghan. It is to be expected
that increasingly the best people, the really superior, will
withdraw from politics, leaving the squalid mess to inferior
types. Will that be good for society, let alone culture?
The really cultivated will withdraw, as with the aristocracy
under the Third Republic (except for the army and diplo-
macy).

'We lunched with the daughter of the Duc de Grammont,
in a grander apartment in the Rue Dominique – but no view
like the Princess's. We passed St Clothilde, *très frequentée* –
naturally in this aristocratic area, for religion has become
largely a matter of class. What a contrast with the eighteenth
century! The Revolution taught the aristocracy the error of
their ways, at least in that respect – they had opened the way
to unbelief among the people, with fatal consequences.' So,
with the *Restauration* the upper classes recovered religion; the
middle classes now took to unbelief, with predictable consequences. Alfred de Vigny, I think, has some illuminating
pages on this dialectic.

'I fell for our hostess – she was natural and unaffected,
intelligent as well as charming, like an English girl in spontaneity of manner, but more taste and finesse, perfection of
breeding. The same was true of my neighbour at lunch, a
young Princesse d'Arembert – half Spanish, her father killed
in 1940. I remembered the name in the earlier form, Arem-
berg, grandees in the Spanish Netherlands, who remained
with Spain against William the Silent; one of them cropped

up in Ralegh's underhand dealings which brought him to book under James I.[4]

'We lunched under a large dominating Nattier of Madame de Vintimille – regular oval, rose-coloured face (or rouge), hand raised in perpetual conscious charm or expostulation – who had been a mistress of Louis XV and had a son. Beneath sat her descendant, the son of the house. How much alive the *ancien* régime still is in these circles! I have always felt that something irreplaceable went out of French life with the monarchy – as Alfred de Vigny, a congenial spirit, thought. At the same time, a devotee of Proust, I reflected that though the Faubourg Saint Germain was impenetrable to outsiders, once one was inside ways were relaxed and easy, spontaneous as with the English aristocracy, rather English in fact.

'One phrase revealed the anti-Americanism, however: our hostess thought the American influence "poisonous" – in so far as it was demotic and populist, it would be disagreeable, Henry Adams or Henry James would agree. The Princess d'Arembert was more open-minded, less emotional; she said that she could well understand foreigners not liking the French. If she were a foreigner she would not like their pride, their self-sufficiency. I did not accept this, and said that any-one who appreciated French history and culture accepted and admired France for herself, and not for something different. I did not say how much I respected the prudent meanness: France had accepted something like £2000 million from the Americans, one way and another, held on to it and made the most of it. So unlike the easy-going English who had got nothing and squandered their resources on others after the war; while it is impossible to respect the wastefulness and extravagance that runs through the American way of life.

'There, all round the apartment were the evidences of French civilization. I have never seen such a superb writing-desk, except the one made by Riesener at Blenheim: this one more simple, rectangular lines, ormolu decorations on the cupboards, opening perfectly with the dull sigh of fine wood. On the desk the leather writing *cahier* had the *poissons* of the

[4] v. my *Ralegh and the Throckmortons*.

Pompadour; another object the arms of Marie Leczinska.[5] In the blue boudoir within were eighteenth-century books that had belonged to the Comtesse Grefulhe, of Proust's adoration, a chief original of the Duchesse de Guermantes.'

In the evening, after a reception at the British Institute, the Director, Francis Scarfe, took me out for a quiet meal before my lecture at the Sorbonne. 'Richelieu's Chapel loomed immensely down as we went up – a very good audience, the Amphithéatre Richelieu three parts full, mostly youngish research students. In the front row sat the Princess with her friends, our hostess's son, the young Comte de Maigret, the Comtesse de Rougemont, her daughter and friend, a young man of immensely old family, de la Falaise.

'Afterwards the Princess gave a small party in her apartment, and I had some pleasant chat with the Rougemont lady, very Anglophile and sympathetic. She told me that the Pompadour, in addition to being beautiful and intelligent, was a kind woman, always doing people good turns, and not so influential politically as people thought. I said the same was true of Mme de Maintenon: she had been blamed for the Revocation of the Edict of Nantes, but the bishops were responsible, not she.

'29 April: lunch with Francis Scarfe in my favourite Place de l'Odéon. Across the street was the Library Benjamin Franklin – all the windows displaying photographs, books, enlargements of MSS of Robert Frost: an effort to impress Paris with American culture. To what effect? At lunch a Cambridge disciple of Leavis expressed the view that D. H. Lawrence was a writer in the same class as Shakespeare. I did not let this Leavis nonsense pass – what bloody fools, humans: they *never* know. Coming back along the Rue Vaugirard, I popped into the church of St Joseph des Carmes, in the crypt of which the September massacres of French aristocrats took place – the people at their fun.

' 30 April. I was to take the Princess out to lunch, and made it early, 12.30, to get in good time to the airport. I shopped in the charming little shops of the Île St Louis: a mass of white flowers, gladioli and tulips, to take the place of the

[5] Louis XV's Queen.

extinguished daffodils; chocolate-liqueurs for Blanche; nothing for the *perroquet vert*. The Princess was not ready. I read Maurois' *Le Monde de Marcel Proust*, fascinating photographs, but not one of Robert de Montesquiou. Still no sign of the Princess. I should have banged on her bedroom door, perhaps have entered. Instead, I grew furious – the old impatience, the familiar complex from childhood at being frustrated. I marched loudly up and down the creaking parquet; I banged books. No one appeared; no sign of life. Time was getting on. I went outside on the staircase and rang the bell. Blanche appeared from nowhere: No, the Princess was not ready. I told her that it was now too late, I had to get to the airport.

'I began to go downstairs; if the taxi had not been waiting I should have walked out on her. I know myself well enough: I have done it before, when anyone keeps me waiting too long and I start walking away. But the taxi was there; I went back, and there she was descending the staircase, nearly an hour late. This succeeded in spoiling my departure.

'While waiting, Blanche had brought out a curious picture to occupy me: a Jacobite portrait of Charles I as Jesus Christ, with a mysterious inscription about the head having been executed by Lentulus and sent to the Senate. I was so beside myself with impatience that I never gave the matter a moment's consideration, or I should have seen that the reference had something to do with Speaker Lenthall, the execution reported to Parliament.

'We hurried along to lunch at the Espadon, the Ritz restaurant – imagine having to rush through a delicious turbotin, fresh woodland strawberries and cream! The day was ruined, and I had an appalling programme of lectures before me in England.' But I had seen another side to my *chère Princesse* and she of me – she never once seemed to resent it – but wrote asking to be forgiven.

On my return I got a letter: 'My Professor, Immediate is the answer with you, always' – she had got the message – with more information about the mysterious picture. It had come to her from her aunt, the Comtesse Odon de Montesquiou; it had belonged to the Château de Courtanvaux, which her aunt had restored with Bibesco money. The *châ-*

teau was the original home of Montluc, author of the military *Commentaires* of which I once (before taxation became penal) possessed an original edition. The picture was known as '*Le Jésus mousquetaire*'. Why?

D'Artagnan of Dumas' *Trois Mousquetaires* was a cadet of the Montesquiou family; the Château d'Artagnan was always the seat of a younger son.

> In my time Robert de Montesquiou – Proust's Charlus – owned the *château*, whence he wrote his letters to me – and the sonnet about my emeralds which is quoted in *Au Bal avec Marcel Proust:*
>
> > Vous portiez sur la robe en satin d'un vieux rose
> > Des émeraudes dont Shakespeare dit l'attrait . . .
>
> But why 'Jésus Mousquetaire'? Everything at Courtanvaux smells of *mousquetaires* – the famous picture of the real D'Artagnan by Philippe de Champagne being on the wall over one of the seventeen staircases. I stayed at Courtanvaux during my honeymoon . . . The picture may have been propaganda for the Stuarts, showing the King as Christ condemned by his own people! . . . All here remember you and wish to see you revisiting Paris very very soon, and often.

Alas, that I did not.

At the end of Shakespeare Year she was writing to her 'dearest Professor' her pleasure at the letter I had received from de Gaulle, for whom she had a fervent admiration and whom she was to meet at a reception for him at the 'Palais Royal facing the Louvre, Mazarin's abode'. She had been a guest at the Académie française at the introduction of Dr Adenauer as honorary member, 'as also when they received *our* beloved Sir Winston, on a very different occasion'. She had been exchanging greetings with him on his ninetieth birthday, and attending the Toulouse-Lautrec Exhibition at the Petit Palais. This had been 'a revelation: I thought I knew, and discovered, as many others did, that I *knew nothing*. What a genius, and from his early boyhood, poor little monster! He had his divine revenge, thank God.' Then, 'bring me back some camellia-seeds from California,' of which she affected to be jealous for taking me away so much. 'P.S. I saw Anouilh's *Richard III*, and to my surprise I loved it. *Your French text is in the program.*'

My Journal records one or two more outings in Cornwall, always best when we were alone. We were to go down to Falmouth, where an All Souls colleague possessed an exquisite Regency house: cream-washed stucco, with two large niches for statues, with a granite colonnade. One of a number of delicious late Georgian houses built round Falmouth for post-captains or officers retired from the Packet Service. Inside, elegant staircase going up to a cupola, honey-coloured mahogany doors brought back from Honduras, drawing room hung with a lovely landscape wallpaper. O the taste of the eighteenth century, and O the horrors of today, the grounds built up with trivia. The stables retained their distinction and were lived in by an Oxford acquaintance, a discriminating bachelor. The Princess used him for chauffeur – she had brought him to lunch at Trenarren – and for company for her daughter when she was away in Paris. The daughter, Princess Ghika, accompanied, submissive, charming, *distraite*, and her taciturn soldier son.

'I drove down the narrow drive of close-planted Cornish elms I used to walk down with my cousins, as children, to Swanpool: the house then belonged to cousins of Charles Henderson. We all infiltrated into the coach-house, which our bachelor friend had made charming: good taste and good china, Sèvres and Chelsea, which he inherited. He keeps house and cooks for himself. He served drinks, but was in no hurry to serve lunch, after twenty minutes in his pretty garden – a fine viburnum, cherry-coloured and rose-red hydrangeas, plenty of pears on the wall.

'The Princess and I chatted together on the sofa, mainly about my little de Gaulle campaign in *The Times* (which much displeased Lord Gladwyn, with whom I had wrangled through lunch with Leola Epstein at Claridge's). With no appearance of, or move towards, lunch, the Princess began to play up. "I am feeling faint . . . I am ill. I must have lunch." She commanded our host to begin lunch at once. I was amused: quite right, it revealed the impatience superior persons feel towards ordinary mortals – a feeling I shared – and perhaps the latent tartar always held in restraint with me. She was in a rage – just like me at being kept waiting in her Paris apartment. Lunch began in an atmosphere of considerable *gêne*, while I worked away papering over the cracks and bringing things round. All went well and lunch ended fairly happily; a crack had, however, appeared.

'After lunch our host took me out into the garden where I learned a few things, more in the car going back with the Princess. She had found a rich wife for him in Italy: he had found her impossible. The lady was a French Singer, who had made a mess of life and reputation, been left by two husbands, and would welcome rehabilitation by a respectable marriage. Very rich, with a villa in Florence and a house in Paris. When he saw the set-up, he decided against. I said, Wouldn't she do for me? Marthe replied, "Too low-brow. Too unintelligent. You would be bored." Then, meditatively but conclusively, "Tous les Singers sont un peu fous."

'This led us on to another of the French Singers, whom we both knew and had taken the measure of – I one weekend at that paradisal house, Compton Beauchamp, under the escarpment of the Berkshire Downs, moat, water-garden, formal forecourt and all. O to live in it – one of the Astor boys subsequently did. Marthe repeated her story of the Singer lady's jealousy at her dancing at a ball with someone she passionately wanted to marry. Off the rebound she had married a cousin of Winston's, a sprig of Blenheim.

'Many stories were told of her – of the handsome young Italian declaring his passion for her, and her saying "Prove it", pointing to the shadowy moat in the twilight. He dived in – it was empty – and the fool smashed his handsome profile against stone. This was the woman who, on the excuse of being in mourning for her husband, killed in the 1914 war, had herself presented at the English Court in black plumes and train, against a forest of white.

'This was the woman who tried to get me to break a public engagement at Bristol to stop a weekend with her to meet Duff Cooper – and would hold up the telephone line to Paris to discuss a chess-game with Duff when ambassador. She did make me break a Codrington rule at All Souls to lend her the *Memoirs* of the Duc Decazes, her great-grandfather and Louis XVIII's boyfriend. People are immoral about books – no sign of her returning it: in the end I made her. With her wonderful taste, exotic and exquisite, she was a full-bloomed specimen of French bitchery. She got no further with me: I expect she found me rather *naïf* and innocent.'

One last Cornish trip, from my Journal: to beautiful Croan, near Wadebridge, a William and Mary manor-house which the taste of an Air-Marshal, Sir John Tremayne, had made still more so. The square farmyard beside the house he had turned into a formal court, rather Italianate, with urns and summer houses. Within, the house was haunted by a Queen Anne lady, Madam Damaris, whose portrait hung in the drawing room; tapestry furniture, *petit-point*, 'the house smells like Hatfield', as one of the Cecils said – that nostalgic fragrance of polished wood, beeswax and wood-smoke which David Cecil describes in his book about Hatfield.

The Princess was working on three books simultaneously, now that she had a full-time secretary: this lady was born a Crèvecoeur, of the 'American Farmer's' family and Sir John had been all the way to Perran-ar-worthal to bring them to lunch. While the joys of family life occupied the conversation, I occupied the French lady, and at intervals observed the golden charm of this Cornish house: three rooms *en suite* all looking across the small forecourt and long lawns to the gate which John had made. I had once observed a striking colour arrangement outside: beds of gold montbretia between the silver boles of the beeches.

'The Princess, troublesome as usual and making a practice of asking for a flower, asked for a magnolia bloom, which necessitated John's going off for long mechanical cutters to get up so high. A trouble – but with his refinement of courtesy he managed with some difficulty to reach two, another for "the pretty French lady", as he had called her in introducing his grandchildren. The demonstration of aristocratic manners was not lost on me; but I was not persuaded by it.

'I drove the ladies back to their lair, since John had brought them. Enough. As we drove into Truro the Princess – another test – wanted to be taken off the road to Alan Bennett's new antique shop. She did not get out of the car: he was summoned to the presence. I took the opportunity for a quick five-minute look round inside. Intensely concentrated on the job, I was subconsciously aware that the unattached widow had taken her opportunity to trail round at my heels – a thing I detest – and corner me. Alone with her on the sofa I had half-registered her pointed inquiries about my house – the Princess must have told her that I was well off and unattached. Having to leave in two or three days, I felt safe and took no notice. Now was the moment: with only five minutes to decide on two Victorian footstools (like those which Nancy Astor had snatched before my eyes), consider a *chaise longue* and exclude a pair of Staffordshire china baskets, the French lady was upon me, forced to call attention to herself. I took no notice of the interruption.

'Going back to the car with my catches, a lot of feminine fuss was made about taking them in and where to stow them away, choc-a-bloc with the ladies' traps. "He travels furthest who travels alone" had always been my motto. Detesting feminine fuss, I crossly stowed one footstool under my feet, rather in the way of the driving, and was tucking the other away at the back of all the impedimenta. But no – the pretty French lady held up the proceedings – she wanted to inspect it: another endeavour to draw attention to herself. By now irritated and impatient – very far from a chivalrous Sir John – I drove them fast home with few words. On taking my leave the French lady gave me only the tips of her fingers for a handshake: she had been shown where she got off, and that evening it gave me, in spite of a little self-reproach, not a few laughs.'

In her last years Marthe had a deal of ill-health – shingles, which went on for months and months: a nervous ailment, perhaps from overwork and certainly overworry, the family, family finances, the strain of keeping up Tullimaar. Gallant old war-horse, she said to me only once, with no accent of complaint, that it fell to her to be the pillar to uphold everything and keep it going. She poured out her books, most of them *livres de circonstance* to make money – about Churchill, about Queen Elizabeth II – while working at her serious book, the second volume of *La Nymphe Europe*. I did what little I could to help, in getting books, small literary commissions.

In 1972 she was sending me her *Le Confesseur et les Poètes*, the correspondence of the Abbé Mugnier with commentary. She had sent her *Échanges avec Claudel* to the French Institute at Oxford inscribed as a present from me: I don't think she knew that I was allergic to Claudel as a writer. He represented what I disliked in French literature – rhetoric, intellectual arrogance, Ultramontane intolerance; his bullying of Gide was intolerable – a kind of French Belloc (but then Belloc *was* French). However, to be just, I had been unexpectedly impressed when young by Claudel's *L'Annonce faite à Marie* at the Odéon.

Now she was writing about 'Le Prince de Galles, le Roi, le Duc de Windsor'. The Princess had a stalwart, and genuine, admiration for the royal family in Britain: not just snobbery or flunkeyism – she was above that – she appreciated what a tremendous factor the monarchy was in ensuring social stability, all the more by contrast with the political instability of France she had lived through. (Miraculously, De Gaulle had remedied that; and, happily, she did not live to see Britain shabbily, unnecessarily, weakened.)

'May I ask you for one more favour, having received so many from you?' Would I receive a nephew of hers now at Oxford, at my old college, Christ Church: Prince Constantin de Brancovan, 'very dear to me and very near' – another historic name from the old Eastern Empire. 'Impatiently waiting for more news of you, I remain, my dearest Professor, your obedient Pupil, regardless of absence and age.'

Her next, from the Île St Louis, May Day 1973, begins:

'Time has no effect on my admiration and affection for you.' She had missed so much a visit from me last year and hers to me 'and *that* garden with the sea as drapery, above in the sky.' She was failing, but lived long enough to hear of my discovery of the Dark Lady, and asked for my *Shakespeare the Man* which announced it. 'If you come to lecture in *La Sorbonne* you will find me an hermit in my island until 14 July.' She went each year for treatment at the baths at Bagnolles sur l'Orme, and would be in the 'Delectable Duchy' in September. 'I am writing you on *le jour du Muguet, porte-bonheur*, and enclose one for you.' There is the little fragment of lily-of-the-valley sticking to the letter still – touching remembrance from one soon to die.

Fortunately I was able to pay her a visit that summer –

> the memory green of your visit to Tullimaar is with me, for ever, every problem solved . . . It was heaven to see you, in your Delectable Duchy which has the honour to have you as its Poet-Son, and Master as well. Hoping to see you in Paris and to hear you again at the Sorbonne, I dream of you in your Cornish garden where the sea is drapery to the lawn. I say *à toujours, à jamais*.

It was her last letter to me. I see her now, very pale and frail, having been placed on the sofa in the drawing-room, by the chimney-piece with the Cousteau horses prancing, afternoon sun filling the room from the western window looking down the drive. Her voice – it is impossible to recapture it – low and a little masculine, with a curious crackle in it, giving it a character all its own.

Gone the old vigour, yet the zest for knowledge, the intelligence, still lit up the dark eyes in the perfect ivory skin. She never quite lost the dark, black lustre of her hair, ringlets a little after the fashion of the Regency. I never knew her in the days of her great beauty – she once, again only once, said a brave, stoical word about that, the futility of women regretting vanished beauty.

Looking back over this friendship, I have now a sense of my own inadequacy. I had done my best – or, not quite – my best within my willed and deliberate limitations. The two great emotional experiences of my life had both come to grief and suffering. Henceforth I was immune. Human beings were always inadequate (hence religion), and my expectations of them were always too high. The Princess was one of those rare beings who do not fail; I have now the obscure and humble feeling that I may have failed her. Could it be expressed in the one word – love? The thought then never occurred to me – I should have thought it presumptuous on my part. There was the difference of age, every sort of difference – and yet, in spite of that, a deeper kinship of spirit than I realized. I regarded her with admiration, deference, a fascination that was partly historic and partly personal. But I did not love her; it never occurred to me that possibly she might have loved me.

All in all, she was the most remarkable woman I have ever known.

8

An Evening with Edmund Wilson

I confess that I have some difficulty in doing justice to
Edmund Wilson: he was not one of my favourite American
writers. I could construct a list of a score of them – from my
favourite in early years, Nathaniel Hawthorne, through Walt
Whitman, Henry James, Henry Adams, Santayana, going on
to Edith Wharton, Willa Cather, Flannery O'Connor – but
Edmund Wilson would not be among them. (My unfavourite
American writers would be no less revealing – Dreiser, Carl
Sandburg, Sinclair Lewis, Steinbeck and such.)

The fact that Edmund Wilson was something of a mentor
to the fashionable Left intellectuals, at Oxford and elsewhere,
did not recommend him to me: I had ceased to be a Left
intellectual myself in my thirties, with the oncoming of the
second German war. Wilson's ambivalence about England
was obvious, a kind of quirk – he was full of quirks – rather
than a fully-fledged complex. I did not much care for his
report on England after all the strain and suffering of the
war, 1939 to 1945;[1] actually rationing of food and fuel went
on for years. The British people were underfed for some years
after the war – not until 1953, coronation year, did things
take an upward turn.

Hence, in this perspective, I was still more unfavourably
impressed by a remark of his that the high estimation of
English literature reflected Britain's ascendancy; with her
decline perhaps her literature might be less highly regarded.
May be. No doubt about the decline, but literary decline does

[1] In *Europe Without Baedeker*.

not necessarily accompany political decline. France, at the apogee of her power under Napoleon, was rather bare of good literature, while the squalid Third Republic witnessed a marvellous explosion of genius in the creative arts, not only literature, but music and painting.

Wilson's judgment seemed to reflect something of *Schadenfreude*, and his was not an historical mind for all that his best work in literary criticism was historical rather than analytical. The best thing about him was his passion for literature, his ever-questing mind for new work; his unfailing nose for anything good. His literary flair was remarkable, his judgment good in this field, certainly not in the field of politics.

He held on for too long to the old American liberal tradition and democratic illusions – he thought T. S. Eliot's political conservatism 'twaddle', though it stands up to the subsequent tests contemporary society has posed far better than Wilson's Jeffersonian liberalism. He later added a flavouring of Marx and Communist sympathies – even defending Stalin, explaining away the purges, massacres of the faithful; but ended up disillusioned, and confessing himself 'alienated' from all the United States stood for.

Literary people are not very good judges of politics, and Wilson was no exception. No, to do him justice we must judge him on his literary showing, rather than his views on politics or history.

As a writer he was singularly uncreative – his ventures into fiction, *I Thought of Daisy* and *Memoirs of Hecate County*, are really autobiographical. A great egoist, he could never transcend himself. He treasured up every scrap concerning himself, scraping the bottom of the barrel to publish adolescent notes and jottings hardly worthy of print in, for example, *A Prelude: Landscapes, Characters, Conversations from the Earlier Years of My Life*.

On the other hand, his literary curiosity was insatiable – though very odd that he should never have read *Don Quixote*, one of the supreme imaginative experiences of the world. His range of reading was immense, his appetite exceptional, the zest and intellectual vivacity admirable.

No work of his, in my opinion, came up to his first book

of criticism, *Axel's Castle*, which had unity of theme, the then Modern movement in literature: Yeats, Valéry, Eliot, Proust, Joyce, Gertrude Stein (for what she counted), Axel, i.e. Villiers de L'Isle Adam, and Rimbaud. The book was dedicated to Wilson's remarkable preceptor at Princeton, Christian Gauss; the dedication proclaimed what was to be the signature tune of Wilson's best work and his statement of 'what literary criticism ought to be – a history of man's ideas and imaginings in the setting of the conditions which have shaped them'.

I am much more sympathetic to that than to the verbal analytics of I. A. Richards or Empson, or the want of proportion and common sense which accompanied the paranoia of Leavis, the acutely personal bias disguised as objective critical discipline, though the disguise was transparent to anyone with any psychological perception. In other words, Wilson's interest was in the history of literature, the works themselves and the personalities of the writers – something more real than to suppose that you need know nothing of that out of which the work of literature sprang, in the mind and experience of the writer or the conditions in which he wrote.

For all that, Wilson was not interested in history as a branch of literature – in that very characteristic of literary critics in general, and an important loss to them. He had read Gibbon and Macaulay with pleasure, but as literary art only. It is curious that there is not a single mention in his *Letters* of Samuel Eliot Morison, a near neighbour when Wilson went to live in Cambridge (Mass.); I suspect that they did not much approve of each other. Prescott is never mentioned, and Parkman only once indirectly via an essay about him by the literary critic Van Wyck Brooks. And it is amazing that the universal reader had not read that most distinguished and beautiful work of American historical writing, Henry Adams' *Mont St Michel and Chartres*.

One consequence of this was that Edmund Wilson tended to follow the bias of a Leftist historian such as Charles A. Beard – in spite of Morison's devastating exposure of him in

'The Shaving of a Beard'[2] – or a crackpot like Harry Elmer
Barnes, who appeared to think that at Pearl Harbour the
Americans attacked the Japanese. Wilson subscribed to their
absurd interpretation of the event. After this one is the less
surprised at his statement that in many ways the United
States was closer to other countries than to England. An
historian like Morison, Nevins or Mattingly would know
that this was nonsense. With Wilson it was his irremediable
Scotch-Irish prejudice.

Ambivalence was similarly characteristic of his attitude
towards my friend, T. S. Eliot. I do not suppose that his
attitude was so simple as that of Carl Sandburg, whom I once
heard denounce Henry James for not being sure whether he
was a citizen of the United States or a subject of a British
monarch. Wilson's judgment was too good to set any store
by a Sandburg, whose vast self-identificatory book on Lincoln, Wilson said, was the worst thing that happened to him
since Booth shot him.

Wilson's essay on the early (i.e. American) Eliot in *Axel's
Castle* is penetrating and just; but, as time went on and Eliot's
experience deepened, his thought matured, Wilson became
querulous. By 1933 he was writing:

> I heard Eliot read his poems the other night. He did
> them extremely well – contrary to my expectation. He is
> an actor and really put on a better show than Shaw . . .
> He gives you the creeps a little at first because he is such
> a completely artificial, or rather self-invented, character
> – speaking English with a most careful English accent as
> if it were a foreign language which he had learned
> extremely well.

Virginia Woolf noticed that Eliot was careful also to pronounce French precisely and correctly.

Why? The answer is simple: Eliot was a perfectionist. A
master of language, he wished to present a language at its
best, in the best way he could. André Maurois noted something psychologically perceptive, that the way a man reads his

[2] In *By Land and By Sea*.

work aloud reveals his ideal conception of himself, the self he has at heart and would be.

By 1957 Wilson was writing to Van Wyck Brooks, 'There is a scoundrel and actor in Eliot. It was the young scoundrel who wrote the good poetry and it is now the old scoundrel who is putting on the public performance.' This is the kind of clever nonsense that intellectuals like to write. Anyone less of a scoundrel than Eliot would be hard to imagine: he was always fastidious, if one wanted to be critical one could say – inclined to be priggish, in the end a good deal of a saint. Still more absurd than Wilson was the view of another literary patriot; he was writing to Van Wyck Brooks, 'I know that you regard him as a more sinister figure.'

Wilson could not understand why in Britain people were so critical of his Irish friend, Cyril Connolly. The answer again is simple: Connolly never fulfilled the talents he had, the 'promise' of *Enemies of Promise*, in any constructive work. Connolly hadn't the character to achieve it; so he became a commentator on other men's work – like Wilson himself. Connolly was a much better stylist; like the Irish (Eugene O'Neill, Scott Fitzgerald, Flannery O'Connor) Connolly had a specific gift for language – there was in him an aborted poet.

The poet, John Hall Wheelock, old-fashioned but authentic, used to make a comparable criticism of Edmund Wilson to me: 'What does it all add up to?' Perhaps we may confront that searching question at the end. Wheelock would compare Wilson unfavourably with Brooks, who – in spite of the disadvantage of having endured years of madness – did in the end accomplish a large constructive work with his successive volumes on the history of American literature.

Altogether, it may be seen that I was rather critical of Wilson, though that was of no importance since I did not enter into his fields of literary criticism or literary journalism. And he would be given no unduly favourable report of me by his informants among the Left intellectuals in Britain. However, when he turned up as a guest of one of them at All Souls – in those days everybody turned up there, sooner or later – I happened to be at the head of the table and did my best to make his evening agreeable. I was able to assure him that he had an elect following in England; this was evidently not disagreeable to him and rather turned his flank.

We got on quite well; he found that I was, though an historian, equally interested in literature, and I promised to send him my *Poems Partly American*, if only because very few English poets had ever responded to the American landscape. When he got back safely to Cape Cod, he wrote to me that he had enjoyed the poems: 'You are good on the American landscape, for which many Europeans have little real feeling.' Then came the reservation. 'But you do run true to type in speaking of "the loneliness that is America". It is natural for a European to get this impression, but, except in the great wilds and waste places, America does not seem lonely to us – especially at East Hampton!' I had experienced this feeling of aching loneliness, not only up in the mountains of California, out on the prairie of Illinois or Nebraska, going through the forests of North Carolina, the deserts of New Mexico and Arizona, but even in Central Park, New York. As for East Hampton, about which I had written a poem (later reprinted for the Music Festival there), there was the loneliness the early settlers had looked out upon in the waste of waters, the ocean that had once broken in and surrounded my friend's house on the coast.

Wilson went on:

> The relation between the people and the country is different from what it is in the closely packed and cultivated countries of Europe. I now live most of the time near the tip of Cape Cod or in a village in the Adirondack foothills, and this seems to me far more normal than living in American cities where I have a good many friends. The difference in this relationship from the European one lies in one's feeling that in order to function – to think, to realize oneself, to do solid work, etc. – one has to *pit oneself against* the country, which at the same time, however, will give one support.

This is very different from England, and – alas! – in both

terms. One does not have to pit oneself against nature, as in America – but one gets precious little support from the country, especially from democratic, popular society, i.e. a society without standards, 'without pride of ancestry, or hope of posterity', in Disraeli's phrase.

Wilson concluded in friendly wise: 'If you should ever be in this part of the world, I hope you will let me return your All Souls dinner.'

So, on my next visit to Boston, in October 1960, I decided to take him at his word, pay him a visit and satisfy my curiosity as to what he was like at home. I find some account of the experience in my Journals.

'As bidden I telephoned Edmund Wilson, and was asked to wait a minute, while I heard the inevitable typewriter clicking. Wilson was hard at it earning his living. The German voice of his young wife – the third (?) – resounded, then the rich, rounded Irish voice came back: would I come to tea at 5.30? I taxied out to 12 Hilliard Street, an ugly house in an old-fashioned street next to famous Brattle Street. In the pleasant lighted room were the sage, his wife and her contemporary, young Mrs Arthur Schlesinger.

'Edmund Wilson sat in his armchair, a generation older, pot-bellied like a Buddha, sipping glass after glass of whiskey. An extraordinary expression of face: inquiring upraised eyebrows, innocent open glassy eyes, marked downward droop of corners of the mouth, querulous, exceedingly irritable. The face of a crotchety, pernickety man, not unkindly. He began bored at the thought of me: I felt for him, and gradually got him completely round. (He *was* innocent, indeed, transparent: no subtlety.)

'We had a fascinating conversation, more or less ignoring the women, who had their own talk. The sage had a low fender of books by him, Angus Wilson's *Zola* uppermost.

'He talked about Compton Mackenzie, whom he wanted to write about – thinks him much underestimated, out of line with London so dominant in our literary affairs. True enough, but less so than had been, I said. He expressed himself interested in the minorities in Britain as opposed to the

English. He has always felt ambivalently about the English, in fact hostile, himself being Scotch-Irish.

'I teased him about this – said that, in spite of his being rather anti-English, there was much admiration for him in England – the English didn't mind. A curiously impervious man, he couldn't resist this line after a little reiteration. He began to melt, in so far as he is capable of melting – 'wilting' would better describe it, or 'blinking'.

'At any rate he warmed, and was complimentary about Cornwall, had been there once and thought it beautiful. Wouldn't I have a whiskey?'

(I declined whiskey, which I abominate; what I longed for was a cup of tea, to which I had been bidden. This was not offered. The ladies were engaged in ardent talk. In England they'd have been making tea.)

'Wilson now said that he wasn't exactly anti-English, but had a love-hate complex, induced by those of his relations who were Oh, so English. And then there were the English Abroad, their official representatives who were – I supplied the word "insufferable", which he grasped eagerly.

'I said that I was completely unEnglish myself, hadn't a drop of English blood, 100 per cent Cornish. But what was wrong with the English? Much as the Celtic minorities complain about them, they like the English better than they do each other. The Scotch and the Irish, for example – look at Ulster! The Cornish and the Irish miners fought like cat and dog in Wisconsin and Montana.[3] The Welsh didn't like the Irish. He was surprised at this last, but agreed that they preferred the English to each other.

'He came back to Compton Mackenzie and these minority themes in his work, and recommended to me the volumes about Greece and his First War experiences. I hadn't read these, or much of Mackenzie, not being much of a novel-reader. But he had been enamoured of Cornwall, blissful as it was in the pre-1914 days; I had gone up to Oxford properly equipped with a reading of *Sinister Street*, and had met Mackenzie once or twice, visited him at his hide-out near Oxford, celebrated in one of the best of his novels, *Guy and Pauline*.

[3] cf. *The Cornish in America*.

'In an intermission with the ladies we talked about the election. This was, like most of Harvard, a Kennedy household – he is "Jack Kennedy" here, a former pupil. I happened to mention old Joe Kennedy's American performance as ambassador in London in 1940, writing an open dispatch to say that we were defeated and had better make the best terms we could. At that – apparently Wilson didn't know the disgraceful episode (I had heard all about it from Winthrop Aldrich) – Wilson's nose wrinkled up, Irish fashion, just like Connolly's, and he tittered. It was an unpleasant surprise: I saw the ineradicable irresponsibility, the malice of the intellectual. I said that it wasn't amusing in 1940, when Britain needed every ounce of its will-power to survive. He said, "No, it wasn't amusing then. But I can't help laffin'."

'That placed him for me. No real judgment about politics, and therefore history. What is good about him is his passion for literature.

'He went on to talk about the Iroquois, and the immense complexity of Indian languages, of which there were something like eight hundred in the New World, with curious criss-cross similarities, likenesses of some Iroquois words to Mayan. I think he said he knew some sixty of them. (Did he expect me to believe that, or was it the whiskey working?) I told him about my Cornish friend, Donald Rickard's acquaintance with Indian life on the last frontier, in northern Ontario, in case he would be any use to Wilson. But, no, he had finished with the subject, and was on with the next.

'That is how he writes his books evidently – gets a craze for a subject, rushes into it, gets a smattering of it, writes a book or an essay or two, and passes on. Something of a sciolist.

'As with his *Dead Sea Scrolls*. He learnt a little Hebrew – brave of him – sploshed into a fearfully technical subject knowing little about it – and with the usual conceit quickly produced a book to catch the market. He is really a highbrow literary journalist – just like so much of the writing that pours out into the literary journals and gains ephemeral attention, tomorrow forgotten: all the Higher Journalism.

'He didn't relish my saying of Isaiah Berlin that, with his

linguistic gifts and Russian background, he should by this time have given us a big solid history of Russian Social Thought, something weighty and significant – indeed three or four of such books.

'He didn't agree (I expect the thought held some reflection upon himself): had I read Isaiah's thing on Moses Hess?

'I had – just a lecture, like his lecture on Inevitability in History, or his essay *The Hare and the Fox*. Mere lectures and essays, nothing of substance.

'Wilson proceeded to be rather illuminating about Berlin: how the core of his mind was essentially, deeply Jewish, with the characteristic passion for justice; how surprised people had been in Israel at his fluency in the language (Isaiah is fluent and inaudible in all languages); that his people had been very important in some movement towards greater strictness in Russian Judaism.

'He, Edmund Wilson, had "gone into the subject". I said that I agreed rather with Isaiah's English empiricism philosophically, his middle-of-the-road position, careful not to commit himself. Wilson didn't much like that, the old ingrained bias peeped out.

'Wouldn't I have some whiskey? (No, I would not have some whiskey; though, a drug-addict, I had given up all hope of tea.)

'*A propos* of history, one could never find out the truth about things anyway. He had "gone into that" too, had been writing history, etc. Now take Churchill's History – he didn't think much of it. He wouldn't, I reflected – and also he wouldn't know. This is a rather A. J. P. Taylor view, I noted – same irresponsibility, same facile dismissal of something that needs thinking about.

'I said I didn't agree. If you took Churchill's life of Marlborough, for example, it was an important contribution to history. The greatest of English soldiers had always been traduced and this tradition fixed by Macaulay: Churchill had corrected all this, and he was right.

'Wilson said he took his view of Marlborough from Swift.

'I said that there was nothing more biased, partisan and

unreliable. I greatly admired Swift as a writer – and had meant to write a biography of him[4] – but not as an historian. Think of his defaming Duchess Sarah by hinting that she was Godolphin's mistress, when everybody knew that Sarah was a prude: nothing but friendship among the three of them. Fancy the obtuseness of Swift, not much more than an unbeliever, the author of the sceptical *Tale of a Tub*, surprised that he wasn't made a bishop! The author of "The Windsor Prophecy", those terrible verses on the Duchess of Somerset, the Queen's friend, implying that she had murdered her husband – and expecting preferment from the Queen! It really was extraordinarily obtuse of him, apart from the irresponsibility as to historical fact – and then hoping to be made Historiographer Royal!

'Wilson was quite excited by all this on my part, at last surfacing. He said that this attitude was just like the English – a very feeble reply – and that Swift was speaking for the Irish minority. (But in these matters he wasn't: it all sprang, understandably, out of furious personal resentment.) I left it at that – perhaps Wilson had had too many whiskies by this time, at least four or five.

'I was getting anxious for a taxi, having promised to be back at my hotel by 7.30 or 8 p.m. Outside there was a downpour. A certain agitation seized on us both: Wilson was plainly fascinated and frightfully anxious to keep me.

' "Won't you stay on for a simple dinner?" he said hospitably, urgent, and to his wife a bit apologetically, "You've got something?" It was rather touching and pathetic, he so much wanted to go on with the conversation. "This is *most* interesting,' he said, all stirred up.

'I was determined to go, to leave at the best possible moment, when he most wanted to go on – having seen, as he had not before or been told by his Oxford informants, what I really was like to talk to. As for Edmund Wilson, I had done my best, and had not liked him – any more than Eliot had. However, I had seen right into him: a smatterer, who had "gone into all this" and that.

'What I respect is the unquestioned vivacity of mind, his

[4] Many years later I wrote *Jonathan Swift: Major Prophet*.

genuine love of literature. Even here his judgments are erratic: Mrs Schlesinger much admired Anthony Powell's sense of style. Wilson flatly contradicted her: he had "no style at a'al" (in Irish brogue). Actually Powell's command of words is one of the best things about him; I don't care for his later novels (one of the Left intellectuals finds them "devitalizing"); but he *is* a stylist.

'I saw something of what the women had to put up with from grandpa. He had told me that he much admired Mary McCarthy, but found her intolerable; I dare say she could say the same of him. And so they parted – as the Athanasian creed might, but does not, say: "And yet there are not two Intolerables, but One Intolerable."

'Edmund Wilson is a pernickety, contradictious and rather pathetic ageing man. Isaiah, who had (according to Wilson), "run down" a young Fellow of St Antony's to him, may have given Wilson a picture of me such that the reality came as rather a surprise. I dare say all the intellectuals had given him a pretty unfavourable report. It was comic – the reluctant invitation that morning to tea at 5.30, no tea – and then the urgent desire to keep me on to dinner.

'But I really had had enough; I had satisfied my curiosity. I passed a more pleasurable, if less intellectual, evening at the hotel.'

However, I think that he never forgave me for refusing his pressing invitation and insisting on leaving. He had expressed an interest in Cornwall and the Cornish, among other minorities under the heel of the English; but when I sent him *Tudor Cornwall* there was no reaction from him. Perhaps it was too historical for him.

What then does Edmund Wilson add up to (in John Hall Wheelock's phrase)?

I think that my ultimate judgment of both the writer and the man must be more favourable than my impression of him that evening. He was a gentleman, not a cad; he was warm-hearted and had kindly impulses, on the whole not malicious.

As a writer, his best critical work, *Axel's Castle*, has permanent value. So also has his conspectus of American literature, *The Shock of Recognition*: anyone who wants a chronological guide to American writing can hardly do better than read that – less biased than Van Wyck Brooks after all. I do not wish to underrate *To the Finland Station*. It would seem that Wilson had read Gabriel Monod's *Renan, Taine, Michelet*, though he does not say so; he has a sensible judgment of Taine, less good on Renan – I expect he found him too sceptical. He has too much respect for Marx – he was a Marxist at the time – anyone would think that Marx was the Law and the Prophets. The deification of Marx is one of the most curious phenomena of the twentieth century; John Stuart Mill would make a better mentor, with his emphasis on the freedom of the individual, with a reasoned sympathy for the working classes, co-operation and a democratic socialism.

At the end, Edmund Wilson was as disillusioned at the way his earlier hopes had been betrayed as the rest of us. It was found that for some years he had not kept up with his taxes; the total sum demanded came as a crushing blow. To help to raise some cash and recoup himself – American taxation is nothing like so confiscatory, so killing to all incentive, as in Britain – he wrote a little book describing his predicament. He also described himself as totally 'alienated' from a society which imposed such burdens.

Here I am wholly sympathetic with him. All his life he had had to work hard to earn a living; while in America, as now in Britain, there are many people who have lived into the second generation on social security and never done a day's work.

So much for his earlier democratic illusions; it seems that T. S. Eliot was right about such a society after all.

9

With Beaverbrook in Canada

Beaverbrook, I confess, I was originally prejudiced against. The matter needs no explaining. After all, I was a straight Labour Party man, loyal to Attlee, Bevin and Herbert Morrison. I was not one of the extreme Leftists patronized by Beaverbrook, supported by him or kept by his newspapers – Aneurin Bevan, Michael Foot, Tom Driberg, for whom I had no respect. When Germany was the overwhelming threat in Europe, to Britain as well as to others, I regarded his preaching of Isolationism as dangerous and ignorant.

It was impossible for Britain to isolate herself from what was happening across the Channel a score of miles away. Ostrich-like Isolation would mean that we should wake up and find the whole Continent under the heel of Hitler – as it very nearly was – and our turn would come next. The only security was in a Grand Alliance, the policy that had been the sheet-anchor of Britain's safety and success in the past three centuries. Beaverbrook was too ignorant of history to know that. In so far as millions read his newspapers they were misled – as he came out with his announcement at New year 1939: 'There will be no war this year.' Good for newspaper circulation, no doubt, but irresponsible.

On the other hand, a straight Labour man, I was strongly in favour of the British Empire; I was not an anti-Imperialist like those on the Left who ate out of Beaverbrook's hand. At All Souls I had been very close to the Empire group who believed in the trusteeship of native races, gradually leading them along the way to better things. A great colonial administrator like Lugard, whom I met there, set a model to be proud of over the vast area of Nigeria, where a man could walk in safety unarmed two or three hundred miles. Today, the blacks in Africa have massacred and murdered each other in hundreds of thousands.

The British Empire meant that under its sovereignty, justice for all and the well-being of its subjects were the prime considerations in governing them – not corruption from top to bottom, and barbarous military dictatorship as the prevailing blue-print of African government. The ideal was to lead these peoples gradually, educate them in government as in medicine, health and welfare services – the take-over would have taken decades and have been given a better chance to take root with more time and at a slower pace.

Not the least of the charges against the Germans for what they have been responsible for in the wreck of this century is that they speeded up the processes of history, advanced the date of a nuclear world, apart from everything else for which we have to thank them.

The British Empire has largely been brought to an end: has this been much benefit to the peoples concerned?

Thus, though I regarded Beaverbrook's campaign for Empire Free Trade as the nonsense it was, utterly out of the question of practical possibility, I was not averse to his Empire enthusiasm, as his Leftist employees were.

I could have been one of his employees myself. Towards the end of the war his right-hand man, George Malcolm Thomson, made me an offer to become a reviewer-in-chief – such as I suppose Arnold Bennett had been – with my reviews syndicated throughout the Beaverbrook Press. I never considered it for a moment – any more than my friend Douglas Jay did, when they made him an offer to write on economic affairs. We were not irresponsible Leftists: we had principles.

I was a supporter of Ernest Bevin, a truly great man, the dominant figure in the Labour Movement after the catastrophe of 1931. Bevin detested Beaverbrook, and regarded him with the greatest distrust. Everyone agrees that – whatever his good qualities, and he had some notable ones – he was a mischief-maker. He had an irresistible itch to throw a spanner in the works; he had charm, generosity, kindness (as well as the reverse), he was even courteous – but he was *méchant*, like a mischievous imp. (I saw this side of him on his native heath in New Brunswick.)

Bevin himself told me that, even in the grave crisis of 1940, Beaverbrook was continually trying to get him out of Churchill's government. At that moment of gravest danger to the nation – the sheer irresponsibility of it! That he was irresponsible is the worst thing I shall say against him. All the same, I regard irresponsibility as a bad mark against a man in politics, where the lives of people are in question (cf Aneurin Bevan's campaign for a Second Front long before it was possible, would have cost hundreds of thousands of lives, and might have lost us the war).

By the same token I detest irresponsibility in historians, for history is past politics, similar issues and persons come up for judgment. If one must have irresponsibility (there is a place for it) let it be on the stage, with dramatists and play-boys like Bernard Shaw and Oscar Wilde (both Irish, by the way).

Beaverbrook recruited to his service an historian in the shape of A. J. P. Taylor, whose book, *Origins of the Second World War*, put forward the striking thesis that Hitler was hardly more – or not much more – to blame for the war than we were. However, we may regard his biography of Beaverbrook as a fine effort; it provides a mass of information on which we may make up our minds. The book received scathing criticism from a fellow Leftist, Richard Crossman; I am more appreciative – Taylor tries to be objective, to point out occasionally where Beaverbrook was wrong or went wrong. The portrait that emerges is vivid and authentic, and one finishes with more liking for the man that one had expected.

It is a good fault in a biographer to err on the side of too much sympathy for his subject. Mr Taylor tells us that 'this old man was the dearest friend I ever had . . . The joys of his company are beyond description. [I shall try to describe them.] I loved Max Aitken Lord Beaverbrook when he was alive. Now that I have learnt to know him better from his records I love him even more.' Mr Taylor adds modestly that he did not suppose that he was important to Beaverbrook 'except perhaps by appreciating his historical works at their true worth.'

This touching friendship began with a rapturous review by Mr Taylor of one of these historical works, and since the great man 'trembled' for the reception of his writings by the public, he was correspondingly grateful. It led to great things.

However, the historian has to admit that, despite the 'true worth' of Beaverbrook's history, his claims are not always accurate. His record of events in the first German war, 1914–18, was presented to the public several times over as a diary written at the time: 'this Diary, in narrative form, was kept all through these dramatic days.' Mr Taylor has to tell us that actually the story of events was recorded subsequently in 1917: 'no diary has survived, and it is as certain as any negative can be that none every existed.' A candid omission.

With regard to a statement of Beaverbrook about George Barnes, the Labour member of Lloyd George's War Cabinet, Mr Taylor has to append a footnote: 'This is not correct.' We are told that 'later in life Beaverbrook claimed that he ran his newspapers for the sole purpose of promoting Empire Free Trade.' The historian has to add the gloss that 'in this publicity campaign of 1925–27 the cause of Empire Free Trade is not mentioned.' The biographer candidly admits that Beaverbrook attached much importance to the trick of 'balancing', in other words, inventing: 'At a late stage in the process of drafting and redrafting he livened up the narrative, whenever he felt that it was becoming pedestrian, with a vivid phrase or an anecdote, sometimes I fear invented for the purpose.' And Mr Taylor conscientiously provides examples.

The historian gives a more important example of the art of balancing – on a crucial subject, the introduction of the Convoy System, which saved Britain in the first German war. Beaverbrook described vividly how Lloyd George, 'the Prime Minister descended upon the Admiralty and seated himself in the First Lord's chair.' When Mr Taylor tackled his master on the subject, 'I got little satisfaction on my specific point. Beaverbrook, when pressed, said: "I'm sure it happened. I'll ask Churchill when I see him next." Of course he never did. And of course the incident never happened . . . It was another balancing act, inserted for vivid effect at the last moment.'

What then are we to think of the 'true worth' of Beaverbrook as an historian? What are we to think of Mr Taylor as a professional historian 'appreciating his historical works at their true worth'?

The worth of an historian's work must depend on (a) his responsibility of mind towards events and facts and (b) his absolute adherence to the truth about them. Otherwise, it is not reliable history, though it may be drama, or journalism.

I do not entirely dismiss Beaverbrook's work as an historian, but I have a more limited, and more wary appreciation of it. It is useful as material for the real historian, with a critical mind, to make use of. Beaverbrook was a sharp observer of men in politics, and his vignettes of them have their utility. Take his thumb-nail sketch of the enigmatic Milner, the power of whose personality and whose influence are difficult to understand. Beaverbrook gives us the key.

> He was born in Germany, and his father, although descended from an English family, was a German by nationality. Milner's claim to British nationality was derived from his grandfather, who settled in Germany in 1805. He was educated in Germany . . . He admired Bismarck's Zollverein . . . frowning on reductions of taxation, and favouring extensions of social welfare.

Also like Bismarck.

In fact Milner had a completely German mentality; an administrator of the highest order, imposing social welfare from above, an authoritarian, something of a state-socialist. He had no English sense of compromise whatever, and as High Commissioner in South Africa, determined on the elimination of the Boer Republics – he was a Bismarckian Imperialist – he was more responsible for the South African war than anyone else, more than the unyielding Kruger (after all it was his country), or even the disastrous Joe Chamberlain. The South African war was a great disaster for Britain, let alone South Africa.

The second German war naturally brought about a general party *rapprochement*, the danger to Britain was so immeasurable. And when the war was over the fact of living in a nuclear world transformed the human condition, may be said to have revolutionized history, changed the terms. Henceforth the human race would live contingently.

What was the point of party divisions under this universal cloud? In this perspective differences between Labour and Tory, Democrat and Republican, Britain and America, melted away: our affairs were reduced to a question of survival. In Churchill's government of 1940–5, which saved Britain, party differences hardly existed. Churchill became Prime Minister through the support of the Labour Party; the twin poles of that historic government were Churchill and Ernest Bevin. For the first time, after years of frustration, exasperation and growing anguish, I was politically content; I ceased to be a party man.

Friendships were made across party fences – I always had been friendly to anti-Chamberlain Tories, L. S. Amery, the Cecils, Eden, Macmillan: anything to get rid of that Old Man of the Sea. At Oxford I even made peace with 'the Prof', Lindemann, now Lord Cherwell (from the view from his rooms looking over Christ Church Meadows to the river), united in our admiration of Bevin.

It was my acquaintance with Churchill that brought me that of Beaverbrook. On 6 May 1958 he wrote to me: 'I have been reading your book *The Later Churchills*. It is a delightful narrative and, if I may say so, a magnificent work. Particularly, I enjoyed your material on Churchill, with which I so heartily agree. Will you let me know, please, when you publish?' He must have seen a proof-copy, or perhaps Winston lent him his.

He sent me a couple of invitations to dine or lunch with him in London, and eventually I lunched with him alone in his penthouse flat at the top of Arlington House. As I waited

for the great man I had time to reflect on the historic associations of that street, Arlington Street. Sir Robert Walpole
had lived there and, I think, Lord Salisbury when he was
Prime Minister. At any rate Beaverbrook was virtually a
nextdoor neighbour of the Cecils, while on the other side his
flat looked across St James's Park to Buckingham Palace.

He must have found the proximity provoking, for he carried on a feud with the Cecils, with whom I agreed over
Appeasement and was actually a 'friend of the family' (as
Bobbety Salisbury wrote to me in his last letter). So I did not
approve of Beaverbrook's sniping at the most distinguished
of our historic families, any more than at snide remarks about
the royal family, in particular the Princess Margaret at that
time. After all, they couldn't answer back. I reflected as I
waited that what provoked him was something that he
couldn't *buy*. He had bought a peerage, so to say; very well,
he should accept the conditions and abide by the rules of the
game. At any rate, he couldn't buy *me*; I was all prepared to
sup with him at the end of a very long spoon.

The moment he appeared the situation was transformed by
a comic episode. Ah! Rowse – Cornwall. 'But I own a place
in Cornwall.' I had never heard of it, never knew that he had
any association with Cornwall or had ever been there – and I
thought I knew everything about Cornwall. 'But I do own a
place in Cornwall. What is the name of it?' Of course I didn't
know, and he couldn't remember the name.

I was tickled by the situation – fancy being so rich as to
own a place you didn't know the name of. He rang for his
manservant. 'What is the name of that place down in Cornwall?' Apparently his daughter lived there during the war.
Happily the man knew: it was Treverbyn Vean; but I had
never heard of it, not the Treverbyn near St Austell which I
had known from childhood, but a large modern house standing out on its bluff in woodland, one sees it well from the
railway line approaching Liskeard.

The *contretemps* bridged the gap – anyway there were few
gaps in talk with Beaverbrook, and I at once felt amused and
at home with him. Two significant things I remember from
that talk. He told me that over India Churchill had at last

come round to Attlee's point of view, and accepted the take-over. Apparently Attlee had persuaded him – this wasn't known at the time, if it is since. One can understand Churchill's holding out to the last: he had always realized that India was the heart of the British Empire; if India went, the Empire went; and India opting out meant a strategic vacuum. (Did the Americans appreciate that when they were so anxious to see the British out of India – and the Russians in both Afghanistan and the Indian Ocean?)

Beaverbrook was appalled. Never in history, he said, had an empire come to an end so rapidly. That was something we agreed about, and in deploring its consequences. He went on to launch an attack on the Americans, which I did not hold with. I had always regarded the anti-Americanism of his papers as dangerous. I thought, mistakenly, that this was conceived for purposes of circulation, but found that it was genuine conviction – all the more deleterious. So I stood up to him and said, Look, with Russia and Eastern Europe all Communist, with Communist China a people of eight hundred million, the only hope for us is for the English-speaking peoples to pull together.

To my surprise he wouldn't accept the argument, which I considered unanswerable – as it is.

Angrily he burst out: '*Lousy* people – wanted to push us out of India', and so on; a flood of emotional invective. I wasn't going to give up, and tried another tack. I said, 'Well, by the end of the century, Canada will be a Great Power in her own right. She will be able to confront the United States on her own level, and perhaps mediate between us.' Whether this was right or not, he saw that I wasn't going to subscribe to his anti-Americanism, though I no more approved of the American attitude towards the British Empire than he did. It was not long after Suez, and the collapse of the British position in the Middle East – largely owing to Eisenhower and the appalling Dulles – with all the consequences for the United States that followed. I hope they appreciate them.

Sometime after this he invited me to come to Canada as his guest, stay with him at Fredericton, and give a few lectures at the university of New Brunswick, of which he was

Chancellor. I gladly accepted for the autumn of 1960, and had a fascinating time of it. Nancy Astor professed to be shocked: 'I am surprised you took anything from the person you did. In fact, it shocks me to the quick! However, I am glad you are having a good time. Let me know when you come back.' Little love was lost between those great newspaper owners; however, that didn't affect me. It was a duty for an historian to see something of Canada, especially under such an aegis, and to observe an historic figure on his native heath, see what he was really like at home. In the event, I saw him at his best.

So far I had had only a brief glimpse of Canada. One year on my way to the United States I decided to go via Canada, by the Canadian Pacific steamship *Britannic* – a beautiful white motor-vessel – which took one up the St Lawrence at the height of the autumn foliage, all aflame with scarlet, crimson, gold. The arrival in the pool opposite Quebec was spectacular, the sun a glowing red plate sinking into the river, the Heights of Abraham – and at that moment the bells began clanging for vespers as in a city in Old France. I felt much at home, and had the good luck that Vincent Massey, loyal Balliol man, was in residence at the Citadel, who showed me round it, historic relics of Wolfe and Montcalm and all.

Thence I paid a brief visit to Montreal, where later I was to give the Bailey Lectures at McGill (still unpublished, so remiss have I been!) On the way to New York that night I had a pleasant encounter with an historically-minded conductor on the train. Crossing the frontier, he inspected my passport; noticing my name, he said, 'Do you know we are just passing Rouse's Point?', apparently some strategic position along the route in the American War of Independence. Rouse had fought on the wrong side – I leave the reader to his own taste as to which that was.

I wished to see more of Canada (I still haven't seen much, neither Toronto nor Ottawa, nor even British Columbia, where part of my family lives). I am always keenest to see what is historic, and the Maritime Provinces were part of old Canada, of more interest to me than any amount of the Mid-West. My Journal brings me close to my experience of it, and of the dynamic figure to which it had given birth – now entered into its history in turn.

12 October 1960. 'A good flight in beautiful clear New England weather from New York to Boston; but the horrid accident last week just outside the Boston airport – near sixty lives lost on an Electra, the type I was in – made me apprehensive. The left swerve from the airport, which gave me a beautiful view of the land – lakes, woods, rivers, seashore, blue, dun, green, no sign of wreckage – at an angle of 33°, gave me no pleasure at all. At Boston I waited two hours, and came on in a Viscount to St John, flying across the Bay of Fundy at 15,000 ft., to Yarmouth in Nova Scotia for Customs, then across to St John.

'Here I was met by a nice Scot, Galloway, Professor of English Literature. We halted in the centre of St John to look at the American Loyalists' burying ground (people who didn't accept the Revolution and wouldn't live under the Stars and Stripes). I noted the names of someone designated an Esquire, from Staten Island in the United States, others from Philadelphia. Most names were of Scots, but one was from the West Country, a master-mariner from Bideford. It was a touching scene – these headstones in the clear sunlight and nippy autumn air of Canada. The atmosphere was Canadian: what makes the difference?

'Oct. 15. After half a week in which to observe, I am in a better position to say. For one thing everything happens later here: in US they get up and go to bed earlier. Then this part of Canada is old-fashioned, a quiet backwater: it is like stepping back, except for motor cars, into the world of before 1914. Fredericton is an agreeable place for a university town, a good deal of charm, trees everywhere, on the slope of the hill with this grand river and the two bridges laid out below. Everything is slower and quieter, people slower on the uptake, slower to move – waitresses in restaurants, boy-pages in hotels, ordinary people in the streets. It is nicer that way.

'I have run up against the old United Empire Loyalist sentiment against the United States. A Loyalist historian, Highlander MacNutt, is quite shocked by my pro-Americanism. Revealing of Beaverbrook: I perceive his roots, he is an unreconstructed United Empire Loyalist. I give MacNutt the reason I gave Beaverbrook why, in a nuclear world, with Russia and China massed under Communism, the English-speaking peoples *must* pull together. MacNutt was displeased by my saying in a lecture that the American Revolution was a very English phenomenon – the determination to have self-government when arrived at the maturity to take over. He said that this cut at the roots of Canada's nationhood, the foundation upon which Canada had been built. To which I replied that *both* the Republican Milton and the Royalist Clarendon were good Englishmen.

'The drive up along the St John River was very fine: clear, golden autumnal sun lighting up the colours of the woods, flaming maples and birches, dark greens of pines and conifers. At one point the river opened out splendidly to make Grand Bay – what a scene in sailing ship days, when the river was the main artery of communication: New Brunswick grew up along it.

'Galloway took me home to dine – an excellent meal, though I was so tired, I'd rather have gone to bed. The house a delightful one of about 1815, roomy, with a fine view of the lights of the town below. Already late, at 10 p.m. we went on to the President's party for new members of the faculty: another Scot, Colin Mackay, a lean greyhound of a young man, already greying, able, successful, overworking – hungry for what? Power, I think. I diagnose that he would make a good Prime Minister of Canada, another bachelor Scot, like Mackenzie King.

'At lunch in the Lord Beaverbrook hotel, I was recognized by two Rhodes Scholars, who took me for a drive further up the river. The scenery became more rugged and Scottish, colours all delicate golds and flushed scarlets, the great river placid, sweet and summery. A Fenimore Cooper world – I could imagine the Indians still in possession, their canoes darting down. What a vast dispossession of peoples North America has witnessed! They exist only in holes and corners of their own land, now static and mission children, living by potato picking. We passed a so-called "Reserve" – really only a dozen houses with a church by the roadside. How extraor-

dinary it would be to be able to look into *their* consciousness
of the great Dispossession!

'14 October: Dean Alfred Goldsworthy Bailey drove me
round the town, a rather prissy character of some distinction,
has written two volumes of verse, comes from Virginian and
New England stocks going back to the 1630s, with a 1780s
admixture of Cornish: from Richard Goldsworthy of
Redruth, builder and surveyor, master of the King's works at
Quebec, where his house still stands. Dean Bailey has several
volumes of this old Cornishman's books – tables of measure-
ments and accounting, with the usual theological junk.

'A master of local lore, Bailey took me to see the house
where Bliss Carman had lived, and Charles Roberts not far
away. Carman had lived many years *à trois* with a friend and
his wife – people said that he was the wife's lover. I suggested that it was all platonic, and Bliss not one for married
bliss. Bailey agreed. Carman had told Bailey's people that
he had been writing all his life and not made enough to buy
a ham sandwich from his poetry, warning young Alfred
against it.

'We went up to Forest Hill cemetery to pay our tribute to
him: a beautiful graveyard, trees in colour in full view of the
blue river, a scarlet maple planted beside the grave. I thought
of Q. (Quiller-Couch, who put a poem of Carman's into the
Oxford Book of English Verse) – they were contemporaries. Q.
born in 1864, the other in 1861. His was a tall granite tomb,
with an open book and all the Loyalists around him. Not far
away was his cousin Charles Roberts, also a poet, but whose
children's and animal stories were better.

'We crossed the bridge to the north side, flat water
meadows, more English except for the immense size of the
river. For the first time I saw a huge log-jam, men working
on the logs in the river, the trunks packed together like sardines silver in the sun. All the property of Mr Irving, Beaverbrook's millionaire buddy down at St John. (All to be
consumed, in faithless, ephemeral newsprint?)

'We went on to Majorville and the first settlers' church,
even before the Loyalists: a Congregational one, where President Mackay's ancestors are buried. So he's deeply rooted

here, going back to the very beginning. A nice young fellow on the road wanted a lift. But Dean Bailey never picks anyone up. Once, when motoring in Wisconsin he was just behind a judge, who had given someone a lift and been shot dead. Never give anyone a lift in the New World.

'That evening I had to make a speech at a dinner of historians, English Literature people, librarians, from New Brunswick, Mount Allison and Acadia Universities. Next morning a symposium at which information was exchanged as to the resources of the various libraries for scholarship. I did my best to make useful suggestions. In the evening, after the dinner Galloway had given, followed a party at which I talked to everybody, hearing about the young men's subjects, etc. while consoling myself on a sofa by holding the charming Galloway cat, Troilus (thinking sadly of Peter at home at Trenarren). Not getting to bed until 2 a.m., when I like to be in bed before 10 p.m., I was so tired that I spent the afternoon in bed.

'At 6.30 p.m. was called for by a nice Scot, offshoot of the Camerons, and taken home to dinner: a family affair with pretty, dark Scots lassie for wife, and two children aged two and one: I came through the ordeal, and so did they, rather better than expected. After dinner people came in, including a Scotch-Australian widow. Lots of laughing and chaffing, which I enjoyed – and on to the next party at the Baileys.

'A different atmosphere: this was upper-class, childless, select, elderly, tasteful. A handsome Jugo-Slav, who had had fearsome adventures in the war, was unfortunately fearful, as a newcomer, of monopolising my attention. I suffered horribly from the heat: *all* the heating on, plus a wood fire on the hearth. I skirted round the company, keeping as clear of the fire as I could. Talked to a middle-aged silvery head of a Woman's Hall, who adored the pure thin cold air of Canada in the snow in winter, came back from Switzerland longing for it, etc. etc.

'I moved on to agreeable banter and argument, chiefly politics, with the men. Toole, Vice-President, beautiful manners of an Irish gentleman, chemist, Catholic become rationalist, reads the *New Statesman*, but of a Left doctrinaire with some of the illusions. I talked too much, but felt that that was what I was there for. Came up against MacNutt's Loyalist anti-Americanism again; then hot coffee – at that hour and in that heat! – the wide eyes of the big Jugo-Slav constantly on me.'

In the intervals of all this I had been reading steadily and neither got in touch with nor been summoned by Beaver-brook. I rather enjoyed the Kafka *Castle*-like atmosphere. There we were both in the Lord Beaverbrook, somewhere on another floor this dynamo of energy, people coming and going: I wanted a day or two's intermission before catching up with him. And was rather surprised to find that I was given it, left to find my own feet. No summons. One sunny morning I saw the little black dynamo stepping out along the river bank with his grand-daughter. There were rumours that 'Lady Jean' was up here with him. Who was Lady Jean?

On the third day I went along to the Art Gallery, where he also has a flat, to announce my arrival. Like Winston, who must have had a strong influence on Beaverbrook's ways, particularly in collecting paintings and founding a gallery, he was in a whirl of energetic direction. People were coming and going carrying pictures for him to look at and away again; he was talking into a dictaphone and/or long-distance telephone, was dictating to a woman secretary, col-loguing with the velvet-coated Director of his Gallery, and yet was prepared to receive me in the midst of this whirl-pool.

'He really is a phenomenon – the speed of his mind, the quite abnormal memory, the pounce, and at eighty-two! Not a faculty is impaired: he is like a man of fifty-two or forty-two. At once he was *au fait* with my movements and, getting off the telephone and the dictation, cleared himself a space of fifteen minutes to take me into the vault and have the Hilliard miniature of Elizabeth I brought out for "the Doctor". I inspected it carefully: it looked to me like her in the later 1570s, rather young-looking. (She must have looked young until later middle age.)

'With all these acquisitions around him – some of the modern caricatures he had bought off his own bat I did not much relish – he said, provokingly: "I make my money in Britain, I spend it over here." But he had made a Canadian fortune – all by fixing and company mergers – before he came to Britain, where he made another.

'Walking out into the Gallery, I was no less impressed by his phenomenal memory for people: one young man among the visitors he addressed by name and knew all about him. This too was rather Churchillian, for I noticed the natural courtesy with which he greeted people going round; and then the magnetism of the man who had called it all into existence and made it live. Here he was – on his home-ground.

'Sunday, 16 October, I dined with him in the Gallery flat. Toole was there, and a New Brunswicker from the West who is a Senator; last came Lady Jean Campbell. "Guess who this is! Who is she?" He was as merry as a cricket. "She's my grand-da'ter. Isn't she exactly like me?" Actually a good-looking girl, black hair, grey-blue eyes, pretty figure all in black plus pearls.

'Beaverbrook was in the gayest mood. Stories flowed. Asquith had said: "Some men think while they talk (i.e. Lloyd George); some men think while they write (i.e. himself); some men think both while they talk and while they write, and they are the salt of the earth." We were to guess whom he meant by this, but were floored. I thought of Arthur Balfour; but I might have guessed, from Beaverbrook's own predilections, it would be Birkenhead.

'He thought Horatio Bottomley [popular orator, fraud and cheat] and Tim Healey [Irish Nationalist] the best wits he had known. Bottomley, M.P., protesting against a new kind of Parliamentary veto. "What is a veto? It is a new kind of vegetable." When aristocratic disapproval was expressed, of the way he exploited the credulity of the people – they wanted to be cheated by him – he threatened to follow the Cholmondeley example and call himself Bumley. Beaverbrook enjoyed having the rogue to dinner – much to Bonar Law's disapproval [incomprehensibly, Beaverbrook's hero – a dull man], who thought it disgraceful. Beaverbrook chuckled impishly at this: one saw the *gamin* coming out. One evening he had Beerbohm Tree to dinner, who monopolized the conversation and had no intention of letting Bottomley score. Tree got the conversation round to the most beautiful woman he had ever seen. It transpired that it was the actress, Lottie Collins. Nothing daunted, Bottomley jumped in with "My Aunt", and won.

'Next came the story of Bottomley in gaol: he was eventually run down by the Astors for cheating thousands of poor people of their savings. Visited by an acquaintance, Bottomley was engaged in sewing bags. "What are you doing – sewing?" "No, reaping," said the old renegade, who had mesmerized so many audiences with his "Prince of Peace" peroration. He would estimate what the audience was good for: if over £1000 they should have the "Prince of Peace"; if not, not.

'Then Healey. When Beaverbrook was Minister of Information in the first German war, he got into some serious Parliamentary trouble; Bonar Law wouldn't come to the rescue, and advised him to try Tim Healey. Beaverbrook got him on the phone; Healey said he would cross from Ireland by the Sunday boat after Mass. Beaverbrook hoped that Mass wouldn't last too long and would meet him for dinner. After dinner Tim was too tired to listen to Beaverbrook's case, or decide on any line of defence; next day at lunch he wouldn't think about it. When the debate came on that day in the House of Commons, Healey began: "This Minister of Information isn't so bad. The Minister before him was Carson" – and went over to the wrongs of Ireland. From that moment nothing more was heard of Beaverbrook in the debate. (I was not amused: I registered inwardly – what idiots.)

'So it went on, all popping like the champagne served. (Beaverbrook on his reviewer, Arnold Bennett: "How I loved Arnold, and how he loved my champagne." He would not be able to say that of this teetotaller. But the dinner was excellent, the fish brought up fresh from St Andrew's, artichokes in leaf (too much trouble), butter sauce, meringues, brandy.

'I was placed by the granddaughter, who politely professed

herself an admirer of my *Churchills*. Beaverbrook sang the praises of A. J. P. Taylor, whom I had known since he was an undergraduate. "Your favourite historian," I said as a challenge. At once: "No; you're my favourite historian. But I like Taylor. He's a brave man." I didn't comment on this, though much might be said of their "elective affinities", in Goethe's phrase.

'The young woman was very engaging, spontaneity and charm under the sophistication of the society she frequents. She adores New York, where she lives up on 94th Street among the Porto Ricans, has a job as *Daily Express* correspondent of the United Nations. Also adores Mr Khrushchev – he has such a funny face, is a first-class comic and makes such fun of the solemn Americans and *their* UN. I recognized the family anti–Americanism or, as she put it, a love-hate complex.

'How like her grandfather's impish irresponsibility! I had been in New York at the time of Khrushchev's visit to the UN Assembly, specifically for the purpose of bringing it into derision, taking off his shoe to beat on his desk with it, uncouth brute. Beaverbrook longed to bring him up to Fredericton to shock Canada. "O that 'twere possible": the idea vastly tickled him; he and his granddaughter chuckled at the jolt it would give to Fredericton's old-fashioned respectability.

'We had a subject in common to mull over – a mutual lawyer acquaintance who had been consulted over the Argyll case – "my family has been much before the courts lately." She was wearing a prehistoric gold bangle, treasure-trove from Inverary, I supposed. [All the talk we had about our well-known lawyer friend can wait till we're all dead . . .] So too with her information about the able, attractive President, whom she had been "studying for years". I was naturally much interested. Apparently he was her grandfather's choice, who knew he was the right man, not the Faculty's; though all agreed now how successful he was, all his celibate energy devoted to building up the university.

'Once or twice I noticed her smiling at my shyness or slowness, or just my old-fashioned manner (a teetotaller, I don't think she observed my observing). Unasked, she gave me her address and telephone in New York, swore me to get in touch, and kindly promised to show me the UN Building, about which she was quite lyrical. [I never did; I had no interest in the UN Building.] Beaverbrook is obviously fond of the girl: "Doesn't she know that she's my favourite gran'child!" etc.

'The brandy circulated. She had two goes, and wanted a third. Grandfather refused. "But who taught me to drink, grandpa?"

'Talk circulated about newspapers and their proprietors. Beaverbrook claimed proudly that only three newspaper groups had been *created* in the last thirty years, all by sons of the Presbyterian manse: the *Express* group, the Henry Luce group, and the Readers' Digest group created by Wallace. On religions, Beaverbrook described himself as a Presbyterian Pagan, Toole said that he was a Catholic Pagan; I refrained from saying that I was an Anglican Pagan.

'At 10.30 we broke up. No more late night sessions as with Winston in old days. The President says that the old man "watches himself like a ha'k." Beaverbrook told me that Birkenhead, dying at sixty-two, had expected to live another twenty years. (The fool, brilliantly gifted as he was, killed himself with drink.)

'17 October: I had my heaviest chore, addressing the student body in a large ecclesiastical-looking hall with a gallery and difficult acoustics. My theme was "The Use of History in Modern Society" (John Wesley recorded his sermon texts: why shouldn't I?).

'The President took me to lunch, and then I got *his* perspective on grandfather and granddaughter. [That also can wait . . .] Rather comically he told me his own experience with the Beaver, whose house looking on to the river he had donated for the use of the President of the University. First year the Beaver had spent two weeks in it; the second, two months; the third threatened to be more than the President could stand, it added two or three hours to his work a day. So, during the seven weeks of vacation he had himself run up the odd little bungalow he occupies on the campus. The Beaver had lost his caretaker, and took to staying in the Lord Beaverbrook hotel, with a flat in the Gallery as a hide-out. The President thought of himself as a sort of Catherine Parr to Henry VIII and sometimes wondered whether he would survive him . . .

'He had the Beaver well weighed up, good qualities as well as intolerable ones. There had been several changes of President; at one time when there was none Beaverbrook stepped in and practically ran the place, keeping some continuity in the administration. At another time *he* had resigned as Chancellor, to be persuaded back as Honorary Chancellor next year. There was his ceaseless interest on their behalf, in addition to all his benefactions – Library, Art Gallery, a vast Skating Rink for the town – and his interferences. Above all was his loneliness: Mackay would get a telephone call from him any time to come down to New York to talk business. It was just that he wanted company.

'19 October. Beautiful day, took an early class for Galloway up the hill. After early lunch togged myself up for Convocation, and up to the familiar gathering, quite impressive. In the robing room – beautiful Mrs Ross, wife of the Lieutenant-Governor of British Columbia, a powerful economic administrator; Monsignor Lussier, fine figure of a man, Rector of the big University of Montreal. Then the vigorous young Premier of New Brunswick, the first Frenchman to be so. We were the four to receive honorary degrees – the others Doctors of Laws, I a DCL.

'The local grandees assembled: the Lieutenant-Governor O'Brien; the Commander in military red, members of the Senate, the Roman Catholic Bishop of Bathurst in purple, skull cap, silk cloak, ribbons and all. Monsignor Lussier swiftly, proficiently kissed his ring; I complimented him, and said how nice it was to see the purple. "It is my uniform," he said and pointed out the Anglican Bishop of Fredericton also in purple and scarlet.

'The long procession gathered and crocodiled brilliantly downhill in the afternoon sun. As we entered the immense Lady Beaverbrook Skating Rink the audience rose, the band played – and I realized that I had just picked up a pebble in my shoe. We mounted the platform, I in a strategic position on the extreme left. For a moment I was touched thinking of the long way I had come from my Cornish village to this, and then laughed to myself at the thought of Hardy's worst line.

Where are we? and why are we where we are?

'The so familiar academic ceremony unrolled itself, the graduates coming up to be capped by the Chancellor – one saw him in a new rôle, *en grand seigneur*. The Public Orator, with his Welsh background, was so eloquent in presenting Mrs Ross, an improbably elegant dictator of fats and oils during the war, that I was quite carried away and forgot my turn. Monsignor Lussier signalled me up, to stand there and receive some flowery compliments on my work – with which I fear the Public Orator was not at all acquainted (he is a devotee of Howard Spring). Capped by his lordship, I received a friendly grin and grasp of the hand, with a large vellum roll to carry about. The Chancellor seemed to enjoy it, a wide boyish grin on his frog-face.

'Out in a huddle into the cold sun, I having a chat in French with the Roman bishop, who turned out to be of Breton stock. Then uphill to the opening of Thomas Carleton Hall, after the early Governor who had set aside an endowment of 6000 acres for the College. "We now have 3000," said the Chancellor; "I recommend the University to ask the government what has become of the other 3000." This for the benefit of the new Premier, who had urged more money for education, etc. Shrewd old Beaver, never missing a point!

'We went in to tea, where a geologist told me that Bathurst had had a colony of Cornish miners, who had now gone over to farming. [Why doesn't someone follow up my book, *The Cornish in America*, with one on the Cornish in Canada?]

'The Chancellor gave a large dinner-party for us all that evening. Before it I had some cosy chat with Lady Dunn, the widow of Beaverbrook's multi-millionaire friend, Sir James Dunn. When he died, she shut herself up and retired from the world; Beaverbrook has now brought her out into the world, got her interested in things again, to give money and pictures to the Art Gallery, scholarships to the University. I was not allowed to get off with her: I was placed as far away as possible, between two boring men, the Lieutenant-Governor and another. Beaverbrook put her carefully between himself and the Bishop. I did not have a chance of speaking to her again. [Later, Beaverbrook married her: a proper cure for his obsessive loneliness.]

'Next morning, before leaving, I had a consoling visit from a young Cornishman, whose family, a familiar name to me, had lived at Killiganoon, near Truro. Good-looking and *simpatico*, he told me his and his family story: *nihil Cornubiense alienum a me puto*. Over here studying forestry, but with a turn and the looks for acting: a Hollywood actor is taken with his talent and is coaching him in a university production. Left Charterhouse at sixteen to go to Dartmouth, where the Navy was cutting down and offered no prospects, he decided on forestry for an outdoor life and worked his passage over to New Brunswick – worked as a waiter in vacation to pay his way.

'Here was the enterprise of a younger generation, but I wonder what will happen to him? How the Cornish do get about the world!

'Next day kind David Galloway drove me to the airport, after my strenuous visit and varied entertainment. The golden autumn over, there was an inch deep of rain on the cement at the airport, and the same at St John. However, I arrived in Boston without disturbance, had my dinner on board, and even enjoyed the spectacle of the lights of the city spread out below, outlining the bay, the harbour front, quays running out into the water where the ghastly disaster to the plane had occurred ten days before.'

I trace only one more slight contact with Beaverbrook, and since it shows him wise, considerate and courteous, I give it – all the more remarkable in the last months of his life.

As I have said, I think that my brief acquaintance with him sprang out of my interest in Churchill and my two books about the family, particularly *The Later Churchills*. When my *William Shakespeare: A Biography* came out in 1963, it was treated to a disgraceful attack by that exemplar of Christian charity, Malcolm Muggeridge. I know quite well that one is not supposed to take any notice of reviews by people who do not qualify to hold a serious opinion on the subject. Very few people do qualify to hold an opinion on Elizabethan subjects, certainly not glib, superficial journalists.

But if people make trouble for a Celt, a Celt is apt to make trouble for them; and I wrote privately to Beaverbrook to protest. He had read the snide review, and consoled me by saying that

> just about the same time I read an attack on myself by the same author, published in a Canadian magazine. On the whole, I have more right to complain than you . . . I was not warned of the Muggeridge review, but I certainly would be warned of a review of any book on Churchill. Now if you decide to instruct Macmillans not to send any of your books for review by the *Standard*, I will make no complaint. But that sort of situation never works out. It is never any good for the author and it does the *Standard* no harm. But it will not be regarded by me as an unfriendly action on your part. I saw the editor of the *Evening Standard* last evening and told him not to submit any of your books to Muggeridge for review. If any of your work comes to the *Standard* in future, Muggeridge will certainly not be the reviewer. It is a great disappointment to me to have to write this letter. I would much rather have read a joyous and happy review of which you would have no reason to complain.

I call that extraordinarily good and generous of him; it shows him in a most favourable light, and yet true to him. As we know, he was exceptionally sensitive about the reception of his own work and deeply appreciative of understanding. I too was sad that my happy acquaintance with him should end on this note – it shows the damage that inferior people, with little sense of responsibility, can do.

However, I hope that, though for many years on the opposite side of the fence, indeed a strong supporter of Ernest Bevin, inveterately hostile to Beaverbrook, I have not given an unjust depiction of this very remarkable, if controversial, figure who made such a mark in our time.

10

The Poet Auden

My relationship with W. H. Auden was a curious one, but not without some significance. It began promisingly, and then was bitten off by a characteristic (in retrospect, comic) *contretemps*. After that, our relations were for a long time rather cool, somewhat sketchy, though we never completely lost touch. When he came over to Oxford after the war I used to see him at All Souls, and we used to meet when I was in New York. When he came back finally to Oxford he spent his first month in All Souls, until our old college, Christ Church, got his cottage ready for him there. I determined to make it up to him for my earlier gaffe and took him under my wing again, as more than forty years before. For, after all, I was his Oxford senior: he was a whole undergraduate generation – three years – my junior, and when we were young that had made all the difference.

I can hardly claim that he was my *protégé* – as he was Nevill Coghill's, who was his sympathetic and very understanding tutor. But the young Wystan used to come round to All Souls and read me his poems: from the very first I had no doubt of his genius, his astonishing originality in one so young, his challenging verbal sophistication.

It is a good thing that I have kept diaries and retained calendars all my life – very properly for a historian – or I might get my facts wrong: mere memory is a shaping instrument. (So much for the third-rate reviewer in the *London Magazine*, who couldn't imagine that there might well be a

Rowse industry *à la* Boswell in the next century from the
mass of papers the historian has accumulated.)

Wystan and I, as House-men, had friends in common at
Christ Church; but, without my calendar, I should not have
known that it was my junior who invited me to lunch with
him there in October 1926, or again in October 1927, for I
have no memory of these occasions. I well remember his
rooms in Peck – Peckwater Quad – and my calendar gives me
the number, Staircase V, number 5 (for the benefit of those
who wish to venerate). Next term, in February 1928 I had
him to lunch with me to meet my friends, the historian K.
B. McFarlane and Richard Best, whose father was Lord
Chancellor of Northern Ireland.

Apparently Wystan refused John Betjeman's invitations to
meet obvious grandees, peers and such; mine were not social,
but by way of being propaganda for Wystan's poetry. In July,
after his Schools, he came to Sunday dinner at All Souls; in
spite of his usually appalling clothes, he must have donned a
dinner-jacket for the occasion – in those days we were rather
particular about that. Next day he came again to tea.

Perhaps he thought terms were getting warmer, for that
week occurred the absurd *contretemps* which Charles Osborne
partially relates in his truthful biography. After reading his
poems to me in the hot July quad, Auden suggested that we
adjourn to his rooms. When we got there I was a little surprised at his 'sporting the oak' (i.e. locking the outer door),
pulling down the blinds and shutting the shutters. I didn't
know about his odd line against sunlight.

Turning on his ugly green-shaded lamp – I can see it now
– instead of reading more poems he proceeded to read me
long extracts from a friend of his in Mexico, with the Mexican Eagle Oil Company, all about his goings-on with the
boys. I sank further and further back into my armchair, wondering what next. I remember registering to myself (God
help me), 'Fellows of All Souls don't do that sort of thing.'
(Little did I know.) Fortunately, at that moment I heard the
bell of Great Tom booming through the quad and, with
'That's four o'clock! I am always in the Common Room at

All Souls for tea at 4 o'clock,' I managed my escape from the awkward situation.

How inept I was! The fact was that I was rather a prig, but, even more, I had none of the sophistication of these Public School boys, years ahead of me in knowledge of the facts of life. What would have happened if I had had their training and Wystan been a handsome young Adonis I tremble to think . . . But he was singularly unappetizing with his nicotined, nail-bitten fingers, his chain-smoking or pipe-sucking, unwashed, his uncombed tow-hair, dirty collars, etc. I was something of a political fanatic in those days, preserving myself for great endeavours and expectations; I was also a good deal of an aesthete, which Wystan never was. In fact he was neither; at this time he had not opened a newspaper. Our sole bond was poetry.

Though three years his senior, I was years behind in *savoir-faire*. I suppose I was precocious intellectually, and hardworking, and winning a prize Fellowship at All Souls in those days, when it was the blue-ribbon of an Oxford career, had given me an elevated idea of my station, certainly of its responsibilities. No doubt my attitude was a bit patronizing; for that I must be forgiven, for I was his senior and a don, and also I was out to do my best for him.

When Stephen Spender printed a small number of Wystan's first little book of *Poems*, in its orange wrappers, I subscribed for a copy and got E. F. Jacob to subscribe too. (It cannot be that all copies were given away, as Osborne says.) Now an item of the utmost rarity – a copy fetched £1750 after Wystan's death – like a fool, I lent mine to an unappreciative young friend who disappeared in the limbo of the war and never saw it again.

Wystan was always a bit careful and cagey with me after that episode; anyway in 1928 he went down and was away from the Oxford scene for years, while I plodded on as a part-time teaching don, part-time researcher, more and more caught up in the anxieties of politics in the thirties – but practically, as a Labour candidate during those despairing years, and getting more and more ill.

Anyway Wystan had got a bad Third in his Schools. I

could not be expected, as a don, to approve of that, and it did make me discount him intellectually. This was not donnish snobbery on my part, though, after a frightful struggle I had had in getting to Oxford, as a working-class man I did disapprove of these bourgeois young men, who had had all the chances, wasting their precious time at Oxford. There they were, having had their wonderful time, going down like ninepins: my exact contemporaries, the most heralded and brilliant of them all, Cyril Connolly with his Third, Peter Quennell sent down, Graham Greene and Evelyn Waugh with their Thirds (Evelyn admitted that his tutor (my friend Cruttwell) scored with 'It is a mistake to go through life with an inappropriate label'); John Betjeman sent down; I don't know what happened to Harold Acton and Stephen Spender – Fourths, I expect.

For all the dismissive face he put upon it, Wystan knew that he had been wrong. 'Beneath the fun I was always conscious of a dull, persistent, gnawing anxiety. To begin with, I felt guilty at being so idle. I knew very well what sort of degree I was going to get and what a bitter disappointment this was going to be to my parents.' I also knew what sort of prospect there would have been for me if I hadn't worked hard to get one of the best Firsts of my year and then a prize Fellowship at All Souls. No such cushy job on the *Architectural Review* such as Maurice Bowra landed for Betjeman; Connolly got the job of companion to old Logan Pearsall Smith, while Desmond MacCarthy took him under his wing on *The New Statesman*. And so on.

But there is a far deeper reason for my disapproval (Connolly regarded me as 'censorious'). It is this: those decisive undergraduate years afforded a precious time, such as would never recur, for one's intellectual development, and one's training – above all, to think. One way and another, what I have noticed about these contemporaries is that, gifted as they were, and they mostly fulfilled their gifts, they were not *trained thinkers*: they were not intellectually disciplined (as Eliot certainly was). Cyril Connolly, for example, had been a History Scholar at Balliol; but when he wrote about history subsequently, it was always uncertain and wobbling.

Similarly with Wystan's criticism and thinking: full of good insights (like Connolly's), but untrained and undisciplined, marred by unreasoned prejudices and flaws. It would have done him good to have worked seriously during those three years at Oxford and emerged with a trained intellectual outfit.

However, his poetry was the thing to him. I continued faithfully to support it, not only buying each volume as it came out (he was always prolific), but putting it across others – my historian friends, for example: Richard Pares, Bruce McFarlane, Charles Henderson, and my German friend, Adam von Trott. Maurice Bowra was inconvertible: he used for years to call Wystan the Martin Tupper of the age – and that put his followers off, like John Sparrow, who wrote a very unsympathetic little book about these contemporary poets. That would have no influence with me. I find from my calendar, what I had forgotten, that in February 1936 I was lending Veronica Wedgwood *The Dog beneath the Skin*, and that that month I saw it in London. I also faithfully went to see *The Ascent of F6*, I forget where.

Even as an undergraduate Wystan was extraordinarily self-confident, would regularly lay down the law like a *Partei-Führer* to his followers. He would then reverse himself, and say to Stephen Spender who took everything solemnly, 'Why do you take everything I say so seriously?' Wystan said a lot of things simply *pour faire effet*. He never did that with me, for he knew it wouldn't be any good. An historian – and Wystan hadn't much historical sense – is interested only in the truth.

His exchange with Eliot about Tennyson, for example, is held up for admiration. Wystan said – and not once only, but wrote it in a Preface – that Tennyson was the stupidest of our poets. Eliot scored by saying that that showed Wystan was no scholar, or he would have been able to think of still stupider poets. I don't think much of their joke, if it was one. Anyone who really knows what Tennyson was like – as revealed by Sir Charles Tennyson, from out under the whited sepulchre of the son's official biography – will know that Tennyson was an utterly independent and original thinker for himself, with an extraordinary range of unexpected and curious reading.

Though continuing to be interested in and to support the work of my immediate juniors, I did not share their German *schwärmerei*. I had had my German phase before them and continued to have my own private line through Adam von Trott. I thought that all that German *Expressionismus* was bad for them, and that it would have been better for them if they had gone to Paris instead of ugly Berlin, or Rügen Island and all that – undergone the influence of French civilization and literature, always good for uncultivated, undisciplined Teutons and Anglo-Americans.

There again I was with Eliot, not with them (and, though Eliot published them and always recognized Wystan's genius, he did not really like their poetry. He once allowed that mine was closer to his – as it was, in its defeatism and despair. He got out of that eventually through religion; I never did: I had no inner beliefs or hopes, and the world grew worse.) Wystan's attitude to everything French was simply childish: 'Italian and English are the language of Heaven. "Frog" is the language of Hell.' How silly, how uncouth! When French is the best-bred of all European languages – the language of Rimbaud and Verlaine, and in Wystan's time of Valéry and Gide, Cocteau and Montherlant, or of a kindred spirit like Radiguet, if they had heard of him: their exact contemporary, and a perfect artist, where they were so flawed and imperfect.

That was just like Wystan: to take up a terrific pose and then with sublime insensibility to adhere to it (he was not the most sensitive of men, unlike Eliot). I never cared for his oracular statements laid down in verse, the rhetoric that made him popular in the thirties. Real poetry is a more subtle and secret affair; I am sure it does damage to a poet's inspiration to create a persona for himself, and then act up to it. This can be proved, or at any rate shown: Wystan's best poetry was written when he was being direct and simple, not fabricating it out of his clever brain with all his verbal and metrical virtuosity (verbosity, too), but writing autobiographically:

Fish in the unruffled lakes
The swarming colours wear,
Swans in the winter air
A white perfection have . . .

Sighs for folly said and done
Twist our narrow days;
But I must bless, I must praise
That you, my swan, who have
All gifts that to the swan
Impulsive Nature gave,
The majesty and pride,
Last night should add
Your voluntary love.

That volume, *Look, Stranger!* of 1936, contains some of his
finest poems, precisely *because* – contrary to his perverse
theory – they are direct and autobiographical.

My purpose is not literary criticism, but notes written at
the end of that volume show just what one was thinking *at
the time*, which is relevant.

Isherwood has told us of the influences entering into the
making of Auden's poetry – the unfashionable admiration for Bridges and Housman: he shares ships with the
former and soldiers with the latter. Note the impression
the depressed areas, the Northern industrial districts
have made; in the Malvern Hills he thinks of the chimneys of Lancashire. The theme of rebuilding has brought
them [his group] into definite political associations:
comradeship and sympathy with the working classes follow from this attitude, consistent and natural, though
slightly forced in expression. He has the makings of a
great patriotic poet in time – in the Shakepearean tradition, not Roy Campbell. [Whom I had fed on as a poet
to Eliot, who thereupon published *Adamastor*. Campbell
became a Fascist, though I continued to admire his
poetry.] An extraordinary eye for English countryside,

particularly the North – fells, mountains, dales – which I as a Westerner, an extreme Westerner, don't know. It makes me jealous for the West – I wish we had some share in his affections. But he has recently described Dover, nobody better, and 'the wide and feminine valleys of the South'. [I always used to think of this line when passing through Winchester in the train.] Wystan a rhetorical poet, not afraid of rhetoric – appropriate vehicle for expression of feelings about 'this island'.

Came the Spanish Civil War, which was rather particularly their war – the war of the Left intellectuals – and they all went off to serve the Republican cause in various capacities. It didn't make much difference to the result: the Spanish Republic was ruined by its own incompetence, the idiot people riven from top to bottom by their own factions. Such people deserved to lose out. I was already thoroughly disillusioned, eating my heart out with 'the sickness of hope deferred'. Wystan wrote some propagandist verses about Spain – which they all did – and which I did not bother to keep.

And Wystan was shortly as disillusioned with it all as I was – but very fly in keeping it quiet. This leads me to a significant point about him: for all the originality of his stance, his independence of mind, the courage of his convictions, he was in a curious way rather prudent and tactful. He never entered into controversy with people: he let them go their own way, as he went his. This was rather clever of him from a literary point of view: he did not get into trouble; he had enemies, but he did not *make* them. Also he was a gentleman (Eliot a great gentleman, almost a saint); Wystan was a good man, with high standards, in spite of external appearances.

It really was astonishingly courageous of him, independent as well as sophisticated, to come to terms with his own nature as a boy of sixteen at school, accept it and go forward on that basis. He simply saw no reason for not accepting the facts of life as they were. (I was in continual revolt, and on every front, private as well as public – not good for duodenal ulcer, exacerbated it until it nearly killed me.) Wystan was rational about all this; I remember how impressed I was when David

Cecil told me that Wystan could always make a pick-up on the train from Oxford before it reached Paddington. And – a tribute of another kind to Wystan's early *réclame* – when a culture-vulture of a lady found that David's sister, the Duchess of Devonshire, had not read Auden, she pushed the point home with 'I suppose you have never read *Alice in Wonderland*!'

The second German war, to which everything in the thirties had been leading, proved the great divide. Wystan was already in the United States when it started, and he stayed there. An appalling attack on him was unleashed by a good many people, some of them former friends; this must have wounded him, though he maintained an extraordinary self-control, never replied, and just went forward on his own way, as he always did.

I never dared to raise the subject with him; and naturally I never joined in the attack – I thought it beneath me. Privately, I realized the situation: Wystan was so physically unattractive that when, at last, he found someone to love him, that was it.

> Lay your sleeping head, my love,
> Human on my faithless arm;
> Time and fevers burn away
> Individual beauty from
> Thoughtful children, and the grave
> Proves the child ephemeral:
> But in my arms till break of day
> Let the living creature lie,
> Mortal, guilty, but to me
> The entirely beautiful.

This is poetry, not rhetoric.

On the public side, Wystan had arrived at the same degree of disillusionment with men and their affairs as I had myself. He wrote: 'To be forced to be political is to be forced to lead a dual life.' This was what had almost done me in: incessant illness, operations, it took me years to recover. To have survived at all was my only triumph. He went on, wisely – and it spoke for me: 'Perhaps this would not matter if one could consciously keep them apart and know which was the real one. But to succeed at anything, one must believe in it, and only too often the false public life absorbs and destroys the genuine private life.' It had nearly killed me; how wise of Wystan it was to diagnose it and eschew it. Resignedly he wrote, 'Artists and politicians would get along better in a time of crisis like the present, if the latter would only realize that the political history of the world would have been the same if not a poem had been written, not a picture painted, nor a bar of music composed.'

So much for all the political writing of the thirties, his own included. Mine too – I have never allowed mine, e.g. *Politics and the Younger Generation* (which Eliot so carefully wet-nursed through the press for me) to be republished; only the essays in *The End of an Epoch*, for the historical record.

So Wystan settled for America.

My attitude to the great divide in his life was entirely different: I have always believed that his own poetry, and our literature in consequence, were the losers by his not being in the country to share the endurance, and the inspiration, of the last heroic period in our history, those wonderful years 1940–5, when the country's exceptional and happy insular history came to an end fighting the battle for civilization.

It will have been seen that I had already perceived that Auden had the makings of a fine patriotic poet in him. He had already derived such inspiration from the landscapes of England:

O love, the interest itself in thoughtless Heaven,
Make simpler daily the beating of man's heart; within
There in the ring where name and image meet,

Inspire them with such a longing as will make his
    thought
Alive like patterns a murmuration of starlings,
Rising in joy over wolds unwittingly weave;

Here too on our little reef display your power,

This fortress perched on the edge of the Atlantic scarp,
The mole between all Europe and the exile-crowded sea;

And make us as Newton was, who in his garden
    watching
The apple falling towards England, became aware
Between himself and her of an eternal tie . . .

In spite of the uncertainty of the syntax, it is a splendid poem;
and there are several fine poems which show his love for
England and its landscapes. It is indeed a dangerous thing for
a poet to break that eternal tie, to sever oneself from the roots
that nourish the imagination. Robert Lowell once said to me
in New York that, in some way, the atmosphere of the
United States (perhaps the prosiness of so much American
life), was not propitious to English poets. And I believe this
to be true: very few English poets have been able to write
poetry in America. Wystan was prodigiously successful in
America, but it was not good for his poetry – at any rate, he
missed the undying inspiration of the war years here, and it
was bad for him in other ways.

Wystan had the warmest of welcomes over there; he made
friends everywhere – he was naturally gregarious, he chain-
smoked and drank, far too much. He took jobs in universities; he gave poetry readings all over the country, for large
fees; he made money – and, though he was generous, he was
prudent about money. And America made him internation-
ally famous – if that was good for him.

I refuse to go into the literary malice that accompanied his
return to Europe with the end of the war, unabashed, an
American citizen in uniform, or the mischievous reporting of
it by such as Edmund Wilson. When he occasionally turned
up at All Souls, he was a bit wary of me – understandably, in
spite of my baiting him with a camp-joke about 'spectacled
sailors' (American of course).

When I was in New York we would meet. He would come
up for a drink (always a Bloody Mary) to my modest hotel,
the Wellington, which was Edmund Wilson's usual refuge,
always hard-up. I wasn't hard-up, by then, but of course we

had no dollars. Our talk was usually about old Oxford days and our friends at the House. He put my name into one of his ephemeral poems, because he wanted a rhyme for our old College; and, always a gentleman, asked my permission when he needn't have done. But I noticed that he never asked me back to his flat down in Greenwich Village – still on the defensive with me. I wouldn't have fitted in, though I knew rather more of the goings-on there than perhaps he suspected. Once the young men of *Time* magazine gave me lunch; they very much wanted to do a profile of Wystan – until they found that the domestic life down at Cornela would hardly be suitable for the great heart of the public. How Wystan got away with it all is really surprising – generally respected and, in some quarters, rather revered.

I remember unwontedly attending a literary party given by my kind, discerning agent down in the Village, when Wystan, recognizing my 'limey accent', came across the room to talk to me. By this time he had adopted his American accent – all part of the pose, I suppose – though the short a's were the same as in the North Country, or, for that matter, my original West Country.

Wystan made up to me – rather condescendingly, I thought, he was now so famous (*Ich nicht!*) – with talk about Cornwall, Cornish mining, the old beam-engines and installations – very much his thing, he said. I didn't need to be told about all that. I responded by asking him about the Pennines and Sedbergh. At that, something of the pathos of his situation came through: 'I could never go back,' he said; 'that was Paradise.' Here was the home-sickness that lies behind one of the better poems written in America, 'In Praise of Limestone':

> If it form the one landscape that we the inconstant ones
>   Are consistently homesick for, this is chiefly
> Because it dissolves in water. Mark these rounded slopes
>   With their surface fragrance of thyme and beneath
> A secret system of caves and conduits; hear these
>   springs
>   That spurt out everywhere with a chuckle

Each filling a private pool for its fish and carving
  Its own little ravine whose cliffs entertain
The butterfly and the lizard . . .

Then the poem goes off into Auden caricaturing himself (as Eliot was apt to do) with talk about 'Mother', and 'the nude young male against a rock displaying his dildo'. However, the poem recovers itself and ends,

      but, when I try to imagine a faultless love
Or the life to come, what I hear is the murmur
Of underground streams, what I see is a limestone
  landscape.

On one of these talks in New York Wystan suddenly interjected, 'Of course, I've always been an Anglican.' What was the purpose of his telling me that, I wondered, slightly put off, when I knew perfectly well what the situation was, and he must have known that I knew. I don't think religion meant very much to him – as it deeply did to Eliot, and even affected me more than it did Wystan. He may have been coming back to Mother, but all the same it had its utility; he knew very well which side his bread was buttered, and this helped him to work his passage back and rendered him respectable. Fancy preaching in St Giles's Cathedral, Edinburgh, of all places! – breaking his false teeth on the Sunday, and having to have them cobbled up, after a fashion, just in time. (He was never very audible, and read his poems badly – again, unlike Eliot, who was a perfectionist.) Preaching later in Westminster Abbey tickled Wystan, for in that he had 'beaten Eliot'. (It was like Edith Sitwell, who became a Roman Catholic to beat Eliot, who was only an Anglo-Catholic. All rather childish.)

What rehabilitated Wystan in England was his election as Professor of Poetry at Oxford; I faithfully supported him – Maurice Bowra not – but was not in on it, for by this time I was a great deal away in America myself, only in Oxford for the summer. So I saw little of Wystan in those years; he was immensely famous (like Eliot) and, sensitive as ever, I did not wish to intrude. I think I a little resented it, having no *réclame* myself, for all my life of achieved hard work, partly I suppose from my secretive way of life. Though Eliot was encouraging and published my poetry, it had little recognition: I was categorized as a historian – and one could not be a historian *and* a poet. Eliot and Betjeman thought well of my poetry but, cagey as ever, I never mentioned the subject to Wystan. They were full-time professional poets.

In my view professional poets are apt to write too much – look at Bridges or Browning; Byron or Shelley or Wordsworth; even Tennyson. And certainly Wystan wrote far too much. A great deal of his later poetry is really prose cut up into metrical form.

In this period fell Shakespeare's Quatercentenary year, 1964, for which I wrote my standard biography, which solved the problems of the Sonnets, though it was some years before I discovered the identity of the Dark Lady. There was nothing surprising about the leading authority on the Elizabethan Age proceeding to write the biography of its leading writer, but it was much resented by the Shakespeare industry. The BBC typically called on Wystan to pontificate on the subject, not me who had written the biography.

The don was immediately shocked by a crass howler Wystan made – worthy of a Third in the Schools – in referring to the young man of the Sonnets' 'exclusive interest in women'. The exact opposite is the case: the whole point of the earlier Sonnets was to try to persuade the young man to take an interest in women. Everybody knows that the young man was ambivalent and as yet unresponsive to women. Shakespeare himself tells us so:

> A woman's face, with Nature's own hand painted,
> Hast thou . . .
> And for a woman wert thou first created;
> Till Nature, as she wrought thee, fell a-doting . . .
> By adding one thing to my purpose nothing.

That is, Nature added a prick, which defeated Shakespeare, who was very heterosexual. The situation is perfectly clear, fundamental to understanding the Sonnets; Wystan got it wrong, and never put it right.

He was blinded by the dogma which C. S. Lewis laid down – and with Ulster dogmatism labelled the converse the 'personal heresy', namely that it is quite unimportant to know the personal facts in question. Wystan repeats the dogma: 'What I object to is the illusion that if the identity of the Friend, the Dark Lady, the Rival Poet, etc, could be established beyond doubt, this would in any way illuminate our understanding of the Sonnets themselves.'

This is rank nonsense: of course it would and does; in fact, one cannot understand the Sonnets fully and intelligibly without that knowledge.

What C. S. Lewis (and Eliot too) meant in extruding the personal and biographical from consideration was that the critical judgment of poetry as poetry is an aesthetic one, and that is unexceptionable, indeed obvious. But, beyond that, to understand a poet's work, or his works, whatever one can find out about him or them helps our understanding of it. Eliot and Wystan both had reasons for wanting not too much known about their personal lives, but anyone who cares about knowledge wants to know all he can. It all has a bearing.

Wystan goes on and on repeating this nonsense, and not only in this essay. 'Even the biography of an artist is permissible,' he says condescendingly, 'provided that the biographer and his readers realize that such an account throws no light whatsoever upon the artist's work.'

A better-trained mind would realize with more discrimination that the importance of biographical knowledge varies very much with the writer: it is immensely important in the cases of Milton and Byron, say, whose egos were so important to their work and whose lives were so much bound up with the events of their time. We might say, less important in the cases of Shakespeare and Dryden, as dramatists – and yet illuminating all the same. As a matter of fact, Wystan contradicts himself in the very next essay. With a bow to the dogma, 'it is not often that knowledge of an artist's life sheds

any significant light upon his work, but in the case of Pope I
think it does.'

I should have thought it less significant with Pope than
with, say, Dr Johnson. Wystan is intellectually rather confused on the subject. Never mind: it is rather amusing to find
him subscribing so loyally to the dogma of the Eng. Lit.
School at Oxford in which he had done so badly.

There were other ways in which America was bad for him:
he became something of a sage, a guru, could lay down the
law about anything and everything, and get away with it,
with an insufficiently critical audience with real standards. So
his later books are filled out with prosy platitudes, if cut up
into verse form:

> The Road of Excess
> leads, more often than not, to
> The Slough of Despond.

> Gossip-Columnists I can forgive for they make no
>   pretences,
>   not Biographers who claim it's for Scholarship's sake.
> Autobiographers, please don't tell me the tale of your
>   love-life:
>   much as it mattered to you, nothing could marvel me
>   less.

Both these thoughts are plain silly: biographies and autobio-
graphies have provided some of the great books of the world.
What about Boswell's Johnson or Lockhart's life of Scott; the
confessions of Rousseau or St Augustine? Wystan's own autobiography would have made a marvellous book, if he could
have written it; I quite understand that he did not want the
tale of his love-life told – but much autobiography is, of
course, in his poems.

At length he became lonely in New York – there are poems
of loneliness – and he longed to return to the Paradise of
those early days, as if one can ever return along the path one
has trodden! Christ Church – the House – was remarkably

agreeable and allotted him a cottage on the premises, with membership of the Senior Common Room etc., such as E. M. Forster had enjoyed at King's, Cambridge.

Wystan came back and spent his first month with us at All Souls, where I was his oldest friend in residence. I welcomed him warmly, took him under my wing, resumed the old relationship of nearly fifty years before, the senior and junior.

His very first night in College he was burgled of all he had in his wallet, and came to tell me next morning. I said, 'Did you sport your oak?' No, he hadn't; he had gone to bed early and left his outer door unlocked. I said, 'You cannot do that. You must realize that Oxford has completely changed since our young days.' In those days we never thought of locking a door; today, in our filthy society, everything has to be kept locked. Even in the fortress of All Souls, I have had valuable rugs stolen, and lately a box of books and papers.

Someone had read in the paper of this famous man's return to Oxford and came to him with a sob-stuff tale about needing money for wife and child. Wystan, as a Christian (a lot of Christians have been had in Oxford that way – not me!), at once wrote out a cheque. That night someone entered his rooms and took all the money in his wallet. We all knew who it was, but the proof could not be brought home. Another characteristic trait of our delightful society.

Wystan and I resumed our talks, warmer, friendlier than before: I felt that he was sad and lonely, he confessed to me that he did not want to go on living. He told me that he was the runner-up for the Nobel Prize: I don't know who the successful candidate was – some second-rater, I suspect, like Steinbeck or Faulkner, instead of Robert Frost or Samuel Eliot Morison. I dare say Wystan would have got it if Hammarskjöld had lived – he was rather on his wavelength (absolutely not on mine: liberal-minded, universal do-gooder, no friend to this country).

In one of our talks Wystan restated his view of the unimportance of the biographical in the understanding of a writer's work – but gently, almost tentatively. I didn't bother to argue the matter, merely gave him my view. Nor did I take him up on Shakespeare. To what point? I have come to

Henry James's point of view and make it my motto: 'Nobody ever understands *any*thing', and leave it at that. All I care about, as a historian, is the truth of the matter in and for itself, no matter what anybody else thinks, or misthinks.

I was rather touched when Wystan gave me his last book, *Epistle to a Godson*, with the inscription 'With love from Wystan'; I wrote beside it, 'How nice, after all the years!' Reading it, I saw how nearly we had come to approximate in our view of the time we had lived through:

> Housman was perfectly right.
> Our world rapidly worsens:
> Nothing now is so horrid
> Or silly it can't occur.

> We all ask, but I doubt if anyone
> Can really say why all age-groups should find our
> Age quite so repulsive.

> Alienation from the Collective is always a duty:
> Every state is the Beast who is Estrangement itself.

This is the way we had set out on together, and after such differing courses in life – yet keeping some touch – had reached the same conclusion. When I was young, I tied myself in knots to make some rational sense of the concept of Equality. Now, towards the end of our course Wystan – altogether more tactful than I – had not hesitated to say that there was immeasurably more inequality between men, in their gifts and abilities and potentialities, than is to be seen anywhere else in the animal kingdom. Think of the difference between a marvellous brain surgeon like Hugh Cairns in our time at Oxford, a physiologist of genius like Sherrington or a physicist like Rutherford at Cambridge, a Newton or an Einstein, and – shall we say – an average shop-steward! Now Wystan was saying:

> My family ghosts I fought and routed;
> Their values, though, I never doubted:

> I thought their Protestant Work-Ethic
> Both practical and sympathetic.
>
> Then Speech was mannerly, an Art,
> Like learning not to belch or fart . . .
>
> Dare any call Permissiveness
> An educational success?
> Saner those class-rooms which I sat in,
> Compelled to study Greek and Latin.

In short Wystan and I adhered to the old Oxford values we had been brought up in – which he had briefly played truant from earlier – and both believed in. He ended by asking:

> Is it Progress when TV's children know all the names
> Of politicians, but no longer play children's games?

I see that my note on that reads: 'Loss of innocence goes with loss of imagination, quality, joy.'

When he died, he left a message in a posthumous volume:

> No summer sun will ever
> dismantle the global gloom
> cast by the Daily Papers,
> vomiting in slipshod prose
> the facts of filth and violence
> that we're too dumb to prevent.

We were at one; and when this light – that had accompanied me, nearer or farther, all my life – had gone out, dear Wystan, I found, somewhat to my surprise, that I had been rather fond of him.

Glimpses
of the Great

To
Kay Halle
in friendship
and with so many memories
we share

Preface

This book is in some sense a sequel to my *Memories of Men and Women*. With regard to the title, I could not resist the alliteration, though not all my subjects (or victims) can be regarded as 'great'. Winston Churchill (in my previous book) was both a great man and a man of genius. Ernest Bevin was a great man, if not a genius. H. G. Wells was a man of genius, but certainly not a great man. Was Bertrand Russell a man of genius? – I suppose so, in mathematical logic and analytic philosophy – as to that I am no judge. Of my other subjects Keynes, John Buchan and Evelyn Waugh were at least touched by genius, as was Elizabeth Bowen. Lionel Curtis and C. S. Lewis? – indefinable, but both thought themselves prophets.

In writing about these people I have confined myself to personal contacts and personal knowledge.

I am honoured by my friend Kay Halle allowing my dedication: she has had her own fascinating glimpses of the great, through her close relationships with the Churchills, Kennedys and Roosevelts – would that she would write about them! I wish to pay tribute particularly to her good work over a lifetime for Anglo-American relations.

A.L.R.

I

Bertrand Russell

Was Bertrand Russell a great man? – Certainly not. Was he a great intellect? Wittgenstein thought not; he considered that Russell had a clever sharp mind, but did not see into the bottom of things. Who are we to differ from the most revered sage among modern philosophers? – who thought that after all there was not much to be said for or about philosophy, and 'as to that about which nothing can be said, nothing is to be said.'

I had more glimpses of and contacts with Russell, over a good many years, than I had with Keynes; and yet I felt closer to Keynes, more sympathy, more in touch with his mind and intellectual concerns. Nevertheless, Russell was a more present figure to me in my younger years. This was partly due to the influence of my Cambridge friends, particularly J. G. Crowther, who had been at Trinity – and Russell was very much a Trinity man. Russell's troubled relations with Trinity make quite a story, and indeed his fellow mathematician, G. H. Hardy, has told it.

My old friend, G. M. Trevelyan,[1] was a contemporary of Russell there, and a fellow Apostle. He knew all about Bertie over a long life, and would say to me: 'He may be a genius in mathematics – as to that I am no judge; but about politics he is a perfect goose.' I think that that was put not unkindly; I came to think worse of him, his influence deplorable.

I did not think that when I was young and innocent; I was rather dazzled by him and admired what he had and retained all through life, one source of great appeal: intellectual vitality and vivacity. His mind genuinely sparkled, sharp like a

[1] For him cf. my *Memories of Men and Women*.

diamond; he was stylish and crisp, not a word wasted; no sentiment or emotion was expressed. All was ratiocination, argument, with sharp summings-up, epigrammatic, never halting or slow or ruminative. Perhaps this was why he was so liable to be wrong – he concluded swiftly and brushed the matter aside without giving it a further thought at the time. When he thought about it another time, he often thought differently. He constantly changed his mind – abruptly: there were no gradual transitions.

There was paradoxically a marked impersonality about him; for, though a striking personality who stood out in any company, he was such an absorbed egoist, with more than a touch of megalomania, that few could get through to him. One of his mistresses, Constance Malleson, with whom he had his longest affair, wrote, with perhaps unintended irony: 'It seems a dreary end to all our years – I see now that your inability to care for anybody, for longer than a rather short time, must be more painful to you than it is to those who are able to continue caring in spite of everything.' I do not think that this caused him much pain – he was not very human.

My first meeting with Russell was when I was no more than an adolescent undergraduate. I was Secretary, then Chairman of the Oxford Labour Club, and it fell to me to invite the speakers. Russell accepted, in his own prim, small hand. I took him out to dinner at a little restaurant, which was all that we could afford. I don't think that Russell was interested in food (as Eliot was); he had no taste and had been brought up in Spartan Victorian fashion. I remember nothing of the evening, except that before we went off to the meeting he said, not unkindly: 'I wish on such occasions that I could fall down and break my leg, or that the earth would swallow me up.'

This struck me so that I never forgot it: I was so nervous at speaking that I felt oddly consoled. If this is what the great man feels before speaking then I ought not to be so nervous, I thought: so innocent that it never occurred to me that he was just plain bored. In subsequent years I have often thought of his remark, girding myself up to speak; and now that I am of his age and experience I suspect that it was boredom, rather than fear, at having to go through the hoop yet again.

Another meeting with him was more in character, for he

told a bawdy story of his brother Frank, Earl Russell – the last peer to be tried by the House of Lords and sentenced to prison for bigamy. Frank was an admirer of *le beau sexe* (poor Santayana was in love with him, in vain),[2] and an ardent supporter of the suffragettes and Votes for Women. At a public meeting one of these ladies declared that people talked about the difference between men and women, but for her part she couldn't see where it came in.

'Couldn't she?', said Frank, who was Chairman.

Bertrand had moved away from the strict high-mindedness in which he had been brought up, the ascetic Stoicism he declared so rhetorically in 'A Free Man's Worship', which he subsequently disclaimed – as he did so much of what he thought all through his life. This essay was much admired; it appeared in his *Mysticism and Logic*, which had been given me to read by my mentor, Crowther. I couldn't make much of it. It didn't occur to me that there wasn't much to make.

Russell had lived with his first wife, Alys Pearsall Smith, of that distinguished Pennsylvanian Quaker family, under the strain of these principles. It was more than flesh and blood could stand. One day, in the course of a bicycle ride – those blissful early days – Bertie decided that he was no longer in love with his wife and came straight home to tell her so, just like that.

Perhaps his experience in prison helped to broaden his experience as to the facts of life. He was not in principle a pacifist in all circumstances – he was not as foolish as that, when you consider the facts of human nature, what humans really are. But he was almost as foolish, in opposing Britain's resistance to Germany's threat to all Europe in the First German War, 1914–18. When it came to Germany's second attempt in 1939–45, Russell at last saw the light and supported Britain's resistance. Very well, he should have seen that the Second was continuous with the First, and that if right over the Second War he had been wrong over the First.

All that distinguished Cambridge circle were wrong about Germany, and Russell maligned Sir Edward Grey's foreign policy with equal injustice and lack of intellectual responsi-

---

[2] Frank, Earl Russell, is recognisably the hero of Santayana's long and somewhat abortive novel, *The Last Puritan*.

bility. The policy of the Entente had been worked out within the Foreign Office by the able brain of Sir Eyre Crowe, who understood Germany and her intentions perfectly, and had a German wife to help him. So indeed did Queen Victoria's intelligent daughter, the German Empress Frederick, and her husband. Bismarck called her 'die Engländerin', because she believed in the proper constitutional development of Germany into a responsible Parliamentary system: she wrote that Hohenzollern Germany was on a course that could lead only to catastrophe. She was right: it has taken two appalling world-wars to force Germany into the decent course of Western civilisation – and even then it took all the might of the United States to do it.

None of that clever circle of Cambridge and Bloomsbury had the historical sense, or even common sense, to see it. Least of all Russell, a paragon of intellectual arrogance. When the United States entered the war in 1917, all too belatedly but in order to save Britain, all that Bertie could say was that the purpose of bringing American troops to Britain was to break strikes! He wrote an article to that effect publicly, and for it he was sent very properly to prison for six months (and Trinity dismissed him from his Fellowship).

Russell was given preferential treatment in prison, pens and paper, reading and writing, and while there he wrote one of his better books – it enabled him to concentrate better. (Evidently prison was good for him.) When he read Lytton Strachey's *Eminent Victorians* – one of that elect circus's performances – it made him laugh so much that a warder had to remind him that prison was supposed to be a place of punishment. What a lot of clever schoolboys they were!

Garsington just outside Oxford, exquisite Jacobean house of Philip and Ottoline Morrell, with its terraces, parterres and peacocks, had been the haven for these people during the war. There they were regarded as martyrs, while braver men were dying for the civilised values Garsington stood for.

As a promising young Fellow of All Souls, I was introduced there by David Cecil, and Ottoline was always kind to me – she was a genuinely kind-hearted woman, for all the things said about her. But, a young fanatic of the Left, serious-minded and prim, I did not like the malicious tone of the circle, and was rather shocked by the outrageous things they said about each other – not used to it in my working-class ambience. Ottoline would tell me how D. H. Lawrence and the awful Frieda (cousin of the German air-ace, Richthofen) beat each other in bed. Though I wasn't interested in their mixed-up, heterosexual goings-on, I regret that I never met Lawrence; by the time I graduated to Garsington he had left England for good.

However, I did meet Desmond MacCarthy, regarded as the most seductive of conversationists (to which he sacrificed his writing, a weak Irish character, like Connolly), whom I treated to a Marxist diatribe all over the terraces of Garsington. He was not amused; however, I was not amused by what *he* had to say: Russell was another matter.

I did not know what Bertie's relations were with Ottoline, and would not have cared to know that she was Bertie's mistress. One day when Ottoline was saying that I should see more of him – I had already met him in Oxford – I said in all innocence that I could not see what people saw so much in him with his scrawny, gander-like neck, active Adam's apple and all. Ottoline replied in her extraordinary way of speaking as if it were Italian – which Lawrence took off so exactly in *Women in Love*: 'O but, my deah, you've no ideah how *ir-res-istible* he is!'

She herself had put up some resistance to Russell, who was very pressing – having emancipated himself from Alys's cold embraces and then married the warmer Dora Black, whom I heard holding forth at Oxford, on women's rights, in the last stages of pregnancy. I youthfully thought that rather unappealing. One thing – or rather another thing – that Russell and Ottoline had in common was that they were both ducal, family-wise.[3]

Russell behaved badly in this affair; for Philip, though rather *égaré* himself, was in love with his wife, and Russell tried to break up the home. And Julian, Philip's daughter, had to threaten legal action to stop Russell years later from writing the whole affair up for money. As for Russell, he wrote, 'what Philip might think or feel was a matter of indifference to

[3] Russell descended from the dukes of Bedford, Ottoline from the dukes of Portland.

me. . . . I have a perfectly cold intellect, which insists upon its rights and respects nothing.'

This is in flagrant contradiction with what Russell laid down in his *Autobiography* as having been a guiding principle in his life. 'Three passions, simple but overwhelmingly strong, have governed my life: the longing for love, the search for knowledge, and unbearable pity for the suffering of mankind.' I regard that as a piece of humbug, or a preliminary puff to his book, and what he really thought expressed by his unrhetorical, 'I am quite indifferent to the mass of human creatures.'

At this very time of the affair with Ottoline took place the episode of the American Professor's daughter, a young girl whom he seduced, when an eldering famous man visiting at an American university. The girl had fallen for him. Others of us have had the experience of being pursued by girl students over there, but if one has an affair with one – affairs with one's own sex are more superficial – doesn't it involve a certain moral obligation? Russell gave her to understand that, if she came to England, he would take her under his wing.

When the girl, of good family and upbringing, followed him hither, Russell cold-shouldered her and put her off on to poor Ottoline. 'I don't think she realises *quite* what you and I are to each other,' he wrote, 'and now there is no reason why she should.' Ottoline, in the goodness of her heart, found the girl a job: Russell was 'amused and pleased to hear you have provided H.D. with work. Never mind if she is hurt.' And then, 'I feel now an absolute blank indifference to her, except as one little atom of humanity. I feel I shall break her heart – but the whole affair is trivial on my side.' It did break the girl's heart; she eventually committed suicide.

I am not so much concerned with morals here – sex makes fools of us all – as with the intellectual self-contradiction in his protestations. He contradicted himself again and again all through his life. Anyone else would condemn him, setting up for a moralist, as a humbug – as he would be, if he were aware of the contradiction between what he set himself up to be and what he was. Russell's case is more curious: he was not aware. George Santayana, who knew both Russells intimately, put his finger on the explanation with his usual perception. He saw that both Russells – Frank so adept at practical science and engineering, and Bertie at mathematical abstractions – had little or no human understanding. There was the gap. The consequence was, as the historian Trevelyan said, that Bertrand Russell might be a genius at mathematics, but was a perfect goose about politics.

History and politics demand above all human understanding, knowledge of men, what they are like and how to handle affairs. Training in abstract mathematics is in itself a disqualification for history and politics. Russell was almost always wrong in his political judgments and should have confined himself to what he really knew about – mathematics, mathematical logic, and analytical (*not* moral) philosophy.

As a comic addendum, it was remarkable that this great-grandson of a duke, who didn't know how anything practical worked, and could hardly make himself a cup of tea, was always prepared to lay down the law how governments should act and the world be run. People were asses to listen to him on these subjects – responsible men of affairs of course never did; it was chiefly Left Intellectuals who took him seriously, with their infallible gift for getting things wrong, forever snatching defeat out of the jaws of victory. It is appropriate that, for Michael Foot, 'Russell is my Man of the Century.'

Was Russell any better then as a guide to Education and Marriage, Morals and Religion? He set up for a guide and wrote prolifically on all of them, books, brochures, pamphlets for the Rationalist Association.

It is not for me to write about the relations between Russell and my friend T. S. Eliot's first wife, Vivienne, in which Russell may not have been much to blame. For she was a psychotic woman whom Eliot should never have married – he realised that on the day he married her. Eliot had been a student in Russell's philosophy class at Harvard. He married and settled in England without much money, to his father's disapprobation, and his allowance was cut off. Bertie, involved with Vivienne, made over the Armaments shares he had inherited and disapproved, as a loan to Eliot, who sensibly had no compunction in holding them. He was convinced that

Bertie's relations with Vivienne were a factor in disturbing her mental balance, precarious anyhow, and Eliot condemned him in the characteristically scrupulous phrase: 'Bertie has wrought Evil.'

Marriage to Dora Black and begetting children in middle age gave Russell a new interest: the Family and children's psychology, which he observed, if at all usefully, as he went along. They set up a school at Telegraph House, on the latest modern principles of freedom, absence of discipline or religion etc. This was a fad at the time – experiments like early Dartington, which I never regarded seriously. An elementary schoolboy myself, proletarian horse-sense told me that all young animals need discipline (I am fond of cats and dogs and donkeys myself), and that it is unfair to them to bring them up without discipline. Especially so for kids – it makes it more difficult for them to learn in school, which is what schools are for, and it ill prepares them for what the world is like and what they will encounter when they go out into it.

On the basis of his and Dora's experience at their school, Russell wrote his book, *Education and the Social Order*. 'Sentence after sentence that could be written in the teacher's golden treasury of wisdom', said *The Observer* with its usual optimism. The school was a flop, and so was the marriage, leaving the oldest child of it a permanent invalid from its strains and stresses.

This did not prevent gallant old Bertie from a third attempt, this time to an Oxford girl, an undergraduette one-third his age – who, to complicate things a bit, was always known as 'Peter' Spens. I knew her as a beautiful, bouncing red-head, bent on becoming the Countess she eventually became.

Russell was also experimenting with history, and wrote *Freedom and Organisation in the Nineteenth Century*. His Preface expressed thanks to Peter Spens for many 'suggestions' in the course of writing it, which sounded well enough to the innocent. Bertie then inserted an erratum-slip: for 'many suggestions' please read 'many *valuable* suggestions'. How many people appreciated the naughty joke? One of the irresistible things about Bertie was his wit, and the stylish humour that played around everything and everybody, except himself.

At this time Russell was out of a job, having blotted his

copy-book in America and been dropped from a chair by a university there. I ran into him one day outside All Souls. Everything about him was memorable, and I can visualise the scene on the pavement in the High Street now: Russell in the gutter, in his shiny old black suit, practically threadbare. He said that the first £1050 of everything he earned went to the upkeep of three women. I thought to myself, 'Serve you right, you old fool.' At the same time I thought it might be a good idea to recruit this eminent Cambridge luminary, one of that most scintillating pre-1914 world, dropped by his own college of Trinity, for Oxford.

At that time All Souls had among its Fellows some five former Fellows of Trinity. I proceeded to approach our then Warden, W. G. S. Adams, with the idea that we make Russell a Research Fellow – a distinguished capture for Oxford: I felt sure that our philosophers, Stuart Hampshire and Isaiah Berlin, would approve. I had no luck with the Warden (he had recruited Hubert Henderson to All Souls), any more than when I had tried to find Ralph Fox, the Communist, a footing in Oxford. Adams was a wise old Scot: he wasn't one for raising a hornets' nest of controversy; also, though he was too shrewd to say so, as a believing Christian he would have disapproved of Russell. (The Warden, I hasten to add, was also a great dear.)

I did not share many of Russell's views – in any case he changed them often, went round like a weathercock; once, lecturing on an important point, in philosophy, 'I changed my mind in the middle', he said blithely. As for his philosophical work, about which so much fuss is made by the fashionable analytic school (Freddie Ayer and others), Bryan Magee concludes: 'whereas most great philosophers seem to have managed to write one or two masterpieces in which their fully developed views are presented, Russell wrote no such masterpiece; but, instead, umpteen flawed and superseded books.'

Russell admitted that the investigation into the logical basis of mathematics, upon which he and Whitehead spent ten years, was abortive. It eventuated in the large abortion, *Principia Mathematica* (shades of Newton, that other Trinity man!). I well recall yet another Trinity man, D. H. Mac-

Gregor at All Souls, chortling over the mouse the mountain brought forth at the end: after some 900 pages establishing, by no means a certainty, but a distinct probability, that 1 plus 1 = 2.

He thought that a great joke: I thought it a great waste of time. Russell considered that never had his mind achieved such acuteness again (he had colossal vanity: a leading clue to him). An historian has little use for philosophical abstractions, and only a limited respect for abstract theorising. He is apt to remember the famous reply, at the Sorbonne, to the guide in the hall where the theologians and philosophers had disputed for 300 years: 'And, pray, what have they settled?'

My own disapproval of Russell, to whom I had looked up when young, grew with time and related to his public stance and statements, on public issues. After all, his private life and its imbroglios – the third marriage, with Peter Spens, came unstuck too (evidently no good guide to Marriage) – were his own affair. I did not know about this apostle of Truth's private habit of lying – the ultimate sin to an historian, whose rule must be 'the truth at all costs'. The full biography by R. W. Clark, based on an immense documentation, catches Russell out again and again, showing how unreliable his *Autobiography* is. His account of his longest *affaire*, with Constance Malleson, for instance: 'an urbane example of his ability to make the best of his own story. The truth is very different.' Clark goes on to show how different.

It was over public and political issues that I grew to disapprove so strongly. Take the crucial one to us all today, the Nuclear Issue. He actually advocated nuclear war against Soviet Russia – and then denied that he had ever done so. In 1948 he wrote: 'Even at such a price, I think war would be worthwhile. Communism must be wiped out.' (So much for his opposition to the war in 1914–18.)

He continually denied that he had urged this evil course. Clark tells us that in a letter denying it to the *Nation*, he 'conveniently ignored his articles in *Cavalcade* and the *Daghens Nyheter*, his letter to Dr Marseille, his talks to the Royal Empire Society and the Imperial Defence College, and the private letters' he wrote urging it. Even 'three years after being driven into an admission that his earlier denials had been completely unjustified,' he wrote in a private letter, in 1962: 'I should be in your debt if you would contribute towards putting the lie to the fiction that I have advocated war against the Soviet Union.'

It was *not* a fiction: he had done so. When faced with this publicly on a BBC interview, by John Freeman (subsequently British ambassador in Washington), 'Is it true or untrue that in recent years you advocated that a preventive war might be made against Communism, against Soviet Russia?', Russell replied without turning a hair, 'It's entirely true, and I don't repent of it.'

What is one to think of such a man, such a philosopher, such a seeker after truth? – A Man of the Century, indeed! What would be said of an historian, Trevelyan or myself, if we had advocated anything so criminally irresponsible? The least we can say is that he was no guide whatever in the dangers of our appalling time.

In fact a dangerous mentor for people silly enough to listen to him – as was proved by the decisive confrontation over Cuba, when Krushchev began placing nuclear missiles there, within sixty to eighty miles of the American coast. If the United States had allowed that to continue, *then* it would have led to war. President Kennedy had to have a showdown and prevent it. The withdrawal of the Russian missiles produced a better mood on the part of Soviet Russia, was actually the beginning of a period of *détente*.

Russell came out on the wrong side as usual, with maximum publicity: Kennedy and Macmillan who supported him were 'about fifty times as bad as Hitler', he trumpeted. What is one to think of such mad irresponsibility? To have allowed Krushchev to put missiles sixty miles from the American coast was the very way to lead to war; to stop it led to peace, and even better relations with Russia.

This is the perspective in which to see the last phase in his life, the Peace Campaign in which he took the lead – processions, sitting out on pavements, clamouring to be taken to prison again – all tremendous publicity, soothing to vanity. The overriding truth is that for one side to go in for disarmament is an invitation to the other side to gamble on aggression

– as we experienced with Hitler's Germany. The proper way is to achieve balance, and *on that basis* to secure peace. Absolute pacifism is, alas, not of this world, and no way to peace.

However, Russell got world-publicity by his campaign, and with it the Nobel Peace Prize. Well, we are all in favour of peace – though we do not expect to get a Nobel Prize for it. Fancy awarding it to so crazy a candidate!

What then is to be said for Russell, what remains of him?

He was an aristocrat, with the moral and intellectual courage of an artistocrat; he spoke out and never minded what he said – like Churchill – and that was something in a world where humbug is common currency, the contemporary universe of discourse. A great-grandson of a Duke of Bedford, grandson of Lord John Russell the Prime Minister, as a Russell he belonged to the most distinguished intellectually of aristocratic clans. So he thought he had a right to say whatever occurred to him; and he said it with style. On his mother's side he belonged to a hardly less remarkable family, the Stanleys of Alderley. They had a vein of doctrinairism indistinguishable from fanaticism: one Lord of that ilk sat in the Victorian House of Lords as a Moslem.

Wasn't there also something slightly dotty about them? I always thought that there was something significant, perhaps a pointer, in the story Russell tells in his *Autobiography*, of setting himself up one day in his youthful Cambridge rooms for God, and getting his friends to kneel down and worship him. A joke typical of the Cambridge Apostles, of course; but wasn't there a streak of megalomania in the later avatar?

Bertrand was certainly no democrat, didn't care what anybody else thought, and didn't subscribe to the demotic humbug of the time. He always had some private means, which help one to independence of mind. 'The Shelleys and Darwins and so on couldn't have existed at all if they'd had to work for their living. And surely one Darwin is more important than thirty million working men and women.' Exaggeration as usual, but there I can agree with him in principle. 'Let us not delude ourselves with the hope that the best is within the reach of all.' Here Bertie deviates into commonsense. Or again, 'I believe in several definite measures – for example,

Infanticide – by which society could be improved.' We should not allow ourselves to be shocked by Bertie: we could meet him half-way – say, only for mongols or congenital idiots; otherwise, birth control – a more civilised way.

Of his philosophy, his mathematical logic, I am not qualified to speak, though I have no very high opinion of the value of philosophising, except as intellectual exercise. Russell certainly had a strenuous athletic mind, always engaged in theorising and arguing, for what that is worth – historians do not think much of it: they prefer to watch facts and what they point to. Russell always spoke with absolute certainty – and then changed his mind; he never learned to speak with less certainty, and then wait for thought, observational and empirical, to mature. His fellow Cambridge philosopher, C. D. Broad, pronounced sentence on him: 'Mr Russell produces a different system of philosophy every few years.'

It was, however, great fun to have known him, and I found him stimulating intellectually, as others did, when I was young. I read almost everything he wrote, even a number of his philosophical lucubrations. Did one profit from them? – in the way that some more reliable thinkers left an enduring mark, a permanent deposit: Frazer's *Golden Bough*, for instance; still more Sherrington's *Man on his Nature*, physiologist of genius, *my* Man of the Century, along with Churchill.

Russell wrote with verve and style, an admirable prose style, brisk and spare, springy and stringy (like him), lean and spare, no poetry about it. His ideal of beauty was mathematics – otherwise no aesthete; and I prefer aesthetes – Keynes for instance collected pictures and books, as well as Duncan and Lopokova. Such are the salt of the earth.

An American admirer of Russell, the Leftist philosopher Sidney Hook, provides a fresh angle from which to regard him. He charges Russell with two main failings, vanity and greed for money. I think we may let Russell off both charges rather lightly, without undue seriousness. No doubt he needed to grab all the cash he could to provide for his women, their alimonies, and his family. Even the vanity had its comic side. Hook's observant little daughter said, 'Daddy, Uncle Bertie's wee-wee is larger than yours', at which the old philosopher was highly gratified. No doubt it had been a factor in his success with women – as also an element in his obsessive need for them.

Hook, when young, had been taken in even as I was earlier. Hook was influenced by 'Russell's cool demolition of the myths about Teutonic frightfulness' in Belgium during the First German War; 'his passionate lucidity and dedication to the truth sustained me in the difficult years after the Armistice.' I had been brought up under the myth put about by H. N. Brailsford, E. D. Morel and the pro-Germans that the Germans were no more responsible for the war than we were. When I came to think things out for myself and could judge from the evidence, I soon appreciated that *that* was the myth – especially after I came to know Germany and the Continent. Not many years after the Armistice I was in Louvain, where the Germans in 1914 had set fire to a quarter of the town; an act of 'Teutonic frightfulness' to intimidate the population. Those who remember the sudden evisceration of friendly Rotterdam in 1940 will have no difficulty in recognising the patent and the pattern.

No: I regard Russell's blithe disregard for truth as far more damaging, and its influence more poisonous. When a world-famous guru could say of the United States, 'Anybody who goes so far as to support equal rights for coloured people, or to say a good word for the United Nations, is liable to a visit by officers of the F.B.I. and threatened with blacklisting and consequent inability to earn a living' – what nonsense, what poisonous nonsense!

We have seen that with him the truth was largely at the mercy of his prejudices – and how silly people were to heed such nonsense, let alone take such a type as guide.

2

J. M. Keynes

Lifelong Oxonian as I am, my glimpses of Keynes were at Oxford, never at Cambridge. Oddly enough, Keynes when young was prejudiced against Oxford, and did not want to come up to Balliol from Eton. This was a pity, for Oxford's essentially historical outlook would have done him a power of good, instead of the mathematical and moral abstractions of Cambridge. And ironically Oxford's historicism was more in keeping with Keynes's later thought, as it developed away from the abstractions of economic orthodoxy. A Cambridge historian, G. M. Trevelyan, never had this rather adolescent prejudice – really a form of irrelevant inferiority-complex from the equipollent daughter university.

My first glimpse of Keynes was a public one, as an undergraduate, when he came to give the Sidney Ball Lecture (Sidney Ball was an early Oxford Socialist of the previous generation). This was in 1924, the subject the rather scandalous one, *The End of Laissez-faire*,[1] in which he announced tentatively his widening breach with economic orthodoxy. Since my generation of intellectuals was attracted by the prospects held out by socialism, we all crowded to hear the great man in the Schools. – Or, not yet a great man, rather a notorious one for the world-wide interest his book, *The Economic Consequences of the Peace*, had created, with its attack on the Treaty of Versailles and its malicious, Stracheyesque portraits of its makers – Lloyd George, President Wilson, Clemenceau – on a par with the caricatures of

[1] Published by Leonard and Virginia Woolf at the Hogarth Press in 1926, the year of the General Strike.

Eminent Victorians.

Keynes's appearance came up to expectations, though he disappointed our further, Leftist hopes. He did however prefigure the end of the economic orthodoxy under which we were restive and about which I already had my doubts. Deep in history, I was ravaged by scepticism about political theories and economic doctrines being 'true' for all times and places: I considered them both historically conditioned. In my last term I openly challenged the Regius Professor, H. W. C. Davis, on this at a lecture (my fellow-historian, Geoffrey Barraclough, witnessed the embarrassing scene). Davis politely rebuked me with, 'That is a degree of historical scepticism with which I do not agree.'

Keynes's challenge was in keeping, one to which I was sympathetic. He said, 'For more than a hundred years our philosophers ruled us, because, by a miracle, they nearly all agreed, or seemed to agree, on this one thing' – Laissez-faire. Keynes summed this up – 'Suppose that by the working of natural laws individuals pursuing their own interests with enlightenment in conditions of freedom always tend to promote the general interest at the same time!' The doctrine held that 'State Action should be narrowly confined and economic life left, unregulated as far as may be, to the skill and good sense of individual citizens actuated by the admirable motive of trying to get on in the world.'

This was the middle-class orthodoxy of the Cambridge sage and mentor, Alfred Marshall, who dominated the subject with an authority largely moral, under which Keynes had been brought up and from which he was with difficulty now emancipating himself. He no longer believed in it. A recruit from the working-class (a rarity at Oxford in those days), I had read a great deal of Carlyle and Ruskin before coming up, and I didn't believe that Laissez-faire was Revealed Truth either, laid up from on high and true for all circumstances and places.

When I got to All Souls – where H. W. C. Davis was good enough to introduce me to my more admired Trevelyan – Keynes came to visit us occasionally. He would complain of the Spartan conditions under which we lived, our Arctic bedrooms. Quite rightly; for one difference between Oxford and Cambridge in those days was that, over there, the dons did themselves so much better. They had sets of three, some even four, rooms, where we mostly had only two; one or two Cambridge dons (R. V. Laurence of Trinity was one) died simply of over-eating. See A. E. Housman on Cambridge life. All Souls provided a combination of public splendour with private squalor.

Keynes came to see Professor Edgeworth in the course of their editing the *Economic Journal* together. Edgeworth was a rare bird, even at All Souls. Anglo-Irish on one side – his great-aunt, Maria Edgeworth the novelist, had instructed him to say Brighthelmstone, never Brighton, like the people – he was Spanish on the other: Francis Ysidro Edgeworth. He kept people at a distance by his oblique courtesy. A distinguished intellect, he had a fabulous memory. On his one journey to America, laid up in his cabin by sea-sickness, he managed to reconstruct about a half of the *Iliad* in Greek. His lectures were only for the elect; a few Fellows attended them out of loyalty: nobody could understand them. He had once proposed marriage to Beatrice Webb, who has a characteristically disparaging account of him. He was a pure mathematical economist, an outpost of Marshallianism in Oxford; from that point of view, *he* should have been at Cambridge, Keynes at Oxford.

It was a joke at All Souls that one could never get Edgeworth to pronounce a definite judgment about anything – his motto might well have been his dictum, 'I like the duplicity of things.' One exception to this was his disapprobation of Karl Marx: Edgeworth condemned him with a moral distaste that was worthy of the sainted Marshall.

They were all supercilious about Marxism, and obtuse as to its real significance. In his Laissez-faire Lecture Keynes spoke of the 'poor quality of its thinking, of inability to analyse a process and follow it out to its conclusion. How a doctrine so illogical and so *dull* can have exercised so powerful and enduring an influence over the minds of men and, through them, the events of history', he could not understand. There was a great deal in the events of history which Keynes did not understand, but which Marx did.

Let us be clear about this. I no more subscribe to the dogmatism of Marx's economic or political doctrines than

Keynes did. I do not think that Marx was a pure economist or political scientist, or 'pure' anything (except a pure egoist); but he had deeper insights into the processes of history and the forces at work in society than Keynes ever had, with his superficial rationalism and his Bloomsbury superciliousness. That is one reason for Marx's influence upon 'the minds of men and the events of history', altogether greater and more 'enduring' than Keynes's.

Of course Keynes was a more generous man, encouraging to other people's work, especially of young men – where Marx was a nasty man, unwilling to recognise quality in others: an envious, recognisably German type. Both men were justifiably arrogant, but Keynes was occasionally willing to admit where he had been wrong. In the *Treatise on Money* he admitted how much he had underestimated J. A. Hobson, who had emphasised the importance of under-consumption in the shortcomings of the economic system. Hobson had been effectively excluded, as a heretic, by the economic establishment and academic economists all hanging tgether, when this solitary thinker was on to something more important than most of them were.

Keynes was good enough to encourage my reviews in his *Economic Journal* of books on political theory – Tawney, Russell, E. H. Carr, Laski – in spite of my obsession with Marxism. He would send me brisk p.c.s to urge me on, and in fact published my first piece of research, on the Dispute concerning the Elizabethan Plymouth Pilchard Fishery, in the *Journal's Economic History Supplement*. This had some relevance as an illustration of the conflict between state regulation and free economic processes.

I knew Keynes only intellectually, not personally, and nothing at all about his rip-roaring homosexuality. So I was much amused when my stockbroker friend, Nicholas Davenport, who had invited me to Covent Garden, told me that Keynes said, 'You can't do that: he's *my* boy.' Actually I was not his boy (or anybody else's either – more's the pity: such relentless repression, when young and rather sexy, cannot have been good for duodenal ulcer).

Naively enough, I was constantly concerned for Keynes's intellectual well-being. I never ceased to be amazed throughout the appalling Thirties at his inability to see the significance of the Marxist approach and insight into the gaping problems of society, the conflicts of class interests – indeed the crucial rôle of Class in history and politics; and his refusal to come to terms with the Labour Movement, make an alliance with it, which would give his views – about Unemployment, economic expansion, etc – the *fulcrum* they needed, and make both the Labour Party and himself more effective. Why couldn't he see it? After all, the Webbs had seen it and formed the most effective alliance with the Labour Movement – which ultimately proved the foundation of the Welfare State.

I wrote a number of articles urging this line upon him, in the *Nineteenth Century* and elsewhere, some of them reprinted for the historical record in *The End of an Epoch*. Reviewing it, Professor Denis Brogan referred to the continuing dialogue I had engaged in during that wasted decade when all went wrong. But there was no dialogue, for Keynes did not reply. Privately, I considered that no reply was possible. Professor Skidelsky reminds me that Labour was out of government throughout the whole of that decade and couldn't do anything anyway.

True enough; but it need not necessarily have been so but for the fatal events of 1931, the turning-point in history between the two German wars. The year 1931 saw a ganging-up of the upper and middle classes, and of their political parties, both Tory and Liberal, against the Labour Movement to keep it out. The long-term effects were disastrous; in some ways Britain was crippled by them.

In terms of immediate policy at that time Ernest Bevin and the Labour Movement were right. The proper way to correct the deficit on the balance of payments in 1931 was a temporary 10 per cent tariff on imports. Keynes was in favour of this (as I was), along with correcting the exaggerated fixation of the pound at 4.86 to the dollar. Keynes had been against this measure – which precipitated the prolonged Coal-Strike and its train of consequences, General Strike and all: see his *The Economic Consequences of Mr Churchill*. Actually, Churchill's instinct had been against the return to the Gold Standard, but he had been overruled by the combined weight of the Treasury and the Bank of England. – As the Labour Movement was – and was kept out of responsibility and power the whole of that disastrous decade. Until 1940.

Bevin had served on the Macmillan Committee (Lord Macmillan, not Harold), to which Keynes had contributed the most important evidence, clean contrary to the paralytic policy of the National Government, and the Bank of England under Montagu Norman, who admitted that he had never 'considered the effect the Return to the Gold Standard might have on Unemployment'! (It naturally contracted exports and increased unemployment.)

Instead of the obviously sensible policy, a moderate amount of expansion, a measure of controlled inflation at the right time (not, as in the 1960s, at the wrong time), the Old Men of the Sea of 1931–9, of whom the most powerful was Neville Chamberlain, went in for a consistent deflationary policy, worsening the situation. The dominant man in the Labour Movement, Ernest Bevin, and Keynes were of one mind in all this. Why could they not have joined together, and worked together, for the right ends in that miserable time? Keynes could have provided intellectual leadership, the Labour Movement the mass backing and support.

Lenin said, 'Politics begin with the masses.' Keynes needed a mass movement behind him to be effective. He had not that Marxist perception. As Skidelsky replies to me today, Keynes thought that he could be more effective as an individual, with no party affiliations, i.e. no movement behind him. A massive imperception – Marx could have told him; a historic mistake, for of course the government of 1931–9, with its enormous majorities – could have done anything, dealt with Hitler too if they had wanted to – did nothing, and Keynes had no effect whatever. Until the Second German War, which they brought down on Britain in the worst possible circumstances.

Keynes realised his ineffectiveness, a lone voice in the wilderness, and at length chose to link up with the wing of the Liberal Party led by Lloyd George, whom he had so much maligned in the *Economic Consequences of the Peace*. Together, he and Lloyd George produced a Yellow Book of constructive proposals for dealing with Unemployment which was better than anything else produced. But what on earth was the point of urging that on the country *without any leverage behind it*?

Anybody with any political sense could have seen from 1931 that there was no future for the Liberal Party; that there would never be a Liberal government again.

Actually I was in favour of bringing together all the elements opposed to the disastrous course of the 'National' government, Appeasement of Hitler, caving in to Mussolini over Abyssinia and Spain, etc – both the Labour Party and the Liberals, and even including Churchill and the Tories who were anti-Chamberlain. When I urged this to Hugh Dalton, who was sympathetic, he replied, 'But – how many Tory MPs can Churchill count on in the House? Only 20 or 25.' Baldwin and Chamberlain had that unspeakable Assembly with them all through that decade, to the edge of disaster: at first with a majority of 450, even after 1935 a majority of nearly 300! They could have done anything. In the long-term they ruined their country. Britain's great days are now over.

In these years the combination of experience and an original inquiring mind was undermining Keynes's belief in the rigid economic orthodoxy in which he had been brought up and which was inflicted on us all. Not to believe it was not only an intellectual but moral deviation; to challenge it was to be rewarded with exclusion from responsible teaching posts and even from notice and discussion of one's ideas. Keynes himself, in his earlier orthodoxy, had refused to review any more of J. A. Hobson's original books, describing his criticism of the quantity theory of Money as 'Mythology intellectualised, brought up to journalistic date, most subtly larded with temporary concessions to reason.'

Unforgivable superciliousness, which Keynes had reason to regret, for he came to see that Hobson had been largely right. In his classic *General Theory of Employment, Interest and Money* he admitted, 'It is astonishing what foolish things one can temporarily believe if one thinks too long alone, particularly in economics, where it is often impossible to bring one's ideas to a conclusive test either formal or experimental' – i.e. as in either mathematics, or in physics, chemistry, etc. That is why it is absurd to insist on a rigid orthodoxy in economics, which is not a 'pure' science like mathematics, but an impure subject of mingled theory and practical affairs. However, as Skidelsky says, 'Authority in economics had come to demand adherence to certain orthodoxies.'

I had observed this in the unnecessary 'crisis' of 1931, which panicked everybody, when not a single economist, except for Keynes, would subscribe to the commonsense remedy of a temporary tariff on imports, let alone a release from the strain of retaining sterling at 4.86 to the dollar. Not one of the academic economists at Cambridge or Oxford (where D. H. MacGregor stood for Cambridge orthodoxy), still less at the London School of Economics, where Lionel Robbins trumpeted the purest milk-of-the-word Free Trade, would allow a temporary departure from it. Events in the real world framed a showdown: Britain was forced off the Gold Standard, and the world did not come to an end.

As an historian, I had never had much belief in economic or political theories as absolute truths, and ever since the experience of the Thirties I have not had much respect for academic economists. Economists with experience of practical affairs, which is what the subject is about, are another matter.

It is hardly surprising therefore that when Keynes completed his revolution in economics with *The General Theory of Employment, Interest and Money*, he should have been greeted with incomprehension and obstruction by his academic colleagues. Skidelsky points out that not one of his eminent *confrères* at Cambridge agreed with him – not Pigou, who as Professor was head of the Faculty. (Keynes was never a professor: he said stylishly, 'I will not have the indignity of the title without the advantage of the emolument.') Nor did Denis Robertson – there was even a breach between them over it. Nor did Hubert Henderson, who never understood Keynes's argument. But he tied himself in knots over it at All Souls, whither he had removed, and could argue the hind leg of a donkey off, as I found to my irritation.

It always irritates me that supposedly intelligent persons, particularly academics, simply cannot think outside the categories their minds have been formed in. When the greatest of our physiologists, Sir William Hervey, conceived his idea of the circulation of the blood, people would not credit it, and his practice as a doctor fell away almost to nothing. He had to wait for a new generation to grow up accustomed to the new idea. Fortunately Hervey lived long enough to see that happen. Something of the same kind happened to Keynes: though he did not live as long as Hervey, the succeeding generation of economists gradually filled up with his disciples.

I have experienced something of this phenomenon myself. The revolution in our knowledge of Shakespeare effected by, after all, a first-rate authority on the Elizabethan Age, background to his life and work, has been met with blinkered incomprehension. So far from wanting to know, the second-rate put up a wall of obstruction and make no effort to go into the new discoveries and findings: it will need a new generation accustomed to them. What is irritating – I am sure Keynes would have agreed – is that it is properly the business of the second-rate to mediate the discoveries of first-rate minds to the third-rate. A further factor today is the *vis inertiae* of an egalitarian society – naturally low-grade intellectually, no standards.

When Keynes's revolutionary book came out, I set myself to grasp its argument and draw out its implications in economic and social policy as a basis for a wide agreement on the Left, against the paralytic hold of Chamberlainism on the nation. (Right up to 1940 they really thought, and even said, that they were indispensable. See the evidence in the Memoirs of the time, the complacent Sam Hoare and Simon – let alone Chamberlain, who wrote down his conviction that he was superior to Lloyd George, the only political figure of genius to compare with Churchill!)

In 1936 I produced my tract, *Mr Keynes and the Labour Movement*. I do not claim to be an economist, but I certainly put enough effort into the small book – long out of print and unobtainable. What I was anxious to do was to draw out the common ground between Keynes and the Labour Movement's line, dotting the i's and crossing the t's. My Preface affirmed that 'there is little or no divergence between what is implied by Labour policy and by Mr Keynes.' I hoped that the booklet was 'a contribution towards clarifying and building up an agreement between various sections of opinion of the Left, *on a wide front*; a body which, if an understanding had

been reached before, might have given this country progressive government for the past ten years, and to Europe an
effective and progressive lead.'

Keynes wrote to me from Bloomsbury, 12 May 1936, 'I
agree with you that there is, or ought to be, little divergence
between the political implications of my ideas and the policy
of the Labour Party. I should officially join that party, if it did
not seem to be divided between enthusiasts who turn against a
thing if there seems to be a chance that it could possibly
happen, and leaders so conservative that there is more to hope
from Mr Baldwin.' But was this true to fact, or an adequate
excuse? The 'enthusiasts' had no real weight, and there was
nothing to hope from Baldwin – look at his record over the
coal-miners, and his declared indifference to foreign affairs.
'Wake me up when that is over', he would say when they were
being discussed in Cabinet – with the danger already looming
from Hitler and Mussolini!

Keynes continued, 'But perhaps it is better for several
reasons that I should remain aloof and stick, for the present, to
my academic standpoint. . . . My book is not, in truth, well
adapted for carrying the gospel beyond academic circles. But
if you can help to get it read more widely, I shall all the same be
very grateful. Those whose heads are already too full of
preconceived ideas sometimes find it harder than more innocent readers do to understand.' Supercilious as this was, it was
true enough of his fellow economists (as I find today with
fellow Shakespeareans).

I followed this up with a pamphlet urging a Popular Front,
as wide as possible, against the Old Men before it was too late.
Keynes wrote in October, 'Some of it makes me blush a little,
and I hope your eulogies won't irritate people too much. It is a
problem how best to bring ideas into relation with politics. I
am, of course, in favour of a popular front. But I should like to
see some group of like-minded people formed which one
could join, and which then could seek affiliation with the
official Labour Party, in the way that the old I.L.P. and the
Fabians used to, I think. To try and make the official Liberal
Party join with the official Labour Party raises unnecessary,
and perhaps hopeless, difficulties.' Why should they not?
Anyone of sense could have seen that there would never be a

Liberal government again, their day was over. The only way to be effective was to join together and co-operate before too late.

He went on, 'I believe the solution may lie in a number of groups, having ideas of their own not wholly along the party ticket, but definitely subordinated to the Labour Party and affiliated to it.' 'A number of groups' – how *ineffective* that would be! Just like an intellectual liberal, I thought; imagine what Lenin would think of that. . . . However, I considered that this, from Keynes, was a step forward, and suggested his standing for a University seat at Cambridge then occupied by a Conservative Chamberlainite.

Keynes replied, 'I hope that next time you are in Cambridge you will let me know. I agree with you that the Next Five Years' Group would be the most hopeful, if they could be persuaded to affiliate with the Labour Party. I fancy that Harold Macmillan would agree, but whether all his Committee would I am not sure. I have, of course, often considered standing for Cambridge University. But I am convinced that it is useless to go into politics except as a whole-time job, and I have so many other avocations that I care about much more.'

No doubt. At this point I gave him up, and turned to another possibility for the Cambridge seat. What was clearly necessary was a non-party man who could collect the widest support against the fraud of a 'National' government. This was the way Arthur Salter had won a seat at Oxford; and for Cambridge I raised a candidate willing to stand in Sir Ralph Wedgwood. I did not let Keynes know when I was next in Cambridge, though I find a message from him dated from King's, 24 April 1938: 'A very excellent letter in today's *M.G.*', i.e. *Manchester Guardian*. What was the point? I suppose it was advocating an understanding with Russia before too late. But Neville Chamberlain, as he said, 'preferred to trust Herr Hitler's word', and we were along the road that led to Munich, and the Second German War, in the worst possible circumstances – virtually no allies. After nearly twenty years of Tory government!

It was heart-breaking to live through the Thirties, if one was intelligent, seeing quite clearly the way things were going and what it was leading to. No-one would take the obvious and sensible steps. All over Europe the parties of the Left, who stood for the right objectives – international peace, freedom, social progress – would not pull together. The idiots preferred to fight each other, like the Social Democrats and Communists in Germany, the Communists even collaborating with the Nazis in the Berlin tram-strike just before Hitler came into power. *He* knew all about power. The evil forces were all too effective: those on the side of good causes all too ineffective. I used to find this maddening in my arguments with Ralph Fox, whom the Communist Party sent to Spain, against his will, to be a martyr.

Neither in Britain would the opposition to the paralytic Old Men of the Sea come together to get rid of them – though Churchill too hoped for such a consummation. In consequence they stuck to power, until the country was in fact overwhelmed in 1940. L. S. Amery, a good Tory who was right about all this, one day said to me at All Souls that, in politics, it is a mistake to walk too far ahead of your following. With a sinking feeling I recognised the truth of that.

I will not resume the argument of *Mr Keynes and the Labour Movement* here – merely say that it was dedicated to my particular leader in it, Herbert Morrison, who had effectively set the model of the semi-public corporation with the London Transport Board. This was in line with what Keynes had proposed in *The End of Laissez-faire:* 'I suggest that progress lies in the growth and the recognition of semi-autonomous bodies within the State.' He went further than this: 'It is true that many big undertakings, particularly Public Utility enterprises still need to be semi-socialised.' This was what Herbert Morrison stood for as our leader in London, and what we in the Labour Movement thought. Why could not Keynes combine with us, to make us both more *effective*?

I was then very active in the Labour Movement: a political candidate throughout that decade, whose uphill work for years in Cornwall eventually brought over my constituency, Penryn and Falmouth, to the Labour Party in 1945 (too late for me); speaking, lecturing, writing in Labour papers, having created one for Cornwall, wearing myself out.

Victor Gollancz was in the lead as socialist publisher at the

time, so I naturally offered my Keynes booklet to him. He
kindly asked me to lunch at the Savoy, into which I had never
penetrated, and capped it with an invitation to his country
villa, with the added attraction of a swimming-pool. Little did
he perceive that his combination of opulence with extreme
Leftism did not recommend itself to my austere and rather
Puritan outlook; nor did I swim. He turned down the book –
insufficiently Leftist for him. He preferred the trash of the Left
Book Club he was promoting – Harold Laski, John Strachey,
Michael Foot, Tom Driberg and such, some of them Communists or fellow-travellers. (I did not know that he had also
turned down George Orwell.) That finished Gollancz for me; I
at once took the book to Keynes's publisher, Macmillan, who
made no difficulty about publishing it.

I saw Gollancz only once again. After the war he made
another name for himself for his more-than-Christian
attitude, falling over backward, with much publicity, to
forgive the Germans for their appalling crime in massacring
six million Jews. This won him much sentimental admiration:
'that Jesus-Christ-like man, Victor Gollancz,' said one of his
employees (female of course). Meanwhile, forced to give up
politics by illness and despair, I found consolation in the past
and was writing history with some success. Gollancz and I
happened to be coming back from America on one of the
Queens, he travelling first-class of course, I second-class, of
course. He kindly invited me up to visit him: 'Friend, come up
higher.' I did not avail myself of the invitation. I did not wish
to know him.

With the Second German War, it was just a question of
survival – all earlier possibilities and hopes, discussions and
arguments put behind us (though I did not forget or forgive).
Keynes moved into his period of greater service to the country
– out of my ken, into the stratosphere of high Anglo-American financial relations.

What had accounted for his refusal to line up with us and
make an effective Opposition – ranging from Stafford Cripps
to Churchill – against disastrous Chamberlainism and
Appeasement of the dictators while there was yet time? He
certainly didn't see the Marxist point that it is a mass move-

ment that provides the backing and the power to move things in politics. He looked to persuasion, in fact produced a book, *Essays in Persuasion*: just the way to be ineffective – as if people were rational enough to be persuadable.

He was a Liberal, and a Cambridge Rationalist. Fancy thinking that men were reasonable! – you need only take a look round the world today: you do not need to go so far as the Lebanon or Middle East, darkest Africa or Central America; Northern Ireland gives the lie to rationalist assumptions. In the Thirties I was constantly attacking in my writings the Rationalist Fallacy that dominated the Left. The Right had no such illusions, they knew that politics were about power. The ineffective fools of the Left denounced this as 'power politics' – their cliché for the facts of political life: what was their alternative, 'powerless politics'? That was in effect what they achieved: their ineffectiveness, all over Europe, Liberals, Social Democrats, decent people, sold the pass to the malign criminals who had no such illusions and were all too effective. Hitler, Mussolini, Stalin had utter contempt for the political idiots the masses are – and the masses rewarded them with devotion, died in millions for them.

If I have ceased to write about politics and given up girding against the Rationalist Fallacy, it is because I no longer care – as I did when I was young – about what happens to people bent on remaining fools. I write now simply for the record that is history – and we know what Gibbon, greatest of our historians, thought that was: 'the register of the crimes, follies and misfortunes of mankind.' As a modern historian, living alas in democratic times, I add – their idiocy, their sheer silliness. (One has only to look at their newspapers, or listen to their media!)

Keynes was a Liberal, and there was an element of snobbish superciliousness in his refusal to line up with a Labour Movement. I had come across that with other Liberals at the time, to whom I urged the historical conclusion, obvious enough, that there was no future for the Liberal Party and that they should throw in their lot with effectively the only two political parties, either of which could have used their ability. As it was, the country was robbed of the ability of a number of good men ploughing the sands.

But Keynes was a Cambridge-and-Bloomsbury Liberal, the *crème de la crème* – and the superciliousness of that lot, though well enough known, is hardly credible. Here is the young Keynes on his first official visit to America, writing to handsome Duncan Grant with whom he was in love: 'The only sympathetic and original thing in America is the niggers, who are charming.' Fancy writing like that – and he a Liberal! No wonder the poor British Ambassador thought him 'really too offensive for words.' This select group, who thought themselves so superior to the mass of humanity – and were – in fact did not know what humanity was like. They were not historians, and Keynes himself had a very naif view of history: they were addicts (and victims) of G. E. Moore's adolescent ethical views – I find him a faintly ridiculous figure. They were utterly taken by surprise by the war in 1914: dear Duncan, a conscientious objector: 'I never considered the possibility of a great European war. It seemed such an absolutely mad thing for a civilised people to do.' But this is precisely what peoples have done all through history, civilised or not, and still do.

That Cambridge group, as Skidelsky points out, were really pro-German, and supposed the Germans – with their record in philosophy and music – the most civilised nation in Europe. There was another side to the coin, of which they were ignorant. Couldn't they *see* what Germany was heading for? Hadn't they noticed what Germany was up to since Bismarck? The leading German historian of these matters today, Fritz Fischer, recognises that Germany meant war and was responsible for the war in 1914.[2] Actually – an historical point no-one notices – the Germans as a whole were more keen on war, *der Tag*, in 1914 than they were in 1939.

That Cambridge circle was childishly confused about Germany – and Cambridge became the centre of a distinguished anti-war, 'conscientious objector' group whose organ was *The Cambridge Magazine*, run from King's Parade by my eccentric acquaintance, C. K. Ogden. The files of that periodical make fascinating reading for the time, the office once raided by patriotic Cambridge men and its contents thrown

[2] The two fundamental works for the reader to study are Fritz Fischer, *Germany's Aims in the First World War*; and *War of Illusions. German Policies from 1911 to 1914*. Both translated.

into confusion. It has now become known that Keynes himself, though working in the Treasury, was also a 'conscientious objector', under the influence of the Bloomsbury *Weltanschauung*. He wrote to dear Duncan, 'I work for a government I despise, for ends I think criminal.' I find this shocking. Was it criminal to resist a militaristic Germany's attempt to subjugate Europe? This was the crest of the first wave of aggression into which retrograde Germany swept Europe, ruining the hopes of the twentieth century – and it would have succeeded, as the second attempt under Hitler nearly did, had not the United States come to the rescue.

Again and again Keynes's judgment is shown to be wrong. In January 1915 he told Woolf 'German finance is crumbling'. He was wrong: in fact Germany managed. Partly through the genius of Walther Rathenau, the head of the electrical industry, who successfully re-organised German industry on a wartime footing. He was a Jew – so, after the war, the Right murdered him. (Another Jew, Balin, creator of the Hamburg-Amerika shipping line – when he saw what Germany was bent on in 1914 – himself in touch with the outside world and more sensitive to world opinion – committed suicide.)

In April 1915 Keynes was predicting financial collapse for Britain; or, if not, then October following. Wrong again. Then he fixed '31 March 1916 for the end of the world, though this had been postponed for a few months.' In fact, Lloyd George – whom Keynes as an Asquithian at this time detested – was usually proved right as against the Treasury experts. Also Lloyd George was the only man with the leadership to win the war – not Asquith, drunken, lazy, spending hours of Cabinet time writing love letters to young Venetia Stanley.

All through 1916–18 Keynes was in favour of a Compromise Peace. That would have meant that Germany's way was clear for a second attempt. This is no biased opinion – the point is proved by the peace of Brest-Litovsk next year, 1917, which Germany inflicted upon Russia, annexing all Eastern Europe up to the threshold of St Petersburg. Hitler's aim was simply continuous with Germany's in 1914–18.

The pro-Germans were appallingly mistaken, and the lightweights of Bloomsbury not to be taken seriously. Those superior intellects had just not thought things through: would it have been a good thing for *them* and their view of life if Germany's aggressive militarism had won? We have more reason to respect the brave men who gave their lives to resist it, and save a society for *them* to be so civilised in. (At the memorials to the fallen all over Britain, particularly at Oxford and Cambridge, I always remember them.)

At the end of the First German War Keynes told Virginia Woolf that he was 'disillusioned. No more does he believe – that is, in the stability of the things he likes: Eton is doomed; the governing classes; perhaps Cambridge too.' More important matters were at stake than Eton or Cambridge, or even the English governing class. The future of a decent, civilised Europe was in the balance (the New World saved us – not only the United States, but Canada, Australia, South Africa, New Zealand, as again in 1939–45). Germany's crime in 1914 portended the end of the old civilised nineteenth-century world, and started the chain-reaction of violence and revolution that has been going on ever since, and ended in the Nuclear Age, that may end us all.

How petty and narrow the want of historical perspective in Cambridge-Bloomsbury and their prophet Keynes!

This is the proper historical perspective in which to consider his *Economic Consequences of the Peace*, of 1919, which brought him fame and a fortune, first made him an international figure – and did so much damage. By far his most historically influential book, it did more than anything to undermine the Peace of Versailles and to give the Germans an alibi for what they had done in 1914–18, and thus prepare the ground for their second attempt. It was of the highest possible value to German propaganda against the Treaty, which never ceased, not merely Hitler's. Worse: it confused the minds of British and Americans over the German question, and helped to fuel the Revisionists in Britain and the USA, and the Appeasement which played straight into Hitler's hands.

We should be historically clear about the Versailles Peace. On the territorial side it was fair enough – and what a contrast with what the Germans would have imposed is quite clear from their record at Brest-Litovsk. Poland was re-created as a nation-state; a great historical injustice rectified. The peoples of Central Europe – Czechs, Slovaks, Slavs – were given the

independence and self-determination they demanded: inevitable, and historically just.

On the economic side, it was again only right that Germany
should pay some Reparations for the enormous damage she
had inflicted on Belgium and on eleven provinces of North-
Eastern France; let alone on other peoples in Eastern Europe
and elsewhere. Wickham Steed, under whom *The Times* was
well-informed about Europe (as under the arch-Appeaser,
Geoffrey Dawson, it was not), put the issue squarely: 'Germany went to war because she made it pay in 1870–1, and
believed she could make it pay again.'

No difference of opinion on the principle – differences arose
on the question of How much Germany could pay?

Keynes's book was chiefly concerned with the economic
issue – which was never satisfactorily settled, because it
transpired that Germany never intended to pay for what she
had been responsible for – and Keynes's book was a great aid in
helping her to get away with it. French economists never
accepted Keynes's arguments. Etienne Mantoux – killed by
the Germans in their Second War – showed that they spent
twice the amount on Re-Armament for it that they paid in
Reparations. As for these, they borrowed largely from Wall
Street and the City of London; and this had the excellent effect
of re-inforcing the pro-German sentiments prevailing in those
quarters. For the rest, Germany deliberately depreciated its
currency. The French felt themselves cheated – as they were.
(No wonder they were not keen to fight for us again in
1939–40!)

Skidelsky points out that 'the constant revision of the
schedules of German payments in the 1920s paved the way for
Hitler's successful assaults on the territorial clauses in the
1930's.' It set the pattern: the economic, and then the territorial, undermining of the Versailles settlement played
straight into Hitler's hands and made the Second War possible.
What fools his opponents were! – as indeed he thought them.
And Keynes bears a heavy responsibility here: *The Economic
Consequences of the Peace* had a greater historic effect, an
influence on events, than anything else he wrote.

Much of its popular success was due to the brilliant, malicious portraits of the men at Versailles – Lloyd George,

President Wilson, Clemenceau – wrestling with the intractable issues. Keynes's wise mother asked him to tone these caricatures down; Brand, the judicious banker, an All Souls man, warned Keynes of the damage the book would do in America – as it did. (Brand said to me during the Crisis of 1931: 'Only two men understand the Gold Standard, Keynes and I – and we don't agree.' Note that Montagu Norman of the Bank of England was not one of them.)

Keynes subsequently retracted something from his deleterious book, but it was too late – the damage had been done. In later years, with more experience of the world if not of history, he retreated from the Rationalist Fallacy I held against him and liberal intellectuals generally. In 'My Early Beliefs' he wrote, 'As cause and consequence of our general state of mind we completely misunderstood human nature, including our own.' So much for Cambridge-Bloomsbury; there could not be a more complete disclaimer. 'The rationality which we attributed to it led to a superficiality, not only of judgment but also of feeling.'

His view of history, however, continued to be naif and superficial. I noticed that, both in the *Treatise on Money* and in what he wrote about Sir Isaac Newton's papers. He was astonished to find that Newton had spent a great deal of his time on trying to make as much sense of Holy Writ as of the Universe; and that Newton was as much a Magus as he was a scientist, seeking the transmutation of metals as well as their analysis. Historians take that sort of thing for granted: the science of chemistry arose along with, if not out of, alchemy; astronomy along with astrology, etc.

Naiveté goes with optimism: historians are not prone to it. Keynes's idealistic liberal optimism arose from the happy circumstances of his early life – Cambridge – Eton – Cambridge again – in those pre-1914 days when it was bliss to be alive (and the world was never the same again).

When the Second German War was coming to an end – with all the devastation it had wrought this time in Britain and the erosion of her resources, the destruction to replace and make good – Churchill asked his economic experts what the country would be able to afford to devote to Social Services. Keynes, over-optimistic as a liberal would be, put in the maximum estimate; his colleague, Hubert Henderson, cautious Scot, suggested a minimum. Though all my admiration, and indeed affections, were with Keynes, I suspect that Henderson's was the better judgment.

3

Ernest Bevin

'The outstanding Trade Union leader produced by this, or perhaps by any other, country', so Bevin's biographer, Lord Bullock, describes him, with justice. Bevin would have agreed, for he had no middle-class false modesty: he described himself as 'a turn-up in a million', as indeed he was. No nonsense about equality in that quarter: he was indubitably a great man, essentially constructive, a builder-up.

And from what wretched beginnings! He was illegitimate – like several of the early Labour leaders: Keir Hardie, Ramsay MacDonald, J. H. Thomas. No-one knew who was Ernie's father; his mother described herself as a widow and, a fine woman, she worked herself to an early death to bring up her children. Bevin was devoted to the memory of his mother, but would never speak about the appalling struggle of his childhood. In his way he was more reticent and reserved than Attlee, who had nothing to be reserved about: all was very normal with him. Someone who had known young Ernie said, 'I'm sure there's no one in this wide world was ever poorer than he and his mother.'

In spite of this depressing background Mrs Bevin did her best for her boy. He scrabbled what intermittent elementary education he could, just reading, writing and arithmetic. He was always unsure of his grammar, but did not let that stand in his way, was a more effective and commanding speaker than those who were perfect in their English. His real training came from the West Country Nonconformist chapels he attended, in the Somerset and Devon countryside, then in Bristol, where he worked as a boy labourer, eventually graduating to driving his own horse and cart. He joined the Christian

Endeavour Society, attended evening classes at the Y.M.C.A. after the day's work, and became a local preacher. Those solid, old-fashioned Nonconformist principles stood him in good stead all his life.

He was an ardent reader, and had a passion for acquiring knowledge and for argument – in this like his later colleague, Attlee, who in his younger days at school was held to be 'self-opinionated'. Ernest Bevin was always that, never had any qualms about expressing his opinion on anything – and justly so. But he did not move his sights from chapel to politics until he was nearing thirty. He was in his sixtieth year when he became a Minister of the Crown. He was late in developing his remarkable potential, naturally enough; but, by the time he arrived at the front rank in politics, a national figure, he had a world of experience behind him – wider than any, except Churchill's.

A remarkable characteristic of Bevin's was his sheer *intellectual* ability. I have remarked elsewhere that I never heard him speak without being intellectually convinced. Most people were unaware that, behind the rough, clumsy, ungrammatical sentences, he was a match for anybody – lawyers or economists, let alone industrialists or politicians. I am astonished to realise how much he *knew*, the range of information he commanded. Another thing: he had no inferiority complex whatever, not a shadow of one – unlike MacDonald (it went with *his* sensitiveness and romanticism, but was a source of weakness). Bevin was a very masculine character; I do not think he had much sensibility or taste – it was hardly to be expected – but immense horse-sense.

My glimpses of him, though not considerable, were fewer than those of Attlee, with whom, after all, there was Oxford in common. Bevin had not much interest in universities and a great distrust of intellectuals. This was unlike his rival Morrison, who liked coming down to Oxford and several times stayed with me at All Souls; he was generous too with his time, was good to Nuffield College in holding seminars on government there, and (I think) accepted a Fellowship. Magdalen tried to corral Bevin – a very large rogue-elephant – as a Fellow; but he made nothing of it, and never came. Was Bevin a generous man? I doubt it.

It is not my purpose even to sketch his achievement, but I must point out that much that was constructive in the Labour Movement, speaking widely – Trade Unions first, the Party second – was of his doing. First, casual labour at the docks he organised into the Dockers' Union. Then he built up the big and efficient Transport Workers' Union; to which he eventually annexed the rather ineffective General Workers' Union (to which my father as a china-clay worker nominally belonged, though nothing of a Trade Unionist). Bevin was an empire builder; he made the Transport and General Workers' Union the biggest and best organised in his time. He built Transport House in Smith Square, and housed the Labour Party head-quarters in it – a significant accommodation. Labour had no voice in the daily press whatever, except George Lansbury's lively *Daily Herald,* which had a small circulation and regularly lost money. Bevin made a deal with Odhams Press to make the *Herald* a big Labour paper, went all over the country putting it across (I attended one or two of his meetings) and helped to build it up to a two million circula-tion: '*My* paper.'

Bevin came to the fore in the aftermath of the disaster of 1931, as if to fill the gap left by the loss of Labour's leaders and to repair some of the damage. In the financial crisis itself, he emerges as the only public figure who knew what to expect and the right measures to take. For this he had been equipped by his experience on the (Lord) Macmillan Committee on Finance and Industry, upon which the other historic figure was Keynes. Meeting throughout 1930 this had a profound effect on Bevin: it gave him a grasp of the working of the financial and economic system such as no other politician had, certainly not Snowden, Chancellor of the Exchequer, fixed in the Gladstonian orthodoxy of Treasury and Bank of England. Keynes challenged this intellectually, though he did not dare to draw out the logical conclusions for practical action. Bevin was not afraid to; it is astonishing how right he was, in the light of all that has happened since. Nobody thought that at the time.

Briefly, Bevin agreed with Keynes that the return to gold parity in 1926, with the pound at $4.86, had been a great mistake, damaging exports, creating unemployment, indirectly responsible for the disastrous Coal Strike, a whole train of ill consequences. (Ironically, Churchill's intuition had been against it, but as Chancellor he had been overborne by the weight and expertise of Bank and Treasury.) It emerged that these experts – Bradbury of the Pound notes and Montague Norman of the Bank – did not consider the effects on industry and employment: their blinkered vision was confined to finance, and the currency, the maintenance of the gold standard, the parity of the pound to maintain the City's prestige as the international money market. The strain on the country and its internal economy was intolerable.

Bevin urged that any necessary sacrifices should not be inflicted alone on wages and unemployment benefit, and the *rentier* class go scot free. He was not afraid to contemplate a temporary tariff (I was in favour of a tariff on luxury imports, e.g. wine, tobacco etc, to correct the imbalance of payments); and he was the only one to envisage the devaluation that was inevitable. His biographer says that Keynes 'shied away' from this, and wonders mildly, in the stagnation of Britain's economy throughout that dreary decade – when the *rentier* class never had it so good – 'whether the untrained layman did not show more understanding than all the experts who sat on or appeared before the Macmillan Committee.' I think he did, and Bevin thought so too. We may except Keynes and Lord Brand of All Souls, who understood the technical minutiae; oddly enough, Brand was less unsympathetic than the rest to Bevin's views. However, he was an international banker.

What should MacDonald have done in the *impasse* of the (to us minimal) crisis of 1931, a mere matter of raising a deficit of £75 millions? He could not throw over the immovable Snowden, plus the Treasury and the Bank of England. Having a majority of Tories and Liberals against him, he should have handed the 'poisoned chalice' to Baldwin, who had the majority with him. Instead of that he allowed himself to be flattered into remaining a figurehead of a bogus 'National' government. He was a lost man, a deserter, never forgiven by any of us.

Already during MacDonald's second Labour government Bevin was moving into the foreground with his revitalisation of the *Herald* as a Labour daily paper. In his agreement with

Odhams he was careful to keep control of political policy, and no less careful to place Trade Union members, not Labour party nominees, on the board. He had a great nose for *power*, the real stuff of politics, himself a figure (and speaker) of tremendous, indeed vehement, power. By 1933 the *Herald* was the first paper in the world to reach a two-million circulation, Bevin beating Beaverbrook.

To supplement it Bevin planned a weekly, a more reliable *New Statesman,* utterly undependable under Kingsley Martin, whom Keynes had placed as editor. This took the form of *The New Clarion*, echoing the title of Robert Blatchford's famous broadsheet, *The Clarion*. It was Bevin's brain-child; he raised the money for it, became the chairman and wrote articles for it anonymously, keeping in the background. I think that at this time he did not want to come forward into politics – though Colonel Wedgwood told him he ought to be Prime Minister. (Would that he could have been in 1931!)

Again he worked hard, this time behind the scenes, to recruit support, and I was invited to write regularly for it. I do not seem to have kept a file of the paper, as I have of the *Cornish Labour News* which I founded. But Bevin's biography tells me that I contributed twenty articles, as also did G. D. H. Cole and H. N. Brailsford, Harold Laski even more. Among other contributors were Morrison, Lansbury, Stafford Cripps, H. E. Bates and Phyllis Bentley – not however Attlee, never much of a writer. I have forgotten my articles, except that, knowing Germany and a friend of Adam von Trott, I was obsessed by the Nazi danger, and saw very early that it was all over with European Disarmament. I have not forgotten that for this foresight, obvious enough, I was occasionally labelled 'Fascist' by some young fool. *The New Clarion,* however, failed to reach a circulation to make it pay; here it was unfortunately outrun by Keynes's *New Statesman and Nation*.

Bevin now made a surprising move. G. D. H. Cole had started the New Fabian Research Bureau and the Society for Socialist Inquiry and Propaganda, and Bevin decided to give the latter his full support. Lord Bullock says, 'with their strong flavour of Hampstead, Bloomsbury, and the University Labour Clubs, neither was the sort of body with which anyone would expect Bevin to be connected.' He even consented to become Chairman of S.S.I.P. and take the lead in it; it showed how much he recognised the need, with the growing economic crisis and the failure of the Labour government to deal with it, a refusal to look at any new ideas, Snowden blocking the way, and MacDonald's faltering lack of decision, which angered even Attlee.

Attlee was a silent member of S.S.I.P. – I never saw him at its meetings – along with Cripps and Pritt, Dick Mitchison and his wife Naomi Haldane, and the deleterious, semi-Communist Postgates. 'Bevin's willingness to join such a group marked a big change of attitude on his part and, if the partnership had proved successful, it might have strengthened the Labour Movement at one of its weakest points, the gap which separated the intellectuals from the trade unionists.'

For Cole it was a chance to repair some of the damage he had done years before by leaving the Fabians – as Beatrice Webb said to me, he had taken with him all their younger generation. Fond as I was of Douglas, especially when later he came across from Univ. to All Souls, I gradually came to distrust the facile way in which he would lay down the law about the running of the coal mines or iron mills – had he ever been in one to know how?

Myself, I wasn't much of a socialist when it came to economics – I always believed in work, and properly differentiated incentives. The old formula of the nationalisation of 'the means of production, distribution and exchange' meant nothing to me; as for nationalisation of the land, could one see the Labour Party running agriculture! I believed only in the extension of public corporations, such as the Port of London Authority, or the BBC, or the London Transport Board – as Morrison and Keynes did. (And why couldn't Keynes work with us to that end?) For the rest, I was obsessed by the growing threat from Germany; while Chamberlain and Co. regularly sold the pass to our enemies as well as the interests of Britain, when we should have supported and gathered together our friends – even reaching an understanding with USSR, with both under threat. Churchill always thought that it need never have come to war – we should simply not have allowed Hitler to re-arm. Fundamentally, it was the ineptitude – worse, the sabotaging of our own interests and those of the democracies – to play the game of Hitler, Mussolini and Franco, that kept me on the Left in all that evil decade.

What was S.S.I.P. supposed to be doing? Bevin himself put the purpose – 'that of projecting ideas. It is not a ginger group to the Party, or anything of that kind; it is an attempt to work out problems and to give the new generation something to grip. A good many of us feel that the younger people are just drifting; there is a kind of apathy which is appalling.' I had just produced my *Politics and the Younger Generation*, in time to have it caught in the disaster of 1931; but there was a good deal of talk about the younger generation and the gap in leadership with a whole generation of the best lost in the holocaust of 1914–18. (What we have to thank the Germans for!)

Oxford was good recruiting ground for the new generation: there Cole was our leader. I brought along my friends from All Souls, Richard Pares and G. F. Hudson (who knew about the Far East), and I recall from our body the beautiful, but serious-minded, Elizabeth Harman, to become well-known later as Lady Longford. We foregathered for several meetings at Lady Warwick's Easton Lodge at Dunmow. This was the inheritance of that extravagant beauty, a Maynard, mistress of Edward VII.

How well I remember it all: the big house with its Edwardian flavour, palms and aspidistras. In the grounds was a summerhouse, the 'temple of friendship', dedicated to those bygone days, photographs of Edward and his 'exotic entourage', to which the favoured were permitted access. There was the old lady herself – she had been converted to socialism years before by the condition of the chain-workers of Birmingham: still beautiful, violet eyes, ample velvety bosom, pneumatic bliss. She and Ernie Bevin sat there peaceably overflowing their armchairs together; I don't know which was fatter.

My mind was distracted by the scene and her, I don't know what we talked about, mostly hot air – 'What I am thinking in terms of . . . ' Cole would begin, Bevin looking benevolently on, saying nothing. When we got back to Oxford, Pares directed my wandering attention to an item in a Brighton book-catalogue: a cheap French novel by Paul de Kock, morocco bound and inscribed 'For lovely Warwick, from

Albert Edward, Xmas 1894.' It inspired me to send her, for her kindness to us, a little book I valued (and could not replace), François Mauriac's *Vie de Province*.

Then misfortune struck S.S.I.P. Among those seeking to give a 'new lead' after the disarray of 1931 was Stafford Cripps. A good deal of a crank himself, for all his forensic ability, he had the faculty of attracting cranks around him, along with them a break-away group from the hopeless I.L.P. The Independent Labour Party had had a distinguished past, as the nursing ground for leaders like MacDonald and Snowden. It had now dwindled into a pathetic faction, with long-haired Jimmy Maxton as leader, going round asking, 'Tell me what I am to do, and I will do it.' Talk about 'making bricks without straw'! – a sickening exhibition of ineffectiveness.

There now came up a proposal to unite the Socialist League they formed with S.S.I.P. Initially Bevin was not opposed, he suspended judgment. I was all along in favour of the widest front possible against the unspeakable Old Men of the 'National' Government. But, an unimportant young man in the ranks, I knew nothing of the negotiations, or that the crackpots of the Socialist League were so hostile to Bevin that they refused not only to have him as Chairman but to accept him in any office at all! Talk about sense of power – lack of it was the endemic disease of the Labour Party, one of the things that had sickened MacDonald, as it was sickening me. (It was also the fatal disease of the Social Democrats in Germany, and enabled Hitler, who knew all about power, to brush them aside with the greatest ease.) Here were the crackpots of the Left alienating the most powerful, and biggest-minded, man in the Trade Union Movement, and Cole – reluctantly – capitulated.

The effect on Bevin was permanent: it confirmed his distrust for intellectuals for good and all. His attempt to work with them in a common effort went by the board. To Cole he wrote, 'How could anyone have followed you in the last ten years?' – referring to Cole's book on the Next Ten Years. 'Really, old man, look how you have boxed the compass.' 'When we have tried to associate with the intellectuals, our experience has been that they do not stay the course very long. . . . You see, the difference between the intellectuals and the trade unions is this: You have no responsibility, you can fly off at a tangent as the wind takes you. We, however, must be consistent and we have a great amount of responsibility.'

As usual, Bevin's case was unanswerable. I was an intellectual myself, but not a middle-class one with no roots in the Movement, and I did 'stay the course' until the bitter end in 1939–40. However, I did not follow Cole again. Margaret Cole wrote me a kind, patronising letter approving my 'loyalty to the Executive' at this juncture; but I was not wholly apprized of what was afoot, and may have been wrong – as they were. Cole should have stayed with Bevin at all costs, instead of allowing himself to be pressured by the semi-Communist Postgates. I always remained on personally affectionate terms with him, and managed to persuade him not to stand for the University seat at Oxford at the election which returned Arthur Salter. I got him to back Salter, with the widest range of support against Chamberlain – anything, anything to get rid of the Old Man before too late. Ultimately it was too late.

There now came up something vastly more important: Mussolini's invasion of Abyssinia and the first crucial test of the 'National' government's sincerity in its foreign policy. Would they allow him to get away with it, or would they make effective the declared policy of Collective Security – i.e. that of the democracies – against an obvious aggressor? The Trade Union Congress was solid on the issue, led by Bevin and Citrine, who declared: 'There is only one way of dealing with a bully, and that is by force. Moral resolutions are no good.' The Government sought the support of the Labour Party, in the cause of unity in case of war.

After 1931 the 'National' government had some 550 MPs in the Commons – they could have done anything in the nation's interest – to 55 Labour MPs. All the experienced leaders of the Party were out of Parliament; the leadership fell by default to George Lansbury, a secondary figure who commanded much affection for his overflowing heart, with Attlee as Deputy Leader, an unknown quantity.

Labour's support in the interest of national unity was responsibly given by the Trade Union Congress, and by the resolutions of the Party Executive. Lansbury as leader had accepted this, and then his 'conscience', his emotions, got the better of him and he went back on his undertaking – really an old Pacifist sheep. He was supported by Stafford Cripps, no Pacifist, but with the clever argument that the 'National' Government, having been given the confidence of the Labour Party, would use it for another snap election and catch the Party at maximum disadvantage. There *was* that danger; nevertheless it was the duty of a responsible Party to incur it if necessary.

The issue came before the Brighton Conference, the most dramatic in the Party's history – until 1940 – and it was debated all day. Bevin was justly angry at Lansbury's exposing a rift in Labour's leadership at a time of crisis – to him it was like 1931 over again with MacDonald. Bevin gave the Conference a lead with a vehement speech which raised protests from sentimentalists, who thought he was brutal to Lansbury – Bevin in effect was giving him notice. 'If he finds that he ought to take a certain course, then his conscience should direct him as to the course he should take. It is placing the Movement and the Executive in an absolutely wrong position to be hawking your conscience round from body to body to be told what you ought to do with it.'

It was a most dramatic moment when this direct challenge to the old man was made: I held my breath, many people were shocked by Bevin's words. But there was no getting away from it: his argument was unanswerable. By the time he finished the Conference did not want to hear any more bleatings from Lansbury: he had to go. Bevin's anger was directed no less at Stafford Cripps; and in his own defence he could argue, 'the great crime of Ramsay MacDonald was that he never called in his Party; and the crime of these people is that they have sown discord at the very moment when candidates want unity to face an election.'

For, of course, Baldwin – a party-politician before anything – having got the green light from the Labour Party took the opportunity to catch it out, as Cripps had foretold. The Tories won another disproportionate majority – some 450 seats to Labour's 155. L. S. Amery was a Conservative figure whom the Old Men kept out during the whole of that decade, because he consistently opposed Appeasing the dictators. He admitted to me that the Election of 1935 was a deception.

Baldwin's government put up a half-hearted token resistance to Mussolini, while privately determined not to topple him over. Hitler immediately drew the conclusion as to what he could get away with, and in 1936 militarised the Rhineland. He was thereupon allowed to get away with that and the aggressions that followed: Austria, then Czecho-Slovakia, which overturned the whole balance of power in Europe. – Until, eventually, it took the might of the United States and Russia to overpower Germany and save us. For – though no one states the fact – in 1940 Britain was defeated as well as France.

It was not merely the ineptitude of the British governing class during that decade, which brought this about: it was their connivance. They sold the pass because of their fear of Communism. Opposition to Communism was understandable and right enough; no one was more anti-Communist than Churchill. But he had the strategic sense to see that the immediate threat came from Germany – Soviet Russia was no danger in the Thirties. We should in fact have joined with her in containing Hitler's Germany, as Churchill thought. Then, as he also thought – he always called the Second German War the 'Unnecessary War' – Hitler would have been unable to break out: the abscess would have burst inside.

In 1940 Labour joined up with Churchill to save the country. He made Bevin Minister of Labour and National Service, and from that moment his enormous career became part of the history of Britain. The story of it is told, possibly in too much detail, in the second volume of Bullock's three-decker biography (two volumes would have been enough). Party politics were over 'for the duration', and the Minister passed out of my ken. I have to offer no more than what those who worked with him have told me, though I did see him occasionally in London and he told me a thing or two in chats with him – I noted them for the record.

Briefly, what Bevin did in 1940–5 was a tremendous job: he re-created the Ministry of Labour to organise bit by bit the whole man-power and woman-power of Britain for the war effort. He did it by his own principle of 'Voluntaryism', as he called it clumsily, against all those, like Beveridge, who wanted industrial conscription. Bevin knew better. Paradoxically this great Trade Union boss was more of a democrat: instinct and experience told him that he would get better results from the workers if he brought them willingly into the war effort, consulted them, kept touch with them, journeyed round over war-scarred Britain, gained their confidence and shared with them what was involved. He was much criticised in Parliament – and always resented criticism personally, especially ill-informed criticism. He was more in touch with the working class, belonged to it, and spoke their language. (His forceful, ungrammatical way of speaking, dropped h's and all, were an advantage in talking to the men in the works: he was one of them.)

His technique worked, and he gradually won his battle. He would content himself with 80 per cent of what he wanted, and at the next opportunity slip in the remaining 20 per cent. He was full of ideas, his civil servants realised that he had more than anybody, and *knew* more of the subject – he had been in it all his life. They too rallied to him with enthusiasm, as later at the Foreign Office, where the eminent civil servants were grateful for a Minister who knew his own mind.

An important point that is overlooked is that Bevin was always a social reformer. Educationally he had had no chances at all – so he was keen on raising the school-leaving age. In his colossal task of organising the whole of British humanity to fight the evil thing – in Germany they did not make use of woman-power to the same extent and the German people fed well enough by starving the rest of Europe – Bevin kept working-class conditions in the front of his mind, food and health, hours and wages, and housing as far as possible in all the destruction going on from the German mania. (Once, he let out that he really hated the Germans – understandably – but that he strove to keep an impartial judgment.)

Bevin had always been concerned about the health and well-being of his men. He once told me that 'his' London bus-drivers had a high incidence of duodenal ulcer (no doubt from strain, irregular meals, stooping over their steering-wheels), and that he had got his Transport Union to vote a considerable sum to the Manor Road (Trade Union) Hospital for research into the causes and conditions of duodenal and gastric ulcers. I noted then how characteristically imaginative of him.

As Minister of Labour his most strenuous battle was with Beaverbrook as Minister of Aircraft Production, who wanted priority for aircraft and, even after he had achieved his targets, pushed to extend his empire at the expense of other urgent necessities. The hostility between the two is well known; Bevin himself told me that Beaverbrook exerted himself all he could to get him out of the government. The irresponsibility of that, and at such a time! Bevin, with the support of the Labour Movement was immovable: it was Beaverbrook who went. Bevin went from strength to strength; Churchill well realised his essential contribution to the war effort, his patriotism and loyalty, his indispensability, and came to lean on him, treating him with exceptional consideration as no one else.

Those two great men balanced each other, each a heavyweight in the scales: Churchill in the conduct of the war, Bevin in home affairs. It is ironical, after the vacuity of the Thirties, that the inner cabinet in charge of home affairs during the war consisted of three Labour men and one civil servant: Attlee, Bevin, Morrison and Sir John Anderson. As the end of Germany's preposterous effort approached, the government became concerned with post-war plans. Rab Butler assured me how much he learned from Bevin, serving under him on the committee to consider these questions. Butler succeeded him as Minister of Labour in Churchill's Conservative government, both men made it clear that Bevin's plans for demobilisation and re-settlement would be adhered to.

The great men who had saved Britain – Churchill, Bevin, Attlee – were all in favour of maintaining the national union until the war with Japan was over, in perhaps six months, and that that was the proper time for an Election. Those three were looking at it from the standpoint of world affairs and Britain's influence in them. The party politicians thought otherwise; and in the Labour Party Morrison and Aneurin Bevan joined forces to precipitate an Election.

From the Party point of view they were proved right: there was an immense overturn in the country, and Labour won a disproportionately large victory to compensate for the historic injustice of the Thirties. Since this is a personal account, personal recollections, I may say that Ellen Wilkinson, 'Red Ellen', told me that when she toured the Occupied Area in Germany and asked British soldiers why they had all voted Labour, they replied blissfully, 'Well, miss, – anything for a change!' In the constituency where I had worked as a candidate for so long, which now went Labour, people told me that they had voted Labour but were 'sorry for Mr Churchill' – decent of them.

Churchill was angry at what he considered the British people's ingratitude. He had, however, warned Stalin that it might happen: in Britain there were two Parties and he might be voted out. Stalin was able to assure him that 'one Party is much better.' At Potsdam Molotov complained to Attlee that he had told them he expected only a small majority. They simply could not understand the working of a democracy, were convinced that it must have been arranged – and what was the explanation? (Like Talleyrand at the Congress of Vienna, when the Russian ambassador died: 'Dear me, I wonder what was his motive?') Churchill met his Conservative Ministers with only one consoling thought: Bevin was going to be Foreign Secretary, and 'he is as firm as a rock.'

Bevin himself wanted, and expected, to be Chancellor of the Exchequer; after his long and formative experience with the Macmillan Committee he considered that he knew 'all about' economic and financial questions. And indeed his hunches, his instinctive understanding of them, were more reliable and sound than those of the economic experts, themselves always divided, often giving contradictory advice. Attlee's chief motive in preferring Bevin to the Foreign Office was that he would be firm as a rock in dealing with the Russians – he had had a lifetime's experience in dealing with Communists and fellow-travellers.

At the Party's Victory celebration Bevin encountered Kingsley Martin, editor of the factious *New Statesman,* mouthpiece of the intellectuals: "ullo, oogly – 'ow long before you'll be stabbin' us in the back?' It was only a matter of weeks. Malcolm Muggeridge, with his usual Christian charity, says that he could not stand Kingsley Martin's physical proximity. Myself, I could not stand his intellectual proximity. Kingsley Martin was not a bad man, nor a Communist; he was just inside-out: whatever his own country did was always wrong, the other side (usually USSR, never the USA) right; and, of course, his own Party under Bevin's leadership always wrong.

Never a good word for, or even an attempt to understand, Bevin's policy the whole time he was Foreign Secretary, and a great one. It sickened me, as it sickened George Orwell. We do not need to go into the record here: Bevin personally turned Marshall Aid – the American offer of help to Europe – into a measure for the complete economic Reconstruction of Europe. Even Molotov inclined to favour it, until Stalin brutally vetoed it. Bevin had the measure of Stalin, and was left alone in the breach to stand up to him, while the Americans still suffered from Democratic illusions about the Russians under a hopelessly ignorant Secretary of State, Byrnes. Not until President Truman himself, new to international affairs, tumbled to the facts, did they get it right.

Stalin complained that Bevin was 'no gentleman': a *petit-bourgeois* himself, he encountered a real working-class man in Bevin. Molotov – a middle-class man, cousin of the composer Scriabin (which was his own real name) – complained that Bevin did not treat Soviet representatives with proper respect. In a good humour Ernest would occasionally slap the monster on the back, though he always called him Mowlotov, even after being corrected. Privately, Ernest regarded him as a murderer, and indeed he had connived at Stalin's multiple murders – though Molotov's own wife was held under arrest for several years. What a society!

In Dean Acheson, Bevin had an opposite number in Washington worthy of himself: a great American Secretary of State. Acheson's tribute to Bevin was that he 'could lead and learn at the same time.' To Ernest the youthful-looking Dean was always 'My boy'.

The Left Intellectuals backed the Communists to win in the Civil War in Greece, and attacked Churchill, then Bevin, bitterly for their resistance. (The Americans were at sea about the issue in Greece also.) Bevin had no illusions, he knew Communists only too well, and the appalling massacres they were perpetrating in Greece (this is not to deny that there were massacres on the other side too). What the Left Intellectuals did not know was that Stalin himself had given over the

Communists in Greece. An utter realist, he had made a deal with Churchill as to respective spheres: Roumania and Bulgaria the Russian sphere, Greece that of the West. Loyal to the agreement, Stalin left the Communists in Greece to their fate.

Their endless nagging abuse of Bevin merely confirmed his distrust of intellectuals. A propos of Dick Crossman, to whom he had given his chances on a Palestinian Commission – during which he crossed sides – Bevin said that he wouldn't have university men in the Cabinet: 'you can't trust 'em.' Loyalty was a keynote of his nature – loyalty and responsibility. Though Attlee was not his creation as Party Leader – as I used to think – Bevin came to appreciate from working with him his exceptional qualities.

These were not obvious to the world outside, for Attlee would never push himself or put himself across: extraordinarily selfless for a politician. In consequence there were several attempts to replace him. Morrison always thought that he ought to be Leader, and several times tried to nudge Clem out. Actually, Attlee did not like Morrison; he liked Aneurin Bevan better, though he gave so much trouble. Nye, as a complete Celt, had a warm, lovable personality. Morrison was the Party's best tactician; Bevin did not appreciate this, he considered Morrison an intriguer. I am bound to own that, though I admire Bevin more, he was unfair to Morrison. He would never serve in government under Morrison, and that effectively excluded him from the leadership. Herbert could never reconcile himself to this and, for all his splendid career of achievement, died a disappointed man – as most politicians do.

There was a funny scene when Cripps and Dalton joined forces to lever Attlee out and get Bevin to take his place. One of them put it to the lumbering old fellow getting out of his car in Downing Street – by this time eyes and face twitching with overwork and strain: 'No. I'm stickin' with little Clem.' When I had a chat with him about this time at the Garrick Club, of which he enjoyed being a member and where he used to lunch companionably, he told me that he hadn't been to bed before 2 a.m. for years. By that time he looked it.

An essentially constructive mind, a builder, Bevin was

often angry at the frustrations and abortiveness of international relations. When one reads Bullock's detailed third volume, devoted to Bevin's five years as Foreign Secretary, 1945–50, one is appalled by the complexity of the events Bevin had to deal with – a world smashed-up by the German mania (Tacitus knew it, *furor teutonicus*) – and the weak hand he had to play. He made the most of it: no-one could have done more, not even Churchill as much, in the conditions that prevailed. As an historian I doubt if any Foreign Secretary before him ever had to operate under such difficulties. For his achievement consult that volume: here I confine myself to my last glimpses of him. In the early complications of the Palestinian issue, he told me that he was within an ace of clinching an agreement between Jews and Arabs, had in fact an understanding with the US State Department, when it was thrown over by Truman, who had an election to consider in New York with its large Jewish electorate. Such are the amenities of politics.

Bevin made a great Foreign Secretary – he grew to that job and had an instinctive grasp of international affairs, as I am afraid my friend, Herbert Morrison, showed that he had not, when he insisted on succeeding Bevin. As with Attlee himself, the extraordinary thing about Bevin was his capacity for growth. His lifelong experience as a Trade Unionist had made him a formidable negotiator; and the international contacts of Trade Unionism, the conferences, had initiated him into world affairs. And he had travelled. Morrison suffered from the disadvantage of lack of education. I knew him better than I did Bevin. It was pathetic that, when Morrison was Foreign Secretary, he was trying to learn French. Ernie would have known better than to try; he had the instinct and the knack for foreign affairs, and the decision. No wonder his officials adored him; one of them described him to me, squaring himself up: 'I won't 'ave it.'

All the same, though Bevin spoke freely and unreservedly to me, one had no sense of intimacy with him. I was never close to him. Few people were. Lord Bullock sums up fairly, 'Even those who agreed with him . . . often found him difficult to approach. He was reserved in private life, suspicious and slow to give his trust or admit anyone as a friend. His ability, his strength of character and determination were obvious and admitted; but he was respected or feared rather than loved, and his position in the Labour Movement, although powerful, left him personally isolated.' I am afraid that he had not the upper-class ethical high-mindedness of Attlee; he was working-class, and apt to be vindictive.

Then, too, 'like Churchill, Bevin enjoyed being a Minister and exercising power with that uninhibited enjoyment which shocked the conventional but was one of the hallmarks of both men's strength.' Why should it be inhibited? Why should the dull and conventional set standards for remarkable people? Practically all remarkable people have a strong ego, the source of their strength. Attlee wrote of Bevin, 'like Stafford Cripps he was a tremendous egotist – Ernest having the egotism of the artist, Stafford the egotism of the altruist.' And then, 'Ernest looked, and indeed was, the embodiment of common sense. Yet I have never met a man in politics with as much imagination as he had, with the exception of Winston.'

Though we all admired him, Bevin did not have a personal following, as Morrison had, and even Dalton, both of whom did their best to encourage young recruits to the Movement. I recall traipsing round the China Clay area in Cornwall as a candidate, with Bevin speaking; but he was there as a Trade Unionist, not as a Labour Party politician, and I do not suppose that he was interested in my candidature (or anybody else's). When I told him some years later that I was giving it up, all he said was, 'Get another constituency.'

By that time I had had enough – or, rather, too much. All the same, as I go over the ground at home today I often think of that great lumbering figure, who became a statesman on the stage of world affairs, coming down to speak to the men in the works, at a street corner, or at the cross-roads, when only half-a-dozen would turn up to hear him in those days, the paralysis of the Thirties over all the land.

4

C. R. Attlee

Attlee has this in common with President Truman that he turns out to have been a much bigger man historically than anyone realised at the time. Of course each of them attained the summit of power to become leader of his nation, as Prime Minister and President respectively; but this was largely by accident – politics is full of accidents – and no-one expected it. Truman did not want to become President of the United States; he was perfectly content to be Senator for Missouri; and Attlee can hardly have expected – perhaps hardly wanted – to become Prime Minister of Great Britain.

Each of them proved himself a greater man in office, and paradoxically each has reached a higher pinnacle of estimation after his death. This is not the usual way with political figures, let alone ordinary politicians. A famous tag of Tacitus may be applied in reverse. A Roman who everybody thought capable of ruling before he came to the job was found to be no good at it: *capax imperii nisi imperasset*. With Truman and Attlee, no-one would have thought beforehand that they would prove so good at it – and now, we know, even better. In fact they grew with the job, coping with events increased their capacity to deal with them. As Churchill put it, in his own way, when someone remarked how much Attlee had developed: 'If you take a wasp and feed it on royal honey, in time it becomes a queen-bee.' This points the contrast with his earlier remark, when someone defended Attlee as a 'modest man', 'He has plenty to be modest about.' Churchill himself was far from modest: why should he be?

Even at the end of Attlee's life – with an historic career behind him and all the events of history into which he had entered – his estimate of himself was absurdly modest. He had got a Second Class in the History School – appropriately awarded, by my old friend Sir Charles Grant Robertson of All Souls. If he had got a First, he would have stayed up at Oxford and tried to become a Fellow of a College. 'I've no regrets, but in fact it has been the second-best thing', he said to an interviewer. 'If I could have chosen to be anything in those days I'd have become a Fellow of Univ.' It was an extraordinary summing up. He was blissfully happy at University College, across the High Street from All Souls; his second year there was the happiest in his life – though he made no impression as an undergraduate, just a quiet, good sort of fellow, whose only prize was for playing billiards.

He remained always loyal to Oxford and loved coming down for a break from the unceasing grind of politics – for he was always a conscientious hard worker. Thus it was at Oxford that I mostly saw him to speak to, a man of few words; I had glimpses of him publicly at Labour Party Conferences, and once or twice he came down to Cornwall to speak for me during the ghastly Thirties when I was the Labour candidate for Penryn and Falmouth. It was an uphill struggle, though the decade of work I put into it (not entirely wasted, for I learned a good deal about politics and people in the course of it) turned it into a Labour seat in 1945. Clem's brother, Tom, lived in the constituency at Perranarworthal. He took no active part in politics but dedicated himself to the W.E.A. (Workers' Educational Association); however, his correspondence with Clem kept his brother apprised of affairs in Cornwall.

It is typical that I cannot remember when I first set eyes on Attlee, for his was an appearance so unstriking as to be almost invisible. Most leaders stand out by their appearance: Ernest Bevin, that huge bulk, once seen never forgotten; Ramsay MacDonald, with handsome looks, mop of waving hair and glowing eyes; George Lansbury, with old-fashioned ginger mutton-chops and Cockney accent, like a Victorian cabman; Philip Snowden, crippled, with narrow, wizened face, marked by pain, sharp chin and hissing s's, with a sudden sweet wintry smile; Mussolini, with the heavy ill-shaven jowl and bald scalp of a convict; Bukharin, copper-red beard. (I never saw Hitler with his mesmeric eyes.) Attlee looked like the Average Man and merged with the background.

One used to see him, one of many on the platform at Party Conferences, smoking his pipe and doodling, hardly ever looking up or listening to the waffle poured forth on such occasions. But, when Ernest Bevin spoke, Clem woke up and was all attention; for Bevin was powerful horse-sense incarnate, and he, with Walter Citrine, another commonsense man, commanded the Trade Union block-vote which held the majority and decided issues. I never heard Bevin speak but I felt it was self-evidently right.

The catastrophic Election of 1931 was decisive for Attlee. Labour was deserted by its leaders – MacDonald, who certainly had charisma; Snowden, generally respected; Jimmy Thomas, the Railwaymen's leader, un-admirable but popular (even with King George V: their language had much in common. 'Your Majesty, I've got an 'orrible 'eadache.' 'Take a couple of aspirates, Mr Thomas.' I do not believe this story: George V would not have known what an aspirate was). The 'National' Government got 550 MPs behind it; Labour's representation in Parliament was reduced by the panic to some 55. The consequences were disastrous. The 'National' government took every wrong course: contraction of social services, increase of unemployment, instead of expansion; severe deflation when a dose of moderate inflation would then have been the right course; a ruinous foreign policy that enabled first Mussolini to get away with aggression, then Hitler following his example and taking the measure of the nerveless lot he was confronted with. Attlee condemns the record wholly and justly in his autobiography, *As It Happened*.

The Parliamentary consequences were hardly less deleterious. The Panic Election of 1931 repeated that of 1924, when the Labour Party was framed by the Red Letter scare. A very young man then, I was astonished that people could be such fools as to be taken in so easily. But again in 1931 – with a mere rump of an Opposition of 55, this unbalanced the working of Parliamentary institutions, and confirmed distrust throughout the Labour Movement. Baldwin, the most powerful man in British politics from 1924 to 1937, claimed that he encouraged the maturing of the Labour Party towards responsibility. In fact, the sequence of fraud Elections, 1924, 1931, 1935, which enabled the Tory Party to hold power through most of the period between the wars, gravely undermined the sense of responsibility and increased distrust of whatever came from the upper classes – even when they were right, as they were (belatedly) over Re-armament. (Neville Chamberlain was mainly responsible for holding it up.)

George Lansbury, a secondary figure in the Labour Party, became Leader of the Opposition in these disheartening circumstances. Major Attlee, a quite unknown quantity, became Deputy Leader and worked doubly hard to cover all the subjects left bare, unprovided of any qualified speakers – they were all out of Parliament. It was this accident that gave Attlee his historic opportunity, and he conscientiously made the most of it. A naturally laconic man, he covered more columns of Hansard in those depressing years than anyone.

In the country at large the Party needed pulling together, reorganising from top to bottom by a first-rate administrator. Herbert Morrison was just the man for that job, when Arthur Henderson stepped down as Treasurer, the key post in the structure – as Morrison showed when Labour won the London County Council and he gave it efficient and inspiring leadership. (I recruited Douglas Jay's wife at this juncture for social services on the L.C.C., to which she devoted years of work.)

Morrison could have done much the same for the Labour Party's organisation in the country. Careful steps were taken to see that he did not get the chance. He was the leader of the constituency parties, i.e. the political wing of the Movement, in which I was his convinced supporter. He was opposed by the Trade Unions, which were determined to hold up his advance; and at the Leicester Party Conference, where I was a delegate, I watched the manoeuvre with a sickening heart.

Before it I had gone over from Oxford to Inkpen to urge Hugh Dalton to back Morrison for Treasurer. To my astonishment Dalton declared himself against – when he must have known that Morrison was the best man for the job. Much disheartened, I privately concluded that Dalton was being careful to keep in step with the Trade Unions, especially with Ernest Bevin, Morrison's inveterate enemy. At Leicester the manoeuvre was worked. The motion brought forward was drafted to exclude anyone of Cabinet stature from being Treasurer – quite obviously designed to exclude Morrison. Laski, popular as a speaker but a light-weight politically, of no judgment, was brought in to speak for the motion; naif as he was, he may not have realised who was pulling the strings. I watched Morrison, white with suppressed anger at the game being played to exclude him. The Party went without the re-organisation it so badly needed, stumbling on as inefficiently as before. The game of 'making bricks without straw' I used to call it biblically, more and more sickened as I watched it.

Attlee had nothing to do with these manoeuvres: he was not that sort of man. Altogether he put in fourteen years of solid good work in the East End, at social services and then administration as Mayor of Limehouse, for which he was elected MP. So that he was a London figure, hardly known in the country at large. As his official biographer (my early protégé), Kenneth Harris, says: 'Few people thought much about Attlee at all.' He was almost H. G. Wells's 'Invisible Man'.

Another accident, or chapter of accidents, made him the Party's Leader. No-one expected it. At the Brighton Party Conference the overriding issue was Mussolini's invasion of Abyssinia: should Labour support the National Government in a showdown with Mussolini, the threat of armed interven-tion if necessary? The responsible elements in the Party – as against the lunatic fringe of pacifists and cranks – brought the Conference round to support a direct confrontation with Mussolini, if it came about. What gave serious trouble was that the Party's leader, George Lansbury, was a declared Pacifist, which played straight into Mussolini's hand, as it did Hitler's.

Attlee himself says the last word on this issue: 'Socialist pacifism was a product of the optimistic Victorian era when the British Navy ruled the seas and when the idea of a world war seemed remote. Liberals and socialists held to this idea.' Again, on the general issue so much debated today in con-nexion with Nuclear Disarmament: 'Non-resistance is not a political attitude: it is a personal attitude. I do not believe it is a possible policy for people with responsibility.' This is put characteristically – not at all controversially, but unanswerably. However much one might wish to be an absolute pacifist, in an ideal world – in the real world, with human beings as they are, it is not practical politics; i.e. as Attlee says, it is an individual attitude, not a political one – really not relevant to politics.

This was what Ernest Bevin meant when he challenged Lansbury's conduct as Party Leader. The conference overwhelmingly supported Bevin; Lansbury resigned and Attlee was elected Leader, again unexpectedly. We of the constituency parties, the political wing, all wanted Morrison. So now did Dalton, too late: he regarded Attlee's election as 'a wretched disheartening result! And a little mouse shall lead them.' Bevin wanted Arthur Greenwood, a good-hearted fellow, but too easy-going. It was the MPs in Parliament, mostly Trade Unionists, who had seen Attlee's day-by-day devotion to his work there, who made him Leader.

That evening I spent mostly alone with him in our hotel. I was far from enthusiastic, all my hopes had been for Morrison. Attlee sat there glumly smoking his pipe and said practically nothing. I thought that he had plenty to worry about; now I realise that he was a great one for not taking his hurdles till he came to them.

Thereupon Stafford Cripps's cynical expectation of the National Government was fulfilled: having been given the trust of the Labour Movement to do justice on Mussolini, Baldwin took the chance to declare a snap election and catch out the Labour Party yet again. The Election of 1935 was just as fraudulent – as a leading Conservative, Leo Amery, admitted to me. The Labour Party returned only 155 MPs; the 'National' Government commanded an overwhelming majority and could have led the nation in accordance with its interests and those of the other European democracies. Instead, it betrayed both, beginning with Italy, continuing with Spain and Hitler's Germany.

Its inner guiding line was, quite simply, anti-Communism, for which it followed what it took to be its class interests, and sacrificed Britain's. It put up a token show against Mussolini, while anxious not to topple him over. His Abyssinian war could have been easily stopped by sinking a ship in the Suez

Canal, then under British control. When this point was put by Sir Reginald Coupland at All Souls to Sir John Simon, then Foreign Secretary, Simon replied, 'But that means Mussolini would fall!' This gives their game away. Attlee knew Simon well – he had served for months with him on drafting a constitution for India (whence Attlee learned much about India for himself). He later summed him up: 'Simon was a lawyer – justify anything, believed in nothing.'

The next crisis that came up was the Abdication of King Edward VIII in 1936. Here the Parliamentary Labour Party, informed of the facts of the case by Baldwin, were in agreement with him and his government. Attlee pays this Old Man of the Sea a generous tribute for the way in which he handled the awkward affair. 'The Party – with the exception of a few of the intelligentsia who can be trusted to take the wrong view on any subject – were in agreement with the views I expressed.'

This was one for the likes of me and my (then) younger generation, who were not informed of the facts, who did not take an old-fashioned moralistic view of the matter and were inclined to think of Baldwin, Archbishop Lang and Co as humbugs. I freely admit now that I was wrong; but my attitude was not a sentimental one. I had no sympathy for Edward VIII and Mrs Simpson; my motivation was political. – Anything, anything at all to get rid of the paralytic Old Men of the 'National' Government, Baldwin, Chamberlain, Simon, Sam Hoare, the lot. This was Churchill's motive too, not simply emotional loyalty to an unsuitable monarch. They, however, stuck to power; Churchill, and the Labour Party, *out*, until in 1940 it was virtually too late.

Hitler's conquest of Western Europe was the culmination of seven years of Appeasement – not even then did the architect of it lose the support of that unspeakable House of Commons, where he still had a majority. Enough of them however deserted him to demand a real national union at the crisis of our fate. The Labour Party would never serve under Chamberlain after the experiences of the Thirties. But who was to lead the nation? The King apparently favoured Halifax, as many Labour people did because of his record in India. Once more we were wrong, and Attlee was right.

He favoured Churchill – as Churchill himself did. The men both on the Left and on the Right, who had been kept out during that dreary decade – Churchill, Eden, Attlee, Bevin, Morrison – came together to save the nation. Attlee became Deputy Prime Minister. During the First German War he had served as an officer in Gallipoli, and was always convinced that Churchill was right over the Dardanelles Campaign – that it was only by accident that it did not succeed, as it should have done. This made for an unspoken bond of understanding between the two. Attlee had been a good officer; a Public School boy, he had enjoyed the discipline and his O.T.C. training. So that he had – unlike most Labour people – a natural habit of command. This is an important clue to his success as leader, presiding over the snakepit of the Labour Party for so many years, when no-one else could have done. This clue most people missed, and wondered how he managed to hold on, when several times challenged. Again, in government, it was important that he was a member of the governing class (as a child he had succeeded to young Winston Churchill's governess).

I once asked Lord Strang of the Foreign Office how Attlee compared as an administrator with Chamberlain, whose chief claim was that he was a methodical, orderly administrator, unlike the indolent Baldwin. Strang answered that Chamberlain was not in the same class: Attlee had a natural instinct for running the machine of government. Montgomery regarded Attlee as far superior to Churchill as chairman of the Cabinet – a man of genius, Churchill had too many ideas and talked too much. And, as Lloyd George noted, Attlee had much safer judgment.

All this was invisible to us. Attlee remained a mole in the background – actually an indispensable link in the machine – though he had none of the magic of Churchill's oratory or was capable of his inspiration. So we continued to underestimate him. I remember a meeting in my rooms at All Souls, where I had succeeded G. D. H. Cole for a time in running his socialist group, the 'pink dons'. Attlee came down, sat with the others on the floor of the crowded room, and never uttered a word – he might as well not have been there. I remember thinking, suppose if Hitler's Deputy, Göring, were here, he would make his presence felt all right!

It was a defect in a political leader to have so little presence, and no charisma at all. MacDonald had had too much, and in Labour's reaction to him in 1931 it was a commendation of Attlee that he had no 'side'. In fact he disliked any 'side' in people, and did not care for that element in Churchill, an essential part of his dramatic personality and of his appeal to the people. On the other hand, it was thus that Attlee conserved his energy and never wasted a word. Though a wiry man, he was not strong physically, and led a controlled, disciplined life – with the bonus of a happy marriage and family background, happy and contented at his Public School (unlike so many rebels who came over to the Left in consequence). Thus he was an exceptionally well-balanced man, no 'personality' troubles; hence his extraordinarily trustworthy judgment (though even he was belated about Re-armament, while Dalton was right).

Attlee had a dislike of volatile intellectuals, like Harold Laski or Dick Crossman. His public rebuke to Laski, with his itch for the limelight, is well known: 'A period of silence from you will be welcome.' After which Laski curled up and eventually faded out. Attlee put paid to Laski's prolific outpourings on politics with a quiet phrase to me: 'He never did get the hang of it.'

Crossman, who once hoped to succeed Laski at the L.S.E., was a more serious case. Actually the Attlees had been friends with his parents. Dick's Achilles' heel was that he had a German grandmother: Richard Pares, who had known him from Winchester days, used to say that his trouble was that he was just a German. He had their daemonic energy and, just like them, no sense of direction: he spun round like a top. Hence Maurice Bowra's soubriquet, 'Double-Crossman' – unfair, it was just that Dick charged round and was liable to change horses in mid-stream. When Hitler came to power, Crossman said to me that National Socialism meant socialism and that Hitler would bring it into being. What judgment! – I was furious with him. At Attlee's College Dick defended Hitler at high-table: 'At least he is sincere.' On one occasion Crossman treated Attlee to a twenty-minute long tirade about foreign policy – at the end of which Attlee said, not unkindly,

'Dick, how's your mother?' He had simply not wasted time listening to it. Another time Dick caught Attlee in the Smoking Room of the House of Commons, and told him that he thought that the Party's latest statement on foreign policy was a very good one. 'And, do you know', Dick reported to Douglas Jay, 'he never said anything at all! I wondered whether he had heard me; so I said, "Mr Attlee, I thought that the Party's statement on foreign policy was very good." And all he said was, "Did you?" '

I hope this gives the reader an idea of what Attlee was like to know – not very encouraging. This kind of thing meant that Crossman hadn't a good word to say for him. Neither had G. D. H. Cole, whom Attlee described as a 'perpetual undergraduate'. Of Stafford Cripps, he is 'no judge of politics' – quite right, as usual. Hugh Dalton slipped up as Chancellor of the Exchequer, by imparting to a journalist on the way into the House to make his Budget speech that there would be no rise in taxation: the news was in the City before his speech was ended. Attlee sacked him at once. Herbert Morrison told me that he was not in favour of this drastic action, but 'the Prime Minister took a different view.' Attlee on Dalton: 'He always was a loud-mouthed fellow.'

I suppose it must have been on that visit that Clem reported to brother Tom at home in Cornwall, 'I saw Rowse the other day at Oxford. He is maturing a bit, but should certainly stick to history.' This was what I was making up my mind to do; in spite of wasting time and health on being a political candidate, I had carried on with historical research and teaching, and was already writing history. In fact, nearly killing myself with overwork and overstrain. Continual ulceration had practically blocked the food passage into my stomach – peritonitis twice – critical operations (when my nurse kindly informed me after a second that she 'didn't expect to see me leave the operating table alive'). I survived; but when I had a severe haemorrhage later, my doctor ordered me to give up an active life and reconcile myself to an invalid's. So I gave up politics – and was happy ever after.

How I had hated the chore of being a political candidate, trying to open the eyes of fools to the idiocy of Chamberlain's Appeasement of Hitler! It had all ended as anyone of sense should have foreseen; but few did. In the Foreign Office itself, Cadogan who had been promoted by Chamberlain to carry out his policy in place of Vansittart: 'It has all happened as Van said it would, *and I never believed it*.' So there need be no further argy-bargy about Appeasement: it was hopeless from the start. The only correct policy was the historic one of a Grand Alliance against the overwhelming threat to us and everybody else which Germany constituted, both the Kaiser's and Hitler's. This both Churchill and Attlee understood; I had been arguing for it, writing for it – all in vain – ever since Hitler came into power in 1933.

Attlee, as a historian, understood clearly and simply who had been responsible for 1914, as Churchill did – another historian. Attlee wrote, 'One can see now that the German and Austrian ruling classes, by their ill-considered action in making war, destroyed the class society which gave them their privileged position'. Few people understood the sinister dialectic between Germany's backward social structure and the threatening policy of her dominant classes: they meant war. Then, as Henry James despairingly said, 'Nobody ever understands *any*thing.' I had had enough, and was willing, though sad, to give up.

In any case, when the nation was fighting for its life, there was no point in party politics any more: it was a question of survival. In a nuclear world, dominated by the appalling danger of the spread of nuclear armaments – the black cloud over all our lives – I have ceased to be interested in mere party divisions, between Labour and Conservative, Democrat and Republican, between Britain and the United States: we are all involved in the human tragedy together.

Up to the turning point of the Second German War and the formation of Churchill's government backed by the whole Labour Movement, I had been a straight Labour Party man, no fringe-man like so many fellow intellectuals, let alone joining the Communist Party as many of them were such idiots as to do, and later repent. Strictly speaking, I was a follower of Herbert Morrison, whom I had hoped to see Leader; I have letters from him saying how sorry he was that I was giving up. I had many twinges of heart when I went round my former constituency and ran into old supporters, particularly when one of the fishermen at Mevagissey said sadly, 'You don't come to see us much now.' More than that, I had had so much to put up with one way and another, that I turned my back on Cornwall: they had had their chance: they would hear no more from me for the next twenty years. Their loss rather than mine.

Active politics being blessedly over – which I made absolute, with the absolutism of my temperament – I nevertheless kept in some touch with the friends with whom I had had so many contacts over those wasted years. (I hated that decade so much that I have written little about it in all my writings; however, the evidences remain *pour servir à l'histoire*, as the phrase has it.) Here is a letter from Attlee, from 11 Downing Street, 15 September 1941: 'Thank you for your admirable suggestion of the O.M. for Beatrice Webb. My general rule is not to recommend for any honours except those which, like Privy Councillorships, are part of our Parliamentary tradition; but this is certainly a justifiable exception. I am, therefore, mentioning the matter to the Prime Minister.' A couple of years later Churchill gave the O.M. to Sidney Webb; he should have given it to Beatrice, the most remarkable woman of the time. But Winston was always rather anti-feminist. Earlier, when the formidable Beatrice had planned to make him her instrument for the expansion of the social services, he 'declined to be shut up in a soup-kitchen with Mrs Sidney Webb.' I still think my suggestion was a right one; so evidently did Attlee.

Next year he wrote of *A Cornish Childhood*, 'It seems to me a most happy conception to give at the same time a picture of past Cornwall and an impression of the journey from Tregonissey to All Souls, which is itself a symbol of the new age.' Actually, that was the way the book had begun – not as an autobiography, but as a picture of the life of the village before I was born, from what my father and mother and old great-uncle had told me; I remember feeling rather self-conscious when, halfway through, I realised that I had to begin on myself. Attlee went on, 'It makes one feel a bit old, for your early days at school coincide with my beginnings in the Labour Movement. I can never escape from the Victorian era in which I grew up – an era which, in the light of the last thirty years, had some points of vantage in the way of tranquillity.'

That was saying a lot for him, always laconic, and also characteristically sober. What a blissful era of security the Victorian age was! We shall never see the like again. Attlee inherited, and carried on into a hideous world the good standards, the devotion to duty and public service, the incorruptible uprightness and honour, of that better age.

Myself, I was now immersed in the still more inspiring Elizabethan age, when we were a small 'people such as mend upon the world' (Shakespeare): we were then going up in the world, at the beginning of that wonderful historic arc of achievement, which has left its traces across the oceans, though we, alas, witness its end. I put together a harmless little book, *An Elizabethan Garland*, to celebrate the coronation of Elizabeth II. Attlee wrote, 'I started reading it in the train this morning and much enjoyed it. I liked the chapter on Coronations. I wonder what kind of celebrations they had in the country in Elizabeth's reign. The street parties were a great feature in London this time. I wonder what the Elizabethans did in the little towns and villages?'

The answer to that was – nothing. A Tudor coronation was a London and Westminster affair, with a procession from the Tower to Whitehall the day before. There grew up spontaneously the custom of celebrating the Queen's Accession day, 17 November, with bell-ringing all over the country, for a century or more, so great was her fame.

In November 1951 Attlee reported to Tom, 'I have read Rowse's last book – very good in parts, with curious little strokes of egotism coming in.' This would have been *The England of Elizabeth*. I don't in the least mind that comment. He wasn't a writer and wouldn't know that a writer's ego is where he gets his inspiration from. The little strokes are there to keep the reader on his toes – irritation, better than sending him to sleep. If they were not there I should deliberately put them in. Nothing of that in Attlee's own writing, like a civil servant's. He was a dull writer, and not inspired as a speaker, unlike Churchill – most egoistic of men, fortunately.

Attlee was a quick and widely read reader, especially of history. At Oxford he had taken the Renaissance as his Special Subject in the History School. Appropriately, in taking possession of 10 Downing Street and Chequers, he quoted Leo X's 'Now that we have the Papacy, let us enjoy it.' And, with all the worries of politics, he never lost a night's sleep over them.

One day after a crucial division in the Parliamentary Labour Party over the Government's Re-armament programme during the first phase of the Cold War, he presided over a debate which was a very close-run thing and would have overthrown his leadership if it had gone against him. His motion was carried by only two or three votes. At once he snapped, 'The motion's carried – meeting's closed.' Not a moment allowed for reconsideration or recrimination. Douglas Jay caught up with him hurrying down the corridor. Not a word about the critical meeting, the narrow shave he had had. All he said was: 'My wife has had a small sum of money left her. How would you advise me to invest it?'

I find, in my immense Archive, a last letter from him in retirement, from Cherry Cottage, his home at Great Missenden, in 1958. 'Thank you so much for sending me your book on the Churchills with such a charming inscription. I always think it is interesting where an old stock suddenly burgeons with brilliant blossom. There is a parallel case in the Cecils, where after the first two nothing happens until we have the old Marquis; and in the next generation what the present Salisbury once described to me as his harlequin set of uncles; and of course himself and David. I suppose a geneticist cannot throw any light on the problem, any more than they can explain the flowering of genius anywhere. I am reading the book with much delight here in bed, but I expect to be out and about by the end of the week.'

During the intervals I had met and chatted with him several times, usually on his visits to Oxford, and each time there was some memorable point in the exchange. One night we were talking about Labour Party figures, in the candlelight over dessert at All Souls. I had been amused by old Trade Unionist Tomlinson, whom Attlee had made Minister of Education, speaking at a Foyle's Literary Luncheon: ' 'amlet – ah've always liked 'amlet.' I thought this rather good from a Minister of Education. Attlee said, 'I always like to hear what Tomlinson has to say.' No doubt he was right: he would get plain, working-class commonsense from old George – Attlee didn't want to hear what the Crossmans had to say.

Curiously enough he was more sympathetic to Aneurin Bevan than he was to Morrison. Attlee wished that Aneurin Bevan could have made a Leader of the Labour Movement: he had the gifts, if it had not been for his irresponsibility and fatal lack of judgment. It was Aneurin, seconded by Harold Wilson, who brought down Attlee's second administration, in 1951. This had very ill consequences. If Attlee had been there, there would have been no Suez fiasco. He was always friendly with Eden, went into 10 Downing Street, and warned him: 'Now, Anthony – no getting caught out on a limb with the French.' This is exactly what happened: the French Prime Minister and Foreign Secretary came over and gave Eden the final push. After the collapse, Eden said to me in Cornwall that it would not have happened if Ernest Bevin had been there. I suppose he meant that Bevin would have rallied Labour behind the government. Doubtful.

I happened to be on a cruise of Lady Waverley's down the Thames on one of her husband's Port of London Authority's vessels. There in the party was Clem, just before he was due to leave for Russia with Aneurin Bevan and others in the delegation. It was obvious that he didn't want to go, but was going to keep an eye on Aneurin and prevent any mischief. An exhausting affair, for they were going across Siberia to Vladivostok, and out via Japan. I hoped that he had had proper inoculation. Yes, he had had inoculations against every sort of thing. He did not need any inoculation against Communism: he had had too much experience all along of what it was and what its leaders really were. He described Stalin, *tout court*, as a 'barbarian'. A barbarian of genius, of course, like Hitler. At the Potsdam Conference Stalin had his first glimpse of Attlee, and said, 'He doesn't look a greedy man.' A sharp insight. The same could not be said of Stalin.

In Moscow, at a reception at the British Embassy, there they were, the people involved in Stalin's crimes; Aneurin engaged in friendly talk with Malenkov, the successor, Clem planted in the middle of the room, alone, stolidly looking on the ground. Wouldn't he like to come and talk with Mr

Malenkov? Or Mr Mikoyan? Or . . . ? Clem: 'No, sick of the lot of them.' When they emerged into the light of day and civilisation, and were interviewed by the world press, Aneurin was able to enthuse about Malenkov: a most intelligent man, he was sure we could reach understanding and do business with him. When Attlee was asked for his opinion, he replied glumly, 'Very able man.' Within a matter of weeks Malenkov was out of power. It offers a typical contrast of judgment between the volatile Celt and the sobersided Englishman: Aneurin was very Welsh and Clem very English, almost to the point of caricature, reserve, shyness, understatement. However, the English are more intelligent than they pretend to be, and that takes others in.

Few other occasions do I remember. Attlee had a close understanding with Edward Bridges of All Souls, secretary to the Cabinet and Head of the Civil Service – to whom the country owes an immense debt for the maximum efficiency with which he ran the machine of government. After a hard day's work, each night he took home work till midnight for next day; every morning Cabinet business ready for decisions in order of priority. Nothing like it at Hitler's headquarters, where all depended on the inspiration of the divine Führer. Attlee persuaded Bridges to stay on after his term – he was expected to come back to All Souls as Warden. I shared rooms with him in College, and one day remarked what secrets of state he had shared; 'Yes, and they will remain in the deep freeze.' Like Attlee – and unlike Churchill – he gave away nothing.

But Bridges did describe to me Churchill's curious way of reaching a decision; he thought it must be something like that of Elizabeth I, for he would delay, and procrastinate, and hum and haw – until eventually the thing came clear to him, emerging as from a pregnancy. With Attlee, I suspect, the process was less intuitive and more rational, crisp and clean from the first. As also with President Truman (in contrast with Roosevelt), whom Churchill described as 'the man most full of decision that I have ever met.' Edward Bridges told me a remarkable dream he had, which tells its own tale as to the burden of responsibility he carried. He took over as Secretary to the Cabinet, from Hailey, under Neville Chamberlain. He

dreamed that at his first Cabinet meeting a man crawled out
from under the green-baize table, ran out of the door and
down the stairs of 10 Downing Street. Bridges pursued him,
but lost him in the street. When he came back, Chamberlain
said, 'But didn't you look under the table? Hailey *always*
looked under the table.'

Attlee came down to Oxford to persuade Oliver Franks to
come back into government service. Franks had made a great
name for himself as a recruit to the civil service, much trusted
by Ernest Bevin, highly thought of by everybody, with an
unrivalled gift in negotiation. After the war he came back to
academic life, and was comfortably installed as Provost of
Queen's, next door to All Souls. I remember this visit too,
where Attlee was successful in persuading Franks to become
Ambassador to the United States.

A later glimpse, on a visit to the gallery of the House of
Lords, revealed the two old rivals, Attlee and Morrison,
retired from the hurly-burly of the Commons, to the plush
dignity of the Upper Chamber. There they were, lounging
side by side, feet up on the bench, nothing to do. What a life!
Last glimpse of all was in the course of some publishing
occasion, at the Tower of London: there was, unexpectedly,
Clem, old and looking frail, taking the opportunity to sit
down, but alert and keeping his interest in what was going on,
to the end. We exchanged a few words; I felt it was a kind of
farewell, and in that historic place.

I hope I have given a fair, recognisable picture of this man not
easy to conjure up, so little was in evidence, so much under the
surface. Where bigger, bulkier men – Bevin or Churchill –
provoked opposition to their ebullient personalities, Attlee
threaded his way like a needle, creating the minimum of
resistance. No doubt theirs were richer and more humorous
natures, Aneurin Bevan's and Gaitskell's warmer and more
eloquent, yet Attlee's was sharp and incisive, with an edge of
wit. Of Chamberlain he said that, where Baldwin gave the
House of Commons an impression of being in touch with
world affairs, with Chamberlain their minds were tuned in to
the Midland Regional. This was his parallel to Churchill's
funnier *mot* that Chamberlain looked at world affairs 'through

the wrong end of the municipal drain-pipe.'

A deeper element in Attlee's achievement was his capacity to grow with events. This is where we had been wrong earlier to underestimate him and prefer Morrison as leader. Attlee had a capacity for growth much beyond Morrison's, as was shown when he insisted on following Bevin at the Foreign Office: 'the worst appointment I ever made', Attlee concluded.

This has become clearer than ever – since the publication of Kenneth Harris's biography, a notable contribution to the history of our time. We used to think that the dominant man in Attlee's government was Bevin: we now know, what was not apparent at the time, that Attlee was the master. He took all the major decisions as they came up himself. I once asked him in the early days of Labour rule what chance there was of planning ahead. He said, none – things kept 'boiling up' the whole time. A good thing he was a pragmatist: he met each problem as it came up; all the same, under his aegis the Welfare State came into being.

He had a vein of idealism in him; as he says in his auto-biography, *As It Happened* – a significant title – his family had a strong tradition of social service. This is the way he came to socialism, that and the reading of Ruskin. His long years of service in the East End undoubtedly determined him to do all he could to improve the lot of the poorest and lowest-paid. He only once made a public plea that they should respond with some sense of service to the community. This was rather upper-class of him; a working-class man would hardly have that idealist expectation. Try it on the highest paid (and most selfish) of the Trade Unions!

He made the big decision to hand over rule in India: whether that was an advantage to the teeming millions of peoples there I doubt, but the end of the Raj was inevitable. He made the decision for Partition between Hindu India and Moslem Pakistan, overriding Stafford Cripps who was under the influence of Congress – Nehru's – demand to keep Moslems under Congress rule. (Nehru succeeded in holding on to Moslem Kashmir, contrary to justice, humbugging the issue: hence the two or three wars since Britain left.) Congress had always played down the inveterate hatred of Moslem and

Hindu, and blamed it on Britain – no longer there to blame. Even Churchill came to accept the inevitability of the hand-over, persuaded by Attlee, so Beaverbrook told me resentfully.

When it came to the decisive issue of an independent Nuclear deterrent for Britain, Attlee again took the onus himself, without consulting either the Cabinet or Parliament in so urgent a matter that had to be kept secret. Finally, he saw to it that Hugh Gaitskell became his successor as Leader of the Labour Party, the right man for the job – his early death a grievous loss to the Party and the nation. For he too had the capacity for development, as well as absolute integrity and public spirit.

These qualities and Victorian standards in Attlee gave him his strength: it was the combination in one man in politics that made him exceptional. No-one else could have held together a government that contained the mutually exclusive Bevin and Morrison as leading members of it. For long it was unknown why Bevin went to the Foreign Office – a surprise to himself, for he had expected to be made Chancellor of the Exchequer, the field in which his interest lay. None of us knew. It eventually transpired that it was a characteristic decision of Attlee's to keep him and Morrison apart: one in home affairs, the other in foreign. It would never have done to have them competing and wrangling in the same field: it would have rent the government. Thus Attlee held the field and himself controlled it.

There is a charming story of the Attlees towards the end of his life. His wife – who had driven him thousands of miles electioneering in their modest car, somewhat unsteadily, but in the end not fatally – came from a Conservative family, like the Attlees themselves. (He always had the old Tory dislike of Gladstone.) 'Clem was never really a socialist, were you, darling?' she said. Clem, preoccupied with *The Times*, mumbled dissent. 'Well, not a rabid one', she said comfortably.

Clem was a good socialist, and a kind, civilised man – unlike his German and Russian contemporaries, who ruined the world we live in.

Lionel Curtis: 'The Prophet'

Of all the eminent men who foregathered at All Souls in the old days – Viceroys of India, Governors-General of Dominions, archbishops, Cabinet Ministers, political figures – Lionel Curtis was perhaps the most remarkable (along with his friend there, T. E. Lawrence). Curtis was to some extent a mystery man, who deliberately chose to keep out of the limelight, while seeking to influence public affairs more effectively as an *éminence grise*. This was not only policy on his part, it became almost an affectation – when, for example, he organised a large dinner of prominent people to advance some cause he had in mind, the one person absent being himself.

His entry in *Who's Who* was similarly characteristic: it doesn't tell one who his parents were or where he was born; it doesn't give his full name, and supplies hardly any dates. All that mattered to him was 'the Cause' – the overriding Cause to which he dedicated his life, and of which he considered himself the Prophet, along with the lesser causes he took up and promoted. He might have said of himself as Napoleon did, 'J'avais le goût de la fondation, et non de la propriété.' He was a promoter, propagandist, constitution-monger, schemer, planner, founder of bodies and institutions – of which Chatham House, the Royal Institute of International Affairs, is perhaps best known.

I remember his coming back from London one evening, throwing himself down on the long bench in our smoking-room (from which they liked to think the affairs of the Empire were governed), with: 'Thank God, Chatham House is safe! I've got Abe Bailey to give it £150,000.' Curtis had a magic wand where big-minded business men were concerned – he had several of them among his submissive followers and disciples; he could do nothing with small-minded dons.

This habit of mystification means that it is hardly possible to write his biography; several people have tried their hands at it and fallen down on the job. Geoffrey Dawson – the notoriously pro-German editor of *The Times*[1] – Curtis's associate for many years from the South African war onwards, once told me that only he could write the Prophet's life. One would think him a pure innocent in the ways of life, Dawson said; not a bit of it, and he retailed an example of Curtis's technique. One follower subscribed a large sum of £25,000 for one of his causes, and was promised an honour for it. Under MacDonald the honour was not forthcoming, nor under the next Prime Minister. The poor rich man began to be restless and to complain; nevertheless, after an interval and yet another administration, it was eventually forthcoming. One element in Curtis's technique was persistence: he never gave up. A more important weapon was his personal disinterestedness: he wanted nothing for himself, and this gave him power with others. I used to think, watching him with affection (for he was also lovable), that with him absolute disinterestedness became absolute interestedness.

Again Dawson was right that, though Curtis was a Christian gentleman, one would think butter wouldn't melt in his mouth – yet he knew the shady side of public life all right, he knew the score and people's price. He told me of some disagreeable transactions regarding a Secretary of State for India and the Indian Princes. He was well informed about the financial dealings of a behind-the-scenes wheeler-dealer in these matters (knighted of course; forgotten today, but not by the historian, whose business it is to remember). He himself was not the least interested in money.

As for Lionel's innocence of the facts of life – he regarded the Johannesburg millionaires of the time of the South African war as a vicious lot. As Town Clerk there he visited the hospitals, where one woman was affected by syphilis in her eye. She had been regularly paid by one of these infected miscreants to ejaculate in her eye. And Lionel knew all about

---

[1] For him v. my *All Souls and Appeasement* (fuller version the American edition, *Appeasement: A Study in Political Decline*).

Lord Randolph Churchill, similarly infected, on his visit to South Africa in his last years, 'crawling in and out of kaffir kraals.' Thus Lionel, by no means the innocent – though a deeply good man – the innocent themselves might think.

In any case he would never write an autobiography, though I wished he would. To my mind his life was far more interesting than the 'Causes' to which he dedicated himself. To people who urged him to write his Memoirs he would reply: 'My job lies with the future, not with the past.' Portentous – he really thought of himself as a prophet; but we see that there were many things in his life that he really couldn't tell.

In his last years he did allow the early Diary he had kept to be published under the title, *With Milner in South Africa*. It turned up unexpectedly, 'and the diary records much which in fifty years had passed from my own memory.' He did not set much store by it – after all, it was the past. To a historian, however, it was the most interesting thing he ever wrote; this would be heresy to him, and I should be excommunicated for saying it – except that our relations were of mutual affection and he allowed me to be a licensed libertine, which was certainly not allowed to his disciples in the faith.

The Diary is not only a fascinating record, but one of the most revealing documents of the South African war, which has had such tragic consequences. One certainly sees the tragedy of it. But there is a great deal else with it: wisdom, insight, foresight; the charm of the handsome boyish young man the photographs show him to have been (he always retained that handsome presence, his distinction of manner, unfailing good temper in fractious circumstances); the generosity and warmth, the good fellowship and camaraderie. On top of everything else Lionel was a good scout, impossible to resist.

I laughed at myself at what happened when I determined to resist, in early days. He had a rambling thatched house beside the Cher at Old Kidlington. There was to be a Kidlington historical pageant. Alice Buchan and various others were writing scenes, and Lionel called on me to write the Elizabethan one. I was quite determined that I would not – I had so much else to do, wasn't sure that I could, etc. Then

Lionel called in Arthur Salter's brother, who was a parson out
there, brought him to lunch – and of course I ended by doing
what Lionel intended I should do. There it all is in print; I do
not remember ever seeing the Pageant.

In addition to everything else, there has been a kind of hoo-
doo about a Curtis biography. Practically all his immense
collection of papers went up in flames when that thatched
house, Hales Croft, burned in 1933. He was stoical about that,
quite unmoved by it. Dermot Morrah, of All Souls, was to
have written the biography, and failed. Then somebody else.
At length a woman scholar collected a great deal of material –
and had her typescript, notes etc in two suit-cases stolen from
her car in a London car-park. (Apparently she hadn't heard of
the new social order, nor taken the proper precautions against
its amenities. As if historical papers were of value to the
depredators so characteristic of it! They must have been
disappointed, but a loss to us.)

Though I lived for thirty years on terms of friendship and
increasing affection with Lionel, and have memories and
stories of him – he was an excellent raconteur, and did have a
sense of humour – enough to fill a booklet, I know that I could
never have written his biography. There was so much that was
missing, and so much that he would not talk about – he would
never betray the technique by which he gained influence with
people, though I watched them fall with amusement. I realised
that the South African experience, over those crucial years
1899–1909, had been the formative one in his life, had fixed
him in what he regarded as his call from God – he did not bore
me with it, or even attempt to. His friends of Milner's
Kindergarten – no less than five of them were Fellows of All
Souls – were constantly coming to and fro; so one was fairly *au
fait* with that part of the story and the characters. But one knew
nothing about his part in the Irish negotiations that led to the
Treaty of 1922 and the setting up of the Irish Free State (that
led to a breach with Kipling, who had donated a large sum for
arms for Ulster). Or about Curtis's invention of Dyarchy for
India, the compromise that held the field for some years,
granting a measure of responsible government in the provinces while retaining authority at the centre in Delhi. Curtis
would be the first person to recognise that historic compro-

mises do not work for long: the Prophet was an Either-Or man (in Keirkegäard's terminology).

Curtis's childhood was spent at Ledbury in Herefordshire – John Masefield's home background: Lionel told me how shocked local people were by *The Widow in the Bye Street*. I suppose Curtis was born there, in 1872, his father an Evangelical hot-gospeller, whose sermons about Hell-fire made the young Lionel quake as a boy – and the Gospel influence remained with him all his life. When he came to marry, lateish, in 1920 it was to the daughter of a Devonshire parson, who exchanged her original name of Gladys for 'Patricia', a handsome piece, fine brown eyes, sexy voice, a rather heavy sense of humour. She had been his secretary. Earlier he had proposed to the eldest daughter of the great Lord Salisbury, though making it clear that marriage to her was not to interfere with his prophetic call. This was not thought good enough for a daughter of the House of Hatfield.

Like Attlee – I don't know whether they knew each other – Curtis was at the Anglo-Indian Haileybury. Then New College, where at evensong in Chapel his eyes fell on the tall upstanding Lionel ('Nel') Hichens. 'It was love at first sight' – Curtis said innocently to me, registering naughtily that one couldn't say such things nowadays. I have often wondered whether there was an unconscious homo-eroticism among Milner's Young Men, the atmosphere was so emotional, and towards the great man, a life-long bachelor until towards the end of his life. Completely repressed and virtuous, of course; though Lionel knew the facts of Public School life, 'in my time perfect sinks of iniquity'. All the same, it is clear from the Diary that Lionel loved and admired Nel Hichens, constant tributes to his charm and comradeship, the ability with which he surmounted all difficulties.

Hichens returned from South Africa to become chairman of the shipbuilding firm of Cammell, Laird and Co. He is almost the only member of the Kindergarten I never met; I regret this the more because he was a fellow Cornishman, from Falmouth. He was killed in 1940, when a bomb hit Church House, Westminster. Lionel wrote biblically of him: 'It was fitting that he should pass from the earth in a chariot of fire.' I think otherwise: one more fine fellow extinguished by the German mania that ruined our century.

Those two had had a wonderful time together in South Africa. If we can forget for a moment that the Boer War was a tragedy, and should never have happened, those young fellows had a high old time, were tested, brought to maturity, and gained large responsibilities in the course of it, and the reconstruction thereafter. Modern Johannesburg owes much to young Curtis, though he never spoke of it. His wider experience in South Africa as a whole was a formative influence upon his mind, and fixed it – the word is deliberate, he had a 'fixation' – upon imperial federation, and later 'world-federation'. It is typical that Bertrand Russell should get a Nobel Prize for his abortive campaign in that direction, while Curtis got no recognition for his – equally abortive.

Curtis's career in South Africa is part of history, and vastly more constructive than anything the useless Russell ever accomplished. I do not need to go in detail into it here. But as Town Clerk Curtis took over the direct administration of Johannesburg when it was a chaos of mine dumps and workings, shacks and slums, dotted with *nouveaux riches* properties on the margins; with no proper water supplies, drainage or sewage systems, etc. No wonder typhoid, enteric, dysentery were widespread. (Lionel's elder brother died of enteric at Ladysmith, Lionel himself contracted dysentery.)

He laid the foundations of the great modern city and brought that kind of thing to an end. On horseback he surveyed the district, following the contours and watersheds to co-ordinate an area equal to that of modern London, laid down what was to be a splendid city park, appropriated sites for schools and hospitals, and set proper municipal government going following the procedure of the London County Council. And in thirty years of constant discourse he never mentioned his extraordinary achievement as a young man!

Lionel Curtis is known as an Imperialist, but a historian should point out that he was also liberal-minded – about the blacks, for example. Indeed, that was an issue in the War itself: the Boers really believed in Biblical slavery, the British did not. John Buchan, as another young man working for Milner, held that the British were 'only just right' in the War. With the advantage of hindsight, I should say that they were 'only just wrong'. Beneath the two immovables, the Boer Kruger and the Germanic Milner, was the conflict for power. The simple fact is that the Boers, the Africaners, regarded – and regard – South Africa as *their* country (they were there before the blacks largely moved south) – and, in spite of a deplorable war, they eventually won the peace.

A considerable number of the British ended up, chivalrously – the young Churchill among them – as sympathetic to the Boers. One is struck by the wisdom and foresight of the young Curtis similarly. After his brother's death, he wrote home that 'we must think of them as given as they gave themselves that, after the War, we might have a South Africa where men have learned to bear with one another.' Alas, for his hopes! At home the Jingo *Times* was then edited by Buckle (another Fellow of All Souls); his brother, a private in South Africa, remarked, 'We who are fighting are mostly pro-Boers. The really bitter people have stayed at home to write articles.' Curtis continually inveighs against the appalling inefficiency of the military and the War Office, the criminal ineptitude of the farm-burnings, the never-to-be forgotten tragedy of the disease-ridden refugee camps.

Curtis – a high-minded Christian gentleman – wrote home with equal distaste for the behaviour of the looting soldiery, 'the sweepings of the Empire', and the Joe-Chamberlain line of *The Times*: '*The Times* seems to me to represent all that mass of respectable moneyed opinion against which Christ came to wage war.' Modern wars come about largely because of ignorance or blindness as to the intentions of the other side; here the Boers and British were equally at fault and should have known better. At home the War was popular with the mob; Curtis understood, 'about fifty years ago it was a common belief that popular government would mean the end of war.' No democratic illusions of that sort with him. Nor did he regard the idea of an 'independent United States of South Africa' as discreditable to the Dutch: 'It may ultimately be realised in the dim centuries to come.'

It has come about in this very century; for, in fact, at the Peace of Vereeniging the British capitulated to the Boers, and the ablest of the Boer leaders, Smuts, dominated the drafting of the constitution of the Union of South Africa – for which Curtis led the propaganda on the British side. In return, Britain gained South African support in the two German wars that threatened her existence; in the first, the quarter-German Milner made an inestimable contribution in the War Cabinet, as Smuts gave invaluable help and counsel in both wars. Such was the reward of politic generosity. Curtis himself brought both Smuts and Herzog to All Souls.

He saw the conflict in South Africa partly in terms of the struggle between North and South in the American Civil War. He points out at the time that Southern 'rebels' were being rounded up in Texas only quite recently. 'Had the South and Slavery prevailed, America would be a decaying nation instead of the most vigorous one in the world. English predominance in South Africa is to save it from the worst, *and that is all*.' Alas, for English hopes, once Boer predominance was re-established! Meanwhile, 'The more one hears of America the more one is inclined to think that she will eventually inherit the earth.' Curtis was writing that in 1901, at the beginning of 'the American Century': good for him.

The South African War was Kipling's apogee, the most famous writer in the world, still young – except perhaps for old Tolstoy at the opposite pole. Curtis told me that on the march they would recite 'Boots':

> We're foot-slog-slog-slog-sloggin' over Africa . . .
> Boots-boots-boots-boots-movin' up an' down again!

The Leftist poets of the Thirties talked about taking poetry to the people – can one imagine them marching to *their* over-intellectualised verse, Auden's 'Spain', for instance? Kipling didn't talk about it, he just did it.

Nor, ardent Imperialist as he was, was he without sympathy for the gallantry of the fighting Boers – many wartime poems like 'Piet' testify to it. Or there is his moving epitaph on the Boer General Cronje:

> With those that bred, with those that loosed the strife,
> He had no part whose hands were clear of gain,

> But subtle, strong, and stubborn gave his life
>   To a lost cause, and knew the gift was vain.
> Later shall rise a people, sane and great,
>   Forged in strong fires, by equal war made one;
> Telling old battles over without hate –
>   Not least his name shall pass from sire to son.

When Curtis accompanied Lord Milner to take possession of Pretoria, the Governor General recited the tribute to Cronje to his companions. Those were the days when the élite figures in public life could be inspired by poetry. (Curtis himself wrote not bad verse, and later gave me a little booklet of verses he had privately printed.)

He continues: 'Then we built castles on the air and on the kopje, and laid out terraces and avenues in imagination. Pretoria lay just at our feet, and we were looking right across it to the Magaliesburg.' Thus came into existence the magnificent Parliament buildings designed by Rhodes's favourite architect, Herbert Baker. The politics of it was that this was a concession to the Boers: if Johannesburg had been chosen for capital they would have regarded the government as being under the thumb of the Uitlanders.

Curtis got characteristic glimpses of Kipling, who, in February 1900, 'came into our camp at Green Point with his nose to the ground for subject matter, and examined every mortal thing from the Maxims to the officers and privates.' Curtis was capable of being critical of the much-publicised writer, who arrived at Bloemfontein, the capital of the Orange Free State, in the wake of the Army. Curtis hoped that the statue of President Brand of 1888 would make Kipling re-think his recent 'hasty' pronouncement – evidently too jingoistic for Lionel. At Cape Town Herbert Baker took him to see the beautiful house he had designed for Kipling, at Rhodes's expense, in an exquisite situation: 'Rhodes's idea was that Kipling would do his best work in such a place rather than living in an hotel.' Actually nothing stopped Kipling from writing wherever he was. A pal of Curtis introduced Kipling to 'a youthful looking commander of a flat iron called De Horsey, and shortly after he wrote "Judson of the Empire". In an abandoned tin hotel Kipling lay a little on all the beds successively looking at the ceiling, and in the morning produced "The Ballad of the *Clampherdown*." '

Curtis was no less critical of Rhodes, whose appearance he remarks on unfavourably, and 'how refreshing for that man of iron will and muddled mind to blunder into a correct opinion.' The greatest blunder of all was the Jameson Raid, which precipitated the war. 'Jameson tried to conquer the Transvaal with 500 men.' That affair was one of monumental ineptitude. (My father's brother and a son, Cornish miners in Jo'burg, sat up all night drinking whisky, waiting for the call which never came.) In the War itself Curtis ran into a detachment of Cornish Volunteers – I suppose miners. In later years he told me a comic story about the mistake the military made in arresting and imprisoning as a rebel, a fellow of the good old Cornish name of Baragwanath (Anglice, Whitbread), which they were convinced was Dutch.[2] Later, when the mistake was cleared up, they had to pay the Cornishman a good sum in compensation, I am glad to say; but I wish I could remember the misunderstandings and complications of the story before this happy consummation was reached.

Naturally Rhodes's Will and his imaginative conception of Rhodes Scholarships, with the foundation of the Trust, more than doubled the pivoting of the Kindergarten and its allied interests upon Oxford. His architect was called in to design Rhodes House, with its domed hall of approach, Zimbabwe bird as totem, and the temple which a friend of mine described as 'the tomb of the Unknown Rhodes Scholar'. When Kipling came to visit it in later years – he who had been so celebrated all over the Empire, and in the United States a special train provided for him – he was shown round by the official Porter, whom the great man thanked, and 'You may like to know whom you have been so kind as to show round: my name is Rudyard Kipling.' It did not register: unrecognised. *Sic transit gloria mundi*.

Among all these Empire grandees whom Curtis brought to All Souls, Kipling did not figure: there had been a breach. Curtis would say of him that, on one side, he was an inspired

---

[2] Today the big hospital in black Soweto is named for a Baragwanath, no doubt people think a black.

prophet; on the other a grousing reactionary. He told me a comic story of Leo Maxse's last illness, a spiritual brother of Kipling, editor of the *National Review*.[3] When Kipling inquired how he was – he had had a blood transfusion – Maxse replied, 'No better: I think they have injected into my veins the blood of a member of the League of Nations Union.' Kipling rushed to send a telegram with the consoling message: 'It's quite all right: no believer in the League of Nations ever gave his blood for anything.'

Working with Milner in South Africa and, after his departure, in accordance with his ideas for the reconstruction of the country, Curtis was in his element: from re-starting, practically re-founding, Johannesburg and giving it proper municipal government to Assistant Colonial Secretary of the Transvaal for Local Government, to Member of the Transvaal Legislative Council. He never talked about that later: it is true that he did not look back – he was no historian.

Though I once and again asked him what was the secret of Milner's extraordinary influence over the variously gifted young men of the Kindergarten – they were all devoted to him – Curtis never answered the question. With his well-developed technique for working people to his purposes, not only instinctively but quite consciously, I do not think that he was interested in them psychologically: he was a Victorian, pre-Freud. It is evident that Milner was a remarkable administrator, with a constructive mind, full of ideas; a non-party man, really contemptuous of party-conflict – he was above all that – he even came to look sympathetically on the Labour Party at the end of his life. I remember his surprising *Observer* articles to this effect. He might have been a Fabian – as, oddly enough, the Tory Amery was.

Amery was another Fellow of All Souls whom Curtis became friendly with in South Africa. It is extraordinary the number of people who made their mark later whose apprenticeship was served in South Africa. Among All Souls men,

---

[3] Milner eventually married Maxse's sister. Were they Germans too? I once met her, a deep-dyed, doctrinaire reactionary, whom nobody could agree with.

Bob Brand, international banker of Lazard's, influential in shaping the constitution of the Union, on which he wrote the standard book. Geoffrey Dawson – who had to change his name from Robinson (hence always 'Robin' to the group) on succeeding to his Yorkshire estate; he served his apprentice-ship in editing the Johannesburg *Star* and as correspondent of *The Times*, of which he became editor. (In his day the paper was hailed as 'the All Souls Parish Magazine'; he recruited several of us to it, and was kind enough to ask me to join – I should have been sacked rather than accept his pro-Appease-ment line.) Dougal Malcolm, who had defeated John Buchan for the Fellowship, most clubbable of men and devoted to College life, became Chairman of the British South Africa Company, Rhodes's great enterprise for Central Africa. Perry, who had been responsible for the native Protectorates, had been personally recruited by Milner and helped to bring Curtis out ('I was dying to get back to South Africa to work under Milner – as we all did'). Perry later hived off to Canada; I saw him only once in College, a handsome, amiable, remote fellow. Lionel did not speak of the deserter.

Philip Kerr – later Lord Lothian – was a close co-operator, the first editor of the group's propagandist journal, *The Round Table*, inspired by Curtis and him. With his facile pen he wrote profusely and, overworked, had a prolonged nervous break-down. (There was mental instability in the family.) Hereditarily a Catholic, he was helped to recovery by Christian Science, a bonus from Nancy Astor with whom he was in love – platonically of course, but a bore to Waldorf. A man of charm, public spirit and generosity, he was hopelessly wrong about Germany, which he did not know. When he died in the Washington Embassy, without medical attendance, Lionel owned to me: 'Philip died in the knowledge that he had been wrong.' What was the good of that? The damage had already been done, and was irretrievable.

It was a tribute to Curtis that he did not go in with Lothian over Appeasement of Hitler's Germany; he never declared himself on the issue, he had more sense, perhaps of political expediency. For some of the friends he wished to keep in line with – or, rather, keep *them* in line – were not Appeasers. Brand was not: he knew Germany, in touch with Schacht.

Amery, who knew Central Europe and the Balkans (he was partly Hungarian) was absolutely sound and had a consistent record on the issue. Even Waldorf Astor at Cliveden was not so sold on Appeasement as the editors on *The Times* and *The Observer*, Dawson and J. L. Garvin, Lothian or the egregious Tom Jones, working away like a mole for Hitler; or Neville Chamberlain and his *éminence grise,* Horace Wilson, another mole; or Chamberlain's Tory Party; or Montague Norman and the City. In the event they wrecked their country. It was not only Lionel Hichens but Britain that went up 'in a chariot of fire'.

Curtis to me, at that appalling moment of the Fall of France, in 1940: 'We must go down with the flag flying.' (I had other ideas.)

Though not a Fellow, Lothian came regularly to College. Occasionally too came the mysterious John Dove, who succeeded as editor of *The Round Table.* He had played his part as Chairman of the Transvaal Land Settlement Board, and subsequently accompanied Curtis to Australia on his fact-finding plus propaganda mission for Imperial Union. Dove was an asthmatic and a valetudinarian: I remember him silently snooping about the papers in our Coffee Room, as if surreptitiously – he didn't belong.

Basil Williams was another of the group, who came to visit us: he became an eminent eighteenth century historian, a precursor of Richard Pares in that field. There turned up too in South Africa the deplorable Duke of Westminster, Churchill's buddy, 'Bendor', recently the subject of a superfluous biography: to Curtis merely 'a gilded youth'. Lionel had no use for him – as he had a use for most of us.

After Reconstruction Curtis devoted all his energy and single-mindedness to the cause of promoting the Union of South Africa. He was a man of an *idée fixe* – of a series of *idées fixes,* one at a time; this was what gave them force. Here the idea was sparked off by his reading F. S. Oliver's book, *Alexander Hamilton.* It is extraordinary to think what an influence that book, by a rich business man in Debenham's – no historian – had on the thinking of the group. 'I shall never forget the effect which *Alexander Hamilton* had on me when I read it', Curtis wrote. 'He came into our lives as a great inspiration at the moment when we most needed it in South Africa. Here we were trying to work out a new philosophy of the State, and behold an unknown linen draper who had done it all for us!' The more intellectually trained Amery realised that Oliver's *Alexander Hamilton* was the Bible of the Kindergarten.

Lionel recommended it to me. To us who were historians this was derisory; Oliver was no historian any more than Curtis was: both were propagandists. This was their point, and perhaps it showed how limited the unappreciative academic mind was, for it is men of a fixed idea who are apt to make the running in history (look at Hitler! look at Lenin!). I suppose Oliver's point was that Alexander Hamilton, even after the American Revolution, wanted to keep what had been the first British Empire together in world affairs. Historians, however, would draw the moral that when dominions arrive at a degree of maturity they want to run their own affairs their own way. This is the moral to us of the American Revolution – applied, perhaps rightly, by Attlee in the hand-over in India; and subsequently, with very questionable results, in Africa.

Oliver, the sage, an elderly man, did not appear at All Souls. But, among colonial administrators, Curtis brought to us one of the greatest, Lugard, under whom Nigeria was a source of pride: one could trek unarmed two or three hundred miles. Look at it today! – massacres running into hundreds of thousands, political and economic collapse, chaos. Similarly with the Sudan, Zimbabwe, or Uganda: black shambles.

Personally considerate as always, Lionel introduced me to Oliver's artistic son, a collector of pictures, who invited me to dine at his house, a fragment of the old Tudor Richmond Palace. There I saw my first Modigliani. But we did not keep up the acquaintance – I was much too busily occupied at Oxford, and one really couldn't keep up with all the people one met in those generous, hospitable days.

Curtis had inspired, and Philip Kerr largely wrote, the journal *State* which made the propaganda for Union in South Africa. Curtis also travelled incessantly in those years before 1914 putting the idea across, as forcefully as he knew how. What effectively brought Union about was the change in political circumstances. The Liberal government at home granted responsible government – prematurely in Milner's opinion, who saw that it would mean Boer predominance, and despaired. The Kindergarten, however, favoured responsible government, and did not despair; Union came about, within the Empire, until ultimately the Afrikaners moved out.

After Union, most of the Kindergarten, their work done, returned to England to their different avocations – Curtis, however, to carry forward the propaganda for Imperial Union. He became the 'Prophet'. Today it is easy for us to see that this was never a possibility, difficult for us to appreciate that anybody thought that it was. True, circumstances were very different. The Dominions had not yet arrived at complete jurisdiction within their own bounds; Canada and Australia had contributed notably to the Empire's effort in South Africa; one half of the Unionist Party supported Joe Chamberlain's campaign for Tariffs, allied with Imperial Protection. A practical politician like Amery saw that the only practicable step in this direction was the latter. Curtis did not declare himself on this issue, for most of his group were Free Traders. He was fixed on the idea of Organic Union. Amery resented his dominating all discussions within the group by his *idée fixe*, and withdrew.

When Curtis made his fact-finding tour, sponsored by the group, to Canada and Australia, he found the prospects more discouraging than he expected, though he managed to set up groups to study the problem and Empire questions generally, to be aired and discussed in *The Round Table*. He was the standard-bearer; but he had the sense to realise the strength of the movement in each Dominion towards self-sufficiency and running their own affairs, if not actual independence. It is true that, at that time, the Dominions were not independent from the point of view of defence: they were dependent on the British Navy. It was not until the Second German War that the United States succeeded to the leadership of the English-speaking peoples. As for an Imperial Parliament – an historian should have known that the Declaration of Independence, of 1776, put paid to that.

Curtis came to realise the strength of the Dominion movements to realise their own separate identities; but, an Either-Or man, he posed the exclusive alternatives of *either* Organic

Union *or* the dissolution of the Empire. Milner, with his Germanic mind, agreed with Curtis at heart. They set too much store by having things set down on paper, framing a constitution, etc, and insufficient store by instinctive, unspoken affiliations, the consoling fact that blood is thicker than water, that all round the globe were Britain's kith and kin, who did not need constitutional formulas to come to her rescue at the two crises in her destiny in the twentieth century – above all from the United States. (It must be gall and wormwood for German historians to reflect upon, but Germany showed herself altogether too uncivilised for any leadership in the world.)

The 1914–18 War ended even discussion, let alone prospect, of Imperial Union. Curtis must have felt that his mission had failed, though his *sense* of mission remained; he had other irons in the fire, causes to promote, people to push forward, followers and disciples. I do not know what his part in the Anglo-Irish negotiations amounted to, though he was closely involved. All he said to me was his oracular: 'The history of Ireland is something all Englishmen should remember, and all Irishmen forget.' (So typical of human affairs, the contrary is what prevails.) It was like his pronouncement that the history of South Africa was 'much too interesting'.

Curtis knew the Irish negotiators, and in South Africa had known Erskine Childers, who adopted the Irish Republican cause and was shot, by former comrades, then in the Free State government. Lionel did tell me that Childers was driven into his desperate extremism by his fanatic of an Irish-American wife, a cripple devoured by hate. Childers was condemned to death by Kevin O'Higgins, who was then assassinated by the Republicans – the usual sickening amenities of Irish politics. I once asked Curtis if the boundaries of Ulster in the Irish Treaty had not been drawn too widely: would it not have been better to include fewer Catholics? He said that only thus was the Province viable. I wonder. In Thrace, only an exchange of populations made peace possible between such humans (Swift is in this regard doubly to the point: he knew Northern Ireland). Or perhaps a Chinese Wall?

In those negotiations W. G. S. Adams proposed the most

promising settlement. Adams, who became our Warden, was a Scot who lived a good deal, and married, in Ireland. He had been secretary to a grand man, Sir Horace Plunket, who created Irish Agricultural Cooperation and did much for the rehabilitation of the land. The Irish Republicans burned down his house for him and destroyed his historic papers.

I must confine myself to Curtis at Oxford, which henceforth became his base with his election to a Fellowship at All Souls. Warden Pember, friend of Grey and Asquith, was really a Little Englander and did not like the 'Empire builders', as we called them. (Though a Labour man, I did.) I fancy that Geoffrey Dawson put Curtis across – as Estates Bursar he wielded much influence at the time. T. E. Lawrence had also been elected, to write his famous book. It is again a tribute to Lionel that Lawrence confided in him more than in anyone. When one reads Lawrence's remarkable Letters, one sees that the most intimate and revealing are those written to Curtis – Lawrence poured out his secret heart-aches to him as to no-one else.

When Lawrence joined the R.A.F. and ceased to live in College, he left his few possessions with Lionel, who exercised a kind of guardianship over his interests. When Lawrence sometimes arrived at night, with Curtis away, he would sleep in his rooms and away again on his fatal motor-bike at daybreak. Lionel was involved in Lawrence's affairs at his death, and was much moved, though he had seen too much of death in South Africa to show it. I remember Lawrence's appearance on the night his Fellowship expired. It was All Souls tide, and my first Gaudy Night. There suddenly appeared in the Smoking Room, crowded with Fellows in dinner jackets and black ties, and Quondams in white ties and tails, a slim lance-corporal in R.A.F. uniform, looking like a boy of eighteen, only his blazing eyes and tortured mouth betraying him. Lionel pushed me forward to meet him: I would not intrude, as usual I was content to watch and record.

Curtis brought the most interesting people to All Souls – I don't remember Brand or Dawson or Malcolm doing so, all much richer: Lionel was the hospitable one, the entertainer. He had some private means, not much, and later he inherited a bit of property; he used his small Fellowship stipend to print his books. As I have said he brought Smuts and Herzog to us, and also Smuts's right-hand man, highly intelligent young Jan Hofmeyr, whom his own Africaners would not have at any price to succeed Smuts: as an Oxford Rhodes Scholar, much too liberal-minded about the blacks. Dick Feetham came over too, by now (I think) Chief Justice in the Union. I do not recall Sir Patrick Duncan, who became Governor-General, whose early promise Curtis had observed admiringly, if patronisingly: 'a great man sprung from a Scotch peasant home.' Lionel was nothing if not a patron.

From Canada he brought the retired Prime Minister, Sir Robert Borden: a fine old-fashioned Canadian gentleman, crinkly curly hair parted in the middle, elastic, springy gait. He was good to me, very much a junior, and on his return kept writing me letters, and sent me the Collected Poems of Archibald Lampman. A terrible highbrow, I could not enthuse over sub-Swinburne – a devotee of Eliot, I didn't much care for Swinburne in the original. It was rather a case of –

> There was a young man in the States,
> Who so greatly admired Mr Yeats
>   That he sent him some books –
>   An edition *de luxe*
> Of Wilcox, with portraits and plates.

Then came André Siegfried, with whom I became more friendly. A tall, harsh Lorrainer, with grey complexion, staring blue eyes and grinding voice, he was distinctly *raide*, but interesting to me as any Frenchman would be. He had made a name in the English world with a book on New Zealand, and followed it up with something of a best-seller, *America Comes of Age*. In France he was regarded as an authority on the Anglo-Saxons. Of a rigid cast of mind, in his way as pontifical as Curtis himself, he had no subtle or flexible understanding of the English, as Elie Halévy or André Maurois[4] had. Siegfried was astonished when I told him that the then Leader of the Labour Party, a Leftist Socialist, George

---

[4] For Maurois v. my *Memories of Men and Women*.

Lansbury, was a practising Anglo-Catholic: unthinkable in France, he said. (However, I remembered that at least the wife of the great Socialist, Jean Jaurès, was a *dévote*.)

Siegfried, a rich man in his own right – the family were manufacturers in Normandy, from which his father had been a Senator of the Third Republic – had political aspirations, but settled for an academic career, becoming a professor at the Collège de France, eventually attaining to the French Academy. He had imbibed Anglo-Saxon habits of hospitality, entertaining me at his home in the Rue de Courty, just round the corner from the Chambre des Députés, where perhaps his heart was.

An interesting example of what Curtis could do with and for a man is provided by the case of Reggie Coupland – to become Sir Reginald. A New College Wykehamist, he was stuck as Ancient History tutor at Trinity, bored in the well-trampled field of Greek history, nothing in mind to write about. Curtis persuaded him into the field of the Empire, and he eventually became Beit Professor of Colonial History. As such, he wrote a series of standard historical works, mainly on the history of East Africa, such as *Kirk of the Zambesi* and its successors. He may be said to have laid the foundations of research in this field, though he wrote also on Nigeria, William Wilberforce and David Livingstone. Somewhat overlooked by the narrower and stricter academics, he produced some of the most creative and fertilising historical work of the time, and in a significant field.

Coupland became a distinguished public figure, member of important government commissions on Palestine and India, and ended up with an ambitious (unfinished) work on the Nationalities within the Empire. A pure academic like Richard Pares derided Coupland's avowed business of bringing colonial governors to Oxford; and there was a *Zwiespalt* between Coupland and E. L. Woodward. (My sympathies were with Coupland. G. N. Clark realised that though I was the protagonist of the Labour Party in college, a supposed Left fanatic, in fact I was more ready to compromise; Pares not, a sea-green incorruptible. Contrary to academic opinion, I also thought Coupland a better historian.)

Then came a sad breach. Coupland refused to follow Curtis

in his last campaign, for World Federation, announced in *Civitas Dei*, and its sequel, subsequently published as *The Commonwealth of God*. Coupland thought, as others did, that the Prophet had gone off the rails. But Prophets are ruthless, and Coupland was never forgiven for his defection. Lesser men were forgiven minor offences, Lionel took no notice; but this was the Ark of the Covenant, he held the key to it. The world must come together, or perish in flames. If Curtis was wrong, he was no more so than Bertrand Russell, who received all the acclaim. Curtis remained, as always, in the background.

We of the younger generation in College were very irreverent about *Civitas Dei*. According to his custom with earlier (influential) memoranda for circulation, Curtis had it printed with a blank page opposite each page for comments by the Chosen whose opinions he sought. Pares and I, like a couple of schoolboys, used to steal surreptitious readings in Lionel's absence. We were convulsed by his introduction to the Problem of India: 'The ground is damp, difficult and dangerous to sit upon.' We felt confirmed by Bernard Shaw's Comment, ending up, 'In short, the British Empire is Christ's Kingdom on earth, and Lionel Curtis is its Prophet.' This was no worse than the Red Dean of Canterbury's conviction that the USSR, *The Socialist Sixth* – a best-seller, which made a fortune for him, already a rich man – was Christ's Kingdom; or Sartre's pronouncement that the USSR was the incarnation of human freedom.

'Lord, what fools these mortals be!' – William Shakespeare was not given to such prognostications. Lionel's brought him a fresh crop of devotees. His book was translated into several languages; gifts were laid at his feet from various countries. I recall a consignment of magnificent sponges from Cyprus; Lionel gave me a huge one, which has lasted me to this day, more than thirty years after. And the faithful turned up – some of them fearful bores – to follow in the steps of the Master.

However much we laughed, he had not ceased to be able to pull off a trick or two. He brought Arthur Salter back, retired from the International Labour Office at Geneva, to become Professor of Political Theory and Institutions. Salter was an eminent civil servant, but he knew no political theory – none the worse for that; so I was given the job of deputising for him and giving his lectures on it, tying myself in knots to square Marxist theory with common sense.

China came up as a chief question on the international chessboard, and these various authorities tootled off to see what they could do to put things right. Curtis went, and wrote his portentous book, *The Capital Question of China*; Salter went, and came back with that curious Chinese look about the eyes, as also did R. H. Tawney. I think Lindsay of Balliol went, so did Warden Adams. The more these great and good men put their shoulder to the wheel, the more the thing fell apart, till it collapsed totally. When I made the point irreverently to Salter, he was nonplussed for a moment, but saw the humour of it.

Another creation of Curtis' was H. V. Hodson (my first election as examiner for the Fellowship). Lionel lifted him on to *The Round Table*, of which he became editor, thence on to *The Sunday Times,* meanwhile writing on the economic aspects of the Empire, and books like *The Empire in the World, The British Commonwealth and the Future* – very much in the idiom of the Master; or a more factual study of disintegration, *The Great Divide: Britain – India – Pakistan*. He ended up as Provost of beautiful Ditchley.

Hodson is descended from the Hodson of Hodson's Horse. His career makes me think of Lionel's charming children's story: of the hunter who spared the life of a baby elephant in Africa. Elephants never forget, and when this one grew up to be a circus elephant, years after, it one day recognised its saviour, extended its trunk and carefully lifted him from the sixpenny seats into the half-crown stalls. There was something elephantine about Curtis, and something of the hunter in Harry Hodson.

Did Curtis recognise defeat? He gave no outer sign of it. There were always minor causes to take up: at one time a campaign against Ribbon development – Kidlington was being ruined, a hideous mess. No doubt he was right, but – a Canute against the tide of modern 'civilisation': in vain. At another time, a campaign against sky-writing. A modern young man with modern tastes, the Duke of Windsor – then Prince of Wales – was all in favour of it. Curtis's campaign got through to old-fashioned King George V, who carpeted the

Prince, and enforced that the Royal House should speak with one voice on the matter. I rather think that the nuisance was abated for the time.

Academe was allergic to Curtis. A typical don, Robin Dundas of my old College, Christ Church, described him to me *tout court* as a 'bore'. Of course Lionel could be a bit of a bore, but he was so much else; Dundas was unaware that he was a bore – and nothing else. And Lionel did good work for Oxford, unbeknownst, and in spite of discouragements.

Among unforgettable scenes at All Souls, some of them comic, here was one that was rather shocking. Lionel brought to dinner rich Mr ffennell of Wytham, woods and all, a valuable lung to the city. Lionel had known him as Schumacher in South Africa, and now had his eye on him for a prospective benefactor. E. L. Woodward was in the chair – I as a junior the only other witness; he held forth against bringing rich people into Oxford, holding out the prospect of honorary degrees, etc, for what they might do for the university. I was rather shocked, though hardly surprised at anything from Woodward – he was lower middle class, envious of his betters, rather ill-bred. Lionel was appalled, but said not a word, except to me afterwards. Patience, persistence, public spirit received its reward: eventually the university got Wytham, park and woods, from generous Colonel ffennell. I think Woodward walked in them.

Another such scene occurred one evening when Lionel was entertaining Tom Jones. 'T.J.' had been immensely influential as secretary to Lloyd George, then to Baldwin, eventually to the Cabinet. He was a regular habitué of Cliveden; I have a photograph of Lionel, T.J., and myself out walking on a winter's day there. I am bound to own that T.J. was friendly, and I liked my fellow-Celt. One evening the three of us were in Lionel's rooms with Douglas Jay, then Junior Fellow, when he launched forth into a violent diatribe against the Welsh – he was really reacting against recent experience with Goronwy Rees, unreliable and undependable as any Celt could be. Again Lionel kept utter silence – always under control, as I was myself (an unpopular trait with juniors).

There were also comic scenes. Lord Faringdon was coming in from Buscot to present a book to the Codrington Library through Lionel: he was never my guest, though I had been his at Buscot. On the other hand, Lord Berners, who lived at Faringdon, was frequently my guest. We were sitting around the smoking-room fire with Quintin Hailsham, not expecting Gavin Faringdon to be brought in.

Lionel, portentously: 'Why am I mixed up between Lord Faringdon and Lord Berners?'

Quintin, wickedly: 'Ask Leslie: he knows.'

Lionel: 'But I don't know. Which is which? Why do I confuse the two?'

Quintin, with a meaning look at me: 'Ask Leslie. *He* knows.'

Lionel, thinking this over, raising his voice: 'Do you mean that he is an Enemy of the Family?'

The butler, appearing round the screen: 'Lord Faringdon to see you, sir.'

– Had he heard the exchange from behind the screen? Lionel hastily arose and scampered off with him; Quintin vastly pleased at his own naughtiness, and both of us tickled by Lionel's old-fashioned phrase, 'an Enemy of the Family', for it.

Lionel's last protégé before the War came down on us was the splendid German, Helmuth von Moltke, grandson of the famous Field Marshal and head of the family with its vast estate in Silesia. Lionel came to know him through his South African connexions, the Rose Innes (of Scottish descent). It fell to me, one sombre autumn evening before dinner in Hall, to introduce those two noble figures to each other: Lionel's friend Helmuth and my friend, Adam von Trott, each of them 6 feet 6 inches tall; Helmuth, dark, erect and glittering, like a sword; Adam fair, blue-eyed, more supple and willowy. I watched them give each other a momentary look of doubt. Both were condemned to death by Hitler after the Generals' abortive plot in July 1944, though Helmuth had no part in it. A devout Christian, he belonged merely to a circle which discussed the shape things should take in Germany *after* the evil thing was defeated – by others. Foreign Office people had a certain sympathy for Hitler at that moment: after all, the

Generals, the German Army and people had supported him all the way, so long as he was successful. Historically, he had done a marvellous job in organising his idiot people for a second attempt at *Welt-Macht*. No wonder Stalin remarked to Eden that he was 'a very remarkable man – only he had no sense of moderation'; and then added, 'I see you think I have no sense of moderation. That is where you are wrong.'

Lionel celebrated his friendship with Helmuth in a booklet, *A German of the Resistance*; I celebrated mine with Adam in *A Cornishman Abroad*: a certain parallelism in our experience. It was General Swinton who first brought Adam, quite young, to All Souls. Lionel had known Swinton in South Africa. I helped to bring Adam to Oxford as a Rhodes Scholar. These things connect up. And what scenes there were at All Souls in those historic days!

Lionel and I were both countrymen, a bond between us; neither of us was urban, and certainly not suburban – where the mass of English people today inhabit suburbia, physically and mentally. At Johannesburg his idea was to ensure 'a girdle of green country around the city.' Then, 'we found a lovely little nest of dead grass on the ground with two warm eggs in it, exactly like lark eggs.' On the veldt 'the flowers defy description, B. & L. were quite carried away, and I, not knowing by what names to address them, remained speechless.' He had an eye for everything country-wise: here 'a mimosa bush with strange green flowers or fruit in the shape of arrow heads hanging downwards. . . . The pendants were the houses of creatures made in imitation of a product of the tree.' Or, there, 'an immense area of drainage amongst the hills all runs down to a narrow neck, which could be blocked at slight expense giving immense storage for irrigation.' Then, 'I went to see the 1500 graves of the English soldiers before we left Bloemfontein. I noticed Tom Hichens' fresh grave with a rough wooden cross.' Both Lionels left a brother in South Africa. I often notice the memorials of the Boer War in English churches: the price of Empire. Had it been worth it?

At Kidlington Lionel created a garden behind the house, planted a whole field of willows beside the Cher beyond, and lived a rural life. I can see him now canoeing alone along those sedgy waterways, looking like a tramp. And indeed, as an undergraduate, he had taken to the roads as a tramp to see what it was like to live as such folks lived. Once he overplayed the part and arrived at a village at night in a downpour, dirty and famished, utterly penniless, and had to throw himself on the mercy of the local vicar for a night's lodging, declare who he was and what he was up to, to help him to get back to Oxford. Sometimes he would organise a Sunday morning tramp across the fields – in those days there were fields – ending up at hospitable Kidlington for lunch.

On our after-lunch walks round Christ Church Meadows or Magdalen Lionel was always first to see spring announced in the rose-flush of the willows, or to admire the first chestnuts coming out in flower. Along the city wall in front of Merton there used to grow clumps of ivy-leaved crowfoot – the French have an imaginative name for it, *les ruines de Rome*. Lionel noticed that the gardeners had scraped it all off (the people never *see* or understand anything). One afternoon in Addison's Walk I pulled down a superb chestnut bloom for him to sniff; at once there popped out a bee, which stung him on the inside of his nostril. He charged me with doing it deliberately, to tease me; but by the time we got back to All Souls his nose, that fine organ, looked like a pudding.

He was not accident-prone, but he told me of a comic happening to him when coming through the Mediterranean on a liner during the 1914–18 War. There was an alarm of a submarine about, and Lionel, going below to console a hysterical old lady, sat plump down on her crochet-bag; the needle hooked on to his bottom and couldn't be got out. So Lionel had to step up the companion-way with the crochet-bag fixed to his backside to get hold of the ship's doctor. Everybody laughed so much that they forgot the submarine for the time.

The most accident-prone of the Fellows was Geoffrey Faber, to whom something similar happened. He was fly-fishing on a stream on the Welsh Border when the wind blew his line back into his face, and the barb hooked itself into the gristle of his nose. The more he tugged at it the worse it got. Nothing for it but to mount his motor-bike into the neighbouring town, riding uphill with rod, line and hook fixed to his face, to seek the doctor, while the boys in the street jeered and cheered.

I have said that Lionel was a good raconteur – I wish I could remember more of his stories. Here is one from South Africa, where Bishop Colenso (a Cornishman) was a doughty defender of the blacks, particularly the Zulus, even of Cetewayo, a rather murderous old barbarian. The Bishop's daughter, a rigid six-footer of an unmarriageable sort, had gone thoroughly to the good. The joke was put about that she was to marry Cetewayo, and she was supposed to have said, 'What? And he a *king*!'

It was Lionel who told me the story of an irrevocable brick dropped at the Bodleian. Bodley's Librarian was Craster of All Souls, of a Northumbrian family so ancient that his name originally had an apostrophe, Cra'ster, and with a cleft palate he had an apostrophe in his speech; his hair sprouting from every orifice, he resembled the sculpted gargoyle of himself over a Bodleian gateway. He was the soul of courtesy. However, one day he was showing round the Bodleian a party which included a former Foreign Office diplomat who had had to resign for dealing in foreign currencies. This gentleman put the question to Craster, who had no idea who he was, 'How did Sir Thomas Bodley come by his money?' To which Bodley's Librarian replied innocently, 'He was – ah – in the diplomatic service.'

Craster came off better when, at the time of the Abdication, Lionel was saying that a statue should be put up to Mrs Simpson for ridding us of an unsuitable monarch. Lionel laid down that what was needed above all in a king was punctuality – and Edward VIII was always late. Craster, who had the Edwardian taste for puns: 'So he became the – ah – late king.'

Curtis had a nice story, which reflected absurdly the conflict between the philosophers over realism and idealism, and put it in its proper perspective. He had come back from more urgent affairs in South Africa, and went to New College to take his former tutor, the philosopher Joachim, out for a walk. Joachim had been a friend of his fellow philosopher, Pritchard. Pritchard was now living in one of those delightful eighteenth-century houses in the Broad, destroyed to make way for the architecturally third-rate New Bodleian. Curtis proposed that he and Joachim should collect their old friend too, but noticed a distinct coolness, and asked why. Going down New College Lane, Joachim pointed to a tree saying, 'He thinks that that tree is *real*!'; and then, his voice rising to a scream, 'And not only real, but *green*!!' Lionel, who had more important things on *his* mind and been through a war, said, 'Come on, now; let's call on Pritch.'

Dear Lionel, his last days of decline were rather sad. He had developed an addiction to snuff, with a little admixture: where had he got the habit from, whence the addiction? I wondered whether it wasn't, at the end, an unspoken admission of defeat, a recognition that the Prophet's mission was over.

6

John Buchan at Elsfield

When John Buchan died, the Editor of *The Times* told me that never had they received so many tributes to a public figure, sheaves of them pouring in from men of all walks and conditions of life, only a tithe of which could be published. That gives us some indication of the man himself; it is testimony to the extraordinary range and variety of his contacts and friendships with people. It also shows that these contacts were not merely formal; John Buchan belonged to the rare class of public figure who comes across to people as a friend, with whom they feel a personal bond, and in whom they feel a care for them and their concerns.

I can testify from my own experience. When he was on his last leave from Canada and already ill – within a year of his death – I was ill in London of the same duodenal complaint of which he was a victim, and he found time amid all the innumerable claims on him and in his own illness to write me encouraging letters in his own hand. Hundreds of people have had similar experiences of his kindness and thought. I appreciated it much then – how much more now; perhaps only a busy author, with writing of all kinds on his hands, knows so well what it means.

No doubt he paid some price in concentration of achievement for his readiness and willingness, his constant services to all and sundry. What he gained in stature was unmistakable; he gave himself away, right and left, with no thought for his own strength, like the man in the fable, *L'Homme à la Cervelle d'Or*.

With that there went – and perhaps from it came – the

catholicism of his sympathy. A Tory himself, his instinctive conservatism rooted in his sense of history – though that did not mean that he was not a progressive – his sympathies and affections were extended in every direction politically. In fact, I believe it was a recommendation with him that one was on the other side. I remember the particular regard in which he held, and always spoke of, Maxton, then much in the public eye as leader of the I.L.P. and a notable figure in Parliament. With one young neophyte of the Left, ardent and touchy, he was patience and courtesy itself.

Alas, with what can one reward his kindness now? Nothing – except to cherish the memory of the man he was: that quick, spare, gallant figure, with the grave face and frosty Northern eyes that could yet sparkle with liveliness and good-humour, with his old-fashioned Scots courtesy and birdlike quickness of movement, walking cap in hand and in loose-fitting tweeds along the lanes and up the hill from Marston to his home on the brow of Elsfield overlooking Oxford; or walking on the terrace in the green shades of a summer evening, looking down upon Otmoor and, in the gathered blue of distance, his beloved Cotswolds; or again, sitting on a low chair in a corner of the library at Elsfield, the firelight leaping up and gleaming in the ranks of books, himself the heart and soul of the talk.

The foundation of his life, I realise now, was the principle of Christian love. He really loved people. Everything, apart from his gifts – though they derived strength from it – sprang from that. There was the secret spring of the two qualities that were so marked in him: the unsleeping sense of duty, the breadth of his sympathy. His devotion to duty was obvious in every sphere of his life. He was stern with himself in his work; always beforehand with his engagements (like Trollope), never failing to perform what he had promised – in that so unlike the ways of authors in general. He was a good deal of a stoic – except that, to balance that strain in him, no one had a greater natural gift for the enjoyment of life. Only someone who knows the physical anguish and pain that accompany that illness from which he suffered, knows what such devotion to work and duty must have cost.

Perhaps I may say something of him as a writer, though it is a disadvantage not to know the Scottish background, the society and tradition out of which he sprang and against which his work must be seen. I appreciate all the more the importance of that background, the inspiration that came from his native region, the memories and associations that went back to his childhood there, since a writer should have roots. His were vigorous and idiosyncratic, at once hardy and nourishing to the life of the imagination; the beginnings in the manse in Fife looking out upon the Forth; the summer holidays in the Border country, that was Sir Walter Scott's own country too, the beloved Tweedside. The memory of those hills and streams is never far away in his writings, and his best books are either inspired by them or somewhere carry their stamp. When he came to sum up his own work in *Memory-Hold-the-Door*, he wrote: 'The woods and beaches (of Fife) were always foreign places, in which I was at best a sojourner. But the Border hills were my own possession, a countryside in which my roots went deep. . . . The dying shepherd asked not for the conventional Heaven, but for "Bourhope at a reasonable rent", and, if Paradise be a renewal of what was happy and innocent in our earthly days, mine will be some such golden afternoon within sight and sound of Tweed.'

One can appreciate what he owed to that distinctive background and the life of its people. For a writer, it was an advantage too to have been born a son of the Manse; he knew what it was to be poor, to share the life of the people; at the same time, the standards that he imbibed from childhood were the educated standards of ministry and gentlefolk. It meant, as with Kilvert or Crabbe, that all doors were open to him, the ways of life of all classes. There was the freshness and vividness of the Border country itself, the sense of the soil, the love of its solitary spaces, above all the historic memories and associations with which it is crowded. Nor should one forget the importance attached to intellect and the things of the mind – which Scots are apt to feel more keenly than English people – to appreciate learning, scholarship, intellect as such. A further strain in him was the tradition of Adam Smith, Lockhart, Caird, and of so many generations of Scots coming up to Balliol. He told me that he should have come up to Balliol in the usual way if it had not been for his intense admiration in his undergraduate days at Glasgow for Walter Pater. Out of that romantic devotion he chose to come up to Brasenose. (By the time he came up Pater had died.)

He started as a follower of, and inspired by, Robert Louis Stevenson. There could be no better school for a beginner; for Stevenson was a careful craftsman and Buchan had a mastery of words – an initial gift which greater writers have sometimes been without and some writers never achieve. His romantic temperament, his preference for the life of action, admiring the heroic and stirring deeds, responded to Stevenson; one sees the influence on his early stories – among his best. Buchan has told us how potent that influence was over the young men of his generation, especially at the universities in Scotland. R.L.S. was 'at once Scottish and cosmopolitan, artist and adventurer, scholar and gipsy. Above all he was a true companion. He took us by the hand and shared in all our avocations. It was a profound and overmastering influence.'

Eventually Buchan grew out of it. In time 'Stevenson seemed to me to have altogether too much artifice about him, and I felt a suspicion of pose behind his optimism and masculinity.' That helps to define a point for us about Buchan's own work: he was an admirable stylist. His own style was the reverse of artificial or affected; it was vigorous and natural, athletic and spare, running beautifully clear like one of his own Border streams, with an occasional coloured pebble in it to arrest the attention, some infrequent word that was yet authentic, coming out of the life of the land and the language of its people. He had a discriminating use of words, sensitive and scholarly. He was, by nature and inclination, a scholarly writer, having both a classical education, with its accompanying training, and strong historical feeling. Since style is a preservative element in literature, his best books will be read so long as we care for good standards.

Of his novels I am not qualified to speak; but to his gifts we must add – what is not very common – the sheer faculty of telling a story. John Buchan was a Tusitala in his own right. He loved the story for its own sake; he understood suspense, the art of excitement, in such stories as *The Thirty-Nine Steps*; that he was sensitive to atmosphere may be seen from a story like 'The Grove of Ashtaroth' in *The Moon Endureth*. In his autobiography he tells us how from early days he told himself stories, or rather stories told themselves in his head; one recognises a born story-teller – just what Trollope says of himself in his *Autobiography*.

Buchan kept a clear distinction in his mind between his lighter efforts, his thrillers and tales of adventure, and his more serious work, whether in fiction, *belles lettres* or in the field which came to weigh most with him, historical biography. I remember him telling me that he wrote his novels at dictation speed; but that he never could write more than fifteen hundred words a day at serious history. He took biography as serious history, devoted himself to it with all the application of his mind, working hard at sources, making himself into a professional historian – a professional who could write: there is the difference.

He says of his *Montrose, Sir Walter Scott, Cromwell* and *Augustus*: 'All these four books were, indeed, in a sense a confession of faith, for they enabled me to define my own creed on many matters of doctrine and practice, and thereby cleared my mind. They were laborious affairs compared to my facile novels, but they were also a relaxation, for they gave me a background into which I could escape from contemporary futilities, a watch-tower from which I had a long prospect, and could see modern problems in juster proportions. That is the supreme value of history.'

Above all, there is the Life of Scott. There he had a magnificent subject, to which all his impulses responded. 'It is a book which I was bound one day or other to write, for I have had the fortune to be born and bred under the shadow of that great tradition.' He had the noble background of Scott's country, Edinburgh – the most striking, the most sharply-etched town in this island, with its mingled sharpness and sweetness, like the cold showers and rare lights of a Northern spring; and the shared experiences of Tweedside: 'Above all, Scott had that kindest bequest of the good fairies at his cradle, a tradition, bone of his bone, a free life lived among clear waters and green hills as in the innocency of the world. . . . The world opened to him as a wide wind-blown country, with a prospect of twenty miles past the triple peaks of Eildon to the line of Cheviot, the homely fragrance and bustle of a moorland farm, the old keep of Smailholm as a background, and a motley of figures out of an earlier age. . . . He had mingled intimately with every class and condition of men, he had enough education to broaden his outlook but not enough to dim it; he was familiar alike with city and moorland, with the sown and the desert, and he escaped the pedantry of both the class-room and the drawing-room; above all, he had the good fortune to stand at the meeting-place of two worlds, and to have it in him to be their chief interpreter.' From the country that gave him birth to the man himself: the poetry, the peopled imagination, the nobility of Scott, one of the most magnanimous of men.

Of his historical biographies, *Montrose* and *Cromwell* have special claims: *Montrose*, because Buchan had a lifelong devotion to that gallant figure out of the Scottish past, and because he had an inner sympathy with his point of view. It is true that he sees the history of that time through the eyes of Montrose, but he gives a just estimate of the character of Montrose's grim opponent, Argyll. In all these books he has a firm hold of the personalities of the historical figures, whether his sympathies are with them or not. This book must be regarded as his chief contribution to historical research; it is written from original sources and he had various additions and corrections of his own to offer in writing it. He had an intimate knowledge of the countryside over which Montrose fought, all those marches and counter-marches in and out the Highlands, the Homeric battles. He had an intimate knowledge of the literature, even of the pamphlet literature, of the seventeenth century; he collected the traditions and stories, what there was of verbal tradition.

The Life of Cromwell covers a less original track, a more trampled field. It is a bigger subject, a larger canvas crowded with figures, and Buchan made of it a fine book. It sprang out of his abiding interest in the seventeenth century, where he was most at home. He read all the sources and authorities; he visited, as an historian should, the places and studied the battlefields. He had a good understanding of military history. (An historian friend of mine, who fought in 1914–18, told me that Buchan's account of trench-warfare in his *History of the Great War* was true to the fact.) He brought something more to his study of Cromwell – his own turn of mind.

We see the breadth of his sympathies enabling him to thread

his way with fairness and understanding through the maze of sects and sectaries, the parties and factions. There is justice of mind in his treatment of the men on both sides, Cromwell and Charles, Laud and Strafford, Ireton and Vane. For Cromwell himself, that extraordinary man, Buchan had an inner feeling that makes him at least clear. Then there is the firm composition of the book, well conceived and built up, the sense of scene, the practised rendering of action, the gift of phrase. Of Cromwell's religion, for example: 'He has been called a religious genius, but on his genius it is not easy to be dogmatic; like Bunyan's Much-afraid, when he went through the River none could understand what he said.' On the constitutional dilemma of the Protector's government, its inner contradiction: 'He was to be a prince, but a prince who must remain standing, since he had no throne.'

I remember meeting Buchan on his way back to Elsfield the afternoon he came down into Oxford to send off the manuscript of *Cromwell*. (He did all his writing in his own hand; hence the high standard he maintained.) It was early summer, June over the Oxfordshire countryside, the long grass lush in the water-meadows, the elms of Marston in their full panoply of foliage. He was feeling sad, he said, at parting with someone with whom he had lived for two years now. Not a word about the immense labour and effort that had gone into it; he took all that for granted.

He lived in the realm of the historical imagination. How naturally it came to him may be seen in an essay, 'Thoughts on a Distant Prospect of Oxford', full of feeling for the place and its memories; printed in a volume in which the sense of history illumines the study of literature, *Homilies and Recreations*.

Of his classical biographies, *Julius Caesar* and *Augustus* – the latter his last big work – I am not able to speak. But they have this element of authenticity, that they go back to his youthful interest in Roman history, to the ambition of his undergraduate days to paint a portrait of Augustus. 'I had already done a good deal of work on the subject,' he wrote amid all the distractions of being a Governor-General – 'and my first two winters in Canada gave me leisure to re-read the Latin and Greek texts.' 'I have rarely found more enjoyment in a task,' he adds, 'for I was going over again carefully the ground which I had scampered across in my youth.' What boyishness, what verve! – and from a man in highest office and often in pain.

It testifies to the width of his reading and culture; a man of a type all too rare in public life today. For he was a great reading man. 'Reading has always filled so large a part of my life', he says disarmingly – as if there were not a score of other interests and avocations: fishing, bird-watching, walking; the Empire – first South Africa, then Canada; publishing, Reuter's, serving on the University Chest at Oxford; becoming a Member of Parliament, Governor-General of Canada. In addition to being one of the most prolific authors of his time. Yet – reading filled a large part of his life. You will get some idea of his powers in this direction – along with a retentive memory – from an essay on Scott in *Homilies and Recreations*. During his serious illness and duodenal operation in 1917 he read through a dozen of the Waverley Novels, the Valois and d'Artagnan cycles of Dumas, then Victor Hugo's *Notre Dame* and the immense *Les Misérables,* almost a library in itself, ending up with half a dozen of Balzac. How he contrived to get through all the reading and writing he did, let alone everything else he accomplished, beats me; though he owed a lot to the watchfulness and care of his wife: a rare comradeship in life, in work and public service.

When in those days one went up to Elsfield, one always found him abreast of contemporary reading as of affairs, interested in all that was being written and thought. Alas, being young, one took so much for granted! It is only now that one knows how remarkable that was, such generosity of spirit in it: he was by nature an admirer, an encourager of others' work. He had nothing of the denigrator about him: I never heard him utter depreciatory words of anyone – a rare attitude in literary circles. He did not move in literary circles; he was by nature a man of action, who happened to have the gifts of a writer. I remember how he won me early on by his warm appreciation of 'Q.' 's novels and stories – absurdly under-estimated.

Now, when one thinks of Elsfield, something rare has gone from the familiar landscape. Everything there reminds one of him; the way up the hill, the little bridge and culvert at the foot, the road winding between the elms and ash trees, the elder I once saw in blossom-time gleaming like a ball of snow in the frozen moonlight, while a parachute-flare slowly descended over Otmoor. There is the little church, hipped up on its platform, with bell-cote at the west end overlooking the road; then around the bend to the tall house with its eighteenth-century core, and something Scottish about its rigid vertical lines – that ever-hospitable house with its friendly welcome for the young.

On Sunday afternoons in those days there was always a crowd and good talk. Out of a kindly thought for my shyness, I used to be asked on quieter occasions, when there was just the inner circle of the family, a few guests, the domesticity and firelit charm which those two, John and Susan Buchan, gathered around them. Evening wore on; the firelight leaped on the hearth and made a comfortable glow in that square shelved room with its cargo of books. Now it is autumn and the trees outside are turning lemon and gold; mellow evening light comes across the green spaces of Otmoor and in at the western windows. Or it is winter and there is a winter stillness outside – darkness in the trees, snow-light upon the slopes, the village street moonlit as in Arnold's poem. At the door one takes leave of that friendly house; it is time to go downhill, back to the spires and colleges waiting down there in the night. As one recalls that so familiar routine, the village on the brow, that hospitable house, time slips away and one is there again, the circle rounded and complete once more.

II

What are we to think of John Buchan today?

When a well known writer dies, his reputation, and even knowledge of him, dip into a trough for a time, perhaps for a whole generation, and the more popular he was in his lifetime the longer and deeper the trough. The most notorious example of this is the case of Trollope, and the more spectacular the recovery. A writer as distinguished as he was popular, Quiller-Couch – properly admired by John Buchan – has not yet emerged from eclipse. Buchan himself, in the shade for a time, has made an early recovery, especially with his thrillers – which he himself set least store by.

My original tribute to him was written under the immediate shadow of his loss. Since then much more has emerged about him. He has had the good luck of one of the best literary biographies of our time, by Janet Adam Smith; and recently a Memoir by his son, William Buchan, hardly less good. Yet neither achieves intimacy; each author, even the son, is conscious of a certain distance from the subject. What was it that was so reserved about Buchan, when so many people thought they knew him? Where was the centre of the man? What made him tick?

His son entitles his concluding chapter, remarkably, 'A Very Queer Fish Indeed?' He says, 'JB had always seemed to me a mysterious person. For all his openness, courtesy, kindness, his geniality, his great knowledge which he was ready to share, his charity and his questing, eager spirit, together with his pains and disappointments and very human foibles . . . I believe that he held always a certain part of himself apart, inviolable and inviolate.'

I don't regard Buchan as a queer fish at all. He was above all a writer; and one answer to his son's question is that a writer instinctively keeps the seed-bed from which he creates secret and inviolate. With no-one was this more obvious than with Trollope, who protected his inner life with a gruff, abrasive manner. John Buchan had beautiful manners, and was courteous to all and sundry; his eminent qualities his son denotes justly, but about his inner life the writer was as close as a clam. Not deliberately, but quite naturally; that was what made him a secret man, the essential man no one knew (except possibly his wife: she understood him).

His inner life was dominated by his imagination. Wherever he was and whatever he was doing – and he was doing a hundred other things besides writing (that was what was so remarkable) – he was telling himself the stories that welled up in him, talking to the characters that came to mind and demanded to have their stories told. Just like Trollope. The characters in his fiction were sometimes suggested by, or had touches of, real people he had known, as with any novelist. Sir

Edward Leithen, especially in *Sick Heart River*, comes closest to himself; and Auberon Herbert has had a distinguished biography under the title, *The Man Who Was 'Greenmantle'*, for his career suggested it. The great men of history and literature were no less real to Buchan – they were heroes to him, Montrose and Sir Walter Scott especially (for they were Scots), but also Cromwell, Ralegh and Augustus; and he wrote about them all.

Paradoxically Buchan started as a writer of the Nineties in the *Yellow Book*, the organ of the decadent aesthetes, and as reader for John Lane, their patron and publisher. Q. distinguished in the Nineties two schools: the writers of action who looked up to Robert Louis Stevenson, and the aesthetic movement around Yeats and Arthur Symons. Q. belonged to the first; when it came to the decadent Symons, 'I could do nothing for him', he said to me, and would not put a single poem of his into *The Oxford Book of English Verse*. In spite of the aesthetic book jackets of Buchan's earliest volumes, poems and essays, he was no aesthete and realised himself in the school of action.

These writers had a view of life in which action came first; their aim was a well-rounded, balanced life, making their contribution to the life of the nation – as both Q. and John Buchan did – in which writing was only a part of the whole. Both of them devoted a large amount of time unsparingly to public causes. This stands in marked contrast to writers who dedicated their whole lives to their writing – contemporaries like Henry James, Hardy, Kipling, Meredith, Conrad; these emerge as greater writers, single-minded, concentrated on their work.

Public life has many disillusionments, and demands sacrifices all the greater from a writer, who has better things to do. Perhaps Buchan's son has this in mind when he writes: 'Contrary to the widely held belief that John Buchan's life was a story of unbroken successes, he had in fact many disappointments. After his failure to win a Fellowship at All Souls, the first real setback of his life, he was to endure many other blows, to feel sometimes a sense of rejection. There was his failure to make the kind of mark in British politics which, once, he must have been sure of making. There was the noticeable lack of recognition of hard and valuable work for his party.'

John Buchan was a small, spare man. I sensed among the bigger, bulkier figures who took up so much more room on the public stage in their day, were so important and self-important – and are now forgotten (as he is not) – a condescending attitude towards him on their part: after all, he was only a writer. They did nothing for him – until Canada asked for him to be Governor-General; Canada and John Buchan put that right: he became the best and best-loved Governor-General Canada ever had.

There remains the question of the man as such. William Buchan tells us: 'The world of my father's family was an innocent one, and the quality in him that I see most clearly is a kind of innocence, a real simplicity of heart. Giving people all his kindness, perception, even his admiration, he was unaware that they were not always so generous in receiving as he was in giving. His faults were the faults of innocence. If he dropped names, or seemed to rejoice in close acquaintance with important people, this was only an expression of his pleasure in the richness and variety of the English society in which he, a Scotsman and a historian, had found a place: to call him a snob would imply that he used his grand acquaintance to impress or humiliate others. . . .'

The important thing here is that Buchan was a historian, and a historian has, in the course of his work, to drop names like Henry VIII and Oliver Cromwell, the Duke and Duchess of Marlborough, the Marquis Curzon, Ernie Bevin or Winston, names like those I am dropping in this book. Not to drop names, to please conventional muffs, would put a historian out of business, and 'name-dropping' can be seen to be an absurd (and very recent) American cliché. It is usually the dull and inferior who resent one mentioning more interesting people than they are.

Once at a dinner of the Annenbergs at the American Embassy, I was engrossed in conversation with the lady on my left, when at length the lady on my right said, 'Are you particularly interested in the lady on your left because she is Curzon's daughter?' I said, 'Of course, Curzon was a historic figure, and I am a historian; one was always hearing about him at All Souls, though I never knew him.' She said, 'Well, I am descended from Sir Gervase Elwes.' I was at once interested, knowing all about the murder of Sir Thomas Overbury in the Tower of London, when poor Elwes was Lieutenant.[1] So then we had an equally interesting conversation on the right, instead of pointless chat.

Snobbery is a wide subject, and again most people think nonsense on the matter. There are intellectual snobs (I am one), garden snobs (not one), social snobs, family snobs, snobs about the royal family; democratic Americans are apt to be luggage snobs. Something is to be said for most forms of snobbery; it testifies to a sense of values and, if the values are good, so is the snobbery. I once came to the defence of Archbishop Lang on this score, against one of his own confraternity, with this: 'It only meant that he found interesting people more interesting than *un*interesting ones.' Logically irrefutable, and anyway interesting people *are* more interesting – though the uninteresting may not like the fact.

This was John Buchan's case: he was so generous-minded that he found almost everybody interesting, a Scotch fisherman or ghillie as much as a duke or T. E. Lawrence. It was part of his inexhaustible human interest – of the greatest value to a novelist – part of his kind nature as a man, and also (like Cosmo Lang) he was a Scots romantic at heart. It was also charmingly naif of him. Early in our acquaintance he asked me at dinner, Did I know the Duchess of Marlborough? Of course this young neophyte from the people replied equally naively, 'Do you mean Sarah?' To John Buchan the Marlboroughs and Blenheim Palace, past *and* present, were part of the romance of English history.

His son concluded his account of his father: 'Yet he eludes me still, as I believe he has eluded everybody.'

John Buchan does not elude me. He was, first and foremost, a man of genius, and that does make a man 'mysterious'. Secondly, he was a normal, even conventional family man; that does not usually go with genius, which is apt to be abnormal, sometimes scandalous. John Buchan was also an innately good man, with the highest standards of conduct,

[1] v. my *The Tower of London in the History of the Nation*.

both public and private. That quality is hard to write about; it is much easier and more exciting to write about a bad man. Then William Shakespeare says,

> They say best men are moulded out of faults
> And, for the most, become much more the better
> For being a little bad.

John Buchan had nothing bad in him whatever; perhaps it is that that makes him more difficult to recapture.

There is nothing that I wish to alter in my earlier tribute, written at the request of his widow, under the immediate impact of his loss. Only one word: I always thought that there was something sad about John's countenance and expression – Susie made me substitute the word 'grave' for 'sad'. But why shouldn't he have looked sad? For all his enjoyment of life he was often in pain from duodenal ulcer; he had had a Calvinist upbringing and knew the tragic side of life – his nearest friends and youngest brother killed in the holocaust of the First German War, so ruinous to English life.

I am proud that G. M. Trevelyan approved of my evocation of him, and should like to add a description of his appearance from a woman's sharp eye, Catherine Carswell's. 'The scar from an accident in childhood drew attention to the strikingly noble contours of his head. The long queer nose, questing and sagacious as a terrier's, was in odd contrast with the lean, scholarly cheeks and with the mouth narrowed as by concentration or the hint of pain subdued.' That tight-lipped mouth speaks to me of inner discipline and determination, a hint of repression, constant exertion of the will, and perpetual strain.

Some things now can be added. I never quite realised how deeply his failure to become a Fellow of All Souls affected him, how much he missed all through life the camaraderie of that unique freemasonry, of which several of his early friends – from Milner's Kindergarten – were lifelong members. He spoke to me of it, told me that he had tried twice, came nearest in the examination on the first occasion; his second attempt came after a year when he was already so hard at work in

London that he could not keep his scholarship, or perhaps examination technique, up to scratch.

He spoke without any rancour or resentment against the College – unlike some people who have failed to be elected. In Buchan's case it was the College rather that failed by adhering too closely to examination marks. Buchan was beaten by a fellow Scot, an Etonian, with a special aptitude for Greek verse – undoubtedly a better classical scholar, but with nothing of Buchan's promise already fully evident. Everyone expected that he would carry it off, like his friend Raymond Asquith.

The Prize Fellowships of All Souls were the Blue Ribbon of an Oxford career, even more so then than today, when there are more of such opportunities about. Naturally, when only one or two of the twenty to thirty candidates are chosen, one could construct a College of as much distinction from those who were not elected. For myself I used to regret that, among all the public and academic figures, there were not more writers. We might have had Belloc, instead of H. W. C. Davis, a better historian but no genius – just a professor; we might have had Aldous Huxley or David Cecil, Namier or John Buchan. It is a consideration that goes against too rigid an adherence to examination papers.

Actually it was at All Souls that I first met the Buchans at lunch with the Pembers in the Warden's Lodgings. Warden Pember was a handsome figure-head for the College, first-class classical scholar, an Harrovian friend of Stanley Baldwin, but a closer friend of Edward Grey and Asquith. Well off, an admirable host and raconteur, Warden Pember was a dear kind man (he did not recover from the loss of his only son in the War, had never believed he would be killed) – it was good of him to include this proletarian recruit to the College so often in the private gatherings at his table.

I used to be asked out a lot, for those were the days when people still had servants, were not taxed to the bare bones, and there was a great deal of hospitable, civilised entertaining. (Today impossible – only trade unionists have the money for that: whether the entertainments are civilised is another matter.)

Shortly I was recruited to Elsfield, the house and company

as I have previously described it. Little to add – except that, as Alice Buchan writes, I felt rather shy there, for Susan herself was shy; tea-time was all very well, but I found dining out rather a chore. In later years I became a devoted friend of Susan in her long widowhood – when she found herself as a writer. While John was alive she had a very full life with the family, beautiful Elsfield to look after, and John to protect. It was the writer who was the magnet for me.

Only on the historical side was I on Buchan's wave-length, for I did not read his thrillers or his novels, and, a Left intellectual, I was devoutly highbrow. In any case he did not go in for literary chatter. In his nostalgic autobiography, *Memory-Hold-the-Door* – no one knows where he got the title from – he says: 'As a writer it was my misfortune to be too little in the society of writers.' Like Kipling, he was all for men of action. He goes on: 'A writer must inevitably keep the best of himself for his own secret creative world.' That corroborates my diagnosis of him.

He was a man for a telling anecdote, perhaps germ for a story. I remember the *frisson* I got from his story about the Old Man of the Cairngorms. Buchan was a tremendous walker, and one day he was on those ominous mountains, late and alone, when he heard footsteps behind him; the faster he went the closer the steps tracked him, and he came down off the mountains right quick! No doubt it was the echo that was following him. All the same those mountains are sinister. The mother and sister of an Oxford contemporary were out on them, when there was a thunder clap and a flash of lightning which threw them to the ground; the sister did not rise again. The month in which I write this, the winter of 1983–4, five men were missing on those hostile hills.

Buchan could never resist a challenge. When Governor-General of Canada, an elderly and a sick man, returning from an exhausting tour in the Arctic, Bear Mountain above the Mackenzie River confronted him. 'The face had never been climbed, and up he had to go.' 'The rock was rotten and slanting the wrong way, but I took it cautiously and had no difficulties, except at the very top where there is an overhang. I managed to drag up an Indian so that he could give me a back, and wriggled my way up. The rest of my staff, including an inspector of police, got stuck on the lower rocks and had to be rescued by ropes!'

Now, why had he to do everything, be everything, taking every challenge and so much out of himself, life such a strain? – that is the question. I suspect the little man had to *show* them. I feel sure that the grandees of political life, the pomposities, disconsidered him, rather looked down on him – until Canada; that showed them all right, made up for everything. Others envied the success he had achieved, entirely by his own gifts and hard work, Scotch grit and will power. He did not allow it to sour him – too Christian a spirit for that – but he knew it well enough, and said one day to Susie: 'It is only when you are successful that you discover the world is not a very nice place.'

I have forgotten most of his anecdotes, but one Scottish one had a characteristic theological flavour. He was out fishing and was engaged hauling in a catch, when his old boatman said something to this effect; in the receiving of Divine Grace, would you say that the initial impulse came from above, or from the believer below? Catch an English fisherman entertaining such thoughts!

Buchan was not in sympathy with the writers of the Twenties and Thirties, whom I did read: Eliot, D. H. Lawrence and Joyce, the whole of Bloomsbury. He writes in a rather stuffy way about them, evidently not able to come to terms with them. 'One section of this class, very vocal in speech and writing, cherished modernity as its peculiar grace, regarding the word as descriptive of quality, and not merely as denoting a stage in time.' A good historian's debating point, this – and as a stylist he was himself equal to the best of them. He clearly detested Lytton Strachey, 'their fugleman', as G. M. Trevelyan did; and then goes on uncomfortably: 'they were much concerned with sex, and found sexual interest in unusual places, dwelling upon it with a slight titter.' This makes me laugh; for of course I was much more in accord with their view of things. Dear John, how innocent he was! Married to Susan, 'the only woman I have ever been in love with, or ever shall love' – it was just like Q., married to the only woman in *his* life. Each of them wrote to his wife every day that he was absent from her. To us and my generation, simply extraordinary: it made for such utter simplicity.

Nor, as a Labour Party man, with my intellectual obsession with Marxism, was I in sympathy with Buchan politically. I realised that he was naturally a romantic, historically minded Tory, but I did not give him credit for being much less of a party man that I was. He was genuinely friendly with the Red Clydesiders, Jimmy Maxton and David Kirkwood. Scotland was a bond, and that held too with Ramsay MacDonald. When MacDonald's eyesight began to fail him, Buchan had the new biography out specially printed in large type, for MacDonald to read on the rest he was ordered to take from politics. I don't suppose that in all Buchan's wide reading he had ever read Karl Marx.

I can see in the mind's eye that comfortable square library at Elsfield, his books all round him; behind his big writing desk was a bottom shelf of the manuscripts of his own books, beautifully bound. When I eventually graduated to a house of my own, I took that tip from him and had my bulky manuscripts similarly bound – John wrote everything longhand, as I do. Above the chimney piece hung a portrait of Sir Walter Ralegh, an early subject of John's – I doubt if he knew how faulty a hero he was. The Victorian chimney piece had been replaced and put away in the attics of that rather gaunt house, with the label – Susie said – 'Disapproved in 1930', perhaps to be rehabilitated in the next century.

I always thought there was a Scottish look about that abrupt Victorian house fronting directly on the village street. The back of it was older, with its magnificent view over all Otmoor, where John loved to walk, and across to the Cotswolds, which he wrote about and in which he placed, I think, *Midwinter*. Later the Buchans added an upper story to the eighteenth-century wing at the back, making a drawing-room and a private study for John's writing, away from the interruptions of family and visitors – for hospitality was incessant. How generous John was, with money, time, people – part of his innate and schooled generosity of mind. Money poured in from his books, though money was neither motive nor objective with him. I suppose he was a good business man, he was so methodical, and was a publisher from early days – when he could keep himself as an undergraduate from his writing. I remember how shocked Lionel Curtis pretended to be, at a publishers' session with John, when masterpieces of literature were swapped and bandied about like saddles of mutton. Money simply accrued, in those good days when a writer could hold on to his own earnings, instead of having them confiscated for people he disapproves and causes he detests.

The library was really the centre of the life of that house. I recall the new grand drawing-room being used only once, on the threshold of the Buchans' departure for Canada, for a dinner-party for Elizabeth Bowen, a friend of Susie rather than of John. We were sad at their impending departure – a consummation for him, a *corvée* for Susie. She was planning how she meant to keep it informal; but, of course, when they got there, in the Thirties, Vice-regal state had to be maintained: one sees it in the photographs – not for nothing was her Excellency a great-grandniece of the Duke of Wellington. Still, kind and warm-hearted as ever, they invited me over – though in those duodenal days I wouldn't dream of going: quite beyond me. A fellow sufferer – fellow member of the Duodenal Club of 'the best people', as a doctor described it, i.e. those who strained themselves working to the limit – John went through all the demands of the job, all the ceremony and ritual, the duties and chores, as he undertook everything, patience, good will, anxious to do his best and prove himself. In the end it killed him.

The historic, the essential, thing that remains is the remarkable way in which John and the whole Buchan family identified themselves with Canada. To be a Scot was a tremendous advantage: there were Scots everywhere. I gather that Buchan was asked for by Mackenzie King – and that would have been agreeable to the romantic Scot in Ramsay MacDonald. Mackenzie King, 'soft-centred spiritualist' in constant touch with his dead mother and a calculating party politician, was a queer lonely man, who expected to find a buddy in his Governor-General, whom he could lean upon for long heart-to-heart talks into the night. That was not to Buchan's mind or taste: those long Canadian winter nights were for work, and he used them to work harder than ever at his writing, free from the incessant calls and interruptions of life in England.

Elsfield was never the same without him, the whole spirit of the place for me had gone. After his death the family dispersed and left, and in later years I have rarely been up that beloved hill from Oxford – each time to watch for a moment beside his grave under the Round Table, to which did he, after all, belong?

7

Rebecca West; H. G. Wells

My subject is really my friendship with Rebecca West over many years, not her famous *liaison* with H. G. Wells. Others have written about that affair, including both principals; it will be seen that Rebecca wrote to me about it, and now their son, Anthony West, has given us his version. Actually I had had a contact with Wells some years before I met her, and the fact that I had known him was a bond with her. Thus I have placed a semi-colon between them to divide them – as early Saints would place a sword between them and their women in bed (far from H.G. and Rebecca in life); my title is not Rebecca West *and* H.G. Wells.

Let us dismiss him first.

I had seen and heard enough of him at various Leftist gatherings in London, New Fabians, or G. D. H. Cole's S.S.I.P. He was singularly unimpressive on the platform: a dumpy, bright-eyed chirpy little man, with an unregulated wispy moustache, and a pipsqueak of a voice. It was obvious that he was no gentleman, and no proletarian either (which I prided myself on being); he was unmistakably lower middle-class. In contrast to Bernard Shaw, ineffably an Irish gent. – at any rate Anglo-Irish; tall, slim, lithe, erect, on many years of vegetarianism; a carefully cultivated appearance to make him look like nobody else in the world, grizzled beard that had been copper-coloured, quirkish eyebrows; courteous manner and a most effective mastery of speaking and of the art of projecting his public persona.

Shaw had all the advantages, and this gave Wells an irritable inferiority-complex in regard to him; for he too had 'an overmastering determination to impress himself upon his time.' Even Rebecca, years after her disillusioning experience with him, wrote of him as 'master of his time'.

Well, he wasn't. He was a man of genius – that may be taken for granted; but he was not a 'master-mind', in the sense of the British Academy's series of lectures on such. On the other hand, before and after the First German War, he was famous, both in Britain and the USA. Those were the days when writers would incur fame (and garner the rewards) – in an elect world where standards counted for something; and where British writers had positive advantages, a bias in their favour in the USA, where we today have to work our passage the hard way.

Wells made something like £120,000 out of his *Outline of History*, when the pound was worth something too, and taxation not confiscation. But he was not a historian, and I did not think much of his history. I was even less interested in his science, more his field. Nor was I responsive to his novels: *Mr Kipps, Love and Mr Lewisham, Tono-Bungay, Ann Veronica*, were not for me: suburban, lower middle-class, Cockney comedy – not my world. I did appreciate *The Invisible Man*; it made me laugh uncontrollably – Wells had a rollicking sense of humour. I remember quite liking *The History of Mr Polly*.

However, a young Marxist on my high horse, I had no opinion of him as a thinker. I thought – and still think – that Marxism gave a clue to society, its structure and conflicts, a penetrating approach to history. The high-minded Christian, R. H. Tawney, was the better as a historian for imbibing a little Marxism. Wells had nothing of this, and was superficial (and supercilious) enough to think it unimportant and could be ignored.

That did for him in my eyes as a social thinker, and somewhere or other in print I said this. Wells was bent on influencing the mind of my younger generation; Leonard Woolf reported my remark to him, and Wells was concerned enough to write to ask me what I meant. Comically enough, it led to a row between Woolf and Wells. Woolf couldn't find the *locus classicus* of this youthful indiscretion, and I had forgotten where I had said it. It wasn't in a book, as Woolf thought; he couldn't find it in an article – had it been in a letter? Eventually, some years later, he did run it down; it appears somewhere in his Autobiography.

Meanwhile, I had to write and explain myself to Wells – and he carefully kept my letter. For, years after, when Gordon Ray was going through the Wells Archive at the University of Illinois, he came upon it and gave me a copy. I don't remember the content, except that I put what I considered the necessary historical approach to the understanding of society, an indirect way of defending what I *had* said.

Wells was interested enough to want to meet me, and began by asking me to lunch at his Reform Club. I was not charmed: he wanted to talk all the time, and I wanted to talk all the time. We were at cross-purposes: he laid down the law about Science and Society – not my subject and I didn't want to hear about it. I tried to lay down the law about Marxism and Society – he didn't listen. I was put off by his studying his plump, pink, well-manicured little hands. Then he made a mistake: he tried to shock my Marxist purism by telling me about the sexual goings-on of Claire Sheridan, sculptress (Winston's cousin), with the Bolshevik leaders. I said that I wasn't interested in the goings-on of men and women. Then Wells thought to score: 'In that case, you are not interested in half the human race.' I could have told him that, an unreconstructed Swiftian, I was not even interested in one half per cent of the human race.

However, he was obviously interested, for he swore me to let him know, when he got back from France, so that we might meet again. (I had no intention of doing so.) He was on his way to Grasse, where he and Odette Keun had neighbouring properties and, for more than neighbourly convenience, he made a communicating door between the two. When they had had more than enough of each other, he tried to close the aperture.[1] She went to law about it and defeated him; he thereupon wrote a novel about her as *Dolores*. I didn't read it; I merely made a *mot* about her having dropped a 't' from the end of her name and gone all over Europe looking for it.

Wells continued to send me inscribed copies of his books: I

---

[1] I leave this as I wrote it for the sake of the joke; but it appears that it was more of a *fracas* than I knew. According to Wells's son, Anthony West, Odette managed to throw Wells out of his own house. What a mug he was about women – another contrast with Shaw.

recall the vast (and boring) *Health, Wealth and Happiness of Mankind*, and various brochures and pamphlets planning the future of society. I set no store by them and used promptly to sell them. In later years I have occasionally felt – or thought that I ought to feel – sorry. After all, he had been kind to me, and he was a man of genius. But he just wasn't my type; I was all for history and poetry, my mentors were G. M. Trevelyan and T. S. Eliot. Perhaps my instinct was right; nothing could have come from an association with him, nor was I in fact very sociable.

This happened some years before I met Rebecca, I do not remember how or where. Her first book, *Henry James*, I bought when I was young and poor, I suppose because it was cheap, but I did not read it – beyond me. Nor did I make much of *The Strange Necessity*, not caring much for Lit. Crit. – I prefer creative writing, poetry and the novel. In later life Rebecca said that, if she had had her time over again, she would have written more novels. Her own early novels passed me by. The best of them was a novella, *The Return of the Soldier*: an original theme – the shell-shocked soldier who could not remember his previous existence or family – and an authentic one of that terrible First German War, with its innumerable casualties: a holocaust from which neither Britain nor France fully recovered. We owe that to the Germans.

Still, I have sometimes wondered whether Rebecca was not too cerebral, too much of an intellectual critic, for a novelist. The first thing about her was that she was extraordinarily clever, and hers was a discursive, argumentative intellect, too much interested in everything to concentrate in one field. Unlike Elizabeth Bowen, or Barbara Pym. (I wonder now what she thought of *them*?)

Thus Rebecca was first and last a journalist, and of the most brilliant – that ill-used word, so often used by American academics of books of leaden consistency. It means shining – and Rebecca's journalism shone and scintillated, spluttering with wit. H.G., as we both referred to him, put his finger on its special and curious quality: it was an *intricate* wit. How she carried those elaborate sentences in her head to their explosive conclusions, I cannot think.

Then there was this young woman's breath-taking impertinence, the dash with which she attacked 'The Gospel according to Mrs Humphry Ward', the *grande dame* of English letters before 1914, standard-bearer of women's rights, niece of Matthew Arnold ('Why, Uncle Matt, will you never be wholly serious?', of Max Beerbohm's caricature), mother-in-law of G. M. Trevelyan, whose wedding-service she composed, because the bridal pair were too high-minded to believe in God; above all, the author of *Robert Elsmere*, so much admired by Mr Gladstone, though its expressed doubts alarmed the bishops. 'Barricaded from the fastidious craftsman behind the solid Tottenham-Court-Road workmanship of her mental furniture . . . Mrs Ward reveals to us the psychology of the clergyman class.' Or, 'Mr Harold Owen is a natural slave, having no conception of liberty nor any use for it. So, as a Freewoman, I review his anti-feminist thesis, *Woman Adrift*, with chivalrous reluctance, feeling that a steam-engine ought not to crush a butterfly. . . . He leaves one wondering whether one can safely lend an umbrella to one's uncle.' The author of a work on Eng. Lit. is 'a bishop *manqué*. He writes in the solemn yet hiccupy style peculiar to bishops, with a "however", or "indeed" interrupting every sentence.' His book must have been written 'in apron and gaiters.'

No apron and gaiters for Rebecca at twenty: she was an 'Emancipated Woman'. 'Life ought to be a struggle of desire towards adventures whose nobility will fertilise the soul. To avoid the ordeal of emotion that leads to the conception is the impulse of death. Sterility is the deadly sin.' Again, 'It is the soul's duty to be loyal to its own desires. It must abandon itself to its master-passion.' She refuses 'to accept the convention that if marriage is denied to her so is motherhood.' As for Shaw, he 'never brought anything so anarchic as an unmarried mother on to his stage.'

One sees that this young woman at twenty was ready for H.G. Wells at forty-six, the prophet – and exponent – of free love, notorious for several affairs which had created scandal. The latest, with Amber Pember Reeves, daughter of the Director of the London School of Economics, forsooth, Beatrice Webb herself told me about. The girl was pregnant;

Blanco White was in love with her, willing to marry her and take on H.G.'s child. Mrs Webb, formidable woman, was determined that the marriage should go forward and the cracks be papered over. She forced Wells, who was reluctant, to drop the girl: she warned him that, if there were a court-case, she would go into court and give evidence against him. This worked: the marriage turned out happily and the bride turned against her former lover.

I used to wonder why women fell for Wells, so physically unattractive. Of course Wells was keen, and the charity of women is inexhaustible. He needed sex, and his otherwise indispensable wife wouldn't have it, so he was impelled to look elsewhere. One of his women told G. D. H. Cole that Wells smelled like honey – and some men, particularly workers on the land, do smell well; women should always wear scent. Wells, odd as it seems, was attractive to women, who often enough took the initiative with him. No doubt fame helped, it seems to go their – hearts. He himself said of Odette Keun, whose eyes devoured him, that she made him feel that his trousers were made of gauze.

I was never convinced by Rebecca's account of her affair with Wells.[2] The 'eternally feminine' of Goethe, she was entirely subjective, and, with her creative mind, inveterately given to fantasying. She was not wholly unobjective but, with her, objectivity was intermittent. Wells, who was already in trouble on several counts, was cautious and held off at first. It is obvious that she took the initiative and dared him to take her on. Wells: 'You're a very compelling person. I suppose I shall have to do what you want me to do.' They became passionate lovers – and sex makes fools of us all.

Rebecca became pregnant, and I have never accepted her account of the responsibility in the matter – which led to so much continuing trouble. We all know that men are held to be alone responsible and have to take the blame. Queen Victoria blamed the Prince Consort for her too numerous children, and we have had recent cases in public life where the men have had

---

[2] cf. Gordon N. Ray, who fell a victim to Rebecca's account in his *H. G. Wells and Rebecca West*. This view is contradicted by Anthony West in his book on his parents.

to carry all the blame. Men are more naif than women, and more easily taken in. Rebecca wanted to make H.G. marry her: that much is admitted. He was determined not to be divorced from his wife (his second); he was dependent on her to manage his affairs (Rebecca, an intellectual, was never a good manager). Mrs Wells was a *femme complaisante*: she told Beatrice Webb, 'I know H.G. is polygamous, and I don't mind.' Much more, he confided his 'affairs' to her and sought her advice on them. Rebecca said later that she would have settled for a *ménage à trois*. Like the Regency Duke of Devonshire, his Duchess Georgiana, and Lady Elizabeth Foster – whom the Duke married when Georgiana died. Mrs Wells died before many years were out. Suppose Rebecca had waited . . . by then H.G. would not have married her anyway. This was what rankled.

Meanwhile, there was the child to be provided for and brought up, a perpetual bone of contention between them, and a life-long complex to Rebecca, as may be seen from her later letters to me. Before the nuisance arrived, it was, from Wells: 'I think of that happy thing cuddled up in your soft flesh and your dear warm blood.' Or, it was, 'Nobody licks his fur properly 'cept her. Nobody yowls back same as she does. Wants to take Handsful of her dear soft hair and stroke her Magnificent Flanks and—. Ssh!' It is extraordinary to think of a grown-up writing like that, vulgar little man. What would Henry James think of it? – indeed did think of Wells the Vulgarian.

Soon enough the tune changed: 'I love being with my work with everything handy.' That was what Jane Wells provided. 'I *hate* being encumbered with a little boy and a nurse, and being helpful.' Odette Keun saw the perhaps inevitable truth about a writer, when the two women ganged up together against the male chauvinist: 'I've never known anybody in my whole life who, fundamentally, can do without others as he can. It's only a pose of his that he needs people: he only needs people to elaborate his ideas and spread them. And, so long as he can work, he'd master every kind of shock, however sorrowful.' There is the woman's point of view, the female freemasonry. Henry James knew the overriding demand of a writer's vocation, and accepted it. Wells was too mixed-up by sex to give himself wholly to his genius, and – everybody agreed, Henry James, Rebecca, Wells himself – his work suffered.

Then came the recriminations. After their separation Wells destroyed practically all her letters, but we may judge what they were from what remains. They nagged and raged at each other, and Rebecca admits that it was her nature to answer rage with rage. Wells: 'The thing goes on and on with you, and I am tired to death with it. I do regret very bitterly that I ever met you, but I have done what I could to make some sort of life tolerable for us. For ten years I've shaped my life mainly to repair the carelessness of one moment. It has been no good and I am tired of it.' And again, 'I do not love you and I do not feel the slightest stirring of jealousy about you.' Really, after all those expressions of love! . . .

Later came Rebecca's complaints. 'He treated me with the sharpest cruelty imaginable for those horrible years' – she was a great one for complaining and exaggerating. 'He has cheated me of all but one child' – after all the trouble that one was to them! It is extraordinary that people should write like that to and about each other – like the letters of D. H. Lawrence (Rebecca was a character out of Lawrence, out of *Women in Love*), or the denizens of Bloomsbury, analysing themselves and each other to bits. The lack of self-control is incomprehensible – very unlike the correspondence of Henry James or G. M. Trevelyan, or even Eliot or mine.

Then there was money, of course, hardly necessary to specify. Wells was generous to his mistresses. Rebecca opened her mouth for £3000 a year; he gave her $20,000 out of his American royalties; then Odette insisted on trusts for the child's education. (What mugs men are about women!) When Wells died, she came out with: 'I loved him all my life and always will, and I bitterly reproach myself for not having stayed with him, because I think I was fairly good for him. . . . The tyranny was the incorrigible part of him – I could not have submitted to it all my life; nor do I think that he could have loved me or that I could have loved him if I had been the kind of person that could.'

What is one to make of that tangle of self-contradiction? It has the maddening feminine quality of inconsistency. Work was what mattered to a man; thus Wells: 'Your output of work has been trivial, my work has suffered enormously.' Rebecca's weakness in regard to him was that she thought – or at least assured him – that he was 'a great man'. Wells, for his part, assured her that '*The Outline of History* is going to change History.' I well remember the enormous *réclame* it had; but that was all. Fancy anybody thinking anything of the sort!

In her letters to me Rebecca gave varying accounts of her affair with H.G. Fairly early in our acquaintance, 'I write to you in a cold sweat of apprehension about a blithering paper I have received, suggesting that as a memorial to H. G. Wells an organisation should be formed to promote the publication of works which might be supposed to be in line with his ideas. I hope you disapprove of this as strongly as I do. H.G. was like Voltaire, he was master of his time, and ran beside it so assiduously that, when he broke with time, there was little to tell us what he would have thought of this world at this moment. I can see a committee being formed which would be indefatigable in their loyalty to H.G.'s ideas of, say 1910, and who make his name dusty in the eyes of a new generation by associating his name with the Joads who are yet to be born. I can see the dowdy progressive line which is bound to be followed. Look at the names on the list – Kingsley Martin, Vera Brittain, G. D. H. Cole, Dame Sybil Thorndike. Oh *God*.'

Twenty years later, after we had become much closer: 'Don't be apprehensive because I answer almost by return. You express wonder that I should have gone off with H.G., because he was so vulgar. But there was a very simple explanation. I had an aching need for affection and reassurance. While my mother and sister Winifred loved me very much, I nevertheless was emotionally starved during my adolescence. One of my family had always scolded and nagged me all day long. My sisters went out into the world, to school and University, and I was left at home with my mother, who then became a victim of Graves Disease (an exophthalmic goitre). She became unkind and ungrateful, and I had to use all my energy to keep her going, and got to school exhausted, upon which my teachers tormented me. When my sisters returned home I got no praise whatever, and indeed was nagged worse than ever. I simply wanted to be loved and cherished – the natural place to seek it was in a man's arms – and what arms I chose! But the point about H.G. that was, when he was not possessed by a devil, he delighted in and perceived one's good points as nobody else. And indeed all would not have been so bad if it had not been for—' and there follows a rocket against her son, which I omit.

It is no secret that Rebecca had a complex about Anthony, and went on about it in other letters; it was no business of mine, and I never reverted to it. I did not know him. I had met him only once, when Gerald Berners was staying with me in Cornwall, and John Betjeman brought Anthony to lunch. All I remember of the occasion was John's exclamation, seeing Johannesberger on the bottle of wine, 'And South African, by Jove!', to Gerald's reproach: 'he should have known better.'

After this meeting Rebecca wrote me a letter to say that she heard that I had taken Anthony's side against her. I was quite innocent in the matter and hardly knew what she was complaining about. (I hate complaints, another boring feminine trait.) Anyway I was able to reassure her of my innocence.

A later letter ended up, 'Thank you for the kind words about *The Birds Fall Down*.' (I thought this remarkable novel her best.) 'I could have been a good writer had I not been torn apart by a horde of devils.' I had been writing about Swift, a lifelong interest of mine. Rebecca was Anglo-Irish like him, and ended, 'An odd thing about Swift is that his biographers always write of the diseases inflicted on him by old age as if they were his normal state in middle age.' This, by the way, is not exact; nor do I suppose that her highly suggestive account of her youth is exact either. Nor perhaps her conclusion: 'People love you very much. I hear them saying so, often and often. Yours ever, with real love, Rebecca.' She was the most generous of women, but I did not count on that assurance – too sceptical and despairing of humans.

An earlier letter, of December 1947, throws light on her attitude towards her own writing. 'I have never been able to write with anything more than the left hand of my mind; the right hand has always been engaged in something to do with personal relationships. I don't complain, because I think my left hand's power, as much as it has, is due to its knowledge of what my right hand is doing.' Precisely: I should have thought that engagement in personal relations is the necessary equipment for a novelist.

She wanted to argue with me about my little *aide-mémoire, All Souls and Appeasement,* of which C. P. Snow had written, 'This is just as it was' – though attacked by a Junior Fellow, one Wolfenden, who had not been through the experience and did not know what he was talking about. Rebecca wrote, 'I am in the main in enthusiastic agreement: I think no analysis of the situation has come near to yours for shrewdness. But since I have been writing on Fascism and anti-Semitism I have wondered if Halifax and Chamberlain were not terribly representative.' She was right: they were; people supported them all the way along, and then were surprised when it landed them in war. She went on, 'The people who live in prefabs are valuable because they are living in houses which are apt symbols for their minds. But the minds of English people are often like that when they live in beautiful houses, large or small.

'There is a fact revealed by my correspondents which has interested me very much. The English correspondents present an extraordinary contrast to the Irish and the Jews, in their attitude to themselves: they do not seem to have any conception of themselves. The Jews write reams on what it is to be a Jew, and how wonderful they are. The Irish write reams on what it is to be Irish, and how much more than wonderful they are. "We are a people the like of which has never been seen," tells one, "for purity, generosity, courage, and simple wisdom." But the English never say what they are; they talk about the Union Jack and wanting to be worthy of England, but they hardly ever express an opinion of what they are. If you ever think of what you are, it is obviously more difficult to mobilise yourself for action, than if you were absorbed in a picture of yourself for twenty minutes out of every half-hour.'

Kipling has a perceptive poem on just this theme, but I doubt if he was a favourite with Rebecca, too much a Left Intellectual for him.

By 1957 I had become her 'favourite dreaming spire', and I would reply flirtatiously, 'Come down, O maid, from yonder mountain height'; for she was now happily married to Henry Andrews, a rich banker, with a large house at Ibstone on a ridge of the Chilterns. When Henry couldn't come down into Oxford and I suggested that she could come alone, it was, 'I couldn't trust myself.' (Dear Rebecca, at her age! And how little perceptive of her: she would have been disappointed.) Or she would bid me up to meet the siren Violet Trefusis, famous Mrs Keppel's daughter. I think she liked to have people think that she was Edward VII's, and indeed she had the figure. I rather think that clever Alice Keppel played the game properly by her husband, the Colonel. I have always been enchanted by the knowing Italian who, seeing them together on the Piazza in Venice, was able to inform his companion: 'See that man – Queen Victoria is his mistress.' I was not able to make much of Violet Trefusis, except to compliment her on her romantic Cornish name. Oh, no; she could never change that, she assured me. I registered 'disingenuous'.

A letter of February 1961 has some autobiographical interest. 'As a woman I have a great grievance on the physical plane, because I was born at a time which meant that the periods when I was young, and not so young that I was miserably shy, and when I had money to spend on clothes, coincided with the period when the best clothes were made by Chanel. The dresses that she made, or that other makers copied, were unbelievably hideous. I had to wear a hat bashed down on my head, and skinny and shapeless sacks that looked bad if one was made like a choirboy, and worse if one was not! Exactly the same thing seems to me to have happened in my time in literature, with T. S. Eliot preaching that you must not have three-quarters of an idea to every ten pages, and Leavis using fastidiousness like a *nouveau riche* who buys asparagus tongs for eating asparagus. All this dreary nonsense has made the world more grey than the Galilean succeeded in doing.'

I remember an earlier *contretemps* of hers with Eliot, to which he had replied with his usual courtesy by inviting her up to 24 Russell Square to discuss the issue over a cup of tea. She did not respond: Eliot was not her cup of tea. Quite right about the dreary Leavis, of course. I was to come up to lunch: 'I have a couple of sphinxes on the terrace that I did not have when you were last here, and I think you might like them.'

Rebecca had married Henry in 1930; he was able to support her in style: not only a largish Georgian country house, with farm attached, but a London life as well. Would I disinter myself from historical research to come up to the Picasso party at the Tate, dinner beforehand? No, I would not: London life was not for me. The domestic life of All Souls was more to my taste.

Both Henry, a New College man, and Rebecca were always willing to come down to All Souls with me. As she got grander and more at ease with society she became more and more interested in her Anglo-Irish descent and, since I was so very West Country, would insist that she had West Country blood through the Champernownes of Dartington. She wrote me reams about it. As time went on her letters show her clearly as Irish, or Anglo-Irish; hardly a word about her Scottish family, though she had been brought up in Edinburgh and very well educated at George Watson's Ladies College. I noticed that she had the Scots-Irish use of 'will' and 'would' for shall and will. (Today hardly anybody has the correct usage, and American writers don't know it.)

In earlier letters she did not mention her father, a typically feckless Irish gent, a Fairfield, apparently gifted and scholarly, a gambler, who could not bear the chains of family life. He deserted it, leaving his wife, an excellent Scots woman, whom Rebecca adored, to bring up three daughters. One sees why Rebecca needed a man so much: she as good as had no father. The ardent feminist all her life had been reared in an exclusively feminine environment. The clue to Rebecca is that, though her brain and *bildung* were Scotch, her temperament and character were Irish. This too is where she got her verbal wit, her sheer gift for words – like Cyril Connolly, who would scarcely recognise it, and claimed to be English, in spite of his all too visible characteristics. One notices this specific gift for words in the best writers of the language in America: Scott Fitzgerald, Flannery O'Connor, Eugene O'Neill, perhaps Edmund Wilson.

On one occasion, when Philip Magnus was staying with me, she was looking forward to discussing her family connexion with Edmund Burke, about whom he had written. In 1962 I had published *Ralegh and the Throckmortons,* based on the invaluable find of the Diary of Ralegh's brother-in-law, Sir Arthur Throckmorton, fullest and most remarkable of all Elizabethan diaries. It revealed the inner story of Ralegh's secret marriage, the birth of a child unknown to history – called after his West Country descent, D'Amory ('Damerei') – along with a great deal of fascinating information which has not yet seeped through into conventional textbooks.

Rebecca's alert mind was all interest. 'I have some interest in the Raleghs, being descended from Joan Champernowne who was Ralegh's aunt; but apart from that interest, I am delighted by the pace and concentration and warmth of your book.' With her rather bawdy mind she was struck by Throck-morton's intimate revelation of the horrors of regular Elizabethan purgations. 'The things which distinguish man from the brutes – the use of the hand, of course, but also surely distress over the bowels.' Who but Rebecca would have thought of that?

She goes on – so characteristic of her discursive mind: 'It has struck me as so odd that the Manichaeans, who were obviously more rather than less intelligent than the mob, were so worried about the discreditable contents of the intestines; and the contemporary African, who *loves* his little children, for their own good drives many of them straight out of this world by driving sin out of their little rectums by castor and even croton oil.' (Here by the way is an example of Rebecca's *intricacy* of mind and style.) 'Throckmorton was obviously trying to rid himself of those Tudor characteristics which he saw were making hell for him and his group, a self-made hell. But what an iron constitution he must have had.' Not so, Rebecca – too clever by half; Throckmorton's Spring purg-ings were just regular habit with Elizabethans. The historic truth was much simpler than Rebecca's fertile fantasyings; but then, I didn't waste time arguing with her, as H.G. had done – it would have been endless, she was all over the place.

There shortly followed a long letter about her Tudor ancestors. 'My collateral ancestress who is said to have been the source of so many peerages was Joyce, the eldest daughter of Sir Edmund Denny, King's Remembrancer to Henry VII, who married as her first husband, Sir William Walsingham, and as her second Sir John Carey, whose brother married

Mary Boleyn. [Correct: that was young William Carey, who became father of Lord Hunsdon, Patron of Shakespeare's Company, and protector of Emilia, *née* Bassano.] The brother of Joyce, Sir Anthony Denny, was my direct ancestor, and he married Joan Champernowne.' I omit more details.

'Her elder son, Henry, married Lord Grey de Wilton' – Spenser's hero in the *Faery Queene*. 'But that line died out in 1660. Henry's son was the original Earl of Norwich, and my cousin, Sir Henry Denny, an alcoholic rector sustained only by pride of birth in that unhappy position, ground his teeth at Duff Cooper for taking that title.' Fancy bothering! old Denny – I had no notion of his being related to Rebecca – used to bore me with fanmail about his ancestry.

Rebecca too. 'Henry's second wife was Elizabeth, daughter of Lord John Grey, and their younger son married a daughter of Piers Edgcumbe [of that Cornish family], and went to Ireland, and vegetated. Then some Denny girl had a daughter who married Charles George Fairfield, originally of County Longford: my grandfather.' – So that's who the Fairfields were. 'All this you know one way and another, but I thought it might interest you to see how it links up with the person who comes to lunch.' I didn't know it, and was interested only in herself the writer.

There followed another long screed, for 'here's a thing that has often seemed to me a wonderful example of the way events and personalities disguise their true nature.' Here was Rebecca the novelist of *The Birds Fall Down*, and her obsessive interest in *The Meaning of Treason*, spies and double-agents. 'There was an Irish General called Sir William Cuppidge, whose cousin was the William Burke who lived with Edmund Burke; the poor chap spent his life bailing out those two financial morons.' (They were worse than that.) 'Cuppidge's sister was my great-grandmother, or great-great. There could be nothing more English-sounding than the name Cuppidge; or more English, I understand, than the Cuppidges, who left Ireland and settled in Vancouver. But the founder of the Cuppidge family was a German soldier of fortune who came to Ireland, and his real name was Faustus Cuppich. The Cuppidges married mostly Scottish immigrants to Ireland, such as the Clydesdale Campbells [her mother's family, Celtic enough], and never any family domiciled in England. So the connection with England was purely institutional, school and army, and cultural.'

Altogether, one sees how un-English Rebecca was. Her obsession with her ancestry and family connexions reminded me of people of good family in the Southern States. There must have been something in this complicated link-up, for later I was to meet a Walter Raleigh Coppedge, when President of Charleston College, South Carolina.

Next month, she brought Curzon's daughter, Lady Ravensdale, down to All Souls. Curzon had been a great figure in the College, and when I was young his legend still lingered. 'Irene was enchanted by the visit to her father's haunts, and to bring enchantment into her sad world is really a deed that will let you off several thousand years in Purgatory. (Where both you and I may, I feel, spend some considerable time).' Note that Rebecca's lifelong habit of exaggerating everything was not an English trait, but Irish. (Nothing could be more English than Clem Attlee, by contrast.)

'I didn't know of the trouble you had mentioned. I knew her well in the Twenties and Thirties, and it was then threatened, but I have seen very little of her in the past fifteen years, and I hoped that like many of our friends she had shed that habit as she came out of those raffish years. My nephew dearly loved you. He is a genius, by the way, and also wildly interested outside his special field. As for Virginia [Cowles] and Bill, obviously Virginia is the attraction, and your frank, free prattle made me reflect that she is the object of deep affection on the part of two highly intelligent women. Polly Kahn, the wife of Gilbert Kahn, whom I think the most wonderful creature, lovely and intelligent, and Barbara Gimbel, the Californian schoolteacher, who married the chairman of Sachs, Fifth Avenue, and is quite something. I hadn't realised the pattern till you spoke of it.'

Well, the innocent historian, with all that feminism about, was alive to the possibility of a spot of Lesbianism. In earlier years, Rebecca had been an intimate of Lady Rhondda and her circle around *Time and Tide*. Why not? With Colette, it had been strokes all round the wicket, in Maurice Bowra's phrase; or in the French, *à voile et à vapeur*.

'What a unique tragedy the Curzon family have acted out – do you realise that Curzon's second and *quelconque* wife got through about half-a-million and there was nothing, nothing, NOTHING, to show for it?' Of course, I knew about it. I had been an undergraduate along with her alcoholic son, Alfred Duggan, whose historical novels Evelyn Waugh had boosted out of Catholic freemasonry. If only all that Duggan money had gone into saving Kedleston and its treasures, as no doubt Curzon intended! All I care about – the vanishing heritage, in our squalid society.

A few days later she received my *Ralegh* book: 'The relative to whom I lent my own copy – bought the day of publication, such was my esurience [what a vocabulary she commanded!] has asked me if she may keep it. Yes, Virginia did fall for the (not at all old) Professor, not that she's bored with Bill – they beat different records all the time of different sorts and respect each other's muscles, if nothing else. But I am sorry if she was too insistent on coming to Oxford. Still, you forgave her, with all your usual sweetness of spirit.' Evidently, my defences were well up: like Arthur Balfour, where women were concerned, I 'fancied a career for myself'.

'How charming of you to think that my nephew has charm. Yes, I think that in the kingdom of heaven everybody will fall for everybody all round. And how lovely it will be, with those enfolding wings, so much better than what Leda got, which I have thought must have been technically so unmanageable.' I fear that I was unresponsive to Rebecca's bawdy streak – all very well for H.G., not for H.J.

At this point came the letter giving her version of why she had 'gone off with' H.G. And later I was to receive an invitation to meet Gordon Ray of the Guggenheim – whom I already knew – who was writing up her account of the affair. She would, if only I would come, put me up for the night: 'No strings.' Nor did another invitation to meet Violet Trefusis lure me out of my defences: 'Violet was so disappointed.' I was more pleased to learn that Rebecca had always adored Hawker of Morwenstow, when I sent her my essay on him. 'I had overlooked the delightful incident when he read the Exorcistic Service over the five farmers. This is not only endearing but really useful information, for I fly to South Africa on January

6th, and I shall now know what to do at any awkward moment. I shall be back in two months and hope to see you if greedy America hasn't snatched you from us.' It had – after various disappointments I wasn't the one to put up with (always from the second- and third-rate, never the first-rate), I was spending half my time there now: a new phase to my life, an altogether new experience, after claustrophobic Oxford (which I had loved), a new world to explore.

Through all these years Rebecca had kept up her journalism. Now she was one of a cloud of vultures from all over the world who settled on South Africa to report the consequences of the Soweto shooting, when the Africaners, who now had their own way in what they regarded as their own country, fulfilled Milner's pessimistic forecast of what would happen when they had. The world's journalists were all of one liberal mind, quite sure that such a state of affairs, the Africaner ascendancy, could not last more than two or three years. Rebecca, always a liberal, subscribed to this illusion like the rest of them. I thought at the time what fools they were. Had they no judgment? Didn't they know how tough the Boers were? They hadn't fought the whole British Empire to see their country become another Nigeria, or Uganda. The liberal illusions of those who suppose themselves to be so intelligent – and sometimes are – are ludicrous to a historian. Dear Rebecca was no exception; but then she was no historian. H.G. had ended in utter despair, with *Mankind at the End of its Tether*. He should never have entertained such superficial hopes of mankind earlier. And how the world's prospects have worsened even in the years since then!

With Henry Andrews I had good relations. A nice but uninteresting rich man, he worshipped Rebecca and made it his prime business to look after her, which was what she needed. When she wrote her book, *The Court and the Castle*, an interpretation of *Hamlet*, he wrote to me privately to vet the typescript: he was afraid for her that she might put a foot wrong. I dutifully read it, but remember nothing of it. I didn't see why she had to write her interpretation of *Hamlet*. There are hundreds of superfluous works on Shakespeare's plays, practically all of them of little value. The play itself is the thing: let it speak for itself. Beyond that, one needs to know its place in Shakespeare's work, when it was written, the circumstances of the time, the personal and topical experience that went into its making. This is precisely what the critics are incapable of providing, and cannot see the significance of when it is provided for them. As the leading Canadian novelist today, though a professor – Hugh MacLennan – writes to me: 'They simply don't understand how plays and novels are written.'

Instead of wasting her time on a critical 'interpretation', Rebecca might have re-written *Hamlet* as a novel – she did know how to write a novel – as Tom Stoppard re-worked the theme of Rosencrantz and Guildenstern in an exciting play. (Louis Auchincloss, with whom I saw the play in New York, missed the point of it – as with my own Shakespeare discoveries.)

On my summer return to All Souls I regularly had lunch parties in that *décor* to mingle my American and British friends, new and old. I find a letter from Henry to tell me how impressed he was by a party for Rouben Mamoulian, the film producer, who had first brought Greta Garbo to the fore in *Queen Christina* (Stalin's favourite film). He was the first too to produce a modern acting version of *Hamlet*. He made the point that, when he was young in Russia, he could always understand Shakespeare in Russian. When he became American, though he had a remarkable command of English, he could not always understand Shakespeare's archaic language. This put an idea into my head.

When Henry died Rebecca gave up the country house near Oxford, and moved back to an entirely London life at Prince's Gate in Kensington. Without Henry she was once more at a loss. In June 1967, 'I am in a welter of distress and incompetence. I do not really suffer from the loss of Henry because the last two years made it a cruelty to wish anything for him but release, it was like an animal caught in a trap. Now what is left for me demands adaptations I find so difficult to make. I should be at home in this place [Kingston House North, where she had a large flat], with which I have long and mystical ties – really strange ones. It was built on the site of the house where the bigamous Duchess of Kingston died – a lovely house – my mother and I used to go on the top of a bus to visit a cousin, who had one of those Regency houses near Chiswick House. I used to point to Kingston House and say, "I will live there when I am grown up" – and it has come about, but *not* as I hoped!

'I could be reasonably happy here if I had not had to break up my library. I could not bring even half of it here, and I have almost no hope of ever arranging it in a usable way. The use I made of it didn't come out so much in my work as in my own personal life. . . . I am speaking on McLuhan to the English Association, and I wanted to illustrate a point by a reference to an odd essay of Valéry on Le Prince et la Jeune Parque (a German prince who was in love with Rachel, do you remember).' She couldn't recall the name of the volume, and so couldn't get it from the library; when she panicked – one knows the feeling – it turned up by miracle.

She wanted to read my 'Cornish Oxford' book, I suppose *A Cornishman Abroad*, for 'I would like to talk to you about Adam von Trott.' She knew what odious German characteristics are, for they are portrayed to the life in her *Black Lamb and Grey Falcon*, a big two-tiered best-seller which must have made her a small fortune. 'I went to Oxford the other day . . . and walked about all Sunday morning, and envied everybody who had been a (male) student there. What is it Oxford does to girls? They all look Kardomah, except the ones I meet with you. Tell me when you are in London and want lunch – I will be [Scotch-Irish usage for 'shall'] fit for receiving the great in about a fortnight. Love from your faithful Rebecca.'

Next summer I came back from the USA to find that Rebecca had returned from Mexico to deal with business concerning Henry's estate, and 'to find my house had been *stripped* by a wicked charwoman during my absence, and as she has elected to be tried by jury this goes on and on. I am so appalled to find that the courts are simply choked by the crime wave. This woman was arrested on February 17, she has not been tried yet [June]. This social crisis is a great deal worse than people realise.' But, of course: I had realised it all along, belonging to the people I know what they are – it was middle-class people, like Rebecca, with their liberal illusions, who hadn't realised. She wanted me to come and comfort her, 'for you are one of the few people I dearly love.' Dear Rebecca, she was full of love; sad that I could not respond more, I see now. However, I did respond to her invitation 'to meet someone whose ancestors you know very well – my cousin, Anthony Denny.'

Next spring she took the chair for me at a lecture at the Royal Society of Literature on Simon Forman; but I could not recognise myself in the description she gave of me. I suppose we think of other people's view of us as subjective, and our own as objective; and men regard themselves as more objective. Virginia Woolf – what did Rebecca think of her? – made a case for feminine subjectiveness as equipment for the novelist: but not for a historian, and Rebecca was given to fantasies. She wrote me after: 'It was such a lovely lecture and you gave it so well and looked so entrancing. (My niece said, "Nothing prepared me for such an absolute *beauty*.")' Well, really: what nonsense! She made me an offer of two whole albums of photographs of astrological material which Henry had had made for the Yale Library. I wasn't interested in astrological nonsense – like Frances Yates who wasted her scholarship on it, Hermeticism, Rosicrucianism and such. As a historian I was concerned with facts, the intimate facts of Elizabethan social and sexual life revealed by Forman. Academic historians, except for Lawrence Stone, have not caught up with it yet. Rebecca's bawdy side was tickled by Forman's code-word for copulation: *halek*. One still doesn't know its derivation, but a musical was devoted to Forman in California under that title. 'What a lovely phrase it sounds now: "The March of the men of Halek." Much affection and admiration, Your devoted Rebecca.'

At last, in 1971, she visited Ireland, and wrote me yards about it; the novelist took charge, and I must contract its exuberance. 'My Anglo-Irish father was elderly when I was born and we had no family to go to there, and so we stayed among our Scottish relatives. My sister Letitia, now 86, and I did a pilgrimage to the homes and tombs of our ancestors in County Cork and County Kerry, and I was staggered by the collision there between the lushness of County Cork and

South Kerry – with its hedges of fuchsias and hydrangeas and wild montbretias – and the mountain wildness of North Kerry. We went to Youghal . . . to see the tombs of our remote ancestors, the Ormondes, in the old Protestant church, and to visit Ralegh's house. We asked the owner, Commander Arbuthnot if we might see the house, as Ralegh was a collateral ancestor of ours.

'We turned up in a car driven by one of the many out-of-work, white-collar Irishmen, very sad and very sensitive and sick at heart over the Ulster business.' (He might well be – much worsened since.) Ralegh's house is 'a long low building, quite small, and it has a gravel sweep in front of it. Round and round the gravel sweep were walking the Commander, his wife and his schoolgirl daughter, not together but isolated, all looking down on the gravel. When we went across they greeted us with the abandonment of ordinary custom one would expect from ghosts. They were not uncivil, they were just hardly there. They all spoke very softly, and never volunteered a remark, or answered one except in monosyllables. They were really extraordinarily like ghosts.'

The novelist describes the interior, the staircase 'ornamented with the most beautiful Victorian flower-paintings from some relative whose husband had been stationed abroad. What acres of flower-paintings the British Empire produced. He told us that this had been the home of Sir John Pope Hennessy's father; and that his sister-in-law was the sister of Claud Cockburn' – famous in the Thirties as creator of *The Week*. (He retired to Ireland, whence I have letters from him: we were Anti-Appeasers together.)

Rebecca noticed the Commander's resemblance to Wellington's delightful Mrs Arbuthnot of the Diary, and a portrait of her was fetched which corroborated it. Rebecca felt the whole atmosphere to smack of the supernatural (but couldn't it have been fear?). At the church the sexton was astonished to hear that they had been inside: 'Nobody went to the house. The incident seemed to me typical of Ireland. It was as if there was a chemical process going on which drained everything off the country and left a precipitate of fear.

'I was so horrified by what had happened to the house in Tralee where my father was born, in Day Place, an exquisite

Georgian terrace. It belongs to a prosperous dentist, and he has gutted the interior.' But of course. 'It looks like a Council-house, while his wife potters about, holding up china cherubs out of no known ceramic stable, and Woolworth pink glass vases and says how she loves anteeks. (Spondee.) How horrible it is to know that the same thing has happened to Ibstone House, which has been mutilated; the present owner runs a chain of dress-shops in the Thames Valley and is a Christian Science practitioner.

'In Tralee we met quite an interesting character, a young man who was risking much by saying that Ireland was a product of Celt plus Englishman; his great-grandfather having come from Cornwall to join the R.I.C. [Royal Irish Constabulary], and his grandfather having followed suit; and his father also, having passed into the service of the municipality, as R.I.C. personnel did when the body was broken up. What an odd situation, how like what must have happened on the fringes of the Roman Empire at a certain time. And how the Catholic middle-class can allure one by its innocence and its sweetness. There was a family we visited in Listowel who had the ideal Quaker sweetness about them.

'But in Dublin I sat next – at a party I got roped into in the Kildare Street Club (which used to be a Protestant stronghold) Erskine Childers, who has, I think, no drop of Irish blood in him, English and American [Irish American and a bit of Scotch, Rebecca], and is a Cabinet Minister. Looking exactly like Beaverbrook, he sat beside me and hissed in my ear denunciations of the wickedness of – who do you think? – who could be most irrelevant to the tragedy of North Ireland? Believe it or not – the Duke of Windsor.' Erskine Childers, whose Republican father was shot as a rebel by the Free State, became President of the Republic. He was a reader of my Elizabethan books, and invited me, when in Dublin, to the former Vice-Regal Lodge I should like to have seen. Next thing he was dead.

'How smartly your familiar goes for the seat of Trevor-Roper's trousers. Your familiar is a very engaging animal. I shall be happy with your book for the next week or two. Longer, of course, but my happiness will be intense during that period. And do see me when you come back. It is such a long time since you came and nearly haleked the debs in my kitchen.' Not so, dear Rebecca: merely polite flirtation.

She followed up with a 'Supplementary' to correct my saying that Belloc's sister had been worldly enough to marry her daughters off very well. 'But she didn't. She let both her daughters, without a protest, marry husbands quite unsatisfactory from a worldly point of view. Elizabeth married Lord Iddesleigh, who had no money at all and gave her no other distinction than that which belongs to the wife of the only known Albino Peer. [However, an earl is an earl is an earl, and a Catholic earl rarer still.] Her other daughter married a Portuguese journalist and – believe me, Leslie, as only your adopted mother – I should be bitterly disappointed if you made such an alliance. It would be as if I had heard you had married Helen Gardner.'

In February 1972, 'I think of you so often now, for I am writing my memoirs and in 100 pages have not got past the year 1800 – my family history has so much affected me. It grieves me very much to pass from the Denny who was a cousin of Swiss[3] Sir Walter and the Gilberts to the Dennys (my great-great grandfather and my grandmother), who handed over all the family fortune to the Plymouth Brethren.' That bespeaks a crazy streak in the family line. She goes over again her visit to the homes of her ancestors and how she so loved the place – 'those hedges of crimson fuchsias and the ancient high crosses, the spitting images of the ones in Macedonia, and Dingle Peninsula which is so like a grey Greece. But oh the JOIN THE IЯA painted across the railway bridges and the children playing with pistols in the market-place, and the grinning woman who said to me, "Aar, they're playin' theyre

---

[3] This is a reference to John Aubrey's bawdy story, how Ralegh 'one time getting up one of the Maids of Honour against a tree in a wood, who seemed at first boarding to be something fearful of her honour – she cried, "Sweet Sir Walter, what do you me ask? Will you undo me? Nay, sweet Sir Walter! Sweet Sir Walter." At last, as the danger and the pleasure at the same time grew higher, she cried in the ecstasy, "Swisser Swatter! Switter Swatter!" She proved with child. . . .' And hence Ralegh's trouble with the Queen. The prig of an editor of the otherwise standard edition of Aubrey's *Brief Lives* – Andrew Clark – omitted this, along with a good deal more fun. One has to look elsewhere.

in Bélfãst!" How I hate the thought of the young soldiers being killed. Denny wrote that queer phrase about Ireland being fitter for mastiffs than for men. I wonder why mastiffs.' I suppose because they were fierce dogs. Swift regarded the Irish as mad.

'My dear Leslie, I hope we meet sometime soon. You have become very retiring – do consider that in these hard times you should shed your light around.' To what point, in such a filthy society? I was more and more determined on withdrawal from it.

At the end of that year, 'Were you in England at Christmas time, would you come to my birthday and watch me gracefully becoming eighty during either lunch or dinner? I should so love to have you there – think of me as your little Champernowne, you don't know many people as thoroughly Tudor as me.' However, I was in Cornwall at Christmas time, so I asked if my celebration might take the form of dedicating a book to her. She replied, 'I can't quite believe it about the dedication – are you not just "leading me in" like a Victorian seducer – will you not turn to me and break my heart with your mocking laughter? – I am still enchanted by your book, in spite of its revelation about my collateral ancestor, Richard Champernowne.' This was merely a rumour at Court, reported by fellow-Devonian Drake, that he was 'a gelder of boys' to preserve their voices. He had a choir at Dartington, and Robert Cecil wanted one of his boys with a fine voice for his choir. This came into *The Elizabethan Renaissance: the Cultural Achievement*. 'What an odd world you suddenly reveal in those pages. I was thinking the other day that the person I would most desire to meet of them all would be Thomas Hariot – but by preference with Walter Ralegh. What a bright vision you give of it all.' Her choice showed her judgment: Hariot was the most brilliant scientific intellect of the time, the most hidden and mysterious.

Simon Forman: Sex and Society in Shakespeare's Age was duly dedicated to her, as 'admirable writer, constant friend', not without a naughty suggestion of the propriety of dedicating so sexy a book to her.

'The wording of your dedication gives me such pleasure. That is the way one would like to be described by someone whom one loves and honours, and, dear, how lovely it is that honour is the word, though you are such fun.' She would pass over more of her 'peculiarly eerie family trouble' – I never entered into that, regarding families (my own especially) as such a bore.

'My egotism gloats over the knowledge that the Dark Lady was kept by an ancestor, but I don't know if direct or collateral, Lord Hunsdon. . . . There was evidently something in Simon Forman's claims to magic powers.' And she told me yet another story of coincidence regarding a book. Her secretary had fetched her a *Who's Who*, to look up an Elton, but her thumb had rested on the only Forman in the book. She wondered whether Simon went as far as a soothsayer, for 'he cannot have been able to concentrate with all that haleking. How beautifully, by the way, do you discern who it was that was Forman's true love.'

This identification, Avice Allen, wife of a London grocer, gave me far more trouble than the obvious identity of Shakespeare's Dark Lady, with the patron of his Company, the Lord Chamberlain, as her protector – so close, along with complete corroboration as to circumstances, characteristics and definite dating. When Avice Allen died, my research helper and I looked through all the London parish registers in print for her burial. In vain: no luck. Then it occurred to me that the reason for her not being there was that she might have been a Catholic. I looked up the Roll of Middlesex Catholic Recusants – and there she was.

'I wish you hadn't told me that Emilia had been converted to her really very touching Christianity – Christ wasn't, she's obviously saying, a bit like all those rude boys that haleked her with their boots on – at Cookham, where later St Spencer painted all those screaming religious paintings – it suggests that places determinate.' She then goes into various odd events and happenings at Cookham. 'Your writing of this book is tighter than some of your other work – and must have been written with great care, and I suppose that's why it has such an effect.' Not much effect on the numb, and dumb, I fear. 'I liked the Life, with its picture of a man in the difficult situation of having a burning passion to practice a science that had not yet been truly invented.'

My sympathy for Forman was for the poor boy who was desperately keen to educate himself, when others who had all the chances gave themselves no trouble. We have reason to be grateful too to the old *roué* for the information that directed me to the Dark Lady, with whom his experience exactly corroborated that of William Shakespeare four and five years before. 'This is indeed my book. Somehow your dedication has given it to me in a special sense. I was so moved by Forman's account of his father's death. And surely it is an extraordinary piece of writing, as well as of feeling.' No one else noticed it, except this woman of genius. Perhaps this is to be expected; but ordinary people need to be, and should have been, told. Simon Forman was a very interesting character, an addition to the gallery of remarkable Elizabethans.

I followed this up by publishing the Dark Lady's long religious poem, *Salve Deus, Rex Judaeorum,* for which we had a celebration thoughtfully laid on by the learned librarian at All Souls, John Simmons. What fun we had in those days, one way and another: he sprang surprise quotations for us under our plates at lunch. Rebecca: 'The Rivers-Scotts are bringing me down to your Dark Lady festival, and we will present ourselves in a state of delight, because we are to be with you, the great Illuminator, the power Exorciser.' One Nigel Dennis had crabbed a book of mine in her paper, and I inquired who he was. 'No, Nigel Dennis is not a Catholic. If he dies and finds there is a God he will sue. He is a gloom-browed congenital sourpuss and is worse now because he is living in Malta.'

In 1975 I was asking her about Mary Renault, whose books I admired, and Rebecca had lived so much in London that she knew, or knew about, everybody. 'She is an ex-hospital nurse of quite a high standing. I think she was a theatre sister at one of the teaching hospitals. She then went to South Africa and lived with another nurse in a most revolting shanty on the edge of the Indian ocean. The breakers pounded down on the rocks only a few yards away from you. It was most alarming. I think she is an extremely good writer and she was also very good-looking in a severe way. I agree with you about Elizabeth Jenkins' – another admiration of mine, who wrote the best letters I have ever received. I have kept them all (she did not keep mine). 'I am being as happy as the world allows me, following your injunction' – this was not to fuss about family troubles, 'a predicament I should have got used to.'

A couple of years later, why had I not let her know beforehand about my *Homosexuals in History*? – she would have reviewed it and 'cheered on the cause'. Now she longed to read it. 'E.M. Forster was simply the largest marshmallow ever created, what a SILLY book *Howard's End* is, and as mascot of King's he was hardly worthy to be in the company of mascots like the Welsh Guards' goat.' We agreed about him, altogether made too much of by the claque, really rather comic; I enjoyed his essays and occasional writings, his novels too namby-pamby, for an obvious reason, a *castrato*.[4] On the other hand, 'I like Oscar Wilde's grandson too much to concede that Oscar was just an Irish Exhibitionist, but loving you too I am also prone to think that I must be wrong.' Of course I did not think that Wilde was 'just' an Irish Exhibitionist, but another writer made too much of by *his* claque. And his exhibitionism brought untold misery and sufferings upon hundreds of people, humans being the idiots they are. He of all people should have known that, and kept his tastes to himself, or to the intelligent. Dear Rebecca, being highly intelligent, had no prejudices regarding those.

Her letters as usual were full of her troubles; she was a regular complainer. Now her 'sister of 91 has had a stroke and had to be found a hospital, and how strange that is; she now looks beautiful as she was when she was young, but as if she were young and made up for the stage.' (Rebecca had fancied herself for the stage when young; but was rejected by a fool who thought she had not enough personality, when her trouble was that she had too much. In fact I think she was given to 'acting up' all through her life; one sees this in her relations with Wells – very Irish of her, and he after all was very English: it must have bored him. It did not bore me, for I kept a safe distance and observed, as Henry James would have done.)

In spite of constant complaints about health, Rebecca was as

---

[4] cf. my essay, 'A Great Writer? – The Case of E. M. Forster', in *Portraits and Views*.

vital and active as ever in her eighties, and as observant. Her sister's paralysis had a 'Byzantine effect' – who would have thought of that? And 'how odd it is that royalty all over the world and all through time imitate the paralysed.' Meanwhile, she had had 'a curious upheaval of my life, of which I will tell you someday'. This did not prevent her from a visit to Rouen, 'which is magnificently rebuilt, and the poorer quarters are no longer poor, everyone looks healthy and is well dressed, and the students look ravishing. But it is hell because of a maze of one-way streets, and coming down from Calais through Picardy I marked a terrible loss – not a Percherin to be seen, and surely they were among the world's most beautiful inhabitants, just scruffy tractors. . . . Did you know what I learned from a votive tablet in the *église abbatiale* of St George in St Martin de Boisselle that Linley Sambourne, the *Punch* cartoonist who succeeded Tenniel, was saved from drowning in the Seine by appealing to the Virgin Mary as represented in that church? – on August 19, 1873.' I was always surprised at how much Rebecca *knew*, if discursively. She was a great reader.

When my book, *Memories of Men and Women*, arrived, 'I have been reading *it* instead of finishing my book on 1900, and I doubt if I shall be able to pick up my Biro again. *Your* book is so charming. I don't agree with you in your estimate of the people you write about in some cases.' I only hope the historian was more objective. 'I was specially amused at your paper on Beaverbrook whom I knew well. The curious thing about him was that he never got a story right, and as he chose as his biographer A. J. P. Taylor, who had the same characteristic, their cooperation must have made a huge rent in reality! I have been writing about Milner and was amused to see Beaverbrook's account of his ancestry on p. 221 of your book. Milner, that detestable man, cannot be laid at the door of the Germans: his soundly English grandfather lived in Germany and married a German lady called Sophie von Rapport.[5] But his mother was English. . . . It's perfectly true he was spiritually German, but not because of Bismarck, because of Treitschke. But all that of course you know.

[5] I do not agree that Milner was 'a detestable man', and his grandmother *was* German, a von Rappard, not Rapport, by the way.

'I was amused to find that Taylor had included in his biography Beaverbrook's story of how, when he was a young MP staying at a hotel in Cannes, he found that Dilke was staying in the same hotel . . . and that they spent hours walking along the Promenade at Cannes talking about politics and the Empire. In fact the year this was supposed to have happened Dilke *did* go to the Riviera, but to Hyères, in an invalid carriage, where he had a house, and he hadn't for some time been able to walk along promenades.' Nothing surprising in this: Taylor admits that Beaverbrook regularly embellished a story or improved on the facts. What is surprising is then to praise Beaverbrook as a brilliant historian. No historian worthy of the name should tamper with the facts.

'Regarding Milner', she continues, 'it irks me how his Kindergarten lived on to be Appeasers from the word go, such as lived long enough. The odious editor of *The Times* for one, who liked Hitler so much.' Of the Kindergarten, Geoffrey Dawson of *The Times* and Philip Lothian were arrant (and errant) Appeasers; Bob Brand and Leo Amery were not; Lionel Curtis lay low. Those are the objective facts.

As for the feminine subjectivism of Rebecca's judgments, I registered a couple of cases from her lively *Sunday Telegraph* reviews. She gave a severe wigging to the celebrated Lady Salisbury, wife of the Prime Minister. Rebecca thought her simply appalling. She was a bit of a dragon, but anyone who knows the history of the family knows how much the great Lord Salisbury owed to his rather middle-class wife. As a young man he had been highly nervous, something of a neurotic; she built him up steadfastly into the steady, monumental statesman he became.

Another case was that of Edith Wharton's lover, Morton Fullerton, whom Rebecca slated the length of a review as an appalling blackmailer. He gave Edith Wharton the satisfaction she did not get from the man she loved, Walter Berry, who was not responsive. Fullerton gave her what she wanted. Ambivalent and not at all well off, he accepted some cash when needed. Not very dignified, but women do for services rendered. I do not call it blackmail.

Incidentally, I several times urged Rebecca to collect some of these amusing later pieces. Her earlier journalism has been admirably collected in *The Young Rebecca*.[6]

'I have not seen you for a long time, but I dearly love you. I have been ill and have had other forms of hell in the last years. My family have been smitten in various ways' – then she goes into detail. (I wasn't interested in people's families: the joys of family life were not for me.) 'The relatives I love – not that I don't love my grand-daughter and my strange son – live in Edinburgh, which is sad. I know you are happy because you are in Cornwall.'

This penultimate letter was typed by a secretary, who gave Rebecca her title: 'Dame Rebecca West, D.B.E.' – a pseudonym after all, and Dame of the no longer existing British Empire. Indeed it was an end. Rebecca was a lady, but not lady-like – she was above all that. Now that she was a Dame, she had become – after those earlier embarrassing years (and she had had a good many embarrassments to put up with) – rather a *grande dame*. It was ironical that by the end she had become, like Mrs Humphry Ward in her day, the *grande dame* of English letters.

She had always been generous about my poetry, buried under – and overlooked on account of – the history. Rebecca was not so compartmented, unimaginatively specialised – she was more Elizabethan. When I sent her my *A Life: Collected Poems* – my life's work in poetry (more important to me than the history, my inner life as opposed to the outer, my secret life) – she was responsive as ever. 'Beautiful affectionate poems, affectionate towards all the right things. Shall I never see you again?'[7]

Alas, we never did meet again. In spite of illness her interest in life remained inexhaustible. 'I am distressed by the Brixton riots beyond measure.' I wasn't – just what one should have

---

[6] *The Young Rebecca: Writings of Rebecca West 1911–1917*. Selected by Jane Marcus.

[7] My verses about the cult of the suicidal Sylvia Plath, making a plain straightforward statement, aroused the ire of a third-rate poetry-resident at a provincial university – typical humbug-job created in our cultivated society – to whom the *Times Literary Supplement* fobbed it off for review, instead of someone qualified to write about it. Rebecca responded with comic verses about the Plath cult. Once before a volume of my verse had been disparaged, by a Miss Phoebe Pool, feeble little fool. Who now remembers who the creature was?

expected from the Macmillan government's leaving the door to immigration irresponsibly open. As with Appeasement, anybody of sense could have seen that it would mount up until it became an almighty problem. And in a small, heavily overpopulated island, at the apogee of power and prosperity at the beginning of the century with a population of 40 million – now towards the end approaching 60 million! What are politicians *for*, if not to think of the long-term interests of their country?

Rebecca's attitude was more subjective. 'I have in recent years constantly passed through Brixton. I had some ties there, with a most charming Negro accountant. He was utterly happy there with his family, till the Left Wing Council on the one hand, and the crime, gave him a nervous breakdown. These riots mean the end of bourgeois happiness for a lot of very nice black people. . . . What horrible times we have lived to see.

'I spent some years of my childhood in the last house we owned, in Streatham – a very pretty little Regency house finally bombed to the ground. My great-great plus grandmother . . . came to live in those parts when she married Richard Fairfield on his return from India in mid-18th century and is buried at Lewisham. And her sister, the mother-in-law of Sydney Smith lived at Cheam.' That seems an appropriate ghost for Rebecca at the end. 'I am full of serious, sad troubles, but thoughts of the people I love such as you bear me up.'

With the end approaching I had asked if she kept my letters, as I kept hers. I hope that I did not hurt her feelings, but that she was only teasing me when she replied: 'I am sending back your letters, but I am heartbroken by the implied lack of trust – of course I would *never* have sued you for breach of promise. But here they are, with all my love.'[8]

Dear, generous, warm-hearted, *great* woman: she was all for love – made for love, as H.G. had well realised. I feel now, reading through her letters again, how somehow inadequate I had been.

---

[8] In the event she decided to keep the originals, and sent me photo-copies, largely illegible.

Elizabeth Bowen; Goronwy Rees

What is curious about my relations with Elizabeth Bowen is that for a considerable time I got her quite wrong. Perhaps that was understandable since, during the early years of a long acquaintance, I did not know her well; later on I came to know her much better. Earlier, I had been wrong on two counts. I thought her a more remarkable woman than she was a writer – the development of her writing, her fulfilment as novelist, in time put that right. Secondly, I thought her too cerebral for a novelist; I put this down to her deracination as Anglo-Irish, that she was somehow cut off from the sources of life, and was perhaps rather sexless.

How wrong I turned out to be! But there was something to be said for my assumptions before I came to know her. My close friend Elizabeth Jenkins, who knew her well, thought that she was 'a writer before she was a woman.' She herself gave a clue, I thought, in a tell-tale phrase, 'her sex is all in her head' (just what I thought); and another clue in her description of Le Fanu, a fellow Anglo-Irish writer, as having Irish infantilism and sexlessness. This became corroborated in her own case in that her sexual interest was rather belated, and, when aroused, was regularly directed to young men years younger than herself.

Her marriage to Alan Cameron – part Scotch, part Cornish (a Lanyon) – was odd, and appeared to be sexless; he was rather ambivalent, and they had no children. She was the closest friend of my oldest Oxford friend, David Cecil and, though that was an emotional relationship, a love affair, it was platonic, apparently non-sexual. Above all, Elizabeth was an aristocrat, with an aristocratic reticence – that would have made a bond between them. Though I had a close friendship with him, neither of them betrayed anything to me, though I was a bit curious. Elizabeth never had the slightest interest of that sort in me (nor I in her): David would have let her know what the score was.

So altogether circumstances conspired to put me wrong. Young, I thought she was a cold woman. I still do not think she was a warm one, though it transpired that she was capable of passion – a different matter. Eventually, she became friendly, well-disposed, appreciative of my own writing, always loyal, never crabbing or malicious – she was above all that. She was a great woman – I always thought that – but not easy to know.

To my mind she was, in those early years, a strange woman. I did not know that her father had been mad, or that she had had an earlier breakdown. She was excessively sensitive; an unfavourable review would send her to bed for a couple of days. Once, when I might have called on her at the tiny cottage where she and Alan then lived up at Headington (he was Director of Education down in Oxford), she was laid up in bed: she had had a bad review. Really! Later on, with success – or, better, fulfilment in her work – she became more normal. I thought of her, perhaps not altogether wrongly, as an over-intellectualised woman, like Virginia Woolf: hence the mental strain.

Her appearance was sufficiently striking, not exactly welcoming. I thought her very handsome: a magnificent head and profile, rather masculine, with beautiful fine red-gold hair; large, unfeminine hands and feet, and what she herself described as an 'androgynous' figure. Then there was her stammer, which in itself put a distance between her and the outside world. The odd thing was that her stammer was very attractive (I don't know if she knew that): it added distinction to everything she said, for it was clearly due to her having so many thoughts in that quick brilliant brain which she could not bring out all at once. But I did not know, another clue, that it started at the time of her father's madness.

Altogether someone very exceptional, most uncommon, not to be familiar with; as time went on, and, in spite of the burden (and danger) of excessive sensibility and intellectuality, she fulfilled herself in her work by sticking to her last, with underlying strength of character. It became evident that she was a woman of genius.

Again, I was not particularly impressed by her early novels. David Cecil thought best of *The Last September*. The historian recognised her obsession that her home in County Cork, Bowen's Court, was in danger of being burned down; three neighbouring country houses were burned by the mad Irish, outposts of civilisation amid mountain and bog – if civilisation of a Somerville-and-Ross character. I was myself critical of *The House in Paris*, with its middle section given up to the unconvincingly clever conversation of children – almost a transcript (did anyone else notice?) from Cocteau's *Les Enfants Terribles*. Agatha Christie, unappreciated by intellectuals, was far better at children's talk.

Elizabeth herself said that she never expected to write novels, but short stories; and in her early work I appreciated those most – she was always a fine short-story writer. *Death of the Heart*, longest of the earlier novels, she condemned as an inflated short story; the kernel of it is an autobiographical episode which gave her a theme – which I happened to be very close to, at the time it was written. I thought that book artistically unintegrated, it did not altogether come together; and she had another reason for liking it least of all her work. The essence of the book went back to a now celebrated house-party at Bowen's Court in 1936, and her relationship with Goronwy Rees, by whom she felt herself betrayed; she had not yet distanced herself from that awkward experience when she wrote the book.

When I read it I recognised his personality – which I knew only too well – at once: a speaking likeness. Various clues are there: he is lower-class for one thing. That made for difficulty in the relationship with Elizabeth, who was not only a lady, but a great lady – difficulties on both sides. I realised these so well, as working-class myself, that I wondered that people should be willing to risk the inevitable misunderstandings in mixing classes, crossing bounds, fences, ditches. True, one can see that there is an element of challenge, and some people are impelled – chiefly by sex – to take risks. But it doesn't come off well in literature, let alone life: Henry James's *The Princess Casamassima* is a failure on this count; so is *Lady Chatterley's Lover*; and Hardy is unconvincing when he tries to portray aristocrats.

I knew the people present at that crucial house party pretty well: Isaiah Berlin from the time he was an undergraduate, Goronwy Rees from the time he became a Fellow of All Souls, Elizabeth less well, Rosamond Lehmann not at all. As usual I observed from the side-lines, not giving myself away. Isaiah and Goronwy had every reason to know me well enough, since I lived with them in College – though Goronwy later gave as reason for his younger generation not wanting me as their Warden that they felt that they did not know me. (I dare say they were right to reject me: I would have seen to it that they did their research – as he had not done his.)

Since I formed an unfavourable, and perhaps prejudiced, view of Goronwy Rees's character, I must in justice say what was in his favour. It goes without saying that he was highly intelligent, or he would never have been elected as a Prize Fellow on the examination; he was cultivated and amusing; he was warm-hearted and spirited; he had courage and a good war record. He was a natural writer and should have stuck to his last. He was very handsome, with an irresistible combination of beautiful curly raven-black hair and blue eyes; well-made and masculine figure, a good footballer. In sum, one of Connolly's 'deadly irresistibles': several people fell for him, and in both sexes (I was not one). Geoffrey Faber was in love with him, and eventually wished him on the College as his successor as Estates Bursar. I had no confidence in his running the business, estates and finance, of the College. When Warden Sumner asked me if I, as Sub-Warden, minded his appointment (I could have stopped it), I said, 'Well, it's your funeral.' It turned out to be so.

For, the fundamental thing lacking in Goronwy, was, quite simply: character. He admits this in his well-written, *A Bundle of Sensations*. 'It has always surprised, and slightly bewildered me', he writes, 'that other people should take it so much for granted that they each possess what is usually called "a character". That is to say, a personality with its own continuous history. . . . I have never been able to find anything of that sort in myself; and in the course of my life this has been the source of many misunderstandings, since other people persist in expecting of one a kind of consistency – which they really have no right to demand.'

Perhaps they have no right to 'demand', but it is only reasonable that they should expect some consistency of conduct and also in the treatment they receive from others. I take it that it is a good thing that we should aim at achieving some consistency, even if we are not very good at it – all the more reason then to try. Goronwy never tried; he is here making a plausible case for his own weakness of character – he was always only 'a bundle of sensations', and himself in the event a chief sufferer from this. A natural writer, he had not the character to stick to his gift and make something of it. (Elizabeth had, and did.) A writer needs not only his original gift of nature but also the strength of character to abide by it, tie himself to his desk and endure the burden and the drudgery.

Goronwy couldn't, or wouldn't; he tried everything else, for he was of an adventurous spirit, a good deal of an adventurer. He wrote two early novels, really long short-stories, which showed some promise, but did not press on to anything better. He fell back on College research – would the College support him in a research project? He hadn't thought of a subject: I thought of a suitable one for him. Our Leftist group was much interested in Marxism and its German affiliations; Lassalle was a significant figure, a fascinating adventurer, a suitable subject for Goronwy. He was keen on going to Germany – they all were, Auden, Isherwood, Spender – and Goronwy was glad of the opportunity. He took it, enjoyed himself there like the rest of them, did no research whatever; then came back and handed in his cards.

That was the end of him as a researcher: he would never have made a historian. However, John Sparrow and I got him a job as assistant literary editor on the *Spectator*. This at least gave him a *stellung* in London, and enabled him to lead a London life, occasional week-ends at All Souls. Then came the *fracas* with Elizabeth Bowen and the fuss over *Death of the Heart*. Elizabeth had already had an affair with a much younger married man at Oxford – small blame to her, she needed sexual experience for her writing.

She then fell in love with Goronwy, a lower-class irresistible some eight or ten years younger – apt to be an humiliating situation, as it turned out to be. His character, or lack of it, is recognisably rendered in the novel, where the young man complains that women 'have a lunatic instinct for picking on another person who doesn't know where he is. How can I keep on feeling something I once felt, when there are so many things one can feel? . . . I may be a crook, but I'm not a fake.' Goronwy was neither a crook nor a fake, but I thought he was something of a cad, and would never trust him after being let down over his research assignment. After all, he had the ability to write a life of Lassalle – why not stick to it and do it? The novelist's comment on the young man in the novel is that he tries to get off with people because he could not get on with them.

He could never have got on with me, though we were both, after all, Celts. I once teased Geoffrey Faber about this, who was publishing us both, but with an emotional fixation on Goronwy; Geoffrey remarked what very different characters we were. I don't think he got much change out of the relationship, Goronwy was so keen on getting off with the other sex. He made this clear at the beginning of his long and close relationship with Guy Burgess. Then what was the basis of this peculiar intimacy? Goronwy was neither a Communist, nor a spy: I think it was just that they were both adventurers, with a very flexible, fluent, free-wheeling and -dealing attitude to life, both cads.

It was utterly contrary to my own view of life. The only time I ever saw Guy Burgess was when Goronwy brought him into our smoking-room after dinner one night. Burgess hadn't been there twenty minutes before the Junior Fellow came up to complain to me that Burgess had made a pass at him. I happened to be the Senior Fellow present: but what was I supposed to do about that? I said sympathetically, 'Well, you can keep away from him' (Burgess remained away at the end of the room). What was the basis of Goronwy's friendship with Anthony Blunt? I suppose, intellectual rather than sexual ambivalence; they belonged to the same circle, and in fact

Goronwy was all over the place.

The affair with Elizabeth received its *coup-de-grace* at that disastrous summer house-party at Bowen's Court. Goronwy and the younger woman not only fell for each other but 'carried on' under the eyes of the *châtelaine*. Reproaches ensued, with Goronwy being hysterical on the drawing-room carpet. Really, one didn't behave like that in a country-house, in front of one's hostess, whatever one's emotions or private relations: Elizabeth was one for upper-class standards, a proper *tenue*. I'll bet she maintained them throughout, though mortally offended; indeed, she felt betrayed – betrayal is the theme of *Death of the Heart*. Apparently she said something frightening to Goronwy at the time: 'My father went mad in this house. Will we?' When I stayed at Bowen's Court later, I felt that the house was overwhelmingly melancholy, even something sinister.

I had made a mistake about Goronwy. With our joint Leftist views I assumed that he was working-class, like myself. He was not: he was Welsh middle-class, his father a well-known Calvinist minister. In College I assumed a leadership of our Leftist group, as a born proletarian and, a few years senior, having helped to elect Goronwy, I may have seemed patronising – though one couldn't very well patronise a chameleon.

When *Death of the Heart* came out, he was at first delighted and told Rosamond how brilliant it was. He then changed his mind completely, wrote Elizabeth bitterly, threatening libel. Again, one doesn't do that between friends – and it was Geoffrey Faber who persuaded him against such caddishness. When Goronwy told me all about it I took very much a senior prefect's line, and said, 'If you give yourself away to the upper classes, this is what you must expect. Why don't you give it up, and devote yourself for five or ten years to a wonderful subject – Tudor Wales?' I was then researching away at what was to become *Tudor Cornwall*. Tudor Wales is a much bigger, richer and more variegated subject – no Welsh historian has yet got round to giving us a picture of it as a whole. I think that Goronwy knew Welsh, and he had the writing ability; what he had not got was the character, the stability or persistency. He was quite candid about it, and gave me the answer: 'My dear Leslie, I couldn't do it.'

As for Elizabeth, her last word on the affair came in a short story: 'Before you came, I was walled in alive. I didn't know where to turn. I was burning myself out.'

Then the war came down on us – in which Goronwy acquitted himself well, and in which Elizabeth reached her apogee as a writer. The war released something in her as it did for all of us – the sense of excitement, the ever-present danger, the leave-takings and homecomings, the heart-breaks, the grief for those who never returned, the joy for those who did, the camaraderie and good fellowship: those were unforgettable years in which Britain's glorious past came to an end in flames. Elizabeth sensed what happened to herself, and expressed it in her own oblique, too clever way: 'It seems to me that during the war in England the overcharged subconsciousness of everybody overflowed and merged.' It seems an odd way of putting it; more directly, love and sex were a free-for-all. Her own phrase 'life with the lid on' was over, and that released her into her finest work.

To my mind *The Heat of the Day* is not only her best novel, but gives the truest picture of wartime London – along with James Lees-Milne's factual Diaries: the bombings, fires, crumps, houses crashing, whole blocks falling, splintered glass everywhere; the glow and glory, the casualties, pain and squalor; the fun and jokes amid the misery; the unspoken bravery. She worked as an air-raid warden, and on her patrols met all kinds of people she would never have met before. Once more she met a much younger man with whom she fell in love – one recognises him, yet another Oxford man, but a Canadian, in the novel; his height, 'the long elegant hands and head', the way he lies on a sofa, 'extended at full length, narrow and Byzantine in a dressing gown.'

Elizabeth was now a famous author, success put her in full control and made money for her; everybody has the phrase that she could 'use' a lot of money, I should regard her as rather extravagant, with Irish notions of hospitality. I was bidden to stay at Bowen's Court, which I was the more glad to do because it gave me a chance to see Spenser's Kilcolman Castle not far away. I had read her book about the house and the history of her family, Cromwellian Welsh by origin – she was a better historian than Goronwy, though he had been trained to it at Oxford. Here was something Elizabeth Bowen and Rebecca West had in common, an absorbing interest in their Anglo-Irish family. Elizabeth's description of her family home was so vivid that I was pleased to discover that I could find my way round that overtall, gawky mansion almost blindfold – and there was a trap in it: the top story, where my bedroom was, did not communicate direct with the main staircase, one had to go round behind. Was that architectural solecism, something unfinished, peculiarly Irish?

The rest of the house was in keeping, rather down-at-heel, a lot of it unfurnished. The big western drawing-room was very sparse; it did not seem that Elizabeth spent anything on furniture. I remember her irritation when a castor came off an old armchair – 'so like everything in Ireland', she said. With a big, semi-vacant Georgian house at hand, I amused myself fantasying how I would furnish it if it were mine – all those sales with lovely eighteenth-century furniture going cheap from emptied houses! The dining room was kept up; one can see what life was like there, now all has gone, from the photographs. Elizabeth sits there again at the head of her hospitable dinner table, extremely *décolletée*, face like a noble thoroughbred; silver candlesticks, flowers, grand guests, family portraits looking down on the improbably intellectual converse.

My fellow-guest was another friend of David Cecil's, Cynthia Asquith, who had won a huge BBC prize by answering all sixty-four questions about Jane Austen correctly. I did not feel altogether at ease in such highly geared society, with two such hypersensitive women, electric as eels. When my heavy-soled country shoes scraped once on the drawing-room floor, Cynthia shuddered from head to foot. (Could one have lived cheek by jowl with that? I would never have made the mistake of trying.)

However, I took the ladies off to dinner at a hotel in Cork, where I had to give a lecture. Elizabeth was convulsed by being led into a room entirely populated by ladies' hats. There must have been some convention or meeting afoot, but she kept referring to the oddity of it – the kind of thing that appealed to her imagination. I remembered her queer short-story of the unruly children, who were inexplicably kept under control – though their complexions suffered – by a governess in charge in the absence of their parents. They were quietened all right, reduced to silence, but debauched. The explanation appeared when the parents returned, to find a cubby-hole stuffed with scores of empty boxes of chocolates.

She made it all sound convincing, but queer; indeed she had a lively sense of the strange and untoward, a distinct gift for rendering fear and the supernatural. (Apparently she did *believe*, as Flannery O'Connor did.) I wonder that she was not frightened to live alone in that big house full of ghosts. While Alan Cameron lived he looked after the place; but he can have done nothing about the rooks. They came back at evening in clouds, overcasting the sky. I said to Elizabeth, 'Don't you shoot them?' Oh no, she loved them, and the sound they made. I said, but surely they ate up the place, the corn in the fields; and, firmly, that they needed keeping down.

I find that we both attended the Coronation, though I did not see her there; she was reporting the event for *Vogue*, I for *The Western Morning News* and a Canadian paper. Nor did I know that she always had a desire to write about Swift – an obsessive figure, one can hardly say patron-saint – to all Anglo-Irish. I too had always wanted to write about him, and eventually did, though we never discussed him. Nor did we exchange many letters (I cannot find hers to me), though she was always characteristically generous in her reviews of my books, and noticed things that others didn't – effects of light on landscape, for one thing.

After the war she took to going to the United States, where she became a distinguished figure in the literary landscape: all quite convenient, a motor drive to Shannon Airport, and next thing she was in New York, where she had publishers to look after her and literary parties to be lionised at. For me things were more difficult. For years I had been ill, endless ulceration deflected by a series of dangerous operations. (I suppose only a sound proletarian constitution underneath pulled me through – to become a reformed character in old age.)

I loved All Souls, and the College constituted my chief sustaining happiness in life. Goronwy Rees played a part in weaning me from it. During the mortal illness of two Wardens in succession I had the burden of running the College as Sub-Warden, responsibility without authority. It was agonising: the group of young men who were elected from and after the war – Isaiah Berlin called them the *sans-culottes* – had got out of hand under Humphry Sumner, who was a dying man (another duodenal) and afraid of them.

I was not in the least afraid of these young men, some of whom owed their election to me (dear Cyril Falls thought that I would always remain 'influential' in the College), but they had me framed as Authority and thought that I wanted to run the place. So far from that, during the agitating nine months when I was left alone in charge, and two elections to the Wardenship to conduct, I never wrote a single sentence of a book of mine. Writing was all in all to me, not endless committees to decide who should cook, or cook up, what. All the College officers, except one, wanted me to go on to become Warden. Privately, I did not want this, but could hardly say so to such loyal supporters and a varied following, from Lionel Curtis to G. D. H. Cole.

The chief exception was Goronwy Rees who, returned like the whole of the younger generation from the war, behaved like a *Partei-Führer* and organised them to a man against the Sub-Warden, simply engaged in doing his duty for the place he loved beyond anything. Rees's partisanship was precisely in keeping with the way he behaved subsequently as Principal of Aberystwyth, which brought him down.

He came to consult me as Sub-Warden whether he should accept the offer (he was Tom Jones's candidate, and he put Goronwy into the job). Though I was longing to get rid of him as our Estates Bursar, I gave him honest advice. He gave every secondary reason for accepting: good salary, healthy climate for the family, cheap schooling for the children (Margie was a wonderful wife, who gave him what stability he had). He gave every reason, except the fundamental question I conscientiously put to him: Could he stand it? He never answered that one, and the event showed that he could never stand it, or they him.

Meanwhile, his candidate for the Wardenship at All Souls won the election by a considerable majority: every single member of the younger generation he had organised, with a sufficient number of seniors, like his old patron Geoffrey Faber, and the Wykehamists – who were almost a majority in themselves – to elect a young Wykehamist. For me it was an almighty deliverance, for which I was not at all grateful. I was incensed that these young people – several of whom owed their Fellowships to me, and a few had been pupils or protégés – should follow the lead of a light-weight irresponsible like Rees, as against mine. Though I did not want the job, I have never put up with being turned down by the second- or third-rate: one does not have to put up with that sort of thing from the first-rate. And, a good Celt, I never forgave it or them.

When the historian Grant Robertson, who should have succeeded the fine Warden Anson who had wished it, was turned down for a classical lawyer from London whom the kindly Oman described as 'a returned empty', Robertson hived off to Birmingham to become an eminent and constructive Vice-Chancellor. I remained a Fellow, but turned my face to America, where I had been invited to become a Research Associate at the Huntington Library. Ambivalent as always, I elected to keep a foot in each camp, free of either and to pursue my own course, with no further obligations to anyone except myself, to research and write. My solipsism was confirmed.

It was typical of Rees's light-headedness and warmth of nature that, the next thing, he should invite me to give a few well-paid lectures at Aberystwyth. This fitted in with my work: I wanted to meet the Welsh historians and gain their help for my chapter on Wales, one of the best, for the next volume of my planned trilogy on the Elizabethan Age, *The Expansion of Elizabethan England*. So I accepted. Goronwy was friendly and hospitable. It did not make any difference to my well-formed and long-tested opinion of him.

In New York I met up with Elizabeth, whom I was glad to see, for I was not yet at home in the brave New World. I came to stay regularly at a cheap hotel on Seventh Avenue, convenient to Central Park and the Carnegie Hall for concerts. I had originally been recommended to it by the Rockefeller Foundation, when it was quite pleasant; over the years I saw it go down and down – little did I care about appearances, so long as

I had a clean bedroom and bathroom to myself. Elizabeth stayed a long way down town, at the Gladstone Hotel, near Henry James's Washington Square – very appropriate for her, I thought. I arranged to go down and take her out to lunch.

In those days after the war British people were very hard up for dollars. All the same, I was a little taken aback when Elizabeth suddenly said, 'Leslie, *could* you lend me ten dollars?' I was just back from a lecture tour, so I could; but said, 'Ten dollars – that's no good; what about thirty?' Then, as an after-thought, 'What about a hundred?' 'O darling, could you? I'll write you a cheque in pounds.'

It was the only time in my life that Elizabeth called me 'darling', and I shortly saw why. She immediately rushed to the machine to get a packet of cigarettes: she was an utter addict, hipped on smoking. As her biographer says, for years she had a smokers' cough, and lung cancer got her in the end. It doesn't so much matter that ordinary folk kill themselves with smoking: they are all too easily replaceable. But I resent it when intelligent people, especially friends of mine, unnecess-arily kill themselves this way. One sees a typical photograph of Elizabeth, out for a walk at Bowen's Court, clutching the inevitable packet of fags in hand.

We went out and up the street to find a restaurant. I thought it characteristic of what a lady Elizabeth was that she led the way into, and would have settled for, a cheap little place which one glance told me wouldn't do at all. I wouldn't have it; we went on to find a place which was, though not expensive, decent and good: more my style.

At Aberystwyth Goronwy went racketing on to his downfall. For one thing, he behaved as he had done at All Souls and became the *Partei-Führer* of the younger generation, the students with whom he was, I believe, popular and who imitated their leader's style in white socks. Imagine the silli-ness of a Principal, who should by definition be the head of the whole institution, becoming the leader of a party! He gave his opponents their opportunity to get rid of him by the bad mistake he made of publishing a couple of notorious articles in a popular newspaper at the time of Burgess and Maclean's escape to Soviet Russia.

There had been much discussion as to Rees's motives in this, whether to clear himself of suspicion, or to forestall charges against him. I am not concerned with any of the *bas-fonds*. It is enough for me that the Principal, who always lived light-heartedly and denied himself nothing, was considerably indebted and that the not inconsiderable sum he raised paid his debts.

The articles, with their revelation of his contacts, finished him at Aberystwyth and in the eyes of his Oxford friends – I don't know about London. Maurice Bowra wrote to him that Judas-trees should be planted around the campus at Aberystwyth, and cut off communications. I was not surprised, I merely felt corroborated; nor did I come forward to take any line, for I had already written him off. In these articles he had spilled a good many beans about that circle of his close friends, ambivalent both politically and sexually. He said nothing about its most eminent member, Sir Anthony Blunt – he may have guessed, if not known, that he was a spy; but he gave the name of a working-class lad in this ambivalent circle. I thought that caddish.

In the first half of his career Goronwy had always fallen on his feet; we were there to help, and he had more than his share of good luck – he was a spoiled child of fortune. In the latter half of his life he had less than his share – fortune turned against him. He relates some of this in a second volume of autobiography, *A Chapter of Accidents*, again well-written, and true so far as it goes. But it is only one side of the story; he omits the other side – as to which I am quite sufficiently informed – and the effect therefore is decidedly disingenuous.

He did indeed have more than his share of accidents; ill luck caught up with him; old friends fell away. It was some years before he dared to show his face again at All Souls and, when he did, I did not speak to him. Not until towards the end, after Margie died – who was his good angel; I felt sorry for that, she was a fine woman, who must have had a difficult job keeping him on the rails. After she died, he went off them, and took to drink, as such people are apt to do.

I don't know whether Elizabeth kept any contact with Goronwy after *The Death of the Heart*. She at any rate went on to fulfil herself in her work, as he never did. I think he mistook himself, as I have seen other gifted young Fellows do at All Souls – as I nearly did myself with my anguished pre-occupation with politics all through the Thirties. Even so, I never let go of my writing, and Providence stepped in to bar the way from deviating from my real vocation – which was, from my boyhood on, to write *und sonst nichts*. Goronwy, with his talents, should have been a writer; what he left are fragments of what he might have accomplished.

Elizabeth was a woman of genius, and that means obsession with one's work. In her last years she moved to Hythe – she wrote to me from there; I fancy that it was partly out of devotion to Henry James, but it was a mistake and she came back to London. She had no illusions about the world, the society, she had lived into – the end of civilisation – for there was Ireland as well as ruined London to remind her. A sympathetic study of her work summed it up. 'The earlier books dealt with a world that has, for all practical purposes, ceased to exist: the crust of civilised life has been cracked in too many places, the abyss beneath our feet can no longer be ignored. What will be her approach as a novelist to the squalid, standardised, and unhopeful world in which we are now living?'

The answer to that, in my view, is – Turn back to the better past, and live in that, if you can. Elizabeth had turned back to it with her book on her family, *Bowen's Court*. After all, Anglo-Irish society had been a civilisation, with standards of culture – something better than the lower middle-class *régime* of the 'gombeen man' which took its place. Myles Dillon described it thus to me, son of the Nationalist leader, John Dillon, who died a bitterly disillusioned man, saying that English rule after all had been better than the outcome he had fought for. George Russell, that statesman-like man – known as a writer as AE – left the country in disgust; Joyce lived in exile; Shaw and Wilde had lived in London when the going was good; Yeats died at Rapallo; I met other members of the diaspora, like James Stephens, in America.

Elizabeth could no longer keep Bowen's Court going. She sold it to a neighbouring farmer, thinking that his handsome children would be running about the vacant rooms, bringing back life to it. Not a bit of it: he pulled it all down – one more country house, island of civilisation, gone. 'The shallow hollow of land, under the mountains, on which Bowen's Court stood', she wrote in her farewell to it, 'is again empty. Not one hewn stone left on another on the fresh-growing grass. Green covers all traces of the foundations. Today, as far as the eye can see, there might never have been a house there.'

Since Elizabeth had lived the life of the mind, it was still there in hers, as it is in mine. 'When I think of Bowen's Court, there it is. And when others who knew it think of it, there it is, also' – illumined by the presence of this woman of genius.

9

How Good Was Connolly?

Cyril Connolly and I were exact contemporaries at Oxford. We came up in the Michaelmas term of 1922; he, with a brilliant reputation from Eton, as Brackenbury Scholar at Balliol; I, an unknown quantity from working-class Cornwall, as Douglas Jerrold Scholar at Christ Church. It may surprise the reader, considering our subsequent careers, that Connolly's scholarship was in Modern History, mine in English Literature. The Eng. Lit. School was regarded as a soft option, mainly for women, and Christ Church, not having an Eng. Lit. don, directed me into the History School, which had a higher standing, second only to Greats (ancient history and philosophy, Greek and Latin).

Having brought myself up in remote Cornwall largely on literature and the poets, I found the History School uphill work.[1] However, I was too poor to have distractions, so at home in vacations I worked (in term time diverting myself with politics and contributing, mostly verse, to *Oxford Poetry, The Oxford Outlook*, etc, along with Graham Greene and Harold Acton. I don't think Connolly did – too idle). In the event I emerged, to my immense relief, with an unquestioned First, Connolly with a Third. He should never have taken the History School; he found it boring and had not the mind for an historian: *he* should have taken Eng. Lit. After all, he had a passion for literature, and was very well read. He came up from Eton with some knowledge of the literatures of five civilisations.

As a Colleger, living in daily contact with other clever boys

[1] cf. *A Cornishman at Oxford,* for the ways and means of self-education.

– they all appear in *Enemies of Promise* – he was years ahead in sophistication. One sees that in the brilliant letters he and Noel Blakiston exchanged as schoolboys and undergraduates. I can only compare those letters with the extraordinary sophistication of the young Flaubert's correspondence with his friend, Alfred Le Poittevin, or the Home Letters of T. E. Lawrence.

Nothing of this in my simple correspondence with my uneducated home, where my parents could barely read or write. (I have rather over-compensated there, in both fields.) All my life I have been competing with these brilliant begonias in literary life, and – when it hasn't been Etonians – it has been sharp-witted Wykehamists at All Souls. And how they looked after each other in the literary papers, pushed one another and wrote each other up! Connolly and Eric Blair, i.e. George Orwell, were at Prep. School together as well as at Eton, and a good deal of the over-estimation of Orwell, writing him up into a veritable cult, came from that. As if Orwell's knowledge of the working-class is to be compared with D. H. Lawrence's or mine! *We* come from the people: he was merely slumming in Wigan, as people there realised quite well, and rather resented it.

Connolly tells us, 'my Oxford generation were all highly successful social climbers. They had no political awareness (I am speaking of the writers): Acton liked the Prince of Wales, Waugh the Lygons, Betjeman Irish peers. How different to [*sc.* from] the political thrusters of the Thirties do these delicate aesthetes seem. Clothes were an intoxication. Waisted suits by Lesley and Roberts, white waistcoats from Hawes and Curtis, monogrammed silk shirts arrived in cardboard boxes, top hats, opera hats, Oxford bags. Credit seemed unlimited, fathers had no idea of what they were in for. Lobster Neuberg, foie gras sandwiches, Yquem daily crossed the quad.' – Not to my rooms, where I daily lunched off bread and jam. 'It appears that those afternoons which I spent under some hot towels in Germers were full of goings-on, lectures, tutorials, Heaven knows what.' Germers was then the fashionable hairdressers where these pimpled youths had their complexions improved under hot towels. I had my hair cut cheaply at home in Cornwall.

Then, Connolly writes, 'I went down. London at last. The

Twenties. Parties, Parties, Parties. And behind them all an aching feeling – Was it worth it?' To my mind it wasn't. But they all had somebody to look after them when they went down with their Thirds. Connolly had Logan Pearsall Smith to put him up – he was always an arch-scrounger – while his fellow Anglo-Irishman, Desmond MacCarthy, got him on to the *New Statesman*.

MacCarthy and Connolly had much in common. In 1927 Connolly notes, 'Asked Desmond about himself, and he spoke of his life at twenty-three. He told me he was as idle as I was, and eventually it made him ill. I said I knew the feeling.' Then why didn't these two Irish Etonians get down to some solid work? – Weakness of character, not want of talent. They talked it away – brilliant conversationalists – in smoke. MacCarthy was one of the first to get on to the new appreciation of Donne, and was to have written *the* book on it – he never did. He was early in on the modern interpretation of Coleridge, and was going to write *the* book on that; he never did, that book was written by Hugh Ianson Fausset. MacCarthy, for all his talent and feeling for literature, merely wrote hundreds of reviews. Connolly similarly, though that was not quite all – he did rather better.

Why didn't Connolly do better with his precocious talent and his evident love of literature? He wrote a book to explain that away, *Enemies of Promise,* largely self-defence under the technique of self-accusation. We need not be taken in by that – Connolly played that card from the beginning to the end of his career. Depreciating oneself is a well known ploy to flatter others' self-esteem – La Rochefoucauld understood that. Only fools are taken in by it, but since most people are such, it is highly successful. 'Trying to be funny', turning the laugh against himself, was the way this Irishman sucked up to the English, and got into Pop – otherwise inaccessible to him – at Eton.

It is the chief theme of *The Unquiet Grave*, his one success: 'I am one of those whom suffering has made empty and frivolous: each night in my dreams I pull the scab off a wound; each day, vacuous and habit-ridden, I let it re-form.' What did he suffer from? So far as I can see, the effects of over-indulgence. The books are full of eating and drinking, the cult of the best food and wine, the grandest restaurants. The last time I saw him he was being lunched at the Ritz by a publisher with an eye, no doubt, to a review of a forthcoming book in the *Sunday Times*.

Since *Enemies of Promise* gives us his views we need not go in detail into what he considered holds writers up. Success, for one – we see the sour grapes in that; but Shakespeare, Balzac, Tolstoy? The book begins with lunch on the French Riviera – omelette, vichy, peaches, and 'I always try to write in the afternoons for I have enough Irish blood to be afraid of the Irish temperament.' (The fact was that he did not get up in the mornings.) A main theme of the book is the obsession with Money: one cannot write unless one has an income of several hundred a year. Well, after being kept a year or two by Logan Pearsall Smith[2] as his secretary – I don't know what secretarial duties were involved, but it was good for Cyril's knowledge of literature (one sees Logan's influence in the book, for he was a scholar) – Cyril married money. This freed him for a bit – I do not know that he wrote any the more for it, except an unmemorable novella, *The Rock Pool*. Then the marriage broke up, as they say, with a good deal of inconsiderateness on his part, and back he came to the drudgery of reviewing.

'Ninety Years of Novel-Reviewing', he put it in an essay of 1929, getting amusement out of despair. 'The reviewing of novels is the white man's grave of journalism. . . . The early expectations of discovering a new writer are perhaps less keen a pleasure than one's later hopes of being able to discredit an old one. . . . Remember that the object of the critic is to revenge himself on the creator, and his method must depend on whether the book is good or bad, whether he dare condemn it himself or must lie quiet and let it blow over. Every good reviewer specialized in that subject on which he has not been able to write a book, and his aim is to see that no-one else does.' *Verb. sap.*

So we need not take seriously the portentous opening of *The Unquiet Grave,* so often quoted and to which too much attention has been unnecessarily paid. 'The true function of a writer is to produce a masterpiece and no other task is of any

---

[2] First in Bertrand Russell's varied collection of brothers-in-law.

consequence.' Silly. William Shakespeare did not think like that; he produced a number of plays that are not masterpieces, and in consequence eventually wrote others that were. It is only one more example of Connolly's sleight-of-hand defence for not tackling a solid piece of work himself. Like other Anglo-Irish writers, when young he hoped to write a brave book on Swift. He never got round to doing it.

It was an odd and unsatisfactory notion to write *Enemies of Promise* in two halves, the first literary criticism, the second autobiography. Connolly could be interesting even when writing criticism, as few can, but much the more interesting is the second half about Eton. That was the seminal and happiest period of his life, the most blissful, the cleverest boys in England (besides those at Winchester, of course) living together in College in that lovely place – the river, the bridges, Lupton's Tower, afternoon sunlight falling like honey on the Chapel walls, looking up to the towers and battlements of Windsor Castle, the history of England in mellow brick and stone.

Lucky boys! How I wish I could have been one of them – the camaraderie, the Library, the music, the Chapel! I mustn't be disloyal to my own background, the little Cornish grammar school where I was happy; but that was a rather lonely affair, where there was no-one of comparable intelligence to those Collegers to keep one company. Edward Marjoribanks, Denis Dannreuther, Roger Mynors, Bobby Longden, Victor Cazalet, Connolly himself (it took me a long time to catch up with them). The cruel disadvantage was that everything that came after that Paradise (as Horace Walpole, Gray and West had found it too) was decline – even Oxford. Connolly writes nostalgically, 'Early laurels weigh like lead and of many of the boys whom I knew at Eton, I can say that their lives are over. Those who knew them then knew them at their best and fullest; now, in their early thirties, they are haunted ruins. When we meet we look at each other, there is a pause of recognition, then a subsequent moment of guilt and fear.'

Exaggeration – typical Connolly: the usual ploy of self accusation to excuse non-fulfilment of promise. Guilt-complex is rather a fashionable mode, too prevalent, partly assumed. But there are worse things than guilt: of those six boys, one committed suicide, one was killed in action in the Second German War, another by a German bomb, a fourth (Denis Dannreuther, with all his promise) died as a young Fellow of All Souls. There remained only two to fulfil that promise.

Myself, I could never understand the cult of misery with which the intellectuals wrote up their time at their Public Schools[3] – Raymond Mortimer, for example, a fellow Etonian promoted with Connolly from the *New Statesman* to the literary pages of the *Sunday Times*. Desmond MacCarthy, who preceded and promoted them, always said that he was 'bird-happy' at Eton. Dick Crossman, who had no reason whatever to be unhappy at Winchester where he was top-dog, used to give as a reason for being in politics the aim of ending the Public Schools (and All Souls, of which he was not a Fellow). I noticed that the declared enemies of the Public Schools were always Public Schoolboys, rebels or misfits, never working-class fellows like Bevin or Morrison or me. The Public Schools provide the best education in the country – I only wish I had been at one (preferably Eton or Winchester). The people who attack them are not interested in education, let alone educational standards, only in levelling down.

I didn't know Connolly when we were undergraduates, but I came to know some of his close friends at Balliol – the favourites of 'Sligger' (Urquhart), whom I did not like, with his lascivious blue lips and hooded erotic eyes (repressed of course). It was not until some years later, when I was in turn contributing to the *New Statesman* that, first, Raymond Mortimer, then Cyril Connolly, tracked me down to my lair at All Souls.

I well remember Cyril's first visit: my dark-panelled rooms in the front Quad, small shuttered windows looking out on the Warden's garden on one side, the spire of St Mary's, Newman's St Mary's, on the other. When Cyril glimpsed *Enemies of Promise* on my table I got no further word out of him. With the usual writer's egoism he was fascinated by the marginalia, the running commentary with which I had accompanied him all through his book, mostly favourable,

[3] cf. *The Old School. Essays by Divers Hands*. Edited by Graham Greene.

sometimes critical.

The year was 1938 or 1939, the time of Munich, the German danger threatening all Europe, the war inevitable. Cyril had the usual flavouring of the intellectuals, lenient to the Germans, not unsympathetic – his London associates were the Berlin boys, Spender, Auden, Isherwood. He was not a pro-German, but intellectually confused on the German Question. He was not a historian, and did not know the German record historically in the past century: the three wars of aggression against Denmark, then Austria, then France; the prime responsibility for 1914–18; the renewal of the attempt. Nor was he a thinker; so he did not know the German intellectual disease, from Fichte onwards to Hegel, which had such a disastrous hold on Germany, and a distasteful influence all over Europe (including Oxford, with Green and Bosanquet; Cambridge, with McTaggart).

When Cyril had finished checking up on himself, I sat him down to a tutorial on the German mind and mentality; concluding by reading to him that marvellously penetrating passage, in Santayana's *Egotism and German Philosophy*, in which he diagnosed and precisely pin-pointed the disease during the First War, long before it became so brutally self-evident in Nazism, the full flowering of it in the popular low standards appropriate to a demotic age.

'The transcendental theory of a world merely imagined by the ego, and the will that deems itself absolute, are certainly desperate delusions. . . . The thing bears all the marks of a new religion. The fact that the established religions of Germany are still forms of Christianity may obscure the explicit and heathen character of the new faith: it passes for the faith of a few extremists, when in reality it dominates the judgment and conduct of the nation. No religious tyranny could be more complete. It has its prophets in the great philosophers and historians of the last century: its high priests and pharisees in the Government and the professors; its faithful flock in the disciplined mass of the nation; its heretics in the Socialists; its dupes in the Catholics and the Liberals, to both of whom the national creed – if they understood it – would be an abomination. It has its martyrs now by the million, and its victims among unbelievers are even more numerous, for its victims, in some degree, are all men.'

That was written in the first years of the 1914–18 war, decades before the German mania had devastated all Europe. At the time Santayana so exactly diagnosed the disease, writing in Oxford, thousands of young fellows were sacrificing their lives to counter it – while Russell, Keynes, and Bloomsbury (but not Eliot: he knew better) were 'conscientious objectors' to fighting it. If those in charge of the nation's affairs between the two German wars had been capable of reading and understanding Santayana, they would have known what they were up against.

Connolly was an intellectual, but not a second-rate one: he immediately got the message, and was visibly impressed. After that exercise he was not taken in by the pro-German intellectuals any more – the insufferable Kingsley Martin, H. N. Brailsford with his German wife, the Headlam-Morleys with their German mother; I never heard Connolly expressing pro-German sentiments thereafter. I will say for him that he was teachable: he learned. The second- and third-rate, of course, not; with them I had the utmost trouble in getting the message across. Perhaps one could not expect them to understand Santayana – and he never seems to have penetrated minds at Cambridge. They would have done far better to listen to him than to a Russell – whom Santayana knew intimately and saw through perfectly.

Connolly made a brilliant periodical of *Horizon* and several times asked me to write a political article for it – I think once I did. Just like Eliot with the *New Criterion*, it was politics that they pressed me to write about – when I was already writing enough about politics for Leonard Woolf's *Political Quarterly*. Raymond Mortimer in the *New Statesman* at least published my poems; so did Joe Ackerley, best of literary editors, in the *Listener*. When it came to the most important of my earlier poems, 'The Old Cemetery at St Austell', I sent it to Connolly with a defensive note to say that the metre was that of Valéry's 'Cimetière Marin', the poem influenced by Yeats. These were admirations of mine, though the poem was not a bit like either of them: it turned out much more after Gray's 'Elegy in a Country Churchyard', similar melancholy tone, same sad concern for and sense of the past. Connolly used my very words to reject the poem – as it if were a pastiche of Yeats and Valéry, of which I was quite incapable.

For long I held this against him. Can he have read it? He certainly had not considered it – and would have been incapable of writing it himself. Actually Gray was a good deal of a historian and scholar, but poet first. Connolly, like all the pure *littérateurs,* had me categorised as historian; and it is a curious thing that, though one may be novelist and poet (Hardy, Meredith), or critic and poet (Arnold, Eliot), one is not allowed to be historian and poet. It is true that it is a very rare combination: I can think only of Macaulay, whose poetry should not be overlooked, and in the Elizabethan age Samuel Daniel, who was poet first, historian second. Actually I was writing poetry from my schooldays, long before I dared to write history. Connolly should have known better – he could have remembered that at Oxford I had been the Eng. Lit. scholar when he was the History scholar (not a very good one). It was Eliot who took my poetry under his wing and published it, and if it was good enough for him, it should certainly have been good enough for Cyril, still more the third-rate reviewers of the *T.L.S.* and the media.

Cyril himself was a poet *manqué.* It is odd that he should not have realised this: he had the eye, and the ear, and the heart. What was missing? It was not that he was too intellectually indolent, that was merely an exterior element in the non-fulfilment creatively; it was something deeper. Sophistication is a dangerous enemy of poetry; in one way, one has to become like a child again, trust to the inner springs, not let self-consciousness get in the way and stop the flow; poetry is written from a deeper level than the cerebellum, from the whole heart and mind, what D. H. Lawrence would call the bloodstream. Hardy was deeply right – and Philip Larkin is right to call attention to it – in saying that poetry is what moves the heart expressed in a way that moves other hearts. That is all: it needs no lit. crit. Neither Hardy nor Larkin, Betjeman nor I, write lit. crit. Self-consciousness stops this most delicate and subtle flow. It is the rarest thing for poetry to be created intellectually, as with Eliot and Valéry; no wonder so much of the verse poured out by inferior intellects today, under that misconception, is not poetry at all.

Cyril wrote a generous obituary tribute to Maurice Bowra: that 'massive head replete with value judgments, innumerable lines of poetry in many languages, seventy-four years of discrimination, affection, love, memories of old battles, all rendered in his unforgettable voice with its fastidious rasping musical glow, an epigram whistling over like an untakeable service, a qualification or a pun woven into the verdict.' Cyril goes on, 'I am convinced that his tragedy, since every man has a tragedy, is that he was not a poet. Such a lifetime's devotion to the critique of poetry must have been the sign of the poet manqué.'

That does not follow; and the Connolly signature-tune, 'since every man has a tragedy', betrays that Cyril was thinking of himself. Everyone who reads or knew Bowra realised that his genius, if genius it was, was a prose genius. I knew Maurice better than his followers, his claque, did: they knew the outer, public man, the noisy, rhetorical Bowra, the natural wit, dominating the company with his cracks, setting the table on a roar, shouting people down. That was not the Maurice I cared for. Cyril had an image which became notorious, that inside every fat man there was a thin one longing to get out (referring to himself as usual). Inside the extrovert Maurice was a sensitive shy man, extremely afraid of ridicule (he had a short, comic figure), and he had been deeply wounded by the 1914–18 war into which he had been thrown as a boy. Beneath the bluster and aggressiveness – it is a familiar enough psychological pattern – Maurice was *afraid*, especially of ridicule. So was Cyril, who took refuge in self-parody. Fancy being afraid of anything the third-rate may say or think! One should be above that: I suspect that this came from their early Prep.-and-Public School exposure to self-consciousness.

Something of Cyril's suppressed poetry comes out in his vocabulary, his love of rare words, his verbal (and visual) intoxication, his images and metaphors, the unexpected or striking connotations that occurred to him as he went along. One of them occurs above, where he compares a Bowra 'epigram whistling over like an untakeable service.' On another visit to All Souls Cyril was sitting with me in our little

Common-room garden, where the fig-trees are trained up the crumbling grey walls. They were leafless, and Cyril at once saw that their intricate bare branches and stems were like the mechanical pipes of an engine-room on board a ship.

One sees this gift again and again. Even when hardly more than a schoolboy, in Switzerland 'the big mountains look as if they had skins like elephants.' On the Piazza in Venice: 'those pigeons! Strutting banality, flying sewers.' In Africa, the elephants – 'their ears flap like canvas on a dinghy, their droppings are like enormous vol-au-vents.' The giraffes have 'creamy suède scrotums, the hyenas faces like sex-tormented scoutmasters.' 'Monotonous as the tap of a lecturer's pole'; or 'a strained voice emerged from his tortured face like a cobra from a snake-charmer's basket.' There are innumerable memorable phrases. Myself a devout lover of cats (and secondarily dogs and donkeys), I never forget that 'affection for animals is the honey of misanthropy.' *Touché*. And the rare words: pericope and pangolin; native fruits such as corassol and darkassou; amniotic, satyriasis – to rival my own addiction to banausic or apolaustic, borborygmic or steatopygous. Cyril had the advantage of a knowledge of botany, and doesn't he display it – as no doubt he did as a member of Pop. Did he collect these words like a conscientious artist, as Pater did adjectives to go with his nouns for future use? Or as Eliot did definitions: a Fellow of All Souls once watched him at work on the dictionary, in the train between Oxford and London. Hence those hair-splitting distinctions in both prose and verse, the refinements of meaning until one reaches the (sometimes) meaningless, so well caught in Henry Reed's parody:

> As we get older we do not get any younger . . .
>   . . . *vento dei venti*
> The wind within a wind, unable to speak for wind.
>   I think you will find this put,
> Far better than I could hope to express it,
> In the words of Kharma . . .

All this equipped Connolly to be a brilliant parodist, and he evidently regarded his masterly parodies of the Thirties as the top of his achievement. Here you have Connolly playing the funny man for the benefit of Pop again. Aldous Huxley was an obvious target: he meant so much to the intellectuals of the Twenties and Thirties, especially if they were Balliol men. He did not speak for me, any more than Wells did, in spite of my knowing Garsington and its denizens, the *décor* and creatures of *Crome Yellow*.

As a schoolboy Cyril was a devotee. 'I bought *Crome Yellow* out of some prize money. After that his novels and stories continued to dominate my horizon, so enormously competent, so clever, sympathetic, on the spot.' I was never on that spot. 'Now that I have been free for a few years I see *Crome Yellow* as his best book, backed up by *Limbo, Antic Hay,* and his short stories.' That was written in 1936. I tried *Crome Yellow* again recently and, in spite of the nostalgic appeal of its rendering of Garsington and Ottoline, I do not think it a good book: not only faded – it does not live, and to me Huxley is a dead writer. He never did appeal to me; Lawrence did: a most uncertain and fallible artist, who wrote a lot of nonsense, he yet *lives*.

Connolly condemned Huxley for over-production, 'for which the present economic system is to blame' – a Leftist sentiment popular at the time. In this guide we have yet another excuse for Connolly's own under-production – one not very good novella. Really great writers have a way of over-producing, evidence of their prolific creative energy, witness Shakespeare, Walter Scott, Balzac, Victor Hugo. Connolly's ideal was a Flaubert, or Gérard de Nerval, Baudelaire. 'As for Lawrence, I really believe he is asleep at last, and I think nothing should be done to disturb him.' That sentence shows how fallible Connolly's literary criticism was. He thought that Evelyn Waugh would find it difficult to continue after *A Handful of Dust*, 'since Tory satire, directed at people on a moving staircase from a stationary one, is doomed to ultimate peevishness.' A wrong judgment again: the finest satire in the language is the Tory satire of 'Hudibras' Butler, Dryden and Swift.

Far better is Cyril 'being funny' at the expense of his own admirations. Even the names in 'Told in Gath' are perfect Huxley: 'Giles Pentateuch, scatologist and eschatologist, as he dubbed himself.' Then there are Luke Snarthes, 'with that splayed ascetic face of his, consulting his guru, Chandra Nandra'; Reggie Ringworm and Mr Encolpius, Roland Narthex and Mary Pippin, 'whose arm had been eaten away by termites in Tehuantepec'; 'Mrs Amp, whose huge wen, like Saint-Evremond's, made her look more than ever like some heavily wattled turkey, a chicken gumbo; for the rest Risi-bisi Mabel Dodge, *bêche de mer*, beer steak, and Capri pie.'

They all meet in a room 'with a few Longhis round the walls, a Lupanar by Guido Guidi, and over the bed an outsize Stuprum Sabinarum by Rubens – civilised people the hosts, evidently.' A few mistakes are carefully planted to catch the uncivilised. ' "But how can you, how can you?" It was Ursula Groyne. "How *can* you when there are two million unemployed, when Russia has re-introduced anti-abortionary legislation, when Iceland has banned *Time and Tide* [the Lesbian weekly of the Thirties], when the Sedition Bill hangs over us all like a rubber truncheon?" ' It is a heavenly caricature of the fatuities we used to have to put up with from progressive women, dedicated do-gooders, in the Thirties.

Even the sainted Orwell, yet another fellow Etonian, gets an irreverent bucketful splashed over him in 'Year Nine'. 'Having some minutes to spare before the Commonmeal and because it was raining slightly, we took shelter in the glorious Artshouse. There were the ineffable misterpasses of our glorious culture, the pastermieces of titalitorian tra, the magnificent Leadersequence, the superstatues of Comradeship, Blatherhood, and Botherly Love, the Leader as a simple special constable. . . . Mr Abject looked at me with profound commiseration till he received a nudge from the other commissar, and said in a loud voice: "This is your man." I was marched out between them while serried ranks of my old beltmates sang the Leaderchorus and cried: "Show mercy to us by showing no mercy to him, the dog and the traitor." Outside the newsboys were screaming, "Long live the Censor. Gumlicking wrecker discovered." '

I fear this is more or less what would have happened to Connolly at the hands of the Writers' Union in the brave new world of USSR, the incarnation of human freedom to Left intellectuals like the asinine Sartre or the criminal Brecht. An intelligentsia, being rootless and without practical responsibility – as Ernest Bevin diagnosed – tends to be Leftist. Didn't Lenin, *after* he had got into power, write a tract on *The Infantile Disease of Left-Wing Communism*? There was Connolly, trapped among his fellow intellectuals of the Left, when I suspect his real feelings were more exactly expressed by his quotation, in *The Unquiet Grave,* from Norman Douglas's *Siren Land*: 'Has any good ever come out of that foul-clustering town-proletariat, beloved of humanitarians? Nothing – never; they are only waiting for a Leader, some "inspired idiot" to rend to pieces our poor civilisation.'

That was written as early as 1911 – it points directly to Hitler, *der Führer*, the Leader years after. Norman Douglas knew his Germans: he was half an Austrian himself.

In the Thirties, when there was some question of returning their former Colonies to Germany, the joke used to go round our circle that we might return the Connollys. And jokes against Connolly recur here and there in the novels of Evelyn Waugh, with whom Cyril's relations were rather ambivalent. I don't think that Evelyn, who was Lancing and Hertford – and a terrible snob about such things – much cared for Cyril's being Eton and Balliol. Of *The Unquiet Grave* – which made Cyril's literary fame and fortune – Evelyn wrote: 'Half commonplace book of French maxims, half a lament for his life. It is badly written in places, with painful psychological jargon which he attempts to fit into services of teleological problems.' Evelyn of course, as a Catholic *dévot*, knew the answer to those. I thought at the time that the book's *réclame* was excessive, partly due to its appearing when it did, in 1944 when the war was nearing its end and we were culture-starved; and for the rest it was stuffed with, mainly written by, Baudelaire, Horace, Pascal, Petronius, Sainte-Beuve, Apollinaire, Virgil, Epicurus and, of course. Flaubert. It was a fascinating example of book-making.

How then do the two dubious friends compare?

Cyril was much the better educated, with far wider range of reading, and altogether fairer judgment. Evelyn's judgment was, to an extreme degree, at the mercy of his prejudices, no notion of justice of mind. Stylistically, though Evelyn may have been a more exact writer, Cyril was the more poetic one, with greater brilliance of colour and phrase – even if his was a poet's eye turned to journalism. On the other hand, Evelyn was inspired by the demon of creative genius, and that is everything.

I fancy that Connolly is a better writer than people think, than perhaps he himself thought and, if not a creator, he has his own inspiration. His best work is not in *The Unquiet Grave,* which had more success, but in *The Condemned Playground* and *The Evening Colonnade,* which had little or none. It is amusing to watch him becoming towards the end an Establishment figure, which Waugh would never have become – too far out on the Right, and he detested everything about contemporary society. Today the Establishment has been taken over by the Left; the Leftists of the Thirties – those who have survived – considerably be-knighted. It is nice to think of Connolly as Sir Cyril – appropriate enough; after all, old Col. Connolly was an Anglo-Irish gent.

After a briefer time than usual lying in a trough of depreciation, the purgatory lying in wait for all writers, Connolly is re-emerging into sympathetic re-appraisal. Peter Quennell, his contemporary at Balliol – and my opposite number as Eng. Lit. scholar (he did not stay the course, any more than John Betjeman did) – has edited a Selection of Cyril's Essays with a very just appreciation of his work. Peter sums him up: 'He and Edmund Wilson, I think, were the most individual critics to appear during the last half of the twentieth century.' To that I append – Connolly was a poet in prose, Wilson was not. 'And Cyril, we must not forget, was also the finest satirist and parodist we have had since Max Beerbohm.' To that I add a third distinction: he was exceptionally gifted as a travel writer, a glutton for seeing places and things – particularly the exotic – as for eating and drinking in them. With his restlessness from childhood, travelling here, there and everywhere, he was really rather rootless – except in literature.

This goes with his Irishry, or Anglo-Irishry. It is odd that he hated being regarded as Irish, when all his characteristics went irreversibly back to the Irishman in him. He was virtually the stage-Irishman, making fun of himself to amuse the English. (It won him his place at Prep. School as well as entry into Pop at Eton: 'Connolly's being funny' attracted the crowd.) He had also the self-indulgence and the self-pity, what the English regard as weakness of character. He had generosity, and a certain seedy gentlemanliness (like Joyce), with a bit of caddishness – witness his, and the Franco-Scot Orwell's, mean disloyalty about the poor Prep. School owners who had done their best for both of them. Connolly certainly had the gift of the gab, a rare and beautiful way with words, like so many writers with the Celt in them – though he never got over the Irish misuse of 'will' and 'would', for shall and should. Did he even notice it? That other stage-Irishman, Wilde, knew that his usage was uncertain, and used to get an English friend to vet his text.

Connolly was no more a scholar than Wilde was – too superficial and impatient. Connolly never noticed that 'Mr W.H.' of Thorp's dedication of Shakespeare's Sonnets was Thorp's man, not Shakespeare's; Wilde simply invented a Willie Hughes, who never existed, under the usual misapprehension, as well as fancying that the Sonnets were homosexual, as he wanted to think, when they are not. Connolly was uncertain about Shakespeare, knowing little if anything about the Elizabethan age. He thought mistakenly that Montaigne gave Shakespeare the idea for *The Tempest*; he reviewed my biography of Shakespeare sympathetically, but couldn't get the facts right.

Nor was he much of a thinker. All things considered, it is remarkable that he was so good a critic. I think this was due to good taste, he had an instinct for quality in literature, as for places and for food and drink. The publication of his biography, with an early Journal, adds little to our knowledge of him – he was such an obsessed egoist that he has told us everything about himself. I learned only one thing of concern to me that I had not known: when we were all undergraduates together Cyril did have a crush on Richard Pares, my chief friend at All Souls. Cyril denied this in a letter to me. Perhaps he had forgotten; or, no historian, he was not very strong on facts. Never mind: he was something better than that, he had a touch of genius – more than the quantitative Edmund Wilson.

Wilson reproached him with spending himself reviewing other people's books, instead of writing his own; and Connolly regretted writing 'brightly' – 'being funny' again – about so many bad books. But what would he have written? Would he have been capable of writing otherwise than he did write? I think not. He fulfilled himself as he was, what he had in him to fulfil, in character pretty exactly.

10

The Infantilism of Evelyn Waugh

Because I propose to deal with Waugh intellectually with some severity, I should make clear that I am an admirer of his genius as a pure writer – of his fiction and satire, his comic gifts in stories, essays, letters, and as a stylist (as against the parsonic didacticism of a Grigson). Of his Letters, which I shall treat as a revelation of the man, I think I have never been so fascinated since reading the Letters of Horace Walpole. Waugh's offer a scintillating picture of our time and of many people whom I too knew, for we were exact contemporaries at Oxford, and of so many whose variegated personalities cross these pages: Graham Greene, Cyril Connolly, Harold Acton, John Betjeman, Peter Quennell, Lord Longford, Lord David Cecil, and others.

Waugh was a mass of crusty prejudices – and these can be amusing, if taken in the right, light spirit. They were not mostly to be taken thus by Waugh, who held to them firmly and constructed his intellectual position, such as it was, out of them. I, of course, never took him seriously as an intellectual: that was not his function or his gift. We do not have to take seriously what even the greatest writers suppose themselves to think. Consider the utter nonsense Tolstoy wrote about both Shakespeare and Beethoven. Much of what Milton thought and believed was nonsense;[1] not the least remarkable thing about William Shakespeare was that he doesn't seem to have thought any nonsense at all.

Not so Waugh. On the anniversary of the Massacre of St Bartholomew (1572) – one of the bloodiest and most dis-

---

[1] cf. my *Milton the Puritan: Portrait of a Mind.*

astrous experienced in French history, when thousands of decent Protestants were killed by their fellow Christians who were Catholics, Waugh writes to Nancy Mitford, 'Today is a glorious anniversary in the sad history of your adopted country. I hope you are keeping it with solemnity and splendour.' This is all very well for a tease – well, no, it is not well, when one considers the lives that were lost to France, a great man like Coligny, an outstanding man like Ramus, etc. But it was not a tease: Waugh really believed this kind of evil nonsense.

He tells us, consistently, that 'for me Christianity begins with the Counter-Reformation' – of which the Massacre of St Bartholomew was an outward, and not uncharacteristic, expression, compare the *autos-da-fe* of the Spanish Inquisition. Imagine beginning the history of Christianity with that, and ignoring the work of early Christianity in civilising the barbarians of Northern Europe, the marvellous expressions of the high-water mark of medieval Christianity in the cathedrals of Europe, in the literature, Dante, St Thomas Aquinas, the deeply moving Latin hymns of Saint Bernard, Abélard, and so on!

Similarly with English history. Elizabeth I 'survived alive because of the high Christian principles of Mary Tudor, when in any other royal family she would have been executed. She was jockeyed into place by a gang of party bosses and executed the rightful heir, Mary Stuart. All the newspapers are full of the glorification of Elizabeth Tudor, the vilest of her sex.' Infantile, of course. It is all very well to lay down the law, if you know the facts. Waugh didn't trouble to learn them, any more than Belloc did. The facts are that, after Wyatt's Rebellion, Mary Tudor sent Elizabeth to the Tower and wanted to have her executed. There would have been revolution in the country if she had done so, and even her husband, Philip of Spain, did not want a French woman to succeed to the English throne, when he was at the time engaged in war with France.

So, too, towards the end of Waugh's life, when reading Churchill's Life of the great Duke of Marlborough, linch-pin of the Grand Alliance which defeated Louis XIV's overweening ascendancy in Western Europe, threatening other nations' independence. Louis had very nearly extinguished the

independence of Holland in 1672, but for the resistance of the
Dutch people under the heroic leadership of William of
Orange. William's whole life was inspired by the aim of
reducing Louis XIV to size, preserving the balance of Europe;
to this end he booted out his stupid father-in-law, James II, to
bring England into her proper place in the Grand Alliance.

Waugh on this: 'I lately read Sir Winston's *Marlborough*.
How he alienates all sympathy. I found myself on every page
praying, "Oh God, do defeat the Grand Alliance."' Well, God
didn't. Nor do I suppose that Waugh knew that the Pope,
Innocent XI, was a supporter of Protestant William and of the
Grand Alliance, having had more than enough of Louis'
arrogance to put up with, even in Rome. It must have been a
Protestant wind that brought William to victory in 1688, as
also presumably against the Spanish Armada in 1588.

Waugh gets no better marks on American history. '*Of course*
the Americans are cowards. They are almost all the
descendants of wretches who deserted their legitimate
monarchs for fear of military service.' Why write such rubbish? Why not get the facts right – it is apt to lead one to such
wrong judgments of contemporary affairs for another thing.
In 1947 it is: 'Big things will happen in Palestine, where the
American Jews have made it possible for the Red Army to
reach its goal in the Mediterranean.' We all know that the exact
opposite was the case.

What accounts for this? Sheer perverseness was very strong
in his make-up and a constant factor from schooldays to the
end. A certain streak of infantilism is apt to go with genius, as
psychologists should be aware: men of genius are often not
well-rounded individuals, sometimes noticeably not grown-
up. In Waugh's case he took up a position out of prejudice,
either of taste or emotion, by an act of will, and then stuck to it
contrary to all reason. Of course he called it 'reason' and said
that he arrived at it by a process of reasoning, like his
conversion. But it was not; he spoke more truly when he said
that that was 'a step in the dark'.

He was no less perverse about religion than about history.
One would have thought it a good step when Christians of
various denominations ceased persecuting each other, to stand
together for common purposes, especially against the chal-

lenge of Communism – or the advance of Islam – around the world. Not so with Waugh. The Jesuit Cardinal Bea had been promoting good relations with the Anglicans and the Greek Orthodox Church. However, 'I was greatly cheered to read yesterday of the rebuffs given to Cardinal Bea at Patras. That should put off Ecumenism for a millennium.'

Again, 'all this talk of ecumenism is exceedingly painful'; and, of Hans Kung, its theologian and promoter, 'in a happier age Kung would have been burned at the stake.' When even his friend Woodruff inclined to ecumenism, it was 'a senile infatuation for a very dangerous clergyman called Kung, a heresiarch who in happier days would be roasted.'

In his last years, when the new vernacular rite was adopted by the Roman Church, though much less moving than that of the Anglican Prayer Book – Waugh is off to Rome for Easter, 'to avoid the horrors of the English liturgy.' Then Rome lets him down. His last letter is pathetic: 'Easter used to mean so much to me. Before Pope John and his Council – they destroyed the beauty of the liturgy. I now cling to the Faith doggedly without joy. Church-going is a pure duty parade. I shall not live to see it restored.' Serve him right for having been so infantilely perverse.

By sheer prejudice, mere wilfulness, Evelyn had taken up an Ultramontane position, like Belloc, and then found that the Roman Church let him down. He expected the Second Vatican Council to repeat the absurdities of the First, with its declaration of Papal Infallibility, etc: 'As in 1869–70 the French and Germans are full of mischief but, as then, the truth of God will prevail', i.e. what Waugh fancies, that is Truth. 'The spirit of that wicked Père Couturier still lives on in France and must be destroyed.' This was a highly intelligent Dominican who disagreed with Waugh. He says that he simply cannot understand why everybody is not a Catholic – but this evidently means his sort of Catholic. Everybody who does not agree is a heretic (as with the equally assertive C. S. Lewis, another intellectual bully, on the other side).

All this comes out in Evelyn's bullying Penelope Betjeman out of the Anglican Church into the Roman (though she had propulsions of her own), and the attempt to bully her husband, John Betjeman. 'It is impossible for someone like

yourself, who is in formal heresy, to realise the horror which
heresy inflames in an orthodox mind. What seems to you a
harmless and amusing speculation is, to me, a denial and
perversion of God's truth', *sc.* Waugh's opinion. And then to
his friend Betjeman himself: 'Awful about your obduracy in
schism and heresy. Hell hell hell. Eternal damnation.' This
gave Betjeman's gentle nature fearful nightmares. Fancy taking Waugh's not very well-developed, not very adult, intellect
so seriously, intellectually – they were all of them, for all their
other gifts, not very strong in the head.

Evelyn persisted with his proselytising: 'I wouldn't give a
thrush's egg for your chances of *salvation* at the moment.'
What does that precisely mean, one might ask? The poor wife
was driven to protest: Betjeman 'is in a dreadful state. He
thinks you are the devil and wakes up in the middle of the
night, and raves and says he will leave me at once if I go over.'
However, it was no use bullying a jelly – it was like Paul
Claudel trying to bully André Gide: same tactics, similar
results. But Evelyn did succeed in driving a wedge between
Penelope and her husband, and creating great unhappiness.
(Was this very Christian? Evelyn was a Catholic, but was he a
Christian?)

After her brother's suicide, Penelope did go over, leaving
that 'Empty Pew' in their village church, where John continued to worship alone – of that touching poem which he
never felt able to publish. From that time the marriage came
apart and the couple began to separate. John had met with an
intellectual bully before in C. S. Lewis, who was his tutor at
Magdalen College – also of no effect, except by way of
reaction. (Lewis set Betjeman against Shakespeare, and he
subsequently went down without a degree.) C. S. Lewis was a
far more formidable proposition than Waugh intellectually,
and both Lewis and Betjeman remained in the bosom of the
Church of England.

Similar bullyings are delivered by Evelyn to others among
his friends – in the case of Lady Eden, reproaches for not
keeping up with Rome. 'Clarissa's apostasy has upset me
more than anything that had happened since Kick's [Kathleen
Kennedy's] death. I can't write about it, or think of anything
else.' To Lady Eden herself: 'I don't suppose you deliberately

chose the vigil of the Assumption for your betrayal, or deliberately arrived in a Catholic capital on the Feast. But I am sure Our Lady noticed. Anyway on your jaunt in Portugal did you never go into a church to glance at the Emanuel style? When you found yourself, then, in the presence of Our Lord, what had you to say to him?' etc. Poor Clarissa Churchill compounded her offence by marrying a Protestant, Sir Anthony Eden – and on her wedding morning received a rocket by telegram such as no friend should dream of sending to another. 'I have been thinking of her with deep compassion, but then she had herself photographed going to a Protestant church, so all my kindness was turned to despair again.'

No compassion for fellow Christians in other churches. 'Many things have puzzled me from time to time about the Christian religion, but one thing has always been self-evident – the bogosity of the Church of England.' The Pope in Canterbury Cathedral must have made him turn in his grave. Lord Longford's 'prurient interest in Protestantism disgusts me.' On a friend's son leaving Eton for a Catholic school, 'I am sure that St Henry in heaven constantly prays for the rescue of the unhappy little victims of his perverted foundation, and that he is to be thanked for this triumph of Grace.' Henry VI was indeed the founder of Eton, but he never achieved the status of a Saint – bad history again. Waugh never seems to have drawn the conclusion from the admission he makes at one point: 'God knows I don't blame the Poles for any shifts they have to resort to; but I have the undeserved privilege of living in a country where compromise is unnecessary.' That is because Britain was neither Communist nor Catholic – hence compromise was of the essence of her successful record in history. Did he never think that out?

Allowing prejudice to determine his intellectual position meant false judgments in literature as well as in history. Proust was a 'mental defective' – a mind far subtler and cleverer than his own. Rose Macaulay 'was, I think, quite devoid of the gift of faith' – she was in fact a believing Anglican. Edith Sitwell's conversion greatly pleased Evelyn – her junior, he became her godfather. Neither conjuncture seems to have done her much good – she was soon as unhappy as before. One motive had been to go one further than T. S. Eliot, in his conversion to

Anglicanism. How childish they were! One finds infantile anti-Americanism all through, not worth going into: 'There is no such thing as an American – They are all exiles uprooted, transplanted and doomed to sterility.'

Wrong too about his friend Maurice Bowra: 'I believe all his pretentions to understand foreign poetry an imposture.' Maurice had a genuine passion for poetry in all the various languages he knew: Cyril Connolly paid generous tribute to that. Nothing generous in Evelyn's judgments about other writers – unless they happened to be Catholics, fellow members of his Club. Maurice knew that trait well in Evelyn: it accounted for his over-estimation of Fr. Ronald Knox ('if he had been an atheist, he would have had the O.M.'), his campaign for the historical novels of the reformed alcoholic, Alfred Duggan, or his public acclaim for Graham Greene's work.

I well remember reproving Greene for his thoughtless statement that, if he had to choose between living in the USA and Soviet Russia, he would choose Soviet Russia. He cannot have meant it, if he had thought about it, or he wouldn't have given such a false lead. Why are these people so unaware? Waugh always presented a firm public front on behalf of his own free-masonry; but, in his Letters, we descry what he really thought of his co-religionists' work. Of Greene's *A Burnt-Out Case*: 'M. Grisjambon Vert [Mr Greene has gone to live in France, understandably for tax-reasons] has written a very sorrowful novel.' Or, 'And now Graham Greene has written a most distressing work.' To Graham on his play, *The Potting Shed*: 'It was an enthralling evening. It seemed to me that all the audience was enthralled.' To his wife Laura (who had much to put up with) he confided: 'The play is great nonsense theologically, and will puzzle people needlessly' – himself being an authority on theology. QED.

When these people make such a statement as that our whole life here is but a preparation for a life elsewhere, a hypothesis, a preparation for the non-existent, do they realise that they are making a non-sense statement? Similarly when Waugh allows that American monasticism may yet 'save' the world, it *means* nothing. To the world at large it means nothing, nine-tenths of which cannot be regarded as Christian. The Chinese alone constitute one-fifth of the human race; there are 100 million Japanese, besides the teeming millions of South-East Asia. India will have a population of a billion by the end of the century. Islam advances in vast numbers in the Middle East and across Northern Africa; then the rest of proliferating Africa, Central and Southern America, to say nothing of Soviet Russia and Communist countries, mainly atheist.

Christianity was really a European export, and Waugh would even subtract from it all that is not Roman Catholic. Methodism is the largest Protestant denomination in the USA, and Waugh would throw over all Protestant Christians.

Evelyn Waugh and Connolly came up to Oxford in the Michaelmas Term of 1922, as I did – both of them with History scholarships, though they should have taken the English School, which I was intended for as a scholar in English Literature. (My opposite number as an Eng. Lit. scholar at Balliol was Peter Quennell.) Evelyn and Cyril were not cronies as undergraduates, and I knew neither then, though I knew Richard Pares – Evelyn's 'dearest friend' – who became my closest friend at All Souls – through the Labour Club. In Waugh's 'First Volume of Autobiography', *A Little Learning*, he writes, 'There was already an active Labour Party to which Richard Pares and many clever men belonged. Indeed it comprised so many of the best brains that I advised a middle-brow socialist acquaintance, before he came up, that he would find the competition too hot and that he had better make his appearance as a Conservative. He took the advice and prospered.' Ingenuous and sincere, I did not think in such terms and did not take such a prosperous course. Moreover, priggish and rather puritanical, I disapproved of the Hypocrites Club to which they belonged, with all that drinking and smoking – Graham Pollard, John Sutro, Terence Greenidge, Evelyn and even dear Richard.

Connolly was already taken up by Maurice Bowra – Evelyn did not make that grade until he began to be known as a novelist. In my early days at All Souls Maurice tried to take me up, arriving in my rooms afternoon after afternoon for a walk; I did not encourage this attention – too frivolous. Evelyn notes that in *Enemies of Promise* Cyril said little of his Oxford life, and

I have noted that he regarded it as a decline from Eton. Evelyn – ambivalent as they were about each other – says that, when Cyril should come to write about those days, 'he was suffering, I think he will tell us, from poverty. At the university he found himself on an inequality of expenditure with his old friends from Pop. This never worried a man in precisely the same position, Christopher Hollis [another contemporary, who wrote an indifferent autobiography, I thought], but Cyril was haunted by an Anglo-Irish ghost of dandyism. Balliol was ill-suited to his mood; it was not a luxurious college; next only to Keble [Evelyn's anti-Anglican feeling comes in here] it was the least luxurious. The architecture is dismal. Cyril would have been happy in Peckwater [the aristocratic quarter of Christ Church; I lived in the Latin Quarter of Meadows] with an allowance of £750 a year.'

Knowing so many of Evelyn's friends, I felt that I knew him quite well enough. I had several periscopes trained on him, even from his schooldays, where Max Mallowan told me how unpopular he was, and Hugh Molson how badly he treated his sentimental old father, whose ninetyish sentimentality the difficult son could not stand. However, what an advantage Evelyn and Alec Waugh started with, with a father already high up in the publishing world.

The fact was that, like many men of genius, Evelyn had a divided, almost a split, personality. We must allow that, on one side, he had great charm and, when he behaved himself, could be irresistible. (I had nothing to complain of from him – better not!) He was fearless and lion-hearted, and always amusing, sometimes even when naughty. Hugh Molson told me that, when young together, those gifted boys, Richard and Evelyn, were like brilliant children with their prattle. I recognise them both as such. Evelyn himself recognised that, on the other side, he had a nasty character and sometimes wondered why. (He was resentful of his appearance, at being so short, and made himself up as an Angry Old Man.) One thing to be said for Protestantism is that it encourages moral effort: Evelyn never tried, but said that, without his Catholicism, he would have been worse. A Catholic, but not a Christian – unlike Pope John, of whom he did not approve. (Randolph Churchill to the Pope: 'Do you know Evelyn

Waugh? He's a Catholic too.')

Waugh had a complex about his tutor at Hertford, C. R. M. F. Cruttwell, whom I knew intimately as an All Souls man. Evelyn's portrait of him in *A Little Learning* is authentic enough, a recognisable description, but only one side of the human being. 'Cruttwell's appearance was not prepossessing. He was tall, almost loutish, with the face of a petulant baby. He smoked a pipe which was usually attached to his blubber-lips by a thread of slime. As he removed the stem, waving it to emphasise his indistinct speech, this glittering connection extended until finally it broke leaving a dribble on his chin. When he spoke to me I found myself so distracted by the speculation of how far this line could be attenuated that I was often inattentive to his words.'

The rest of Evelyn's account of Cruttwell is caricature. It is true that he offered a target for caricature, and Richard and I used to study him from this point of view. Richard described him as 'the Dong with the luminous Nose', which was more accurate than Evelyn's 'petulant baby'. Cruttwell had a comic vocabulary for colleagues, which made us laugh: dons were 'hacks', women–dons were 'hags' or 'breast-heavers'. It was highly inventive – I wish I could remember it all. Once, walking in the Meadows, we passed 'Nippy' Williams, an oleaginous Canon of Christ Church, strutting beside his large wife: 'There go Mr Spiritual Pride with his wife, Mistress Carnality', said Cruttwell – Evelyn himself could not have done better. Or Maurice Bowra, on my friend David Mathew, an enormously fat Roman ecclesiastic: 'A perfect specimen of the Word made Flesh.'

It is true that Cruttwell's table manners were bad; I never can understand why hearty masculine types can't eat their food neatly and not plaster crumbs over their faces, let alone pipe-spittle. I detest smoking – and Evelyn himself was a filthy cigar-smoker. However, I did understand the whole man in Cruttwell. He had had an appalling war in the trenches on the Western Front, and emerged a wounded man, physically and psychologically. Before the war he had been a good athlete, a fine heavy-weight footballer; after it he was lamed, and crippled with rheumatism. He was a believing Christian, who gave surreptitious financial help to many an undergraduate, though barking at them if they fell down on their work – as he did not, in spite of his physical disabilities.

The most impatient of men, he was extraordinarily patient with me and my Leftism. I had been brought up under the influence of the Russell and Brailsford nonsense that the British were as responsible as the Germans for the war in 1914, and was maddeningly persistent in arguing this line when I first arrived at All Souls. Cruttwell, himself a victim of the Germans, scarred by his ordeal, was astonishingly patient with me; all he said in reply to me about the Armistice of 1918 (it proved to be no more than an armistice in the long career of German aggression) was: 'It was an almighty deliverance.'

Mentally, he was a victim of sex-repression. As I became more and more ill, we became companions on our afternoon walks for exercise. He had a gruff tenderness towards me. I confess that I had begun by being afraid of his whiplash of a tongue, but once I stood up to him all that vanished. He showed more forbearance towards Evelyn as his tutor than I should have done. After all, he had given Waugh his scholarship, a good one, and expected him to work; Evelyn was a slacker and a drunkard. He tells us how he behaved. 'It was Terence who imaginatively imputed to Cruttwell sexual connection with dogs and purchased a stuffed one, which we set in the quad as an allurement from his return from dining in All Souls. For the same reason we used rather often to bark under Cruttwell's windows at night.'

On Evelyn's last night as an undergraduate he says that he climbed into Hertford from the garden of All Souls. I don't know how that was possible, he may have been let in by Richard Pares, or he may have been mixed up. I remember him dining with Richard only once, and then drunk. He seems to have realised that Cruttwell scored with his valedictory notes: 'I cannot say that your Third does you anything but discredit: especially as it was not even a good one; and it is always at least foolish to allow oneself to be given an inappropriate intellectual label. I hope you will soon settle in some sphere where you will give your intellect a better chance than in the History School.'

Fair enough: that shows that Cruttwell realised that Evelyn was capable of better things; but for the time it meant a series of undignified jobs in disreputable Prep. schools, from whence he emerged with *Decline and Fall*, and after that found himself. In subsequent novels Waugh worked off his grudge by using Cruttwell's name for various shady characters, male or female. I suppose Cruttwell could have had him up for libel: he never bothered, and all he said to me about his unsatisfactory pupil was, peaceably, 'I could have sent him down.'

I do not know if Cruttwell knew about Evelyn's love-affair with Richard Pares; though Richard was my greatest friend, he never spoke of it to me. Nor would I mention it, if it were not now in print in Evelyn's Letters. In 1954 'I went to Oxford and visited my first homosexual love, Richard Pares. At 50 he is quite paralysed except his mind and voice, and waiting deterioration and death. . . . He would have been Master of Balliol if he had not been struck down. A very harrowing visit.' Unaware as usual, little did he realise that he sickened poor Richard – patient, resigned, heroic, never a word of complaint – by puffing cigar-smoke over him.

It marks a sad contrast with the old gay days just after going down. In November 1925 it is: 'I went to Oxford and contrary to my intentions stayed the night. John's [Sutro] party consisted of Harold Acton, Mark Ogilvie-Grant, Hugh Lygon, Robert Byron, Arden Hilliard and Richard Pares. After luncheon which was hot lobster, partridges and plum pudding, sherry, mulled-claret and a strange rum-like liqueur, I left Hugh and John drinking . . . and then to the New Reform where I found Terence and Elmley drinking beer. I drank with them, and went to dinner with Robert Byron in Merton Hall. I found Billy (Clonmore) and after dinner went to the rooms of a hunting man and drank beer. . . . Next morning I drank beer with Hugh and port with Preters [Molson] and gin with Gyles Isham, lunched with Hugh and Desmond Harmsworth. Harold and Billy saw me off at the station feeling woefully tired.' It is the world – and some of the characters – of *Brideshead Revisited*.

Evelyn writes of Richard, 'the first friend to whom I gave my full devotion did not enjoy drinking and as a result we drifted apart. He was Richard Pares, a Balliol Wykhamist [*sc.* Wykehamist], with an appealing pale face and a mop of fair hair, blank blue eyes and the Lear-Carroll-like fantasies of many [?] Balliol Wykhamists [sic]. I loved him dearly, but an excess of wine nauseated him, and this made an insurmountable barrier between us . . . He withdrew, or was withdrawn, from our company' – and into mine, I may say. John Sutro, a rich dilettante, regarded it as 'a defection to All Souls' – where I occasionally met him, with his remarkable talent for mimicry, dining with Richard. 'Once, before his withdrawal, he had a dream in which one of us was convicted of the unknown vice of "vanoxism". . . . We founded a club named the Vanoxists who met for breakfast now and then at the Trout at Godstow, all of us united in nothing but affection for Richard.'

Evelyn goes on to an account of his next affair under a pseudonym. Not until twenty-one did he graduate, as Connolly did too – to the girls. As an undergraduate Evelyn had three satisfying homo affairs. Then why the later vicious attacks on homosexuals? I find this yet another strain of unawareness – odd in one who had been one himself. My old friend Cecil Roberts, the novelist, complained to me of Evelyn's appalling behaviour to him in the *foyer* of the Grand Hotel in Rome. Evelyn came up to him and said, 'You old bugger, I thought you were in prison years ago.' I told Cecil, 'You must forgive him. Don't you realise he was mad?' – as he was: he had gone off his head with drink and drugs. That passage in his life he characteristically turned to good account with *The Ordeal of Gilbert Pinfold*. On board ship he was persecuted by voices accusing him of being a homosexual – as he had been. Why should that be a subject for paranoia, when it is normal enough, common enough surely?[2]

It was just after the publication of this remarkable book that I met Evelyn, when I was staying at Dunster Castle with hospitable Alys Luttrell, its *châtelaine*. At the end of September 1959 he writes to his daughter, 'Did I tell you we went to luncheon at Dunster on Sunday? It was to meet a reformed socialist Fellow of All Souls named Rowse.' Evelyn was on his best behaviour – he had better be – ear-trumpet and all. He was still animadverting against Trevor-Roper, with whom he had had a controversy, at the end of which Evelyn advised him to

[2] cf. my *Homosexuals in History*.

change his name and go to Cambridge. Trevor-Roper followed the advice on both counts, with results that were yet to be seen. We did not speak of the controversy, though I had followed it closely and thought of intervening on Trevor-Roper's side.

Evelyn and Laura had come over from Combe Florey, which I did not visit until after his death. The place was touchingly full of his presence, the possessions he had gathered around him, the atmosphere he created. The spacious Georgian house was full of the Victoriana he affected: in the rather shabby drawing-room the big carpet he had bought from the proceeds of a libel-action he had won, and a large Burgess bureau. Upstairs was a yet more complicated piece of Burgess furniture, which I think Betjeman had given him: combined dressing table and washstand with metal apparatus (I think now in a Museum). In the hall a bust of himself, his Captain's cap of *Officers and Gentlemen* stuck on at a jaunty angle. In the dining room a picture of travel in the Victorian age – the interior of a railway compartment; with a companion piece he had had painted of air-travel, the space-age.

Then into the beautiful library, with painted shelves, which he had created: the heart of the house. Here one had one's finger on the pulse of the dead man yet alive in his work. On the shelves inscribed copies of the books of his friends: from Harold Acton, 'To gallant Evelyn, away at the war', from Maurice Bowra, Edith Sitwell, Graham Greene, fellow campaigner. (Curious how all that anguished concern about religion has vanished. No-one thinks about it in the social revolution that has overwhelmed us.) And at last the writing-desk, pens, ink and paper; the Diary open in that academic-artistic handwriting – he wrote everything longhand – for me to see. The firm squat figure might be seated there at the desk, puckered, angry expression, hand poised ready to throw his dart.

The Personality of C. S. Lewis

C. S. Lewis was an odd and gifted man, much odder than his numerous disciples knew. Those who observed him from close at hand, like an historian friend of mine who was for years a colleague of his at Magdalen College, Oxford, and observed him closely, knew how odd. It is the business of historians to watch and observe – not dogmatise, like Lewis – and the first thing that my friend observed was that Lewis's Academy-prized book, *The Allegory of Love*, was not in keeping with the facts of medieval life. K. B. McFarlane was a medievalist, the leading authority on the fifteenth century: he knew that Lewis was theorising as usual and not getting it right. Lewis had an idealised view of chivalric and courtly love which was not in keeping with the *facts*, which have prime authority with historians. As an historian I clashed with Lewis, the theorist, at Oxford on similar grounds.

I am reminded of this by Lewis's autobiography, *Surprised by Joy*, a rather noble book, for Lewis was a good man with the highest standards. Then I knew from my friend's intimate information what Lewis was referring to in a crucial gap in the autobiography, an omission of 'one huge and complex episode.' This refers to the domestic circumstances of his life away from college in the cottage he inhabited with two women at Headington. He did not live in college as Fellows who were bachelors almost all did at that time.

One day a couple of the Fellows walking on Shotover were caught in a downpour of rain, and sought shelter in Lewis's cottage nearby. No-one was at home, but they were surprised to see women's clothes lying about, and drew the obvious conclusion. So this was Lewis's secret! They were wrong in their conventional assumption: the truth was much more odd.

Lewis lived there with *two* women – the mother and daughter of his closest friend, who had been killed in the war of 1914–18 and wished the care of them upon him. He took on what he regarded as a duty, a burden which bore more and more heavily upon him as the years went on. For he had nothing in common with these commonplace people. Bearing it must have appealed to the masochistic element in his make-up.

McFarlane noticed another, rather analogous, element. Lewis was full of *fear*: he had something wrong internally, but was afraid of an operation. His autobiography confesses to the fears and terrors of his childhood, his 'terror' of his father, though that may have been a rhetorical exaggeration.

The rhetoric and the exaggeration he got from his Welsh-Irish father – 'that fatal bent towards dramatisation and rhetoric: I speak of it the more freely since I inherited it.' Another trait which he inherited was an inability to listen to other people – his father never listened and always answered at cross purposes, showing that he had not understood what was being said to him. 'He could never empty, or silence, his own mind to make room for an alien thought.' Neither could the son; he never tried; he was a dogmatist, equally cocksure both when he was an atheist, and when he became a kind of fundamentalist Christian. I had a couple of instances with him when he simply didn't, or wouldn't, take in the point. 'Words came to him and intoxicated him', he says of his father; something of this was true of the son. A little more scepticism, a little less cocksure, both of his atheism and of his Christian belief, would have been salutary and more cogent.

To return to the point of Fear. McFarlane was convinced that it was the terror of war approaching once more that unnerved Lewis and brought him to the Christian faith. This was understandable, especially for the men who had been not much more than boys in the First German War and had known the horrors of the trenches on the Western Front. It was so with Maurice Bowra, who could not bear to think of it, it had been such a cruel experience. I don't see why Eliot should have made such a cult of 'The horror! The horror!', when he wasn't caught in that.

*

For all Lewis's fulminations against the 'Personal Heresy' – it would be 'heresy' if he didn't agree with it (like his dogmatic father) – he is very much to the fore personally in all his writings. Naturally in an autobiography; but there he reveals himself in lights he wouldn't suspect, for though an able man intellectually, he was not a subtle or perceptive one.

There is the constant trick of writing himself down. This is very popular with readers who do not realise that it is a way of writing oneself *up*. Self-depreciation is inverted pride. I prefer taking oneself plain, simply and directly, with a proper opinion of oneself (which, of course, should be justified in work).

'Whatever I know – it is not much – of courtesy and *savoir faire*' . . . he does not need to write himself down: Lewis was always, and in every relation of life, a gentleman. 'I was, no doubt, and was blamed for being, a conceited boy.' He always had a good conceit of himself, and rightly. He immediately justifies himself with, 'but the blame was usually attached to something in which no conceit was present.'

'Up till now I had committed nearly every other sin and folly within my power, but I had not yet been flashy.' Here is the parental tendency to exaggerate – how absurd to write like that of a boy of sixteen, a Public School boy too: what else? It is hardly sinful for a boy to be flashy. He goes on about all his 'slips from virtue', which he would not impute to a young schoolmaster, who 'made sad work of certain humble and childlike and self-forgetful qualities which (I think) had remained with me.' There is a note of smugness in that, which became characteristic of him – one saw it in the expression on his face. 'I began to labour very hard to make myself into a fop, a cad, and a snob.' Exaggeration again, to condemn a mere schoolboy in this fashion – but it is a way of recommending himself to an imperceptive reader.

Speaking of the two sins he was never tempted to commit, 'impure love' of his own sex at school, and gambling – 'This means then,' the reader (of whom he is very conscious) is supposed to object, 'that all the other vices you have so largely written about . . . Well, yes, it does, and more's the pity.' I just don't believe it: Lewis was a naturally good man, and evidently an exceptionally innocent boy at school. Exaggeration again – to impress the reader.

He condemns himself for not worrying about the war, putting off thinking about it: 'No doubt, even if the attitude was right, the quality in me which made it so easy to adopt is somewhat repellent' . . . I find this moralising about oneself distasteful. 'In the depth of my disgraces, in the then invincible ignorance of my intellect, all this was given me without asking' . . . I do not detect any disgraces. 'There was a humility in me, as a reader, which I shall never recapture.' I knew him well enough, but I never detected any humility – not that that is a count against him, for I regard humility as an exaggerated virtue, if a virtue.

What everyone could see was his father's dogmatism – that did not take much detecting. He always thought Bacon, for example, 'a solemn, pretentious ass.' An absurd judgment to anyone who can appreciate that tolerant, all-comprehending, ecumenical intellect. Lewis, always too ready to condemn what he has no fancy to, thinks keeping a diary 'a time-wasting and foolish practice.' Absurd again, especially to an historian who reflects how much we should be impoverished without the diaries of Pepys and Evelyn; or to a person of literary sensibility, who can appreciate Dorothy Wordsworth or Kilvert. But, then, Lewis – who disapproved too readily what he did not like – seemed to think that English poetry had reached its term with Chesterton (!) and, like his older colleagues in the English School at Oxford, conventional academics, depreciated Eliot.

'The moment good taste knows itself some of its goodness is lost.' One should ask, why? The reason for his laying down the law about this is that he was anti-aesthete. To anyone who thinks that the apprehension and experience of beauty offer the redemption of man from the slime, this *is* a sin – in my sense of the word, not Lewis's, which would be merely theological. He goes on further about 'good taste', 'Even then, however, it is not necessary to take the further downward step of despising "the Philistines" who do not share it.' Why 'downward'? It is a duty for anyone who knows the redeeming quality of aesthetic values – for all people, not only the elect, in so far as they can apprehend them – to disapprove of Philistinism in any form.

Actually, there was an element of Philistinism in Lewis – hence his word of defence: all that beer-swilling, pipe-smoking, pub-crawling heartiness of the Inklings, C. S.'s cronies at Oxford. I thought it vulgar.

'Hymns are extremely disagreeable to me' – that is no recommendation, simply a defect; and an aesthetic defect when one considers the haunting beauty of the Latin hymns of the medieval Church, by some of its greatest spirits too – St Thomas Aquinas, Abélard, St Bernard or Adam of St Victor: the nostalgic evening hymn, shutting the shutters upon daylight and the day's work, 'Te lucis ante terminum.' Or,

O quanta qualia sunt ista sabbata.

Lewis, by way of self-promotion, to show that he is 'with it' will condemn 'the wicked institution of Church Parades.' What is there wicked about Church Parades? They may very well do some people some good. It was just that he didn't like them, either at school or in the Officers' Training Corps. Once again, what he didn't like is generalised into a proposition if not a rule. This becomes important intellectually, when it is carried over into the fields of literature, philosophy or theology.

He was unhappy at his Public School, which his brother, a year or two older, simply loved. Why couldn't C.S. take it in his stride? The Public Schools were geared to ordinary fellows, *l'homme moyen sensuel*; he was odd man out, a misfit.

He makes an important point when he says: 'For the last thirty years or so England has been filled with a bitter, truculent, sceptical, debunking and cynical intelligentsia.' This is true – and it is even worse today, with the lowering and vulgarisation of standards. Lewis rightly pin-points the fact that 'a great many of them were at Public Schools and I believe very few liked it.' I never had this difficulty to contend with, since I went as a dayboy to a grammar-school and loved every moment of it: for me it was a liberation from, and an enrichment of, the cultural waste-land of working-class life (as with D. H. Lawrence). The grammar-schools, of which the great Education Act of 1902 created a nation-wide system, have been dealt a destructive blow in the interest of monochrome egalitarianism, no matter about education or educational standards. Lewis and I would agree about that.

What I did not like was his perpetual disputatiousness, seeing everything in terms of argument. Whatever his success with readers – who, for the most part, I suspect, ignore the arguments – not all his pupils and colleagues at Oxford would stand for it, any more than I would. John Betjeman, a gentle soul on his way to being a good poet, could not bear it, wilted before the intellectual bullying, did no work and was sent down. Ironic flecks of Betjeman's experience appear in his early work:

> 'Objectively, our Common Room
> Is like a small Athenian state –
> Except for Lewis: he's all right
> But do you think he's *quite* first rate?' –

inquires one don of another. While in the Preface to *Ghastly Good Taste* Betjeman pays tribute to his old tutor, 'whose jolly personality and encouragement to the author in his youth have remained an unfading memory for the author's declining years.'

John Cooper, a tougher spirit, refused to go to Lewis for political theory tutorials. Magdalen College asked me to take him on; he was the best pupil intellectually that I ever had, a very difficult, cross-grained individual of great promise. He had had a bad time in the Second German War, and lost the one person he loved in it, his only brother. He became a distinguished historian before he died, still young. But he wasn't taking C. S. Lewis, any more than I was.

My disagreement with Lewis, and his with me, was an intellectual one: we were at opposite poles in war-time and post-war Oxford. Lewis was essentially un-historical, in one sense anti-historical. His mind was philosophical, in the old-fashioned way in which he had been trained. The old Greats School at Oxford believed in the primacy of metaphysics – the situation is different today, in the wake of Wittgenstein, with the philosophers busily engaged in sawing off the bough upon which they formerly sat, showing up metaphysical problems

as largely due to confusions in the meaning of words, superfluous if not positively bogus. Even while Lewis was at
Magdalen the College had an original philosopher in J. L.
Austin, devoted precisely to this business of analysis, a solvent
of so much metaphysics. If anything is 'a waste of time' I
regard metaphysics as more so than keeping a diary is.

Lewis misunderstood the issue between us, just as his father
would have done. He insists, quite rightly, that a view or a
theory may be out of date, but that 'tells us nothing about its
truth or falsehood.' This is obvious. He tilted against the
'chronological' heresy, mistakenly equating it with historical
relativism, as if that were all there was to it!

I was the proponent of historical relativism, and Lewis pin-
pointed it as the enemy (one of them). He gave it a special
name, which no one knows now – 'bulverism'. I cannot here
expound what historical relativism means: I did so at the time
in the central chapter of *The Use of History*. This attitude of
mind is a solvent of the claims of most abstractions – in
politics, economics, philosophy, theology – to absolute truth.
That is not to say that the abstract propositions of mathematics
do not possess self-certifying truths; but abstractions in most
fields are apt to be determined by extraneous considerations,
historical, sociological, etc and have no absolute validity.

This was anathema to Lewis, for it undercut the ground
upon which he pontificated – and pontificate he did, laying
down the law all round. It was the disputatiousness that I
disliked, and the cocksureness it led to even more. (All
historians are impelled towards scepticism, and apt to become
moral indifferentists, like Gibbon, another Magdalen man.)
Lewis got this disputatiousness – as if this led one to knowledge! – from both his father and Kirk, the tutor who so much
shaped his adolescence. 'The most casual remark was taken as
a summons to disputation.' When the propositions referred to
mathematics, 'I grasped the principles but my answers were
always wrong.' We may apply this to some of his conclusions
in other fields, and ask then to what point the principles?

Not all of them were wrong. When Lewis went to Cambridge and wrote his *Experiment in Criticism* he dislodged
Leavis from his position with singularly little fuss. Nothing
surprising in this, for Lewis *was* a first-rate mind, where Leavis

was a second-rate one. Lewis was an excellent scholar, Latin and Greek, French, German, Italian, Anglo-Saxon and Middle English. Leavis knew hardly any other language but English, and that badly.

It was, however, possible to catch out Lewis on a point of scholarship. When he wrote his volume in the *Oxford History of English Literature* on the sixteenth century, I gave the book a warm welcome in a review. I had some reservations to make – Lewis wrote of Cardinal Allen as one of the best of Elizabethan prose-writers. Now he hardly wrote anything of any significance at all. But the famous Jesuit, Robert Parsons, was a prolific and important writer, whom Jonathan Swift considered one of the best masters of English prose.

Lewis came up to my railway compartment, on my way to Cambridge, to thank me for my review – always polite and gentlemanly. I asked him why he had so over-estimated Cardinal Allen, who wrote hardly anything, and ignored Father Parsons who wrote so well and so much. Lewis astonished me by saying that he didn't think Parsons important! He simply didn't know. The significant thing is that he wouldn't take telling by someone who did – his father's trait coming out again.

I think I have read most of his books: I doubt if he had read a single book of mine. We once were invited to debate on the issue between us, in an upper room in St Mary's, the University church.[1] Lewis spoke first, and after my speech he had to go, leaving me in possession of the field, if not of the argument. In any case, nothing would have persuaded him: he was impermeable, at bottom insensitive.

Take his attitude to Renaissance humanism. He was prejudiced on the subject, because Renaissance humanism undermined the transcendental authority of religion. Not that the greatest of scholars, Erasmus, was irreligious: he was deeply, but undoctrinally, religious. He cut away all the superfluous accretions of late medieval Catholicism, especially scholastic logic-chopping, to concentrate on single-minded devotion to God.

That was not good enough for Lewis: he insisted on the

[1] I have described this in *A Man of the Thirties*.

doctrine, the more unbelievable the more he insisted, in his Ulsterman's bullying way. The chaplain at All Souls went to hear a sermon in which Lewis insisted on belief in every little circumstance of Jesus' 'resurrection' – as our chaplain protested, 'nails and all.' I hardly think it did the chaplain's faith much good – Lewis's absurd book on *Miracles* is enough to undermine anyone's faith.

In his autobiography he says dismissively, 'I do not much believe in the Renaissance as generally described by historians.' No, because he did not like it, and did not hold with historians. Humanist scholars like Erasmus presented the texts in themselves, not overlaid by theological argy-bargy. But the latter was precisely what Lewis liked. No matter – the significant point is that his theological preconceptions warped his literary judgment. He preferred medieval obscurantists.

There were besides specific judgments on Elizabethan writers and poems I did not much care for, on Marlowe or on 'Venus and Adonis'. I do not think Lewis was at his best on Shakespeare: he had a heavy preference for the epic and the allegorical, which I do not share, but where I am content to learn from him. (Would he learn from me? No, but he was eager to commend such a second-rate work as Chesterton's *The Everlasting Man,* because it fitted in with his prejudices.) In any case, I am chary of summary critical *judgments*: I prefer critics to interpret rather than to judge. And too much literary criticism strangles the appreciation of literature.

The importation of so much heavy theological speculation leads to sometimes ludicrous results. In his *Preface to Paradise Lost* there is a passage about an erection (sexual) – can blame be attached to the object, if involuntary, etc? This led one innocent girl in a class at Oxford to ask what an erection was. A passage nearby discusses what the sexual relations of Adam and Eve were before the Fall: Lewis, is for once, uncertain but thinks that they were something ineffably beautiful!

He is always very certain about Hell, and the Enemy – the Devil. 'Divine punishments are also mercies.' Are they? Even if, assuming them to be divine, they might sometimes be to others observing them, are they to the persons afflicted? To a little child dying already of cancer, for instance? Flannery O'Connor, another religious, thought so in the case of a young girl she knew, dying of cancer in the face. Not so brave myself, I cannot think so.

The problem of pain is insoluble to anyone who believes in a personal God, who knows us personally, loves and cares for us – and afflicts his creatures with incurable suffering. Not a hair of your head but God knows; the 'fall of a sparrow' gave me a spasm of unbelief, when quite young. The belief in an impersonal God, soul of the universe, involves no such strain; while to those of no belief the problem does not exist.

Lewis was always ready to attack an extreme position with an even more extreme assertion, or with paradox, or to mount an unconvincing argument which his fellow-philosophers would not accept, riding his high horse in *The Problem of Pain*. At All Souls we possessed the copy that had been owned by another Magdalen man, a young R.A.F. officer who was killed in the Second German War. It was fascinating to read his marginal comments, affronted by the perverse ingenuity of the arguments, as I am by those of the book on *Miracles*, where Lewis insists on the literal fact of Jesus' Walking on the Water, the Feeding of the Five Thousand with a few loaves and fishes, the Raising of Lazarus from the dead, etc. Common sense and historical sense alike tell one that Jesus was a healer, a not unnatural phenomenon; it also tells one that ordinary humans will believe anything. Lecky, the historian of European Morals, tells us that humans will believe against the evidence, or in spite of the evidence; but hardly ever what is in accordance with the evidence.

Lewis, no historian, really anti-historian, was not bothered by that. Because he wanted to believe he accepted the infantile beliefs of primitive fishermen, and then used his logic-chopping propensity to put them across the public. Of course, they too want to believe, want re-assurance or consolation or whatever their *guru* gives them. In all the suffering of wartime thousands needed such solace and comforting. Stoicism, the real creed of most of the men fighting, was no creed for their dependents at home or their women. That time was the apogee of Lewis's *réclame*.

We come to the core of Lewis's religious position with his statement: 'Theology says to you in effect "Admit God and with Him the risk of a few miracles, and I in return will ratify your faith in uniformity as regards the overwhelming majority of events." ' Give us this ha'porth of tar and we will save the ship. 'Theology offers you a working arrangement, which leaves the scientist free to continue his experiments and the Christian to continue his prayers.'

I do not object to this bargain, which is the central demand of all Lewis's religious books. There may well be a spirit of the universe, working in and through it; or why not take the cosmos itself for base? But there is no evidence of Its being personal to us – It is far and away beyond us and our petty concerns. There is no evidence that It cares for our pain and suffering. And the mystery of it all is beyond human comprehension.

In his autobiography Lewis makes a case, step by step, for such a belief, a God-inspired universe. But what led him to go further and accept the Christian myth? He unaccountably skips over that leap he made, apparently in a bus going up to Headington – like Paul Claudel's by his pillar in the nave of Nôtre Dame. The fact is that he *wanted* to believe, he was '*intérieurement préparé*', to accept.

Having submitted his reason, Lewis – like the Welsh-Ulsterman he was – went the whole hog, to swallow illusions that are unnecessary to reasonable belief. His dogmatism actually diminishes his credibility, the sensible part of his argument.

We can go some way to meet him by agreeing that there are phenomena as yet unexplained. But the area of rational explanation of such is being constantly extended. That is the rational way to further knowledge, not subjecting the reason to the illusions of primitive minds, apt to take things literally, when it is quite unnecessary, even for believers, to do so.

Since this book is intended as one of personal memories and associations, rather than rebarbative arguments, perhaps I may conclude with an Oxford story revealing of both Lewis and Eliot. Both were Christian believers, defenders of the faith before the public, but had not met each other – and Lewis, who would have liked most of all to be a poet (he wrote verse), did not think well of Eliot's poetry. Charles Williams, whose work Lewis preached up because he was a fellow believer, knew both and invited Eliot down to meet Lewis at lunch, appropriately, at the Mitre.

Eliot was a sensitive man, apt to fumble a move on the board from shyness; Lewis was neither sensitive nor shy. Eliot, who had prepared his opening move on the way down in the train, began nervously:

> You are a younger man than I thought – judging from your photographs.

Lewis did not encourage this approach, though both absurdly condemned 'the personal heresy', the biographical approach. Lewis remained silent, so Eliot tried again:

> I have been reading your book about Milton . . . The passages about *Virgil* are very good.

This was not well received: Eliot was heretical about Milton. Eventually Eliot gave up, before the waters closed over his head, with the modest

> Well, speaking as a publisher . . .

Lewis did not help him out. It is often a mistake to bring two luminaries together: their lights are apt to put each other out.

12

The Real Betjeman

Betjeman has been so much written about by people who did not really know him, or thought they knew him, or did not know him at all, that it is as well that someone who knew him on the intimate side for forty years, more than half a lifetime, should have a go at delineating his elusive personality. For – naturally, with a man of genius – all was not as meets the eye. There was much ambivalence about him, much that was paradoxical, ironical, not easily penetrable, given to guying things that he really held seriously – and this took simpletons in.

It didn't at any time take me – and I don't think that John supposed for a moment that it did: essential basis for friendship. I have paid tribute elsewhere to his poetry, which I love.[1] (And loved him for writing it. When I said this at a joint Christie Minstrels turn we did at Port Eliot, to raise money for Historic Cornish Churches, I added that I hoped that at our age that was all right; only one clergyman in the audience appreciated the joke.) Here I shall confine myself to the personal, as elsewhere in this book, remember associations that were idiosyncratic, like no other – an enrichment of life.

John Betjeman was from his schooldays an 'original', and always recognised as such: there was, and never has been, anybody quite like him. Where on earth he came from, that personality utterly *sui generis*, heaven only knows. There is ambivalence at once in the very name. It was never mentioned, obviously the source of a deep complex, going right back to Prep. school days in the first of our German wars,

---

[1] 'The Poetry of John Betjeman', in *Portraits and Views*.

when he was persecuted by the other boys with shouts of 'Betjeman's a German spy/Shoot him down and let him die.' I was led to believe, in the usual manner after the impression the Germans made in this century, that his ancestry was Dutch. His biographer tells me that the family was not Dutch, but German from the Bremen area: 'The Dutch smoke-screen must have been put up in the First World War . . . I think, however, that J. B. sincerely believed he was of Dutch ancestry to the end.'

So he was not all that English, the persona he so successfully – and genuinely – projected upon the public through his writing, prose as well as poetry, and latterly most effectively through television. He loved England with the self-conscious passion of one who does not inwardly belong, when the purely English take that kind of thing for granted.

Similarly with the assumption of Cornishry. Some public prints would refer to him as Cornish – fancy the idiocy of anybody supposing that a name like Betjeman could possibly be Cornish! Betjeman was passionately devoted to that bit of the north coast of Cornwall around Padstow, Trebetherick and Rock, which was bound up with his happiest childhood memories, on which he had a life-long fixation and about which he wrote some of his best and most moving poems.

That is not the same thing as being Cornish, though we are grateful to him for his love of Cornwall. In writing to me – and I have a wad of his letters from the 1940s – he would often sign himself 'Jan Trebetjeman', once 'Jan Killigrew Trebetjeman', and draw a shield of the fifteen bezants (arms of the Duchy) with our motto 'One and All'.

More important, he was projected upon the people as one of them. What a joke! There was hardly anyone who was less like the ordinary boring human being. He was put across them as a cult folk-figure, a kind of sugar-daddy whom everybody recognised and thought they knew. That was one side, genuine enough, the kindly, sentimental family man, with kiddies and their interests at heart (also genuine enough, for like many men of genius he never grew up, remained a child at heart). Inside, he was much odder and queerer: religious, but given to doubt and depression; in company cheerful and gay, full of jokes, but when alone given to melancholy, needing solace and support.

There were other ambivalances. The more sensitive of those who have had the advantage of sex-education at a Public School are apt to know about bisexuality, and the doubled perception, intuition and receptivity it gives – as against the limitations of the unisexual. One can see the understanding and the sympathy in a number of the later poems, though there exist adolescent poems as a surprise for the imperceptive. (Henry James: 'Nobody ever understands *anything*.') John, with an Oriel crony of his with whom he used to go church-crawling, took me up to the Trout Inn at Godstow to peer in at a beautiful, blue-eyed kitchen boy whom they called 'Chick-abiddy.' Anything for a lark, or larks! Not having their sense of humour, I didn't see much fun in *that*.

Actually, I didn't know John as an undergraduate and, rather prim (not having been to a Public School – wish I had!), I would have disapproved of him wasting his time, careering around in a motor-car his grandmother had given him, dining at the George, neglecting his tutorials, and getting sent down for failing Divvers (Divinity, of all things). People hardly realise what a gulf there is between one brief undergraduate generation and the next: only two or three years, and there is all the difference – one has a completely different lot of friends. My contemporaries were Harold Acton, Graham Greene, Cyril Connolly, Richard Pares; as already a young Fellow of All Souls I didn't know John's, Hugh Gaitskell, John Spar-row, Douglas Jay, Frank Pakenham – I came to know them later, and sooner if they came to All Souls. I knew Maurice Bowra quite well, who took up John and to whom John owes so much: Maurice gave him his start on an architectural review, base for a career. But my later friendship with Maurice (I wouldn't be taken up or become a member of his circle) was a private, not a public one.

Significantly enough my first contacts with John were architectural. Any good historian should have an interest in architecture – 'frozen history', in which periods of time so eloquently reveal their spirit. John took me to see things in Oxford I had never seen before. I had never penetrated into the splendid eighteenth-century interior of Oriel Library, with its grand scagliola columns; we trespassed into the Senior Common Room below to see the drawings of Tractarians like Newman, delicate feminine features, and the admirable historian Froude, who learned how to write from him. John took me into the beautiful chapel of the Cowley Sisters, not open to the public, pointing out the Scottish-Gothic inflexion of his friend, Sir Ninian Comper: 'dear Sir Niminy-Piminy', finest church decorator of the century.

Then to pretty little Stockcross church near Newbury, which Comper had entirely re-decorated, with his unerring and eclectic sense of beauty – Jacobean-style rood screen, stained glass window with its modern touch of a handsome young sailor we did not fail to appreciate. Quite lost on the heavy Teutonic Pevsner, of course, with his dogmatism and fixation on the toneless expressionism of the modern German school. He never missed an opportunity to depreciate Comper. All that he has to say about this beautiful work is – 'almost entirely re-fitted by Sir Ninian Comper. Comper's anaemic E. window replaces that which is now blind and hard to see.'

John brought Comper to lunch with me in Hawksmoor's oval buttery at All Souls. I recall Sir Niminy-Piminy telling me that he had been asked to design vestments for the Cardinal Archbishop of Paris, and 'I absolutely powdered them with fleur-de-lys.' He at any rate had a sense of humour to add to his lively sense of beauty; and I remember still his rich Scottish pronunciation of 'churrch'.

Upon occasion John and I went church-crawling in Cornwall. I can see him now, the schoolboy excitement with which he fitted the key into the south door, bending down with 'What *will* it be like inside?' Or, again, his popping down quite un-selfconsciously on his knees to say a prayer, leaving me standing. His attitude was really nearer than people think to Hardy's 'hoping it might be true'. Alas, if only it were! A North Coast man, he didn't know the Victorian churches around St Austell, so when he came over from Trebetherick I took him to the little barn-like church of Biscovey, with its Street spire, and the 'Good Shepherd' at Par; also the pretty church of my poem, 'Passion Sunday in Charlestown Church', which he specially liked, for in addition to Oxford, Cornwall, and architecture, we had poetry in common – though I was rather cagey about that, he a full-time professional, not averse to baring his soul in public.

His visual memory was extraordinary. He knew every one of the Wren churches of the City, before so many of them were damaged or destroyed by the barbarian Blitz on London. He could remember individually a dozen or fifteen churches seen in one day, when I could visualise only five or six. He would come over to lunch, sometimes with Penelope, both at Polmear Mine above Charlestown and later at Trenarren. At one such occasion he was fascinated by the very unfascinating character of a failed painter with a raging inferiority-complex – he was no good and a great bore – whom an early girl-friend of mine had incomprehensibly married. This was not mere politeness: John was fascinated by dimness – partly genuinely, though it was also, like so much with him, a comic turn. At Oxford he had a line in dim peers, especially if they were Irish, like Lord Wicklow. He introduced me to the Earl of Huntingdon whom he had taken up, a very rare bird for he was also a Labour man: 'Meet the dimmest peer in Britain.' (John, luckily, had no politics and no comprehension of them.) Similar remarks about Kolkhorst, the eccentric Anglo-Portuguese don at Oxford, whom John had a cult of: he always called him 'the Colonel' – I never acclimatised myself to the derogatory remarks to him. I suppose John himself could be called an eccentric – another of those ambivalences the great heart of the public was not alerted to.

It was John who introduced me to the beauties of Victorian Cheltenham. We jogged across the Cotswolds in his tumbledown ramshackle, grimy old car, painted and patched but totally unwashed – like John himself in those days, until Elizabeth Cavendish kindly took him in hand and tidied him up. ('We have ruled sex out.') I dare say Penelope got tired of keeping him in order – a full-time job – and rather fancied a career for herself. In those days John had an objection to taking a bath. Ordered upstairs by Penelope to take one, he went up, filled the bath with water, went on talking, swishing the water with his hand, 'Ooh! lovely bath', etc, and after a decent interval came down again never having got in.

His appearance was no less *sui generis*. Someone wrote of his green complexion; carious teeth, full lips, dribbling a little with enthusiasm; large and beautiful brown eyes, full of varying expression, puzzled, swivelling, sympathetic, kind, amused; rich, plummy clerical voice, like an archdeacon, which later turned out such an asset on TV; then giggles, gales of laughter, always finding or creating something funny. Never serious for long – at any rate with others: he thought it good manners to be light in conversation. He was a card.

Eccentricity was the order of the day. He and Penelope, neighbours of Gerald Berners at Faringdon, would often come over, Penelope bringing her white horse into the drawing-room to tea. There is a charming photograph of that hospit-able tea-table, the horse quite at home, muzzle hovering over the sugar basin. Then there was Archie, John's teddy bear whom he had always slept with from childhood and continued to do into his married days. One day, when there were 'words', Penelope threw Archie out of the bedroom window – then there nearly was a Divorce! Archie was either a Strict Baptist or a Paedo-Baptist, I forget which – John has written a book about him.

Where ordinary people's children grew up saying 'dear doggie', or 'my pussy cat', or whatever, their children were brought up to say 'Sarum Use' or 'Immaculate Contheption'. No wonder that, when John and Penelope went inside to view a church, the children remained firmly entrenched in the car reading their Penny Dreadfuls. Everything was in inverted commas, turned to fun, guyed, but with poker face – you could easily be taken in. I remember John saying solemnly to me, of a high-brow don at Balliol, John Bryson who collected pictures: 'He's cultivated', then a giggle. Penelope cultivated a Cockney accent (John genuinely was Cockney, witness the Cockney rhymes in his poems), and this rather flummoxed people in a Field-Marshal's daughter. (Socially, John always knew which side his bread was buttered.) He had some talent for drawing. I remember one of a grand luncheon at Longleat, with Penelope in schoolgirl pig-tails electrifying the table with ''ow, Lord Bath [the old Marquis], 'ow do you do these stoofed eggs?' She was a very good cook.

Anything for a lark – larks all the time. When David Cecil became Professor of English Literature at Oxford, he announced an Inaugural Lecture on 'Reading'. On the morn-ing of the lecture there arrived by post a little book labelled

Reading: it turned out be a specially bound book on the topography of the town. An envelope would be addressed to one 'First Class Male.' I don't think he called me by any other than my name in family and College, Leslie – unattractive in itself and wrong for a Cornishman. But, then, I dislike all three of my names: I should like something recognisably Cornish, 'by Tre, Pol, or Pen.' Not that I want to go too far and be called Penaluna or even Penhaligon.

I always loved John's topographical poems about North Oxford, territory which he made especially his, and hardly ever go there without thinking of his laburnum and red-may flowering gardens and 'St C. S. Lewis's church' – the dogmatic Lewis had been John's tutor at Magdalen, whom he could not abide – and 'Goldylocks' Myfanwy Piper bicycling around those dear suburban pavements. Very early in our friendship John bought for me Piper's beautiful *gouache* of the derelict fifteenth-century chapel at Hall, above Bodinnick Ferry – I'll bet it is a complete ruin now, original wagon-roof, bell-cote and all. It was through John that I came to know 'Mr' Piper, as he always was – John had names for everybody. At All Souls his old friend John Angus Hanbury Sparrow was 'Spansbury', my friend Geoffrey Hudson was 'Chinese Hudson', after 'Chinese Gordon'.

Cornwall and poetry were far more intimate bonds between us than architecture or people, and most of his letters to me are about the first two. Very early on he took the trouble to copy out two passages from Robert Ross's *The Georgian Revolt*, which represented what he himself thought and felt about poetry. 'At some times there are more great poets than at others. But there are always poets . . . and they will go quietly on their way, saying nothing where they have nothing to say and, when they cannot help saying something, saying it in a form they cannot help.'

This was by Gerald Gould, who in Lansbury's days was literary editor of the *Daily Herald*, when the paper had some quality and of course a small circulation. John reviewed novels for it – in dozens, wasting his time on trash, though he used to get some of the reading done for him by girl-friends. He told me at the time, 'my energy is terrific'.

From Ross John quoted for me: 'For most poets [in the 20s] it was simply a case of fight or die, coterie warfare or poetic oblivion. The slow, often halting development of the individual poetic genius along lines determined by its own uniqueness, which had been the priceless jewel of English poetry for generations, seemed likely by 1920 to become a thing of the past, a sacrifice to the collectivist urge and the relativist spirit of the onrushing twentieth century.'

These two statements must have spoken for John, who stuck to his last, his own original inspiration all the way along, without caring tuppence for what literary critics thought, or what ephemeral poets wrote to keep in with temporary fashions. John was wise never to write 'criticism' of poetry: it is dangerous to be self-conscious about, and tamper with, the seed-bed from which real poetry is created. That is why so much of the 'poetry' patronised by the media and the literary modes today is bogus – as John and I knew, no less than Philip Larkin or Kingsley Amis who has dismissed it as not being poetry 'in any sense of the word sense.'

John was writing to me on the day of 'St Loy, Cornish Calendar, 1944, that great agnostic Saint the Rev. J. M. Thompson, the only nice man in Magdalen, tells me you have his topographical poem. If you can find it – and I know how one loses mss and also what hell it is putting things into envelopes, hence this post card – I wd. be v. glad to see it.' This was a rarity. Thompson had been 'inhibited', or whatever, by the minatory Bishop Gore – who was very censorious about his clergy – and Thompson became, more usefully, a good history tutor at Magdalen and wrote a book on Robespierre for my series, 'Men and their Times'.

In August 1945 came a characteristic coloured post card written in antique capital letters from 'Skimmery, Oxford' – was that St Mary Hall, part of Oriel? This must have been the time of his illness recorded in the poem, 'Before the Anaesthetic, or A Real Fright.' 'N°T AT ALL Al. I C°VLDNT M°VE F°R A L°NG WHILE & THEN WENT TO BEAULIEV. [That would be when he wrote 'Youth and Age on Beaulieu River, Hants.'] W°VLD LIKE T° SEE Y°VR NEW PO°EM. G°ING T° ABERYSTWYTH °N XIVTH F°R A F°RTNIGHT (D.V.) AT°MIC B°MB A BIG

ADVANCE IN CIVILISATIᵒN. JᵒHN B.'

That was how he thought about the horror of the age we live in, as all pereceptive people do – compare my poems of the Thirties, clearly realising the approach of war, when the blind and stupid wouldn't or couldn't see. John, no politician, saw well enough and was terrified by what he saw: no cosy comfortable illusions such as ordinary people – his later addicts – cherished: 'Come, friendly bombs and rain on Slough', etc. I wrote to the same effect in '1937':

> A day will come when there shall descend on them
> From the skies they do not observe, some stratagem
> Of fate to search and sear their flesh with fire . . .
> Liquid fire will rain down from the air,
> Will suddenly arrive upon them there
> And lick their bodies up and burn their bones . . .
> For these are they who, warned of what's to come,
> Walk blindly on to their appointed doom.

They would not take warning: they went on supporting Chamberlain in thinking that he could appease Hitler.

Next thing, a missive framed like a picture, 'To A.L.R. Called in to say how much I enjoyed THE USE OF HISTORY & that I have cracked it up in this week's *Daily Herald*. A little friend of mine – his mother is the Emily of my poem on Ireland – Peter Patrick Hunphill, son of a drunk Irish baron of that name is coming up from Downside to BNC [Brasenose College] today for an entrance examination. I am taking him out to luncheon at George. Do come if you can, 2 o'clock.' What a time! I rarely went out to lunch anyway; he gave me his new home telephone number, but I never ring up either, if I can help it.

Another invitation to lunch came on a post card of beautiful Farnborough Old Rectory under snow, high up in the Downs above Wantage. I never went up there, but Gerald Berners told me what an exquisite Queen Anne red-brick house with cupola it was; and how inconvenient, no water laid on and no electric light, John coming to the door with a lighted candle in hand.

I find a number of letters thence from 1948–9. 'I have taken to drink and am much better. Brandy-&-Soda. It all came about through reading one of the GREATEST ENGLISH NOVELISTS – G. J. Whyte-Melville whose Hussars and hunting men always have a B-&-S. when discussing their chops. Read Whyte-Melville (not old Herman–Whyte) [*sic*] – a most upper-class writer & *Kate Coventry* & *The Brookes of Bridlemere* are the two I've liked best so far. Read Whyte-Melville & take to drink.'[2]

I followed neither piece of advice. There followed more helpful advice I wanted for projects of my own, an illustrator for some Oxford book in mind. Sharp's Plan for post-war development of the city was not yet out, but he 'has taken offices under Ye Olde Payntedde Roommie so I'll see the plan before anyone. Dom Julian Stonor has identified the beehive between Brown Willy and Rowtor as St Petroc's hermitage and written a delightful account of it and my beloved St. P. in the Downside Review. What on earth is all this about Herefordshire? Is it to be bombed out of existence?'

Evidently I had been ill again, and thinking of a Cornish slate slab with good lettering, like that which John had put up to his father in St Enodoc church. 'Monuments are better done by someone you can trust – leave it to me to look after in your will, and in the event of my pre-deceasing you, I can give you a few good reliable names of younger men.' Dear John, alas!

Next was from Trebetherick, August 1948. 'Here I am on the eve of my 42nd birthday amid the tamarisks, slate, mesembryanthemum, hunting wasps, tennis, golf, shorts, baked bald heads of my contemporaries, greying hair of my seniors, sherries, churchbells, cliffs, cars, hard wet sand of the only place I ever want to be in.' I had put up a proposal for a book of his essays to Odhams, which I was then advising.

[2] This Victorian author, who was killed in the hunting field, had 'considerable literary powers, which he himself was inclined to underrate, and would have brought him greater fame', according to the *D.N.B.* Locker Lampson says that 'Whyte-Melville never sought literary society, preferring the companionship of soldiers, sportsmen and country gentlemen. Had he been more assiduous in cultivating literary men, his reputation might have stood higher with the general public, though he could scarcely have been a greater favourite with readers of his own class.' No doubt. An interesting case, and a suitable subject for John's admiration; while myself I have never played the literary game.

'YES. I can collect the essays and they fall into the headings you enumerate, i Lit. ii Arch. iii Top . . . Lit. might be made to include sentimental-pious, e.g. Christmas Nostalgia of last year. Please put the matter to Odhams. Terms suit me fine. They will lose on it. But they can afford to do so . . . No petrol. We could get over.'

It then transpired that, while I was away, he made 'this sad discovery that I was committed to Murray's about the book of essays, and since then a contract which I signed ten years ago and forgot all about has turned up. Murray's and I are now engaged in trying to find periodicals in which I have written articles. I am always so disgusted with what I write after it is printed that I keep very few specimens of past work. I think the best thing to do is to wait and see what is left over that is worth printing. Murray's want a volume that is entirely topographical; that should leave an immense amount of material over which is not, and which is about poetry and literature. Ah! to see you again would be nice. Would you ever come out here for a meal, if I came and fetched you. You have never been here.' In fact there *is* an immense amount of John's dispersed prose, some of which is worth bringing to light: not the novel-reviews, but material from *Time and Tide*, and I used to like his miscellaneous bits and pieces in the *Spectator*.

May, 1949: 'I shall, I fear, be in Newcastle-on-Tyne (D.V.) on Saturday next when I should, if I followed my own inclinations, be having luncheon with you and your distinguished guests. Blast. I should have loved it. I have *never* been to Launcells. It is an ambition I have never had the petrol to realise. Is it as good as the photographers say? [Better: quite unspoiled.] I have put in Parson Hawker's account of Ship-wrecks in 1858 into my readings for Victorian Provincial Life in the West of England. I am nervous of not living up to the fine and flattering description you gave of me in that stimulating and excellent opening broadcast for the series.[3] I go to HAYLING ISLAND tomorrow. Ever been there? Nor have I. That poem of yours "Alfoxden" haunts me. Do propose yourself here for a meal. I will come and fetch you.' Alas, I never went.

---

[3] This was a BBC series I had arranged, published as *The West in English History*, to which John contributed 'Victorian Provincial Life'.

By 1951 the Betjemans had descended from the hills to the pleasant 'The Mead', Wantage – nearer to Wantage church-bells – and I had dedicated *The English Past* to the two admirable Johns, Betjeman and Piper, 'whose genius re-creates something of the English past.' I had realised earlier than most that the great days of England were over, had come to an end in the flames and glory of the heroic years 1940–1945, and that the past of this country was far more interesting than its future was likely to be.

'How can I enough thank you for the unexpected and generous dedication and present of your book, for? You cheer and encourage me at the very moment when I most need cheering, for I feel that the Pevsners who kill every object they classify, are in the ascendant. "First class", "important", "fully documented" are the only adjectives which they use in commendation. They see things only in terms of things not of people. Your essay on All Souls is a glorious condemnation of Pevsnerism and the crashing specialists. What people don't recognise about you is how good you are as a prose-writer, how imaginative and <u>melodious</u> a writer. That is because you are a poet.

'I am really honoured, old top, by sharing with Mr Piper (whom I saw this morning) this dedication. Ta ever so. And I really mean it. We are allies against the professionalising of what is art. You are an artist. Proud to know you, old top. Notice my new address THE MEAD (an ugly small Victorian villa in a nice site), WANTAGE. Come and see us. Will telephone. Yours till death.'

Actually 'The Mead' was quite a pleasant house: I include John's remark merely to show that he was not uncritically fixed on everything Victorian. He knew well enough that Georgian architecture was better. There was an element of the comic in his cult of Victorian extravaganzas like the piece of Burgess furniture he gave to Evelyn Waugh, who also pre-ferred Victorian to much that is modern. John had a great influence in opening our eyes to what was good in Victorian architecture and art – we may discount the jokes about 'dear Sir Gilbert' [Scott, of course] that took in solemn asses. Ian Fleming made a collection of first editions of books that exerted an historic influence; alongside of John Locke and

Darwin, John Ruskin and Karl Marx were two or three books of Betjeman's.

Penelope set up her rest, in the Elizabethan phrase, in the birthplace of King Alfred, and opened a little cake shop, 'King Alfred's Kitchen'; but refrained from advertising 'Burnt Cakes a Speciality.'

In September 1952 he was at Bodare, Trebetherick 'but, ALAS, only till next Monday.' I had been away in Dublin lecturing: 'v. pleased to have your Oirish post card. I'm glad you like I.C. churches, as Church of Ireland churches are called by the Irish Churchmen. But I was particularly delighted to have your Presidential Address to the English Association. It is most stirring. What a dim organisation to take such a deal of trouble for. . . . I am honoured to be mentioned. Who wrote that splendid bit of blank verse about asphalt roads and golf balls? I ought to know, but don't.'

It was of course a line from Eliot's Church-pageant, 'The Rock' – dear John's education at Marlborough and Magdalen was oddly patchy. 'See you next term. Joe Lynam and Philip Landon are here': the one an old schoolmaster from the Dragon School at Oxford, the other a rather dim don such as John adored to cultivate – like the unknown Pembroke don of whom he wrote a virtuoso poem when he died. John had a cult of Pembroke, not the most scintillating of Oxford colleges – Balliol wouldn't have been in it, not a word about that institution of 'plain living and high thinking'. Besides, little Pembroke had the best cellar in Oxford.

His next letter came on *Time and Tide* notepaper, where he had a job as literary editor, under the supposedly liberal but really autocratic Lady Rhondda, the owner. Its printed heading described it as a strictly 'Non-Party Weekly Review', but John had inked this out to read, 'A jolly Party Weekly'. 'I am horrified by what happened to your review. We are printing your letter in full.' Some fool of a girl had cut several sentences, omitting a 'not', which made me say the exact opposite of what I had written – the kind of thing that often happens when the third-rate think they can improve on the first-rate. What one has to put up with as a reviewer, from cuts and inserts and silly captions missing the point!

'I have had written up in huge letters in the book room "NO

REVIEWER, HOWSOEVER MILD, MUST BE CUT OR ALTERED IN ANY WAY WITHOUT CONSULTING THE REVIEWER FIRST." I was away the last fortnight at the death-bed and then funeral of my old mum. Had I been up here, this tragedy could never have happened – the altering of your review I mean, not my mother's death. Buried at St Enodoc, sea mist lifting over Stepper, waving tamarisks, granite—: very moving. [With all my experience of Elizabethan handwriting, I often find it difficult to read John's: he would apologise for it as illegible.] Happy Christmas. Come and see us at Vintagia if you are in Oxford. Love.' – Alas, I have never been at Oxford for Christmas.

John's job with *Time and Tide* did not last long, for all that he enlivened that dim periodical with his jokes and bright ideas for competitions, etc. There was a certain liberal-minded, broad-bottomed fatuity about Lady Rhondda – and one day she took him out to a good lunch and suddenly sacked him. A poem on the manner of it takes her off to the life:

> 'I'm making some changes next week in the organisation,
>   And though I admire
> Your work for me, John, yet the need to increase
>   circulation

[It never did: circulation went down and under her administration]

>   Means you must retire:
> An outlook more *global* than yours is the qualification
>   I really require.'

True enough, John's outlook was anything but *global*, silly woman. Fancy losing him, just like that!

> I stood on the pavement and wondered which loss was
>   the greater –
>   The cash or the pride.
> Explanations to make to subordinates, bills to pay later
>   Churned up my inside.

In the end, I think that that Lesbian millionairess got her comeuppance.

I must have had a lunch-party at All Souls, for next, 'We all enjoyed ourselves *immensely* and Philip Landon, so silent usually, has been full of it all today – especially the bit about the last of the Trevannions (Trevanyons? Trevanion?) of Caerhays.' Third time lucky – he got it right. I must have told them the extraordinary story of the end of the family there, in a riot of extravagance, and their incestuous fixation on the Byrons, which I did not write up until years later in *The Byrons and Trevanions*. Not until I had retired from heavy historical research at All Souls had I time to do the more literary books I had had in mind to do all along. John ended, 'Penelope and Aunt Elsie were full of it all too. Ta muchly, as we say on the North Coast.' There followed a bit of Old Irish I cannot translate: 'Jan Treb:'

In 1953 he was giving me the name of a sculptress in Berkshire 'who would fill the bill nicely for St Mabyn's statue.' That fine church had had its interior completely scalped by an aristocratic Rector, bloody fool, in the early nineteenth century; rood-screen, bench-ends, monuments, everything. I could scalp him for the destruction he wrought. John wanted me over for a lunch party, holding out enticingly a 'Mrs Villiers-Stuart, Greta Hellström of one of my poems, a girl from Oxford (Trebetherick)', somebody from Boar's Hill and a nice young man who is given the mysterious label Q. (which always means Quiller-Couch to me). The mystery is resolved by a P.S.: 'Have you read *The Heart in Exile* by Rodney Garland. It goes farther than any novel heretofore *on a certain subject.*'

Not much of a modern novel reader, I had not heard of the book. In those days people were absurdly more cagey about that subject, one of the simple facts of life about which people have become more sensible since. Subsequently, I was to write a straightforward book, *Homosexuals in History*, to say how natural it all was and how silly to make such a fuss about it – historians had known the facts all along. The book was to be attacked by the Gay Lib. people in America as being unsympathetic, [!] and because I laughed, was insufficiently solemn – when so much about sex is comic and makes fools of us all.

With his ambivalent nature, his doubled sensibility, John was always sensible on that subject – anybody who belonged to Maurice Bowra's circle would be more than sympathetic. (I kept out of it, and Maurice too thought that I was unsympathetic. How imperceptive people are!) John's sympathies are quite clear in his poems, as in mine: I realised all along that one can express everything in verse, for people are so obtuse they don't know what you are saying. Very early on John had written 'The Arrest of Oscar Wilde at the Cadogan Hotel' – *there* was a fool, flaunting his vulgar exhibitionism, bringing trouble and suffering down upon hundreds of poor innocents, instead of going abroad for a breath of fresh air as Bernard Shaw advised.

Towards the end there is a moving poem:

> . . . and that you did with said intent procure
> the aforesaid Sidney Alexander Green
> being at the time a minor . . . [etc.]

John understood all about the subject and its literary ramifications. His son Paul, for instance, was always called Pauli – after the good-looking young lawyer with whom Samuel Butler was hopelessly in love. One day John said to me of another couple, who got into trouble with conventional types, that at least they loved each other. John was a Christian, and had charity.

October 1954: 'I am very happy indeed to have *A Cornish Waif's Story*.' This was an astonishing story of a poor child who had been *sold* to a sailor: they made a living by travelling the roads with a barrel-organ and a monkey. I think the book may have been sparked off by my *Cornish Childhood*, for it came to me out of the blue a mass of semi-literate manuscript. I made a book of it, cutting it down, shaping it up into chapters and paragraphs: it was simply the story that was so extraordinary, and *Nihil Cornubiense alienum a me puto*. But the sequel gave any amount of trouble with the (perhaps understandably) psychotic character of the authoress. 'I suppose the convent she went to was St Faith's at Lostwithiel. The nuns are obviously Anglo and I should think they are Wantage Sisters. I

wish you would let me know if this is true. [I think not.] I wish
you'd come out and have a meal with us, old top. Give us a
tinkle on the telephone and I'll come along and fetch you.
How often do you see Philip Landon? He loves Cornwall like
you and I do. Yours Jan Trebetjeman.'

I hardly knew Philip Landon – he had no allure for me,
though Trinity was Q.'s old college; I didn't go out much to
other colleges – none had the interest of All Souls, not even my
undergraduate college, Christ Church, which thought itself so
grand and with which I had broken: mistakenly, no doubt.
After so much illness and wasting time on politics I had little
time for anything but work. And, alas, though John was
always urging me to come out to see him – as Eliot had urged
me earlier to come up to London – I hardly ever did. I once
took Gervase Mathew out to Wantage, a close friend for years:
a totally unwashed Dominican from Blackfriars, a regular
consumer of my sherry, a conjurer with my match-boxes and
a great converter of souls, to whom both Graham Greene and
Frank Pakenham owe their salvation. Gervase was my *protégé*,
whom I was for ever feeding and sherrying; only in that
respect was I his victim. In any other he would have had no
more luck that Father D'Arcy – who did for Evelyn Waugh –
had had earlier. I was impressed equally by Penelope's delicious cooking and John's collection of Victorian illustrated
and architectural volumes.

From Wantage 'I have sent a sub for 1 copy of the *lovly*
book' – this was a joke, because I had said that one could
always tell homos by their constant use of the word 'lovely'
(and heteros by their halitosis). 'The Historic Churches
Preservation Trust have made a large loan to Par for the Street
job to be repaired' – I had been largely concerned in founding
the Cornish branch. His next p.c. from Trebetherick, on his
return from Sicily in 1966: 'Bright sun here, green Atlantic and
sailors in blue shirts on the cliffs . . . I am vastly flattered by
your kind, generous and perceptive remarks about me . . . on
my work for an Arsse at BBC programme.'

Next year, 'Have written you a three-page (both sides)
letter of praise and thanks for *Cornish Stories*. They are magnificent – much better than my poems. [Rubbish, dear John.
My stories are the kind I like to read, but I *love* your poems.]

"Death of a Principal", though not necessarily Cornish, is agony and deeply moving.' It was, in fact, based on the agony of George Gordon, President of John's own college, Magdalen, which I had heard all about from Bruce McFarlane. 'Your descriptions of Tamar and other valleys and of the china clay district are so good I feel myself there *and* you have narrative power and can sketch character. Love. Jan Treb:'

If my stories were good enough for Betjeman, they are good enough for other people and to be reprinted. . . . He was sufficiently moved to write again next day, a long letter. 'The *Cornish Stories* are marvellous. Never mind my verse, these stories of yours *are* Cornwall and flecked all through with description that makes me inly stirred.' He then gives chapter and verse, taking trouble to go into detail. 'Do you think Lambethow could be Laneast? or Launcells?' No: 'The Advowson of Lambethow' is based on the authentic parish story of Blisland, and today the Rector tells me that old folk there recognise it as such. Blisland on the edge of Bodmin Moor was a favourite church of John's, about which he wrote a beautiful piece, with its dedication to St Protus and St Hyacinth. (Who on earth were they?)[4] 'What I also enjoy about them is their warmth and humanity and your beautiful ear for Cornish dialogue. The curse Mrs Slade gives is terrific.' It meant more to me that it was authentic.

'I started the book this morning, resumed it waiting for the dentist – Mr Graham of Beaumont Street – and now can't get on with a mountain of letters for joy of reading it. I read a story between each letter and have reached "The Squire of Reluggas". I very much enjoy the subtlety of the difference between Higher Quarter and down there by the sea. I fancy "All Souls Night" was an early one.' It was: nothing to do with All Souls College – where it was a favourite with Halifax, a connoisseur of ghost-stories – it was based on authentic experiences at Wardour Castle, staying with John Arundell,

[4] Apparently they were third century martyrs in Rome, two brothers, one of them executed, the other burned, in the kindly human way. But how on earth did Blisland church come to be dedicated to these obscure Saints? – the only church in Britain to be so. That is the problem. I can only suggest that some medieval patron was responsible, perhaps a bishop of Exeter who had been to Rome and seen their tombs or whatever.

who died after years of prison camp with the bestial Germans at Colditz.

'It has a Doidge-like quality about its plot – do you remember Doidge's Western Counties Annual?' I did not: it never penetrated my illiterate working-class home. 'Some of the Doidge stories are Hardyesque melodrama and Hardy might well have contributed to it, as did his secretary Lois Deacon who is still alive. But *the* story in your book so far is the "Death of a Principal." It couldn't be old Murray, but how right was that dying man's advice and how moving your picture of his death.' George Gordon dying had urged McFarlane, then Vice-President, *not* to become President: he himself had been 'meant for literature', but had wasted his life on college chores. Happily Bruce missed this unhappy consummation, largely by the efforts of A. J. P. Taylor whom I had urged upon him as a colleague. Nevertheless, Bruce left all his written work to be produced by his pupils, unable to produce it himself. (Hence his psychotic attitude to my work – hard to take from a close friend; but that is what academics are like, John not, himself creative.)

' "Trespittigue's Vote" is a very subtle piece and oh how sad.' It is based on a true Cambridge story, as John Sparrow recognised. 'Is Lansillian Luxulyan?' Indeed it is: 'The Wicked Vicar of Lansillian' is the authentic eighteenth-century parish folklore; it was not much appreciated by my friend, the Vicar at the time, who had seen the apparition in the haunted drive. He lived in that granite vicarage alone: I shouldn't have much cared for that.

'*Indeed* I went to Trewithen and have since been down your way with Sir John Tremayne, looking at the filthy scum of china clay on Pentewan beach, and how many more streams than the St Austell White River are white.' We came to call it the White River, but its old name was the Cober, which simply means stream, represented still by the place-name Gover at the head of it. I did my best to be an honest broker between Air-Marshal Tremayne and Sir Alan Dalton of English China Clays, both my friends. In the end the militant Air-Marshal won; English China Clays are very public-spirited and conservation-minded, and the streams are now flowing clearer. 'On the moor, they're pumping the stuff away artificially and not polluting.' China clay detritus is completely harmless anyway, merely white granitty sand; and English China Clays, under Lord Aberconway and Alan Dalton, both gardeners, have planted trees galore and covered sand-burrows with rhododendrons and lupins, purple and gold, bless them.

'All the same I prefer polluted streams to streams of visitors. I suppose you're safe in Trenarren but I don't go down in Summer at all. I'm going to Spain with the C. of E. Ramblers next month but hope to look in between lets at Daymer Bay in May. You and I love the same places, Oxford and Cornwall, and really for me there are no other places so good. It is good to read a book like yours. I must now go on and read some more. God bless you dear and great Cornish writer for these stories and your remembering your old chum.'

'St George's day 1967, *Cornish Poems* have now arrived. I have read them all with pleasure. Of course the American ones mean less to me as I don't know the places they are about, but they are vivid enough for me to *imagine* the places. You have a piercing eye for significant detail. I have read out aloud the Cornish ones several times to 2 different lots of friends. That last poem in the book is v. good simplicity – but *the* poem, yes *the* poem is the Charlestown Mass. I didn't realise you have been brought up "High".' I wasn't: I brought myself up High Church – I couldn't bear Low or Broad, let alone Nonc. There follows more I can't quite make out, except that by now John was 'v. busy on Telly in London.'

This was followed by a p.c. of the White Horse at Uffington, not wholly legible, with characteristic news: 'All noisy on the Wanton front. Trees going. Villas increasing. Martin Bell is a good poet. So are you.' Was John being too generous? Even so, it was clear that, apart from Cornishry and Oxford, he liked my poetry – he especially liked the poem about my mother's death-bed, which I could never read to anyone. Here again, it is the general point that is important, not the particular one. If my poetry was good enough for him and Eliot, who published it and wrote the blurbs, for Edith Sitwell and Kathleen Raine, Edmund Blunden or Philip Larkin who chose one poem (not the best) for the *Oxford Book of Modern Verse,* then it is certainly good enough for the hack reviewers.

I know as well as the next man that one is not supposed to say such things. John had the Public School technique, like Connolly, of deflecting criticism by writing himself down: he would say to me 'I'm an emmet, a worm.' It is only too obvious a game to write oneself down – Larochefoucauld and the French epigrammatists knew two to that one. Not a Public School man, I think it beneath me, and am always willing to tell the inferior their rating. It is a duty to do so in an egalitarian society where they think they know as well as their betters – how otherwise are they to learn (if at all)? So when I hear nonsense about Shakespeare or the Elizabethans, Marlowe, Bacon or Richard III, or about England's record in history, or Germany's, or Appeasement, etc, I have no compunction in telling them that they do not qualify to hold an opinion – any more than I would on nuclear strategy or science in general. Anyway, I never waste time on ordinary people's opinions – almost always nonsense, whether about religion or sex, politics or economics; with *them* I exchange only facts. There are very few people in all the world with whom one can discuss the things that matter: there is so little to discuss *with*.

A historian knows that there is a sociological point involved. All expert knowledge is by definition élitist, and only the elect know it. In a properly organised society, hierarchically, this is obvious and accepted. In a squalid society like today's, run by egalitarian humbug – though more humbug than any real equality – the truth about these things is evaded, slobbered over by smoothies. It is the historian's duty always to tell people the truth, whether they like it or not (contrast a Churchill with a Baldwin). John knew these things well enough, though too smooth to say anything about it – so he got away with it, and became a folk-figure to the great heart of the people, to whom he did not at all belong. Unlike D. H. Lawrence and me – and see what we think! No one was more élitist really than John. Like all the creative spirits of our time: they hate its guts and the society that engulfs us, whether Akhmatova or Shostakovich, Pasternak or Solzhenitsyn; whether Yeats or Eliot, Lawrence or Evelyn Waugh, Joyce or Connolly. Myself, I have found an answer: withdrawal into solipsism. Contemporary society? – They can get on with it.

John's next letter was from 'Roscarrock Manor Farm, Port Isaac: Look where I am writing from. I return to horrible London on Sunday.' His hosts who ran the place were Cornish, 'but brought up by the Revd Sabine Gould at Lew Trenchard.' John told them of a paper I had written on Nicholas Roscarrock: had I a copy for them? It was published in a *Festschrift* for G. M. Trevelyan, now out of print.[5] Roscarrock was an Elizabethan Catholic antiquarian who left an immense manuscript Lives of the Saints, into which he had collected information about the Cornish Saints and the old rites and usages. The Cambridge University Library had kindly deposited the vast folio in the Bodleian for me to work at, conveniently across the street from All Souls.

In capital letters across the top: 'YOUR ANTHOLOGY IS SUPERB [of Cornwall] NEVER CAN BE BETTERED.' It proved a favourite bedside book of John Sparrow at All Souls, since it had not been written by me, merely compiled. Oddly enough, it gave me a great deal of trouble. I had thought of it nearly forty years before, and wrote to Q. suggesting that he do it. He passed the buck back, and suggested that I do it. For years I simply couldn't; in the end I discovered that the only way to do it was to think out a logical scheme, partly by subject and time, and partly geographical by place, working naturally from east to west, as one would exploring Cornwall.

John sometimes took the trouble to write me by airmail to America. In 1968 he was writing from his hide-out in the City – a very open one, though I never visited him there – 43 Cloth Fair, E.C.1. 'My sec. has flu. Penelope is in New York and hating it.' She loved India, where her father had been Commander-in-Chief – and what a marvellous job the British did for India, and how many of them were in love with it! Kipling is a far better guide than E. M. Forster, as Indians know – Left intellectuals, as usual, not.

'I am well and thankful not to be P.L. [Poet Laureate], and

[5] *Studies in Social History*. Edited by J. H. Plumb.

writing hymns à la D-Day Lewis, as Osbert Lancaster calls
him.' Perhaps it was his Leftist sympathies of the Thirties,
expressed in demotic adjurations, that promoted him. It is fair
to say that his later poetry is better than his poems of the
Thirties. The letter is mostly concerned with some question of
conservation at St Austell, which I had raised, I forget what –
some piece of destruction. John had now become a public
figure, when I had ceased to be one, since I dropped my long
and excruciating candidature for Penryn and Falmouth. (After
a decade of hard work, it went Labour in 1945 – an almighty
deliverance that I was out of it: I should have been killed by it.)
Television made John a public man, and nobly he took up
causes of preservation, continually trying to save relics of
better days from destruction – and how hard he worked at it!
He should have been made an earl for his pains. He couldn't
pronounce 'without going down to the site – of course I agree
with you about it – which I am proposing to do in mid-Feb.' I
was chagrined by what the County Council was doing at his
Wadebridge: destroying the finest medieval bridge, fifteen
arches, in the West Country and building a new one. They
might have kept the fine old one for one-way traffic, and built
a new one for the other way. But I had given up hope, John
not, more credit to him. 'What about the pollution of river and
sea by the China Clay Co.? I feel for Sir John Tremayne.' As I
said, he won, with the agreement of the excellent Company.
Oddly enough, sometimes the right course even prevails – but
I no longer care; I grieve privately, not publicly; I live in the
Elizabethan Age, not this. John concludes, 'Oh it's a joy to
hear from you and to know that you are back with the
Elizabethans.'

I next sent him, for his interest in Ireland, my abridged
version of Froude's remarkable novel, *The Two Chiefs of
Dunboy*. Froude was an historian of genius, who fell into no
conventional categories and so has been overlooked, when
people have gone on and on writing about Macaulay and
Carlyle. Froude was a better stylist than either – he got that
from Newman – where I find Carlyle's intolerable. He is the
last great Victorian awaiting revival, when so many inferior
to him have been regurgitated. As a young Fellow of All
Souls I hoped to produce a Life and Letters of Froude follow-

ing in the wake of G. O. Trevelyan's Life and Letters of Macaulay, a delightful book. I was frustrated – a curious story.[6] Nor did my more readable version of Froude's novel – the original was too long and discursive – have the least effect in reviving him. (How unimaginative can you be?) 'I've asked Batsford to send you a bit of bookmaking of mine, of old photographs of London, a poor return for your kindness.'

During my absence in America I had been taken advantage of and framed as Patron of the Appeal to finish the spire and furnish the bells for Charlestown Church, where my poor parents were married way back in the early 1890s. Folklore said that the Victorian vicar had drunk up the funds – and certainly when he died a large consignment of bottles surfaced from the vicarage. 'Penelope is in India. Wantage is let to Americans. My house here [Cloth Fair] is to be pulled down and rebuilt next summer. I am in a bad way financially, so all I have been able to do is to order from Jock Murray two copies of Summoned by Bells [he had told me that he was coming down to Trebetherick for peace and quiet to concentrate on it], which I'll inscribe especially for the Appeal and send to the Honorary Treasurer, so that he may be able to get rid of them at some sale. I think it is marvellous of you to give a thousand pounds to the Bells, and I pray that before you die they will be ringing across the water to Trenarren.'

Thereupon Noël Coward wrote me fan-mail to say how much he admired A Cornish Childhood, and that it brought back vividly the summer holidays he used to spend as a boy at Charlestown. I took my opportunity to tell him that he could then give a bell – I was giving three. He sent me £350 for one by return of post, generous fellow. So we called the top bell Noel, for he was born in Christmas week; when he died, the ringers rang a muffled peal for him out to sea. They make a beautiful light peal of six, but, alas, I cannot hear them from Trenarren: perhaps they will ring a muffled peal for me out across the bay.

In December 1971, 'I've just come back from Australia,

---

[6] I have told it in my Introduction to the novel.

where Cornwall meets one at every turn in place names[7] and in mining, and it is lovely to find all this about Trecarrel. How beautifully your Commemoration address is worded. How sad its concluding paragraphs. I have just heard from Arthur Bryant that he is willing to come to St Albans for some discussion you and he and and I are to have there. . . . I shall be delighted to do so. It will be a meeting of old friends. I am now dotty about Australia and now find the green of England rather strident and vulgar after all those glorious olive silvery light-fretting gum trees and those huge skies and suns on copper-coloured earth. Penelope is back from Injer and I may see her tonight. I am glad we are all still alive.'

We three duly turned up for our goggling turn for the St Albans Festival. We were tied up and gagged for recording in huge black dentists' chairs, blinded by fierce TV lights, to face a vast dark pit where one could see nothing. For once I felt distinctly nervous; John was completely at home with this sort of thing, and I felt relieved when he led off with a piece about St Albans. He had done his homework and broken the ice: that was the way to do it, I registered, impressed. After that he had little to contribute and left the running to Arthur, suave and smooth, and me. One ass there regarded my forthrightness as 'controversial', the usual conventional cliché nowadays; but that it was appreciated by the audience – as it always is – is clear from the fact that I was the one invited for the next year and again a third. Never pay any attention to what the critics say! In this a contrast with John, a gentle, sweet nature, a prey to constant depression; criticism wounded him and got him down, made him grieve and undermined his confidence. Not so this Cornishman: fortified by contempt, I get stimulated

---

[7] For years I had been trying to incite Australian professors to follow up my *The Cornish in America*, with which I had blazed the trail for the remarkable story of the Cornish in Australia. For all that it made a significant subject, with plenty of research material, for a book – where there can not be very much – I could not get any of them to move. People are so slow in the uptake. At last, a couple of decades later – with a pure Cornishman, Bob Hawke, as Prime Minister – they are beginning to wake up and take notice. There should be similar studies of the Cornish in New Zealand, South Africa and Canada – so far no response, as usual – to complete the picture; for most of the Cornish people are overseas.

and take the offensive. My substitute for drink?

'Monday after Trinity Sunday [which I always keep: St Austell parish feast], Hill Farm, Oaksey, Malmesbury: Penelope and I are staying here with the famous jockey John Lawrence, now Lord Oaksey, and coming through in the train I saw "lanterned Uffington" – exactly the right adjective for the tower and the position of the village below the White Horse. I had not realised how very good a topographical poet you are, not just of Cornwall – where you are unbeatable, and all the Cornish ones in this book are the best you have done. But I also can appreciate the American ones without having been to the places you describe. Tell the Warden to read "Ardevora Veor" and "Distant Surf".' I did not waste time doing so: precious little appreciation of my poetry in that academic quarter.

'I absolutely understand about an unbelieving "Anglo-Catholic". So am I. I *hope*, that is all. Faith, Hope and Charity – and the greatest of these is Hope.' There is a difference between the two old friends: I am without hope, I despair. 'Thank you and Thank you for *Strange Encounter*. Let us have another.'

Ambassador Walter Annenberg inspired a grand *livre-de-luxe* about Westminster Abbey, and public-spiritedly financed it. Architecture, monuments, works of art all specially photographed; sculpture, frescoes, mosaics written up by experts; Prologue by John, Epilogue by Kenneth Clark; the main body of the book, the story of the Abbey, I was called on to do. Once more John wrote with enthusiasm: 'I always knew you were a great historian, but your essay on Westminster Abbey is SUPERB – Learning so lightly worn – Every period alive – Such insight – such humour – such *poetry*. I am proud to be near you in that funny, American-inspired book. I had thought there were enough books on the Abbey what with Dean Stanley's, but your essay adds a new dimension and inspired your old chum. . . . Once more thanks and thanks and thanks for your genius.'

Why quote these tributes to one's work all through a hard-working life, starting with nothing? After all, John did not need to write a fellow-contributor at all, unless he felt an urge to do so. I quote them, from a fellow man of genius, to teach the unimaginative, the mean and ungenerous, a lesson. After all, if they are not told, how can they tell?

Next year, 1973, 'Batsford's and I have made a selection of old photographs of Cornwall, trying to cover all aspects of life in the Duchy. We *may* have failed. I feel sure that something important has been left out. You will know.' So John wanted me to come in on this, as his knowledge of Cornwall, considerable as it was, was mainly North Coast and there are at least – people may not realise – half-a-dozen different landscapes in the small but elongated county (not Duchy, by the way: that is something different). Thus came about the illustrated book, *Victorian and Edwardian Cornwall*, which goes on selling through the magic of the Betjeman name.

We have had Daphne du Maurier's *Vanishing Cornwall*, Winston Graham's *Poldark's Cornwall*, and eventually *Betjeman's Cornwall* – none of them Cornish, all of them having adopted Cornwall. I am the real thing, 100 per cent Cornish: when is someone going to see that a 'Rowse's Cornwall' would be a rather different matter – history, antiquities, villages, crevices, holes and corners, relics, what is beneath: the *real* Cornwall?

Next, generous as ever, a word from Tonbridge. 'Staying here with the very rich and well-appointed – with the garden of England all round changing to deep blues in the gloaming, gratitude rises in my breast. Chiefly it rises to you for your really doing the CORNWALL book and giving me the credit. I wish they hadn't said I was a Cornishman in the blurb. I am and always have been a furiner. But I am proud to be linked with you.' The selection of photographs was entirely John's, but I rather think that I did all the letter-press.

There follows another tribute, largely illegible and unidentifiable, to a poem about a character who 'grasped once in his full cruelty is TERRIFIC. Who was he? I know what he was like and have met such. But I don't know this one's name. I loved Encaenia but missed C. S. Lewis. Ta ever so and love yours Jan Trebetj', accompanied by a drawing of the shield with fifteen bezants, derived from the arms of Richard, Earl of Cornwall and King of the Romans. (He thought to buy the crown of the Empire with the wealth extracted from poor little Cornwall, an exploited people: hence Cornish Nationalism, a forlorn cause.)

Encaenia is the honorary-degree ceremony at Oxford, when All Souls gives a grand luncheon in the Codrington Library – all the College plate out, flowers, scarlet gowns, ladies in their best: a splendid scene. John, now a famous public figure, had been awarded a D.Litt.: there he was in all his glory, spruced-up and arrayed in scarlet, the old look of nervous anxiety gone from the bland, clerical features, beaming on us all. He said to me that he had seen the heavens open and C. S. Lewis, his old tutor whom he could not abide, looking down: it must have been a shock for Clive Staples, undoubtedly in Heaven.

Maytime 1975: 'When I got back here from Cornwall I found your magnificent book on Oxford. It could not be better for balance and wise selection of pictures. All my favourite things are in it and all my unfavourite are not in it. You are quite right about your poetry being overlooked. I am going to take your *Poems of Cornwall and America* to Derbyshire tomorrow [i.e. with Elizabeth Cavendish to Chatsworth], and to Penelope in the Black Mountains, when I'm back from Canada. Poetry reads differently in different places. Really it's best where it was born; but Wordsworth brings the Lakes to us and I am certain you are going to bring Cornwall to Derby and Hereford. There are no things more enjoyable than discovering a good poet in an old friend. I thought that the American poems in the book you gave me in Cornwall deliciously effective and depressing' (in some of them I cast a cold eye upon demotic civilisation).

A pretty coloured photograph shows little St Enodoc church in its hollow, bent spire, churchyard with graves, blue Daymer Bay and Stepper Point beyond. 'Expect *Summoned by Bells*, a Cockney Childhood, next week. I *loved* the poem, particularly the 6th verse. Would I were worthier.' This was the poem 'Easter at St Enodoc', with its little tribute:

> Up the lane the poet lives,
> Flowering currant at his door:
> Inspiration receives, and gives,
> From hill and valley, stream and shore.

That spring, 1975, 'I much like the idea of seeing you, even if it has to be the BBC.' We did a joint reading of poems, mainly Cornish, from Plymouth. 'I like your poems. I like Charles Causley's and him and Ted Hughes's and him. Poets are more than pen counters (?). Poor Griggers. Not good enough, but he does know about good and bad.' (Not always: he could not recognise that John and Dylan Thomas and Edith Sitwell were good poets, himself not so good. Nor can one stand the parsonic didacticism.) 'Penelope's garden in the Black Mountains is full of hippies under canvas. She is their Queen and loves them.'

After the recording, 'I thought your poems came over splendidly the night before last. Beautiful, haunting, and very Cornish. Elizabeth Cavendish and I are here [Trebetherick] till Tuesday week. Give us a "tingle" (Australian for "tinkle") if you are free to come over. You are wisely not in the directory, but then nor is your devoted old fellow poet.' Not content, he followed this up with another St Enodoc post card: 'And, of course, "Distant Surf" is *a great poem*.' It is a sad, nostalgic, but authentic one – unlike most contemporary verse, simply not authentic.

Next year, 'My sight gets worse and worse. I think that Patrick Garland, who did the Kilvert programme, would make a lovely Hawker programme with you.' (Parson Hawker of Morwenstow's centenary was coming up.) 'In fact he ought to make several programmes with you. He is a brilliant producer. Literate and loving his subjects . . . He did that production of Aubrey's *Brief Lives* in London some years ago. His father was sent by my father to Paris with me to teach me about sex with ladies, but it failed because I fell ill.' (Not only, I should say.) Nothing came of the programmes either. Marooned on my headland in Cornwall I had never heard of the great BBC producer. As another TV star, A. J. P. Taylor, says of his experience, you need to be 'in' with these people, and I lacked the Public School technique of 'sucking up'. So I turned my back to them and my face to America – more responsive in every way.

There followed a series of John's coloured Underground post cards, his writing hardly legible. There was Elizabeth now to help with his typing – and what a chore: TV had made him so popular that he would get some thirty letters a day. I wouldn't answer them, sheer waste of time, but I suppose a public figure has to. A typed p.c. says, 'Would you be free to have Evelyn Duchess's grand-daughter and the adventurer to luncheon at Trenarren? . . . It would be lovely to see you and have a laugh.' Elizabeth's grandmother, whom I knew as Dowager Duchess of Devonshire, had been a good friend to me: had me to stay several summers at historic Hardwick, most exciting of Elizabethan houses, got over original mss from Chatsworth, for me to work on, of Bess of Hardwick, a comparably formidable personality, her predecessor.[9]

We did have several laughs, exchanging reminders of the Duchess's ducal – or should it be, duquessal – *dicta*: 'I always say, when in doubt plant an avenue', for one. If only one could! We also had some serious talk about poetry. I quoted Paul Valéry's saying that one was *given* a line, and from that one went on – a *donné*: it might be one or two lines, one doesn't know where they come from, from on high or from the depths, rather, of the subconscious. I don't think John read much in any foreign language, and earlier his line was that he hated 'Abroad'. But he agreed: a line or lines came into one's head involuntarily, and 'the rest is hard work', an act of will. Verses can be made by the will, an intellectual process; poetry comes from something deeper, welling up from the depths of one's being. I cannot write a poem unless moved emotionally; I can hardly ever write just verses. Nevil Coghill told me that he had written thousands of lines of verse – his modernisation of Chaucer, for example – but not one line of poetry. John was most excited by this: 'Did he really say that?' I said that John had the right qualification for Poet Laureate in that he could write both poetry *and* verse. He then said the most serious thing he ever said to me, emphasising it quite solemnly: '*I have never compromised.*' The only claim he ever made for himself.

It meant that he had never fallen in with any of the prevailing poetic fashions at any time, Yeats or Eliot in the 1920s, or his contemporaries Auden and the Boys of the Thirties: he simply held on his way, being his own unique and original self, true to his own inspiration and intuition, taking

[9] v. 'Bess of Hardwick' in *Eminent Elizabethans*.

no notice of what anyone else might say. That is the right way. And he certainly reaped his reward: for long a poet of only a few, an esoteric taste, he eventually came across to thousands, the most popular Poet Laureate since Tennyson – though Kipling also was a poet with the widest public.

Tennyson was John's great love. I remember, when first taking part in a broadcast programme with him, being slightly shocked at his not caring for Shakespeare: he had been put off the Elizabethans by C. S. Lewis for good (or bad) and all. When he gave a reading at Port Eliot – the candle-lit house crowded with his fans – he began with a long piece from Tennyson. Eyesight was failing, I had to find the places for him in his own poems; the enthusiasm was no less. John wanted me to read my poems, but I had only the poem I had written for his seventieth birthday with me, 'Marytavy'. Some farming gent came up to compliment me on the clever 'pastiche' of Betjeman he thought it: I am incapable of pastiche, but for once let the well-meaning ass get away with it. We made over £1000 that night for the Cornish Churches Trust.

'The pale but strong white fingers of Elizabeth are typing this because I cannot write legibly. Our journey back after the paradise of Trenarren was another paradise through Rowseland.[10] We came a mysterious way through St Austell and then suddenly on the horizon, like an illustration in a Walter Scott novel, rose Roche Rock. After that the more familiar lanes and shacks to Wadebridge and those thin elms that "tug at the heart" [quoting me]. We read out to each other seven of your poems, the Cornish ones, on our return. They go right home, and you must never lose your poetic fire. You must be the only historian who has written truly topographical poetry. Macaulay's is geographical, but not such haunting poetry. Hawker may have tried history but I don't think of him as an historian.' Nor was he: a good folklorist, rather.

'Elizabeth continues to speak of the wonder of your house and view, and I of that Paul Sandby, the Gainsborough and Tilly Kettle, and poor Elizabeth liked the Kit Wood best of all. Your Piper is one of his best. You buy on eye not names; so does your grateful old friend, Jan Trebetjeman, pp Passmore

---

[10] Pun on Roseland, of course.

Edwards. P.S. Tregonetha is a dream village on our route.'

Passmore Edwards was a Victorian-Edwardian philanthropist who gave libraries to Cornwall early this century. Tregonetha is indeed a queer, haunted place: a tiny ring of tumbledown, derelict cottages round a green, one little Bible Christian chapel, the road virtually shouldering its way between two houses. Atmosphere of the last century, sad and forgotten.

In *Blackwood's* 1978 I wrote an essay about John's poetry, about which he wrote to the editor: 'I am delighted with the trouble dear Leslie Rowse has taken over it, and the discernment it shows. . . . I was glad to see *Blackwood's* keeps its tidy and traditional typography: just as I remember it from when my father subscribed to it.' Of course, this historic literary journal, going right back to the Edinburgh of Sir Walter Scott and all the famous contributors throughout the nineteenth century, has had to close down.

To me John wrote: 'I cannot thank you enough . . . It makes me feel less of a fraud than usual, and quite encouraged to try and write about my Irish friend, the least known peer in the world, Lord Clonmore (Wicklow) who has just died. Kindly keep alive yourself.' Billy Clonmore was one of the Bright Boys of the Twenties at Oxford, whom one reads about now in Evelyn Waugh's Diaries and Letters, and in John's poems: Basil Dufferin and Ava (killed in Burma), Patrick Balfour, later Lord Kinross, Hugh Lygon (of *Brideshead Revisited*), Robert Byron (drowned in the Mediterranean); members of the Bullingdon set, regulars of the George, Fothergill dinners at the Spread Eagle out at Thame. What a time they had while the going was good!

March 1978: 'I re-read your poems all yesterday.' Then, 'I am fascinated by the autobiographical honesty of your poems and the love of landscape they display.' Well, my poetry contains all my inner life and secrets, where the prose books, history, literature, politics, deal mainly, not wholly, with the outer. 'And now I must top writing to you, and write about them for *Books and Bookmen*.' Another Underground post card followed: 'When I saw it in *B. and B.* I thought it too short and not generous enough. I should have added "all your Cornish poems" should be put into one book, and a record made of you reading your favourites of them.' This has yet to occur to someone!

'I was much intrigued by John Edwards. I suppose he is the — Edwards of Colvin's *Biographical Dictionary of English Architects*.' I couldn't find out anything about him, and I don't think John knew either. But he was the builder of one of the most beautiful late Georgian houses in Cornwall – Carclew, consumed by fire in the 1930s, and the grander mansion of the Bassets – Tehidy, burned down in the 1920s. Two casualties of the hideous, destructive age we live in.

In August, 'I am so pleased to have "Withiel Church". I suppose the Rector must be the grandfather of Nancy Trethewey, a real breath of the Twenties and the toast of the Bodmin tennis tournament when I was a boy. Of course Withiel and its rectory were the remotest Cornwall I ever found in my bicycling days, and that lichen-crusted area of steep hills and little farms and deep woods seemed full of witches. I wonder why Griggers can't do it. He has the feelings and the eye, but something gets in between.' It is easy to see what – self-consciousness and didacticism. 'I am off to Derbyshire, the home of witches and Keltic survival. I have left you a shell-model of St Mary's, Penzance, in my will, if you survive me – which I hope you do.'

February next year: 'It was very nice seeing you in that Wren church by Bodley yesterday. It was good of you to talk to me as I was wearing the wrong tie, which Frank Pakenham noticed – I could feel it – but his wife kindly ignored. Frank is no longer red. The craze among vicars for pulling down screens is all part of the kitchen table which is being substituted for the altar, and making things simple for the kiddiz, which is getting rid of mystery. It is Pevsnerism as opposed to Tractarian. It is out of date, which the C. of E. is so afraid of becoming. . . . Pray God for a bit of mystery. It was kind of Bodley to have left that City church for us to eat in. . . . Penelope is in India conducting a cruise. I am in Chelsea misconducting myself, or would that I were.'

On a visit to lecture in Dorset I entered a church with a very fine tower, and noticed a decorative chancel screen, late Victorian and of considerable beauty, flowing lines and tracery. Thereupon I learned that an ignorant and tasteless vicar was intending to remove it to the back of the church to make way for a nave altar. Actually it would make a very good background for his nave altar; all he need do would be to remove the front pew to make room for it. So I wrote to the Bishop, who proved to be more interested in ski-ing. I alerted John, who forwarded my protest to the Council for the Places of Worship. 'Pevsner of course does not mention the screen, which means that it must look very well as he has no eye or feeling for mystery. As there is glass by Kempe in the church, the screen is possibly Bodley. How good it would be if you went into this matter.'

How good it was of John to take it up – he had scores of calls like this on his time, in the never-ending struggle to prevent clerics and vandals from destroying things of beauty. He was a public figure, and never spared himself in what he regarded as a duty. I do not know what transpired. I gathered the advisory committee on churches in that diocese was neither well informed nor instructed. A scholarly cleric of the older generation tells me that the younger have little knowledge of or interest in architecture or history. I'll bet that, if I go back to that church, I shall find that fine screen shoved away at the back where it can't be seen, or possibly got rid of altogether.

A letter, of September 1980 from Derbyshire, reads, 'A lovely poem on Endellion. We must save it from being amalgamated with Port Isaac. It is a holy kingdom on its hilltop. Your *Road to Oxford* poems are a constant pleasure to me – so are your vigour and Cornishness.' A last letter to me commented on the final poem in my *A Life: Collected Poems,* 'Intimations of Mortality'. This poem summed up my own belief with which I had lived my life: from one moment of vision to another, holding on to a secret trail from a source unknown, whatever it may mean:

> What to make of it? I cannot say.
> Here and now we cannot know. I know
> Only that these moments have sustained me,
> Given food to the spirit, nourished mind
> And imagination in the forlorn spaces,
> Shafts of light into the heart of things
> Though the mystery remain immutable.

John wrote back that he had often felt just that.

Providentially he died at his beloved Trebetherick, when they
were thinking of taking him back in an ambulance to London.
He was buried in the churchyard of his poem, 'Sunday
Afternoon Service in St Enodoc Church, Cornwall', on a day
of raging Atlantic rain and wind. The parson said that the
huddled figures crossing the sand-dunes looked like a lot of
Cornish wreckers coming up with their findings.

On a Sunday afternoon not long after I went to visit his
grave: a day that somehow seemed more in keeping. Sun-
drenched dunes, people picnicking, figures further off on the
sands, boats bobbing white on the blue of Daymer Bay, the
loved vision of Stepper Point across the estuary opening out to
sea. There was the little bent spire, the church itself hidden,
crouching in the hollow sheltered by Bray Hill. As I went
down the slope, keeping the grey spire in view, phrases from
the poem floated hazily in mind:

> Sand in the sandwiches, wasps in the tea,
> Sun on our bathing dresses heavy with the wet . . .
> Blessèd be St Enodoc . . .
> Blessèd be the springy turf, we pray, pray to thee . . .

In at the gate, the enclosure surrounded by tamarisks, the
newly made grave dug out of sand and rock on the right,
flowers wilting in the hot sun, a plain wooden cross: JOHN
BETJEMAN. Across the path to the church-porch, on the
western verge of the little place is his mother, not far off. Into
the church, Sunday afternoon service just over, there on the
right is the Cornish slate tablet to his father, beneath which
John sat or knelt in church: 'Ernest Edward Betjemann of
Underdown in this parish.' There is the ambivalence: the two
German nns, one of which the family dropped when the father
died.

From what curious ancestry did John come, where on earth
did his spirit come from? I think in the end of the image from
the early Anglo-Saxon poem, of the bird flying from the dark
into the lighted hall and out again into the night.

Biographical Notes

Astor, Nancy, Viscountess (1879–1964). American by birth, she was the first woman MP to take her seat in the House of Commons. She was MP for Plymouth (Sutton Division) 1919–45.

Attlee, Clement Richard, 1st Earl (1883–1967) was educated at Haileybury and University College, Oxford. He was called to the Bar in 1906; Secretary of Toynbee Hall 1910. Lecturer at the London School of Economics 1913–23. He served throughout the war 1914–19. He was Mayor, 1919, 1920 and MP for Stepney 1922–50. Deputy prime minister in Churchill's war-time government and Labour prime minister 1945–51. His publications include *The Labour Party in Perspective* (1937), *The Labour Party and Twelve Years Later* (1948), *Purpose and Policy*, *As It Happened* (1954) and *Empire into Commonwealth*.

Auden, Wystan Hugh (1907–73) was educated in Birmingham, at Gresham's School and Christ Church, Oxford. His first collection of poems was published in 1930 and many other collections followed. He was Professor of Poetry at Oxford 1956–61.

Bevin, Ernest (1881–1951) was born in Somerset, and was largely self-educated. He was Assistant General Secretary of the Dockers' Union; General Secretary of the Transport and General Workers' Union 1921–40; member of the General

Council of Trades Union Congress 1925–40; MP for Central
Wandsworth 1940–50 and for East Woolwich 1950–51;
Minister of Labour and National Service 1940–45; Secretary of
State for Foreign Affairs 1945–51.

Beaverbrook, William Maxwell Aitken, 1st Baron
(1879–1964) was born in Canada and educated at Newcastle,
New Brunswick. He made his fortune as a promoter and came
to England in 1910 for a political career. He became better
known as a newspaper proprietor; in 1916 he bought the *Daily
Express*, launched the *Sunday Express* and in 1923 gained control
of the *Evening Standard*.

Betjeman, Sir John (1906–84) was educated at Marlborough
and Magdalen College, Oxford. His publications include
Collected Poems (1958, expanded 1962) and his autobiography,
Summoned by Bells. He was appointed Poet Laureate in 1972.

Bibesco, Marthe, Princess (1888–1973). Of French and
Romanian parentage, author of many books, Member of the
Belgian Royal Academy.

Bowen, Elizabeth (1899–1973). An Anglio-Irish novelist and
short story writer. Her works include *The Last September*
(1929), *The House of Paris* (1935), *The Death of the Heart* (1938),
The Heat of the Day (1949), and an autobiographical account of
her home in Ireland, *Bowen's Court*.

Buchan, John, 1st Baron Tweedsmuir (1875–1940) was
educated in Glasgow and at Brasenose College, Oxford. He
combined a literary career with public life and was Governor
General of Canada 1935–40. He wrote lives of Montrose (1913)
and Scott (1932); his novels include *The Thirty-nine Steps*
(1915), *Greenmantle* (1916), *Mr Standfast* (1918), and *Sick Heart
River*. He wrote an autobiography, *Memory Hold the Door*.

Christie, Dame Agatha (1890–1976) was born at Torquay and
educated at home. *The Mysterious Affair at Styles* (1920) was the

first of her sixty-six detective novels. Not merely a thriller writer, she was a good novelist and playwright. She wrote also *An Autobiography*.

Churchill, Sir Winston Leonard Spencer (1874–1965) was born at Blenheim Palace, and educated at Harrow and Sandhurst. He was commissioned in 1895 and became a war correspondent before beginning his political career. He entered parliament in 1900, and held many Cabinet posts, but was out of office 1929–39. He became prime minister 1940–45 and 1951–5. He was awarded the Nobel Prize in 1953. His publications include: *The Life and Times of John Churchill, Duke of Marlborough* (four vols.), *The World Crisis* (four vols. 1923–9), *My Early Life* (1930), *The Second World War* (six vols. 1948–54) and *A History of the English-speaking Peoples* (four vols. 1956–8).

Connolly, Cyril Vernon (1903–74) was educated at Eton and Balliol College, Oxford. Essayist and critic, his publications include *Enemies of Promise* (1938) and *The Unquiet Grave* (1944).

Curtis, Lionel (1872–1955) was educated at Haileybury and New College, Oxford; he became a fellow of All Souls College, Oxford in 1921. He had a great influence on the creation of the Union of South Africa, the progress of India towards self-government and the Irish Treaty of 1922, as well as the founding of the Oxford Society and the Oxford Preservation Trust. His publications include *Civitas Dei* (Vol. 1 1934, Vols. 2 and 3 1937).

Keynes, John Maynard, 1st Baron (1883–1946) was educated at Eton and King's College, Cambridge. Economist and publicist, he first became famous with *The Economic Consequences of the Peace* (1919). He also wrote *The General Theory of Employment, Interest and Money* (1936) and *Treatise on Money* (1930). He founded the Arts Theatre, Cambridge and was first chairman of the Arts Council of Great Britain.

Lewis, Clive Staples (1898–1963), of Welsh and Ulster parentage, was educated privately and at University College, Oxford. He was fellow of Magdalen College, Oxford 1925–54 and Professor of Medieval and Renaissance English at Cambridge 1954–66. His works include: *The Allegory of Love* (1936) and *English Literature in the Sixteenth Century* (1954); religious writings: *The Problem of Pain* (1940) and *The Screwtape Letters* (1940); also *Out of the Silent Planet* (1938), *Surprised by Joy* (1955), and for children *The Lion, The Witch and The Wardrobe* (1950).

Maurois, André (1885–1967) was educated at the Lycée de Rouen and became a Member of the French Academy. Author of many novels, he also wrote important biographies of Victor Hugo, George Sand, Dumas and Proust.

Morison, Samuel Eliot (1887–1976) was born in Boston, Massachusetts and educated at Harvard University, where he was Professor of History 1925–55. He was the first Professor of American History at Oxford. His many publications include *History of US Naval Operations in World War II* (15 vols. 1947–62), *Oxford History of the United States* (1927), *Oxford History of the American People* (1965), biographies of Otis and Columbus and the autobiographical *One Boy's Boston* and *Mount Desert*.

Russell, Bertrand, 3rd Earl (1872–1970) was educated privately and at Trinity College, Cambridge, of which he became a Fellow. He wrote voluminously on philosophy, logic, education, economics and politics. He was awarded a Nobel Prize in 1950. His publications include: *Principles of Mathematics* (1903), *Principia Mathematica* (1910) (with A. N. Whitehead), *The Analysis of Mind* (1921), *An Inquiry into the Meaning and Truth* (1940), *Human Knowledge, Its Scope and Limits* (1948), and an autobiography in three vols.

Trevelyan, George Macaulay (1876–1962) was educated at Harrow and Trinity College, Cambridge. He became Regius

Professor of Modern History at Cambridge in 1929 and Master of Trinity College in 1940. His many publications include *English Social History* (1944), *The History of England*, a quartet on Garibaldi and Italy, and *England under Queen Anne*, (three vols.).

Waugh, Evelyn Arthur St John (1903–66) was educated at Lancing and Hertford College, Oxford. After a spell as a schoolmaster he pursued a career as a journalist and writer. His novels include *Decline and Fall* (1928), *Vile Bodies* (1930), *Black Mischief* (1932), *A Handful of Dust* (1934), *Scoop* (1938), *Put Out More Flags* (1942), *Men at Arms* (1932), *Brideshead Revisited* (1945), *Officers and Gentlemen* (1955), and *Unconditional Surrender* (1961).

Wells, Herbert George (1866–1946) was educated in Bromley, Kent, and at the Royal College of Science. His publications include *The Time Machine* (1895), *The Invisible Man* (1891) and *The War of the Worlds* (1898). He wrote both novels of social comedy and science fiction, prolifically; also an *Outline of History*, and the autobiographical *World of William Clissold* (three vols.).

West, Dame Rebecca (1892–1983) was born Cecily Isabel Fairfield. She was educated at Edinburgh and became a journalist and publicist. Her novels include *The Return of the Soldier* (1918), *The Judge* (1922), *The Strange Necessity* (1928), *Harriet Hume* (1929), *The Thinking Reed* (1936), *The Fountain Overflows* (1956) and *The Birds Fall Down* (1966). She wrote also critical works, and on public affairs.

Wilson, Edmund (1895–1972) was born in New Jersey and educated at Princeton. He was a critic and author of *Axel's Castle* (1931), *The Triple Thinkers* (1938), *The Wound and the Bow* (1941), *To the Finland Station* (1940), *The Shores of Light* (1952) and *The Dead Sea Scrolls* (1955).

THE QUIET PINT

Drew Dunford

Josephine Dempster

THE QUIET PINT

A GUIDE TO PUBS WITH NO PIPED MUSIC

Fifth Edition
Compiled and edited by
DEREK and JOSEPHINE DEMPSTER

AURUM PRESS

This edition first published 2002 by Aurum Press Ltd
25 Bedford Avenue, London WC1B 3AT

Cover painting: Original pen and ink wash by Alan Palmer
Cover design by Don Macpherson

A catalogue record for this book is available from the British Library.

ISBN 1 85410 835 2

10 9 8 7 6 5 4 3 2 1
2006 2005 2004 2003 2002

Designed by Don Macpherson
Typeset by M Rules
Printed and bound by Bookmarque Ltd, Croydon

Contents

N.B. A 'Q' symbol on the maps means Quiet pubs – fully described in the relevant
county sections. 'B' stands for Best of the Rest: worthwhile, sometimes outstanding
pubs with very quiet music (not pop), of which there are brief descriptions at the end
of each county section. 'W' shows the location of Wetherspoon pubs – some fully
described within the county chapters; the rest listed in the J.D. Wetherspoon section
at the back of the book.

Foreword by Rowan Pelling

Editor of *The Erotic Review*

I like to say that I was born and bred in a pub. The actual facts do not quite bear this out – I was born in Sevenoaks Hospital and bred in Ghana – but the spirit of the statement is true. My parents took up the tenancy of the Fox & Hounds in the beautiful Kent hamlet of Toys Hill in 1968, shortly after their return from the Gold Coast. I was born in the January of that year. Of the five Pelling siblings, I am the one who can exactly measure her life against the number of times 'Last orders' has been called – scratch the surface of my editor persona and you will quickly find the barmaid. I even took my first steps behind the bar, tottering over to the beer trays. From that day to this, my parents' inn has barely changed. The sofas and armchairs that have distinguished their reign are still in situ, *Country Life* and *Private Eye* can be found on the counter, and the animated buzz of chatter fills the bar. The only dramatic innovations have been the addition of *Hello!* magazine to the other periodicals and the repositioning of the gents' lavatory (something still regretted by spartan types).

My sympathy for the traditional pub lifestyle is therefore absolute, and my rage against the new order – the theme bars with cheap Sauvignon, ten lagers, blaring music and vomiting clientele – knows no bounds. I grew up with the idea that a pub is somewhere you go to combine two exquisite pleasures: conversation and drinking. And as the drinking continues, the conversation becomes ever more philosophical. War and peace, love and hate – the metaphysical boundaries of these hardy perennials are extended in saloon bars everywhere. I learnt as much about life as I did from books by pressing my ear to the door that divided the pub from the house. The opportunity to eavesdrop was considerable: for my entire school career I did my homework at a desk that was tucked right behind this door. And because there was no piped music, no jukeboxes or fruit machines, I could overhear every last thrilling word of these adult dramas. Even better, when I started pulling pints myself, I was able to contribute my own ill-informed opinions.

It breaks my heart to tell you that the glory days are over. After 34 years behind the bar, my mother called 'Last orders' for the final time last December. (Understandably, she wanted to avoid my father's fate of being carried from the Fox in his coffin, after serving pints well into his 78th year.) Two hundred and sixty people attended her leaving party and there wasn't a dry eye in the house.

As one customer put it, 'We will not see her like again'. Which is true. Who else would be so outraged that a nationwide poll named *The Lord of the Rings* as the book of the millennium that she would set up her own survey in the pub? Who else would take such a robust stance against the evils of mobile phones? A retired headmaster who has driven a round trip of 35 miles at least once a week over the past 34 years, solely to enjoy a quiet pint, summed up the Fox & Hounds as follows: 'the most exclusive of clubs, with no membership fee and anyone who wanted to was free to join and would be made to feel welcome and special'. The value that people of discernment attach to the custodians of decent beer and conversation is beyond measure. We can only hope that the Fox & Hounds' new licensee steps into my mother's size-eight Clarks flatties. Only one way to find out, of course: by checking the next edition of this excellent guide.

Introduction

You'll find some changes in this edition of *The Quiet Pint*. The maps have been reworked to be more attractive and informative; they now show the topography of Britain's counties so that you can see the ups and downs of the land around the pubs you're calling on; the Wetherspoon list continues to grow, in keeping with Wetherspoon's aim to have a pub in every town; and we have introduced a new category of pub.

Our new category comes under the heading 'Best of the Rest'. These pubs come highly recommended, but they have been segregated and described only briefly because they do play music. However good they are, if they play pop or any other music that calls for eardrum protection they are out of the main listings. Very soft – you can hardly hear it – background music, mostly classical, is the norm. Of course, you're entitled to clench your fists and cry 'Heresy!' But please hear me out. We have good reason for allowing them a place in this book.

Pubs are closing down all over the country at an alarming rate. We have lost a considerable number from the last edition. Those that have not closed but are no longer in the book have usually been taken over by managers brought up surrounded by the loud, constant beat of muzak – mainly pop. They are inured to the sound and feel deprived if it's not blaring out – even if they're not listening to it, which most admit they don't, excusing it with the explanation: 'The customers like it.' If you're travelling around, though, there is nothing more depressing than finding lovely-looking and alluring old pubs pumping out the pop charts' latest hits. So we thought there should be more choice for our readers. The Best of the Rest category lists pubs that are as good as you are going to get anywhere, but with the addition of a little light music.

Several counties are seriously deprived of piped-music-free pubs. Some have always been deficient. Surprisingly, for example, Hertfordshire, Berkshire, Surrey and Bedfordshire are among them. If you know better, we'd like to hear from you.

Food in pubs does seem to have taken a great leap forward, although there are still a vast number of landlords who take the easy way out. When you see a long menu you know the catering has been done elsewhere. You are going to get bought-in frozen meals that find their way to your table via a microwave. Even though some menus look interesting, you know the landlord wouldn't in a million years have introduced deep-fried Brie, or duck breast on a plum compôte in a port-wine jus, not to mention wild mushrooms or Parmesan flakes. Next time you see a whole lemon sole with a choice of sauces listed on a pub menu, send it back to the kitchen for it to be taken off the bone – you'll soon find out whether there is anyone there who knows what they're doing with the ingredients. Sometimes I'm reminded of a notice I once saw years ago on the window of a Wimpy Bar opposite London's Olympia Exhibition Hall: 'Wanted: Chef – no experience necessary'. Having said that, the volume caterers do us a sort of favour by giving the customer a greater choice in a pub that might be located in the prettiest, most appealing place but has a staff that wouldn't normally know their Caesar salad from their gravadlax, although both could well be on the menu.

Naturally, there are horses for courses. We have tried to give you all the information you could possibly need. Many pubs serve the most delicious food, have well-compiled, reasonably priced wine lists, the beers are excellent, and all in all they are wonderful places to be. Some are bloke-ish, serving just beer and maybe a sandwich; some only serve beer; some are just totally eccentric. In some places you can find a welcome even with muddy boots and an equally muddy dog; others have moorings for your boat; one has a bookie's office in the car park; another has somewhere to park your helicopter. Whatever you are looking for, we know there will be a pub to suit you.

We receive dozens of testimonials, typical among them being: 'Your book has become our bible.' What we tell you about our pubs originates from personal observations, recommendations and contact with the licensees themselves. We have a loyal touring band of Pipedown Campaign members who keep us as up to date as possible – and on matters well beyond the presence of piped music. Their reports have usefully exposed fabulists keen on maintaining their listings in *The Quiet Pint* when, quite clearly, they cease to qualify the moment our backs are turned. The reports of many independent readers have also been incorporated into our descriptive narratives. To all who have taken the trouble to think and do something about adding value to this guide, my grateful thanks.

As I write this at the start of 2002, I would like to blame poor management for the continuing closure of pubs throughout the land – some six a week. It's true that you don't have to go far to find a scruffy, unfriendly, unattractive, badly run pub with a surly landlord serving indifferent beer and truly awful food who frankly deserves to go out of business. However, it is encouraging that other, more traditional pubs, which don't deserve to close, are making themselves more appealing to a wide cross-section of the community. They have anticipated Prince Charles's campaign to put the pub back at the centre of a community by becoming a pub, post office and village store rolled into one. Some are included in *The Quiet Pint* and, as we have remarked elsewhere in the book, they have sown the seeds of what we would like to think will become a popular excuse for slipping out for a pint: 'I'm just off to buy a stamp!'

However, it is not only to take on the roles of rural post offices and village stores that the country pub is so well suited. As the centre of the community, it is also the centre of local fun – cricket, football, skittles, even *pétanque*. Which takes me back to the first edition of this guide, where we defined our vision of what a pub should be: it is a community centre where people usually go to be sociable. It is a place where patrons need to be mindful of their fellow customers' varying ages, persuasions and tastes. The whole idea of going to a pub is to have a drink, seek company if you are on your own, exchange a few jokes with friends, talk to the bar staff, nurse a depression in a quiet corner if that is how you feel, play darts or shove ha'penny, perhaps eat and generally relax. If there is background music it is bound to irritate if you have not chosen it yourself – for one person's harmony is another person's discord.

Rowan Pelling echoes this philosophy, as you can see from the Foreword she has written for this edition. Perhaps I should say that we echoed her philosophy, because at the time the first edition of *The Quiet Pint* was published in 1995 – before she acquired her fame and we got to know her – she had already grown up at the delightful Fox & Hounds in Toys Hill, Kent, which her parents ran, a stone's throw from Chartwell, Sir Winston Churchill's old home, and thus absorbed the essential ingredients of a good pub.

Derek Dempster

Pipedown: The Campaign for Freedom from Piped Music

by Nigel Rodgers, Honorary Secretary

One of the chief reasons for founding Pipedown almost ten years ago was the increasing difficulty of finding a pub that was *not* filled with blaring, obtrusive piped music. All too often I would enter a decent-looking pub, order a drink and a bite to eat, sit down in what seemed like a quiet corner – only to find a loudspeaker pelting out music non-stop just above my head. This made conversation very difficult and relaxation quite impossible. Oddly, few other drinkers appeared to want the music, but the management insisted they had to have it, making it seem as essential as oxygen to human existence. This was utter nonsense, as survey after survey has since shown that more people hate piped music than love it, but it was the received wisdom of the day.

It was therefore wonderful news when Derek and Josephine Dempster decided to compile the first edition of *The Quiet Pint*. Since then, the guide has grown both bigger and better, filled with information about what sort of place each pub is, what type of food you can expect, whether dogs and children are welcome – even if it has a resident ghost! It makes a very entertaining guide just to leaf through, crammed with historical and architectural details as it is.

Pipedown, the campaign for freedom from piped music (by which we mean any sort of music piped around a place where people go for other purposes than listening to music), fights piped music everywhere. We fight it in pubs, shops, restaurants, hotels, airports, on the beaches even, and especially down the telephone. (I used to love Vivaldi's *Four Seasons* until I had heard it, tinnily mutilated, a thousand times while being kept on hold!) We have a sub-campaign against excessive muzak on television and radio programmes, and we are setting up local groups. Members receive five different types of protest card to hand out or post, stickers, posters, fact sheets, and a quarterly newsletter detailing the fight around the world and listing 'Quiet Corners', which may include anything from a hotel to a ferry company. Recently, a concerted letter-writing campaign has stopped Marks & Spencer from installing piped music throughout its stores, and we are pushing for a bill in Parliament to ban piped music in hospitals.

Membership costs £12 per annum. For more details, please send an SAE to Pipedown, PO Box 1722, Salisbury SP4 7US, or visit our website: www.btinternet.com/pipedown/index

QUIET PINT
Areas

J·D·WETHERSPOON

SCOTLAND

NORTHUMBRIA

CUMBRIA

YORKSHIRE

LANCASHIRE, MANCHESTER & MERSEYSIDE

CHESHIRE

STAFFORDSHIRE & DERBYSHIRE

LEICESTER, LINCOLNSHIRE & NOTTINGHAMSHIRE

NORFOLK

WALES

HEREFORDSHIRE, SHROPSHIRE & WORCESTERSHIRE

MIDLANDS

SUFFOLK

CAMBRIDGESHIRE & BEDFORDSHIRE

GLOUCESTER-SHIRE

OXFORD-SHIRE

WARWICKSHIRE

HERTFORD-SHIRE

ESSEX

BERKSHIRE

LONDON

WILTSHIRE

SURREY

KENT

SOMERSET

HAMPSHIRE

SUSSEX

DEVON

DORSET

CORNWALL

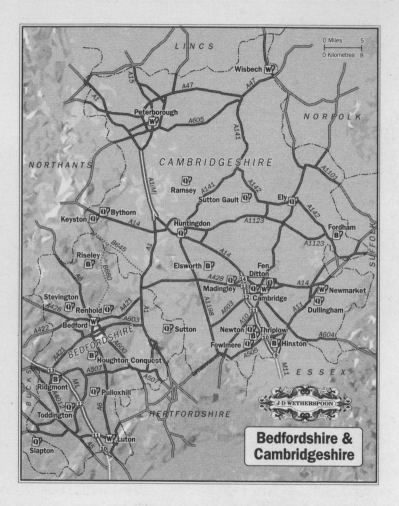

Bedfordshire & Cambridgeshire

Bedfordshire & Cambridgeshire

BYTHORN

White Hart
Tel: 01832 710226

Bythorn, Nr Huntingdon, Cambs PE18 0QN
Free House. Bill & Pam Bennett, licensees.

This 17th-century village inn on the Huntingdon to Thrapston road is more a restaurant than a pub – Bennett's at The White Hart. Still able to have a pint or two though, or a glass of wine to go with your nut or crisp. But when you see what is on the imaginative and popular menu, I'm sure you'll suddenly find an appetite. Food is served in the bar as well as the restaurant and no-smoking dining room: home-made soups, ploughman's, duck-liver terrine, fresh scallops, venison casserole, game in season, loin of pork in orange sauce, steaks and home-made puddings. Big Sunday lunches. Greene King IPA, Abbot ales, Everards Tiger, Guinness and lagers. Wines by the glass. Seats and tables in the garden.

> OPEN: 11–3. 6–11. Closed Sunday eve and all day Monday.
> Real Ale. Restaurant. No-smoking dining room.
> Children welcome. No dogs.
> Occasional Morris dancers.

CAMBRIDGE

Champion of the Thames
Tel: 01223 352043

King Street, Cambridge
Greene King. Nick Elmer, licensee.

Atmospheric, busy and friendly. It has just two bars – one no more than a tiny snug. This town pub fills up quickly with university dons, students, businessmen and anyone else wanting to enjoy a quiet pint. Lunchtime snacks Monday to Friday only: filled rolls, that sort of thing – no hot food. As the landlord says, 'we're a pub, and pubs sell beer', which they do very well. All the beers are from the Greene King range.

> OPEN: 11–11.
> Real Ale.
> No children. Dogs: yes, if the landlord likes the look of you.
> N.B. Lunchtimes are always quiet, but blues tracks are played some evenings.

CAMBRIDGE

Cambridge Blue
Tel: 01223 361382

85–87 Gwydir Street, Cambridge CB1 2LG (side street off Mill Road)
Free House. Chris Lloyd, licensee.

All change in Cambridge. Chris Lloyd has come here from the Free Press to take over the popular Cambridge Blue. Part of a long town terrace, one of the attractions of this late-Victorian pub is its unexpectedly large garden. Inside is a no-smoking, no-mobile-phone area. Rowing memorabilia and other pictures cover the walls; daily papers and local magazines are available to read while you enjoy your drink. Traditional, sustaining food is served in the conservatory: filled ciabatta rolls, sausage and mash with onion gravy, filled baked potatoes, salads and other cold dishes from the cold cabinet; daily specials too. On the first Tuesday evening of each month they hold a speciality night when food from a special region or country is featured. Seven real ales from local small brewers as well as Guinness, Weston Cider, Cassels Cider and wines by the glass or bottle. The Cambridge Blue has been the Cambridgeshire CAMRA pub of the year.

> OPEN: 12–2.30. 5.30–11 (12–3. 6–11 Sat. 12–3. 6–10.30 Sun).
> Real Ale.
> Children in conservatory area. Dogs on leads.
> Wheelchair access (not WC).

CAMBRIDGE

Eagle
Tel: 01223 505020

Bene't Street, Cambridge CB2 3QN
Greene King. Alistair Morrison, manager.

The first mention of an inn on this site was in the late 17th century, although the land on which this pub was built was bequeathed to Corpus Christi College in 1525. Much of the original interior is still here to be admired: 17th-century fireplaces, some mullioned windows, wall paintings and pine panelling. Originally known as the Eagle and Child, this handsome, lively, rambling old pub was once a very important coaching inn: in 1834, 20 pence would get you a seat on the fast coach from Cambridge to London. More up to date are the names of British and American airmen written on the 'RAF ceiling' in lipstick, candle smoke or whatever else came to hand during the Second World War. A simple, good range of bar food – a variety of salads, quiches, pasties, roast lamb, chicken, seafood pancakes etc. Lunchtime and dinner menus served in any of the five bar areas. Greene King ales on hand pump. Wines – mulled wine at Christmas – including champagnes, by the glass. There are seats and tables in the cobbled, galleried yard at the entrance to the pub.

> OPEN: 11–11.
> Meals/snacks 12–2.30. 5.30–8.45 (not Fri, Sat or Sun eves).
> Real Ale.
> Children inside. No dogs, except guide dogs. Wheelchair access.

CAMBRIDGE

Free Press
Tel: 01223 368337
Prospect Row, Cambridge CB1 1QU
Greene King. Donna & Martin Thornton, tenants.

The best of back-street pubs – a delightful place. The pub, originally a terraced house, gets its unusual name from a failed local temperance newspaper. You have to admit that's novel and ironic. With new tenants, the decor reflects its printing connection instead of its old sporting leanings. The Free Press is still totally non-smoking and building a reputation for serving good home-made food: tomato and roasted-pepper soup or Tuscan bean soup, both with crusty bread, filled toasted ciabatta bread, hot home-made Scotch eggs with salad, stuffed sweet pepper with a hot chilli sauce, a ploughman's and delicious puds. The menu changes daily. Ales change regularly, there is a range of malt whiskies and a good wine list. Seats in the small, sunny, sheltered terrace where honeysuckle and roses flourish.

> OPEN: 12–2.30. 6–11.
> Real Ale.
> Children welcome. Dogs on leads. Wheelchair access (not WC).
> Cards: Maestro, MasterCard, Solo, Visa, Visa Electron.

DULLINGHAM

Kings Head
Tel: 01638 507486
50 Station Road, Dullingham, Cambs CB8 9UJ
Pubmaster. Erich Kettenacker, tenant.

In an attractive village south of Newmarket and off the B1061, the Kings Head is washed a perfect pink. Inside are two bars – with cosy winter fires – serving a good choice of bar food, daily specials, some vegetarian dishes and a children's menu. Tollys Original and Flowers IPA. Lots of seats outside, some overlooking the village green.

> OPEN: 11–2.30. 6–11 (11–3. 6.30–10.30 Sun).
> Real Ale. Restaurant.
> Children welcome. No dogs.
> Cards: Amex, MasterCard, Visa.

ELY

Prince Albert
Tel: 01353 663494
62 Silver Street, Ely, Cambs CB7 4JB
Greene King. E.M. Hunt, tenant.

A handsome, smart, well-painted town pub with an award-winning garden (with seats) and exuberant window boxes and hanging baskets. If things look good on the outside, everything will be just as it should be on the inside; just the sort of place to make a beeline for. Menus change according to the seasons: home-cooked hot dishes, soups, quiches, their 'famous' egg and bacon dribbler sandwich and a variety of toasted and freshly made sandwiches to go with the beer. Greene King IPA, Abbot Ale, Mild, seasonal ales and two guest beers.

> OPEN: 11–4. 6–11 (12–4. 7–11 Sun).
> Real Ale.
> Children in garden only. Dogs on leads. Wheelchair access (not WC).

FEN DITTON

Ancient Shepherds   Tel: 01223 293290
High Street, Fen Ditton, Cambs CB5 8ST
Pubmaster. John Harrington, tenant.

Named after the Ancient Order of Shepherds, who used to meet in this charming 16th-century pub, the Ancient Shepherds is a comfortable old place, where they make you feel at home. A warm, welcoming interior serving a traditional menu with the addition of a few more exciting dishes. Bar food includes sandwiches and ploughman's, steak baguettes, steak and ale pie, perhaps a rack of lamb or liver and bacon. Menus change regularly. Beers are Flowers IPA, Tetleys Bitter and Benskins Best Bitter. No-smoking dining room. Seats in the garden.

> OPEN: 11–3. 6–11.
> Real Ale.
> No children. No dogs. Wheelchair access. Car park.
> N.B. Classical music may be played during quiet early evenings.

FOWLMERE

Chequers   Tel: 01763 208369
High Street, Fowlmere, Cambs SG8 7SR
Free House. Norman Rushton, licensee.

The Chequers, a very civilised old 16th-century coaching inn, has a fascinating history. It was a stopping place for post-chaise passengers, and it is recorded that on 24 February 1660, Samuel Pepys spent the night here on his way to Cambridge. Not long after it was built, the inn was used as a coffin stop – a halfway chapel of rest between London and Cambridge. Regarding a different sort of transport: it was a favourite with pilots stationed at Fowlmere during the First and Second World Wars. Still a good place to stop, it has a considerable reputation for serving an interesting variety of food: home-made soups, a warm salad with thin strips of fried pancetta and prawns, garnished with chopped dill and served with garlic bread, grilled Dover sole, grilled venison steak on rosti potatoes with red-wine onion compote, garnished with pink peppercorns and served with a green salad. Lots more chef's specials, vegetarian dishes, cheeses and home-made puddings too; the blackboard menu changes daily. Wide range of wines by the glass; Adnams Bitter and a good choice of malt whiskies, ports and brandies. Seats in the pretty, flowery garden.

> OPEN: 12–2.30. 6–11.
> Real Ale. Restaurant.
> Children welcome – if parents are well behaved! No dogs. Wheelchair access.

HUNTINGDON

The Old Bridge Hotel
1 High Street, Huntingdon, PE29 3TQ
Free House. Martin Lee, chef/patron.

Tel: 01480 424300
Fax: 01480 411017

Huntingdon is twinned with Godmanchester; they are as one. Among the fine Georgian buildings in the town is this handsome, classy, creeper-covered hotel with moorings on the River Great Ouse. You can have everything here: just a drink in the panelled bar, a varied lunchtime buffet or something from the imaginative menu, a proper tea, stay the night, or enjoy the attractive gardens and watch the river flow by. The menus change monthly; a lot of the ingredients are from local sources. There could be wonderful soups, Caesar salad, pot-roast breast of chicken in a tarragon sauce, baked cod under a herb crust and very good puds. Adnams Bitter, a changing guest beer and an excellent, wide-ranging wine list.

> OPEN: 11–11 (12–10.30 Sun).
> Real Ale. Restaurant.
> Children in lounge area and restaurant. No dogs. Car park. Twenty-four bedrooms – all en suite. Fishing.
> Cards: Amex, Delta, Diners, MasterCard, Switch, Visa.
> N.B. Music once a month on themed evenings.

KEYSTON

Pheasant
Village Loop Road, Keyston, Nr Bythorn, Cambs PE18 0RE
Free House. John Hoskins & Clive Dixon, licensees.

Tel: 01832 710241
Fax: 01832 710464

Run by the same group as The Old Bridge Hotel at Huntingdon, this is a well-kept, pretty, heavily beamed, big thatched pub. Inside, its one room is divided into two distinct areas. Clive Dixon uses the best local produce, including fresh fish and game in season, for his interesting, monthly changing menus. There is an extensive list of starters and light snacks: leek and potato soup with crème fraîche; salad of baby leeks, mozzarella, radish, shaved fennel and piquillo peppers; Parma ham with rocket and Parmesan; fishcakes on buttered spinach; poached and grilled guinea fowl with mashed potato, buttered cabbage and foie gras sauce; chunky pork sausage on mashed potato with onion and thyme sauce; European farmhouse cheeses; and wonderful puds. One menu serves both the casual (paper napkins) and the more formal (linen napkins) sides of the pub. Adnams Best and three guest beers. An interesting wine list; 16 house wines, all available by the glass. Tables outside.

OPEN: 12–3. 6–11.
Real Ale. Restaurant with a no-smoking area.
Children welcome. No dogs. Wheelchair access (not WC).
Cards: Amex, Delta, Diners, Mastercard, Switch, Visa.

MADINGLEY

Three Horseshoes
High Street, Madingley, Cambs CB3 8AB
Free House. R. Stokes & John Hoskins, licensees

Tel: 01954 210221
Fax: 01954 212043

Really a dining pub, in the same group as The Pheasant at Keyston and The Old Bridge Hotel at Huntingdon – all members of The Huntsbridge Group – lucky Cambridgeshire. So you wouldn't really think of it as a pub – more an informal restaurant – though you can still get a pint. It's delightful: whitewashed and thatched and said to have been burnt down three times but not recently! The emphasis is on Mediterranean-style food, both in the conservatory and in the bar. Home-made soup; toasted bread with the new season's Tuscan olive oil; baked aubergine with tomato, mozzarella and pesto; pan-fried halibut with seaweed, lemon grass and butter sauce; fillet of beef marinated in thyme, garlic and Chianti with a red-onion tarte tatin; tomato and basil tart; and lots more. Interesting cheeses and good puddings. Three-quarters of the customers of this pub are wine buffs, so I don't have to tell you that it has an enviable, imaginative, wide-ranging wine list. Adnams Best and three guest beers are on hand pump. Tables in the flowery garden during the summer.

OPEN: 11.30–2.30. 6–11.
Real Ale. No restaurant Sun eve.
Children welcome. No dogs. Wheelchair access (not WC).
Cards: Amex, Delta, Diners, MasterCard, Switch, Visa.

NEWTON

Queens Head
Newton, Nr Cambridge, Cambs CB2 5BG
Free House. David & Juliet Short, licensees.

Tel: 01223 870436

What more could you want in a country pub than an unspoilt, charming, traditional 17th-century village inn with a small, well-beamed saloon bar with a big log fire in winter, and a larger, simply furnished, Victorian public bar with a difference – not many have a very dead goose in pride of place. The painting of the goose on the pub sign depicts poor Belinda, one-time keeper of the car park, now in residence in the public bar – stuffed. Good, simple bar food complements the fine ales and country wines. Wide choice of sandwiches, all cut to order, home-made soup (a firm favourite), along with the roast beef or smoked ham sandwiches, or platter of mixed cheeses. Evenings and Sunday lunchtime there is a selection of cold meats, salads, etc. Adnams Bitter and Broadside and Regatta with Adnams Fishermans Ale in winter – all tapped from the cask. Organic apple juice, freshly squeezed orange juice and farm cider. Seats at the front of the pub or on the green.

> OPEN: 11.30–2.30. 6–11.
> Real Ale.
> Children in games room and dogs on leads – well behaved – both of them.
> Wheelchair access into pub only.

PULLOXHILL

Cross Keys   Tel: 01525 712442
High Street, Pulloxhill, Beds MK45 5HB
Charles Wells. Peter & Sheila Meads, tenants.

The Cross Keys is known for its ghost: a Cavalier from the Civil War stalks the pub by night, but as he's in a little village off the A6 Luton to Bedford road and nowhere near an obvious battle site, he had perhaps lost his way. Anyway, here he is, in this white-painted, flower-bedecked pub. A typical English country pub with a heavily beamed interior and large log-filled fireplaces. A lunchtime bar-snack menu provides satisfying soups, egg mayonnaise, trout with salad, fresh mushrooms in garlic butter, chicken Kiev, Cajun chicken, mixed grill, grilled steaks, two plaice fillets, haddock royale, ploughman's, salads, vegetarian dishes and a children's menu; daily specials too. More substantial dishes are available in the restaurant. A comprehensive wine list, Charles Wells and Adnams ales. Serious jazz sessions on Sunday nights.

> OPEN: 11–3. 6–11.
> Real Ale.
> Restaurant. Specially priced lunches for senior citizens Monday–Friday.
> Children in own room. No dogs. Wheelchair access. Jazz every Sunday eve.
> Cards: Access, Switch, Visa.

RAMSEY

Jolly Sailor   Tel: 01487 813388
43 Great Whyte, Ramsey, Cambs PE26 1HH
Pubmaster. Michael Rogers, licensee.

Ramsey is an ancient market town in an area known more for its vegetables than jolly sailors. But the Great Whyte River does flow under the road, and you can moor your boat on the nearby High Lode, so it really is quite nautical. Jolly and cosy it may be, but the Jolly Sailor has no food – well, a crisp and a nut if you're peckish – but plenty of beer:

Greene King Abbot, Charles Wells Bombardier, Batemans XB, Tetley Bitter, a weekend guest beer and a garden in which to sit and enjoy them.

> OPEN: 11–3. 5.30–11 (11–3. 6–11 Sat. 12–3. 7–10.30 Sun).
> Real Ale.
> Children in one bar. Dogs on leads. N.B. Two bars are quiet, one has music.

RENHOLD

Three Horseshoes   Tel: 01234 870218
42 Top End, Renhold, Beds MK41 0LR
Greene King. Mr L. Hobbs, licensee.

In the country, off the A428, near Bedford – John Bunyan's birthplace – and on the way to St Neots, the traditional Three Horseshoes is somewhere to stop when you are making your own pilgrim's progress along the lanes of North Bedfordshire. It's an area of streams and rivers and small villages surrounded by pastureland and water meadows. Good open fires welcome you; also well-kept ales and good value food: filled sandwiches, steaks, gammon and a choice of fish. Greene King Dark Mild, IPA, Abbot and occasionally Triumph or another guest beer.

> OPEN: 11–3. 6–11 (12–10.30 Sat & Sun).
> Real Ale.
> Children allowed in. Dogs – yes-ish.

SLAPTON

Carpenter's Arms   Tel: 01525 220563
Slapton, Nr Leighton Buzzard, Beds LU7 9DB
Vale Brewery. Andrew Loft, licensee.

Only half a mile from the Grand Union Canal – in the rolling countryside on the borders of Bedfordshire/Hertfordshire – this delightful 16th-century village pub and restaurant provides not only good cask ales and an extensive menu to choose from but the house specialities: large home-made pies with fillings such as pigeon breasts in red wine, salmon, cod and scallops, and aubergine and mushroom with fresh coriander. Lots of salads, steaks, poached salmon, home-made soups, pâté and Italian cold meats. The Vale Brewery, which always supplied the beer, are now the landlords and this means the second-hand bookshop in the Maltings next door has gone. As it kept pub hours, it will be missed. Now, if you think you are going to be in for a long wait, or if you want a book to read with your pint, you'll have to bring your own.

> OPEN: 12–3. 7–11. No food Sunday eve.
> Real Ale.
> Quiet children welcome. Quiet dogs on leads. Wheelchair access (not WC).
> STOP PRESS: Doubts were expressed after going to press about the future of the Carpenter's Arms.

STEVINGTON

The Red Lion   Tel: 01234 824138
1 Park Road, Stevington, Bedford MK43 7QD
Greene King. Hilary & George Williams, tenants.

Just the sort of pub you would expect in the centre of a village. A comfortable, friendly place full of chatty locals where you'll get a short, satisfying, traditional menu offering freshly made sandwiches, ploughman's, filled jacket potatoes, various omelettes, ham, egg and chips, battered cod and chips and some home-made daily specials. The well-kept ales are Greene King IPA and Abbot. Outside, the sheltered garden has picnic tables and two *pétanque* pistes for the slightly more energetic. The pub is at the end of a circular walk past the remains of an old mill.

> OPEN: 12–2.30. 5–11 (open all day Sat and Sun).
> Real Ale. No food Monday.
> Children welcome. Dogs on leads. Bedrooms.

SUTTON

John O'Gaunt Inn   Tel: 01767 260377
30 High Street, Sutton, Sandy, Beds SG19 2ND
Greene King. Les Ivall, tenant.

The pink-washed, 18th-century John O'Gaunt is in a delightful village near a 13th-century packhorse bridge and ford, which, since the weather pattern seems to have hit a rather damp phase, should still be full of water. Not just a simple pub: it has an investment club, two quiz teams, a golf society and serious boules players in the local league. The bar is no smoking, as is a part of the lounge. Well-kept ales. An extensive bar menu offers, among other things, sandwiches or baguettes, filled jacket potatoes, toasted sandwiches, shepherd's pie, beef-in-ale casserole, balti dishes, fish, vegetarian dishes and daily specials. Sunday lunches too. Greene King IPA and Abbot ales, plus guests such as Gales HSB, draught Bass or Old Bailey.

> OPEN: 12–3. 7–11.
> Real Ale.
> Well-behaved children over ten years old welcome. Dogs in public bar.

SUTTON GAULT

Anchor Inn   Tel: 01353 778537
                                                    Fax: 01353 776180
Bury Lane, Sutton Gault, Cambs CB6 2BD
Free House. Robin Moore, licensee.

Here's another place that you could call an informal restaurant. Translated, that means you are going to experience some wonderful, imaginative food without losing touch with the ethos of a pub. This 17th-century place, on the banks of the New Bedford River, has four heavily beamed rooms with sturdy pine tables and chairs, old settles and big log fires. Cooking is the best of modern British; wonderful soups, crab tart with chicory and potato salad, chorizo and buffalo mozzarella salad, open lasagne of char-grilled vegetables with red-pepper sauce and herb oil, breast of chicken, tarragon and wild-mushroom sauce, parsnip mash and roast new potatoes, British cheeses, desirable puddings and a good-value wine list. And the beers: Hampshire King Alfred, Black Sheep Bitter, City of Cambridge Hobson's Choice and Hoegaarden. You can sit in the garden or watch the wildlife from the riverbank.

> OPEN: 12–3. 7–11 (12–3. 6.30–11 Sat. 12–3. 7–10.30 Sun).
> Real Ale. Restaurant.
> Children welcome. No young children after 8.30pm. No dogs. Wheelchair access to all parts of the pub. Car park. Accommodation.
> Cards: Amex, Delta, MasterCard, Switch, Visa.

TODDINGTON

Sow & Pigs   Tel: 01525 873089
19 Church Square, Toddington, Nr Dunstable, Beds LU5 6AA
Greene King. Roger Martin, licensee.

This is one of the more eccentric pubs. Built in the Victorian era, it has a narrow bar and a theme: pigs – some even flying – and very well-kept beer. Not many concessions to comfort in the minute public bar, nor in the lounge either, but you do have an unusual collection of furniture to sit on from where, if you're comfortable, you can enjoy freshly filled rolls and sandwiches to go with seasonal guest beers and ales from Greene King.

> OPEN: 11–11 (12–10.30 Sun).
> Real Ale.
> Children welcome. Dogs on leads. Occasional musical evenings. They have a function room which is used more and more for banquets, but they say this doesn't interfere with the pub – you will still be well looked after.

BEST OF THE REST

ELSWORTH, Cambs

George & Dragon   Tel: 01954 267236
Near Cambridge, this well-kept, well-run pub in a pretty village serves interesting food: bar snacks – soup, sandwiches, ploughman's, that sort of thing – plus pork ribs in a barbecue sauce, salmon topped with prawn and anchovy butter, mixed grill and daily specials. Greene King and Ruddles County, decent wine. Closed Sunday evenings.

FORDHAM, Cambs

White Pheasant
Tel: 01638 720414

Big sign, big pub. A large, white-painted 17th-century inn set back off the main road. A good mix of pub and restaurant. On the pub side there is quite an extensive choice of dishes listed on the blackboards; plentiful country cooking: liver and bacon, lamb chops, Norfolk chicken and home-made puds. Dishes are more elaborate in the restaurant. Tolly Cobbold and Foresters beers and a good choice of international and country wines.

HINXTON, Cambs

Red Lion
Tel: 01799 530601

Pink and 16th-century. Regularly changing, really imaginative chef's specials in either the bar – with parrot accompaniment – or the restaurant – without. Adnams, Greene King and guests.

HOUGHTON CONQUEST, Beds

Knife & Cleaver
Tel: 01234 740387

A very attractive pub opposite the church; panelled, polished and comfortable. Food is really good; it is regarded as more of a restaurant than a pub. Though having said that, it still has a bar, real ales, lots of malt whiskies and some good wines.

RIDGMONT, Beds

Rose & Crown
Tel: 01525 280245

Once part of the Duke of Bedfordshire's estate, this 17th-century pub has a lovely sunny garden. Just a pub serving pub food and real ale from Charles Wells.

RISELEY, Beds

Fox & Hounds
Tel: 01234 708240

In the High Street, this is a pub that has had a facelift, been enlarged and upgraded. A delightful place where they serve some rather good steaks and imaginative specials, as well as the more usual pub food. Charles Wells range of beers and some guests.

THRIPLOW, Beds

Green Man
Tel: 01763 208855

Tastefully decorated and full of collectors' bits and pieces; the surroundings are certainly not dull. Good, filling, classic bar food to go with quietly playing classical music. Evening menu jumps up a notch or two. Timothy Taylor's Landlord, about four guests from smaller breweries and some interesting wines.

Berkshire

ALDWORTH

Bell
Tel: 01635 578272

Aldworth, Nr Reading, Berks RG8 9SE
Free House. H.E. Macaulay, licensee.

On the rolling Berkshire Downs, this is a gem of a place. An unspoilt 14th-century inn, it has been in the same family for two centuries, during which nothing much has changed – well, some things have, but all to the good – the essentials of modern living, that sort of thing. As you would expect, the Bell is heavily beamed, with panelled walls and traditional furnishings. It has no bar counter, just a hatch through which you are served. The bar menu lists hot crusty rolls filled with ham, cheese, ox tongue, corned beef, smoked salmon, salt beef, Devon crab, or spicy prawns; a nice crisp salad tossed in a garlic mayonnaise; ploughman's; home-made soup during the winter. Ales are West Berks Ol' Tyler, Dark Mild and a monthly guest from the brewery, also Arkells BBB and Kingsdown. Wines from Berry Bros. A good claret and a house medium-dry white always on offer by the glass. Seats in the attractive garden next to the cricket pitch.

> OPEN: 11–3. 6–11. Closed Mondays except Bank Holidays.
> Real Ale.
> Well-behaved children in tap room. Dogs on leads. Occasional Morris dancing.
> Wheelchair access (not WC).

BRACKNELL

The Old Manor
Tel: 01344 304490

Grenville Place, High Street, Bracknell, Berks
Wetherspoon.

The Old Manor House probably has many a tale to tell: when the builders were renovating the old building several years ago, they found some interesting escape tunnels and hidey-holes dating back to the Reformation. But apart from some ancient beams, all has changed inside; the Old Manor is now a town-centre pub with a large drinking area, a third of which is no smoking. There will be a choice of five or six reasonably priced beers, plus a changing guest from one of the smaller breweries. As in all Wetherspoon establishments, the food is good and reliable.

> OPEN: 11–11.
> Real Ale.
> No children. No dogs. Wheelchair access.

CHEAPSIDE

The Thatched Tavern   Tel: 01344 620874
Cheapside Road, Ascot SL5 7QG
Free House. Rick Mileham, manager.

Things have changed here since our last edition; as you can see, it is no longer a tied house
and new people are in charge. Still hugely popular, it's busy and handy for the Guards polo
club in Windsor Great Park if your interests lie in that direction. Not a straw to be seen
on the roof, though you still have low ceilings, beams, flagstone floors, an inglenook fireplace and a general feeling of wellbeing inside this fine old pub. The food ranges from filled
baguettes and home-made soup to steak and kidney pudding, local game, wild salmon, fish
(various) and vegetarian dishes. Proper puds too. Greene King Abbot, Fullers London
Pride and Brakspears Bitter and a choice of wines. Seats outside on the sheltered lawn.
Parking tricky, so instead of starting your walk from here, make it the stopping-off place –
there is a car park about a mile away!

> OPEN: 12–11.
> Real Ale. Restaurant. Bar meals and snacks lunchtime only.
> Children: not in the bar. Dogs welcome. Car park – gets very busy.

COOKHAM DEAN

Jolly Farmer   Tel: 01628 482905
Church Road, Cookham Dean SL6 9PD
Free House. Simon Peach, licensee.

Cookham, Cookham Rise, then Cookham Dean and the Jolly Farmer: one on the river,
the others in its embrace. A small 18th-century pub on the other side of the village green.
Cosy rooms with fires, a charming dining room and a bar. Good filling bar food to go with
the Courage Best and guest beers. Lots of room in the big garden.

> OPEN: 11.30–3. 5.30–11.
> Real Ale. Dining room.
> Children away from bar. Well-behaved dogs allowed. Wheelchair access.

CRAZIES HILL

Horns   Tel: 0118 940 1416
Crazies Hill, Wargrave, Berks RG10 8LY
Brakspears. Andy & Clare Hearn, tenants.

Just follow the signposts to Crazies Hill and the Horns. Painted white, with beams outside,
beams inside, big open fires and stag's antlers above the front door. The bar is part of the
original Tudor hunting lodge and the old barn is now the restaurant. The menu is varied
and imaginative and might include: warm salad with bacon, mushrooms, avocado and
Stilton served with 'the Horns' salad dressing; garlic bread with herbs and melted cheese;

calves' liver pan-fried with onions and bacon served with gravy; pancakes filled with smoked salmon and topped with a feta cheese and coriander sauce; rack of lamb with redcurrant jelly, rosemary and mint gravy; and something from the 'fresh fish of the day' on the specials board. Vegetarian dishes, a selection of puds and cheeses too. Home-made soup, and filled baguettes for the not so hungry. Sunday lunch is comprehensive: a choice of roasts, fresh fish, beef, mushroom and Guinness pie or just a bar snack. Meals are served in the restaurant every weekday evening. Brakspears ales and lots of malt whiskies. Good choice of wines. Lucky them: the pub has a big garden of several acres.

> OPEN: 11–2.30. 6–11.
> Real Ale. Food served every lunchtime and evening except Sun eve.
> Brasserie meals Fri and Sat eves: must book.
> Children at lunchtime only. Doubtful about dogs – you have to ask. Wheelchair access.
> Cards: Delta, Diners, MasterCard, Switch, Visa.

FRILSHAM

Pot Kiln   Tel: 01635 201366
Frilsham, Nr Hermitage, Berks RG18 0XX
Free House. Philip Gent, licensee.

Tucked away down a country lane, it's popular with locals and passing ramblers. A bit tricky to find; if you approach from the wrong direction you think you never will. There is a counter you can lean on in the small public bar – and take the dog, otherwise service is through a hatch in the tiny entrance hall. Plenty of space, though, in the 'big room'. Good fires to keep the customers warm in winter and a simple bar menu to sustain them. Home-made soup, filled rolls, ploughman's and daily specials. Ales include Morlands Original and Arkells BBB. There is also Brick Kiln ale and Gold Star, a beer brewed with local honey, which Dave Maggs brews for the Pot Kiln at the back of the pub. Tables in the big, sheltered garden. Good walks nearby.

> OPEN: 12–2.30. 6.30–11. Closed Tues lunchtimes and no food Tues eves.
> Real Ale. Limited food Sun and Tues.
> Children in back room. Dogs on leads. Wheelchair access (not WC).
> Live music 1st Sun of month.

GORING-ON-THAMES

Catherine Wheel   Tel: 01491 872379
Station Road, Goring-on-Thames, Reading RG8 9HB
Brakspears. Diana Kerr, tenant/licensee.

The Catherine Wheel, the oldest pub in the village, is small, cosy, beamed and panelled. Goring is in a historic area on the very edge of the county – Berkshire becomes Oxfordshire in the middle of the river – and the ford at Goring is where the ancient

Icknield Way and Ridgeway joined to cross the Thames. All the food is freshly made; specials are on the blackboard, but from the regular menu you could choose grilled giant New Zealand mussels stuffed with garlic, herb and tomato butter, calamari alla Romana, filled jacket potatoes, chicken Diana, liver and bacon Dijonnaise, or Sam's Boston cheese steak submarine sandwich (tender rump steak, grilled with cheddar cheese, topped with fried onion and mushrooms in a French roll and served with salad) – that should keep you quiet for a bit! Also a choice of eleven different fillings for the brown or white rolls. Brakspears Mild, Bitter, Special, Old Ale and Brakspears seasonal beer. Plenty of room in the large garden.

> OPEN: 11.30–3. 6–11 (12–3. 7–10.30 Sun).
> Real Ale.
> Children in restaurant area. Dogs on leads. Wheelchair access (not WC). Public car park behind the pub.
> Cards: MasterCard, Solo, Switch, Visa.

HOLYPORT
Belgian Arms   Tel: 01628 634468
Holyport Street, Holyport, Maidenhead, Berks SL6 2JR
Brakspears. Alfred Morgan, tenant.

This pub has been owned by Brakspears since the end of the 19th century. It's as pretty as a picture when the wisteria is out and the garden is in full flower. Illustrations of Belgian army uniforms – what else? – and other military prints adorn the low-ceilinged bar. A friendly, busy place, the pub has a dining area in the conservatory, which often doubles as an overflow for the lunchtime trade. Bar food includes sandwiches, plain and toasted, pizzas with various toppings, ham and eggs and daily specials; Sunday lunches too. Brakspears ales and several malt whiskies are available. Seats in the garden overlook the pond and village green.

> OPEN: 11–3. 5.30–11 (6–11 Sat).
> Real Ale. No food Sun eve.
> Children in conservatory. Dogs on leads. Wheelchair access (not WC).
> Cards: all major credit cards.

KINTBURY
Dundas Arms   Tel: 01488 658263
53 Station Road, Kintbury, Nr Newbury, Berks RG17 9UT
Free House. David A. Dalzell Piper, licensee.

It was Lord Dundas who opened the Kennett and Avon Canal in 1810 and who gave his name to this attractive 18th-century pub on the edge of the canal. As you would imagine, it is very popular in summer; from the terrace and dining room you have a view of the canal and passing horse-drawn canal barges. The chef is skilled and enthusiastic, and the luncheon menu and à la carte dinner might include: home-cured gravadlax with a mustard and dill sauce, grilled scallops with black pasta and saffron sauce, baked sea-bass fillets, roast breast of duck with cider and apple sauce, and of course delicious puddings and a selection of British cheeses. However, you can eat less ambitiously in the small bar: home potted shrimps, avocado and 'hot' smoked-salmon salad or baked cod fillet. A wide variety of wines from the cellar. Butts Barbus Barbus and Greene King IPA are the permanent ales; Burcombe Bitter, Ruddles County and Ringwood Best and True Glory are the guests.

> OPEN: 11–2.30. 6–11.
> Real Ale. Restaurant.
> Children to stay. No dogs. Wheelchair access (not WC). Car park. Five bedrooms.
> Cards: Amex, Delta, MasterCard, Switch, Visa.

READING

Sweeney & Todd   Tel: 0118 958 6466
10 Castle Street (off St Mary's Butts), Reading, Berks
Free House. Mrs June Hayward, licensee.

Presumably named after the well-known Fleet Street barber who had a predilection for pies with more macabre ingredients! It is situated at the back of the pie shop – down a couple of steps and into a railway-carriage-shaped room with lots of tables and proper waitresses. Here you can a choose from a vast range of home-made pies with adventurous fillings. Soups, sandwiches and other dishes too. Exceptionally busy at lunchtimes during the week. Wadworths 6X, Adnams Bitter, Eldridge Pope Royal Oak and a guest beer.

> OPEN: 11–11. Closed all day Sun.
> They serve breakfast from 8–10.30 a.m.
> Real Ale.
> Children welcome. No dogs.

SLOUGH

Moon & Spoon   Tel: 01753 531650
86 High Street, Slough, Berks
Wetherspoon.

The bigger, the better; by now you all know that size is everything to Wetherspoons. Originally a building society, now a big pub with a giant 'spoon man' to welcome you. Always five very reasonably priced beers; always a good reliable menu with daily specials; always a no-smoking area; and this Wetherspoon has real draught cider.

> OPEN: 10.30–11 (12–10.30 Sun).
> Real Ale.
> No children. No dogs. Wheelchair access to all areas.

STANFORD DINGLEY

Old Boot Inn
Tel: 0118 974 4292

Stanford Dingley, Berks RG7 6LT
Free House. John Haley, licensee.

To emphasise the name, a giant boot stands next to the fireplace – holding the fire irons.
A delightful white-painted 18th-century building in a pretty village in an 'area of outstanding natural beauty'. Two bars, a restaurant and no-smoking conservatory in this
popular dining pub. You can choose well-filled baguettes or a ploughman's from the bar
menu, as well as home-made pies, lasagne, sausage and mash, curries and beef stroganoff.
The à la carte menu is constantly changing and there is a fresh-fish board every day and
some comforting puds. Beers are draught Bass and something from Brakspear, Youngs and
the West Berks brewery. Over 40 bottles on the wine list, about six by the glass.

> OPEN: 11–3. 6–11
> Real Ale. Restaurant.
> Children welcome, dogs too. Wheelchair access (not WC). Car park.
> Cards: Delta, MasterCard, Switch, Visa.

WALTHAM ST LAWRENCE

The Bell
Tel: 0118 934 1788

The Street, Waltham St Lawrence, Berks
Free House. Ian Glenister & Rachel Young, licensees.

Black and white, beamed, panelled and popular. The Bell, in the middle of the village and
behind hanging baskets – well, it is in summer! – is an important Wealden hall house well
over 500 years old. In 1723, for the grand rent of £8 per annum, a building 'known as The
Bell' was taken by a victualler called John Cumber; this was the first mention of it being
used as licensed premises. Little altered externally over the years, it is still a very handsome
building. Good log fires to keep you warm in winter, and when the weather improves you
can sit in the attractive garden. Home-made soups and a wide selection of English, continental, oriental and vegetarian dishes, bar snacks and daily specials. Brakspears PA,
Wychwood Beers, Marlow Rebellion and others. An extended range of whiskies and malts.

> OPEN: 11.30–3. 5–11 (12–10.30 Sun).
> Real Ale.
> Children welcome in eating areas.

WARGRAVE

The Bull
Tel: 0118 940 3120

High Street, Wargrave, Berks
Brakspear. Jayne Worrall, tenant.

As with Goring, this is another village on the Thames where the county boundary does a
quick change in mid-river. Below Shiplake, this is an area popular with walkers and

anyone on the river. In the centre of the village is the well-beamed, 15th-century Bull; a favourite old coaching inn with lovely log fires, two non-smoking bars serving well-kept beer and good food. Brakspear Bitter and Special. Seats in the walled garden.

OPEN: 11–3. 6–11 (12–4. 7–10.30 Sun).
Real Ale.
Children in the dining room. Dogs in garden only. Wheelchair access. Bedrooms.

WOKINGHAM WITHOUT

Crooked Billet
Tel: 0118 978 0438
Honey Hill, Wokingham Without, Berks RG40 3BJ
Wootton Inns. Robert Warren & Abi Chrisp, managers.

Due for a complete refurbishment during 2002, so you will have to avoid the builders for a time. On the edge of Wokingham, the Crooked Billet has had a licence for the last 130 years; before that it was a private house. Low-beamed ceilings and real fires with plenty of room for eating and drinking. A choice from any of the menus – à la carte, table d'hôte, bar menu and the two specials boards – can be eaten anywhere in the pub including the no-smoking restaurant. Lots to choose from – anything from soup to a T-bone steak, home-made pies, curries, pastas, various fish dishes, vegetarian meals and puds. Brakspears range of ales, and one guest. Seats in the garden.

OPEN: 11–11.
Real Ale. Restaurant.
Children in restaurant and garden. Dogs in bar and garden. Ample car parking.

BEST OF THE REST

BURCHETTS GREEN

Crown
Tel: 01628 822844
A popular pub with a small bar serving snacks and light lunches, also a bigger bar-cum-dining room. The blackboard menu changes twice a day, ranging from the usual pub favourites to chicken in a wine sauce, or poached fillet of salmon. Ruddles, Charles Wells Bombardier and a decent selection of wines.

CHIEVELEY

Blue Boar
Tel: 01635 248236
Difficult to find but it is only 2 miles from Junction 13 on the M4. A 'Cromwell was here' pub and when you manage to find it, you can be too. Rather isolated, with views over the surrounding country, this 17th-century thatched pub serves better-than-average bar food to go with Fullers London Pride and Wadworths 6X.

STANFORD DINGLEY

Bull
Tel: 0118 974 4409

Seats at the front and the side of this old pub. Straightforward bar food: soups, sandwiches, filled baked potatoes, that sort of thing, as well as daily specials. Brakspears Bitter and something from the West Berkshire Brewery.

Buckinghamshire

J D WETHERSPOON CO

NORTHANTS

BEDFORDSHIRE

HERTFORDSHIRE

OXFORDSHIRE

BERKS

Newport Pagnell
Moulsoe
Milton Keynes
Buckingham
Thornborough
Waddesdon
Aylesbury
Easington
Ford
Bledlow
Great Hampden
Prestwood
Great Missenden
Little Missenden
Chesham
Chenies
Great Kingshill
Amersham
West Wycombe
Coleshill
Forty Green
High Wycombe
Turville
Beaconsfield
Frieth
Hedgerley

0 Miles 5
0 Kilometres 8

Buckinghamshire

AMERSHAM

Kings Arms
Tel: 01494 726333

30 High Street, Old Amersham, Bucks HP7 0DJ
Free House. John Jennison, licensee.

Originally two separate timber-framed open hall houses, this handsome black-and-white, flower-bedecked building has been altered, added to and improved virtually every century since it was built in 1450. The Georgians formalised one frontage, but inside, the Kings Arms still has a wealth of beams, supporting timbers, inglenook fireplaces and lots of the little nooks and crannies so typical of a 15th-century building. Traditional bar snacks: home-made soup, ploughman's, lots of fillings for the baguettes, Cumberland sausages with mashed potato, vegetables and onion gravy, chicken-tikka kebabs with rice and popadoms, steak and kidney pie, roasted vegetable lasagne, daily specials on the black-board and no chips; if you are really pushing the boat out, you can order from the restaurant à la carte menu, which changes every three months, or three courses from the table d'hôte, changing every four to five weeks. Benskins Bitter, Ind Coope Burton, Rebellion IPA and a weekly guest ale. Wines by the glass. Seats in the flowery courtyard or on the lawn.

> OPEN: 11–11 (12–10.30 Sun).
> Real Ale. Restaurant.
> Children welcome – they have their own area. Dogs on leads. Wheelchair access (not WC). Car park.
> Cards: Amex, MasterCard, Visa.

BEACONSFIELD

Greyhound
Tel: 01494 673823

33 Windsor End, Beaconsfield, Bucks HP9 2JN
Free House. John & Clare Flippance, licensees.

Thought to date back to the 15th century and originally a drover's pub, the Greyhound is all you would expect. At the older end of Beaconsfield, near the old coaching road and opposite the parish church, it is unspoilt, with low ceilings, beams, open fires and loads of atmosphere. Two bars and a dining room, serving reliable and interesting food – ranging from a sandwich to elaborate fish, steak and chicken dishes, home-made pies and a daily changing blackboard menu. Courage Best and Fullers London Pride; two guest ales change weekly. Seats in the garden. Good walks are not far away.

OPEN: 11–3. 5.30–11 (12–3. 7–10.30 Sun).
Real Ale.
No children. No dogs. Wheelchair access (not WC).

BLEDLOW

Lions of Bledlow   Tel: 01844 343345
Church End, Bledlow, Bucks HP27 9PE
Free House. Mark McKeown, licensee.

The hills and beechwoods that surround this village are a walker's paradise. There is also the 13th-century church, a cross cut into the hillside that they say dates back to the 7th century and, of course, the 16th-century Lions of Bledlow. If you're in your walking boots, this pub is hard to miss as all the best-used tracks seem to end up here, not quite in the bar, but near enough, making it an ideal place to start or finish a long walk. In summer, you can relax on the sheltered terrace and admire the views; in winter, warm yourself by the fire in the comfortable beamed bars. On the menu are home-made soups, filled baguettes, salads, steak and Guinness pie, some fish dishes and about ten daily specials. Brakspear, Courage Best, Marstons Pedigree and Wadworths 6X ales on hand pump and one guest beer.

OPEN: 11.30–3. 6–11 (12–3. 7–10.30 Sun).
Real Ale. No-smoking dining room.
Children: if well supervised. Dogs very welcome; water and biscuits for them! Car park.
Cards: Amex, Delta, Diners, MasterCard, Switch, Visa.

CHENIES

Red Lion   Tel: 01923 282722
Chenies Village, Rickmansworth, Herts WD3 6ED
Free House. Heather & Mike Norris, FBII, owners/licensees.

(We have returned Chenies to Bucks because that is where it strictly belongs; Chenies is in Bucks, Rickmansworth is in Herts.) On the edge of the village, look for a summer floral display and this delightful old pub will be right behind it. Inside is a large main bar and a small dining area in what was the original 17th-century cottage. A varied selection of very popular home-cooked bar food might include soup of the day, hot or cold fillings for the French sticks, lots of interesting fillings for the jacket potatoes, home-made pâté, sardines marinated in lime and coriander served with a tomato salad, pork, chilli and lentil casserole, Caribbean chicken breast with glazed mango served with couscous and mint yoghurt, the special 'Chenies lamb pie' and lots of other dishes to choose from. They serve oven-baked lamb with a port-and-redcurrant gravy, also rump steaks, cooked however you like them. All dishes come with fresh vegetables, but no chips. Daily specials from the blackboard. Wadworths 6X, Benskins Best, Notley Ale and Lion Pride, brewed for the pub by The Rebellion Beer Co. They have a short wine list, and house wines by the glass. If you want a little culture, Chenies manor house – a Tudor manor built by the Earl of Bedford in 1526 and still with its original Tudor garden – is not far away.

OPEN: 11–2.30. 5.30–11.
Real Ale.
No children. Dogs on leads. Wheelchair access. Car park.
Cards: Amex, Delta, Diners, MasterCard, Switch, Visa.

COLESHILL

Red Lion
Tel: 01494 727020
Village Road, Coleshill, Bucks HP7 0LN
Alehouse Company. Christine & John Ullman, lessees.

Don't worry: it's not a villa built circa 1930! It really is a pub – and a popular one at that with all age groups for its well-kept beers and reliable bar food: freshly made sandwiches, ploughman's, salads (real ham – off the bone), smoked salmon with scrambled eggs is a favourite, also daily seasonal specials such as braised pheasant, oxtail in winter, cold salmon with prawns and salad and warm crab tartlets with avocado salad in summer. There will be a choice of roasts on Sundays. Good selection of puddings. Greene King IPA, Brakspear and Rebellion ales. A selection of wines by the glass. Tables at the front of the pub in summer and barbecues in the garden at the back.

OPEN: 11–3.30. 5.30–11 (11–11 Sat).
Real Ale. No food Sun eve.
Children welcome. Dogs on leads. Wheelchair access (not WC).

FORD

Dinton Hermit
Tel: 01296 747473
Water Lane, Ford, Nr Aylesbury, Bucks HP17 8XH
Free House. John Bingham-Chick, licensee.

Still here, thank goodness. The change of ownership, late in 2000, has transformed this 15th-century stone-built village inn with open log fires, stone floors and rustic furniture – all is as it should be – including a portrait of John Bigg, secretary to Simon Mayne who signed the death warrant of King Charles I. Distraught by his connection with the death of the king, he became a hermit – hence the Dinton Hermit. The extra good news here is that food is back on the agenda in a big way. One end of the pub is a formal dining room where the menus have more than a lean towards the Mediterranean, though you can still find a good variety of bar food: good home-made soups, ploughman's and open sandwiches from the bar as well as more substantial dishes, such as a pheasant casserole in a port sauce or beef stroganoff. Adnams, Hook Norton and Brakspear plus more guests in the busy season. Fifty wines on the list and some by the glass. There's a big garden with lovely views of the surrounding countryside and lots of walks nearby.

> OPEN: 11–2.30. 6–11 (12–3. 7–10.30 Sun).
> Real Ale.
> Children by arrangment. Dogs in garden. Car park.
> Cards: Amex, Delta, MasterCard, Switch, Visa.

FORTY GREEN

Royal Standard of England   Tel: 01494 673382
Forty Green, Nr Beaconsfield, Bucks HP9 1XT
Free House. Cyril & Carol Cain, licensees.

There really is a royalist connection here. Charles II hid in the pub's rafters to escape the Parliamentarians after the Battle of Worcester. Once Charles II was back on the throne – in 1661 – the landlord decided it was safe to change the name in honour of their late royal guest. Gloriously atmospheric interiors: splendid carved-oak panelling, big fireplaces with roaring log fires in winter and magnificent oak beams. There is a wonderful choice of food, from home-made soup and exciting fillings for the sandwiches and ploughman's to sautéed chicken with bacon strips in garlic-cream sauce, pork loin steak with an apricot glaze, chicken, leek and mushroom pie, beef and Owd Roger ale pie, a vegetarian sweet-potato, spinach and rosemary bake topped with Parmesan; daily specials too. A good selection of cheeses, chutney made to a centuries-old secret recipe, and various continental breads. Marstons Pedigree, Morlands Old Speckled Hen, Brakspears and regular local guest beers. Good choice of malt and Irish whiskies; also fruit wines and a decent wine list. Lots of seats in the garden.

> OPEN: 11–3. 5.30–11 (12–3 or later. 7–10.30 Sun).
> Real Ale. No food Sun eve.
> Children in three special areas. Dogs in garden only. Wheelchair access.

FRIETH

Prince Albert   Tel: 01494 881683
Moors End, Nr Henley-on-Thames, Bucks RG9 6PX
Brakspears. Steve & Irene Anderson, licensees.

It's a small, friendly village pub, 250 years old, with fires to warm you and local guide-books to read. Moreover, the Prince Albert has a reputation for serving good-quality bar food and beer. New tenants have taken over, so changes will have been made. The menu has a considerable range of food: sandwiches with different fillings, ploughman's, the usual bar food as well as specials from the blackboard – and lots of it. Brakspears Bitter and Special on hand pump. Good choice of wines and decent whiskies. In lovely countryside, surrounded by attractive woodland with lots of wonderful walks.

OPEN: 12–2.30. 5.15–11.
Real Ale.
Children welcome. Dogs on leads. Wheelchair access (not WC).

GREAT HAMPDEN

Hampden Arms   Tel: 01494 488255
Great Hampden, Nr Great Missenden, Bucks HP16 9RQ
Free House. Terry & Barbara Matthews, licensees.

John Hampden, who lived in Hampden House in the 17th century (and after whom the pub is named), was killed during the Civil War and buried in the churchyard. It's not a big pub – just two rooms: one with the bar – you can eat and drink in both – that's if you can find the space. Standing room only in summer; you must book if you want to sit and eat inside. Outside there are lots of tables, so if you hit a busy period, hope that the weather is fine. Lots of dishes to choose from – so there should be something for everyone – plus a range of starters, snacks, vegetarian and low-fat specials. Abundance all round. You can start with deep-fried Brie in a seasonal sauce, tomato soup, prawn and mushroom pot, stuffed mushrooms, proper ham, sea-fish medley, steak Diane or duck moderne (breast of duck in a brandy and orange sauce) and finish with profiteroles. Lots and lots more. Adnams, Brakspears, Addlestones draught cider and a small wine list.

OPEN: 12–3. 6.30–11. Closed all day Sunday and Monday eves.
Real Ale.
Children welcome. Dogs on leads – ask first. Wheelchair access. Car park.
Cards: Amex, Delta, Diners, MasterCard, Switch, Visa.

GREAT KINGSHILL

Red Lion   Tel: 01494 711262
Missenden Rd, Great Kingshill, High Wycombe, Bucks HP15 6EB
Pubmaster. Pepe Rivero-Cabrera, tenant.

This isn't the sort of place where you can loll on a bench with a beer mug in your hand, though having said that, they do still serve beer. But it is really more of a restaurant; all the tables are set for dining. Señor Cabrera is not just the tenant but also the chef, and his speciality is fish – all sorts, and lots of it, from fresh sardines to skate: calamares a la Romana, coquille St Jacques, fillets of smoked trout, grilled sardines, and for a main course you could choose grilled sole, halibut au gratin, grilled fillet of turbot or sole bonne femme; lots more on the menu and you can even order a take-away traditional paella. You can be sure the only relationship between the fish here and the fish from your average fish and chip shop will be the word fish. Even the chips are properly made. Benskins and Tetleys ales; Murphys and wines by the glass.

> OPEN: 12–2. 6–10. Closed Sun eve and all day Mon.
> Real Ale. Restaurant.
> Children welcome. No dogs.

GREAT MISSENDEN

George   Tel: 01494 862084
94 High Street, Great Missenden, Bucks HP16 0BG
Free House. John & Susan Holmes, licensees.

Pockets of delight still remain in Great Missenden; the George, an old coaching inn built towards the end of the 15th century as a hospice for the nearby abbey, is one. Grade II listed, the bars still have their original heavily beamed ceilings. New owners have taken over, and things have swung to the east on the culinary front: all is authentic Thai. Still some vegetarian dishes and Adnams, Flowers, Youngs, Morlands Old Speckled Hen and two guest beers, also mulled wine in winter. There is a lovely large garden.

> OPEN: 11–11 (12–10.30 Sun).
> Real Ale. No-smoking restaurant.
> Children in eating areas. Dogs on leads. Six bedrooms.

HEDGERLEY

White Horse   Tel: 01753 643225
Village Lane, Hedgerley Village, Nr Slough, Bucks SL2 3UY
Free House. Kevin Brooker & Dot Hobbs, licensees.

A nice old country local with its original small public bar and larger lounge bar. At the end of the village, this pleasing pub hides behind some extravagant window boxes. The White Horse serves home-cooked food; the cold bar menu has a refrigerated cold tray that keeps the salads fresh. Hot food could include steak and mushroom pie, chilli, home-made fish cakes, quiches and some chicken dishes. The menu frequently changes. Always six ales available; they change too from day to day. Lovely views from the big garden. Good walks nearby.

> OPEN: 11–3. 5.30–11 (12–10.30 Sun).
> Real Ale.
> Children allowed in the garden. Dogs in public bar and garden.

HIGH WYCOMBE

Chequers   Tel: 01494 883070
Bullocks Farm Lane, Wheeler End, High Wycombe, Bucks HP14 3NH
Fullers. S. Warner & A. Kaiser, licensees.

A 300-year-old, white-painted village pub on the edge of Wheeler End Common; between
the two Wycombes. Situated in well-kept gardens and looking very rural, friendly and welcoming, the Chequers is a pleasing, unspoilt pub with good winter log fires in the big
inglenook fireplace. The bar-snack menu is available lunchtimes only: filled baguettes or ciabattas, freshly made sandwiches, mussels cooked in cumin, ginger, white wine and cream. Thai
fishcakes, warm avocado and smoked-bacon salad, and from the specials menu: roast partridge
with a sweet-potato rosti and leek and mushroom stuffing, or grilled fillets of lemon sole with
king prawns in a white-wine and chive butter sauce. There is also an à la carte menu and
Sunday roast lunch. Fullers range of ales, and a good selection of wines. Plenty of walks nearby.

OPEN: 11–3. 5.30–11 (12–10.30 Sun).
Real Ale.
Children welcome. Dogs on leads.
Cards: all major cards except Amex and Diners.

LITTLE MISSENDEN

Crown   Tel: 01494 862571
Little Missenden, Nr Amersham, Bucks HP7 0RD
Free House. Trevor How, licensee.

So many of these charming Buckinghamshire pubs were cottages in their previous lives,
including the Crown. Owned by the same family for about 70 years, the building dates back
to the 17th century and has just one bar decorated with old farm implements. Snack menu
at lunchtime: simple home-made food, steak and kidney pies, salads, ploughman's, sandwiches – that sort of thing. Hook Norton Best Bitter, Adnams and one weekly changing
guest beer. Little Missenden gets its name from the River Misbourne which runs (except in
a drought) along the bottom of the pub garden, eventually flowing into Shardloes Lake.

OPEN: 11–2.30. 6–11 (12–2.30. 7–10.30 Sun).
Real Ale. No food Sunday.
No children. Dogs on leads.

NEWPORT PAGNELL

Bull Inn   Tel: 01908 610325
33 Tickford Street, Newport Pagnell, Bucks MK16 9AE
Free House. Terry Fairfield, licensee.

Home of the Aston Martin – the town, not the Bull! But they are geared up, if you excuse
the pun, to the speed of modern life. Service by fax: if you are in a hurry you can fax your

lunch order and they'll have it ready and waiting for you when you arrive. Very sensible, if you know what you want. This old coaching inn is typically 17th-century inside, unmodernised and haunted. Outside? Well, you can see for yourself, those Victorians couldn't leave well alone! Even so, it's a haven for beer drinkers: when the Bull says that eight real ales are continuously on tap, they don't mean the same eight; they really range around the country. Lots of good sustaining food to go with the beer: trout stuffed with prawns, a seafood platter, seafood pasta, cauliflower and broccoli bake, vegetable lasagne or, if you really must, a cheeseburger and chips. As for the beers – go and be surprised. Reasonable wine list. Seats in the garden.

OPEN: 11.30–2.30. 5–11 (11.30–11 Sat. 12–10.30 Sun).
Real Ale.
Children if they are eating. Dogs on leads. Wheelchair access. Car park.

TURVILLE
Bull & Butcher   Tel: 01491 638283
Turville, Nr Henley on Thames, Bucks RG9 6QU
Brakspear. Nicholas Abington Abbott, licensee.

Next to the 13th-century church, this is another film star – TV's *The Vicar of Dibley*, *Goodnight Mr Tom* and other series. First licensed in 1617, the black-and-white timbered pub was built in the middle of the 16th century. Inside this charming old pub all is as it should be; low-beamed ceilings, big log fires – one in the inglenook – and unusually, a 50-foot-deep well with a glass cover. Their very own emergency water supply! The Bull and Butcher has had a lot of praise in the national press because they serve seriously well-cooked food from a short, clever menu. As a starter you could have seafood terrine with fresh pesto, coarse chicken-liver and pork-belly pâté served with toast and seasonal chutney, or anti pasto – Parma ham and Milana salami with marinated vegetables and Parmesan. Main courses include sausages, mash, roast shallots and gravy, Italian seafood stew with rosemary crostini and mascarpone or a chargrilled lamb gigot steak with ratatouille and Lyonnaise potatoes. A Brakspear pub, so Brakspear beers plus a guest, Weston's cider – one still scrumpy – 38 wines on the list, 38 by the glass.

OPEN: 11–3. 6–11 (11–3. 6.30–11 Sat. 12–5. 7.30–10.30 Sun).
Real Ale. Restaurant.
Children by arrangement. Dogs on leads. Wheelchair access. Car park.
Cards: Delta, MasterCard, Switch, Visa.

WEST WYCOMBE
George & Dragon   Tel: 01494 464414
West Wycombe, Nr High Wycombe, Bucks HP14 3AB
Inntrepreneur. Philip & Cass Todd, lease.

In this village of fine 15th- and 18th-century houses, owned by the National Trust, the George, a former coaching inn on the old London to Oxford road, is full of atmosphere.

Built in the 15th century, extended and modernised in 1720, it is full of huge beams, sloping walls, big log fires and the ghost of a servant girl said to haunt the handsome staircase. Well-prepared food: home-made soup, seafood platter, satay chicken with a spicy peanut dip, salad niçoise with fresh tuna, venison pasty, chicken and oyster pancakes, five different chicken dishes, beef Wellington or fillet steak, a choice of home-made puddings and a selection of English cheeses. Menus change with the seasons. Fullers London Pride, Charles Wells Bombardier and guests. As the owners have opened a wine shop on the premises, you can expect a choice wine list, all by the glass. Interesting walks close by.

> OPEN: 11–2.30. 5.30–11 (11–11 Sat).
> Real Ale. Restaurant.
> Children in own room. Dogs on leads. Wheelchair access to the pub difficult but possible – lots of cobbles. Car park. Bedrooms.
> Cards: Amex, Delta, Diners, MasterCard, Switch, Visa.

BEST OF THE REST

EASINGTON

Mole & Chicken   Tel: 01844 208387

From Long Crendon, go up Carters Lane and follow the signs to Easington. A very pretty country pub that is leaning hard towards being a restaurant, but as they still serve beer, it is a pub with a difference; the dishes you choose are from an à la carte menu – no bar snacks – and what you get will have distanced itself from the average pub menu. How about grilled crostini of smoked salmon, trout and halibut over cream cheese with basil oil, or chicken breast basted in mixed herbs, stuffed with cream cheese and wrapped in smoked bacon and puff pastry with a smoked-cheddar and spring-onion sauce. Try to leave plenty of room for scrummy puds. Greene King IPA, Morlands Old Speckled Hen and Strongbow cider.

MOULSOE

Carrington Arms   Tel: 01908 218050

Big and built of brick to house Lord Carrington's estate manager; now a small hotel. Lots of steaks, game, other meat and lots of fish – all displayed for you to choose. Sold by weight, you can pick and mix and watch it cooked in front of you. Real ales, good wine list and champagne by the glass.

PRESTWOOD

Polecat Inn   Tel: 01494 862253

This pub is on the busy Great Missenden to High Wycombe road, but with luck you should find room in the car park. A delightful pub in a lovely garden. Very food-orientated, so you will find some interesting dishes on the menu: leek and potato soufflé baked in filo pastry and served on mixed leaves with chive sour cream and a fillet of beef

Wellington are among the main courses. Lots more; you can see delights await. Marstons Pedigree, Theakstons Best, Ruddles County, Wadworths 6X and Morlands Old Speckled Hen. About a dozen wines by the glass.
N.B. Closed Sunday evening.

THORNBOROUGH

Lone Tree   Tel: 01280 812334
Unusual real ales, some unusual English cheeses and decent food as well. Just off the busy A421; well, the 'off' bit is that the road has been straightened, so it's not quite on the road. Small, well kept, well polished and popular. Good wine list, farm ciders, country wines and whatever ales are currently on offer.

WADDESDON

Five Arrows   Tel: 01296 651727
Built in the late 19th century as part of the Rothschild estate, this is a rather smart small hotel with a good bar and a restaurant serving interesting, stylish food. Adnams Bitter, Fullers London Pride, a really good wine list, champagne by the glass and anything else you might want – within reason. From here you are poised for a visit to Waddesdon Manor. Note that they don't serve bar snacks on Sundays.

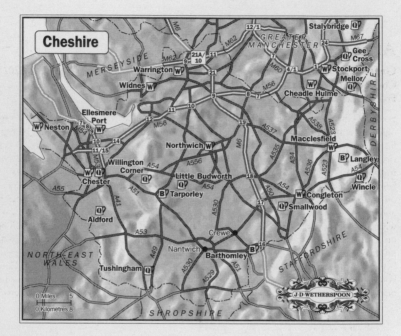

Cheshire

MERSEYSIDE

GREATER MANCHESTER

DERBYSHIRE

STAFFORDSHIRE

SHROPSHIRE

NORTH-EAST WALES

Stalybridge
Gee Cross
Stockport
Mellor
Cheadle Hulme
Macclesfield
Langley
Wincle
Congleton
Smallwood
Little Budworth
Tarporley
Willington Corner
Chester
Aldford
Tushingham
Nantwich
Barthomley
Crewe
Northwich
Ellesmere Port
Neston
Widnes
Warrington

M6 M62 M67 M60 M56 M53 M54 M53/54
A537 A538 A523 A535 A34 A536 A523 A54 A50 A556 A54 A530 A529 A51 A49 A53 A41 A55 A556

12/1 24 21A/10 11 9 10 21 4/1 1 8 7 19 18 17 16 11/15 14 12 7 8 9 10

0 Miles 5
0 Kilometres 8

J.D.WETHERSPOON

Cheshire

ALDFORD

Grosvenor Arms
Tel: 01244 620228

Chester Road, Aldford, Cheshire CH3 6HJ
Free House. Gary Kidd, licensee.

South of Chester and not far from Eaton Hall, the Duke of Westminster's estate, it's a large, dignified building thought to have been built for the estate – it's certainly been given the family name. Cosy is not a word one would use; formal would be more to the point – just right for the classy area it's in. Inside is more redolent of a country house: comfortable seating areas and a smart, flowery, no-smoking conservatory. That said, there is a bar serving beer where you can also order a sandwich with a difference: open egg and watercress mayonnaise on sun-dried tomato bread, rare roast beef with horseradish or open smoked salmon and cream cheese on walnut bread. From the menu: layered crab, guacamole and tomato with a red-pepper dressing, Caesar salad, garlic and lemon stuffed chicken breast served hot on a niçoise salad, medallions of beef fillet cooked in a mustard, brandy, cream and wild-mushroom sauce, maybe pear tarte tatin to finish. Batemans XB and Flowers IPA are the beers; there are over 100 single malts, 30 bourbons and 25 Irish whiskies which could keep you happily occupied for a considerable time, as well as a good, reasonably priced wine list, many by the glass. You do rather well here. Outside is an attractive terrace and gardens.

> OPEN: 11.30–11 (12–10.30 Sun).
> Real Ale.
> Children welcome. Dogs in one bar only. Wheelchair access. Car park.
> Cards: Amex, Delta, MasterCard, Switch, Visa.

CHESTER

Albion
Tel: 01244 340345

Park Street (off Newgate Street), Chester CH1 1RN
Inn Partnership. Michael Mercer, licensee.

Chester's medieval buildings, galleried streets, glorious Tudor houses and magnificent cathedral make it one of the treasures of the country. You'll find the Albion tucked under the walls of the best-preserved walled city in England, friendly and unchanging. The landlord has a fascination with the First World War and has collected a quantity of memorabilia and contemporary pictures – as well as a number of artifacts from the 1940s and

Best Cellars

OLD STOCKPORT (3.5% ABV)
- rich golden body with a refreshingly hoppy taste and lightish alcohol content.

XB (4.0% ABV)
- a smooth bitter ale with a malty taste. First brewed in the Lake District.

HATTER'S (3.3% ABV)
- brewed from quality hops and barley and cask conditioned to produce a mellow, well balanced brew.

OLD TOM (8.5% ABV)
- smooth, dark and mellow. Brewed from a recipe almost as old as the brewery itself.

FREDERICS (5.0% ABV)
- light and golden in colour and packed with flavour. Named after the brewery's founder. Also available in bottles.

BEST BITTER (4.2% ABV)
- pale and bright with a full bitterness derived from choice aroma hops.

FREDERIC ROBINSON LIMITED, UNICORN BREWERY, STOCKPORT, CHESHIRE SKI IJJ
TELEPHONE: 0161 480 6571 FAX: 0161 476 6011
Website: www.frederic-robinson.com

1950s, all displayed in the Edwardian-style rooms. An interesting choice of bar food, an inventive menu and no chips. No butter in foil packets either. From the changing menu you could choose lamb's liver and smoked bacon with onions in a rich cider gravy, home-baked spiced honeyed gammon in a rich port-wine Cumberland sauce, award-winning haggis and tatties, Staffordshire oatcakes served with broccoli and Stilton with smoked bacon, individual cottage pie with a crisp leek and cheese crust served with pickled red cabbage, filled butties (doorstep size) and lots more. Greenalls Mild and Original, Cains Bitter, a weekly guest beer and a large selection of malt whiskies.

OPEN: 11.30–3. 5.30–11 (11–11 Fri).
Real Ale.
Children not encouraged. No dogs.

CHESTER

The Old Harker's Arms   Tel: 01244 344525
1 Russell Street, Chester CH3 5AL
Free House. Barbie Hill & Catryn Devaney, licensees.

There is still plenty of activity on the canal, but now it is mostly pleasure craft, so what was once a busy Victorian canal warehouse is now a spacious, successful pub. A well-run place serving pub grub with a difference: sandwiches, toasted ciabattas and ploughman's, as well as mushrooms in herb-cream sauce, focaccia bread, chorizo sausage, tomato, Mediterranean vegetables and melted mozzarella, salmon and dill fishcakes, linguini pasta with sun-dried tomatoes, courgettes and peppers with creamed basil sauce, or chicken breast marinaded in garlic and rosemary with a wild-mushroom sauce. Daily specials on the blackboard. Daily papers to read if you're kept waiting, and plenty of things to drink: Boddingtons, Thwaites ales and six changing guests: eight cask beers always on; 27 malt whiskies and a good, small wine list, featuring many New World wines – 16 available by the glass. No music, no fruit machines, no pool table – just a friendly, jolly pub, with a view of the watery comings and goings.

OPEN: 11.30–11 (12–10.30 Sun).
Real Ale.
Children before 7pm. No dogs. Wheelchair access.
Car parking after 5.30 and all weekend and Bank Holidays. No garden.
Cards: Amex, MasterCard, Visa.

GEE CROSS

Grapes Hotel   Tel: 0161 368 2614
Stockport Road, Gee Cross, Hyde, Cheshire SK14 5RU
Robinsons. Brian Samuels, tenant.

Edwardian through and through, this is a gabled, bay-windowed building, with leaded lights and engraved Edwardian windows, four large carpeted rooms with red ceilings, brass light fittings, and tiles from bar top to floor. It's on the corner of a steep hill in the old village of Gee Cross, opposite an imposing Victorian-Gothic church. It has cheerful, friendly staff and customers. Robinsons traditional ales stocked, including Bitter and Best Mild. A bowling green is attached to the pub so you can while away the time encouraging the experts.

OPEN: 12–3. 5–11.
Real Ale.
No children. No dogs. Occasionally stabling for your horse.
Wheelchair access (not WC).

LITTLE BUDWORTH

Shrewsbury Arms   Tel: 01829 760240
Chester Road, Little Budworth, Nr Tarporley, Cheshire CW6 9EY
Robinsons. Tim Gandy, tenant.

On the 'Cheshire Fine Food Trail', this 16th-century old farmhouse has had a lively past. Inside are framed articles reporting on the days when it was just a beer house very near local races; the pub's cellars got somewhat crowded on race days when local bookmakers hid there to escape irate Irish navvies who had foolishly bet, and lost, their wages. Now, in less fraught times, this is a friendly, relaxed place with well-kept ales and better than usual pub food, including several vegetarian choices, fresh fish and specials: chicken tikka masala, or diced pork in a cider and apple sauce; extra specials of medallions of lamb with Dijon mustard and tarragon or duckling à l'orange, and of course bar snacks and freshly made soup, egg mayonnaise, steak casserole and ocean pie. Robinsons Best Bitter and seasonal ales. Short, wide-ranging wine list. You are very near good local walks – the Whitegate Way and Delamere Forest – also the interesting Winsford salt mines and, if you're so inclined, Oulton Park motor racing circuit.

OPEN: 11.30–2.30. 6–11 (12–2.30. 7–10.30 Sun).
Real Ale.
Children welcome, so are dogs. Wheelchair access. Car park.
Cards: MasterCard, Switch, Visa.

MELLOR Nr Stockport

Oddfellows Arms   Tel: 0161 449 7826
73 Moor End Road, Mellor, Cheshire SK6 5PT
Free House. Robert Cloughley, licensee.

It looks as a 300-year-old country pub should: flagstone floor, low ceilings, open fire. A fine old building with a first-floor dining room and a handsome bar on the ground floor. Famous locally for its fish dishes – there is usually a choice of eight – bar food as well, all prepared 'in pub': soup, mussel chowder, medley of cured fish, cherry-tomato bruschetta, Moroccan lamb casserole, Catalan pork tenderloin, also steaks, curries, hot and cold sandwiches, salads, ploughman's or something from the specials board: tender chunks of lamb cooked in ale, duo of tuna and swordfish brochettes, haddock poached in white wine and laced with a light prawn, parsley and white-wine cream sauce. The restaurant is no smoking and there are some tables outside. Adnams Best, Marstons Bitter, Pedigree and a rotating guest beer.

> OPEN: 12–3. 5.30–11 (12–3. 7–10.30 Sun).
> Real Ale.
> Children until 8.30pm. Wheelchair access into bar only.
> Cards: all major credit cards.

SMALLWOOD

Blue Bell Inn
Tel: 01477 500262

Spen Green, Smallwood, Nr Congleton, Cheshire
Greenalls. Robert Slack, tenant.

Away from the industrial centres and Cheshire is like a huge glorious park: grassy slopes, woodland and small rivers. In the midst of all this is the 16th-century Blue Bell – only 3 miles from Congleton and Alsager. A gem of a pub with beamed bars and big log fires – just as you imagine it ought to be. Bar food, available every lunchtime, is limited, but there is always soup, toasted sandwiches, home-made pies, filled baguettes, cheese and pâté platters and filled jacket potatoes. They have won a CAMRA award for their beer so you know it is tiptop: Greenalls Bitter, Timothy Taylors Landlord, Bass and weekly guests. Keg beers too. Outside is a picturesque garden.

> OPEN: Winter (Oct–May) 12–3. 5.30–11 (12–3. 7–10.30 Sun).
> Summer (June–Sept) 12–3. 5.30–11 (11–11 Sat & Sun).
> Real Ale.
> Children welcome. Dogs on leads.

STALYBRIDGE

Stalybridge Station Buffet Bar
Tel: 0161 303 0007

Stalybridge Station, Rassbotham Street, Cheshire SK15 1RF
Free House. Sylvia Wood & John Hesketh, licensees.

Here is an old Victorian station buffet going great guns; they have even expanded into the ladies' waiting room and the stationmaster's quarters – without the stationmaster! Nostalgia is fully catered for. All the original fittings are still here: the conservatory, bar and coal fire, railway memorabilia and photos of the glory of steam and the working station. Newspapers and magazines to read and seats on the platform where you can sip your freshly made tea or coffee. Home-cooked food: sandwiches, ploughman's and two or three daily specials. Boddingtons beer, Flowers IPA, Wadworths 6X and constantly changing guests – over 3250 in four years – increasing all the time. Traditional scrumpy or perry available too. Regular beer festivals with jazz on the platform.

> OPEN: 11–11 (12–10.30 Sun).
> Real Ale.
> Children welcome. Dogs too. Wheelchair access. Car park.

TUSHINGHAM

Blue Bell Inn   Tel: 01948 662172
Tushingham, Whitchurch, Shropshire SY13 4QS
Free House. Patrick & Lydia Gage, licensees.

There isn't any music at this 17th-century Blue Bell, but there are plenty of children. So if you want to go out for the evening 'en famille' this is the place for you, near the Shropshire border, on the A41, 3 miles north of Whitchurch. It is a pub with a ghost; no ordinary ghost though: one duck. This wartime duck had attitude and met an untimely end. Fed up with customers complaining about his aggressive bird, the then landlord disposed of him, walling up his body under the pub stairs. Years later his skeleton was found during restoration work and carefully returned to his burial place. But he still haunts the pub. Built as a coaching inn in 1667, it has some foundations dating back to around the 14th century, making it possibly one of the oldest buildings in Cheshire. Black and white – typical Cheshire timbering – the inside still has beams, sloping floors, and crooked doors with not a right angle between them. Good home-cooked food, all freshly prepared, including the vegetables and the curries. As the landlord says, 'You may note that our food benefits from the nationality of the owners. As an American, I see to the quantity and my Russian wife sees to the quality.' Take the home-made soup. This comes in two sizes: normal – one roll and butter, and large – and this means large – with two rolls and butter! Or you could have garlic mussels served hot with toast, local trout (big) and other fish dishes from the specials board, locally bought meat, Cumberland sausages and fresh chickens. Three hand pumps, always Drawwell Bitter, probably Hanby's Ales, another from a local Cheshire brewery and a guest: Coach House, Woods, Beartown, etc. Lots of room in the extensive gardens for you, the children and everyone else.

> OPEN: 12–3. 6–11 (7–10.30 Sun).
> Real Ale. Restaurant.
> Children welcome. Dogs on leads. Wheelchair access. Car park.
> N.B. Occasional Classic FM in one room – quiet elsewhere.

WILLINGTON

Boot Inn   Tel: 01829 751375
Boothsdale, Willington, Nr Tarporley, Cheshire CW6 0NH
Tied to Nomura. Michael Gollins, licensee.

In Cat Lane, the Boot, known locally as the Cat, is a delightful country pub. This area, known as 'Little Switzerland' because of its grassy slopes, woodlands and wooded ridges, has also played a significant part in the history of the country, scattered as it is with the remains of Iron Age forts and Roman ramparts. Tucked in the shelter of the hill is the Boot. Originally a row of cottages, it has some fine old beams inside, plus big fires and quarry-tiled floors. On Cheshire's Fine Food Trail, the Boot's interesting menu is served in either the bar or restaurant: home-made soup, anchovy bake, devilled kidneys in a port-wine sauce, warm smoked trout, traditional steak and kidney cooked in ale, escalopes of chicken, calves' liver, bacon and onions, steaks, salad platters, filled warm baguettes or even a freshly made sandwich; specials and vegetarian dishes too. Traditional roast on Sundays. Greenalls, Bass Cains, Flowers IPA, the local Weetwood ales and regular guests. Over 35 malt whiskies and a good wine list. A booklet with details of six circular walks from the Boot is available in the pub. Tables on the terrace.

OPEN: 11–3. 6–11 (11–11 Sat. 12–10.30 Sun).
Real Ale. Restaurant.
Children with well-behaved parents. No dogs. Car park.

WINCLE

Ship   Tel: 01260 227217
Wincle, Nr Macclesfield, Cheshire SK11 0QE
Free House. Mr Steven & Mrs Sally Simpson, licensees.

The comfortable old Ship is deep in lovely Cheshire countryside. You are surrounded by excellent walking country and many a footpath ends close to this 16th-century stone pub – as do the walkers, still in their boots – but in the tap room. The Ship was named in 1850 after a ship owned by the local Brocklehurst family of nearby Swythamly Hall was lost on an expedition with Sir Philip Brocklehurst on board. Inside they offer a good range of bar food, from soup and sandwiches to grilled trout, steaks, venison casserole and always the very popular gammon and eggs. Wednesday is fish day and there is a regularly changing specials section on the blackboard menu. Titanic Bitter from Burslem and changing guests – Timothy Taylors Landlord is the most regular guest of about 100 different ales per year. The wine list has been extended and includes specialist wines at sensible prices.

OPEN: 12–3. 7–11. Closed Mondays.
Real Ale.
Well-behaved children in family room. Dogs on leads. Wheelchair access (not WC). Car park.
Cards: Delta, MasterCard, Switch, Visa.

BEST OF THE REST

BARTHOMLEY

White Lion   Tel: 01270 882242
A very traditional, black-and-white, thatched, 17th-century inn, opposite the 15th-century village church where Robert Corke, landlord of the time, must have witnessed the Barthomley massacre during the Civil War. Ghosts may roam, but not during lunch. Newly painted, but nothing much else has changed, still wonderfully beamed, panelled and full of atmosphere. Reasonably priced bar food: soups, cheese and onion oatcakes, ham or cheese ploughman's and daily specials. Burtonwood Bitter and Top Hat plus a guest. Sunday roast lunch – do book.

LANGLEY

Leathers Smithy   Tel: 01260 252313

If you're a walker you probably know this place; if you're not – well, here it is. Not far from Macclesfield Forest, Teggs Nose country park and the Ridgegate Reservoir. A well-run, cosy old pub serving good value, interesting bar food to go with the real ale, cider and a choice of Irish or Scotch whiskies. No food Monday evenings.

TARPORLEY

Rising Sun   Tel: 01829 732423

In the High Street, this is a jolly, friendly village pub looking very pretty when the flowers are in bloom. Traditional bar food: sandwiches, toasties, filled jacket potatoes, lasagne, home-made pies and a restaurant menu. Robinsons range of ales.

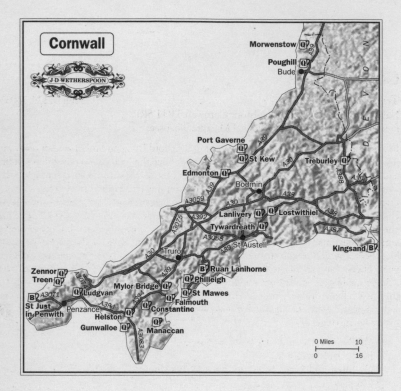

Cornwall

CONSTANTINE

Trengilly Wartha
Tel: 01326 340332

Nancenoy Constantine, Nr Helston, Cornwall TR11 5RP
Free House. Nigel Logan & Michael Maguire, licensees.

In acres of glorious garden, near a creek of the Helford River and in an area of outstanding beauty, this delightful old place has been here since the 18th century. Inside you'll find a low-beamed main bar, a lounge, an eating area off the bar, a no-smoking family conservatory and, outside, picnic tables so you can appreciate your surroundings. Lots of home-made bar food: soups – on the board by the bar – ciabatta garlic bread and cheese, chicken-liver and port pâté with home-made chutney. Perennial favourites: leek and cheese soufflé, crab cakes, smoked-chicken strudel, a traditional Cornish pasty as well as various ploughman's with home-made pickles, salads, steaks and daily specials from the blackboard, which usually features a number of fish dishes. Don't forget the delicious puds. There is also an imaginative restaurant menu. On Wednesday evenings you can have a home-made steak and kidney pudding and a pint of Sharp's Coaster for considerably less than usual. Exmoor Ale, Cotleigh, Tawny and Sharp's Doom Ale; other guests from small independent breweries. Ciders, a big selection of malt whiskies, and a good choice of wines by the bottle or glass.

> OPEN: 11–2.30. 6–11 (6.30–11 in winter).
> Real Ale. Restaurant.
> Children welcome. Dogs on leads. Wheelchair access (not WC). Bedrooms.
> Car park.
> Cards: Amex, Delta, Diners, MasterCard, Switch.

EDMONTON

Quarryman
Tel: 01208 816444

Edmonton, Nr Wadebridge, Cornwall PL27 7JA
Free House. Terry & Wendy de Villiers Kuun, licensees.

The Quarryman, built around a courtyard, originally the quarrymen's quarters, is now part of a sport and holiday complex. Three pleasant rooms – one of which is no smoking – where they serve good, sustaining bar food: sandwiches, filled ciabattas, lasagne, lots of fresh, locally caught fish and daily specials. Sharp's Doom Bar Bitter, Skinner's Knocker and Coastliner and guest beers. Handy for the Camel Trail and there's also a good walk from Wadebridge to Padstow along a path that follows the abandoned railway line. Other good walks too, and you're near the County Showground.

OPEN: 12–11 (12–10.30 Sun).
Real Ale. Restaurant.
Children in eating area. Dogs on leads. Wheelchair access (not WC).
Cards: MasterCard, Switch, Visa.

FALMOUTH

Seven Stars   Tel: 01326 312111
1 The Moor, Falmouth, Cornwall TR11 3QA
Free House. Rev. Barrington-Bennett, licensee.

After walking along the spectacular cliffs above the ancient port and admiring the glorious wooded countryside, you can make your way to the Seven Stars, a blissfully quiet pub built in 1660 and owned by the landlord's family since 1873. Also on The Moor is a monument celebrating the 150 years that the 'Falmouth packets', fast, light, ships, privately owned but contracted to the Post Office, delivered the mail to Europe and as far away as the West Indies. With a fine natural harbour, deep enough for big ships to moor as far inland as King Harry Ferry, Falmouth was for 200 years the first and last port of call for all Atlantic shipping. No food except crisps and nuts. Refreshment of the liquid kind only: draught Bass and Sharp's Own from the cask and guest beers. Tables on the forecourt.

OPEN: 11–3. 6–11.
Real Ale.
No children. Dogs in the back bar. Wheelchair access (not WC).

GUNWALLOE

The Halzephron   Tel: 01326 240406
Gunwalloe, Helston, Cornwall TR12 7QB
Free House. Angela Thomas, licensee.

Halzephron, a Cornish name meaning 'hell cliffs', is the only pub on the coastal path between Mullion and Porthleven. It is aptly named as much of the wood in this solidly built, 500-year-old stone pub comes from ships that were wrecked in the waters below. This is an area that had more than a nodding acquaintance with the smuggling and wrecking that went on in the past; a shaft connected to an underground tunnel still exists. Surrounded by dramatic scenery, small fishing villages and near the glories of the Helford river, this is a very popular place packed to the gunnels during the summer, not only for its well-kept beers, but for its food, which is above the ordinary. One menu for both bar and no-smoking restaurant ranges from the usual pub favourites to home-cooked dishes from the daily-changing specials board: seafood chowder with basil aioli, smoked-trout pâté with toasted brioche, boeuf bourguignon or pan-fried salmon steak on linguini, mussels and with a fennel and saffron cream sauce. Evening specials could include: terrine of guinea fowl confit with a fine bean, potato and shallot salad or lamb, lemon and honey tajine with chilli and apricot couscous, pan-fried cod steak on mustard lentils and crispy potatoes with an anchovy and caper dressing. Food here is creative and tempting. Sharp's Own, Doom Bar, a guest and an interesting wine list. Outside there are seats on the terrace and in the garden. Next to National Trust land, the pub has wonderful views across Mount's Bay towards Penzance and Land's End.

OPEN: 11.30–3. 6–11 (6.30–11 winter eves).
Real Ale. Restaurant.
Children in family room and restaurant. No dogs.
Wheelchair access possible but not easy.
Car park. Two en-suite double rooms.
Cards: Amex, Delta, MasterCard, Switch, Visa.

HELSTON

Blue Anchor   Tel: 01326 562821
50 Coinagehall Street, Helston, Cornwall
Free House. Kim Corbett & Simon Stone, licensees.

There is every possibility that this old place is the oldest brewery in the country, as local monks started brewing ale here about 500 years ago and continued even after the Dissolution of the monasteries. The strong own-brew Spingo Ale is a feature in this unspoilt 15th-century pub. Locally very popular, the Blue Anchor has two bars and a family room. Home-made soups, filled rolls, toasted sandwiches, fish pie, liver and bacon hotpot, different pies, home-made Cornish pasties and a changing selection of specials make up the menu. Ales here are in-house so to speak: Middle, Best, Spingo Special and Extra Special. You are allowed to see around the brewery some lunchtimes – by arrangement of course.

OPEN: All day.
Real Ale.
Children in family room. Dogs on leads.
Jazz 1st Mon and folk 2nd Mon in the month.

LANLIVERY

Crown Inn   Tel: 01208 872707
Lanlivery, Nr Bodmin, Cornwall PL30 5BT
Free House. R.D. Williams, licensee.

We are always interested in ghosts and this 12th-century longhouse, which must be one of the oldest buildings in Cornwall, has somehow managed to gather a couple of friendly spirits of the ethereal kind. They serve, the staff that is, the usual variety of bar snacks, including chef's specials from the blackboard, which changes twice a day. There is also a frequently changing à la carte menu in the restaurant. Always fresh fish and shellfish – the straight-out-of-the-sea-into-the-kitchen sort – and a comprehensive vegetarian menu. The vegetables are all freshly steamed and the bread rolls are made in the pub. Lots of sandwiches and bar snacks. All Sharp's ales at the moment. Picnic tables in the garden. Lovely views. Lanlivery is just off the Lostwithiel road, on the Saintsway, an ancient path that goes from coast to coast.

> OPEN: 11–3. 6–11.
> Real Ale. Restaurant.
> Children welcome. Dogs too. Wheelchair access. Two double en-suite bedrooms with own gardens.

LOSTWITHIEL

Royal Oak   Tel: 01208 872552
Duke Street, Lostwithiel, Cornwall PL22 1AH
Free House. Malcolm Hine, licensee.

There are many rumours of tunnels connecting pubs and other buildings, but not much in the way of evidence. The Royal Oak is a case in point; this very old pub has, they say, a smugglers' escape tunnel to Restormel Castle. Well! When you realise that the castle is about a mile away, it does seem a rather tall story. The Royal Oak, a town-centre pub in this old market town, serves a good choice of food from either the printed menu or the home-cooked daily specials on the blackboard: French onion soup, stuffed mushrooms, smoked-fish platter, salmon steak poached in a dill and cucumber sauce, sauté chicken in red wine, salads, vegetarian options and fruit pies for puds, not forgetting the clotted cream. At least six real ales including Fullers London Pride, Marstons Pedigree, draught Bass, guest beers from the smaller breweries and lots of unusual bottled beers. Seats on the terrace.

> OPEN: 11–11 (12–10.30 Sun).
> Real Ale. Restaurant.
> Children welcome. Dogs on leads. Car park. Bedrooms.
> Cards: Amex, Delta, Diners, MasterCard, Switch, Visa.
> N.B. Jukebox in public bar.

LUDGVAN

White Hart   Tel: 01736 740574
Ludgvan, Nr Penzance, Cornwall TR20 8EY
Inn Partnership. Dennis Churchill, tenant.

This is an unspoilt, quiet and appealing 14th-century village pub with rugs on the floor, two big wood-burning stoves for warmth and fine old seats and tables. The White Hart's small beamed rooms are full of interesting objects, pictures and photographs. They serve good, reasonably priced bar food: sandwiches, home-made soup and real Cornish pasties, salads, omelettes, steaks, daily specials and fresh fish. There is a no-smoking section in the eating area. Flowers IPA and Marstons Pedigree from the barrel, plus one guest ale during the season.

OPEN: 11–2.30. 6–11.
Real Ale. Restaurant. No food Mon eves Oct–May.
Children in restaurant. Dogs on leads.
N.B. The music you hear will probably be the local male voice choir practising, though the radio may be on.

MANACCAN
New Inn
Tel: 01326 231323
Manaccan, Helston, Cornwall TR12 6AJ
Greenalls. Penny Williams, licensee.

Only one bar in this cob-built thatched pub. Small and friendly, it can just about seat 29 – more can get in if everyone stands up. They serve home-cooked food: ploughman's and sandwiches of course, fresh-salmon pie, gammon in cider, steaks and some chicken dishes, daily specials too. Flowers IPA from a barrel behind the bar, Castle Eden, Wadworths 6X and a guest beer. A beer garden at the rear takes the overflow.

OPEN: 12–3. 6–11.
Real Ale.
Children: if very well behaved. Dogs welcome.

MORWENSTOW
Bush Inn
Tel: 01288 331242
Morwenstow, Nr Bude, Cornwall EX23 9SR
Free House. Mrs B. Moore, licensee.

All the land from Morwenstow church to the spectacular Vicarage Cliffs is now owned and protected by the National Trust. In this isolated village, the Bush Inn joins those listed as 'one of the oldest pubs in Britain'. Once a monastic rest house, it is thought to date back to the 10th century. Near the coastal path, this little pub is full of fascinating items, including a propeller from an old De Havilland Gypsy Moth aeroplane. Lunchtime bar food only: home-made soup and a home-made stew in winter, crab and smoked mackerel with rolls and garnish in the summer are specialities of the house. You will also find pasties, ploughman's, daily specials and good substantial puddings such as spotted dick. Beers include St Austell HSB on hand pump and guests. Draught Guinness and cider. Seats outside in the courtyard. There is a ship's figurehead in the churchyard, surrounded by the graves of 40 unknown men who drowned in one of the ferocious storms that blow up in this part of Cornwall.

OPEN: 12–3. 7–11. Closed Mon Oct–Apr except Bank
Holidays.
Real Ale. Lunchtime food only but not Sun.
No children. No dogs.

MYLOR BRIDGE

Pandora   Tel: 01326 372678
Restronguet Creek, Mylor Bridge, Nr Falmouth, Cornwall TR11 5ST
St Austell. John Milan, tenant.

From Mylor Bridge there is a lane which brings you to Restronguet Creek and the Pandora. This wonderfully sheltered creek is a haven for the small boats and yachts. You can't get much closer to the creek than the Pandora; with a very high spring tide, it isn't so much near the water as in it. It has a jetty where you can tie up under the eyes of a jovial audience who, drinks in hand, could be trying to be helpful. Having said that, you'll find that this very pretty 13th-century thatched pub – with showers for visiting yachtsmen – has three bars, a no-smoking restaurant and two no-smoking areas. Bar food includes home-made soup, stuffed pancakes, Restronguet fish pie, crab cakes, lots of local fish, and daily specials. There is an evening à la carte menu when you could have local Helford mussels (when available) steamed in white wine and flavoured with herbs, breast of chicken stuffed with wild mushrooms, sage and bacon in a Marsala sauce, roast rack of lamb in a port and rosemary sauce and lots more fish. St Austell's ales and Bass on hand pump. Malt whiskies and a large selection of wines. If you are coming by road, remember parking can be a bit tight at the height of summer.

> OPEN: 11–11 summer. 11–2.30. 6–11 winter (11–11 winter weekends).
> Real Ale. Food till 10pm summer; restaurant open all year.
> Children in eating area. Dogs on leads. Wheelchair access (not WC). Car park.
> Bedrooms.
> Cards: Amex, Delta, MasterCard, Switch, Visa.

PHILLEIGH

Roseland   Tel: 01872 580254
Philleigh-in-Roseland, Truro, Cornwall TR2 5NB
Freehouse. Colin Phillips, licensee.

Long, low, white-painted and nearly hidden behind a glorious summer floral display; there is just one low-ceilinged bar inside this typically 17th-century pub with a big log fire in winter. In summer there is a sunny courtyard for you to enjoy. Home-made food includes rich Stilton and port pâté, apple, celery and mussel cocktail, filled baked potatoes, plough-man's, sandwiches, real Cornish pasties, local clams in summer, Philleigh shank of lamb braised with cranberries, red wine, mint, rosemary, garlic and bitter orange, seafood pan-cakes and, as you might expect, lots of fish dishes. There is a greater selection in the evenings. In summer there is even more fish on the menu. Greenalls Bitter, Morlands Old Speckled Hen, Marstons Pedigree and draught Bass. Farm cider in summer; a good range of malt whiskies. Short, reasonable wine list, some by the glass. Certainly no muzak, no jukebox or one-armed bandits, but they do entertain the local rugby club – singers all – and the choir has a practice a couple of times a week.

> OPEN: 11–3. 6–11 (11.30–3. 6.30–11 winter).
> Real Ale.
> Children welcome. Dogs on leads. Wheelchair access. Car park.
> Cards: MasterCard, Switch, Visa.

PORT GAVERNE

Port Gaverne Inn   Tel: 01208 880293
Port Gaverne, Cornwall PL29 3SQ
Free House. Mrs M. Ross, licensee.

Port Gaverne was a flourishing fishing village in the 19th century. Now it's a delightful place to stay. White-painted, the inn is close to the sea and just what you would expect a 300-year-old pub to be. It has beams, big log fires and comfortable bars serving a good choice of bar food: home-made soup, freshly filled sandwiches, ploughman's, lasagne, wonderful fish dishes and daily specials. Sharp's Doom Bar, Bass and Flowers IPA. A good-size wine list and malt whiskies. If you're feeling energetic you can walk over the headland to Port Isaac, and, if the weather is favourable, clearly see Tintagel.

> OPEN: 11–11 (12–10.30 Sun). Closed early Jan–mid Feb.
> Real Ale. Restaurant.
> Children in restaurant. Dogs on leads. Bedrooms in converted cottages. Parking can be difficult.
> N.B. New licensees were due to take over during January 2002, and we couldn't find out their policy on music before going to press.

POUGHILL

Preston Gate Inn   Tel: 01288 354017
Poughill, Nr Bude, Cornwall EX23 9ET
Free House. N. Rice, licensee.

Two miles inland from Bude, this cosy, welcoming local is especially popular in summer. Lunchtimes are busy, the locals joining the holidaymakers in the evening. Satisfying bar food: marinated mussels, crispy-coated king prawns in garlic and herbs, potato skins with dip, seafood platter, chicken Kiev with mushrooms, grilled plaice, basket meals, ploughman's, lunchtime sandwiches and, of course, daily specials off the blackboard. They tell us that they have two specialities here: a 250-gram fillet steak washed down with a couple of pints of Marstons! Also Flowers IPA, Boddingtons and a local bitter. Water for the dog. Seats on the terrace.

> OPEN: 12–2.30. 6.30ish–11.
> Real Ale.
> No small children. Love dogs. Wheelchair access. Car park.

ST KEW

St Kew Inn   Tel: 01208 841259
St Kew, Nr Wadebridge, Cornwall PL30 3HB
St Austell. Des & Ginny Weston, tenants.

Next to the church, in a peaceful wooded valley. This stone-built 15th-century inn has what must have been an impressive stableyard – now the pub's car park. Inside are two bars and two dining rooms, both with very extensive menus which could offer home-made soup, sandwiches, seafood lasagne, beef in Guinness with herb dumplings, steaks and king prawns in garlic, not forgetting the Sunday roast and a children's menu. The beers are St Austell Tinners, Hicks, Cornish Cream, Duchy served from casks behind the counter and one guest in summer. There is a large garden for lounging in.

> OPEN: 11–2.30. 6–11 (July–Aug 11–11).
> Real Ale. Restaurant.
> Well-behaved children allowed in restaurant and own room; none under 14 in bar; none under six in eves. No dogs.

St Mawes

The Rising Sun
Tel: 01326 270233
Fax: 01326 270198

The Square, St Mawes, Nr Truro, Cornwall TR2 5DJ
St Austell. R.J. Milan, tenant.

This small holiday resort has a sheltered harbour, sandy beaches and a mild climate – all you could wish for. St Mawes, built on a steep slope, is in a delightful setting on the 'Cornish Riviera' and just across the road from the harbour wall is the small, elegant, beautifully cared-for Rising Sun. The cooking is exceptional; there could be a crab and celery soup and a saddle of rabbit in a red-wine sauce, salmon or corn-fed chicken. The blackboard in the bar lists more simple dishes. The well-thought-out menus go with the well-kept St Austell's range of ales and good wine list, about 18 by the glass. Seats on the sunny terrace facing the harbour.

> OPEN: 11–11.
> Real Ale. Restaurant.
> Children welcome. Dogs too. Wheelchair access. Bedrooms. Car park.
> Cards: Amex, Delta, Diners, MasterCard, Switch, Visa.

Treburley

Springer Spaniel
Tel: 01579 370424

Treburley, Nr Launceston, Cornwall PL15 9NS
Free House. Colin Philips, licensee.

On the A388 between Callington and Launceston, this cream-painted, popular pub has a reputation for serving some imaginative food. The menu, available in both the bar and restaurant, could offer home-made soup, seafood chowder, fillet of smoked trout served with apricot chutney, a plate of smoked salmon, tagliatelle with cream and mushrooms topped with grated Parmesan, also several fish dishes, home-made pies and Cornish crab pasties, breast of chicken served with a white-wine, cream and mushroom sauce, vegetables and cheese en croute, beef stroganoff and lots more, as well as filled French bread rolls, cold meats with pickles and a choice of fish and salads. Wonderful puds. Sharp's Doom Bar and Springer Ale, brewed especially for the pub, and occasional guest beers. New World wines to go with the good food.

OPEN: 11–3. 5.30–11.
Real Ale. Restaurant.
Children welcome. Dogs on leads. Wheelchair access (not WC).
Cards: Delta, MasterCard, Switch, Visa.

TREEN
Gurnard's Head Hotel   Tel: 01736 796928
Treen, Zennor, St Ives, Cornwall TR26 3DE
Free House. Ray & Joy Kell, licensees.

The hamlet of Treen is on the spectacular Atlantic coast between St Ives and St Just. The Gurnard's Head Hotel, close to the North Coastal Path, actually stands on Gurnard's Head, a rocky promontory among massive granite cliffs embracing sheltered, hidden coves. A traditional Cornish country pub, properly modernised, with a welcoming, cosy bar. Not surprisingly, as the sea is on the doorstep so to speak, the emphasis is on fish. The same menu, available in both the bar and dining room, always has some favourites such as their own Cornish seafood broth, the catch of the day, a 'walker's platter' – for encouragement – maybe Cornish crab claws with a garlic mayonnaise, Moroccan-style grey mullet fillet or sautéed duck breast with pine nuts and balsamic jus. Evenings there could be a smoked-fish medley, rillettes of pork, supreme of chicken Normandy style, or Aberdeen Angus steak, delicious puds and daily specials. Flowers Original, Skinner's Cornish Knocker ale and Fullers London Pride. Short wine list. Don't confuse this Treen with Treen in south Cornwall, near St Leven.

OPEN: 11–3. 6–11 (12–4. 7–10.30 Sun).
Real Ale.
Children welcome, dogs too. Wheelchair access. Bedrooms. Car park.
Cards: Amex, MasterCard, Switch, Visa.

TYWARDREATH
New Inn   Tel: 01726 813901
Fore Street, Tywardreath, Cornwall
St Austell. Mr & Mrs Hill, licensees.

All you have to do when you get here is ask for the pub and this is where you will end up, as it's the only pub in this small village. Built in the 18th century of stone under a slate roof, the New Inn originally had two bars but the saloon bar is now a family area. Bar snacks are served at lunchtime but you're really here for the beer; people come from miles around for the draught Bass tapped straight from the barrel. Other beers are St

Austell XXXX Mild, Tinners and the seasonal Winter Warmer. Near a safe beach at Par Sands.

> OPEN: 12–3. 6–11 (11–11 Sat. 12–4. 7–10.30 Sun).
> Real Ale.
> Children welcome. Dogs on leads.

ZENNOR

Tinners Arms   Tel: 01736 796927
Zennor, Cornwall TR26 3BY
Free House. David Care, licensee.

Overlooked by St Senara's Church, the Tinners Arms is in a wild landscape 300 feet above the sea. Over 400 years old, with a granite face set to the ferocious weather that sometimes pounds this part of the Cornish coast, this pub used to be the tin-miners' local. As with many Cornish pubs, it was rebuilt on the same site as the original 12th-century hostelry which housed the masons working on the local church. Continuing the tradition of feeding and watering the populace, this comfortable old pub offers good simple bar food: smoked mackerel, lasagne, ploughman's, chicken and ham pie and some vegetarian dishes. The menu changes with the season. Sharp's ales from the barrel – as well as Sharp's Special during the winter and Cornish Coaster in the summer.

> OPEN: 11–3. 6.30–11 (11–11 summer).
> Real Ale.
> Children, but not in main bar. Dogs on leads.
> N.B. Occasional Classic FM.

BEST OF THE REST

KINGSAND

Halfway House   Tel: 01752 822279
Between the two conservation villages of Kingsand and Cawsand, the South West Coast Path passes this attractive village and its equally attractive twin at Cawsand. So if you're thinking of stopping off, they serve some interesting bar food: fish soup, chicken supreme with wild mushrooms, venison casserole with port and Guinness, filled French bread and ploughman's to go with the Boddingtons, Sharps and Bass. Decent wines.

RUAN LANIHORNE

Kings Head   Tel: 01852 501263
Where the River Ruan meets the Fal, this delightful pub is opposite the village church. Beamed and comfortable inside, they serve a good choice of bar food including home-made soup, potted shrimps, fillet steak, vegetarian dishes and daily specials. Wine by the

bottle, carafe or glass and Hardy and Sharps ales. Views of the Fal estuary from the sunny garden.

ST JUST IN PENWITH

Star   Tel: 01736 788767
At 1 Fore Street. Unchanged for years, the L-shaped bar with its mining memorabilia reminds the visitor that you are in what was once a prosperous tin-mining area. Food is served all day, but only pasties and rolls between 3 and 6, otherwise: soups, pasties, fresh crab sandwiches (when there is a fresh crab), home-made pies, good bacon sandwiches and daily specials. St Austell ales from the cask. Mulled wine in winter, cider in summer. Seats on the pretty back terrace.

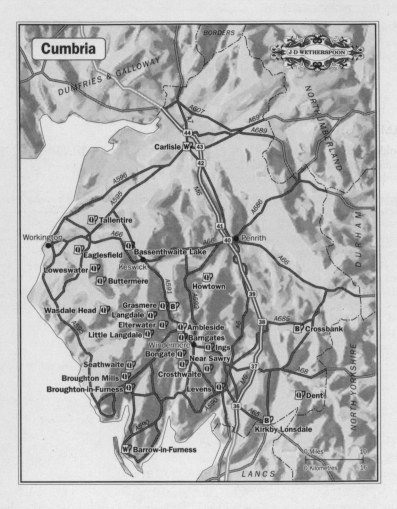

Cumbria

J D WETHERSPOON

BORDERS

DUMFRIES & GALLOWAY

NORTHUMBERLAND

A607
A69
A689

44
Carlisle W 43
42

A596

A595

M6

A686

DURHAM

Tallentire
A66

Workington
Eaglesfield
Loweswater
Keswick
Buttermere
Bassenthwaite Lake

Penrith
A66
A66
41
40

39

Howtown

A591
A592
38
A685
Crossbank

Wasdale Head
Grasmere B
Langdale
Elterwater
Little Langdale
Ambleside
Barngates
Windermere
Bongate
Near Sawry
Ings

NORTH YORKSHIRE

A595

A68
37
A686

Seathwaite
Broughton Mills
Broughton-in-Furness
Crosthwaite
Levens

Dent

A590
36
A65
Kirkby Lonsdale

A590

W Barrow-in-Furness

LANCS

0 Miles 10
0 Kilometres 16

Cumbria

AMBLESIDE

Golden Rule
Tel: 01539 432257

Smithy Brow, Ambleside, Cumbria LA22 9AS
Hartleys (Robinsons). John Lockley, tenant.

You'll find the Golden Rule tucked away down a side street in this very popular Lake District town, largely developed by the Victorians. Ambleside is a favourite base for serious and casual walkers – walking boots and backpacks of various sizes to the fore. This is an area really geared to the tourist and the climber. You can even hire a guide, along with those essential bits of rope and tackle to help with the rock climbing. It's at the centre of the glorious Lake District, so if you are out for one of those character-building walks or climbs, the Golden Rule is in just the place for a welcoming, refreshing drink. Only filled rolls or a pork pie to fill a gap, but you will find Hartleys XB, Robinsons Hatters Mild, Stockport Bitter, Best Bitter and Frederics on hand pump. Seats outside in the secluded yard.

> OPEN: 11–11.
> Real Ale.
> Children welcome until 9pm. Dogs on leads. Wheelchair access and to ladies' WC, not gents'. Parking difficult (very).

BASSENTHWAITE LAKE

The Pheasant
Tel: 01768 776234

Bassenthwaite Lake, Nr Cockermouth, Cumbria CA13 9YE
Free House. Matthew Wylie, licensee.

With Skiddaw as a backdrop, Bassenthwaite Lake, fanned by gentle breezes, is a firm favourite with the local sailing fraternity; not that you can actually see the lake from the Pheasant, but it's there, and because they've banned motorboats from this 4-mile-long stretch of water, it's quiet. The Pheasant is a solid, comfortable Cumbrian inn. The bar quickly fills at lunchtime for the home-made soup, cheese or meat platter, potted Silloth shrimps, Cumberland sausages, Cumberland pork and ham pie, smoked local trout, local lamb and much more. If you want to have a full meal there is an à la carte menu in the no-smoking restaurant. Theakstons Best, Jennings Cumberland and Bass on hand pump. Wines by the glass and half-bottle and a choice of whiskies. Walks lead from the garden into the surrounding woodland.

> OPEN: 11.30–2.30. 5.30–10.30 Mon–Thurs. 11.30–2.30. 5.30–11 Fri & Sat. 12–2.30. 6–10.30 Sun.
> Real Ale. Restaurant.
> Children in eating area. Dogs in bar only. Wheelchair access.

BONGATE

Royal Oak   Tel: 01768 351463
Bongate, Appleby-in-Westmorland, Cumbria CA16 6UN
Free House. Hugo Broadford, licensee.

A fine white-painted old coaching inn, to the south of Appleby, close to the River Eden's gently wooded valleys and opposite Bongate's old church. Inside you will find beamed and panelled rooms where you can enjoy a well-kept pint, and choose a dish from the imaginative menu: home-baked bread to go with the soup, home-cooked ham and beef to go in the sandwiches, potted shrimps, Royal Oak smokie – a selection of home-smoked morsels served with a cranberry and orange relish – filled crêpes, beef in ale, fillet of codling baked with a herb crust, pork fillet in cream and Madeira sauce, more fresh fish, steaks, vegetarian dishes, daily specials and good puds. A children's menu too. There are two restaurants, one of which is no-smoking. Ten beers are kept on hand pump; guests include interesting beers from lesser-known small breweries in the north of England and Scotland. In summer there are seats among the flower-filled tubs at the front of this attractive old place. Lots of lovely walks nearby; you are also near the Settle–Carlisle Railway, which is well worth a visit.

> OPEN: 11–11. Food served all day.
> Real Ale. One of the restaurants is no smoking.
> Well-behaved children welcome. Dogs: not in public rooms but they can stay. Wheelchair access (not WC). Nine bedrooms.

BROUGHTON-IN-FURNESS

Manor Arms   Tel: 01229 716286
The Square, Broughton-in-Furness, Cumbria LA20 6HY
Free House. David Varty, licensee.

Though not much bigger than a village, Broughton is a Charter Town on the edge of the Duddon Valley. The Charter is read out in front of the Manor Arms every year telling residents what they can and can't do – disobey and the stocks could be dusted off and used again. This is a small, handsome town with a delightful Georgian square, in which you will find the contemporary Manor Arms. Convenient for the western lakes, it is just the place for an excellent, well-kept pint of beer in a comfortable bar warmed by two blazing fires. A favourite with CAMRA members, so you know the beers are perfectly kept. Quite a choice, always a minimum of seven beers on hand pump including two or three guests. Currently Yates Bitter, Dent Aviator, Timothy Taylors Landlord and Coniston Bluebird. Food is limited to hot snacks: pizzas, toasties, sausages and a pot of home-made soup kept hot in the bar when the weather turns chilly.

> OPEN: 12–11 (12–10.30 Sun).
> Real Ale.
> Children welcome (must be over five if staying overnight). Dogs welcome too.
> Wheelchair access. En-suite bedrooms.

BROUGHTON MILLS

The Blacksmiths Arms   Tel: 01229 716824
Broughton Mills, Broughton-in-Furness, Cumbria
Free House. Margaret Blackburn, licensee.

A delightful, very attractive pub; out-of-the-way, unspoilt and traditional, serving the local farming community and everyone else nearby. Situated in the Lickie Valley, one of the prettiest in the Lakes, the Blacksmiths Arms has tremendous character – 300 years old, hung about with lots of hanging flowers; inside the beams and uneven flagstone floors reflect its age. Very popular with climbers and walkers as well as ordinary travellers. A full 'traditional English' menu is on offer seven days a week, as well as sandwiches and plough-man's, Blacksmith's steak pie in a suet pastry, steaks in sauces – devilled, Stilton or pepper. Extensive specials board with local fish and meat, including local Herdwick lamb dishes – all you need to sustain you. Jennings ales and local guests. This is a very special place – the only pub in Cumbria listed on CAMRA's National Inventory as having a pub interior of outstanding heritage interest. Do go and see it. Seats among the flowers at the front of the pub.

> OPEN: 12–2.30. 5–11 (11–11 weekends). Closed Monday mornings.
> Real Ale. Children's menu.
> Children welcome. Dogs too.

BUTTERMERE

Bridge Hotel   Tel: 01768 770252
Buttermere, Cumbria CA13 9UZ
Free House. Adrian McGuire, managing director.

If you're caught out by the erratic Cumbrian weather, help is at hand. The Bridge Hotel is ready for you – it has a drying room! Muddy boots? Make for the walkers' bar. Over the years, what was a simple two-storey alehouse has been extended and improved, result-ing in the handsome, comfortable hotel you find today; even the walkers' bar is smart and caters to your every need. The selection of bar food from the walkers' snack corner ranges from simple soups, sandwiches and ploughman's to puff-pastry ricotta-cheese and spinach parcels, Cumberland hotpot, chicken breast cooked in herbs and garlic, grilled chicken supreme, spicy fruit lamb curry, chef's daily specials and vegetarian dishes. Sunday roast. There is a table d'hôte menu which changes daily: you could choose poached Borrowdale trout with hot caper butter, prime sirloin chargrilled to order, and lots more. Black Sheep Best Bitter and a summer guest beer. Wines by the glass and a selection of malt whiskies. Seats outside on the terrace and wonderful views and walks.

> OPEN: 10.30–11. Food served from 12 noon–9.30pm.
> Real Ale. Evening restaurant.
> Children welcome. Dogs on terrace and sometimes they can stay. Self-catering apartments.
> Cards: Access, Switch, Visa.

CROSTHWAITE

Punch Bowl Inn   Tel: 01539 568237
Crosthwaite, Cumbria LA8 8HR   Fax: 01539 568875
Free House. Steven Doherty, licensee.

Next to the church and sharing the same car park, this 17th-century, solidly built old place looks like a pub and indeed still sells beer, but you would more likely be coming here knowing they serve some seriously good food in both the bar and dining room. If you're lunching during the week, you will appreciate the very reasonably priced two-course lunch. There could be pea and ham soup, baked garlic mushrooms, braised oxtail, lamb with ratatouille, fillet of salmon with a lobster and basil sauce, delicious puds too. A good, short wine list includes half-bottles and some by the glass. Beers: Theakstons Best, Jennings Cumberland, Black Sheep and Morlands Old Speckled Hen.

> OPEN: 11–11. 12–10.30 Sun.
> Real ale. Restaurant.
> Children welcome. Car park. Bedrooms – all en suite.
> Cards: MasterCard, Switch, Visa.

DENT

Sun Inn   Tel: 01539 625208
Main Street, Dent, Sedbergh, Cumbria LA10 5QL (village off A683)
Own Brew. Martin Stafford, licensee.

Cobbled streets aren't all that common these days, but they survive in this small town in the Yorkshire Dales Great Park. You'll find the Sun in one of them, and just up the road is their very own Dent Brewery, providing it with Bitter, Ramsbottom, T'Owd Tup beers and a strong ale called 'Kamikaze'. Inside are lots of beams, comfortable furnishings and home-cooked bar food. This includes the stalwarts, also pasties, chicken curry, lasagne, chilli, steak and kidney pie, Cumberland sausage, salads and specials. Seats outside in summer.

> OPEN: 11–2. 6–11 (6–10.30 Sun).
> Real Ale.
> Children welcome until 9pm. Dogs on leads. Wheelchair access into pub and, if you're a gent, to the WC. Bedrooms.
> N.B. Jukebox in the separate pool room.

EAGLESFIELD

Black Cock   Tel: 01900 822989
Eaglesfield, Nr Cockermouth, Cumbria
Jennings. Mrs Annie Sterkie, licensee.

It was in this village, not far from Cockermouth, that John Dalton, the father of modern chemistry, was born in 1766. Things have changed a bit in the Black Cock since then, but it is still an unspoilt gem of a pub that just serves beer. It's a crisp and nut place, with a fire in the bar and a garden to sit in; somewhere to go whatever the weather. Well worth a special visit.

> OPEN: 11–3.30. 6–11 (11–11 Sat).
> Real Ale.
> Children welcome. Dogs on leads.

ELTERWATER

Britannia Inn   Tel: 01539 437210
Elterwater, Ambleside, Cumbria LA22 9HP
Free House. Judith Fry, licensee.

Overlooked by the Langdale Pikes, the Britannia is ideally placed to sustain you while you admire the surrounding countryside or recover from walking the peaks and fells. Painted black and white and opposite a pretty village green, it is at the very centre of the Lake District. The inn has small, friendly bars with beams and log fires and they serve a wide-ranging menu which always features the local Langdale Herdwick lamb, served as either a rack of lamb, a leg, saddle, or braised – all very popular; also the usual favourites: soups, filled baps, baked potatoes, ploughman's, some unusual alternatives and daily specials. Good breakfasts and afternoon teas, too. Well-kept Jennings Bitter, Coniston Bluebird and Dent Aviator, plus guest ales and a good wine list, including fruit wines. Lots of garden chairs and tables on the attractive terrace in front of the pub so you can admire the view.

OPEN: 11–11.
Real Ale. No-smoking dining room.
Children and dogs welcome. Nine guest bedrooms and four in the annex.
Cards: Amex, Delta, MasterCard, Switch, Visa.

GRASMERE

Dove & Olive Branch   Tel: 01539 435592
Wordsworth Hotel, Grasmere, Cumbria
Free House. J.G. van Stipriaan, manager. .

In the middle of Grasmere, next to St Oswald's churchyard where the poet William
Wordsworth is buried, this is an 'in-house pub' attached to the smart Wordsworth Hotel.
On the menu are tasty bar snacks, home-made salmon cakes, filled rustic rolls, freshly
cooked fish and chips, ploughman's and daily specials served both in the bar and conservatory. Well-kept Tetley Cask Smooth-Flow, Jennings Cask Cumberland Ale and one
guest beer.

OPEN: 11–3. 6–11.
Real Ale.
Children welcome, but no infants. No dogs. Wheelchair access. Bedrooms in the
Wordsworth Hotel.

Nr HAWKSHEAD

Drunken Duck   Tel: 01539 436347
Barngates, Nr Hawkshead, Ambleside, Cumbria LA22 0NG (off B5286 Hawkshead to
Ambleside road)
Free House. Stephanie Barton, licensee.

Sheltered from the worst of the weather with views towards Lake Windermere from the
veranda at the front of the pub, you are surrounded by magnificent scenery; some of it the
Drunken Duck's very own 60 acres. Travellers have been dropping in for over 400 years and
how the Barn Gates Inn became the Drunken Duck is worth a journey for the telling alone.
Full of atmosphere, walls covered with pictures and interesting bits and pieces, well beamed,
cosy and with good winter fires. Lunchtime food includes lots of fillings – hot and cold – for
the sandwiches, game pie with roast vegetables and red-wine jus, baked aubergine with
pesto, roast flat mushrooms and grilled goat's cheese, red-onion and blue-cheese tartlet with
new potatoes and herb salad and sautéed Thai chicken strips with Caesar salad. The
evening menus go up a notch or two with lots of delicious puddings and local cheeses. The
home of Barngates Brewery, they serve their own Cracker Ale and Chesters Strong and
Ugly – all named after dogs that have been part of the pub over the years; also Jennings Best
Bitter, Theakstons Old Peculier, Yates, and other guest beers. Over 60 malt whiskies. Seats
on the veranda, which has opulent hanging baskets in summer.

OPEN: 11.30–11.
Real Ale. Restaurant.
Children in eating area. Dogs on leads. Wheelchair access. Car park.
Very stylish bedrooms include two suites across the courtyard.
N.B. Sometimes background music in restaurant.
Cards: Amex, Delta, MasterCard, Switch, Visa.

HOWTOWN (Ullswater)

Howtown Hotel   Tel: 01768 486514
Howtown, Ullswater, Cumbria CA10 2ND
Free House. Mrs Jacqui Baldry and son David, licensees.

It is approached along a narrow lane – on foot if possible as there is no car park, or, as it's
by the lake, by boat. This unspoilt hotel is in a quiet little village on the sheltered southern shore of Ullswater lake and surrounded by dramatic scenery, sweeping tree-clad lower
slopes above which are tree-less crags and fells affording you every type of walk from the
gentle to the very difficult. It is around here that the poet Wordsworth saw and admired
those daffodils – or so they say. The walkers' bar at the back of the hotel is a favourite
meeting place for those still in their boots, while the less energetic of us gather in the hotel
bar. A delightfully old-fashioned place serving freshly filled sandwiches, good filling
lunches and all the usual things you get from a welcoming hotel – coffee and afternoon
tea. No real ale, only a keg beer, but you can get a decent glass of wine.

OPEN: 11–11. Closed from beginning of November to end of March.
No children. No dogs. Wheelchair access, but not into the public bar.

INGS

Watermill Inn   Tel: 01539 821309
Ings, Nr Stavely, Kendal, Cumbria LA8 9PY (east of Windermere)
Free House. Alan & Brian Coulthwaite, MBII, licensees.

The Watermill, an ivy-covered stone building, is in a quiet backwater only 2 miles from
Windermere. In its previous life it was where they made shuttles and bobbins for the
Lancashire cotton industry. Now it's a comfortable, family-run inn with friendly bars, log
fires and no jukebox or noisy machines. All bar favourites and constantly changing chef's
specials feature on the blackboard. Among the dishes there could be Italian-style meatballs
in a basil sauce, medley of shellfish, pan-fried chicken with a lemon and pepper marinade,
finished with cream, leeks au gratin and peppered pork with rice, lots more fish, steaks and
other good things on the menu. Up to 16 real ales on hand pump, among them Black
Sheep Special, Jennings Cumberland, Coniston Bluebird, Theakstons Old Peculier, also
farmhouse scrumpy and Hoegaarden wheat beer, plus continental and English bottled
beers. The River Gowan, which used to power the old mill, runs through the grounds.

There is a viewing area into the cellar so you can keep an eye on the beer. Seats in the sunny beer garden.

> OPEN: 12–2.30. 6–11 (12–3. 6–10.30 Sun).
> Real Ale.
> Children in lounge. Dogs on leads in bar. Wheelchair access.
> Seven bedrooms

LANGDALE

Old Dungeon Ghyll   Tel: 01539 437272
Great Langdale, Ambleside, Cumbria LA22 9JY
Free House. Neil Walmsley, licensee.

Converted from a farmhouse in 1885 and named The Middlefell Inn, it was extended, renamed, sold for £4100 in the early 1900s and given to the National Trust. Situated at the foot of the Langdale Pikes, the road from Chapel Style on the Great Langdale beck comes to an abrupt end at the Old Dungeon Ghyll Hotel. Here it really is 'on with your boots' to climb the steep path that leads you to the spectacular Dungeon Ghyll waterfall which drops into an abyss 100 feet below. Back at the hotel the Hikers Bar serves refreshing beer and good food. Home-cooked meals and snacks – soups, sandwiches, Cumberland sausages, chicken dishes, local trout, steaks, etc. A four-course dinner is served in the no-smoking restaurant. Jennings Cumberland, Theakstons XB, Old Peculier and Yates Bitter plus some guest beers. The pub is opposite a National Trust campsite, which can get very jolly and busy at weekends.

> OPEN: 11–11.
> Real Ale. Evening restaurant.
> Children welcome. Dogs on leads. Bedrooms.
> Occasional live music.

LEVENS

Hare & Hounds   Tel: 01539 560408
Causeway End, Levens, Kendal, Cumbria LA8 8PN
Pubmaster. Colin Burrow, licensees.

Dating back to Georgian times, the Hare and Hounds still retains some of the original features. In a popular village overlooking the Kent Estuary and the Lyth Valley and not too far from Sizergh Castle and its wonderful gardens. The pub is well known for serving good reliable food: home-made soup of the day, garlic mushrooms, lasagne, Cumberland sausage, gammon steak, chicken Kiev, filled jacket potatoes, a vegetarian dish or two and a choice of sandwiches, plain or toasted (lunchtimes only). Daily-changing home-made specials board which features dishes using fresh, local produce including meat and vegetables. Tetley, Theakstons and a regular guest ale, Guinness and a good selection of malt whiskies. Seats on the terrace with views of the estuary.

OPEN: 11.30–3. 6–11 (6–10.30 Sun).
Real Ale. Dining room.
Children welcome. Dogs in bar only. Wheelchair access. Car park.
N.B. Music in pool room well away from the bar and dining area.

LITTLE LANGDALE

Three Shires Inn   Tel: 01539 437215
Little Langdale, Ambleside, Cumbria LA22 9NZ
Free House. Ian Stephenson, licensee.

Little Langdale is not even on the same road as Great Langdale, so please don't think
Little leads to Great: it doesn't. This Langdale, on an old packhorse route, is a few miles
west of Ambleside in the pretty Little Langdale valley – in the direction of, but not very
near, Hardknott Pass. Aptly named, the Three Shires is a 19th-century slate inn built
near the meeting point of the three shires of Cumberland, Westmorland and Lancashire;
somewhere to rest before climbing the high passes of Wrynose and Hardknott en route
to Ravenglass. An attractive building in a wonderful setting, it has seats under the
veranda at the front of the hotel, which is hung with flowering baskets in summer.
Inside, in the slate-floored beamed bar, you can enjoy a bar snack or a more substantial
dish of home-cured marinated salmon in a sweet dill and whisky sauce, rich chicken-
liver parfait with Cumberland sauce, marinated venison, pan-fried and served with a
port and Stilton sauce, locally made Cumberland sausage with onion rings and home-
made chutney, the popular beef and ale pie, vegetarian dishes or something from the
specials board. All dishes are cooked to order from fresh ingredients. Jennings
Cumberland Ale, Old Man Ale, Coniston, Jennings Best Bitter, Black Sheep Bitter,
Marstons Pedigree as a guest and an extensive wine list. Tables in the streamside garden.
Lots of walks.

> OPEN: 11–11. (N.B. Restricted opening hours in Dec & Jan and no evening meals
> during those months.)
> Real Ale. Restaurant. Packed lunches provided.
> Children until 9pm. Dogs in bar. Wheelchair access. Car park.
> En-suite bedrooms.
> Cards: MasterCard, Switch, Visa, Visa Debit.

LOWESWATER

Kirkstile Inn   Tel: 01900 85219
Loweswater, Cockermouth, Cumbria CA13 0RU
Free House. Richard Humphreys, licensee.

Another inn that has wised up to the variable Cumbrian weather: it too has a drying room.
Opposite the church, it's an attractive, white-painted, slate-roofed inn in spectacular
countryside. Outside are peaks, fells and woods – and the Cumbrian weather, so if you

want to dry off after a wet walk this is the place to be. Not only are they ready to look after you if you're soaked to the skin, but however you arrive. Inside, a warm, beamed bar serves good sustaining food. Freshly baked wholemeal rolls served with a salad and filling of your choice, or a Loweswater Ploughman's which would keep any ploughman going for some time, filled baked potatoes or a cheeseburger. Lots of home-made daily specials from the blackboard – starters, main courses, puddings and a cheese and wine selection. Jennings Bitter and Cumberland, draught Guinness, Coniston Blue Bird, 16 malt whiskies and 18 different wines. Seats on the enclosed veranda from where you can admire the view.

> OPEN: 11–11.
> Real Ale. Restaurant (piped music in here Thursday, Friday & Saturday).
> Children welcome. Dogs on leads. Car park. Bedrooms are geared up to hikers as well as the non-energetic.

NEAR SAWREY

Tower Bank Arms   Tel: 01539 436334
Near Sawrey, Hawkshead, Cumbria LA22 0LF
Free House. Philip Broadley, licensee.

Next to Beatrix Potter's Hill Top Farm – preserved by the National Trust – and between the medieval village of Hawkshead and the western shore of Lake Windermere. The countryside is wonderful and the Tower Bank Arms is in the right place to greet you after you have made the long journey around the lake. This pub is a literary star, known in Beatrix Potter's *The Tale of Jemima Puddleduck* as 'The Small Country Inn'. A friendly old place with a comfortable beamed bar and winter log fires serving traditional bar food of home-made soup, filled rolls, ploughman's, a pie of the day, salads, something for the veg-etarian and a pudding or two. More substantial dishes are available during the evening. Theakstons ales, a guest beer, Belgian fruit beers and a good selection of malt whiskies. There are seats outside and good walks nearby. Thimble Hall, in the centre of Hawkshead, houses an exhibition of Beatrix Potter's life and work.

> OPEN: 11–3. 5.30–11 (6–11 winter).
> Real Ale. Restaurant. N.B. Tapes played in restaurant.
> Children lunchtimes only. Dogs on leads. Wheelchair access (not WC). Bedrooms.
> Cards: Amex, JCB, MasterCard, Switch, Visa.

SEATHWAITE

Newfield Inn   Tel: 01229 716208
Seathwaite, Duddon Valley, Broughton-in-Furness, Cumbria LA20 6ED
Free House. Paul Batten, licensee.

Walkers might take some solace when they come in from a dampish hike over the fells that this isn't the Seathwaite that is the wettest place in Britain; this Seathwaite is the next wettest, with only 90–100 inches of rainfall (in a good year, that is). In a small hamlet on a narrow road in the Duddon Valley – one of Wordsworth's favourite places – it is some-what remote, so it's no wonder this old Lakeland pub is a popular and very welcome stopping place for fell walkers. An interesting slate floor in the main bar shows different levels of volcanic activity, and legend has it that the old beams in the pub came from ships of the Spanish Armada. Hmm: all I can say is that they must have been a bit desperate for some wood. Homely bar food of soups, sandwiches, Cumberland sausages, home-cooked gammon and steaks, plus a vegetarian dish or two; there is a more extensive evening menu. Ales from Jennings and, during the summer, guest ales, which could be Marstons Pedigree and Theakstons Old Peculier. An additional ale will be Coniston Brewery Bluebird Bitter. Interesting selection of malt whiskies. Tables in the garden, from where you can admire the dramatic scenery.

OPEN: 11–11 (11–10.30 Sun).
Real Ale. Restaurant.
Children welcome if well behaved. Dogs on leads. Wheelchair access (not WC). Self-catering flats available. Very occasional folk music.

TALLENTIRE

The Bush Inn   Tel: 01900 823707
Tallentire, Nr Cockermouth, Cumbria CA13 0PT
Free House. Mr & Mrs Alan Wilkie, licensees.

'By Royal Appointment once removed.' We hear that a member of Prince Charles's staff calls in here for a welcome break when journeying to and from Scotland. Only a small vil-lage, so this pub wears two hats. Not only is the 17th-century Bush the local pub, it is also the post office and Mr Wilkie is the sub-postmaster. And that is one of the best and most novel excuses anyone can think of for going to the pub – 'Just off to buy a stamp!' A very relaxing and welcoming pub serving an interesting variety of home-cooked food including several vegetarian dishes. Quality and value are of high order we are told. Theakstons XB, Youngers Scotch Bitter, McEwans lager and a guest beer.

OPEN: 12–3. 7–11.
Real Ale.
Children welcome. No dogs. Wheelchair access (not WC).

WASDALE HEAD

Wasdale Head Inn   Tel: 01946 726229
Gosforth, Seascale, Cumbria CA20 1EX (north-east of lake)
Free House. Howard Christie, licensee.

At the head of the dramatic Wast Water – the deepest lake in England – it is, as you can imagine, a popular refuge. Wasdale Head joins several others in being one of the more remote places in the Lake District, as it is approximately 8 miles from the nearest habitation;

someone described the area as a collection of sheep pastures and an inn. This particular inn is a wonderfully sturdy, handsome three-storey building with a good selection of well-prepared bar food ranging from home-made soups, fisherman's crumble and vegetable curry to the ever-popular beef-in-ale pie and local lamb casserole. There is also an evening restaurant. Well-kept ales: up to nine real ales – all local, including Jennings Cumberland, Yates Bitter, Hesket Newmarket and Dents Ramsbottom on hand pump. But they should soon have their very own microbrewery up and running which will mean a wider choice of ales. Dramatic scenery. No need to say there are wonderful walks round here because that is probably why you are here anyway.

OPEN: 11–11 (Jan & Feb 11–10).
Real Ale. Restaurant.
Children and dogs welcome – both on leads. Wheelchair access. Bedrooms (12) and seven self-catering apartments.

BEST OF THE REST

GRASMERE

Travellers Rest   Tel: 01539 435604
About half a mile north of Grasmere, tucked under Helvellyn. There are wonderful views, a welcoming landlord and plenty of good things on the menu: home-made soup, honey-baked ham, steak and kidney pie and daily specials. Jennings range of ales as well as Marstons Pedigree.

KIRKBY LONSDALE

Snooty Fox   Tel: 01524 271308
In one of the most beautiful towns in south Cumbria, the imposing, Jacobean, white-painted Snooty Fox serves a good, varied menu, everything freshly prepared: home-made soups, filled baguettes, pan-fried lamb's kidneys flamed with sherry served in a filo nest, twice-baked three-cheese soufflé with garlic cream, vegetarian dishes and lunchtime daily specials on the blackboard. Hartleys XB, Theakstons Best and Timothy Taylors Landlord on hand pump. New World wines.

RAVENSTONEDALE Nr Crossbank

Fat Lamb Country Inn   Tel: 01539 623242
Rather remote, this attractive, stone-built 17th-century inn is situated in the most glorious countryside at Crossbank, off the A683. Well-chosen dishes on the menu as well as local trout. Tetleys beers. You can also stay.

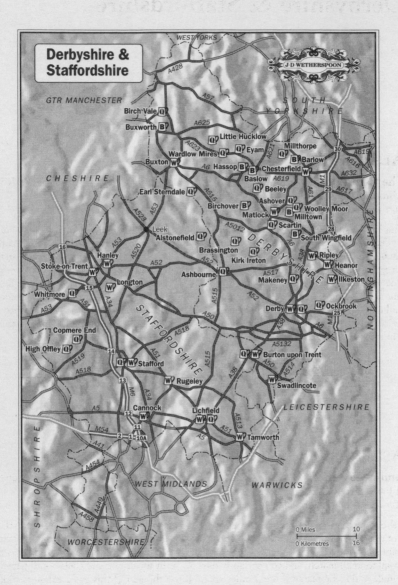

Derbyshire & Staffordshire

J.D WETHERSPOON

WEST YORKS

GTR MANCHESTER

SOUTH YORKSHIRE

CHESHIRE

NOTTINGHAMSHIRE

Birch Vale
Buxworth
Little Hucklow
Wardlow Mires
Eyam
Millthorpe
Buxton
Barlow
Hassop
Chesterfield
Baslow
Earl Sterndale
Beeley
Birchover
Ashover
Woolley Moor
Matlock
Milltown
Alstonefield
Scartin
Leek
Brassington
South Wingfield
Kirk Ireton
Ripley
Hanley
Heanor
Stoke-on-Trent
Longton
Ashbourne
Makeney
Ilkeston
Whitmore
Derby
Ockbrook
Copmere End
High Offley
STAFFORDSHIRE
Stafford
Burton upon Trent
Rugeley
Swadlincote
Cannock
LEICESTERSHIRE
Lichfield
Tamworth
SHROPSHIRE
WEST MIDLANDS
WARWICKS
WORCESTERSHIRE

0 Miles 10
0 Kilometres 16

Derbyshire & Staffordshire

ALSTONEFIELD

The George
Tel: 01335 310205

Alstonefield, Ashbourne, Derbyshire DE6 2FX
Burtonwood. Richard & Sue Grandjean, licensees.

The 17th-century George, in a small village between Ashbourne and Buxton, is just what a village pub should be, with beams and open fires and an interesting bar, said to be the smallest in either Derbyshire or Staffordshire. It has an amazing turnover, so size isn't everything. They serve a good selection of bar food: home-made soup, pâté, ham or cheese ploughman's, different fillings for the sandwiches, meat and potato pie, lasagne, quiche, plus about eight home-made puds; daily extra bar meals and puddings are shown on the wall in the passage. Burtonwood's range of ales. Children have a separate room and there are seats in the garden. Alstonefield is on the edge of Dove Dale in a lovely area in the southern part of the Peak District National Park.

> OPEN: 11–3. 6–11 (11–11 Sat. 12–10.30 Sun). Closed Christmas Day.
> Real Ale. No-smoking restaurant.
> Children welcome. No dogs. Wheelchair access from the rear car park.
> Cards: MasterCard, Switch, Visa.

ASHBOURNE

Smiths Tavern
Tel: 01335 342264

St Johns Street, Ashbourne, Derbyshire DE6 1AE
Marstons. Paul Mellor, tenant.

Ashbourne is an attractive market town on the fringe of the Peak District National Park. Not only surrounded by glorious scenery, this wonderfully old-fashioned tavern possesses a unique string to its bow – or its goalposts I should say. Every year there is a annual free-for-all football match, and you certainly have to be fit for this, as the goals – mill wheel spindle and stone plaque – are 3 miles apart! If the thought of this game exhausts you, recover in Smiths Tavern, a town pub that concentrates on running the sort of place we all make a beeline for. Relax with a newspaper while you wait for something from the good traditional bar menu – sandwiches, ploughman's, home-made pies, vegetarian dishes and much more. Three-course Sunday lunch in the restaurant. Marstons range of ales and one guest.

> OPEN: 11–11 (12–10.30 Sun).
> Real Ale.
> Children in one room and restaurant. Dogs on leads.

ASHOVER

Crispin Inn   Tel: 01246 590591
Church Street, Ashover, Derbyshire S45 0AB
Mansfield. David Spittal, tenant.

The scenery in parts of the Derwent valley is quite dramatic; lovely wooded valleys open up into rolling stone-walled fields. The Crispin, between Matlock and Chesterfield, is off the A632 but you might have to get the map out to find it – another hunt-the-pub game. The Crispin, one of the oldest inns in the area, dates back – well, bits of it do – to the mid-15th century. A popular local, serving traditional pub food and a very reasonable three-course Sunday lunch to go with the Mansfield ales: Riding Bitter, Mansfield Mild and Mansfield Pedigree.

> OPEN: 12–3 Mon, Wed & Fri. 12–11 Sat. 12–10.30 Sun.
> Real Ale.
> Children welcome. Dogs allowed in bar. Wheelchair access. Car park.
> Bedrooms, four with TV.

BEELEY

Devonshire Arms   Tel: 01629 733259
Beeley, Nr Matlock, Derbyshire DE4 2NR
Free House. J.A. Grosvenor, MBII, licensee.

At the gateway of Chatsworth House, the Devonshire Arms is a popular, charming, well-kept village inn, catering for locals and visitors to the lovely Derbyshire Peak District. Originally three separate cottages, they were converted in 1747 to become a prosperous coaching inn on the road between Bakewell and Matlock; coaches from London would stop here to rest the horses. Charles Dickens and, it is rumoured, Edward VII were frequent visitors but for entirely different reasons. The Devonshire offers an interesting bar menu that ranges from hot toasted baguettes with inventive fillings, ploughman's, vegetarian dishes and salads to devilled whitebait, chicken ballantine, beef and horseradish suet pudding, salmon hollandaise, venison in plum sauce, steak au poivre and a mixed grill. Friday night is fish night so you could start with a seafood taster platter or a well-dressed crab, then grilled halibut in an orange and lemon butter as a main course. Specials on the blackboard, also a wide range of home-made puds. Sunday mornings they serve a 'Victorian breakfast', with Bucks Fizz, from 10am until 12 noon, for which you must book. Theakstons XB, Old Peculier, Black Sheep Best, Special and a guest beer. About 30 single malt whiskies and a short wine list. At the southern end of Chatsworth Park – an outstanding area for walking and cycling.

OPEN: 11–11.
Real Ale. Restaurant.
Children welcome – family room upstairs. No dogs. Wheelchair access (not WC).
Cards: Access, MasterCard, Visa.

BIRCH VALE

Waltzing Weasel   Tel/Fax: 01663 743402
New Mills Road, Birch Vale, Derbyshire SK22 1BT
Free House. Michael Atkinson, licensee.

From the restaurant of this appealing old inn you have views of the spectacular Derbyshire countryside and the crowning glory of the Peak District, Kinder Scout – all 2088 feet of it. Inside, the Weasel is very comfortable with well-decorated bars, open fires and interesting pieces of furniture. Still a pub, but the food's the thing: English with a touch of the continental and North Africa in the slips. As they say, they are working on three culinary fronts – new and exciting vegetarian dishes, peasant casseroles and stews (at least one a day) and touches of Italy – the lunchtime 'Fantasia Italiana' is a firm favourite. Marinated anchovies or black-olive pâté as a starter, then sea trout, Moroccan vegetable casserole or marinated and roasted leg of lamb Italian style. Beers are Marstons Pedigree and Best; wines are mainly French with a soupçon from the New World. Outside is a pretty garden and terrace – with the view.

OPEN: 12–3. 5.30–11 (12–3. 5.30–10.30 Sun).
Real Ale. Restaurant.
Children welcome. Wheelchair access (not WC). Car park. Bedrooms – all en suite.
Cards: Amex, Delta, MasterCard, Switch, Visa.

BRASSINGTON

Ye Olde Gate   Tel: 01629 540448
Well Street, Brassington, Derbyshire DE4 4HJ (north-east of Ashbourne)
Wolverhampton & Dudley. Paul Burlinson, tenant.

We are in Civil War territory now. Dating back to 1616, this is an unchanging country pub. Ye Olde Gate is very ye olde; the panelled dining room was used as a temporary hospital during the Civil War. To add to the atmosphere, they have a resident ghost: unfortunately nothing to do with the Civil War – this one is quite a youngster, dating no further back than the Victorian era! Even so, the ghost story has featured in

Carlton's *Heart of the Country* programme – a famous ghost, this. In spite of all the 'happenings' there is a very jolly ambience in the beamed bars. Bar food changes by the day, but baguettes with varied and interesting fillings are available at lunchtime as well as home-made curries, Cajun chicken, seafood dishes, roasts, steaks and good puds available. No chips with anything! No-smoking dining room. Marstons Pedigree, Owd Roger at Christmas and a guest, plus lots of malt whiskies. Seats in the sheltered garden.

> OPEN: 12–2.30 (12–3 Sat). 6–11.
> Real Ale. Summer barbecue.
> Children over ten in dining room. Dogs on leads. Wheelchair access.

BURTON-ON-TRENT

Burton Bridge Inn   Tel: 01283 536596
24 Bridge Street, Burton-on-Trent, Staffs DE14 1SY
Own Brew. Kevin McDonald, tenant.

You could well 'only be here for the beer', as the beer is brewed on site. So popular are the own-brews that they created a new room to give a greater bar area; oak panelled with a feature fireplace, it looks out onto the brewery. With more space in the pub, one room is now totally non-smoking. Lots of bits and pieces here relating to brewing: notices, awards and so on. If you're getting a bit peckish, the menu lists quite a range of bar snacks: filled cobs and filled oatcakes, Yorkshire puddings with faggots and peas, roasts, and hot bacon and egg rolls. A skittle alley, which seems to be booked months ahead, is available for private parties. Burton Bridge Bitter, XL Bitter, Porter and Festival plus seasonal varieties. Selection of malt whiskies and fruit wines.

> OPEN: 11.30–2.15. 5.30–11 (12–2. 7–10.30 Sun).
> Real Ale. No food Sun.
> Children over ten in eating area. Dogs on leads.

COP MERE END

Star   Tel: 01785 850279
Cop Mere End, Eccleshall, Staffs SP21 6EW
Free House. Mike Davis, licensee.

Well known for well-presented, freshly made food, the Star is a traditional, two-room country pub opposite Cop Mere Pool and a great favourite with walkers and the local cycling club. On the menu are well-filled sandwiches, ploughman's, a large selection of fish dishes and steaks. They serve a popular roast for Sunday lunch. Draught Bass and always a guest ale. Lovely garden to sit in.

> OPEN: 12–3. 7–11 (12–11 Sat. 12–3. 7–10.30 Sun).
> Real Ale. No food Sun eves.
> Children welcome. No dogs. Car park.

DERBY

The Flower Pot   Tel: 01332 204955
25 King Street, Derby DE1 3DZ
Free House. Michael John Evans, licensee.

The Flower Pot, built in the early 18th century as a private house, was first licensed in about 1750. Within walking distance of the cathedral and shopping centre, it provides not only refreshment for the inner man, but also offers the opportunity to improve the mind with interesting photographs of old Derby and a small library – mostly of books donated by the customers with which you can while away the time, or even take home to read. There is a wide choice of traditional bar food: sandwich platters served with salad and spicy potatoes, filled jacket potatoes, home-made soup, lots of meat or fish dishes, a selection of vegetarian meals and some bar snacks such as chip butties and cheeseburgers. Fruit crumble or bread-and-butter pudding are among the puds. Sunday lunches too. Timothy Taylors Landlord, Bass and Marstons Pedigree are the regular ales; there are also guest beers and quite a selection of malt whiskies. Small walled garden at the back of the pub, where there is also a children's play area.

> OPEN: 11–11.
> Real Ale.
> Children welcome. Dogs on leads.

DERBY

The Smithfield   Tel: 01332 370429
Meadow Road, Derby DE1 2BH
Free House. John Evans, Lawrence Steveson, licensees.

Originally the Cattle Market Hotel, it was built to serve the old Derby cattle market which has long since gone. The market site is now occupied by the *Derby Evening Telegraph* and the bus station, so you know you are close to the city centre. Still offering a warm welcome, the Smithfield has fine ales and a good selection of traditional bar food. Ten ales on hand pump include draught Bass, Marstons Pedigree and beers from Derbyshire breweries. Food is served all week. Sunday lunches are a speciality. Seats in the large garden by the river and on the new terrace at the water's edge. Large car park.

> OPEN: 11–11 (12–10.30 Sun).
> Food served 12–2 Tues–Sat. No food Sun.
> Real Ale.
> Children welcome. Dogs on leads.

DERBY

Ye Olde Dolphin   Tel: 01332 267711
6–7 Queen Street, Derby DE1 3DL
Enterprise Inns. Terry & Nina Holmes, licensees.

The Romans had a camp here and the city traces its origins back to the Norman Conquest, but the greatest early influence was Danish. Derby comes from the Danish *deoraby*, meaning 'the place of the deer'. Not much Danish influence in the Olde Dolphin – not many deer around either. This is a very English, timbered 16th-century inn, close to the cathedral and the pedestrianised area of the city; a traditional old pub serving traditional pub fare: sandwiches, plain or toasted, filled jacket potatoes, fish and chips, grills, omelettes and sizzlers – rump steak, mixed grill or gammon. Beers are Black Sheep, Greene King Abbot, Marstons Pedigree, Adnams, Bass and John Smith Smooth plus four weekly, rotating guests. Seats on the patio.

OPEN: 10.30–11 (12–10.30 Sun).
Real Ale. Restaurant.
Children welcome. No dogs. Wheelchair access. Car park. Quiz night Sunday.

EARL STERNDALE
The Quiet Woman   Tel: 01298 83211
Earl Sterndale, Nr Buxton, Derbyshire
Free House. Ken & Jen Mellor, licensees.

When you see the pub sign you realise why the poor woman is so quiet: she is headless! Part of the scenery for many a year, an unchanging village local; well-scrubbed tables, beams, tiled floors and a good coal fire. Walkers always get a warm welcome here and sustaining food. Not a huge choice on the menu: toasties, Wardles pork pies, and winter stews, enough to keep your strength up for the onward march across some of the prettiest countryside in the Peak District. The well-kept ales are Marstons Pedigree, Bitter, Mansfields Dark Mild, Everards Tiger Bitter and guest ales: Adnams, Hartington Ales, Slaters, Stonehenge and Timothy Taylors Landlord. The large garden has a picnic area and donkeys, geese, pigs, hens, ducks and turkeys – all for your entertainment and not for lunch! But you can buy free-range eggs. Nine walks start from here. They have parking for three touring caravans, also a large park for caravanettes and somewhere to pitch your tent. There is a new kitchen, and interesting postcards of the pub and sign for you to buy.

OPEN: Moveable hours – usually 12–3. 7–11.
Real Ale.
Children welcome. No dogs.

EYAM
Miners Arms   Tel: 01433 630853
Water Lane, Eyam, Derbyshire S32 5RG
Free House. John & Michele Hunt, licensees.

Eyam, in a picturesque part of Derbyshire, has a tragic history. When the plague struck in September 1665, the village isolated itself from the outside world. By October in the following year the epidemic was all over, but out of a population of 350 souls only 33 were left alive. Built in 1630, before the village was struck by the disaster, the Miners Arms still has the original inn's stone over the lintel. The pub also boasts a couple of ghosts, thought to be two unfortunate girls who perished in a fire on the same site before the present inn was built. There are three quiet rooms in the pub and a very good choice of home-made dishes, a lot of them prepared from local seasonal produce. Bar lunches, which change daily, might include home-made soups, crispy roast duck, Cumberland sausages in onion gravy, haddock mornay, chicken breasts in cream and Parmesan sauce, braised beef, quiche, ploughman's, sandwiches and a selection of home-made puds. There is also an à la carte menu in the evening, when the selection of dishes goes up a notch. A traditional roast on Sunday. Stones ales, Bass and one guest. Seats outside the front of the inn and in the courtyard at the back.

> OPEN: 12–11.
> Real Ale. Evening restaurant.
> Children welcome. No dogs. Wheelchair access.
> Cards: all credit and debit cards except Amex and Diners.

HIGH OFFLEY

Anchor   Tel: 01785 284569
Old Lea, High Offley, Staffs ST20 0NG
Free House. Mrs Olive Cliff, licensee.

Built during the Crimean War, this is a little treasure of a pub, unchanged and delightful. You can get here in various ways but the best is by water, clutching a canal map, as the pub is alongside Bridge 42 on the Shropshire Union canal. Easier to reach by towpath than by car, the Anchor, which has been in the same family for over 100 years, is a two-bar pub with a gift shop selling painted canal-ware and a beer garden to sit in on sunny days. Simple snacks usually available to go with the Wadworths 6X, Marstons Pedigree, Owd Roger and real ciders brought up from the cellar.

> OPEN. 11–3. 6–11 (12–3. 7–10.30 Sun).
> Real Ale.
> No children. Dogs on leads. Wheelchair access to WCs; two steps into pub. Touring caravan site, camping and caravans to rent.

KIRK IRETON

Barley Mow   Tel: 01335 370306
Main Street, Kirk Ireton, Ashbourne, Derbyshire DE6 3JP
Free House. Mary Short, licensee.

An imposing, 17th-century, tall, gabled building, the Barley Mow has been catering for villagers and visitors since it became an inn over 200 years ago. Largely unspoilt, it has antique settles, open fires, panelling and mullioned windows. The small bar serves limited food; only filled rolls are available at lunchtime. Evening meals are served, but only for residents. Well-kept beers from the cask: Hook Norton Old Hooky, Pedigree, Hartington IPA; others changing weekly. Thatchers draught cider and a speciality single apple cider in the bottle, Carlsberg Export lager. Seats in the garden and at the front of the pub.

> OPEN: 12–2. 7–11.
> Real Ale. Filled rolls at lunchtime.
> Children welcome by arrangement. Dogs on leads. Wheelchair access. Bedrooms (five en suite).

LICHFIELD

Queens Head   Tel: 01543 410932
Queen Street, Lichfield, Staffs WS13 6QD
Marstons. Roy Harvey, tenant.

Known as the 'Ale and Cheese House', the Queens Head, which became Marston's first real alehouse, has over 20 different cheeses on offer; also pâtés, breads, pickles and tracklements. Lichfield, a delightful, small cathedral city, was the birthplace of Dr Samuel Johnson in 1709 and, interestingly, the last place in England where, in 1612, a man accused of heresy was burnt at the stake; a memorial to Edward Wightman is in the market square. Beers are Marstons Pedigree, Timothy Taylors Landlord and Adnams Southwold Bitter. Two regularly changing guests.

> OPEN: 12–11 (12–3. 7–10.30 Sun).
> Real Ale.
> Children welcome. Dogs on leads.

LITTLE HUCKLOW

Ye Olde Bulls Head   Tel: 01298 871097
Little Hucklow, Tideswell, Derbyshire SK17 8RT
Free House. Julie & Peter Denton, licensees.

At the centre of the Peak District, what you have here is an attractive, unspoilt old pub in a small limestone village, surrounded by sheep pastures. Another Ye Olde that really is olde: 700 years roughly – the fifth oldest in England, and they've been busy since the start! Inside are two welcoming rooms, both with open fires. The Bulls Head is famous for serving huge, juicy gammon steaks topped with either an egg or pineapple; you can also choose home-made vegetable soup, assorted sandwiches, filled jacket potatoes, chicken supreme in white wine with apricots and walnuts, filled Yorkshire puddings and vegetarian dishes. John

Smiths and Tetleys beers plus a guest and a selection of malt whiskies. Seats in the garden, and lots of walks nearby.

> OPEN: 12–3. 6–11.
> Real Ale.
> Children welcome. No dogs. Wheelchair access. Car park.

MAKENEY

Hollybush Inn   Tel: 01332 841729
Hollybush Lane, Makeney, Derbyshire DE56 0RX
Free House. John Bilbie, licensee.

There are two bars, a cosy snug and a conservatory in the Hollybush, a delightfully unspoilt village pub where some of the beer is brought up from the cellar in jugs, just as it used to be. They serve traditional pub food plus bar snacks. Five beers available: Marstons Pedigree, Ruddles County and guests. Lots of jollifications at the annual beer festival when there are plenty of new beers for you to try. To avoid confusion be warned: Makeney is near Milford off the A6. There's another Milford across the border, in Staffs.

> OPEN: 12–3. 4.30–11 (12–11 Fri & Sat. 12–10.30 Sun).
> Real Ale.
> Children welcome. Dogs on leads.

MILLTHORPE

Royal Oak   Tel: 0114 289 0870
Millthorpe, Holmesfield, Dronfield, Derbyshire S18 7WJ
Free House. R.H & E. Wills, licensees.

Stone walls, beams and good fires create a warm atmosphere in the bar of this attractive, friendly, 17th-century roadside pub. A welcoming walkers' pub – which, roughly translated, means you don't have to take your boots off. As well as the usual bar snacks – to help keep your strength up – there could be fresh salmon fishcakes, fisherman's pie, beef in red wine and some vegetarian dishes, not forgetting good ploughman's lunches. Bread-and-butter pudding and treacle tart to follow. Real, freshly percolated coffee too. Tetley Cask, Tetley Smoothflow, Marstons Pedigree, Carlsberg Export, Castlemaine XXXX and a wide range of malt whiskies. There is a very pleasant garden and seats on the terrace. You are in good walking country here.

> OPEN: Closed all day Mon, Tues & Wed lunchtimes and Sun eves, otherwise 11.30–2.30. 5.30–11.30.
> Real Ale.
> Children in garden. Dogs: not at meal times.

SCARTIN

The Boat Inn
Tel: 01629 823282

Scartin, Nr Cromford, Derbyshire DE4 3QF
Free House. Kevin & Debbie White, licensees.

Not far from the High Peak Trail, the village of Scartin attracts visitors from far and near. This is a delightful walking area and walkers are very welcome in the pub (but mind the carpets). Located off Cromford Square, the 18th-century Boat has a comfortable long bar with a low-beamed ceiling and exposed stone and brick walls. Bar food is listed on the blackboard and varies daily. Marstons Pedigree, Blue Moon from Norfolk and Springhead Bitter are the beers, plus two constantly changing guests.

OPEN: 12–3. 6–11 (12–11 Sat. 12–3.30 Sun).
Real Ale.
Children welcome. Dogs on leads.

STAFFORD

Picture House
Tel: 01785 222941

Bridge Street, Stafford ST16 2HL
Wetherspoon.

A listed Art Deco cinema that has been imaginatively converted into a flourishing Wetherspoon establishment. The ornate contemporary plasterwork is still in situ, the bar is on the stage, the stalls and circle are more organised seating areas and there are old film posters for you to admire. You will be as well looked after here as you invariably are at Wetherspoon. There is something for everyone on the menu, from light bites, filled baps and jacket potatoes, wraps and salad bowls to main meals, steaks and vegetarian meals. Egon Ronay works with Wetherspoon, helping to maintain quality and variety. Beers are consistently cheaper, wines are sourced from all over the world – something for everyone. Unusually for a converted cinema, they have an outside drinking area.

OPEN: 11–11.
Real Ale.
No children. No dogs. Wheelchair access.

WARDLOW MIRES

Three Stags Heads
Tel: 01298 872268

Wardlow Mires, Tideswell, Derbyshire SK17 8RW
Free House. Geoff & Pat Fuller, licensees.

When open (note the new hours), this is just the place for all those energetic, serious walkers, as the sensible flagstone floors in the charming, very unspoilt, 17th-century Three Stags mean that they will allow you in with your muddy boots. They draw the line at backpackers though; they are not encouraged – they take up too much room. Not only the right sort of floors for a pub, but sustaining bar food too. The menu ranges from home-made soups, seasonal game, steak and kidney pie, cottage pie and chicken and aubergine curry to fillet steaks with garlic butter – it all depends on what is available and what inspires the cook. Home-cooked food on home-made plates – there is a pottery in the barn. The ales are from the Abbeydale Brewery in Sheffield: Matins, Best Bitter, Absolution and Black Lurcher, which is exclusive to the pub. A number of continental and British bottled beers. Lots of local dogs enjoy the fire – their owners too – and there is an interesting mummified cat well out of harm's way – in a case.

OPEN: Limited opening hours. 7–11 Fri. 12–11 Sat & Sun and Bank Holidays.
Real Ale.
Children until 8.30pm. Dogs on leads.
Live music Sat eve.

WHITMORE

Mainwaring Arms   Tel: 01782 680851
Whitmore Road, Whitmore, Nr Newcastle-under-Lyme, Staffs ST5 6HR
Free House. James & Sara Froggart, licensees.

South-west-ish of Newcastle-under-Lyme, in an attractive village seemingly surrounded by well-known gardens, this is a popular old place. Rambling and full of character, it has a single bar and three interconnected comfortable rooms, each with log fires in winter. A favourite with all sections of the community, it's a friendly place with an interesting tale to tell – if you can get someone to explain the history of the photographs in the snug. Good-value sandwiches and a reliable blackboard menu. Boddingtons, Marstons Pedigree, Bass and regular guest beers. Seats on the terrace.

OPEN: 12–11 (12–10.30 Sun).
Real Ale. Food served lunchtimes Tues–Sat.
Children in eating areas and not after 8pm. Dogs allowed when no food being served.

WOOLLEY MOOR

White Horse   Tel: 01246 590319
Badger Lane, Woolley Moor, Derbyshire DE5 6FG
Free House. Graeme Jones, licensee.

Ideally placed for the enthusiastic walker. In a truly rural setting, the White Horse is a lively and very busy pub in more ways than one. Sometimes there may be classical music playing in one of the bars, so go carefully; but there are plenty of opportunities to get away from it if you want to. In winter, you can tuck yourself into a corner of one of the bars and in summer spread yourself out in the big garden. The pub has a printed menu with the usual selection of traditional bar food and quite a number of daily blackboard specials: sandwiches – hot or cold, toasted paninis, crispy-duck pancakes, Thai crab rosti fish-cakes, salads, seafood paella, game and ale pie, Greek moussaka, bangers and mash, poached salmon and prawn salad, vegetarian dishes and lots more. Much of the food is from very local sources: butcher, baker and an enthusiastic vegetable grower. They hold a beer carnival weekend. Draught Bass, and four guest beers – one weak, one medium, one strong and one dark, all on hand pump; these change weekly. Excellent walks nearby and you can hire a local guide. They have their own boules piste if you feel energetic but don't want to go too far, and there's an adventure playground for energetic children.

> OPEN: 11.30–2.30 (11.30–3.30 Sat). 6–11 (11–10.30 Sun).
> Real Ale. Restaurant (possibly classical music in here).
> Children in eating area or restaurant.
> Dogs in public bar. Wheelchair access.
> Cards: all major cards.

BEST OF THE REST

BARLOW, Derbyshire

Trout   Tel: 0114 289 0893

North-west of Chesterfield, this is one of those places that can be all things to all people. A typical pubby bar on one side serves Bass, Boddingtons and Marstons Pedigree – as well as something from the menu; on the other is a popular restaurant serving good home-made food.

BASLOW, Derbyshire

Cavendish   Tel: 01246 582311

Classy and desirable. Overlooking the Chatsworth estate, this hotel is a lovely place to be. You can eat informally – comparatively speaking – in the conservatory, or in the dining room. Interesting food, beautifully served in wonderful surroundings.

BIRCHOVER, Derbyshire

Druid Inn   Tel: 01629 650302

A creeper-covered old stone pub in a glorious part of the Peak District. Lots of walkers end up here to enjoy rest and recuperation. Beers are Marstons Pedigree, Morlands Old Speckled Hen, Mansfield Bitter and Druid, brewed for the pub. But if you're here to eat, and most people are, there is a wide choice of imaginative dishes on the blackboard menu; the best of English cooking with a touch of the Far East.

BUXWORTH, Derbyshire

Navigation
Tel: 01663 732072

As you might guess from the name, a canal pub. Built in the 18th century, the bits and pieces inside celebrate the glories of the canal age. Flagstone floors, warm fires and good wholesome food is served – home-made soup, Cumberland sausages, bubble and squeak, that sort of thing – to go with the Marstons Pedigree, Timothy Taylors Landlord, Websters Yorkshire and a couple of guests.

HASSOP, Derbyshire

Eyre Arms
Tel: 01629 640390

We have moved this pub from a main entry because it does occasionally have music playing. An unspoilt village pub, certainly here at the time of the Civil War – a ghostly Cavalier soldier has taken up residence. Known for serving popular, wholesome food and well-kept ales. Don't ask for a little taste of a new beer, as they have been known to refuse.

MILLTOWN, Derbyshire

Miners Arms
Tel: 01246 590218

Closed Monday and Tuesday, and you probably have to book to eat in the evening. Not far from Ashover, you are in a lovely part of Derbyshire with lots of good walks. They serve some imaginative food, Mansfield ales and decent wines.

SOUTH WINGFIELD, Derbyshire

Old Yew Tree Inn
Tel: 01773 833763

Don't turn up here during the week before 5 o'clock; this place is only open weekday evenings and weekends. In a village 6 miles from Matlock, the Yew Tree is a stone-built, 16th-century local serving traditional pub food. Home-made soup, salads, sandwiches, plain or toasted, vegetable lasagne, chicken Kiev, grills, a 'Yew Tree Mighty Grill', steak au poivre and three different sizes of steak. Roast lunch on Sunday. Marstons Pedigree always on tap, so to speak, but Greene King Abbot and Fullers London Pride are popular.

Devon

Lundy Island

East Down

Barnstaple

Molland

SOMERSET

Burrington

Dolton

Iddesleigh

Sheepwash

Tiverton

Broadhembury

Crediton

Thorverton

Stockland

Sticklepath

Broadclyst

Colyton

Newton St Cyres

Whimple

Drewsteignton

Woodbury

Sidford

Lydford

Wonson

Exeter

Salterton

Branscombe

Chagford

Doddiscombsleigh

Topsham

Lower Ashton

Lustleigh

Exmouth

Haytor Vale

Widecombe in the Moor

Holne

Stokenteignhead

Lutton

Woodland

Torquay

Hemerdon

Rattery

Paignton

Plymouth

Dartington

Brixham

Harberton

Tuckenhay

Holbeton

Dartmouth

Blackawton

Kingston

Stokenham

Bantham

Southpool

0 Miles 10

0 Kilometres 16

J·D·WETHERSPOON

Devon

BARNSTAPLE

Corner House
Tel: 01271 343528

108 Boutport Street, Barnstaple, N. Devon
Free House. Louise Oldfield, licensee.

One of the oldest towns in Britain and an important market for the wool trade, Barnstaple also minted its own coins in the 10th century. The sheltered moorings on the River Taw helped the town develop into what was a bustling port – now but a memory. However, on Friday, market day, it's as busy as ever; crowded with people coming to see what's on offer. The Corner House, built on the site of the old East Gate, will be crowded too. A traditional town alehouse – a drinking man's pub with an unspoilt interior – it is popular with locals and office workers. Sustaining, simple bar snacks, sandwiches and filled rolls to go with the excellent draught Bass and the weekly changing guest beer.

> OPEN: 11–11 (12–10.30 Sun).
> Real Ale.
> Dogs on leads. Wheelchair access.

BLACKAWTON

The George Inn
Tel: 01803 712342

Main Street, Blackawton, Devon TQ9 7BG
Free House. Mr & Mrs S. O'Dell, licensees.

This quiet village is about 4 miles, as the crow flies, from the glories of the Devon coast and the historic Slapton Sands where American troops trained for the assault on Normandy in 1944. The George is an interesting pub serving a selection of beers from distant breweries. It has a warming fire in the bar where you'll find a good selection of bar food: deep-fried whitebait, garlic mushrooms with bacon and cream, steak and kidney pie, pork loin with Devon cider, freshly made pizzas, curries and vegetarian dishes – fish and steaks on the blackboard. Beers are always changing and they also have regular small beer festivals, so you'll have to go to see what is on offer.

> OPEN: 12–2.30. 7–11 (12–10.30 Sun).
> Real Ale.
> Children in eating area. Dogs on leads. Bedrooms.

BRANSCOMBE

Fountain Head
Tel: 01297 680359

Branscombe, Nr Seaton, Devon EX12 3BG
Free House. Mrs Catherine Luxton, licensee.

Find the church and the pub isn't far away. Incorporating the old blacksmith's shop, this is a small, delightfully cosy pub. Some fishy things are on the bar menu – cockles, mussels and crab sandwiches as well as home-made lasagne, cottage pie, salads and occasionally fried sardines and salmon steaks with fresh herbs as daily specials. Friday is fish and chips night; speciality food nights are held at other times. Mrs Luxton's husband runs his own brewery a mile away and the own-brew beers include Branoc, Jolly Geff, Hells Bells in the winter, Yo Ho Ho brewed for Christmas and Summa' That during the summer. Farm cider. Seats outside on the terrace. A jolly beer festival is held over three days in mid-summer: barbecues, Morris men, over 30 ales, farm ciders – a good time is had by all.

> OPEN: 11.30–2.30. 6.30–11 (11.30–2. 7–11 winter).
> Real Ale.
> Children in own room lunchtimes and, if over ten, in eating area eves. Dogs on leads.

BRANSCOMBE

Mason's Arms
Tel: 01297 680300

Main Street, Branscombe, Nr Seaton, Devon EX12 3DJ
Free House. Murray Inglis & Christopher Painter, licensees.

You are only a ten-minute stroll from the beach, so it is not surprising that this place was used by smugglers; most of the coastal pubs in Devon were. Another thing they have in common is that many are thatched, but not many run to thatched umbrellas over the tables – well, here they do, and there are thatched hats over the doors too. At the bottom end of the village, which is scattered over the slopes of a steep green bowl, the Mason's Arms can't be missed. The rambling, beamed bar has a roaring log fire, complete with a spit that is regularly used for roasting beef, lamb, pork, sometimes goose and occasionally a whole shark. The menu now offers dishes from Italy, France, South America and the Caribbean. Bar food includes soups, sandwiches, ploughman's, Caribbean chicken, chicken piri piri, steak and kidney pudding, grilled fish, mullet, sea bass, plaice, or whatever is available. There is a bar specials board listing some vegetarian dishes; this changes every day. On Sundays: only sandwiches, ploughman's and a roast. Part of the restaurant is no smoking, and there is a no-smoking bar in place of the top dining room. Always five real ales: Otter Bitter, Bass and Dartmoor, plus two guest beers. Eighty wines on the list, 18 by the glass. Twenty whiskies; a beer festival in July and a whisky festival in December. Last but not least, two draught ciders and in summer a local farmhouse cider.

> OPEN: 11–11 (11–3. 6–11 winter).
> Real Ale. Restaurant.
> Well-behaved children may be allowed away from bar. Dogs on leads. Wheelchair access. Car park.
> Cards: Delta, MasterCard, Switch, Visa.

BROADCLYST

Red Lion
Tel: 01392 461271
Broadclyst, Nr Exeter, Devon EX5 3EL
Free House. Stephen & Susan Smith, licensees.

A really nice old pub in an idyllic situation on the green near the church. This quiet village is largely owned by the National Trust and the Red Lion is on the recommended list when you visit the Trust's Killerton House nearby. Inside, in the beamed bar, they offer a good traditional snack menu and interesting specials: Tanglefoot rabbit braised in a whisky and cream sauce, or whole red mullet oven-baked in an orange and ginger sauce. Bass, Eldridge Pope Royal Oak, Worthingtons Best, Wadworths 6X and a changing guest. Good range of house wines by the glass. Seats at the front of the pub, and in the garden.

> OPEN: 11–3. 5.30–11.
> Real Ale. Restaurant.
> Children in own room. Dogs on leads. Wheelchair access (not WC).
> Cards: all major cards.

BROADHEMBURY

Drewe Arms
Tel: 01404 841267
Fax: 01404 841765
Broadhembury, Devon EX14 0NF
Free House. Nigel & Kerstin Burge, licensees.

A 15th-century cob and thatch pub looking just as you imagine a country pub would: cream-washed with flagstone floors, beamed ceilings, comfortable furnishings and decorative bits and pieces. The Drewe Arms specialises in wonderful fish dishes: using crab, brill, red mullet, sea bass, salmon, langoustines and anything else that's fresh and available. Other than fish, there are some open sandwiches, a chicken dish or two, fillet of beef, but the emphasis is on fish. This is still a pub where you can relax and have a drink, ordering your food from the blackboard. Beers are from the Otter range, and there is a good wine list with about 12 by the glass.

> OPEN: 11–3. 6–11 (12–3. 7–10.30 Sun).
> Real Ale. Restaurant.
> Children welcome in eating areas. No dogs. Wheelchair access. Car park.
> Cards: Delta, MasterCard, Switch, Visa.

BURRINGTON

Portsmouth Arms
Tel: 01769 560397
Burrington, Nr Umberleigh, N. Devon EX37 9ND
Free House. Mrs Maureen Casey, licensee.

Over 300 years old, the Portsmouth Arms is in a delightful village overlooking the River Taw on the Exeter to Barnstaple road. Yet another haunted Devon pub; haunted, they think, by just one female ghost, but a visiting psychic maintains there are actually two watching over the diners. So if the plates move, it isn't the strong ale – more likely an ethereal spirit or two. Two beamed bars, with big log fires and a dining room decorated in medieval style – suits of armour and other period pieces. Home-made bar food: soups, well-filled sandwiches, local trout and salmon and roast lunches. All the vegetables are grown locally. Draught Guinness, Tetleys Best, Portsmouth Arms Bitter and a varying real ale. Local dry and sweet ciders. You can sit in the garden and enjoy the views of the glorious Taw valley.

> OPEN: 11.30–2.30. 6.30–11.
> Real Ale.
> Children welcome. Dogs on leads.

COLYTON

Kingfisher   Tel: 01297 552476
Dolphin Street, Colyton, Devon EX13 6NA
Free House. Graeme & Cherry Sutherland, MBII, licensees.

In the 16th century Colyton was a prosperous wool town owned by the Marquis of Exeter who carelessly lost his head and his land when he had a little argument with Henry VIII. Still an attractive small town, it has some fine Georgian houses and a handsome church. The Kingfisher is a friendly pub with a comfortable bar and family room. There is a full menu of home-made specials, salads, filled jacket potatoes, bar snacks, sandwiches and home-made puddings. Badger Best, Tanglefoot and several guest beers on hand pump. An extension built onto the back of the pub is used as a no-smoking dining area and family room. Seats on the terrace overlooking the garden.

> OPEN: 11–2.30. 6–11.
> Real Ale.
> Children in family area. Dogs on leads. Wheelchair access.

DARTMOUTH

Windjammer   Tel: 01803 832228
Victoria Road, Dartmouth, Devon TQ6 9RT
Free House. Mary Coombe & Andy Coombe, licensees.

An elegant townhouse opposite the market square in historical Dartmouth – a port since Roman times. The family-run Windjammer is easily recognisable during summer months: the hanging baskets will be putting on a grand show. Inside is one room with a big log fire in winter, decorated with shipwright's tools, charts and other nautical memorabilia, as befits a pub in a town steeped in naval tradition. It's surrounded by rich agricultural land and much of the produce used is very local; as well as sandwiches and filled baguettes, there will be smoked fish and meats, West Country cheeses, local sausages and wines. From the light-meal menu you could choose savoury stuffed mushrooms served with mango chutney, grilled whisky garlic prawns served with crusty bread or deep-fried West Country cheeses served with home-made tomato and pepper ketchup, and for a main meal a mixed-bean cassoulet with parsnip chips, breast of hickory-smoked chicken grilled with pineapple and hoisin sauce, or a loin of pork with honey and mustard sauce; the very local fish on the menu are caught in nearby Start Bay and vary according to the catch. Ales are the local Princetown Dartmoor IPA, draught Bass, a continually changing guest beer and Luscombe organic cider. Short, wide-ranging wine list.

OPEN: 11–3. 5.30–11 (12–3. 6.30–10.30 Sun).
Real Ale.
No children. Dogs welcome. Wheelchair access with help – one step.

DODDISCOMBSLEIGH

Nobody Inn   Tel: 01647 252394
Doddiscombsleigh, Nr Exeter, Devon EX6 7PS (turn left off the A38 at Haldon Racecourse, signposted Dunchideock, and follow the signs to Doddiscombsleigh, 3 miles)
Free House. Nick Borst-Smith, MBII, licensee.

You'll probably need a map to navigate the deep Devon lanes to find the Nobody Inn. Very secluded, but you'll know that you've arrived when you see an inn sign, almost hidden by foliage, near a notice saying 'Unsuitable for Motor Vehicles'. Ignore it and carry on. At first glance it looks more like a village house than an inn – it has a proper front garden and gate – but once inside you'll find an impressive wine list, 250 different malt whiskies, varied, well-thought-out bar food and a changing blackboard menu. Widely acclaimed for their imaginative dishes: specials could be wild-boar casserole, fresh salmon in a dill, chive and mayonnaise sauce, beef cooked in red wine, cold duck pie with salad, red-onion flan served with salad or a layered terrine of white fish and smoked salmon served warm with a dry vermouth sauce; from the bar menu, the ultimate toasted sandwich – ham, cheese, tomato, onion, herbs and sweet pickle all together in brown bread. But that's not all: if you are a cheese buff, you have about 30 to choose from, many from the county. Not difficult to find a good wine to go with the cheese as between 700 and 800 are stocked in the pub cellar; about 20 by the glass. Nobody's Beer (brewed by Branscombe), Teign Valley Tipple, Bass and other guest beers on hand pump or from the cask. Farm ciders. Seats outside from where you can look at the view and appreciate the peace and quiet.

OPEN: 12–2.30. 6–11.
Real Ale. Restaurant open evenings only (not Sun).
No children under 14. No dogs. Car park. Bedrooms. Stabling.
Cards: Delta, MasterCard, Switch, Visa.

DOLTON

Union Inn   Tel: 01805 804633
Fore Street, Dolton, Devon EX19 8QH
Free House, Ian & Irene Fisher, licensees.

Dolton is a quiet, south-facing village above the Torridge river, ideally placed to explore the North Devon countryside. Someone took good care of the Union Inn over the centuries. An old Devon longhouse has always been vulnerable as the cob walls (a mixture of clay and straw) risk crumbling in wet weather, so dry foundations and a good roof were essential for it to survive the ravages of time. 'Georgianised' in the 18th century and converted into the small hotel you see today, the Union has a cosy bar with a big log fire, a comfortable lounge bar and a no-smoking restaurant. Food is important here; a keen interest is taken in providing game and fish for the menus. From the bar you could have home-made soup, spinach and feta pie, sardines grilled with sea salt and olive oil, moules marinières, local sausages with bubble and squeak, or fish mixed grill – fish dishes are a speciality. Sharp's Doom Bar Bitter, Jollyboat, Clearwater Cavalier, St Austell Tribute – two are chosen from these ales – and a decent wine list. Some tables at the front of the pub.

> OPEN: 12–2.30. 6–11 (12–2.30. 7–10.30 Sun).
> Real Ale.
> Children: questionable. Dogs on leads. Car park. Bedrooms.
> Cards: Delta, MasterCard, Switch, Visa.

DREWSTEIGNTON

Drewe Arms   Tel: 01647 281224
The Square, Drewsteignton, Devon
Whitbread. Colin Sparks, tenant.

In a village high above the Teign valley, this old thatched pub next to the church has hardly changed since the 19th century. The social life of the village revolves around it. The ales and draught ciders are still kept on racks in the tap room: Flowers IPA, Gales, Greene King and Morlands Old Speckled Hen. A fairly traditional menu, with a few interesting additions; fish dishes and daily specials on the blackboard. Life at the Drewe Arms goes on. An unspoilt alehouse – a delight to see. (We hope the opening hours and so on are correct; getting any information out of Mr Sparks is akin to pulling teeth.)

> OPEN: 11–3. 6–11 (12–3. 7–10.30 Sun).
> Real Ale. Restaurant.
> Children welcome. Dogs on leads. Wheelchair access.

EAST DOWN

Pyne Arms   Tel: 01271 850207
East Down, Nr Barnstaple, N. Devon EX31 4LX
Free House. Jurgen & Elizabeth Kempf, licensees.

A very attractive, well-kept old pub. Horse harnesses and horse-racing prints adorn the walls of the low-beamed bar, which has a wood-burning stove to keep you warm, a flag-stone-floored games area and no-smoking gallery with tables and chairs. You'll find varied pub food: home-made soup, sandwiches, pâté, ham and eggs, scampi provençale, fresh grilled trout, roast chicken in a mushroom sauce, steak Diane, beef stroganoff, half a roast duckling in a mushroom, cream and wine sauce, lots of steaks and a daily specials board, which will include some vegetarian dishes. Selection of puddings. Ind Coope Burton draught ale, the local Barum Brewery XTC Bitter. A choice of wines, some by the glass. Seats among the tubs of flowers in the pretty paved garden.

> OPEN: 11–2.30. 6–11.
> Real Ale.
> No children. Dogs: maybe, you have to ask.
> Cards: Delta, MasterCard, Switch, Visa.
> N.B. As we go to press we hear this pub is up for sale, so telephone first if you are making a special journey.

EXETER

Imperial   Tel: 01392 434050
New North Road, Exeter, Devon EX4 4HF
Wetherspoon.

Next to St David's railway station, in its own private park, the Imperial – originally the old Imperial Hotel and before that a private house built at the beginning of the 19th century – is again a landmark in the city. Much of the original 'grand' decor, as befitted the building's standing in Exeter society, still exists. There is a wonderful view across the city from the huge old orangery, originally built to house a collection of tropical plants. Now fully restored, it is now one of the Imperial's three bars. Always six, reasonably priced, cask-conditioned ales. A full menu is available throughout the day, seven days a week. Tables in the courtyard and in the grounds.

> OPEN: 11–11 (12–10.30 Sun).
> Real Ale.
> No children; no under 18s. No dogs. Wheelchair access.

HARBERTON

Church House Inn   Tel: 01803 863707
Harberton, Nr Totnes, Devon TQ9 7SF
Free House. David & Jennifer Wright, licensees.

Gloriously atmospheric, with an interior reflecting its age, Church House Inn, very near the church, is thought to have been built around 1100 AD. It is full of oak beams and has what is said to be one of the oldest oak screens in the country, a huge inglenook fireplace of great antiquity and some very ancient glass. Food here is up to the mark – a choice of 'little eats': devilled whitebait, mushrooms in garlic butter, their own chicken-liver pâté, ploughman's and various sandwiches; the lunchtime specials could include fillet of plaice marinated in white wine, garlic and lemon, steak and kidney pie, home-made soups, locally made sausages, curries and grills. Virtually all the vegetables are fresh, and they use free-range eggs from the village, local pork and lamb; even the rabbits have a Devon accent. Draught Bass plus two weekly changing guest beers. Good selection of wines.

OPEN: 12–2.30. 6–11 (11.30–3 Sat).
Real Ale. Restaurant.
Children in family room and eating area. Dogs on leads.
Bedrooms. Wheelchair access (not WC). Morris dancers in summer.

HAYTOR VALE

Rock   Tel: 01364 661305
Haytor Vale, Nr Newton Abbot, Devon TQ13 9XP
Free House. Christopher Graves, licensee.

Another pub for your list of haunted places. Belinda the ghost has been seen by several customers. Legend has it that she was having an affair with a coachman and was murdered by the coachman's wife on the stairs of the pub. A former coaching inn, the Rock, a mere junior in the scale of things – just 200 years old – is a friendly local serving a small, rural community. It has two panelled rooms, both with big log fires, a no-smoking dining area and a restaurant. Good choice of bar food: home-made soup, ploughman's, local rabbit in mustard sauce, curries, poached Devon salmon, steaks and daily specials. Also home-made puddings and a Sunday roast. Dartmoor Best, Royal Oak and Thomas Hardy on hand pump. Malt whiskies. A pretty garden and an adjoining terrace are in high favour in summer. On the edge of the Dartmoor National Park, so there are some wonderful walks.

OPEN: 11–3. 6–11 (11–11 Sat).
Real Ale. No snacks Sundays or Bank Holidays.
Children in eating area of bar. No dogs. Wheelchair access (not WC). Bedrooms.
Cards: Amex, Delta, Diners, MasterCard, Switch, Visa.

HEMERDON

Miners Arms   Tel: 01752 343252
Hemerdon, Nr Plymouth, Devon PL7 5BU
Free House. David Honey, licensee.

Run by the same family since about 1850, the Miners Arms has been serving, as the name suggests, the old tin mines and the local community. Now the tin mines have closed, this is just a friendly local on the edge of Dartmoor. Food is of the 'fill you up and keep you going' kind, as the pub is predominantly a drinking establishment. Draught

Bass, Ushers, Boddingtons, Sutton XSB (a local brew) and one guest. They sometimes have a really local farm cider.

> OPEN: 11–2.30. 5.30–11 (12–3. 7–10.30 Sun).
> Real Ale.
> No children. Dogs welcome.

HOLBETON

Mildmay Colours   Tel: 01752 830248
Fore Street, Holbeton, Plymouth, Devon PL8 1NA
Free House. Louise Price, licensee.

This pub has seen a few changes in its time. When it was first licensed it was called the George, but before that it was a 17th-century manor house. White-painted and looking very smart, it was renamed in 1967 after the death of Anthony Mildmay, Lord Mildmay of Flete; the sign is painted in his racing colours. Bar food includes home-made soup, sandwiches, ploughman's, filled baked potatoes, beef-in-ale pie, Mexican chicken enchilada and daily specials from the large blackboard. They have a popular curry night on Wednesdays, fish night on Fridays and a carvery Sunday lunchtime. The beers, brewed in Truro, are SP and Colours Best; they also have other guest beers. Plenty of tables outside at the front of the pub, high above the street, and in the garden at the back.

> OPEN: 11–3. 6–11 (occasionally all day summer).
> Real Ale. Carvery restaurant closed Mon–Thurs.
> Children welcome. Dogs on leads. Eight en-suite bedrooms in the old brewery.
> N.B. Background music in restaurant only.

HOLNE

Church House   Tel: 01364 631208
Holne, Nr Ashburton, Devon TQ13 7SJ
Free House. Tony Skerritt, licensee.

Church House is in the centre of this village on the southern edge of Dartmoor, on the border of the National Park. At the time of the Civil War, Cromwell is said to have used the 14th-century Church House as a stopping-off place on the way to encourage his troops, who were fighting bitter and bloody battles around Totnes. Inside is a pine-panelled bar, a comfortable, carpeted lounge – both with big log fires in winter – and a no-smoking restaurant. Lovely views over the moors from the front of the pub. Fresh, locally produced organic vegetables, some of them home-grown; fish from Brixham, carefully chosen local meat; only the very best ingredients find their way into the kitchen. Lunchtime snacks could include mushrooms in garlic butter, filled baked potatoes, various ploughman's, sandwiches, omelettes, vegetarian dishes and there are daily specials and a weekly changing menu in the bar and also the à la carte menu in the restaurant. Tanglefoot, Butcombe

Bitter, Gold plus two lagers, Murphys and varying guest ales. Farm cider and a good choice of house wines, 14 by the glass.

OPEN: 12–3. 7–11 (12–3. 7–10.30 Sun).
Real Ale. Restaurant.
Children and dogs welcome. Bedrooms. Wheelchair access (not WC).

IDDESLEIGH

Duke of York   Tel: 01837 810253
Iddesleigh, Winkleigh, Devon EX19 8BG
Free House. Jamie Stuart & Pippa Hutchinson, licensees.

In this isolated village, the long, low, 14th-century, thatched Duke of York is well liked by local and visitors. A few of the regulars can still be found pulling their own pints when the landlord is busy elsewhere, a tradition dating back to the last landlord. Home-made food is listed on the blackboard in the main bar: soup of the day, crab mayonnaise with salad, Stilton and port pâté, fish of the day, fillet of salmon with a creamy dill sauce, beef and Guinness casserole, pork chop with apple gravy, steak and kidney pudding, always some vegetarian dishes and something interesting on the restaurant menu: duck parcels, a selection of four or five fish dishes and a variety of smoked seafood from Dartmouth. Locally made ice-creams. Cotleigh Tawny, Adnams Broadside and Sharps Doombar Bitter from the cask. Farm ciders and guest beers, a good number of New World wines, some by the glass and a pretty back garden to sit in.

OPEN: 11–11 (12–10.30 Sun).
Real Ale. Restaurant. Food served 11–10 all day and every day.
Children welcome. Dogs on leads. Limited wheelchair access.
Bedrooms.
Cards: Delta, MasterCard, Switch, Visa.

KINGSTON

The Dolphin Inn   Tel: 01548 810314
Kingston, Nr Bigbury, Devon TQ7 4QE
Ushers. Mr & Mrs R.N. Williams, tenants.

The Dolphin is within walking distance of the beach at Wonwell and stands out as the building with the most flowering pots in this very flowery village. A well-beamed 16th-century pub offering good, imaginative bar food. Menus change frequently but you could choose a tomato and basil soup, crab bake with brown bread, deep-fried Camembert and gooseberry sauce, seafood chowder with garlic bread, coq au vin, freshly poached salmon, plaice fillets with a spinach and mushroom stuffing in a cream and wine sauce, grills, vegetarian meals or even a sandwich or ploughman's. Wash that down with Courage Best Bitter, Ushers Founders and Abbot Ale, or even something from the wide-ranging wine list. Tables in the garden, where you can sit with your dog. Lovely walks to the beach or along the River Erme.

> OPEN 11–2.30. 6–11 (12–3. 6–10.30 Sun).
> Real Ale.
> Children welcome. Dogs in garden only. Wheelchair access. Three en-suite bedrooms.

LOWER ASHTON

The Manor Inn   Tel: 01647 252304
Lower Ashton, Teign Valley, Nr Exeter, Devon
Free House. Clare & Geoff Mann, owners/licensees.

Glorious views across the Teign Valley from this well-run old place. Creeper-covered, you really can't miss this – well, you might do soon if the creeper covers any more of the pub. Then it will be: spot the creeper with the red door! The owners tell us that they concentrate on their ales and one of the rooms in the pub is, you could say, themed: beer mats, brewery advertisements and beer – Teignworth Reel Ale, RCH Pitchfork (a Somerset brewery), Princetown Jail Ale (a Taunton brewery), and regularly changing guest ales. Good choice of food, home-made soup, sandwiches and ploughman's, filled jacket potatoes, spaghetti bolognese, home-made 8oz beefburger, ratatouille topped with cheese, home-cooked ham and a changing specials board which could feature beef bourguignon, ragout of lamb, beef and red-wine casserole, salmon and prawn au gratin. There are always three specials boards with at least three vegetarian dishes, ten meat and eight fish – something for everyone. Picnic tables in the garden on the other side of the road.

> OPEN: 12–2.30. 6–11 (7–11 Sat. 12–2.30. 7–10.30 Sun). Closed Mon except Bank Holidays.
> Real Ale.
> No children. Dogs welcome. Car park.
> Cards: all debit cards.

LUNDY ISLAND

Marisco Tavern   Tel: 01237 431831
Lundy Island, Bristol Channel, Bideford, Devon EX39 2LY
Free House. Paul Roberts, licensee.

Owned by the National Trust and managed by the Landmark Trust, Lundy Island is 12 miles off the north Devon coast. The lucky Marisco Tavern has a captive clientele, so to speak, as it is the only place on the sparsely populated island – about 20 residents, plus thousands of birds – where you can get a pint of beer and something to eat. The 15,000 or so visitors each year make the inconvenience of living on an island worth the effort of it all. The Marisco, a solid, stone-built old place, serves breakfast, morning coffee, lunch, afternoon tea and dinner. Light bar meals at lunchtime and a greater choice in the evening. The very traditional pub food includes something for everyone: home-made soup, sandwiches, mushrooms au gratin, deep-fried whitebait, chicken and black-bean stir fry, steak and Lundy ale pie, omelettes, specials on the blackboard, children's meals and four vegetarian dishes. Two ales on hand pump – Bass and Exmoor Bitter (Lundy Experience), also Guinness, Celtic Smooth and lagers. Good wine list. The business of the pub is largely dependent on the weather and what and who the boat brings in. Weather forecasts are all important here; otherwise a bunch of seaweed outside the back door used to do the trick. Sea views from the main bar. On Lundy there are lots of delightfully restored cottages and houses to stay in – all well managed and beautifully furnished by the Landmark Trust. Reaching Lundy takes about two hours by boat – depending on the weather – from either Ilfracombe or Bideford.

> OPEN: 12–2. 6–11 (officially – it depends on boat arrivals). Closed winter lunchtimes except weekends.
> Real Ale.
> Children welcome. No dogs.
> Cards: MasterCard and Visa only.

LUSTLEIGH

Cleave   Tel: 01647 277223
Lustleigh, Nr Newton Abbot, Devon
Heavitree. Alison Perring, tenant.

Sheltering from the moor, this picturesque village nestles in the Dartmoor foothills. The granite cottages, many of them thatched and creeper-covered, and the attractive 15th-century thatched Cleave cluster around the 13th-century village church. Inside the pub is a charming, low-ceilinged bar with a really huge inglenook fireplace. Bar meals are available lunchtimes and evenings: home-made soups, chicken-liver and brandy pâté, tomato and mozzarella salad, cornets of smoked salmon with cream cheese, sandwiches, hot sandwiches, hot cheese and onion flan, 'Cleave' steak, kidney and stout pie with a light puff-pastry crust, local butcher's sausages with mash and onion gravy, or half a duckling roasted with honey and served with an orange and Grand Marnier sauce. Sunday roast lunches. A good short restaurant menu; home-made puddings too. Bass, Wadworths 6X and Flowers Original on hand pump. Farm ciders. Short wine list, many by the glass. Morning coffee.

> OPEN: 11–3. 6–11 (11–11 Sat and every day during the summer).
> Real Ale.
> Children in no-smoking family area. Dogs on leads. Wheelchair access to pub and gents' WC. Car park.
> Cards: Delta, MasterCard, Switch, Visa.

LUTTON

Mountain Inn   Tel: 01752 837247
Old Church Lane, Lutton, Nr Cornwood, Ivybridge, Devon PL21 9SA
Free House. Charles & Margaret Bullock, licensees.

Up a steep hill, the Mountain, a traditional village pub, is near the Dartmoor Wildlife Park on the edge of the Dartmoor National Park. The Mountain always has some interesting beers to go with well-presented bar food: home-made soup, sandwiches, hot rolls, chicken Kiev, prawn, mackerel, crab and other salads, Cornish pasty, cottage pie, or ham cooked in cider. The beers are Suttons XSB, Darkside of the Mountain (brewed especially for the pub) and two weekly changing guest beers. Seats on the large terrace with views across the National Park.

OPEN: 11–3. 6–11.
Real Ale.
Children welcome. No dogs. One step up for wheelchairs (not WC). Car park.

LYDFORD

Castle Inn & Hotel   Tel: 01822 820242
Lydford, Nr Oakhampton, Devon EX20 4BH
Free House. David & Susan Grey, licensees.

Past the church, the delightful, pink-washed Castle Inn is in a secluded village dominated by a 12th-century castle, built not for defence, but as a prison. The licensees who made this pub so successful are back from the Cott in Dartington to work their magic yet again. Lots of room in this well-kept, well-polished old place; low-beamed bars, filled with antique settles and interesting bits and pieces collected over the years, including some Lydford pennies dating back to King Ethelred the Unready. A good choice of food from the daily changing blackboard menu: home-made soups, mussel chowder served with garlic bread, a Devon cheese platter – four local cheeses – smoked haddock in a creamy cheese sauce with a cheese and potato topping, fresh salmon and trout fishcakes with a wine and prawn sauce, casserole of pheasant in a cream and brandy sauce, plus home-made puddings and local ice-creams. The evening restaurant is à la carte. The pub supports local growers and farmers, most of the supplies coming from within the county. Well-kept Fullers London Pride, Flowers IPA and Morlands Old Speckled Hen on hand pump. Wines by the glass and a list of about 40 wines. Hot toddies and mulled wine when appropriate. Seats on the terrace. The restaurant is no smoking. Within walking distance, along a twisting path from the Castle Inn, are two of the most spectacular waterfalls in Devon: the White Lady waterfall which slides 100 feet down a rocky shute to join the River Lydd in a wooded valley below, and the Devil's Cauldron where the river crashes through a narrow gap down a vertical, mossy cliff.

OPEN: 12–3. 6–11 (12–11 Sat. 12–10.30 Sun).
Real Ale. Restaurant.
Accompanied children in snug and lounge by day, in the restaurant in evening. Dogs on leads in bar areas. Wheelchair access (not WC). Car park. Nine individually designed bedrooms.
Cards: Delta, MasterCard, Switch, Visa.

MOLLAND

The London Inn   Tel: 01769 550269
Molland, South Molton, Devon EX36 3NG
Free House. Michael Short, licensee.

The church in this village on the edge of Exmoor has a very interesting Georgian interior, including a three-decker pulpit – well worth seeing. Next to the church, this thatched

15th-century coaching inn is still largely unspoilt, though the interior has been rearranged over the years. The dining room is where the original inn used to be, and the bar is in the old brewhouse. The food is good value and ranges from bar snacks to full meals in the dining room. Bar snacks could include savoury pancakes and Welsh rarebit topped with bacon and mushrooms; specials are on the blackboard, but from the weekly changing evening menu you could choose a crispy salad with bacon, red peppers and croutons, or Somerset pork tenderloin in a cider cream sauce. Well-kept Cotleigh and Exmoor Ale from casks behind the bar. Sunny garden to sit in. Next to the pub, the village church has links to the legend of Lorna Doone.

OPEN: Coffee from 11. Bar opens 11.30–2.30. 6–11 (12–2.30. 7–10.30 Sun).
Real Ale. Dining room.
Children welcome. Dogs too. Wheelchair access. Car park. Bed and breakfast accommodation.

NEWTON ST CYRES

Beer Engine   Tel: 01392 851282
Newton St Cyres, Exeter, Devon EX5 5AX
Own Brew. Peter Hawksley, FBII, licensee.

They are as proud of their glorious summer floral displays at the Beer Engine as they are of their beers. Not many trains pass through here now but this old station pub, now brewing its own beers, hasn't forgotten its past. All the beers have a railway theme: Rail Ale, Piston Bitter, Sleeper (rather strong) and occasionally a special brew. You can see through to the brewery from the Boiler Room Bar. Reasonably priced bar meals include cod and parsley pie, speciality sausages, lasagne, casseroles, a selection of fresh fish, at least three vegetarian dishes and a vegetarian soup. Roast lunches every Sunday. Rumour has it that there is a female ghost walking the pub, but as the only people who have seen it are the chaps who have had a few beers, it could be a case of a vivid imagination and strong ale! There are tables in the large sunny garden.

OPEN: 11–11 (12–10.30 Sun).
Real Ale. You can take home up to 20 litres of beer from the brewery.
Children in eating area. Dogs on leads. Wheelchair access difficult.
Function room.

RATTERY

Church House   Tel: 01364 642220
Rattery, South Brent, Devon TQ10 9LD
Free House. Mr B. & Mrs J. Evans, licensees.

Another very old building with ecclesiastical roots. It is also said to be connected to the church by a tunnel – a short cut for early-morning prayers? All these secret tunnels beg the question: has anyone actually found one? Huge beams inside Church House hold up this listed building, which dates back to about 1028. Thought to be the oldest pub in Devon, it is also a strong contender for being the oldest in the country. Good range of bar food, soups, filled rolls, home-baked ham, smoked salmon, chicken, Algerian lamb and home-made puddings. Venison and chicken casserole and the beef and coconut balti are two of the favourites from the menu. Children's menu too. Furgusons Dartmoor Best, Abbot Ale, Marstons Pedigree and a guest beer on hand pump. Range of old malt whiskies. Farm cider. Between 50 and 60 wines to choose from. Lovely views of the wooded countryside from the pub.

> OPEN: 11–2.30. 6–11.
> Real Ale.
> Children in eating areas. Dogs on leads. Wheelchair access with help.

SHEEPWASH

Half Moon   Tel: 01409 231376
Sheepwash, Nr Hatherleigh, N. Devon EX21 5NE
Free House. Nathan & Lee Adey, licensees.

This thriving fishermen's pub and hotel is totally geared up for all eventualities: a rod room, somewhere to dry yourself when you fall in, and a shop where you can buy all those bits and pieces you thought you had packed. Between Hatherleigh and Holsworthy, the Half Moon is surrounded by miles of glorious fishing on the River Torridge and has plenty of room at the bar for the 'one that got away' stories. Bar snacks at lunchtime are all you could wish for: home-made soup, pasties, home-cured ham, salad, ploughman's. At night, the dinner menu includes roasts, steaks and fresh fish. Courage Best, Ruddles Best, Marstons Pedigree, and one locally brewed ale as a guest on hand pump. Selection of malt whiskies. Impressive wine list.

> OPEN: 11.30–2.30. 6–11.
> Real Ale. Evening restaurant. Lunchtime snacks.
> Children lunchtimes only. Dogs on leads. Wheelchair access.
> Fourteen bedrooms, 12 en suite.

SOUTHPOOL

Mill Brook   Tel: 01548 531581
Southpool, Kingsbridge, Devon TQ7 2RW
Free House. Liz Stirland, licensee.

This pub is tiny and one of the few whose opening times are governed by natural forces, not the local licensing authority. The state of the tide dictates the opening times. High tide in the creek, which runs into the middle of the pretty little village, means that you can virtually sail straight in and order drinks – so it's very popular with the local sailors and visiting yachtsmen. And inside is a charming, comfortable bar with lots of fresh flowers on the tables where they serve good, dependable bar food such as soup, filled potatoes, cottage pie, smoked mackerel, fish pie and chilli. Daily specials with Devon Apple Cider Cake to finish. Fullers London Pride, Bass and Wadworths 6X plus a guest ale on hand pump. Farm ciders.

> OPEN: 11–3. 5.30–11 (summer). 11.30–2.30. 6.30–11 (winter). All times approximate; may open longer in summer.
> Real Ale.
> Children in family room. No dogs. Wheelchair access difficult.

STICKLEPATH

Devonshire Inn   Tel: 01837 840626
Sticklepath, Oakhampton, Devon EX20 2NW
Free House. John & Ann Verner-Jeffreys, licensees.

Relaxed and friendly, this 17th-century thatched pub has a low-beamed, slate-floored bar with comfortable furnishings, big log fires in winter and something to read if you're waiting for someone. The food is reasonably priced and freshly cooked to order; they also cater for small dinner parties on request. Booked meals only in the evening. Real ales include St Austell's Tinners, Bass and some guest beers. Farm cider. Next to Finch's Foundry, now a National Trust property, where three huge water wheels drive the forges, grindstones and polishing wheels which, in the past, made tools for Devon miners and farmers.

> OPEN: 11–3. 5–11 (11–11 Fri & Sat and summer weekdays. 12–3. 7–10.30 Sun).
> Real Ale.
> Children: if under control. Dogs on leads always welcome. Wheelchair access (not WC). Bed and breakfast available – for dogs too (with human in tow).

STOKENHAM

Tradesman's Arms   Tel: 01548 580313
Stokenham, Kingsbridge, Devon TQ7 2SZ
Free House. John & Elizabeth Sharman, licensees.

Between Dartmouth and Kingsbridge, this partly thatched pub is in a delightful area. The pretty thatched end dates back to the 15th century; the unthatched bit was built a little later. Named after the tradesmen who collected their wares from Dartmouth, made their way around the coast with a loaded donkey and stopped at this pub for rest and refreshment. Inside, the bar is heavily beamed and warmed by a wood-burning stove. Off to one side is a no-smoking room. All the tables can be reserved (very advisable at the weekend), but if you just want a drink, you are very welcome to come and lean on the bar. Food is the thing here: interesting and creative. The menu, displayed on the blackboard, is the same throughout the pub. There is always a choice of about six starters:

traditional fish soup with garlic flutes, gravadlax with a dill sauce, smoked chicken and melon on a bed of green leaves with a walnut dressing, salade niçoise or wild-duck pâté, and for a main course, baked local sea bass, wild pigeon breast finished with cream and chorizo, sauté of rabbit with fresh horseradish. For vegetarians, spinach and lentil bake with tomato and basil sauce, or aubergine, courgette, avocado and rice mould. Utterly scrummy puds too. Adnams Southwold and guests from Exmoor, Otter, Badger or Summerskill. Heron Valley cider, organic apple juice and a fine range of malts. Small, carefully chosen wine list.

OPEN: 6.30–11 Tues–Sat (12–3-ish Sun).
Real Ale.
Children welcome for Sunday lunch only. Dogs in bar. Wheelchair access (not WC). Car park.
Cards: Delta, MasterCard, Switch, Visa.
N.B. Closed one week after Easter, one week at beginning October, two weeks in November.

THORVERTON

Exeter Inn   Tel: 01392 860206
Bullen Street, Thorverton, Exeter, Devon EX5 5NG
Free House. John Mann, licensee.

Nobody knows quite how old the Exeter is – just that it is very old. Only one main bar and a room for those important local meetings, but, to be different, there's a well in the bar, topped with glass and unused at the moment but that could probably all change if the water rates keep going up! Though I bet they'd charge you for that too. A crisp and nut place, this, to go with the Fullers London Pride, Exe Valley's Devon Glory, draught Bass and a guest.

OPEN: 12–3. 5.30–11 (12–3. 7–10.30 Sun).
Real Ale.
Children: well, maybe – there is a play area. Dogs welcome. Wheelchair access.

TOPSHAM

Bridge Inn   Tel: 01392 873862
Bridge Hill, Topsham, Devon EX3 0PQ
Free House. Mr N. Cheffers & Mrs C. Cheffers-Heard, licensees.

This glorious pub is in an area with a fascinating history. Topsham is a salutary lesson in why it does nobody any good starting a legal battle (except for the legal profession). Four miles south-east of Exeter, Topsham was, until the 16th century, the main port for the city. A weir constructed downstream in the late 13th century prevented access to Exeter and started a legal battle that went on for three centuries. However, by the time it had been finally settled, the River Exe had silted up, making it totally unnavigable anyway!

Built after all the legal squabbling, the pink-painted Bridge Inn is a handsome 16th-century Grade II-listed building, with even earlier foundations. It has been in the same family for five generations. Inside are panelled walls and huge settles to settle in. Traditional pub food only – three different ploughman's, soup, sandwiches and hot meat and potato pasties – but lots of different beers. Years ago they used to brew their own; now they just keep trying different ones, but you could find Adnams Broadside, Branscombe Vale Branoc, Exe Valley Devon Glory and about nine others. Occasionally draught Bass.

> OPEN: 12–2. 6–10.30 (12–2. 6–11 Fri & Sat. 12–2. 7–10.30 Sun).
> Real Ale.
> Children welcome. Dogs in the tap room.

TORQUAY

Crown & Sceptre   Tel: 01803 328290
2 Petitor Road, St Marychurch, Torquay, Devon TQ1 4QA
IPL Co. R.D. Wheeler, licensee.

You can thank Napoleon and the Napoleonic wars that stopped people travelling to the continent for turning Torquay into the important resort it is today. Surrounded by high wooded hills, the glorious expanse of Tor Bay, subtropical trees and a mild climate make the town the nearest thing we have to the French Riviera. So you know the Crown & Sceptre is in a very desirable area. A friendly old coaching inn serving good beer and sustaining pub fare of sandwiches, plain or toasted, ploughman's, pasties, ham, egg and chips, seafood platter, filled jacket potatoes and specials. Courage Best Bitter and Directors, Youngs Special, Morlands Old Speckled Hen, Fullers London Pride, Wychwood Hobgoblin, Bass and a different guest ale every week.

> OPEN: 11–3. 5.30–11.
> Real Ale.
> No children. Dogs welcome.
> N.B. Live music – folk and jazz – Tues, Sat and Sun eves.

TUCKENHAY

Maltsters Arms   Tel: 01803 732350
Tuckenhay, Nr Totnes, Devon TQ9 7EQ
Free House. Denise & Quentin Thwaites, licensees.

Bow Creek, off the River Dart in this lovely part of Devon, is of tremendous appeal to tourists, sailing enthusiasts and walkers. The 16th-century waterside Maltsters Arms serves some really satisfying food as well as ploughman's: home-made soups and double-decker sandwiches, cockles and mussels in cream, vanilla and onion sauce, pan-fried pigeon breasts with a spicy redcurrant glaze, leek, potato and Stilton pie, steak, kidney and

Dartmoor ale pie, fish from Brixham harbour, dishes using locally caught and raised game and desirable puddings; both the lunch and evening menus change daily. Blackawton Special, Princetown Dartmoor IPA, a changing guest and a good wine list. You can sit by the creek and watch all the comings and goings. Moorings for your boat. Barbecues at the weekend.

OPEN: 11–11. Christmas Day: bar only 12–2.
Real Ale.
Children in certain rooms. Dogs on leads. Wheelchair access (not WC). Bedrooms overlook the river.
Cards: Access, MasterCard, Switch, Visa.
Live music 1st and 3rd Friday of each month.

WIDECOMBE-IN-THE-MOOR

Rugglestone Inn   Tel: 01364 621327
Widecombe-in-the-Moor, Devon TQ13 7TF
Free House. Lorrie & Moira Ensor, licensees.

There's a huge granite stone called the Rugglestone south of the village and it has given its name to this popular inn, a favourite stopping place for walkers and anyone enjoying the surrounding countryside. Stone floors – just the thing for all those walking boots – and open fires. Food is freshly prepared and cooked on the premises: home-made soup of the day, filled rolls, jacket potatoes, ploughman's, traditional pasties, local beef casserole with dumplings and home-made 'pot-meals'. Daily changing specials are on the blackboard. The pub deliberately excludes children and chips! Bass and Butcombe Bitter. Seats in the large garden. Plenty of dogs come here; there are three in the pub – two Jack Russells and a flat coat retriever. Plenty of room and shelter for children in the garden. Uncle Tom Cobleigh and the well-known song 'Widecombe Fair' made the village famous; Widccombe Fair is still held on the second Tuesday in September and Uncle Tom Cobleigh puts in an appearance on his grey mare.

OPEN: 11–2.30 (11–3 Sat). 7–11 (6–11 summer. 12–3. 7–10.30 Sun.)
Real Ale.
No children inside. Dogs welcome. Wheelchair access (not WC).
Cards: MasterCard, Visa.

WHIMPLE

New Fountain Inn   Tel: 01404 822350
Church Road, Whimple, Exeter, Devon
Free House. Paul Mallett, licensee.

A well-beamed, attractive, friendly pub where they serve good-value food: freshly made sandwiches, ploughman's, garlic mushrooms, chef's choice of pâté, whitebait, home-made steak and kidney pie, locally cooked ham, mini steak in a crusty roll with onions and mushrooms, home-made chicken curry, daily specials such as a Brixham crab salad, plus a vegetarian dish or two. Teignworthy Brannock Ale and a guest beer. Seats in the beer garden. Another place for you to visit is the craft centre that has been set up in the redundant railway station.

> OPEN: 12–2.30. 6.30–11.
> Real Ale.
> Children welcome. Dogs too. Wheelchair access (not WC). Car park.
> Cards: Switch, Visa.

WONSON

Northmore Arms
Tel: 01647 231428

Wonson, Nr Throwleigh, Devon BX20 2JA
Free House. Maureen Miles, licensee.

A small, unspoilt, cottagey pub, tucked away down a maze of narrow, leafy Devon lanes, in an area rich in prehistoric stone circles. South-west of Drewsteignton, it's open all day so you can take your time to find it. Beams and good fires inside and traditional simple bar food: sandwiches, ploughman's, filled baked potato, steak and kidney pudding and roast lamb. Changing ales, some of them from local breweries – Cotleigh Tawny Bitter, Exe Valley Dob's Best Bitter, Adnams Broadside and two guests. Some house wines. There is a garden to sit in from where you can appreciate the peace of the countryside. Good walks.

> OPEN: 11–11.
> Real Ale.
> Children welcome. Dogs on leads.

WOODBURY SALTERTON

Diggers Rest
Tel: 01395 232375

Woodbury Salterton, Nr Exeter, Devon EX5 1PQ
Free House. Sally Pratt, licensee.

This 14th-century thatched village pub is tremendously popular for lunch. In the heavily beamed bar they serve a variety of bar food including filled pancakes, steak and kidney pie, liver and bacon, home-cooked gammon, curries, sandwiches, soups and daily specials. Always fresh vegetables and home-made puddings too. Sharps Doom Bar and Bass on hand pump, keg Tetleys. It all sounds very jolly, with a summer skittle alley and a games room – music in here. Splendid views over the local countryside from the terrace.

> OPEN: 11–2.30. 6.30–11.
> Real Ale.
> Well-behaved children in family area. No dogs.

WOODLAND

Rising Sun   Tel: 01364 652544
Woodland, Ashburton, Devon TQ13 7JT
Free House. Heather Humphries, licensee.

Just in case you are wandering off into the hinterland, you might want to know that the
Rising Sun is here – deep in the Devon countryside between the A38 and the A381. Well
worth finding as they provide some really good bar snacks, including home-made pasties
(which you can also order to take home), soup, local sausages, local venison and home-
made chutney to go with the ploughman's. Princetown Jail Ale and maybe two guests. A
couple of family areas in the pub, so there's somewhere to park the little darlings.

> OPEN: 11–3. 6–11 (12–3.30. 7–10.30 Sun).
> Real Ale. Restaurant.
> Children in eating areas and restaurant. Dogs on leads.
> Bedrooms.

BEST OF THE REST

BANTHAM

The Sloop Inn   Tel: 01548 560489/560215
This is an interesting old smuggling inn, once owned by one of the most famous smugglers:
John Whiddon. Traditional pub grub on the bar menu, also a variety of fishy things – all
very fresh: sea bass, monkfish, lobster – also local steaks and good home-made puddings.
Draught Bass, Ushers Best and bottled beers. Comprehensive wine list and lots of malt
whiskies. Children and dogs welcome, and there's wheelchair access. Sorry to demote this
one from the main list, but they do occasionally turn on the music.

CHAGFORD

Ring o' Bells   Tel: 01647 432466
This pub has had a very colourful past: over the years you could have been sentenced,
banged up, laid out or you could have bought a lamb chop – all at very different times!
Now beamed and panelled, it leads a more settled life in a delightful village just off the
moors. Open for morning coffee with the daily papers, and the rest of the time for a good
choice of bar food, home-made puds and Butcombe beers. Children in eating area and
dogs welcome. Bedrooms.

DARTINGTON

Cott Inn   Tel: 01803 863777
Predominantly white, with touches of black, the 14th-century thatched Cott looks solid
and prosperous. Inside are beams, flagstone floors, big fireplaces and lots of room. At
lunchtime there is a choice of salads, cold meats, Dart salmon, quiches, and so on.
Otherwise you could have a rough country terrine with Cumberland sauce, tenderloin of

pork with bacon, mushrooms, green peppers in a mustard sauce; the menu changes daily. Otter Ales, Wadworths 6X and an interesting wide-ranging wine list. Children and dogs on leads welcome. Bedrooms. Wheelchair access but not to bedrooms.

SIDFORD

Blue Ball   Tel: 01395 514062
North of Sidmouth; big, thatched and family-friendly. Run by the same family since early last century, they serve a fairly traditional pub menu of sandwiches, ploughman's, locally made sausages, steak pie and daily specials. Boddingtons, Flowers, Otter and a guest beer – all well kept.

STOCKLAND

Kings Arms   Tel: 01404 881361
Off the Chard to Honiton road, a 16th-century, white-painted, thatched inn with an interesting interior. A well-used bar for the locals; otherwise they concentrate on some seriously good food – but no bar snacks in the evening or Sunday – king-prawn thermidor, pigeon rossini, lamb Siciliano, prawn curry, steak au poivre and more-ish puds. Courage Directors, John Smiths, Otter and Exmoor ale. Good wine list, some by the glass and farm ciders. Children welcome if eating, dogs in bar. Wheelchair access. Bedrooms.

STOKEINTEIGNHEAD

Church House   Tel: 01626 872475
A really old – well, most of it – thatched pub in an unspoilt village north of Torquay. Some interesting additions (seafood pancakes, chargrilled chicken, breast of duck) to the usual menu to go with the Bass, Flowers and Wadworths. Farm ciders too. Children welcome.

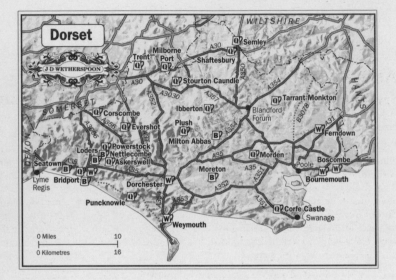

Dorset

ASKERSWELL

Spyway Inn
Tel: 01308 485250

Askerswell, Nr Bridport, Dorset DT2 9EP
Free House. Alan Dodds, licensee.

Deep in glorious Dorset countryside, off the Bridport to Dorchester road, is the old, rambling Spyway Inn, complete with beams, scrubbed pine tables, settles and a fine collection of decorative rural objects. All the food is freshly cooked and the menus change daily: there could be soup, rabbit, or steak and onion pies, mushroom, leek and courgette bake, ploughman's, omelettes, home-cooked ham, steaks and lots of salads. Adnams Southwold Bitter, Greene King IPA, Abbot and Branscombe Vale's Branoc. Wines by the glass, country wines and a large selection of malt whiskies. A pretty garden to sit in and admire the view. There is a good walk to Eggardon Hill, 827 feet high, with an Iron Age hill fort and Bronze Age barrows at the summit.

> OPEN: Closed all day Mon and Sun eve, otherwise 11–2.30. 6–11 (12–3 Sun).
> Real Ale.
> No children. No dogs. Wheelchair access (not WC). Bed and breakfast.

BOURNEMOUTH

Moon in the Square
Tel: 01202 314940

4–8 Exeter Road, Bournemouth BH2 5AD
Wetherspoon.

Unusually for a town-centre pub, this one has an outside drinking area – where you can smoke. A bit too much hot air caused the demise of the previous occupants of this site: the Forte coffee house roasted one coffee bean too many. The burnt-out shell was rebuilt and is now a very large, thriving town-centre pub. On two floors; the top floor is non-smoking. As with all Wetherspoon outlets, there will be five or six cask ales and a big selection of guest beers from the smaller breweries. One beer will be considerably cheaper than elsewhere. Consistently reliable bar food: ploughman's, filled jacket potatoes or baps, different burgers, a vegetarian dish, haddock and chips, bangers and mash – that sort of thing.

> OPEN: 10.30–11 (12–10.30 Sun).
> Real Ale.
> No children. No dogs.

BRIDPORT West Bay

The Bridport Arms Hotel   Tel: 01308 422994
West Bay, Bridport, Dorset DT6 4EN
Palmers Brewery. John & Carla Jacobs, licensees.

West Bay used to be known as Bridport Harbour. Built in 1740, more than 500 ships a year used it in its heyday and it continued to be in use until the 1870s; it's quiet now – though you can still hire a rowing boat! The Bridport Arms is a big, low-beamed, 16th-century thatched building with flagstone floors, two bars – one quite small – and a restaurant. On the edge of the beach at West Bay, and as you might expect, being by the seaside, there are lots of fish dishes on the menu; also home-made lasagne, cottage pie, salads and delights such as chicken with a peppercorn and lemon sauce, grilled fillet of salmon with hollandaise sauce, steaks and specials on the blackboard. Palmers ales and a varied wine list. A separate family room for children and seats outside.

> OPEN: 11–11 (12–10.30 Sun).
> Real Ale. Restaurant.
> Children in the family room and restaurant. Dogs on leads.

CORFE CASTLE

Fox Inn   Tel: 01929 480449
West Street, Corfe Castle, Dorset BH20 5HD
Free House. Miss A. Brown & Graham White, licensees.

Corfe Castle, destroyed during the Civil War in 1646, dominates this village in the Purbeck Hills. The ruins are a dramatic part of the scenery visible from the attractive, sheltered and sunny garden of the old Fox Inn. Medieval architectural remains have been found within the pub and these have blended well with the changes made over the years. Traditional bar food from the varied menu, plus daily specials; vegetarian dishes always available. Sunday roasts in winter. Morlands Old Speckled Hen, Marstons Pedigree, Youngs Special, Fullers London Pride, Greene King Abbot, Wadworths 6X and Burton Ale. Look for the old well inside the pub which was found during restoration work. Good walking country.

> OPEN: 11–3. 6–11 (11–2.30. 6.30–11 winter).
> Real Ale.
> Children in the garden only. Dogs welcome.

CORSCOMBE

Fox Inn
Tel: 01935 891330

Corscombe, Dorset DT2 0NS (off A356 south of Crewkerne going towards Dorchester, take the left turn to Corscombe and Halstock, NOT the one just to Corscombe. Pub at bottom of hill)

Free House. Martyn & Susie Lee, licensees.

Along a quiet country lane, you'll know you've arrived when you see a cream-painted building with a thatched roof, thatched hats over the doors, climbing roses, hanging baskets and a general air of wellbeing. Slightly difficult to find but well worth the effort. This is just the sort of pub we would all like as our local. Really good things are happening in the kitchen; the food is all you could wish for: seafood risotto with mussels and prawns, French beans with bacon, garlic and olive oil, mushroom and bacon filled filo baskets, medallions of tuna au poivre, herb-crusted fillets of brill with red pesto, rabbit braised with mustard, cream and rosemary, Moroccan leg of lamb tagine, braised venison with wild mushrooms, thyme and red wine, beef braised with bacon, mushrooms and red wine, Burmese beef curry, imaginative vegetarian dishes and desirable puddings. All vegetables are fresh and are freshly cooked. Exmoor Ale, Exmoor Fox and Fullers London Pride beers. Good, well-chosen wine list – only house wines by the glass; home-made damson vodka, sloe gin and elderflower cordial. Tables outside and by the stream; there is also a conservatory full of flowers and a large oak table to seat 22.

> OPEN: 12–2.45. 7–11-ish.
> Real Ale. Restaurant.
> Well-behaved children. No dogs. Wheelchair access (not WC). Car park.
> Four bedrooms.
> Cards: Amex, Delta, MasterCard, Switch, Visa.

EVERSHOT

The Acorn Inn
Tel: 01935 83228

Fore Street, Evershot, Dorchester, Dorset DT2 0JW

Free House. Martyn Lee, owner/licensee.

In a pleasing, time-has-stood-still village, handsome and comfortable, the Acorn, owned by the same family as the Fox at Corscombe, is everything it should be. Beamed and polished, it offers an interesting bar and dinner menu. Dishes change from day to day but there could be a freshly made soup of the day, home-made salmon fishcakes with lemon butter sauce, wild-mushroom risotto, brill with mussel and saffron sauce, cod steak with smoked-cheese mash and chive sauce, local-estate game casserole with port and junipers, home-made steak and kidney pie and roast rack of lamb with rosemary gravy. To complete your meal, English cheeses, vanilla ice-cream, almond crème brûlée, apple crumble or chocolate fudge tart with orange sauce. The beers are Fullers London Pride and Butcombe Bitter. You'll find a comprehensive wine list, home-made damson vodka, sloe gin and a non-alcoholic elderflower cordial for the driver. A small garden to sit in and lots of good walks in the surrounding area. Midway between Yeovil and Dorchester, so it's not far from the Fleet Air Arm museum at Yeovilton and the Thomas Hardy memorabilia museum in Dorchester.

> OPEN: 11.30–2.30. 6.30–11.
> Real Ale.
> Children welcome. Dogs too. Wheelchair access (not WC). Car park. Nine classy bedrooms – all en suite. Well-behaved dogs can bring their suitcases too.
> Cards: Amex, Delta, MasterCard, Switch, Visa.

IBBERTON

Crown   Tel: 01258 817448
Church Lane, Ibberton, Nr Blandford, Dorset DE11 0EN
Free House. John Wild, licensee.

Here in the Crown you are below Bulbarrow Hill, in the heart of the densely wooded and beautiful Blackmoor Vale, well watered by the Stour and Lydden rivers. It's a small, attractive pub with flagstone floors, a big inglenook fireplace and historic photographs of times past. Traditional bar food ranges from soup and sandwiches to pies, chicken dishes, fresh fish and grills. They serve a local cider, draught Bass, M & S Brew XI and a changing guest.

> OPEN: 11–2. 7–11 (5.30–11 summer).
> Real Ale.
> Children welcome. No dogs. Wheelchair access (not WC). Car park.

MILBORNE PORT

Queens Head   Tel: 01963 250314
High Street, Milborne Port, Nr Sherborne, Dorset DT9 5DQ
Free House. John & Glenda Thomas, licensees.

The 'Port' in the name means that this small place was a borough that at one time returned two members of Parliament – electioneering probably got a bit rough! Built in Elizabethan times, but now mainly early Georgian, the Queens Head is in an area that has been settled since 871 AD. The food is Elizabethan – modern Elizabethan that is – with specials from the blackboard. On Mondays they serve a very reasonable two-course meal for £5.25; on Tuesdays you get a free bottle of wine if the order is over £17.50; Wednesday evening is curry night; Thursdays, two steaks for the price of one! Somebody is doing some serious marketing here – otherwise, traditional pub fare. Seven real ales include the regulars: Fullers London Pride, Butcombe Bitter, Charles Wells Bombardier, Greene King Abbot and two different ciders to choose from. You can dine in the conservatory.

> OPEN: 11–2.30. 5.30–11 (11–11 Sat & Sun).
> Real Ale.
> Children welcome. No dogs.
> N.B. Background music in public bar.

MORDEN

Cock & Bottle
Tel: 01929 459238

Morden, Nr Wareham, Dorset BH20 7DL
Badger. Pete Meadley, licensee.

Cosy and welcoming with lovely wood fires in winter. Food is plentiful and varied, rang-ing from interesting bar snacks and meals – with a good choice of fish and game – to dishes with an international bias: crab and ginger tartlet, roast partridge wrapped in bacon with port wine, ragout of seafood with white-wine sauce. Always very busy, so you should book if you want to eat. Badger Dorset Best, Tanglefoot and King & Barnes Sussex. Short wine list, some by the glass. Outside there are seats on the terrace and in the beer garden with views across the open country.

    OPEN: 11–2.30. 6–11 (12–3. 7–10.30 Sun).
    Real Ale. Restaurant.
    Children welcome. Dogs too. Wheelchair access. Car park
    Cards: Delta, MasterCard, Switch, Visa.

PLUSH

Brace of Pheasants
Tel: 01300 348357

Plush, Dorchester, Dorset DT2 7RQ
Free House. Jane & Geoffrey Knights, licensees.

Plush, a peaceful hamlet in the Piddle Valley near Piddletrenthide, has its own babbling brook as well as this pleasant old pub. Many years ago an attractive group of 16th-century thatched buildings – two cottages and the village blacksmith – were joined to create the Brace of Pheasants. Today, a brace of stuffed pheasants welcomes you into the pub, where their cousins feature on the menu (when in season). Inside, all is as it should be: beamed, traditionally furnished and with big log fires in winter. Good, popu-lar bar food with imaginative 'extras': oak-smoked and home-honey-cured salmon, seared scallops set on chorizo and orange salad, grilled chicken salad with Parmesan shavings, breast of pheasant with Calvados and apple cream, glazed tenderloin of pork with Stilton and sherry cream, steak and kidney pies, fish pies and a specials board with more exciting dishes. The Brace holds three special evenings each week: Tuesday is pasta night, Thursday curry night and Friday the surf and turf evening. Once a month they host 'The Brace Wine and Dine Club'. Children's menu too. Both the restaurant and family room are no smoking. Tisbury's Stonehenge, Fullers London Pride and a guest beer available at peak times. All ales are served straight from the cask. Lovely walks nearby.

    OPEN: 12–2.30. 7–11 (10.30 Sun). Food served 12–1.45 and 7–9.45.
    Real Ale. Restaurant.
    Children in family room – not in the bar. Dogs on leads. Wheelchair access (not
    WC). From spring 2002 new bedrooms should be ready.
    Cards: Delta, MasterCard, Switch, Visa.

POWERSTOCK

Three Horseshoes
Tel: 01308 485328

Powerstock, Dorset DT6 3TF
Palmers. Mark & Susan Johnson, tenants.

Rebuilt from local stone after a fire in 1906, the pub, set in large gardens, is surrounded by glorious countryside. Next to the church, the Three Horseshoes is an important part of this working village. A busy, friendly place, with a reputation for good, imaginative food served in both the bar and the attractive panelled dining room. Fresh fish from local fishermen, Dorset lamb and local game, maybe grilled Cornish scallops, Portland crab gratin or sea bass with roasted peppers and delicious puddings. Good short wine list; up to ten by the glass. The ales are Bridport Bitter and Palmers IPA. Fine views over the Dorset countryside from the large garden.

> OPEN: 12–3. 7–11.
> Real Ale. Restaurant.
> Children in bar until 8.30pm only. Dogs on leads. Wheelchair access. Car park.
> Bedrooms.
> Cards: MasterCard, Switch, Visa.

PUNCKNOWLE

Crown Inn
Tel: 01308 897711

Church Street, Puncknowle, Nr Dorchester, Dorset DT2 9BN
Palmers. Mike Lawless, tenant.

Even though you are about 2 miles inland, Puncknowle village was a favourite haunt of smugglers from Chesil Beach – that 10-mile strip of banked shingle fringing the Dorset coast. In this quiet and lovely honey-coloured village you'll find the Crown, a very likely meeting place for the smugglers. A spacious, well-run 16th-century thatched inn, it offers a wide and imaginative choice of well-prepared food: home-made soup, freshly made sandwiches, ploughman's, filled jacket potatoes, smoked peppered mackerel, gammon steak topped with pineapple and chicken Kiev, as well as home-cooked steak and kidney pie cooked in Guinness, chicken and smoked-bacon casserole cooked in white wine, beef stroganoff, vegetarian dishes, grills and more besides. Children's portions and a traditional Sunday lunch. Palmers Copper, IPA and Tally Ho! when available, plus 200 (the Anniversary Ale) and a selection of country wines. Seats in the big garden, where they sometime erect a marquee for large functions. Outside bars. Delightful area with lots of walks.

> OPEN: 11–2.30. 7–11.
> Real Ale.
> Children welcome. Dogs on leads in the public bar, and to stay. Wheelchair access.
> Bedrooms.
> Once a month, during the summer, the Wessex Military Band gives a Sunday-lunchtime concert.

SEMLEY

Benett Arms   Tel: 01747 830221
Semley, Shaftesbury, Dorset SP7 9AS
Free House. Joe Duthie, FBII, licensee.

Just one bar in this old place opposite the village green. Pleasantly furnished with a good fire in winter, you'll find well-tried favourites on the bar menu: soups, ploughman's and various sandwiches, leek and cheese bake, omelettes, Wiltshire ham served with either salad or chips, scampi royale, avocado and seafood salad, venison pie, grills, steaks and occasionally bouillabaisse; also interesting daily specials from the blackboard. Table d'hôte Sunday lunch. Home-made puddings. Brakspear, Adnams Bitter and Youngs Special ales. Good extensive wine list. Lots of liqueurs. Inchs ciders. Seats in the small garden.

> OPEN: 11–3. 6–11.
> Real Ale. Restaurant.
> Children in upper bar. Dogs on leads. Wheelchair access (not WC).
> Five en-suite bedrooms.
> Cards: Amex, Diners, MasterCard, Visa.

SHAFTESBURY

Ship Inn   Tel: 01747 853219
Bleke Street, Shaftesbury, Dorset SP7 8JZ
Badger. Gregg & Sarah Noble, tenants.

This is Hardy country and this historic town was used by Thomas Hardy in his novels. Built on the edge of a 700-foot-high plateau, Shaftesbury has some very handsome buildings, including the 17th-century Ship Inn, which has an interesting panelled interior reflecting its age, an elegant small restaurant, an eight-seat snug, public bar and pool table. Bar food includes the pub stalwarts of home-made soup, sandwiches, pâté, lasagne and daily specials which sometimes lean towards the continental. Booking is advisable if you want to eat in comfort. Badger Dorset Best and Tanglefoot, also Newtimer in the winter and Champion Gold in the summer. Farm ciders. The Ship has an outdoor boules pitch and there are seats on the terrace.

> OPEN: 11–3. 5–11 (11–11 Thurs–Sun).
> Real Ale. Restaurant.
> Children in eating areas. Dogs on leads.

SHAFTESBURY

Ye Olde Two Brewers   Tel: 01747 854211
24 St James Street, Shaftesbury, Dorset SP7 8HE
Free House. Richard Pearce, MBII, licensee.

You look down on much of Shaftesbury from the top of the incredibly steep, cobbled Gold Hill, and someone has made sure you know where to aim for – he's painted the pub's name on the roof! Now you know where you're going, you'll find a large, open-plan, comfortable, carpeted bar with several different drinking areas. All the food is freshly produced and there's something for everyone on the menu, which lists soup, whitebait or crispy-coated mushrooms, omelettes with various fillings, sandwiches, ploughman's, toasties, fish dishes, filled jacket potatoes, chilli con carne, lasagne, steaks, mixed grill, even a late breakfast and a vegetarian dish or two. Good puds. Well-kept Theakstons XB and Courage Directors are the permanent beers and there are quite a number of frequent guests. From the front door of the pub you look directly at the hill site of the ruined abbey, founded in 880 AD by King Alfred the Great. Wonderful views from the garden too.

> OPEN: 11–3. 6–11 (12–3. 7–10.30 Sun).
> Real Ale.
> Children welcome. No dogs. Wheelchair access (not WC).

STOURTON CAUNDLE

Trooper Inn
Tel: 01963 362405
Stourton Caundle, Nr Sturminster Newton, Dorset DT10 21W
Free House. Larry & Sue Skeats, licensees.

Enjoyed by all, this stone-built inn is between Stalbridge and Sherborne in an attractive village, deep in the Dorset countryside. Run by an ex-shepherd and shepherdess, they have a fascinating collection of old country tools and artifacts displayed on the bar walls – their own private museum. Traditional bar snacks are served to go with Cottages Champflower, Hampshire's King Alfred, Oakhill Best, Otter Bitter and something from Exmoor. Various traditional ciders – Thatchers or Burrow Hill. Tables at the front of the pub and a small beer garden.

> OPEN: 12–2.30. 7–11. Closed Mondays.
> Children if under control.
> Real Ale. Well-behaved dogs welcome. Wheelchair access difficult (not WC).

TARRANT MONKTON

Langton Arms
Tel: 01258 830225
Tarrant Monkton, Nr Blandford, Dorset DT11 8RX
Free House. Mrs Barbara Cossins, owner/licensee.

Built around a courtyard, thatched and looking very flowery at the height of summer, the Langton Arms is nearly 300 years old, with beams, an inglenook fireplace, good food and well-kept beers – all you could possibly want. From the bar you could have filled baguettes, ploughman's, baked potatoes, lasagne, liver and bacon, fillet of salmon, wild-boar sausages, pot-roast rabbit, or a lamb and rosemary stew. An evening menu is served in the no-smoking dining room, which is in a converted stable: fan of melon with fresh fruits, baked tartlet of goat's cheese, mixed olives and redcurrants, tempura of king prawns scented with ginger and coriander, breasts of pigeon marinated in Pernod and star anis, pan-fried sirloin steak, or breast of barbary duck honey-roasted with grain mustard on home-made chutney. Home-made puddings to finish. A changing number of wines by the glass and Flashmans Clout, Smiles Best and Ringwood Fortyniner ales. Seats and play area in the garden. Good walks nearby.

OPEN: 11–11 (12–10.30 Sun).
Real Ale. Restaurant.
Children welcome. Dogs on leads. Wheelchair access. Bedrooms. Car park.
N.B. Jukebox in the snug and background music in restaurant but bar quiet.
Cards: MasterCard, Switch, Visa.

TRENT

Rose & Crown   Tel: 01935 850776
Trent, Nr Sherborne, Dorset DT9 4SL
Free House. Charles Marion-Crawford, licensee.

Partly thatched and traditional, the Rose and Crown is a 15th-century village pub with an 18th-century addition and roses around the door. It has one big bar with smaller rooms leading off it, flagstone floors, three open fires and a dining room/conservatory at the back. A good choice of well-cooked bar food, full menu and daily specials which could be a hot leek and potato soup, fish soup, brioche filled with roasted pepper, spinach and ricotta cheese, boiled mutton in a caper sauce, beef or chicken enchilada with Mexican salsa and jalapeno peppers, spaghetti alla vongole (clams, olive oil, garlic and parsley sauce), Louisiana 'blackened' swordfish with a roasted-pepper mayonnaise. Good puds and interesting cheeses, some of them local. Shepherd Neame Spitfire and three varying guest ales. Lovely views from the large garden. You will see when you arrive that this pub really does have a sign outside saying 'Dogs welcome, children on leads'. Swings and slides in the hope that children will stay outside.

OPEN: 12–2.30. 7–11 (12–3 Sun. Closed Sun eves).
Real Ale. Conservatory/restaurant.
Children preferably in garden but there is a special room. Dogs welcome.
Wheelchair access.

BEST OF THE REST

BRIDPORT

George   Tel: 01308 423187
Opposite the Guildhall, this handsome Georgian town pub will take good care of you. They serve everything from morning coffee to something better than usual from a menu including home-made dishes, fresh fish and a choice of English cheeses. Palmers ales as well as decent wines.

LODERS

Loders Arms   Tel: 01308 422431
North of Bridport, in the depths of the countryside, Loders is an attractive village full of thatched cottages off the A3066 with an attractive pub serving traditional bar food as well as some inspired options and home-made puddings. Palmers ales. Children and dogs welcome – in certain areas. Wheelchair access. Two bedrooms.

MILTON ABBAS

Hambro Arms   Tel: 01258 880233
Surrounded by unspoilt countryside, the Hambro Arms and Milton Abbas are a delight. Standard bar snacks and a selection of hot dishes, as well as daily specials on the blackboard and a choice of fresh fish. There is a popular Sunday-lunchtime carvery. Boddingtons and Flowers Original ales. Seats outside on the terrace. There is a jukebox in the pool room which you can sometimes hear. No children or dogs.

MORETON, Nr Dorchester

Frampton Arms   Tel: 01305 852253
T.E. Lawrence is buried in Moreton churchyard and inside the church are some wonderful etchings by Lawrence Whistler. The Frampton Arms has a quiet lunchtime restaurant with a timeless ambience, and a charming conservatory. Home-made soups, freshly filled sandwiches, casseroles, seafood and fish specialities, a small selection of daily specials and vegetarian dishes on the blackboard. Boddingtons and Flowers IPA and a short wine list. Music in evenings.

NETTLECOMBE

Marquis of Lorne   Tel: 01308 485236
In a peaceful setting, this 16th-century farmhouse is a well-run, busy pub. Lots of things to choose from the bar menu, much of it home-made, daily specials and interesting soups. Palmers range of ales and a good wine list, several by the glass.

SEATOWN

Anchor   Tel: 01279 489215
Another village of thatched cottages and a beach of golden shingle, not far from Chideock. Very busy during the season, but all year round they serve a good choice of bar food including daily specials. Palmers beers and small wine list.

Essex

Map labels:
CAMBRIDGESHIRE
SUFFOLK
0 Miles 10
0 Kilometres 16
B1039
M11
B1052
B1054
B1053
B105
A101
A131
Radwinter
Great Yeldham
Arkesden
Saffron Walden
Blackmore End
Rickling Green
Gosfield
Earls Colne
Harwich
B1038
Shalford
A134
A137
A120
Stansted Mountfitchet
Braintree
A1124
Colchester
Wivenhoe
A120
A12
Young's End
A106
A130
A131
Pleshey
Witham
Peldon
A133
Clacton
HERTFORDSHIRE
M11
B184
Chelmsford
Maldon
Coopersale Common
High Ongar
A414
A414
7
M25
Mill Green
Ingatestone
Purleigh
Stow Maries
26
6/2
A12
A130
Burnham-on-Crouch
Loughton
A128
Stock
5
Billericay
Paglesham Eastend
28
A129
Basildon
GREATER LONDON
A127
A13
Leigh-on-Sea
South Ockenden
A128
Southend-on-Sea
Dagenham
30
Horndon on the Hill
31
A13
Tilbury
KENT

J.D.WETHERSPOON

Essex

ARKESDEN

Axe and Compasses
Tel: 01799 550272

Arkesden, Essex CB11 4EX
Greene King. Themis & Diana Christou, lease.

The 'occasional stream' that runs down the main street in this pretty village was more likely to be described as a 'raging torrent' during the wet spells the country has experienced over the last year. On the main street, at the centre of the village, you'll find the delightful Axe and Compasses. You can relax at the Axe, a spacious, 17th-century, mostly thatched pub, which has been added to over the years. Hung about and surrounded by a wonderful floral display – where the flowers stop, the pub stops. Meals are served in both the bar and the restaurant: home-made soup, grilled sardines, smoked mackerel, cannelloni with a salad and garlic bread, tenderloin of pork in breadcrumbs topped with ham and cheddar on a wholegrain-mustard sauce, pan-fried breast of duck with parsnip quenelle and cranberry gravy, chargrilled supreme of chicken finished with a port and Stilton sauce, a choice of fresh fish, some vegetarian dishes or one of the daily specials. A wider choice is available in the restaurant. Greene King beers and a very good wine list. Seats on the terrace among the hanging baskets.

> OPEN: 11–2.30. 6–11.
> Real Ale; Cask Marque award. Restaurant.
> Children in eating areas. No dogs. Car park.
> Cards: Delta, MasterCard, Switch, Visa.

BLACKMORE END

The Bull
Tel: 01371 851037

Blackmore End, Nr Braintree, Essex CM7 4DD
Free House, London. Sidney Morris, licensee.

Good food and good wines – beer too of course. The word has got out and people come from miles around to sample something from the regularly changing menu at the Bull, a 17th-century timbered pub with a good reputation for food. If you want a quick snack, you will find the usual sandwiches, ploughman's, salads, interesting home-made soups and pâtés. An à la carte menu and more dishes on the changing blackboard menu: fillet of steak in a port sauce, venison cutlet in a red-wine sauce, all served with fresh vegetables,

delicious home-made puds too. Adnams, Greene King IPA and a guest beer. A selection of European and New World wines.

OPEN: 12–3. 6–11.
Real Ale. Restaurant.
Children in eating area of bar. No dogs.

Burnham-on-Crouch

Olde White Harte   Tel: 01621 782106
The Quay, Burnham-on-Crouch, Essex CM0 8AS
Free House. John Lewis, licensee.

Known as the 'Cowes of the East Coast', Burnham has a largely Georgian High Street that runs parallel to the river, and a quay only wide enough for pedestrians, so walk past the yacht builders until you get to the elegant, 17th-century Olde White Harte. You can't quite sail into the hotel, but it does have its own jetty. When the tide is high, you can get really close, and believe me, this is one of the places you get really close to during Burnham Week, when everyone who is anyone in sailing fills the town to the gunnels. Enjoy a drink on the jetty, or inside among the beams in the comfortable bar. The bar menu has something for everyone; the restaurant has both a table d'hôte and an à la carte menu. Bar food varies daily, but there could be roast pork, liver Lyonnaise, pan-fried skate, locally caught cod, grilled plaice or steak and kidney pie. Specials change weekly: fresh asparagus tips, poached salmon in a mushroom, chive and cider sauce, or duck à l'orange. Tolly Cobbold Bitter, Adnams Bitter, Crouch Vale IPA and a good wine list.

OPEN: 11–3. 6–11 (11–11 Sat).
Real Ale. Restaurant.
Children if well-behaved. Dogs on leads. Wheelchair access (not WC). Eleven bedrooms en-suite, eight others. Car park.
Cards: all except Amex and Diners.

CHELMSFORD

Endeavour   Tel: 01245 257717
351 Springfield Road, Chelmsford, Essex CM2 6AW
Gray & Sons. Walter Jenkins, MBII, tenant.

On the old London to Colchester road and on the site of a former smithy and forge, the Endeavour is an oasis in a noisy desert. Built in 1810 as a private house, it was first licensed in 1844. The inn sign is fascinating: Captain Cook's sailing ship *Endeavour* on one side and NASA's spaceship of the same name on the other. Inside this quiet three-roomed pub you will find a convivial, chatty atmosphere. All the food is cooked on the premises and the menu is full of nice surprises with a touch of English and a soupçon of Mediterranean. Always a selection of real ales including a dark mild. A popular local that is well known for its successful charity fund-raising events.

OPEN: 11–11 (12–2.30. 7–10.30 Sun).
Real Ale.
Dogs on leads. Wheelchair access to public bar only.

DAGENHAM

The Lord Denman   Tel: 020 8984 8590
270–272 Heathway, Dagenham, Essex
Wetherspoon.

Another large space converted into a successful and always popular Wetherspoon outlet. Photos of 'local boys made good' are on the walls, among them Dudley Moore and Terry Venables. Named after the first Lord Denman, Lord Chief Justice of England, who lived in Dagenham from 1850 to 1852. There is a bust of Lord Denman in the bar. Reliable bar food and always six real ales, one of which is invariably cheaper than usual. The pub is on two levels; they have a special stairlift for wheelchairs. Seats in the garden.

OPEN: 11–11.
Real Ale.
No children. No dogs. Wheelchair access to all parts.

EARLS COLNE

Bird in Hand   Tel: 01787 222557
Coggeshall Road, Earls Colne, Colchester, Essex CO6 2JX
Ridleys. Colin & Lesley Eldred, lessees.

Opposite the old airfield, used by the U.S. Army Air Corps from 1942 to 1944, the Bird in
Hand lies at the end of a disused runway between the villages of Earls Colne and Coggleshall.
During the war the roof was regarded as a potential hazard, so, to stop it being inadvertently
rearranged by low-flying aircraft, the Americans lowered its profile. Restored to its full height,
you can see the 'before and after' photographs displayed in the saloon bar. Not a 'foody' pub,
it has, nevertheless, a full menu of favourite dishes – some of which are home-made, and
these, understandably, are the most popular, and could include steak and mushroom pie, beef
lasagne or chicken curry. Six different fillings for the jacket potatoes. Basket meals; specials on
certain days. Ridleys range of ales; draught and bottled. Seats in the large garden.

> OPEN: 12–2. 6–11 (7–10.30 Sun).
> Real Ale.
> No children under 14. Dogs: perhaps. Wheelchair access.

GOSFIELD

Green Man   Tel: 01787 472746
The Street, Gosfield, Essex CO9 1TP
Greene King. Janet Harrington, lease.

It may be called the Green Man, but it's pink and quite unmissable. Warm, friendly service and imaginative food are the hallmarks of this pub just a few miles north of Braintree.
Inside are two small bars, a dining room and separate function room. As well as bar snacks
and an exceptional lunchtime cold table, a full à la carte menu is available both at
lunchtime and in the evening. Always lots of interesting things on the blackboard menu:
home-made soups, home-made curries, fresh fish, lamb chops (done pink), steak and
kidney pudding and home-made puddings. Good, reasonably priced wine list. Greene
King IPA and Abbot on hand pump.

> OPEN: 11–3. 6.30–11 (7–10.30 Sun).
> Real Ale. Restaurant (no food and no restaurant Sun eves).
> Well-behaved children in eating area. Dogs if very restrained. Wheelchair access.
> Cards: Amex, Delta, MasterCard, Switch, Visa.
> N.B. Jukebox in public bar.

GREAT YELDHAM

White Hart   Tel: 01787 237250
Poole Street, Great Yeldham, Halstead, Essex CO9 4HJ
Free House. John Dicken, manager.

This is a 'beat a path to the door' place. Outside, it's a 16th-century, half-timbered inn on the
edge of Great Yeldham with a spectacular display of hanging baskets and tubs of flowers.

Inside are low-beamed ceilings and panelling, both restored to their former beauty, big log fires and some very interesting menus. There is still a warm welcome if you want something informal – just a beer and a snack, but you will find far more culinary delights in the no-smoking restaurant. From the snack menu you could have home-made soup, which varies with the season, a sandwich of mozzarella, plum tomato and salami, grilled rainbow trout, or a ploughman's with pâté, cheese and plum chutney. The full menu offers spiced figs with red onion and walnuts and fillet mignon of lamb with dauphinoise potato and a basil jus, chocolate and pecan nut tart with crème fraîche to finish, other delicious puds and a selection of cheeses. The à la carte menu changes about every two weeks. An extensive wine list; some wines by the glass. Two or three ales on permanently and guests including seasonal and speciality ales from regional brewers. Large gardens running down to the River Colne.

> OPEN: 11–3. 6–11 (12–3. 7–10.30 Sun).
> Real Ale. Restaurant (not Sun eves).
> Children welcome. Dogs in garden only. Wheelchair access. Car park.
> Cards: Amex, Delta, Diners, MasterCard, Switch, Visa.

HIGH ONGAR

Wheatsheaf
King Street, High Ongar, Essex CM5 9NS
Free House. Graham Milo & Patricia Fleming, licensees.

Tel: 01277 822220

'Ongar' is the Anglo-Saxon word for grazing land, and this ancient farming area is full of Ongars, including Chipping Ongar, an old market town with some interesting 17th-century buildings, and High Ongar with the Wheatsheaf. Newly decorated outside, and with an impressive flower display, this well-beamed old pub has good log fires and serves a satisfying choice of bar food. Always a home-made soup, freshly filled sandwiches, ploughman's, filled jacket potatoes, a good selection of vegetarian dishes and daily specials: sea bass with ginger and spring onion, whole lemon sole stuffed with prawns or rack of lamb with red-wine jus. Greene King IPA, Abbot and Courage Directors beers. There is a large garden with all sorts of play equipment to keep the children happy and out of the pub.

> OPEN: 12–3. 6–11 (11–11 Sat & Sun).
> Real Ale.
> Children in garden only. No dogs.
> Cards: all accepted.

HORNDON ON THE HILL

Bell Inn
High Road, Horndon on the Hill, Essex SS17 8LD
Free House. John Vereker, CMBII, licensee.

Tel: 01375 642463

You can't help but notice the magnificent floral display of hanging baskets and flowers at the front of this handsome 15th-century coaching inn. Run by the same family for well over 50 years, this is a charming place. Only one bar in the Bell, and a restaurant serving exceptional food: a choice of interesting soups, such as creamed corn soup with red-onion bhaji, crayfish, pea and goat's cheese risotto with tarragon, roast chicken with butter beans and cheese and parsley sauce, pot-roast lamb shank with parsnip cream and basil – these are just few dishes from the changing menu. Home-made puddings as well. Good selection of wines, many by the glass or half-bottle. The landlord has produced notes on what to drink with what; you can buy wine from him too. Draught Bass and Greene King IPA on hand pump, plus weekly changing guest beers such as Crouch Vale Brewers Gold. Seats outside in the courtyard. (John Vereker won Pub Operator of the Year 2001.)

> OPEN: 11–2.30 (12–3 Sat). 6–11. Closed all Bank Holidays, Christmas Day and Boxing Day.
> Real Ale. Restaurant.
> Children in eating area. Dogs on leads. Wheelchair access. Car park. Fourteen en-suite bedrooms.
> Cards: Amex, Delta, MasterCard, Switch, Visa.

INGATESTONE

Cricketers   Tel: 01277 352400
Mill Green, Ingatestone, Essex CM4 0DS
Gray & Sons. Mrs E. Marriage, tenant.

Overlooking Mill Green Common, which was the old cricket field, there's a lot of cricketing memorabilia in this aptly named and interesting old building. Two bars, one of which is used for a no-smoking restaurant. Bar snacks include filled baguettes, ploughman's, also fresh fish, steaks and daily specials on the snack board. Greene King IPA and Abbot. A good choice of wines. Seats on the terrace overlooking the old cricket green and in the garden at the back of the pub.

> OPEN: 12–3. 6–11.
> Real Ale. Closed Sun eves.
> Children welcome. Dogs on leads. Wheelchair access.
> Cards: MasterCard, Visa.

LEIGH-ON-SEA

Crooked Billet   Tel: 01702 714854
51 High Street, Leigh-on-Sea, Essex SS9 2EP
Six Continents. Wayne Bowes, manager.

Leigh, with its narrow high street, still has its old fishermen's cottages, a sailing club, cockle boats and a small beach with a slipway. The Crooked Billet, unsurprisingly, flourished as a smugglers' haunt. With sea views and in a bracing position against the sea wall, the 16th-century pub is still flourishing – only now with a more law-abiding clientele. Full of character: some interesting Tudor beams and plasterwork were found when restoration work was carried out. From the lounge bar you can sit and look out to sea, warmed by a solid fuel stove, and think about what you would like to try from the choice of over four different beers from the barrel. A beer festival is held annually when more than 30 beers are served from casks in the cellar, which is then open to the public. Bar food consists of home-made soups, freshly baked baguettes, ploughman's. A seafood platter is a speciality of the house, but there are also daily specials and some vegetarian dishes. The pretty hanging baskets and window boxes feature on the big terrace during the summer, from where you can enjoy a view of the working harbour.

OPEN: 12–11. Lunchtime meals and snacks only.
Real Ale. No food Sun lunchtimes.
No children. No dogs. Occasional live music.
Cards: all credit cards.

MILL GREEN
Viper   Tel: 01277 352010
Mill Green, Nr Ingatestone, Essex CM4 0PS
Free House. Roger Beard, licensee.

Nearly hidden by an exuberant floral display, this unchanging little pub has been run by the same family since 1938. A 14th-century building with a pretty flowery garden in an enchanting wooded setting, it has four bars, two with carpets, two without (for those still in their walking boots). The food is simple but varied, bar food of the fill-a-gap variety: soup, sandwiches, ploughman's, chillis and, at weekends, home-made pies – that sort of thing. Between three and four weekly changing beers from the smaller, less well-known breweries. Seats outside in the attractive garden.

OPEN: 12–3. 6–11 (12–3-ish. 7–10.30 Sun).
Real Ale. Lunchtime snacks.
Dogs on leads. Wheelchair access difficult.

PELDON
The Peldon Rose   Tel: 01206 735248
Mersea Road, Peldon, Colchester, Essex CO5 7QJ
Lay & Wheeler Bars. Mr & Mrs John & Claire Riddleston and Alex Scarfe, licensees.

The 600-year-old, rambling Peldon Rose once served the three old ports of Maldon, Colchester and Mersea. Turn off the main road on the way to Mersea and you will find that with its rose-pink walls, the pub is aptly named. The 1884 earthquake, which must have made headlines in the Essex papers, had its epicentre at the front of the pub and gave the place a bit of a jolt, which explains some of the crooked doors and uneven floors in the two heavily beamed bars. Plenty of room in the bars and a big log fire to make you welcome. All the food is prepared and cooked 'in house': sandwiches and light snacks are available all day until 4.30pm, otherwise the varied menu will include lots of fresh local fish, and vegetarian dishes. On Sundays they serve roast sirloin of beef and home-made puddings. Daily cream teas in summer. Adnams, Greene King and Fullers

London Pride beers. Good number of wines to choose from. Seats in the garden in the summer.

OPEN: 11–11.
Real Ale. Restaurant.
Children welcome away from bar. Dogs on leads. Wheelchair access (not WC).
Bedrooms.

PLESHEY

White Horse   Tel: 01245 237281
Pleshey, Chelmsford, Essex CM3 1HA
Free House. Michael & Jan Smail, licensees.

Whichever bar you're in – the modern 20th or the original late 15th century – they offer an extensive bar menu listing ploughman's, filled jacket potatoes, huffers (a local bread roll) with a variety of fillings, fish dishes, steak and something for vegetarians. A full à la carte menu is provided in the no-smoking restaurant. The pub also holds speciality months, during which they offer varying menus from different countries. You will need to telephone for details. A range of beers is available, selected from the best of British brewing. Nethergate Best and Tolly Original and regularly changing guest beers which could include Crouch Vale and Ridleys. There is an extensive list of wines from various parts of the world. This is another ghostly pub: three pub ghosts. One is a lady in blue with a cat. Seats on the terrace and in the garden during the summer.

OPEN: 11–3. 7–11.
Real Ale. Restaurant.
Children welcome. No dogs.

PURLEIGH

The Bell   Tel: 01621 828348
The Street, Purleigh, Essex CM3 6QJ
Free House. B. Mott, licensee.

Purleigh is between two rivers, the Crouch and the Blackwater, that provide sheltered moorings and are well used by sailors. Sailing barge races on the Blackwell are held in August, and at the end of August/early September you have the highlight of the east-coast yachting calendar – Burnham Week. Next to the church, the Bell is an interesting old pub. Rambling, beamed, cosy and with a good log fire in the big inglenook fireplace – just what you want when the sea mists roll in from the estuary. Good home-made lunchtime food to go with the Adnams Bitter, Greene King IPA and a guest beer. Seats outside and views across the marshes towards the Blackwater. Purleigh, off the B1010, is east of Danbury.

OPEN: 11–3. 6–11 (12–3. 7–10.30 Sun).
Real Ale.
No children, but allowed if over 14 and with an adult. Dogs on leads.

RADWINTER

The Plough Inn   Tel: 01799 599222
Sampford Road, Radwinter, Saffron Walden, Essex CB10 2TL
Free House. Tony Burdfield, licensee.

This 17th-century, white-painted, weatherboarded pub has now been joined to a thatched annex with en-suite accommodation – so there's no need to worry about the breathaliser here! East of the village of Radwinter and 4 miles from Saffron Walden, the Plough, built high on the hill, has westerly views over open farmland. It offers lots of good things from lunchtime snacks to three-course main meals. Bar snacks include ploughman's, freshly cut sandwiches, filled jacket potatoes, pasta dishes, daily specials and home-made puds. During the week there are also home-made pies, steaks, grills and vegetarian dishes; fresh fish in beer batter is on the menu from Wednesday to Saturday. An ever-changing range of ales from Greene King IPA, Hook Norton, Batemans, Brakspear, Timothy Taylor, Nethergate, Crouch Vale, Dark Horse, Smiles and whatever else they can get hold of. Keg ciders and draught scrumpy in the summer. Short, interesting wine list. Seats on the lawn and on the clematis-covered patio.

> OPEN: 11.30–3. 6.30–11 (12–4. 7–10.30 Sun).
> Real Ale.
> Children and dogs welcome if both on their best behaviour. Wheelchair access (not WC). Car park. Self-contained accommodation. Holiday car parking for residents using Stansted airport.
> Cards: MasterCard, Solo, Switch, Visa.

RICKLING GREEN

Cricketers' Arms   Tel: 01799 543210
Rickling Green & Quendon, Saffron Walden, Essex CB11 3YG
Free House. Tim Proctor, licensee.

Overlooking one of the oldest cricket greens in north-west Essex, this rambling old pub grew out of a terrace of 16th-century cottages. It has a fascinating collection of cricketing memorabilia and hundreds of cricketing cigarette cards. The green is still used by the county club once a year. There is an extensive menu in both the bar and the elegant restaurant: sandwiches, ploughman's, filled jacket potatoes or a traditional French fish soup, a dish of smoked fish, their own chicken-liver pâté, chicken in apricot and cream sauce, a traditional cottage pie, medallions of lamb, liver and bacon, steaks cooked in various ways, a number of vegetarian dishes, mussels in five various guises – a speciality of the house, balti curries, home-made puddings and much more. Whatever can be home-made on the menu, is. Apart from Flowers IPA, the beers are nearly all from local breweries and change regularly; the only rule is that they have one strong bitter, a dark mild and one other bitter. Good wine cellar. Delightful terrace from where you can watch the cricket, or just relax and do nothing.

> OPEN: 12–11 (12–10.30 Sun).
> Real Ale. Restaurant.
> Children welcome. Dogs on leads. Bedrooms. They also have a parking and transfer facility for people flying from Stansted.
> Live music Thurs and Fri.

SAFFRON WALDEN

Kings Arms
Tel: 01799 522768

Market Hill, Saffron Walden, Essex CB10 1HQ
Free House. Debbie Bell, licensee.

Originally Chipping (Market) Walden, it was renamed Saffron Walden after the discovery that the profitable saffron crocus grew well in the local soil. It's a lovely old town, full of wonderful 15th- and 16th-century timber-framed houses and a tree-lined high street. As a settlement, Saffron Walden is much older, dating back to the 12th century, when the original market was established under the castle walls. Not far from the market you'll find this comfortable, friendly pub serving traditional home-cooked lunches with no surprises. Menus change every day but you could expect to find pâté and toast, Newmarket sausages with salad or mash, liver and bacon with fresh vegetables, steaks, ploughman's and freshly filled sandwiches. Greene King IPA, Bass, Scrumpy Jack cider and lagers. Seats in the garden.

> OPEN: 11–4. 5–11 (11–11 Fri & Sat).
> Real Ale. Restaurant.
> Dogs on leads. Live jazz on the first Sunday of every month.

SHALFORD

The George
Tel: 01371 850207

The Street, Shalford, Essex CM7 5HH
Free House. Ken & Elaine Lavery, licensees.

In a lovely part of Essex – with its wide-open skies and river valleys – the George is in a pretty village by the River Pant. Dating back to the 15th century, the George is heavily timbered with low beams and a huge log-filled inglenook fireplace. A friendly old place serving plenty of pub favourites and a full restaurant menu – something for everyone. Adnams Broadside, Greene King IPA, Caffreys and an occasional guest beer. Outside there are tables on the large terrace.

> OPEN: 11–3. 7–11 (12–3 Sun).
> Real Ale. Restaurant.
> Children only if eating. No dogs.

STANSTED MOUNTFITCHET

Dog & Duck
Tel: 01279 812047

58 Lower Street, Stansted Mountfitchet, Essex CM24 8LR
Greene King. Eric Wrighton, licensee.

In an area rich in historic buildings, the town was at the forefront of the battle against the building of Stansted Airport. Fifty yards from away from the Dog & Duck is Mountfitchet

Castle, which was built in Norman times and destroyed by King John. A busy place, the town is noisy with traffic, but the quiet side streets have some interesting buildings. The Dog & Duck, over 400 years old, weatherboarded and beamed, is a fine traditional Essex pub. Two bars, public and saloon, plenty to drink but not a crumb to eat between them. Greene King ales and some guest beers. Tables in the garden.

> OPEN: 11–2.30. 5–11 (7–10.30 Sun).
> Real Ale.
> Children preferably in garden. Dogs very welcome, bowls of water for them.

STOCK

Hoop   Tel: 01277 841137
21 High Street, Stock, Ingatestone, Essex CM4 9BD
Free House. Albert Kitchin, licensee.

As well as an all-day menu, the Hoop offers, on average, 500 different ales over the year, some on hand pump, some straight from the cask. The pub provides a good selection of dishes – at least two fresh fish dishes and five or six other specials, such as braised steak and dumplings, braised oxtail, lamb and barley stew, also soups, omelettes, ploughman's, sandwiches, filled jacket potatoes, fish pie with trout and prawns, chicken and ham pie and hotpots. The range of ales, including some from the tiny independent breweries, is so extensive that it is best to go and see what's on offer. There is a beer festival over the May Bank Holiday each year which goes on for about ten days, offering a choice of 150 ales. Farm cider, wines by the glass, mulled wine in winter. Seats outside, either in the pretty garden or in the pagoda-like extension, which has a bar and about 40 seats.

> OPEN: 11–11.
> Real Ale. Meals and snacks served 12–9 (Sundays 12–8.30).
> Children in garden. Dogs on leads.
> Cards: MasterCard, Switch, Visa.

STOW MARIES

Prince of Wales   Tel: 01621 828971
Woodham Road, Stow Maries, Essex CM3 6SA
Free House. Rob Walster, licensee.

A beer-taster's heaven: this pub is run by a real-ale fanatic who changes his selection of beers every week. The Prince of Wales, a marsh pub on a main road from Basildon to the yachting mecca of Burnham-on-Crouch, is part of a well-restored group of weatherboarded buildings which includes an old Victorian bakery; the oven is still used for bread and pizzas. Small, with cosy rooms where they serve a good selection of home-made bar food and an ever-changing range of five or six beers, a selection of Belgian beers, malt whiskies and a farm cider. The beer is very special here; the landlord is very enthusiastic about it and searches out the more unusual brews for the benefit of his customers and local beer festivals.

> OPEN: 11–11 (12–10.30 Sun).
> Real Ale.
> Children – maybe. Dogs very welcome. Car park.

WIVENHOE

Rose and Crown   Tel: 01206 826371
The Quay, Wivenhoe, Nr Colchester, Essex CO7 9BX
Punch Retail. Roger Wormull, licensee.

A steep little street of old houses leads down to the old quay. Nothing much has changed in the last 200 years; the shipbuilders who were here since Elizabethan times have gone and the fishing boats have virtually disappeared, but the 250-year-old Rose and Crown is still an important part of the scenery. So if you're in a boat and aiming for the Rose and Crown, you need to be on the Colne river, sailing in the direction of Colchester. By car, turn off the A133 and head south. It is a small place with tables outside on the quayside, where you can enjoy your drink and watch the nautical comings and goings when the tide is in – lots of mud and wildfowl when it's not. Newly refurbished with a new kitchen, cellar and back bar, and traditional bar food is served every day now: filled baguettes, a proper ploughman's, open sandwiches, home-made soup, steak and kidney pie and specials on the blackboard. On Sunday there is a roast lunch as well as the usual menu. Adnams, Greene King Abbot, Friary Meux, Bass, IPA and Mild. Small, interesting wine list – some by the glass.

> OPEN: 11–3. 6–11 winter. 11–11 summer (12–10.30 Sun).
> Real Ale.
> Children allowed. Dogs too, with well-behaved owners.
> You can catch a ferry from Wivenhoe to Fingeringhoe – depending on the tide.

BEST OF THE REST

COOPERSALE COMMON

Theydon Oak   Tel: 01992 572618
If you look at a map, you will see Coopersale Common is south of North Weald airfield and north of where the M11 crosses the M25 – by Epping. Weatherboarded and hung about with flowery baskets outside, the Theydon Oak is beamed and cosy inside. The landlady is in charge of cooking the traditional menu, fresh fish and daily specials. Bass, Whitbread Best, Greene King IPA, Wadworths 6X and Black Sheep Bitter. Beers vary but 6X seems to be a fixture. (No music, but too late to include in main entry.)

PAGLESHAM EASTEND

Plough & Sail
Tel: 01702 258242

Not sure there is much in the way of ploughing – sailing, yes. As remote as you can get; next stop the River Roach. If you're a sailor, you know the pub is here, if you're not, now is the chance to be adventurous. Old, weatherboarded and charming. You will find familiar bar food and some creative daily specials. Lots of fish, and oysters when available – the oyster beds are very near. Greene King beer and a guest.

YOUNG'S END

Green Dragon
Tel: 01245 361030

On the A313, near Braintree. White-painted and well known for its food; the restaurant is in the big, brick-built barn alongside. The menus are more imaginative than usual. Fish dishes are something of a speciality. Greene King ales and a guest.

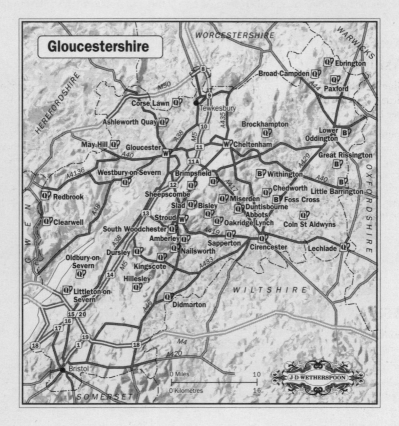

Gloucestershire

Gloucestershire

AMBERLEY

Black Horse
Tel: 01453 872556

Littleworth, Amberley, Stroud, Glos GL5 5AD
Free House. Patrick O'Flynn, licensee.

South of Stroud and close to 600 acres of National Trust land at Minchinhampton Common, the Black Horse is a friendly local with two bars and a conservatory where they serve value-for-money food: soup, ploughman's, sandwiches, Mexican dishes, pasta, steaks, fresh fish and seafood; fish and chips on Fridays. Tetleys Bitter, Smooth, Archers Best, Golden, Fullers London Pride, Wickwars Brand Oak Bitter and Black Rat Cider and guest beers. Permanent barbecue area. They have a no-smoking family room. Seating on the terrace and in the large, pretty garden. Spectacular views over the Stroud valley.

OPEN: 12–11.
Real Ale.
Children welcome. Dogs on leads.

ASHLEWORTH QUAY

Boat Inn
Tel: 01452 700272

Ashleworth Quay, Glos GL19 4HZ
Free House. Jaquie Nicholls, licensee.

Sadly, Mrs Jelf died just before we went to press, so the Jelf name will no longer be over the door. Granted a licence during the reign of Charles II, the Boat, a small 15th-century pub on the banks of the River Severn, has been run by the Jelf family since the 17th-century. But they will still give you the sort of welcome you would expect from a pub with centuries of experience serving travellers. Inside are two timeless, simply furnished rooms and a small back tap room with a couple of settles and casks of ale. Locally baked rolls for lunch are filled with proper ham or mature cheddar and served with home-made pickle. Beers include RCH Pitchfork, Arkells 3B, something from Wyc Valley and various others. Westons Farm cider. Seats in the flowery, sunny courtyard.

OPEN: 11–2.30. 6–11 summer. Between Oct and April closed Mon & Wed lunchtimes, otherwise 11–2.30. 7–11 winter.
Real Ale. Lunchtime snacks.
Children welcome. No dogs in the pub.

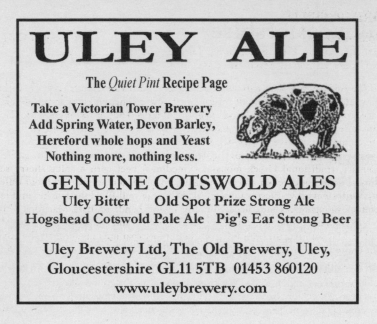
BISLEY

Bear Inn   Tel: 01452 770265
George Street, Bisley, Glos GL6 7BD
Pubmaster. S.N. Evans, MBII, tenant.

High on a hill in the Cotswolds – apparently known locally as 'Bisley-God-help-us' when the winter wind blows – the Bear is where you go for comfort. All is as it should be in this lovely 16th-century inn, parts of which date back to the 14th century. Architecturally very attractive, the colonnaded front supports an upper storey under which is a small flagstoned sitting area. Menus change daily and include a lot of fresh local produce: you'll find filled French sticks with salad, fried potatoes with garlic and herb butter, stuffed aubergines, venison steak in an orange and brandy sauce, venison sausages, Mediterranean fish pie, rabbit in cider, vegetable pasties, home-made burgers and other dishes. The daily specials, selection of local cheeses and home-made puds are listed on the blackboard. Bass, Flowers IPA, Tetleys, Charles Wells Bombardier and Wadworths 6X on hand pump. Seats in the garden too.

OPEN: 11–3. 6–11.
Real Ale. No food Sun eves.
Children in own room. Dogs on leads. Irish folk music during Cheltenham Gold Cup week.
Cards: Access, Barclaycard, Solo, Switch.

BRIMPSFIELD

Golden Heart
Tel: 01242 870261

Nettleton Bottom, Brimpsfield, Birdlip, Glos GL4 8LA
Free House. Catherine Stevens, licensee.

Off the A417 Ermin Way, this well-beamed, extended 16th-century country inn is all you could wish for. An unspoilt interior with low ceilings and a huge inglenook fireplace, traditional furnishings, and exceptional food. They are winners of the Booker prize for excellence – Pub Caterers of the Year 2001 – so you are going to find some interesting, innovative dishes: wild-boar terrine with Armagnac, filo prawns and prawn crackers, red-mullet provençale terrine, lamb steak marinated in garlic and rosemary, traditional Greek moussaka, medieval beef with a spicy sherry sauce, Chinese-style hot chicken and bacon salad, poached-salmon salad and four different ways with steak. If you just want a snack, there are well-filled sandwiches and jacket potatoes, ploughman's and salads. Timothy Taylors Landlord, Bass, Marstons Pedigree on hand pump, or from the barrel, as well as Murphys and Guinness. Beer festivals are held in May and August. Guest barrels behind the bar are changing all the time. A well-chosen, wide-ranging wine list. Scrumpy and wine by the glass. Seats outside on a sunny terrace.

> OPEN: 11–2.30. 6–11 (11–11 Fri & Sat. 11–10.30 Sun).
> Real Ale.
> Children welcome in their own room. Dogs on leads.

BROAD CAMPDEN

Bakers Arms
Tel: 01386 840515

Broad Campden, Nr Chipping Campden, Glos GL55 6UR
Free House. Ray & Sally Mayo, licensees.

In a quiet village south of Chipping Campden, the Bakers Arms welcomes you with a big log fire in the beamed bar during winter, and seats outside on the sunny terrace in summer. A reasonably priced bar menu lists soups, pâté, ploughman's, a very popular cottage pie, smoked-haddock bake, liver and onions, chicken curry and mariner's pie. Several vegetarian dishes and daily specials are on the blackboard; these can include peppered pork, salmon and broccoli bake, duck breast, rainbow trout, lamb shank or coq au vin; fruit crumbles, steamed puddings and other favourites for afters. Ales change all the time but five usually on hand pump, mainly from independent breweries such as Donnington, Hook Norton and Stanway Bitter. You are surrounded by wonderful walks in wonderful countryside.

> OPEN: April–Oct 11–11. Nov–March 11.30–2.30. 6–11 (12–3. 7–10.30 Sun).
> Real Ale.
> Children welcome. No dogs in pub. Wheelchair access.
> Folk night 3rd Tues in month.

BROCKHAMPTON

The Craven Arms
Tel: 01242 820410
Brockhampton, Nr Cheltenham, Glos GL54 5XH
Free House. Dale Campbell, licensee.

Just a couple of miles north of the A436, this rambling, stone-built, 17th-century village pub with flagstone floors and low beams is a popular lunchtime meeting place. They serve a wide choice of good-value, wholesome food in attractive surroundings. Ales are Wadworths 6X, Hook Norton Best Bitter, Butcombe Bitter, Goff's Jouster, Fullers London Pride, draught Bass and a guest ale. Big garden for sitting in.

> OPEN: 11–2.30. 6–11 (12–3. 7–10.30 Sun).
> Real Ale. Restaurant.
> Children welcome. No dogs, except in the garden in summer.

CHEDWORTH

Seven Tuns
Tel: 01285 720242
Chedworth, Cheltenham, Glos GL54 4AE
Smiles. Kevin Dursley & Anthea Saunders, licensees.

Close to the well-preserved Roman Villa at Chedworth, a particularly des res at the time, with under-floor heating, two types of bath and a water shrine still filled by an ancient spring. Keeping up the watery theme, this attractive 17th-century pub – once a billet for Cromwell's troops – has a working waterwheel in the garden. Always popular, especially in the summer walking season, it's the big log fire in the lounge bar that's popular in winter. The menu changes daily and everything is freshly cooked; they specialise in steaks and fish, but there is a popular bar menu as well. Sunday roasts. Smiles Best and Bitter from the Bristol Brewery, one guest and Guinness on draught. Skittle alley and games room to hire if you're so inclined. Plenty of tables outside. Big welcome for families, walkers and dogs.

> OPEN: 11–11.
> Real Ale.
> Children and dogs welcome.
> Cards: all credit cards accepted.
> N.B. Music in public bar.

CIRENCESTER

Corinium Court Hotel
Tel: 01285 659711
12 Gloucester Street, Cirencester GL7 2DG
Free House. Tim McGrath, licensee.

Situated in the oldest part of this ancient town, what was a 16th-century wool merchant's house is now an attractive hotel. This hotel has been aptly named, as I'm sure you all know that Corinium was the Roman name for Cirencester. Make for the courtyard bar where they have a short, satisfying menu of Mexican chilli tortillas served with a tossed salad, lasagne verde, chicken and vegetable stir fry, omelettes, grilled steak with salad garnish or something from the specials board. If you want to push the boat a little further out, the hotel has a rather smart restaurant serving imaginative, reasonably priced food. Beers are changing all the time, but there will always be some from the local breweries. Lots of malt whiskies. Seats in the courtyard or in the big garden.

> OPEN: 11–11 (12–10.30 Sun).
> Real Ale. Restaurant.
> Children welcome. Dogs too. Wheelchair access. Fifteen en-suite bedrooms, including some on the ground floor for disabled guests. Car park.

CLEARWELL
Wyndham Arms
Tel: 01594 833666
Clearwell, Nr Coleford, Glos GL16 8JT
Free House. John, Rosemary & Robert Stanford, licensees.

A village surrounded by some glorious Gloucestershire countryside: the Royal Forest of Dean, Symond's Yat and the Wye valley. Interesting architectural buildings abound, and below ground are the Clearwell caves mined for iron and ochre since at least the Bronze Age, over 4000 years ago. Though mining ceased in 1945, the caves are now an amenity for mining and caving enthusiasts, geologists, historians and sightseers. So, if you want a base to explore all these attractions, this is the place to be: the 600-year-old Wyndham Arms, a charming small hotel, with a wonderfully atmospheric interior. They serve an excellent choice of bar snacks and starters: chicken-liver pâté, pan-fried oysters in a creamy sauce with onions and bacon, grilled Portuguese sardines, pasta dish of the day, poached smoked haddock, a choice of open sandwiches, egg and prawn mayonnaise, whitebait, smoked local salmon and a lot more. Chef's specials too. They have a very reasonable two- and three-course table d'hôte lunch and dinner menu. Most of the vegetables, fruit and herbs, are home-grown. All food is cooked to order, so expect a little delay. Delicious ice-cream sundaes to finish. There is a greater choice of dishes in the no-smoking dining room and the Forester grill room. Seats outside on the terrace during the summer. If you are lucky enough to be staying here and exploring the countryside, the Wyndham Arms can provide you with a well-packed hamper. Bass on hand pump, a good wine list and an excellent choice of malt whiskies.

> OPEN: 11–11.
> Real Ale. Restaurant.
> Children welcome. Dogs on leads. Good wheelchair access. Car park.
> Eighteen bedrooms.
> Cards: Delta, MasterCard, Switch, Visa.

COLN ST ALDWYNS
The New Inn At Coln
Tel: 01285 750651
Coln St Aldwyns, Nr Cirencester, Glos GL7 5AN
Free House. Brian Evans, licensee.

This fine Elizabethan Cotswold village inn, originally built as a coaching inn, has tremendous appeal and it's not just visual: big, beautiful and creeper-covered, it has a spacious, beamed bar where they serve well-kept ales and a top-class restaurant with a chef to match. From the impressive Courtyard Bar menu: baked couscous with Mediterranean vegetables, salad of boiled egg, bacon, croutons, French beans and parsley, Thai vegetable spring roll with a soy vinaigrette, New Inn fish and chips with peas and tartare sauce, casserole of guinea-fowl leg with tarragon, mushrooms and smoked bacon, or roasted red peppers stuffed with cherry tomatoes, basil and feta cheese. The fixed-price menu is thought out daily and might include gazpacho with tapenade croutons, salad of bacon, anchovies, black pudding and chives, roast rack of lamb with Mediterranean vegetables, or pan-fried calves' liver with asparagus, wild mushrooms and balsamic red-wine sauce, with a tart of Mirabelle plums covered with meringue and fruit coulis to finish; a selection of cheeses too. If after all that you want more excitement, you might catch sight of the resident ghost; you can hear him first – jangling keys herald his arrival. Hook Norton, Butcombe, Wadworths 6X ales and other guest beers on hand pump. A round-the-world wine list, about eight by the glass. Seats in the garden. The walk along the river to Bibury is not to be missed.

> OPEN: 11–11.
> Real Ale. Restaurant.
> No children under ten in restaurant. Dogs on leads. Wheelchair access. Car park.
> En-suite bedrooms – very classy.
> Cards: Amex, Delta, MasterCard, Switch, Visa.

CORSE LAWN

Corse Lawn Hotel   Tel: 01452 780771
Corse Lawn, Glos GL19 4LZ (near Tewkesbury but actually in Worcs)
Free House. Denis Hine, licensee.

Corse Lawn takes its name from the wide, mile-long green either side of the road. The original Tudor inn, burnt down early in the 18th century, was rebuilt in 1745 as a Queen Anne-style coaching inn. Corse Lawn House still has the old 'coach wash' at the front of the hotel which has been retained as an unusual ornamental pond. The proprietor is French, the staff English, and the atmosphere Franglais. The menu in the bar/bistro in this relaxed and welcoming hotel might include chilled gazpacho soup or hot vichyssoise, Mediterranean fish soup, marinated sardine fillets with olives, capers and tomatoes, prosciutto ham, melon and grilled figs with mint dressing, cold whole crab in the shell with salad and mayonnaise, crispy pancake of mushroom with wild-mushroom sauce, seared tuna fillet with tomato dressing and provençale mash, pigeon breast with red wine, lentils and black sausage, grilled rib eye of beef with bourgignon sauce and horseradish mash and lots more; fish and shellfish are a speciality here. There are also sandwiches, baguettes, omelettes, creative vegetarian dishes and good puddings. Worthington Best and Caffreys. Hine cognac and over 300 wines.

> OPEN: 12–2. 6–11.
> Children welcome. Dogs on leads. Wheelchair access. Car park.
> Nineteen bedrooms – all en suite.
> Cards: Amex, Delta, Diners, MasterCard, Switch, Visa.

DIDMARTON

Kings Arms   Tel: 01454 238245
The Street, Didmarton, Glos GL9 1DT
Free House. Nigel & Jane Worrall, licensees.

Close to the year-round delights at the Westonbirt Arboretum, the Kings Arms is a fine
traditional Cotswold inn on a lease that has certainly beaten inflation. I doubt when nego-
tiating a lease today that anyone would be as lucky as they were in 1745, when the Kings
Arms was leased from the Beaufort Estate for a thousand years at sixpence a year! Inside,
there is a restored, comfortable interior, well beamed and garlanded with hops, plus the
added bonus of menus featuring good, creative food: home-made soup, seafood gumbo,
smoked goose breast with an apple and cider brandy chutney, salmon and cod fishcakes
with a citrus mayonnaise, baked sea trout with a fennel aioli, chicken breast cooked with
Moroccan spices and served with a honey sauce, pork and hop sausages with bubble and
squeak and onion gravy as well as game, pasta and vegetarian dishes, and a more elaborate
menu in the restaurant. House beers are Uley's Hogshead Bitter and John Smiths plus two
guests. They have an interesting wine list, a few by the glass. A true local – everyone
comes here, including crowds during Badminton week when it's standing room only.
Large garden with a boules pitch.

> OPEN: 12–3. 6–11 (12–3. 7–10.30 Sun).
> Real Ale. Restaurant.
> Well-behaved children welcome. Dogs on leads. Wheelchair access (not WC).
> Car park. Bedrooms. Three self-contained holiday cottages.
> Cards: Delta, MasterCard, Switch, Visa.
> N.B. There may be CDs playing in the back bar during the evening; also occasional
> live music.

DUNTISBOURNE ABBOTS

Five Mile House   Tel: 01285 821432
Old Gloucestershire Road, Duntisbourne Abbots, Glos GL7 7JR
Free House. Jo Carrier, licensee.

There is an abundance of Duntisbournes in this Cotswold valley: four of them, as you
would expect, are spread along the River Dunt. This is a very special place; Five Mile
House has been beautifully restored so that you can hardly see the join, and you might
like to know that the small bar has a listed interior. They are very firm as to where you
drink and eat: drinkers stay one side; anyone eating on the other. The twain can mix but
only in the lounge bar – not a crumb in the bar, please. The restaurant is smart and there
is a no-smoking cellar bar – which you can hire, and where they can, if asked, put on the
music. You'll find specials on the board and a good choice of lunchtime bar snacks:
home-made soups, open sandwiches, ploughman's, home-cooked gammon; in the
evening, stuffed shoulder of lamb, steaks, chicken in a cream sauce, nice puds and a

good, varied wine list. Archers Village Bitter, Timothy Taylors Landlord and one rotating guest ale.

> OPEN: 12–3. 6–11 (12–3. 7–10.30 Sun).
> Real Ale. Restaurant.
> Children: not in bar. Dogs on leads. Wheelchair access (not WC). Car park.
> Cards: no charge cards accepted.

DURSLEY
Old Spot Inn   Tel: 01453 542870
Hill Road, Dursley, Glos GL11 4JQ
Free House. Ric Sainty, licensee.

Rather tucked away, so you need to find the bus station and the handy car park before you spot the Old Spot. White-painted, built as a farmhouse in 1776, a school throughout the 19th century – now an appealing local. Here you will get, as well as a friendly welcome, good lunches from the bar menu, daily specials – using fresh local produce – and well-kept ales from regional brewers including Uley – made with Uley's own spring water – Wickwar, Bath Ales, Smiles and a weekly guest beer. They serve a traditional Sunday lunch. The pub has its own boules pitch and a beer garden.

> OPEN: 11–3. 5–11 (11–11 Fri, Sat & Sun).
> Real Ale.
> Children at landlord's discretion. Dogs on leads. Wheelchair access.
> The Old Spot has been Gloucestershire Pub of the Year and runner-up in CAMRA's Pub of the Year contest.

EBRINGTON
Ebrington Arms   Tel: 01386 593223
Ebrington, Nr Chipping Campden, Glos GL55 6NH
Free House. Gareth Richards, licensee.

In a good walking area, a firm favourite with those in walking boots, and a favourite for all the locals since 1764. The Ebrington has one beamed, flagstoned bar and an adjoining dining room with handsome fireplaces. The display of fine trophies bears witness to an enthusiasm for dominoes – on the whole a nice quiet game, though things can get a bit tense on match days. Obviously no music and no machines either, but the TV goes on for the Six Nations Rugby Match – Wales versus England only! The menu, written on the beams of the bar, can take some time to read, but somewhere on it you will find traditional bar food including sandwiches, local sausages, lasagne, chicken Kiev, egg and chips, omelettes, steak and kidney pies and steaks; fresh cod is a speciality. Hook Norton Best,

Donnington SBA and guest beers on hand pump. Farm cider. Seats outside on the sheltered terrace.

> OPEN: 11–2.30. 6–11 (7–11 winter). 12–3. 7–10.30 Sun.
> Real Ale. Restaurant.
> Children in eating area. Dogs on leads.

HILLESLEY

The Fleece   Tel: 01453 843189
Chapel Lane, Hillesley, Nr Wotton-under-Edge, Glos GL12 7RD
Interbrew. Mr & Mrs Kim Williams, licensees.

This unspoilt, Grade II-listed local is an essential part of village life, still with the definite demarcation between public and saloon bar, just as it was years ago. Inside the Fleece are low ceilings and open log fires in both busy bars. The bar menu and daily specials board give you a lot of choice: ploughman's, steak pies, gammon, steaks and scampi on the bar menu; the specials could be a salmon dish, fillet steak in a sauce or steak Diane. Whitbread ales and guests. Seats in the garden. Surrounded by glorious countryside and near the Cotswold Way, so there are good walks nearby.

> OPEN: 11.30–3. 6.30–11 (12–3. 7–10.30 Sun).
> Real Ale.
> Children welcome. Dogs in the public bar. Three bedrooms.

KINGSCOTE

Hunters Hall   Tel: 01453 860393
Kingscote, Tetbury, Glos GL8 8XZ
Free House. Miss Stephanie Ward, licensee.

An eye-catching, creeper-covered 16th-century inn; a popular local. You need to know that this place is very family-minded. The back room has a pool table, darts and jukebox and there is a no-smoking family gallery above the bars; the garden is also planned for children. Inside is full of character: beams, flagstone floors, stone walls and open fires, three bars and a no-smoking dining room. Bar food changes daily; there will be a cold buffet in the dining room at weekends, otherwise dishes may include tian of prawn with mango and apple topped with marie rose sauce, homemade chicken and duck-liver pâté, chicken breast stuffed with Brie and wrapped in bacon with a port-wine sauce, braised lamb shank with a thyme and redcurrant jus, cod in beer batter and steak, kidney and Guinness pie. Also à la carte and table d'hôte menus; three roasts on Sundays. As they say, 'traditional English cuisine with a continental flair'. Beers are Bass, Ruddles Best, Marstons Pedigree, Uley Hogshead.

Wines by the glass, and a selection of malt whiskies. A summer barbecue in the children-oriented garden.

> OPEN: 11–11.
> Real Ale. Restaurant (no sandwiches Sun).
> Live music every Sun eve.
> Children welcome. Dogs on leads. Wheelchair access to pub and bedrooms.
> Twelve en-suite bedrooms in what was once the stables and blacksmith shop. Cards: all except Diners accepted.
> N.B. Music (very low) in restaurant.

LECHLADE

Trout Inn   Tel: 01367 252313
Lechlade-on-Thames, Glos GL7 3HA
Nomura. Bob & Penny Warren, lease.

An important watery crossroad, where the Leach and Coln rivers join the youthful Thames. Among the handsome Georgian buildings in Lechlade is the Trout. The pub's foundations are several centuries older and date back to the 13th century. Inside are two pleasant, low-beamed bars, one over 350 years old, the other a mere stripling of 100. An extra outdoor bar functions during the summer. In both the restaurant and the bar the menu is dependable: home-made soups, pâté, salmon, steaks, locally produced sausages, daily specials and home-made puds; the pub does get very busy. John Smiths Yorkshire and Courage Best ales, Smiles Best and Wadworths 6X are the changing guests. They have their own boules pitch. On a warm day you can sit in the big garden or on the riverbank.

> OPEN: 10–3. 6–11 (all day Sat in summer).
> Real Ale. Restaurant with no-smoking area.
> Children in eating area of bar. Dogs on leads (not in dining or children's room).
> Wheelchair access.
> Live jazz Tues and Sun eves. Music in outdoor bar on occasions – never in the main pub.

LITTLETON-ON-SEVERN

White Hart   Tel: 01454 412275
Littleton-on-Severn, Glos BS12 1NR
Youngs. Howard & Liz Turner, licensees.

Very near the Severn Bridge; sometimes, depending on the weather, a bit too near the river – or rather, the river gets too near the pub. Originally a 16th-century farmhouse, it is now a fine and well-cared-for old pub where you will find plenty of room. Four bars and a family room serving a wide choice of bar food ranging from home-made soup, filled crusty rolls, ploughman's, steak and kidney pie, fish pie, vegetarian dishes to special seafood and game dishes – all at pub prices – and daily specials. Smiles range of ales and two guests, one of which is Wadworths 6X. The others change regularly. Seats at the front in the pretty, cottagey garden and on the terrace at the back of the pub; on a good day you get a good view of Wales and the Welsh mountains.

> OPEN: 11.30–3 (12–3. 6–11 Sat. 12–4. 7–10.30 Sun). N.B. Closed eves Mon–Fri.
> Real Ale.
> Children in the garden room. Dogs on leads.
> Four en-suite bedrooms in the converted barn.

MAY HILL

Glasshouse Inn
Tel: 01452 830529

May Hill, Longhope, Glos GL17 0NN
Free House. Steven Pugh, licensee.

Time has not changed the Glasshouse, a country inn with glorious hanging baskets, old flagstones and log fires in the big inglenook fireplace. May Hill, nearly 1000 feet high, is on the edge of the Vale of Gloucester and was planted with trees to celebrate Queen Victoria's diamond jubilee. From the hill on a clear day there are fantastic views over the surrounding counties. The pub serves a good, short, traditional menu all cooked 'in pub'; cod and chips is a speciality. Popular with shooting parties – steak and kidney pie for them – and with Irish supporters during Gold Cup week at Cheltenham. The well-kept beers are Butcombe Bitter and various guests. Seats outside on the lawn near an old cider press. Lots of walks nearby.

> OPEN: 11.30–3. 6.30–11 (12–3. 7–10.30 Sun).
> Real Ale. No food Sundays.
> Children: tolerated. Dogs on leads at lunchtime only. Wheelchair access.

MISERDEN

Carpenter's Arms
Tel: 01285 821283

Miserden, Glos GL6 7JA
Free House. Johnny Johnston, FBII, licensee.

In this unspoilt village, roughly equidistant from Cirencester, Cheltenham and Stroud, in the great estate of Miserden Park, the 18th-century Carpenter's Arms is a friendly, welcoming place, with not even a gaming machine to disturb the sleeping dogs. The old carpenters' workshop at the back is still being used, but only as a storeroom. A typical bar menu could include home-made soup, chicken and bacon Caesar salad, garlic mushrooms topped with melted Stilton, home-made pie of the day, honey-roast ham with egg and chips, fresh poached salmon steak and cauliflower and leek bake, and from the blackboard menu you could choose a quarter lamb shoulder slowly roasted in rosemary and honey, seafood platter, home-made beef lasagne or curry of fresh vegetables with poppadoms and mango chutney. The beers are Goffs Jouster, Wadworths 6X and a guest, and there is an extensive wine list. Tables in the garden.

OPEN: 11–3. 6–11.
Real Ale.
Children welcome until 8.30pm. Dogs in bars. Car park.
Cards: Amex, MasterCard, Switch, Visa.

NAILSWORTH

Weighbridge Inn   Tel: 01453 832520
The Longfords, Minchinhampton, Glos GL6 9AL
Free House. Simon Hudson, licensee.

Between Nailsworth and Avening on the B4014, this pub is really, really old; there has
been a building on this site since 1220. Next to the old packhorse route to Bristol – now
a footpath and bridleway – and alongside the old turnpike road. During the 19th century
the landlord was responsible not only for running the inn, but also for the weighbridge,
which weighed the raw materials going into the local mills. Inside are four traditionally
furnished rooms housing an interesting collection of country artifacts. No restaurant food,
just good, seasonal pub grub. Two-in-one pie is a speciality of the house – half cauliflower
cheese and the other half a filling of your choice from the menu, topped with a short-
pastry crust; they serve a mini version of the latter – so you can leave room for a pudding –
also bangers and mash, pasta bake, moussaka, chicken casserole, comforting puddings
and a selection of English cheeses. The guest ales change frequently, but there will be a
range of local Uley beers and Wadworths 6X. A good number of wines by the glass or
bottle. Seats outside in the sheltered garden.

OPEN: 12–11 (12–10.30 Sun).
Real Ale.
Children in rooms away from bar. Dogs on leads.
Wheelchair access into pub and soon to WC.

OAKRIDGE LYNCH

Butchers Arms   Tel: 01285 760371
Oakridge Lynch, Nr Stroud, Glos GL6 7NZ
Free House. Peter & Brian Coupe, licensees.

There is a pub signpost pointing you in the right direction on the main road, otherwise you
can easily get lost in a confusion of lush, high-sided Gloucestershire lanes. It is well worth
hunting out the Butchers Arms for its good-value home-cooked food including bar snacks
and daily specials. They serve a three-course Sunday lunch – for which you must book.
Archers Best, Wickwar Bob, Tetleys and Greene King Abbot ale are among the ales kept.
Plenty of room to park in the detached car park and there are seats in the garden from
where you can enjoy views over the village to the valley below. Not far from good walks
along the old Thames and Severn canal.

OPEN: 11–3. 6–11 (12–3. 7–10.30 Sun).
Real Ale.
Children in anteroom and restaurant only. Dogs on leads.

OLDBURY-ON-SEVERN

Anchor Inn   Tel: 01454 413331
Church Road, Oldbury-on-Severn, South Glos BS12 1QA
Free House, Michael Dowdswell & Alex de la Torre, licensees.

Not easy to miss, as the first thing you'll notice if you arrive in summer is the floral
display. Flowers hang from windowsills and baskets and somewhere behind all the
opulence is the pub. Comfortably furnished, with old beams, open fires (when needed)
and window seats. You can eat in either lounge, bar or no-smoking dining room.
Traditional English cooking and the best of continental cuisine are reflected in the
menus. Local meat, fruit and vegetables – all the produce is as fresh as can be. They have
delicious ways with potatoes but there are no chips; however, on offer are 14 different
salads, a leek and potato bake, Oldbury chicken – chicken breast cooked in apple juice
with brandy, cream and mushrooms, locally reared pork and garlic sausages cooked on
the charcoal grill, Yorkshire pudding with a generous filling, or there's fresh salmon in
a cream and wine sauce and Caribbean pork cooked with ground coconut, ginger,
mango, raisin, pineapple and lime juice. Amazing puds and home-made ice-cream.
Theakstons Best Bitter, Old Peculier, draught Bass, Butcombe Bitter, John Smith,
Guinness and three different lagers. Over 75 malt whiskies, an extensive wine list,
Frobishers fresh fruit juices and lots of sparkling water. Large garden at the back of the
pub. Surrounded by attractive walks.

OPEN: 11.30–2.30. 6–11 (11–11 Sat. 12–10.30 Sun).
Real Ale. Dining room.
Children welcome in dining room and garden only. Dogs on leads – not in dining
room. Wheelchair access and disabled WC. Car park.
Cards: MasterCard, Visa.

PAXFORD

Churchill Arms   Tel: 01386 594000
Paxford, Nr Chipping Campden, Glos GL55 6XH   Fax: 01386 594005
Free House. Leo Brooke-Little, licensee.

Once a tied and basic village pub opposite the church, the Churchill Arms has come a
long way since then. It still has its cosy, traditional bar, but the restaurant is now the
thing here. Open-plan, spacious and furnished with scrubbed wooden furniture, here
you can experience some really imaginative cooking. Normally a selection of six starters
to choose from: saffron-marinated mackerel with cucumber sauce, chicken cooked in
herbs and olive oil with asparagus, aubergine and tomato dressing, pan-fried scallops,

spring-onion mash and crisp pancetta; for a main course, John Dory with red-wine risotto, capers, spring onions in olive oil and tapenade, loin of rabbit filled with spiced aubergine, lentils and mustard dressing, or brill with creamed leeks, beurre blanc and smoked salmon; and always some inventive puds to follow. Menus are constantly changing. Arkells BBB, Hook Norton Best and a guest, all on hand pump. Reasonable wine list, some by the glass.

OPEN: 11.30–3. 6–11 (12–3. 6.30–10.30 Sun).
Real Ale.
Children not in bar. Dogs in garden only. Wheelchair access (not WC).
Four bedrooms – all en-suite.
Cards: MasterCard, Switch, Visa.

REDBROOK

Boat Inn
Tel: 01600 712615
Lone Lane, Penalt, Monmouth, Gwent, South Wales
Free House. Donald & Pat Ellis, licensees.

Clinging to the bank of the River Wye, the Boat is strictly speaking in Wales, but the car park is in Gloucestershire, so that is where we have put it. Very popular with our energetic friends, so walking boots and hairy socks are the norm. You will find a genial bar serving good, familiar bar food; all the food is home-cooked and even though there has been a change at the top, they still cook the house dish of Panhaggerty, the Boat's shepherds pie and a steak and Guinness pie. There is a garden (parts of which are perpendicular), from where you can watch the river. Up to ten ales from casks behind the counter, Wadworths 6X and Greene King and others according to availability; they change all the time. There is a footbridge across the Wye connecting the pub to its Gloucestershire car park!

OPEN: 11–11 (12–10.30 summer Sundays. 12–3. 6–9 winter).
Real Ale.
Children welcome, so are dogs. Live music Tues & Fri eves.

SAPPERTON

Bell Inn
Tel: 01285 760298
Sapperton, Cirencester, Glos GL7 6LE
Free House. Paul Davidson & Pat Lejeune, licensees.

Sapperton, a lovely village at the head of the Frome valley, is where the 2½-mile Sapperton Tunnel was cut through the hill in 1789 to link the Thames and Severn rivers. The restored eastern entrance is well worth a visit. After the walk, or the sightseeing, head for the bars of the Bell Inn, which over the past year has been done up and looks very smart. Not only can you 'eat in', they do takeaways too. Very interesting things are going on in the food line. The menu might include antipasto of Mediterranean vegetables and provençale olives, carpaccio of beef fillet, chilli and ginger dressing and Chinese radish, breast of free-range chicken, Parma ham and dolcelatte, roasted courgettes filled with oregano, tomato and ricotta cheese, or a cassoulet of duck confit, Toulouse sausage and beans. Home-made puddings. Fresh fish and specials will be on the boards. Uley Old Spot, Bath Ales and others – all on hand pump as well as scrumpy cider. A considerable number of wines by the glass from a wide-ranging wine list. Tables at the front of the pub and in the garden at the back.

OPEN: 11–2.30. 6.30–11.
Real Ale.
Children and dogs welcome. Wheelchair access.
Cards: MasterCard, Visa.

SAPPERTON

Daneway Inn   Tel: 01285 760297
Sapperton, Cirencester, Glos GL7 6LN
Wadworth. Liz & Richard Goodfellow, licensees.

The old Daneway Inn, originally built to accommodate the canal workers, is at the western end of the Sapperton tunnel, which takes the canal under the A419. There's a canal museum in an old lock-keeper's cottage in nearby Chalford. The Daneway has a wonderfully grand Dutch fireplace in the lounge bar which came out of the long-since-demolished Amberley House. Lunchtime bar food ranges from filled rolls, baked potatoes and ploughman's to lasagne and a beef-in-ale pie; additional dishes are on the evening menu. Wadworths 6X and Henry's Original IPA, plus seasonal ales and Westons Old Rosie cider from the cask. Tables in the pretty garden overlook the canal and the river valley.

OPEN: 11–3. 6.30–11 (12–3. 7.30–10.30 Sun).
Real Ale.
Children in no-smoking family room. No dogs.

SHEEPSCOMBE

Butchers Arms   Tel: 01452 812113
Sheepscombe, Nr Painswick, Glos GL6 7RH
Free House. Johnny Johnston, FBII & Hilary Johnston, MBII, licensees.

You drive along narrow lanes to reach this quiet village, tucked away in a deep valley, and the 17th-century Butchers Arms. It's so sheltered that you can sit outside the pub in comparative comfort in the early spring. Facing south, it's a traditional pub with a timeless atmosphere: huge log fires, walls covered with old pictures and prints, no fruit machines or jukebox, just lots of chat. Plenty of choice on the bar menu: home-made soup of the day, chef's home-made chicken-liver pâté with hot toast, pan-fried mushrooms in garlic butter topped with melted Brie and served on a toasted crouton, mixed game cooked in a cranberry and red-wine sauce topped with puff pastry, poached salmon served cold with prawns and salad, home-cooked honey-roast ham served with parsley sauce, filled jacket potatoes, filled rolls, ploughman's and daily specials from the blackboard. Specials such as braised lamb in a leek, mint and red-wine sauce, home-made beef stew with braised vegetables, fresh tuna steak on a bed of stir-fried vegetables, mixed grills and home-made puds. Hook Norton Best, Timothy Taylors Landlord and guest beers. Farm ciders and a good wine list. Wonderful panoramic views over the surrounding countryside.

> OPEN: 11–11 (11–2.30. 6.30–11 winter. 12–10.30 Sun).
> Real Ale. Restaurant.
> Children in eating areas. No dogs. Wheelchair access into pub and restaurant.
> Cards: Amex, Diners, JCB, MasterCard, Switch, Visa.

SLAD

The Woolpack   Tel: 01452 813429
Slad, Nr Stroud, Glos
Free House. Mark Henriques, Daniel Chadwick & Dawn Cullen, licensees.

High on a hill, the village and the Woolpack look across the glorious Slad valley to the woods opposite. A delightful village pub – the late Laurie Lee's local – in a beautiful area immortalised in Lee's book *Cider with Rosie*. But things have moved on. Most of the food is home-cooked, and they serve a wide range of reasonably priced dishes. Worth a trip for Uley's locally brewed Old Spot, Bitter and Pig's Ear; also Old Rosie cider.

> OPEN: 12–2.30. 6–11 (7–10.30 Sun).
> Real Ale.
> Children welcome. Dogs on leads. Wheelchair access (not WC).

SOUTH WOODCHESTER

Ram Inn   Tel: 01453 873329
Station Road, South Woodchester, Nr Stroud, Glos GL5 5EL
Free House. Michael & Eileen McAsey, licensees.

South of Stroud, this is Gloucestershire at its best. Traditionally furnished, the beamed bar in the stone-built Ram Inn has no less than three log fires during winter. An interesting, regularly changing menu includes the usual sandwiches and ploughman's, maybe spinach roulade with a cream-cheese and smoked-salmon filling, plaice with a prawn and mushroom stuffing, Italian beef casserole, spicy pork loin with a brandy and apricot sauce, fillet of steak with a cream and pepper sauce, venison in red wine and always fresh vegetables. The well-kept ales change frequently, but there are usually eight or nine on hand pump; serious beer drinkers flock here. This is another pub with the most spectacular views.

> OPEN: 11–11 (12–10.30 Sun).
> Real Ale. Restaurant.
> Children welcome. Dogs on leads. Wheelchair access (not WC).
> Cards: MasterCard, Switch, Visa.

WESTBURY-ON-SEVERN

Red Lion   Tel: 01452 760221
Westbury-on-Severn, Glos GL14 1PA
Free House. Wayne Duplessis & Colin Smith, licensees.

If you are keen on baseball this is the place to be, as the Red Lion has a definite baseball
theme, with a large collection of caps brought back by customers and friends from all over
the world. A fine, traditional pub. The extensive menu of freshly cooked food is popular,
so it's better to book to be sure of your peppered chicken breast in garlic cream, fresh
salmon with cream and dill mayonnaise, pork medallions in port and cranberry or fresh
cod and chips, among others – and lots of puds. Thatchers Wickwar Ale, Brains SA,
Everards Tiger, Buchanans Original, Mansfields Old Baily and Wye Valley Brew. Good
selection of malt whiskies, South African and New World wines. Seats in the garden.

OPEN: 11–2.30. 7–11.
Real Ale.
Children welcome. No dogs. Car park.
Four en-suite bedrooms. Good full English breakfasts.

BEST OF THE REST

FOSS CROSS

Hare & Hounds   Tel: 01285 720288
South of Fossbridge and north of Cirencester, this is a lovely old place. Exciting things
were uncovered during recent renovations, including a spiral staircase and a working fireplace with a bread oven. A beamed interior with three large, log-burning fireplaces;
wonderfully cosy. Delicious food such as salmon and potato terrine on a warm bed of pickled cucumber and dill cream sauce, a fillet of beef Wellington with a rich port jus, daily
specials, or filled ciabattas if you just want a snack. Arkells 2B and 3B, ciders and a short
wine list. Children and dogs welcome. Wheelchair access.

GREAT RISSINGTON

Lamb   Tel: 01451 820388
Overlooking the Windrush valley, between Oxford and Cheltenham. A smartened-up
17th-century pub. You can stay here and you can eat well. Lots of home-made dishes on
a traditional bar menu; even more choice in the restaurant. Fullers London Pride,
Wadworths 6X, Ruddles and a good wine list.

LITTLE BARRINGTON

Inn for all Seasons   Tel: 01451 844324
If you are on your way to the Cheltenham races you might like to know you can park
your helicopter here, avoiding all the traffic jams. What you will definitely want to
know is that the food here is worth a detour. They specialise in fish but also have a

clever, inventive, non-fishy menu. Wadworths 6X, something from Wychwood and an impressive wine list.

LOWER ODDINGTON

Fox   Tel: 01451 870555
Such an attractive village pub – inside and out – where they serve some very good food: watercress soup, beef stew with parsley dumplings, a warm chicken, bacon and avocado salad – that sort of thing. Badger Tanglefoot, Hook Norton Best, Marstons Pedigree and a really good wine list. A very popular place.

WITHINGTON

Mill Inn   Tel: 01242 890204
Quite delightful: the inn stands alone in a little wooded valley with its very own river running through the garden. They serve good traditional bar food: ploughman's, vegetarian lasagne, roast beef and Yorkshire pudding, daily specials too. Sam Smiths range of ales.

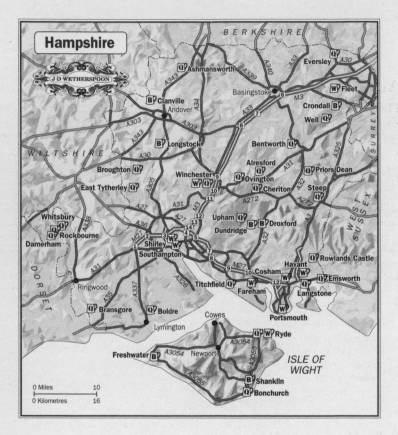

Hampshire

J D WETHERSPOON

BERKSHIRE

WILTSHIRE

Ashmansworth
Eversley
Basingstoke 6
Fleet
Clanville
Crondall
Andover
Well
Bentworth
Longstock
Alresford
Priors Dean
Broughton
Winchester 9
Ovington
Cheriton
East Tytherley
Steep
Whitsbury
Upham
Rockbourne
Droxford
Damerham
Dundridge
Shirley
Southampton
Havant
Rowlands Castle
Cosham
Emsworth
Ringwood
Titchfield
Langstone
Fareham
Bransgore
Boldre
Portsmouth
Lymington
Cowes
Ryde
Freshwater
Newport
ISLE OF WIGHT
Shanklin
Bonchurch

SURREY

WEST SUSSEX

DORSET

0 Miles 10
0 Kilometres 16

Hampshire

ALRESFORD

The Globe on the Lake
Tel: 01962 732294

The Soke, Broad Street, Alresford, Hants SO24 9DB
Free House. Marc Conway & Emma Duveen, licensees.

A village of great charm. Broad Street, lined with Georgian houses, leads to Old Alresford ponds; these were created in the 12th century by Godfrey de Luce, Bishop of Winchester. This stretch of water teems with wildlife, and the Globe, as near as can be, has its own lakeside garden. This fine old pub has been considerably renovated, structurally improved, painted and got ready for another successful century. The garden and dining room both look over the lake – you can eat with a view. From the daily changing menu you could have wild-mushroom soup or a smoked-salmon and dill tartlet with lemon cream sauce, spinach and Brie flan with salad, local smoked trout, Thai-style chicken curry with rice, peppered sirloin steak with French fries and delicious puds to follow. Brakspear Bitter, Courage Best, Directors and Wadworths 6X are the beers. Well-chosen, reasonably priced wine list, many by the glass. Lots of room to sit outside and appreciate the watery surroundings.

> OPEN: 11–3. 6–11 (12–3. 7–10.30 Sun). 11–11 summer weekends.
> Real Ale.
> Children in garden, garden room and dining room until 7.30pm. Dogs on leads in garden. Wheelchair access (not WC).
> Cards: Amex, Delta, MasterCard, Switch, Visa.

ASHMANSWORTH

The Plough
Tel: 01635 253047

Ashmansworth, Nr Newbury, Berks RG20 9SL
Free House. Oliver Davis, licensee.

South of Newbury and south of Highclere, the Plough, built in 1778, has for all its long life been a beer house. Brick and flint, previously thatched but now with a slate roof. According to the map, the pub has always been firmly in Hampshire, so we have put it there too, though as you see from the address, the post office confuse matters by putting it in the next county. A small, simple place with just one quarry-tiled bar; the bottles and the cheery landlord face you as you come in. Too small to do much with food, but there are sandwiches, beef cooked in beer and scampi, that sort of thing – all the familiar bar favourites to go with the beer. Archers Village, Best, Golden and one guest, served from the barrel. Seats in the small side garden.

> OPEN: Closed Mon and until 6pm Tues, otherwise 12–2.30
> (12–3 Sat and Sun). 6–11.
> Real Ale.
> Children at lunchtime and until 8pm if well behaved. Dogs welcome. Wheelchair access (not WC). Small car park.

BENTWORTH

Sun Inn   Tel: 01420 562338
Bentworth, Nr Alton, Hants GU34 5JT (at Sun Hill off A339 from Alton)
Free House. Mary Holmes, licensee.

The Sun Inn is especially appealing in winter. On a dreary day there is nothing quite so welcoming as walking into a pub to find big log fires in equally big fireplaces. On the edge of the village, this cosy place has been extended, allowing more people to enjoy the praiseworthy catering: daily specials on the blackboard could be watercress or asparagus soup, a choice of pasta dishes, smoked-haddock pancakes, Mediterranean lamb casserole, Somerset pork, sweet and sour chicken, as well as sandwiches, ploughman's, filled baked potatoes, ham and eggs, salads and home-made puddings. Eight real ales including Bunce's Pigswill, Badger Best, Brakspear Bitter, Ringwood Fortyniner and Timothy Taylors Landlord. Gales country wines. When summer comes there are tables outside among the flowering tubs.

> OPEN: 12–3. 6–11.
> Real Ale.
> Children in garden room. Dogs on leads. Wheelchair access.
> Occasional Morris dancers.

BOLDRE

Red Lion   Tel: 01590 673177
Ropehill, Boldre, Nr Lymington, Hants
Eldridge Pope. Vince Kernick, lease

You can't really see the join but it is still evident that this pub was once two cottages on the edge of the New Forest. This smart, black-and-white 17th-century pub is a riot of colour in summer; not only are there flower-filled tubs, hanging baskets and window boxes, but a redundant farm cart has been pressed into service to hold even more flowers. Inside is a collection of all those artifacts you associate with past country life displayed around its four well-beamed rooms. They serve a range of familiar bar food: home-made soup, fishcakes in a white-wine and cream sauce, liver and bacon, beef and mushroom pie, excellent ploughman's and triple-decker sandwiches, some vegetarian dishes and quite a choice of puddings, daily specials on the blackboard. Menus change with the seasons. Websters Green Label, Eldridge Popes Hardy Country and Royal Oak ales. Wines by the glass. Seats in the attractive garden. Good walks nearby.

> OPEN: 11–11 (12–10.30 Sun).
> Real Ale. Restaurant.
> No children under 14 inside pub. No dogs. Wheelchair access.

BRANSGORE

Three Tuns
Tel: 01425 672232

Ringwood Road, Bransgore, Nr Christchurch, Hants BH23 8JH
Whitbread. Steve Biss, lessee.

A delightful 17th-century thatched pub hung about with exuberant hanging baskets. If you're too late for the summery baskets, a cheery open fire will welcome you on cooler days. The comfortable beamed bar has a wide choice of freshly cooked dishes listed on the blackboard: home-made soups, savoury choux buns stuffed with Stilton served on a red-pepper, tomato and rosemary coulis, home-made venison terrine, filo wrap filled with wild mushrooms, asparagus, baby spinach and savoury rice served with a sweet chilli dressing, braised Scotch beef and kidney in a rich stout, mushroom and herb jus with a pastry case, whole fresh brill – puddings too. The restaurant has been extended – eating here is popular. Whitbread Best, Ringwood Fortyniner, Gales HSB, Boddingtons and one extra guest ale each week. Good range of wines by the glass. Lots of room to sit outside.

> OPEN: 11–2.30. 6–11 (12–3. 7–10.30 Sun).
> Real Ale. Restaurant.
> No children. Dogs on leads. Car park. Wheelchair access.

BROUGHTON

Tally Ho!
Tel: 01794 301280

High Street, Broughton, Nr Stockbridge, Hants SO20 8AA
Free House. Trevor Draycott & Patricia Witts, licensees.

Comfortable, well restored and totally redecorated throughout, this pub is in a pretty village full of timbered houses on the Wallop Brook. Opposite the 13th-century Norman church, the Georgian Tally Ho! has good winter fires and serves reliable, home-made bar snacks and a wide variety of daily specials including vegetarian dishes. The ales change all the time so there will always be something new. There is a lovely, colourful walled garden at the back of the pub. Near the Clarendon Way, so you are in good walking country, and you might like to know it is not far from the Test valley, which has one of the best trout rivers in the country.

> OPEN: 12–3. 7–11 (12–11 Sat. Sunday breakfast 10–11.30, otherwise 12–4. 7–10.30).
> Real Ale. No food Sunday eves or all day Tuesday.
> Children welcome. Dogs on leads. Wheelchair access at the back.

CHERITON

Flower Pots   Tel: 01962 771318
Cheriton, Alresford, Hants SO24 0QQ
Own Brew. Joanna & Patricia Bartlett, licensees.

Bought in the early 19th century by the retired head gardener of Avington Park, the pub, with its past horticultural leanings, is aptly named. On the other side of the road is their very own brewery – The Cheriton Brewhouse – opened in 1993 (tours can be arranged), where they keep up the horticultural theme naming their popular, reasonably priced beers Cheriton Best, Diggers Gold and Pots' Ale. You will find good-value bar food: well-filled jacket potatoes, sandwiches – plain and toasted – nine different fillings for the large baps, six varieties of ploughman's and a number of hotpots. Seats outside at the front and the back of the pub.

> OPEN: 12–2.30. 6–11 (12–3. 7–10.30 Sun).
> Real Ale. No food Sun eves or Bank Holiday Mon eves.
> No children. Dogs on leads. Wheelchair access (not WC). Car park. Bedrooms.
> Cards: no cards accepted.

DAMERHAM

Compasses Inn   Tel: 01725 518231
Damerham, Nr Fordingbridge, Hants SP6 3HQ
Free House. James Kidd, licensee.

The two bars – a traditional public bar and delightful lounge – in this attractive old coaching inn both have good winter fires. Well-thought-out menus: the emphasis is on fresh local produce, the extensive menu and daily specials have something for every-one, both in the bar and the dining room. Soup of the day, ploughman's with home-made pickles from the bar and from the specials board there could be John Dory and salmon with an orange salsa, pork tenderloin with prunes in a white-wine sauce, king prawns, mussels and pasta with herbs, garlic and cream or a gammon and leek pie and home-made puds to follow. They have their own Compasses Ale: Ringwood Best, Wadworths 6X, Hopback Summer Lightning and frequently changing guest beers. Varied selection of wines, many from the New World, and 120 malt whiskies. To go with the malts, cheese. The pub is recommended by the British Cheese Board for the excellence of its cheeses. Delightful gardens with views of the surrounding countryside.

A notice on the pub door reads: 'Clean wellies, boots and dogs are allowed in the public bar'.

> OPEN: 11–3. 6–11.30.
> Real Ale.
> Children welcome. Dogs in public bar. All disabled facilities.
> Six en-suite bedrooms.
> Award-winning toilets here; they have won the 'Loo of the Year' award for several years running.

EAST TYTHERLEY

Star Inn
Tel: 01794 340225

East Tytherley, Nr Romsey, Hants SO51 0LW
Free House. Paul & Sarah Bingham, licensees.

In a quiet area, away from main roads but not far from the Roman road that linked Winchester and Salisbury, the Star is a welcoming place with big log fires in the bar, a separate no-smoking bar and a restaurant. New licensees, who have won 'Hampshire Chef of the Year', will mean a new approach to the menus; everything is prepared 'in house', so you must be patient. There could be home-made soup of the day, as well as pan-fried scallops with creamed leeks and smoked salmon, saffron couscous with hara masala and curried mushrooms – as a starter or main course – and lamb's liver, bacon and mash, grilled sea bream with ratatouille, tapenade and basil oil, faggots with pea and potato purée and onion gravy, pan-fried fillet of beef with potato, bacon and lentil cake with red-onion confit, something from the specials board and always a choice of vegetarian dishes and good, proper puds. Gales HSB, Ringwood Best and one other. Seats in the garden where there is a children's play area.

> OPEN: 11–2.30. 6–11 (12–3. 7–10.30 Sun).
> Real Ale.
> Children welcome – if under control. Dogs allowed.

EMSWORTH

Kings Arms
Tel: 01243 374941

19 Havant Road, Emsworth, Hants PO10 7JD
Gales. Adrian & Penny White, tenants.

Easy to find in summer: all you need to do is look for the exuberant flower display and the black-and-white Kings Arms will be right behind it. On the Havant road (A259) westward out of Emsworth, 50 yards from the mill pond and the ducks, this is a 'sometimes' pub. If it is very quiet, the landlord will sometimes put on a little light classical music to take the chill off the early-morning silence, but it quickly fades out as the customers move in. Just one bar with a no-smoking area; ploughman's, salads, steaks etc on the bar menu; home-made fresh crab gratin, Moroccan chicken, cheese and vegetable pie and pineapple upside-down pudding from the blackboard. Daily specials could include Stilton and bacon mushrooms, cauliflower moussaka or Victorian beefcake and a Hampshire six-cup pudding. A selection of wines by the glass and the bottle. Well-kept Gales beers and guest ales. Gales country wines. Outside there is a prize-winning garden.

OPEN: 11–2.30. 5.15–11 (12–2.30. 7–10.30 Sun).
Real Ale.
No children in bar. Well-behaved dogs on leads. Wheelchair access (not WC).
Cards: all major credit cards.

EVERSLEY

White Hart   Tel: 0118 973 2817
The Street, Eversley, Hants RG27 0PJ
Unique Pub Company. Doug Page, tenant.

As soon as you arrive, it is clear that they run a happy ship and get rid of all their surplus energy by fielding a rugby team who tour as 'The White Hart Marauders'. Photos of the rugby club at various celebratory moments in their career cover the walls of the main bar. Built in the 16th century, originally thatched but now with a slate roof, the building is otherwise untouched: the beams in the bars are still as they were – in some places the height of the ceiling is a hazard for anyone much over 6 feet. There's more room in the small Village Bar at the back of the pub, where they keep a television set for sporting events. Food is served at lunchtimes only: usually soup, different ploughman's, lots of fillings for the sandwiches, rolls and jacket potatoes, or you could have something more substantial such as beef in Guinness, bangers and mash or steak and Stilton pie with onion gravy, to go with the Courage Best and Hobgoblin, Fullers London Pride and John Smiths Smooth (a keg beer). Lagers and some wines. Seats in the small garden.

OPEN: 11–11 (12–10.30 Sun).
Real Ale. Lunchtime bar food only.
Children – if you must. Dogs on leads. Wheelchair access difficult. Big car park.
Cards: all credit cards.

LANGSTONE

Royal Oak   Tel: 023 9248 3125
19 Langstone High Street, Langstone, Havant, Hants PO9 1RY
Whitbread. Chris Ford, manager.

Opposite Hayling Island, which divides the tidal waters of Langstone and Chichester Harbour, this tiny village, once a medieval port, overlooks a huge marshy expanse designated an area of special scientific interest. The 16th-century Royal Oak is on the edge of a natural harbour; an extra high tide – when the water nearly reaches the front door – and local swans could join you for a drink. Warm and comfortable in winter with open fires, it is appealing in all seasons. A traditional range of bar food with home-made soups, well-filled cottage cobs, a vegetarian dish, moules marinière, a Royal Oak infamous sizzler, local fish and something from the two daily specials boards. Flowers Original, Gales HSB, Boddingtons, Wadworths 6X, Morlands Old Speckled Hen on hand pump and Bulmers traditional cider. Seats at the front of the pub or in the garden behind – you have views over Chichester harbour from the pub.

OPEN: 11–11.
Real Ale.
Children in eating area. Dogs on leads in part of pub.

OVINGTON

Bush Inn   Tel: 01962 732764

Ovington, Nr Alresford, Hants SO24 0RE
Wadworths. Nick & Cath Young, managers/licensees.

Down a winding lane, just south of Alresford, the village is on the south side of the fast-flowing River Itchen where it is joined by two other streams – the Arle and the Candover. Noted as an excellent trout stream, the Itchen also has some wonderful riverside paths; you can either work up an appetite before arriving at the Bush, or walk off your meal afterwards. Inside the 400-year-old pub are three comfortable bars, each with roaring log fires in winter. Traditional bar meals are readily available; daily specials are on the blackboard, which lists a small number of more adventurous dishes such as Thai-spiced crab cake with rocket salad and peanut dressing, or pork medallions with grain-mustard mash, fennel and juniper sauce, also home-made puds. Wadworths range of ales plus seasonal beers. Various country wines. Seats overlooking the river and, naturally enough, lovely walks.

OPEN: 11–2.30. 6–11.
Real Ale.
Children in eating area lunchtimes only. Dogs on leads.
Limited wheelchair access.

PRIORS DEAN

White Horse Inn   Tel: 01420 588387

(Known as The Pub with No Name)
Priors Dean, Nr Petersfield, Hants GU32 1DA (clutching a good map, you go up a track past East Tilstead/Privett crossroads, between Petersfield and Winchester)
Gales. Janet & William Egerton, licensees.

High on the Downs with views all round of the surrounding country, it's simple and tra-ditional. Think of a country pub 20 or so years ago and that will give you some idea of what to expect when you see this 17th-century farmhouse with an empty inn sign stand-ing outside; then you'll also know why they call it 'the pub with no name'. Menus vary with the seasons – as do the specialities – and everything is cooked to order. You can always get sandwiches, soup (in winter made on the Aga), and ploughman's. Ballards Best, Courage Best and Directors, No Name Best, No Name Strong, Fuggles, Bass, Theakstons

Old Peculier, Gales Festival Mild, Butser and IPA are among the ales on offer, plus guest ales. A considerable number of country wines, including wine from a local vineyard. There are occasional visits from those wonderful old steam road rollers and the pub is a meeting point for vintage cars and motorbikes. If you want to pitch your tent, you can do that here too.

> OPEN: 11–2.30 (11–3 Sat). 6–11.
> Real Ale. No meals or snacks Sun lunchtimes.
> No children. Well-behaved dogs on leads. Wheelchair access.

ROCKBOURNE

Rose & Thistle   Tel: 01725 518236
Rockbourne, Fordingbridge, Hants SP6 3NL
Free House. Tim Norfolk, licensee.

On the border of three counties: Hampshire, Dorset and Wiltshire. Rockbourne has one long village street with a mix of Georgian and Tudor houses and thatched cottages. A chalk stream flows through the middle of the village; small bridges give access to the houses on the north side. The thatched, 16th-century Rose and Thistle is part of this delightful place. Inside it has the ambience you would expect. There is a short, well-chosen menu of freshly prepared food: bacon and mushrooms on toast, cheese, ham or rare-roast-beef ploughman's, medallions of pork fillet with a wild-mushroom and Marsala sauce, three lamb cutlets on a celeriac and potato rosti with redcurrant sauce; there will always be a daily pasta dish, fish and specials on the blackboard. Over a period of time there could be a seafood tagliatelle, pork and apple casserole with a sage scone, venison steak in a spring-onion and chestnut sauce, seafood platter of crab, prawns, smoked trout, crevettes, rollmop herring and marinated salmon. Fullers London Pride is on permanently, Hopback Brewery beers are the guests. Wide-ranging wine list, ten by the glass. Surrounded by lovely countryside; the Romans thought so too – over 50 years ago a substantial Roman villa was excavated east of the village. A museum on the site contains all the fascinating objects found there.

> OPEN: 11–3. 6–11 (12–3. 7–10.30 Sun).
> Real Ale. Restaurant.
> Children welcome, dogs too. Wheelchair access (not WC). Car park.
> Cards: Delta, MasterCard, Switch, Visa.

STEEP

Harrow Inn   Tel: 01730 262685
Steep, Petersfield, Hants GU32 2DA
Free House. Eileen McCutcheon, licensee.

North of Petersfield along a minor road, the Harrow, probably 15th-century, is beamed and hung with hops and dried flowers. There are old oak benches in the public bar and a big inglenook fireplace. Steep is well named – the pub is perched on a ledge. Slightly difficult to find: first locate Sheet Church, turn left, follow the sign to Steep – over the motorway bridge – and hey presto, there's the Harrow! Beer is served through a hatch from the barrels behind. Unchanging, wonderfully traditional – a place to be treasured. Generous portions of the home-cooked ham (cooked by the landlady), Scotch eggs, soups, salads and, an added bonus, treacle and Bakewell tart to follow. Ringwood Best, Cheriton Pots, Diggers Gold and Ballards Trotton beers. Country wines. Tables in the wild garden.

OPEN: 12–2.30 (11–3 Sat). 6–11 (12–3. 7–10.30 Sun). Closed Sunday nights Oct–April.
Real Ale.
No children. Dogs on leads. Always help for the wheelchair.

TITCHFIELD

Fishermans Rest   Tel: 01329 845065
Mill Lane, Titchfield, Hants PO15 5RA
Laurel Pub Company. Dave Roseby, licensee.

The Fishermans Rest, on the banks of the River Meon, is opposite the remains of Titchfield Abbey. As you would expect with a name like the Fishermans Rest, there are lots of fishing bits and pieces on the walls of its comfortable, flagstone-floored bars. The pub serves a good choice of freshly prepared food including ever-popular filled baked potatoes, fish and chips, steak and kidney pie and ploughman's. Daily specials are listed on the blackboard. Wadworths 6X, Flowers Original, Gales HSB, Bass and Boddingtons. Wines by the glass. Seats in the large waterside garden.

OPEN: 11–11 (12–10.30 Sun).
Real Ale.
Children: under protest! Dogs welcome.

UPHAM

Brushmakers Arms   Tel: 01489 860231
Upham, Nr Bishops Waltham, Hants SO32 1JJ (village signposted from Winchester)
Free House. Tony Mottram, licensee.

This Upham is a village deep in the country between Bishops Waltham and Winchester – do not confuse it with Lower Upham which is near the main Winchester to Bishop's Waltham road. As you might imagine with a name like this, you'll find brushes for most occasions – there is quite a collection hanging around the pub, which has a comfortable, good-sized bar divided by a wood-burning stove in a central fire-place. Better-than-average choice of bar food and a Sunday roast; the menus are all on blackboards now, so things are constantly changing. Bass, Ringwood and Charles Wells Bombardier plus regular guest beers to wash it all down. A choice of malt whiskies, Addlestone cider and country wines. Seats outside on the terrace and the lawn.

> OPEN: 11–3. 5.30–11 (12–3.30. 7.30–10.30 Sun).
> Real Ale.
> Children welcome away from bar. Dogs on leads. Wheelchair access (not WC).

WELL

Chequers Inn   Tel: 01256 862605
Well, Odiham, Hants RG29 1TL
Hall & Woodhouse. Kieran Marshall & Clare Baumann, licensees.

Beamed and panelled with shelves of books to read if you are waiting for someone, or just want a book to browse with your beer. This delightful 17th-century pub in deepest Hampshire is a perfect place to be. The menu chalked on the blackboard in the bar is quite enterprising and changes daily. There could be pasta, coronation chicken, seafood vol-au-vents, smoked salmon and scrambled eggs and other dishes. Badgers Best, Fursty Ferret and Tanglefoot are the ales. Good range of wine. Tables in the garden, at the back and on the vine-covered terrace at the front of the pub.

> OPEN: 11–3. 6–11 (12–3.30. 7–10.30 Sun).
> Real Ale. Restaurant. Food is served until 8.30pm Sun eves.
> Children welcome. Dogs on leads.

WHITSBURY

Cartwheel   Tel: 01725 518362
Whitsbury Road, Nr Fordingbridge, Hants
Free House. Patrick Lewis, licensee.

Rather remote, this place; but although it's deep in the country, lots of people seem to find it – so out with the map and keep an eagle eye on the signposts. Aptly named as it was built originally for wheelwrights who have long since gone. Now it is a very pleasant, beamed country pub serving good imaginative food. So when you finally get here you'll find freshly filled sandwiches, ploughman's, steaks, salads, local trout and daily specials; there are usually about six ales on offer which are continually changing, so what is here today may not be there next week – you'll have to go and see what they've got. Good-size garden with children's play area.

> OPEN: 11–2.30. 6–11 (12–3. 7–10.30 Sun).
> Real Ale. Restaurant.
> Children in eating areas. Dogs welcome. Car park.

WINCHESTER

Wykeham Arms
Tel: 01962 853834

75 Kingsgate Street, Winchester, Hants SO23 9PE
Gales. Peter & Kate Miller, managers.

South of the Cathedral Close, the Wykeham Arms is a handsome, old-fashioned place –
in a beautifully run sort of way. High standards in every department are what you get. Six
rooms radiate from a central bar (where the serious drinking goes on), so there is plenty of
space for you to sample the extremely popular bar food. They change the lunchtime
menu daily so you should get there early to avoid disappointment as all Winchester seems
to beat a path to the door. Specials on the blackboard could include cream of mushroom
and thyme soup, chicken-liver and Madeira pâté, Wyke cottage pie, pork, apple and sage
casserole, or a hot or cold open sandwich. There is also an interesting restaurant menu
along with an impressive wine list. Several no-smoking areas. Draught Bass and Gales
range of ales. Seats on the terrace and small lawn.

> OPEN: 11–11. No snacks Sun.
> Real Ale. Evening restaurant.
> No children. Dogs on leads. Car park. Thirteen bedrooms.

ISLE OF WIGHT Bonchurch

Bonchurch Inn
Tel: 01983 852611

The Shute, Bonchurch, Ventnor, Isle of Wight PO38 1NU
Free House. Ulisse & Aline Besozzi, licensees.

When, and if, we find more quiet pubs on the island, we will give the Isle of Wight a separate section, but until we do, we'll keep it attached to its big neighbour. I just hope they
don't mind. Bonchurch, a delightful village with its own tiny beach, is in one of the prettiest areas of the island and the Bonchurch Inn is a delight. Ulisse is Italian but has been
in England since 1956 and has created a remarkably old-style English pub full of interesting junk – statues, pottery and all sorts of other stuff that fills up any odd space. Even the
floors are interesting, having come from a ship's deck, and as for the chairs, they're from
an ocean liner! As well as the traditional English pub fare you'll find several Italian specialities in the Italian restaurant and on the wide-ranging bar-snack menu: tagliatelle
carbonara, seafood risotto, lasagne – and the lasagne here really is home made, scampi
cooked in butter with an onion, cream, mushroom and Pernod sauce, or chicken cooked
in a tomato, mushroom and white-wine sauce, other fish, shellfish and steaks. Good,
small wine list, also Courage Directors, John Smith's Best and local beers. Morland's Old
Speckled Hen is the summer beer.

> OPEN: 11–3. 6–11 (12–3. 7–10.30 Sun).
> Real Ale. Italian restaurant.
> Children over seven years old welcome. Dogs in public bar. Wheelchair access.
> Car park. Self-catering holiday flat.
> Cards: all credit cards.

ISLE OF WIGHT Ryde

S. Fowler & Co   Tel: 01983 812112
41–43 Union Street, Ryde, Isle of Wight
Wetherspoon.

Aficionados of Ryde will recognise the name as that of the old department store. Mindful of social history, Wetherspoon kept the name of the well-known shop and just changed the fittings. Haberdashery out, beer pumps in. As usual it looks wonderful; they have done the old place proud. Ryde is a hugely popular resort; the building of the pier in 1813 was the start of a love affair with tourists which has continued to this day. Here, as with all Wetherspoon's pubs, you will get a very reasonably priced pint of beer (they say about 30 per cent less than in other places). No wonder all the customers are happy. Seasonally changing menus and always a big no-smoking area.

> OPEN: 11–11.
> Real Ale.
> No children. No dogs.

BEST OF THE REST

CLANVILLE Nr Andover

Red Lion Country Inn   Tel: 01264 771007
What was once a modest brick-and-flint coaching inn has been hugely extended – there is even room for you to land a helicopter. That said, they welcome you however you arrive – by bike if you wish. Inside you'll find an intimate bistro, and you can certainly get a pint in the bar. Different menus in different places: 'light bites', daily specials in the bar or an à la carte menu in the bistro, also a traditional Sunday lunch. Fullers London Pride and Brakespear ales and whatever else you could ever want. Children and dogs welcome. All disabled facilities.

CRONDALL The Borough

Plume of Feathers   Tel: 01252 850245
A 500-year-old pub on the site of a building mentioned in the Domesday Book in 1085, so something here is very, very ye olde. Beamed and full of character; you will be well looked after. They serve a familiar bar menu: home-made soup, ploughman's, steak sandwiches, lasagne, terrines and fresh fish, steak, ale and mushroom pie, also game in season from the specials board. Ruddles Best, Greene King range, Charles Wells Bombardier as a guest and a choice of wines. Children and dogs welcome.

DROXFORD South Hill

White Horse Inn   Tel: 01489 877490
Inside, this family-run old coaching inn is a bit of a mixture so be warned: it has a quiet, beamed lounge bar and a no-smoking restaurant, however, it does have a public bar with

games, jukebox and music. The good selection of bar food includes a home-made soup, filled French sticks, locally smoked fresh salmon pâté, steak pie cooked in Guinness, fish pie and various game pies. Home-made fruit pies and crumbles to finish. Morlands Old Speckled Hen, Flowers Original, Burton Bridge, Guinness, also Morlands IPA, Kaliber and White Label bitter.

DUNDRIDGE

Hampshire Bowman   Tel: 01489 892940
Near Bishops Waltham, but you need to ask directions as it is a bit out of the way. We have been told there is no music, but we don't have enough information to put it in the main category. A friendly, cosy old place that welcomes everyone – children, walkers and dogs. They serve good wholesome food to go with the cask ales.

LONGSTOCK Nr Stockbridge

Peat Spade   Tel: 01264 810612
An elegant Victorian pub in a pretty village. An inn since the middle of the 19th century, it has grown from a pub serving 'luncheons and teas' to a place offering a wide range of freshly prepared, original food without losing the charm of a warm and comfortable pub. From the regularly changing menu: salad of smoked eel and smoked mackerel, rillette of duck with apple chutney, breast of Gressingham duck with damson sauce, home-made ravioli of mushrooms, cream cheese and smoked baby tomatoes, home-made faggots and mash, and well-filled sandwiches. Carefully selected wine list. Ringwood Best, Fortyniner, Hampshire King Alfred or Strong ales. Lovely garden and terrace which you share with some Scottish Grey chickens. Children and dogs welcome. Wheelchair access. Two bedrooms.

ISLE OF WIGHT Freshwater

Red Lion   Tel: 01983 754925
Any pub with its own herb garden has a culinary head start over the opposition in my book. Near the church and extremely popular during the holiday season – particularly weekends. Really old, this comfortable pub serves an interesting, varied menu to go with Flowers Original, Fullers London Pride, Wadworths 6X and a local guest beer. Decent wine list; about 15 by the glass. Close to the River Yar, this is a good area for walks.

ISLE OF WIGHT Shanklin

Fishermans Cottage   Tel: 01983 863882
It probably was one too, as this thatched cottage is actually on the beach, very close to the fish! A short walk through the delights of Shanklin Chine will get you to the pub. Fairly simple bar food, but location is all. Courage Directors and some country wines. Only open during the holiday season. Lunchtimes are quietish, but the promise of live evening entertainment is always suspicious.

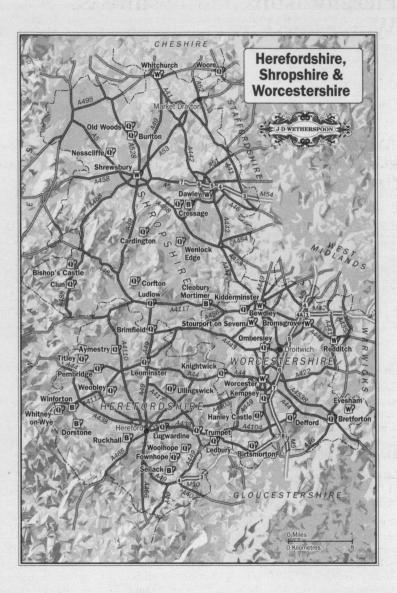

Herefordshire, Shropshire & Worcestershire

J·D·WETHERSPOON

CHESHIRE

STAFFORDSHIRE

WEST MIDLANDS

WARWICKS

SHROPSHIRE

HEREFORDSHIRE

WORCESTERSHIRE

GLOUCESTERSHIRE

Whitchurch
Woore
Market Drayton
Old Woods
Burlton
Nesscliffe
Shrewsbury
Dawley
Cressage
Cardington
Wenlock Edge
Bishop's Castle
Clun
Corfton
Ludlow
Cleobury Mortimer
Kidderminster
Brimfield
Bewdley
Stourport on Severn
Bromsgrove
Ombersley
Droitwich
Redditch
Aymestry
Titley
Knightwick
Pembridge
Leominster
Ullingswick
Worcester
Weobley
Kempsey
Winforton
Evesham
Whitney-on-Wye
Hanley Castle
Defford
Bretforton
Dorstone
Hereford
Trumpet
Ruckhall
Lugwardine
Woolhope
Ledbury
Fownhope
Birtsmorton
Sellack

0 Miles 5
0 Kilometres 8

Herefordshire, Shropshire & Worcestershire

AYMESTREY

Riverside Inn
Tel: 01568 708440

Aymestrey, Herefordshire HR6 9ST
Free House. Steve & Val Bowen, licensees

You really can't miss this place as there is quite a lot of it; big, 16th-century, heavily timbered, black and white and very near the bridge over the River Lugg. The picnic tables are on the banks of the river – you can't get much closer than that. Inside the Riverside Inn are beams, hops, scrubbed tables, bits of antiques, country artifacts and good fires, a 'how a well-run country pub should be' sort of place. The daily changing bar menu could include home-made soup, rack of local lamb, pheasant in red wine, steak and kidney in the local ale and lunchtime daily specials. Very local Woodhampton ale: Kingfisher, Jack Snipe, Raven's Head and Wagtail, local farm cider and a good wine list.

> OPEN 11–11 (10.30 Sun).
> Real Ale. Restaurant.
> Children in eating area. Dogs welcome. Wheelchair access (not WC). Car park.
> Bedrooms.
> Cards: Visa, MasterCard, Switch, Delta.

BEWDLEY

Little Pack Horse
Tel: 01299 403762

31 High Street, Bewdley, Worcs SY12 2DH
Inspired Pubs plc. Michael Gaunt, licensee.

A fine old town, with many 18th-century houses, on the edge of Wyre forest. Low-beamed, well-timbered and cosy, the 16th-century Little Pack Horse is a town pub with tremendous appeal; busy, cheerful and slightly eccentric, it is full of fascinating objects, including an incendiary bomb. It is also the meeting place for the Bewdley and District Mountaineering Club and The Little Pack Horse Golf Society – they are obviously an energetic lot here. The pub is the home of 'Desperate Dan Pies' – these come in two sizes; otherwise the food ranges from the traditional pub menu (sausage and mash) to the more exotic (Cajun marinated salmon fillet, chargrilled with roasted pepper and garlic). Always about five vegetarian dishes on the evening menu. Ind Coope Burton and Ushers beers. Note: there is no parking nearby.

> OPEN: 12–3. 6–11 (11–11 Sat. 11–10.30 Sun).
> Real Ale.
> Children in back bar or stable room.
> Cards: MasterCard, Visa, Switch, Solo, Electron.

BIRTSMORTON

Farmers Arms   Tel: 01684 833308
Birts Street, Birtsmorton, Nr Malvern, Worcs WR13 6AP
Free House. Jill & Julie Moore, licensees.

This family-run (mother and daughter), friendly, black-and-white timbered pub, with its low-beamed, convivial, rambling interior, offers a good range of familiar bar food. This includes sandwiches, ploughman's, salads, steak and kidney pie, trout and almonds, steaks and good puddings. Hook Norton Old Hooky and some guest beers on hand pump. Seats in the garden during summer. Good walking country.

> OPEN: 11–2 (3 Sat). 6–10.
> Real Ale.
> Children welcome. Dogs on leads. Wheelchair access.

BISHOP'S CASTLE

Three Tuns   Tel: 01588 638797
Salop Street, Bishop's Castle, Shropshire SY9 5BW
Three Tuns Brewing Co. Ltd. Janet Cross, licensee.

Nothing much of the castle is left now – just a pile of stones with a bowling green on top. But the castle was built by a bishop – the Bishop of Hereford in 1127 – to help beat back the Welsh raiders who were after the ecclesiastical sheep. The Three Tuns, originally granted a licence to brew beer over 350 years ago, is still going strong. The brewery, a listed building, was rebuilt in Victorian times on the site of a brewery licensed in 1642. The inn, and a black-and-white malt store, probably date from that time too. Inside, the pub retains many original features, including heavy oak beams and a good Jacobean staircase. The bar menu includes a number of fish and vegetarian dishes – all freshly prepared, using local and, where possible, organic produce – and pub specials such as beef in Three Tuns ale. From the brewery comes XXX Bitter, Sexton and seasonal beers – Michaelmas and Old Scrooge in winter. The pubs own bottled beer is Clerics' Cure. They have an interesting small wine list. Seats on the terrace and in the sheltered summery garden. Lovely walking country.

> OPEN: 11.30–11.
> Real Ale. Dining room. Brewery tours by arrangement.
> Children welcome if well behaved. Dogs in bar and snug. En-suite rooms available in the converted stable block. Occasionally there is live music in the Victorian Assembly Room attached to the pub.

BRETFORTON

Fleece   Tel: 01386 831173

The Cross, Bretforton, Nr Evesham, Worcs
Third Room Ltd Small Pubs Group. Peter Clarke, licensee.

Once a medieval farmhouse, the Fleece became an inn during the 19th century. During its long life it has been added to and extended and these alterations are indicated by the changes in the timber framing at the front of the pub. Once completely thatched, the roof is now a mixture of thatch and stone. Beer was brewed in the back kitchen well into the 19th century. The same family lived here for over 500 years, and when Miss Taplin died in 1977 she left the Fleece and all its wonderful contents to the National Trust. Inside remains much as it was: the family collection of antique furniture, pewter, china and other ornaments and artifacts are still in their place. A unique interior which must be seen to be appreciated (don't miss the witch's marks still on the flagstones in front of the fire). It seems a bit mundane to talk about food and beer, but special as this place is, it is still the village local and as such provides good ales and an equally good choice of generous, varying bar food; a full menu is served both at lunchtime and in the evening. Hook Norton, Uley Old Spot, Pig's Ear, Ansells Bitter and two guests. Country wines and farm ciders. Seats outside in the orchard.

> OPEN: 11–2.30. 6–11.
> Real Ale. Food served all day summer Sun.
> Children welcome. No dogs.
> Occasional live entertainment. Visiting Morris men and silver band.

BRIMFIELD

Roebuck   Tel: 01584 711230

Brimfield, Nr Ludlow, Shropshire SY8 4NE
Free House. David & Sue Wilson-Lloyd, licensees.

This has the best of all worlds. A fine, well-loved local with very lively bars and an exceptionally well-regarded restaurant in the newer part. Everything really is home-made and the choice of food is considerable – there will be something for everyone, including chicken breast stuffed with garlic and fresh herbs, home-made sausages, salmon fillet, old-fashioned steak and kidney pie, venison and pigeon pies, their very own fish pie, a fantastic choice of puddings and 15 different English farmhouse cheeses. An even more extensive menu features in the restaurant, where they also do set three-course lunches. Woods ales, Morlands Old Speckled Hen, Tetleys and a weekly guest. Local ciders, and some half-bottles of wine from a wine list featuring French and New World wines.

> OPEN: 12–2.30. 7–11.
> Real Ale. Restaurant.
> Children welcome. Dogs in the snug bar. Wheelchair access (not WC). Car park.
> Bedrooms.
> Cards: Visa, MasterCard, Switch, Delta.

BROMSGROVE

Golden Cross Hotel   Tel: 01527 870005
20 High Street, Bromsgrove, Worcs B61 8HH
Wetherspoon.

An old, run-down commercial hotel has been knocked about and transformed into a busy, popular pub. Standards are high, the beer is a reasonable price, facilities are good and the food is reliable. The menus throughout the Wetherspoon chain change three times a year, but there will always be some daily specials on offer. As for the beers: six regulars, including Courage Directors, Theakstons Best & XB, Youngers Scotch Bitter, Banks Mild, Morlands Old Speckled Hen and guest ales. The new long bar has 21 hand pumps! They drink a lot of beer here.

> OPEN: 11–11 (12–10.30 Sun).
> Real Ale.
> No children. No dogs. All wheelchair facilities.

BURLTON

Burlton Inn   Tel: 01939 270284
Burlton, Nr Shrewsbury, Shropshire SY4 5TB
Free House. Ann & Gerry Bean, licensees.

In this tiny village between the small market town of Ellesmere and the glories of Shrewsbury is the delightful, beautifully kept, beamed Burlton Inn, without a gambling or cigarette machine in sight. The general air is of comfort with a touch of class. They serve interesting, home-cooked food seven days a week; anything from a light snack to a four-course meal. Always filled rolls, sandwiches, ploughman's and specials from the blackboard. To start you could have a platter of Scottish smoked salmon, New Zealand mussels, giant king prawns with a piquant mayonnaise or garlic bread topped with red onions and melted cheddar, and as a main course: grilled field mushrooms topped with pesto and Parmesan crumb served with a garlic croute, steak, kidney and beer pie, or cider chicken tagliatelle, more fish dishes and steaks too. Always four real ales: Banks's Bitter and Camerons Strong Arm the regulars. Short wine list, some by the glass. Seats outside on the terrace and in the lovely garden. The pub has won awards for its displays of hanging baskets and flowers.

> OPEN: 11–3. 6–11 (12–3. 7–10.30 Sun).
> Real Ale. Limited food Mon lunchtime: only soup, rolls or ploughman's.
> Children welcome. Dogs on leads. Wheelchair access. Car park.
> There is an annex with six en-suite bedrooms, one with disabled facilities.
> Cards: Visa, MasterCard, Switch, Delta.

CARDINGTON

Royal Oak   Tel: 01694 771266
Cardington, Nr Church Stretton, Shropshire SY6 7JZ
Free House. Mike & Dawn Carter, licensees.

Between Church Stretton and Cardington is Caer Caradoc, 1500 feet high, and the story is that the British chieftain, Caractacus, made his last stand against the Romans on the western slopes of this hill in 50 AD. That might just be a persistent rumour, but the Roman road does pass Church Stretton. In the quiet village of Cardington, behind the church, the delightful, creeper-covered 15th-century Royal Oak – reputed to be the oldest pub in Shropshire – has a rambling, well-beamed bar with a good log fire in the big inglenook. The varied, reliable bar food at lunchtime includes the traditional plough-man's, soups and filled baguettes, traditional Shropshire Fidget, steak and onion and chicken and vegetable pies, all freshly baked, steaks, mixed grill and specials on the board. Bass, Hobsons and Woods Parish Bitter. Tables on the terrace at the front of the pub with views over the glorious undulating countryside.

OPEN: 12–3. 7–11 (6–11 Fri).
Real Ale. Closed Mon except Bank Holidays.
Children welcome. No dogs.

CLUN

Sun Inn   Tel: 01588 640559
Clun, Craven Arms, Shropshire SY7 8JB
Free House. Mr & Mrs McHale, licensees.

This is the Sun at Clun, a 15th-century, cruck-framed building in one of the most ancient settlements in the country – Bronze Age, and that is old! Close to the border, the town is dominated by the ruins of the 12th-century castle built by the Normans to keep out the troublesome Welsh. The age of the building is not obvious from the outside, but inside it is full of beams, flagstones and huge fireplaces. The atmosphere is wonderful. Food is plentiful and good, much of the produce locally sourced. The bar menu lists some famil-iar dishes: home-made cottage pie, steak and kidney pudding, lasagne and daily specials, vegetarian options too. Beers are Banks, Hobsons and Woods Shropshire Lad. The glori-ous Clun valley is the most wonderful area for walking: Clun forest, Long Mynd and the surrounding hills.

OPEN: 11–11 (12–3. 6–11 Sat. 12–3. 7–11 Sun).
Real Ale. Restaurant.
Children only allowed when dining. Dogs on leads. Car park.
Bedrooms.

CORFTON

Sun Inn   Tel: 01584 861239
Corfton, Nr Craven Arms, Shropshire SY7 9DF
Free House. Teresa & Norman Pearce, licensees.

Close to the market towns of Ludlow, Bridgnorth and Much Wenlock. First licensed in 1613, the 17th-century Sun is thought to be the oldest licensed premises in Corvedale. Inside, the lounge bar has a dining area where you can choose either bar snacks, some-thing à la carte or even a children's menu; the daily offerings are written on the blackboard in the lounge. There is a regularly changing selection of dishes: local lamb and leek pie, beef in ale, smoked haddock, prawn and pasta bake, lamb Shrewsbury, gammon, and various steaks; a fish menu, vegetarian menu, steak menu, and somewhere there is bound to be a pudding menu. Eggs are free range, vegetables from local growers and meat from the local butcher. Four real ales from the pub's own microbrewery are permanent, but approximately 1200 guest ales have been tried. Seats in the garden. They hold small beer festivals with 15-plus ales to try at Easter and the August Bank Holiday.

OPEN: 12–2.30. 6–11 (12–3. 7–10.30 Sun).
Real Ale.
Children welcome. Dogs on leads.
Wheelchair ramps to all parts of pub. Disabled toilets.
They have won the 'Open to All' award for services to the disabled.
Cards: All cards except American Express.
N.B. Music in the public bar. Lounge and dining area quiet.

CRESSAGE

Cholmondeley Riverside Inn   Tel: 01952 510900
Cressage, Nr Shrewsbury, Shropshire SY4 1DB
Free House. John Radford & John Wrigley, licensees.

Open fires, beams and flagstone floors in this well-run, renovated, 17th-century coaching inn. It has an interesting menu ranging from home-made soups and filled baguettes to chicken breasts in a mushroom and cream sauce and fillet steak. Delicious puds to follow. Interesting wine list, Marstons Best, Pedigree plus some weekly changing guests. On an attractive stretch of the River Severn; and if you are staying, you can fish for free. Seats in the garden from where you can appreciate the charms of the river.

OPEN: 11–11 (12–3. 7–10.30 winter Sun).
Real Ale.
Children welcome. Dogs on leads. Bedrooms.
N.B. Music in the tiny reception area, but not throughout the pub.

DEFFORD

The Cider House (Monkey)   Tel: 01386 750234
Woodmancote, Defford, Hereford, Worcs WR8 9BW (no pub sign; it's the last cottage after Oak Public House)
Free House. Graham Collins, licensee.

One of the last traditional cider houses. A notice near the door saying they sell cider and tobacco will let you know you're in the right place; otherwise you could be forgiven for thinking this black-and-white cottage was just someone's home. Cider is served from a barrel into a jug, through a hatch, into a mug – an experience not to be missed. Simple and unspoilt, there are only a few of these unique places left in the country. Beer available in cans; nuts and crisps. They will let you bring your own picnic to enjoy with the cider.

> OPEN: 11–2.30. 6–10.30 (6–11 Fri & Sat).
> Closed Mon eves, all day Tues and Wed, and Thurs lunchtimes.
> Cider. No food. No dogs. Wheelchair access.

FOWNHOPE

Green Man
Tel: 01432 860243

Fownhope, Nr Hereford, Herefordshire HR1 4PE
Free House. Arthur & Margaret Williams and family, proprietors.

A handsome black-and-white timbered 15th-century inn with a fascinating history: dating from 1485, the first year of Henry VII's reign, and then named 'The Naked Boy'. During the Civil War the Roundheads stopped here for the night, a fact which hasn't been forgotten! Then it became an 18th-century petty sessions court; after that a coaching inn, and now a hotel where everyone is welcome. Wonderfully comfortable, this old place has big log fires, a no-smoking dining room and a residents' lounge. Good-value bar food: soup, filled baguettes, toasted sandwiches, egg mayonnaise, a 'Tom Spring' steak sandwich with mushrooms and onions, which should set you up for the day, a choice of salads, fish dishes, vegetarian menu, seafood platter, a carvery on Sundays, and children's meals. Well-kept ales: Hook Norton Best, Courage Directors, Marstons Pedigree and farm ciders. Overlooking the river, the attractive garden has lots of room for drinks and afternoon tea and the Indoor Leisure Complex. A unique sign, which was commissioned decades ago, hangs over the entrance to the coach-house yard and reads in part: 'You travel far, you travel near, it's here you find the best of Beer. You pass the East, you pass the West, if you pass this, you pass the best'.

> OPEN: 11–11 (12–10.30 Sun).
> Real Ale. Two restaurants.
> Children welcome. Dogs on leads. Wheelchair access. Car park.
> Twenty bedrooms, all en suite.
> Cards: Visa, MasterCard, Solo, Switch, Delta.

HANLEY CASTLE

Three Kings
Tel: 01684 592686

Hanley Castle, Worcs WR8 0BL (north of Upton-upon-Severn off B4211)
Free House. Mrs Sheila Roberts, licensee.

Attractively timbered, this 15th-century building has several small rooms, each with its own atmosphere. Run by the same family for 90 years, this is a wonderfully unspoilt pub. There is always a good choice of bar snacks, ranging from soups and sandwiches to ploughman's and omelettes. Gammon and egg and a toasted bacon and mushroom sandwich are the most popular items. Specials, which can take half an hour to prepare, include grilled trout and steaks. Beer is served through a hatch and includes Thwaites and Butcombe Bitter plus three guest beers. Over 50 malt whiskies and one farm cider. Seats at the front of the pub overlook the village green.

OPEN: 12–3. 7–11.
Real Ale. No food Sun eves.
Children in family room. Dogs: do ask. One letting bedroom.
Live music Sun and some Sat eves.

KEMPSEY

Walter de Cantelupe Inn   Tel: 01905 820572
Main Road, Kempsey, Worcs WR5 3NA
Free House. Martin Lloyd Morris, manager/owner.

A name you can't forget, and there'll only be the one as the unusual name is that of the Bishop of Worcester, Walter de Cantelupe, who lived in Kempsey in the 13th century. A little more recently, the inn has acquired an enviable reputation for its food; customers are definitely beating a path to this door. When possible, locally produced vegetables, meat and cheese are used to create a reasonably priced, well-chosen menu. Home-made soup, usually vegetarian, smoked Scottish salmon cornets filled with prawns, grilled gammon, wild-mushroom and fennel stroganoff, locally reared chicken breast stuffed with Stilton, wrapped in smoked bacon and covered in a mushroom and Calvados sauce, baked sea-bass fillet, freshly filled sandwiches, curry, steaks and other dishes. During the six-week asparagus season, they have a special menu featuring locally grown asparagus. A favourite pudding is a banana-filled pancake served with toffee sauce and crème fraîche. Quality wines by the glass; they hold regular free tasting sessions. Everards Beacon, Timothy Taylors Landlord and a guest ale, usually from one of the smaller breweries. Seats in the flowery hidden garden.

OPEN: 12–2.30. 6–11 (12–3. 7–10.30 Sun). Closed Mon lunchtimes except Bank Holidays.
Real Ale.
Children welcome at lunchtime & until 8.15pm. Well-behaved dogs allowed.
Wheelchair access (not WC). Car park. Two bedrooms, one on ground floor.
Cards: Amex, Visa, MasterCard, Switch, Delta.

KNIGHTWICK

Talbot Inn   Tel: 01886 821235
Knightwick, Nr Worcester, Worcs WR6 5PH (at Knightsford Bridge off A44 Worcester–Bromyard)
Free House. Ann & Wizz Clift, licensees.

What else could you possibly want? A beamed, comfortable 14th-century coaching inn with its own brewery and a reputation for serving imaginative, well-cooked food, well-kept ales (their own) and good wines. A daily changing menu for both bar and restaurant features interesting and adventurous dishes using local farm produce; many of the vegetables are home grown; happy hens are out the back; as much as possible is locally sourced. Mostly within the Teme Valley area – organic if possible. From the bar menu you could choose mushroom and cheese timbale, pork orange and cognac pâté, or saffron fish soup, beef carbonara with rice and mushrooms, roast breast of lamb with damsons, or sea-bass fillet with salsa to follow. Proper puddings too, such as gooseberry tart, plum jalousie and spiced bread and butter pudding. Home of the Teme valley brewery which brews four beers: 'This', 'That', 'T'other' and 'Wot' – all on hand pump. Good wine list and wines by the glass. Seats outside and opposite the pub. Lots of walks nearby.

OPEN: 11–11.
Real Ale. Restaurant.
Children in eating area until 7.30. Dogs: ask first. Wheelchair access is just possible. Car park. Bedrooms. Now in its 4th year, a Teme Valley Farmer's Market is held on the 2nd Sunday of every month at the pub. Morris dancers winter Wednesdays.
Cards: Amex, Visa, MasterCard, Switch, Delta.
N.B. Jukebox in the back bar.

LEDBURY

Feather's Hotel
High Street, Ledbury, Herefordshire HR8 1DS
Free House. D.M. Elliston, licensee.

Tel: 01531 635266

Ledbury is a delightful small market town surrounded by some of the best of the Herefordshire countryside. Little changed over the centuries, still with narrow lanes and cobbled streets and in the midst of the half-timbered buildings the handsome, 16th-century Feathers is an example of timber-framed building at its best – architecturally a jewel. Inside is a big, well-beamed, attractive bar (Fuggles) and an elegant restaurant (Quills). Good lunchtime dishes from the brasserie: chargrilled vegetable terrine with mixed leaves, warm salad of button mushrooms and smoked bacon with hazelnut dressing, baked cod fillet with white wine, tomato and basil, chive fishcakes with French fries, tournedos of Herefordshire beef fillet with thyme, wild mushrooms, burgundy and glazed shallots, or tenderloin of pork with fresh sage, Marsala and lemon jus. Lots of fish – sea bass, hake, tuna, Cornish plaice or lemon sole, escalopes of local pork fillet with a green-peppercorn and brandy sauce, rosettes of local beef fillet with a wild-mushroom, thyme and Madeira sauce, vegetarian dishes, grills, and imaginative home-made puddings. Three-course Sunday lunch. Fullers London Pride, Worthington BB and Bass on hand pump plus two guest beers. Large wine list and choice of malt whiskies and farm ciders.

OPEN: 11–11.
Real Ale. Restaurant.
Children in eating area. Dogs on leads. Wheelchair access (not WC). Bedrooms.
Cards: Amex, Visa, Switch, Delta.

LEOMINSTER

Grape Vaults
Tel: 01568 611404

Broad Street, Leominster, Herefordshire HR6 8BS
Free House. Mrs Pauline Greenwold, licensee.

In this old wool town at the junction of the River Lugg and Pinsley Brook, with fine Georgian buildings the length of Broad Street, the well-restored Grape Vaults is one of the nicest small 17th-century pubs you could come across. No fruit machines, computer games or jukebox. Just the hum of conversation and the clink of glasses. All the advantages of an English country inn, but in town. Wide-ranging bar menu of home-cooked food: soups, deep-fried Brie in ale batter, steak and kidney pie, cottage pie, ham and leek pie with potato topping, ham on the bone and fresh cod in their own beer batter – using Marstons Best! Ales could be Banks's Mild, Marstons Bitter, and Pedigree, but these change very regularly.

> OPEN: 11–3. 5–11 (12–3. 7–10.30 Sun).
> Real Ale.
> No children. Dogs on leads. Wheelchair access just possible.

LUDLOW

The Unicorn
Tel: 01584 873555

Corve Street, Ludlow, Shropshire SY8 1DU
Free House. Alan, Elizabeth & John Ditchburn, licensees.

Ludlow is a town full of architectural treasures. Not far from the centre is the half-timbered Unicorn. Dating from 1635, the oak-panelled, beamed bar reflects its great age. Two dining areas in the pub; one has a view over the flood meadows on the other side of the river. Better-than-average pub grub with daily additions listed on the blackboard – ham served with a parsley sauce, black pudding with a cider and mustard sauce, always some vegetarian dishes. Chicken wrapped in bacon in a cream and mushroom sauce is on the restaurant menu as well as half a chicken roasted in ginger wine and apple sauce, fillet of cod with crab and prawn bisque and lots more well-thought-out, well-cooked dishes. Beers are draught Bass and Hancocks HB. Seats on the terrace of this attractive old place with views over the River Corve (quite small, fringed with willows), which merges with the River Teme in Ludlow.

> OPEN: 12–2.30. 6–11 (12 until empty. 7–10.30 Sun).
> Real Ale. Restaurant.
> Children welcome. Dogs on leads. Wheelchair access to the back of the pub.

LUGWARDINE

Crown & Anchor
Tel: 01432 851303

Cotts Lane, Lugwardine, Hereford HR1 4AB (off A438 east of Hereford)
Free House. Nick & Julie Squire, licensees.

When the Gloucester to Hereford canal opened in 1845, barge traffic on the nearby River Lugg slowly declined and business dropped off at the Crown & Anchor. Ironically, the Hereford and Gloucester Canal Preservation Society still hold their meetings here.

Old and timbered, the pub has comfortable, friendly bars, plus one room especially for families. They offer a good variety of traditional bar food and well-kept ales. Plenty to choose from in the bar: avocado and prawns with fresh green-herb mayonnaise, garlic mushrooms, spiced chicken wings with tomato and garlic sauce, poacher's pie – flaked salmon in cream sauce with potato and cheese topping, chicken with lemon and sweet-pepper sauce, roast guinea fowl with apple and walnut stuffing, game sausages in Madeira wine with button onions and mushrooms, pot-roast partridge with brandy, white-wine and parsnip purée, grills, vegetarian dishes, vegan dishes and either a ploughman's (cheese, pickle and crusty bread) or a squire's lunch (a selection of cold meats, salad, pickle and crusty bread – definitely more upmarket). More salads, children's menu and puddings. A daily changing specials board too. Worthington BB, Butcombe Bitter, Timothy Taylors Landlord and a weekly changing guest beer all on hand pump. A range of wines.

OPEN: 11.30–11.
Real Ale. Sandwiches are only served Mon to Sat lunchtimes.
Children welcome. Dogs on leads. Wheelchair access.

NESSCLIFFE

Old Three Pigeons   Tel: 01743 741279
Nesscliffe, Nr Shrewsbury, Shropshire SY4 1DB
Free House. Dillon Brooks, licensee.

There were some very determined builders around when this place was built. Local trees must have been in short supply as they have used ship's timbers in its construction. The question you have to ask is: where from? You are a long way inland here; perhaps they floated up the Severn – not far away – and were hauled inland. All a little eccentric, then, and now. Things have moved on a bit over the centuries, but having bits of military hardware dotted around – very big bits too that can be hired out to any interested party – a seat that belonged to a highwayman, and more understandably, a collection of feathered friends, some of which lay eggs – are not the first things that come to mind when you think of a village pub: an old, 17th-century stone place with two bars and a good-size restaurant serving food that is just that little bit different. Everything is written on the huge blackboard, where you'll find lots of fresh fish and locally raised meat, all cooked to order. Inspiration changes all the time – so does the menu. Three real ales change each week; there is a good wine list, some by the glass.

OPEN: 11.30–3. 6–11 (11–11 Sat & Sun). Closed Mon and Tues during winter.
Real Ale. Restaurant.
Children welcome. Dogs on leads in the bar. Wheelchair access (not WC).

OLD WOODS

The Romping Cat   Tel: 01939 290273
Old Woods, Shrewsbury, Shropshire SY4 3AX
Free House. Mr G. Simcox, licensee

You're only here for the beer. It's a small pub in a small hamlet about 5 miles north-west of Shrewsbury. Just one room with an open fire and a snug. Both very cosy and decorated with a collection of framed prints and photographs. Ales could be Boddingtons, London Pride and four guest beers, but they change all the time.

OPEN: 1–3. 7–11.
Real Ale. No food.
Children welcome. Dogs too.

OMBERSLEY

Kings Arms
Tel: 01905 620142
Ombersley, Droitwich, Worcs WR9 0EW
Quintessential English Pub Co. David Pendry, manager.

Black and white with a definite lean to one side; big, beamed and aptly named. Another 'the king was here' pub: Charles II supposedly took refuge here after his defeat at the Battle of Worcester in 1651. He probably did too; they have put his coat of arms on the ceiling in one of the rooms. No music and no machines either in this rambling old place, just handsome beamed rooms with good log fires in the inglenook fireplaces. Plenty of choice from the changing menus; these could include roast goat's cheese with sherry-vinegar onions, wild-rocket and plum-tomato risotto with Parmesan flakes or corned-beef hash with a fried egg as a starter or light meal. Main courses might include home-made steak and kidney pie, seared duck breast with Thai noodles or corn-fed chicken wrapped in bacon with a garlic and lemon cream sauce. Fish from the daily changing blackboard, puddings and English cheeses. Draught Banks's Bitter, Marstons Pedigree or Morrels Varsity. A range of malt and Irish whiskies and a good wine list, a dozen by the glass. Tables in the walled garden among the summer flowers.

OPEN: 11–2.45. 5.30–11 (12–10.30 Sat).
Real Ale. Food all day Sun.
Children: not after 8.30pm. No dogs. Wheelchair access. Car park.
Cards: Delta, MasterCard, Switch, Visa.

PEMBRIDGE

New Inn
Tel: 01544 388427
Market Square, Pembridge, Herefordshire HR6 9DZ
Free House. Jane Melvin, licensee.

You're in a tiny medieval village of half-timbered houses where the 'new' inn meant new in the 14th century. Contemporary with the Market Hall and the village church, the pub is charming and traditional. Flagstones and heavily beamed bars inside, without a right angle between them. Well-chosen home-cooked food: haddock, mussel and sweetcorn chowder, apple, leek and pork sausages with mustard dumplings, lamb fillet in redcurrant sauce and interesting puddings. Ruddles Best or County, Fullers London Pride, draught Bass; local Kington Bitter, Woods, Black Sheep and Timothy Taylors Landlord as guests, New World wines and a considerable range of malt whiskies. Tables outside with views of the church; the separate bell tower, with arrow slits, was used as a refuge during the Welsh border wars.

OPEN: 11–3. 6–11 (6.30–11 winter).
Real Ale. Restaurant (not Sun evenings).
Children in eating area until 9pm. No dogs. Wheelchair access (not WC).
Car park. Bedrooms.
Cards: Amex, Delta, MasterCard, Switch, Visa.

TITLEY

Stagg Inn
Tel: 01544 230221
Titley, Herefordshire HR5 3RL
Free House. Steve Reynolds & Nicola Holland, licensees.

This is not only the local pub but also a local pub serving fantastic food in appealing surroundings. If you haven't found it yet, now is your chance. There is always a welcome if you just drop in for a pint of their well-kept ale, but the food's the thing: organic meat and dairy produce, fish from Cornwall, fruit and vegetables from local growers, cheese from small producers, elderflowers and sloes from the hedgerows and anything else local and edible able to find its way into the kitchen. You may not be able to afford Le Gavroche, but this is the next best thing – Steve Reynolds trained with the Roux brothers. There is a choice of ten local cheeses for the ploughman's, locally smoked free-range chicken and ham hock salad from the bar menu, or fillet of organic salmon with Swiss chard and lemon beurre blanc, rack of local lamb with olive mashed potato and thyme sauce, Herefordshire rump steak with pepper sauce, fish and specials on the blackboard and some desirable puddings. Hobsons Best and Town Crier beers plus various guests, list of over 60, mainly French and eight house wines.

OPEN: Tue–Sat 12–3. 6.30–11 (12–3. 7–10.30 Sun).
Closed Mondays, first two weeks November and Christmas Day.
Real Ale. Restaurant.
Children welcome. Dogs in bar. Wheelchair access bar only (not WC). Car park.
Two en-suite bedrooms.
Cards: Delta, MasterCard, Switch, Visa.

TRUMPET

The Verzons
Tel: 01531 670531
Hereford Road, Trumpet, Nr Ledbury, Herefordshire HR8 2PZ
Free House. David Roberts, licensee.

Two miles from Ledbury, this was originally a country house of some importance. Big, and built of brick in 1790, this is a Georgian building of note, difficult to miss. The Hop Bar, which reflects its rural attachment – hops, farming implements, Hereford cattle, apple orchards, is where the locals and everyone else meet for a drink and something from the bar menu. On the blackboard there could be a selection of continental salamis and meats with a spicy tomato relish, sauté chicken with Italian-style vegetables, chorizo and garlic-sausage risotto, fillet of cod and sesame ginger prawns with cucumber and wasabi nori rolls and lemongrass sauce, as well as soup, filled rolls, sandwiches, wraps and more-ish puddings. There is also a more formal restaurant. Beers are Hook Norton, Bass and Wye Valley; the wine list is all embracing. From the Garden Room restaurant you have views of the Malvern Hills.

> OPEN: 11–11 (12–3. 7–10.30 Sun)
> Real Ale.
> Children welcome. Dogs by arrangement. Wheelchair access. Car park.
> Eight en-suite bedrooms.

ULLINGSWICK

Three Crowns Inn   Tel: 01432 820279
Ullingswick, Herefordshire HR1 3JQ
Free House. Derrick & Sue Horwood & Brent Castle, licensees.

Not far from the village – well, about a mile – is this simple brick and timber building, 300 years old and one of the county's few remaining original public houses. No nasty modern gimmicks to shatter the quiet, just the happy hum of a pub doing everything as it should be done and better than most – an ideal combination of good pub and good restaurant. All the vegetables are organic, either from local growers or out of the pub garden, fish from Cornwall, and other supplies as local as they can be. Brent Castle, who is also a partner in the pub, is the busy chap in the kitchen creating all the delights. For a starter you could have: fish soup with rouille and croutons or carpaccio of Marches beef with chicory tart and black truffle oil. For a main course: roast rack of Marches lamb with garden vegetables and Madeira sauce or breast of duck with Victoria-plum sauce, golden chard and wild rice; and maybe plum tart with clove ice-cream to follow. Always some additions to the lunchtime menu, vegetarian dishes too, interesting cheeses and more delicious puds. Hobsons Best ale and one or two guests. Short wine list, mainly New World, house wines by the glass, two ciders and a choice of malts and brandies.

> Food served: 12–2. 7–9 (12–2. 7–9.30 Sun). Closed Tues.
> Real Ale. Set lunch menu not available on Sunday.
> Children – yes, but no special room. No dogs. Wheelchair access with help. Car park.
> Cards: Delta, Electron, JCB, MasterCard, Maestro, Solo, Switch, Visa.

WENLOCK EDGE

Wenlock Edge Inn   Tel: 01746 785678
Hilltop, Wenlock Edge, Shropshire TF13 6DJ
Free House. Stephen Waring, licensee.

The inn – two converted cottages – was first licensed in 1925. When you realise that the cottages were built in the 18th century on the top of a 400-million-year-old coral reef, you have to think they are positively youthful. Run by the Waring family, the inn has a reputation for creating a very friendly, welcoming atmosphere and for serving English cooking at its best. All the dishes are listed on the blackboard, and there could be freshly made soups, celeriac and tomato or celery, apple and lovage, marinated Orkney herrings, spicy prawns, smoked salmon with herbed cheese; popular pies include venison, rich beef and vegetable, farmhouse chicken and savoury flans. Also salmon baked with peppers, prawn and salmon gratin, a chicken and duck dish, excellent cuts of organically raised beef, ham served with interesting sauces, at least one roast is served at weekends and there are some imaginative vegetarian dishes. Children's menu too. More-ish puds. Two locally brewed ales, Hobsons Best and Town Crier, plus one guest. Selection of malt whiskies and wines by the glass. On the second Monday of the month there are storytelling evenings when a local group swops stories from 'the Edge'. Ask about Ippikin, a thief who lived in a cave opposite the pub.

OPEN: 11.30–2.30. 6–11 (6.30–11 winter). Closed Mon lunchtimes.
Real Ale. Restaurant. No meals Mon except Bank Hols.
Children in restaurant (not under ten after 8pm). Dogs on leads in bar. Car park.
Bedrooms. There is a Festival of the Edge every July.
Cards: Amex, Delta, MasterCard, Switch, Visa.

WEOBLEY

The Salutation Inn   Tel: 01544 318443
Market Pitch, Weobley, Herefordshire HR4 8SJ
Free House. Chris & Frances Anthony, licensees

Black and white and handsome; visually, it epitomises one of the best examples of an age-old country inn, although, without losing its timelessness, it is firmly in the 21st century. With a growing reputation for serving some imaginative food, the pub doesn't forget that it is still the village local where you can meet for just a drink and a chat. You have the choice of an informal bar menu or something from the elegant Oak Room Restaurant. From the bar menu you could choose a wild-mushroom and spinach tartlet, grilled goat's cheese, supreme of pheasant with red wine, onions, mushrooms and herbs, tagliatelle and smoked bacon in a spicy tomato sauce, lamb's liver casserole, or fillet of coley served with prawns and lemon and parsley butter. If you just want a quick snack, they have ploughman's, hot filled baguettes and a variety of salads. Seasonal specials, vegetarian dishes and interesting puds to finish. An à la carte menu is available in the no-smoking restaurant and a very popular three-course lunch on Sundays. Wye Valley Butty Bach, Hook Norton Best, Westons cider and a guest ale. Over 120 different wines and 20 malt whiskies. Seats on the terrace at the back of the pub.

OPEN: 11–11.
Real Ale. Restaurant.
Children in eating areas. No dogs. Wheelchair access to eating area only.
N.B. Jukebox in public bar only.

WHITNEY-ON-WYE

The Rydspence Inn   Tel: 01497 831262
Whitney-on-Wye, Herefordshire HR3 6EU (1½ miles west of village on A438)
Free House. Peter & Pamela Glover, licensees.

You really couldn't get much nearer the Welsh border, as the stream in the garden marks the boundary between England and Wales. Until the coming of the railways, the handsome Rydspence was an assembly point for drovers en route to the English market towns, even as far as London. The 140 acres surrounding the inn were divided up into penny, ha'penny and farthing fields, so if you didn't have many animals for overnight grazing, a farthing field would do. Overlooking the Wye valley and Black Mountains, this is a comfortable, charming inn. Two bars, one with a big log fire, are in the heavily beamed, 16th-century part of the building; both serve bar meals lunchtime and evenings. There is also a very attractive restaurant. From the bar menu you could choose from ploughman's platters with crusty bread, tortilla pancakes filled with vegetable chilli, fresh pasta with smoked chicken and courgettes in a white-wine sauce, beef lasagne, Heal's Farm organic Devon sausages, steak and kidney pie, grills, vegetarian dishes – all this and more – everything freshly prepared. Good selection of home-made ice-creams and sorbets. Robinsons Best Bitter, draught Bass and Brains SA. Interesting wine list. Local cider. Seats on the sunny terrace and in the large garden.

> OPEN: 11–2.30. 7–11.
> Real Ale. Restaurant.
> Children welcome. No dogs. Wheelchair access (not WC). Bedrooms. Car park.
> Cards: Amex, MasterCard, Switch, Visa.

WOOLHOPE

Butchers Arms   Tel: 01432 860281
Woolhope, Herefordshire HR1 4RF
Free House. Mrs S. Vallely, licensee.

Just outside the village, with the glorious countryside for company, the black and white, half-timbered, 14th-century Butchers Arms has two low (very) beamed bars with log fires in winter and windows opening onto a flowery terrace in the summer. Lots of traditional pub favourites on the menu: sandwiches, ploughman's, salads, lasagne, chillis, steaks, also Woolhope pie, made with wild rabbit, bacon and cooked in cider. There is a vegetarian dish or two and some home-made puds. The menu is constantly changing. The separate restaurant is only open on Saturday evenings. Hook Norton Best, Old Hooky and guest beers. Short wine list, a few by the glass. A stream borders the garden and there are very good walks nearby.

> OPEN: 11.30–3. 6.30–11.
> Real Ale. Restaurant.
> Children welcome. Guide dogs only. Wheelchair access (not WC). Two bedrooms.
> Cards: All major cards except Amex.

WOORE

The Falcon   Tel: 01630 647230
London Road, Woore, Nr Crewe, CW3 9SF (really in north Shropshire)
Marstons. Ian Swan, tenant.

An old coaching inn with a fascinating sporting history and a bookie's office in the car park – there are not many of these! Not surprising really, as this inn was licensed to keep 12 horses during the day, six at night, so they are just keeping in touch with their equine past. A really sporty place, this. Until recently, the Falcon had its own cricket field, and during the 19th century prize fights used to take place in the field at the back, the organisers often bringing fighters over from America. One such fight started in Newcastle-under-Lyme, was stopped by magistrates, only to be restarted at the Falcon, 10 miles away, watched by 7000 spectators. The beer sales must have shot up. Now the only argument will be over who has what from the menu. Specialising in fish, the landlord is never certain what will be available from the Manchester fish market, but there will be about 25 different dishes, anything from haddock in batter to lobster thermidor. Famous for his food, fish in particular, in past years he has been voted 'Pub Chef of the Year', so you know he can cook! Marstons Bitter and Pedigree are the regular ales, and every two weeks there is a Head Brewer's choice as a guest. Nearly 50 different whiskies, and wine to go with the fish. Seats in the garden.

OPEN: 11.30–3. 5–11 (11–11 Sat. 11–10.30 Sun).
Real Ale. Restaurant.
Children – but not young children and not in the evening. No dogs.

BEST OF THE REST

DORSTONE Nr Hay-on-Wye, Herefordshire
The Pandy   Tel: 01981 550273
In the outstandingly beautiful Golden Valley where the River Dore meanders between the villages of Dorstone and Pontrilas, parts of the Pandy are thought to date back to the 12th century; others say 15th. Stout beams everywhere and a big welcoming fire in a fireplace built to accommodate half a tree. Substantial bar food: soups, sandwiches, filled pancakes, steak and kidney pie and steaks from a local supplier. Bass, Wye Valley HPA and lots of malt whiskies.

RUCKHALL, Herefordshire
Ancient Camp Inn   Tel: 01981 250449
Off the A465 west of Hereford, and built on the site of a very ancient camp – an iron age fortress. They knew a thing or two then; glorious, fertile country and ample fresh water full of fish. The inn owns a stretch of that fish-filled water. They serve really competent food: local lamb, crab and spinach ravioli, home-cured gravadlax – that sort of thing. Interesting puddings, fine wines, and last but not least, Hook Norton Best and one or two guest beers – some local.

SELLACK, Herefordshire
Lough Pool   Tel: 01989 730236
Towards Ross-on-Wye, the pub is black and white with colourful hanging baskets in summer. Inside: beams, flagstone floors – just as it should be. Better-than-average bar menu with some interesting dishes and daily specials. Local farm ciders; Bass, Wye Valley and John Smiths ales and a decent wine list.

WINFORTON, Herefordshire

Sun Inn
Tel: 01544 327677

A quiet village in unspoilt Welsh border country. The Sun is very old, with a rustic interior – stone walls and beams; the cooking, however, is very up to date. Their award-winning ploughman's comes with home-made pickles, chutneys and a choice of local cheeses. Other dishes could be fennel, leek and parsnip soup, caramelised-onion tart with chilli and balsamic dressing, roast Welsh Marsh March lamb with hedgerow jus, or rib-eye of local beef with a Stilton sauce. Daily specials and delicious puds. Flowers, Hook Norton, Jennings and Felinfoel Double Dragon beers, ciders and a sizeable wine list.

CLEOBURY MORTIMER, Shropshire

Kings Arms
Tel: 01299 270252

On the Ludlow to Bewdley road. Beamed and ancient inside, formally Georgian outside. They feed you well: warm bacon and avocado salad, chicken breasts with leeks and Stilton, daily specials – all well above average – to go with the Hobsons Best.

CRESSAGE, Shropshire

Cholmondeley Riverside
Tel: 01952 510900

As the name suggests, you are alongside the River Wye. A 17th-century coaching inn, all beams, flagstone floors and open fires. The varied menu ranges from home-made soup to home-cured gravadlax, cassoulet and fillet steak in a cream and brandy sauce. Marstons Best, a couple of weekly guests and a good wine list.

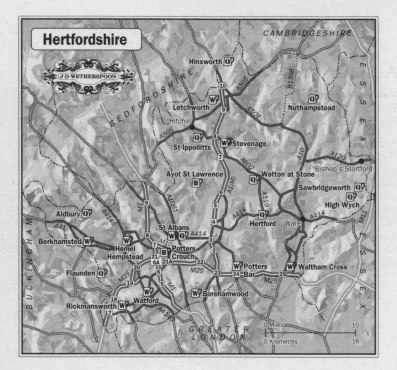

Hertfordshire

ALDBURY

Valiant Trooper   Tel: 01442 851203
Trooper Road, Aldbury, Nr Tring, Herts HP23 5RW
Free House. Tim O'Gorman, licensee.

A delightful village with a village green and stocks, which were last used to clamp a drunken villager in 1835. Close to the Ridgeway Path, so it's handy for serious walkers. It's also near the National Trust's Ashridge Estate – 6 square miles of glorious countryside. The Valiant Trooper is ready to serve a good pint and something from either the short bar menu or the blackboard specials, which could include roast sea bass with garlic prawns, chicken stir fry, kidneys turbigo, venison and wild-boar sausages and fresh fish – always three or four choices on the board; all home-cooked using fresh ingredients – no chips. Always a number of vegetarian options. Morrells Oxford Blue, Fullers London Pride and Becks plus three weekly changing guest beers. Strongbow and Scrumpy Jack ciders. Charming cottagey garden to sit in.

> OPEN: 11–11 (12–10.30 Sun).
> Real Ale.
> Restaurant (not Sun eve); no meals or snacks Sun or Mon eves.
> Children in one room lunchtimes. Dogs on leads.
> Cards: all except Amex and Diners.

ALDBURY

Greyhound   Tel: 01442 851228
19 Stocks Road, Aldbury, Nr Tring, Herts HP23 5RT
Free House. Martin Roberts, licensee.

Tucked under the Chiltern Hills, this creeper-covered pub is another TV star. *Inspector Morse* and *Pie in the Sky* have both been here and so should you. There are ducks in the duck pond for you to admire and the stocks and village whipping post to remind you of the times when you took the law into your own hands and a quieter life was had by all. Surrounded by some wonderful walking country; for the truly energetic, forget the 172 steps to the Bridgewater monument – try instead the Ivinghoe Beacon, 756 feet up, a well-known viewpoint. Created by the Elizabethans, these beacons were signalling posts: pans filled with pitch and set alight. Back on earth, the Greyhound serves a good selection of food from blackboard menus ranging from soup, ploughman's, filled baked potatoes and sandwiches to fillet steak and grilled salmon. Aldbury Ale and changing guests. Walkers are allowed in, but don't bring the mud with you.

>OPEN: 6am–11.30pm (8am–11.30pm Sun) – well, they do have bedrooms, 11 of them.
>Real Ale. Restaurant.
>Children welcome, as are well-behaved dogs.

FLAUNDEN

Bricklayers Arms   Tel: 01442 833322
Hogpits Bottom, Flaunden, Herts HP3 0PH
Free House. Peter Frazer, licensee.

Low beams and big fires; a tremendously popular, appealing place, filled to overflowing at weekends. Generous bar food is served at lunchtime and ranges from soups and filled baked potatoes, ploughman's and sandwiches to different fillings for the Yorkshire puddings, beef and ale pie and a selection of home-made pies. The bar specials change daily and the à la carte menu in the dining room is changed weekly. Marstons Pedigree, Fullers London Pride, Ringwood Old Thumper and five guest beers. Good selection of wines. Seats in the lovely cottagey garden. Good walks nearby.

>OPEN: 11–2.30 (11–3 Sat). 6–11.
>Real Ale. Restaurant.
>Children in restaurant. Dogs on leads. Wheelchair access (not WC).
>Cards: all major credit cards.

HERTFORD

White Horse   Tel: 01992 501950
33 Castle Street, Hertford SG14 1HH
Free House. Nigel Crofts, licensee.

In what is a fairly unspoilt county town, the very old – 14th-century in parts – beamed and timbered White Horse is just a small old-fashioned local that serves a wide variety of real ales from the smaller breweries and range of country fruit wines. Opposite the castle grounds, this traditional pub – no frills here – serves straightforward pub food every lunchtime: venison and pheasant casserole, seafood pie or their very own cheesey hammy eggy. Very busy at weekends. Upstairs they have a no-smoking area where supervised children are allowed; there's somewhere to sit outside too.

>OPEN: 12–2.30. 5.30–11 (12–11 Sat. 12–10.30 Sun).
>Real Ale. Food served 12–2 daily.
>Children welcome upstairs. Dogs on leads. Wheelchair access (not WC).
>Cards: all major credit cards.

HIGH WYCH

Rising Sun   Tel: 01279 724099
High Wych, Nr Sawbridgeworth, Herts CM21 0HZ
Free House. Stephen Prior, licensee.

The Rising Sun is one of those pubs that belongs to several different periods; bits have been added over the years, resulting in a classic layout of small public bar, saloon bar and tap room (without carpet). A friendly local pub with friendly locals which has been run by the Prior family since 1929. No food – a crisp and nut place, this – just beers. Well-kept Courage Best and a guest beer from one of the smaller breweries. Relax in the quiet garden at the back of the pub.

> OPEN: 12–2.30 (12–3 Fri & Sat). 5–11.
> Real Ale.
> Children welcome in tap room. Dogs on leads.

HINXWORTH

Three Horseshoes   Tel: 01462 742280
High Street, Hinxworth, Herts SG7 5HQ
Greene King. Paul Ockleford, tenant and licensee.

They have a reputation at this pub for serving some interesting food. A lot of the emphasis is on fish. Menus are decided on the fin so to speak; the choice of fresh fish offered by his wholesaler will inspire the landlord to create some inventive fish dishes. His expertise is acknowledged by an award from the Seafood Industry Authority. You'll also find traditional bar snacks in this fine old place, as well as daily specials, all using as much local produce as they can and game in season. Greene King range of ales and Guinness. Good selection of wine. Big garden to sit in and to lose the little darlings in.

> OPEN: 11.30–2.30. 5.30–11 (12–2.30. 7–10.30 Sun).
> Real Ale.
> Children welcome. Dogs on leads. Wheelchair access to WC.

NUTHAMPSTEAD

The Woodman   Tel: 01763 848328
Nuthampstead, Nr Royston, Herts SG8 8NB
Free House. Ian & Sandra Johnson, licensees.

If you are interested in the history of the Second World War, then you would be fascinated by the memorial outside the Woodman: it commemorates members of the United States Air Force who lost their lives in the last war. The 398 Bomb Group flew Flying Fortresses out of Nuthampstead airfield and the Association regularly returns for a reunion. This pub, externally much altered, is basically a 16th-century building; thatched and weatherboarded outside, beams and an inglenook fireplace inside. The bar-snack menu includes basket meals, local ham and sausages and daily specials on the blackboard. An à la carte menu features in the restaurant – mainly grills, steaks, salmon and chicken – very traditional fare. Wednesday is fresh-fish night. Ales vary, usually four cask-conditioned ales are available. It is a favourite place for those pursuing country sports or just having an energetic walk.

> OPEN: 11–3. 5.30–11 (11–11 Sat. 12–4. 7–10.30 Sun).
> Real Ale. Restaurant.
> Children welcome. No dogs. Wheelchair access. Bedrooms.
> Cards: Access, Amex, MasterCard, Switch, Visa.

St Albans

Rose & Crown   Tel: 01727 851903
10 St Michael Street, St Albans, Herts AL3 4SG
Greenalls. Neil Dekker, tenant.

This is an area that has seen constant development and change for over 2000 years. An important part of the history of the town, the 300-year-old Rose and Crown was built in the shadow of the 9th-century abbey. Bringing you right up to date, the landlord specialises in American-style sandwiches with names such as Clark Gable, Lucille Ball, Johnny Appleseed and others, including many-layered double 'Dekker' sandwiches – try these and you know you have had a sandwich. 'Serf's' sandwiches available too (roast beef, pâté, ham or cheese) plus hot pub dishes such as moussaka, lasagne, broccoli and creamy cheese, tuna with pasta or chilli con carne. They have a lunchtime no-smoking area. Adnams, Tetleys, Courage, Directors and guest beers, ciders and choice of malt whiskies. Plenty of tables outside in the garden among the flowers. The car park is built over the gates of the old Roman town.

> OPEN: 11.30–3. 5.30–11 (6–11 Sat).
> Real Ale. Food Mon–Sat lunchtimes only. No food Sunday.
> Children in eating area. Dogs on leads. Wheelchair access.
> Live music Thurs and Mon eves.
> Cards: MasterCard, Switch, Visa.

St Albans

Lower Red Lion   Tel: 01727 855669
34–36 Fishpool Street, St Albans, Herts
Free House. David Worcester, licensee.

Some of the town's inns are 15th-century, some have medieval foundations, and in one the King of France was held after the battle of Poitiers in 1356, so you will see that the Lower Red Lion is somewhat youthful – a 17th-century coaching inn, still able to offer you a bed for the night, decent home-cooked food at lunchtime and a choice of ale. JHB from the Oakham brewery and Fullers London Pride are the regular beers, plus ever-changing guest beers from microbreweries. Delightful, good-size garden for you to sit in.

> OPEN: 12–2.30 (12–3 Sat). 5.30–11.
> Real Ale. Lunchtime food only.
> No children under 14 years old. Dogs on leads but preferably in the evening when no food is served. Car park. Bedrooms.
> Cards: MasterCard, Switch, Visa.

St Ippollitts

Greyhound   Tel: 01462 440989
London Road, St Ippollitts, Herts SG4 7NL
Free House. Roy Pearce, MBII, owner/licensee.

During the Middle Ages, if your horse wasn't feeling too good, you would bring him into the mainly 14th-century church in the hope that the patron saint St Hippolytus – a Roman martyr and horse doctor – would cure him. It was St Hippolytus who gave his name to this small village. Unconnected with horses, the Greyhound does have an unusual facility – for a pub – and this one is really different: if you happen to be staying here you can park your car and get free transfer to Luton Airport, about ten minutes away. Set in attractive countryside, it has one comfortable beamed bar with two fires and a small dining room. They serve an extensive range of food including sandwiches, bar snacks, vegetarian dishes and daily specials. They will even cook something especially for you – give them a bit of notice though! Very popular Sunday lunches too. Adnams and Greene King IPA are the beers, plus two guests. Picnic tables at the front of the pub and a beer garden at the side. You are in good walking country.

> OPEN: 11.30–2.30. 5–11.
> Real Ale.
> Children welcome. No dogs. Wheelchair access with assistance. En-suite bedrooms. Car park.

Sawbridgeworth

King William IV   Tel: 01279 722322
Vantorts Road, Sawbridgeworth, Herts
Courage. Derek Tunmore, FBII, tenant.

Voted 'Friendly Pub of the Year', so you know you have an affable host and clientele. All the food is locally supplied, freshly cooked and good value. The special 'Willie's Sausages' are made by the local butcher 100 yards or so from the pub. No jukebox, just a TV in the snug, off the main saloon, which is normally only switched on for major sporting events.

Well-kept Courage beers, Guinness and a guest. No garden, but there are seats outside the front of the pub where you can watch the world go by.

OPEN: 11–11.
Real Ale. No food Sunday.
Children welcome. Dogs on leads.
Occasional live music.

WATTON AT STONE

George & Dragon   Tel: 01920 830285
High Street, Watton at Stone, Herts SG14 3TA
Greene King. Peter & Jessica Tatlow, lease.

If you want a relaxed, civilised pub, complete with daily newspapers, proper napkins, interesting pieces of furniture and a reputation for good, imaginative food, then this is where you want to be. Pink-washed and on the main road – 16th-century, tall and proud, you can't really miss the George and Dragon, nor should you. From the menu there could be a tomato, basil and prawn salad with olive-oil dressing, chef's pâté, puff-pastry tart filled with a mix of mushrooms in cream and garlic sauce, diced chicken breast cooked in white wine with cream and chopped leeks, poached fresh salmon fillet in a white-wine and sorrel sauce, roast duck breast in a cognac and plum sauce, or an Aberdeen sirloin steak. Light snacks and home-made puddings too. The blackboard specials could be fresh fish, seasonal game or whatever inspires the chef. Very popular with everyone from near and far. Greene King ales, wide choice of wines and choice of malt whiskies. Some tables in the restaurant are non-smoking.

OPEN: 11–2.30. 6–11 (11–11 Sat).
Real Ale. Restaurant.
Children in family room and restaurant. No dogs. Wheelchair access difficult but just possible with help.
Car park. Occasional live entertainment.

BEST OF THE REST

AYOT ST LAWRENCE

Brocket Arms   Tel: 01438 820250
Among the timbered village cottages, the 14th-century Brocket Arms appears largely unaltered. The interior is well beamed, with good fires and rustic furniture. A popular bar menu includes soup, sandwiches, home-made curries, game pie and specials on the blackboard. Adnams Broadside, Greene King IPA and Fullers London Pride, plus a guest ale; short wine list. A suntrap of a garden has a children's play area. There is also a house ghost – a monk.

POTTERS CROUCH

Holly Bush
Tel: 01727 851792

A short distance outside St Albans, white-painted and creeper-covered, this is a classy little place, all primped and polished. Traditional bar food at lunchtime only. A Fullers pub, so Fullers range of ales. A big, attractive garden to sit in.

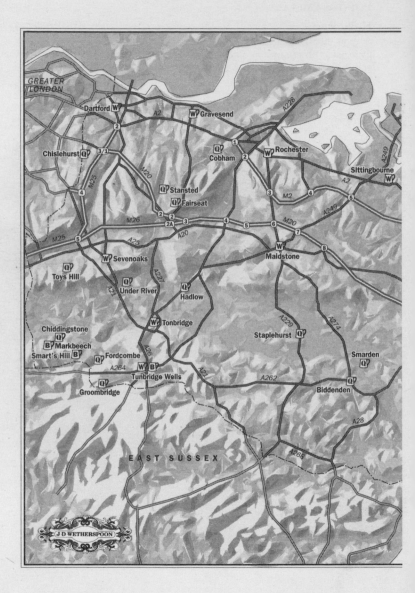

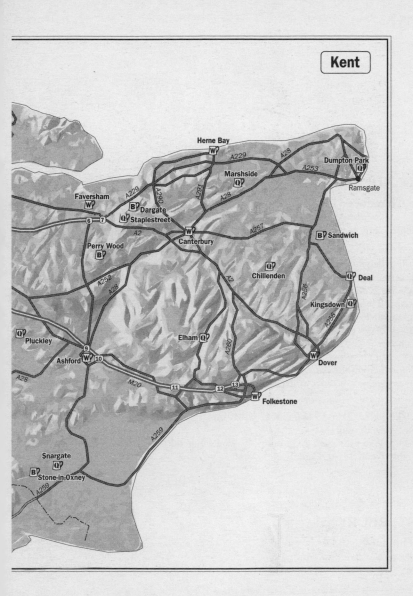

Kent

Kent

BIDDENDEN

Three Chimneys
Tel: 01580 291472

Biddenden, Nr Ashford, Kent TN27 8HA (1 mile west of village on A262)
Free House. Craig & Jackie Smith, licensees.

Since our last edition there has been a change of ownership – not that we could see the join. Still as delightful and as popular as ever, and the food is just as good. This is a gem of a place; black and white, 15th-century, rambling, with low-beamed bars and huge log fires. Leaving Biddenden, it is easy to drive past as it is slightly below road level, on the right at a road junction a mile and a half west of the village. Good, imaginative food on offer: home-made soups, crab cakes with varied dressings, pan-fried chicken breast with roasted vegetables and leek and ham mornay are just a few examples. The blackboard menus change every day; puddings change daily too. There is a restaurant and tables in the pretty garden, which is filled with shrubs, roses and nut trees. The range of ales, tapped from behind the bar, could include Shepherd Neame, Flowers Original, a strong local cider, local wines and a varied wine list; mostly French. Wines by the glass and half-bottle.

> OPEN: 11–2.30. 6–11 (12–2.30. 7–10.30 Sun).
> Real Ale. Restaurant.
> Children in restaurant. Dogs on leads. Wheelchair access (not WC). Car park.
> Cards: Delta, MasterCard, Switch, Visa.

CANTERBURY

The Thomas Ingoldsby
Tel: 01227 463339

5–9 Burgate, Canterbury, Kent
Wetherspoon.

There has been a settlement in Canterbury since 300 BC; largely medieval until 1940, when one-third of the city was destroyed by German bombers. Canterbury's loss was the archaeologists gain, as they were able to trace the occupation of Canterbury from the Stone Age, through Roman to medieval times. The miracle is that the cathedral survived the destruction. Wetherspoon's Thomas Ingoldsby, close to the cathedral, is in the rebuilt area. A big, airy place; very like a French brasserie. Lots of satisfying food on the menu and daily specials board. You're really spoilt for choice if you want a beer – they have about eight on the go – or you could have a glass of scrumpy or the house wine. Wetherspoon establishments are never cosy and intimate but they are friendly places; this one has a particularly nice atmosphere.

> OPEN: 11–11.
> Real Ale. Always a no-smoking area.
> No children. No dogs. Disabled facilities.

CHIDDINGSTONE

Castle   Tel: 01892 870247
Chiddingstone, Nr Edenbridge, Kent TN8 7AH
Free House. Nigel Lucas, licensee.

Originally a private house built circa 1420, this property was then known as Waterslip House. Bought early in the 18th century by Thomas Weller, who took out a licence in 1730, it was then renamed the Castle Inn. In a row of spectacular timbered houses opposite the church, this is considered to be one of the finest village streets in Kent, a significant part of the unspoilt Tudor village bought from the Streatfield family by the National Trust in 1939 for £25,000. The Castle's heavily beamed saloon and public bar can get very crowded in summer, so arrive early to be sure of room to eat. Two highly regarded chefs have joined the Castle team, so you know the food will be first class. An extensive 'Fireside Menu' is available in the saloon bar: home-made soup, a Caesar salad with strips of Cajun chicken, timbale of smoked mackerel, supreme of chicken on a nest of mustard-and-coriander-scented carrots, or pan-fried cod on spinach drizzled with a seafood and tomato dressing. Pub stalwarts too on the lunchtime bar menu: local pork sausages, a daily pasta (read the blackboard), lots of different salads, a very hot chilli con carne, filled jacket potatoes, sandwiches, ploughman's, and of course daily specials. Some very interesting Spanish and French ice-creams to follow, plus good old Walls and other home-made puddings. More elaborate two- or three-course meals available in the restaurant, also an à la carte menu. Tea too. No cucumber sandwiches, but you'll find something desirable on the menu and the choice of teas ranges from rosehip to Darjeeling. The ales are Larkins Traditional (Porter in winter), Harveys Best and usually Youngs Ordinary as the guest ale. There is an extensive wine list featuring wines from all over the world. Outside is a very pretty vine-hung courtyard, with tables and its own bar, beyond that a lovely garden. Not far from Hever Castle, Anne Boleyn's home.

> OPEN: All week for coffee and soft drinks at 10.30am, otherwise 11–11. On Sundays, from 11am for coffee, otherwise 12–10.30.
> Real Ale. Restaurant; not open Tues lunchtimes.
> Children welcome. Dogs on leads.
> Cards: Amex, Diners, Electron, MasterCard, Solo, Switch, Visa.

CHILLENDEN

Griffins Head   Tel: 01304 840325

Chillenden, Nr Canterbury, Kent CT3 1PS (off Eastry to Nonington Road)
Shepherd Neame. Mark J. Copestake, tenant.

In a tiny hamlet off the main road consisting of about 20 houses, a farm and the pub, the Griffins Head is an old Wealden hall house dating back to 1286. It is just how you imagine a country pub to be; heavily beamed, rambling and with two big inglenook fireplaces. The rooms are decorated with old photographs and a collection of oil-pressure lamps and heaters; a formidable number of unusual beer bottles and artifacts relating to the brewing trade are displayed in a side room, between the bar and dining room. Only one bar serving three different areas and a dining room. Food is the usual pub fare: very variable, but the weekend summer barbecues are good; otherwise there could be home-made soup, chicken-liver pâté, beef stew, minute steak, grilled sea bass or seasonal game on offer. You also have a choice of champagnes and a list of bin ends on a blackboard. Shepherd Neame ales: Spitfire, Master Brew, Best Bitter and Bishops Finger. Lots of picnic tables in the large garden; a barbecue in the middle of the car park is lit at weekends during the summer. On the first Sunday of every month the local vintage-car enthusiasts meet and admire each others' vehicles. The Griffin has its own cricket pitch, cricket eleven, and keen followers.

> OPEN: 11–11.
> Real Ale. No food Sunday eves.
> No children. Dogs on leads. Car park. Annual jazz festival.
> Cards: Amex, Delta, MasterCard, Switch, Visa.

CHISLEHURST

Ramblers Rest   Tel: 020 8467 1734

Mill Place, Chislehurst, Kent BR7 5ND
Scottish & Newcastle. Peter Grierson, tenant.

Chislehurst, east of Bromley, is built around a large wooded common, home to the Chislehurst cricket ground and golf club. The clubhouse, Camden Place, built on the site of a 17th-century house, was home to the French Imperial family, Napoleon II and Empress Eugenie. On more down-to-earth matters: the pub isn't far away. You have to keep your eyes peeled, as you could easily miss the turning; access to the pub is along a driveway off the Chislehurst to Bromley road (A222). The Ramblers Rest is just what you would expect of a 17th-century Kent building – painted clapboard under a Kent peg-tiled roof. Outside is bedecked with flowers during the summer, inside is a wealth of beams and a warm welcome. Familiar, well-tried bar food served at lunchtime only: steak and kidney pie, spaghetti bolognese, chilli, fisherman's pie, toasties, sandwiches, salads and ploughman's. Courage ales plus guest beers. Seats in the secluded garden.

> OPEN: 11–3. 5.30–11 (11–11 Sat. 12–10.30 Sun).
> Real Ale. Bar menu. No food evenings or Sunday.
> Children in eating area. Dogs on leads.

COBHAM

Darnley Arms
Tel: 01474 814218

The Street, Cobham, Kent DA12 3BZ
Free House. Trudie Mockrie, licensee.

South-east of Gravesend, Cobham village stands at the gates of Cobham Hall, once the residence of the Earls of Darnley – hence the name of the pub – and the home of the Hon. Ivo Bligh, the 19th-century cricket captain of Cobham, Kent and England. Everyone who was anyone, including W.G. Grace, played cricket at Cobham Hall. Not only sporting but literary connections too, as one of the other historic inns in Cobham featured in Charles Dickens' *Pickwick Papers* – but it wasn't the Darnley Arms, though the pub, among others, is known as a 'notable building'. Quite youthful – this building only dates back to the 18th century – but there has been an inn on this site for over 600 years and rumour has it that there is a tunnel connecting the pub to the nearby church. Good range of bar food: sandwiches, ploughman's, home-made pies, egg mayonnaise, tiger prawns, various fish dishes, grills and daily specials. Steamed pudding or ice-cream for afters. Courage ales on hand pump and a selection of wines and liqueurs.

OPEN: 11–3. 6–11. N.B. Closed Sun eves.
Real Ale.
Children: if well behaved. No dogs.

DEAL

The Three Compasses
Tel: 01304 374661

129 Beach Street, Deal, Kent CT14 6JS
Free House. K. & F. Mayr, owners/licensees.

The shingle beach saved Deal from being developed into a seaside resort by the Victorians, so the majority of the town is still as it was – mainly 18th century. Beach Street is just that; next stop the sea wall, the pebble beach and the Channel. What was originally just a corner pub on the seafront is now a 'continental pub/restaurant' but with very limited opening hours. A small, well-run, beautifully kept, smart restaurant with a drinking area. If you only want a drink you are very welcome, but there is only one beer: Ruddles County, plus Murphys Stout on hand pump – lagers too. But if you're here in the evening, you will want to eat – the smell of cooking is so tempting. Home-made pâté and toast to start, or some smoked salmon, different salads, oven-baked Kentish lamb in Madeira sauce, grilled fillet of turbot, fillet steak in a creamed brandy and pepper sauce or game in season – all served with potatoes and fresh vegetables. There is a very good wine list and excellent coffee. Bracing walks along the seafront or along the pier only a few hundred yards away.

OPEN: 7–10.30 Wed–Sat. 12–3 Sunday. Closed Mon, Tues and during November.
Food only served in the evenings.
No children. No dogs.

DOVER

The Eight Bells
Tel: 01304 205030

19 Cannon Street, Dover, Kent
Wetherspoon.

A port since Roman times and an increasingly important route to the continent, Dover has had a long and eventful history. Lots of good things are happening here now and there are many things to see; the town is making a great effort. Wetherspoon took over a redundant bingo hall in Cannon Street and transformed it into the Eight Bells. Only five minutes' walk from Dover Castle, Dover Museum, the medieval boat (now on view) and the Roman Painted House, the Eight Bells is surrounded by Dover's past and future. Always reliable food in these establishments, always a reasonably priced beer and usually about nine guest ales.

> OPEN: 11–11.
> Real Ale. No-smoking area.
> No children. No dogs. Wheelchair facilities.

DUMPTON PARK

The Brown Jug
Tel: 01843 862788

204 Ramsgate Road, Dumpton Park, Broadstairs, Kent CT10 2EW
Thorley Taverns. Jennifer Skudder, tenant.

On a corner site towards Broadstairs and Dumpton Park is this small, early-18th-century flint pub with a giant brown jug above the door. An utterly charming, timeless place with some interesting original fittings. Two small rooms at the front, and in one, which could probably accommodate about ten people standing, is a very handsome carved settle. The other, larger room has some 18th-century fitted cupboards either side of the fireplace. A teeny bar but quite a lot of space in the back room, which has a fine collection of jugs and leads into the exuberant garden and *pétanque* pitch. They really are keen players, all playing in a local team. No food, just something to drink. Greene King cask ales, Whitbread Mild, Guinness and a good number of malt whiskies – these are greatly appreciated, particularly by the Scottish customs men.

> OPEN: Fluid opening hours. 11.30–3. 6–11 (Sat & Sun 11–11).
> If busy during the week, they stay open all day.
> No food.
> No children – no licence. Dogs on leads. Car park. Toilets outside.

ELHAM

The Kings Arms
Tel: 01303 840242

The Square, Elham, Nr Canterbury, Kent CT4 6TJ
Whitbread. Edward Walsh, licensee.

In a valley of chalk hills, this very attractive village – a market town in the 13th century – has some interesting buildings. The Kings Arms, the church, Georgian and earlier houses form a delightful square just behind the main street. A favourite with locals having a pre-prandial drink, the Kings Arms is also a very popular place for lunch. Jolly, friendly, blissfully quiet except for contented chat and the thump of darts. A fairly extensive menu: freshly made sandwiches, filled potatoes, salads, beef stroganoff, poached salmon, whole grilled trout, chicken Kiev, steaks, devilled kidneys, vegetarian dishes and many more. More real ales now, always Whitbread, and there could be Flowers Original or Harveys Sussex, perhaps Fullers London Pride. Choice of wines. Seats in the garden and a couple of tables at the front of the pub overlooking the square. Parking in the square can be difficult at weekends and in the evening.

OPEN: 11–3. 6–11 (12–3. 7–10.30 Sun).
Real Ale. Restaurant.
No children in public bar. Dogs on leads, water for the dog.

ELHAM

Rose and Crown
Tel: 01303 840226
High Street, Elham, Kent CT4 6TD
Free House. Gerard McNicholas, licensee.

A handsome old coaching inn with an interesting tale to tell. During the French Revolution, the man on whom the fictional Scarlet Pimpernel was based used to dine at the Rose and Crown while waiting for a fresh horse to take him to the coast to catch the boat to France. Horses out, beds in: the stables are now six letting bedrooms. Inside the pub is a huge inglenook fireplace surrounded by comfortable sofas and chairs. Traditional pub snacks and hot and cold open sandwiches are available, but the menu leans towards fish dishes. These are on the comprehensive, daily changing blackboard and could include baked sea bass, lemon sole, crab and salmon fishcakes with a fruit salsa, steak and kidney pudding, pot-roast lamb shank on parsley mash, or a vegetarian Wellington in a wine, tomato, garlic and basil sauce, also local sausages in an onion gravy. Hopdaemon Brewery Golden Braid, Ruddles Best and Rother Valley Level Best and guest beers.

OPEN: 11–3. 6–11 (12–3. 7–10.30 Sun).
Real Ale. Non-smoking restaurant.
Children in eating areas. Dogs on leads. Wheelchair access (not WC).Car park.
En-suite bedrooms.
Cards: MasterCard, Solo, Switch, Visa.

FAIRSEAT

Vigo Inn
Tel: 01732 822547
Fairseat, Nr Wrotham, Sevenoaks, Kent TN15 7JL
Free House. Mrs P.J. Ashwell, licensee.

Mostly liquid refreshment at the Vigo, unless you count crisps and nuts as food. The old saloon bar is now a no-smoking area. Quite a selection of well-kept ales: Youngs Bitter, Ordinary, Special, Harveys Mild and Best Bitter, also Flagship Ensign Beer from the

Chatham Dockyard Brewery. Addlestons draught cider, lots of local fruit juices plus wine by the glass. An old drovers' inn, it has room for your livestock, so if you've parked your horse or cattle, you can keep an eye on them from the garden at the back of the pub. Good walks in the nearby country park. The pub game is Dadlums – an old table skittles game that is so unusual it has been listed in the *Guinness Book of Pub Games*.

OPEN: 6–11 Mon–Fri. (12–3. 6–11 Sat. 12–3. 6–10.30 Sun).
Closed weekday lunchtimes except during holidays and Christmas.
Real Ale.
Children under supervision. Dogs on leads.

FORDCOMBE

Chafford Arms   Tel: 01892 740267
Fordcombe, Tunbridge Wells, Kent TN3 0SA
Whitbread. Barrie Leppard, licensee.

The landlord has been running this pub for over 35 years, so there is a very steady guiding hand on the beer pump at the Chafford Arms. Very near the village green and cricket club, this flowery, attractive and comfortable village pub was designed by George Davey, a noted Victorian architect. Behind the horticultural expertise and inside the spacious pub you'll find an extensive bar menu which includes speciality fish dishes. As well as the home-made country soup, you could have smoked-salmon pâté, Greenland prawns, local Weald-smoked trout, fresh Dover sole, dressed crab and prawns, grilled local trout, prawn provençale, a selection of vegetarian dishes, ploughman's, sandwiches or a salad. That should set you up for the day. Larkins Traditional and Gales HSB ales. Outside there is a large, award-winning garden, with lots of secluded areas in which to enjoy your drink.

OPEN: 11–3. 6.30–11 (12–4. 7–10.30 Sun).
Real Ale. No food Sun and Mon eves.
Children welcome, well-behaved dogs as well. Wheelchair access to pub and else-where with help. Car park.
Cards: Delta, MasterCard, Switch, Visa.
N.B. Live jazz and Broadway standards 3rd Sunday eve in the month.

GROOMBRIDGE

Crown   Tel: 01892 864742
10 The Walks, Groombridge, Kent
Free House. Peter & Pauline Kilshaw, licensees.

A divided village on the Kent–Sussex border: only old Groombridge, which includes the Crown, and a charming terrace of tile-hung, 18th-century cottages, are in Kent; all the rest is next door in Sussex. The Tudor Crown is in an enviable position: on the edge of the sloping village green, with views towards the village below. Inside the pub are beams, ancient timbers and winter log fires in the inglenook fireplace. The new licensees have brought in new lunch and evening menus as well as a new wine list. For a starter you could choose: home-made soup, Norwegian prawns in garlic butter or smoked duck breast with apple and celeriac salad; for a main course: seared salmon on stir-fried vegetables, home-made steak and mushroom pie, or grilled lamb cutlets with garlic and herb butter, some vegetarian dishes and daily specials on the blackboard. Harveys IPA, Courage Directors and Harveys Armada, but this changes two or three times a year, local farm cider and house wines by the glass. Groombridge Place is very near and well worth a visit.

> OPEN: 11–2.30 (11–3 Sat). 6–11 (11–11 Sat & Sun in summer).
> Real Ale. Restaurant (evenings). No food Sunday eve.
> Children in restaurant. Dogs on leads in bar only. Wheelchair access into pub just possible. Four bedrooms. Endless Morris dancers!
> Cards: all major credit cards.

HADLOW

Artichoke Inn   Tel: 01732 810763
Park Road, Hampton, Hadlow, Kent TN11 9SR (off Hadlow–Plaxtol road)
Free House. Terence & Barbara Simmonds, licensees.

The centre of Hadlow is a conservation area, and among the village's historic buildings is the church, where you can see the marks of crusaders' crosses on each side of the Saxon doorway. The Artichoke, in the delightful hamlet of Hampton, is surrounded by hop gardens and orchards. Part of the Hampton Estate until 1950, the Artichoke has been here since the late 16th century. Only two small beamed rooms in the pub, so it can be quite a squeeze when they're busy, but in the summer you can spread out on the covered front terrace, enjoy your drink and admire the surrounding countryside. Good, reliable home-made bar food: pork in a garlic and cider marinade, casseroles, vegetable pies, steak and kidney pies, king prawns, steaks and a number of pasta dishes. Youngs Ordinary and Fullers London Pride on hand pump.

> OPEN: 12–3. 7–11 (closed Sun eve and all day Mon).
> Real Ale. Restaurant (not Sun eves or Mon).
> Children in eating area. No dogs. Wheelchair access. Car park.
> Cards: all major cards except Amex and Diners.

KINGSDOWN

Zetland Arms   Tel: 01304 364888
Wellington Parade, Kingsdown, Deal, Kent CT14 8AF (at the sea end of South and North Roads)
Unique Pub Co. T.J. Cobbett, licensee.

Nothing much changes here – not even the paint! Years ago, this used to be just a pub at the end of two unmade-up roads bordered with small fishermen's cottages; the pub is still there, largely unchanged, the roads are still unmade and bumpier than ever, but the cottages have been gentrified – the fishermen would be amazed. The Zetland is in a wonderful position to take full advantage of glorious summer days, as you are virtually on the beach – well, where the pub stops, the pebbles begin and so does the car park – on the pebbles. When a north-easterly gale is blowing, you can watch the waves crashing against the sea defences from the safety of the bar. Nothing much to look at – weather-beaten is a good description. Just one bar with helpful, friendly staff. Food is traditional: dishes such as quiche, fish and chips, a pint of prawns, a huge bowl of mussels cooked in wine and garlic (highly recommended), rib-eye steak, curries and crab or prawn sandwiches. Shepherd Neame Master Brew, Morlands Old Speckled Hen, Youngs Bitter, Charles Wells Bombardier, Guinness on hand pump. Carlsberg and Holstein lagers also on draught. Water for the dog. There is a path along the coast into Deal and, about half a mile away, a wonderful walk over the cliffs to St Margaret's Bay.

> OPEN: 11–3. 6–11 (12–3. 7–10.30 Sun). 11–11 summer.
> Real Ale.
> Children welcome. Dogs on leads.

MARSHSIDE

Gate Inn   Tel: 01227 860498
Boyden Gate, Nr Marshside, Canterbury, Kent CT3 4EB (off A28 Canterbury–Margate road near Upstreet)
Shepherd Neame. Christopher Smith, tenant.

A very 'local' local: an unspoilt country pub surrounded by farmland and marshes with a very loyal following. Inside are just two connecting rooms warmed by a big log fire in the central fireplace. The Gate offers a well-cooked, simple menu and has a thriving trade based on fresh local produce whenever possible. Sandwiches – they do a prize-winning black-pudding sandwich, hot torpedoes (filled French bread), filled jacket potatoes, Gateburgers, lots of home-made pickles, spicy sausage hotpot, home-made flans and puddings. At lunchtime the dining area is no smoking. Shepherd Neame ales, tapped from the cask. In summer you can sit outside by the stream and feed the assortment of ducks and geese that have made their home there.

> OPEN: 11–2.30 (11–3 Sat). 6–11 (12–3. 6–10.30 Sun).
> Real Ale.
> Well-behaved children in eating area and family room. Dogs on leads.

PLUCKLEY

Dering Arms   Tel: 01233 840371
Pluckley, Ashford, Kent TN27 0RR (near station)
Free House. James Buss, licensee.

Reputed to be the most haunted village in Britain, but who last saw a ghost? Originally a hunting lodge for the Dering family, who lived in the district for over 900 years, the imposing Dering Arms has the distinctive arched 'Dering' windows that can be found on all the estate houses, as well as distinctive Dutch gables. Inside the Dering Arms, the main beamed bar has high ceilings, stone floors and a huge fireplace. There is also a more intimate restaurant serving some interesting dishes. The pub provides imaginative menus, using local ingredients where possible. Look for specials on the blackboard; dishes may include mussels in cider and cream sauce, potted shrimps, pasta with Stilton and basil sauce, whole crab salad, rack of lamb with herb crust, pheasant casserole with red-wine sauce, many more fish dishes such as potted crab, fillet of halibut and local trout, home-baked pies, steaks, selected cuts of pork and lamb, and scrummy puds. Every meal is prepared to order. Gourmet evenings are held several times a year. Ales include specially brewed Dering ale and Goachers Maidstone ale. Extensive, wide-ranging wine list and local farm cider. Garden parties and musical evenings are sometimes held in the large garden. Telephone for details.

> OPEN: 11–3. 6–11.
> Real Ale. Restaurant (closed Sun eve and all day Mon).
> Children in restaurant and eating area.
> Dogs on leads. Wheelchair access (not WC). Three bedrooms.
> Cards: all cards except Diners.

SMARDEN

The Bell   Tel: 01233 770283
Bell Lane, Smarden, Nr Ashford TN27 8PW
Free House. Jackie Smith, licensee.

Tile-hung, by itself, with a very big sign first hung in the late 18th century. Before that, after they received their beer and cider licence in 1630, it was an inn without a name. Even earlier than that, this building was leading a totally blameless existence as an ordinary farmhouse on a country lane about 3 miles from Headcorn on the approach to Smarden. Spacious and rambling, very rustic, with low beams, exposed, creaking timbers, flagstone floors and inglenook fireplaces – all the requirements for a traditional country inn. Food too. Good filling fare, from sandwiches and ploughman's to the daily specials on the blackboard, using seasonal and local produce; always fresh fish, vegetarian dishes, an interesting à la carte menu and six home-made puddings. Always between eight and 10 real ales: Shepherd Neame Master Brew, Morlands Old Speckled Hen, Harveys IPA, Marstons Pedigree, Flowers Original, Fullers London Pride, Rother Valley Level Best, Wadworths, Boddingtons Bitter and a guest beer. About 40 wines, some by the glass. Seats in the secluded garden among the fruit trees.

> OPEN: 11.30–2.30. 6–11 (11.30–3 Sat. 12–3. 7–10.30 Sun).
> Real Ale. Restaurant area. No-smoking bar.
> Children welcome in two bars only. Dogs on leads. Wheelchair access. Car park.
> Classic cars meet here on the second Sunday in each month.
> Cards: MasterCard, Switch, Visa.

SMARDEN

The Chequers
Tel: 01233 770217

The Street, Smarden, Nr Ashford, Kent
Free House. Charles Bullock, licensee.

Along with Tenterden and Cranbrook, this village was one of the centres of the Flemish cloth trade, but unlike them it didn't grow but stayed just as it was, a small, delightful village. Three roads lead into Smarden, and as the Chequers takes up a biggish corner site, two of them nearly end up in the pub, the third in the churchyard. Apt really, as part of the pub used to be the village meeting place; it still is, of course, but in a totally different way. Just the sort of place you wish you lived near: 14th-century, comfortable and welcoming with lots of beams, two bars, two dining areas – one a no-smoking dining room – two open fires and an general air of prosperity. A pub serving some really good food, but plenty of local support for the beer. Daily specials on the blackboard could be tempura prawns with a sweet-chilli dip, leek and potato soup, poached salmon with a wholegrain-mustard sauce, home-made steak and kidney pudding, fillet or T-bone steak; also a reliable bar-snack menu: a hotpot, something with pasta, fisherman's pie and a vegetarian dish or two. Always draught Bass, Harveys Best, maybe Hardy and Hansons Frolicking Farmer plus guests from microbreweries. A wide-ranging wine list to go with the good food. Outside the courtyard has seats for 40. The car park at the back of the pub has been enlarged; beyond that, well-landscaped gardens, lawns, seats, and a pond with ducks.

> OPEN: 10–3. 6–11 (12–3. 7–10.30 Sun).
> Real Ale. Restaurant.
> Children: if well behaved. Dogs on leads. Wheelchair access (not WC).
> Disabled toilet in the village. Car park. Bedrooms.
> Cards: Delta, MasterCard, Switch, Visa.

SNARGATE

Red Lion
Tel: 01797 344648

Snargate, Kent (on B2080 Brenzett–Appledore road)
Free House. Doris Jemison, licensee.

If you're interested in a little bit of social history, this is the place for you. A totally unspoilt, unchanging, timeless treasure a couple of miles from Brenzett. Even though they say they open at 12, don't expect the door to be unlocked on the dot, even if a couple of thirsty farm-workers are impatiently waiting to hear the lock turning. When you do get in, you walk straight into the bar, large enough to accommodate at most six people sitting down, and only a few more than that standing. This bar is also the passageway to the other two, equally small rooms. Time has stood still here; beers from the barrel, crisps from the box, maybe a nut to keep you going – and coal fires in winter. The Red Lion has been run by the same family since 1911; it was last 'done up' in 1890! The gaslight fittings are still there, and even oil lamps that come into their own when they run out of candles – their main source of light. Electricity has, however, crept in: there is a spotlight over the dartboard. Nothing much has changed – not even the paint! You come here for the experience, the good ale, not the comfort. Goachers Light Ale is on permanently, Rother Valley Level Best (brewed at Northiam) is the guest. Double Vision cider from Staplehurst.

> OPEN: Roughly from 12–3. 7–11 (12–3. 7–10.30 Sun).
> Real Ale.
> No children. No dogs inside and heaven only knows where the toilets are.

STANSTED

Black Horse   Tel: 01732 822355
Tumblefield Road, Stansted, Nr West Malling, Kent
Free House. Ian Duncan, licensee.

High on the chalk downs above Wrotham (pronounced Rootam), about 5 miles from West Malling. The yew tree in the grounds of the much restored, 13th-century St Mary's Church is reputed to be 1000 years old. The Black Horse is not quite so old but is at the centre of things in this village. Beers are Larkins, Youngs Special, two guests and two draught lagers. Food will be filling pub favourites. As this is a good walking area, you need to be well stoked up for the onward march. In the second week of July they hold a Kent Fair Week on land belonging to the Black Horse. The Fair promotes all Kent produce: wine, cheese, beer, fruit, vegetables – everything grown in Kent. During that week they also hold a vintage-car rally.

> OPEN: 10–11 (12–10.30 Sun).
> Real Ale.
> Children under control. Dogs on leads. Wheelchair access.
> Four en-suite bedrooms.
> Cards: all major credit cards except Amex and Diners.

STAPLEHURST

Lord Raglan   Tel: 01622 843747
Chart Hill Road, Nr Staplehurst, Kent TN12 0RN
Free House. Andrew Hutchison, owner/licensee.

If you're on the right road, you can't really miss the Lord Raglan; it is virtually the only building on a road bordered by orchards. Lots of people seem to find it, so you can too. In Staplehurst take the right turn at the timber yard and keep going. An unspoilt country pub, the oldest bit is 17th-century, full of old beams and open log fires. There is one long bar and a dining area, but you can eat wherever you can find a table. An unusual and interesting addition to the usual pub furniture is slumped in a chair by the door into the car park – a full-size model of a man dressed in 18th-century clothes. About to be chucked on a bonfire, he was rescued to spend his days in happy company in the corner of the pub. The bar menu offers various sandwiches and ploughman's, and the blackboard may list king prawns in garlic and ginger, stir-fried beef and peppers, guinea fowl in a red-wine sauce, grilled fillet steak or poached salmon in a sorrel sauce, though the menu changes all the time – it depends on what is available. Harveys Best Bitter, Goachers Light plus a guest beer – two in summer. As befits the area, there is an orchard garden.

> OPEN: 12–3. 6–11. Closed all day Sunday.
> Real Ale. Dining room.
> Children welcome. Dogs on leads. Wheelchair access. Car park.
> Cards: MasterCard, Switch, Visa.

STAPLESTREET

Three Horseshoes   Tel: 01227 750842
Staplestreet, Hernehill, Faversham, Kent
Shepherd Neame. Mike Skipper, licensee.

A village pub as you remember them. Unpretentious, beamed, plain floorboards to cope with boots; cricketing trophies (they're all cricket mad; they even play expats in France – and lose!), a bar billiards table, upholstered benches and chairs, and gas lighting that is still used when they have power cuts. In a small hamlet near Boughton (between Canterbury and Faversham) and the start of the M2 motorway, this pub is the centre of a village community. Jolly things go on and are arranged: there is an onion competition and general auction on the first Sunday in September in aid of the cricket club, and we mustn't forget the very keen cricketers, who meet for lots of matches. Toasted sandwiches, steak pie, ploughman's – good home-made, traditional food to go with the Shepherd Neame range of ales. The garden is in use again and the window boxes are in place – things are on the up. In 1749 Samuel Shepherd purchased the pub and started the Shepherd Neame empire.

> OPEN: 12–3. 5–11 Mon–Thurs. 12–11 Fri & Sat. 12–3. 7–10.30 Sun.
> Real Ale. No food Sundays.
> Children: if well behaved. Dogs welcome. Car park.

TOYS HILL Nr Westerham

Fox & Hounds   Tel: 01732 750328
Toys Hill, Nr Westerham, Kent
Greene King. Tony & Shirley Hickmott, licensees.

Not far from Chartwell, Sir Winston Churchill's family home for over 40 years. Hazel Pelling, who retired as licensee in December 2001, was a very special landlady. We hope that Tony and Shirley Hickmott won't sweep away all the appealing things about this pub. It was too early to say what was going to happen at the time of going to press, so our description of the Fox must date from Hazel's regime, when it was rather like a front room, cosily furnished with well-loved sofas and chairs. The logs were outside ready to go on the fires and there was a notice warning about 'unofficial stoking' – moving logs with a tentative toe was not tolerated. Mobile phones were banned; if one was heard the owner was likely to be evicted to the car park. Kindly eccentricity was the norm. Food was limited to lunchtime snacks: filled rolls, cauliflower cheese etc. Sundays and Bank Holidays, rolls only. Greene King IPA, Abbot Ale, Guinness on hand pump, cider and lager. Obviously no music, except at Christmas, when they played carols from Kings College, Cambridge.

OPEN: 12–2.30. 6–11 Mon–Fri. 12–3. 6–11 Sat. 12–3. 7–10.30 Sun.
Real Ale.
Children with parents in special area, lunchtimes only.
Dogs – do please ask, as it is only a small pub. Wheelchair access difficult but possible with help.

TUNBRIDGE WELLS
The Opera House   Tel: 01892 511770
48–60 Mount Pleasant Road, Royal Tunbridge Wells, Kent
Wetherspoon.

The final curtain fell years ago at the Opera House in Tunbridge Wells; the building was a sorry sight – very unloved. Now that it has been rescued by Wetherspoon, it is flaunting its finery again. Go and gaze at the lovely interior – the stalls are still in situ, so is the grand chandelier – then settle down to a cheaper-than-usual pint or something from the menu; these change twice a year and are standard throughout the chain. One thing worth noting is that they have a good selection of vegetarian dishes. Always about eight real ales on the go, cider, and anything else you want really, including a reasonably priced champagne.

OPEN: 11–11.
Real Ale.
No children. No dogs. All disabled facilities.

UNDER RIVER
The White Rock   Tel: 01732 833112
Carters Hill, Under River, Nr Sevenoaks, Kent TN15 0SB
Free House. Frank Scott, licensee.

Tucked under the high ridge overlooking Tonbridge and the Weald of Kent, between Sevenoaks and Hildenborough. Under River means 'under the hill', river being a derivation of *rither*, the Anglo-Saxon word for hill. The White Rock, a pleasing pub, is brick-built with a weather-boarded wing to the side. Inside is a small, quiet bar with beams, comfortable seating and a log fire. Noisy bits – pool table and games – are in the bigger bar. There is a separate restaurant. Traditional bar snacks and daily specials including fresh fish and seafood on the menu, as well as freshly prepared vegetarian dishes and traditional puddings. Harveys BB, Fullers London Pride and Swale's Kentish Pride. Big garden to sit in and good walks from the village.

> OPEN: 11–3. 6–11 (12–3. 7–10.30 Sun).
> Real Ale. Restaurant.
> Children in summer. No dogs. Wheelchair access. Car park.

BEST OF THE REST

DARGATE

Dove   Tel: 01227 751360
In the country between Whitstable (oysters) and Faversham (beer), off the A299. Unspoilt in a very civilised way, just as a country pub should be, catering for the thirsty locals and the discerning traveller. Really enjoyable, imaginative food – way above the usual – the sort of place to make a detour to. Shepherd Neame range of beers and a good wine list.

MARKBEECH

Kentish Horse   Tel: 01342 850493
South of Edenbridge; there is only one Kentish Horse in the country and this is it. In the middle of the village, a Victorian pub with a long main bar and a blackboard menu. Unpretentious but excellent-quality home-made soups, local sausages, filo prawns, home-cooked ham, steak and ale pie, Thai red chicken; simple, but done with care. Well-kept Fullers London Pride, Harveys, Larkins, a guest and a modest wine list.

PERRY WOOD Nr Selling

Rose & Crown   Tel: 01227 752214
To find this place you might like to sign up for an outward-bound course first; if Kent has a hinterland, this must be it. Once you get here, it is a delight. The garden is lovely and if you have the dog with you, the walks are wonderful. Traditional bar food with a few surprises. Local cider and four changing ales on hand pump.

SANDWICH

Red Cow   Tel: 01304 613243
Very near the market and you might like to know that Thursday is market day. A gloriously atmospheric pub, as medieval as the town itself. Heavily beamed, comfortable and inviting. Usual pub food, well-filled sandwiches, soup, sausages and daily specials – that sort of thing. What they do, they do well. Currently the beers are Greene King Abbot IPA, Morlands Old Speckled Hen, Fullers London Pride and draught Bass.

SMARTS HILL Nr Penshurst

Bottle House Inn
Tel: 01892 870306

You'll need to know you're aiming for Coldharbour Lane and a 15th-century pub. Inside, this is a comfortable, well-beamed old place; outside, you get views of the Kent country-side. Dishes are more imaginative than the usual pub food – lots of fresh fish served here and dishes such as fillet of beef Wellington. Harveys Best and Larkins beers, local cider and local wine.

STONE-IN-OXNEY

Crown
Tel: 01233 758789

Just in case you're thinking of coming here for a meal on Monday, don't – there'll be no food at all. It's nice inside, with a big inglenook fireplace and old wooden pews. Food ranges from filled baguettes to dressed Scottish crab or roast duck with blackcurrant sauce; puds include Eton Mess! Shepherd Neame Masterbrew and two guests on handpump.

TUNBRIDGE WELLS

Beacon
Tel: 01892 524252

Find Rustall Common and Tea Garden Lane to reach this Victorian pub. Very popular at lunchtime, when they serve an extremely reasonable two-course lunch or anything else you want from the bar menu: poached-salmon salad, game terrine, braised rabbit or cod in batter – that sort of thing. More elaborate dishes are available. Fullers London Pride, Harveys Best and Timothy Taylors Landlord beers.

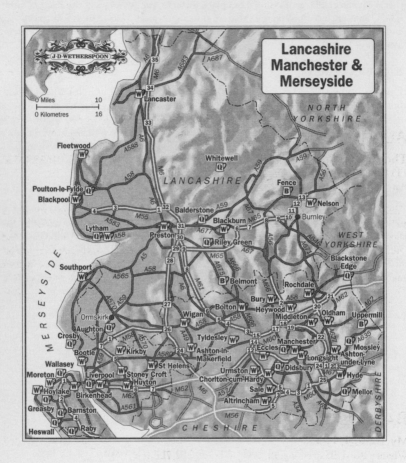

Lancashire Manchester & Merseyside

Lancashire, Greater Manchester & Merseyside

AUGHTON

The Dog & Gun Inn
Tel: 01695 42330

233 Long Lane, Aughton, Ormskirk, Lancs L39 5BU
Burtonwood Brewery. Mrs Shirley Davies, tenant.

There are two Aughtons in Lancashire; the one you want is south of Ormskirk and is an important market town surrounded by good farming country. There are seasonal displays of hanging baskets and tubs of flowers at the front of the mock-Tudor Dog and Gun – a couple of benches too. You can sit, admire the flowers and watch the world go by while clutching your pint of well-kept Burtonwood Mild, Bitter or Forshaws Bitter and munching a nut or two. Not a TV or fruit machine in the place – no food either. Darts and quiz teams in the winter; bowls in the summer. Extra seats in the pub garden.

> OPEN: 5–11 weekdays. 12–2. 6–11 weekends.
> Real Ale.
> Quiet children welcome. No dogs. Wheelchair access. Car park.

BALDERSTONE

Myerscough Hotel
Tel: 01254 812222

Whalley Road, Balderstone, Blackburn, Lancs BB2 7LE (on A59)
Robinsons. Ian Riddock, licensee.

If you're motoring along the M6 near Preston and looking for a welcome break from driving, swing off the motorway at Exit 31 and head for the A59 towards Clitheroe. When you see a Canberra bomber and Lightning fighter parked by the side of the road, you'll know you have reached the Myerscough: it's opposite the two jets. In the Ribble valley and only 2 miles from the M6, this friendly country pub is a favourite place for lunch during the week, particularly with businessmen and families from the nearby British Aerospace plant. Spacious, comfortable bars where they serve good traditional bar food. Robinsons ales and

Hartleys XB plus a good selection of malt whiskies. Picnic tables and assorted livestock in the garden.

> OPEN: 11.30–3. 5.30–11 (12–10.30 Sun).
> Real Ale.
> Children in front room till 8.30pm. No dogs except guide dogs.
> Wednesday quiz night. Bedrooms.

BARNSTON

Fox & Hounds   Tel: 0151 648 7685
Barnston Village, Wirral CH61 1BW
Free House. Ralph Leech, licensee.

You might think when you look at the map that you are in the middle of the industrial North-West – totally urbanised from Ellesmere Port to Wallasey – but the Wirral Peninsula is an area of many parts, the south being full of delightful villages. Situated in one of the very pretty areas, this pub, built early last century to replace the old original 18th-century Fox and Hounds (pictures of which can be seen in the bar), offers a good choice of home-cooked pub food: soup, open sandwiches, ploughman's; the lasagne, quiche and coronation chicken are very popular; lamb hotpot, country casserole, glazed supreme of salmon, well-filled baked potatoes, salads and changing specials from the blackboard – it all depends on what inspires the chef. Puds on the blackboard too. Sunday lunch always includes four roasts and a fish dish. Theakstons Best, Old Peculier and Cool Cask, Websters Yorkshire, and two guests. They have a flowery courtyard, an outside bar and lovely garden. Attractive surroundings and good walks.

> OPEN: 11–11.
> Real Ale.
> Children welcome. Dogs on leads. Wheelchair access (not WC). Car park.

BLACKSTONE EDGE

White House   Tel: 01706 378456
Blackstone Edge, Little Borough, Rochdale OL15 0LG
Free House. Neville Marney, licensee.

This lonely stretch of moorland is up in the clouds, 1450 feet high. The Roman road running across the moor is one of the best-preserved sections in the country, and the whole area is a favourite with walkers – the Pennine Way crosses the road outside this windswept old pub. If you want to take a break from your onward march, the White House is an excellent stopping-off place. Make a beeline for the main bar and warm yourself by a glowing coal fire. From another room you have far-reaching views over the moors. Daily specials, as well as traditional bar food: soup of the day, sandwiches, garlic mushrooms, quiche, steak and kidney pie, sirloin garni and salads. Children's portions. Moorhouse Pendle Witches' Brew, Theakstons Best and Black Sheep Bitter. Farm ciders and several malt whiskies. Remove the muddy boots and leave them in the porch; only clean shoes or socks inside the bars.

> OPEN: 11.30–3. 7–11 (12–10.30 Sun).
> Real Ale. Restaurant.
> Children welcome. No dogs. Wheelchair access.

CHORLTON-CUM-HARDY

Beech Inn
72 Beech Road, Chorlton-cum-Hardy, Greater Manchester
Whitbread. Edna Thomas, manager.

Tel: 0161 881 1180

Nothing to eat, just great beer. A popular pub near the village green on the western edge of Greater Manchester. Naturally you'll find a crisp and nut or two, but you'll be here to enjoy the beer: Boddingtons, Whitbread Trophy Bitter, Timothy Taylors Landlord, Best and Morlands Old Speckled Hen. Beer garden at the back of the pub.

> OPEN: 11–11 (11–10.30 Sun).
> Real Ale.
> Children until 5pm. Dogs: small ones only.

CROSBY

Crow's Nest
63 Victoria Road, Crosby, Liverpool, Wirral
Scottish & Newcastle. David Hughes, licensee.

Tel: 0151 924 6953

A town pub and a popular local, with bar, snug and lounge. They keep a tight grip on things here; a notice reads: 'No music, no pool, no fruit machines, no footballers and no food'. It is just serious drinking, in fact so serious you have to go early in the week to try the guest beer before it runs out – sales are booming. A combination of good traditional beer and conversation. Frequented largely by professionals – teachers, barristers and the like. Five cask ales on every day, various lagers, stouts and cider. There is a garden ready to be enjoyed.

> OPEN: 11.30–11.
> Real Ale.
> Children allowed if well behaved. No dogs.

DIDSBURY

Royal Oak
729 Wilmslow Road, Didsbury, Greater Manchester M20 0RH
Marstons. June Brunton, manager.

Tel: 0161 434 4788

You don't immediately associate a pub with cheese – well, you might, but this place is in a different league: truly knowledgeable, a specialist. The selection wouldn't disgrace

Selfridges' food hall. For a lunch snack you can have any two cheeses from the many available – a hunk of cheese with a chunk of bread, an olive or two and salad. You should get yourself over there rapidly. What you don't finish, you can take home – doggy bags provided. If you're not into cheese, you can usually get soup and choice of pâté. Marstons Pedigree Bitter, Banks's Original and a guest beer, plus sherries and port from the barrel – delicious with cheese.

OPEN: 11–11.
Real Ale. Lunchtime snacks, not weekends or Bank Holidays.
No children. No dogs.

GREASBY

Irby Mill   Tel: 0151 604 0194
Mill Lane, Greasby, Wirral, Merseyside L49 3NT
Scottish & Newcastle. Anthony Carr, licensee.

South of Birkenhead, Irby Mill is a small, delightful sandstone pub covered in hanging baskets. Long and narrow – they compare it to drinking in a railway carriage. Until 1980 it was the old miller's cottage. Unfortunately, the mill blew down in 1898, but in the bar you can see old photographs of the working mill in its heyday. Traditional pub food: sandwiches, ploughman's, Cumberland sausages, lasagne and (the favourite) a hot bacon and cheese baguette; reliable pub fare. They're in the process of changing the beers around, but there will always be ten bitters and two guest beers. Irby Mill backs onto National Trust land, so it's surrounded by good walking country.

OPEN: 12–11 (12–10.30 Sun).
Real Ale. Food all day until 8pm
Children allowed. Dogs too, but not in eating areas.

HESWALL

Black Horse   Tel: 0151 342 2254
Village Road, Lower Heswall, Merseyside P60 0DP
Free Trade Breweries. John Mitchell, owner.

Well over a hundred years old, this is the sort of place that customers come to for a chat; they think of the Black Horse as a 'talking pub', so be prepared for some lively repartee. Inside is a big lounge and a conservatory where they serve standard pub fare of sandwiches, jacket potatoes, crusty rolls with hot fillings, sizzling steaks, and mixed grills – all with chips. Daily specials and vegetarian dishes – all good, filling food. Worthington BB, Stones BB, M&B Brew XI and varying guest ales. No garden and only a very small car park.

OPEN: 11.30–11.
Real Ale. No food Sundays.
No children. No dogs.

LIVERPOOL

Roscoe Head Tel: 0151 709 4490
24 Roscoe Street, Liverpool L1 2SX
Punch Taverns. Carol Ross, licensee.

The larger of the two parlours in this mid-Victorian city pub – which has been described as 'a tiny little pub, with a little snug, two little parlours and a little bar' – is known as the tie room. They started collecting the occasional tie, and then it caught on. Customers bring in ties that mean something or have a history. Now they have over 190, including one for Japanese prisoners of war. Each one is numbered and identified on a chart – it is quite a sight. People come on pilgrimages to view them. So remember, if you happen to turn up here with a tie representing an unusual club, or one with its own interesting story, you could well lose it. Food, which you can pre-order if you are pushed for time, is served at lunchtime only – reliable pub grub of filled baguettes, jacket potatoes, curries, steak pie, chicken pie, sausages – that sort of thing. Ind Coope Burton, Old Speckled Hen, Jennings Bitter, Adnams Broadside, Tetleys Mild and Bitter and guest beers. Stellar, Skol and Carlsburg Pilsner lagers. No outdoor drinking area. A conversation pub.

> OPEN: 11.30–11 (12–11 Sat).
> Real Ale.
> No children. No dogs.

LYTHAM

The Taps Tel: 0151 709 4365
12 Henry Street, Lytham, Lancs FY8 5LE
Whitbread. Ian Rigg, manager.

A basic alehouse. It might have been refurbished in the last few years, but the Taps has always existed for the true beer enthusiast. It's not far from the beach, so there's a seashore theme running through the pub (fish, boats and things), but the real interest here is in the beer. So far, they've tried well over a thousand different varieties of ale – not all at once! No doubt the others being brewed will be tasted by the Taps' patrons in due course. At that rate you take pot luck (if that's the expression with beer), as who knows what's on offer and when. A basic sort of place serving traditional bar food with home-made daily specials.

> OPEN: 11–11.
> Real Ale. Lunchtime meals and snacks except Sunday.
> Children in eating area at mealtimes. No dogs.

MANCHESTER

Circus Tavern Tel: 0161 236 5818
86 Portland Street, Manchester M1 4GX
Tetley Walker. Steven Campbell, licensee.

Searching for the smallest pub in Manchester? Here it is – well known for being small, a timeless little gem. You might have to knock! It isn't really closed, it just sometimes looks as though it is. So small there is only room for one beer – Tetley Walker Bitter. No room to cook – certainly nowhere to put a plate! So a bag of crisps and a nut, neither of which take up much space, is all you will get.

OPEN: 11–11.
Real Ale.
Children welcome. Dogs – well, yes, if well behaved and not too big!

MANCHESTER

Moon under Water   Tel: 0161 834 5882
68–74 Deansgate, Manchester M3 2FN
Wetherspoon.

Now you know where to find the smallest pub in Manchester, well, this one is said to be the biggest one in the country – and it probably is. It's not what you would call intimate; beer is cheap though. Situated in the heart of the city, the Moon under Water was built on the site of the old ABC cinema. There are three separate bars on two levels and a passenger lift. Not many of our pubs have one of those. Decorations include pictures, photographs and, slightly unnervingly, specially commissioned sculptures of Manchester's famous five. They sit in cinema seats on the first floor: Ena Sharples from Coronation Street, Sir Robert Peel, Emily Pankhurst, Hattie Jacques and horror actor Christopher Lee. Console yourself with the five or six real ales and the guest ale this chain always provides. Bar snacks, or, if you're hungry, a full menu of good solid reliable fare, plus a daily special or two.

OPEN: 11–11.
Real Ale.
No children. No dogs.

MELLOR

Devonshire Arms   Tel: 0161 427 2563
Longhurst Lane, Mellor, Nr Marple, Greater Manchester SK6 5PP
Robinsons. John Longworth, tenant.

Once you've got here, make sure you are in the right Mellor – there are two Mellors. The Devonshire Arms is a cheerful, friendly pub with a reputation for serving some imaginative home-made food. The constantly changing menu leans towards curries and spicy dishes, varied soups, steamed fresh mussels, chicken and peppers in spicy sauce, smoked sausage, vegetarian dishes, steaks and home-made puds. Robinsons ales including the occasional Robinsons Stockport's Arches ale – 'a splendid pint' according to one customer – lots of malt whiskies and a good selection of wine. This Mellor is very near the Cheshire border, between the A626 and the A6015.

OPEN: 12–3. 6–11 (11–10.30 Sun).
Real Ale.
Well-behaved children in eating area. No dogs.
N.B. Live jazz every other Tuesday evening.

MELLOR

Oddfellows Arms   Tel: 0161 449 7826
73 Moor End Road, Mellor, Nr Marple, Greater Manchester SK6 5PT
Free House. Robert Cloughley, licensee.

Very near the Cheshire border, this is a splendid old country pub. As you would expect, low ceilings, flagstone floors and good fires. The emphasis might be on food, but it is still a pub and pubs serve beer, so you are still welcome to lean on the bar with a pint in your hand. From the bar menu there is home-made soup, ploughman's, usually a good choice of fish served with imaginative sauces, curries, chicken in garlic and yoghurt, steaks and puddings. Varied, imaginative and appealing. Upstairs is a no-smoking restaurant. Adnams and Marstons Pedigree are on permanently, plus one guest ale.

OPEN: 12–3. 5.30–11 (12–3. 7–10.30 Sun).
Real Ale. Restaurant.
Children welcome. Dogs in bar. Wheelchair access into bar only.

MOSSLEY

Tollemache Arms   Tel: 01457 832354
415 Manchester Road, Mossley, Ashton under Lyne, Lancs OL5 9BG
Robinsons (Stockport). Frank Varey, licensee.

Very much a local pub attracting an interesting cross-section of the local populace: actors, stage managers, journalists and company directors, they all come here, as well as the rest of us. An old roadside pub looking over the restored Huddersfield canal, it is highly civilised. The Tollemache Arms has no music or gaming machines. There is a small, cosy tap room where you can play darts, dominoes and cards, and, when you feel a bit peckish, they have various fillings for the giant Yorkshire puddings, five different curries and home-made pies; there also a barbecue going full tilt in the garden during the summer months.

OPEN: 12–11 (12–10.30 Sun).
Real Ale.
Children and dogs welcome. Wheelchair access. One bedroom.

POULTON-LE-FYLDE

The Thatched Public House   Tel: 01253 891063
Ball Street, Poulton-le-Fylde, Lancs FY6 7BG
Scottish & Newcastle. Brian Ballentine, manager.

The thatched roof of this very traditional pub just off Market Square, next to the Norman Church, disappeared in 1906. It's now tiled. No food – just one bar and four rooms where you can enjoy your drink and a few crisps and nuts. No pool table; there's a game machine, but with the sound turned off – this is a talking pub and very busy serving well-kept Boddingtons Bitter, Theakston Cool Cask and rotating guests.

OPEN: 11–11.
Real Ale.
No children – a child-free zone. No dogs. All wheelchair facilities.

RABY

Wheatsheaf Inn   Tel: 0151 336 3416
The Green, Rabymere Road, Raby, Wirral CH63 4JH
Free House. Thomas Charlesworth, licensee.

Still with its thatched roof, the inn is known as 'The Thatch'. The Wheatsheaf, found among a row of farm buildings, looks just as a traditional country pub should look. Thatched roof, black and white and hung about in summer with wonderful baskets of flowers. Seats outside the door so you can while away the time, admire the flowers and enjoy your drink. Inside is a single bar with a big inglenook fireplace and, opposite, a small snug. Lunchtime snacks: 46 varieties of toasties (you name it, they do it!), bacon baps and sandwiches – but the toasties are the favourites. In the restaurant, called 'The Cowshed', they serve far more elaborate dishes: dressed Cornish crab, asparagus tartlet, poached chicken breast wrapped in Parma ham served with a tomato and hollandaise sauce, vegetarian dishes; they also play MUSIC. There is a good choice of real ales: Thwaites Bitter, Theakstons Best and Old Peculier, Cains Bitter, Tetleys and guests. Seats on the terrace and in the beer garden

OPEN: 11.30–11 (12–10.30 Sun).
Real Ale. Restaurant open every evening except Sun and Mon.
Children at lunchtime only. Dogs in pub, not in restaurant. Ramp and disabled facilities for restaurant. Car park.
N.B. Music in restaurant.

RILEY GREEN

Royal Oak   Tel: 01254 201445
Blackburn Old Road, Riley Green, Hoghton, Nr Preston, Lancs PR5 0SL
Daniel Thwaites PLC, Blackburn. Eric Hargreaves FBII, licensee.

Being so near Hoghton Tower, a historic house rebuilt in the 17th century and restored in the 19th, the Royal Oak became a well-used coaching inn, an important stopping place. Still a good place to stop, this low-ceilinged country pub has stripped stone walls, beams and open fires, comfortable armchairs to lounge in and settles to sit in. Not a jukebox, radio, TV, pool table or gaming machine to be seen. Reliably good food is served every day. To start you could have home-made soup, black-pudding slices with a wholegrain-mustard dip, home-baked cheese and onion pie, grilled gammon or grilled fillet steak, lasagne with garlic bread, freshly filled sandwiches, filled jacket potatoes, a ploughman's or something from the specials board such as a beef pot roast, casserole of lamb with Stilton dumplings or halibut with prawns and dill. Vegetarian dishes too, children's portions and a big selection of hot and cold puds. Very well-kept Thwaites Best Bitter, Mild and Morning Glory on hand pump, also Thwaites Smooth, Guinness and Strongbow cider; about three dozen single malt whiskies. The large garden looks towards Hoghton Tower. Very popular with walkers as you are only about 800 yards from the towpath of the Leeds and Liverpool canal.

OPEN: 11.30–3. 5.30–11 (11.30–11 Sat. 12–10.30 Sun).
Real Ale.
Children welcome – on leads until 9pm. Dogs too – no time limit. Two big car parks with CCTV.
Cards: All major credit cards except Amex.

WALLASEY

Cheshire Cheese   Tel: 0151 630 3641
2 Wallasey Village Road, Wallasey, Wirral
Pub Estates Co. Steve Carless, licensee.

Beer has been sold on this site for hundreds of years but the Cheshire Cheese only dates from the Victorian era. As so frequently happens, you find a new-ish pub on ancient foundations. At the heart of Merseyside and surrounded by miles of sandy beaches, this is a popular place with one large lounge divided up into three distinct areas, and a separate bar. The only food available is a roast on Sundays; crisps and nuts the rest of the time. Seats in the beer garden, and a lovely walk to the promenade at New Brighton.

OPEN: 12–11.
Real Ale.
Children welcome. No dogs. Wheelchair access.

WALLASEY

Magazine Hotel   Tel: 0151 637 3974
7 Magazine Brow, Wallasey, Merseyside CH45 1HP
Six Continents Retail. Martin Venables, manager.

An 18th-century black-and-white pub dating back to the days when sailing ships had to unload their gunpowder before being allowed to dock. The gunpowder was put into the magazine 50 yards away – which is why the pub is so named. On the banks of the river, overlooking what was once the busiest shipping lane in Europe, the Magazine was originally a hotel, but when the unloading of gunpowder ceased and the hotel trade died out, it survived by becoming a simple pub. One main bar and lots of small rooms full of beams and shiny brass where they serve home-made soups, steak and kidney pies, lasagne, mixed grills and daily specials. Food is served every lunchtime. Evenings are devoted to the serious drinker. Draught Bass and one guest ale.

OPEN: 11–11 (12–10.30 Sun).
Real Ale. Food served 12–2.30 Mon–Sat and 1–4 Sun.
Children allowed. Dogs in garden. Wheelchair access.

WHITEWELL

Inn at Whitewell   Tel: 01200 448222
Whitewell, Forest of Bowland, Clitheroe, Lancs BB7 3AT
Free House. Richard Bowman, licensee.

An inn of many parts: owned by the Queen, it is also a hotel, a pub, a wine merchant's and an art gallery with pictures for sale. Lots of magazines and guidebooks to read and a piano to play to while away the time. Deep in glorious rolling countryside this lovely 14th-century coaching inn next to the village church overlooks the River Hodder. Traditional, well-cooked bar food and a more adventurous selection from the restaurant menu. From the bar menu: interesting soups, sandwiches, salads and ploughman's, roast Mediterranean vegetables served in an Indian pastry basket with curry fondue and mango raita, pressed duck and pistachio-nut terrine with peach and ginger chutney, the popular Whitewell gourmet fish pie, honey-glazed joints of chicken and lots more; specials of the day are on the blackboard. Grouse, partridge and pheasant in season. Home-made puds and a good cheese selection. Marstons Pedigree and Boddingtons ales. Extensive, interesting wine list. Views of the river from the restaurant and the seats in the garden.

OPEN: 11–3. 6–11.
Real Ale. Restaurant (not Sun lunchtimes).
Children welcome. Dogs on leads. Car park. Bedrooms.
Cards: Amex, Delta, Diners, MasterCard, Switch, Visa.

BEST OF THE REST

BELMONT, Lancashire

Black Dog   Tel: 01204 811218
Views of the moors from this delightful old farmhouse full of interesting bits and pieces. Welcoming and popular, they serve a good selection of filling bar food varying from home-made soup to pork in a Cumberland sauce. Holts range of beers. Walks onto the moors and a garden to sit in. Bedrooms.

FENCE, Lancashire

Forest   Tel: 01282 613641
On the A6068, near the Forest of Pendle, this beautifully decorated place is an acknowledged 'dining pub', which loosely translates as 'you eat very well here'. You can of course

have a sandwich – it is, after all, a pub – but there could also be king prawns in filo pastry with a coriander and mint dressing, or pavé of Scottish salmon with a spring-onion and dill velouté; home-made puds too. Ruddles and Theakston Best plus a couple of guests and a good wine list. Weekends are busy; you need to book.

UPPERMILL, Lancashire

Church Inn
Tel: 01457 820902

Upper it is too. Find the village and keep on going – up! Worth it for the eccentricity of the place, their 'own brew' beer and a traditional menu – home-made soup, sandwiches, steak and ale pie and daily specials.

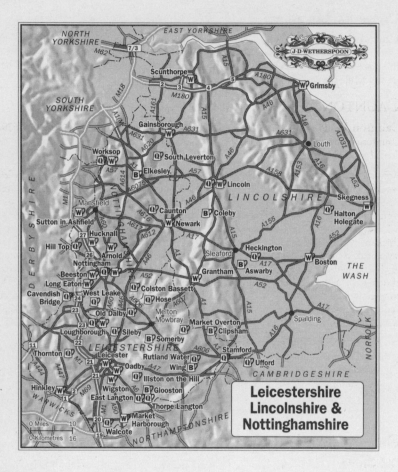

Leicestershire
Lincolnshire &
Nottinghamshire

Leicestershire, Lincolnshire & Nottinghamshire

CAUNTON

Caunton Beck
Tel: 01636 636793

Caunton, Newark, Notts NG23 6AD
Free House. Mrs Julie Allwood, licensee.

Admirably run by the same people who run the Wig and Mitre in Lincoln. From an early breakfast to a late supper, nothing is too much trouble – a cross between a perpetual restaurant and a pub; just turn up and they will look after you. Once just a 16th-century cottage, it has been wonderfully restored using the old Elizabethan timbers and reclaimed oak and pitch pine. Menus could offer smoked mussels or a lightly curried mussel soup, chicken-liver pâté with chutney and toast, pan-fried breast of pheasant in a port-wine sauce, baked fillet of cod with herb crumbs and butter sauce and lots more. A good choice of cheeses and interesting puds; Blue Mountain coffee with home-made fudge or bitter chocolates. There is a viewing window into the original cellar where the cask-conditioned ales are racked up on two levels; Timothy Taylors, Adnams and Marstons Pedigree are the permanent beers. They also have a considerable wine list. Outside are a lawn, a rose arbour and plenty of places to sit to enjoy your surroundings.

> OPEN: 8am–11pm everyday and food served all day.
> Real Ale. Restaurant.
> Children welcome. Dogs: not usually, but if you and your dog are very nice they might let you into the garden. Wheelchair access. Car park.

CAVENDISH BRIDGE

Old Crown
Tel: 01332 792392

Cavendish Bridge, Leics DE72 2HL
Free House. Peter Morton-Harrison, licensee

A pub and a few houses. Blink and you could miss it, but try not to. Older than it looks; it's been here since the 17th century, but everything else is bang up to date, especially the cooking. Substantial pub food of filled baguettes, fish and chips and vegetarian dishes. But it is the wildly imaginative specials that will catch your eye. Draught Bass and Marstons Pedigree and the regular beers, plus guests and usually something from the local Shardlow brewery set up in the old Cavendish Brewery stables across the road. Short wine list with a few by the glass.

> OPEN: 11.30–3.30. 5–11.
> Real Ale.
> Children welcome. Dogs too. Wheelchair access. Car park.
> Cards: Delta, MasterCard, Switch, Visa.

COLSTON BASSETT

Martins Arms   Tel: 01949 81361
School Lane, Colston Bassett, Notts NG12 3FD
Free House. Lynne Strafford Bryan & Salvatore Inguanta, licensees.

Surrounded by interesting buildings and opposite the Market Cross, the handsome Martins Arms started life in the 17th century as a farmhouse with a licence to brew beer. Not until the early 1800s did it become a proper pub, taking the squire's name – hence the Martins Arms. A touch of bygone formality remains in the smart interiors and uniformed staff. The above-average bar menu includes speciality sandwiches that are offbeat and different: poached salmon, basil mayonnaise and pickled peppers, grilled chicken, watercress and plum tomatoes, bacon, lettuce and tomato – all on ciabatta bread; or if you don't want a sandwich, there could be a classic Caesar salad with barbecued chicken strips, grilled tuna and salad niçoise, or a ploughman's which would keep any ploughman going all day – Melton Mowbray Pork Pie, Colston Bassett Stilton or Cheddar, home-cured ham and pickles, slices of apple, roll and garnish – wonderful. Inventive vegetarian dishes, pasta dishes and for a main course, fillet of beef with braised cabbage or breast of guinea fowl with puy lentils, roasted garlic and baby onions are just a few examples from the menu. Lots more: daily specials on the blackboard, home-made puddings and proper coffee to finish. Restaurant menu too. Own Label Beer, Timothy Taylors Landlord, Marstons Pedigree, Bass, Black Sheep Bitter, Fullers London Pride and Batemans XB are among the ales they keep. Interesting wine list, including champagnes and sparkling wines. Tables outside in the large garden with views over National Trust parkland.

> OPEN: 12–3. 6–11 (12–3. 7–10.30 Sun).
> Real Ale. Restaurant (no food Sun eves).
> Children in garden. No dogs. Wheelchair access. Car park.
> Two bedrooms.
> Cards: All cards except Amex and Diners.

EAST LANGTON

The Bell   Tel: 01858 545278
East Langton, Nr Market Harborough, Leics LE16 7TW
Free House. Alistair Chapman, licensee.

Overlooking the quiet village and well-kept cricket field – which hosts Leicester league matches – the Bell is an ideal place to spend a little time between overs. The 16th-century, creeper-covered Bell is comfortable and friendly. All the food is freshly prepared: home-made soup, filled baguettes, a Bell's steak sandwich; or as a starter you could choose a lemon chicken salad, or chicken-liver and garlic pâté served with crusty bread; valentine pork steak, sirloin or fillet steaks and lots more. Quite a choice of vegetarian dishes too. Specials on the blackboard. Senior citizens' lunches from Monday to Saturday. Sunday lunches for which you should book a table. Greene King IPA and Abbot are the main beers with regularly changing guests. The Bell has opened a microbrewery and brews Caudle Bitter, Bowler Strong Ale – to encourage the cricketers! – and two seasonal beers: Boxer and Bankers Draught. Good short wine list. Seats in the lovely walled garden.

> OPEN: 10–2.30. 7–11 (12–3. 7–10.30 Sun).
> Real Ale.
> Children until 8.30pm. Dogs welcome. Wheelchair access (not WC). Car park.
> Bedrooms.
> Cards: Delta, Diners, MasterCard, Switch, Visa.

HALTON HOLEGATE

Bell Inn   Tel: 01790 753242
Firsby Road, Halton Holegate, Lincs PE23 5NY
Free House. John & Irene Clayton, licensees.

Flat with wonderful, uninterrupted views is how you would describe the country around here. The Bell Inn and the interesting carved bench-ends in the church share the same date – early 16th century. In the pub is one big bar, low-beamed ceilings, inglenook fireplace and the ghost of a Labrador dog. No one knows for sure, but maybe he was a Lancaster bomber pilot's pet who pined for his master when he failed to return. Interesting variety of food, both in the bar and restaurant: home-made fish soup, seafood au gratin served in a scallop shell, sandwiches, salads, lots of steaks, chicken Kiev, the Bell special steak, onion and mushroom pie in a rich Madeira sauce, lots more and a vegetarian menu. Sunday roasts. Batemans XB, Tetleys Cask, Calders Premium Cream and occasional guests. Tables and chairs at the front of the pub. Several walks around the pub, one to the River Lymn.

> OPEN: 12–3. 7–11 (12–3-ish. 7–10.30 Sun).
> Real Ale. Restaurant.
> Children in restaurant. Dogs on leads. Car park.
> Cards: Amex only.

HECKINGTON

Nags Head   Tel: 01529 460218
34 High Street, Heckington, Lincs NG34 9QZ
Pubmaster. John & Theresa Clark, lease.

Quite a number of Nags Head pubs in the vicinity, but this is the one you want in Lincolnshire – a 17th-century coaching inn with the emphasis on food. White-painted, overlooking the village green, and reputedly the haunt of Dick Turpin and presumably his horse Black Bess. He did seem to do a lot of visiting in this area, although one thing I do know for certain is that he was arrested at the Green Dragon Inn, Welton, in 1739. Inside you'll find a comfortable two-roomed bar with a coal fire, friendly landlord and well-presented bar food. The changing blackboard menu could list celery and cheese soup, garlic mushrooms on toast, warm smoked mackerel with horseradish, roast gammon and pineapple, fresh crab salad, grilled sea bass, sausage and smoked-bacon quiche, vegetarian dishes and sandwiches too. An unusual favourite is the avocado and prawn hotpot – pieces of avocado with prawns in a cream and garlic sauce topped with cheese and served with French bread. Daily specials and home-made puds. Sunday roasts. Tetleys, John Smiths Smooth, Adnams Broadside and a changing guest beer. Wines by the glass. Tables in the garden. Heckington has a very attractive 14th-century church and an interesting eight-sail windmill, circa 1830 – the last in the country.

> OPEN: 11–3. 5–11 Mon–Thurs. 11–11 Fri & Sat. 11–10.30 Sun.
> Real Ale.
> Children welcome. No dogs. Wheelchair access to part of the pub.
> Quiz night Sunday. Bedrooms.

HILL TOP

Nags Head Inn   Tel: 01332 850652
Hill Top, Castle Donington, Notts DE74 2PR
Wolverhampton & Dudley. Ian Davison, tenant.

Painted white outside, gently colourwashed inside; beams, open fires and friendly staff give this old place a wonderful ambience; the food is in a league of its own. So near the border that it is a bit of a toss-up as to where you want to put it – Derbyshire or Leicestershire. It's not far from East Midlands airport and the motor-racing circuit at Castle Donington, so the pub is kept very busy. Something for everyone on the blackboard. Sandwiches are re-interpreted: imaginative fillings for baguettes and ciabattas, chicken-liver parfait with toasted ciabatta, seared scallops with balsamic vinegar, Lincolnshire sausages with mashed potato and onion gravy, beef, mushroom and red-wine casserole, monkfish with stir-fried oriental vegetables, maybe fillet of beef in Cajun spices with tzatziki. All the more-ish puds are home-made – fruit crumbles, treacle tarts – that sort of thing. Beers are Marstons Pedigree, Mansfield Bitter and Banks Mild. Thirty wines on the list, six by the glass.

> OPEN: 11.30–2.30. 5.30–11 (12–3. 7–10.30 Sun).
> Real Ale. Restaurant.
> No children. Dogs in bar. Wheelchair access. Car park.
> Cards: Amex, Delta, MasterCard, Switch, Visa.

HOSE

Black Horse   Tel: 01949 860336
21 Bolton Lane, Hose, Nr Melton Mowbray, Leics LE14 4JE.
Tynemill Group. Mike Aram, tenant.

On the edge of the rich farmlands in the Vale of Belvoir, this traditional, busy village pub has just three rooms: an unspoilt flagstoned tap room, a lounge-bar-cum-snug and a small restaurant. The menu changes weekly, but there could be melon, egg mayonnaise or prawn cocktail to start with, a range of steaks, the pub's very own way with a chicken – chicken sunrise: chicken breasts cooked in cornflakes with a sweet-and-sour sauce, rack of lamb with a redcurrant sauce, swordfish and a vegetarian dish or two. Six real ales: Brains Dark, John Smiths Bitter, Bass, Castlerocks Farriers Gold and three guests. Seats in the garden.

> OPEN: 12–2.30. 6.30–11 (12–3. 7–10.30 Sun).
> Real Ale. Restaurant. No food Mondays or Tuesdays.
> Children welcome. Dogs on leads. Wheelchair access. Car park.
> N.B. Music in restaurant, not in bar.

ILLSTON ON THE HILL

The Fox & Goose   Tel: 0116 259 6340
Main Street, Illston on the Hill, Leics LE7 9EG
Everards. George Bullers, tenant.

A small, white-painted village pub; delightfully quiet, the Fox and Goose is in a country village off the Market Harborough to Melton Mowbray road. You would come here for the beer and the freshly made sandwiches. Everards Beacon, Tiger, Old Original and always one guest beer as well as Guinness, Carling and Strongbow. Seats among the flowers at the front of the pub.

> OPEN: 12–2.30 (only on Fri, Sat & Sun in winter). 5.30–11 (12–2.30. 7–10.30 Sun).
> Real Ale.
> Children welcome. Dogs on leads.

LINCOLN

Pyewipe Inn   Tel: 01522 528708
Fossebank, Saxilby Road, Lincoln LN1 2BG
Free House. Mr & Mrs R.L. Pickles, licensees.

Originally surrounded by a considerable acreage, it still has 4 acres of grounds and enough room to land a helicopter – should you be so inclined. The Pyewipe (it's the local word for the lapwing) is a substantial three-storey building built in the late Georgian period – an alehouse by the end of the 18th century and an inn by 1823. On the Fossedyke canal (boat trips from Lincoln land here), the Pyewipe has some imaginative dishes on the menu; for a starter you could choose a pâté of Stilton with apricots and almonds, or melon with ginger and white wine. For a main course, fillet of lamb with onion mash or sirloin steak with prawns in a garlic sauce. The daily specials boards will list fresh fish, home-made puds and vegetarian dishes. The à la carte menu will change three times a year. Tetley, Greene King Abbot Ale, Bass, Flowers Original, Bass and Wadworths 6X. Views towards Lincoln Cathedral, just 2 miles away.

> OPEN: 11–11 (12–10.30 Sun).
> Real Ale.
> Children welcome but not after 7pm. Dogs on leads. Wheelchair access. Car park.
> Twenty bedrooms in a new, purpose-built lodge.
> Cards: all major cards except Amex.

LINCOLN

The Victoria   Tel: 01522 536048
6 Union Road, Lincoln LN1 3BJ
Free House. Neil Renshaw, manager.

Busy and unpretentious, this is a two-room city pub by the west gate of the Norman
castle. Here you can expect some very good beer and, to go with it, good-value home-
cooked food; nothing deep-fried, nor any chips. Usually a soup of the day, filled rolls,
ploughman's, bacon butties, an all-day breakfast (Saturday only), curries, pies and stews.
At least five guest beers available – always a dark mild – also draught Belgian beers and ten
bottled ones. They hold two yearly beer festivals: in June and December. There's a beer
garden tucked under the castle walls.

> OPEN: 11–11 (12–10.30 Sun).
> Real Ale.
> No children. Dogs on leads. Limited wheelchair access.
> Cards: Electron, JCB, MasterCard, Solo, Switch, Visa.

LINCOLN

Wig & Mitre   Tel: 01522 535190
30–32 Steep Hill, Lincoln LN2 1LU
Free House. Toby Hope & Valerie Hope, licensees.

From here, on the Pilgrim's Way below the cathedral, you can keep an eye on all the comings
and goings in this part of the bustling city. Dating back to the 14th century, many of the original timbers were reused when the old building was restored 20 years ago. Food is in perpetual
motion throughout the day from an early breakfast to tea or dinner in the evening. The menu
changes regularly but there will always be a 'daily fish' and possibly sun-dried-tomato pasta
with Parma ham, spring onions and Parmesan cheese, baked cheese soufflé, or sirloin steak
with cracked black peppercorns, brandy and cream; puddings and a piece of cheese too.
Nothing is too much trouble. Wines (nearly 100 and many by the glass), ales and spirits are
available from 11 in the morning until midnight. Morrels Varsity and Marstons Pedigree ales
on hand pump, and also, as you would expect, freshly squeezed orange juice and coffee.

> OPEN: 8am–midnight. Food served continuously.
> Real Ale. Restaurant.
> Children in eating area and restaurant. No dogs.
> Cards: Amex, Delta, Diners, MasterCard, Switch, Visa.

LOUGHBOROUGH

Swan in the Rushes   Tel: 01509 217014
21 The Rushes, Loughborough, Leics LE11 5BE
Free House. Ian Bogie, licensee.

Solidly Victorian. A tile-fronted, serious town pub, with no frills; a good, plain, matter-of-
fact sort of place with a reputation for simple, good-quality, home-cooked bar food,

complementing its extensive range of European bottled beers, whiskies and the nine or more beers on hand pump. These could include Archers Golden, Tetley Bitter, Castle Rock Hemlock and up to seven guests. There is also a selection of farm ciders which change periodically. With all this on offer, it is not surprising that the pub is very popular and can get crowded. Service does, nevertheless, remain friendly and efficient.

OPEN: 11–11 (12–10.30 Sun).
Real Ale. No food Sat and Sun eves.
Children in dining room and no-smoking room. Dogs on leads.
Wheelchair access. Jukebox in public bar. Folk music every two weeks.

MARKET OVERTON

Black Bull   Tel: 01572 767677
Teigh Road, Market Overton, Rutland LE15 7PW
Free House. John & Val Owen, licensees.

An atmospheric thatched old pub in a quiet village. It combines the ideals of a thriving local with a restaurant serving some really good country cooking. Low-ceilinged and beamed, it is very cosy – a place to linger. All the food is listed on the blackboard: there could be French onion soup, game pie or fresh fish; puddings are of the nostalgic kind, such as treacle sponge and apple tart. Beers are Charles Wells Bombardier, Hook Norton, Marstons, John Smiths and Theakstons Black Bull Bitter. Short wine list, only two by the glass.

OPEN: 12–2.30. 6–11.
Real Ale. Restaurant.
Children welcome. Dogs on leads. Bedrooms.
Cards: Delta, MasterCard, Switch, Visa.

NOTTINGHAM

Ye Olde Trip to Jerusalem   Tel: 0115 947 3171
Brewhouse Yard, Castle Road, Nottingham NE1 6AD
Hardy & Hansons. Claire Underdown, manager.

Of tremendous architectural interest, this old place was probably rebuilt on the site of the original inn during the 17th century, and reputed to be – or at least the foundations are – the oldest pub in England. Previously named 'The Pilgrim', it, or the remains of it, stands on what was apparently the meeting point for crusaders before they sailed to deal with the heathen hordes. Architecturally of interest, the panelled rooms have alcoves cut into the rock and the cellars are in rock caves. Tunnels, staircases, hidden rooms are all hewn out of the sandstone rock below the castle. An upstairs, impressive, part-panelled, part-rockface, high-ceilinged bar is open every day and well worth seeing. Traditional, sustaining food in the stone-floored bar: steak and kidney pudding, garlic and herb chicken, filled giant Yorkshire puddings – that sort of thing, plus daily specials and a good choice of vegetarian dishes. Hardy and Hansons have introduced a

'Cellarman's Cask' range of ales which changes every two months. Seats outside in the courtyard.

> OPEN: 11–11 (12–10.30 Sun).
> Real Ale. Meals served from 11–6 (12–6 Sun).
> Children until 6pm. No dogs. Wheelchair access (not WC).
> Cards: Delta, MasterCard, Solo, Switch, Visa.

OLD DALBY

Crown   Tel: 01664 823134
Debdale Hill, Old Dalby, Nr Melton Mowbray, Leics LE14 3LF
Free House. Lynne Busby, licensee.

Creeper-covered and really quite smart, the Crown, a converted 16th-century farmhouse, has small, comfortable, beamed rooms with open fires, all well kept and prosperous-looking. The food really is home-made, and these are the type of dishes you could find on the daily menu: a warm salad of smoked chicken, bacon and pear with blue-cheese dressing, fresh linguini, and potato cakes filled with Stilton or Cheddar cheese served with mango chutney. Also speciality sandwiches served on warm ciabatta with a dressed salad and a venison sausage or two. The Crown ploughman's – Melton Mowbray pork pie, Colston Bassett Stilton or Cheddar, home-cured ham and pickles with slices of apple, wholemeal roll and garnish – should keep you quiet for a bit! Lots more, several vegetarian dishes, specials on the blackboard. Delicious puds. There is a separate menu in the no-smoking dining room. Ales are always changing, some served from a cask behind the bar. Choice of malt whiskies and a good wine list. Tables on the terrace overlook the large garden. There is also a *pétanque* pitch and a landlady who is a very skilled player. The Midshire Way Pennine walk nearby offers plenty of scope for healthy exercise.

> OPEN: 12–3. 6–11.
> Real Ale. Restaurant (not Sun eves).
> Children over ten in restaurant only. Dogs on leads welcome. Wheelchair access.

RUTLAND WATER

Barnsdale Lodge Hotel   Tel: 01572 724678
The Avenue, Rutland Water, Nr Oakham, Rutland LE15 8AH
Free House. Robert Reid, owner/licensee.

Rutland, the smallest county in England, has a county town mentioned in pre-Norman records. But Rutland as a county was only created in the reign of King John. It was eliminated when the government redefined county boundaries in 1974 but restored at the end of the last century after persistent lobbying by its inhabitants. This farmhouse hotel overlooks Rutland Water and all rooms have views over the surrounding countryside. The famous gardens at Barnsdale are nearby – just down the avenue – as are historic Oakham,

Uppingham and Stamford in Lincolnshire. Lots to do near here, whether on or off the water. In the hotel there is a welcoming bar and conservatory where they serve bar meals and snacks, also two dining rooms for more formal eating. Outside is a colourful courtyard and well-planted gardens. Interesting choice of food and a good wine list. The beers are Grainstore Oakham Best and Courage Directors.

> OPEN: All day; the bar is open until midnight for residents.
> Children and dogs welcome except in main eating areas – guide dogs excepted. All wheelchair facilities.
> N.B. There is a pianola playing in the bar area. Tell us if you think it is 'too much'.

SILEBY

White Swan   Tel: 01509 814832
Swan Street, Sileby, Leics LE12 7NW
Free House. Bob & Theresa Miller, licensees.

Atmosphere is all in some pubs, usually created by the feeling of antiquity, of being part of continuing hospitality. This comparative newcomer has a few centuries to make up but it's on the right track; not all pubs need to be 15th-century. Not only well-kept beer but good-value home-cooked food too. You can either eat in the attractive book-lined restaurant or in the bar. Lots of fillings for the baguettes, jacket potatoes and rolls, or you could choose a hot Mediterranean vegetable tartlet with a garlic and herb cream-cheese topping; Parma ham, goat's cheese and walnut salad; baked chicken breast wrapped in bacon with home-made sausage; pan-fried sirloin steak in red wine; or deep-fried lemon sole fillet in breadcrumbs with battered squid rings. Ansells Bitter, Mansfield Cask, Adnams, Banks plus a guest. A glass or two of wine, a garden to sit in and a skittle alley to hire. They have their own dog, Leo, a finalist in the UK's naughtiest dog competition, so they don't want any outside influences!

> OPEN: 11.45–3. 7–11. No food Sun eves or all day Mon.
> Real Ale. Restaurant.
> Children welcome. No dogs. Wheelchair access. Car park.
> Cards: All cards except Amex.

SOUTH LEVERTON

The Plough Inn   Tel: 01427 880323
Town Street, South Leverton, Notts DN22 0BT
Free House. J.B. Bell, licensee.

A small, simple place – scrubbed tables and benches and well-kept beer. Just a beer pub, this; no food, no excesses in the interior-decoration line. 'Them what think they know' say it is the smallest pub in Nottinghamshire, but the pub has managed to find room for the stamps and postal orders as the Plough leads a double life as the local post office. When you're not posting a letter you can enjoy the Ruddles Best Bitter and whatever guest is on that day.

> OPEN: Closed weekday mornings, otherwise 2–11 (12–11 Sat. 12–4. 7–10.30 Sun).
> Real Ale.
> No children. Dogs on leads. Wheelchair access poor, but the locals manage to force their way in.

STAMFORD

George of Stamford   Tel: 01780 750750
71 High Street, St Martins, Stamford, Lincs PE9 2LB
Free House. Ivo Vanocci & Chris Pitman, licensees.

Behind the handsome Georgian façade, the London and York bars – which face each other just inside the building – were the waiting rooms for the 40 coaches that stopped here each day for a change of horses and to allow the passengers some refreshment. It is still a focal point for the local community, whether dining or enjoying a glass of wine or pint of ale in the comfortable bar. Go into the York Bar for a quick, light snack: soup of the day with Italian bread, Cheddar and Stilton platter with ciabatta, open toasted sandwiches, lots of fillings for the ciabatta bread, or if you want to fill more than a corner, a Daniel Lambert sandwich – ciabatta bread, sirloin steak, fried onions, tomato and mushroom. The Garden Lounge menu, available all day, ranges from a warm salad of chicken strips, smoked bacon, avocado, spinach and cherry tomatoes to a Grand Brittany Platter which includes half a lobster, crab, langoustine, mussels, king prawns, oysters, clams, shell-on prawns and whelks. Much, much more, and a restaurant menu. Adnams ales, a guest ale, a considerable wine list, many by the glass and all the other niceties you associate with a well-run establishment – freshly squeezed orange juice, good coffee and afternoon teas. An attractive cobbled courtyard at the rear of the creeper-covered George is filled with tables and chairs among flowering tubs and hanging baskets.

> OPEN: 11–11.
> Real Ale. Restaurants (two).
> Children welcome. Dogs in garden. Wheelchair access. Bedrooms.
> Cards: All major credit cards.

THORNTON

Bricklayers Arms   Tel: 01530 230808
Main Street, Thornton, Leics LE67 1AH
Everards. T. Swyers, tenant.

If you're planning to come here on a Monday and you want something to eat, forget it: there's not a crust to be had. If you're a local you'll know how to get here, but if you're on the M1 motorway and want to get to the pub you will have to come off at Exit 22 and work backwards. When you do arrive, you'll find an unspoilt, 16th-century village pub, still with a basic, stone-floored bar and a more comfortable lounge, both with good open fires. Two-course special Tuesday, Wednesday and Thursday: mince and dumplings, toad in the hole, seven vegetables to choose from – no skimping on the portions here – and a pudding to follow. All home-cooked comfort food and it's very popular. Well-kept Everards Tiger, Old Original and a guest beer.

> OPEN: 12–3. 6–11 (12–11 Sat. 12–10.30 Sun). Pub opens one hour earlier during the summer except on Sunday.
> Real Ale. No food Mondays.
> Children welcome. Dogs on leads. Wheelchair access.

THORPE LANGTON

Bakers Arms   Tel: 01858 545201
Main Street, Thorpe Langton, Leics LE16 7TS
Free House. Kate Hubbard, licensee/manageress.

Lots of little Langtons – Church, East and Thorpe; even a Langton Hall – but to find this small, quiet village you need to take a left turn off the B6047. The thatched Bakers Arms, mostly 16th-century but extended and refurbished, has over the last few years built up an excellent reputation for serving fine food accompanied by a knowledgeable wine list. There is a constantly changing menu – all on blackboards. You could start with a warm salad of new potatoes, black pudding and bacon or grilled goat's cheese with roast cherry tomatoes, and for a main course, roast shank of lamb with cumin, honey and roast parsnips, or whole baked sea bass with mussels, leeks and saffron. Scrummy puds to follow. It's wise to book a table. That said, they do still serve a pint or two: Tetleys ales and Guinness. The pub piano is brought to the fore on Friday evenings, so if you don't appreciate a little night music, you know when to avoid it.

> OPEN: 6.30–11 Tues–Fri (12–2. 6.30–11 Sat. 12–2 Sun). Closed Mon, Sun eves and every lunchtime except Sat and Sun.
> Real Ale.
> No children under 12 – ever. No dogs. Wheelchair access (not WC). Car park.
> Cards: Amex, Delta, MasterCard, Switch, Visa.

UFFORD

Olde White Hart   Tel: 01780 740250
Main Street, Ufford, Lincs PE9 3BH
Scottish & Newcastle/Youngers. Glenis Garner & Beverly Harrison, tenants.

The White Hart's large, attractive garden is big enough for you to set up camp if you have brought your tent. This pretty 17th-century pub has two comfortable bars and a cosy snug.

Lunchtime snacks include a variety of exotic dishes which change from week to week. The usual sandwiches, maybe stuffed pancakes or rump steak with a garlic sauce, daily specials and, on Sunday, a roast lunch and hot beef rolls. Theakstons Best, XB and Old Peculier. Guest beers and lots of imported bottled beers. Wines by the glass and farm cider. Good walks nearby.

> OPEN: 11–2.30 (11–3 Sat). 6–11.
> Real Ale. No food Sunday eves or Monday.
> Children in eating areas. Dogs on leads.

WALCOTE

The Blackhorse Inn   Tel: 01455 552684
Lutterworth Road, Walcote, Leics LE17 4JU (only a mile from Junction 20 on the M1)
Free House. Mrs Saovanee Tinker, licensee.

You can experience a mix of cultures here: East meets West. On the one hand, you have a Thai landlady serving wonderful, authentic Thai food; on the other hand, to remind you that you're still in England, they serve a selection of well-kept ales, usually Hoskins, Oldfield Hob Bitter plus T.T. Landlord and Fullers London Pride as guests and maybe a real cider.

> OPEN: 7–11 Mon–Thurs. 12–3. 7–11 Fri. 12–3. 7–11 Sat. 12–3. 7–10.30 Sun.
> Closed Mon–Thurs mornings.
> Real Ale.
> No children. No dogs. Wheelchair access. Car park.

WORKSOP

The Greendale Oak   Tel: 01909 489680
Norfolk Street, Worksop, Notts S80 1LE
Free House. Jan Parry & Jon Aspinall, licensees.

The ancient town of Worksop on the River Ryton is known as the 'Gateway to the Dukeries': grand estates created for sport, north of Sherwood Forest. The pub, built about the same time as the delightful Clumber Park and created by the Duke of Newcastle in the late 18th century, might be as old but is certainly not as grand; the Greendale Oak is just a small, gas-lit terrace pub, serving good traditional pub food. The changing menu offers 14 specials a day, also roasts, home-made pies, all kinds of fish and all served at your table. This is proper sit-down food. For the serious drinker, Stones Bitter, Theakston Mild and a changing guest bitter and mild from microbreweries, are all cask ales.

> OPEN: 12–4.30. 7–11 (11–11 Fri & Sat. 12–3. 7–10.30 Sun).
> Real Ale.
> No children. Dogs – yes, except at mealtimes.

WEST LEAKE

Star Inn   Tel: 01509 852233
Melton Lane, West Leake, Nr Loughborough, Leics
Enterprise Inns. Linda Collins, licensee.

Inside this lovely old coaching inn the beamed bars are comfortably furnished and kept warm in winter by open log fires. Food is home-cooked and the menu changes daily, but there could be soup, mushrooms in cream and garlic sauce, pâté, roast leg of pork, chicken chasseur and a choice of puddings. They have beers from many of the small breweries, currently something from: Harviestoun, Adnams, Robinsons, Charles Wells and Black Sheep but these do change, and there is always draught Bass. Over a dozen malt whiskies. Seats and tables outside during the summer. You are surrounded by beautiful countryside.

> OPEN: 11–3. 6–11.
> Real Ale.
> Children in family room. Dogs on leads. Wheelchair access.
> Cards: MasterCard, Solo, Switch, Visa.

BEST OF THE REST

ASWARBY, Lincolnshire

Tally Ho   Tel: 01529 455205
In a pleasing rural situation, with apple trees to sit under and sheep in the park to look at. As well as the usual bar food, there are always some exciting dishes on the menu: chicken in a pepper and orange sauce, warm duck salad, pork with olives and delicious puds. Batemans, a guest and a good wine list. Bedrooms.

COLEBY, Lincolnshire

Bell   Tel: 01522 810240
In this village south of Lincoln, the busy 18th-century Bell has a comfortable, beamed and panelled main bar with a big log fire. From the reasonably priced menu you could choose crostini with garlic mushrooms, a lightly poached selection of fresh fish in a saffron sauce, Suffolk-cured gammon with free-range eggs, daily specials and lots more – something for everyone. Thursday night is fish night. Flowers Original, Bass and Tetleys ales; Marstons is the guest. Range of malt whiskies and a short wine list. Seats in the garden. Bedrooms (3 Crown rated).

CLIPSHAM, Rutland

Olive Branch   Tel: 01780 410355
Just a collection of cottages and the pub. The lucky locals have a little treasure on their doorstep. It's looking very smart since it reopened three years ago, and you are going to be extremely well fed from either the short bar menu or the delights of the *prix fixe* lunch;

beers are from the Grainstore Brewery in Oakham and other small eastern breweries. Wine is taken very seriously here, as reflected in the interesting offers on the wine boards.

SOMERBY, Rutland

Stilton Cheese   Tel: 01664 454394

Between Melton Mowbray and Oakham, this is a 16th-century pub in a pretty village where they serve good pub food. Simple things, well cooked and presented: home-made soups such as Stilton and onion, Rutland trout, sausage and mash, steak and kidney pie and daily specials. Marstons Pedigree, Tetleys and the local Grain Store Ten Fifty, as well as weekly changing guests from small breweries. Wide-ranging wine list, and a number of malts. Muzak is on but hardly audible at lunchtime.

ELKESLEY, Nottinghamshire

Robin Hood   Tel: 01777 838259

Here is a possible refuge to break a relentless journey on the A1: a village local with some better-than-usual offerings on the food front. As well as home-made soup and well-filled rolls there could be a courgette, mushroom and cheese bake, chargrilled chicken with Mediterranean vegetables, duck breast on potato rosti with a port-wine and cherry sauce – daily specials too. Wines to go with your meal as well as Boddingtons and a guest beer.

GLOOSTON, Leicestershire

Old Barn   Tel: 01858 545215

Unfortunately we have had to demote the Old Barn as the new owners have introduced music – quiet, but still there. The 16th-century Old Barn is still worth finding – the menus are imaginative. There is a bar menu, or from the à la carte you could have a terrine of fresh salmon and chive mousse garnished with prawns to start, and then strips of pork loin with mixed peppers, tomatoes and leeks cooked in cider and cream; home-made puddings to follow. In addition there will be fish, local game in season and chef's specials. Always four ales on draught: Tetley Bitter, Green King IPA and two guests; also several European bottled beers and a more extensive wine list. Closed Monday lunchtimes.

WING, Leicestershire

Kings Arms   Tel: 01572 737634

Not far from Rutland Water, this stone-built 17th-century pub with beams, flagstone floors and huge fires offers reasonably priced bar food, along with something a little different from the specials board. The local Batemans and other beers. Bedrooms.

The Midlands

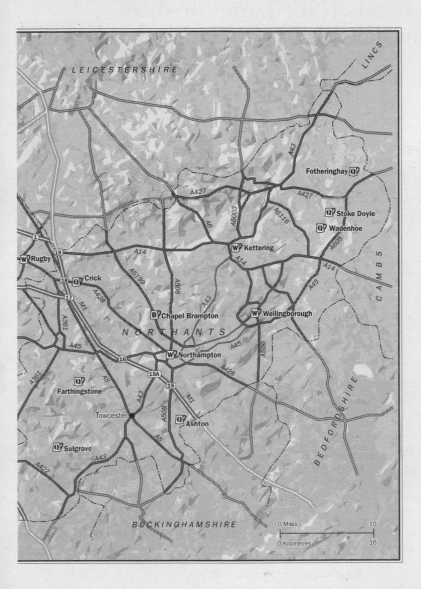

Midlands (Northamptonshire, Warwickshire & West Midlands)

ASHTON

The Chequered Skipper
Tel: 01832 273494

Ashton, Oundle, Nr Peterborough, Northants PE8 5LE
Free House. Colin & Ian Campbell, licensees.

Outwardly a traditional thatched country pub in an idyllic village; inwardly a more minimalist look. After being gutted by fire the interior was completely rebuilt ready for the 21st century. The young staff are helpful and friendly and it is still patronised by the locals, muddy boots, dogs and all. Food is plentiful and inventive. For a starter you could have grilled whole sardines served with a tomato, oregano and garlic sauce; terrine of roasted peppers; wild mushrooms, sweet potato and asparagus with fresh herbs, wrapped in spiced cabbage leaves. For a main course there are some interesting fish dishes – red mullet, lemon sole or halibut steak all done in different ways; paupiette of chicken with creamed mango sauce; sautéed venison steak served with a fig sauce and game chips, lots of steaks and grills, vegetarian dishes and delicious puddings to finish. Draught Bass, Oakham JHB and Shepherd Neame Spitfire.

> OPEN: 11–3. 6–11 (11.30–11 Sat. 12–10.30 Sun).
> Real Ale.
> Children welcome. Dogs yes, but not in dining area.

BIRMINGHAM

Briar Rose
Tel: 0121 634 8100

25 Bennetts Hill, Birmingham, West Midlands B2 5RE
Wetherspoon.

This is definitely different. Converted from offices in the centre of the city, decorated with more than a nodding acquaintance with Art Deco. Not only can you eat and drink well but you can stay here too; you really might be 'going out for the night', as this is one of the new branches of Wetherspoon: a Wetherlodge – with bedrooms – 41 of them. Standards are high – as reliable and as reasonable as you would expect.

> OPEN: Hotel hours.
> Real Ale.
> Children if staying. No dogs. Wheelchair access.

BRIERLEY HILL

Vine   Tel: 01384 78293
10 Delph Road, Brierley Hill, West Midlands DY5 2TN
Bathams. Melvyn Wood, manager.

Glassmakers have been in this area from Roman times to the present day, as you can see from the number of local museums dedicated to their art. The Vine, known locally as the Bull and Bladder, is associated with the Royal and Ancient Order of Buffalos, not the glassmakers, though they do have a stained-glass front window depicting a bull's (buffalo's?) head and a bunch of grapes. Plenty of room in this bustling pub; there is an award-winning extension into the brewery offices – not quite a permanent beer line to the brewery, but as it is next door there could well be! Popular, well-made and reasonably priced lunchtime snacks, freshly filled sandwiches and lots of salads. Bathams Bitter and Mild on hand pump, also Delph Strong Ale in winter.

> OPEN: 12–11.
> Real Ale. Lunchtime snacks (not Sun).
> Children in own room. Dogs on leads. Disabled WC but no access into the pub with wheelchair.
> Live music Sunday and Monday: blues/jazz/folk.

BUBBENHALL

Three Horseshoes   Tel: 024 7630 2108
Spring Hill, Bubbenhall, Warwickshire CV8 3BD (between Coventry and Leamington Spa)
Punch Taverns. Mary Jones, licensee.

The Three Horseshoes, an old coaching inn, is in a pretty village on the way to Leamington Spa, south of Coventry, in countryside as varied as it is beautiful. You are very near the geographical centre of England – in Shakespeare country. A cheerful and popular place; inside are several small rooms with tiled and flagged floors and log fires. They serve good plain food to go with the ales: draught Bass, Brew XI and Caffreys. Picnic tables outside the front and back of the pub. Surrounded by good walks.

> OPEN: 11–2.30. 5–11 (11–3. 5–11 Fri. 11–11 Sat. 12–10.30 Sun.)
> Children welcome. Dogs too. Wheelchair access. Car park.

CRICK

Red Lion   Tel: 01788 822342
52 Main Road, Crick, Northants NN6 7TX
Free House. Tom Marks, MBII, lease.

Only a mile from Junction 18 on the M1, so if you're out of familiar territory and wanting a break from the boredom of driving, slip off the motorway and search out the Red Lion – rest and recuperation is not far away. In winter this comfortable thatched pub has log fires in the low-ceilinged bar; in summer you can relax on the terrace at the back and admire the floral display. Reasonably priced lunchtime snacks – 17 hot dishes to choose from, some changing daily: sandwiches and ploughman's, steaks, chicken Kiev, trout, lamb cutlets, moussaka. Over ten vegetarian dishes are available on the evening menu. Beers change regularly, so what is on today could be off next week. Go and be surprised.

> OPEN: 11.30–2.30. 6.30–11 (12–3. 7–10.30 Sun).
> Real Ale. Sunday lunches but no food Sunday eves.
> Children in family room lunchtimes only. Dogs on leads. Wheelchair access.
> Cards: all except Amex and Diners.

DORRIDGE

Railway Inn   Tel: 01564 773531
Grange Road, Dorridge, Solihull, West Midlands B93 8QA
Punch Lease. Philip (Joe) Watson, licensee.

A friendly and unchanging pub with only public and lounge bars. On the edge of the village: village one side, green fields the other. The bar menu ranges from sandwiches (plain and toasted), filled baguettes, ploughman's and salads to smoked salmon, rump-steak toasted sandwich (with fried onions) to a mixed grill, gammon steak or T-bone steak to go with the draught Bass, Brew XI, Highgate Mild and a selection of guest beers. There is a choice of wines. Seats in the garden,

> OPEN: 12–3. 4.30–11 Mon–Fri. 11–11 Sat. 12–10.30 Sun.
> Real Ale.
> Children at meal times only. Dogs in public bar only.
> Cards: MasterCard, Solo, Switch, Visa.

EARLSDON

Royal Oak   Tel: 024 7667 4140
Earlsdon Street, Earlsdon, Coventry, Warwickshire CV5 6EJ
Free House. Ray Evitts, licensee.

Another pub for those who appreciate their beer. Search out the hanging baskets; the pub is somewhere behind them. Immensely popular with those who appreciate good beer served in pleasing, unfussy and friendly surroundings. Large wooden communal tables and comfortable chairs. Waiter service in the rear bar. House rules are rigorously applied – no dogs, no music, no noisy, rowdy behaviour and no food! Ansells Mild, Bass, Tetley, draught Guinness and guest beers.

> OPEN: 5–11 Mon–Sat (12–3. 7–10.30 Sun).
> Real Ale. No food.
> No dogs. Wheelchair access (not WC).

FARTHINGSTONE

The Kings Arms
Tel: 01327 361604
Farthingstone, Nr Towcester, Northants NN12 8EZ
Free House. Paul & Denise Egerton, proprietors.

You naturally assume that pubs are open at lunchtime, but this one isn't – except at the weekend. So no refreshing drinks and snacks here; it is open during the evening but food is only served Saturday and Sunday lunchtimes. Opposite the church (some of the same stone seems to have found its way into the walls of the pub). The Kings Arms is mostly 18th-century with the most wonderful windows, lots of nooks and crannies, beams, an inglenook fireplace, log fires – all just as it should be. The home-cooked food, served for weekend lunches in both the bar and lounge, could include home-made soup, well-filled baguettes and sandwiches, specials such as vegetable and Stilton tartlets, pork steak with mustard and bacon, game casserole, venison with bacon and prunes, also Hooky beef. They have quite a selection of British cheeses to take away or nibble on. Hook Norton Old Hooky and weekly changing guests.

> OPEN: Closed weekday lunchtimes and all day Monday and Wednesday. All other evenings 7–11, otherwise 12–3. 7–11 Sat. 12–3. 9–11 Sun.
> Real Ale. Food Saturday and Sunday lunchtimes only.
> Children welcome. Dogs in garden. Car park.

FIVE WAYS

Case is Altered
Tel: 01926 484206
Case Lane, Five Ways, Hatton, Nr Warwick, Warwickshire CV35 7JD (north of Warwick)
Free House. Jackie Willacy, licensee.

Liquid refreshment only. An old-fashioned, basic pub with a beamed bar, red tiled floor, old wooden tables and chairs and a good log fire during the winter. Popular with locals as well as walkers and cyclists at weekends. No food, except for a crisp or nut. Hook Norton Old Hooky, Greene King IPA, Jennings Mild and one regular guest ale.

> OPEN: 12–2.30. 6–11 (12–2. 7–10.30 Sun).
> Real Ale. No food.
> No children. No dogs. Wheelchair access.

FOTHERINGHAY

Falcon Inn
Tel: 01832 226254
Fotheringhay, Nr Oundle, Northants PE8 5HZ
Free House. Ray Smikle, chef/patron.

This village has an enduring place in history. It was here in Fotheringhay Castle that Mary Queen of Scots was executed in 1587; a grassy mound and a few stones are all that is left. The Falcon, a busy and informal village pub (darts and dominoes and all) has a very classy conservatory as a dining room. Here they serve good-value, imaginative food: tomato, fennel and garlic soup, spicy crab and salmon cake with peanut, chilli and cucumber dressing, fillet of salmon with courgettes, minted new potatoes, lemon butter sauce and salsa verde, Jamaican jerk chicken with crushed sweet potato and plantain, spinach and red-wine shallot sauce with marinated cherries layered with meringues, lemon, mascarpone and biscuit to follow gives you some idea of the delights on the menu. Snacks are on the blackboard. You can eat what you like; there is no minimum order. Greene King, Adnams, and guest ales. Wide-ranging, inspired wine list, 17 by the glass. Tables in the garden.

> OPEN: 11.30–3. 6–11 (7–11 Mon in winter. 12–3. 7–10.30 Sun).
> Real Ale. Restaurant (not Mon lunchtimes) and conservatory are no smoking.
> Children welcome. No dogs. Wheelchair access. Car park.
> Cards: Amex, Diners, MasterCard, Switch, Visa.

GREAT WOLFORD

Fox & Hounds   Tel: 01608 674220
Great Wolford, Nr Shipston-on-Stour, Warwickshire CV36 5NQ
Free House. Wendy Veal & John Scott Lee, licensees.

The directions to find this pub are as varied as the ways to get here, but we think it is a right turn off the A34 Shipston-on-Stour to Long Compton Road, or it could be a turn off the A44 north of Moreton in the Marsh, or it could be … I'm sure you've got a very good map. Well worth the finding. A wonderful, atmospheric country pub at its best. Stone-built, dating from about 1499 with polished flagstone floors, old wooden settles, open log fires – when we are not having a heatwave – and lots of bric-à-brac to admire. Lots of compliments about the food, so to give you some idea what could be on the menu, these are a few of the dishes: home-made soups and pâté, warm duck starter salad with lardons of bacon, croutons, sauté potatoes and mixed seasonal leaves tossed in a Caesar dressing. For a main course you could have paupiettes of lemon sole stuffed with prawns, wrapped in smoked salmon and served on a bed of creamed leeks with new potatoes and lemon-balm sauce, tournedos, fillet or sirloin steaks served with delicious fresh vegetables. Local traditional food on the blackboard. Good wine list, about six by the glass and quite a list of beers: Hook Norton, Fullers London Pride, Hobgoblin, Ruddles County, Wadworths 6X, Boddingtons – and more. Over 200 malt whiskies to try. Seats outside on the terrace.

> OPEN: 12–3. 7–11. Closed all day Mon and no food Sunday eves.
> Real Ale. No restaurant – now there are smoking and non-smoking areas.
> Children in eating area. Dogs on leads. Wheelchair access. Car park. Bedrooms.
> Cards: none accepted.

ILMINGTON

Howard Arms
Lower Green, Ilmington, Nr Shipston-on-Stour, Warwickshire CV36 4LT
Free House. R. Greenstock & M. Devereux, licensees.

What more could you possibly want when searching for your ideal pub but a rambling, handsome, 16th-century stone Cotswold pub that overlooks the village green? Altered and renovated since our last edition, it still has plentiful beams, polished stone floors, a fireplace big enough to burn a tree, comfortable furnishings and a general air of well-ordered house-keeping – and as an added bonus it is in a very desirable area if your interest leans towards the horticultural. Ilmington is near two of the most famous gardens in the country: Kiftsgate and Hidcote; what's more you can stay here and do one garden a day. The food is imaginative and out of the ordinary; it is all cooked to order, which means there can be delays but it is worth the wait. To start with you could have grilled sardines, roasted cherry tomatoes and tomato relish, crisp pancetta, French-bean and warm potato salad with pesto dressing; to follow, pan-fried calves' liver, buttered onions, crisp bacon with balsamic dressing or grilled salmon, lemon and garlic pappardelle, a couple of vegetarian dishes, and delicious home-made puds. Beers from a local North Cotswold Brewery – Genesis, Everards Tiger and one guest, a short wine list with European and New World wines, ten served by the glass. There is a delightful garden and good walks.

OPEN: 11–2.30. 6–11.
Real Ale. Restaurant.
Children welcome. Dogs on leads. Wheelchair access (not WC). Car park.
Bedrooms – all redecorated, looking very smart.
Cards: MasterCard, Switch, Visa.

LAPWORTH

Navigation Inn
Tel: 01564 783337
Old Warwick Road, Lapworth, Warwickshire
Bass. Andrew Kimber, lease.

You can be entertained by the locals in this pub in more ways than one, as anything can be going on in the garden, from a barbecue to visiting Morris dancers, even a theatre company bringing a bit of culture. If you just want to sit down and stare, you can do that too, as you can sit on the lawn of this canalside pub and watch the water flow by. They serve some appetising bar food: filled rolls, lasagne, a beef, Guinness and mushroom pie, rack of lamb, noisettes of lamb, fresh fish, steaks, curries and some vegetarian dishes. Draught Bass, Brew XI and Strongbow, Woodpecker and guest ciders. Seats on the lawn which runs down to the water's edge.

OPEN: 11–2.30. 5.30–11 (all day summer Sats).
Real Ale.
Children in eating area before 9pm. Dogs on leads.
Occasional Morris dancing/folk music.

LEAMINGTON SPA

Benjamin Satchwell
Tel: 01926 883733
112–114 The Parade, Leamington Spa, Warwickshire
Wetherspoon.

Leamington Spa, on the River Leam, discovered the famous spring waters as early as 1586 and acquired the Royal prefix in 1838 after a visit by Queen Victoria. You can still take the waters at the Royal Pump Room in the town centre. After that you can wander into the Benjamin Satchwell, which is on the main shopping street of the Royal Spa, for a refreshing drink. Always six real ales if you are interested in the beer, and anything else you could possibly want if you're not. Good reliable food always available.

OPEN: 11–11.
Real Ale.
No children. No dogs except guide dogs. Full disabled facilities.

NEWBOLD ON STOUR
White Hart Inn
Tel: 01789 450205
Stratford Road, Newbold on Stour, Nr Stratford-upon-Avon, Warwickshire
Punch Taverns. Mr & Mrs J. Cruttwell, lease.

Picnic tables and glorious hanging baskets are the first things you see at the front of this pub; you sit amid the flowers. Inside is one spacious main bar, with a public bar with all the noisy bits, including the jukebox, behind. Chat a lot in the main bar and with any luck you may not hear it. A popular local, offering a good selection of reasonably priced food; it gets very busy on Friday and Saturday evenings. You should book if you want Sunday lunch. The rest of the week there could be home-made soups, ploughman's, braised lamb in wine and herbs, poached salmon in cream herb sauce and paella among other dishes. Worthingtons Best and Adnams Bitter on hand pump.

OPEN: 11–2.30 (11–3 Sat). 6–11.
Real Ale. Restaurant (no food Sun eves).
Children welcome. Dogs on leads.

SHIPSTON-ON-STOUR
The Horseshoe
Tel: 01608 661225
Church Street, Shipston-on-Stour, Warwickshire CV36 4AP
Inntrepreneur. Lorain Stinton, licensee.

Among the very pretty houses in the centre of Shipston is the 17th-century Horseshoe; low-ceilinged, well-beamed, and with panelling in both the lounge and public bars. Bar food ranges from home-made soup and sandwiches to a mixed grill. Currently the most popular dish from the restaurant's à la carte menu is a leg of lamb for two – very hearty eaters here! There is a carvery on Sunday. Ruddles Best, Courage Directors, and Hook Norton Mild as the guest beer. Seating for 40 on the terrace, so you should be able to find somewhere to rest your pint pot and half a leg.

OPEN: 11–3. 6–11 (11–11 Fri & Sat. 12–3. 7–10.30 Sun).
Real Ale. Restaurant.
Children welcome. Dogs on leads outside eating hours.
N.B. Jukebox and live music.

STRATFORD-UPON-AVON

Black Swan (The Dirty Duck)
Tel: 01789 297312
Waterside, Stratford-upon-Avon, Warwickshire CV37 6BA
Laurel Pub Co. Sam Jackson, licensee.

A tourist and theatregoer's heaven; members of the Royal Shakespeare Theatre regard it as their own local. Overlooking the River Avon, near the theatre, Shakespeare's house and Holy Trinity Church, where he is buried, this is the place to go to spot the famous. A lovely old pub dating back to Shakespeare's day, catering for the theatre trade. If you dine here, timing is everything. It's a before-the-performance or after-the-performance place. Beams and panelling throughout; photos of famous thespians decorate the walls. The wide selection of bar food includes substantial open sandwiches, traditional fish and chips, home-baked pies and filled jacket potatoes. In the restaurant you could have roast beef, honey-roast duck, smoked salmon and scrambled egg or one of the daily specials. Flowers Original, Wadworths 6X and Morlands Old Speckled Hen. Wines by the bottle and glass. No garden, though the terrace, complete with ancient mulberry tree, overlooks the theatre gardens.

> OPEN: 11–11 (12–10.30 Sun).
> Real Ale. Restaurant.
> Children in restaurant area only. Dogs in bar. Wheelchair access difficult.

SHUSTOKE

Griffin Inn
Tel: 01675 481205
Nr Coleshill, Birmingham, West Midlands B46 2LB (at Furnace End east of Shustoke)
Own Brew. Michael Pugh & Sydney Wedge, licensees.

This 17th-century village pub used to have its own small brewery in what was a coffin shop, but the brewery outgrew its space and moved to larger premises. You'll be pleased to know that there are still about ten or more beers for you to try. Inside, the pub has a large beamed bar with two effective fires and a roomy conservatory – children are allowed in here. The good choice of bar food ranges from sandwiches, various fish dishes, steak and kidney pie to steaks (large portions), plus daily specials on the blackboard. The dozen or so hand pumps allow a wide choice of beer – the guests change every couple of days. The Griffin's own beers have an ecclesiastical ring about them: Cuthbert's (name of the church), Vicar's Ruin, Fallen Angel, Choir Boy, Grave Diggers Mild and Old Pal. Car enthusiasts might like to know that the Sunbeam Alpine Tiger Club meets here monthly. Seats outside in the garden and on the terrace.

> OPEN: 12–2.30. 7–11 (7–10.30 Sun).
> Real Ale. Lunchtime meals and snacks (not Sun).
> Children in conservatory. Dogs on leads. Wheelchair access.
> Cards: none accepted.

STOKE DOYLE

The Shuckburgh Arms
Tel: 01832 272339

Stoke Doyle, Nr Oundle, Peterborough, Northants PE8 5TG
Free House. Paul & Jayne Kirkby, owners/licensees.

A great place for families, if that is what you want, as they are very child-friendly here. In a tiny village, 2 miles west of Oundle, a creeper-covered, 17th-century, stone-built inn with a comfortable panelled bar complete with inglenook fireplace and Chesterfield sofas. They serve a lunchtime bar-snack menu, a choice of ploughman's or garlic pâté, home-made soup of the day, sausage Creole – diced sausages in a tomato, garlic and sweet-chilli sauce – devilled kidneys, garlic mushrooms, egg, cheese, ham or tuna sandwiches and a short children's menu. From the main menu you could have duck casserole with white wine, Calvados, apples, herbs and garlic, pork in cider, grilled trout, chicken and apricot curry, boeuf bourguignon and much more. Delicious puds too. Good short wine list. Greene King Abbot, IPA and Everards Tiger. The usual guest is Wadworths 6X but this can change. Large enclosed garden. Barbecues in the summer.

OPEN: 12–3. 7–11 (12–3. 7–10.30 Sun).
Real Ale. Restaurant.
Children welcome and there is an extensive children's play area. No dogs.
Wheelchair access. Car park. Five en-suite bedrooms.
Cards: Amex, Delta, MasterCard, Switch, Visa.

SULGRAVE

Star Inn
Tel: 01295 760389

Manor Road, Sulgrave, Northants OX17 2SA
Hook Norton Brewery. Andrew Willerton, MBII, tenant.

On the border of Oxfordshire and Northamptonshire, this old farmhouse has considerably changed outside, but inside it is just as it should be – gloriously beamed, beautifully kept, with open fireplaces, flagstones and decorated with some interesting artifacts dating back to pre-war days. Looking like everyone's ideal of a 17th-century country pub, it is a very civilised establishment. An interesting addition to the decor is 'George the Skeleton' – still waiting for his lunch! All the food is freshly cooked and promptly served. Lots of home-made dishes on the blackboard menu, from a wide variety of hors d'oeuvres and filling sandwiches to a mixed grill; leek and potato soup, chicken-liver pâté, pork escalope with a gorgonzola sauce, half a roast duck with apple jus and seasoning, breast of smoked chicken with Caesar salad and lots more. Sunday roasts and good home-made puds. Hook Norton range of ales, a regular guest beer, Symonds Scrumpy Jack and good house wines. Seats in the delightful garden and on the terrace. Within walking distance of George Washington's ancestral home – Sulgrave Manor – and not too far from Silverstone.

OPEN: 11–2.30. 6–11 (12–3. 7–10.30 Sun).
Real Ale. Restaurant.
No children. Dogs outside only. Wheelchair access into bar only. Car park. Four en-suite bedrooms.

WADENHOE

The Kings Head
Tel: 01832 720024

Church Street, Wadenhoe, Oundle, Nr Peterborough, Northants PE8 5ST
Free House. Louise Rowell & Richard Sponton, licensees.

Wadenhoe – thought by many to be the prettiest village in Northamptonshire – is looked after by a charitable trust which ensures that the architectural and aesthetic qualities which make up the village are not ruined by insensitive 'modernisation and rebuilding'. Wouldn't we all like one of those. No one has done any disastrous meddling with the old Kings Head. Built in 1662, it still has the original quarry-tiled and oak floors, inglenook fireplaces and beams. In the public bar, you can play Northamptonshire skittles as well as other pub games; relax and eat in the lounge bar or the no-smoking dining room. The menus change with the seasons, but as well as the lunch snack menu, there could be Thai-style chilli crab cakes on leaves with a honey and mustard dressing, venison casserole in Broadside ale and port, roast aubergine with Stilton and tomato stuffing, or fillet-steak strips in brandy and cream, vegetarian dishes, lots of fresh fish and delicious puds too. Sunday lunch menu will have a roast as well as fresh fish and casseroles. Outside are seats in the sheltered courtyard, on the terrace or in the paddock which leads down to the navigable, willow-fringed river Nene. Adnams Southwold, Broadside and guest beers, and a wide-ranging wine list.

> OPEN: Summer 12–3. 6–11 (11–11 Sat & Sun). Winter 12–2.30. 7–11 (12–2.30. 6–11 Fri & Sat).
> Real Ale. Dining room. Evening meals Wed–Sat eves only.
> Children welcome. Dogs on leads. Wheelchair access. Car park.

WELFORD-ON-AVON

The Shakespeare
Tel: 01789 750443

Chapel Street, Welford-on-Avon, Nr Stratford-upon-Avon, Warwickshire CV37 8PX
Laurel Pub Co. Mark & Georgina O'Carroll, licensees.

The River Avon does a big loop around the lovely village of Welford before flowing on towards the Severn in Tewkesbury. This is Shakespeare country and here is the Shakespeare, a traditional pub with an award-winning garden, and a library of paperbacks to read while waiting for your food or to borrow to read at home. Traditional pub food and a daily changing specials board. The soup is home-made, the sandwiches are made to order and you have a choice of ploughman's. A wider choice is available in the evenings. Always five real ales, three lagers, a rotation of guest ales as well as seasonal ales such as 12 Days and Haymaker. Ten house wines. Lots of seats in the lovely big garden.

> OPEN: 12–3. 5–11 (12–4. 6.30–10.30 Sun).
> Real Ale.
> Children welcome; dogs too. Wheelchair access. Car park.

BEST OF THE REST

ALDERMINSTER, Warwickshire

Bell   Tel: 01789 450414

This old coaching inn near Stratford serves some very good food. On the monthly changing menu there may be home-made soups and pâté, also tomatoes stuffed with prawns, lamb moussaka or lemon and ginger chicken. Lots of other good things to try; wines by the glass and Greene King Abbot and IPA beer. Bedrooms.

LONG COMPTON, Warwickshire

Red Lion   Tel: 01608 684221

Not far into Warwickshire, north of Chipping Norton and the Rollright Stones, this is a fine old coaching inn with a newly done-up, but unspoilt, interior and warming log fires. The pub serves a choice of freshly prepared food from sandwiches and ploughman's to daily specials. Courage Directors, Websters Yorkshire and something from Hook Norton.

WARWICK, Warwickshire

Zetland Arms   Tel: 01926 491974

Gloriously situated on the banks of the River Avon, this small town has an interesting mix of Tudor and Georgian buildings and historic Warwick Castle – now owned by Madame Tussauds. The Zetland, a cosy, friendly town pub on Church Street, serves a good traditional choice of bar food from filled jacket potatoes and sandwiches to home-made dishes. Outside, the interesting, well-planted garden has been a television star. Ales are a well-kept Tetleys and Guinness as well as guest ales – these change fortnightly – and a good selection of wines.

CHAPEL BRAMPTON, Northamptonshire

Brampton Halt   Tel: 01604 842676

A Victorian stationmaster's house that is now something entirely different. Waiting for a train will never be the same. The Northampton steam-railway trains stop here at the weekend and while you're waiting (on Saturdays) you can stoke up with some filling bar food to go with the Adnams, Fullers London Pride, Everards and whatever guest beer is on that week. Decent wines. Note there is no bar food on Sunday.

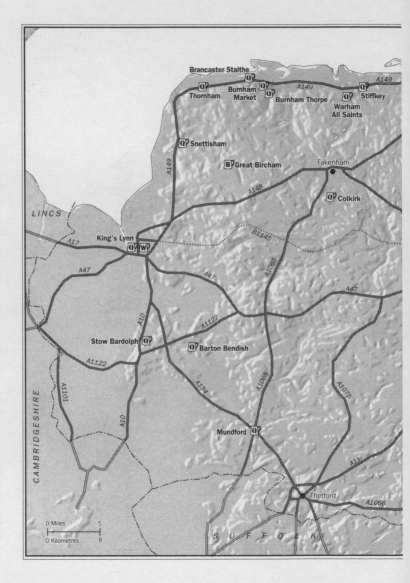

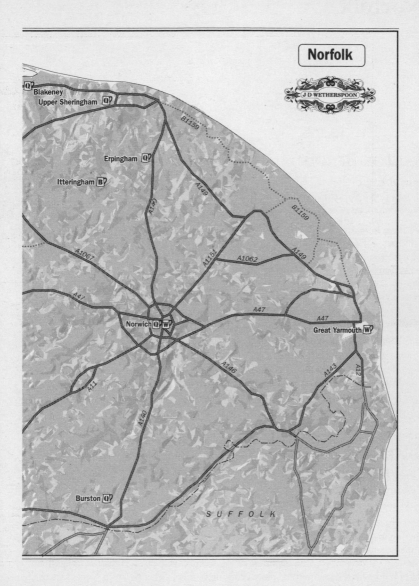

Norfolk

J·D·WETHERSPOON

Blakeney
Upper Sheringham

B1159

Erpingham

Itteringham

A149

A140

A1067

B1159

A151

A1062

A149

A47

A47

A47

Norwich   Great Yarmouth

A146

A143

A122

A41

A140

Burston

S U F F O L K

Norfolk

BARTON BENDISH

Spread Eagle   Tel: 01366 347295
Church Road, Barton Bendish, Norfolk PE33 9DP
Free House. Carole & Lucie Gransden, licensees.

You have here a well-kept pub in a class of its own, a well-kept village off the A1122 Swaffham to Downham Market road, and a fairly empty bit of Norfolk. The bar is full of the most amazing collection of bits and pieces, most of them with a price attached. When you've finished looking for a bargain, there are two dining rooms with different personalities – you take your choice. A printed menu lists the more traditional pub offerings; daily specials are on the blackboard. Expect well-cooked, above-average pub food, nothing too exciting. Greene King IPA always available plus a guest ale. The village is off the A1122 Swaffham, Downham Market road.

> OPEN: Odd opening hours – 12–2.30. 7–11 Wed–Sat (12–3. 7–10.30 Sun). Closed Mon & Tues.
> Real Ale. Restaurant.
> Children in dining room. No dogs. Wheelchair access. Car park. Bedrooms.
> Cards: Amex, Delta, MasterCard, Switch, Visa.

BLAKENEY

Kings Arms   Tel: 01263 740341
Westgate Street, Blakeney, Norfolk
Free House. Howard & Marjorie Davies, licensees.

Once three fishermen's cottages, this place was first licensed in the 18th century. A popular pub in one of East Anglia's picturesque coastal villages, it is simply furnished, the walls of the bars decorated with photographs from the licensees' theatrical careers and original paintings by local artists. A wide range of bar food is available: a variety of ploughman's, lots of fillings for the sandwiches (plain or toasted), filled jacket potatoes, local crabs in the summer, Blakeney mussels in winter, fish, steaks, vegetarian dishes and daily specials. Websters Yorkshire, Marstons Pedigree, Morland Old Speckled Hen, Adnams plus the local Woodfordes Wherry Bitter. Fosters, Holstein and Carlsberg export lagers. Seats on the terrace at the front of the pub and in the large garden. There are three no-smoking areas in the pub and a separate children's area.

OPEN: 11–11.
Real Ale.
Children welcome. Dogs on leads. All disabled facilities. Self-catering flatlets.
The new extension has four en-suite bedrooms and a large dining area leading into the garden.

BLAKENEY

White Horse Hotel
4 High Street, Blakeney, Norfolk NR25 7AL
Free House. Daniel Rees, licensee.

Tel: 01263 740574
Fax: 01263 741303

When the tide is out in this popular sailing village, there isn't much water to go sailing in. So, while you wait for the tide, the 17th-century White Horse waits for you. Originally a coaching inn built around an attractive old courtyard and stables, this delightful old place was Blakeney's first hotel. The redundant stables have been converted into a smart restaurant overlooking the plant-filled courtyard and walled garden. Much more than good sustaining pub fare here: home-made soups (some fishy ones, as you would expect), deep-fried herring roes on toast, cockle chowder served with granary bread, fisherman's pie with a flaky-pastry crust, cheese and vegetable pie, lots of salads, freshly made sandwiches and dishes of the day on the bar blackboard. They have a great chef doing good things in the kitchen; the à la carte restaurant menu might include local crab with Thai mayonnaise with cucumber and radish, grilled smoked salmon on avocado salsa and for a main course, fresh-herb-marinated chicken breast in provençale sauce with black olives or chargrilled medallions of beef fillet topped with flat mushrooms and ginger butter. Additional seasonal dishes will be on the restaurant blackboard. Vegetarian dishes too. Good home-made puds. Adnams Southwold Bitter, draught Bass, Woodfordes and Guinness; a well-chosen wine list supplied by Adnam's Wine Merchants. Seats in the sunny courtyard.

OPEN: 11–3. 6–11.
Real Ale. Restaurant 7–9pm (last orders) Tuesday to Saturday. Bar food all week.
Children in restaurant. No dogs. Wheelchair access (not WC). Car park. Ten en-suite bedrooms.
Cards: Amex, Delta, MasterCard, Switch, Visa.

BRANCASTER STAITHE

The Jolly Sailors
Brancaster Staithe, Norfolk PE31 8BJ
Free House. Darren Humphrey, licensee.

Tel: 01485 210314

You have to wait for high tide to be a jolly sailor; when the tide's out, there isn't much more than a narrow channel of water between banks of mud. But in the middle of this delightful village, on the main road halfway between Hunstanton and Wells-next-the-Sea, is the Jolly Sailor, 200 years old, just a few hundred yards from the harbour and, as you can imagine, popular with visiting sailors. Inside this white painted old place are a spacious beamed bar and separate, elegant restaurant. The chef grows his own herbs, so lots of fresh herbs are used in the cooking. You could choose home-made soup, goat's cheese en croute, deep-fried whitebait, ploughman's, Brie and roasted vegetables, steak and ale pie, at least six fish dishes with the local mussels, crab, lobster and oysters being very much in demand; other goodies from the blackboard. Woodfordes Wherry, Adnams Bitter, Iceni Fine Soft Day and guest beers. Very drinkable wines. Seats on the sheltered patio and in the garden next to the tennis court: that's a first – not many pubs have one of those.

> OPEN: 11–11.
> Real Ale. Restaurant – music in here.
> Children welcome. Dogs in garden and patio. Wheelchair access (not WC). Car park.
> Cards: Delta, MasterCard, Switch, Visa.

BURNHAM MARKET

Hoste Arms
Tel: 01328 738777
The Green, Burnham Market, Norfolk PE31 8HD
Free House. Paul Whittome & Jo Race, licensees.

A large, handsome 17th-century building overlooking the green in the Georgian village of Burnham Market, once the manor house of Burnham Westgate, now an elegant hotel. Inside are two very welcoming bars offering excellent lunchtime and evening menus using a combination of British, French and Oriental influences; the menu changes twice a day. Food served in the two panelled dining rooms and the conservatory might include: local fish, half a dozen Burnham Creek oysters with crushed ice, red wine and shallot vinegar, or spiced lamb meatballs, saffron and onion relish; and for a main course pot-roasted ham hock with green-pea purée and parsnip crisps, or chargrilled rump steak. To finish, dark-chocolate cheesecake, warm blueberry tart with creme fraîche, or a selection of British cheeses. In the evening, the restaurant, which is mostly no smoking, serves an à la carte menu and has a really good, reasonably priced wine list. Woodfordes Wherry, Greene King IPA, Abbot and Beamish Red. There is an art gallery on which to feast your eyes and you can sit and enjoy your drink in the walled garden or at the front of the hotel among the flower tubs.

> OPEN: 11–11.
> Real Ale. Restaurant for lunch 12–2 and dinner 7–9.
> Dogs most welcome. Wheelchair access. Car park. En-suite bedrooms.
> Cards: MasterCard, Switch, Visa.

BURNHAM THORPE

Lord Nelson
Tel: 01328 738241
Walsingham Road, Burnham Thorpe, Kings Lynn, Norfolk PE31 8HN
Greene King. Lucy Stafford, lease.

Apt when you think of it: Horatio Nelson, born only 300 yards away in 1758, held a party in this old pub, then called the Plough, before he sailed off to do his duty against the French in 1794. Nelson, as everyone knows, was killed at the victorious Battle of Trafalgar in 1805; his body was returned to England preserved in a barrel of brandy. A spirited send-off, and a very spirited return. It was soon after his death that they renamed the 350-year-old Plough in his honour. A charming, unchanging little place, with four rooms – two of which are non-smoking – but no bar and a collection of Nelson memorabilia. They serve a better-than-usual bar menu and have a daily changing specials board which could feature lemon sole, grilled lamb chops in a rosemary and red-wine sauce, fresh crab and salmon. The beers, drawn from the barrels in the tap room, are Greene King, Abbot, IPA and Mild, plus Woodfordes Nelson's Revenge. All the real ales are gravity-fed from the barrel. The parish Church of All Saints has some Nelsonian mementoes, including a lectern and crucifix made of timbers from his flagship, the *Victory*.

OPEN: 11–3. 6–11 (12–3. 7–10.30 Sun).
Real Ale.
Children welcome. Dogs on leads. Wheelchair access.
Cards: All major cards over £25, otherwise Delta, Switch.

BURSTON

Crown Inn   Tel: 01379 741257
Crown Green, Burston, Norfolk IP22 3TW
Free House. Mrs V. Whitehead, licensee.

The interior of this fine old pub had to be restored by the present owners to regain its original charm. Insensitive modernisation in the 1970s had resulted in a less-than-perfect 16th-century pub. All that has changed for the better. This is one of those places you come across when you're meandering around the countryside. The public bar, better known as Harvey's Bar – Harvey being a Great Dane who made it his own after arriving as a puppy with his owners. The specials change according to the availability of fresh local produce. The bar menu is limited to sandwiches and ploughman's. All the beers are from local breweries; only Adnams Bitter is permanent.

OPEN: Closed Tuesday, otherwise 11.30–2.30. 5.30–11 (12–3. 6.30–10.30 Sun).
Real Ale. Restaurant.
Children welcome in restaurant, not bar. Dogs in bar. Car park.

COLKIRK

Crown   Tel: 01328 862172
Crown Road, Colkirk, Fakenham, Norfolk NR21 7AA
Greene King. Roger & Bridget Savell, tenants.

Standards are high in this delightful, friendly, well-run old pub with a reputation for serving good, interesting food. Cosy welcoming bars, both with open fires and a non-smoking dining room. The menu includes soup, hot herby mushrooms, chef's pâté of the day, ham and cheese pancakes, Scotch beef, lots of fresh fish, home-made casseroles, curries and salads. Good puds too. The specials board might include braised steak in cream and garlic sauce, baked cinnamon duck leg with Cumberland sauce, fresh skate-wing provençale and a vegetarian spicy-bean casserole. Around 50 wines to choose from, either by the bottle or the glass. Greene King Abbot and guest ales. Tables outside on the sunny terrace and in the garden.

> OPEN: 11–2.30. 6–11.
> Real Ale.
> Children in lounge and dining area. Dogs on leads.
> Reasonable wheelchair access.

ERPINGHAM

Saracens Head   Tel: 01263 768909
Wolterton, Nr Erpingham, Norfolk NR11 7LX (off A140 near Wolterton Hall)
Free House. Robert Dawson-Smith, licensee.

Knowing that delights await will improve your map reading no end. Just accept, as everyone does, that you may get lost in the lanes of Norfolk while trying to find the Saracens Head. Even the pub's publicity gives you lots of directions, heading them 'Lost in North Norfolk'! Between Erpingham and Calthorpe, or you could say between Erpingham and Itteringham – whatever, you need a good map to find the Saracens Head, possibly a mobile phone and a torch as well, but persevere: the hunt is worth it. The secret is to locate Wolterton Hall; the pub is close by. When you get there you'll find interesting, unusual snacks and a selection of main dishes. Monday to Friday there is a special, very reasonably priced two-course lunch with, I quote, 'no chips, peas or fried scampi'. Also a special 'Two Choice' Sunday supper. Feast nights are held throughout the year: a Mediterranean feast night, for example, or one for Empire Day. You can even organise your own if you are so inclined. The everyday-changing menu could include parsnip and spring-onion soup, red-onion and goat's-cheese tart, a dish of Morston mussels cooked in cider and cream, crispy fried aubergine with garlic mayonnaise; and for a main course: baked Cromer crab with mushrooms and sherry, grilled salmon with mango and cider, pan-fried breast of chicken with rosemary and cream, or wok-sizzled strips of sirloin with olives and tomatoes. Also puddings such as a chocolate pot with a rich orange jus or old-fashioned treacle tart. Roast lunch on Sunday. You can even enjoy a special evening garden menu served either in the delightful courtyard or walled garden. Adnams Bitter, Woodfordes Blickling and several guest beers; a good choice of wines from Adnams Wine Merchants.

> OPEN: 11–3. 6–11 (12–2. 7–10.30 Sun).
> Real Ale.
> Well-behaved children welcome. No dogs. Wheelchair access possible. En-suite bedrooms.
> Cards: All major cards.

KING'S LYNN

Duke's Head Hotel Tel: 01553 774996
Tuesday Market Place, King's Lynn, Norfolk PE30 1JS
Free House. Adele Fisher, general manager.

King's Lynn has two markets: the 14th-century Tuesday and the even older Saturday market which was probably founded when the town was first mentioned in the Domesday Book. The handsome Duke's Head is difficult to miss; not only is it painted pink, it is also rather large. Built in 1683 to replace the demolished 16th-century Griffin Inn, it was named the Duke's Head in honour of the Duke of York, who later became James II. The main entrance was originally an open carriageway enabling the coaches to drive into the stableyard. The place you are making for is the panelled Lynn Bar, where you will find an interesting bar menu. A good selection of beers – Woodfordes Nelsons Revenge, Adnams Best Bitter and Flowers Original. If you want a reasonably priced two-course lunch – a duo of fish mousses and chef's steak and mushroom pie, for example – you will have to listen to music; the bar, lounge and cocktail bar, however, are quiet.

> OPEN: 11–3. 6–11 (12–3. 7–10.30 Sun).
> Real Ale. Two restaurants.
> Children to stay. No dogs. Car park.

MUNDFORD

Crown Hotel Tel: 01842 878233
Crown Street, Mundford, Thetford, Norfolk IP26 5HD
Free House. Barry Walker, lease.

Breckland is about 300 square miles of heathland, villages and some coniferous woodlands between Norfolk and Suffolk. Mundford, on the edge of Thetford forest, was a 17th-century hunting inn. Not many pubs in this part of Norfolk, so head for the Crown. Built on a hillside – not many of those in Norfolk either – the kitchens and restaurant are upstairs; the beamed lounge bar (gracious) with a big open fire, and the public bar (more basic), are on the ground floor. Three menus available virtually all the time: the bar menu, specials board and the à la carte (the latter never on Sundays). Interesting bar food includes home-made soups, filled baguettes and sandwiches, ploughmans, tiger prawns in filo pastry, or a Roquefort and walnut tartlet, and for a main course: honey-fried chicken, grilled steak, rump of lamb marinated with thyme and garlic and served roasted upon gratin potatoes with a parsley and lentil sauce, always a fish dish and steaks. From the specials board you could have devilled kidneys in red wine served with saffron rice or Chinese-style chicken – boned whole spring chicken baked in sweet chilli with prawns mixed with a noodle and vegetable stir fry. Good puds too. Woodfordes Wherry, Courage Directors, Nethergate and local Iceni ales. House wines, a wide-ranging wine list and over

50 malt whiskies. Woodland walks in Emily's Wood on the road between Mundford and Brandon.

> OPEN: 11–11 (12–10.30 Sun).
> Real Ale. Restaurant.
> Children welcome. Dogs on leads. Wheelchair access. There is a jukebox in the public bar. Bedrooms.
> Cards: Amex, Delta, Diners, MasterCard, Switch, Visa.

NORWICH

The Bell Hotel   Tel: 01603 630017
5 Orford Hill, Norwich NR1 3QB
Wetherspoon.

Don't even think you can stay. It might still be called a hotel, but the beds have definitely moved out. Wetherspoon took over this old place and gave it a new life, rearranged the inside, installed the mod cons and created two bars – upstairs and downstairs. Full menu available all day – this is standard in all Wetherspoon outlets – changing three times a year. Every day at the Bell you have four different daily specials – no gastronomic fantasies, just good honest fare to go with the cask-conditioned beers. Youngers Scotch Bitter, Courage Directors, Theakstons Best, a local regional beer and guest beers from small breweries.

> OPEN: 11–11 (12–10.30 Sun).
> Real Ale
> Children between 12 and 7pm. Guide dogs only. All wheelchair facilities.

NORWICH

The Fat Cat   Tel: 01603 624364
49 West End Street, Norwich NR2 4NA
Free House. Colin Keatley, licensee.

This is a traditional alehouse and looks it. Simple, with uncomplicated furnishings and only filled rolls at lunchtime. So, if it's a vast choice of beers you want, this is the place. The customers all thoroughly enjoy tasting lots of different ones: usually more than 20 on the go from all over the UK and Ireland. What isn't on hand pump will be in barrels at the back. Also lagers, stouts and four draught Belgian beers. You really are only here for the beer and the like-minded company. A permanent beer festival all year round. Wonderful.

> OPEN 12–11 (12–10.30 Sun).
> Real Ale (lots).
> No children. No dogs.

SNETTISHAM

Rose & Crown Inn   Tel: 01485 541382
Old Church Road, Snettisham, King's Lynn, Norfolk PE31 7LX
Free House. Anthony Goodrich, licensee.

Over the years this 14th-century building has been changed and extended to create the rambling place you see today. Near the church, built as a hostel for the church builders, it is as pretty as a picture in summer when decked out with exuberant hanging baskets. Well-beamed with big fireplaces and three bars, four including the recently opened no-smoking cellar bar, and the garden room, made warmer and cosier with the addition of a fireplace. Very popular with families; it is geared up to accommodate children and keep them happy. Well-served bar food in ample proportions: home-made gazpacho soup, locally smoked salmon with cucumber and dill salad, honey and lime crème fraîche, Greek tapas selection served with warm pitta bread, open-flamed rib-eye steak, warm tomato and balsamic salad, breast of Barbary duck served pink, dauphinoise potatoes, black pudding and chocolate jus, plus freshly filled baguettes, traditional fish and chips or a choice of vegetarian dishes and grills. There is a specials board, a children's menu and a selection of barbecue dishes. Adnams, Bass and guest beers on hand pump and a well-chosen wine list. Seats on the terrace and in the walled garden. Family room, and a well-equipped children's play area outside.

> OPEN: 11–11.
> Real Ale. Restaurant.
> Children in own room and eating areas. Well-behaved dogs. Wheelchair access.
> Car park. Eleven en-suite bedrooms.
> Cards: Access, Switch, Visa.

STIFFKEY

Red Lion   Tel: 01328 830552
Wells Road, Stiffkey, Wells-next-the-Sea, Norfolk NR23 1AJ
Free House. Matthew Rees, licensee.

A path opposite the village church leads to the National Trust's Stiffkey Marshes, an area of tremendous interest to birdwatchers. This straggling village has a partly ruined Elizabethan hall, an interesting church with 15th-century brasses and the white brick and flint Red Lion, a busy, jolly place, well-used and homely, furnished with pine tables and settles, serving good home-cooked food. The blackboard menu is changeable but there are always generously filled sandwiches, pâté, ploughman's, fresh local fish, mussels, lobster, crab and seasonal local game pie. Woodfordes Wherry, Abbot and guest beers; short wine list. Seats on the terrace.

> OPEN: 11–3. 6–11.
> Real Ale.
> Children welcome. Dogs on leads. Wheelchair access (not WC). Car park.
> Cards: Delta, MasterCard, Switch, Visa.

STOW BARDOLPH

Hare Arms   Tel: 01366 382229
Stow Bardolph, Norfolk PE34 3HT
Greene King. Trish & David McManus, tenants.

Once the ancestral home of the Hare family – hence the name – this creeper-covered, friendly old pub is at the heart of the village. They serve a wide range of food throughout the week. Bar food could include sandwiches and rolls with a choice of fillings, soups and home-made pâté; the daily specials might be lemon sole fillets with prawn sauce, salmon fillet with a mushroom, lemon and herb sauce, chunks of tender steak in a black peppercorn, cream and brandy sauce topped with shortcrust pastry, pork steak with orange and sage sauce, local sausages with mash and red-wine and onion gravy and lots of steaks. The à la carte restaurant menu is inspired. There is also a table d'hôte and separate vegetarian menu. All the dishes are home-cooked using local seasonal produce, local game, fresh fish, lamb and beef. Imaginative puds too. Greene King ales. Good selection of wines. Tables in the garden among the peacocks and the other feathered residents.

> OPEN: 11–2.30. 6–11.
> Real Ale. Restaurant (not Sun eves).
> Children in conservatory. No dogs. Wheelchair access (not WC). Car park.
> Cards: Delta, MasterCard, Switch, Visa.

THORNHAM

Lifeboat Inn   Tel: 01485 512236
Ship Lane, Thornham, Norfolk PE36 6LT
Free House. Charles & Angie Coker, owners & licensees.

Between the inn and the sea is marshland; on one side the RSPB's Titchwell Marsh Reserve, on the other, further to the left and nearer the coast, the Holme Bird Observatory – a birdwatcher's paradise, though in the 16th century this area, and the pub, were the haunt of smugglers and their wicked ways. The Lifeboat, a charming, rambling inn, has low-beamed ceilings, quarry-tiled floors, old oak furniture, blazing fires in winter and tempting home-cooked food. The bar menu ranges from soup, ploughman's, Cromer crab salad and filled baguettes to pan-fried liver with smoked bacon, roasted vegetables and mash, game pie, Brancaster mussels, a choice of fish and their own Lifeboat fish pie; daily specials are on the blackboard. The dishes go up a notch on the extensive restaurant menu. Greene King ales, Adnams, Woodfordes Wherry and guest beers. Good range of wines. Fairly near sandy Thornham beach and lots of wonderful walks.

> OPEN: 11–11.
> Real Ale. Restaurant.
> Children welcome. Dogs too. Wheelchair access. Car park. Bedrooms.
> Cards: MasterCard. Switch, Visa.

UPPER SHERINGHAM

Red Lion   Tel: 01263 825408
Holt Road, Upper Sheringham, Norfolk NR26 8AD
Free House. Suzanne Prew, licensee.

Upper is, as you might guess, above Lower. Lower Sheringham was the old fishing village that became a popular resort during the latter part of the 19th century. Upper,
once dependent on agriculture, is now residential. The 300-year-old flint cottages are
a recent conversion into what is now The Red Lion. With two attractive bars and a
reputation for serving reliable home-cooked food, the pub is a busy, popular place. The
blackboard menu changes frequently, but there could be home-made soups, hot
smoked mackerel fillets and salad, fresh spicy baked Sheringham crab salad, pork with
cider, apple and thyme, or home-made steak and kidney pie; also lots of fresh fish.
Sunday roasts. Greene King IPA and Woodfordes Wherry, Murphys and Scrumpy Jack
cider; Woodfordes Great Eastern is the guest ale, Stella and Guinness on draught and
over 30 malts to try. After all that, you can gather yourself together in the sunny
walled garden, or go and see the old sail-powered Sheringham lifeboat kept in a shed
by the shore.

> OPEN: 11.30–3. 6.30–11 (pub quiz Sun eves winter).
> Real Ale.
> Children in eating area. Dogs on leads. Wheelchair access possible – willing helpers
> on hand. Three bedrooms.

WARHAM ALL SAINTS

Three Horseshoes   Tel: 01328 710547
The Street, Warham All Saints, Norfolk NR23 1NL
Free House. Iain Salmon, licensee.

This 18th-century brick and flint pub at the crossroads of this pretty North Norfolk village retains an interior from a different age, with an atmosphere redolent of the 1920s.
But, in contrast to the 1920s, you'll now find a good, interesting choice of home-cooked
bar food based on fresh, local produce. As well as assorted sandwiches, filled rolls, ploughman's and lots of fillings for the potatoes, there could be a marshman's shellfish bake of
local mussels, cockles and prawns in a Cheddar sauce grilled until golden, farmhouse terrine, garden-herb and garlic-cream mushrooms, a game and wine pie – local game cooked
in wine with onions under a shortcrust-pastry lid, cod in cheese sauce and a Norfolk beef
pie – beef, mushrooms and onions cooked in beer and topped with flaky pastry. A daily
selection of dishes on the blackboard complements the printed menu; everything is
cooked to order. Half-portions too for those with smaller appetites, and no chips. A
selection of English cheeses to finish or something from the pudding menu on the blackboard. Greene King IPA, plus guest ales. House wines and eight country wines including
a medium-sweet Silver Birch – I have never tried that! Tables on the grass outside. Lots
of things to see in Warham: St Mary's Church still has its original Georgian box pews and
pulpit; Warham Camp, an iron-age fort, is not far away; and Warham Marsh is one of

Europe's largest salt marshes. If you feel energetic, you can join the Norfolk coastal path for a brisk walk.

OPEN: 11.30–2.30. 6–11.
Real Ale. No-smoking restaurant.
Children in eating area. Dogs on leads. Wheelchair access. Car park.
Bedrooms and rooms in the Old Post Office next door.
Occasional live music Saturday evenings.

BEST OF THE REST

GREAT BIRCHAM

Kings Head   Tel: 01485 578265

Big and white – a village hotel you really can't miss. You can either eat in the bar or restaurant. Always good, the menu ranges from sandwiches, fresh fish and seafood to steak and kidney pudding. Both the bar and restaurant menus have a touch of the Italian – from the licensee, so the pasta will always be just as it should be. Adnams, Bass and Greene King IPA and a decent wine list.

ITTERINGHAM

Walpole Arms   Tel: 01263 587258

Inside this 18th-century pub is a spacious, attractive bar where they serve well-prepared dishes. The menus change daily so there are always some surprises. The pâté and soups are home-made; they home-smoke the salmon and sausages and make delicious puds. Adnams Bitter and Broadside as well as draught Bass, Woodfordes Nelson's Revenge and seasonal beers. Wines by the glass.

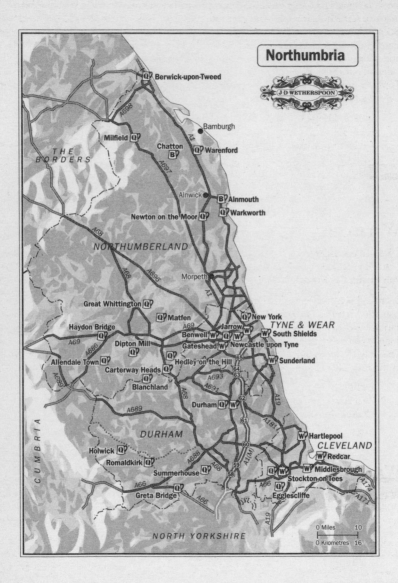

Northumbria

J·D·WETHERSPOON

Berwick-upon-Tweed

Bamburgh

THE
BORDERS

Milfield

Chatton

Warenford

Alnwick

Alnmouth

Newton on the Moor

Warkworth

NORTHUMBERLAND

Morpeth

Great Whittington

Matfen

New York

TYNE & WEAR

Haydon Bridge

Benwell

Jarrow

South Shields

Dipton Mill

Gateshead

Newcastle upon Tyne

Allendale Town

Hedley on the Hill

Sunderland

Carterway Heads

Blanchland

Durham

Holwick

DURHAM

Hartlepool

CLEVELAND

Romaldkirk

Redcar

Summerhouse

Middlesbrough

Greta Bridge

Stockton-on-Tees

Egglescliffe

CUMBRIA

NORTH YORKSHIRE

0 Miles   10

0 Kilometres   16

Northumbria (Cleveland, Durham, Northumberland, Tyne & Wear)

ALLENDALE TOWN

Kings Head
Tel: 01434 683681

Market Place, Allendale Town, Hexham, Northumberland NE47 9EG
Free House. Mr & Mrs Slater, licensees.

If you want to find the geographical centre of Britain – this is it. The town is built on a steep 1400-foot-high cliff overlooking the East Allen River – hence its name. The tall, imposing Kings Head, one of the oldest pubs in the town, is in the tree-lined Market Place. Originally a coaching inn, the cosy hotel bar is the place to head for, and here you have a huge choice of freshly made sandwiches, daily specials, a glass or two of wine, coffee, even afternoon tea and daily papers to read while you wait. Let's not forget the beer: Jennings Cumberland, Best Bitter and several guests; usually a selection of seven real ales and 75 malt whiskies. There are some good walks through magnificent scenery.

> OPEN: 11–11 (12–10.30 Sun).
> Real Ale.
> Children welcome at mealtimes. Dogs in bar. Live music once a week. Bedrooms.

BERWICK-UPON-TWEED

Rob Roy
Tel: 01289 306428

Dock Road, Tweedmouth, Berwick-upon-Tweed, Northumberland
Free House. Keith & Julie Wilson, licensees.

The handsome bridge connecting the town with Tweedmouth on the other side of the river was built by order of James I in 1611. Once a busy port and fishing town, it's here you'll find what remains of Berwick's fishing boats and the Rob Roy; a place strong on fish. Indeed, it's called a 'Seafood Restaurant with a Bar'. The bar menu offers a soup of the day, freshly made sandwiches, Lindisfarne oysters, salad of sweet pickled herrings, peppered farmhouse pâté with melba toast, North Sea scallops in a cream and fennel sauce, monkfish in garlic butter and lots more. From the restaurant menu: sea bass fillet, grilled Dover sole, tournedos of beef in a cream and green-peppercorn sauce, a warm salad of scallops with bacon and mushrooms or something from the speciality blackboard menus, such as creamed shellfish soup, salmon Limoux (poached in wine – you drink the rest of the bottle), sirloin steak Rob Roy cooked in a sauce of onions, mushrooms, whisky and double cream, or a chateaubriand for two. If you have any room, puds too. They only serve wild salmon: fresh during the season, otherwise frozen in preference to farmed fish. The à la carte menu is changed regularly depending on the fish, shellfish and game available; wild Tweed salmon and sea trout during the season and lobsters and crabs if the weather is favourable. Sounds like a place to be treasured.

> OPEN: 11.30–2.30. 6.30–11 (12–2.30. 7–10.30 Sun). Closed Tuesdays.
> Keg beers and wines only. Restaurant.
> No dogs.

BERWICK-UPON-TWEED

The Free Trade   Tel: 01289 306498
75 Castlegate, Berwick-upon-Tweed, Northumberland TD15 1LF
Free House. Edward Collins, licensee.

This place is for those of you keen on their beer, as it's liquid refreshment only; a crisp and nut too perhaps, certainly biscuits for the dog. You are in an ancient border town that was fought over many times by the Scots and English between the 12th and 15th centuries; changing hands 13 times before finally becoming part of England in 1482. The Free Trade, an unchanging Victorian drinking pub in Castlegate, is beyond the Elizabethan walls and near the railway station. An old-fashioned bar with a pool table for the youngsters. The landlord says he can stock any beer he likes: Federation Founders, Buchanan and Buchanan Original at the moment, and he's aiming to have Fullers London Pride.

> OPEN: 11–11 (12–10.30 Sun). Those are the published times – actually they're quite flexible!
> Real Ale.
> Children: if well behaved. Dogs very welcome – biscuits provided.
> N.B. Jukebox.

BLANCHLAND

Lord Crewe Arms   Tel: 01434 675251
Blanchland, Nr Consett, Co. Durham DH8 9SP (near Derwent Reservoir)
Free House. A. Todd, Peter Gingell & Ian Press, licensees.

Planned in the 18th century, Blanchland is one of England's unspoilt villages and the handsome Lord Crewe Arms one of England's oldest pubs. Well, the building is, as it was formerly the abbot's house, part of the 13th-century Blanchland Abbey, which, until the Dissolution of the monasteries, dominated the surrounding area. Much remains of its historic past; the layout of the 18th-century village follows virtually the same boundary lines as the destroyed abbey. The cloister garden is still evident and now listed as an ancient monument. Another of our haunted pubs: the Lord Crewe Arms has a tragic ghost – Dorothy Forster, a heroine of the Jacobite uprising whose family lived here, haunts the building, asking people to deliver a message to Tom, her long-dead brother. On that cheerful note, make your way to the Crypt Bar for a reviving drink and something from the menu: tagliatelle verde with creamy wild mushroom sauce and Parmesan cheese, tossed salad of Stilton cheese, beans, croutons, bacon, pine nuts and cherry tomatoes, chef's dish of the day; lots of fillings for the rolls, daily specials and Sunday lunches. Castle Eden, John Smiths, Boddingtons Bitter and Guinness. Seats in the enclosed garden.

OPEN: 11–3. 6–11.
Real Ale. Evening restaurant. Also Sunday lunch.
Children welcome. Wheelchair access (not WC). Bedrooms.
Cards: Amex, Diners, MasterCard, Switch, Visa.
N.B. There is sometimes music in the restaurant but not the bar.

CARTERWAY HEADS

Manor House Inn   Tel: 01207 255268
Carterway Heads, Shotley Bridge, Consett, Northumberland DH8 9LX (on A68 between Corbridge and Consett)
Free House. Chris & Moira Brown, licensees.

On the edge of the North Pennines, this long, stone-built 18th-century village pub is about 4 miles from the Derwent Reservoir. Rebuilt after a fire in 1999, it is still friendly, efficient and well run, with a more-than-interesting blackboard menu for both the bar and restaurant. Food could include a leek and courgette soup with French bread, smoked chicken and Brie croissants, moules marinières, baked sea trout, duck breast with orange and coriander, or medallions of beef in a Madeira sauce. Home-made puddings and a choice of local cheeses. Theakstons Best Bitter, Ruddles County, Westons Beamish and guest ales. Wide-ranging wine list. Seats in the garden (wind permitting!).

OPEN: 11–3. 6–11.
Real Ale. Restaurant – no music in here.
Well-behaved children welcome. Dogs in small bar only. Wheelchair access – help always available. Car park. Four en-suite bedrooms.
Cards: Amex, Delta, MasterCard, Switch, Visa.
N.B. Music in the public bar.

DIPTON MILL

Dipton Mill Inn   Tel: 01434 606577
Dipton Mill Road, Nr Hexham, Northumberland NE46 1YA
Free House. Geoff Brooker, licensee.

In peaceful countryside 2 miles from Hexham, by West Dipton Burn, what was once a 17th-century farmhouse and adjoining cottages was extended about a hundred years ago into what you see today: a small pub, with a single bar – and off it a room with a bar-billiards table. Food is served at lunchtimes and in the evenings. A typical menu is soup, beef-in-ale pie, chicken breast in a sherry sauce, always salads and sandwiches, a choice of savoury flans and a selection of puddings. Ales are mainly from the local brewery where they brew four beers: Devil's Elbow, Shire Bitter, Devil's Water and Whapweasel (Whapweasel is named after a burn on the fells). Very beautiful countryside. The old mill stream runs through the garden, and another stream runs alongside the pub. Seats in the attractive garden. You are in good walking country.

> OPEN: 12–2.30. 6–11 (7–10.30 Sun).
> Real Ale. Lunches and evening meals.
> Children welcome. No dogs. Wheelchair access.

DURHAM
Shakespear Tavern   Tel: 0191 386 9709
Saddler Street, Durham City DH1 3NU.
Newcastle/Courage. Mark Charlton, leasehold.

Very friendly, popular and full of character – apart from the television set above the door, this pub has remained unchanged since the 1950s, and is close to everything that matters in this ancient city: the castle, cathedral and the oldest of the university colleges. The television is only on at news time and on Saturdays, but there is a quiet lounge and snug bar behind the main bar – the only one left in the city with original 18th-century panelling. No food at all; a crisp and nut, though, to go with the Theakstons, McEwans 80/–, Newcastle Exhibition, John Smiths Extra Smooth, Guinness and lagers. Cask ales change three times a week.

> OPEN: 11–11 (12–10.30 Sun).
> Real Ale.
> Children welcome. Dogs on leads

EGGLESCLIFFE
Pot and Glass   Tel: 01642 651009
Church Road, Egglescliffe, Cleveland TS16 9DP
Enterprise Inns. Dave Bunyan, tenant.

As you would expect from the address, the 11th-century church and the Pot and Glass aren't far apart. This charming village pub is in a lovely setting, with a public bar, lounge and small side room for meetings and private parties. Low ceilings, beams and panelled walls but no open fires. There used to be, but, the pub being small, the rise in temperature was more than the customers could take. Lunchtime food is served six days a week: home-made steak pies, lasagne, fish and chips and a scampi or two. Evening food Tuesday to Sunday only. Well-kept draught Bass, John Smiths, Guinness, cider and two guest ales. Carling and Stella on pump. Just a small garden where you'll have to sit if you take your dog.

> OPEN: 12–3.30. 5.30–11 (12–10.30 Sun).
> Real Ale. No food Monday.
> Children welcome in side room until 9pm. Dogs in garden.

GREAT WHITTINGTON

Queen's Head   Tel: 01434 672267
Great Whittington, Northumberland NE19 2HP
Free House. Ian Scott, licensee.

If there is a Little Whittington it must be extremely small, as this Great is a very little Great
Whittington – a small village of about 160 inhabitants near Hadrian's Wall. You can combine a bit of sightseeing with a bracing walk and a good lunch at the Queen's Head; lunch
first probably. The Queen's Head is more of a restaurant than a pub, but it has two comfortable beamed bars, both with log fires. A bistro blackboard menu features in the bar offering
lamb's liver with bacon and onion, breast of chicken with broccoli, goujons of fresh haddock
or salmon with lemon and dill sauce and really good home-made puds. There is an à la carte
menu in the restaurant and a choice of over 30 wines to go with the food. Hambleton Bitter,
Black Sheep Special, Bitter and their own Queen's Head Bitter are the beers. Picnic tables
in the garden. Near the Devil's Causeway, an area popular with walkers and cyclists

> OPEN: 12–2.30. 6–11 (12–3. 7–10.30 Sun). Closed Mon except Bank Holidays.
> Real Ale. Restaurant – music in here.
> Well-behaved children at lunchtime only. Dogs in garden. Wheelchair access.
> Car park.
> N.B. Music in restaurant.

GRETA BRIDGE

Morritt Arms   Tel: 01833 627232
Greta Bridge, Rokeby, Nr Barnard Castle, Co. Durham DL12 9SE
Free House. Barbara Anne Johnston & Peter Phillips, licensees.

A fine, appealing 18th-century coaching inn with a strong Dickens connection. Charles
Dickens stayed here in 1834 while researching his novel *Nicholas Nickleby*. The model for
that dreadful school Dotheboys Hall is probably near at hand. By the old stone bridge and
the gates to Rokeby Park, the Morritt Arms has comfortable, panelled lounges, a 'pubby' bar
and an elegant restaurant. The bar has some very jolly 'Dickensian' murals, creating a solid,
prosperous Victorian feel. The food has moved on, though – it's English cooking with a twist.
Good hearty soups, king-prawn and oyster-mushroom spring roll scented with fresh ginger,
garlic and spring onion on a plum and pink-peppercorn sauce, Greta terrine – a layered
watercress, chicken and carrot terrine studded by fresh garden vegetables with a vichyssoise
sauce, fillet steak in a wild-mushroom and brandy cream sauce; daily specials too, all with a
certain *je ne sais quoi*; filled baguettes and other dishes from the menu in the lounge bar; an
extensive wine list, a dozen or so by the glass. Black Sheep Bitter plus the house beer on
hand pump. John Smith Smooth is the keg beer. Lots of room in the large garden.

> OPEN: 11–11 (12–10.30 Sun).
> Real Ale. Restaurant.
> Children welcome. Dogs too. Wheelchair access. Car park. Twenty-three en-suite
> bedrooms.
> Cards: MasterCard, Switch, Visa.

HAYDON BRIDGE

General Havelock Inn
9 Ratcliff Road, Haydon Bridge, Northumberland NE47 6ER
Free House. Gary Thompson, licensee.

Tel: 01434 684376
Fax: 01434 684283

The Havelocks were a local family, and General Havelock is remembered for his exploits during the Indian Mutiny. This is a roadside inn with tremendous appeal. It is family-run, and the licensee is a first-class chef, so food is really the thing here – the restaurant looks seriously professional. But they haven't forgotten that there are other people to cater for; the inn has a traditional bar serving some exceptional food cooked to perfection and presented with style: beef, Guinness and wild-mushroom stew, chicken, leek and Cheddar pie, or fish crumble, with bread-and-butter pudding or apple and bramble crumble to finish. The bar food is important but the emphasis is on the restaurant (only yards from the river). Here there is a reasonable two-, three- or four-course menu which might offer a trio of fish hors d'oeuvre with tossed salad, rack of lamb on roast Mediterranean vegetables or sea bass on a spicy mussel stew to follow. This menu changes every five to six weeks. Always real ales to maintain the ethos of a pub, Timothy Taylors Landlord, Adnams Broadside, Mordues Workie Ticket and Big Lamp Prince Bishop. Wide-ranging wine list, some by the glass.

> OPEN: Closed Monday, otherwise 12–2.30 7–11 (12–2.30 Sun).
> Real Ale. Restaurant.
> Children welcome. Dogs too. Wheelchair access.
> Cards: Delta, Diners, MasterCard, Switch, Visa.

HEDLEY ON THE HILL

Feathers
Hedley on the Hill, Stocksfield, Northumberland NE43 7SW
Free House. Marina Atkinson, licensee.

Tel: 01661 843607

High on the hill, the Feathers is an evening and weekend place; not open during the day except at weekends and Bank Holidays. We have all done it – turned up at the right place at the wrong time. But when this stone-built pub in the middle of the village is open, they serve an interesting selection of popular vegetarian dishes. The menus change twice a week and there could be crab and ginger pot with toast, fresh coriander houmus, tzatziki, olives and pitta, spinach and ricotta filled pancake, smoked-salmon, leek and white-wine risotto, beef and kidney in stout with fresh-herb dumplings, roast fennel, orange and pork casserole, always some vegetarian dishes and at least one for vegans. Yummy puds and children's meals. Local ales – Mordues Workie Ticket and Radgie Gadgie, Butterknowle Bitter and Conciliation could be among the guests; Boddingtons always available. A choice of 30 malt whiskies and a short wine list.

> OPEN: 6–11 weekdays. 12–3. 6–11 Sat. 12–3. 7–10.30 Sun.
> Daytime opening weekends and Bank Holidays only.
> Real Ale. Meals every evening except Mon. Lunch served Sat and Sun.
> Children in eating area and family room till 8.30pm. Dogs on leads. Wheelchair access (not WC). Car park.
> Cards: none accepted.

HOLWICK

Strathmore Arms   Tel: 01833 640362
Holwick, Middleton-in-Teesdale, Northumberland DL12 0NJ
Teesdale Traditional Taverns. Helen Osborne & Joseph Cogden, licensees.

Just off the Pennine Way, in the hills above Middleton-in-Teesdale, this attractive town
is set on a steep hillside above the River Tees. You are in fairly serious walking country, surrounded by wild landscapes and tremendous waterfalls. In the midst of all this wildness is
the Strathmore Arms, on a narrow lane leading nowhere in particular. Inside the pub
there's an attractive bar with a roaring log fire on cold days, and behind the main bar, a
comfortable snug. The bar menu offers home-made soup, grilled local trout, Cumberland
sausages, steak and kidney pie, gammon and eggs – all served with fresh vegetables – vegetarian dishes too. Theakstons Best, Black Bull, Ruddles Best and a guest ale, also
Hedgerow wines and mead. The bar has an old but well-kept piano.

> OPEN 12–11 (12–10.30 Sun).
> Real Ale.
> Children welcome until 9.30pm. Dogs on leads. Four en-suite bedrooms.

MATFEN

Black Bull   Tel: 01661 886330
Matfen, Newcastle-upon-Tyne, Northumberland NE20 0RD (off B6318 north-east of
Corbridge)
Free House. Colin & Michele Scott, licensees.

Find the wonderful floral display and somewhere behind it will be the creeper-covered
Black Bull. When a pub has been awarded Best Pub in the Northumbria in Bloom contest
for several years running, it is worth making a special effort to see the wonderful summer
display. Inside you'll find nicely presented bar food: soups, duck-liver pâté, herb pancake
filled with spiced prawns, home-made steak and mushroom pie cooked in ale, honey-
glazed chicken with toasted almonds and various salads. There is also an extensive,
changing restaurant menu. Part of the restaurant is no smoking. Black Bull Bitter only.
Seats outside at the front of the pub among the flowers.

> OPEN: 11–3. 6–11 (11–11 Sat).
> Real Ale. Restaurant.
> Children in eating area. No dogs. Wheelchair access.

MILFIELD

Red Lion Inn   Tel: 01668 216224
Main Road, Milfield, Nr Wooler, Northumberland NE71 6JD
Free House. John Logan, licensee.

This old coaching inn provided a fresh team of horses for the mail coach from Edinburgh
to London via Coldstream and Newcastle. The cost to travel this route in those days was

13 guineas (£13.60) and according to the Bank of England that is equal to £576.94 in today's money; I think we should all stop complaining about the train fares. The 18th-century Red Lion, the oldest building in the village, has moved on, but the fireplace where the locals used to sharpen their knives is still there; the stone pillars are quite worn away. With all those years of experience behind it, the changing pub menu will have something for everyone: battered mushrooms, deep-fried potato skins, tagliatelle carbonara, filled Yorkshire puddings, steaks and vegetarian dishes. If you are an overnight guest, a full Northumbrian breakfast sets you up for the day; you can have this even if you're not staying as it is served during opening hours. Draught Bass, Black Sheep and two guests.

OPEN: 12–2. 6–11 Mon–Fri. 11–11 Sat. 10–10.30 Sun.
Real Ale.
Children welcome. Dogs on leads. Wheelchair access.
Two double bedrooms; two static caravans to sleep eight people.

NEW YORK

Shiremoor Farm   Tel: 0191 257 6302
Middle Engine Lane, New York, North Shields, Tyne & Wear NE29 8DZ
Sir John Fitzgerald Ltd. C.W. Kerridge, licensee.

Popular with local businessmen during the week, this well-appointed pub caters for everyone – not only someone wanting a pint and bar snack, but also for the family who want high chairs, bottle warmers, etc. For grown-ups there is a traditional bar menu, plus dishes such as roast duck julienne, breast of chicken in garlic and brandy sauce, beef stroganoff, steaks, daily specials and home-made puddings. Timothy Taylors Landlord, Theakstons Best and Mordues Workie Ticket are the beers; brewed in Wallsend, Workie Ticket has been voted 'Champion Beer in Britain'. Wines by the glass. Tables on the grass by the farm courtyard among the flowers.

OPEN: 11–11.
Real Ale. Food served all day, every day.
Children in eating areas. No dogs.

NEWCASTLE-UPON-TYNE

Crown Posada   Tel: 0191 232 1269
31 The Side, Newcastle-upon-Tyne NE1 3JD
Free House. Malcolm McPherson, manager.

The unusual name comes from its 19th-century owner, a sea captain; not quite with a girl in every port, but certainly a wife in Spain and a girl in his pub. It was then called the Crown, but he added Posada, the Spanish word for inn or place of rest, as this was where he felt he was most at home. The Crown Posada, in the shadow of the Tyne Bridge, is an interesting old city-centre pub with magnificent Victorian stained-glass windows, screens, tulip lamps and painted ceilings. Just one long bar, with a snug to one side, serving lunchtime sandwiches. The ales are Theakstons Best, Boddingtons Bitter, Butterknowle Conciliation Ale, Jennings and guest beers. If you want to catch up on the day's events, the daily papers are kept in the snug for you to read.

OPEN: 11–11 (11–4. 7–11 Sat).
Real Ale. Lunchtime snacks (not Sun).
No children. Dogs on leads if well behaved.

NEWTON ON THE MOOR

Cook & Barker Inn   Tel: 01665 575234
Newton on the Moor, Felton, Morpeth, Northumberland NE65 9JY
Free House. Lynn & Phil Farmer, owners/licensees.

If you are wanting some creative food in a comfortable, solid, stone village pub, this is the place to be. High on the moor, with views of the coast, this family-run place with a large beamed bar, dining area and smart restaurant serves good home-made soups, beef with ginger and spring onions, hot beef and onion sandwiches, lamb's liver with vegetables, warm salad of wood pigeon with hedgerow berries, braised lamb shanks with leek and puy lentils, stir-fried Thai beef with spring onions and lemongrass, mixed grills, steaks, and home-made puddings. For the vegetarian, a freshly baked croissant filled with creamy garlic mushrooms. Daily specials are on the blackboard; there are always some exciting dishes for you to try. There will always be three or four local beers as well as Wadworths 6X, Timothy Taylors Landlord, Theakstons ales, Ruddles County and Directors Bitter. Extensive wine list. Seats in the garden.

OPEN: 11–3. 6–11.
Real Ale. Evening restaurant.
Children in eating area. No dogs. Wheelchair access. Car park.
Bedrooms.
Cards: Amex, Delta, MasterCard, Switch, Visa.

ROMALDKIRK

Rose & Crown   Tel: 01833 650213
Romaldkirk, Barnard Castle, Co. Durham DL12 9EB
Free House. Christopher & Alison Davy, licensees.

Here's a fine old 18th-century coaching inn overlooking one of three greens – the one with the village stocks – in an enchanting village in Upper Teesdale. Tall and imposing outside, beamed, panelled, polished and attractive inside, with the bonus of interesting menus in the bar and in the no-smoking restaurant. The weekly changing lunchtime menu offers filled baps and ploughman's, or you could choose a baked Cheddar-cheese soufflé with chive-cream sauce, Queenie scallop and prawn risotto with Parmesan, or, for a main course, fresh pasta with wild-mushroom and cream sauce and blue Stilton served with a salad, roast slice of Scotch salmon with capers, prawns and nut brown butter or beefsteak, kidney and mushroom pie with Theakstons ale under a crisp short-pastry crust. The evening bar menu is more extensive. Imaginative daily lunchtime specials; home-made puddings on the blackboard. Good-value three-course Sunday lunch in the restaurant. Bread will be home-made, as are the chutneys and pickled onions accompanying the ploughman's. Regional cheeses, meat from the local butcher, game from the surrounding moors and fish from the East Coast ports. Black Sheep Bitter and Theakstons Best on hand pump. Wide-ranging wine list – some half-bottles, and some by the glass. Tables outside overlook the village green. You are surrounded by paths to the moors above the village and the river valley below.

> OPEN: 11.30–3. 5.30–11.
> Real Ale. No-smoking restaurant (not Sun eves).
> Children welcome. Dogs on leads. Car park.
> Twelve bedrooms, all en suite, two with private sitting rooms.
> Cards: MasterCard, Switch, Visa.

STOCKTON-ON-TEES

The Masham
Tel: 01642 580414
79 Hartburn Village, Stockton-on-Tees, Cleveland TS18 5DR
Punch Taverns. Dennis & John Eddy, tenant and manager.

Like so many small villages that started out on the edge of a large town, Hartburn village has become attached to its big neighbour. Strangers have difficulty telling where one ends and the other begins. Once you find the Masham, you're in for a friendly welcome in what is a popular local meeting place. It has a bar, a bar area, three small rooms and a garden at the back. Well-chosen bar food is available every day. The Bass and Black Sheep on hand pump are particularly well kept. House entertainment (apart from the customers) is a TV in one of the small rooms for the big sporting events: rugby, cricket, etc. You can't hear the TV anywhere else in the pub – but the customers sometimes get carried away with enthusiasm! Seats and tables on the paved area in the garden, where there is a secluded children's play area.

> OPEN: 11–11.
> Real Ale.
> Children allowed in beer garden. Dogs on leads.

SUMMERHOUSE

Raby Hunt Inn
Tel: 01325 374604
Summerhouse, Durham DL2 3UD
Free House. Michael Allison, licensee.

Surrounded by a wild landscape and the remains of castles and abbeys, the pub is not far from the 14th-century Raby Castle, which was restored in the 18th century and meddled with in the 19th century; it's still very impressive. Stone-built and homely, the Raby

Hunt is a refuge from the rugged moors. You will be well fed here; they serve an uncomplicated menu of pub favourites with the addition of daily special highlights. Mansfield and Marstons beers plus varied guests from local microbreweries. Short wine list.

> OPEN: 11.30–3.30. 6.30–11 (12–3. 7–10.30 Sun).
> Real Ale.
> Children welcome. Dogs too. Wheelchair access (not WC). Car park.

WARENFORD
Warenford Lodge   Tel: 01668 213453
Warenford, Belford, Northumberland NE70 7HY
Free House. Raymond Matthewman, licensee.

Two things you need to know: first, Warenford Lodge is closed on Monday and only open for lunch on Saturday and Sunday. Second, if this is the first time you have been here, you need to know that it isn't any good looking for an inn sign – there isn't one. This place appears to be someone's private house, with lots of parked cars. Stone-built, with mullioned windows, it is a very popular place to eat – but you do have to book to be sure of a table in the evening. Menus change twice a year, but there are usually lots of fishy dishes, which could include the famous Northumbrian fish soup, or the very popular kipper pâté, grilled herb mussels and salmon fillet, Italian shank of pork roasted with wine and herbs, seaside fish platter (large portion), or cannelloni with home-cured ham, lean beef and fresh tomato sauce. As they say, 'all main dishes are complete and fairly substantial' – or you could just have a steak or a pair of kippers. Home-made puddings and a choice of ice-creams. John Smiths, Theakstons and McEwans Scottish ales, plus a varied wine list.

> OPEN: 7–11 (12–2. 7–11 Sat & Sun). Closed all day Monday and all weekday lunchtimes. Closed Mondays except Bank Holidays.
> Evening restaurant & weekend snacks & meals.
> Children in restaurant. No dogs. A few steps for wheelchairs, but there are willing helpers.

WARKWORTH
Black Bull   Tel: 01665 711367
19 Bridge Street, Warkworth, Alnwick, Northumberland NE65 0XB
Free House. J. Morton, licensee.

The delightfully named River Coquet serves as a natural moat, protecting both the village and the impressive ruined castle. The castle, birthplace of Henry Percy (Hotspur), was even mentioned in Shakespeare's *Henry IV*, who was very insulting, calling it a 'worm eaten hold of ragged stone'. Ragged it may be, but it's the place to be in spring when the grassy slopes around the castle walls are covered with daffodils. When you've admired the scenery, make your way to the Black Bull, a delightful pub with seasonal menus that are strong on fish, home-made pizzas and with a definite lean towards the Italian. Beers are draught Bass, Black Sheep Bitter and a guest, plus John Smiths Smooth, Beamish Stout and Strongbow cider.

> OPEN: 11–2.30. 5.30–11 (12–3. 7–10.30 Sun). The opening hours are more flexible during the tourist season.
> Real Ale. Small restaurant.
> Children and dogs on leads. Wheelchair access.
> Cards: none accepted.

BEST OF THE REST

ALNMOUTH

Saddle Hotel   Tel: 01665 830476

Lovers of sailing and golf are well catered for here as there are two golf courses and a yacht haven in the sheltered estuary of the River Aln. A place of some importance before the port silted up; now just a handsome reminder of what it once was. In the Saddle Hotel you will find a well-prepared, unpretentious selection of dishes, ploughman's, Northumberland sausages, steak and kidney – that sort of thing. Ruddles Best, Theakstons, Wadworths 6X and a decent wine list. Bedrooms.

CHATTON

Percy Arms   Tel: 01668 215244

An 18th-century building once owned by the Duke of Northumberland. In an area known for vigorous walks and fishing, this attractive small hotel offers a good choice of bar food: home-made soups, local fish, salmon in a creamy sauce, seafood platter, steaks and specials on the blackboard. Always one real ale, mainly Theakstons, plus good wines. If you stay, the Percy Arms has 12 miles of private fishing for you to enjoy. Bedrooms.

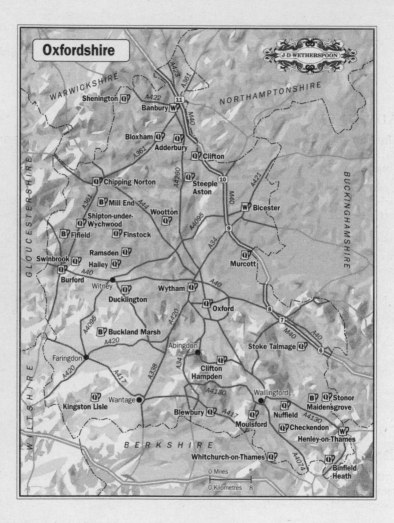

Oxfordshire

J·D·WETHERSPOON

WARWICKSHIRE

NORTHAMPTONSHIRE

Shenington

Banbury

Bloxham
Adderbury
Clifton

Chipping Norton
Steeple Aston
Bicester

Mill End
Wootton
Shipton-under-Wychwood
Fifield Finstock

Ramsden
Swinbrook Hailey
Burford
Witney
Wytham
Ducklington
Oxford
Murcott

Buckland Marsh
Abingdon
Stoke Talmage

Faringdon
Clifton Hampden

Kingston Lisle Wantage
Blewbury
Wallingford
Stonor
Maidensgrove
Nuffield
Moulsford
Checkendon
Henley-on-Thames

Whitchurch-on-Thames
Binfield Heath

GLOUCESTERSHIRE

BUCKINGHAMSHIRE

WILTSHIRE

BERKSHIRE

0 Miles 5
0 Kilometres 8

Oxfordshire

ADDERBURY

The Bell
Tel: 01295 810338

High Street, Adderbury, Banbury, Oxon OX17 3LS
Hook Norton. Tim Turner, tenant.

If, with memories of your childhood, you came through Banbury hoping to find the Banbury Cross of the nursery rhyme, you would be disappointed; the original was destroyed in 1602, and the one you see today is a reproduction. Here in the Bell, at least, things are as they were; no reproduction this. The 18th-century pub, in a village of mainly 17th-century houses, is built in the warm stone so typical of the area. Very traditional, old, beamed, full of atmosphere and friendly – the focus for many village activities, including the local bellringers, theatre workshop and Morris men. They serve a wide range of food from simple bar snacks to home-made steak pie, local rabbit in juniper and cider, breast of duck in a spicy fruit sauce, to fish and chips, daily specials or something from the extensive à la carte menu in the restaurant. They do a very reasonable three-course Sunday lunch complete with fresh coffee served with fudge and mints. Hook Norton range of beers.

OPEN: 12–3. 6.30–11.
Real Ale.
Children welcome. Dogs too. Wheelchair access possible but there are steps – and help. Twin-bedded room. There is a folk club, and occasional live-music sessions.
Cards: Delta, MasterCard, Switch, Visa.

BINFIELD HEATH

Bottle & Glass
Tel: 01491 575755

Harpsden Road, Binfield Heath, Henley-on-Thames, Oxon RG9 4JT
Brakspears. Mike Robinson, tenant.

Between Henley-on-Thames and Reading – the indirect way. Binfield Heath is on an old drovers' road on the edge of the Chilterns. The handsome, 15th-century, black-and-white, thatched Bottle & Glass is just as you hope it will be: flagged floors, antique tables, settles, large log fires in winter, no gaming machines and a friendly ghost – age unknown. An interesting choice of traditional food, all prepared and cooked 'in house' from fresh ingredients: pâté, Cumberland sausages, rump steak, mussels in garlic, fresh fish, lunchtime sandwiches and other dishes; the portions are more than ample – you need a good appetite. The house specialities change from day to day. Outside is a large garden with 24 tables, each with its own thatched canopy to protect you from the noon-day sun. Brakspears ales on hand pump and a good choice of malt whiskies and wines.

> OPEN: 11–3. 6–11.
> Real Ale. No food Sun eves.
> Children and dogs on leads in garden! Wheelchair access (not WC).
> There is a dining room you can hire for a private lunch or dinner.
> Cards: Amex, MasterCard, Switch, Visa.

BLEWBURY

Red Lion   Tel: 01235 850403
Nottingham Fee, Blewbury, Didcot, Oxon OX11 9PQ
Brewery Corporate Catering Co.

This is under totally new management and they say things will stay much the same, but that is all we know at the moment. If you're off for a walk on the Berkshire Downs, this is a good area to start from. So, when you find a lane with a tree in the middle, you know that the 17th-century half-timbered Red Lion isn't far away. This pretty, peaceful village is off the A417 Reading to Wantage road. Menus are on the blackboard and they specialise in fish: seafood soup, mussels, sea bass and lobster, also chicken in a mushroom and tarragon sauce, or pork with apricots. The menus change regularly. Brakspears Ordinary, Special and seasonal ales. Seats in the garden.

> OPEN: 11–2.30. 6–11 (7–10.30 Sun).
> Real Ale. No-smoking restaurant.
> Children in eating areas only. Dogs in the garden. Full wheelchair facilities. Bed and breakfast.

BLOXHAM

Elephant & Castle   Tel: 01295 720383
Bloxham, Nr Banbury, Oxon OX15 4LZ
Hook Norton. Charles Finch, tenant.

If you are involved in a pub quiz, the question 'How did the Elephant & Castle get its name?' will frequently occur. And the answer we all think that is right – 'Infanta of Castile' – is actually wrong! The likely answer is that it has something to do with the sign of the Cutlers' company. Be that as it may, this particular Elephant & Castle is a Cotswold stone pub with a friendly welcome. Just two bars, one a simply furnished public bar, the other a more comfortable lounge – both with big winter log fires, both serving good, straightforward bar food: smoked haddock and leek chowder, minty lamb pie, Thai chicken, lasagne verde, cod in crispy batter and daily specials. In summer there are seats in the flower-filled courtyard and a flourishing barbecue on Saturday evenings and Sunday lunchtimes. Hook Norton ales and a changing monthly guest beer from small independent breweries. Good choice of malt whiskies.

OPEN: 11–3. 6–11 (5–11 Sat. 11–11 Sun).
Real Ale. Restaurant. Bar food lunchtimes only (not Sun).
Children in restaurant. Dogs on leads. Wheelchair access (not WC).

BURFORD
Lamb   Tel: 01993 823155
Sheep Street, Burford, Oxon OX18 4LR
Free House. Richard de Wolf, licensee.

A jewel of a town full of honey-coloured stone houses, shops and inns. Tourists from around the world come to admire it and you can watch them, glass in hand, from a bench outside the Lamb. Inside, the Lamb has flagstone floors, log fires, comfortably furnished bars and a pretty pillared restaurant. Bar lunches could include a cream of watercress and almond soup with granary bread, sautéed chicken livers with bacon, caramelised onions with French bread, fillet of salmon in puff pastry with tarragon, creamed spinach and vegetables, rib-eye steak with pink-peppercorn sauce, garlic potatoes and vegetables, ploughman's, lots of exciting fillings for the baguettes or sandwiches, and delicious puds too. Restaurant meals in the evening: you could start with a terrine of brill, scallops and tiger prawns in a dill and anchovy mayonnaise; for a main course, roast rack of English lamb with fondant potato and broad-bean purée in a smoked garlic and port sauce; to finish, a warm peach and pineapple crumble with vanilla cream. Sunday lunch is something else – if I say you start with Bucks Fizz and end with a pot of coffee and truffles, you will get the drift. Wadworths 6X, Hook Norton Best, Badger Brewery Dorset Bitter on hand pump, plus Old Timer in winter. The wine list includes many classic marques. Behind the inn is a courtyard and a very attractive walled garden.

OPEN: 11–2.30. 6–11.
Real Ale. Restaurant open eves and for Sunday lunch; bar food lunchtimes Mon–Sat.
Children welcome. Dogs too. Fifteen bedrooms – all en suite.
Cards: Delta, MasterCard, Switch, Visa.

CHECKENDON
Black Horse   Tel: 01491 680418
Checkendon, Nr Reading, Oxon RG8 0TE
Free House. Martin & Margaret Morgan, owners/licensees.

Beyond the village, among beech woods and farmland, and next to a farm, the Black Horse is a homely, welcoming, old-fashioned place. It has been in the same family for nearly a hundred years. The beer is drawn from barrels in the still room, just as it has always been. Nothing much has changed over the years. A good fire keeps you warm; freshly filled rolls keep hunger at bay; fresh coffee, Brakspears Bitter, West Berkshire's Good Old Boy and one other from this brewery to quench your thirst. You can sit outside in the pleasant garden and appreciate the unchanging quality of the place.

> OPEN: 12–2 (12–3 Sat). 7–11 – approximately; flexible closing times.
> Real Ale.
> Children welcome. Dogs? Yes-ish – do ask first. Wheelchair access (not WC). Car park.
> Cards: none accepted.

CHIPPING NORTON

Chequers   Tel: 01608 644717
Goddards Lane, Chipping Norton, Oxon OX7 5NP
Fullers. Josh & Kay Reid, tenants.

Several roads converge on this old market town, the highest in the county – 700 feet up and busy too. Originally just Norton, the Chipping was added in the 13th century. Adjoining the Chipping Norton Theatre; this is a well-run, friendly, old-fashioned place with low ceilings, beams and winter log fires. Bigger inside than it looks, with four different drinking areas and a new restaurant (with music). Bar snacks and meals are served every day; the good-value food is prepared from fresh ingredients, much of it with a Thai influence as the landlady went to two cookery schools in Bangkok: vegetable spring rolls with a plum dip, Thai fishcakes with sweet and sour relish, chargrilled and marinated pork-loin steaks, duck-breast and cashew-nut stir fry with rice or noodles. Quite a lot of fresh fish, but the home-cooked ham is so good it pulls them in from miles around. On Sunday they do a traditional roast. Cask Marque accredited; the award-winning Fullers range of beers is very well kept (the Chequers has been a Fullers Pub of the Year); they also have a good small wine list, many available by the glass.

> OPEN: 11–11.
> Real Ale. Restaurant.
> Children welcome. No dogs. Wheelchair access (not WC).
> Cards: Switch, Visa.
> N.B. Music in restaurant area.

CLIFTON

Duke of Cumberlands Head   Tel: 01869 338534
Main Street, Clifton, Nr Deddington, Oxon OX15 0PE
Free House. Nick Huntington, licensee.

Very near the Buckinghamshire border, in an area that saw considerable activity during the Civil War. Apparently Charles I stayed in Deddington after his victory at Copredy Bridge and I'm quite sure the troops found their way to the nearest tavern – probably this old place where I expect the weekly takings shot up! Sixty years old at the time of the battle, it is still thatched, beamed, with huge fireplaces and a comfortable lounge bar. It offers the added bonus of a French restaurant – no smoking – and a constantly changing blackboard menu in the bar. Dishes vary, but there could be a good home-made soup, tomato and mozzarella salad, Iverawe smoked trout, wild-salmon steak with lemon butter, venison in a port and orange sauce, beef bourguignon and lots more, as well as salads and vegetarian dishes. Two- or three-course Sunday lunch. Good range of wines by the glass. Tables outside in the garden. Adnams, Hook Norton, Hampshires King Alfred and guest ales from Easter throughout the summer.

> OPEN: 12–3. 6.30–11.
> Real Ale. Restaurant.
> Children until 9pm. Dogs on leads. Disabled facilities. Car park. All bedrooms en suite.
> Cards: MasterCard, Switch, Visa.

CLIFTON HAMPDEN

Plough
Tel: 01865 407811

Clifton Hampden, Nr Abingdon, Oxon OX14 3EG
Free House. Yuksel Bektas, licensee.

Looking very smart and bright white under a thatched roof, at first glance you wouldn't think that you could pack so much into a building this size. In a village close to the Thames, the 16th-century Plough is one classy pub, run in the best traditions of a public house: the landlord believes in service and in good food too. Food is served throughout the day – one menu throughout the pub, informally in the comfortable beamed bar, and more formally in the attractive restaurant. The menu could include a variety of smoked fish, a pasta dish or two, salmon in mustard and white-wine sauce, beef fillet with wild mushrooms, specials on the blackboard and home-made puddings. Wonderful coffee (several varieties). Directors and John Smiths ales. A very Francophile wine list. A special place this, with a ghost too – a local lad, John Hampden. Absolutely no smoking at all throughout the pub. If you want a quick puff, it's out to the car park.

> OPEN: 11–11. Supper licence until 12pm.
> Real Ale. Restaurant (no smoking). Food served all day.
> Children welcome. Guide dogs only. Wheelchair access. Car park. Ten bedrooms – all en suite; eight in the pub, two in the annex.
> Cards: Amex, Delta, MasterCard, Switch, Visa.
> N.B. Occasional music in the restaurant.

DUCKLINGTON

The Bell
Tel: 01993 702514

Standlake Road, Ducklington, Nr Witney, Oxon OX8 7UP
Greene King. Danny Patching, tenant.

Another flower display with a pub somewhere behind it. Partly thatched, the Bell, in a village alongside the A415, is not far from Witney (famous for those blankets). This is a country pub that specialises in real ales and flower displays. They have been placed in the Pub in Bloom contest for many years, winning it too. They don't have piped music, but the Bell is the headquarters of the local Morris dancers, so you may find them doing a practice session. They do have live folk-music nights; all very rural. A complete range of bar food is served, plus daily and weekly specials; an à la carte menu is served in the restaurant. Always five real ales: the Greene King range, Morlands Old Speckled Hen, Charles Wells Bombardier, Abbot Ale, Triumph Bitter and others; also a full range of wines and spirits. The bedrooms are in a converted brewery and the water source that was used for brewing is still visible in the bar.

> OPEN: 12–3. 6–11 (12–4.30. 6–11 Sat. 12–4. 7–10.30 Sun.)
> Real Ale. Restaurant.
> Children welcome (well behaved and supervised). Dogs too. Wheelchair access into pub just possible (small steps). Car park. Seven en-suite bedrooms.

FINSTOCK

Plough Inn   Tel: 01993 868333
The Bottom, Finstock, Oxon OX7 3BY
Free House. Keith & Nigel Ewers, licensees.

Thatched, with a cosy beamed bar, a log-burning stove in the big inglenook fireplace, comfortable furnishings, doggy bits and pieces and a no-smoking dining room. Good for dogs here; lots of good walks from a pub run by very doggy people – one shows at Crufts. Dog visitors are welcome in the garden (on a lead) or in the public bar – where there is music. Bar food could include grilled bass, crab and avocado gratin, vegetarian pie, steaks and home-baked ham. Their speciality is a steak and mushroom pie with stout and a crusty top, but menus change all the time. Marstons Pedigree, Hook Norton Best, Morlands Old Speckled Hen, Timothy Taylors Landlord, Fullers London Pride, draught Guinness, Scrumpy Jack cider and guest beers. Also farm ciders, a choice of wines and a range of malt whiskies. Tables outside in the garden full of old-variety, wonderfully scented roses.

> OPEN: 12–3. 6–11 (11–11 Sat. 12–4. 7–10.30 Sun).
> Real Ale. Restaurant. Food served 12–2. 7–9.30 Mon–Sat. 12–2.15. 7–9 Sun.
> Children welcome. Dogs on leads. One letting bedroom.
> N.B. Music in public bar, but not in restaurant.

HAILEY

King William IV   Tel: 01491 681845
Hailey, Nr Ipsden, Wallingford, Oxon OX10 6AD
Brakspears. Neil & Mandy Frankel, tenants.

You have to watch out as there are two Haileys in Oxfordshire. The other is miles away, not far from Witney. This is the one you want. Here you'll find a delightful, small, old-fashioned 16th-century pub, with beams and a big log fire in the traditionally furnished bar. Two menus: the one on the specials board changes daily, depending on what is available from the market; the other blackboard menu stays more or less the same and includes steak pies, lemon sole fillets, poached salmon and sausages. An extension gives extra dining space and there is a barbecue outside – weather permitting. Brakspears ales drawn from the cask, farm ciders and a new wine list. Seats outside at the back of the pub with a view of the rolling countryside.

> OPEN: 11–2.30. 6–11.
> Real Ale.
> Children in eating area at lunchtime. Dogs on leads; they have to wipe their feet first – no muddy paws. Wheelchair access and facilities.

KINGSTON LISLE

Blowing Stone Inn   Tel: 01367 820288
Kingston Lisle, Nr Wantage, Oxon OX12 9QL
Free House. Mr & Mrs G.F. Snelson, proprietors.

You all know the old saying 'you can't judge a book by its cover' – well, this pub is a case in point. If the picnic tables weren't outside, you could be forgiven for thinking it was someone's substantial suburban villa. On the Ridgeway near Lambourne on the Berkshire Downs, surrounded by racing stables and serious walks, it's an area full of people on four legs or using their own two. The period of the exterior is reflected in the bar and lounge, while the restaurant is in a modern conservatory. Bar snacks and dishes from the blackboard served at lunchtime; in the evening, it's the à la carte menu only. From the menu there could be a home-made soup, potted shrimps, a mixed salad with anchovies and artichoke hearts, rack of English lamb with herb and garlic crust, pan-fried supreme of chicken with garlic mushrooms and a fresh-fish selection – they are well known for the excellence of their fish. Specials of the day are on the blackboard. They serve a very reasonably priced three-course Sunday lunch. Courage Best Bitter, Wadworths XXX and Fullers London Pride are the beers. European and southern-hemisphere wines. Lots of room in the attractive garden and no bouncy castle!

> OPEN: 11–2.30. 6–11. Closed Mon mornings.
> Real Ales. Restaurant.
> Children in restaurant with parents. No dogs. Wheelchair access. Bedrooms. Car park.

MOULSFORD

Beetle & Wedge Restaurant & Hotel   Tel: 01491 651381
Ferry Lane, Moulsford, Oxon OX10 9JF
Free House. Richard & Kate Smith, licensees.

Wonderfully situated on the River Thames, this is an exceptional place combining the elegance of a well-run hotel with a more informal atmosphere in the boathouse bar. It is another one of those places where you can arrive by water if you're so inclined. From where you tie up you can make for the beamed old boathouse bar, which in summer opens out onto the terrace, only feet from the river. Only one ale served, but there is everything else you could possibly want to drink and a menu that's a pleasure to read. Among the delights you could choose from are home-cured gravadlax with blinis and creamy dill dressing, home-made duck terrine with warm toasted brioche and red-onion compote, and supreme of sesame chicken with wild mushrooms and creamy curry sauce, or from the charcoal grill: fresh scallops with celeriac purée and balsamic vinegar, calves' liver and bacon, or rump steak with wild-mushroom sauce. Interesting and unusual cheeses, plus amazing puds. More formally you would make a beeline for the elegant dining room, where each table has a view of the Thames. If you are looking for a very civilised day by the river, then this is the place to be. Only the finest, freshest local produce is used in this very appealing riverside hotel. Wadworth 6X on hand pump. Extensive, mainly European wine list. For the truly energetic who want to work up an appetite for lunch, rowing boats are for hire nearby.

> OPEN: 11.30–2.30. 6–11. N.B. You must reserve a table if you want to eat – it is very popular.
> Real Ale. Restaurants: one no smoking.
> Children welcome. No dogs. Wheelchair access. Ten en-suite bedrooms – some with river views.
> Cards: Amex, Delta, Diners, MasterCard, Switch, Visa.

MURCOTT

The Nut Tree   Tel: 01865 331253
Main Street, Murcott, Nr Kidlington, Oxon OX5 2RE
Free House. James Wood & Andrew Sparkes, licensees.

Murcott is on the other side of Ot Moor, and the Nut Tree is listed as one of the meeting places for the Ot Moor Rioters who rioted against the Enclosures Act in the 1700s – no doubt triggering another leap in the beer sales! When you reach the 15th-century thatched Nut Tree, you'll find not only a duck pond and ducks, but also golden pheasants, peacocks and donkeys in the 6 acres surrounding the pub. But you're not just here to admire the livestock; you're here for the pub. A conservatory extension houses the restaurant and there is one lounge bar with low ceilings, oak beams, creaking floors, log fires and a ghost: a little girl about 11 or 12 years old in a smock and bonnet. She has been seen several times and it is thought she may have perished in a fire many years ago. Back in the present day, you'll find an extensive menu ranging from sandwiches and locally made sausages to beef Wellington and daily specials. Lots of fresh fish is delivered three times a week from Billingsgate. Nothing is frozen except the scampi. Four ales are available all the time: Hook Norton, Timothy Taylors Landlord, Batemans and other guests. Good range of wines and malt whiskies. Lots of seats outside in the attractive garden.

> OPEN: 11.30–3. 5–11 (11–11 Fri & Sat. 12–10.30 Sun).
> Real Ale. Restaurant.
> Children in garden or conservatory, not in bar. Dogs in garden.
> Wheelchair access. Car park.

NUFFIELD

Crown
Tel: 01491 641335

Nuffield, Henley, Oxon RG9 5SJ
Brakspears. Liz Young & Steve Gunn, licensees.

This traditional old pub, with heavily beamed bars, blazing winter fires and seats outside on which to bask in summer sunshine, is in a village on the edge of the Chilterns on the ancient Ridgeway Path along which countless travellers have walked to reach it. New licensees have taken over so we don't have food details, but expect good-quality home-made bar food. Brakspears ales on hand pump and a good choice of wines.

OPEN: 11.30–3. 5–11 (11–11 Fri & Sat. 12–10.30 Sun).
Real Ale.
Children and dogs welcome. Wheelchair access into pub only.

OXFORD

Turf Tavern
Tel: 01865 243235

4 Bath Place, off Holywell Street, Oxford OX1 3SU
Laurel Pub Co. Darren Kent, manager.

Many famous people have crossed the threshold of this old place: William Shakespeare, Thomas Hardy (*Jude the Obscure*), some film stars: Richard Burton and Elizabeth Taylor and one American President – Bill Clinton. It was *Inspector Morse's* favourite pub too – and it should be one of yours. Glorious Oxford is full of nooks and crannies, and this is a nook in the guise of an attractive courtyard. Here you'll find the Turf Tavern with two comfortable, low-beamed rooms and an ample supply of beer. Known for always having five regular and between eight or nine different guest ales on offer. They get through about 500 different beers in a year. The uncomplicated bar menu lists soup, sandwiches with various fillings, roasts, steak and mushroom and other pies, salads and a vegetarian dish or two. Seats in the courtyards which have heaters to keep you warm. The ales change all the time. Country wines and farm cider also available. A beer festival is held from time to time.

OPEN: 11–11.
Real Ale.
Children in own room. Guide dogs only.

OXFORD

Rose and Crown
Tel: 01865 510551

North Parade Avenue, Oxford OX2 6LX
Inn Business. Deborah & Andrew Hall, tenants.

An old-fashioned local built in the latter half of the 19th century. Inside are three rooms with a bar in two of them, a proper pub piano (in tune) and a friendly, popular landlord. A substantial pub menu lists lots and lots of fillings for the baguettes, whole grilled trout, omelettes, gammon or rump steak, filled baked potatoes – good sustaining fare, and they serve a roast on winter Sundays. Adnams Southwold Bitter, draught Burton Ale, draught Guinness and draught lagers. Good range of wines and an interesting selection of alcohol-free drinks for all of us who drive. The large courtyard at the back of the pub has a retractable awning – and big heaters, which means it can be used all year.

OPEN: 10–3. 5–11 (12–3. 7–10.30 Sun).
Real Ale.
Children: if well-behaved, weekend lunchtimes only. No dogs.
Narrow wheelchairs can get in (not WC).
Cards: Amex if you're eating.

OXFORD

Kings Arms   Tel: 01865 242369
Holywell Street, Oxford OX1 3SP
Youngs. David Kyffin, manager.

This is an old coaching inn in touch with everything that's going on in Oxford. Surrounded by colleges, near the university library buildings and Blackwells bookshop, popular with members of the university, locals (they're the ones still propping up the bar in the vacations) and cosmopolitan visitors. Very busy at lunchtime, but service is fast. Food ranges from predictable pub grub – home-made soups, sandwiches, filled rolls and an Oxford ploughman's featuring an award-winning local blue cheese – to a Kings Arms pie made with chicken and mushrooms cooked in Youngs oatmeal stout. Vegetarian dishes too, and specials on the blackboard. Youngs range of ales, Wadworths 6X, over 20 malt whiskies and a choice of over 20 wines by the glass, including champagne. Tables outside in summer so you can enjoy watching Oxford on the move.

OPEN: 10.30–11 (12–10.30 Sun).
Real Ale. Dining room is no smoking.
Children and dogs welcome if accompanied by well-behaved people!

RAMSDEN

Royal Oak   Tel: 01993 868213
High Street, Ramsden, Oxon OX7 3AU
Free House. Jonathan Oldham, FBII, licensee.

Opposite the war memorial and the village church, the honey-coloured 17th-century Royal Oak is known for its first-rate ales and the excellence of its food. The chef is the owner and licensee of this comfortable, unassuming, 17th-century old coaching inn. A lunchtime bar menu lists sandwiches, ploughmans, smoked Scottish salmon with scrambled egg, baked avocado, cheese and prawn gratinée, fillet of Scottish salmon served

with crevettes and lemon and lime velouté, chargrilled haunch of venison steak marinated in red wine and served with a red-berry sauce, Moroccan chicken tajine cooked
with honey, dried fruit and capsicum served with couscous, a vegetarian dish or two, and
even a special club sandwich. You can choose a dish from either the printed or blackboard menus, or there will always be daily specials. Home-made puds too. Three
cask-conditioned ales are on all the time: Hook Norton BB and two guests. Wide-
ranging wine list. Seats in the sunny courtyard between the pub and four converted
holiday cottages.

> OPEN: 11.30–2.30. 6.30–11 (12–3. 7–10.30 Sun).
> Real Ale. Restaurant.
> Children welcome. Dogs on leads. Wheelchair access. Car park. Four holiday cot-
> tages.
> Cards: MasterCard, Switch, Visa.

SHENINGTON

Bell Inn   Tel: 01295 670274
Shenington, Nr Banbury, Oxon OX15 6NQ
Free House. Jennifer Dixon, licensee.

The welcoming 18th-century Bell is a honey-coloured stone cottage with a well-beamed
traditional interior, some pine panelling and good fires. All the food on the changing
blackboard menu is home-cooked, using local produce whenever possible. Good soups,
well-filled sandwiches, salmon in watercress sauce, devilled sausages on toast, pan-fried
fillet steak and good puds. Boddingtons, Hook Norton and Flowers ales. A good wine list.
Seats at the front of the pub overlook the village green.

> OPEN: 12–2.30. 7–11 (12–3. 6.30–11 Sat).
> Real Ale. Restaurant.
> Children welcome. Dogs on leads. Three bedrooms.

SHIPTON-UNDER-WYCHWOOD

Shaven Crown Hotel   Tel: 01993 830330
High Street, Shipton-under-Wychwood, Oxon OX7 6BA
Free House. Robert & Jane Burpitt, licensees.

This 14th-century hotel, originally the hospice for the nearby Bruern Abbey, was built
around a medieval courtyard garden, an attractive place to sit enjoying a drink or meal on
a summer's day. The Wychwood, later a royal hunting forest, was then as big as the New
Forest in Hampshire; only 1500 acres remain and a large portion of that is now a nature
reserve. The architecturally minded among you should look out for the medieval hall in
the Shaven Crown, now the residents' lounge, with its double-collar braced roof, still in
perfect condition after 600 years. The beamed Monk's Bar, with a log fire in winter, offers
a wide range of bar snacks: sandwiches and filled baguettes, devilled kidneys on a crispy

crouton, deep-fried whitebait and brown bread, Cotswold lamb cutlets, chicken breast wrapped in smoked bacon, steak and mushroom pie and much more. Vegetarian dishes and puddings too. There is a more extensive menu in the evening restaurant: pancakes filled with salmon and spinach in white-wine sauce, deep-fried Camembert, Normandy pheasant, chicken with apricot stuffing and fennel sauce, fish dishes, steaks and more puddings. Hook Norton ale and guest beers. The wine list varies from week to week.

> OPEN: 12–2.30. 5–11 (11.30–11 Sat. 12–10.30 Sun).
> Real Ale. Restaurant.
> Children welcome but no under-fives in evening restaurant.
> No dogs. Wheelchair access to all parts of the hotel.

STEEPLE ASTON

Red Lion   Tel: 01869 340225
South Side, Steeple Aston, Oxon OX6 3RY
Free House. Colin Mead, licensee.

Not only are you guaranteed to get a decent glass of wine in the 17th-century Red Lion, but intellectual stimulation too. Newspapers, an eclectic collection of books and someone to discuss them with. Bar food is limited to lunchtimes only: home-made soups, ploughman's with local cheeses, sandwiches, winter hotpots and summer salads. There's a more ambitious and creative menu in the evening restaurant. On Sundays the Red Lion is a proper pub – a place to go and have a leisurely drink before wending your way home for lunch – just as it should be. Hook Norton Bitter and guest beers only. Over 100 wines are kept; the landlord is very keen on his wines and keeps an interesting, inimitable cellar. Seats on the sunny terrace at the front of the pub among the flowers.

> OPEN: 11–3. 6–11.
> Real Ale. Evening restaurant (closed Sun and Mon).
> Lunchtime meals and snacks (not Sun).
> Children in restaurant. Dogs on leads.

STOKE TALMAGE

Red Lion   Tel: 01844 281343
Stoke Talmage, Thame, Oxon OX9 7ES
Free House. Stephen Wilkins, licensee.

Off the A40 south of Tetsworth – keep an eye out for the signpost to the village. A family-run pub for over 60 years, this 200-year-old former farmhouse is an unpretentious village local, cheerful and welcoming. Warm fires, two rooms – one with comfortable chairs – where you can enjoy something from the wide selection of beers and ciders. No food served except for a few things to nibble Sunday lunchtimes – but you can bring your own sandwiches if you ask first. You are surrounded by some wonderful countryside with well-signposted walks, and the birdwatchers among you might like to know that red kites and buzzards are there to be spotted. Outside, next to the pub's own smallholding, the garden has a play area to keep the children amused, an Aunt Sally for the grown-ups and picnic tables if you just want to enjoy your drink. Beers are from Brakspears, Greene King, West Berkshire Brewery, Nethergate and many others; ciders too: Westons, Inches, Royal County and Thatchers.

> OPEN: 6–11 Mon–Thurs. 12–2.30. 6–11 Fri & Sat. 12–2.30. 7–10.30 Sun. Closed Mon in winter.
> Children welcome. Dogs too. Wheelchair access – new loos! Car park.

STONOR

Stonor Arms Hotel & Restaurant
Tel: 01491 638866
Stonor, Henley-on-Thames, Oxon RG9 6HE
Free House. Sophia Williams, licensee.

Near the Oxfordshire Way and Stonor Park, it is 5 miles north of Henley-on-Thames. Mainly, as you see from the name, a hotel with an award-winning restaurant, it does have a very welcoming bar where you can get a sandwich if that is all you want. The informal bar, called 'Blades' (oars, and other rowing memorabilia) is very comfortable, with sofas to sit on, polished flagstones, pictures on the walls and a log fire to stare into. In this bar you can get a bowl of home-made soup, Cumberland sausages with creamed potato, fish of the day, steak and pitta bread with a tomato and red-onion relish, well-filled sandwiches or a salad. If you want something more substantial, you have a choice of a two- or three-course table d'hôte or an à la carte menu in the very attractive conservatory or the elegant dining room. Brakspear Special and Fullers London Pride. A lovely hotel this; lots of tables in the well-planted walled garden, in glorious countryside with lots of good walks, and, however smart this looks, walkers are very welcome.

> OPEN: 11–11.
> Restaurant.
> Children welcome. Dogs too. Ten bedrooms, all en-suite, some on ground level with doors opening onto the garden.

SWINBROOK

Swan Inn
Tel: 01993 822165
Swinbrook, Nr Burford, Oxon OX18 4DY
Free House. Mr & Mrs A. Morris, licensees.

This unspoilt, unchanging little place has only a small bar but they seem to pack in the locals and walkers. Wisteria-covered – and looking as if it could also soon disappear under the Virginia creeper – this delightful 15th-century inn is near the bridge over the Windrush River. Traditionally furnished with stone-flagged floors and winter fires. Home-cooked bar food and a more ambitious evening menu. The home-made steak and kidney pie is very popular at lunchtime, as is creamy seafood tagliatelle, English lamb cutlets with onions in a mint and cranberry sauce, fish, salads, omelettes and filled baguettes; in the evening there is pork tenderloin pan fried in butter and onions served with sweet apricot, cider and ginger, or fillet steak served as you like it. The specials and puddings are on the blackboards. Archers of Swindon, Wadworths 6X, Morlands Bitter and cider from Somerset. Benches outside – muddy boots outside too.

> OPEN: 11.30–3. 6.30–11.
> Real Ale.
> Children welcome. Dogs on leads. No dirty boots in dining room. Wheelchair access (not WC).
> Cards: MasterCard, Switch, Visa.

WHITCHURCH ON THAMES

Greyhound   Tel: 0118 984 2160
High Street, Whitchurch on Thames, Nr Reading, Oxon RG8 7EL
Pubmaster. Stuart Brackley-Pattison, licensee.

Not far from the river. The comfortable bar in this pretty white-painted little pub serves good, freshly cooked food. Always well-filled sandwiches, ploughman's, a variety of salads, Cromer crab salad in the summer, steak and mushroom pie, pork ribs in barbecue sauce, a pasta dish, filled jacket potatoes and their very own way with prawns. Well-kept Flowers Original, Wadworths 6X, Greene King IPA, Marstons Pedigree, Guinness, Strongbow cider and three lagers. Pleasant garden to sit in and some good walks.

> OPEN: 12–2.30. 6–11 (12–2.30. 7–10.30 Sun).
> Real Ale.
> Children in garden. Dogs on leads. Wheelchair access.

WOOTTON BY WOODSTOCK

Kings Head Inn   Tel: 01993 811340
Chapel Hill, Wootton, Oxon OX20 1DX
Free House. Tony & Amanda Fay, licensees.

This 17th-century stone pub is in an attractive village north of Woodstock. Inside, the Kings Head has plenty of beams, a big log fire and comfortable sofas and settles. You can eat in the bar or in the no-smoking restaurant. Bar snacks, available at lunchtime only, are on a separate board, but from the lunchtime menu you could choose a home-made soup, roasted trio of tomatoes topped with toasted goat's cheese and a drizzle of basil pesto, muscovado-and-lime-cured Scottish salmon with a coriander vinaigrette, a tower of Orkney fillet with wild mushrooms on a potato rosti with a black-pepper dressing, Scottish mussels cooked with fennel in a cream and white-wine sauce, or grilled medallions of pork loin topped with a crust of mascarpone cheese and served with a red-pimento coulis. Much more on the dinner menu, plus English and Irish cheeses and scrummy puds. Marstons Pedigree, Ruddles Best and Wadworths 6X on hand pump, a good wine list and a wine board listing 'wines of the month'. Well known for their food – this place is worth a special trip.

>OPEN: 11–3. 6–11 (12–3. 7–10.30 Sun).
>Real Ale. Restaurant.
>Children welcome if very well behaved. No dogs. Wheelchair access (not WC).
>Bedrooms.
>Cards: MasterCard, Visa.

WYTHAM

White Hart   Tel: 01865 244372
Wytham, Nr Oxford, Oxon OX2 8QA
Bass Six Continents. John Clark, manager.

Another of our film stars. We've already listed the late *Inspector Morse's* town pub in Oxford – this was one of his country pubs. The village of thatched stone houses overlooks the River Thames. The White Hart, an attractive creeper-covered pub, has a part-panelled bar with flagstone floors and an open fire. Bar food includes a huge choice of salads, filled baked potatoes, lots of fish dishes – swordfish, halibut, tuna and others. Most of the food is prepared to order; there are also daily specials and some vegetarian dishes. The barbecue is barbecueing during all opening hours Tuesday to Sunday, weather permitting of course. Adnams Bitter, Morlands Old Speckled Hen, a guest every two weeks and Tetleys Smooth Flow beers – these do change. Seats in the very lovely walled garden. The village is totally owned by Oxford University.

>OPEN: 12–3. 6–11 (12–11 Sat. 12–10.30 Sun). In summer 11.30–11 (12–10.30 Sun).
>Real Ale. Food served every day.
>Children in own room. Dogs on leads in garden.

BEST OF THE REST

BUCKLAND MARSH, Nr Faringdon

Trout at Tadpole Bridge   Tel: 01387 870382
This is one of those pubs that should be on everyone's main list, but because of the music (very quiet), it has to be in this category. That said, there are so many good things about the Trout that maybe you should just grit your teeth and accept it. Find the river and there's the pub. Small, with no excesses in the interior-decoration line, but the beer's well kept: Fullers London Pride and Archers Village Bitter and summer guests, a very comprehensive wine list and some really inventive, worthwhile food: dishes like home-smoked pigeon breast with a celeriac salad and whole roast partridge served with cherry onions, smoked bacon and almond potato give you a flavour of what to expect. Closed winter Sunday evenings. Children allowed, dogs too and you can stay.

FIFIELD

Merrymouth   Tel: 01993 831652

A right turn off the A424 from Burford. Don't confuse this Fifield with Fyfield just over the border in Gloucestershire. It's an ancient stone-built pub with a cosy, beamed bar where they serve freshly made bar food, as well as some imaginative dishes and home-made puds – you won't be disappointed. Hook Norton Best, a guest and a small, decent wine list.

MAIDENSGROVE

Five Horseshoes   Tel: 01491 641282

In the glorious Chiltern beech woods, the Five Horseshoes caters very sensibly for all serious walkers – they have given them their own bar so they can keep their boots on. In the rest of the pub they welcome travellers all (as you can see from the banknotes stuck to the ceiling) to sample something from the menu or daily changing blackboard specials: home-made soups, stuffed pancakes, warm salad of scampi and crab, lamb braised in a provençale sauce, delicious puds. Brakspear ales and an extensive wine list.

MILL END, CHADLINGTON

Tite Inn

Straight away you need to know this pub is closed on Mondays, except Bank Holiday Mondays. The Tite name comes from the spring that feeds the trough (in past times the only water supply) at the front of this 17th-century stone pub on the edge of the village. Friendly and family-run, they have lunch and evening menus. Sandwiches at lunchtime, as well as lamb and apricot pie and caramelised onion and goat's-cheese tart. In the evening, possibly a mixed-seafood salad or boeuf bourgignon by way of examples. Well-kept Archers Village, Charles Wells Bombardier, guest beers, draught cider and a wide-ranging wine list. Children, dogs and wheelchairs all OK.

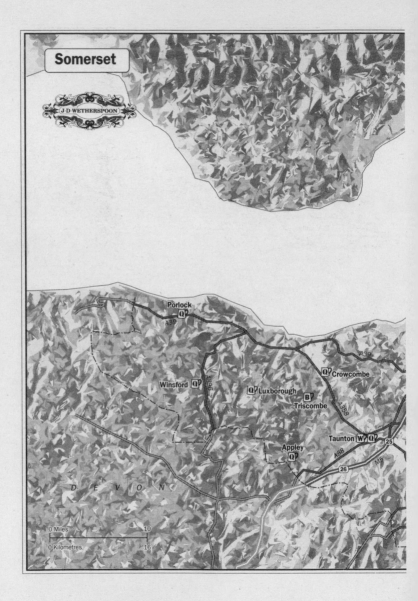

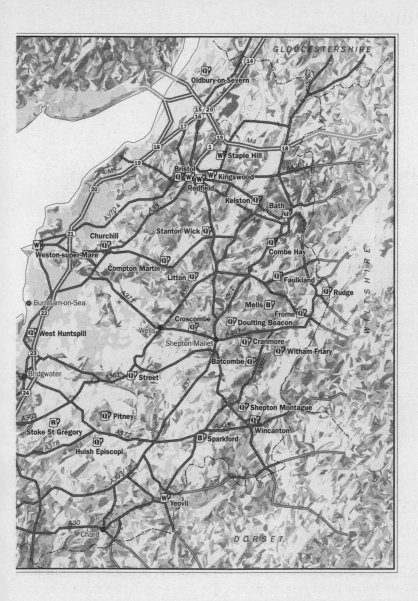

Somerset

APPLEY

Globe
Tel: 01823 672327

White Ball Hill, Appley, Wellington, Somerset
Free House. A.W. & E.J. Burt, licensees.

In an area of scattered hamlets and farms close to the Somerset–Devon border, the 500-year-old Globe is a gem of a place. Cosy rooms lead off the brick corridor, where you'll find a serving hatch for the beers. They have a reputation for really good home-made food. On the bar menu you could find home-made fish soup with chunks of fresh fish cooked in white wine, saffron and garlic; smoked-haddock and bacon chowder; gravadlax served with fresh dill, mustard and brandy dressing; and for the main course, a home-made steak and kidney pie cooked in stout with a puff-pastry top. Add to that casseroled venison with bacon, mushrooms, shallots, garlic, tomato and red wine in a pie; a vegetarian pasta, seafood pancake, more fish and lots more; great puds too. Cotleigh Tawny is the main beer, along with local guests. Local cider too during the summer. Climbing frames, swings and things to keep the little darlings happy. Very busy and very popular.

> OPEN: 11–3. 6.30–11 (12–3. 7–10.30 Sun). Closed Mon all day except Bank Holidays.
> Real Ale. Restaurant.
> Children in eating areas. No dogs.
> Cards: MasterCard, Switch, Visa.

BATCOMBE

Three Horseshoes
Tel: 01749 850359

Batcombe, Nr Frome, Somerset BA4 6HE
Free House. Tony Lethbridge, licensee.

Find the village first, then find the church and there is the Three Horseshoes. It's the village that's the difficult bit, so out with the map again. Very atmospheric this place; the interior decor is warm, cosy and very welcoming. Food is good and popular but there is still a welcome for anyone wanting to lean on the bar with a drink. All dishes are on blackboards and are supplemented by daily specials. Butcombes, Adnams and Wadworths 6X are the beers; wines are mainly French with a touch of the New World, over ten wines by the glass. Tables in the garden where there is a children's play area.

OPEN: 12–3. 6.30–11 (12–3. 7–10.30 Sun).
Real Ale. Restaurant.
Children welcome, dogs too. Wheelchair access. Car park.
Cards: Delta, MasterCard Switch, Visa.

BATH

Old Green Tree
Tel: 01225 448259

12 Green Street, Bath, Somerset
Free House. Nick Luke, licensee.

Among the delights of Bath is this small, mid-18th-century town pub, still with a panelled interior; a delightful, chatty place. One of the most popular places to be, particularly at lunchtime, when food is available. Dishes definitely lean towards the continental at the Green Tree; you'll find tapas and paella as well as the familiar short menu that lists smoked-trout terrine, well-filled Green Tree rolls, good-sized ploughman's with home-made chutney, pasta dishes, seafood platter and salads. The home-made soup and daily specials of freshly cooked seasonal dishes are all listed on blackboards. Local breweries supply the five ales, the choice varying considerably. There are also a number of unusual wines. Pimms is served during the summer; hot punch in winter.

OPEN: 11–11 (7–10.30 Sun). Doors close at 10pm Saturday – entry by doorbell.
Real Ale. Lunchtime meals and snacks (not Sun).
Children over ten if eating at lunchtime only. No dogs.

BRISTOL

Highbury Vaults
Tel: 0117 973 3203

164 St Michael's Hill, Kingsdown, Bristol BS2 8DE
Youngs. Bradd Francis, manager.

There is a timeless and appealing atmosphere in this old pub. A Georgian building with a later interior, it has an intimate snug with a bigger, cosy bar at the back from where you can glimpse the flowery and secluded garden; a favourite place at all times. Reasonably priced traditional bar food changes daily. All dishes are freshly cooked and might include a spinach and mushroom lasagne, pork and apples in cider, and lamb and rosemary casserole. No fried food and no chips with anything. Since the change of ownership to Youngs the ales are Youngs Bitter, AAA, Special and the seasonal ale, Smiles Best and Brains SA. Three guest ales change each week and these could include London Pride, Adnams Broadside, Bishops Finger, Barn Owl, Double Dragon and many more. Seats in the terrace garden which is heated in winter. Blissfully free of jukeboxes and fruit machines. The bars on some of the windows aren't to keep the customers in – they were to keep the prisoners in! For a time this place was part of the local jail.

> OPEN: 12–11.
> Real Ale. No food Sat or Sun eves.
> Children welcome until 9pm. Dogs only in the front bar.

BRISTOL

Commercial Rooms   Tel: 0117 927 9681
43–45 Corn Street, Bristol BS1 1HT
Wetherspoon.

At the heart of Bristol, this building was, for over 100 years, a club for local businessmen. It has now been lovingly restored into the place you see today. The Grand Coffee Room, which had been used for coffee auctions, now has an island bar and is the main drinking area. Two no-smoking rooms are at the end of the bar. Six cask-conditioned beers at all times – Youngers Scotch Bitter, Courage Directors, Theakstons Best, XB, Wadworths 6X and a local regional beer. Guest beers from the smaller breweries. Reliable bar food, with a choice of daily specials, served all day.

> OPEN: 11–11 (12–10.30 Sun).
> Real Ale.
> No children. No dogs, except guide dogs.

CHURCHILL

Crown Inn   Tel: 01934 852995
The Batch, Skinners Lane, Churchill, Somerset BS25 5PP
Free House. Tim Rogers, licensee.

If you're here in summer, you could well be entertained by the local Morris Men. At the base of the Mendip Hills, this small, stone, 16th-century pub is delightfully unspoilt. Beams, stone and slate floors, open fires – all that you would expect. They serve simple, home-made bar food to go with some unusual beers. Draught Bass and Palmers IPA, as well as the constantly changing guests.

> OPEN: 11–11 (12–10.30 Sun).
> Real Ale.
> Children in eating area. Dogs in garden.

COMBE HAY

Wheatsheaf   Tel: 01225 833504
Combe Hay, Nr Bath, Somerset BA2 7EG (off the A367 Exeter road out of Bath)
Free House. Peter Wilkins, owner/licensee.

On a clear day the views from the attractive pub garden are of the English countryside at its best. Inside the black-and-white 17th-century pub are cosy low-ceilinged rooms, country furnishings, a big log fire in winter and a huge blackboard menu. As well as the familiar bar snacks, there are some interesting dishes: they have a creative way with pheasants and pigeons and also serve locally caught trout; the specials board might include king prawns in garlic butter or venison in red-wine sauce, and several fish dishes, including crab and lobster, are among the specialities of the house. Home-made puddings too. There is also a full à la carte menu. Courage Best and Morlands Old Speckled Hen as the guest beer. Seats in the terraced garden – ablaze with colour all summer. Good walks.

OPEN: 11–3. 6.30–10.30 (6.30–11 Fri & Sat).
Real Ale. Restaurant. Barbecue.
Children welcome. Dogs on leads. Wheelchair access to all parts of pub with a bit of help. Three en-suite bedrooms.

COMPTON MARTIN

Ring O' Dells   Tel: 01761 221284
Compton Martin, Nr Bath, Somerset BS18 6JE
Free House. Roger Owen, licensee.

In a village tucked under the Mendip Hills, this pub is popular with walkers, visitors and locals alike. It's a white-painted stone building with flagstone floors and big log fires, making it inviting in winter. The usual sandwiches, ploughman's, filled jacket potatoes, beef in ale, grills and lasagne plus some original specials keep the wolf at bay. Roast lunches are available on Sundays. Wadworths 6X, Butcombe Bitter and Gold plus a guest. Thatchers local cider on draught and a short list of wines to try. Seats in the garden among the apple trees, and a play area for children. Lots of things to do around here: caves to explore, Blagdon and Chew Valley Lakes to admire and the Devil's Punchbowl to wonder at – the Punchbowl is a significant 'swallet', a hole in the limestone that temporarily swallows up streams.

OPEN: 11.30–3. 6–11.
Real Ale. Restaurant.
Children in family room. Dogs away from eating areas. Wheelchair access (not WC). Car park.
Cards: Delta, MasterCard, Switch, Visa.

CRANMORE

Strode Arms   Tel: 01749 880450
Cranmore, Nr Shepton Mallet, Somerset BA4 4QT
Free House. Rodney & Dora Phelps, licensees.

Large, stone-built, handsome and opposite the duck pond. Not far from the East Somerset Railway, so along with all its other goodies, the 15th-century Strode Arms houses an interesting collection of railway memorabilia. Inside are country furnishings, big log fires in winter, daily papers and a smart restaurant. Bar food includes the usual range: home-made soup of the day, Dora's herb toast, a very popular egg mayonnaise à la Strode, smoked Dorset trout, scallops and bacon served on a warm salad, home-made pies, smoked haddock and cod fishcakes, breast of chicken filled with cheese, pan fried and covered in a white-wine sauce, venison sausages, steaks, fish dishes, plus five daily specials on the blackboard, and four or five delicious puds, which could include apple dumplings and Dora's sticky toffee pudding. Oakhill Best, Wadworth 6X, Henry's Original IPA, guest beer, a farm cider and a selection of fine wines. Seats on the terrace at the front of the pub overlooking the village pond, and in the beer garden at the back.

> OPEN: 11.30–2.30. 6.30–11. Closed Sun eves Oct–end of March.
> Real Ale. Restaurant.
> Children in restaurant. Dogs in bar on leads. Wheelchair access. Car park.
> Cards: MasterCard, Switch, Visa.

CROSCOMBE

Bull Terrier   Tel: 01749 343658
Croscombe, Nr Wells, Somerset BA4 4QJ
Free House. Barry Vidler, licensee.

First licensed early in the 17th century, the Bull Terrier was originally the priory and home of the Abbot of Glastonbury. Three bars inside the pub: the lounge, called the 'Inglenook', which still has its original beamed ceiling, the 'Snug' and the 'Common Bar'; also a no-smoking family room. Bar food ranges from ploughman's, filled sandwiches (plain or toasted), home-made pâté and vegetarian dishes to fillet steak, chicken and mushrooms in a tarragon sauce, gammon steak, home-made steak and kidney pie, salads and specials such as lemon sole with a crab and seafood sauce. Good puddings. Varying ales, but mainly Bull Terrier Best Bitter brewed for the pub; also Butcombe Bitter, Greene King Abbot, Theakstons XB and Smiles Best. Local cider and a good wine list. The walled garden backs onto the village church and – continuing the ecclesiastical theme – a footpath from the village leads to the Bishop's Palace in Wells.

> OPEN: 12–2.30. 7–11. Closed Mon in winter.
> Real Ale. No food winter Sun eves or all day Mon.
> Children in family room. Dogs: if they like the look of them.
> Wheelchair access (not WC).
> Cards: Delta, MasterCard, Solo, Switch, Visa.

CROWCOMBE

Carew Arms   Tel: 01984 618631
Crowcombe, Taunton, Somerset TA4 4AD
Free House. Simon & Sheila Jones, proprietors.

At the foot of the Quantock Hills, the 17th-century Carew Arms has only had four land-lords in the past 100 years. The bar is warmed by a wonderful fire in a massive inglenook fireplace that was hidden for many years. Flagstone floors, medieval windows and the old benches are part of the history of this genuine old place, as are some of the locals! In this well-liked, busy pub you will find good food, using a lot of locally grown produce, at sensible prices; the pub is, after all, in an area that can provide some of the best meat and vegetables in the south-west of England. All the food is freshly cooked: home-made soup, filled baguettes, sirloin steak with mushrooms, freshly caught plaice with either parsley or prawn butter, local ham and eggs, locally made sausages with onion gravy and home-made steak and kidney pie – no chips. Exmoor Ale is always available, plus one, soon to be two, guests. Ales are kept to a very high standard – the Carew Arms was CAMRA Pub of the Month in August 2001. The whole area is a mecca for walkers, so walkers and their dogs are encouraged – the flagstone floor is muddy-boot-friendly.

OPEN: 11.30–3. 6–11 (12–3. 7–11 Sun).
Closed Sun eves in winter. No food Sun eves or Mon.
Real Ale.
Well-behaved children. Dogs: yes, encouraged. Wheelchair access – just. Car park.
Skittle alley. Three reasonably priced bedrooms.

DOULTING BEACON
Waggon & Horses
Tel: 01749 880302
Frome Road, Doulting Beacon, Shepton Mallet, Somerset BA4 4LA
Ushers. Francisco Cardona, lease.

Between Frome and Wells and deep in hunting country, you know you are in the right place when you find a car park big enough to turn a horsebox without much effort. Señor Cardona is an enthusiast about horses, art, music and of course this wonderful old coaching inn. Inside is a comfortable, rambling beamed bar with big log fires where they serve quite delicious food; a combination of Central European, Mediterranean, Latin American and the best of British – prime Scottish beef and lots of fresh fish. You can always order a sandwich, or you could have a full meal starting with devilled mushrooms on toast or Greek salad, followed by breast of chicken in white-wine, cream and tarragon sauce, or salmon fishcakes with dill mayonnaise, and a steamed ginger and lemon pudding to finish. As a special treat, if there are four of you, a paella or pot au feu can be ordered in advance. The specials board reflects the seasons and availability of produce. The walls of the pub are used as a gallery for a number of local artists, works are for sale and the turnover is quite brisk on concert nights. Three real ales from Ushers – one seasonal, Blackthorn cider, Murphy's stout and Somerset Royal Cider Brandy. A modest wine list includes a local white, champagne and sparkling wines. The old hayloft, reached by an outside staircase, has been converted into an art gallery, concert hall and function room. This isn't any old concert hall; there is a concert grand piano upstairs and the concerts are the real thing – all professional artistes. Outside is a delightful, well-planted walled garden, Señor Cardona's pride and joy; also exotic chickens – for the eggs – waiting to be admired. If you want to celebrate in a very special way, they will even arrange a concert just for you.

OPEN: 11–3. 6–11 (12–3. 7–10.30 Sun).
Real Ale.
Children if very good. Dogs if under control. Wheelchair access. Car park.
Cards: MasterCard, Switch, Visa.

FAULKLAND

Tuckers Grave   Tel: 01373 834230
Faulkland, Nr Bath, Somerset BA3 5XF
Free House. Ivan & Glenda Swift, licensees.

This cider house is very small and basic and was named after poor Tucker who in 1747 hanged himself at a nearby farm and was buried at the crossroads where this old stone pub now stands. Only three little rooms in the pub. Imagine a pub that has been serving the local community for centuries and you have a picture of this unspoilt little place. Casks of Bass and Butcombe Bitter where you can see them, also Cheddar Valley cider. A skittle alley for fun, seats in the garden for relaxation and a ploughman's or a sandwich for lunchtime sustenance.

> OPEN: 11–3. 6–11.
> Real Ale. No food Sundays.
> Children welcome. No dogs. Wheelchair access.

FROME East Woodlands

Horse & Groom   Tel: 01373 462802
East Woodlands, Nr Frome, Somerset BA11 5LY
Longleat Estate. Kathy Barrett, licensee.

An engaging 17th-century pub on the edge of the Longleat estate. Inside is a cosy, flag-stoned bar with an open fire, a lounge and big restaurant/conservatory. All the food is home-cooked: soup, savoury crumbed cheeses and vegetables, poached-egg florentine, noisette of lamb in basquaise sauce, roast-vegetable filo tart, freshly cooked liver, bacon and onions in a rich gravy (a great favourite), filled baguettes, ploughman's, a fish dish or two and always inspired vegetarian dishes. Beers are Butcombe Bitter, Wadworths 6X, Branscombe Vale Branoc and guests. Wines by the glass. Seats at the front of the pub and in the beer garden.

> OPEN: 11.30–2.30 (12–3. 7–10.30 Sun).
> Real Ale.
> Children welcome under control in lounge and restaurant. Dogs on leads in public
> bar. Wheelchair access.
> Cards: all major credit and debit cards.

HUISH EPISCOPI

Rose & Crown   Tel: 01458 250494
Huish Episcopi, Langport, Somerset TA10 9PU
Free House. Mrs Eileen Pittard, licensee.

Known as Eli's after Mrs Pittard's father, Eli Scott – you'll find 'Eli' in brackets on the inn sign. This year the pub will have been run by the same family for 140 years; even longer if you count the landlady before Mrs Pittard's grandfather, as she was a distant relation. The heart of the pub is the flagstoned central still room; it is one of our national treasures – nothing much has changed. No bar; you go into the still room and they'll draw your beer, cider or stout from the cask. The floor of the large room is 2 feet higher than the rest of the pub. Until about 20 years ago flooding was a regular occurrence; the extra 2 feet at least kept your feet dry. There are still winter floods, but now they don't reach the pub. A very welcoming place. Food is good simple fare – all home-made: soup, sandwiches, plain or toasted, ploughman's, steak and ale pie, pork, apple and cider cobbler, spinach lasagne, cottage pie, cauliflower cheese and daily specials, home-made puds too. Always Teignworthy and three guest ales. Julian Temperley's Burrow Hill Cider (he also makes Somerset Cider Royal Brandy). Tables in the garden; children have a separate play area. Good walks nearby.

OPEN: 11.30–2.30. 5.30–11 (11.30–11 Fri & Sat. 12–10.30 Sun).
Real Ale.
Children welcome. Dogs allowed.

KELSTON

Old Crown   Tel: 01225 423032
Bath Road, Kelston, Nr Bath, Somerset BA1 9AQ
Butcombe Brewery. Chris Cole, licensee.

Only about 4 miles from Bath; everything you would expect a pub to be: traditionally furnished, with polished flagstone floors, hop vines hanging from the beams, good fires, two bars and two small attractive dining rooms. Bar food ranges from the usual sandwiches and light snacks to a three-course meal; there is also a daily changing specials board. Well-kept ales include Bass, Butcombe Gold, Wadworths 6X and Bath Gem. Tables under the fruit trees in the orchard at the back of the pub. You have to be careful when you visit this old pub, as the car park is on the other side of the busy old Bath to Bristol road.

OPEN: 11.30–2.30. 5–11 (11–11 Sat. 12–10.30 Sun).
Real Ale. Restaurant closed Sunday and Monday evening.
No children under 14 except in garden. Dogs on leads. In a building next to, and owned by, the pub are four new bedrooms.

LITTON

Kings Arms   Tel: 01761 241301
Litton, Somerset BA3 4PW
Free House. Roger Barlow, licensee.

Beamed, with polished flagstones and a huge fireplace, this picture-book 15th-century Mendip pub is filled with friendly conversation. There is quite an extensive menu listing ploughman's, smoked mackerel, whitebait, garlic crevettes, crispy sweetcorn and lots more for starters; then a choice of fish platters, six different fish dishes, salad snacks and even a slimline platter or sandwiches. The beers are beautifully kept and served at near room temperature: Bass, Courage Best and Wadworths 6X. Quite family-orientated with lots of play equipment in the gardens – everything to keep the children happy and out of the pub.

OPEN: 11–2.30. 6–11.
Real Ale.
Children in own room. Dogs welcome.

LUXBOROUGH

Royal Oak
Tel: 01984 640319
Luxborough, Nr Dunster, Exmoor National Park, Somerset TA23 0SH
Free House. Cecil Barrow, licensees.

Next to a stream in a village at the bottom of a valley in the Bredon Hills, this is a friendly, unspoilt, 14th-century thatched country pub with heavily beamed bars complete with flagged floors, inglenook fireplaces and an assortment of country furniture. Surrounded as you are by wonderful countryside, you might want to stay – and you can do that too. If you're just passing, you could be tempted by well-kept local ales and good, hearty country cooking. The choice ranges from sandwiches to rabbit stew or roast wild boar. The specials board may have game pies, fish dishes or venison. Home-made puds and local cheeses to follow. Roast lunches on Sunday. Cotleigh Tawny and Thatchers Cheddar Valley are among the ales you may find; also Palmers 200 as a guest beer and Rich's Farmhouse Cider. Good list of wines. Seats outside in the garden.

OPEN: 11–2.30. 6–11 (12–2.30. 7–10.30 Sun).
Real Ale. Restaurant.
Children in dining room and rear bar. Dogs in bar. Car park. Ten en-suite bedrooms.
Folk music every 2nd Friday in the month, quiz night Thursday.
Cards: MasterCard, Switch, Visa.

OLDBURY-ON-SEVERN

Anchor
Tel: 01454 413331
Church Road, Oldbury-on-Severn, Somerset BS12 1QA
Free House. Alex de la Torre, licensee.

If you are walking the area in a bracing westerly, the Anchor, near the river and the tidal flats, is a welcome sight. Inside is a cosy beamed bar, window seats – so you can keep an eye on the weather – traditional furnishings and big log fires. The bar food, all cooked by the landlord, uses lots of local produce and is as fresh as can be. From a very interesting menu, the favourite dishes include fettucine pescatore – salmon, prawn, crab and mussels on a bed of pasta covered in a crab sauce, fresh salmon in a white-wine and cream sauce, snorkers – locally reared pork and garlic sausages cooked on a charcoal grill, and a cod and broccoli bake. Two vegetarian dishes are included in the daily menu and there are lots of other dishes – raspberry crème brûlée to finish or treacle tart. A selection of good cheeses.

Plates of rare roast beef and locally produced sausages are always available. No chips; instead you have a choice of dauphinoise or 'Don Quixote' potatoes. The separate no-smoking dining room allows you an extra choice of starters; otherwise the menu is the same throughout the pub. Bass from the cask, Butcombe Bitter, Theakstons Best Bitter and Old Peculier on hand pump. A short wine list, 12 by the glass. A whisky aficionado? Seventy-five of them for you to try. Seats outside in the attractive garden. If you want a game of boules they have a large pitch at the end of the back garden and their own boules league.

> OPEN: 11.30–2.30. 6.30–11 (11.30–11 Sat. 12–10.30 Sun).
> Real Ale. Restaurant.
> Children in restaurant. Dogs welcome. Wheelchair access. Car park. Occasional live entertainment.
> Cards: MasterCard, Visa.

PITNEY

Halfway House
Tel: 01458 252513
Pitney, Nr Langport, Somerset TA10 9AB
Free House. Julian & Judy Lichfield, owners/licensees.

The Halfway House has been a CAMRA Somerset Pub of the Year; South-West England Pub of the Year and Great Britain National Pub of the Year. So I think you could say those are big votes of confidence. It's simply furnished and friendly with good log fires and newspapers to read. Lots of real ales, mostly from small local breweries – Teignworthy Reel Ale, Cotleigh Tawny, Butcombe Bitter, Hopback Summer Lightning and many more. At lunchtime there is home-made soup, sandwiches, and ploughman's with home-made pickle, and in the evenings they serve the speciality of the house – really good home-made curries. There is a garden for you to enjoy.

> OPEN: 11.30–2.30. 5.30–11.
> Real Ale.
> Dogs and their walkers welcome. Wheelchair access.
> Cards: all major credit and debit cards.

PORLOCK

Ship Inn
Tel: 01643 862507
High Street, Porlock, Somerset TA24 8QD
Free House. Mr & Mrs Cottrell, licensees.

New owners and a smartened-up pub. However, don't get confused with the pub in Porlock Weir – same name but not one of ours. This 13th-century Ship, at the bottom of Porlock Hill and originally a coaching inn, has several literary connections. It was mentioned in *Lorna Doone* and it is said that it was here that Southey and Coleridge used to meet to write their poetry. Hmm ... quite a way to come for a poetry reading, as Coleridge was then living in Nether Stowey. Still partially thatched; inside, heavily beamed, flag-stoned and traditionally furnished. The well-chosen bar food includes the familiar favourites: soups, ploughman's, pâté and local sausages. Daily specials and fresh fish when available. Children's menu too. Cotleigh Old Buzzard in winter, Barn Owl in summer, Courage Best and a local guest beer. Steep garden at the back of the pub with a children's play area. Not far from the sea and open moor.

> OPEN: 10.30–11 (12–10.30 Sun).
> Real Ale.
> Children welcome away from bar. Dogs on leads. Lots of help for wheelchairs.
> Bedrooms. Morris dancing and occasional folk music.

RUDGE

The Full Moon   Tel: 01373 830936
Rudge, Frome, Somerset BA11 2QF
Free House. Patrick Gifford, licensee.

Opposite the green in a quiet hamlet on the Somerset–Wiltshire border, at the crossroads of the old drovers' route to Frome Market, the attractive, gloriously rambling 16th-century Full Moon has gardens front and back, glorious views outside and good food inside. The home-made bar food and fresh fish is listed on the daily changing blackboard along with daily specials and vegetarian dishes; carvery on Sundays. You could start with the house special – Arbroath smokies, mushrooms and onions grilled to perfection, or a braised leg of lamb with mint and redcurrants. The fish can be exotic. They bake their own bread and the puds are all home-made. Wadworths 6X, Butcombe Moonshine and cider (including a local rough one). Seats in the garden to enjoy the countryside.

> OPEN: 12–11 (12–10.30 Sun).
> Real Ale. Restaurant.
> Children welcome. Dogs on leads. Wheelchair access. Car park. Bedrooms.
> Cards: Amex, MasterCard, Switch, Visa.

SHEPTON MONTAGUE

The Montague   Tel: 01749 813213
Shepton Montague, Somerset BA9 8JW
Free House. Mrs Elcock, owner/licensee.

The Montague, a well-run, well-restored country pub, does what the best country pubs do: it serves well-kept ales and creative food in delightful surroundings. Bar snacks and light lunches are served in the bar, otherwise you eat in the Red Room or the Old Snug. Menus change regularly but you could get a tomato mousse with thyme and basil on a raw-tomato coulis, fresh fish of the day, roast breast of guinea fowl on a chervil sauce with asparagus, or a grilled fillet steak topped with a confit of shallots and coarse-grain mustard. Among the ales you will usually find Greene King IPA, Otter Ale, Butcombe

Bitter and Fullers London Pride, all served from the cask. There is a short list of wines by the glass on the blackboard, and a list of wines from regional and New World to fine classic growths. There's everything you could wish for here, including a no-smoking dining room, seats on the delightful flowery terrace and somewhere to stay (four diamonds for their accommodation). Lots of things to do – visit the gardens at Stourhead or Hadspen, go racing at Wincanton or look at aeroplanes at the Fleet Air Arm Museum, Yeovilton.

> OPEN: 12–2.30. 6.30–11 (12–3 Sun). Closed Sun eves and Mon lunchtimes.
> Real Ale. Restaurant.
> Children – not keen. Dogs on leads in bar. Wheelchair access. Car park. Two double bedrooms and one twin, all en suite.
> Cards: Delta, MasterCard, Switch, Visa.

STANTON WICK

Carpenters Arms
Tel: 01761 490202
Stanton Wick, Nr Bath, Somerset BS39 4BX
Free House. Simon Pledge, licensee.

Very smartly done up but without taking away the ethos of a pub. Beams, stripped walls, a big log fire, comfortable settles and good food. You can eat anywhere you can find a table. Bar food could include a home-made soup, filled French bread, fishcakes with home-made tomato sauce, or baked mushrooms on a bed of roasted aubergines. More intricate dishes find their way on to the specials board. Bass, Butcombe Bitter and Wadworths 6X are on hand pump; they also have Addlestones cider and a French-leaning wine list.

> OPEN: 11–11 (12–10.30 Sun).
> Real Ale. Dining room.
> Children in dining room. Dogs in bar. Car park. Bedrooms.
> Cards: Amex, Delta, Diners, MasterCard, Switch, Visa.

STREET

The Two Brewers
Tel: 01458 442421
38 Leigh Road, Street, Somerset BA16 0HB
Free House. Richard & Maggie Pearce, licensees.

You're in a busy town here, on an old Roman road. The Romans quarried stone in this area and you can see some Roman shoes in Clark's Shoe Museum in Street, where there is a fascinating collection of footwear from Roman times to the present day. The licensees of this Two Brewers also own the Two Brewers in Shaftesbury, Dorset; both pubs are run in a similar, successful way, a mirror image of each other, even down to the collection of pump clips. Lots of things to choose from on the menu: freshly filled sandwiches, giant baps, jacket potatoes, omelettes, grilled ham, steaks, home-made soup, at least four fish dishes and a home-made lasagne; pasta and chicken dishes are listed on the blackboard.

No need to tell you about the beers – people travel miles to sample the guest ales. The regulars are Theakstons XB, Courage Best and Directors; after that it is anyone's guess – they try lots.

> OPEN: 11–3. 6–11 (12–3. 7–10.30 Sun).
> Real Ale. Restaurant.
> Children welcome. No dogs. Wheelchair access. Car park.

TAUNTON

Masons Arms
Tel: 01823 288916

Magdalene Street, Taunton, Somerset
Free House. Jeremy Leyton, licensee.

On the river Tone, the county town of Somerset is a thriving commercial centre. In the shadow of St Mary Magdalene Church, which is in the centre of Taunton, the Masons Arms, home of the local rent collector before 1855, is a friendly, busy town pub. Just a small, well-chosen menu with a good selection of hot and cold food. Using mainly local produce, this could include warming soups, various home-made pâtés, plus daily specials such as beef cooked in local beer, chicken cooked in the local cider, also 'grill-stones' – a special stone heated to a very high temperature on which you can cook your own choice of steak. Draught Exe Valley Bitter, Juwards Bitter, draught Bass, local Oakwood and Kingston Black ciders. No garden, but for the energetic among you, a skittle alley awaits.

> OPEN: 10.30–3. 5–11 (10.30–11 Sat. 12–4 Sun). Closed Sun eves.
> Real Ale.
> Children: rather not. Well-behaved dogs on leads welcome.
> Wheelchair access tricky but manageable with help. Self-contained holiday flat for three available to rent.

WEST HUNTSPILL

Cross Ways Inn
Tel: 01278 783756

West Huntspill, Nr Highbridge, Somerset TA9 3RA (on the A38 and only 3 miles from Exit 22 on the M5)
Free House. Michael Ronca & Tony Eyles, licensees.

A 17th-century pub with a touch of the Dutch – architecturally speaking. The Cross Ways Inn, with its low beams, log fires and traditional furnishings, is friendly and welcoming. There is an extensive menu with something for everyone – including children. Pub specials include smoked-sausage and bean stew, garlic mushrooms, chicken and ham mornay, chicken breasts stuffed with mushroom pâté, lamb shank braised in wine with root vegetables, Thai crab cakes, rack of lamb with redcurrant and rosemary jus, salads, a vegetable bake and sandwiches or ploughman's. The menu changes regularly. Flowers IPA, Original and Royal Oak plus varying guest ales – could be Smiles Best, Butcombe Bitter, Bass or

Oakhill. Choice of malt whiskies and Rich's Farmhouse Cider. Seats in the large garden among the fruit trees.

OPEN: 12–3. 5.30–11 (6–11 Sat. 12–3. 7–10.30 Sun).
Real Ale. Restaurant Fri and Sat only.
Children welcome (except in main bar). Dogs on leads.
Occasional live music. Three en-suite bedrooms.
Cards: all except Amex.

WINCANTON

Stags Head Inn   Tel: 01963 440393
Yarlington, Wincanton, Somerset BA9 8DG
Free House. Bryan & Carole Minto, licensees.

Just to be different, the inn sign is hanging on the side of the pub that at first glance could be mistaken for a solid, stone-built, private house with a long, low garden wall and front gate. But you are in the right place. It is the small and very friendly Stags Head. Inside are two bars serving wholesome, varied, bar food: soup of the day, ploughman's, sandwiches, smoked-trout pâté, pork in cider and apple, sausages cooked in red wine and juniper berries, fisherman's pie, steak and kidney pie and steaks. Puds too, and they do special Sunday lunches. Always three real ales and a local guest, Greene King IPA, draught Bass, Guinness and draught Lowenbrau and Hoegaarden, also Stowford Press cider. Seats in the garden.

OPEN: Closed Mon and Sun eves, otherwise 12–2.30. 5.45–11 (12–3 Sun).
Real Ale. Restaurant (no food Mon).
Dogs on leads. Wheelchair access.

WINSFORD

Royal Oak Inn   Tel: 01643 851455
Winsford, Exmoor National Park, Somerset TA24 7JE
Free House. Charles Steven, licensee.

On the river Exe, this picturesque village is on the edge of the Exmoor National Park. Among the stone and thatched cottages is the smart, cream-washed, thatched 12th-century Royal Oak. Well, it was 12th-century but it had to be rebuilt, so shall we say originally 12th-century but still with some fine oak beams, panelling and big open fires. Bar meals include home-made soup, sandwiches, ploughman's, hot steak sandwich, fish or seafood of the day, steak and kidney pudding, chargrilled chicken fillet with tomato butter on a bed of tossed salad leaves, grilled steak or trout, also bar specials and dishes of the day such as salmon in a white-wine and butter sauce, bacon, onion and mushroom quiche with salad, oven-baked guinea-fowl breast. The dishes of the day are cooked in small quantities, so when they are sold that's it – it will be something new for the next day. You know everything is as fresh as can be. All food is home-cooked, including the bread. Puds too. A full menu is served in the elegant restaurant. Small, select wine cellar. Three barrels of real ale in the bar which change every few weeks; Guinness and Stowford Press cider from Hereford. The River Winn, on which the Royal Oak has its own beat, runs through the village and fishing can be arranged.

OPEN: 11–2.30. 6–11.
Real Ale. Restaurant.
Children welcome except in front bar. Dogs on leads.
Eight comfortable en-suite bedrooms in the inn, six more in the annexe. Dogs can be accommodated too.
Cards: Amex, Diners, MasterCard.

WITHAM FRIARY

Seymour Arms   Tel: 01749 850742
Witham Friary, Frome, Somerset BA11 5HF
Free House. Jean Douel, licensee.

In Witham Friary itself there is an interesting building: the remains of a Carthusian monastery which was founded by Henry II to atone for the death of Thomas à Becket in 1170. Much, much later, and solidly Victorian, the Seymour Arms – surrounded by fields – was built as a public house in 1867. An unspoilt old place, 7 miles from Frome off the B3092. Just two rooms, stone flags on the floor, beer from the barrel served through a hatch, and no food. There is a garden where you can sit to enjoy Ushers Best Bitter and Rich's Cider. There are lovely views of the surrounding countryside from the garden. Good walks nearby.

OPEN: 11–3. 6–11.
Real Ale. Real Cider. No food.
Dogs on leads.

BEST OF THE REST

MELLS Nr Frome

Talbot   Tel: 01373 812254
Equidistant from Bath and Wells, this is a substantial 15th-century coaching inn with a classy restaurant, an unusual public bar – it's in the old tithe barn, a lovely garden and seriously good food. Dishes like fresh shellfish soup with toasted cheese muffins, hot Brixham-crab tartlet with fresh Parmesan and mixed-leaf salad, oven-roast noisettes of English lamb with a lamb stock, herb and tomato sauce or chargrilled fillet steak with wild mushrooms, bacon and button onions in a shallot and red-wine sauce give you some idea of the delights you could expect. Butcombe Bitter, Wadworths 6X and Fullers London Pride are the beers; an eclectic wine list, a few by the glass. A lovely place; you can stay too.

SPARKFORD

Sparkford Inn
Tel: 01963 440218

You can't fail to miss this fine old building in the centre of the village – you nearly fall over the picnic tables and flower tubs at the front of it. Inside is full of atmosphere – and well cared for; so will you be. Well-prepared, straightforward bar food ranging from sandwiches to beef-in-Guinness casserole, pork tenderloin in a port and sage sauce, steaks, also daily specials and a daily carvery. Bass, Butcombe Bitter, Morlands Old Speckled Hen, Sharps Cornish Coaster and other more unusual beers. Comprehensive wine list – something for everyone.

STOKE ST GREGORY

Rose & Crown
Tel: 01823 490296

This delightful pub is in a village near the West Sedgemoor nature reserve, an important woodland and wetland area – birdwatchers to the fore. Delights outside and plenty in the pub. Lots of fresh local produce is used in the cooking; their own eggs, fish from Brixham, local lamb and ducks. Food goes up a gear in the restaurant, which has a very reasonably priced menu. Exmoor Ale, Hardy Country and Royal Oak, farm ciders and a good wine list. Bedrooms.

TRISCOMBE

Blue Ball Inn
Tel: 01984 618242

Between Taunton and Minehead, this long, low, thatched 18th-century building is waiting to welcome you. It has an appealing menu of lunchtime filled baguettes, home-made soup and fish and chips; dishes using locally sourced meat and game are on the specials board; also fish from Brixham and home-made puds. Local Cotleigh beers, two guests and farm ciders. The most discerning wine buff will find something on the extensive wine list. Children welcome. Dogs – maybe.

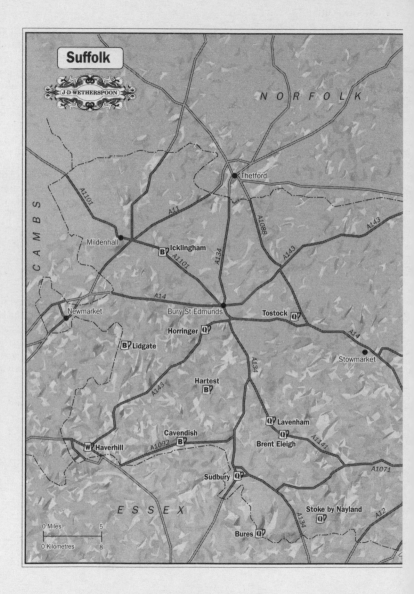

Suffolk

J·D·WETHERSPOON

N O R F O L K

C A M B S

E S S E X

A1101

A11

A1101

A1134

A134

A1088

A143

A143

A14

A14

A143

A134

A1092

A1141

A1071

A12

Thetford

Mildenhall

B Icklingham

Newmarket

Bury St Edmunds

Tostock **Q**

Horringer **Q**

B Lidgate

Stowmarket

Hartest **B**

Q Lavenham

Cavendish **B**

Q Brent Eleigh

W Haverhill

Sudbury **Q**

Stoke by Nayland **Q**

Bures **Q**

0 Miles 5

0 Kilometres 8

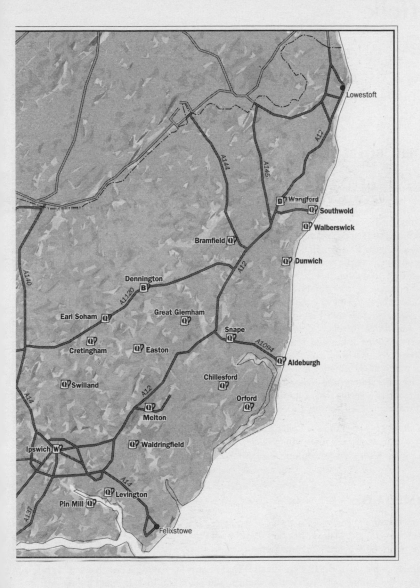

Suffolk

ALDEBURGH

Cross Keys
Tel: 01728 452637

Crabbe Street, Aldeburgh, Suffolk IP15 5BN

Adnams. M.G. Clement, licensee.

Three hundred years ago Aldeburgh was a prosperous shipbuilding town, but the encroaching shingle beach buried the houses of the men who sailed in the ships. Built on the ever-changing East Anglian coast, Aldeburgh, a settlement since Saxon times, was developed to replace the nearby medieval fishing village of Slaunden, destroyed by the sea in the 19th century. Basically a 16th-century building, the Cross Keys is ideally placed; only the promenade separates the courtyard at the back of the pub from the beach. Sitting here you can have a drink or a meal and watch the world go by. Inside, the two bars, each with a cosy stove to warm things up, are a refuge from the cold easterly winds that blow during the winter. Regularly changing menus are on the blackboard: good open sandwiches, vegetarian dishes and lots of fish – fresh from the beach – scallops in bacon, fisherman's pie, lobster, fresh crab, mussels à la crème and whatever else is available will find its way onto the menu; fish dishes are their speciality. Adnams Traditional ales. There are some interesting things to see in Aldeburgh. The church has a John Piper window commemorating Benjamin Britten, the founder of the Music Festival, and there's the half-timbered 16th-century Moot Hall, now a museum.

> OPEN: 11–3. 6–11 (11–11 Sat). From July to September they are open all day.
> Real Ale. No food winter Sun eves.
> Dogs on leads. Three bedrooms – all en suite and two with sea views.

BRAMFIELD

Queens Head
Tel: 01986 784214

The Street, Bramfield, Halesworth, Suffolk IP19 9HT

Adnams. Mark & Amanda Corcoran, tenants.

No ordinary pub this, as the Queens Head is well known for having a creative way with food – a noted 'dining pub'. Inside this well-run old place is a high-beamed lounge bar warmed by a big log fire. No separate restaurant, but plenty of room for you to rest your plate. All meat and vegetables come from local suppliers whenever possible, the emphasis being on organic ingredients. Members of 'The Campaign for Real Food', the Queens Head was the first establishment outside the capital to offer wholly organic dishes – even the bread comes from an organic baker. The menu might list inventive soups, ramekin of marinated olives, chicken-liver and brandy pâté with Cumberland sauce and toast, seafood crumble, free-range chicken supreme in spicy barbecue marinade with rice, or pork steaks in brandy and cream sauce, locally made sausages, English cheeses, home-made puds and ice-creams. Adnams Bitter, Broadside and seasonal beers, organic cider and a good wine list. Outside, the delightful garden is overlooked by the church.

    OPEN: 11.45–2.30. 6.30–11 (11–3. 7–10.30 Sun).
    Real Ale.
    Children welcome. Dogs: if well behaved. Wheelchair access (not WC). Car park.
    Cards: Amex, Diners, MasterCard, Solo, Switch, Visa.

Brent Eleigh

The Cock
Tel: 01787 247371
Brent Eleigh, Sudbury, Suffolk CO10 9PB
Free House. Charles Lydford, licensee.

Just two bars in this unspoilt, 15th-century thatched building, a basic Suffolk drinking pub with large tables in each bar to support all the beer mugs. A firm favourite with the locals, the Cock is worth a visit for the well-kept beer and local cider with a nut and a crisp as a side order. Greene King IPA and Abbot, Adnams Bitter, guest beers from time to time, also a regular supply of the organic Castlings Heath cider, made in an orchard a few miles up the road. Seats in the small garden at the front of the pub.

    OPEN: 12–3. 6–11 (12–3. 7–10.30 Sun).
    Real Ale. No food.
    Children – iffy – allowed Sundays in smaller bar. Dogs on leads. Wheelchairs difficult, but help available. Small car parks, front and back. The old wash house has been converted into comfortable letting accommodation.
    No credit cards, or euros!

Bures

Lamarsh Lion
Tel: 01787 227918
Bures, Lamarsh, Suffolk CO8 5EP
Free House. John & Jackie O'Sullivan, licensees.

The Essex–Suffolk border, overlooking the rolling landscape of the Stour valley from Flatford Mill to Sudbury, is very much Constable country. It was Constable's great-great-grandfather who crossed from Essex early in the 18th century to make his home in Suffolk. The Red Lion, built in the 14th century, is amply beamed; flowers decorate the bar and friendly, helpful staff are there to serve you. The menu is changeable as it depends on what inspires the chef that day. Be assured that it will be imaginative, varied and well cooked. Beers include Adnams The Wherry, Cottage Brewery, John Smiths, Marstons Pedigree, Suffolk Ale and Wadworths 6X, but they change regularly. Wines by the glass and a selection of malt whiskies. This is a particularly attractive place to be on a summer's evening. Life on the River Stour can get very exciting when the young farmers hold their annual raft race on Whit Bank Holiday weekend.

OPEN: 11–3. 6–11 (11–11 Sat).
Real Ale. Restaurant.
Children in eating area. Dogs in barn. Occasional live music.
Bed and breakfast.

CHILLESFORD

The Friars Inn (known as The Froize)   Tel: 01394 450282
The Street, Chillesford, Near Woodbridge, Suffolk IP12 3PU
Free House. Mrs Moira Smart, licensee.

Solidly built of brick and on a quiet country road east of Chillesford. Aptly named, as the 15th-century Friars Inn is on the site of Chillesford Friary. Tremendously popular, and not just locally. Inside is one heavily beamed bar and a 60-seater restaurant. Between Woodbridge and Orford, the Froize, which under the previous regime has been Suffolk Dining Pub of the Year, now has someone new at the pump. The old regime were keeping an eye on the cooking so they should still be going in the right direction, but we haven't any menu details. The speciality is local fish, so there are lots of fish dishes, bar stalwarts and daily specials. On Sundays they serve two different roasts. There will be four alternating real ales and an all-embracing wine list.

OPEN: 11–3. 6–11 (11–3 Sun). Pub closed Sun eves.
Real Ale. Restaurant closed Thurs eve.
Children welcome. Dogs on leads. Wheelchair facilities. Car park. Three bedrooms.
You can park your caravan or pitch your tent too.

CRETINGHAM

Cretingham Bell   Tel: 01728 685419
The Street, Cretingham, Nr Otley, Woodbridge, Suffolk IP3 7BJ
Free House. Vic Llewellyn, licensee.

Between Framlingham and Otley, the rambling, heavily beamed Bell is all a fine Tudor building should be. Inside is a lively snug, lounge bar and no-smoking restaurant. The delights of the day are written on the blackboards, where you will find plenty of choice, either from the traditional menu or the daily specials. They also have vegetarian dishes and children's meals. Beers from Adnams, Mauldons and Earl Soham; the pub concentrates on local brews. Quite a selection of malt whiskies. Plenty of room in the large garden. There is a wonderful 16th-century house at Otley with lovely gardens – well worth a visit.

OPEN 11–2.30 (11–3.30 Sat). 6–11 (12–2.30. 7–10.30 Sun).
Real Ale. Restaurant.
Children welcome. Dogs in the snug. Wheelchair access. Car park. Three en-suite bedrooms.
Cards: Barclaycard, Delta, Electron, Eurocard, MasterCard, Solo, Switch.

DUNWICH

Ship Inn
Tel: 01728 648219

St James' Street, Dunwich, Nr Saxmundham, Suffolk IP17 3DT
Free House. Stephen & Ann Marshlain, licensees.

It is said that on stormy nights you can hear the bells of drowned churches tolling away. A solitary gravestone is all that remains of medieval Dunwich. In the 12th century old Dunwich had a flourishing shipbuilding industry. The village you see today is all that remains, the rest having been gradually washed away by the sea over the intervening centuries. An old smugglers' haunt, the handsome brick-built Ship Inn has a big comfortable bar with plenty of fishing and nautical bric-à-brac distributed throughout the pub. As well as a dining room, it has a family conservatory. Bar snacks are served at lunchtime only. During the evening the restaurant menu applies throughout the pub. The Ship is renowned for its fish and chips and other fish dishes, but you can still get soups, chicken and cider pie, salads, ploughman's and good puddings. Adnams ales. Seats on the terrace and in the sheltered garden, which has a huge fig tree.

OPEN: 11–3 (11–3.30 Sat). 6–11 (6.30–11 winter).
Real Ale. Evening restaurant.
Children not in bar. Dogs on leads. Wheelchair access (not WC). Car park.
Bedrooms – some with a sea/marsh view.
Cards: MasterCard, Switch, Visa.

EARL SOHAM

Victoria
Tel: 01728 685758

Earl Soham, Suffolk IP13 7RL
Own Brew. Paul Hooper, licensee.

A place to make for if you are keen to try the local brew – very local: these beers are brewed at the back of the pub. Not only can you sample the goods on the premises, you can even take some home with you. Inside you'll find pine panelling, tiled floors, big open fires and pictures of Queen Victoria and Victorian life. They have a good selection of bar food, soups, curries, chilli, salads and vegetarian dishes, plus a Sunday roast. They have named the beers: Victoria Bitter, Albert – that's the strong one – and Gannet, a mild. Seats at the front of the pub and on the lawn at the back.

OPEN: 11.30–2.30. 5.30–11.
Real Ale.
No dogs. Folk music Tues eve.

EASTON

White Horse Inn
Tel: 01728 746456

The Street, Easton, Suffolk
Pubmaster. Pip & Sally Smith, licensees.

A lot of pubs have a speciality. Here, in this delightfully unchanging 16th-century, pink-washed village pub overlooking the village green, as well as the beer, it is pies. All the food, including the home-made pies – steak and kidney, chicken and game or chicken and leek – is listed on blackboards. There could be a mixed grill, sirloin steak in a brandy and peppercorn sauce, crab and prawn thermidor, poached salmon in a champagne sauce, king prawns in a salsa sauce, rack of lamb in rosemary and garlic, gammon and three kinds of stir fry. Flowers IPA, Adnams and Greene King IPA. Beer garden at the back of the pub.

> OPEN: 11–3. 6.30–11.
> Real Ale. Restaurant.
> Children in eating areas. Dogs in bar only.
> Wheelchair access (not WC).

GREAT GLEMHAM

Crown   Tel: 01728 663693
The Street, Great Glemham, Nr Saxmundham, Suffolk IP17 1DA
Free House. Barry & Susie Coote, licensees.

Situated in the lovely Suffolk countryside and alongside aristocratic neighbours, the pub has the best of views overlooking Great Glemham Park, the seat of Lord Cranbrook. The Crown, parts of which are early 17th-century, has a large beamed bar and two huge fireplaces filled with blazing logs during the winter. A changing menu ranges from well-filled sandwiches to a mushroom and spinach lasagne, home-made steak and kidney pie, large cod fillet with a home-made beer batter, large East Anglian pork chop with apple sauce, vegetarian dishes and a children's menu. Adnams, Greene King IPA, Morlands Old Speckled Hen and guest ales. Choice of wines and a selection of malt whiskies. Tables on the lawn at the corner of the pub during the summer.

> OPEN: Closed Monday, otherwise 12–2.30. 6.30–11.
> Real Ale.
> Children welcome, and dogs. Wheelchair facilities. Bedrooms.

HORRINGER

Beehive   Tel: 01284 735260
The Street, Horringer, Suffolk IP29 5SD
Greene King. Gary & Dianne Kingshott, tenants.

The Beehive – and there is one at the front of the pub – is a cottagey sort of place built of flint in the 19th century. It has lots of low-beamed, rambling little rooms in which to sit and sample the imaginative food. Menus change daily so these are just examples of what you might find: shellfish chowder with home-made bread, terrine of chicken, coriander and ginger with lime dressing, and for a main course, saffron poached haddock on a leek and tomato fondue, or braised shank of lamb with a redcurrant reduction, then ginger crème brûlée or orange custard tart to follow. Greene King IPA and Abbot ales plus a short, interesting wine list. Seats on the terrace at the back of the pub and in the garden. The village shares a boundary with Ickworth Park, which is well worth a visit.

> OPEN: 11.30–2.30. 7–11.
> Real Ale. No food Sun evenings.
> Children welcome. Dogs on leads. Wheelchair access (not WC). Car park.
> Cards: Delta, MasterCard, Switch, Visa.

LAVENHAM

Angel Hotel   Tel: 01787 247388
Market Place, Lavenham, Suffolk CO10 9QZ.
Free House. Roy & Anne Whitworth & John Barry, licensees.

Lavenham is one of the most perfect towns. It prospered from the rise of the wool trade in Tudor England. Full of wonderful medieval buildings, among them the Angel in the Market Place. It might not look as old as the surrounding buildings, but it has held a licence since the early 15th century and inside you will see all the evidence of a building that has been carefully looked after since then. Something for everyone on the menu: game terrine with Cumberland sauce, smoked salmon and smoked trout with lemon mayonnaise, warm salad of smoked chicken, bacon and red onions, and for a main course, pork medallions with Calvados sauce, fillet of sea bass with saffron and red peppers, or steak and ale pie. English cheeses and delicious puds to follow. The menus change daily but there will always be home-made soups, pies, casseroles, fresh fish, game in season and vegetarian dishes. Adnams, Nethergate, Greene King IPA and Abbot; comprehensive wine list. Seats at the front of the Angel for people-watching and in the sheltered garden at the back. Lots of things to see in Lavenham. Just a wander round the town is a feast for the eyes.

> OPEN: 11–11 (12–10.30 Sun).
> Real Ale. Restaurant.
> Children welcome. Dogs in bar only. Wheelchair access (not WC). Car park.
> Cards: Amex, Delta, MasterCard, Switch, Visa.

LEVINGTON

The Ship Inn   Tel: 01473 659573
Church Lane, Levington, Nr Ipswich, Suffolk IP10 0LQ
Pubmaster. William & Shirley Waite, MBII, tenants.

On the foreshore below this pretty village is a large marina, Suffolk Yacht Harbour, and close by is the handsome, white-painted and thatched Ship Inn. Outside are lots of flowers and picnic tables; inside, as befits its location, it is decidedly nautical: prints, pictures, nets and even a compass under the counter. Popular with locals, townies and visiting yachtsmen, it offers a traditional bar menu listing ploughman's, quiche, sausages in cider sauce, lots of salads and a vegetarian dish or two. More substantial dishes and puds are on the daily specials board. Flowers Original, Tolly Cobbold Bitter, Bass, Wadworths 6X and Greene King IPA drawn from the cask. Country wines and some wines by the glass. Seats in front of the pub overlook fields and the River Orwell.

> OPEN: 11.30–3. 6–11.
> Real Ale. Restaurant.
> No children under 14. No dogs. Wheelchair access.

MELTON

Wilford Bridge   Tel: 01394 386141
Melton, Nr Woodbridge, Suffolk IP12 2PA
Free House. Steve Lomas, licensee.

The pub gets its name from the quaint old bridge over the River Deben that was modernised 20 years ago to carry heavier traffic. This Georgian pub, built in 1750, is on the road to Bawdsey, where the radar that helped the RAF to defeat the Luftwaffe in the Battle of Britain was developed. Run by the same family, and on the same lines, as the Butt and Oyster at Pin Mill, there will be traditional bar food: soups, various ploughman's, sandwiches, lots of fish, steak, Guinness and mushroom pie, vegetarian dishes and steaks to go with the Adnams Best, Broadside and Morlands Old Speckled Hen. Wide-ranging wine list.

> OPEN: 11–11.
> Real Ale.
> Children welcome. No dogs. Wheelchair access. Car park.
> Cards: all major credit cards.

ORFORD

Jolly Sailor   Tel: 01394 450243
Quay Street, Orford, Nr Woodbridge, Suffolk IP12 2NU
Adnams. Philip Attwood, tenant.

North of the village the river is called the Alde, south, it is the Ore. Simple really! Orford was quite important during the heady days of the 12th century. It was in 1165 that Henry II built his castle to help control the local population, and you can see by the size of the castle keep that they must have been an unruly lot – it was obviously a considerable building. Over the years the build-up of the huge spit of shingle – Orford beach, which cut the village off from the sea – meant the gradual decline of Orford as a sea port. Now, this attractive village is not much more than a small square and a road leading to the quay. An old smugglers' inn, the Jolly Sailor is reputed to be built out of the timbers of ships wrecked nearby. Inside are several small rooms warmed by a big stove in winter. As you would expect there is local fish and chips on the menu as well as home-cooked ham, omelettes and ploughman's to go with Adnams ales. The dining room is no smoking and there are tables in the large garden. The 90-foot-high castle keep is open every day; there are magnificent views from the battlements. Havergate Island, just below Orford, is an RSPB bird sanctuary. Boats to the island leave from Orford quay.

> OPEN: 11.30–2.30. 7–11.
> Real Ale.
> Dogs on leads in middle bar. Bedrooms.

PIN MILL

Butt & Oyster   Tel: 01473 780764
Pin Mill, Nr Chelmondiston, Ipswich, Suffolk IPN 1JW
Deben Inns. Steve & Louise Lomas, tenants.

Another pub you can sail right up to. A high tide and you don't even have to leave the yacht to order a drink. If you're not sailing in, you reach this favoured spot on the River Orwell along a lane from Chelmondiston. A delightful place to be; a classic 17th-century riverside pub popular with everyone. During July there is the Pin Mill barge match to watch; otherwise you can sit outside, safely anchored to your seat, watching the comings and goings on the river. Traditional bar food: deep-fried garlic mushrooms, chicken-liver pâté, wholetail Whitby scampi, fish and chips, vegetarian dishes and blackboard specials. The ploughman's is very generous and there's always a vegetarian dish or two. Well-kept beers: Adnams Best, Broadside and guests; Tolly Best and Original still available.

> OPEN: 11–11.
> Real Ale.
> Children welcome away from main bar. No dogs. Occasional piano & folk dancing.
> Cards: MasterCard, Visa.

SNAPE

The Crown   Tel: 01728 688324
Bridge Road, Snape, Nr Saxmundham, Suffolk IP17 1SL
Adnams. Diane Maylott, chef/tenant.

When smuggling was rife along the east coast, they chose their favourite inns with care; this was one of them. A fine, rambling old place, dating back to the 15th century, with only one small bar and dining room, but full of nooks and crannies, low-beamed ceilings, a big inglenook fireplace and huge settles to settle in. Wherever you are in the Crown they serve interesting food. No sandwiches, but ploughman's, course game pâté and home-made chutney, crayfish tails in Thai mayonnaise served with crisp poppadoms, sea bass with prawn butter and new potatoes, pan-fried calves' liver, fillet steak, steak and kidney suet pudding, home-made puds and ice-creams; the menu changes every day. Adnams Best

Bitter and Adnams seasonal ales. A long and enterprising wine list. A big front garden to sit in.

> OPEN: 11–3. 6–11 (12–3. 7–10.30 Sun).
> Real Ale. Dining room.
> No children. No dogs. Wheelchair access. Two double rooms, one twin room, both en suite. Lots of car-parking space.

SNAPE

Golden Key   Tel: 01728 688510
Priory Road, Snape, Suffolk IP17 1SG
Adnams. Max & Susie Kissick-Jones, tenants.

In 2002, the tenants of the Golden Key will be celebrating 34 years behind the pumps of this fine old place; a beer house since 1480, it has had several identities over the centuries. For its first 300 years it was 'The Sign of the Cock', then for 80 years 'The White Lion'; it became the Golden Key at the beginning of the 20th century. No music, no machines either, just a charming 15th-century pub. Inside is a large main bar divided into public (tiled floor), lounge (carpeted) bars and a dining area. Lots of sustaining, well-prepared bar food: home-made soups, pâté, filled rolls, sausage and onion pie, smoked haddock, quiche, lots of fresh fish and game in season, steaks and roast on Sunday. Adnams ales, local farm ciders and a choice of malt whiskies. Seats at the front of the pub, also in the colourful garden at the back.

> OPEN: 11–3. 6–11 (extended opening hours during the Aldeburgh Festival).
> Real Ale.
> Children in eating area. Dogs on leads. Wheelchair access.
> Double and twin en-suite rooms.
> Cards: all except Amex and Diners.

SNAPE

Plough and Sail   Tel: 01728 688413
Snape Maltings, Nr Saxmundham, Suffolk IP17 1SR
Free House. G.J. Gooderham, licensee.

The Victorian Maltings were built to process barley. Now most of the space is converted for use not only by the Aldeburgh Festival in summer, but antique fairs, concerts, lots of shops and a pub – the Plough and Sail. Inside is a bar, dining area and restaurant. A choice of home-made soups on the blackboard, as well as freshly made sandwiches, smoked-salmon or chicken-liver pâté, grilled sardines, smoked sprats, grilled sea trout with linguini, tomatoes and melted mozzarella, seared swordfish, sweet potato and tropical-island salsa, supreme of chicken chasseur and pasta, seared sirloin steak, vegetarian dishes and, as you would expect, plenty more fish dishes, plus everything you would find on a good restaurant menu. Adnams Southwold Bitter, Broadside and Barley Mow in summer, Tally Ho in winter, guest beer Wychwood Hobgoblin. Good wine list, some by the glass. Tables in the enclosed courtyard at the back of the pub.

> OPEN: 11–3. 5.30–11 (12–3. 6.30–10.30 Sun. 7–10.30 Sun in winter). During August: 12–11.
> Real Ale. Restaurant.
> Children in restaurant. No dogs. Wheelchair access (not WC). Disabled facilities at the Maltings. River trips up the River Alde.

SOUTHWOLD

Crown Hotel
High Street, Southwold, Suffolk IP18 6DP
Adnams. Michael Bartholomew, manager.

Tel: 01502 722275

You have everything you could wish for here. A historically interesting building in an elegant little town. The Crown is a handsome Georgian townhouse combining pub, wine bar, restaurant and small hotel. It has an extensive wine list, imaginative weekly changing bar food, and a restaurant where they serve a good, creative, reasonably priced three-course menu. From the bar you could choose a cream of leek and potato soup, chicken-liver parfait with melba toast and plum chutney, Shetland mussels in white-wine, garlic and tomato sauce, chargrilled sirloin of beef with a basil and garlic glaze and horseradish relish, market fish in a coconut laska curry with crispy shallots and fragrant rice. Lots more including good puds and cheeses from Neal's Yard. The flagship of the nearby Adnams Brewery – the ales are kept in the very best condition. They have an impressive wine list (Adnams are wine merchants as well). Lots of wines by the glass, including classic vintages selected monthly. Do note the wonderful wrought-iron inn sign attached to the front of the Crown Hotel.

> OPEN: 10.30–3. 6–11 (closed first week Jan).
> Real Ale. Restaurant.
> Children in eating area and restaurant until 7pm. Dogs in one bar. Wheelchair access to bar. Bedrooms.
> Cards: Amex, Delta, Diners, MasterCard, Switch, Visa.

SOUTHWOLD

The Lord Nelson
East Street, Southwold, Suffolk IP18 6EJ
Adnams. John Illston, tenant.

Tel: 01502 722079

Virtually surrounded by water – the sea in front and Buss Creek at the back – Southwold is nearly an island. A prosperous fishing port as far back as the 11th century, it is now a delightful, elegant town full of Georgian townhouses and cottages. It is full of sea-going history, so why not have a pub named after one of Britain's best-known naval commanders – we'll forget that he was born in the next county. This is a delightful late-Georgian pub not far from the sea. Friendly, well run and popular, with a cosy, low-ceilinged bar, panelled walls and an open fire. Freshly prepared traditional food to go with the range of Adnams beers. Seats in the garden at the back of the pub which is sheltered from the brisk sea breezes.

> OPEN: 10.30–11 (12–10.30 Sun).
> Real Ale.
> Children welcome. Dogs if well behaved. Easy wheelchair access (not WC).

STOKE-BY-NAYLAND Nr Colchester

Angel Inn   Tel: 01206 263245
Polstead Street, Stoke-by-Nayland, Suffolk CO6 4SA
Horizon Inns. Mike Everett, licensee.

The tower of Stoke-by-Nayland church features in several Constable paintings. This is an area of picturesque villages and wide-open skies in the heart of 'Constable country'. The Angel, an attractive 16th-century inn, is at the main crossroads of this quiet village. The casual drinker is still catered for in the small bar, but on the whole it is a serious eating pub. A blackboard menu serves both bars and restaurant; the selection of reasonably priced dishes can change twice a day. A hugely popular place, so if you are eating in the restaurant (called the Well Room – it does have a 52-foot-deep well!) it is best to book to be sure of a table. Lots of fish dishes, such as freshly dressed crab with home-made mayonnaise, steamed mussels in white wine and brochette of scallops wrapped in bacon, as well as local game in season and home-made steak and kidney puddings. They also cook traditional Sunday roasts. Home-made puddings too. Greene King Abbot ale, Adnams Bitter, Greene King IPA and a guest bitter. Lots of interesting wines. Seats outside in the well-planted, very attractive courtyard. You might be interested to know that the church in nearby Nayland houses one of the very few religious paintings by Constable.

> OPEN: 11–2.30. 6–11.
> Real Ale. Restaurant.
> No children in the bar. No dogs. Wheelchair access.
> Six en-suite bedrooms.

SUDBURY

The Angel   Tel: 01787 379038
Friar Street, Sudbury, Suffolk
Greene King. Brenda Rowe, tenant.

In the middle of Sudbury, the Angel was built in the mid-17th century on top of cellars dating back to the 10th century. An attractive, low-ceilinged, well-beamed structure, creaking with the effort of it all – there isn't a right angle in the place. Varied bar snacks are served: sandwiches and ploughman's, or poached salmon, scampi, Cajun chicken, roast chicken, gammon steaks and a large vegetarian menu. You can eat in the bar or restaurant. Greene King-related beers. Outside is a small, pretty patio. The painter Thomas Gainsborough was born here; there is a statue of him in the market place and his father's Tudor house is a museum and exhibition centre.

OPEN: 11–11.30 (12–10.30 Sun).
Real Ale. Restaurant.
Children welcome. Plenty of dogs.

SWILLAND

Moon & Mushroom Inn
Tel: 01473 785320

High Road, Swilland, Nr Ipswich, Suffolk IP6 9LR
Free House. Clive & Adrienne Goodall, licensees.

This is a unique little place with a very 1930s/1940s feel (the same age as the landlord – their words, not mine!). A very cosy, genuine local in the best possible way. The name dates from the owners' takeover in 1966: the Half Moon became The Moon, and the addition of Mushroom reflects the owners' interest in exotic fungi, used as often as possible in their dishes. A simply furnished, friendly place serving beer as local as you can get and genuinely home-made casseroles: venison with dumplings, pork loin in Stilton sauce or Adrienne's minted lamb, all sitting on a hot plate in the dining area along with freshly cooked vegetables. The contents of the casseroles are constantly changing and there are always fresh fish and vegetarian dishes as alternative options. The beers, from East Anglian microbreweries – normally seven or eight – are in the long line of barrels behind the bar. A varied wine list with about nine by the glass.

OPEN: 11–2.30. 6–11 (12–2.30. 7–10.30 Sun).
Real Ale. No bar food Monday or Sunday.
No children inside. Dogs in bar. Wheelchair access. Car park.

TOSTOCK

Gardeners Arms
Tel: 01359 270460

Church Road, Tostock, Nr Bury St Edmunds, Suffolk IP30 9PA
Greene King. Reg Ransome, FBII, tenant.

An example of a village pub at its best; friendly and unspoilt. Just two bars: a lounge and a public bar – with darts, pool table and games. They serve well-presented, home-made bar food and well-kept ales. There is the usual selection of bar snacks and daily specials written on the beams of the pub: a Thai king-prawn curry with stir-fried vegetables on rice, lamb balti, chicken and broccoli bake and various vegetarian dishes. A greater variety of grills and other dishes are available during the evening, when it can get very busy. Greene King Abbot, IPA and seasonal beers. Seats in the attractive garden.

> OPEN: 11.30–2.30 (11–2.30 Sat). 7–11.
> Real Ale. Restaurant (not Sun lunch). No snacks Mon or Tues eves.
> Children in eating area of bar. Dogs on leads.

WALBERSWICK

Bell Inn   Tel: 01502 723109
Ferry Road, Walberswick, Southwold, Suffolk IP18 6TN
Adnams. Sue Ireland-Cutting, tenant.

Once a flourishing port at the mouth of the River Blyth, Walberswick is now a favourite with leisure sailors, and the Bell Inn a firm favourite with everyone. The 600-year-old Bell is at the end of a 3½-mile cul de sac, close to the old harbour and the beach. Inside it is as you would expect: beamed with flagstones and huge log fires in winter. Fish and seafood feature largely on the menu: marlin steak with garlic butter, salmon and pesto en croute, sea bass en papillote with butter, white wine and thyme, as well as tenderloin of pork in green-pepper sauce, pan-fried lamb's kidneys in garlic and red wine, vegetarian dishes, daily specials and home-made puds. An à la carte menu features on Friday and Saturday evenings. Menus change frequently, but you will also find soups, ploughman's, sandwiches and salads if you just want a light snack from the bar. Adnams range of ales include the seasonal Fisherman (winter) and Regatta (summer); Adnams, with their wine-merchant hat on, supply the wine.

> OPEN: 11–3. 6–11 (11–11 Sat. 12–10.30 Sun).
> Real Ale.
> Children welcome. Dogs on leads. Wheelchair access. Car park. Bedrooms.
> Cards: JCB, MasterCard, Solo, Switch, Visa Delta, Visa.

WALDRINGFIELD

Maybush Inn   Tel: 01473 736215
The Quay, Cliff Road, Waldringfield, Suffolk IP12 1QL
Free House. Steve Lomas, licensee.

Downriver from Woodbridge, a drive along narrow country lanes will bring you to the Maybush. The inn is in a most picturesque position on the bank of the River Deben, with a view over the yacht masts to a sandy island beyond. The river is a popular mooring for yachtsmen; when the tide is out the beach is muddy shingle, but firm enough to launch your dinghy. A busy sailing centre and a good area for birdwatching. This friendly, popular pub is used to catering for the hungry hordes and serves generous, well-cooked traditional food to go with Adnams and other ales.

> OPEN: 11–11.
> Real Ale.
> Children welcome. No dogs. Wheelchair access. Big car park.
> Cards: all major credit cards.

BEST OF THE REST

CAVENDISH

Bull
Tel: 01789 280245

This is a delightful pub in a pretty village. One of the Adnams stable, so Adnams range of beers and wines, as well as some imaginative dishes on the specials board: lots of fresh fish, and there could also be crispy duck with Chinese pancakes, salmon stuffed with prawns, or baked lamb with herbs and red-wine sauce; home-made puds too. Bedrooms.

DENNINGTON

Queens Head
Tel: 01728 638241

Next to the church and once owned by them. Handsomely beamed inside, reflecting its great age. As well as soup, sandwiches and ploughman's, there are some more imaginative additions to the menu: prawns in filo pastry, braised sausages in red wine, or salmon and prawn au gratin. The beers are Adnams Bitter, Morlands Old Speckled Hen and Wadworths 6X.

HARTEST

Crown
Tel: 01284 830250

Heavily beamed, this 15th-century building had a grander former existence when it was Hartest Hall. A popular village pub doing some interesting things with food. They have the usual bar snacks but the accent is on fish – lots of creative dishes. Greene King Abbot and IPA beers and some decent wines to go with the fish.

ICKLINGHAM

Red Lion
Tel: 01638 717802

Not far from the delightfully named River Lark, this thatched 16th-century pub has lots of appeal. There are the usual bar snacks on the blackboard menu, as well as more substantial dishes such as chicken breast stuffed with spinach, pork chops in a barbecue sauce, or local sausage and mash. Greene King range of beers, one guest and country wines.

LIDGATE

Star
Tel: 01638 500275

Here's an ancient village pub with a difference. It was in existence at the time of the Spanish Armada – but all that has been forgiven, as you have a Spanish landlady producing some delicious Spanish dishes; the warmth of the Mediterranean is taking the chill off the cold east of England. Greene King beers and some good wines.

WANGFORD

Angel
Tel: 01502 578636

North-west of Southwold, a comfortable village pub where you will be well fed and you can stay the night. The menu lists the traditional bar snacks as well as French bread with hot fillings, fish pie, beef stroganoff and steaks. Adnams and Charles Wells Bombardier beers and wines from Adnams.

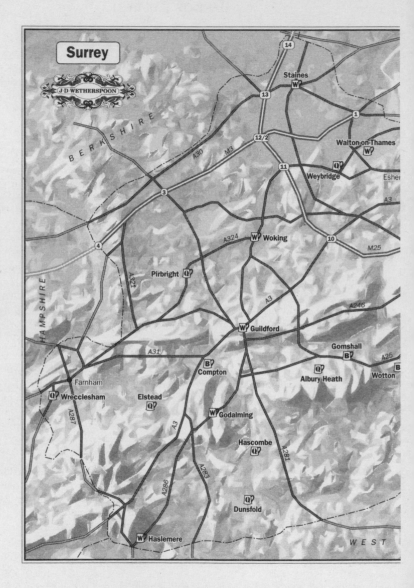

Surrey

J·D·WETHERSPOON

BERKSHIRE

HAMPSHIRE

14

Staines
W

13

12/2

1

Walton-on-Thames
W

11

Q
Weybridge

Esher

A30

M3

A3

3

A324

W Woking

10

M25

4

A321

Pirbright
Q

A3

A246

W Guildford

Gomshall
B

A31

A25

B
Compton

Q
Albury Heath

B
Wotton

Q Wrecclesham

Elstead
Q

W Godalming

A287

A3

Hascombe
Q

A286

A283

A281

Q
Dunsfold

W Haslemere

WEST

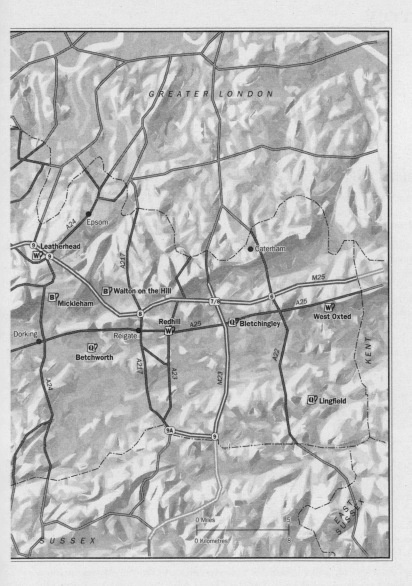

Surrey

ALBURY HEATH

William IV
Tel: 01483 202685
Little London, Albury Heath, Nr Guildford, Surrey GU5 9DG
Free House. Giles Madge, licensee.

This is commuter land, but venture off the main roads and you are in some wonderful countryside – open commons, sandy heaths and many footpaths. Here, south of the Dorking to Guildford road, is an uncomplicated, straightforward little pub, an ideal stopping place for a quiet pint and something to eat. The small rooms have flagstone floors and in one there is a huge inglenook fireplace with an equally huge log fire in winter. The short, reasonably priced bar menu lists a good selection of sandwiches, home-made pies, stews, fish and chips on Friday, steaks, pasta, a Sunday roast and always a vegetarian dish or two. Five real ales, two regulars and three guests among them: Flowers IPA, Wadworths 6X, Badger Tanglefoot, Fullers London Pride, Shepherd Neame Spitfire, Hook Norton BB, Greene King IPA, draught Bass and the local Hogs Back ales. Seats in the pretty front garden.

> OPEN: 11–3. 5.30–11 (11–3. 7–10.30 Sun).
> Real Ale. Restaurant.
> Children welcome. Dogs on leads. Wheelchair access. Car park.
> Cards: MasterCard, Visa.

BETCHWORTH

Dolphin Inn
Tel: 01737 842288
The Street, Betchworth, Surrey RH3 7DW
Youngs. George Campbell, manager.

Another good area for walking, but this time you can vary it as you are near a watery walk – along the banks of the River Mole. The Dolphin, a popular, unspoilt 16th-century village pub, is full of beams, flagstones in the front bar, carpets in the saloon and panelled walls. They cope admirably with the rush; the traditional bar menu lists sandwiches, six varieties of ploughman's, filled baked potatoes, potato waffles with bacon topped with cheese, honey-roast ham, steak and mushroom pie, salads, grills, daily specials and filling puddings. Youngs range of ales, including the seasonal Winter Warmer; wines by the glass. Seats at the front, side, and back of the pub. Excellent walking country.

OPEN: 11–3. 5.30–11 (11–11 Sat. 12–10.30 Sun).
Real Ale.
No children. Dogs on leads. Wheelchair access. Car park.
Cards: most major cards.

BLETCHINGLEY

William IV   Tel: 01883 743278
Little Common Lane, Bletchingley, Surrey RH1 4QF
Lease. Brian Strange, licensee.

If you're caught up in the interminable traffic on the M25 and feel it's time for a break, salvation isn't far away. The William IV, a welcoming country pub, is only a few miles from Exit 6. On a pretty lane just outside the village, what started out as a pair of mid-Victorian cottages has for years been a friendly and well-run pub. Outside, half tiled and hung with weatherboarding; inside, small, charming rooms and a separate no-smoking dining room. The generous, home-cooked bar food includes vegetarian dishes and an à la carte menu. Beers are Harveys Best, Adnams Best, Shepherd Neame Spitfire and Greene King IPA. Seats in the sheltered garden.

OPEN: 11.30–3. 6–11 (12–4. 6.30–10.30 Sun).
Real Ale.
Children welcome in dining room and garden. Dogs on leads.
Reasonable wheelchair access.
N.B. Radio is sometimes on in the bar.

DUNSFOLD

Sun Inn   Tel: 01483 200242
The Common, Dunsfold, Surrey GU8 4LE
Greaves Leisure. Ian Greaves, lease.

In an empty-ish bit of Surrey – well, as empty as Surrey can get – off the B2130, south of Godalming, this attractive, brick-built 18th-century coaching inn is, as the address would suggest, opposite the common. Inside the comfortable beamed interior are three open log fires and a cottage restaurant. Table d'hôte and à la carte menus are available in the restaurant. Everything is freshly cooked: home-made soups, well-filled sandwiches, ploughman's, the speciality of the house – local Dunsfold quail, other game in season, fresh fish and good puds. Daily specials on the blackboard; roasts on Sunday. Marstons Pedigree,

King & Barnes Sussex, Friary Meux and the occasional guest beer. Range of malt whiskies. Seats at the front of the pub.

> OPEN: 11–3. 6–11 (12–10.30 Sun).
> Real Ale. Restaurant.
> Children welcome. Dogs on leads. Wheelchair access (not WC). Car park.
> Cards: Delta, MasterCard, Switch, Visa.

ELSTEAD

Woolpack   Tel: 01252 703106
The Green, Elstead, Surrey GU8 6HD
Carlsberg Tetley. S. Askew, lease.

With a name like this you are bound to think there is a woolly connection and so there is. Built some time in the 18th century to store the wool bales after shearing, the building was later licensed and became the pub you see today. No more sheep shearing, but the main bar is decorated with a number of artifacts relating to its agricultural past. You'll find some real favourites on the blackboard menus: king prawns in filo pastry with a sweet chilli sauce, deep-fried whitebait, smoked trout with horseradish sauce, pork-fillet medallions with mango, brandy and a touch of chilli, beef-in-ale casserole, grills, home-made pies, a duck and spicy-sausage cassoulet, daily specials and Sunday lunches. The menu is constantly changing – it depends on what is available and what inspires the chef. The puddings are another inspiration – really home-made! Children's portions available. Greene King Abbot ale and one other from the cask. A selection of wines by the bottle and by the glass. A family room opens onto the garden and a children's play area. Seats in the garden for the grown-ups.

> OPEN: 11–2.30. 6–11 (12–3. 7–10.30 Sun).
> Real Ale. Restaurant.
> Children in family room and restaurant. Dogs on leads.
> Wheelchair access (not WC).
> Cards: all major cards except Amex and Diners.

HASCOMBE

White Horse   Tel: 01483 208258
Hascombe, Nr Godalming, Surrey GU8 4JA
Allied Domecq. Susan Barnett & James Ward, lease.

Some of the Surrey villages are an utter delight and this is one of them. On the edge of it you'll find the attractive 16th-century White Horse. Food in the beamed bar ranges from well-filled sandwiches and ploughman's to burgers, curries, grilled steaks and daily specials. There is also a separate restaurant. All the food is freshly cooked to order, so be patient. Popular, well run and busy, this is just the sort of pub you need to aim for, particularly if you are keen on walking. Hascombe is surrounded by serious walks – well, they are a few miles away, but what are a few miles between walking boots. You have a choice of the Greensand Way – that is the nearest one – the Sussex Border Path and the Downs Link, which in turn joins (eventually) the South Downs Way. Beers are from the Adnams range and there is a short wine list. Seats in the large garden.

> OPEN: 11–3. 5.30–11 (11–11 Sat. 12–10.30 Sun).
> Real Ale.
> Children welcome, dogs too. Wheelchair access difficult but staff willing to help.
> Cards: Amex, MasterCard, Visa.

LINGFIELD

Blacksmiths Head   Tel: 01342 833697
Newchapel Road, Newchapel, Lingfield, Surrey RH7 6LE
Free House. Celia Hall & David French, licensees.

Off the A22 at the Newchapel roundabout, this nice old-fashioned country pub is handy for the racecourse at Lingfield, with its all-weather racetrack. Inside, one L-shaped bar divides naturally into two distinct areas and a no-smoking restaurant – with an open fire and wood-burning stove. They serve full bar and à la carte menus at lunchtime and in the evenings; food is English with a touch of the Spanish. The well-kept beers are Fullers London Pride, Timothy Taylors Landlord, Brakspear and a changing guest. They have a good wine list. There are seats in the delightful gardens.

> OPEN: 11–3. 5.30–11 (12–3. 6–11 Sat. 12–3 Sun).
> Real Ale.
> No children. Dogs on leads. Wheelchair access with help – one step into the pub (not WC). Five bedrooms should be ready early in 2002.
> Cards: Electron, MasterCard, Solo, Switch, Visa.

PIRBRIGHT

Royal Oak   Tel: 01483 232466
Aldershot Road, Pirbright, Aldershot, Surrey GU24 0D4
Laurel Pub Co. Geoff Middleton, manager.

On a glorious summer's day it would be a good idea to make a beeline for this pub. You'll soon see why the Royal Oak is so frequently placed in the Guildford in Bloom competition. Force your way past the flowers into the beamed, rambling 16th-century Royal Oak and you'll find they serve a good selection of bar food: fresh fish, something with chicken, a vegetarian and a meat dish from the specials board, seasonal salads and traditional bar snacks. Things were changing on the beer front when we went to press and they hadn't yet decided on a policy, so you take your chances. Seats among the flowers at the front, or in the quieter garden at the back. Good walking country.

> OPEN: 11–11 (12–10.30 Sun).
> Real Ale.
> Children to dine only if room is available in no-smoking area. No dogs. Full disabled facilities. Car park.

WALTON-ON-THAMES

Regent   Tel: 01932 243980
19 Church Street, Walton-on-Thames, Surrey
Wetherspoon.

Cinemas always look like cinemas irrespective of what has changed inside. So it is with this building, but it knocks spots off the original – a successful total rebuild. Just off the High Street, this is one big space with a very long bar, always with a no-smoking area. They serve about eight real ales – one is competitively priced – as well as good, reliable food and daily specials.

> OPEN: 11–11 (12–10.30 Sun).
> Real Ale.
> No children. No dogs. Disabled facilities.

WEYBRIDGE

The Old Crown   Tel: 01932 842844
83 Thames Street, Weybridge, Surrey KT13 8LP
Free House. Mark Redknap, licensee.

Long, low – well, most of it – and painted a smart white, this is the place to come if you want some reliable pub food, much of it freshly cooked for you. A friendly, old-fashioned pub, family-run for over 40 years. Three bars inside, a snug and an air-conditioned non-smoking conservatory. Lots of interesting fillings for the sandwiches, plain and toasted, filled jacket potatoes, steaks, gammon steak, ham, egg and chips – sustaining pub fare. The specials board is changing all the time but there will always be a good choice of fish. Courage Best, Directors and revolving guest ales. Seats on the patio and in the secluded riverside garden, which is hidden from the road.

> OPEN: 10.30–11 (12–10.30 Sun).
> Real Ale.
> Children in lounge bar and conservatory only. Dogs on leads. Car park.
> Cards: all major credit/debit cards.

WOKING

Wetherspoons   Tel: 01483 722818
Chertsey Road, Woking, Surrey
Wetherspoon.

There isn't ever anything very much that is new about a Wetherspoon establishment. Beers change, the menu changes with the seasons and there are daily specials, otherwise they simply exist for you and me. This one is in a converted Woolworth store, but it does have a theme – H.G. Wells, relating to his book *The War of the Worlds*. A model of a time machine is attached to the ceiling! At ground level, three ales are on permanently with at least three regional ales as guests. They hold regular beer festivals.

OPEN: 11–11 (12–10.30 Sun).
Real Ale.
No children. No dogs. Always a big no-smoking area and disabled facilities.

WRECCLESHAM

Sandrock   Tel: 01252 715865
Sandrock Hill, Wrecclesham, Farnham, Surrey
Free House. Andrew & Caroline Baylis, licensees.

Eight pumps on all the time, and the beers change every week. This is a place well known for serving the more unusual beers in its one large and one small bar. The small bar, which is used as the games room – for bar billiards – leads into the garden. A straightforward bar menu is served at lunchtime – sandwiches, club sandwiches, ploughman's, ham and eggs, chilli, that sort of thing. Filled rolls only in the evening to go with the range of well-kept ales: Simpkiss Bitter from Enville and Banthams Best, both small breweries in the Midlands, and others from the local breweries. Lots of chairs and tables in the garden.

OPEN: 11–11 (12–10.30 Sun).
Real Ale. No food Sunday lunchtime.
Children welcome. Dogs on leads. Wheelchair access (not WC). Small car park.

BEST OF THE REST

COMPTON

Withies Inn   Tel: 01483 421158
Full of atmosphere and beautifully kept, the Withies is a popular rendezvous. Low beams and huge fires inside the small bar where they serve an uncomplicated snack menu: fisherman's broth, ploughman's, quiche, Cumberland sausages with mashed potato, onions and gravy, seafood platter, sandwiches and filled jacket potatoes. If you want to push the boat out, they have an interesting, more extensive restaurant menu. Fullers London Pride, Bass, King & Barnes Sussex and Greene King IPA are the beers. A comprehensive wine list. Children welcome. No dogs.

GOMSHALL

Compasses Inn   Tel: 01483 202506
Conveniently placed on the main Guildford to Dorking road, it's a good place to drop into as they serve reasonably priced food in generous portions. Inside, the no-smoking restaurant is a delightful symphony in yellow, all very cheery and happy; the ingredients are fresh

and all the dishes are cooked 'in pub', as are the bar snacks. Adnams, Morlands, Hopback Summer Lightning, Fullers London Pride – two beers change monthly. Plenty of tables in the riverside garden.

MICKLEHAM Nr Dorking

King William IV   Tel: 01372 372590

High on Byttom Hill with wonderful views from their own glorious garden towards the Mole valley, the King William IV once had rather grand connections – with Lord Beaverbrook, who extended it for use by his staff. An appreciative public flock here to sample well-known favourites as well as more creative dishes, including fish and vegetarian specials. Adnams, Badger Best Bitter, Hogs Back and a monthly changing guest beer. Short wine list, some by the glass. You are surrounded by lots of walks. Children over 12; no dogs.

WALTON ON THE HILL

Chequers   Tel: 01737 812364

Just to be different, the Chequers' front door seems to be at the back. You get into the bars from the car park and through an enclosed garden. There is a traditional bar menu: sausage, mash and onion gravy, grilled Mediterranean vegetables, fresh cod fillet, several salads, sandwiches, ploughmans and filled paninis. Weather permitting, the barbecue will be going full pelt from the end of April to the end of September. Full Youngs range of ales plus seasonal ales and guests from Smiles brewery. Plenty of room in the garden for you and the barbecue.

WOTTON

Wotton Hatch   Tel: 01306 732931

Not to be missed, though it could be, as this old place is on a bend on the Dorking–Guildford road. The reliable bar food changes with the seasons, but there will always be a good, varied choice of dishes. The evening menu is more extensive. Bass, Fullers London Pride, a guest beer and wines by the glass. You can see the Surrey countryside at its best from the pub garden.

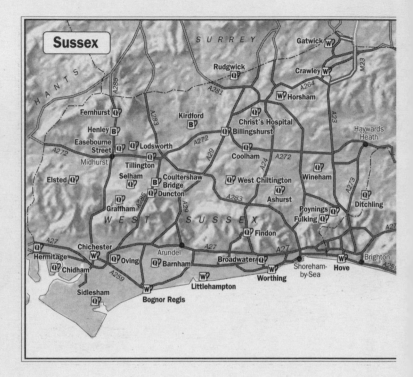

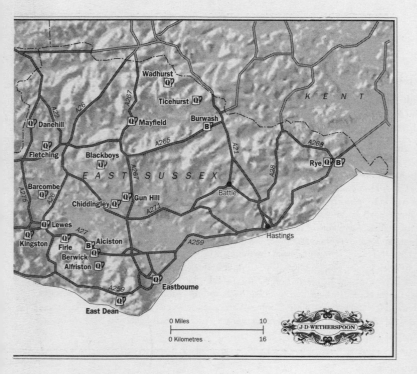

East Dean

0 Miles 10
0 Kilometres 16

J·D·WETHERSPOON

Sussex, East & West

ALFRISTON

Ye Olde Smugglers Inn
Tel: 01323 870241

Market Cross, Alfriston, Polegate, E. Sussex BN26 5UE
Leased, free of tie. Mrs Maureen Ney, licensee.

The old smuggler who owned this place during the early 19th century may have long gone but his notoriety lingers on. He and his lawless companions used to bring their ill-gotten gains from the secluded bay at Cuckmere Haven to this old building, then known as Market Cross House and owned by Stanton Collins, chief of the famous Alfriston gang. Caught in 1831, Stanton was sentenced at Lewes Crown Court and deported to Tasmania for stealing sheep and corn. The old place was full of hiding places; secret passages led under the streets, connecting houses and, rumour has it, a cave near the Long Man of Wilmington. Aptly renamed and more law-abiding these days, you can relax in the low-beamed bar and enjoy something from the menu. Always a soup of the day, a countryman's lunch, huntsman's or ploughman's, several double-decker sandwiches, lots of smuggler's sandwiches or a choice of toasted ones, rump-steak platters, Albert's sausages, gammon steak with pineapple, fresh grilled trout, spinach and mushroom lasagne, cod in batter or a wholemeal-base vegetarian flan. Courage Directors, Harveys Best Bitter and local seasonal ales. Beyond the lounge bar is a conservatory which in turn leads to a brick courtyard and garden.

> OPEN: 11–2.30. 6.30–11 (11–3. 6.30–11 Sat. 12–3. 7–10.30 Sun).
> Real Ale.
> Children welcome, but not in bar. Dogs on leads. Wheelchair access.

ASHURST

Fountain Inn
Tel: 01403 710219

Ashurst, Nr Steyning, W. Sussex BN44 3AP (north of Steyning on the B2135)
Free House. Mark & Christopher White, licensees.

Lots of good things have been going on both inside this 16th-century farmhouse and outside in the garden. For years the oldest part of the inn had been hidden from the public, but all that has changed. The beamed snug has flagstone floors and a huge inglenook fireplace to match the one in the tap room. A wide variety of interesting food is listed on both the printed and the blackboard menus. From the specials board will be fresh fish such as lemon sole, grilled halibut and black bream, and from the printed menu the usual choice of bar food – soup, freshly made sandwiches, ploughman's, steak, ale and mushroom pie, chargrilled steaks, chicken breast marinated in garlic and fresh herbs and vegetarian meals. Very popular, and therefore very busy. Seats on the terrace and in the pretty garden, which has had an improving makeover. There are usually six ales available, among which could be Fullers London Pride, Harveys Best, Shepherd Neame Master Brew, Flowers Original and two changing guests served from the barrels behind the bar. If you are feeling energetic there is a skittle alley in the stables.

OPEN: 11–2.30. 6–11.
Real Ale. No food Sun or Mon eves except sandwiches.
Children over 14 in restaurant. Dogs welcome.

BARCOMBE

Anchor Inn   Tel: 01273 400414
Anchor Lane, Barcombe, Nr Lewes, E. Sussex BN8 5BS
Free House. Peter & Michael Harris, licensees.

As you would expect with a name like the Anchor, there are bound to be some watery connections somewhere. Built in the 18th century to cater for the barges travelling up the River Ouse from the coast at Newhaven, this was the place to stop for a little light refreshment before floating off. An excess of rain and you can float in too; the approach road to the pub has been known to flood, but the kind landlords tend to leave a boat somewhere so they don't lose any custom. Two cosy little bars inside, and a separate restaurant. They are willing to cater for every eventuality and function; you can get married here too (plenty of room outside for the marquee). So if you hear the wedding march it isn't necessarily a permanent state of affairs. There is an à la carte menu in the restaurant and a range of freshly made bar food such as home-made soups, filled baguettes and baked potatoes, steak and kidney pie, sausages in an onion gravy and daily specials. Harveys Best, Badgers Best and Tanglefoot are the beers; they also have a good, short wine list. Seats in the garden and boat trips upriver.

OPEN: 11–3. 6–11 (12–10.30 Sun).
Real Ale.
Children – preferably in summer only. Dogs on leads. Wheelchair access (not WC).
Bedrooms.

BARNHAM

Murrell Arms   Tel: 01243 553320
Yapton Road, Barnham, Bognor, W. Sussex PO22 0AS
Gales. Mervyn Cutten, tenant.

North of Bognor, this is a delightful old place both inside and out. Outside is a flower-filled courtyard and seats in the enclosed garden. Inside, this unchanging place is filled with all those bits and pieces that one collects over the years – all the treasures that help to make the pub friendly and welcoming. The two small bars, both with open fires, are where they serve the proper bar food. Just a short menu, so you know everything is freshly prepared for you: ploughman's, sausages – that sort of thing, and a couple of daily specials such as a boiled bacon pudding or a rabbit and pork casserole – good, honest pub food. No puddings. They know what they can do and they do it well. Barrels of Gales ales and a guest are kept in the still room on the ground floor. Swings in the garden for the children and seats for the grown-ups.

> OPEN: 11–3. 6–11 (11–11 Sat. 12–10.30 Sun).
> Real Ale.
> Children if controlled. Dogs on leads. Wheelchair access possible. Car park.

BERWICK
Cricketers Arms   Tel: 01323 870469
Berwick, Polegate, E. Sussex BN26 6SP
Harveys. Peter Brown, tenant.

There is a homage to cricket in the Cricketers: a collection of cricket bats are hung about and there are plenty of old cricket-related photographs, past and present, for you to enjoy. West of Polegate on the A27, Berwick, a village at the foot of the South Downs, is near the South Downs Way. Four hundred years old, this interesting, unspoilt country pub was formerly two flint-built cottages. It became an alehouse about 200 years ago. Friendly, busy, well loved, it has heavily beamed bars and good log fires in winter. Home-made pub food: soup, garlic mushrooms, oak-smoked salmon, local cod in batter, locally cured ham with eggs and chips, filled jacket potatoes, various ploughman's, vegetarian dishes and daily specials on the blackboard. Fresh fish comes in daily and there is always a vegetarian special on the blackboad. Harveys Bitter and seasonal ales from the cask. A wine of the month – guest wines from around the world. Plenty of seats in the attractive gardens at the front and back of the pub.

> OPEN: April–September 11–11 (12–10.30 Sun). Winter 11–3. 6–11 (11–11 Sat.
> 12–10.30 Sun).
> Real Ale.
> Children allowed in certain areas. Dogs welcome with well-behaved owners.
> Wheelchair access. Car park.
> Cards: Delta, MasterCard, Switch, Visa.

BILLINGSHURST
Blue Ship   Tel: 01403 822709
The Haven, Billingshurst, W. Sussex RH14 9BS
King & Barnes. J.R. Davie, tenant.

Rather off the beaten track, the Ship is another unspoilt pub. Built in the 15th century and with Victorian additions, it's a charming, unchanging place. In a hamlet surrounded by the glories of the Sussex countryside, the pub is particularly popular at weekends. They serve a good choice of traditional bar food – ploughman's, sandwiches and home-made soups, a fish dish or two, cottage pie, steak and kidney pie and good puds. King & Barnes Sussex, Best Bitter and Winter Old from the barrel. Tables in the garden and in front of the pub by the honeysuckle.

> OPEN: 11–3. 6–11.
> Real Ale. No food Sun or Mon eves.
> Children in rooms without bar. Dogs on leads.

BLACKBOYS

Blackboys Inn   Tel: 01825 890283
Lewes Road, Blackboys, Nr Uckfield, E. Sussex TN22 5LG
Harveys. Edward Molesworth, tenant.

Set back off the road, this is an old, rambling pub, full of interesting bits and pieces, antique furniture, big log fires in winter and a good view of the pond if you manage to grab a window seat. An imaginative choice of bar food is listed on the blackboard; sometimes there will be home-made fish soup with croutons and aioli, mushrooms baked in a port and Stilton sauce, scallop of seafood gratinée, fillet of cod in prawn, mussel and scallop sauce, pheasant braised with red wine and sweet chestnuts, fillet steak in a mush-room, cream and brandy sauce or a green-peppercorn and garlic sauce, even a steak butty, sausage, egg and chips, ploughman's or a filled baked potato. Fantastic puds, real ice-cream or fresh-fruit sorbets. Seats outside and by the pond. Harveys ales – usually a choice of three.

> OPEN: 11–3. 6–11 (12–3. 7–10.30 Sun).
> Real Ale. Restaurant (no smoking).
> Children in restaurant. Dogs on leads. Wheelchair access (not WC). Car park.
> Cards: Delta, MasterCard, Switch, Visa.
> NB. There is a jukebox.

BROADWATER

Cricketers   Tel: 01903 233369
66 Broadwater Street West, Nr Worthing, W. Sussex BN14 9DE
Punch Taverns. Mr J.A. Sinsbury, licensee.

You can work out how popular the game of cricket is in a county by the number of crick-eting pubs. The game was probably thought of as a passing fancy here, as this particular Cricketers – formally the Brewers' Arms – was only renamed in 1878, even though cricket had been played on the green since early in the 18th century. Now firmly established, the pub is the home of the local team. Absorbed into the boundaries of Worthing, the parish of Broadwater dates back to Saxon times and once governed the villages of Broadwater, Worthing and Offington. Always a popular meeting place, especially for the home-cooked bar food, table d'hôte and à la carte menus; they specialise in seafood. Greene King IPA, Youngs Special, Bass, Fullers London Pride, Harveys and Bass Worthington are the beers.

> OPEN: 11–3. 6–11.
> Real Ale. Restaurant every lunchtime and Wed to Sat eves.
> Children in family room. Dogs on leads.

CHIDDINGLY

Six Bells   Tel: 01825 872227
Chiddingly, Nr Lewes, E. Sussex BN8 6HE (off A22 Uckfield–Hailsham)
Free House. Paul Newman, licensee.

There is a lot of music here but it is live and you know when it's coming, so if you're definitely not into folk or jazz you'll know when not to be here. A jolly, unassuming 18th-century pub, I don't have to tell you it's not the quietest of places when the bands play. Opposite the church, it serves the best of pub grub – all good and home-made and very reasonable: French onion soup, tuna pasta bake, cheesy cauliflower and broccoli bake, chicken and mushroom pie, spare ribs in barbecue sauce, rack of ribs, steak and kidney pie, lasagne, filled potatoes, etc. Puddings too. John Smiths, Harveys Best and Courage Best Bitter on hand pump. Seats out in the large garden, which has a fishpond. Good long walks nearby.

> OPEN: 11–3. 6–11.
> Real Ale.
> Children in family room. Dogs on leads. Wheelchair access. Car park.
> Cards: all cards except Amex.
> There is live music Tues, Fri and Sat eves and Sunday lunchtimes – in a separate building, admittedly, but it does reverberate. Folk and blues evenings every other Tues; live jazz etc Fri, Sat and Sun eves. The Sunbeam MCC meet the 1st Thurs of every month.

CHIDHAM

Old House at Home   Tel: 01243 572477
Cot Lane, Chidham, Nr Chichester, W. Sussex PO18 8SU
Free House. Cliff Parry & Terry Brewer, licensees.

This is a Chichester harbour village between two tidal creeks, the Bosham and Thorney Channels. You are surrounded by tidal flats, water, small boats and lots of birds. A little out of the way, but worth finding if you want to enjoy the good home cooking and well-kept beers of this pub. The bar snacks range from home-made soups, filled baguettes, ploughman's, filled baked potatoes and pie of the day to chef's specials on the blackboard, lots of fresh fish, steaks and other dishes; there will be more to choose from on the evening printed menu: mango, pawpaw and avocado salad with exotic leaves and an orange and raspberry dressing, oven-baked supreme of chicken served on spinach with a port and basil jus, fish of the day, a choice of vegetarian dishes and a separate pudding menu. Keeping a well-stocked cellar, they also have their own Old House beer – Guest Session Bitter, also Ringwood Best, Badger Best, Old Thumper and Premium Guest Bitter. Seats on the terrace and in the garden. The pub can get extremely busy, so to be sure of a table you should book, particularly in the evenings.

OPEN: 11.30–2.30 (12–3 Sat). 6–11.
Real Ale. Restaurant.
Children welcome. Dogs on leads. Wheelchair access.

CHRIST'S HOSPITAL

Bax Castle
Tel: 01403 730369
Two Mile Ash Road, Southwater, Horsham, W. Sussex RH13 7LA (on the Christ's Hospital–Southwater road)
English Country Inns. Mike Porteous, licensee.

Find the old railway bridge that once carried the Guildford–Shoreham line and behind it you'll find this small country pub in its own big garden, surrounded by trees and good walks. Before the coming of the railways, the building was a 15th-century weaver's cottage. The disused railway track has become the Downs Link, connecting with the South Downs Way. If you're walking or cycling, the Bax Castle is an ideal place to stop. Inside, the bar leads into a dining area; an old cowshed – minus the cows – serves as a function room. There is quite a choice on the menu: soup, deep-fried whitebait, Greek salad, gammon steak, fresh cod fillet in real-ale batter, steak and kidney pie with a shortcrust-pastry top (these last two are currently the most popular dishes), fisherman's platter, lots of fish – halibut, trout, salmon, tuna and swordfish, or you could have a mixed grill, fillet steak or half a shoulder of lamb, perhaps a daily special or two from the blackboard, such as a minted lamb casserole. Harveys Sussex Bitter, Kings Red River, Horsham Bitter and a guest beer.

OPEN: 12–2.30. 6–11 (12–3. 6.30–10.30 Sun).
Real Ale. Restaurant.
Children welcome in their own room. Dogs in bar. Wheelchair access. Car park. Children's play area.
Resident guitarist on Tuesdays. Other musicians from time to time.

COOLHAM

George & Dragon
Tel: 01403 741320
Dragons Green, Nr Coolham, W. Sussex
Hall & Woodhouse. Roger Nash, tenant.

As you approach Coolham from the west on the A272, look out for the signpost to the George & Dragon on your side of the road. It's down a lane, and is a typical tile-hung cottagey Sussex pub – an attractive method of building that has been a feature of south-east England since about the 17th century. Hugely popular at weekends, there is plenty of room in the big garden, but on a wet day it could be quite a squash inside. The beams in the bar are massive – obviously whatever was on hand was used – and there is a huge fireplace and a screened dining area. They serve good traditional pub food, properly cooked and very much appreciated. Home-made soups, ploughman's, steak and kidney pie, they cook their own ham and also make proper chips with real potatoes – rarer than you might think. Sunday roasts. On hand pump they have King & Barnes Sussex (Old in winter), Hall and Woodhouse Badger, Tanglefoot and Champion beers. A delightful place with a glorious garden.

> OPEN: 11–3. 6–11 (11–11 Sat. 12–10.30 Sun). Winter weekdays 11–3. 6.30–11.
> Real Ale.
> Children and dogs welcome if under control. Good wheelchair access.

DANEHILL

Coach & Horses   Tel: 01825 740369
Danehill, Nr Forest Row, E. Sussex RH17 7JF
Free House. Ian Philpots, licensee.

On the outskirts of the village, this cottagey local has some wonderful views towards the South Downs from the pub garden. Inside are public and saloon bars, plus a dining area, each with its own log fire. Bar snacks include soup of the day, sandwiches and grilled ciabatta or focaccia bread with different toppings; from the à la carte menu, whole roast poussin served with Mediterranean vegetables and mushroom and pesto carbonara are examples of the style of cooking. Always fish dishes and home-made puddings. There is an evening menu too. Harveys Best and a weekly changing guest beer. Champagne-method cider during the summer. A choice of 30 wines, five by the glass. There is an enclosed children's play area.

> OPEN: 11–3. 6–11 (12–4. 7–10.30 Sun).
> Real Ale.
> Children welcome. Dogs on leads away from dining area.
> Cards: most accepted.

DITCHLING

Bull Inn   Tel: 01273 843147
2 High Street, Ditchling, E. Sussex BN6 8TA
Free House. Paul Day, owner.

Before this fine 16th-century building became the local coaching inn, it served a far darker purpose: it was the courthouse for the Society for the Prosecution of Thieves. Many a felon left here to be taken to the gallows on Ditchling Common. The gruesome past forgotten, this is now a popular, cheerful place, recently refurbished. Two well-beamed bars inside the Bull, with some fine old furniture and good log fires in winter, also a no-smoking area. Wholesome bar food is served along with specials from the daily changing blackboard. From the menu there are sandwiches and baguettes, ploughman's, filled baked potatoes, traditional steak kidney and Guinness pie, chef's fish pie, cauliflower cheese, bangers and mash, always steaks and vegetarian dishes; Sunday roasts. Harveys Sussex Bitter with two or three guests and a short wine list. Seats outside on the terrace and in the large, pretty garden, which has fine views towards Ditchling Beacon.

OPEN: 11–11.
Real Ale. No-smoking area.
Children welcome. Dogs on leads.
Double and single en-suite bedrooms.

DUNCTON

Cricketers
Tel: 01798 342473

Main Road, Duncton, Nr Petworth, W. Sussex GU28 0LB
Free House. Tamsin Corbett, manageress.

On a well-trodden route at the foot of the South Downs, on the main road from Petworth to Chichester, this pleasant 15th-century pub is as popular with locals as with travellers. In winter you'll find a big log fire in the comfortable bar, and there is cricketing memorabilia in the two split-level eating areas – to remind you of summer. They offer a simple range of bar food from filled rolls and ploughman's, to freshly prepared chicken, local game and fish dishes from the full menu; simple ingredients put together to create something interesting and worthwhile. Good puds too. Archers Golden and Village, Youngs IPA and guest ales, a number of malt whiskies and a good selection of wines. Seats in the attractive garden. The pub has its own skittle alley in an adjacent building.

OPEN: 11–2.30. 6–11 (12–3. 7–10.30 Sun). Closed Sun eves in winter.
Real Ale.
Children over 14. Well-behaved dogs. Wheelchair access to all parts of the pub. Car park.
Cards: Delta, MasterCard, Switch, Visa.

EASEBOURNE STREET

Holly Tree
Tel: 01730 813388

Easebourne Street (off A272), Midhurst, W. Sussex GU29 0BE
Free House. G.D.H. Damerell, licensee.

Up a pretty lane outside Midhurst. Looks belie: inside, the Holly Tree is modern; it wasn't, but it is now. Though done up and undone at the same time, it is still a favourite with the retired locals. Very welcoming and friendly. Inside is a spacious bar and a restaurant. The lunchtime bar menu is supplemented with specials such as fresh salmon mayonnaise, curried prawns and rice or whole grilled plaice. The dinner menu is more extensive and could include whitebait, smoked salmon or trout, smoked-fish pâté, pan-fried trout fillets (caught by the landlord), roast Aylesbury duckling, grilled Dover sole, gammon or fillet steak. Badger Best, Guinness, Carlsberg Export – anything you want really, plus a good wine list and a range of malt whiskies. On the edge of the South Downs, this is good walking country.

> OPEN: Closed Monday, otherwise 11–2.30 (12–3 Sun). 6.30–11.
> Real Ale. Restaurant.
> Children welcome. Dogs on leads. Wheelchair access.
> Cards: MasterCard, Switch, Visa.

EASTBOURNE

The Lamb   Tel: 01323 720545
36 High Street, Old Town, Eastbourne, E. Sussex BN21 1HH
Harvey & Son. Steve Hume, tenant/licensee.

Eastbourne spreads in all directions. Three miles along the sea, and nearly 5 miles inland towards Polegate, but the Lamb is in the old quarter, less than a mile from what is now the centre of the Victorian expansion of the town. The Lamb, licensed as an inn since 1603, has cellars dating from the 12th century. It also had an underground passage connecting the pub to the Old Parsonage, reputed to have been used by the local smugglers, now unfortunately closed. The low-beamed main bar was once a ballroom, and the carved chairs are believed to have been acquired from the German Embassy in London – all very grand. Sandwiches or ploughman's are served in the bar, or you can have a light meal of Indian savouries, or deep-fried salmon and prawn delights, pasta dishes, fish, grills, steak and kidney pie, braised breast of duck and vegetarian dishes. Daily specials on the blackboard; puddings too. Harveys Best Bitter, Pale and their seasonal ales. No garden, but tables on the adjoining terrace.

> OPEN: 10.30–3. 5.30–11 (10.30–11 Fri & Sat. 12–4. 7–10.30 Sun).
> Real Ale.
> Children in lower bar. Dogs on leads.

EAST DEAN

Tiger Inn   Tel: 01323 423209
The Green, East Dean, Eastbourne, E. Sussex BN20 0DA (village off A259 Eastbourne–Seaford)
Free House. Nicholas Denyer, licensee.

The white-painted old pub is among cottages bordering the green in East Dean, a village in the hollow of the South Downs. You know there are some seriously invigorating walks – to Birling Gap, the lighthouse at Belle Tout (the one that moved) and Beachy Head – as there are a lot of people with serious walking boots around looking at folded maps. The picnic tables at the front of the pub fill up quickly in summer. Inside, the Tiger is a comfortable, low-beamed bar with good winter fires and a family room upstairs. An interesting, ever-changing blackboard menu could include venison casserole, garlic mushrooms, macaroni cheese with tomatoes, ploughman's or fish and chips; local fish, cheeses, vegetables and fresh game will feature too. Beers do change but could include Flowers Original, Harveys Best, Adnams Best and Timothy Taylors Landlord as a guest. There is also a good choice of bin-ends of wine on the blackboard and seven or eight wines by the glass.

OPEN: 11–3. 6–11 (11–11 Sat. 12–10.30 Sun).
Real Ale.
Children in family room. Dogs on leads. Bank Holiday Morris dancers.

ELSTED

Three Horseshoes
Tel: 01730 825746
Elsted, Midhurst, W. Sussex GU29 0JX (west of Midhurst off the A272)
Free House. Andrew Beavis, licensee.

Lots of good walking country in Sussex, and the Three Horseshoes is a good place to start from – or end up at – as you're not far from the South Downs Way (good walks) and Beacon Hill, 793 feet up on the Downs (good views). The pub serves generous quantities of regularly changing bar food to help keep up the energy levels of all the walkers and cyclists who drop in. A very traditional 16th-century pub, originally serving the drovers travelling the South Downs. Cosy, low-beamed rooms, full of old furniture and big fireplaces, blazing with logs in the winter. A changing blackboard menu could offer home-made soups, ploughman's, casseroles, steak pies, fresh fish and filling puddings. Ales, which are kept behind the bar, could include Ballards Best, Fullers London Pride and Cheriton Pots Ale. They often have ales from smaller independent breweries. Seats in the pretty garden, which has a marvellous view of the South Downs.

OPEN: 11–3 (11–2.30 in winter). 6–11. Closed winter Sun eves.
Real Ale. Restaurant.
Well-behaved children in eating areas. Dogs on leads.

FERNHURST

The Kings Arms
Tel: 01428 652005
Midhurst Road, Fernhurst, W. Sussex GU27 3HA
Free House. Michael Hirst, licensee.

An early-17th-century stone building between Midhurst and Haslemere. Just a small bar, with seats around a big table piled with the daily papers, low beams and big inglenook fireplace. The bar is first and foremost a bar: bar food is served here at lunchtime, but no crumbs allowed during the evening – then you eat in the restaurant. Family-run, with a very friendly atmosphere, serving good traditional bar food with a touch of the cosmopolitan: modern British is how they describe it. The menu leaps from local sausages and mash to a carpaccio of peppered beef fillet with Stilton and red-onion salad. Fish is bought fresh from the coast so there are at least four fish dishes a day. Menus change monthly and dishes depend on what is available and in season. Everything is home-made, including salad dressings, pasta, ice-creams and sorbets. Delicious puds. Five real ales including two weekly changing guests and real Guinness; this still has a Dublin accent. A comprehensive wine list includes half-bottles and bin-ends.

OPEN: 11.30–3. 5.30–11. Closed Sun eves.
Real Ale.
Children welcome – but no children under 14 after 7pm; dogs too. Wheelchair access (not WC). Car park.
Cards: Electron, MasterCard, Solo, Switch, Visa.

FINDON

Gun Inn   Tel: 01903 873206
High Street, Findon, W. Sussex
Free House. Nick Georgiou, licensee.

Firmly settled in its new role as a free house after a lifetime tied to one of the big breweries, the Gun is a homely and welcoming port of call. Dating from the 16th century, this ancient place is in a charming, unspoilt downland village surrounded by woods and rolling hills. The low-beamed lounge bar contains beams that are reputed to be from old sailing ships. The sea is not far away, nor is the great earthwork of Cissbury Ring, an iron-age hill fort which rises 600 feet above sea level. They serve generous helpings of home-cooked food in both the bar and restaurant and up to five real ales, among them Adnams, Fullers London Pride, Summer Lightning and Harveys HSB. Forty wines on the list.

OPEN: 11–11.
Real Ale.
Children in family room. Dogs on leads. Wheelchair access (not WC).

FIRLE

Ram Inn   Tel: 01273 858222
Firle, West Firle, Lewes, E. Sussex BN8 6NS (off A27 Lewes–Polegate)
Free House. Michael & Keith Wooller, licensees.

The Ram is a well-run traditional pub, unusual in that you really can get something to eat all day; food is in perpetual motion and they even serve afternoon tea. So here you are in the midst of plenty. Lots to see and do: Glyndebourne, little more than an interval away, and Firle Place, an imposing and apparently 18th-century mansion disguising an old Elizabethan house. And when you have had your pint and lunch, a quick dash up Firle Beacon, 713 feet up on the Downs, should put you right for the rest of the day. When you get here after all the refreshing exercise, you'll find a daily changing blackboard menu to tempt you. Using fresh, local produce, the dishes include good home-made soups, spicy chicken wings, salmon steaks, home-cooked ham and interesting puddings.

Harveys BB plus three other guest beers. A good choice of wines and a big walled garden to sit in.

> OPEN: 11.30–11 (12–10.30 Sun).
> Real Ale.
> Children in non-serving bars. Dogs on leads. Wheelchair access. Four bedrooms.
> Live folk music twice monthly.

FLETCHING

Griffin   Tel: 01825 722890
Fletching, E. Sussex TN22 3SS (village off A272)
Free House. Nigel Pullan, James Pullan & John Gatti, licensees.

There seems to be something for everyone in this old village dating back to Saxon times: interesting architecture, indications of religious persecution, and a fascinating historical rumour. In the particularly fine church, which has a Norman tower that can be seen for miles around, it is said that some of the knights killed in the Battle of Lewes in 1264 lie buried in full armour below the nave. The 16th-century Griffin is all a village local should be, with that little extra touch: a priest hole – essential in times of religious persecution. Inside the pub, reflecting its age, is a heavily beamed main bar, creaking floors defying the horizontal, big log fires with griffins, what else, guarding the fireplace, a public bar with pool table and other games for those so inclined, and an attractively decorated restaurant which expands onto the terrace during the summer. The very popular bar food changes daily and there is an à la carte menu in the restaurant. The bar menu could include home-made soups, warm chicken and bacon salad, marinated herring and warm potato salad, Italian sausages with beans and polenta, salmon fishcakes, grilled fish, toad in the hole, a vegetarian or fish risotto and some pasta dishes. Harveys, Hall & Woodhouse Tanglefoot, Rother Valleys Spirit Level, also Kronenbourg 1664 lager and a very good wine list. Splendid views towards Sheffield Park from the 2 acres of garden.

> OPEN: 12–3. 6–11.
> Real Ale. Restaurant (not Sun eves).
> Children welcome. Dogs on leads. Wheelchair access. Car park.
> Eight bedrooms: seven with four posters, some in the main building, some in the converted coach house. Pianist Fri and Sat eves and Sun lunchtime.
> Cards: all major cards.
> N.B. Very quiet music in public bar only.

FLETCHING

Rose & Crown   Tel: 01825 722039
High Street, Fletching, E. Sussex TN22 3ST
Free House. Roger & Sheila Haywood, licensees.

An interesting old pub with even older foundations. The brick 15th-century Rose & Crown you see today is on the site of a 12th-century building. This is verified by a piece of daub and wattle on display just inside the side entrance of the pub, dated circa 1150. Even so, something built in the 1400s and still standing is an achievement. Inside, the comfortable, heavily beamed bar has a splendid inglenook fireplace and the restaurant offers a choice from either à la carte or table d'hôte menus. Bar snacks too: home-made soup, grilled jumbo prawns in garlic butter, leek and mushroom puff, omelettes, macaroni cheese, ploughman's, toasted sandwiches and several vegetarian dishes. Also daily specials and home-made puddings and ice-creams. The à la carte menu in the restaurant changes to reflect availability and the seasons. Harveys Ales and Ind Coope Burton. Choice of wines, some by the glass and half-bottle. Seats in the garden.

OPEN: 11–2.30. 6–11 (12–2. 7–10.30 Sun).
Real Ale. Restaurant.
Children in restaurant only. Dogs in bar only. Wheelchair access. Bed and breakfast accommodation.

FULKING

Shepherd & Dog   Tel: 01273 857382
Fulking, Nr Henfield, W. Sussex BN5 9LU
Hall & Woodhouse. Geoff Chapman, manager.

Dogs yes, shepherds no. There aren't any of the latter around any more, only locals, visitors and enthusiastic walkers at this constantly popular 14th-century pub. Inside is a cosy bar with rustic artifacts where you can enjoy a regularly changing menu. There could be a home-made soup, ploughman's, double-decker granary sandwiches, several vegetarian dishes, venison casserole, moussaka, chicken curry, fresh fish, steak and kidney pie and home-made puddings. Harveys Best, Badgers Dorset Best and Tanglefoot, Guinness – also draught Scrumpy Jack and Dry Blackthorn ciders. There are seats in the pretty garden. If you have had too good a lunch, there are some energetic walks on the South Downs nearby.

OPEN: 11–11 (12–10.30 Sun).
Real Ale.
Dogs on leads. Wheelchair access.

GRAFFHAM

Foresters Arms   Tel: 01798 867202
Graffham, Nr Petworth, W. Sussex GU28 0QA
Free House. Lloyd F. Pocock, licensee.

Close to the South Downs Way and all those invigorating walks, you'll find a warm, friendly atmosphere in the picturesque 17th-century Foresters Arms, gloriously colourful in summer when it is hung about with the most opulent hanging baskets. Bar snacks such as large baguettes filled with cheese, bacon, lettuce, tomato and egg mayonnaise or brown baguettes with smoked salmon are served in the heavily beamed bar. The attractive restaurant offers an à la carte menu of English country cooking, with game a speciality. Harveys

Pale Ale, a varying number of interesting guest beers, plus a range of Belgian beers and a good wine list. The well-stocked garden is particularly attractive.

OPEN: 11–2.30. 5.30–11 (12–3. 7–10.30 Sun).
Real Ale. Restaurant.
Children at landlord's discretion. Dogs on leads. Wheelchair access.
Cards: MasterCard, Switch, Visa.

GUN HILL

Gun Inn   Tel: 01825 872361
Gun Hill, Nr Horam, Heathfield, E. Sussex TN21 0JU
Free House. K. Western, licensee.

The Gun, built when the Ashdown Forest really was a forest, is an attractive, flower-bedecked country pub with rambling, beamed rooms, popular with walkers from the Wealden Way – muddy boots and all. Inside you'll find big fires, a no-smoking area, good-value food and well-kept beers. The bar menu includes soups, French-bread snacks, salads, ploughman's, seafood platter, lasagne and beef Wellington. The specials board usually has another 15 dishes to choose from, including fresh fish, various pies and vegetarian dishes. Boddingtons, Adnams and Harveys Sussex. Merrydown cider and wines by the glass. Outside is a big sheltered garden with seats and a children's play area. There are tables at the front so you can sit and admire the glorious award-winning floral display.

OPEN: 12–3.6–11.
Real Ale.
Children until 9pm. Dogs on leads. Wheelchair access via portable ramp to pub.

HERMITAGE Nr Emsworth

Sussex Brewery   Tel: 01243 371533
36 Main Road, Hermitage, Nr Emsworth, W. Sussex PO10 8AU
Free House. Malcolm & Pamela Roberts, licensees.

It started out as a real brewery, and after tasting their delicious brew, the founders probably got things a bit muddled about whether they had set up shop in Hampshire or Sussex. So if you are looking for Emsworth, you will find it in Hampshire, but Hermitage, and the Sussex Brewery, are here in West Sussex. As the name suggests, this 17th-century building used to brew Hermitage bitter. Along the flagstone passage and up the staircase, the place where the hops were mashed is now a cosy, heavily beamed small dining room. Downstairs, the bar floor is covered in fresh sawdust, not only to protect the floor from spilled pints, but also – as the pub occasionally floods – to soak up the water. The printed menu offers a wide range of snacks. A more comprehensive list of specials, such as mussels in wine and garlic, whole rack of lamb, Dover sole, or local plaice with home-made chips, is also available. However the *pièces de résistance* are the special sausages made for the pub. Bill O'Hagan, a freelance writer and famous sausage maker, provides a remarkable range of 41 pork, lamb, beef, speciality and vegetarian sausages – guaranteed lean, with freshly blended seasoning, no preservatives or monosodium glutamate. Not surprisingly, the Sussex Brewery is called the 'sausage pub'. Hermitage Best is still available, brewed by Poole Brewery in Dorset, also Timothy Taylors Landlord and Mild, Youngs PA and Special Bitter, Tanglefoot, Dorset Best, Golden Champion and Brakspears Special. Nine real ales always on, one of which changes monthly. Outside is a secluded walled courtyard filled with hanging baskets and tubs of flowers.

> OPEN: 11–11 (12–10.30 Sun).
> Real Ale. Restaurant.
> Children welcome. Dogs too, but not in restaurant. Wheelchair access. Car park.

KINGSTON Nr Lewes

Juggs   Tel: 01273 472523
Kingston, Nr Lewes, E. Sussex (off A27 west of Lewes)
Shepherd Neame. Pete & Sandy Smith, licensees.

There is a path called Juggs Way over the Downs from Brighton to Lewes along which the women walked to market. The interesting name is short for jugget; a vessel for fish that the local women carried on their heads. This small, delightful, half-tile-hung, rose-covered pub dates back to the 15th century. Inside is a rambling, beamed main bar with a log fire, and two restaurants, one smoking, one no-smoking. One menu is shared by all; the food includes a variety of sandwiches, locally made sausages, a vegetarian dish, pitta bread with a selection of fillings, steak and kidney pie, daily specials and a children's menu. They specialise in fresh-fish dishes. Shepherd Neame cask ales – Spitfire, MasterBrew and seasonal ales. Tables outside in the courtyard, on the sunny terrace and on the lawn.

> OPEN: 11–11 (12–10.30 Sun).
> Real Ale. Restaurant.
> Children in restaurant. Dogs on leads. Wheelchair access possible – one step into pub.

LEWES

The Lewes Arms   Tel: 01273 473152
Mount Place, Lewes, E. Sussex BN7 1YH
Greene King. Clair Murray, licensee.

From the Normans to the present day, a thousand years of history have created the Lewes you see today. As well as the remains of the Norman castle, the town is full of fine buildings from all periods. Situated on a steep hill overlooking the River Ouse, the Lewes Arms is off the busy main street and just below the Castle Mound. Built at the beginning of the 18th century, it is a pleasant, friendly, old-fashioned town pub with two bars and a cosy snug. Food is all home-made, from the sandwiches to the interesting hot snacks; the menu is constantly changing. Well-kept Harveys Best, Old and Greene King Abbot, plus seasonal beers.

> OPEN: 11–11 (12–10.30 Sun).
> Real Ale. Lunchtime food only.
> Children in games room. Dogs on leads. Limited access for wheelchairs.

LEWES

Shelley's Hotel Bar
Tel: 01273 472361

137 High Street, Lewes, E. Sussex BN7 1XS
Free House. Gary Lupton & Graeme Coles, licensees.

Lewes High Street is full of Georgian shops and houses leading down to the River Ouse. Among them is Shelley's, a hotel with an interesting history. This splendid 16th-century building has turned full circle over the years. Originally an inn called the Vine, it was sold to the 4th Earl of Dorset, who turned it into a fine manor house, and then sold it to the Shelley family, who lived in it for some years before selling it for conversion into a 'grander' inn. The hotel, retaining the Shelley connection, still has a Victorian bar where they serve a selection of interesting bar snacks: home-made soup, a seasonal fish stew, seafood platter, moules marinière, grilled goat's cheese salad, chargrilled chicken, Hungarian goulash, tortellini filled with cream cheese with a tomato and basil sauce, interesting continental salads, sandwiches, filled baguettes and toasted sandwiches. There is a new chef so menus will change on a regular basis. One real ale – the local Harveys; all other beers are bottled. Choice of wines. Seats in the garden.

> OPEN: 11–3. 6–11.
> Real Ale. Lunchtime snacks only.
> Children: not in bar. No dogs. Wheelchair access to bar.

LODSWORTH

Halfway Bridge
Tel: 01798 861281

Lodsworth, Nr Petworth, W. Sussex GU28 9BP (off the A272)
Free House. Sheila, Simon & James Hawkins, licensees.

As its name suggests, halfway between two glorious estates: Petworth and Cowdray Park. An 18th-century coaching inn with a reputation for really imaginative food served in delightful surroundings. Many of the tables will be laid for meals, but there is always room and a welcome in the comfortable, spacious bars for you to enjoy a pint and something from the bar menu. The extensive blackboard menu lists food ranging from mushrooms in cream and tarragon on toast, Welsh rarebit, calves' liver and bacon, grilled salmon with a coriander and Dijon-mustard sauce, and niçoise salad with grilled fresh tuna steak to daily changing specials on the blackboard and home-made puds. Sunday roasts. Cheriton Brewhouse Pots Ale, Fullers London Pride and Gales HSB on hand pump. Also changing guest beers, a porter, old or stout in winter and something from one of the local independent breweries in summer. Farm cider and wine by the glass. Lots of traditional pub games played – shut-the-box, bagatelle, backgammon, dominoes and more. Tables in the garden and on the sheltered terrace at the back of the pub.

OPEN: 11–3. 6–11.
Real Ale. Restaurant.
Children over ten in restaurant. Dogs on leads. Wheelchair access (not WC). Eight bedrooms in the converted barn, one with disabled access.

MAYFIELD

Rose & Crown Inn   Tel: 01435 872200
Fletching Street, Mayfield, E. Sussex TN20 6TE
Free House. Duncan Paul, manager.

This pretty 16th-century coaching inn overlooks a small, peaceful green. Inside, it has low beams, big fireplaces and bars on different levels, also a dining room and candlelit restaurant. The food is well cooked and well served. In addition to the chef's daily specials you could find hot Sussex smokie au gratin, Shrewsbury lamb, lamb fillets in redcurrant and rosemary, aubergine and tomato au gratin, Mediterranean pasta twists, steak and ale pie, chicken, ham and mushroom pie, something from the charcoal grill and, last but not least, filled baguettes, jacket potatoes and ploughman's. They stock Harveys Best Bitter, Flowers IPA and a guest ale. Small patio garden. Built on a high ridge, so there are wonderful views over the Rother valley towards Eastbourne.

OPEN: 11–3. 6–11 (11–11 Fri & Sat. 11–10.30 Sun).
Real Ale. Restaurant.
Children welcome, but not in bar. Dogs in middle bar only.
En-suite bedrooms.
Cards: all credit cards except Amex and Diners.

OVING

Gribble Inn   Tel: 01243 786893
Oving, Chichester, W. Sussex PO20 6BP (east of Chichester)
Woodhouse Inns. Microbrewery. Brian & Cyn Elderfield, managers; Rob Cooper, brewer.

Many would think this was paradise on earth: a local with its very own brewery. All that and good looks too. A delightful, rose-covered 16th-century thatched pub in an attractive cottage garden. Inside are a heavily beamed bar with big log fires, and a no-smoking family room where they serve familiar, home-cooked bar food of soups, ploughman's, sandwiches, salads, ham and eggs, steak, also Sunday lunches. Specialities are Reg's pie – steak and mushrooms cooked in Reg's ale, fisherman's pie, home-made steak and kidney puddings, home-made suet, bacon and onion roly-poly, and supreme of chicken filled with asparagus and Austrian smoked cheese. Also fish dishes and a fish of the day from the blackboard such as fresh cod with watercress sauce, 'Old Favourites' and vegetarian dishes.

The specials board changes at least once a day. Seats outside among the apple trees. The pub's own skittle alley, along with the brewery (tours can be arranged), is on the other side of the car park. Their own-brews Pig's Ear, Gribble Ale, Reg's Tipple, Oving Bitter, Black Adder II and the 'new' Fursty Ferret are the beers.

> OPEN: July–Sept 11–3. 5.30–11 (11–11 Sat. 12–10.30 Sun).
> Rest of year 11–3. 6–11 (11–3. 5.30–11 Sat. 12–3. 6.30–10.30 Sun).
> Real Ale – brewed on the premises.
> Children in family room. Dogs on leads in garden and bar. Wheelchair access to pub and to ladies' WC.
> Cards: Access, Amex, Delta, Switch, Visa.

POYNINGS

Royal Oak
Tel: 01273 857389

The Street, Poynings, W. Sussex BN45 7AQ
Free House. Paul Day, licensee.

The Royal Oak is at the foot of the Devil's Dyke, and from the garden there are far-reaching views of the South Downs. The Dyke, a deep hollow in the weald above Brighton, is supposedly where the devil tried to create a gap in the downs to allow the sea to flood the surrounding land, halting the spread of Christianity – one does wonder where these legends come from. On much firmer ground, the Royal Oak has the comfort of two big log fires and, if you want something to eat, a well-chosen menu. There is a daily specials board, but from the printed menu you could choose home-made soup, scallop and bacon brochette grilled with garlic butter, a duo of smoked salmon and smoked halibut with tarragon sauce and, for a main course, a traditional steak and ale pie topped with puff pastry or grilled Scotch fillet steak on a bread crouton with a wild-mushroom sauce. Always ploughman's, filled jacket potatoes and freshly filled sandwiches. The beers are Harveys, Courage Directors, Morlands and Old Speckled Hen. There is a comprehensive wine list. You are surrounded by good walks so they are very welcoming to walkers and their dogs.

> OPEN: 11–11 (12–10.30 Sun).
> Real Ale. No-smoking area.
> Children welcome. Dogs on leads. Wheelchair access. Car park.

RUDGWICK

Blue Ship
Tel: 01403 822709

The Haven, Rudgwick, Horsham, W. Sussex
King & Barnes. John Davie, tenant.

One more house and Rudgwick would be in Surrey as it's so close to the border. On entering the public bar you could be forgiven for thinking things hadn't changed much over the years: flagstone floors, scrubbed deal tables, in winter a roaring fire in the big inglenook fireplace and farm dogs waiting patiently under the benches – wonderfully unspoilt. No bar as such in the Blue Ship; your drinks are served through the hatch, just as they used to be. Food is all home-cooked and the blackboard menu changes constantly – ham, egg and chips is a speciality. Everything they serve is very wholesome. King & Barnes Broadwood and Sussex ales; Old is available during the winter. Views over the surrounding countryside from the garden. This is a very popular place.

> OPEN: 11–3. 6–11 (12–3. 7–10.30 Sun).
> Real Ale.
> Children welcome. Dogs on leads.

RYE

Mermaid Inn   Tel: 01797 223065
Mermaid Street, Rye, E. Sussex TN31 7EU
Free House. Robert Pinwill, licensee.

Probably dating back to the 12th century; certainly by 1300 the Mermaid was brewing its own ale and charging a penny a night for accommodation. Rebuilt in 1420, the pub looks much the same today as it did then. A steep cobbled street leads to the Mermaid, the largest medieval building in the town and one of the loveliest smugglers' inns in the county – and there are lots of them. The smugglers really were in control here. Even during the Georgian period they used to drink in the inn with their pistols on the table, untouched by the law. Wonderfully beamed and panelled with a really vast inglenook fireplace, two very comfortable lounges, a bar and restaurant. Traditional bar food and a more elaborate restaurant menu. Marstons Pedigree and Morlands Old Speckled Hen on hand pump. House wines and sherries. Brass-band concerts occasionally in the car park during summer.

> OPEN: 11–11.
> Real Ale. Restaurant.
> Children welcome. No dogs. Bedrooms.
> N.B. Classical music in one bar. Lounges and restaurant quiet.

SELHAM

The Three Moles   Tel: 01798 861303
Selham, Nr Petworth, W. Sussex GU28 0PN
Free House. Mrs Val Wingate, licensee.

Once a station hotel, but it's now without a station – or a railway line. Not that it makes much difference to this solid and unpretentious country pub south of the A272 between Petworth and Midhurst, because it is so friendly, popular and successful. Unmissable, although there's no food, just a range of crisps and nuts. But when you know how many awards The Three Moles has won in the past – including National Runner-up Pub of the Year and second place in CAMRA's National Pub of the Year – you know you can be sure of an excellent pint; you can take your own picnic or even your barbecue if you give them fair warning by telephoning first. No chance of driving straight past this place, sitting as it does high on the bank with a distinctive white porch; the very prominent inn sign is detached and on the edge of the road. As I write the ales are King & Co's Horsham Best, Skinners Betty Stog and Ballards Mild; always a strong ale and a seasonal one from an unusual microbrewery. You know that a new experience will be waiting for you from the beer pump. You can eat your picnic or set up the barbecue (don't forget to telephone first) in the garden or on the covered terrace – and there is no hamper charge! Lots of old and new pub games and an old fashioned sing-song, with accordion, on the first Saturday of the month – either to be avoided like the plague or a fixed date in your diary.

> OPEN: 12–2. 5.30–11 (11.30–11 Sat. 12–10.30 Sun).
> Real Ale.
> No children in the bar. Dogs: yes, but beware of the pub cat.
> If you're on horseback, there is a hitching rail under the tree in the car park.
> Cards: none accepted.

SIDLESHAM

Crab & Lobster
Tel: 01243 641233
Mill Lane, Sidlesham, Chichester, W. Sussex PO20 7NB
Free House. Brian Cross, licensee.

Sidlesham has spread itself along the main road, but the Crab & Lobster is firmly in the old area of this attractive backwater. The 18th-century purpose-built pub backs onto Pagham Harbour, whose tidal mud flats are now a 1000-acre bird sanctuary. Inside the pub are two bars, both with fine log fires in winter and no jukebox or fruit machines anywhere. Total bliss. Bar food includes a variety of the usual bar snacks. During the summer the menu includes crab, lobster and prawns, also a lasagne and two vegetarian dishes; in winter, steak and kidney pie, beef in Guinness and fish pie, plus home-made puddings. Seats in the very pretty garden at the back of the pub. Cheriton Pots, Arundel 1999, Ballards Best and Itchen Valley Fagin on hand pump.

> OPEN: 11–3. 6–11 (7–10.30 Sun).
> Real Ale. Food served Sat until 2.30pm.
> Children in the garden. Dogs on leads. Wheelchair access.
> Cards: MasterCard, Switch, Visa.

TILLINGTON

Horse Guards Inn
Tel: 01798 342332
Tillington, W. Sussex GU28 9AF
Free House. Paul Brett, licensee.

Just outside Petworth on the Midhurst road, a delightful, welcoming pub serving some really good food. Here the mix is effortless: diners and drinkers have their own spaces and everyone is happy. About 300 years old, well beamed, well polished and prosperous. High off the road so, if you're lucky enough to have a seat in the bay window, there is, on a good day, a view over the glories of the Sussex countryside. With inventive bar food and à la carte menu, this is cooking at its best. The menus change frequently but delights abound – you won't be disappointed. Fullers London Pride and Youngs ales. The wine list shows the same quality as the cooking; half-bottles and some by the glass. Seats outside in the garden.

> OPEN: 11–3. 6–11 (12–3. 7–10.30).
> Real Ale.
> Children in bar eating area. No young children in evening. Dogs in bar. Car park.
> Bedrooms.
> Cards: Amex, Diners, MasterCard, Switch, Visa.

TICEHURST

Bell Hotel   Tel: 01580 200234
High Street, Ticehurst, Wadhurst, E. Sussex
Free House. Mrs Pamela Tate, licensee.

There is no chance you will forget the name of this hotel once you've seen the amazing collection of bells in the lounge bar. Over the years they have gathered between 300 and 400 to put on show. In the middle of the village, this 14th-century coaching inn has been run by the same family for well over 40 years. Inside, as befits its age, are lots of ancient timbers and a huge inglenook fireplace ablaze with logs in the winter. Two bars: the lounge with the bells, and the public bar with the pool table, but all you'll hear is friendly chatter and the clink of glasses. Bar snacks and meals are always freshly cooked to order from the menu. Harveys and Whitbread ales. Seats in the garden.

> OPEN: 11–3. 6–11.
> No food Sun eves.
> Children welcome. Dogs on leads. Wheelchair access. Bedrooms.

WADHURST

The Greyhound   Tel: 01892 783224
St James' Square, Wadhurst, E. Sussex TN5 6AP
Free House. Jonathan & Emma Harrold, licensees.

Wadhurst spreads out in all directions, but there is a centre and that's where the Greyhound is – a handsome, white-painted, well-kept village pub, beamed, polished and panelled with a huge inglenook fireplace and an equally huge log fire in winter. Like many Sussex pubs it has a smuggling history: in the mid-18th century the infamous Hawkhurst gang used it as one of their safe houses. Later, probably due to a change of landlord, the inn became a posting house where the mail was sorted before being distributed around the locality by post boys. Today you will always find a good choice of bar food as well as an à la carte menu and daily specials: fish soup, smoked-salmon salad, fillet steak with grain-mustard and pepper sauce, grilled lemon sole, baked avocado, prawn and smoked-salmon tartlet or chicken provençale on a bed of pasta. Menus change daily. Bar billiards, darts and Ring the Bull's Nose in one corner, a game apparently brought over by the Romans. The only other pub with this particular game is one in Kent. Harveys Sussex, Bass, Morlands Old Speckled Hen and a guest beer. About eight house wines by the glass and about 30 bottles on the wine list. There is an upstairs meeting room for hire, regularly used by art and yoga classes, and a garden, also seats at the front so you can watch Wadhurst on the move.

> OPEN: 12–2.30. 6–11 (11–11 Sat. 12–3. 7–10.30 Sun).
> Real Ale. Restaurant.
> Children – only in restaurant if very well behaved. Dogs on leads. Wheelchair access. Car park.
> Cards: Electron, Maestro, MasterCard, Solo, Switch, Visa.

WEST CHILTINGTON

Elephant & Castle
Tel: 01798 813307
Church Street, West Chiltington, W. Sussex RH20 2JW
King & Barnes. Charles Hollingworth, AMBII, Sue Gauntlett, tenants.

A pub with its own golfing society – there aren't many of those. It's a 16th-century building behind the church, popular and friendly. Bar snacks include ploughman's, sandwiches, filled baked potatoes and quite a choice of main dishes: liver and bacon, steaks, grilled trout, gammon, salmon and steak and kidney pie, as well as daily specials. Amid the conventional English fare you will find a few South African dishes. The King & Barnes range of beers: Festive, Sussex and all seasonal ales. Wonderful views from the large garden, which has swings and slides for children, large ponds with koi carp and ornamental ducks, also an aviary with exotic birds and tame owls.

> OPEN: 11–5. 6–11 Mon–Thurs. 11–11 Fri & Sat. 12–10.30 Sun.
> Real Ale.
> Children welcome. Dogs on leads. Wheelchair access.

WINEHAM

Royal Oak
Tel: 01444 881252
Wineham Lane, Wineham, Nr Henfield, W. Sussex BN5 9AY
Punch Taverns. Tim Peacock, tenant.

Delightfully unchanging, a well-cared-for family pub: attractive, part-timbered, part tile-hung, 14th-century, with low beams, a huge inglenook fireplace and a cosy back snug. Food is limited to a good range of freshly made sandwiches, plain or toasted, ploughman's and home-made soups in winter. Ales straight from the cask in the still room –

Wadworths 6X and Harveys BB. Tables on the lawn at the front of the pub next to the old well.

OPEN: 11–2.30. 5.30–11 (6–11 Sat).
Real Ale.
Children in family room. Dogs on leads. Wheelchair access.

BEST OF THE REST

ALCISTON

Rose Cottage   Tel: 01323 870377
Utterly delightful. All a village inn should be; full of village life, past and present, quite a lot of it attached to the walls! Way above average bar snacks and changing specials on the blackboard. Locally caught fish, locally grown vegetables and very local eggs – their own. The menu could feature lamb cooked in red wine, rosemary and garlic, pork in cider or Thai-style curries. Harveys Best and Rother Valley Best, good wines, some by the glass, and proper cider.

BURWASH

The Bell   Tel: 01435 882304
A village of mainly 16th- and 17th-century houses. Opposite the church, this is a popular pub looking its flowery best in the summer. They serve reliable bar food; there is something for everyone on the menu from sandwiches to steak in a peppercorn sauce. Local Arundel, Batemans and Harveys as well as Greene King IPA beers.

COULTERSHAW BRIDGE Nr Petworth

Badgers   Tel: 01798 342651
The emphasis tends more towards eating than drinking; you can still join a local or two leaning on the bar but you would really be here to enjoy the food. Known for their imaginative bar snacks and restaurant menu. The dishes change all the time but from the bar there could be pasta with scallops, prawns and basil, tapas or a shellfish stew. Badger and Theakstons Best beers and a good list of wines.

HENLEY

Duke of Cumberland Arms   Tel: 01428 652280
North of Midhurst, this is a small, charming country pub in a fascinating garden. Inside are two beamed rooms where they serve very desirable food and some extremely fresh fish. Gales, Ballards, Hopback and Adnams ales from the cask; farm ciders.

KIRDFORD

Half Moon   Tel: 01403 820223
Another pretty Sussex village with an attractive pub. This one is a little special – if you like fish, that is. Known for its fish: lots of different fish, wonderfully cooked, whatever is

in season could be on the menu. Other delights too, for the non-fish-lovers among you. Local beers too: Arundel, Ballards, King & Barnes as well as Greene King Abbot; wine to go with the fish and local cider.

RYE

Ypres Castle
Tel: 01797 223248

High in Rye; well, Rye is on a hill and so is the pub, with views over the muddy River Rother out to sea. A very straightforward town pub with some interesting dishes on the menu. Delicious ways with fish, much of it local, and some very local lamb. Daily specials too, such as grilled sardines or chicken in a white-wine sauce. Badger Tanglefoot, Harveys Best, Charles Wells and Youngs beers; wines by the bottle and glass, also proper cider.

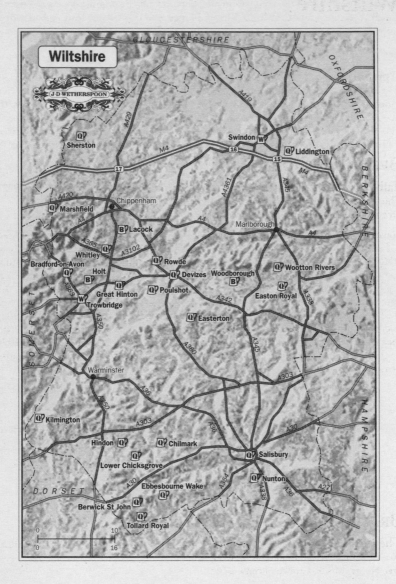

Wiltshire

J·D·WETHERSPOON

GLOUCESTERSHIRE

OXFORDSHIRE

BERKSHIRE

HAMPSHIRE

SOMERSET

DORSET

Sherston

Swindon
Liddington

Marshfield
Chippenham
Lacock
Marlborough

Whitley
Rowde
Bradford-on-Avon
Holt
Devizes
Woodborough
Wootton Rivers
Great Hinton
Poulshot
Easton Royal
Trowbridge
Easterton

Warminster

Kilmington

Hindon
Chilmark
Lower Chicksgrove
Salisbury
Ebbesbourne Wake
Nunton
Berwick St John
Tollard Royal

0   10
0   16

Wiltshire

BERWICK ST JOHN

Talbot Inn
The Cross, Berwick St John, Shaftesbury, Dorset SP7 0HA
Free House. Chris & June Eason, licensees.

Tel: 01717 028222

You can't really blame the post office for confusing addresses as, for efficiency, they need to keep you close to the nearest sorting office. Having said that, the Talbot is firmly in Wiltshire – well, 3 or 4 miles from the county boundary – so I reckon that's pretty firm. Just one big bar in this old village pub, with a big inglenook fireplace – always a roaring fire in winter – and separate dining room. Most of the food is home-made; the excellent steaks come from the local butcher. They also do beef and chicken curries, steak and kidney pie, soups, ploughman's, home-made treacle tart, bread-and-butter pudding, apple and blackberry pie or crumble, or spotted dick – good, comforting puds. Bass and Wadworths 6X, guest beers and a local cider. Good selection of wine available by the bottle, carafe or glass; mulled wine in winter. Tables in the garden. Good walks nearby.

> OPEN: 12–2.30. 6.30–11 (12–4 Sun). Closed Mon (except Bank Holidays) and Sun eves.
> Real Ale.
> Children, with adult, in eating area at lunchtime. Well-behaved dogs on leads in main bar.
> Cards: Access, Amex, MasterCard, Switch, Visa.

BRADFORD-ON-AVON

The Beehive
263 Trowbridge Road, Bradford-on-Avon, Wilts
Free House. Mrs C. Crocker, licensee.

Tel: 01225 863620

Most pubs have a past, but not many have a past like this one. Originally called Mrs Kelly's – obviously a woman who could see an opportunity for profit – this building was formerly a brothel frequented by the navvies working on the Kennet and Avon canal.

Its salubrious past forgotten, it's now a lively, bustling pub on the nearby Widbrook bridge, which crosses the canal less than a mile from Bradford-on-Avon. Interestingly, the canal was the fallback line in the event of an invasion during the Second World War. The pub is ideal for those sailing the canal, towpath walkers and anyone else wanting a warm and friendly place with no muzak, no TV and no gaming machines. The Beehive has just one room with a bar, scrubbed wooden tables, chairs to match, a settle and real log fires in the stone fireplace; if you're so inclined, you can sponsor a log – no prize for the longest-lasting log, though that could be a new twist. The menu changes daily and most of the food is home-cooked; you can choose from filling winter soups served with crusty bread, the ever-popular traditional steak and kidney pie, cheese and onion pie, the Beehive's acclaimed cold beef and home-cooked hams, a selection of vegetarian dishes and for the really hungry, huge portions of sausages, egg and chips. Always Butcombe and a minimum of five well-kept real ales from a changing selection on hand pump or gravity-fed. A well-chosen list of reasonably priced wines and champagnes. On Wednesday evenings in the summer the boules team are practising their skills – you can join in too.

OPEN. 12–2.30. 7–11 (12–3. 7–10.30 Sun).
Real Ale. No food Mon and Sun eves.
Children welcome. Dogs on leads. Car park.

CHILMARK

Black Dog Inn
Tel: 01722 716344

Chilmark, Nr Salisbury, Wilts
Free House. Alaric Campbell Hill, licensee.

As well as being the name of the village, Chilmark is a cream-coloured stone quarried locally since Roman times and used to build Salisbury Cathedral. With three bars in the old Black Dog you're spoilt for choice: there is a restaurant in an old baronial hall, arm-chairs and magazines by the fire in the lounge bar, fossils in the second (no, not necessarily the locals!) and games in the third. Reasonably priced food on the blackboards; the usual snacks are on offer in the bar. In the restaurant the menu always features five or six fish specials – fishcakes are a speciality. Beers are revolving guests. Large garden. This is a delightful village full of stone-built 17th-century houses.

OPEN: 11–3. 6–11 (12–3. 7–10.30 Sun).
Real Ale.
Children welcome. Dogs too.

DEVIZES

Bear
Tel: 01380 722444

The Market Place, Devizes, Wilts SN10 1HS
Wadworths. W.K. Dickenson, tenant.

Sir Thomas Lawrence, the 18th-century portrait painter, lived here when his father ran this old coaching inn. But it had been in business for hundreds of years before that. The first mention of a licence for the Bear was in 1599, but that was just to renew the sign; it is much older than it looks. An attractive, dependable-looking old place, at its glorious best in summer – when wonderful flowery eyebrows bloom extravagantly over the bay windows and handsome pillared doorway. Inside it is as you would expect – beamed, panelled and pol-ished. Traditional bar food, plus hot sausage sandwiches, French-bread toasties, filled jacket potatoes, all-day breakfasts, omelettes, ordinary ploughman's and speciality-sausage plough-man's. Danish open sandwiches and daily specials too. A more extensive menu is served in the two restaurants, the Lawrence Room and Master Lambton restaurant. Wadworths ales, which are brewed locally, and a guest. Morning coffee. Tables in the courtyard.

OPEN: 10–11 (10–3. 7–10.30 Sun).
Real Ale. Restaurant (closed Sun eves).
Children in eating area. Dogs on leads. Wheelchair access into bar only.
Bedrooms.

EASTON ROYAL

Bruce Arms
Tel: 01672 810216

Easton Royal, Nr Pewsey, Wilts SN9 5LR
Free House. Jackie & John Butler, licensees.

Just off the Pewsey road, an old-fashioned country pub – charming and unspoilt. A new games room and skittle alley have been added but nothing else has altered much. Built in the 1840s, it still has a brick floor, old wooden benches and long tables – visually the same except for the central heating. None of the good things about the pub have been changed. Well-filled cheese and onion rolls and home-pickled eggs to go with the Fullers London Pride, Wadworth 6X and guest ale. Seats in the garden.

> OPEN: 11–2.30. 6–11 (12–3. 7–10.30 Sun).
> Real Ale.
> Children welcome, not in the bar. Dogs on leads.

EASTERTON

Royal Oak   Tel: 01380 812343
11 High Street, Easterton, Wilts SN10 4PE
Wadworths. C. Warren, licensee.

On the edge of Salisbury Plain – about 240 square miles of undulating chalk downland, most of it farmed, but some taken over by the military. The small and perfectly formed thatched Royal Oak, built in 1595, has only two rooms with five tables in each. Even so, it concentrates more on food than beer; the menu is seasonal and all the food is home-made: avocado, prawns and smoked salmon, goat's cheese and leek tart, duck breast with a blackberry sauce, salmon fishcakes with a lemon and caper dressing, and rack of lamb with rosemary and garlic crust and red-wine gravy are just a sample of what is on the menu. Wadworths range of beers and some guests. Seats in the small, gated front garden.

> OPEN: 11–3. 5.30–11 (12–3. 7–10 Sun).
> Real Ale.
> Children over five allowed. Dogs in public bar only.
> All disabled facilities. Car park.
> Cards: all major cards except Amex.

EBBESBOURNE WAKE

Horseshoe Inn   Tel: 01722 780474
Ebbesbourne Wake, Nr Salisbury, Wilts SP5 5JF
Free House. Anthony & Patricia Bath, licensees.

Always popular, the delightful Horseshoe Inn, tucked into a fold of the Wiltshire Downs, is covered in rambling honeysuckle and roses. Traditionally furnished, it has open fires and walls that are decorated with country artifacts. Good-value bar food – all 'cooked that day' – is listed on the blackboard: pies, quiches, pâtés, fresh fish, plus the stalwarts: sandwiches, ploughman's and a hot dish or two. On Sundays they serve a roast lunch. Adnams Broadside, Ringwood Best and Wadworths 6X from casks behind the bar, plus farm ciders and a choice of malt whiskies. Seats in the pretty, flowery garden overlook the Ebble Valley.

> OPEN: 12–3. 6.30–11.
> Real Ale. Restaurant. No meals/snacks Mon.
> Children in eating area of bar. No dogs. Bedrooms.

GREAT HINTON

The Linnet
Tel: 01380 870354

Great Hinton, Trowbridge, Wilts BA14 6BU
Wadworths. Jonathan Furby, landlord/chef.

East of Trowbridge, this cosy old village pub has been given a new lease of life. Outside there is a showy flower display; inside, a comfortable bar and a more formal dining area. They do a very reasonable two- or three-course lunch, or you could just dive into the menus and create your own delights: lots of different salads with a variety of dressings, warm smoked salmon and caper blini with a cucumber and dill relish, duck spring roll 'Thai style' on a mango salsa with a plum sauce, and to follow, grilled rib-eye steak with baked kidney and truffle pastry purse on a port and rosemary sauce, or medallions of monkfish on a prawn and lemon risotto with a saffron sauce. Wadworths range of ales and a full wine list.

OPEN: 12–2.30. 6–11.
Real Ale. No-smoking restaurant
Children welcome; dogs too. Wheelchair access. Car park.

HINDON

Grosvenor Arms
Tel: 01747 820696
Fax: 01747 820869

High Street, Hindon, Wilts SP3 6DJ
Free House. Penny Simpson, licensee.

If you are westward bound, you need only slip off the A303 at Chicklade and travel a short way to where delights await. At the crossroads in this quiet Wiltshire village, the Georgian Grosvenor Arms is a pub, restaurant and hotel rolled into one – three parts making one successful whole. The emphasis is on food, but the ethos of a pub isn't forgotten; it is still a popular meeting place for the locals who manage to find room to lean on the bar to enjoy a beer or a glass of wine – 14 by the glass – or warm themselves by the log fires. Bar snacks and meals are served in the bar and courtyard garden; there is also full restaurant service. The food is as fresh as fresh can be and all cooked to order. Fish arrives daily. The favourites are grilled Cornish plaice with a lemon and caper brown butter, deep-fried cod in beer batter, or a dressed crab salad in summer. Dishes range from the welcome favourites – sausage and mash with onion gravy – to breast of guinea fowl with creamed lentils, wild mushrooms and salsa verde, as well as delicious puds. The à la carte menu is interesting and creative; cheeses are from Neal's Yard. Beers are Bass, Wadworths 6X and Henry's IPA; the wine list is mainly French with a touch of the New World.

OPEN: 11–3. 6–11. Closed Sun eves.
Real Ale. Restaurant.
Children welcome. Car park. Ten en-suite bedrooms.
Cards: Amex, Delta, MasterCard, Switch, Visa.

HINDON

Lamb Inn   Tel: 01747 820573
Hindon, Salisbury, Wilts SP3 6DP
Youngs. Adrian Ricketts, licensee.

A handsome old building taking up a considerable corner site in this favoured village, it might look like a 17th-century old coaching inn, but the Lamb is considerably older than its Georgian frontage. Pre-dating the coaches, it served as a courthouse for the local assizes in the 15th century. A bit later on, the local smugglers – the very men that would have been sentenced here – were using it to divvy up the spoils. More law-abiding now, the big old beamed bar with its huge inglenook fireplace has plenty of room for you to enjoy a drink and sample the seasonally changing, well-chosen bar menu. Listed on the blackboard you could find leek and broccoli soup, smoked-trout salad, seafood and leek au gratin, sausage platter, leg of lamb steak, ploughman's, pâté and toast, and much more. There is a no-smoking restaurant with an evening table d'hôte menu. An à la carte menu is available at lunchtime. Now the Lamb has changed hands, all the ales are from the Youngs range. Picnic tables outside in an attractive courtyard.

> OPEN: 11–11 (12–10.30 Sun).
> Real Ale. Restaurant.
> Children welcome. Dogs on leads. Wheelchair access.
> Fourteen bedrooms.
> Cards: Amex, Delta, MasterCard, Switch, Visa.

KILMINGTON

Red Lion   Tel: 01985 844263
Kilmington, Warminster, Wilts BA12 6RP (on the B3092, 3 miles north of Mere (A303) and half a mile from Stourhead Gardens)
Free House. Chris Gibbs, FBII, licensee.

In a lovely part of Wiltshire, well-wooded, well-watered and prosperous, the Red Lion, near the gardens at Stourhead – one of the finest 18th-century landscapes in the country – is on the National Trust estate and is an ideal base for the good country walks that radiate from it. An unpretentious, creeper-covered old pub with cosy, appealing bars, winter log fires and simple but satisfying bar food, daily specials on the blackboard could include home-made soups, the Red Lion's home-cooked ham, plough-man's, filled baked potatoes, popular toasted sandwiches, game, chicken casserole, steak and kidney pie, shepherd's pie in the winter, maybe a creamy fish pie and a vegetarian dish or two. Butcombe Bitter and two changing guest beers. Farm ciders. Seats in the large garden.

> OPEN: 11.30–2.30. 6.30–11 (12–3. 7–10.30 Sun).
> Real Ale.
> Children in eating area until 9pm. Dogs on leads. Wheelchair access (not WC).
> Bedrooms.

LIDDINGTON

The Village Inn   Tel: 01793 790314
Bell Lane, Liddington, Swindon, Wilts SN4 0HE
Arkells Brewery Ltd. Peter & Jo Collins, licensees/managers.

Originally four cottages at the centre of the village, the pub is in two of them; the other
two are used for staff. Well cared for (and that includes the customers), it has an extensive blackboard menu with reasonably priced dishes ranging from home-made soup and
deep-fried crispy whitebait to steak and ale pie, roast loin of pork with apricot stuffing and
a mixed grill. Everything is prepared and cooked on the premises. They say there is no
quick move from the freezer to the microwave here. Sunday roasts – must book. All this
is washed down with Arkells Best Bitter, 3B, Kingsdown and guest ales. They have a
garden to sit in to enjoy the quiet (no bouncy castles) and country air.

> OPEN: 12–2.30. 6.30–11 (12–2.30. 7–10.30 Sun).
> Real Ale
> No children. No dogs. Prize-winning loos. All disabled facilities.
> Cards: all cards accepted.

LOWER CHICKSGROVE

Compasses Inn   Tel: 01722 714318
Lower Chicksgrove, Tisbury, Nr Salisbury, Wilts SP3 6NB
Free House. Jonathan Bold, licensee.

A village with a fine 12th-century church on a steep slope above the River Nadder, which
meanders along to join the young River Avon in Salisbury. The thatched and popular 14th-
century Compasses has plenty of room in the beamed main bar, where lots of country and
farming bits and pieces hang from the beams and walls. They offer a well-chosen, regularly
changing menu of home-cooked bar food, and a good selection of beers: Bass and Wadworths
6X, plus two guest beers. Seats in the garden and courtyard and there is a children's play area.

> OPEN: 12–3. 6–11. N.B. Closed Mon except Bank Holidays; closed the Tues fol-
> lowing a Bank Holiday Mon.
> Real Ale.
> Well-behaved children in certain areas. Dogs under the table on leads. Bedrooms.
> Cards: Delta, MasterCard, Solo, Switch, Visa.

MARSHFIELD

Catherine Wheel   Tel: 01225 892220
High Street, Marshfield, Wilts SN14 8LR
Free House. David Field, licensee.

Gentrified by the Georgians, who were as keen as the Victorians to hide period features
that were currently unfashionable, the original Elizabethan building was hidden

behind an 18th-century frontage. They couldn't leave the inside alone either, particularly the dining room, which reflects the Georgian period more than the Elizabethan. The beamed main bar, with its big fireplace, pine tables and country chairs, is friendly and welcoming. Traditional bar food, plus imaginative additions, fresh fish from Cornwall and daily specials, all freshly cooked to order. Wadworths 6X, Courage Best, Abbey's Bellringer, Brains Bitter, Scrumpy Jack and Dry Blackthorn ciders and a good wine list.

> OPEN: 11–3. 6–11. Closed Mon lunchtime except Bank Holidays.
> Real Ale. Restaurant. No meals Sun eves.
> Children in eating area until 8.30pm. Dogs on leads.
> Five en-suite bedrooms.

NUNTON

Radnor Arms   Tel: 01722 329722
Nunton, Nr Salisbury, Wilts SP5 4HS
Free House. Mr & Mrs Gelfs, licensees.

Creeper-covered and charming, as attractive inside as it is out. Inside the 17th-century pub are low-ceilinged, beamed bars and an eating area in what was the old shop. You'll find extensive, imaginative, home-cooked menus for both the bar and restaurant. Changing daily, the blackboard will have a good selection of fish: plaice, cod, haddock, salmon, squid, gravadlax, scallops or langoustines; there is also venison, game in season, rack of lamb or a curry. Badger Tanglefoot, Dorset Best and Guinness. A large wine list and a good selection of malt whiskies. The extensive garden at the back of the pub has plenty of tables and country views.

> OPEN: 11–3. 6–11.30.
> Real Ale.
> Children welcome. Dogs on leads. Wheelchair access. Large car park.

POULSHOT

Raven   Tel: 01380 828271
Poulshot, Nr Devizes, Wilts (take a left turn off the A361, Devizes to Seend road)
Wadworths. Susan & Philip Henshaw, tenants.

Opposite the village green, the Raven is small, well kept and full of charm, with beamed bars and a separate, no-smoking dining room. The menu is chosen with care and just that little bit more unusual. Everything that can be is made 'in pub'. The menu leans towards the European: risotto, stroganoff, tagliatelle, lamb in red wine, hotpot; a little something from everywhere including a home-made soup, salmon pâté, roasted red peppers stuffed with vegetable risotto served with a fresh tomato sauce, home-made spicy crab and prawn cakes served with lobster sauce, Normandy pork and beef Madras; daily specials too.

Exceptionally well-kept Wadworths ales served from the wood, a home brew and other guests. They have a large walled garden.

OPEN: 11–2.30. 6.30–11 (12–3. 7–10.30 Sun).
Real Ale.
Children in dining room only. Dogs on leads. Wheelchair access difficult but possible.

ROWDE Nr Devizes

George and Dragon
High Street, Rowde, Nr Devizes, Wilts SN10 2PN
Free House. Tim Withers, licensee.

Tel: 01380 723053
Fax: 01380 724738

Small car park, small garden, small pub and not many tables, so if you are thinking of doing any serious eating, you really must book. A very handsome interior and inventive cooking make this old place doubly appealing. The bar and restaurant menus at the small, beamed George and Dragon are one and the same, and just to emphasise how good it is, they have won awards for the standard of their cooking: Greek salad, oysters, provençale fish soup, mussel and oyster soup, smoked-salmon tart, crab pancakes, spicy chick-pea stew, chicken salad with pine nuts and raisins, lamb's kidneys with mushrooms and sherry vinegar; home-made puddings too – marmalade sponge pudding with a whisky sauce and custard should fill any remaining gap. They are 'big on fish' here; fish dishes on the blackboard are based on daily deliveries fresh from Newlyn, so there could be roast hake and aioli or monkfish with bacon served with a mustard and cream sauce. Well-kept beers too: Wadworths 6X and beers from Butcombe, Bunces, Hopback and Ashvine. A glass of wine or two, and port to finish.

OPEN: 12–3. 7–11. Closed Mon lunchtimes.
Real Ale. Restaurant. No food Sun or Mon.
Children welcome. Dogs on leads in bar.
Cards: Delta, MasterCard, Switch, Visa.

SALISBURY

Haunch of Venison
1 Minster Street, Salisbury, Wilts SP1 1TB
Courage. Arnaud Rochette, manager.

Tel: 01722 322024

Outside the Cathedral close, near the Poultry Cross and the 13th-century St Thomas's Church, this inn is one of the outstanding black-and-white buildings in Salisbury; it is really old – well, bits of it are – over 600 years old. Not only do they have their own 'Grey Lady' wandering the pub at night, there is also a gruesome reminder in the Haunch of Venison that it doesn't pay to cheat at cards. Next to the 600-year-old fireplace, which probably dates back to the pub's early days, is a mummified hand, discovered earlier this century, holding some 18th-century playing cards. It appears that someone got a little cross at the card table, though walling up a cheat seems a bit extreme. On a lighter note, the pub is as you would expect: heavily beamed, with timbered and panelled walls and open fires. Good choice of bar food: sandwiches (doorsteps), home-made soup, calves'-liver parfait with red-onion marmalade, pavé of venison with swede mash and red-wine sauce, and the very popular Haunch of Venison platter (venison sausage, potted venison, cobbler and black pudding with garnish and apple sauce) served with a free glass of wine or a pint of Courage Best – that should keep you quiet for a bit! Delicious puds too. Lunch and dinner menus are quite separate. Over 80 malt whiskies. Courage Best and Directors ales served from a pewter bar counter. Comprehensive wine list. A charming pub, not to be missed.

OPEN: 11–11.
Real Ale. Restaurant. No meals/snacks Sun eves Jan–March.
Children away from bar. Dogs on leads. Wheelchair access (not WC). Jazz evening every other Thursday.
Cards: all cards except Amex and Diners.

SHERSTON

Rattlebone Inn   Tel: 01666 840871
Church Street, Sherston, Wilts SN16 0LR
Youngs. Emma & John Williams, licensees.

There was, apparently, a John Rattlebone buried on this very spot – hence the name. On top of the bones you have this wonderful local, well known for the excellence of its food – the perfect combination. The 16th-century Rattlebone is an attractive, rambling place with something for everyone. Among the inspired dishes on the menu there could be home-made duck-liver and bacon terrine served with apricot and ginger chutney, or fresh tagliatelle with mushrooms, oregano, garlic and cream. For a main course, fresh salmon and prawn pancakes grilled topped with mature Cheddar cheese, slices of roast chicken breast with fresh sage, garlic and crème fraîche, roast leg of lamb with baby onions, white wine and apricots; and delicious home-made crumble, crème brûlée or fruit sorbet to finish. Proper coffee and cheese too. Smiles Best, Youngs Triple A, Special, Bitter and guests. Fruit wines, cider, lots of malt whiskies and decent wines. If you feel some exercise wouldn't go amiss, there are four boules pitches and a separate skittle alley. Small, pretty, flowery garden.

OPEN: 11–11 (12–10.30 Sun).
Real Ale. Restaurant.
Children in eating areas. Dogs in bar. Wheelchair access.
N.B. Jukebox in the public bar. Otherwise no music.

TOLLARD ROYAL

The King John Inn   Tel: 01725 516207
Tollard Royal, Nr Salisbury, Wilts SP5 5PS
Free House. Tim & Michelle Birks, licensees.

Cranborne Chase – the former royal forest – is an area of outstanding natural beauty. On the edge of the Chase, tucked away in a wooded hollow, is the King John, opened in the middle of the 19th century as a watering hole for the locals working at the Tollard Royal iron foundry – all very thirsty work. Still refreshing the locals and everyone else, this attractive, creeper-covered building is hung about with flowering baskets and surrounded by tubs of flowers in spring and summer. Inside you will find a good choice of food, all prepared from fresh ingredients. Wonderful cheeses for the ploughman's. Also a three-course evening menu. For Sunday lunch, roast leg of English lamb (local) with onion sauce and a choice of puds. Smiles Best, Fullers London Pride as well as two or three guest ales, usually from a local brewery, and wines by the glass. Lots of picnic tables outside.

OPEN: 12–2.30. 6–11.
Real Ale. Restaurant.
No children. Dogs welcome. Wheelchair access difficult. Car park. Bedrooms – all en suite.

WHITLEY

Pear Tree
Tel: 01225 709131
Top Lane, Whitley, Nr Melkesham, Wilts SN12 8HB
Free House. Martin & Debbie Still, licensees.

This has all the appearance of an appealing, stone-built 18th-century farmhouse, but whatever it might have been, the Pear Tree has become a very successful restaurant without forgetting it is still a pub. A tremendous amount of reorganising and redecoration has taken place and a conservatory has been built, but the old flagstones and open fireplace are where they should be and the bar is still there to lean on. The same menu is available throughout the pub; the style of cooking extends from smoked-haddock and butter-bean soup or deep-fried crispy-duck parcel with celeriac and pumpkin-seed salad to rib-eye steak with pan-fried button mushrooms and red onions cooked in red wine, Stilton and garlic butter, or seared tuna loin with sesame sautéed potatoes and coriander oil. That's not all: how about a dark-chocolate terrine with blackcurrant sorbet and pear purée to finish? Fine cheeses too, and all the bread is made in their own bakery. Wadworths 6X, the local Oakhill Best Bitter, and Gem and Barnstormer from Bath Ales. The comprehensive wine list has wines from local vineyards, ten by the glass. Delightful gardens for you to enjoy.

OPEN: 11–3. 6–11.30.
Real Ale. No-smoking restaurant.
Children welcome. Dogs, other than guide dogs, only in bar. Wheelchair access.
Car park.
Cards: Delta, MasterCard, Switch, Visa.

WOOTTON RIVERS

Royal Oak
Tel: 01672 810322
Wootton Rivers, Nr Marlborough, Wilts SN8 4NQ
Free House. John Jones, FBII, licensee.

The Newbury to Bath section of the Kennet and Avon canal, which passes through a lock at the lower end of the village, was finished in about 1810, which meant that the navigable waterway from Newbury to Bristol, started 1728, was at last complete. I'm telling you this just in case you decide you want to travel here by boat – you can float on by. Half-timbered and thatched, the Royal Oak is in a delightful village deep in the Wiltshire countryside, and near the canal. Inside you'll find a wealth of beams holding up the walls and ceilings, polished tables, flowers and a general feeling of wellbeing. Four different eating areas, so you can be sure you'll find somewhere to rest your plate. Freshly made sandwiches and several different ploughman's – even seasonal ones – available at lunchtime only. Otherwise you could order home-made soup, pan-fried sardines with tomato and basil sauce, prawn and quail-egg mayonnaise with lumpfish caviar, chicken-liver and brandy pâté, roast rack of English lamb, beef and Burgundy casserole, or roast chicken with leek and prune stuffing; lots of fish – lemon or Dover sole, sea bass, scallops, red mullet, salmon steaks; changing daily specials and lots of good puds. Whitbread Best, Wadworths 6X and guest ales. Comprehensive wine list. Small sitting-out area near the car park.

OPEN: 11–3.30. 6.30–11 (12–10.30 Sun).
Real Ale. Restaurant.
Children welcome. Dogs on leads. Car park. Bed and breakfast accommodation in adjoining house.
Cards: Access, Amex, Visa.
N.B. Jukebox in public bar.

BEST OF THE REST

HOLT

Tollgate Inn   Tel: 01225 782326
In Ham Green, a tiny place between Melksham and Bradford-on-Avon. Very interesting things going on in the food department in this sprawling old place. Cosily pubby in the bar with sofas and a big fire. The restaurant is upstairs. On both the bar and restaurant menu you'll experience some very good English cooking with an imaginative edge from a first-class chef. Weekly changing ales, maybe farm ciders and a short wine list, four by the glass. Note that they are closed on Monday.

LACOCK

George Inn   Tel: 01249 730263
There are many reasons to be in Lacock and one of them should be the George, a pub that has held a beer licence since the time of the Civil War. Full of beams, horizontal and vertical, a huge inglenook fireplace with a dog wheel which turned the roasting spit still in situ, and plenty of cosy corners. Traditional bar food includes a good choice of fish – salmon and seaweed roulade with a herb and pesto sauce, marlin steak with a creamy wine and Pernod sauce – as well as beef-fillet medallions pan fried in red wine, onions and garlic. Wadworths range of beers and wines from around the world.

WOODBOROUGH

Seven Stars
Tel: 01672 851325

A little bit of France in Wiltshire. The cooking has a definite Gallic influence – not surprisingly as the landlord is French. Good relaxed atmosphere where you can appreciate the imaginative cooking: French onion soup, boeuf bourguignon, filled baguettes. Mostly French wine on the list but they don't forget the beer. Usually something from Badger, Bunces, Wadworths 6X and a guest.

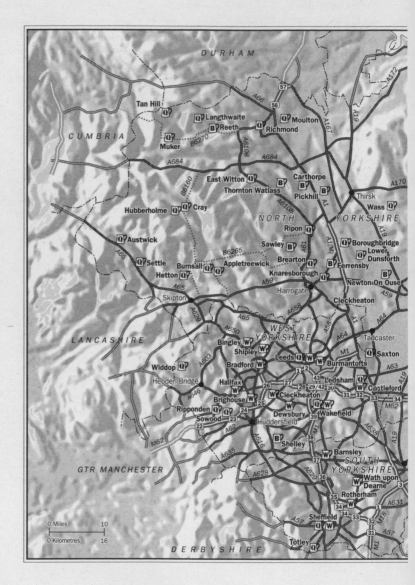

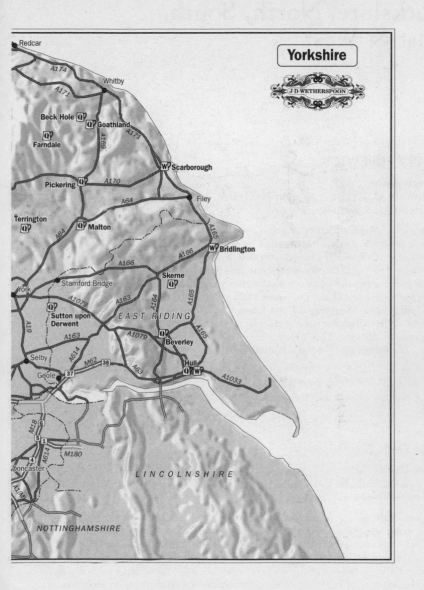

Yorkshire, North, South, East & West

APPLETREEWICK

Craven Arms   Tel: 01756 720270
Appletreewick, Nr Skipton, N. Yorks BD23 6DA
Free House. Linda Nicholson, licensee.

Between the Wharfdale valley and the moors, this village is as pretty as its name. The stone-built Craven Arms, a traditional Dales pub, is typically furnished, with cosy beamed rooms and winter fires. Popular with everyone, including walkers enjoying the high moorlands, steep valleys and fast-flowing streams in the wonderful North Yorkshire countryside. Ample portions of pub food: soups, sandwiches, ploughman's, Cumberland sausages with onion gravy, steak and kidney pie, lasagne, fish, vegetarian dishes and daily specials on the blackboard. Black Sheep Special and Bitter, Theakstons Best and a guest beer, lagers, stouts and ciders. Choice of wines and a selection of malt whiskies. Seats at the front of the pub to admire the view. This hillside village has some exceptionally fine buildings, such as the 17th-century Mockbeggar Hall and nearby Parcevall Hall with its terraced gardens.

> OPEN: 11.30–3. 6.30–11.
> Real Ale.
> Children welcome. No dogs. Wheelchair access (not WC).

AUSTWICK

Game Cock   Tel: 01524 251226
Austwick, Nr Settle, N. Yorks LA2 8BB
Thwaites. Richard Lord, tenant.

Overlooking the main street, the pub has a beamed, simply furnished, friendly bar, a separate dining room and a glassed-in terrace to shelter you from the prevailing wind. Amid the wildness of the Yorkshire dales, off the A65 about 8 miles from Settle, this is a favourite stopping place for walkers and villagers alike. All the food is made 'in pub'. As well as sandwiches and 'light bites' there could be rare fillet of beef marinated, sliced thinly and served on a bed of mixed leaves, or a black-pudding salad on French leaves with raspberry dressing, and for a main course, steak cooked slowly with mushrooms and an oyster sauce under a puff-pastry lid, or a slow-roasted lamb shoulder stuffed with garlic, rosemary, wild mushrooms and lemon served on a bed of onion mash, a chef's lasagne, vegetarian ratatouille or wild-mushroom risotto, and, last but not least, more-ish puddings. The changing specials board always has a few culinary surprises. Thwaites range of ales. There is a play area for children in the garden.

OPEN: 11.30–3. 6–11.
Real Ale. No-smoking restaurant.
Children in restaurant. No dogs.
Cards: all major cards except Amex.

BECK HOLE

Birch Hall Inn   Tel: 01947 896245
Beck Hole, Goathland, Whitby, N. Yorks YO22 5LE
Free House. Colin Jackson, licensee.

If you get here before opening time you can stock up on the other essentials of life, as the 17th-century Birch Hall Inn wears two hats: pub and village shop. Inside are two small bars, one of them with a serving hatch and an open fire. Between the two bars the shop sells sweets, ices and soft drinks; just what a village pub should be – all things to all people. They serve good sustaining food, local pork, turkey and ham pies, Beck Hole butties with generous fillings of ham, cheese, pâté or corned beef. Home-baked scones and their famous beer cake for tea. Theakstons Black Bull Bitter, Black Sheep, local beers and guests – all from the cask. Family room and seats in the garden. A delightful hamlet in a natural wooded valley in a lovely part of Yorkshire. Good walking country.

OPEN: 11–11 May–end Aug. 11–3. 7.30–10.30 winter. Closed Mon eves in winter.
Real Ale.
Children in small bar and garden. Dogs on leads.

BEVERLEY

White Horse Inn   Tel: 01482 861973
22 Hengate, Beverley, N. Yorks
Samuel Smiths. Philip Elliott, manager.

During the 15th century, Beverley was a completely walled town with five medieval gates. Only one – the brick-built North Gate – remains at North Bar. On the corner of North Bar Within and Hengate you'll find the 14th-century church of St Mary's, and having found that landmark, you'll find the White Horse Inn nearby. Full of market squares, old alleyways and courts, this handsome town has changed little over the years; the same can be said of the White Horse Inn. Known as 'Nellies' – after a redoubtable landlady – the pub has a timeless quality which is much appreciated (the gas lighting here is original). Reasonably priced traditional bar food, improving all the time, plus a roast on Sundays. There is a no-smoking room behind the bar. Sam Smiths ales; no guest beer.

OPEN: 11–11 (12–10.30 Sun).
Real Ale. Lunchtime meals and snacks (not Mon).
Children welcome (not in main bar). Dogs on leads.

BOROUGHBRIDGE

Black Bull
Tel: 01423 322413

6 St James' Square, Boroughbridge, N. Yorks YO51 9AR
Free House. Tony Burgess, licensee.

This is a significant historical area. Nearby are ancient monoliths; obvious signs of Roman occupation; Edward II fought a battle here in 1322; and, in a local hotel, rebel earls met in 1569, plotting to depose Elizabeth I and put Mary Queen of Scots on the throne of England. At the black-and-white 13th-century Black Bull, in the centre of town, they kept their heads down and led a quieter life. Inside this listed building are a number of comfortable beamed bars and a popular restaurant serving good, interesting food. From the bar menu you could choose crab and salmon fishcakes with a lemon-butter sauce, strips of chicken and pasta tossed with smoked bacon and mushrooms in a tomato, herb and red-wine sauce, home-made pork and sage sausages with creamy mashed potato; fresh seafood and seasonal specials are on the blackboard; freshly filled sandwiches are available at lunchtime only. There is an à la carte menu in the restaurant. Ales – all on hand pump – are John Smiths, Black Sheep and one guest; over 50 wines on the list, ten of them by the glass.

> OPEN: 11–11 (12–10.30 Sun).
> Real Ale. Restaurant – classical music in here.
> Children in eating area. No dogs. Bedrooms in the modern bit.

BREARTON

Malt Shovel
Tel: 01423 862929

Brearton, Harrogate, N. Yorks HG3 3BX
Free House. Les & Charlotte Mitchell, licensees.

Ignore the address, as you're really nearer Ripley, on a road off the B6165. If the road peters out and you suddenly find yourself on the moor, you know you've missed it – but you were going in the right direction! An unspoilt 16th-century, family-run pub serving really good food in a small North Yorkshire village, it's cosy, heavily beamed, with panelled rooms and good winter fires. The Malt Shovel is a popular meeting place with a reputation for well-chosen, well-cooked food, with the attention to detail that lifts it above the ordinary. Daily changing blackboard menus could include the current favourites of liver, bacon and black pudding with mash and red-wine gravy and a warm chicken salad – chargrilled breast of chicken on a bed of mixed leaves with a warm potato and chorizo salad in a lemon and caper dressing, also seared tuna steak, lamb shanks braised in white wine with garlic and mint, and a seafood gratin. For vegetarians, Cajun bean casserole or wild-mushroom stroganoff. Very good sandwiches. A third of the menu will be meat dishes, a third fish and the rest vegetarian – something for everyone. All the puddings – seven or so – are home-made. Three regular beers, Theakstons Bitter, Daleside Nightjar, Black Sheep Bitter, two others from a microbrewery – Durham Magus, Roosters Special or Rudgate Battleaxe. Interesting wine list and wines by the glass. Farm ciders. Seats on the terrace at the back of the pub.

> OPEN: 12–3. 6.45–11 (6.45–10.30 Sun). Closed Mon.
> Real Ale. No food Sun eves.
> Children welcome. Dogs on leads. Wheelchair access (not WC).

BURNSALL

Red Lion

Burnsall, Skipton, N. Yorks BD23 6BU
Free House. Elizabeth Grayshon, licensee.

Tel: 01756 720204
Fax: 01756 720292

Once a ferryman's inn on the banks of the River Wharfe, the Red Lion has a panelled main bar, a no-smoking lounge bar where they serve good, interesting bar food and a more formal restaurant. You could find queen scallops baked in garlic butter, Gruyère cheese and bread-crumbs, carpaccio of beef, Parmesan biscuit, rocket and olive oil, salmon and coriander fishcake with spiced mango chutney, and for a main course, calves' liver, pan-fried blue-cheese dumplings, sautéed spinach and mashed potato, or 'posh' pigeon pie – breast of woodpigeon, smoked bacon, wild mushrooms in a puff-pastry case; lots of other goodies to choose from. Soups and lunchtime sandwiches, locally smoked chicken, fresh Irish oysters, local cheese for the ploughman's, gammon with free-range eggs. All the food is freshly prepared and nearly all the meat – beef, lamb and pork – is local, some raised by the family, the rest from farms across the river; this is a place that believes in supporting local farmers (we hope they are still in business to support). Theakstons Best, Black Bull, Old Peculier, Morlands Old Speckled Hen, Black Sheep and a guest beer. At least 12 wines by the glass, a further 90 bins by the bottle. Choice of malt whiskies. Seats outside at the front and at the back of the pub.

> OPEN: 11.30–11 (12–10.30 Sun).
> Real Ale. Restaurant.
> Children welcome. Dogs on leads (no dogs in hotel rooms). Wheelchair access.
> Bedrooms.
> Cards: all credit cards accepted.

CRAY

White Lion

Cray, Buckden, Upper Wharfdale, N. Yorks BD23 5JB
Free House. Kevin Roe, licensee.

Tel: 01756 760262

You can't get much more 'upper' than this, as the White Lion, an old drovers' pub at the foot of Buckden Pike, is the highest pub in Wharfdale. A welcoming, traditional Dales pub in won-derful country between Wharfdale and Bishopdale in the Yorkshire Dales National Park. An excellent place to stop and refresh the parts your walking boots have tired out..Flagstone floors, beams, an open fire and filling home-cooked meals including soups, chicken-liver pâté with toast and salad garnish, warm fillet of mackerel with a lime mayonnaise and salad, home-made steak and mushroom pie in rich beer gravy, or pork Madeira – chunks of pork cooked in a Madeira and paprika sauce; also filled Yorkshire puddings and jacket potatoes, sandwiches, a children's menu, vegetarian dishes and puddings on the blackboard. Moorhouses Pendle Witches Brew, Premier, Black Sheep, Timothy Taylors, Roosters and guest beers. Seats on the sunny terrace at the front of the pub overlook the beck on the other side of the road.

> OPEN: 11–11 (12–10.30 Sun). Closed Christmas Day.
> Real Ale.
> Children in specific areas. Dogs on leads. En-suite bedrooms.
> Cards: Delta, MasterCard, Switch, Visa.

EAST WITTON

Blue Lion   Tel: 01969 624273
East Witton, Nr Leyburn, N. Yorks DL8 4SN   Fax: 01969 624189
Free House. Paul Klein, lease.

Looking much as it did when it was built at the end of the 18th century in one of the most beautiful wooded areas of the Yorkshire Dales, this old stone coaching inn is in a delightful Wensleydale village. Extensively renovated without losing an ounce of its charm, it has two bars full of interesting bits and pieces, comfortable chairs, high backed settles and big log-filled fireplaces. The home-made bar food is seriously good: provençale fish soup with garlic crostini, Caesar salad with pancetta and chargrilled chicken, an onion and blue Wensleydale tart with tomato chutney, cassoulet of pork rib, duck, Toulouse sausage and pancetta served with mashed potato, coq au vin with creamed potatoes and sautéed escalope of guinea fowl with a tomato and spinach compote are just a few of the dishes on the menu; lots more to choose from, all with a dash of imagination, and a vegetarian menu too. The à la carte menu goes up a notch in the elegant candle-lit restaurant. Theakstons Best, Black Sheep Bitter and John Smiths on hand pump. There is an extensive wine list including half-bottles – some by the glass – and old English liqueurs. Seats outside the front of the pub and in the big attractive garden at the rear.

> OPEN: 11–11.
> Real Ale. Restaurant (closed Sun eve).
> Children welcome. Dogs on leads. Disabled facilities.
> Car park. Bedrooms.
> Cards: MasterCard, Switch, Visa.

EAST WITTON

Cover Bridge Inn   Tel: 01969 623250
East Witton, Nr Leyburn, N. Yorks DL8 4SQ
Free House. Mr & Mrs N. Harrington, licensees.

Little changed over the years – well, you know what I mean, of course it has changed, but it hasn't been ruined – so it still has that certain atmosphere. Things have inevitably moved on, as this inn was flourishing when Henry VIII's troops destroyed Jervaulx Abbey, so we know it pre-dates 1536. Within easy reach of Ripon and Harrogate, the historic Jervaulx Abbey, remains of the castles at Richmond, Middleham and Bolton, racing, fishing, golf – there are lots of things to keep you out of mischief and bring you here to stay. As the name suggests, you are next to the bridge over the River Cover. When you get inside – and one of our readers says that 'getting past the door handle is quite a challenge'! – you'll find a well-beamed bar, a large log fire and wooden settles to settle in. A range of home-made snacks and meals are available in both the bar and the dining room: traditional ham and eggs, home-made steak pie, chicken, ham and mushroom pie, lasagne or a mixed grill are the favourites. If you're a vegetarian, leek and Gruyère crown, Indian balti or cannelloni are top of the list, washed down with Theakstons, John Smiths, Black Sheep and Timothy Taylors Best Bitters. Lots of room in the beer garden so you can watch the river flow by. Walks along the river and to Jervaulx Abbey.

> OPEN: 11–11.
> Real Ale. Restaurant.
> Children welcome. Dogs too. Wheelchair access (not WC). Car park. Three en-suite bedrooms. Day fishing permits can be obtained at the inn.

FARNDALE

Feversham Arms   Tel: 01751 433206
Church Houses, Farndale, N. Yorks (near Kirkby Moorside)
Free House. Fran Debenham, licensee.

The River Dove runs through Farndale, and in April the riverside path along the upper reaches of the river will take you to what is thought to be the inspiration behind 'the host of golden daffodils' in Wordsworth's poem, as the banks are carpeted with wild miniature daffodils. The Feversham Arms, a delightful, beautifully kept old pub, serves food in the bar and has an à la carte menu in the restaurant – a handsome converted old barn. Hearty appetites are a necessity as the portions are very generous in both the restaurant and the bar. One of the specialities in the restaurant is the fillet of pork en croute stuffed with garlic and shallots, also the tournedos Rossini. Sunday lunches (must book). Full Yorkshire breakfast if you stay. Tetleys ales, also stouts and lagers. Seats in the garden. The path along the loveliest section of the River Dove runs for 1½ miles between Church Houses and Low Mill.

> OPEN: 11–3. 5.30–11 summer. 12–2.30. 7–11 winter.
> Closed Mon Jan–March.
> Real Ale. Restaurant.
> Children welcome. Dogs on leads. Disabled facilities. Bedrooms.
> Cards: all credit cards accepted.

GOATHLAND

Mallyan Spout Hotel   Tel: 01947 896206
Goathland, Whitby, N. Yorks YO22 5AN
Free House. Judith Heslop, licensee.

If you're a fan of the TV series *Heartbeat*, you might like to know that the cast hangs out here. More of a hotel than a pub, but you don't quibble about that when you're out in the wilds of North Yorkshire. Named after the waterfall, this ivy-covered hotel is on a pretty village green where the local sheep (we hope there are some left), are very efficient lawnmowers. Inside are three lounges, which overlook the garden, a comfortable bar serving well-kept ales and a very attractive restaurant. Bar food includes home-made soups, pâtés, home-made chutneys with the ploughman's, their own hand-raised pork and chicken pie, local salmon trout (in season) and fresh fish from Whitby which could be monkfish, sea bream, turbot, brill, prawns or mussels; also daily specials. They host special gourmet weekends. Theakstons Best, local

Malton Best Bitter, Black Dog Scallywag and Black Dog Bitter are the beers, and they have an extensive wine list and choice of malt whiskies. The Coach House shop sells Mallyan Spout chutneys, pickles, jams, home-cured ham and beef, lots of other goodies and Christmas puddings. Starting at the hotel, a 20-minute walk down a steep track will bring you to the Mallyan Spout, a 70-foot waterfall over a mossy cliff into the Esk valley below. Not far away, a lane leads to Beck Hole. This is a wonderful area for walks.

> OPEN: 11–11.
> Daily bar snacks 12–2. 6.30–9. Evening restaurant. Lunch in restaurant only on Sunday. Afternoon teas.
> Real Ale.
> Children welcome until 8.30pm. Dogs on leads. Disabled facilities. Bedrooms.

HETTON

Angel Inn
Hetton, Nr Skipton, N. Yorks BD23 6LT
Free House. Denis Watkins, licensee.

Tel: 01756 730263
Fax: 01756 730363

This is one of those very special places where you can combine the conviviality of a well-run pub with the appreciation of really good food. The Angel has a reputation as a well-known dining pub, though you can definitely still get a pint and sandwich – sandwiches that are something else entirely! You can eat in the informal bar brasserie, or in the elegant restaurant, which has a greater choice of dishes on its fixed-price menu. Food here is not just sustaining, it's an experience: seafood filo parcels in a lobster sauce, crab spring rolls with sauce vierge, grilled chicken sandwich with pancetta, pappardelle with mixed wild mushrooms, chargrilled Yorkshire lamb steak and roasted breast of guinea fowl with pomme purée, forestiere sauce, button onions, bacon lardons and wild mushrooms are some of the delights on the menu. Yummy puds and advice on which dessert wine to drink with them. Special gourmet evenings are organised throughout the year. Black Sheep, Timothy Taylors Landlord and Tetleys beer. Quite an impressive wine list, over 20 by the glass, a couple of champagnes for when you want to celebrate and a choice of malt whiskies. There is a no-smoking snug and seats outside on the terrace.

> OPEN: 12–2.30. 6–10.30 (6–11 Sat).
> Real Ale. Restaurant (closed Sun eves).
> Well-behaved children welcome. Dogs outside only. Wheelchair access (not WC).
> Car park.
> Cards: Amex, MasterCard, Switch, Visa.

HUBBERHOLME

George Inn
Kirk Gill, Hubberholme, Nr Skipton, N. Yorks BD23 5JE
Free House. Terry & Jenny Brown, licensees.

Tel: 01756 760223

Many pubs have had a previous existence, some racier than others, but the George, once owned by the church, has, as far as we know, had a blameless past – although you might like to know that the hamlet of Hubberholme takes its name from a marauding Viking king: Hubba the Beserker! The George, on the banks of the River Wharfe and virtually on the Dales Way, is a solid stone building ready to withstand all the weather this part of the world can throw at it. It's in the right place to sustain the traveller and, understandably, a favourite with the big-boot and hairy-sock brigade – i.e. very keen walkers – and anyone with an appreciation for good, sustaining pub food. In the traditional beamed, stone-walled bars they serve soup, filled rolls, ploughman's, substantial steak and ale pies, chicken, leek and ham pie, fish lasagne, filled Yorkshire puddings, vegetable terrine, fillet of cod, steaks and daily specials. More specials and vegetarian dishes are available during the evening. The breakfast room is no smoking. Tetleys Bitter, Black Sheep Bitter and Special. Twenty malt whiskies and a choice of nearly 40 wines. Seats outside for the view and for gazing at the river.

OPEN: 11.30–3. 6–11 (11–3. 6–11 Sat).
Real Alc.
Children in eating area. Dogs on leads. Wheelchair access (not WC). Car park.
Seven letting rooms.
Cards: MasterCard, Solo, Switch, Visa.

HULL

Ye Olde White Harte
Tel: 01482 326363
25 Silver Street, Hull, E. Yorks HU1 1JG
Free House. Mr B. & Mrs J. Cottingham, licensees.

This 16th-century building has played an important part in the history of Hull. In an alley off Silver Street, in what remains of the medieval sea port of Hull founded in the 12th century by the Cistercian monks of Meaux Abbey, Ye Olde White Harte – not to be confused with Ye Moderne White Hart not far away – is genuinely ye olde, with the beams, panelling, two huge sit-in fireplaces and all the architectural features you would expect of a building that has been here for over 400 years. Here in 'Ye Plotting Parlour', now part of the restaurant, the decision was made by the then Governor of Hull, Sir John Hotham, to lock the gates of the City against Charles I. Not that it did him much good – he was beheaded by the Parliamentarians soon afterwards. Almost destroyed by fire in the 19th century, this exceptional old building has outlived the owner of the mysterious skull it houses and which has been passed down through the generations. Very busy during weekday lunchtimes. The bar food includes all the traditional dishes: sandwiches, pâté, pies, salads, chicken and ham pie, beef-in-ale pie, plus regularly changing specials and Ye Olde White Harte's special mixed grill. An excellent Sunday lunch – all the normal roasts, an à la carte menu and jam roly-poly or bread-and-butter pudding for afters. The dining area is up a fine old staircase. McEwans 80/–, Theakstons XB and Old Peculier and Courage Directors, plus a weekly changing guest beer. Selection of malt whiskies. There is a local ghost walk that the pub is involved in, and it also organises murder mystery evenings for large parties.

> OPEN: 11–11.
> Real Ale. Lunchtime restaurant.
> Children in room upstairs to eat (not in bar). No dogs. Disabled facilities.

KNARESBOROUGH
Blind Jacks   Tel: 01423 869148
19 Market Place, Knaresborough, N. Yorks HG5 8AL
North Bay Ltd. David Llewellyn, manager/licensee.

You would only come here for the atmosphere and the beer – there's not a crumb to be had. Blind Jacks, a fairly new creation wrapped in an 18th-century building, is at the heart of this market town full of Georgian buildings, steep steps and alleyways leading down to the River Nidd. Close to the Market Place are the ruins of the 14th-century castle, partly demolished by the Roundheads in the Civil War. The 'new' Georgian Blind Jacks was named after a John Metcalfe who was blinded by smallpox at the age of six and grew up to be a famous local road builder. A charming, friendly place serving a good selection of unusual beers including the Village Brewer White Boar Bitter and Dalesides Green Grass as well as Timothy Taylors Landlord and Black Sheep Bitter. Gales fruit wines and four changing guest ales, but alas, no food.

> OPEN: 5.30–11 Mon. 4–11 Tues–Thurs. 12–11 Fri & Sat. 12–10.30 Sun.
> Real Ale. No food.
> Children welcome. Dogs on leads.

LANGTHWAITE
Red Lion   Tel: 01748 884218
Langthwaite, Arkengarthdale, Richmond, N. Yorks DL11 6RE
Free House. Mrs Rowena Hutchinson, FBII, licensee.

There is clearly something very special about the Red Lion. It is another one of our film stars, and not just once – repeat performances go on here. The cosy beamed bar has been the location for many TV and film scenes; signed photos of the talented and famous adorn the walls. So, not just a delightful pub, but also a pub with a very glamorous life. Famous it might be, but it is still as it should be: entirely unspoilt. Good, very reasonably priced, sustaining food to go with the beer; a selection of toasted sandwiches, but the beef casserole in beer and the lamb pie with salad are two of the most popular dishes on the menu. Black Sheep Bitter and Riggwelter on hand pump, also Worthington Smooth, John Smiths, Guinness, Tetleys Bitters, Bulmers Original cider, Carling lager. Still very much a local. An oasis in a desert.

> OPEN: 11–3. 7–11 (10.30 Sun for coffee, otherwise 12–3. 7–10.30).
> Real Ale.
> Children at lunchtime. No dogs. Wheelchair access (not WC).
> Cards: Delta, Solo, Switch, Visa (cashback available).

LEDSHAM

The Chequers Inn   Tel: 01977 683135
Claypit Lane, Ledsham, Nr South Milford, W. Yorks LS25 5LP (turn left where the A63 joins the A1)
Own Brew. Chris Wraith, licensee.

If you are thinking of coming to the Chequers on a Sunday – don't. It isn't open. This pub still has a six-day licence: a situation that you can blame on a little local difficulty in around 1836 when the Chequers was open on a Sunday. The story is that some well-tanked-up clay-pit worker shouted abuse at Sir Granville Wheeler as he returned home after church. That was it: he'd had enough, so he used his influence to create this quirky local licensing law. Since then it has closed on Sundays. Not to worry; they make up for it the rest of the week. A creeper-covered, well-kept village local with beams, a bit of panelling, log fires and a nice old-fashioned air. Familiar, reliable bar food: home-made soup, sandwiches, ploughman's, scrambled eggs and smoked salmon, home-baked hams, that sort of thing, plus several daily specials. This pub has plenty of time to brew its own beer and also serve Youngers Scotch, Theakstons Best and John Smiths. Outside is a flowery, two-level beer garden.

OPEN: 11–3. 5–11 (11–11 Sat). Closed Sun.
Real Ale. Restaurant.
Children in own room. Dogs welcome.

LEEDS

Whitelocks   Tel: 0113 245 3950
Turks Head Yard, off Briggate, Leeds LS1 6HB
Youngers. Toby Flint, manager.

The Industrial Revolution of the 19th century changed the face of Leeds – and Whitelocks – forever. The magnificent Victorianisation of Whitelocks makes you forget that the building is really very early Georgian, established in 1715. In an alley off the main shopping centre you'll see the Victorian lamps, hanging baskets, the seats and converted barrels – used as tables – where you can sit and enjoy a drink in fine weather, or, if you're really desperate, sit and wait for the doors to open. This is Victorian pub architecture at its best: stained-glass windows, fine mirrors, red banquettes, marble tiles on the bars and a panelled dining room at the back of the pub. Good choice of traditional bar food: sandwiches, pies, sausages, filled Yorkshire puddings, Scotch eggs, deep-fried whitebait, Yorkshire pudding with onion gravy, Whitelocks fish pie, farmhouse mixed grill, roast lamb, grilled gammon or beefsteak pie. Home-made roly-poly or fruit pie to finish. Wallow in nostalgia by reading the pre-War prices which are still etched on the mirrors. Theakstons Bitter and guests including Wychwood and John Smith ales. A selection of wines. Seats in the beer garden.

OPEN: 11–11.
Real Ale. Restaurant (not Sun eves).
No children. Guide dogs only. Wheelchair access.

LOWER DUNSFORTH

Angler Inn   Tel: 01423 322537
Lower Dunsforth, Ouseburn, N. Yorks YO26 9SA
Free House. Robert Chrystal, licensee.

There has been an inn on this site since the 13th century, and before this became the Angler, it was the Anchor. Rebuilt in 1920 to blend in with the rest of the village – which has had starring roles in the TV series *Frost* and *Heartbeat* – it is less than half a mile from the River Ouse. Years ago, when the bell rang in the bar, the landlord would switch from publican pulling pints to ferryman pulling people across the river on a cable and raft system. Today's landlord is happy that duty is in the past so he can concentrate on the wants of his customers. Robert Chrystal was head chef at the pub his mother owned at Boroughbridge before he took over the Angler Inn. Dishes are well prepared and varied, ranging from crevettes in white wine and garlic seasoned with coriander and black pepper and a ragout of button mushrooms flavoured with lardons of crispy bacon in a creamy garlic sauce served in a pastry casket to pasta tossed with black pepper, onions and button mushrooms in a tomato and herb sauce glazed with Brie and Parmesan and chargrilled sirloin topped with stir-fried vegetables flavoured in an oriental sauce accompanied by basmati rice, and a brandy-snap basket filled with fresh fruits on a lake of fruit coulis and fresh cream to finish; that should stop any hunger pangs. Lots of other dishes on the menus, daily specials too. Beers are John Smiths and Black Sheep, Guinness, John Smiths Smooth, lagers and Strongbow cider. Eight wines by the glass, 27 on the list; also a connoisseur's selection. There are picnic tables in the attractive garden.

> OPEN: 11–11 (12–10.30 Sun).
> Real Ale.
> Children welcome. Car park. Wheelchair access.
> Cards: all except Amex accepted.

MALTON

Crown Hotel (Suddaby's)   Tel: 01653 692038
Wheelgate, Malton, N. Yorks YO17 0HP
Free House. Neil Suddaby, licensee.

The market town of Malton grew up on the site of a Roman fort. Situated in the old part of town, the present Crown, the Georgian replacement for the original coaching inn, which sadly burnt down, has been in the same family for 120 years. Neil Suddaby is the fifth generation, his son will be the sixth. An old-fashioned place. Only sandwiches are served during the week, a full menu Saturdays. Food is served in either the bar or the conservatory – the menu gives you a choice of home-made soups, which could be carrot and coriander or fish chowder, home-made lasagne and lots of daily specials. The family are brewers too: they brew Malton Golden Chance, Double Chance, Pickwicks Porter, Auld Bob and Stone Trough Bitter. When the spirit takes them they produce some special brews. They also have John Smiths and some guest beers. Sounds as though you're spoilt for choice.

> OPEN: 11–11 (12–4. 7–10.30 Sun).
> Real Ale.
> Children welcome. Dogs on leads. Wheelchair access.
> Nine bedrooms.
> Cards: Access, MasterCard, Visa, etc.

MOULTON

Black Bull Inn
Moulton, Nr Richmond, N. Yorks DL10 6QJ
Free House. Audrey & Sarah Pagendam, licensees.

Tel: 01325 377289
Fax: 01325 377422

A very special place in a pretty village about a mile from Scotch Corner. Behind the cottagey front you'll find something for everyone: a bar (with a lovely log fire in winter) serving hot and cold snacks, a seafood restaurant which opens in the evenings – no booking necessary, a Pullman carriage from the *Brighton Belle* with just eight tables for two, one (the coupé) for four – booked for Fridays and Saturdays weeks in advance – and an à la carte menu. And for small parties there is a flowery conservatory complete with grapevine. All very impressive. On the menu are oysters, home-made soups, smoked-salmon pâté, seafood pancake thermidor, poached halibut on bok choi with chilli jam and soy dressing, and a peppered fillet steak with cream and wine sauce. You'll find an impressive, very reasonable – £15.50 – three-course menu. Lots more on offer in the restaurant, a quite wonderful selection of fish dishes and some well-chosen meat dishes. The evening menu is served in all the restaurants. Bookings essential except in the fish bar. Theakstons and John Smiths ales. Good choice of wines and sherries. Seats outside in the courtyard.

> OPEN: 12–2.30. 6–10.30 (11 Sat). Closed Sun eves.
> Restaurant. No meals at all Sun.
> No children under seven in restaurant. No dogs. Wheelchair access.
> Cards: Amex, Connect, MasterCard, Switch, Visa.

MUKER

Farmers Arms
Muker, Nr Richmond, N. Yorks DL11 6QG
Free House. Chris & Marjorie Bellwood, licensees.

Tel: 01748 886297

In the heart of Swaledale – convenient for walkers on the Pennine Way or those of you exploring the Yorkshire Dales – an unspoilt popular village pub, still with its flagstone floors, which means your walking boots are allowed in – with you inside! One big room, traditionally furnished with a welcoming fire. Excellent-value bar food lunchtime and evenings: soups, filled baps, baked potatoes, home-made steak pie, gammon and egg, other home-made dishes and a children's menu. John Smiths and Theakstons ales on hand pump.

> OPEN: 11–3. 6.30–11 (11–11 Sat). 7–11 winter eves.
> Real Ale.
> Children in eating area. Dogs on leads.
> Self-catering flat for two available all year.

PICKERING

White Swan Hotel
Tel: 01751 472288

Market Place, Pickering, N. Yorkshire YO18 7AA
Free House. Victor Buchanan, licensee.

Apart from the White Swan, there are lots of interesting things to see in this town. The Church of St Peter & St Paul has some fascinating medieval frescoes showing the death of King Edmund, and the ruined 12th-century castle was where Richard II was imprisoned after being deposed. Pickering, a delightful town at the southern edge of the North York Moors, has been in existence since Celtic times. The White Swan, a small, traditional hotel, originally a coaching inn, was reputedly at the centre of some energetic salt-smuggling between Pickering and Whitby. In the very heart of the town, the panelled bars in the White Swan are a popular meeting place. You'll find well-thought-out, traditional menus: home-potted shrimps, dressed Whitby crab with mayonnaise, Thai chicken curry, Yorkshire pork sausage with mash and onion gravy, 'posh' fish and chips with mushy peas and daily specials. Vegetarian dishes too. There is a set-price lunch menu in the elegant restaurant. Black Sheep Best Bitter and Nick Stafford's Stallion are the beers, plus a guest. Wines by the glass and a considerable wine list, mostly Bordeaux from the St Emilion region of France.

> OPEN: 11–3. 5.30–11 Tues–Fri. 11–11 Mon & Sat. 12–3. 7–10.30 Sun.
> Real Ale. Restaurant. You must book for Sunday lunch. They have an AA rosette for food.
> Children's room. Dogs on leads. Wheelchairs – one step from the street. Car park. Bedrooms.
> Cards: Amex, Delta, MasterCard, Switch, Visa.

RICHMOND

Black Lion Hotel
Tel: 01748 823121

Finkle Street, Richmond, N. Yorks DL10 4QB
Pubmaster. Nicola Buscall, tenant.

There is a big cobbled marketplace in this ancient market town with an imposing 18th-century obelisk at its centre. Tucked down a side street is the Black Lion Hotel, an old coaching inn with comfortable, heavily beamed bars, big fires, good familiar bar food and well-kept ales. The bar menu includes soups, pâté, ploughman's, salads, leek bake, steaks, quiche and roast of the day. As the restaurant has music, stay in the bars. Camerons Strong Arm, Flowers Original and Tetleys Imperial beers. Yorkshire wines and a choice of malt whiskies. The ruins of the Norman castle dominate the skyline above the town. From the top of the castle keep you have magnificent views over the Dales to the Vale of York. Good walks from the town along the banks of the River Swale.

> OPEN: 10.30–11.
> Real Ale. Restaurant – music in here.
> Children welcome. Dogs on leads in bar only.

RIPON

One Eyed Rat   Tel: 01765 607704
51 Allhallowgate, Ripon, N. Yorks HG4 1LQ
Free House. Les Moon, licensee.

Just a small pub devoted to beer in a row of terraced houses. Inside is a long room with two open fires and usually a few local characters guaranteed to give good verbal accounts of themselves, all enjoying either the well-kept beers – Timothy Taylors Landlord, Black Sheep Bitter and weekly changing guests – or the German draught beers. Outside, the large garden has an outdoor pool table – probably the only place they could put it! No food; crisps and nuts only.

> OPEN: 6–11 Mon–Wed. 12–3.30. 6–11 Thurs. 12–3.30. 5.30–11 Fri. 12–11 Sat.
> 12–3.30. 7–10.30 Sun.
> Children welcome, as are dogs. Wheelchair access.

RIPPONDEN

Old Bridge Inn   Tel: 01422 822595
Priest Lane, Ripponden, Nr Sowerby Bridge, W. Yorks HX6 4DF
Free House. Timothy Walker, licensee.

First search for the packhorse bridge; the inn, a fine 14th-century cruck-framed building, reputedly the oldest in Yorkshire, is next to it. Inside, in keeping with its great age, are antique tables, rush chairs and pictures, prints and interesting artifacts hung on the thick stone walls. During weekdays they do a reasonably priced buffet luncheon of home-made soup or fruit juice, rare roast beef, Virginia ham, home-made Scotch eggs, quiche, other goodies and salads; very popular – you simply must book if you want to sit and eat. Blackboard specials on weekday evenings and weekend lunchtimes. There is no food Saturday or Sunday evenings. Everything is excellent value for money. Beers are all from independent brewers: Black Sheep, Timothy Taylors and one weekly guest. Bottled beers include White Shield Worthington, others from around the world, and several imported lagers. Over 30 malt whiskies, six wines by the glass and a well-chosen wine list. Seats on a paved area at the front of the inn. High on the lonely moor, about 5 miles west of Ripponden off the A68 and beyond Batings reservoir is Blackstone Edge. Built about 1800 years ago, this is the best-preserved section of Roman road in Britain.

OPEN: 12–3. 5.30–11 (12–11 Sat. 12–10.30 Sun).
Real Ale.
Children in limited area. No dogs. Wheelchair access (not WC). Car park.
Cards: MasterCard, Switch, Visa.

SAXTON

Greyhound Inn   Tel: 01937 557202
Main Street, Saxton, N. Yorks LS24 9PY
Samuel Smiths. Mr & Mrs McCarthy, managers.

You are in a region that witnessed a momentous change in the history of the English people. Between Towton and Saxton, on 29 March 1461, the blood of our ancestors helped decide the fate of the English throne; the Lancastrians and Henry VI were on one side, the Duke of York, later Edward IV, and the Yorkists on the other. Blinded by a snowstorm, the Lancastrian army was destroyed and the history of England changed for all time. The Greyhound doesn't date back quite that far, but it is still an old-fashioned, tiny village pub, thought to be one of the smallest in England, and time has not changed it – nor should it. Not only the local inn, but also the post office (before opening times). Beer is still in casks and sandwiches have to be ordered during the week, although they're readily available at weekends; crisps and nuts too. The ale is Samuel Smiths Old Brewery Bitter. You can sit in the courtyard next to the church; very pretty when the roses are out.

OPEN: 12–3. 5.30–11 (11–11 Sat).
Real Ale.
Children in games room. Dogs in tap room only.

SETTLE

Royal Oak   Tel: 01729 822561
The Market Place, Settle, N. Yorks BD24 9ED
Whitbread. Stuart & Jan Rigby, tenants.

There are a handsome square, 18th- and 19th-century houses and lots of small courts and alleys in this old market town at the foot of the limestone cliffs that form the side of the Aire Gap – the only true gap through the Pennines. The 16th-century Royal Oak, a big, low, stone building, newly done-up, has plenty of space in the roomy bars, where you can enjoy home-made soups, sandwiches, baguettes, warm avocado and bacon salad, steak and kidney pie, fish and chips, Cumberland sausages, filled Yorkshire puddings, fish, vegetarian dishes and other traditional fare. Extensive chef's specials board. Full à la carte and table d'hôte menus are served in the restaurant. Children's menu available. Black Sheep,

Timothy Taylors Landlord and Best Bitter, plus one guest ale. Range of malt whiskies. N.B. Music is occasionally played in the restaurant.

OPEN: 11–11 (for coffee from 9am)
Real Ale. Restaurant.
Children welcome. Dogs on leads. Wheelchair access. Bedrooms.

SHEFFIELD

Fat Cat   Tel: 0114 249 4801
23 Alma Street, Sheffield S3 8SA
Own Brew. Steven Fearn, licensee.

Not only can you appreciate the beers on the premises, they have a takeaway service too. This is Sheffield's first real alehouse, where they started brewing their own Kelham Island beer in premises next door to the pub in 1990. So you will probably be here for the beer, as this place was a first and is still up there with the best. Very reasonably priced food; the full menu is available Monday to Friday evenings as well as every lunchtime – filling home-made soups, stews, pies and daily specials, plus a number of imaginative vegetarian dishes and usually one fish dish. Good English puddings – crumbles and pies with cream or custard. Ten draught ales always available: Timothy Taylors Landlord, three from Kelham Island and six guest beers. Draught Belgian beers are available together with Belgian fruit jenevers and draught cider. Country fruit wines and small barrels of Kelham Island Beer can be ordered in advance to take away. Seats in the courtyard at the back of the pub. The Fat Cat has been a CAMRA South Yorkshire Pub of the Year, so you know the beer is excellent.

OPEN: 12–3. 5.30–11 (12–3. 7–10.30 Sun).
Real Ale.
Children in beer garden and upstairs room. Half of the pub is no smoking. Dogs on leads. Wheelchair access.

SKERNE

The Eagle   Tel: 01377 252178
Wansford Road, Skerne, Driffield, E. Yorks YO25 9HS
Free House. R. Edmond, licensee.

The Eagle hasn't changed for years. It still has no bar, no music – hooray! – and no one-armed bandits. Small and unspoilt, this village pub has two small rooms with coal fires and a friendly landlord who delivers the drinks to your table. One beer – Cameron Bitter – kept in the cellar near the entrance. There is a garden.

OPEN: 7–11 weekdays. 12–3. 7–11 Sat. 12–3. 7–10.30 Sun.
Real Ale. No food.
No children. Car park.

Sowood

Dog & Partridge Inn   Tel: 01422 374249
Forest Hill Road, Sowood, Holywell Green, Nr Halifax, W. Yorks HX4 9LB
Free House. Frank Collins, licensee.

Very rural, known as 'Mabel's' after widow Mabel, who ran the pub, which she bought 46 years ago, until her death aged 95 in April 2001. Her son Frank, who helped her, is now the landlord. The original pub, which dated from 1600, was called The Upper Park; the present building dates from 1760 and the name was changed in 1880 by the then landlord. Used by shepherds moving their flocks from the Dales to Derbyshire via Marsden, it had no trouble accommodating them: then they had a barn and 25 acres, now only the barn and 2½ acres. A small, friendly place, it has a bar, lounge and 'best room'. Customers come from miles around, which is just as well as there are only six neighbours to enjoy the general bonhomie and the landlord's sense of humour! A popular walkers' pub, television companies like it too, and so will you. No food, just a crisp, nut and Timothy Taylors Landlord, Golden Best and Black Sheep Bitter. Come at the right time and you may see the ghost of a black sheepdog.

> OPEN: 7–11 (12–4. 7–10.30 Sun).
> Real Ale.
> Children welcome. No dogs, except guide dogs. Wheelchair access. Car park.

Sutton-upon-Derwent

St Vincent Arms   Tel: 01904 608349
Main Street, Sutton-upon-Derwent, N. Yorks YO4 5BN
Free House. Philip Hopwood, licensee.

This really is a family-run business: they all have a hand in making the old place run well. Lots of room in the comfortable panelled bar with an open fire, the main restaurant and a small no-smoking dining room. Just one menu for the bar and restaurant, but there are always a number of specials on the board, which could feature peppered steak, fillet steak with wild mushrooms, steak and kidney pie, half a chicken or scampi; freshly made sandwiches too. Always nine or ten beers on the go, among them John Smiths, Timothy Taylors Landlord, Fullers London Pride, Chiswick and ESB, Boddingtons and Exmoor Gold. Well-chosen wine list. Seats in the pleasant garden.

> OPEN: 11.30–3. 6–11 (12–3. 7–10.30 Sun).
> Real Ale. Restaurant.
> Children welcome. Dogs in garden only. Car park.

Tan Hill

Tan Hill Inn   Tel: 01833 628246
Tan Hill, Keld, Nr Richmond, N. Yorks BL11 6ED
Theakstons. Margaret Baines, licensee.

From Keld – the nearest civilisation – a minor moorland road brings you to England's highest inn. Grouse, sheep (we hope) and the Tan Hill Inn are 1732 feet above sea level –

up in the clouds. Cold and bracing in winter; just bracing in summer. It must be one of the few pubs to keep a fire burning all year. Isolated – 4 miles to the nearest neighbour, and 11 to the corner shop – it lies on what was once an important drovers' route, now just a lane next to a disused mine. However, what you lack in drovers, you gain in walkers; the Pennine Way passes the door, so many pairs of accompanied boots have gratefully found the shortest way across the flagstones to the welcoming bar. They have their own water and electricity supply, freezers full of food and parking for the snow plough that helps them through the year. No need for extra ice – even the beer barrels have been known to freeze! Hearty food from sandwiches to giant Yorkshire puddings filled with Tan Hill sausages and gravy. Theakstons XB, Best and Old Peculier. Hugely popular place in summer. In the depths of winter, the odd lonely traveller finds a very welcome refuge in its rarefied air. Hundreds of acres of moorland to get lost in.

OPEN: 11–11 (12–10.30 Sun).
Real Ale.
Children welcome. Dogs: yes-ish – you have to keep an eye on the resident Jack Russell. Seven en-suite bedrooms. You can get married here too.

TERRINGTON

Bay Horse Inn   Tel: 01653 648416
Terrington, N. Yorks YO6 4PP
Free House. Mike Wilson, licensee.

This is another of our TV stars, albeit some time ago. When *Brideshead Revisited* was being filmed – quite a bit of it at Castle Howard – they also featured this unpretentious village pub. So those of you who like to tread in the footsteps of the stars can tread this way too. The white-painted Bay Horse, a traditional inn not far from Castle Howard, lies west of Malton. They serve a traditional menu: home-made soup, filled baguettes, ploughman's, steak and kidney pie, vegetarian dishes, steaks and daily specials. Roast lunches on Sundays. Bass, Timothy Taylors Landlord and Black Sheep. About 100 malts and blended whiskies, and a garden to sit in.

OPEN: 12–3. 6.30–11.
Real Ale. Restaurant.
Children welcome. Dogs: maybe – if they like the look of them.
Disabled facilities. Car park.

TOTLEY

Crown Inn   Tel: 0114 236 0789
Hillfoot Road, Totley, Sheffield, S. Yorks S17 3AX
Punch Taverns. John Hicklin, licensee.

South-west of Sheffield, towards Baslow, it's stone-built and 16th-century. Very old, very warm and very welcoming. Low doors, all extremely quaint and tiny. A one-room pub with a central bar. The fireplace is opened up and the food is freshly cooked, not bought in – rabbit hotpot, steaks, fish, all written up on the blackboard. Four ales on hand pump and guest beers.

> OPEN: 12–3. 5.30–11 (12–3. 7–10.30 Sun).
> Real Ale. No food Sun or Mon eves.
> Children welcome. Dogs on leads. Wheelchair access into pub only.
> Cards: all credit cards accepted.

WAKEFIELD

The Redoubt   Tel: 01924 377085
28 Horbury Road, Wakefield, W. Yorks WF2 8TS
Punch Taverns. M. Grady, lessee.

Wakefield prospered as the centre of the clothing trade and is still a city full of elegant Georgian houses reflecting that prosperity. The Redoubt, a wonderfully unspoilt town pub next to St Michael's Church, has four rooms (one of which has music) off a central corridor full of Rugby League photographs – keen supporters all. Plenty of beer but no food; if you want to come to enjoy the pub, you can bring your own – and there's no hamper charge. The beers are Tetleys Traditional Bitter and Mild and Timothy Taylors Landlord, and they stock a good selection of malt whiskies. Outside there is a beer garden so you can sup your pint in the fresh air.

> OPEN: 12–11.
> Real Ale.
> Children until 7pm in one room and beer garden. No food – but you can bring your own. Dogs in the tap room. Wheelchair access.

WASS

Wombwell Arms   Tel: 01347 868280
Wass, N. Yorks YO6 4BE
Free House. Andy & Susan Cole, licensees.

A delightful 18th-century inn at the foot of the Hambleton Hills, not far from the ruins of the 12th-century Byland Abbey. Inside, the bar is invitingly cosy and there are beamed dining areas, one of which is no smoking. New licensees have taken over, so the menus have changed, but you will always find some imaginative home-made soups, local game, steak and ale pie, salmon, vegetarian dishes and lunchtime sandwiches. The menus change daily. Black Sheep Bitter, Timothy Taylors Landlord and a guest beer. Choice of wines.

> OPEN: 12–2.30. 7–11. Closed Sun eves.
> Real Ale. Restaurant.
> Children welcome. No dogs. Wheelchair access (not WC). Bedrooms.

WIDDOP

Pack Horse Inn
Tel: 01422 842803

The Ridge, Widdop, Hebden Bridge, W. Yorks HX7 7AT
Free House. Andrew Hollinrake, licensee.

A haven for walkers throughout the summer, the route can be difficult in winter, though when you arrive you'll find a warm welcome (if they're open) in this sturdily built 17th-century converted farmhouse. You are in a remote area, high in the hills, on a moorland road between Hebden Bridge and Colne, near Slack Top, Widdop Reservoir and 300 yards from the Pennine Way. You'll find lots of good sustaining food on the menu: soup, filled baguettes, ploughman's, gammon and eggs – that sort of thing. Draught Thwaites Traditional Bitter, Black Sheep Bitter, Morlands Old Speckled Hen and Theakstons XB. Good range of wines with New World additions. One hundred single malts for you to try.

> OPEN: 12–2. 7–10. Closed weekday lunchtimes and all day Mon from October to Easter.
> Real Ale.
> Children until 8pm – under control. Dogs on leads. Disabled facilities. Car park.

BEST OF THE REST

CARTHORPE, N. Yorks

Fox & Hounds
Tel: 01845 567433

You have the best of both worlds here: a friendly village pub that serves some really good food. You can still get sandwiches, home-made soup and pâté, but from the specials board there could be halibut steak with a lobster and prawn sauce or lamb's liver with bacon and parsley mash. Puds are inventive too. Only John Smiths beer, but there will be something to tempt you from the extensive wine list.

FERRENSBY, N. Yorks

General Tarleton
Tel: 01423 340284

A handsome 18th-century coaching inn. Inside this comfortable, well-polished old place they serve interesting and imaginative dishes in the brasserie-style bar. There is also a more formal restaurant. Think of this as a dining pub, but still a place for a bowl of soup – provençale fish. Black Sheep and Tetley beers and a very good wine list. Seats in the sheltered garden and in the no-smoking courtyard.

NEWTON-ON-OUSE, N. Yorks

Dawnay Arms
Tel: 01347 848345

An 18th-century riverside pub with gardens down to the water's edge. This comfortable old place is beamed and spacious. Bar food is good and varied and as well as the usual bar menu there could be beef bourguignon, lamb's liver in a red-wine sauce, grilled fish or rack of lamb. Home-made puds too. Boddingtons, Flowers Original, Morlands and Tetleys beers.

PICKHILL, N. Yorks

Nags Head   Tel: 01845 567391

Hotel, pub and restaurant all rolled into one and rolling along very nicely too. You can get all the dishes you would expect from a bar menu, as well as smoked salmon and scrambled egg, rack of lamb with honey and rosemary and perhaps steak, mushroom and oyster pie. Beers are Black Sheep, Theakstons, Hambletons, John Smiths and one guest. Decent wines, some by the glass.

REETH, N. Yorks

Black Bull   Tel: 01748 884213

Swaledale and Arkengarthdale seem to converge here; you are in Herriot country – upland moors sweep onward. A very individual, traditional old place in an attractive situation, extended over the years and renovated. Inside the beamed and flagstone-floored bar they serve reliable, reasonably priced bar food to go with the Theakstons and Timothy Taylors Landlord. Bedrooms.

SAWLEY, N. Yorks

Sawley Arms   Tel: 01765 620642

Somewhere behind the wonderful floral display is an old stone pub serving English food at its best: home-made soups, pâté, salmon mousse, roast duck and apple pie with cream could be on the menu. Theakstons and John Smiths beers and house wines. Near the remains of Fountains Abbey.

SHELLEY, W. Yorks

Three Acres   Tel: 01484 602606

Something for everyone at this old coaching inn. You can stay, eat extraordinarily well and stock up with goodies from their own delicatessen. Here you will get imaginatively filled sandwiches, maybe French onion soup or moules marinière, steak, kidney and mushroom pie and a wide choice of fish from the fish bar. There will be a greater variety of dishes on the evening menu. Maybe Adnams, Mansfield, Morlands and Timothy Taylors Landlord beers; also a good list of wines. Bedrooms.

THORNTON WATLASS, N. Yorks

Buck Inn   Tel: 01677 422461

In a pretty village between Bedale and Masham, a pleasant unspoilt village inn so close to the cricket pitch that netting has been erected to prevent straight-driven sixes from breaking the pub windows. The blackboard menu for both bar and dining room lists well-presented, interesting pub cooking at its best to go with the Theakstons, Black Smith Bitter, John Smiths and guests. Bedrooms.

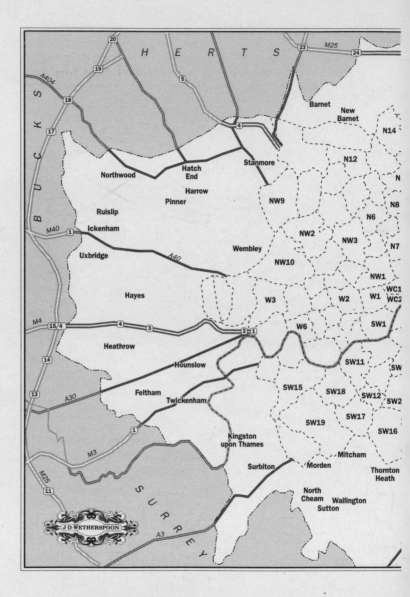

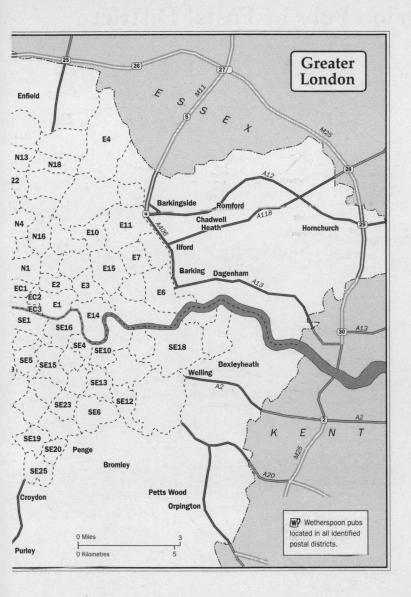

Greater London

Enfield

ESSEX

M11

25
26
27/
5
M25

E4

N13

N18

28

22

N4

E11

Barkingside   Romford
Chadwell
Heath
A118

Hornchurch

29

N16

E10

A406

Ilford

E7

Barking   Dagenham

N1

E15

A13

EC1
E2
E3

30   A13

EC2
E1
E6

EC3

SE1

E14

SE16

SE4   SE10

SE18

SE5
SE15

Bexleyheath
Welling

SE13
A2

SE23
SE12

SE6

2   A2

KENT

M25

SE19
SE20   Penge

SE25

A20

Croydon

Bromley

Petts Wood

Orpington

Purley

| 0 Miles | | 3 |
| 0 Kilometres | | 5 |

W? Wetherspoon pubs
located in all identified
postal districts.

London Pubs by Postal District

E11	The George
E15	The Goldengrove
EC1	Olde Mitre
EC2	Hamilton Hall
EC3	Lamb Tavern
EC4	Ye Olde Cheshire Cheese
EC4	Blackfriar
N7	Coronet
N19	The Dog
NW1	Man in the Moon
NW8	Clifton
NW10	Coliseum
SE1	The George
SE3	British Oak
SE10	Richard 1st
SW1	Bulls Head
SW1	Fox & Hounds
SW1	Grenadier
SW1	Lord Moon of the Mall
SW1	Star
SW3	Coopers Arms
SW3	Phene Arms
SW3	Surprise
SW6	White Horse
SW7	Anglesea Arms
SW10	Chelsea Ram
SW10	Fox & Pheasant
SW13	Ye White Hart
SW18	Alma
SW18	Ship
SW19	Hand in Hand
SW19	Rose & Crown
SW20	Sporting Page
W1	Coach & Horses
W1	Red Lion
W6	Dove

W6	Anglesea Arms
W8	Windsor Castle
W9	Warrington Hotel
WC1	Princess Louise
WC1	Calthorpe Arms
WC1	Lamb
WC2	Lamb & Flag
WC2	Seven Stars
Enfield	Moon under Water
Pinner	Queens Head
Richmond	White Cross Hotel

BEST OF THE REST

E1	Town of Ramsgate
E14	Grapes
NW3	Spaniards Inn
SE13	Horniman
SW1	Westminster Arms
SW13	Bulls Head
WC2	Cheshire Cheese

If the pubs indicated on the map are not fully described in the main section of *The Quiet Pint*, you will find them in the complete Wetherspoon list at the back of the book.

London

The area within the M25.

LONDON SW18

Alma
Tel: 020 8870 2537

499 Old York Road, Wandsworth
Youngs. Charles Gotto, MBII, tenant.

You don't have to be a rugger fanatic to appreciate this place, although it does help, as most other people here – before and after any match – will be. Ideally placed near Wandsworth Town railway station, this is a favourite stopping place for the keen rugby follower – rowdy and exuberant but well behaved. The opulent Victorian decor and the mirrors are still in one piece. Away from match days, when you have room to appreciate your environment, you are in a well-restored, prosperous Victorian pub. Here you get friendly service in attractive surroundings. From the 'light lunches' menu you could choose a toasted muffin with field mushrooms, crab blini hollandaise and poached egg or a gado-gado Indonesian vegetable salad with peanut sauce. Otherwise, grilled-pepper and aubergine soup, crisp chicken-liver risotto, spicy salmon fishcake on warm potato salad, marinated beef stir fry, noodles and mange-tout or steak frites, garlic and green-peppercorn butter, steaks, fresh fish, salads, daily specials and desirable puds. Whenever possible, all of the meat is sourced from their own farm in Surrey; if that's not possible, they always know where it has come from. Youngs range of ales and a good choice of wines by the bottle or glass. Both espresso and ordinary coffee. Youngs Brewery and their magnificent shire horses are just around the corner.

> OPEN: 11–11.
> Real Ale. Restaurant.
> Children in eating areas. Dogs on leads. Wheelchair access (not WC).
> Cards: all credit cards.

LONDON SW7

Angelsea Arms
Tel: 020 7373 7960

15 Selwood Terrace, London SW7 3QG
Free House. Andrew Ford, manager.

Atmosphere is all. A well-loved, early-Victorian pub in prosperous South Kensington. Comfortable armchairs and settles, all plumped and polished; the Anglesea is friendly and reassuring. Not too big, but when it does get crowded, the party continues outside, as it does with so many other popular London pubs, only here they don't need the pavement – they have their own spacious forecourt. Service is very efficient, even with all those al fresco drinkers. Bar food is good pub grub – basically, filled baguettes, sausage and mash, home-baked ham – that sort of thing. An à la carte menu is offered in the evening dining room seven days a week, and there is a Sunday roast in both the bar and dining room. A good range of ales: Fullers London Pride, Adnams Broadside, Brakspear SB – all on hand pump and one guest. A selection of fine wines.

> OPEN: 11–11 (12–10.30 Sun).
> Real Ale.
> Children welcome. Dogs on leads.
> Cards: all except Amex, Diners and JCB.

LONDON W6

Anglesea Arms   Tel: 020 8749 1291
35 Wingate Street, London W6 0UR
Free House. Dan & Fiona Evans, licensees.

The popularity of any pub, its food and the quality of its beer depend so much on who is running it and how. With this particular Anglesea, you can experience the best of all worlds. Have a drink in the cosy panelled bar (with fire) or eat extremely well in the restaurant. The clever, inventive menus are guided by inspiration and change twice a day. They don't take bookings, so unless you get there early enough to grab a table, you just have to be patient and have a drink while you wait for one to become free. It is, after all still a pub. Morlands Old Speckled Hen, Fullers London Pride, Marstons Pedigree and a reasonably priced wine list – a choice of about 15 by the glass.

> OPEN: 11–11.
> Restaurant.
> Children welcome. No dogs. Wheelchair access (not WC).
> Cards: Delta, MasterCard, Switch, Visa.

LONDON EC4

Black Friar   Tel: 020 7236 5474
174 Queen Victoria Street, London EC4 4DB
Nicholsons (Allied). Mr Karl Becker, MBII, manager.

There isn't anything much better than this: one of the finest examples of Art Nouveau decoration in London – marble and monks everywhere – a favourite pub on the tourist route. Built in the 1870s and redecorated at the turn of the century in a flamboyant Art Nouveau style, the pub is full of the most wonderfully florid Edwardian decorations:

mosaics, marble walls, pillared fireplaces, mirrors and a bronze bas relief of monks to remind you that you are on the site of the old Blackfriars monastery. They have a full self-service lunchtime menu and bar food – filled rolls, baked potatoes with various fillings, and a few hot dishes in the evenings. This is a pub with its very own rush hour; a favourite place in the early evening for thirsty hordes refreshing themselves before the journey home. Tetleys, Brakspears, Adnams, Wadworths 6X and Nicholsons – which is brewed by Allied – all on hand pump. No garden, but there is a good pavement for standing on.

OPEN: 11.30–11 weekdays.
Real Ale.
No children. No dogs.

LONDON SE3

British Oak   Tel: 020 8858 1082
109 Old Dover Road, Blackheath, London SE3 8SU
Scottish & Newcastle. Mr P. Jeffery, tenant.

From the 13th to the 17th century, Blackheath witnessed some of the major events in this country's history. It was here that the rebel leader Wat Tyler assembled his men in 1381, where Londoners met Henry V after his victory at Agincourt, greeted Charles II on his way into the city of London to reclaim the throne, and where, more importantly to some, James I introduced the game of golf to the nation in 1608. The open common is all that remains of old heathland either side of the main road to Dover. The patriotically named British Oak is a popular local known for its bitters, and also for the good-value food they serve during the day – an all-day breakfast of double sausage, egg, bacon, tomato and chips, or steak and chips, served until 7pm Monday to Saturday. Courage Best and Directors are the beers, plus two guests. You can sit in the sheltered, paved walled garden at the back of the pub.

OPEN: 11–11 (12–10.30 Sun).
Real Ale.
Children in garden. Dogs on leads.
N.B. TV in one bar.

LONDON WC1

Calthorpe Arms   Tel: 020 7278 4732
252 Grays Inn Road, London WC1X 8JR
Youngs. A. Larner, tenant.

A pleasant, comfortable neighbourhood pub serving lunchtime food in the bar or the upstairs restaurant. On the fringe of Bloomsbury, an area of London developed by the Earl of Southampton – the Duke of Bedford's ancestor – in 1661, a favourite with office workers and television news staff catching up with the local gossip and in between keeping an eye on world events; low-volume TV is on most of the time. Youngs Bitter, Special and Winter Warmer. Seats on the pavement – for people-watching.

> OPEN: 11–11 (12–10.30 Sun).
> Real Ale.
> No children. Dogs – maybe the odd one!

LONDON SW10

The Chelsea Ram
Tel: 020 7351 4008
32 Burnaby Street (off Lots Road)
Hop-Vine. Nick Elliot, licensee.

If you're a stranger to London and you want to find Burnaby Street, head in the direction of Lots Road – you can't go far wrong. The old power station is a significant landmark and the Chelsea Ram is not far away. Many changes have gone on here over the years. Built as a pub in the 19th century, it was refused a licence – it would lower the tone, you see. At last, in 1984 it did become a pub – but it took time to gain popularity. Now it is hugely popular – a bright, cheerful place with pine tables and chairs and a good fire; an 'of the moment' atmosphere for what is a pub-cum-restaurant. Well known for the quality of their imaginative, well-presented food, the menus change daily, but they always have vegetarian dishes, pasta, chicken in different delicious sauces and several fish dishes. On Sunday they do a very popular roast lunch. All Youngs beers. About 25 wines and three champagnes.

> OPEN: 11–11 (12–10.30 Sun).
> Real Alc
> Children welcome. Dogs on leads. Wheelchair access (not WC).

LONDON NW8

Clifton
Tel: 020 7372 3627
96 Clifton Hill, St John's Wood
Nicholsons. Sharon Smedley, manager.

There are several stories as to how this Georgian building became a public house in the early 19th century. The best, which goes with the decor, is that Edward VII met Lillie Langtry here in a private bar. When it was restored and redecorated, the owners created a very Edwardian atmosphere: panelling, polished floors and rugs, pictures of Edward VII, his mistress, Lillie Langtry, and his wife, Queen Alexandra. Inside, the U-shaped bar serves three attractively decorated rooms. The restaurant – which seats about 25 – is in the conservatory. One menu, for both the bar and restaurant, lists among other dishes a soup of the day, filled jacket potatoes, filled baguettes, deep-fried mushrooms with dips, lasagne, a selection of pies, steaks and the two most popular dishes, haddock with chips and sausage and mash. Ales are Tetleys, Fullers London Pride, Bass and possibly two changing guest beers. Seats on the leafy terrace at the front of the pub and on the sunny terrace at the back.

OPEN: 11–11 (12–10.30 Sun).
Real Ale. Restaurant.
Children welcome. Dogs on leads.

LONDON W1

Coach & Horses   Tel: 020 7437 5920
29 Greek Street
Taylor Walker. Norman Balon, MBII, tenant.

Do not be put off by any rumours that the landlord here is the rudest in the capital – he probably is, but for many reasons he is also one of the most famous. Here is a serious drinking pub and one of London's most well known. We have film stars but this is a stage star. This is the pub where the late Jeffrey Barnard did most of his drinking. When the play *Jeffrey Barnard is Unwell* is staged, the Coach & Horses is the main set; the strong personality of Norman Balon, the landlord, making his presence felt offstage. On the corner of Romilly Street and Greek Street, the Coach & Horses has become synonymous with its tenant and is called 'Norman's' by the regulars. Immortalised as 'The Regulars' in the *Private Eye* column, it is where *Private Eye* staff meet every other Wednesday for their fortnightly editorial lunches, and the other customers come for their sandwiches of ham, cheese or egg and tomato. Burton Ale, Fullers London Pride and Marstons Pedigree.

OPEN: 11–11 (12–10.30 Sun).
Real Ale.
No children. No dogs. Wheelchair access (not WC).
Cards: all except Amex and Diners.

LONDON NW10

The Coliseum   Tel: 020 8961 6570
Manor Park Road, Harlesden
Wetherspoon.

Stars of the silver screen take pride of place in what used to be one of the local cinemas before Wetherspoon snapped it up. A 20-foot mural recreating a scene from the film *The Cowboy and the Lady*, starring Gary Cooper and Merle Oberon, is the main feature; other bits and pieces of film memorabilia are used to decorate the interior. Food all day, and always six different, reasonably priced beers and one guest.

OPEN: 11–11.
Real Ale.
No children. No dogs. Wheelchair access.

LONDON SW3

Coopers Arms
Flood Street, Chelsea
Youngs. Mr & Mrs S. Lee, managers.

Tel: 020 7376 3120

Not far from the King's Road and Chelsea Register Office, this is an important lunchtime meeting place for shoppers, professionals and frequently, the bride and groom and wedding guests. The Quiet Pint had its launch party here in 1995, attended by Joanna Lumley and Julian Lloyd Webber, both firm supporters of quiet pubs. Inside this civilised place are framed drawings by the cartoonist Jak to amuse you, and a selection of daily newspapers to let you know what is happening in the big wide world. The interesting, imaginative menu changes daily, but there could be Thai hot and sour prawn soup, Japanese teryaki chicken salad with sesame seeds, seared king scallops in créme fraîche and sweet chilli, garlic and chilli tiger prawns served on spaghetti, or lemon balsamic chicken with coriander and olive mash; desirable desserts too. Youngs range of ales. Also a good selection of New World, French, Italian, Spanish and other wines listed on the blackboard.

> OPEN: 11–11 (12–10.30 Sun).
> Real Ale.
> Children welcome. Dogs on leads. Wheelchair access into pub and gents' WC.
> Cards: Amex, Electron, MasterCard, Solo, Switch, Visa.

LONDON N7

The Coronet
338–346 Holloway Road, London N7 6NJ
Wetherspoon.

Tel: 020 7609 5014

Wetherspoon don't do anything by halves. We have here a big, big drinking area, a sort of 6000 square foot translocated bier kellar. You can fit a lot of pint pots into that. This was yet another redundant cinema. Originally the Savoy, then the ABC, finally the Coronet, before being converted into this huge, popular Wetherspoon outlet. Keeping an eye on things is a lifesize statue of Fred Astaire. Between five and six real ales, one guest and an extensive, reliable menu served all day.

> OPEN: 11–11.
> Real Ale.
> No children. No dogs. Wheelchair facilities.

LONDON N19

The Dog
17–19 Archway Road
Wetherspoon.

Tel: 020 7263 0429

Never ones to let a building go to waste, Wetherspoon started its empire building here, until they outgrew the space and put it to the most obvious use – one more pub. Lots of pictures and references to dogs all around, but not a real one to be seen. Only a few minutes from Archway Underground station. Being one of the chain's smaller pubs, it is a more personal kind of place, attracting a loyal band of local regulars. The usual reliable beers, guest beer and menu.

OPEN: 11–11.
Real Ale.
No children. No dogs. Wheelchair facilities.

LONDON W6

Dove   Tel: 020 8748 5405
19 Upper Mall, Hammersmith
Fullers. Martin Delves, manager.

To reach the Dove you have to go down a quiet alley by Hammersmith Bridge in the footsteps of some of the literary giants who frequented the pub. Ernest Hemingway, Graham Greene, Charles Kingsley and the designer William Morris all knew the place well. The 17th-century Dove is one of the most perfect riverside pubs, and probably one of the oldest tied houses in London. Fullers have owned the place since 1796. The Guinness Book of Records says the Dove has the smallest bar in England; it's on the right as you go in. Measuring just over 4 feet by 7 feet 10 inches – five people, elbows well tucked in, are a crowd – it seems to be permanently full! The main bar is much bigger, beamed and panelled, retaining much of its old charm and character. Lunchtimes are quiet-ish, but come evening, space is at a premium, not only in the Dove, but also, depending on the weather, on the terrace overlooking the river. Well-cooked lunchtime bar food of filled baked potatoes, various pies, salads, ploughman's and changing daily specials on the blackboard. Very well-regarded Thai food is served during the evening. Fullers London Pride and ESB ales. Those patriotically minded among you might like to know that a copy of the score of 'Rule Britannia' is on a wall of the bar. James Thompson, who wrote it, had a room here. Outside drinking area overlooking the river.

OPEN: 11–11 (12–10.30 Sun).
Real Ale.
No children. Dogs on leads. Wheelchair access (not WC).

LONDON SW1

Fox and Hounds   Tel: 020 7730 6367
29 Passmore Street (corner of Graham Terrace)
The Establishment Ltd. James Symington, licensee.

When this small place opened for business, it was only licensed to sell beer, cider and wine. A situation left over from Victorian thinking that the working man should be kept away from the temptation of spirits. Now with a spirit licence – well, for limited spirits: they confine themselves to one gin, one vodka, two whiskies, one rum and one brandy – all classy brands. Anyway, how many do you need? The Fox and Hounds is just a tiny corner pub, with two small panelled rooms, at the end of an early-19th-century terrace on the edge of the Grosvenor Estate. The menu, which changes weekly, usually has home-made soup, a risotto, something with pasta, salads, chicken in various guises, something fishy and whatever else they think the customers would like. A choice of five red and six white wines, four of each by the glass, also Youngs range of ales.

OPEN: 11–3. 5.30–11 (6–11 Sat. 6.30–10.30 Sun).
Real Ale.
Children welcome. Dogs too.

LONDON SW10

Fox and Pheasant
Tel: 020 7352 2943
1 Billing Road, off the Fulham Road
Greene King. Lyn & Ben Asher, tenants.

Situated on a private side road off the Fulham Road, this pub was created by knocking two cottages together in 1848. This area, known as The Billings, is lucky having this very country-ish pub, looking very pretty with flourishing hanging baskets. Inside, it's well-polished with traditional furnishings and there is a nicely mellowed atmosphere in both the public and saloon bars; not a great difference between them, except that the saloon has a square of carpet and the public bar a dartboard. This lucky place has its own garden with room for about 60 people; very popular on a balmy summer evening, and in winter there is a covered, heated outside area. The menu, which changes daily, lists hot and cold dishes as well as sandwiches and filled jacket potatoes. Ales are Greene King IPA and Abbot. Water for the dog. Chelsea football ground is quite near. On match days the pub could well be closed to avoid the over-enthusiastic football crowds.

OPEN: 11–11 (12–10.30 Sun).
Real Ale.
Children in garden. Dogs on leads.
Cards: none accepted.

LONDON E11

The George
Tel: 020 8989 2921
High Street, Wanstead
Wetherspoon.

No point in wasting space! Wetherspoon really believe in packing them in. Before conversion, this was a furniture showroom. Now it's a large, friendly, comfortable pub. All the usual Wetherspoon attributes: a no-smoking area, food served all day and the attraction of between one and two thousand books on display which anyone can read. Full menu, the usual drinks and Theakstons XB, Best, Courage Directors, Youngers Scotch Bitter and a guest.

OPEN: 11–11.
Real Ale.
No children. No dogs. Wheelchair facilities.

LONDON SE1

George   Tel: 020 7407 2056
77 Borough High Street, Southwark
Laurel Pub Co. George Cunningham, manager.

A place that is a must on your list of places to visit – as long as you keep your back to the modern awfulness around it. The architecture is familiar; it played a part in many films depicting London's past. Stagecoaches coming in and out, skulduggery in the dark corners; that is how it was. What we have now is what remains of the magnificent, 17th-century George. Saved from almost certain destruction when, in 1937, the National Trust accepted this wonderful old coaching inn as a gift from London & North Eastern Railway. The original pub was destroyed by a fire that swept through Southwark in 1676 – ten years after the Great Fire of London – and what you see today is the replacement built in that year. Early in the 19th century it had become one of the most important inns in Southwark, with huge stables and yards. It was these that attracted the LNER's predecessor, the Great Northern Railway, to buy the George in 1874 to use as a depot. By 1937, they had pulled down or sold off many of the old buildings, leaving the inn, a couple of houses within the structure, and only one of the magnificent galleries to posterity. Today the George caters for a totally different traveller. The remaining galleries of the south range look over the courtyard where you can sit and enjoy your food and drink, occasionally entertained by visiting Morris men or players from the nearby Globe theatre – all quite medieval. There is a simple bar menu of soup, filled baguettes, filled jacket potatoes, roasted-vegetable lasagne, steak, mushroom and Guinness pie, sausage and mash with onion gravy, omelettes, fish, salads and a cheese platter. The menu goes up a notch in the Coaching Room restaurant. Boddingtons, Fullers London Pride, Morlands Old Speckled Hen, Flowers Original, Greene King Abbot, George Inn Restoration Ale and a guest beer. If you don't know the pub, search it out, as it is not clearly visible behind the huge gates on Borough High Street.

OPEN: 11–11 (12–10.30 Sun).
Real Ale. Restaurant (not Sun); lunchtime meals and snacks.
Children in eating area. No dogs.

LONDON E15

The Goldengrove   Tel: 020 8519 0750
146–148 The Grove, Stratford
Wetherspoon.

The name 'Goldengrove' is taken from one of Gerard Manley Hopkins' poems; he was born in Stratford Grove in 1844 and lived there for the first eight years of his life. Framed poems, some obscure in meaning, hang on the walls of the pub. Less poetically, before being converted into the place you see today, this site housed London's largest discount jeans store. Big, open-plan, with a bar at the front and ample seating. A full menu is served all day: good, satisfying fare and daily specials. They also have a Curry Club on Thursday evenings featuring eight different curries. Shepherd Neame Spitfire, Courage Directors, Theakstons Best and Greene King Abbot ale plus a guest beer. A large beer garden overlooks the nearby Theatre Royal.

OPEN: 11–11.
Real Ale.
No children. No dogs. Wheelchair facilities.

LONDON SW1

Grenadier   Tel: 020 7235 3074
18 Wilton Row
Scottish & Newcastle. Patricia Ann Smardon, manageress.

As the name suggests, the Grenadier leans towards the military; in the 18th century the Duke of Wellington's officers used it as their mess and this pub has lost none of its charm or character over the years. Tucked away in a mews off Wilton Crescent, behind what used to be St George's Hospital, now the Lanesborough Hotel. Painted patriotically in the colours of the Union Flag, a sentry box stands next to the front door and a Guards' bearskin guards the bar. There is a small bar and small candlelit dining room where, naturally enough, you can order beef Wellington. Good hearty bar food: soup, ploughman's, fish and chips, sausage and mash, scampi and chips and a vegetarian dish or two. The beers change frequently; there is always a guest beer and they stock quite a range of lagers, cider, bottled beer and Guinness. The Grenadier has its own very special Bloody Mary, which wins awards; the recipe for it is passed on from landlord to landlord. When possible, the mews becomes the outside drinking area.

OPEN: 12–11.
Real Ale. Restaurant.
Children in restaurant. Dogs on leads.

LONDON EC2

Hamilton Hall   Tel: 020 7247 3579
Liverpool Street Station
Wetherspoon.

One of the glories of Wetherspoon pubs is that they are usually somewhere convenient and Hamilton Hall certainly is. It also has the added bonus of something spectacular to look at. So, if you're waiting for a train or to meet a friend, wanting something simple to drink and a sandwich or a full meal, go and admire Hamilton Hall. On the station concourse, built at the turn of the century as the grand ballroom of the Great Eastern Hotel, now with its splendid, soaring Baroque decor restored, it is still grand. The hotel was closed with the outbreak of war in 1939. Wetherspoon converted the ballroom to create a huge, renovated, sumptuous space with a comfortably furnished mezzanine floor, a great part of which is no smoking. Reliable bar food, with a choice of daily specials and puddings, is served from 11am to 10pm every day. Beers at this chain are frequently cheaper than elsewhere. Courage Directors, Theakstons Best, Fullers London Pride, Shepherd Neame Spitfire and a guest beer are all on hand pump.

> OPEN: 11–11.
> Real Ale.
> No children. No dogs. Wheelchair facilities.

LONDON SW19 (Wimbledon)

Hand in Hand   Tel: 020 8946 5720
6 Crooked Billet
Youngs. Sally Marley, licensee.

Crooked Billet is actually a tiny hamlet on the edge of Wimbledon Common. Originally just an alehouse, the Hand in Hand still has a timeless atmosphere and is now a popular family pub with a no-smoking family room. A cottagey sort of place, hung about with flowering baskets and window boxes, its sunny front courtyard looks over a small green, much used for lolling on during balmy summer evenings. The traditional pub menu features burgers, pizzas and pasta dishes that satisfy the inner man and accompany Youngs range of beers. Wide selection of wines from many countries of the world.

> OPEN: 11–11.
> Real Ale.
> Children in family room. Dogs on leads. Wheelchair access (not WC).

LONDON WC1

Lamb   Tel: 020 7405 0713
94 Lamb's Conduit Street
Youngs. David Hehir, manager.

Much altered since it was built in 1720, the Lamb now has fine etched windows and comfortable leather seats; a wonderful example of a Victorian pub hiding a much older building, but still full of atmosphere. The odd street name commemorates a very philanthropic gesture by an Elizabethan engineer, William Lamb, who paid for a conduit to be built to carry water to all the houses in the street – a charitable act forever remembered. Inside, the pub retains some of the original Victorian fittings. The U-shaped bar and glass snob screens are worth noting, also the photographs of the old Holborn Empire, a famous music hall bombed in the last war. Traditional bar food is served every lunchtime and evening except on Sunday. The most popular dishes are the home-cooked steak and ale pie and lamb's liver and bacon, or you could choose something from the specials board. They serve a full menu and a roast on Sunday. For the health conscious, there is a small no-smoking room where you can enjoy your pint without a fug. Youngs Bitter, Special and AAA, the seasonal Waggledance and Winter Warmer and Smiles guest beer. Some seats in the small courtyard.

> OPEN: 11–11 (12–4. 7–10.30 Sun).
> Real Ale.
> Children in eating area. No dogs. Wheelchair access (not WC).
> Cards: MasterCard, Visa and debit cards.

LONDON EC3

Lamb Tavern   Tel: 020 7626 2454
Leadenhall Market
Youngs. David & Linda Morris, managers.

In the heart of the City of London, the Victorian Leadenhall Market (poultry, fish and game) has hidden depths. Underneath it are the remains of our past – a huge basilica and forum – an important market and meeting place in Roman London. Built on this piece of history and in the entrance to the market itself, the Lamb has height rather than depth: four floors of it; it became so busy that another floor was squeezed in to accompany the other three. The wine bar and smoking room in the basement stayed the same, as has the top floor no-smoking bar that overlooks the market. Note that both the market and the pub are closed at the weekends. But if you are in the area, you could go by and see what is happening – film crews have been known to move in and take over this wonderfully photogenic place. During the week it is full of city types drinking gallons of beer – draught bitter, mostly – and enjoying slices cut off roast ribs of beef and slapped between two pieces of French bread. Four large joints of beef are consumed each day. Youngs range of beers and some lagers to accompany the hearty food.

> OPEN: 11–9.30 Mon–Fri only.
> Real Ale.
> No children. Dogs on leads. Wheelchair access (not WC).

LONDON WC2

Lamb & Flag   Tel: 020 7497 9504
33 Rose Street
Free House. Terry Archer & Adrian Zimmerman, licensees.

When it was first built, Rose Street was a residential area, lived in by local merchants and other people of 'quality'. The first mention of this pub was in 1772 – then known as the

Coopers Arms. Dickens knew this place when he was working in nearby Catherine Street, and he would still recognise it. Situated in a 17th-century Covent Garden alley between Floral and Garrick Streets, the Lamb and Flag is the oldest tavern in Covent Garden. It retains much of the character and atmosphere of that time: low ceilings and panelled walls, the original built-in benches, one long bar downstairs and one upstairs. Frequently crowded in early evening, you'll find the customers spilling out onto the pavement to enjoy their pre-prandial drink. Bar food includes soup, roast-beef-filled baps, roast pork or lamb with the trimmings, quiche, Thai lemon chicken with salad and daily changing hot dishes. Courage Best and Directors, Youngs PA Bitter and Special, Greene King Abbot, Marstons Pedigree and various guest beers. They have a selection of malt whiskies.

> OPEN: 11–11 Mon–Thurs. 11–10.45 Fri & Sat. 12–10.30 Sun.
> Real Ale. Lunchtime meals only but snacks from 11am–5pm.
> No dogs. Wheelchair access (not WC). Live jazz Sunday eves.

LONDON SW1

Lord Moon of the Mall   Tel: 020 7839 7701
16–18 Whitehall
Wetherspoon.

Once upon a time this was Martin's Bank, but before it became Martin's and, even later, the more commonplace Barclays, it was one of the 'grander' banks: Cocks, Biddulfs and Co., bankers to the good, the famous and Edward VII. It was built by a pupil of Sir Gilbert Scott in the 1870s, and Wetherspoon spent a huge amount of money converting it into a spacious, elegant drinking house, retaining the original soaring ceilings, arched windows and exit onto the Mall (emergencies only), but now with granite counters, comfortable chairs, books, a big no-smoking area and the usual Wetherspoon attractions: well-run, reasonably priced beer, food all day and a happy atmosphere. Always five beers and a weekly changing guest.

> OPEN: 11–11.
> Real Ale.
> No children. No dogs. Wheelchair facilities.

LONDON NW1

Man in the Moon   Tel: 020 7482 2054
40–42 Chalk Farm Road, Camden
Wetherspoon.

One of those places that heaves with customers, particularly at the weekend – they do after all serve the cheapest pint in the area. Opposite Camden Market, the pub is also on the tourist route. Full menu with at least four daily specials; they offer two meals for the price of one – Monday to Saturday from 11am until 10pm. They also feature a beer, food and wine of the month, five or six real ales and one guest.

OPEN: 11–11.
Real Ale.
No children. No dogs. Wheelchair facilities.

LONDON EC4

Ye Olde Cheshire Cheese
Wine Office Court (off Fleet Street)
Sam Smiths. Gordon Garrity, licensee.

Tel: 020 7353 6170

Among the most famous places in London. This is the Ye Cheshire Cheese the tourists want. Probably 200 years old when it had to be rebuilt in 1668 on the foundations of the original building, burnt to the ground in the Great Fire of London in 1666. Three hundred years later it was feeling its age and in need of support, so it was made more secure and extended to cope with the demands of the next couple of hundred years. Still very much a typical 17th-century chophouse, with cosy rooms, open fires, settles and sawdust on the floor. There are a formidable number of dining rooms, four ground-floor bars and the original panelled chop room which has famous literary connections. Anybody who was anybody in the literary world crossed the threshold of this charming, timeless old pub. Only sandwiches are available in the cellar bars (these are the original cellars but they do have loud music); elsewhere in the pub there is quite a choice of places to sit and eat. Good hearty English fare on offer: soups, cornet of smoked salmon and crab, avocado and artichoke salad or savoury casket of chicken livers encased in puff pastry with a port-wine sauce as a starter; supreme of chicken with lobster and sorrel on a light muscadet sauce, Ye famous steak, kidney, mushroom and game pudding, chef's speciality sausage, vegetarian crêpes filled with mushrooms, onions and courgettes served on a tomato and basil sauce, fish and chips and various puddings. Sam Smiths beers on hand pump.

OPEN: 11.30–11 (11.30–3. 5.30–11 Sat. 12–4 Sun).
Closed Sun eve.
Real Ale. Restaurant (closed Sun eve).
Children welcome. No dogs.

LONDON EC1

Olde Mitre
Ely Court, off Ely Place
Allied Domecq. Don O'Sullivan, manager.

Tel: 020 7405 4751

The Olde Mitre, only open during the week, is in a very narrow alley off Hatton Garden. The pub, named after an earlier tavern, was built in the 16th century to provide for the

Bishop of Ely's staff. Rebuilt during the mid-18th century, it remains much as it was, a picturesque, delightful pub near the bishop's 13th-century St Ethelreda's Church. The small panelled rooms are crowded during weekday lunchtimes when they serve a variety of sandwiches – simple but good. Ind Coope Burton and Tetleys on hand pump. There are wooden casks for tables in the delightful small yard between the pub and the church. Until a few years ago you could still claim sanctuary in both the pub and the church but – fortunately for the police, if not the local villains – somebody spotted this glaring error and had the right rescinded.

> OPEN: 11–11 (Closed Sat, Sun & Bank Holidays).
> Real Ale.
> No children. No dogs.

London SW3

Phene Arms   Tel: 020 7352 3294
9 Phene Street
Free House. Wesley & Carmen Davis, licensees.

There was a definite, and believable, rumour going around early last summer that the Phene Arms was closing to become a private house – something about the locals objecting to sounds of jollity emanating from the pub! The rumour was unfounded: the Phene has a new lease of life. Named after Dr John Phene, who in the 19th century developed this area, built the pub and planted the trees, creating one of the most delightful and desirable areas in Chelsea. The lucky Phene has its own front garden, a popular place to be on a balmy summer evening. Inside, a bar and dining room. French, bistro-like cooking and a good selection of wines. Roast lunch on Sundays. Fullers London Pride, Adnams Best and Broadside and Morlands Old Speckled Hen.

> OPEN: 11–11.
> Real Ale.
> Children welcome. Dogs on leads. Wheelchair access (not WC).
> Cards: most cards accepted.

London WC1

Princess Louise   Tel: 020 7405 8816
208 High Holborn
Samuel Smith. Timothy Buck, licensee.

To appreciate the glories of this pub fully you need to visit it during its quieter moments – evenings or Saturdays – otherwise it is busy and exuberant. Named after the fourth daughter of Queen Victoria, the pub, built in 1872, didn't become licensed until 1891 when it was bought and decorated by Arthur Chitty. Just escaping the demolition squad in the 1970s, it is now listed Grade II*, making it a building of considerable note. The interior is a monument to the very best in late-Victorian decoration: polished granite pillars, gilt mirrors, ornate plasterwork, elaborate tiling and a huge mahogany U-shaped bar. The gents' lavatory has a separate listing! Downstairs, in the bar, a variety of well-filled, freshly made sandwiches are available from 11am to 10.30pm every day except Sunday. Upstairs from Monday to Saturday they serve a selection of daily specials and home-cooked food from the à la carte menu in the lounge bar. All the beers are from Sam Smiths range of ales, also wines by the glass.

OPEN: 11–11 (12–11 Sat). Closed Sunday.
Real Ale.
No children. Dogs on leads.

LONDON Pinner

Queen's Head   Tel: 020 8868 9844
31 High Street, Pinner HA5 5PJ
Punch Taverns. Jill & James Tindall, licensees.

Soon after George I ascended the English throne in 1715, the Crown Inn was renamed The Queen's Head – probably in honour of its most illustrious customer, Queen Anne, who would change horses here on the way from Hatfield to Windsor. Built on the site of a 14th-century alehouse, the Queen's Head, as beamed and panelled as you would expect, is Pinner's oldest inn. Well run and very atmospheric, it is the focal point of the village. Good-value bar snacks: breakfast in bread – bacon and fried egg in a sandwich, steak and twelve other fillings on the sandwich menu, filled jacket potatoes, ploughman's, mixed grill, bangers and mash, and daily specials. Beers are draught Bass, Youngs, Greene King Abbot and Adnams. European, Australian and New World wines. Seats outside in the beer garden.

OPEN: 11–11.30 (12–11 Sun).
Real Ale.
No children. Dogs: welcome except between 12–2 when food is served. Car park.

LONDON SW1

Red Lion   Tel: 020 7321 0782
Duke of York Street
Bass Charrington. Michael Brown, FBII, manager.

Just off Jermyn Street, this is a very small, popular, delightful pub, handy if you're doing a little shopping in either Piccadilly or Jermyn Street. Only limited bar snacks are on offer weekday lunchtimes, except Friday and Saturday when they serve home-made fish and chips – a tremendous favourite with tourists. On the small side for a gin palace, but a Victorian gem. Virtually unspoilt, the cut glass twinkles away in the sunlight. Ales are constantly changing; most of them are guests from the smaller breweries and some are especially brought in for the regulars. This is another pub that has a loo worthy of note.

'Going to the loo is an adventure in itself,' says Michael Brown. 'We tend to count the customers going down to make sure we don't lose them!'

> OPEN: 11.30–11. Closed Sun.
> Real Ale.
> No children. No dogs.

LONDON W1

Red Lion
Tel: 020 7499 1307

1 Waverton Street
Scottish & Newcastle. Grieg Peck, manager.

Built 300 years ago, the Red Lion has changed with the ebb and flow of the area. Originally it was on a muddy lane alongside the very grand Chesterfield House, which was unfortunately pulled down in the 1930s. An alehouse, it was frequented by the 'rougher' local traders from Shepherds Market, servants and, later, the 18th- and 19th-century builders and masons who were slowly transforming the area into the London you see today. Its humble past forgotten, the Red Lion is now a very smart pub in a smart part of London. The small panelled bar serves food all day – home-made sausages and mash, char-grilled burgers and Cajun chicken sandwiches are very popular, also the salads and hot daily specials. The food in the restaurant goes up a notch; three different set menus to choose from, or you could have Dover sole, grilled wild Scotch salmon, half a roast duck, best end of lamb or fillet of beef Wellington. Greene King IPA, Courage Best and Directors and Theakstons Best, You could of course have the house special, the Red Lion's very own Bloody Mary.

> OPEN: 11–11 (6–11 Sat).
> Real Ale. Restaurant.
> Children in eating area. Only guide dogs allowed. Wheelchair access.
> Cards: Amex, Delta, MasterCard, Switch, Visa.

LONDON SE10

Richard 1st
Tel: 020 8692 2996

52–54 Royal Hill, Greenwich, London SE10 8RT
Youngs. Bill Wood, manager.

In a delightful street, mainly residential but with a few interesting shops, the Richard 1st is unspoilt, with a panelled interior and books to read if you're kept waiting. An exclusive address in a fascinating part of London, forever connected with the might of British sea power. In a dry dock near the pier is the Victorian clipper ship *Cutty Sark*. On the banks of the river is the Royal Naval College, known as Greenwich Hospital, which was designed by Sir Christopher Wren; behind that is the National Maritime Museum, the oldest part of which is the Queen's House built by Inigo Jones in 1633, and to crown it all, 130 acres of glorious park laid out by Le Nôtre for Charles II. The menu lists hearty pub fare, the current favourite being the hot toasted paninis with a variety of fillings. At weekends, if the weather is fine, you can enjoy a barbecue in the garden. They stock the full range of Youngs beers: Bitter, Special and Ramrod plus the seasonal Wheat Beer and an extensive range of Young's speciality bottled beers and lagers. Lots of seats in the walled garden.

> OPEN: 11–11 (12–10.30 Sun).
> Real Ale.
> Children in garden. Dogs on leads.

LONDON SW19

Rose & Crown   Tel: 020 8947 4713
55 High Street, Wimbledon
Youngs. Jeff Messitt, tenant/manager.

This 17th-century building started off innocently enough as an elegant brick-built house but later became a coaching inn – the London coach starting and finishing here – and one of Youngs Breweries' first properties. Walter Swinburne, the poet, who died in 1909, used to walk across the common to the Rose & Crown, which he regarded as his local. Brought up to date without losing any of its charm, it is still a comfortable place with open fires, maps of old Wimbledon and Hogarth engravings decorating the walls of the bar, a small no-smoking area and a conservatory. There is a varied menu – all home-made – and a roast on Sunday. They have the full range of Youngs beers including Youngs Triple A. There are seats in the paved, walled coachyard.

> OPEN: 11–11 (12–10.30 Sun).
> Real Ale.
> Children in certain areas. Dogs on leads.

LONDON WC2

Seven Stars   Tel: 020 7242 8521
53 Carey Street
Adnams. Roxy Beaujolais & Nathan Silver, free of tie lease.

Not only one of the smallest, but one of the few early-17th-century pubs in London. Built in 1602, facing the back of the Royal Courts of Justice, many a tear must have been shed into the beer here. A delightfully unchanging place, all flowery outside – opulent hanging baskets – and snugly intimate inside, with just two small rooms. The building might not have changed much but everything else has: Adnams are the new owners and Roxy Beaujolais – author of the pub cook book *Home from the Pub Contented* – has moved from the Three Greyhounds in Greek Street to be another star. A favourite meeting place for litigants – they could be the ones weeping in their beer, lawyers thinking of their fees, reporters and musicians appreciating the musical quiet, all enjoying the good food. Just a small, regularly changing menu: cured herrings in dill with potato salad, Welsh rarebit, vegetarian fare, or rib-eye steak cut into strips on a chunk of bread. Adnams range of ales,

Guinness and Bitburger and guest ales including Youngs. Bottled lagers. Decent house wines. The law courts' stone balustrade provides an extra bar and beer garden – weather permitting. The gents' loos are a talking point here – if you're a gent; they are up extremely narrow Elizabethan stairs.

OPEN: 11–11. Closed Sundays.
Real Ale.
No children. No dogs.
Cards: Amex, Delta, MasterCard, Switch, Visa.

LONDON SW18

Ship
Tel: 020 8870 9667
41 Jews Row, Wandsworth
Youngs. Charles Gotto, MBII, Desmond Madden, licensees.

Jews Row is very near the south side of Wandsworth Bridge, with a cement works and car park as unexciting neighbours. It is difficult to find; nobody lives in Jews Row and nobody seems to know where it is, but you'll find it in the A–Z. There is nothing nicer on a summer Sunday than to come here to enjoy a barbecued lunch, a pint, and watch the Thames slip by – along with hundreds of others who've had no trouble finding it. An outside pavilion bar has been built to give you easier access to the beer. Weather permitting, anything that can be barbecued will be; if the barbecue is off, it's back inside for the bar menu. This features soups, baguettes, steak sandwiches, chargrilled chicken, Caesar salad, fishcakes with pecan sauce, ploughman's with a choice of British cheeses, and daily specials from the blackboard. All the pork is free range and, along with the lamb, comes from the Gotto farm. Good puds too. Youngs range of well-kept ales, a guest beer and a good selection of wines, many by the glass. Fantastic evening celebrations for the Last Night of the Proms; a huge television screen gives an opportunity for everyone to join in the singing and for all budding conductors to practise like mad. And the firework display on Guy Fawkes Night is enough to satisfy all pyrotechnophiles. Even though it has a car park, walk if you can, as parking can be a bit of a problem.

OPEN: 11–11.
Real Ale. Restaurant.
Children in eating area. Dogs on leads. Wheelchair access (not WC).

LONDON SW10

Sporting Page
Tel: 020 7349 0455
6 Camera Place, Chelsea
Courage. Tonia Ogilvy, manager.

Painted white, tucked down a side street off Park Walk, a smart area between the Fulham and King's Roads, this is really more of a wine bar than a pub. Here they sell huge quantities of Bollinger champagne, more than any other pub in the country. Quite stylish, decorated as you would expect with panels, prints and pictures depicting 'sporting greats'. The television will be on for all the big sporting events. Well-chosen bar food could include soup, pasta, hot chicken salad, smoked salmon and scrambled eggs, home-made salmon fishcakes and lemon mayonnaise, and specials such as pan-fried salmon with artichoke purée and a chunky tomato provençale sauce. Roasts every Sunday. Shepherd Neame Spitfire and Charles Wells Bombardier, a fine wine list, a choice of house wines and lots of Bollinger – the house champagne. No garden, but there are tables outside.

> OPEN: 11–11 (12–10.30 Sun).
> Real Ale.
> Children outside. Dogs on leads. Wheelchair access (not WC).

LONDON SW1

Star
Tel: 020 7235 3019

Belgrave Mews West

Fullers. Chris & T.J. Connell, managers.

A delightful flowery pub in an attractive flowery mews off Belgrave Square; always a haven from the noisy frenetic life of London just a few yards away. Built at the same time as the surrounding squares, the Star was originally used by the staff of the grand houses nearby. They all knew their place and had their own bars as befitted their position in the servants' hierarchy. Now there is no more division of labour and no division of space; we can all go wherever we like. Comfortable and well kept: three rooms downstairs with open fires, and an upstairs room if it gets too crowded. Bar food includes lunchtime sandwiches, salads and favourite hot dishes such as fish and chips and steak pie. There is a greater choice of dishes on the evening menu. Well-kept Fullers Chiswick, London Pride, ESB and seasonal ales. On summer evenings you spread out into the mews.

> OPEN: 11.30–3. 5–11 (6.30–11 Sat). 11.30–11 Fri & daily for two weeks before Christmas.
> Real Ale.
> Children if eating. Dogs on leads. Wheelchair access (not WC).

LONDON SW3

The Surprise
Tel: 020 7349 1821

6 Christchurch Terrace, Chelsea, London SW3 4AJ

Bass. Kip Evans, manager.

King Charles II escaped to France after the Civil War in the frigate *Surprise*, which is featured on the inn sign and, in keeping with this maritime theme, the walls of the bars are hung with reproductions of nautical paintings. In complete contrast, the pub, well favoured by the racing fraternity, celebrates the sport of kings by festooning the rail over the bar with assorted members' badges from Newbury and other racecourses. An unchanging sort of place, it has two bars: the saloon bar with the carpet, the public bar without. The TV is on, tuned into the racing. Food is served Monday to Saturday. You choose from gammon and eggs, pies cooked in the pub and a selection of pasta dishes. When winter sets in, steaks are added to the menu. If the kitchens are closed you can get toasted sandwiches from the bar. Ales are Fullers London Pride, Bass and occasionally a guest beer in the winter.

OPEN: 12–11.
Real Ale.
Children: not encouraged. Dogs on leads.
Live bands occasionally.

LONDON W9

Warrington Hotel   Tel: 020 7286 2929
93 Warrington Crescent, London W9 1EH
Free House. John Brandon, licensee.

The Warrington is a wonderful relic of the Victorian Naughty Nineties – only the owners didn't know it at the time. Listed Grade II, the ceramic pillars at the entrance, mosaic steps, semicircular marble bar, sweeping staircase, high ceilings, cherubs and Art Nouveau decoration created what they used to call a gin palace – once owned by the Church of England. Happily for the church, they didn't know that at its naughtiest it was a success-ful brothel, which explains the naughty murals upstairs. A favourite with Marie Lloyd – and a favourite today. Bar meals at lunchtime only. During the evenings the food is Thai, and they say it's good – you have to book. Ales are Fullers London Pride, ESB, Brakspears Special, Youngs Special Bitter and guests. The Warrington is lucky to have a garden with 20 tables. Arrive early if you want one on a summer's day.

OPEN: 11–11 (12–10.30 Sun).
Real Ale.
No children. Dogs on leads.
Cards: MasterCard, Switch, Visa.

LONDON Richmond

White Cross Hotel   Tel: 020 8940 6844
Water Lane, Richmond
Youngs. Mr & Mrs Heggie, licensees/managers.

A good place to start if you want a day out on the Thames; a little lunch and a leisurely trip – there is no better way to see the wonderful gardens, parks, riverside inns and villages than from the river. Just watch where you park your car though – study the tides carefully or you could find it floating past you. The White Cross really was originally a hotel; now it's just a pub, but a pub in a super setting, with a garden overlooking the Thames. The building dates back to the early 19th century and has one large bar with two fireplaces, one of which is directly under the picture window overlooking Richmond Bridge, which always begs the question, 'Where's the chimney?' Also a family room on the mezzanine floor with a balcony overlooking the river. Occasionally during the summer there is live music in the garden. Food is all self-service from a buffet in the bar: cream of garlic soup, home-made pâté – partridge and pistachio, squid in lemon and garlic, venison and pork burgers, Greek-style lamb with spinach, various pies, vegetarian dishes, salads, lamb's liver in sherry sauce, chicken in a mushroom sauce and venison casserole with juniper berries are among the dishes on offer. Traditional puddings too – rhubarb crumble, bread and butter pudding and a chocolate sponge. Youngs Bitter, seasonal ales and 30 wines by the glass or bottle. Their motto is 'real ale, real food and real fires'.

> OPEN: 11–11 (12–10.30 Sun). Food served over an extended lunchtime – not evenings.
> Real Ale.
> Children in garden or family room. Dogs very welcome.

LONDON SW6

White Horse   Tel: 020 7736 2115
1–3 Parsons Green, Fulham
Bass. Mark Dorber, manager.

With a wonderfully sunny terrace, this is just the place for lunch, weekend brunches and relaxation in the early evening. An old coaching inn on the edge of Parsons Green; your last stop before the rigours of your journey westward, now probably your first stop, and there's no hurry to go anywhere else. Inside, the big comfortable bar is hugely popular – so popular that a no-smoking restaurant was opened in the renovated coach house at the back of the pub a year or two back. They extended the kitchen too, just to keep pace. So arrive in good time if you want a meal and somewhere to put the plate. The food is very 'upmarket' – they even have waitress service with drinks brought to your table. An à la carte menu features during the evening. The upstairs gallery, where they serve Sunday lunch, can be used for private meetings and dinner parties. They hold an annual Old Ale Festival towards the end of November each year, so that is worth putting in your diary. The rest of the year they have a good selection of well-kept ales: Adnams Extra, Bass, Harveys Sussex, Highgate Mild and two guest beers, including one from the Rooster Brewery, plus 55 Belgian, Dutch and German beers and 80 different wines.

> OPEN: 11–11 (11–10.30 Sun).
> Real Ale.
> Children in eating area. Dogs on leads.
> Occasional jazz nights. Wheelchair access (not WC).

LONDON SW13 (Barnes)

Ye White Hart   Tel: 020 8876 5177
The Terrace, Barnes
Youngs. John Lockwood, landlord; Stewart Sell, manager.

On the banks of the Thames between Barnes Bridge and Mortlake Brewery, it's an ale-house that has stood on the site since 1662; the present building, dating from 1780, was extended in 1898. A more recent addition is an outside terrace and gazebo overlooking the river. If you can squeeze in, the balcony at the back of the White Hart gives you an excellent view on Boat Race day. In the one spacious bar there is a collection of old photographs and prints of the race. Traditional hot and cold bar food is served at lunchtime only; there are sandwiches, salads, jumbo sausages, fish and chips – that sort of thing – an evening tapas bar (not Sunday) and menu. Excellent, imaginative, regularly changing wine list including 20 wines by the glass. This pub has the full range of Youngs beers, including their Wheat Beer. It won Youngs Wine Pub of the Year for two years running.

OPEN: 11–3. 5.30–11 Mon–Thurs. 11–11 Fri & Sat. 12–10.30 Sun.
Real Ale.
No children. Dogs on leads.

LONDON W8

Windsor Castle
114 Campden Hill Road, Holland Park
Bass. Carole Gabbour, manager.

Tel: 020 7243 9551

When the pub was built in 1828, there was an uninterrupted view across open country to Windsor Castle, nearly 20 miles away to the west. Now all you can see is very smart, expensive real estate, but this charming old pub is still the same. Inside are three panelled bars – each with its own entrance and customers – and a small dining room. The pub fills up rapidly on summer evenings and the attractive, shady walled garden comes into its own. Interesting pub grub is served all day: sandwiches on focaccia herb bread, chicken Caesar, oysters and mussels, Mediterranean lamb with roasted vegetables, linguini with tomatoes, olives and capers, steamed mussels, sausage and mash and a tremendously popular roast beef and Yorkshire pudding or roast lamb shank for lunch on Sunday. Ales are Bass, Adnams and Fullers London Pride. There are also house wines, a very reasonable champagne and various malt whiskies.

OPEN: 12–11.
Real Ale.
No children. Dogs on leads (not in garden!). Wheelchair access to garden.

BEST OF THE REST

LONDON SW13
Bulls Head
Lonsdale Road, Barnes

Tel: 020 8876 5241

Weekday lunchtimes are blissfully silent – musically – while they gird themselves for another jazz session. This very well-run pub (Innkeepers of the Year for 2001) is a haven for modern jazz groupies. The top jazz groups who come here to play do have their own room, but playing jazz is not a quiet occupation. Lunchtime bar food is all home-made; there is a popular carvery and a selection of other hot dishes. In the evening they have some wonderful Thai food, freshly cooked to order. Youngs Bitter, Special, and over 80 malt whiskies. A really comprehensive wine list – over 220 bottles, 34 by the glass. Weekday lunches are quiet. The rest of the time you either like jazz or wear your earplugs. Live jazz every evening in own room with bar.

LONDON WC2

Cheshire Cheese   Tel: 020 7836 2347
5 Little Essex Street

Frequently a case of mistaken identity, but this is not to be confused with Ye Really Olde Cheshire Cheese. This pub is quite olde (and it has a ghost) but is not as olde as the famous Ye Olde; that one is just a short walk away. Only the main bar is free of music. They do serve cheap and cheerful food all day: as they say, 'red-hot value, fast, no frills and cheap'. Beers are Scottish & Newcastle cask ales and Fosters lager. They organise a ghost walk around the area which you can join in.

LONDON E14

Grapes   Tel: 020 7987 4396
76 Narrow Street

A watery, 16th-century pub with Dickensian connections. Not the easiest place to find; feet are better than wheels, or if the tide is right you could probably still row in as there are steps leading up from the shore. Old and leaning to one side, this is a place to come to soak in the atmosphere. Good, simple bar food; a fish restaurant upstairs. Adnams, Tetleys, Ind Coope Burton and a changing guest beer.

LONDON SE13

Horniman   Tel: 020 7407 3611
Hays Galleria, Nr London Bridge

Tea, rather than ale, is what the name of this pub conveys; Hornimans have been tea merchants since 1826 and the decor reflects this. It has a set of clocks made for the founder, Frederick, that show the time in various places around the world, and a frieze illustrating tea from bush to pot. Spacious and comfortable, it has wonderful views over the Thames and Tower Bridge. Lots of different beers to go with the usual bar food and daily changing dishes. They close at 5 o'clock weekend evenings.

LONDON W11

Ladbroke Arms   Tel: 020 7727 6648
54 Ladbroke Road

A pub with lots of things going for it: they serve some interesting home-made food, about five different beers, and you can buy some works of art if you are so minded; the landlord deals in art and uses the pub walls as an art gallery. Lastly, on a balmy evening you can sit outside and enjoy your drink.

LONDON NW3

Spaniards Inn   Tel: 020 8731 6571
Spaniards Lane, Hampstead

Since the 16th century this has been an interesting place. Variously a tollhouse and the home of a Spanish ambassador, this splendid, well-restored building was certainly known to Dickens, Keats and Byron. A hugely popular pub, they serve home-made traditional dishes and a roast on Sundays. Fullers London Pride, Bass and a guest beer. Outside is a big, well-planted garden for you to enjoy.

LONDON E1

Town of Ramsgate   Tel: 020 7264 0001
Wapping High Street

There really is a connection with Ramsgate in Kent. It was here at Wapping Old Stairs (not to be confused with Wapping New Stairs) that the Ramsgate boats would come to sell their catch of fish. Inside the pub you'll find a fine panelled bar with prints of old Limehouse. Good, familiar bar food plus Fullers London Pride and perhaps one other beer. There is a flowery terrace and platform by the stairs with a limited view of the Thames.

LONDON SW1

Westminster Arms   Tel: 020 7222 8520
Storey's Gate

This is as close to the seat of government most of us will get – fraternising with government staff and researchers while they down a few well-deserved drinks in the small panelled bar. Five beers on the go here, plus a guest; these include Westminster Best brewed by Charringtons. They also have a decent wine list. Food is served in the downstairs bar – steak and kidney pie, fish and chips, that sort of thing; also in the restaurant upstairs.

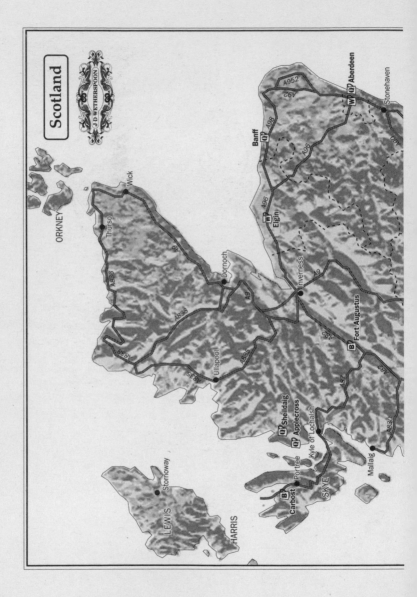

Scotland

J D WETHERSPOON

ORKNEY

Wick

Thurso

A9

A836

A838

A835

Dornoch

A9

Ullapool

A835

A832

A890

Sheildaig

Applecross

Kyle of Lochalsh

Portree

SKYE

Carbost

Mallaig

A87

Fort Augustus

A82

A86

A830

Inverness

A9

A96

Elgin

Banff

A96

A98

A952

A90

Aberdeen

Stonehaven

A90

LEWIS

Stornoway

HARRIS

Scotland

ABERDEEN
Atholl Hotel
Tel: 01224 323505
54 King's Gate, Aberdeen, Grampian AB15 4YN
Free House. Gordon Sinclair, licensee.

Known as Devana by the Romans, granted a charter in 1179, burnt to the ground by Edward III, Aberdeen rose, phoenix-like, from the ashes to become New Aberdeen. Then gradually, from the 13th century, it spread northwards to meet Old Aberdeen. The granite city, as it is known, prospered during the 18th century to become the city you see today. Make your way to the lounge bar in this substantial West End hotel, popular with discerning clients wanting a quiet drink and something from the bar menu. The well-kept beers are changing all the time, so you will have to go and see what's on offer.

> OPEN: 11–2.30. 5–11 (12–2.30 Sun).
> Real Ale.
> Children welcome. No dogs. Bedrooms.

ABERDEEN
Prince of Wales
Tel: 01224 640597
7–11 St Nicholas Lane, Aberdeen, Grampian AB10 1HE
Free House. Peter Birnie, licensee.

In a cobbled lane, just off the main shopping centre, the Victorian Prince of Wales is known to have the longest bar in the city, all 60 feet of it, and at busy times every inch is taken. Comfortable and popular, this is just the place for a pint of well-kept ale and a generous lunchtime snack: home-made soup, steak and ale pie, chicken Kiev, oven-roasted vegetables and rice, fresh breaded haddock, cold meats from the salad bar, filled baguettes, baked potatoes and various sandwiches. The menu listing the home-cooked food changes daily. No distractions from jukebox or TV; it's blissfully quiet, so you can chat to your neighbour and enjoy either the draught Bass, Caledonian 80/–, Orkney Dark Island, Theakstons Old Peculier or Isle of Skye beers. Guest beers and fresh coffee too.

> OPEN: 11–midnight.
> Real Ale.
> Children in eating area. No dogs. Wheelchair access (not WC).
> Live music Sunday afternoons.

ABERDEEN

St Machar's Bar
Tel: 01224 483079

High Street, Old Aberdeen, Grampian AB24 3EH
Free House. James Alexander, owner/licensee.

St Machar's Bar, which takes its name from the twin-towered, 14th-century St Machar's Cathedral, was once named the best licensed corridor in the world. Not far from the oldest inhabited house in the old city – Chaplains Court, built in 1519 – and the medieval Kings College in the High Street. The bar, deep in Aberdeen University territory, can on occasion be overrun by students. When the university is not in session, you can spend an idyllic few hours relaxing with a pint of McEwan's 70/– and one of the generously sized sandwiches that cross the bar for extremely reasonable prices. McEwans Export 70/–, 80/–, John Smiths, Guinness and Theakstons.

> OPEN: 11–11 (12.30–10.30 Sun).
> No children. No dogs. Wheelchair access. No garden. No car park.

APPLECROSS

Applecross Inn
Tel: 01520 744260

Shore Street, Applecross, Highland IV54 8LR
Free House. Judith Fish, licensee.

On the west coast of the Applecross peninsular, the Applecross is the only pub in this remote, isolated community; until the new, single-track road was built in the 1970s this was one of the most inaccessible places in Scotland. The original road – the scenic route – follows an old cattle pass round hair-raising hairpin bends, climbing to over 2000 feet, eventually joining the road to Ardarroch. Suitably terrified and relieved, you should make your way to the inn to recover. Here there is a true communal atmosphere, with lively repartee between locals, staff and visitors. In spite, or because, of its remoteness, the bar is very well stocked with bottled beers and over 50 single malts, and the food is ample and excellent. Fish and seafood take first place on the menu: as well as soup and sandwiches, there could be local oysters, prawns, smoked salmon, crabs, scallops in a creamy sauce, haggis, steak pie, or a chicken dish if you're not wanting fish. Short wine list.

> OPEN: 11.30–11.30 (12–11 winter).
> Children before 8.30pm. Dogs in bar. Wheelchair access. Car park. Bedrooms.
> Cards: MasterCard, Switch, Visa.

ARDUAINE

Loch Melfort Hotel and Restaurant
Tel: 01852 200233

Arduaine, By Oban, Argyll PA34 4XE
Free House. Nigel & Kylie Schofield, licensees.

Next to Loch Melfort are the glories of the National Trust's Arduaine Gardens. If you are staying here, walk down to the shore – where the hotel has its own pots and nets – and you might see what the sea has provided for supper; you'll know the fish on the menu is as fresh as can be. Also on the menu will be venison sausages served with caramelised onions, fillet of salmon en croute, a home-made soup, sandwiches, ploughman's and some interesting specials. Comprehensive wine list (they have won the Scottish Wine Pub of the Year award) and a good selection of malt whiskies. Mooring facilities if you are bringing your yacht, showers for sailors, a drying room too if you need it and plenty of walks for landlubbers. From the hotel there are wonderful views of Loch Melfort and the 'Slate Islands' – islands whose slate quarries had been worked for hundreds of years.

OPEN: 9.30–11.
Restaurant (no-smoking). Two AA Rosettes.
Children welcome. No dogs in the main hotel but they are allowed in the extension.
Wheelchair access. Car park. Mooring. Bedrooms.

BALERNO

Johnsburn House   Tel: 0131 449 3847
Johnsburn Road, Balerno, Lothian EH14 7BB
Free House. Martin & Linda Mitchell, licensees.

Over the years the pub has won awards for all sorts of things, 86 to date, including lots for food and beer. They say it's Britain's most awarded pub. Originally an 18th-century gentleman's baronial mansion, it's now a country pub – comfortable, panelled and beamed. Martin Mitchell is a Master Chef, Master Cellarman and Master Restaurateur. Linda looks after the front of house while Martin conjures up delectable dishes – some of Scotland's best food – in the kitchen. From the menu you could have red-pepper, red-lentil, tomato and carrot soup with tarragon cream, seafood goujons, fried-aubergine and spiced-egg risotto, salmon with lobster sauce, grilled swordfish with fricassee of seafoods, sirloin steak with Diane sauce; from the bar menu, light meals, filled crêpes, toasted sandwiches, even an omelette. Luscious puds too. Five changing cask ales. As they have won two silver medals for Wine Pub of the Year, you will find an interesting wine list.

OPEN: Closed Mon, otherwise 12–3. 5–11 (12–12 Sat. 12–11 Sun).
Real Ale. Restaurant.
Children and dogs welcome. Wheelchair access.

BANFF

Ship Inn   Tel: 01261 812620
8 Deveronside, Banff, Grampian AB45 1HP
Free House. Moire MacLellan, owner/licensee.

This area of coastline is known as the 'garden of the north'. Surprisingly, the climate is on the whole dry and mild. Banff, built at the mouth of the River Deveron, boasts some fine

Georgian architecture, built when it was a favourite winter resort. The Ship Inn overlooks the harbour, which, having largely silted up in the 19th century, is now mainly used as a sailing centre. You would come for the view and the beer; no food, only a crisp and a nut. If you are really desperate they could probably rustle up a sandwich, but nothing fancy. Courage Directors, McEwans 80/–, Murphys and various guest ales.

> OPEN: 11–12 Mon–Thurs. 11–12.30 Fri & Sat. Closed Sun morning, otherwise 7–12 during the summer.
> Real Ale.
> Children in the lounge bar. Dogs on leads. Wheelchair access.

BROUGHTY FERRY

Fishermans Tavern Hotel   Tel: 01382 775941
10–14 Fort Street, Broughty Ferry, Dundee, Tayside DD5 2AD
Free House. Jonathan Stewart, licensee.

In an old extended fisherman's cottage in what was just a fishing village on the eastern side of Dundee, the small, rambling Fishermans Tavern Hotel is known for its well-kept ales and good traditional bar food, which could include a home-made soup of the day, beefsteak roll with onions, toasted sandwiches, steak or chicken and mushroom pie, filled jacket potatoes and daily specials. Belhavens 60/–, 80/– and St Andrew's, Maclays 80/– and a daily changing guest beer. If you look upriver from the harbour you see 'the bridge over the glorious River Tay', as William McGonagall, Scotland's famous versifier, described it. The 15th-century Broughty Castle, which overlooks the busy harbour, is now a museum.

> OPEN: 11–midnight Mon–Wed. 11–1am Thurs–Sat. 12.30–midnight Sun.
> Real Ale. Limited bar food Sun.
> Children in eating area. Dogs on leads. Wheelchair access.
> Bedrooms. Folk music Thurs eves.

CLEISH

Nivingston House Hotel   Tel: 01577 850216
Cleish, Nr Kinross, Tayside KY13 7L5
Free House. Niall Thompson, manager.

An attractive, solid, small, faintly baronial country hotel with a very comfortable bar (carpets and upholstered furniture) and friendly staff. Set at the foot of the Cleish Hills, it serves well-presented bar food at lunchtime and in the evenings. The menu ranges from soup and home-made pâté to a dish of smoked salmon and prawns, plus daily specials. It has a very elegant restaurant with a reputation for serving imaginative, creative dishes: French onion and coriander soup, prawns and sweet-herring platter with a small salad and curry mayonnaise, Scottish sirloin in a red-wine sauce or breast of wild duck roasted and coated with a tomato and port sauce. Calders 80/– Ale, over 50 malt whiskies and, naturally, a good wine list. The seats at the front of the hotel overlook sweeping lawns to the hills beyond.

> OPEN: 12–2.30. 6–11 (6–11.45 Sat).
> Real Ale. Restaurant – CDs played in here.
> Children welcome. Dogs on leads. Wheelchair access. Car park. Bedrooms.
> Cards: all major credit cards.

CRINAN

Crinan Hotel   Tel: 01546 830261
Crinan, By Lochgilphead, Argyll PA31 8SR
Free House. Nicholas Ryan, licensee.

Tucked under wooded cliffs at the north end of the Crinan Canal, the Crinan Hotel is in a spectacular position looking out over Argyll's rugged coastline. From upstairs there are wonderful views of the entrance to the busy canal – with its 15 locks – from the windows. If it's a very light lunch you're after, you can either eat in the public bar or the coffee shop/bakery by the fishing-boat dock. Lots of fresh fish included in the bar menu: local mussels, whole Loch Crinan jumbo prawns, Loch Fyne undyed kippers, trout, princess clams, seafood stew; also honey-roast ham, local butcher's sausages with mashed potatoes and black-pudding bread, and chicken stuffed with leeks and mushrooms. Lots of salads and daily specials. Tennents 70/–, 80/–, and Worthington Cream Flow. A choice of malt whiskies and a good wine list. During the evenings, when there is a shift of emphasis towards the restaurant, the atmosphere does become more formal. Seats outside on the terrace from where you can enjoy the view.

> OPEN: 11–11 (11–2.30. 5–11 winter).
> Restaurant. Bar meals lunchtimes.
> Children in eating area of cocktail bar. Dogs on leads. Wheelchair access. Car park.
> Bedrooms.
> Cards: Amex, MasterCard, Switch, Visa.

EARLSFERRY

The Golf Tavern   Tel: 01333 330610
5 Links Road, Earlsferry, Fife KY9 1AW
Free House. Douglas Duncanson, licensee.

A holiday resort on the Firth of Forth that, as well as wonderful beaches, has two golf courses. The Golf Tavern, an old Victorian-style pub, is beside the course at Earlsferry, near the 19th hole. Facing south with sheltered beaches, the old fishing port of Elie and the ancient market town of Earlsferry are as one. Years ago there actually was a ferry across the Forth to Dunbar, but now the pub sustains just golfers, locals and land-bound travellers. Home-made soups in the bar, also steak sandwiches with a side salad, toasties – that sort of thing. Caledonian Deuchars IPA, Guinness, Tennents Lager and a guest beer. No garden but you can admire the golf course.

> OPEN: 11–12 Mon–Thurs. 11–1am Fri & Sat. 12.30–1am Sun. From October to Easter, 11–2.30. 5.30–12 Mon–Fri.
> Real Ale.
> Children and dogs welcome.
> N.B. Sometimes music in lounge but not in bar.

EDINBURGH

Bow Bar
Tel: 0131 226 7667
80 West Bow, Edinburgh EH1 2HS
Free House. H. McLoughlin, licensee.

Just below the castle, this is a traditional drinkers' bar representing the heyday of the late 19th century – all glass mirrors, mahogany panelling, gas fires, and barmen in long white aprons; even the beer pumps are well over 90 years old. Always Deuchars IPA, Belhaven 80/– and Timothy Taylors Landlord, but more than eight well-kept ales at any one time during the peak season, chosen from the 80 that are tried during the year. Well over 130 malt whiskies and a choice of gins, rums and vodkas. Cheap and cheerful bar snacks of the filled rolls and pies variety.

> OPEN: 12–11.30.
> Real Ale. Lunchtime snacks.
> No children. Dogs on leads. Wheelchair access possible – one small step.

EDINBURGH

Starbank
Tel: 0131 552 4141
64 Laverockbank Road, Edinburgh EH5 3BZ
Free House. Valerie West, licensee.

Well liked; a friendly place where you can get a taste of Scotland's best beer and whisky. An elegant little stone pub on a corner site with wonderful views over the Firth of Forth. Ales change all the time but the Starbank keeps about ten on hand pump, so you can always be assured of a well-chosen range. There is also a good selection of bar food: home-made soup, pâté, trout fillet with tarragon-cream sauce, mixed seafood salad, roast lamb, boiled-ham salad, steak and ale casserole, ploughman's, a vegetarian dish of the day and daily specials. Wines by the glass and a selection of malt whiskies. Seats on the terrace, out of the prevailing wind.

> OPEN: 11–11 Mon–Wed. 11–midnight Thurs–Sat. 12.30–11 Sun.
> Real Ale. No-smoking restaurant.
> Children welcome. Dogs on leads. Wheelchair access.
> Cards: MasterCard, Visa.
> N.B. TV sometimes on.

ELIE

Ship Inn
Tel: 01333 330246

The Toft, Elie, Fife KY9 1DT
Free House. Richard & Jill Philip, licensees.

This is a 'joining in' sort of place – not for the fainthearted. Immensely popular and very family-minded, you will be surrounded by people who like to watch and do energetic things, recovering in the Ship Inn. Every water sport you can think of seems to go on here: windsurfing, water-skiing and sailing in the bay. On a dryer note, the pub organises its own cricket fixtures and even rugby matches on the sandy beach beyond the beer garden. There is also a local golf course. Licensed since 1838, the Ship has perfected the art of catering for the traveller. Inside is a big downstairs bar, three dining areas – one upstairs – where they serve lunchtime and evening bar food, also a three-course lunch, à la carte dinner and a children's menu. In July and August the beer garden is covered with a marquee in which they have a bar and barbecue and hold occasional beer and jazz festivals. The menu could include: chef's chicken-liver pâté, potted shrimps, smoked haddock and broccoli pie, steak and Guinness pie, bangers and mash, vegetarian and children's dishes. There is also a roast Sunday lunch. Belhaven 80/-, Belhaven Best, Theakstons Best Bitter, draught Guinness, Blackthorn cider, Tartan Special and a draught lager. Choice of wines and malt whiskies. The big beer garden overlooks a sandy bay, any cricket or rugby match taking place, and the Firth of Forth.

> OPEN: 11–midnight (12.30–11 Sun).
> Real Ale. Restaurant (not Sun eve).
> Children in restaurant and lounge bar. Dogs on leads.
> Wheelchair access. Occasional jazz outside.
> Cards: Access, Delta, Switch, Visa.

GLASGOW

Babbity Bowster
Tel: 0141 552 5055

16/18 Blackfriars Street, Glasgow G1 1PE
Free House. Fraser Laurie, licensee.

The city you see today is the result of the prosperity of the Industrial Revolution: a medieval city buried under Victorian commercial success. In a quiet pedestrianised street in the business centre, this elegant renovated Adam townhouse is understandably popular with journalists, businessmen, students, or anyone wanting a refreshing drink, from a cup of tea to a glass of the Babbity Bowster's very own beer. It's really more a café/bar with a restaurant and hotel attached than a pub. Breakfast is served from 8.30am and bar snacks from noon until 9 at night. Bar food includes filled baguettes, spicy chicken and haggis, neeps and tatties. Specials from the blackboard include lots of fish dishes: langoustines, oysters, prawns, fresh fish – all with home-baked bread. Barbecued dishes in the summer. Maclays 80/- and a guest beer. This is the only pub in the city centre that has an outside drinking area with seats and tables on a small terrace.

> OPEN: 8–midnight.
> Real Ale. Restaurant.
> Children in restaurant. No dogs. Bedrooms.

GLASGOW

Counting House
Tel: 0141 225 0160

2 St Vincent Place, Glasgow G2 1EG
Wetherspoon.

Overlooking George Square in the centre of Glasgow, the square, named after George III, was laid out at the end of the 18th century and has over the centuries gathered more statues than any other in Scotland. The Counting House is a clever conversion; a redundant Royal Bank of Scotland hit the dust and underwent a change into a Wetherspoon personality. The building was wonderful and the conversion was sensitive. It all looks solid and prosperous – just as an ex-bank should. All the usual Wetherspoon attributes: a selection of local, reasonably priced real ales and a reliable, something-for-everyone menu, plus daily specials.

> OPEN: 11–12.
> Real Ale.
> No children. No dogs. All wheelchair facilities.

GLASGOW

Press Bar
Tel: 0141 552 5142

199 Albion Street, Glasgow G1 1RU
Free House. Mr McEntee, licensee.

As you rightly imagine from the name, the Press Bar is surrounded by newspaper offices and caters largely for thirsty reporters who come in here to relax and gossip. It's a small, no-frills sort of place, dominated by its regulars escaping the high-tech bustling newsrooms. Usual range of bar snacks, plus some chicken dishes and lasagne. Belhaven Best, Caffreys, Guinness, Tennents lagers, Dry Blackthorn and Strongbow ciders.

> OPEN: 11–midnight (12.30–midnight Sun).
> Real Ale.
> No children. Dogs on leads.

GLASGOW

Three Judges
Tel: 0141 337 3055

141 Dumbarton Road, Partick Cross, Glasgow G11 6PR
Maclay-Alloa. Helen McCarroll, manager.

A place for those beer aficionados among you. A couple of thousand beers have been brought in as guests over the last few years; the numbers go up all the time but they've stopped counting. A no-nonsense sort of local where they say more Gaelic is spoken than in the Western Isles. But you probably won't want to be here for the language lessons, nor the simple bar snacks – toasties, pork pies, that sort of thing – but the beer. Nine beers plus a draught farm cider. Good range of whiskies: they feature a 'malt of the month'. Very near the university and the Kelvingrove Art Gallery; the Botanical Gardens are 200 yards away and the Transport Museum just 100 yards along the road. CAMRA award winners since 1992, so you know the beers are in tiptop condition.

>OPEN: 11–11 (11–12 Fri & Sat. 12.30–11 Sun).
>Real Ale.
>No children. Dogs on leads.

GLASGOW

Ubiquitous Chip
12 Ashton Lane, Hillhead, Glasgow G12
Free House. Ronnie Clydesdale, licensee.

Tel: 0141 334 5007
Fax: 0141 337 1302

Originally a Victorian coach house, it is now a well-known restaurant, bistro and bar, where you are served some memorable food. In place of the old wine shop they have opened the 'Wee Pub at the Chip'. Frequented by university lecturers, students and anyone else who knows a good thing when they find it, the Ubiquitous Chip is on a cobbled lane in the very heart of Glasgow. There is a daily changing menu but there could be home-made soup, oak-smoked fillet of mackerel, chicken and ham pâté with Cumberland sauce, honey-roast ham, rare roast Scotch beef, vegetarian haggis with neeps and tatties, roast chicken piri piri, a fish dish, choice of salads and home-made puddings. A two- or three-course lunch is served in the restaurant next to the pretty courtyard. The wine selection is reputed to be the best in Scotland; they have 120 malt whiskies and, last but not least, real ales: Caledonian 80/– and Deuchars IPA. Draught Guinness, Addlestone Cask cider and Furstenberg lager.

>OPEN: 11–12 Mon–Sat (12.30–12 Sun).
>Real Ale. Restaurant.
>No children. Dogs on leads in bar. Wheelchair access to WC.
>Cards: Amex, Diners, MasterCard, Switch, Visa.

KILLIECRANKIE

Killiecrankie Hotel
Killiecrankie, Nr Pitlochry, Tayside PH16 5LG
Free House. Colin & Carole Anderson, licensees.

Tel: 01796 473220
Fax: 01796 472451

Now owned by the Scottish National Trust, the hotel is in a very beautiful area of Perthshire, midway between Pitlochry and Blair Atholl. Built as a manse for the local vicar in 1840, now a handsome hotel in 4 acres of its own land overlooking the River Garry and the Pass of Killiecrankie. Inside the hotel they provide bar lunches and suppers in the attractive panelled bar and a noted, creative table d'hôte menu in the elegant dining room. Bar food includes soups, sweet-cured herrings with salad, home-made chicken-liver parfait with Cumberland sauce and toast, tapas, houmus, olives, tapenade and air-cured ham, home-made chicken goujons served with curried mayonnaise, chargrilled leg of lamb steak with garlic butter, rib-eye steak with garlic and peppercorn butter, Cumberland sausage with onion chutney, ploughman's, honey-roast ham with salad, smoked-salmon and prawn open sandwich, good puddings and cheese to follow. Good-size, varied wine list and a selection of malt whiskies. You are surrounded by lovely countryside with lots of things to see. The 17th-century mill at Blair Atholl is still working and the smallest distillery in Scotland is north-east of Pitlochry. Pitlochry also has a theatre festival every year. Go at the right time of the year and you can watch the salmon struggle up a 'fish ladder' at the southern end of Loch Faskally.

OPEN: 11–2.30. 6–11 (closed from 3 January until mid-February).
No-smoking evening restaurant.
Children welcome. No dogs where food is served. Wheelchair access (not WC).
Ten en-suite bedrooms.
Cards: Delta, MasterCard, Switch, Visa.

KINNESSWOOD

Lomond Country Inn   Tel: 01592 840253
Main Street, Kinnesswood, By Loch Leven, Perthshire KY13 7HN
Free House. Mr & Mrs Martin Bald, licensees.

Solidly built, cosy and friendly, this is a combination of local pub and hotel. Inside it has big open log fires in the bar where they serve bar snacks and meals all day; the food is simply prepared, using fresh ingredients. Plenty of game on the winter menus: pheasant, local venison and wild salmon are frequently featured. There is a separate menu for the 'up a notch' restaurant. Tetley Bitter, three guests and a reasonably priced wine list. Seats in the garden to enjoy your surroundings. There are magnificent views over Loch Leven and the sunsets are spectacular – weather permitting! Loch Leven Castle on Castle Island is where Mary Queen of Scots was imprisoned and, in 1568, made her escape.

OPEN: 11–11 (11–11.45 Fri & Sat).
Real Ale. Restaurant.
Children welcome. Dogs in bar area. Wheelchair access. Bedrooms.
Cards: Amex, Delta, Diners, MasterCard, Switch, Visa.

KIPPEN

Cross Keys Hotel   Tel: 01786 870293
Main Street, Kippen, Stirlingshire FK8 3DN
Free House. Marjorie Scoular & Gordon Scott, licensees.

This small, well-run, 18th-century hotel on the road to Loch Lomond has new licensees, but everything promises to be easily as good as before. Inside, the comfortable lounge bar has a good fire and you can eat here or in the beamed restaurant. Home-cooked food includes soup, fresh filo-pastry parcels filled with haggis served with a whisky sauce, home-made lasagne, their own-recipe steak pie, fresh liver with bacon and onions, poached breast of chicken with a lemon and tarragon sauce, home-made lamb stovies served with crusty brown bread and butter, fried fillet of haddock, pancakes filled with smoked haddock and prawns in a cream sauce, plus daily specials, vegetarian dishes and a choice of puddings. Children's portions. The real ales change on a rota system, there are lots of malt whiskies and a short wine list. Seats in the garden. N.B. Good news: the jukebox and pool table have been given the heave-ho!

> OPEN: 12–2.30. 5.30–11 (12–11.30 Sat. 12.30–11 Sun).
> Real Ale. Restaurant.
> Children in restaurant/family room only. Dogs on leads. Wheelchair access into hotel and ladies' WC. Bedrooms.
> Cards: Delta, MasterCard, Switch, Visa.

MELROSE

Burts Hotel
Tel: 01896 822285

Market Square, Melrose TD6 9PL
Free House. Graham Henderson, licensee.

This small town on the banks of the River Tweed is surrounded by wonderful scenery and is the centre of Sir Walter Scott country. Melrose Abbey, founded in the 12th century, suffered from some very unwelcome attention during border wars between the Scots and the English. Repeatedly damaged, it was rebuilt in 1385, only to be ruined again in 1544; it is thanks to the efforts of Sir Walter Scott and the Duke of Buccleuch that any of the abbey is still standing. Now that Robert the Bruce's heart has been found on the site, the abbey is even more unforgettable. So with all these places to see, Burts Hotel is a good place to start from. Originally an early Georgian private house, it is now a well-run hotel where you have the best of both worlds: a relaxing bar and a more formal restaurant. Consistently good, some dishes reflect the area: Loch Fyne mussels in garlic cream, local lamb and haggis in various guises; others have a more cosmopolitan touch. Deuchars IPA and Caledonian 80/– are the regular beers. They have enough varieties of whisky to keep you happy for a very long time, plus an extensive wine list.

> OPEN: 11–2. 5–11 (12–2. 6–11 Sun).
> Real Ale. Restaurant.
> Children welcome. Dogs in bar. Car park. Bedrooms.
> Cards: Amex, Delta, MasterCard, Switch, Visa.

MOUNTBENGER

Gordon Arms Hotel
Tel: 01750 82232

Yarrow Valley, Mountbenger, Selkirk TD7 5LE
Free House. Mr Krex, licensee.

Surrounded by empty moorland, the Gordon Arms, near St Mary's Loch and the River Yarrow, is in remote, rolling border hills, ready to welcome any traveller on the Southern Upland Way, or on the direct route between Land's End and John O'Groats. Friendly, accommodating, with open fires in the bars in cold weather, the Gordon Arms offers a range of home-cooked meals and a choice of real ales. Breakfast is served all day. Bar snacks include soups, sandwiches, filled baked potatoes, grills, fish and traditional puddings. Children's portions, and in summer, high tea in the lounge. Particularly geared up to the walker/cyclist/birdwatcher, it has a cleverly converted bunkhouse which offers clean, warm, basic accommodation. So, not only big boots and hairy socks but huge backpacks too. Broughtons Greenmantle Ghillie is the beer. Over 50 malt whiskies. Trout and salmon fishing can be arranged. Fantastic wild scenery.

OPEN: 11–11 (11–midnight Sat).
Real Ale. Restaurant.
Children in eating area of lounge and dining room. Dogs on leads.
Accordion & Fiddle Club 3rd Wed each month.
Literary Club meets occasional Wednesdays.

PERTH

Old Ship Inn
Skinnergate, Perth, Perthshire PH1 5JH
Free House. Andrew A. Allwell, licensee.

Tel: 01738 624929

Situated in the heart of this historic city, the Old Ship should be renamed The New Old Ship – it is not as old as it seems. The original inn was pulled down by the Victorians with the excuse that it should be 'reconstructed and brought up to modern requirements'. So in 1860, 200 years of Perth's history was demolished and rebuilt as the Old Ship you see today. This is an area that until fairly recently was the place for buying boots, shoes and gloves. Skinnergate evolving from the word skynnere – skins as in 'Ye Olde Skynneres and Glovers of Perth'; now just 'The Glovers Incorporation of Perth'. Time moves on, but the two things that haven't changed at the Ship are the range of well-kept ales and the dependable, traditional menu. Always fresh haddock, homemade steak pie, roast of the day and a York ham salad. The beers, which can change, could include Caledonian IPA, Fullers London Pride, Timothy Taylors Landlord, Marstons Pedigree, Youngs Special, Greene King Abbot, Burton Ale and Morlands Old Speckled Hen. Six malt whiskies.

OPEN: 11–2.30. 5–11 (11–11.30 Fri & Sat). Closed Sun.
Real Ale. Restaurant.
Children in restaurant only. Dogs in bar.

PITLOCHRY

Moulin Hotel
11–13 Kirkmichael Road, Moulin, Nr Pitlochry, Perthshire PH16 5EW
Free House. Heather Reeves, licensee.

Tel: 01796 472196

This old coaching inn is a warm and friendly place with a good local atmosphere. The oldest section of the inn is 300 years old, so it was certainly here when Bonnie Prince Charlie passed through Moulin on his way to the battlefield of Culloden in 1746. The village of Moulin, on the outskirts of Pitlochry, is at the foot of the 2760-foot-high Ben Vrackie. Inside the inn you'll find well-produced and reasonably priced food: homemade soups, grilled salmon, Angus steaks, haggis of course, lasagne, various fish dishes and specials. From their own microbrewery there will be a Light Ale, Old Remedial, Moulin Ale of Atholl, Braveheart, and maybe a guest beer. Folk music on Friday evenings, but apart from that music-free.

> OPEN: 11–11. 12–11 Sun.
> Real Ale. Restaurant.
> Children welcome. Dogs too. Wheelchair access. Car park.
> Bedrooms in the new part of the hotel.
> Cards: MasterCard, Visa.

SHEILDAIG

Tigh an Eilean Hotel   Tel: 01520 755251
Sheildaig, By Loch Torridon, Ross-shire
Free House. Mr & Mrs C. Field, owners/licensees.

A very rugged area of the western Highlands; spectacular scenery surrounds this small village and its hotel. The huge sandstone mountains on the far side of Loch Torridon are over 750 million years old. The village of Sheildag, however, was only created by the Admiralty in 1800. This is a small, unassuming hotel on the edge of the loch. The non-residents' side has a bar whose windows look out to sea. The well-chosen, daily changing menu ranges from sandwiches, soups, salmon and seafood to hot daily specials which could include lamb baked in hay served on a mixed-bean cassoulet, chicken korma, hare or game casserole, always a choice of fresh fish, a seafood stew and good puddings. The fish dishes depend on what is available. There is also an evening restaurant and comprehensive wine list. Tables and chairs in a front courtyard overlook the loch. Excellent walking country.

> OPEN: 11–11 (11–10 Sun). In winter 11–2.30. 5–11 (11–11 Sat. 12.30–10 Sun).
> Evening restaurant April–October. Bar food all year.
> Children until 8pm. No dogs. Wheelchair access. Bedrooms.

STRATHTUMMEL

The Loch Tummel Inn   Tel: 01882 634272
Strathtummel, By Pitlochry, Perthshire PH16 5RP
Free House. Michael & Liz Marsden, owners/licensees.

From here you can explore the wonderful Perthshire countryside, fish in the loch, attend the festival theatre at Pitlochry, visit Blair Atholl or just have a good long walk. This handsome, comfortable old coaching inn is on the banks of tree-fringed Loch Tummel. The bar, in the old stables, serves Braveheart Ale from the brewery at Moulin, and Guinness; the restaurant is in the old hayloft. Whatever you've been doing, you are bound to have an appetite for the freshly prepared dishes: soup of the day with home-made bread, home oak-smoked salmon with brown bread, chicken-liver pâté with oatcakes, haggis with creamed turnip, baked Arbroath smokie with bacon, game pie or griddled Angus rib-eye steak with mushrooms and onions. Vegetarian dishes are available and the specials and puddings are on the blackboard. Fantastic views from most of the rooms.

> OPEN: 11–11 (12.30–11 Sun). Closed from 1st week after New Year until March.
> Real Ale. Restaurant.
> Children welcome. Dogs on leads. Wheelchair access (not WC). Car park.
> Six bedrooms, some with log fires.

St Mary's Loch

Tibbie Shiels Inn
Tel: 01750 42231

St Mary's Loch, Selkirk, Borders TD7 5NE
Free House. Jill Brown, licensee.

A favourite stopping place for walkers on the long distance Southern Upland Way which passes the door. Built on the finger of land that separates St Mary's Loch and the Loch of the Lowes, it was named after Isabella Shiel, a redoubtable 19th-century landlady who supported herself and six children by taking in 'gentlemen lodgers'. Thirteen beds were somehow distributed between what is now the bar and the attic – increasing to 35 in the shooting season! The inn has been somewhat extended since then, so there is a little more room to move around. Bar food includes soups, ploughman's, Holy Mole chilli salad and garlic bread, and spicy chicken. Fresh local Yarrow trout, salmon, escalope of pork with ginger-wine sauce and queen scallops with a bacon and cream sauce are among the favourites. Some vegetarian dishes and a variety of puddings. Broughton Green Mantle and Belhaven 80/– on hand pump. A selection of wines and over 50 malt whiskies. Lots of sailing and fishing on St Mary's Loch; walks too.

> OPEN: 11–11 (11–12 Sat. 12.30–11 Sun). Closed Mon, Tues & Wed from November to Easter.
> Real Ale. Restaurant.
> Children welcome. No dogs. Wheelchair access throughout the inn.
> Bedrooms, all en suite.
> Cards: Delta, MasterCard, Solo, Switch, Visa.

St Monance

Seafood Restaurant & Bar
Tel: 01333 730327

16 West End, St Monance, Fife KY10 2BY
Free House. Tim Butler, licensee.

There is a definite leaning towards the nautical here, the local mariners feel very much at home in the cosy, windowless bar, behind which is an excellent seafood restaurant. The harbourside restaurant overlooks the Isle of May, Bass Rock and the small working harbour, busy with boat building and repairs. As you have gathered, the emphasis is on seafood: home-made soup, oysters, smoked fish, langoustines, and, well, just lots and lots of fish. Duck, chicken and pork in various guises feature too. Justly very popular. If you want a beer, they have Belhaven 80/–, St Andrews and a changing guest. A modest wine list and a good selection of malt whiskies. There are tables on the terrace; you eat with a view.

> OPEN: Closed Monday, otherwise 12–3. 6–11 (12.30–11 Sun).
> N.B. Closed for three weeks in January.
> Real Ale. Restaurant food only in evening.
> Children in restaurant. Dogs on leads.

STRACHUR

Creggans Inn   Tel: 01369 860279
Strachur, Argyll PA27 8BX
Free House. Robertson family, owners.

Gloriously situated, with uninterrupted views over Loch Fyne and the northern hills. By land or by sea, however you arrive, you will be able to park yourself here. There is the usual car park, and, as the pub garden is just 15 feet from the water's edge, five yacht moorings too. Built as a small coaching inn in 1800, it is located at the end of Strachur pier on the shores of the loch. Painted white, with a slate roof and touches of dark-green wood, the Creggans, a typical Scottish inn, is surrounded by the 3000-acre Strachur estate. Extended over the years, not only do you have somewhere to eat in comfort, but also somewhere to stay. There is a wonderful variety of dishes to choose from. In the smart bar (music and fire in here), the daily changing specials are on the blackboard, but you could order soup of the day, Loch Fyne oysters, Rothesay smoked salmon, steak and ale pie, or fresh cod from Tarbert – with chips. The dinner menu will be more creative and extensive. Delicious puds and Scottish cheeses. The ales are McEwans 70/–, 80/– and revolving guests. A choice of malt whiskies and an interesting wine list.

> OPEN: 11–1am.
> Real Ale. Restaurant.
> Children welcome, dogs too (in the bar). Car park. Yacht mooring.
> Eighteen bedrooms, all en suite.
> Cards: Delta, MasterCard, Switch, Visa.
> N.B. Music in the bar, but the rest of the hotel is music-free.

SWINTON

Wheatsheaf Hotel   Tel: 01890 860257
Main Street, Swinton, Borders TD11 3JJ   Fax: 01890 860570
Free House. Alan Reid, licensee.

Stone-built and facing the village green, the Wheatsheaf is popular with everyone: locals, tourists and fishermen. Warm and friendly, food is a very important feature. The landlord, a dedicated chef, offers a changing bar menu which could include – as well as the usual lunchtime favourites – a choice of two soups, devilled whitebait, creamed mushrooms and bacon in a filo-pastry basket, breast of corn-fed chicken served on a toasted sesame seed, coconut and carrot remoulade, or pork, apple and leek meatballs in a cider gravy with bubble and squeak. Other dishes are shown on the blackboard. Imaginative puddings and Scottish cheeses to follow. Deauchars IPA, Caledonian 80/- and one guest beer. An extensive wine list, six house wines and a choice of malt whiskies. This is a very touristy area. Lots of things to do and see: Abbotsford, Sir Walter Scott's home is nearby, racing at Kelso, fishing on the River Tweed and you're not far from the historic city of Berwick-on-Tweed or Coldstream (Battle of Flodden Field, 1513).

> OPEN: Closed Monday, otherwise 11–2.30 (11–3 Sat). 6–11. Closed Sun eves Nov–March. Closed first two weeks Jan and last week Oct.
> Real Ale. Restaurant. McAllan's Taste of Scotland Hotel of the Year.
> Children welcome. Dogs on leads. Car park. Six en-suite bedrooms.
> Cards: Delta, MasterCard, Switch, Visa.

TAYVALLICH

Tayvallich Inn   Tel: 01546 870282
Tayvallich, By Lochgilphead, Strathclyde PA31 8PL
Free House. Andrew & Jilly Wilson, owners/licensees.

Not really a conventional inn, more a restaurant and bar in an attractive village on the edge of a perfect natural harbour on Loch Sween. In good weather the glass doors in the conservatory are opened onto the terrace so you can sit and admire the view and any yachts at anchor. The bar and restaurant menus offer a wonderful variety of shellfish. They specialise in seafood, so there could be Loch Sween moules marinière, Loch Sween oysters, pickled herring with a dill and mustard mayonnaise, pan-fried Sound of Jura scallops, whole-jumbo-prawn salad with lime mayonnaise, seafood platter and, of course, smoked salmon. Not forgotten though, is the honey-and-mustard-glazed rack of lamb with rosemary jus, grilled prime Scottish sirloin or fillet steak, vegetarian dishes and, last but not least, scrummy home-made puddings on the blackboard and Scottish blue cheese to finish. Choice of wines and malt whiskies plus keg beers: Calders 70/-, Calders 80/-, Calders Cream Ale, Carlsberg lager, Strongbow cider and Guinness. There are walks along the edge of the loch, and to Knapdale Forest. During the year they hold a seafood festival.

> OPEN: 11–midnight (11–1am Sat). Closed Mon Nov–March.
> Restaurant.
> Children in eating areas. Dogs on leads. Wheelchair access (not WC). Car park.
> Cards: Delta, JCB, MasterCard, Solo, Switch, Visa Delta, Visa.

BEST OF THE REST

BRIG O'TURK, Stirling

Byre Inn   Tel: 01877 376292
As the name would suggest, this is a converted Victorian cow byre; now cosy, with a fine open fire. Good, generous home-cooked dishes using lots of local produce, creating a varied menu: haggis of course, maybe chicken, bacon with a whisky and mustard sauce or

venison with port and redcurrant sauce. Maclays 70/– and Wallace IPA, also Guinness and a good choice of malt whiskies. N.B. Closed Mon–Thurs winter.

CARBOST, Isle of Skye
Old Inn   Tel: 01478 640245
Several things to attract you to this old stone inn. First, it is on the shores of Loch Harport, so is a useful spot to refresh walkers, climbers and yachtsmen; they also serve good, filling bar food, including home-made soup and some fine Scottish cheeses; and, last but not least, they are very near a malt-whisky distillery – guided tours available in summer complete with samples of their craft. Bedrooms.

EDINBURGH
Guildford Arms   Tel: 0131 556 4312
This city pub is a place to admire. They have a tremendous range of beers for you to try – 11 usually, mostly from Scottish breweries – but you are also here to appreciate your surroundings: an exuberant Victorian pub interior at its best. Filling bar food of the chargrilled beefburger, fish and steak pie variety, but it is always busy – one of the most popular in Edinburgh.

FORT AUGUSTUS, Highland
Lock Inn   Tel: 01320 366302
Six locks bring the Caledonian Canal into Loch Ness; the inn is next to the first one. With stone walls, beams and open fire, this old post office is a popular, welcoming place. The good, interesting menu could include Loch Fyne mussels, grilled trout, venison casserole, seafood stew or something from the specials board. Always very fresh fish. The beers are from Scottish breweries and there are about 100 malts for you to work through.

GLENDEVON, Perth & Kinross
Tormaukin Hotel   Tel: 01259 781252
An extended 18th-century drover's inn where you will be well looked after and very well fed. Home-made soup, pâté and ploughman's and there could be a fish casserole, pork and pineapple, steaks, or a beef and Guinness pie. Daily specials too. Harviestoun beers, a decent wine list and several malts. Lots of places to walk. Bedrooms.

INVERNARNAN, Stirling
Invernarnan Inn   Tel: 01301 704234
There's no mistaking which country you're in when you go through the doors of the Invernarnan. Tartan, kilts, bagpipes, deerskins and a golden eagle – dead and stuffed. No identity crisis here. Hearty bar food: Scotch broth, toasted sandwiches, steak pie – that sort of thing – and they can put their hands on over 100 malts for you to try. Bedrooms.

KILBERRY, Argyll
Kilberry Inn   . Tel: 01880 770223
A traditional, white-painted, single-storey inn 16 miles around the single-track road from Tarbert (overlooked by the stronghold of Robert the Bruce) and Lochgilphead (B8024).

Feast your eyes on the spectacular views across the loch to Gigha and work up an appetite for the delights on offer at the Kilberry Inn. New licensees have taken over and they are keeping up the good work. They have a constantly changing menu, but favourites can always be found. Scottish bottled beers and a choice of malt whiskies. Bedrooms.

KILMAHOG, Stirling

Lade Inn   Tel: 01877 330152

In the glorious Pass of Leny – a comparatively empty bit of Scotland – Kilmahog and the Lade is where the A821 meets the A84 north of Callender. When you've finished admiring the scenery you will find some really good, freshly home-made food here. Always soups, lunchtime sandwiches and daily specials. On the menu there could be vegetable pancakes, game casserole and grilled trout. Heather Froach (when available), Broughton Greenmantle and Orkney Red MacGregor beers and a good wine list.

MINNICAFF, Dumfries & Galloway

Creebridge House Hotel   Tel: 01671 402121

This handsome place, surrounded by acres of glorious gardens and woodland, was built in the mid-18th century for the Earl of Galloway. Much to admire, and they do pretty well on the food front too. An interesting menu lists the bar usuals and could include a crispy-duck salad, fillet of sea bass or beef stroganoff with wild mushrooms and brandy, daily specials and good puds. Orkney Dark Island, Tetley and Marstons Pedigree beers as well as a very good selection of malts. Bedrooms.

PORTPATRICK, Dumfries & Galloway

Crown   Tel: 01776 810261

By the harbour. A busy, friendly old place that has a good choice of fish on the menu as well as the usual bar favourites. No beer to speak of, but they have over 200 malts and a decent wine list. Bedrooms.

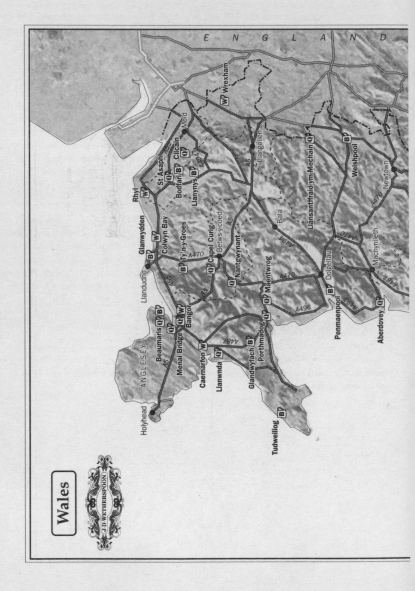

Wales

J.D. WETHERSPOON

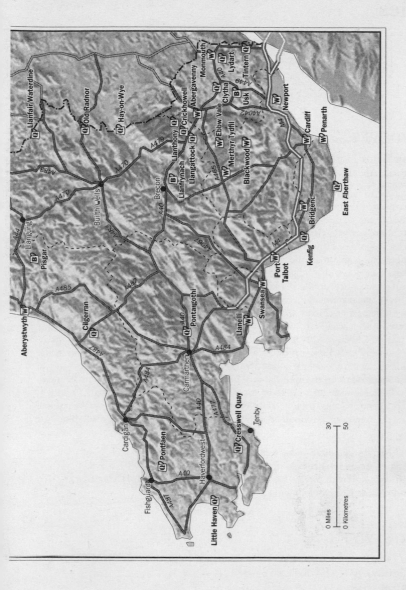

Wales

ABERDOVEY

Penhelig Arms Hotel
Terrace Road, Aberdovey, Gwynedd LL35 0LT
Free House. Robert & Sally Hughes, licensees.

Tel: 01654 767215
Fax: 01654 767690

The white-painted Penhelig Arms has everything you could wish for: comfortable bars, imaginative lunchtime and evening bar menus, an excellent restaurant, above-average accommodation, fantastic views and, last but not least, good ales. Built in the 18th century and then known as 'The Little Inn', it has expanded to become the hotel you see today. They are really big on fish and so are the customers; always a considerable variety to choose from: seared fillets of salmon with a hollandaise sauce, fillet of plaice baked with a Parmesan crust served with tartare sauce, or fillets of local mullet grilled with chilli, ginger and garlic. Food is served in the bar and restaurant; menus change daily and apart from the fish there could be a chicken roulade with a chicory salad, a mixed-leaf salad with Italian salami and mozzarella cheese served with a spicy tomato vinaigrette, grilled lamb cutlets served with a rosemary gravy, or pan-fried fillet steak with a peppercorn sauce; also a variety of puddings. An imaginative, reasonably priced two-course lunch and three-course dinner are available in the no-smoking restaurant; also a three-course Sunday lunch. If it's just a snack you want there will always be home-made soup and sandwiches. Champagne by the glass if you want to be indulgent. A well-chosen wine list with 15 by the glass. Greene King Abbot, draught Guinness, Bass, real cider and changing guest beers. In warm weather you can sit outside on the sea wall and admire the view or tuck yourself up near the fire in the bar if the Welsh winds blow.

> OPEN: 11–3. 6–11.
> Real Ale. Restaurant. Sunday lunch in bar or restaurant.
> Children in restaurant. Dogs in bar.
> Bedrooms – all with private bathrooms, most with views of the Dyfi estuary.
> Cards: MasterCard, Solo, Switch, Visa.

ABERYSTWYTH

Yr Hen Orsaf
Alexandra Road, Aberystwyth, Dyfed SY23 1LN
Wetherspoon.

Tel: 01970 636080

If your Welsh isn't quite as perfect as it might be, you would probably like to know that the literal translation of this pub's name is 'the old railway station', and with that information, you'll know where to make for. Still part of the Great Western complex, this unwanted section has been given a new life. Trains do still run and you can watch the comings and goings from a very civilised covered terrace. As with all Wetherspoon places, you will find something for everyone on the menu: salads, light bites, filled baps and jacket potatoes, curries, vegetarian dishes, and traditional main dishes – bangers and mash, Aberdeen Angus pie, fish and chips – all well cooked and enjoyable. Always reasonably priced beer, a short wine list, champagne and anything else you might fancy.

> OPEN: 11–11.
> Real Ale.
> No children. No dogs. Wheelchair access.

BANGOR
Union Hotel
Garth Road, Bangor, Gwynedd LL57 2SF
Burtonwood. John Duggan; tenant.

Tel: 01248 362462

They may just be right when they claim to be the only quiet pub in this ancient city, founded by the Cistercians in the 6th century – nearly a century before Canterbury. Known as the Union Garth, the pub is next to the local boatyard and the yacht basin. It has a distinctly nautical atmosphere; the view of Snowdonia from the small garden at the back of the pub is seen through a forest of yacht masts. This wide sweep of Conwy Bay is a favourite sailing area. Good, traditional bar food of soups, ploughman's, pâté, smoked mussels, salads, omelettes, grilled gammon, steaks, filled baked potatoes and home-made steak and kidney pie served throughout the year, and seafood salads in summer. Burtonwood Ales and a guest beer. Seats in the small garden. You might like to know that The Bishop's Garden in Bangor has a collection of all the plants mentioned in the Bible – well, those that can survive a Welsh winter. Well worth a visit.

> OPEN: All permitted hours.
> Real Ale. No food Tues evenings.
> Quiet children welcome, but not in bar. Dogs on leads. Wheelchair access (not WC).
> Bedrooms.

BEAUMARIS
Ye Olde Bulls Head
Castle Street, Beaumaris, Anglesey LL58 8AP
Free House. David Robertson, licensee.

Tel: 01248 810329
Fax: 01248 811294

The name Beaumaris evolved from Edward I's Norman French description of the area – *beau marais*, meaning beautiful marsh. His ruined moated castle dominates the town. Younger by two centuries than the castle, the interior of the 15th-century Bulls Head reflects its long history: oak beams, open fires and interesting artifacts, including the town's original ducking stool. One of Cromwell's generals knew when he was on to a good thing. He commandeered the inn so as to be close at hand while his troops laid siege to the castle. Charles Dickens also stayed here. The bar is for drinking only; you eat in the brasserie (music played here in the evening) or the restaurant. The brasserie menu changes every two months but there are always specials on the blackboard – and the food here really is special. You could choose a home-made soup, carpaccio of beef with a roquette salad, walnut oil and Parmesan, bruschetta of chargrilled chicken with roquette, tapenade, peppers and pesto, cassoulet of seafood in a cream, saffron and dill sauce, braised Welsh lamb with vegetables and mint gravy, or chargrilled rib-eye steak with garlic mash and black-peppercorn sauce, pasta, salads, vegetarian dishes and freshly filled sandwiches. Delicious puds too. There is a very good, inventive restaurant menu. Known for the excellence of its food, the Bulls Head has become *the* place to eat in Beaumaris. Bass, Worthingtons and a guest beer. Broad selection of wines, some by the glass.

OPEN: 11–11.
Real Ale. Brasserie open seven days a week for lunch and dinner. Restaurant (not Sun). Children up to 8pm (none under seven in restaurant). No dogs. Wheelchair access to brasserie only. Car park.Bedrooms.
Cards: Amex, Delta, JCB, MasterCard, Switch, Visa.

CAERNARVON

Tafarn Y Porth   Tel: 01286 662920
5–9 Eastgate Street, Caernarvon, Gwynedd
Wetherspoon.

The ceremonial capital of Wales. Edward I built the castle, and his son, born here in 1284, was the first Prince of Wales. Next to the castle, this place has some very ancient roots: the foundations of the building are resting on the remains of the original bridge leading to the castle entrance. As you would expect from Wetherspoon, everything else is firmly in the 21st century. The menu lets you choose anything from a filled bap to a curry or a mixed grill. Always reasonably priced beer and a choice of wines. Outside is a spacious terrace and garden.

OPEN: 11–11.
Real Ale.
No children. No dogs. Wheelchair access.

CAPEL CURIG

Bryn Tyrch Hotel   Tel: 01690 720223
Capel Curig, Betws-y-Coed, Conwy LL24 0EL
Free House. Rita Davis, licensee.

This is a village between two mountains in the Snowdonia National Park, a region of wild landscapes, rocky peaks, well-wooded valleys and rushing streams – an area of importance to both climbers and walkers. Equally relevant is this welcoming country pub. For over a hundred years it has been catering for the energetic lot that make this area their base, with huge fires, appealing menus, good beer and fruit wines for you to try. One thing makes this place stand out from the rest, its speciality: vegetarian and vegan cooking – though they also cater for the carnivores among us. The changing menus are inventive and use whole-foods, seasonal fruit and vegetables and fresh herbs. There will be a choice of two soups, one always vegetarian, hot or cold fillings for the sandwiches, spicy chick pea and vegetable curry served with rice, poppadom and salad, broccoli, cauliflower and Stilton crumble, naturally smoked haddock, prawns and mushroom pie, Moroccan lamb casserole with couscous and salad, or lamb and leek sausages with a port-wine and redcurrant-jelly sauce flavoured with rosemary. All the puddings, including the vegan ones, are freshly made. Flowers IPA, Boddington 6X and Castle Eden are the beers, and they have a well-balanced wine list.

> OPEN: 5–11 Mon–Thurs. 12–11 Fri–Sun.
> Real Ale.
> Children and dogs welcome. Car park. Bedrooms.
> Cards: MasterCard, Switch, Visa.

CILCAIN

White Horse   Tel: 01352 740142
The Square, Cilcain, Flintshire CH7 5NN
Free House. Peter Jeory, licensee.

An attractive country pub deep in the Welsh countryside, the creeper-covered White Horse has several bars, low beams, a big inglenook fireplace and settles to settle in. You have to go into the back bar if you have your dog with you. Mostly local produce (including free-range eggs and organically grown vegetables) is used to create a varied selection of home-made bar food: filled rolls, omelettes (using three free-range eggs), the ham to go with the salad is home-baked, fillet of pink trout, home-made hot Madras prawn curry and a mild chicken curry, grilled steaks, breaded fillets of haddock, vegetarian dishes and a variety of puddings. Their very own steak and kidney pies, generally thought the best anyone has ever had, are made with their own butter shortcrust pastry. The home-made specials change weekly. Banks Ale plus two weekly changing guests; a CAMRA pub of the year, so you know the beers are well kept. A selection of wines and farm ciders. Seats at the side of the pub.

> OPEN: 12–3. 6.30–11 (12–11 Sat. 12–3.30. 7–10.30 Sun).
> Real Ale.
> No children inside pub. Dogs on leads. Wheelchair access (not WC).
> Cards: MasterCard, Solo, Switch, Visa.

CILGERRAN

Pendre Inn   Tel: 01239 614223
Cilgerran, Nr Cardigan, Dyfed SA43 2SL
Free House. Mr R.J. Warren, licensee.

In a lovely wooded area near the River Teifi, Cilgerran is overlooked by the remains of a 13th-century castle built about 100 years before the Pendre. The pub, low-beamed with polished slate and flagstone floors, has loads of atmosphere. The very reasonably priced menu constantly changes – what inspires one day may not the next – but there could be home-made vegetable soup with cheese on toast, poached prawns with sesame toast, roasted chicken with spiced cabbage and onions served with a mild-mustard sauce, or peppers baked with a trio of cheeses served with tomato and basil sauce. All the food is home-made, including the ice-cream; no frozen food passes the door. Worthington BB, something from Tomas Watkins' brewery in Llandeilo and draught Bass are the ales. There are seats outside in the big garden.

OPEN: 11.30–3. 6–12 (6–10.30 Sun).
Real Ale. Restaurant.
Children welcome. Dogs on leads. Car park. Bedrooms.

CLYTHA

Clytha Arms   Tel/Fax: 01873 840206
Clytha, Nr Abergavenny, Monmouthshire NP7 9BW
Free House. Andrew & Beverley Canning, licensees.

Once the dower house for Clytha, this charming place is in beautiful countryside on the old Abergavenny–Raglan road. Inside, the Clytha has a good-sized country bar – with a dartboard – favoured by the locals, a smaller lounge bar with log fires and a well-behaved restaurant. They serve good, reasonably priced country dishes on the bar menu: the usual sandwiches and ploughman's, faggots and peas with beer and onion gravy, smoked salmon and scrambled egg, liver, bacon and onions, wild-boar sausages with potato pancakes, grilled queen scallops, a dish of cockles, as well as specials from the blackboard. The no-smoking restaurant (with napkins, candles and fresh flowers) has a separate, more expensive menu featuring regional specialities including Welsh beef and local lamb. Excellant three-course Sunday lunch. Felinfoel Double Dragon, Bass and Bullmastiff Gold Brew ales, plus an interesting selection of three guest beers, Old Rosie Scrumpy and a guest cider. An extensive wine list includes some Welsh wines and eight house wines. Lovely gardens and wonderful walks along the banks of the River Usk, not too far away, and through the grounds of Clytha Castle.

OPEN: 11.30–3.30. 6–11 (11–11 Sat). Closed Mon lunchtimes except Bank Holidays.
Real Ale. No bar snacks or restaurant Sun or Mon eves.
Children welcome until 8pm. No dogs. Car park.
Cards: Amex, Delta, MasterCard, Switch, Visa.

CRESSWELL QUAY

Cresselly Arms   Tel: 01646 651210
Cresswell Quay, Kilgetty, Dyfed SA68 0TE
Free House. Maurice & Janet Cole, licensees.

Some way inland from the estuary at Milford Haven and by the edge of the River Cresswell. If the tide is in your favour you can sail up to the timeless, creeper-covered Cresselly Arms, little changed since the early 19th century. Not too far from Carew, its ruined 13th-century castle (open most days) and the only 19th-century Welsh tidal mill on the Carew River (restored, and open daily during the summer). Your pint is still served from the cask into large jugs. A jolly, friendly, traditional pub serving good beer as well as a crisp or a nut. Worthington BB, a local ale, also Guinness, Two Cannons Xtra or Heineken. Seats outside to watch the watery coming and goings.

OPEN: 11–3. 5–11 (11–11 Sat).
Real Ale. No food.
No children. No dogs.

CRICKHOWELL
Nantyffin Cider Mill
Tel/Fax: 01873 810775
Brecon Road, Crickhowell, Powys NP8 1SG
Free House. Glyn Bridgeman & Sean Gerrard, licensees.

About 1½ miles from Crickhowell, a market town in the Usk valley at the foot of the Black Mountains, the Nantyffin is an appealing building – more a restaurant than a pub. Converted from a 16th-century cider mill, it still keeps some real cider for you to try and the old cider press remains in the barn – now the no-smoking restaurant. As well as the restaurant there is a bar and a more informal eating area. Very well known for serving excellent, imaginative food. You could have a bowl of home-made soup, an open prawn sandwich, a delicious omelette, fishcakes such as you have never had before, oak-smoked salmon or something more substantial, such as roast rack of Welsh lamb. Always three real ales – Buckley IPA and two guests – and always three draught ciders. Keen on developing their wine list; they have about 90 to choose from – mostly New World vintages. Views towards the River Usk from the garden.

OPEN: 12–2.30. 6–11 (12–3. 7–10.30 Sun). Closed Mon and Sun eves in winter.
Real Ale. Restaurant – music in here.
Children welcome. Dogs in the bar only – do ask first. Wheelchair access. Car park.
Bedrooms.
Cards: Amex, Delta, MasterCard, Switch, Visa.

EAST ABERTHAW
Blue Anchor Inn
Tel: 01446 750329
East Aberthaw, South Glamorgan CF62 3DD
Free House. Jeremy Coleman, owner/licensee.

Slate, not thatch, is the roofing material you usually associate with Wales, but here you have a 14th-century thatched and creeper-covered smugglers' inn. Inside are lots of low beams, flagstones, a huge fireplace in the main bar and two other fireplaces in the small interconnecting rooms. At the centre of what was then a thriving 15th-century port, rumour has it that a secret tunnel connects the pub with the shore (those smugglers again!). Run by the same family for over 60 years, this extremely popular place has evolved from a 1980s CAMRA flagship into a thriving dining pub. People flock from miles around to sample something from the menu. They take food very seriously here. Specialising in local produce – much of it grown on their own 2 acres by Mr Coleman senior – the reasonably priced bar menu could offer salmon and ginger fishcakes with a lemon and cream sauce, sautéed Isle of Lewis mussels in white wine and garlic, beef and ale casserole with herb dumplings, or grilled minted lamb chops with a red-wine and rosemary sauce, delicious home-made puds and a selection of Welsh cheeses. Local steak, lamb and pheasant on the well-thought-out restaurant menu; the rabbits probably have a Welsh accent too. Marstons Pedigree, Wadworths 6X, Buckleys Best and Theakstons Old Peculier beers. A well-balanced wine list. Seats at the front of the pub and in the garden.

OPEN: 11–11 (12–10.30 Sun).
Real Ale. Restaurant – very quiet music in here.
Children and dogs welcome. Car park. Wheelchair access.

HAY-ON-WYE

Old Black Lion   Tel: 01497 820841
Lion Street, Hay-on-Wye, Herefordshire HR3 5AD
Free House. Vanessa King, resident proprietor.

You have to focus on books when you think of Hay, the capital of Britain's second-hand-book trade. There are more than a million books here, all waiting for the right buyer. On the River Wye – over which the Old Black Lion has fishing rights – and surrounded by glorious countryside, the town grew up around the now ruined Norman castle. Outwardly appearing to be a 17th-century coaching inn, the white-painted Old Black Lion has been here since the 13th century. Near the old Lion Gate, this comfortable hotel has an attractive beamed bar serving home-prepared food – anything from a sandwich to a seafood vol-au-vent or Welsh lamb stew; there are about half a dozen dishes to choose from. There is an à la carte menu in the Cromwell Restaurant (yes, he was here too) featuring fresh fish – roast monkfish, salt and pepper squid – local meat, wild-boar steaks, venison and guinea fowl. Three-course Sunday lunches. Wye Valley's Cask ales and an interesting choice of wines. Chairs and tables on the terrace during the summer.

OPEN: 11–11 (12–10.30 Sun).
Real Ale. Restaurant.
Children over five restricted to eating areas. No dogs. Car park. En-suite bedrooms.
They can arrange fishing on the Wye.
Cards: MasterCard, Switch, Visa.

KENFIG

Prince of Wales Inn   Tel: 01656 740356
Ton Kenfig, Mid Glamorgan CF33 4PR (off the M4 at Junction 37, Kenfig is about 2½ miles further on off the A4229 towards Porthcawl, signposted Mawdlem/Kenfig)
Free House. Richard Ellis, lease.

Sand dunes, a 100-acre lake, castle ruins and the Prince of Wales Inn – until the 16th century Kenfig was a thriving community, but the shifting sands virtually overwhelmed the town. The Prince of Wales, however, was made of sterner stuff. Five hundred years old, the inn has seen many changes and has many tales to tell, most of them ghostly. Lots of strange noises emanating from the limestone walls in the 'ghost room' were recorded for a BBC programme on the supernatural. Troubled spirits there may be here, but this is still a popular, successful pub. Only a small bar area, but it has a number of rooms full of old-fashioned settles and three real fires. All the vegetables are home-grown. The pub has an acre of land across the road, so there are fresh vegetables to go with the home-made steak and onion pie, chicken and mushroom pie, daily roast or fresh fish. Bar snacks too: ploughman's, sandwiches and basket meals. Draught Bass, Worthington BB and several guest beers. Large sitting-out area. Just in case you and your friends want to ghost watch, the 'ghost room' is also the function room and can be hired.

> OPEN: 11.30–4. 6–11 (flexible and longer hours Sat & Sun, probably 11–11).
> Real Ale. Restaurant.
> Children welcome. Dogs in card room only.

LITTLE HAVEN

Swan Inn   Tel: 01437 781256
Point Road, Little Haven, Haverfordwest, Pembrokeshire SA62 3UL
Free House. Glyn & Beryl Davies, licensees

The Pembrokeshire Coastal Path passes through Little Haven, so if you're out on a character-building walk you will want to know that this is a very special place to stop. However you arrive, the Swan is in a delightful location by the sea wall with views towards St Bride's Bay. Plain and traditional inside, the food is a cut above the usual. From the bar menu: traditional Welsh lamb and vegetable soup, crab bake (a hot snack of crab, mayonnaise, herbs and cheese), Swan Upper (sardines, spinach and egg topped with mozzarella and grilled), all served with wholemeal bread and a side salad, and for a main course, home-made chicken korma, ham salad or locally smoked salmon. More formal dishes in the restaurant include roast rack of Welsh lamb, grilled fillet of Welsh beef or scampi provençal. Shepherd Neame Spitfire, Greene King Abbot, Morlands Old Speckled Hen, Brains Reverend James, Worthington Best and wines by the glass.

> OPEN: 11.30–2.30. 6.30–11.
> Real Ale. Restaurant – open Wed–Sat evenings.
> No children. No dogs.

LLANFAIR WATERDINE

The Waterdine   Tel: 01547 528214
Llanfair Waterdine, Nr Knighton, Powys LD7 1TU
Free House. Mr K.H. Adams, licensee.

Opposite the church in this small hamlet in the glorious Teme Valley, the black-and-white Waterdine is a 16th-century Welsh longhouse built as a drovers' pub in the architectural style of Shropshire, just the garden and river's width away. Though some people think it is in Shropshire already, we put our faith in the owners of the pub – we're sure they know where they are! Wales or Shropshire, this is a delightful place. The pub has a comfortable lounge bar with a log-burning stove, and a bistro for lunch. The conservatory and the stone-floored, beamed tap room – the oldest part of the building – both have the most fantastic views and are used for dining. The cooking here is expert and clever and based on the freshest of locally grown organic produce, including eggs from their own hens. Every lunchtime there is a blackboard menu including filled home-made baguettes and bread, chutneys for the ploughman's, plus pan-fried foie gras on caramelised-onion tarte tatin, roast chicken and almond soup, mushroom and vegetable ragout, partridge roasted with herbs, beetroot risotto and parsnip mousse, fillet of brill, spinach, shallots and beurre blanc, scrummy seasonal puds and British cheeses. On Sundays there is a very good-value prix fixe three-course lunch; there's also an equally good-value Saturday dinner. Woods Parish Bitter, Woodhamptons Jack Snipe and Westons traditional cider. Wide-ranging wine list.

OPEN: 12–2.30. 7–11. Closed all day Mon and Sun eves.
Real Ale. Bistro and restaurant.
Children welcome. No dogs. Wheelchair access. Bedrooms. Car park.

LLANGATTOCK

Vine Tree Inn   Tel: 01873 810514
The Leger, Llangattock, Crickhowell, Powys NP8 1HG
Free House. I.S. Lennox, licensee.

In the Usk valley, by the medieval bridge over the river to Crickhowell, and surrounded by glorious countryside, the Vine Tree is efficient and busy; a pub where food is all important. Freshly cooked, using local produce and fresh fish from Cornwall, the menu is extensive: mackerel pâté, smoked trout, smoked venison with cranberry sauce, oriental pork in a sweet and pungent sauce, venison casserole cooked in red wine, chicken Cymru – in a creamy white-wine, tomato and mushroom sauce, salmon in a creamy leek sauce wrapped in filo pastry, vegetable curry, steak and ale pie, home-boiled ham, steaks, fish, a variety of vegetarian dishes, Sunday roasts. Even the bread is home-made. Wadworths 6X and Fullers London Pride. Wines are mostly French. Seats outside overlook the river. Wonderful walks along the Monmouth–Brecon Canal and River Usk.

OPEN: 12–3. 6–11.
Real Ale. Restaurant.
Children welcome. No dogs. Willing hands for the wheelchairs.

LLANSANTFFRAID-YM-MECHAIN

The Lion Hotel   Tel: 01691 828207
Llansantffraid-Ym-Mechain, Powys SY22 6AQ
Free House. Mr Ron Edwards, owner/licensee.

Built in 1740 in a lovely part of Wales, the Lion lies off the A483 Oswestry–Welshpool road. Inside is a country bar, public bar, lounge and a dining room, which serves well-chosen, home-made food: ratatouille topped with cheese, garlic mushrooms or deep-fried Camembert, honey-baked ham, chicken à la crème and duckling. For afters, fruit puddings and crumbles. The bar menu gives you a choice of sandwiches, ploughman's, plaice and chips, lasagne, scampi and home-made steak pie. Bass Special and Worthington Best Bitter from the cask. Draught lagers, Guinness and ciders.

OPEN: 12–2.30-ish. 6.30–11 (6.30–10.30 Sun).
Real Ale. Restaurant.
Children welcome. No dogs except guide dogs. Six en-suite bedrooms.

LLANTHONY

Abbey Hotel
Tel: 01873 890487
Llanthony, Nr Abergavenny, Monmouthshire NP7 7NN
Free House. Ivor Prentice, licensee.

Among the ruins of a 12th-century Augustinian priory – a truly magical setting – the hotel contains part of the Norman church, the prior's house and a Norman staircase. The dining room was originally the prior's outer parlour and meeting room; the cellar has been turned into the atmospheric vaulted crypt bar. In the main, simply furnished, flagstoned bar, you can find home-made soups, toasted sandwiches, ploughman's, home-made burgers, veggie ones too, filled jacket potatoes, fish and chips, Moroccan chicken spiced with cumin and coriander, spicy bean goulash. Evening dishes include casseroles, local lamb with garlic, wine and mushrooms – or a nut roast. Draught Bass, Flowers Original and guests such as Ashvine Hop and Glory, Brains Rev James and Shepherd Neames Bishops Finger. Farm ciders too. Glorious setting with wonderful walks.

OPEN: 11–3. 6–11 (11–11 Sat & summer hols). Closed weekdays beginning Nov–end March. Open Christmas and New Year week.
Real Ale.
No children inside. No dogs. Bedrooms.

LLANWNDA

Goat Hotel
Tel: 01286 830256
Llanwnda, Caernarvon, Gwynedd LL54 5SD
Free House. Anne Griffith, licensee.

Well-kept beer, lots of local atmosphere but no food. The Goat, a friendly little local, is in a tiny hamlet not far from Caernarvon. Polish up your Welsh so that you can greet the landlady and the villagers. The Goat has a fair-sized main bar and a no-smoking parlour; no food unfortunately, so it's out with the crisps. Draught Bass, Whitbread and Boddingtons Bitter. Tables on the terrace at the front of the pub.

OPEN: 11–4. 6–11.
Real Ale. No food.
Children welcome. Dogs on leads.

LYDART

Gockett Arms
Tel: 01600 860486

Lydart, Monmouth, Monmouthshire NP5 4AD
Free House. Ken Short, licensee.

A congenial, family-run old country pub and restaurant in an attractive part of South Wales where it's easy to get lost. So it's out with the local map. You should be between Monmouth and Trellech on the B4293. Jolly, cheerful staff serve a good choice of well-cooked food in either the spacious bar or small restaurant. From the bar menu you could choose a shank of Welsh lamb braised in a red-wine sauce, freshly poached salmon, fillet steak with mustard and whisky sauce, steak and kidney pie, lemon and ginger chicken with rice, or vegetarian Brie and broccoli rosti; ploughman's too. They have a particularly well-kept Bass and Hook Norton Best Bitter. French doors lead you from the bar to seats in the pleasant garden.

OPEN: 11–3. 5–11 (12–3. 6–10.30 Sun).
Real Ale.
Children welcome. Dogs in garden. Wheelchair access.
Cards: MasterCard, Visa.

MAENTWROG

Grapes
Tel: 01766 590208

Maentwrog, Blaenau Ffestiniog, Gwynedd LL14 4HN
Nelson Williams Leisure Group. Gruff Jones, licensee.

This handsome, popular old coaching inn, a 19th-century building with a 13th-century cellar, has a musical ghost. If you're staying and you hear a little night music, it could be one of the two resident spirits: one stays below stairs, the other provides the musical entertainment, playing a piano on the hotel landing! Solidly comfortable, well-polished pine-panelled bars, big fires, and they serve well-presented bar food. This could include lunchtime soups – changing daily – seafood pancakes, a medley of mushrooms in garlic butter, filled jacket potatoes, their very own proper beefburgers, French bread filled with steak and mushrooms or onions, smoked bacon or veggie sausage, steak and kidney pies, salads, rack of Welsh lamb, lots of fishy specials and some vegetarian dishes. Everything is cooked to order. The restaurant is no smoking and there is a children's menu. Bass and Worthingtons Best, about five guest beers from a total of 30 or 40 rotating throughout the year. Farm cider. Seats on the verandah which looks over the garden to the mountains beyond. Nearby is the Vale of Ffestiniog and the Ffestiniog Railway. Using 1860 locomotives, it travels through 14 miles of breathtaking scenery, and is well worth a ride.

OPEN: 11–11.
Real Ale. Restaurant.
Children in family room and on the veranda. Dogs on leads.
Wheelchair access. En-suite bedrooms.

MENAI BRIDGE

Liverpool Arms   Tel: 01248 712453
St George's Pier, Menai Bridge, Anglesey, North Wales
Free House. Glynwen Thickett, licensee.

If you are a newcomer to the area, the address can be confusing. There is actually a place called Menai Bridge next to the Menai Bridge – that graceful suspension bridge Thomas Telford built in 1826 to link the Welsh mainland with the island of Anglesey. The Liverpool Arms, a friendly, welcoming, stone-built early-19th-century pub, is full of nautical artifacts, prints and pictures. There are two comfortable bars, a dining room and west-facing conservatory. The dishes on the menu in the restaurant and the bar are all home-made and could include leek and ham mornay, cod and prawn mornay, baked ham salad, sirloin steak, salmon, prawn and fresh Cromer-crab salads. The beers are Flowers Original, John Smiths, Morlands Old Speckled Hen, Courage Directors and Marstons Pedigree and various guests during the week. No garden – just a patio.

> OPEN: 11–11 (12–3. 7–10.30 Sun).
> Real Ale.
> Children welcome. No dogs except guide dogs. Wheelchair access (not WC).

NANTGWYNANT

Pen-y-Gwryd Hotel   Tel: 01286 870211
Nantgwynant, Gwynedd LL55 4NT (at junction of A498 and A4086)
Free House. Jane Pullee, licensee.

There are several routes to the top of Mount Snowdon to suit every level of experience. Among the better known, Watkin Path, on the south side near the village of Nantgwynant, is initially a picturesque climb that gets really difficult later on. The other well-known route is Pig Track. Easier and more interesting, it starts on the Llanberis side of Snowdon, near the Pen-y-Gwryd Hotel in the wooded area of the Snowdonia National Park. If you do make it to the summit, 3560 feet later, and the visibility is good, you can see both the Derbyshire peaks and the Wicklow Mountains in Ireland. Keen climbers often base themselves at this hotel; they are made to feel at home in the climbers' bar, which houses an interesting collection of boots that have made famous (accompanied) climbs. A jolly, friendly inn serving hearty, energy-giving, home-made food, including special pies – a different pie each day, casseroles in winter, soups, sandwiches and home-made bread to go with the home-made pâté and local cheeses for the ploughman's. No bar food in the evening, just meals in the no-smoking restaurant. Bass and Boddingtons ales.

> OPEN: 11–11. Closed Nov–New Year. Open weekends only Jan–Feb.
> Real Ale. Evening restaurant.
> Well-behaved children welcome, but not in residents' bar. Dogs on leads.
> Wheelchair access. Bedrooms.

OLD RADNOR

The Harp Inn
Tel: 01544 350655

Old Radnor, Presteigne, Powys LD8 2RH
Free House. Heather Price & Erfwl Protheroe, licensees.

Overlooking the village green, next to the church (one of the finest in Wales, with a megalithic stone as a font), the Harp has a cosy old-fashioned feel, with beams, slate floors, some nice pieces of antique furniture and log fires in both public and lounge bars. Old Radnor, which is over 2 miles from New Radnor, is older than New (that's only 700 years old!) and stands on a hill 840 feet high. In the Harp the menus change regularly and everything is home-cooked. Beers change too; new ones come in every week, so who knows what's on offer. There are wonderful, panoramic views from the 15th-century Harp, with lots of outside seating so you can admire the view. Good walking country too.

OPEN: 12–11.
Real Ale. Restaurant.
Children and dogs welcome. Bedrooms.

PONTARGOTHI

Salutation Inn
Tel: 01267 290336

Pontargothi, Carmarthenshire SA32 7NH
Felinfoel. Mr & Mrs Richard Potter, tenants/licensees.

On the road between Carmarthen and Llandeilo, the 19th-century Salutation is the place to experience some really worthwhile cooking. A welcoming beamed bar and open fire give the pub a homely atmosphere, and the blackboard menu will give you some idea of the delights that await – traditional cooking with a twist: sausage and mash with crispy onions and gravy, lamb and mint suet pudding, and from the à la carte menu, a mixed grill of fish with herb salad, breast of duck with red cabbage and roast parsnips, breast of chicken wrapped in Parma ham stuffed with mozzarella and sun-dried tomatoes. Felinfoel Dragon and Double Dragon ales, and a comprehensive wine list, some by the glass.

OPEN: 12–3. 6–11.
Real Ale. Restaurant.
Children welcome. No dogs. Car park.
Cards: MasterCard, Switch, Visa.

PONTFAEN

Dyffryn Arms
Tel: 01348 881305

Pontfaen, Dyfed SA65 9SE
Free House. Bessie Davis, licensee.

The Dyffryn Arms is an unchanging Welsh country pub in the Gwain valley, between Preseli and Fishguard. Pontfaen seems to be in the middle of a fairly empty bit of Wales but it is actually only a mile or so off the B4314. Surrounded by woodland and lots of rushing water, the Dyffryn Arms – a tiny, unspoilt pub with just two rooms – has been in Bessie Davis's family for over 150 years. Very well-kept draught Bass or Burtons still served from the jug. Only one real beer; the rest are bottled or canned. To eat? Well, crisps, nuts and a pickled egg!

OPEN: 12–11.
Real Ale.
Children in the garden. Dogs on leads. Car park.

PORTHMADOG
The Ship   Tel: 01766 51299
Lombard Street, Porthmadog, Gwynnedd LL49 9AP
Free House. Robert & Nai Jones, licensees.

Porthmadog and its twin town of Tremadog, built on reclaimed land in the 19th century, form the gateway to the Lyeyn peninsula and its dramatic terrain. In this part of Wales you are surrounded by spectacular scenery: rocky coves, windswept countryside and the sheer sides of mountains disappearing into the sea. The Ship is a popular local near the harbour and, as befits its position, has decidedly nautical decorations. Traditionally furnished, with good fires, they serve a home-made soup, casseroles and lots of seafood, including sea bass. There is a varied, regularly changing menu, maybe gammon hock with a white-bean sauce, braised shoulder of lamb provençale, chicken in a smoky barbecue sauce, salmon and spinach in a tarragon sauce and at least five vegetarian dishes. At lunchtimes they offer two main courses for the price of one – the cheapest main dish is free; that sounds like an offer you can't refuse. Roast lunch on Sunday. Always six different cask beers, lots of malt whiskies and they have a beer festival in March.

OPEN: 11–11 (12–4 Sun). Closed Sun out of season.
Real Ale.
Children lunchtimes only. Dogs when food not served. Wheelchair access.
Cards: all cards accepted.

ST ASAPH
Farmers Arms   Tel: 01745 582190
The Waen, Nr St Asaph, Clwyd (on the B5429 between the A55 expressway and Tremeirchion)
Free House. B. Seaman, licensee.

Lots of interesting things to see around here. Little St Asaph has the smallest cathedral in Britain, founded in the 6th century by St Kentigern. Some of it is Norman, but it's mostly 15th-century, and considerably restored. Cefn caves, south-west of St Asaph, contain prehistoric bones of bears, bison and reindeer. When you've done the sights, you can make your way to the Farmers Arms, a delightful country pub where you can always get a drink and something to eat from the well-thought-out bar menu. Fractionally borderline in our case, but the noisy public bar is well away from the main lounge. There certainly isn't any piped music, but early in the evening, when the bar is still fairly empty, there could be very quiet 'cocktaily' music on tape. This is turned off as the pub fills up, and the landlord, a classically trained musician, can sometimes be persuaded to play the grand piano in the lounge bar. The home-cooked food, including some regional specialities, is available in the bar and on the elaborate à la carte menu in the dining room. Theakstons is the main ale, and two others are chosen by the landlord.

> OPEN: 12–3. 7–11 (12–3. 7–10.30 Sun).
> Real Ale.
> No children. No dogs. Wheelchair access.

TINTERN

Cherry Tree Inn   Tel: 01291 689292
Devauden Road, Tintern, Nr Monmouth, Monmouthshire NP16 6TH
Free House. Steve Pocock, licensee.

Situated west of the main village of Tintern near the River Wye and the glories of ruined Tintern Abbey (founded in the 12th century by the Cistercians and sacked in the 16th by Henry VIII). Nothing much has changed here; the beer is still brought up by hand from the cellar. The Cherry Tree doesn't have a river, but it does have a little tumbling stream and a pretty garden. Only Hancocks HB, a guest beer and a draught cider. After years of just crisps and nuts they now feed you too: there is a traditional menu and bar snacks.

> OPEN: 11.30–2.30. 6–11 (12–11 Sat & Sun).
> Real Ale.
> Children: under control. Dogs in garden only.
> Cards: all cards accepted.

BEST OF THE REST

BEAUMARIS, Church Street, Angelsea

Sailors Return   Tel: 01248 811314
Any returning sailor would be happy in this friendly, jolly town pub, as they look after you very well. Comfortable and popular, it serves some interesting, better-than-usual bar food as well as grilled fish, steaks and daily specials to go with the Morlands and Tetleys beers.

BODFARI, Clywd

Dinorben Arms   Tel: 01745 710309
Several things make this pub stand out from the rest, though when I tell you they have the full range of McCallan's malts as well as over 200 others for you to try, standing perhaps

is not the word to use. Whisky aside, here is a delightful old pub in a wonderful position – clinging to the side of a mountain – where they serve a very popular Sunday-lunchtime smorgasbord, plus the more familiar bar food; daily specials too. If it's beer you want, they have Tetleys, Aylesbury Best and a changing guest.

GLANWYDDEN, Conwy

Queens Head
Tel: 01492 546570

A village pub not far from Llandudno. More of a place to eat than to stop for a quick pint. You can do that too, but you would really have to be here to appreciate something interesting from the weekly changing menu. Bar snacks such as home-made soups, chicken-liver pâté and stuffed pancakes, as well as mussels in garlic butter, loin of pork with a whisky, leek and cream sauce and good puddings. They do serve beer: Benskins, Tetleys and Ind Coope Burton.

GLAN DWYFACH, Gwynedd

Goat Inn
Tel: 01766 530237

A quiet country pub with lots of character, halfway between Caernarvon and Portmadog, on the A487. Our informant was impressed by the way the new landlord of two days had managed to get everything running so smoothly. Hot roast beef sandwiches were delicious, pot-roast lamb in redcurrant gravy and the sweet and sour chicken were nicely done and the portions were generous. Well-kept Robinsons range of ales and a comprehensive wine list.

LLANFRYNACH, Monmouthshire

White Swan
Tel: 01874 665276

If you're looking for a friendly, newly renovated village pub south-east of Brecon where you can eat well, here it is. Flagstone floors, open fires and plenty of room so you can enjoy the beef and mushroom pie, lasagne, fisherman's pie, steaks, grilled trout and much more. Flowers and Brains beer.

LLANYNYS, Clywd

Cerrigllwydion Arms
Tel: 01745 890247

If you're driving from North Wales to Ruthin on the country roads, you might like to know this place exists: an old, rambling village pub serving the usual reliable bar snacks (not Mondays), as well as more substantial dishes such as pork in an apple and cider sauce or a mixed grill. Bass and Tetleys and a fair choice of wine.

PENMAENPOOL, Gwynedd

George III
Tel: 01341 422525

This hotel is just about the lynchpin of the village, as is the old bridge over the estuary. Fantastic views, walks and a wildlife centre in the old signal box of the disused railway line (now a footpath). All this means the hotel bar is a popular place. Always good things on the menu: quite a lot of fish and always daily specials. Ruddles Best, John Smiths and a changing guest.

PISGAR, Nr Aberystwyth

Halfway Inn
Tel: 01970 880631

West of Aberystwyth towards Devil's Bridge. Depending on what you can stand listening to in the way of inoffensive music, you need to know that it's classical at lunchtime and country and folk in the evening. In the Rheidol valley and in a wonderful position to take full advantage of the glorious views, this is a nice old-fashioned place serving filling, familiar bar food. About four real ales and the same number of ciders to quench your thirst. Family-orientated; you can camp if you're a customer and it is a much-used stop on the pony-trekking circuit. No lunchtime food during winter months.

TUDWEILOG, Gwynedd

Lion Hotel
Tel: 01758 770244

Comfortable, friendly, and quieter now that the lively public bar – which has a well-used jukebox – has been moved to create a quieter lounge (we'll wait to hear how this works in practice). On a largely unspoilt stretch of coast with sandy beaches and good windsurfing seas running north-east to Caernarvon. The bar menu includes home-made soups, lunchtime baguettes, ploughman's, baked potatoes with various fillings, local lamb, local beef, fresh sea bass, freshly poached salmon, and several vegetarian dishes. Daily specials too. Forty or more malt whiskies. Theakstons Best and Mild and Boddingtons are on all the time; Marstons Pedigree and guest beers during spring and summer.

TY'N Y GROES, Gwynedd

Groes
Tel: 01492 650545

Thought to be the oldest licensed house in Wales; certainly it's on an old bit of road the Romans used on their way to Anglesea. A classy, rambling old place where they feed you well. Lots of local produce imaginatively cooked: Welsh lamb, local fish, Welsh cheeses, delicious puds. Tetleys, Ind Coope Burton and a choice of wines. Bedrooms.

USK, Monmouthshire

Nags Head
Tel: 01291 672820

A 500-year-old coaching inn in a delightful small market town with its own 12th-century castle. This is a comfortable, well-kept old place serving some good home-made food, much of it local. There will be the usual bar food such as sandwiches and soup, also seasonal game, local rabbits made into a pie and, of course, salmon. Brains range of beers. You are near the River Usk, surrounded by some wonderful scenery and good walks.

WELSHPOOL

Royal Oak Hotel
Tel: 01938 552217

Once the home of the Earl of Powis, the handsome, Georgian-pillared Royal Oak on Severn Street has been a hostelry for over 350 years. This historic border town is full of medieval and elegant Georgian houses. The bar menu and specials board offer excellent variety, including vegetarian dishes and a full three-course traditional Sunday lunch. Worthington Best always available, along with two weekly changing guest beers and a wide selection of wines and bottled beers. Bedrooms. N.B. The two bars – musical Ostler and quiet Oak – have different opening times: the Oak is only open during the evening.

J.D. Wetherspoon

From a 1979 acorn planted in Muswell Hill, North London, the mighty Wetherspoon oak has grown. And, as you can see from the new list of Wetherspoon outlets, it is growing all the time. There soon won't be a town of any size in the country that doesn't have a Wetherspoon – and a good thing too.

They are doing us all a favour by establishing welcoming, reasonably priced, reliable places for you to aim for. They might still be called pubs, but because of their size and function, they are really more like French brasseries: appealing to a wide cross-section of the community and providing them with whatever they want to drink and eat all day (with Egon Ronay keeping an eye on the food).

Cosy is not a word you associate with Wetherspoon; it's size that matters. Space and lots of it are what they are after, which means a substantial turnover of customers; they are the saviours of many a redundant building, thus improving the local environment (we all know a sad, disused building that has been rescued). It is a formula that works.

Everything is standardised, but that is no bad thing. They are there to provide the type of service that at certain times we are all looking for. Their continuing success means they do it very well.

A few Wetherspoon 'pubs' are described at length in this book; all the ones we know about are marked on the maps. So, if they're not listed among the other pubs in a county, they will be on the main Wetherspoon list that follows. All Wetherspoon outlets have disabled facilities; some, but not many, allow children; none allow dogs except guide dogs.

There is a new branch growing on the Wetherspoon tree: Lloyds No. 1. We haven't listed these twigs as they are for the musically hip, or indifferent, depending on your viewpoint – anyway, you need to know that they all have music.

Wetherspoon Free Houses within the M25

BARKING & DAGENHAM

BARKING – The Barking Dog
51 Station Parade
Tel: 020 8507 9109

DAGENHAM – The Lord Denham
270–272 Heathway
Tel: 020 8984 8590

BARNET

BARNET – Moon under Water
148 High Street
Tel: 020 8441 9476

NEW BARNET – Railway Bell
13 East Barnet Road
Tel: 020 8449 1369

COLINDALE – Moon under Water
10 Varley Parade, London NW9
Tel: 020 8200 7611

NORTH FINCHLEY – Tally Ho
749 High Road, London NW12
Tel: 020 8445 4390

BEXLEY

BEXLEY HEATH – The Wrong 'Un
234–236 The Broadway
Tel: 020 8298 0439

WELLING – New Cross
55 Bellgrove Road
Tel: 020 8304 1600

BRENT

KINGSBURY – JJ Moons
553 Kingsbury Road, London NW9
Tel: 020 8204 9675

NEASDEN – The Outside Inn
312–314 Neasden Lane, London NW10
Tel: 020 8452 3140

HARLESDEN – Coliseum
26 Manor Park Road, London NW10
Tel: 020 8961 6570

WEMBLEY – JJ Moons
397 High Road
Tel: 020 8903 4923

BOW

BOW – Match Maker
580–586 Roman Road, London E3
Tel: 020 8709 9760

BROMLEY

BROMLEY – Wetherspoons
Unit 23, Westmorland Place
Tel: 020 8464 1586

ORPINGTON – Harvest Moon
141–143 High Street
Tel: 01689 876931

PENGE – Moon and Stars
164–166 High Street, London SE20
Tel: 020 8776 5680

PETTS WOOD – Sovereign of the Seas
109–111 Queensway
Tel: 01689 891606

CAMDEN

CAMDEN – Man in the Moon
40–42 Chalk Farm Road, London NW1
Tel: 020 7482 2054

CRICKLEWOOD – Beaten Docket
50–56 Cricklewood Broadway, London
NW2
Tel: 020 8450 2972

HAMPSTEAD – Three Horseshoes
28 Heath Street, London NW3
Tel: 020 7431 7206

FARRINGDON – Sir John Oldcastle
29–35 Farringdon Road, London EC1
Tel: 020 7242 1013

HOLBORN – Penderels Oak
283–288 High Holborn, London WC1
Tel: 020 7242 5669

HOLBORN – Shakespeare's Head
Africa House, 64–68 Kingsway, London
WC2
Tel: 020 7404 8846

CITY OF LONDON

LONDON EC3 – Crosse Keys
9 Gracechurch Street
Tel: 020 7623 4824

LIVERPOOL STREET STATION –
Hamilton Hall
Unit 32, The Broadgate Centre, London
EC2
Tel: 020 7247 3579

LONDON EC2 – Green Man
1 Poultry
Tel: 020 7248 3529

LONDON EC3 – Liberty Bounds
15 Trinity Square
Tel: 020 7481 0513

CROYDON

CROYDON – George
17–21 George Street
Tel: 020 8649 9077

CROYDON – Skylark
34–36 Southend
Tel: 020 8649 9909

CRYSTAL PALACE   Postal Order
33 Westow Street, London SE19
Tel: 020 8771 3303

NORBURY – Moon under Water
1327 London Road, London SW16
Tel: 020 8765 1235

PURLEY – Foxley Hatch
8–9 Russell Hill Road
Tel: 020 8763 9307

SOUTH NORWOOD – William Stanley
7–8 High Street, London SE25
Tel: 020 8653 0678

THORNTON HEATH – Wetherspoons
2–4 Ambassador House, Brigstock Road
Tel: 020 8689 6277

WEST CROYDON – Ship of Fools
9–11 London Road
Tel: 020 8681 2835

SELSDON – Sir Julian Huxley
152–154 Addington Road
Tel: 020 8657 9457

DOCKLANDS

DOCKLANDS – The Ledger Building
4 Hertsmere Road, London E14

EALING

ACTON – Red Lion and Pineapple
281 High Street, London W3
Tel: 020 8896 2248

ENFIELD

ENFIELD – Moon under Water
116–117 Chase Side
Tel: 020 8366 9855

ENFIELD – Picture Palace
Howards Hall, Enfield, Middx
Tel: 020 8344 9690

SOUTHGATE – New Crown
80–84 Chase Side, London N14
Tel: 020 8882 8758

PALMERS GREEN – The Whole Hog
430–434 Green Lane, London N13
Tel: 020 8882 3597

EDMONTON – Gilpin's Bell
50–54 Fore Street, London N18
Tel: 020 8884 2744

FOREST HILL

FOREST HILL – Capitol
11–21 London Road
Tel: 020 7291 8920

GREENWICH

ELTHAM – Banker's Draft
80 High Street, London SE10
Tel: 020 8294 2578

WOOLWICH – Great Harry
7–9 Wellington Street, London SE18
Tel: 020 7249 6016

HACKNEY

STOKE NEWINGTON – Rochester
Castle
High Street, London N16
Tel: 020 7249 6016

HAMMERSMITH & FULHAM

HAMMERSMITH – William Morris
2–4 King Street, London W6
Tel: 020 8741 7175

HARINGEY

HARRINGAY – Old Suffolk Punch
10–12 Grand Parade, Green Lanes,
London N4
Tel: 020 8800 5912

HORNSEY – Tollgate
26–30 Turnpike Lane, London N8
Tel: 020 8889 9085

HIGHGATE – Gatehouse
1 North Road, London N6
Tel: 020 8340 8054

WOOD GREEN – Wetherspoons
5 Spouters Corner, High Road, London
N22
Tel: 020 8881 3891

HARROW

HARROW – The Moon on the Hill
373–375 Station Road
Tel: 020 8863 3670

HARROW – The New Moon
25–26 Kenton Park Parade, Kenton Road
Tel: 020 8909 1103

HARROW – Sarsen Stone
32 High Street, Wealdstone
Tel: 020 8863 8533

PINNER – Village Inn
402–408 Rayners Lane
Tel: 020 8868 8551

STANMORE – Man in the Moon
Buckingham Parade
Tel: 020 8954 6119

HATCH END – Moon and Sixpence
250 Uxbridge Road
Tel: 020 8420 1074

HAVERING

ROMFORD – Moon and Stars
99–103 South Street
Tel: 01708 730117

ROMFORD – Colley Row Inn
54–56 Collier Row
Tel: 01708 760633

HORNCHURCH – JJ Moons
46–62 High Street
Tel: 01708 478410

HILLINGDON

NORTHWOOD – Sylvan Moon
27 Green Lane
Tel: 01923 820760

UXBRIDGE – The Good Yarn
132 High Street
Tel: 01895 239852

RUISLIP MANOR – JJ Moons
12 Victoria Road
Tel: 01895 622373

NORTHWOOD HILLS – William Jolle
53 Joel Street
Tel: 01932 842240

ICKENHAM – Titchenham Inn
11 Swakeleys Road
Tel: 01895 678916

HAYES – Botwell Inn
25–29 Coldharbour Lane
Tel: 020 8893 7506

HOUNSLOW

FELTHAM – Moon on the Square
Unit 30, The Centre, Wilton Road
Tel: 020 8893 1293

HOUNSLOW – Moon under Water
84–86 Staines Road, Hounslow, Middx
Tel: 020 8572 7506

ISLINGTON

ISLINGTON – Angel
3–5 High Street, London N1
Tel: 020 7837 2218

ISLINGTON – White Swan
255–256 Upper Street, London N1
Tel: 020 7251 4195

HOLLOWAY ROAD – Coronet
338–346 Holloway Road
Tel: 020 7609 5014

OLD STREET – The Masque Haunt
168–172 Old Street, London EC1
Tel: 020 7251 4195

STROUD GREEN –
White Lion of Mortimer
125–127 Stroud Green Road, London N4
Tel: 020 7281 4773

KINGSTON-UPON-THAMES

SURBITON – Coronation Hall
St Marks Hill
Tel: 020 8390 6164

SURBITON – Cap in Hand
174 Hook Rise, Surbiton, Surrey
Tel: 020 8397 3790

KINGSTON-UPON-THAMES –
Kings Tun
153–157 Clarence Street
Tel: 020 8547 3827

LAMBETH

BRIXTON – Beehive
407–409 Brixton Road, London SW9
Tel: 020 7738 3643

STREATHAM – Crown & Sceptre
Streatham Hill, London SW2
Tel: 020 8671 0843

STREATHAM – Holland Tringham
107–109 High Road, London SW16
Tel: 020 8769 3062

LEWISHAM

CATFORD – Tiger's Head
350 Bromley Road, London SE6
Tel: 020 8698 8645

CATFORD – London & Rye
109 Rushey Green, London SE6
Tel: 020 8697 5028

LEWISHAM – Watch House
198–204 High Street, London SE13
Tel: 020 8318 3136

LEE GREEN – Edmund Halley
25–27 Leegate Centre, London SE12
Tel: 020 8318 7475

BROCKLEY – Brockley Barge
184 Brockley Road, London SE4
Tel: 020 8694 7690

MERTON

MITCHAM – White Lion of Mortimer
223 London Road
Tel: 020 8646 7332

MORDEN – Lady St Helier
33 Aberconway Road
Tel: 020 8540 2818

WIMBLEDON – Wibbas Down Inn
6–12 Gladstone Road, London SW18
Tel: 020 8540 6788

NEWHAM

EAST HAM – Millers Well
419–421 Barking Road, London E6
Tel: 020 8471 8404

STRATFORD – Golden Grove
145–148 The Grove, London E15
Tel: 020 8519 0750

FOREST GATE – Hudson Bay
1–5 Upton Lane, London E7
Tel: 020 8471 7702

REDBRIDGE

BARKINGSIDE – New Fairlop Oak
Fencepiece Road
Tel: 020 8500 2217

WANSTEAD – George
High Street, London E11
Tel: 020 8989 2921

ILFORD – Great Spoon of Ilford
114–116 Cranbrook Road
Tel: 020 8518 0535

CHADWELL HEATH – Eva Hart
1128 High Street
Tel: 020 8597 1069

GOODMAYES – Standard Bearer
7–13 Goodmayes Road
Tel: 020 8597 7624

RICHMOND-UPON-THAMES

TWICKENHAM – Moon under Water
53–57 London Road
Tel: 020 8744 0080

SOUTHWARK

DENMARK HILL – Fox on the Hill
149 Denmark Hill, London SE5
Tel: 020 7738 4756

ROTHERHITHE – Surrey Docks
185 Lower Road, London SE16
Tel: 020 7231 2915

SOUTHWARK – Pommeler's Rest
196–198 Tower Bridge Road, London SE1
Tel: 020 7378 1399

PECKHAM – Kentish Drovers
77–79 Peckham High Street, London SE15
Tel: 020 7277 4283

ELEPHANT & CASTLE –
Wetherspoons
Metro Central Heights, Newington
Causeway, London SE1
Tel: 020 7940 0890

SUTTON

NORTH CHEAM – Wetherspoons
552–556 London Road
Tel: 020 8644 1808

SUTTON – Moon on the Hill
5–9 Hill Road
Tel: 020 8643 1202

WALLINGTON – Whispering Moon
25 Ross Parade, Woodcote Road
Tel: 020 8647 7020

TOWER HAMLETS

BETHNAL GREEN – Camden's Head
456 Bethnal Green Road, London E2
Tel: 020 7613 4263

MILE END – Half Moon
213–233 Mile End Road, London E1
Tel: 020 7790 6810

WALTHAM FOREST

CHINGFORD – King's Ford
250–252 Chingford Manor Road, London E4
Tel: 020 8523 9365

LEYTON – The Drum
557–559 Lea Bridge Road, London E10
Tel: 020 8539 6577

LEYTONSTONE – Walnut Tree
857–861 High Street, London E11
Tel: 020 8539 2526

WANDSWORTH

PUTNEY – Railway
202 Upper Richmond Road, London SW15
Tel: 020 8788 8190

TOOTING – JJ Moons
56a High Street, London SW17
Tel: 020 8672 4726

BALHAM – Moon under Water
194 Balham High Street, London SW12
Tel: 020 8673 0535

BATTERSEA – Asparagus
1–13 Falcon Road, London SW11
Tel: 020 7801 0046

SOUTHFIELDS – Grid Inn
22 Replingham Road, London SW18
Tel: 020 8874 8460

WANDSWORTH – Rose and Crown
Putney Bridge Road, London SW18
Tel: 020 8871 4497

WESTMINSTER

CHARING CROSS ROAD –
Moon under Water
105–107 Charing Cross Road, London
WC2
Tel: 020 7287 6039

VICTORIA STATION – Wetherspoons
Unit 5, Victoria Island, London SW1
Tel: 020 7931 0445

SOHO – Moon and Sixpence
181–185 Wardour Street, London W1
Tel: 020 7734 0037

WHITEHALL – Lord Moon of the Mall
16–18 Whitehall, London SW1
Tel: 020 7839 7701

LEICESTER SQUARE –
Moon under Water
28 Leicester Square, London WC2
Tel: 020 7839 2837

MARYLEBONE – Metropolitan Bar
7 Station Approach, Marylebone Road,
London NW1
Tel: 020 7486 3489

CHANCERY LANE –
Knight's Templar
95 Chancery Lane, London WC2
Tel: 020 7831 2660

MARBLE ARCH – Tyburn
20 Edgware Road, London W2
Tel: 020 7723 4731

VICTORIA – Willow Walk
25 Wilton Road, London SW1
Tel: 020 7828 2953

Wetherspoon Free Houses outside the M25

BEDFORDSHIRE

BEDFORD – Pilgrim's Progress
Midland Road, Bedford
Tel: 01234 363751

LUTON – White House
1 Bridge Street, Luton
Tel: 01582 454608

BEDFORD – Pilgrim's Progress
115–117 High Street
Tel: 01234 342931

BERKSHIRE

BRACKNELL – Old Manor
Church Road
Tel: 01344 304490

CAVERSHAM – Baron Cadogan
Prospect Street
Tel: 0118 947 0626

READING – Back of Beyond
104–108 Kings Road
Tel: 0118 959 5906

READING – Hope Tap
99–105 Friar Street
Tel: 0118 958 2266

READING – Monks Retreat
163 Friar Street
Tel: 0118 950 7592

SLOUGH – Moon and Spoon
86 High Street
Tel: 01753 531650

SLOUGH – Wetherspoons
230 High Street
Tel: 01753 518723

BUCKINGHAMSHIRE

CHESHAM – Last Post
77 The Broadway
Tel: 01494 785622

HIGH WYCOMBE – Falcon
9 Cornmarket
Tel: 01494 538610

MILTON KEYNES – Wetherspoons
201 Midsummer Boulevard, Bouverie
Square
Tel: 01908 606074

MILTON KEYNES – The Seclow
Hundred
Midsummer Boulevard

CAMBRIDGESHIRE

CAMBRIDGE – The Regal
38–39 St Andrews Street
Tel: 01223 366459

PETERBOROUGH – College Arms
40 The Broadway
Tel: 01733 319745

NEWMARKET – Golden Lion
44 High Street
Tel: 01638 672040

WISBECH – Wheatsheaf Inn
18–22 Church Terrace
Tel: 01945 469890

CHESHIRE

CHESTER – Wetherspoons
78–92 Foregate Street
Tel: 01244 312281

CHEADLE HULME – King's Hall
13 Station Road
Tel: 0161 485 1555

CONGLETON – Counting House
18 Swan Bank
Tel: 01260 272654

ELLESMERE PORT – Wheatsheaf
43 Overpool Road
Tel: 0151 356 7454

MACCLESFIELD – Society Rooms
Park Lane

NESTON – Lodestar
Brook Street
Tel: 0151 353 0485

NORTHWICH – Penny Black
110 Witton Street
Tel: 01606 42029

STOCKPORT – Calverts Court
Saint Petersgate

WARRINGTON – Friar Pinkeph
4 Barbould Street

WIDNES – Widnes
93–99 Albert Road
Tel: 0151 422 4920

CLEVELAND

HARTLEPOOL – King John's Tavern
1 South Road
Tel: 01429 274388

MIDDLESBROUGH – Isaac Wilson
61 Wilson Street
Tel: 01642 247708

REDCAR – Plimsoll Line
138–142 High Street East
Tel: 01642 495250

STOCKTON ON TEES –
Thomas Sheraton
4 Bridge Road
Tel: 01642 606134

CUMBRIA

CARLISLE – Woodrow Wilson
48 Butchergate
Tel: 01228 819942

BARROW-IN-FURNESS –
Furness Railway
Abbey Road
Tel: 01229 820818

DERBYSHIRE

BUXTON – Wye Bridge House
Fairfield Road
Tel: 01298 709324

CHESTERFIELD – Spa Lane Vaults
34 St Mary's Gate

CHESTERFIELD – The White Horse
West Bars
Tel: 01246 245410

DERBY – Standing Order
28–32 Irongate
Tel: 01322 207591

DERBY – Babington Arms
11–13 Babington Lane
Tel: 0113 238 3647

HEANOR – Red Lion
Derby Road
Tel: 01773 533767

ILKESTON – Observatory
14a Market Place
Tel: 0115 932 8040

MATLOCK – Crown
Crown Square
Tel: 01629 580991

RIPLEY – Red Lion
Market Place
Tel: 01773 512875

SWADLINCOTE – Sir Nigel Gresley
Market Street
Tel: 01283 227560

DEVON

BARNSTAPLE – Panniers
33–34 Boutport Street
Tel: 01271 329720

BRIXHAM – Vigilance
4 Bolton Street
Tel: 01803 850489

CREDITON –
General Sir Redvers Buller
37 High Street
Tel: 01363 774381

EXETER – Imperial
New North Road
Tel: 01392 43405

EXMOUTH – Powder Monkey
2–2a The Parade
Tel: 01395 280090

PAIGNTON – Isaac Merritt
54–58 Torquay Road
Tel: 01803 556066

PLYMOUTH – Britannia Inn
1 Wolsey Road, Milehouse
Tel: 01752 607596

PLYMOUTH – Union Rooms
19 Union Street
Tel: 01752 254520

TIVERTON – White Ball Inn
Bridge Street
Tel: 01884 251525

TORQUAY – London Inn
15–16 The Strand
Tel: 01803 380003

DORSET

BOURNEMOUTH –
Moon in the Square
4–6 Exeter Road
Tel: 01202 314940

BOSCOMBE –
Sir Percy Florence Shelley
673–675 Christchurch Road
Tel: 01202 300197

BRIDPORT – Greyhound
2 East Street
Tel: 01308 421905

DORCHESTER – Royal Oak
High Street West
Tel: 01305 755910

FERNDOWN – Night Jar
94 Victoria Road
Tel: 01202 855572

WEYMOUTH – Swan
41–43 St Thomas Street
Tel: 01305 750231

ESSEX

BASILDON – Moon on the Square
15 Market Square
Tel: 01268 520360

BILLERICAY – Blue Boar
39 High Street
Tel: 01227 655552

BRAINTREE – Wetherspoons
Fairfield Road
Tel: 01376 550255

CHELMSFORD – Globe
65 Rainsford Road
Tel: 01245 261263

CLACTON – Moon and Starfish
Marine Parade East
Tel: 01255 222998

COLCHESTER – Playhouse
St John's Street
Tel: 01206 571003

LEIGH-ON-SEA – Elms
60 London Road
Tel: 01702 74687

LOUGHTON – Last Post
227 High Road
Tel: 020 8532 0751

SAFFRON WALDEN – Temeraire
55 High Street
Tel: 01799 516975

SOUTHEND-ON-SEA – Last Post
Weston Road
Tel: 01702 431682

SOUTH OCKENDEN –
Moon under Water
Broxburn Drive
Tel: 01708 855245

TILBURY – Anchor
Civic Square
Tel: 01375 850560

WITHAM – Little Elms
Dorothy Sayers Drive
Tel: 01376 510483

GLOUCESTERSHIRE

CHELTENHAM – Moon under Water
16–28 Bath Road
Tel: 01242 583945

GLOUCESTER – Regal
33 St Aldate Street
Kings Square
Tel: 01452 332344

STROUD – Lord John
15–17 Russell Street
Tel: 01453 767610

GREATER MANCHESTER

ALTRINCHAM – Unicorn
1–7 Ashley Road

BOLTON – Spinning Mule
1–2 Nelson Square
Tel: 01204 533339

BURY – Robert Peel
5–10 Market Place
Tel: 0161 764 7287

CHORLTON-CUM-HARDY –
Sedge Lynn
21a Manchester Road
Tel: 0161 860 0141

ECCLES – Eccles Cross
13 Regent Street
Tel: 0161 788 0414

HEYWOOD – Edwin Waugh
10–12 Market Street
Tel: 01706 621480

HYDE – Cotton Bale
212–25 Market Place
Tel: 0161 351 0380

LONGSIGHT – Sir Edwin Chadwick
587 Stockport Road
Tel: 0161 256 2806

MANCHESTER – Paramount
33–35 Oxford Street

MANCHESTER –
Moon under Water
68–74 Deansgate
Tel: 0161 834 5882

MANCHESTER – Wetherspoons
49a Piccadilly
Tel: 0161 236 9206

MIDDLETON – Harbord Harbord
17–21 Long Street
Tel: 0161 654 6226

OLDHAM – Up Stairs Inn
17–23 High Street
Tel: 0161 627 5001

ROCHDALE – Regal Moon
The Butts
Tel: 01706 654334

SALE – JP Joule
Northenden Road
Tel: 0161 962 9889

STRETFORD – Bishop Blaize
708 Chester Road
Tel: 0161 873 8845

TYLDESLEY – George Dragon
185–187 Elliott Street
Tel: 01942 897426

URMSTON – Tim Bobbin
41 Flixton Road
Tel: 0161 749 8239

WIGAN – Brocket Arms
Mesnes Road
Tel: 01942 820372

WIGAN – Moon under Water
5–7a Market Place, The Wiend
Tel: 01942 323437

HAMPSHIRE

COSHAM – First Post
42 High Street
Tel: 01705 710331

FAREHAM – Lord Arthur Lee
100–108 West Street
Tel: 01329 280447

FLEET – Prince Arthur
238 Fleet Road
Tel: 01252 622660

HAVANT – Parchment Makers
1 Park Road North
Tel: 01705 474023

PORTSMOUTH –
Isambard Kingdom Brunel
2 Guildhall Walk
Tel: 023 9229 5112

PORTSMOUTH – Sir John Baker
80 London Road, Northend
Tel: 023 9262 7960

PORTSMOUTH – John Jacques
78–82 Fratton Road
Tel: 023 9277 9742

SHIRLEY – Bright Water Inn
370–372 Shirley Road
Tel: 023 8077 6717

SOUTHAMPTON – Standing Order
30 High Street
Tel: 023 8022 2121

SOUTHAMPTON – Giddy Bridge
12–18 London Road
Tel: 023 8033 6346

WINCHESTER – Old Gaol House
11 Jewry Street
Tel: 01962 850095

HERTFORDSHIRE

BERKHAMSTED – Crown
145 High Street
Tel: 01442 863993

BOREHAMWOOD – Hart and Spool
148 Shenley Road
Tel: 020 8953 1883

HEMEL HEMPSTEAD – Full House
128 The Marlowes
Tel: 01442 265512

LETCHWORTH – Three Magnets
18–20 Leys Avenue
Tel: 01462 681093

POTTERS BAR – Admiral Byng
186–192 Darkes Lane
Tel: 01707 645484

RICKMANSWORTH – Pennsylvanian
115–117 High Street
Tel: 01923 720348

ST ALBANS – Cross Keys
2 Chequer Street
Tel: 01727 839917

STEVENAGE – Standing Order
33 High Street
Tel: 01438 316972

STEVENAGE – Standard Bearer
Unit 1, The Plaza, New Town
Market Square
Tel: 01438 731450

WATFORD – Wetherspoons
Bridlington Road, South Oxhey
Tel: 020 8421 7580

WATFORD – Moon under Water
44 High Street
Tel: 01923 223559

WALTHAM CROSS – Moon and Cross
104–106 High Street
Tel: 01992 700761

ISLE OF WIGHT

RYDE – S. Fowlers
41–43 Union Street
Tel: 01903 228070

KENT

ASHFORD – County Hotel
10 High Street
Tel: 01233 646891

DARTFORD – Paper Moon
55 High Street
Tel: 01322 281127

DOVER – Eight Bells
19 Cannon Street
Tel: 01304 205030

CANTERBURY – Thomas Ingoldsby
5–9 Burgate
Tel: 01227 463339

CANTERBURY – West Gate Inn
1, 2 & 3 North Lane
Tel: 01227 464329

FAVERSHAM – Leading Light
20–22 Preston Street
Tel: 01795 535075

FOLKESTONE – Wetherspoons
213 Rendezvous Street
Tel: 01303 251154

GRAVESEND – Robert Pocock
181–183 Windmill Street
Tel: 01474 352765

HERNE BAY – Saxon Shore
78–80 Central Parade
Tel: 01227 370316

MAIDSTONE – Muggleton Inn
8–9 High Street, Maidstone
Tel: 01622 691527

ROCHESTER – Golden Lion
147–149 High Street
Tel: 01634 880521

SEVENOAKS – Sennockian
139–141 High Street
Tel: 01732 469010

SITTINGBOURNE – Summoner
High Street
Tel: 01795 410158

TONBRIDGE – Humphrey Bean
94 High Street
Tel: 01732 773850

TUNBRIDGE WELLS –
The Opera House
88 Mount Pleasant Road
Tel: 01892 511770

LANCASHIRE

ASHTON-UNDER-LYNE – Ash Tree
18 Wellington Road
Tel: 0161 339 9670

ASTON-IN-MAKERFIELD –
Sir Thomas Gerard
Gerard Street
Tel: 01942 713519

BLACKBURN – Postal Order
15 Darwen Street
Tel: 01254 676400

BLACKPOOL – Auctioneer
235–237 Lytham Road
Tel: 01942 713519

FLEETWOOD – Sir Thomas Drummond
London Street

LANCASTER – Sir Richard Owen
4 Spring Garden Street

LYTHAM ST ANNES – Trawl Boat Inn
36–38 Wood Street

NELSON – Station Hotel
Hibson Road
Tel: 01282 877910

PRESTON – Grey Friar
144 Friargate
Tel: 01772 558542

LEICESTERSHIRE

HINCKLEY – Baron of Hinckley
5–7 Regent Street
Tel: 01455 890169

LEICESTER – Last Plantaganet
107 Granby Street
Tel: 0116 255 5492

LEICESTER – High Cross
103–105 High Street
Tel: 0116 251 9218

LOUGHBOROUGH – Moon & Bell
6 Wards End
Tel: 01509 241504

MARKET HARBOROUGH –
Sugar Loaf
18 High Street
Tel: 01858 469231

OADBY – Lord Keeper of the Great Seal
96–98 The Parade
Tel: 0116 272 0957

WIGSTON – William Wygston
84 Leicester Road
Tel: 0116 288 8397

LINCOLNSHIRE

BOSTON – Moon under Water
6 High Street
Tel: 01205 311911

GAINSBOROUGH – Sweyn Forkbeard
22–24 Silver Street
Tel: 01427 675000

GRANTHAM – Tollemache Inn
17 St Peter's Hill
28 Catherine's Road
Tel: 01476 594696

GRIMSBY – Yarborough Hotel
29 Bethlehem Street
Tel: 01472 268283

LINCOLN – Forum
13–14 Silver Street
Tel: 01522 518630

LINCOLN – Ritz
High Street
Tel: 01522 512103

SCUNTHORPE – Blue Bell Inn
1–7 Oswald Road
Tel: 01724 863921

SKEGNESS – Red Lion
Roman Banks, Lumley Road
Tel: 01754 612567

MERSEYSIDE

BOOTLE – Wild Rose
2a & 1b Triad Centre
Stanley Road
Tel: 0151 922 0828

BIRKENHEAD – Brass Balance
39–47 Argyle Street

BIRKENHEAD – John Laird
Europa Centre
Tel: 0151 650 0620

HOYLAKE – Hoylake Lights
52–54 Market Street
Tel: 0151 632 1209

HUYTON – Oak Tree
Liverpool Road
Tel: 0151 482 1337

KIRKBY – Gold Balance
6–10 New Town Gardens
Tel: 0151 548 7939

LIVERPOOL – Thomas Frost
177–187 Walton Road

LIVERPOOL – Wetherspoons
Unit 1–2 & 3 Charlotte Row
Tel: 0151 709 4802

LIVERPOOL – The Raven
72 Walton Vale
Tel: 0151 524 1255

MORETON – Mockbeggar Hall
239–241 Hoylake Road
Tel: 0151 678 5659

ST HELENS – Glass House
Market Street

SOUTHPORT – Wetherspoons
93–97 Lord Street
Tel: 01704 530217

STONEY CROFT – Wetherspoons
694 Queens Drive
Tel: 0151 220 2713

MIDDLESEX

STAINES – George
2–8 High Street
Tel: 01784 462181

NORFOLK

GREAT YARMOUTH – Troll Cart
7–9 Regent Road
Tel: 01493 332932

KINGS LYNN – Lattice House
Chapel Street
Tel: 01553 769585

KINGS LYNN – Kings Lynn
King Street

NORWICH – Bell Hotel
5 Orford Hill
Tel: 01603 630017

NORWICH – Whiffler
Boundary Road, Hellesdon
Tel: 01603 424042

NORWICH – City Gate
5–7 Dereham Road
Tel: 01603 661413

NORWICH – Queen of Iceni
Unit 6, Riverside Development

NORTHAMPTONSHIRE

KETTERING – Earl of Dalkeith
13–15 Dalkeith Place
Tel: 01536 312589

NORTHAMPTON –
Moon on the Square
The Parade, Market Place
Tel: 01604 634062

NORTHAMPTON – Wetherspoons
7a St Peter's Way
Tel: 01604 887420

WELLINGBOROUGH – Red Well
16 Silver Street
Tel: 01933 440845

NOTTINGHAMSHIRE

ARNOLD – Ernehale
149–151 Nottingham Road
Tel: 0115 967 4945

BEESTON – Last Post
Foster Avenue/Chilwell Road
Tel: 0115 968 3100

HUCKNALL – Pilgrim's Oak
44–46 High Street
Tel: 0115 963 2539

LONG EATON – Twitchel Inn
Clifford Street/Howitt Street
Tel: 0115 972 2197

NEWARK – Sir John Arderne
1–3 Church Street
Tel: 01636 671334

NOTTINGHAM – Roebuck Inn
9–11 St James Street
Tel: 0115 979 3400

NOTTINGHAM – Wetherspoons
11–12 South Parade, Market Square
Tel: 0115 947 5034

SUTTON-IN-ASHFIELD –
Picture House
Fox Street
Tel: 01623 554627

WORKSOP – White Lion
Park Street
Tel: 01909 476450

OXFORDSHIRE

BANBURY – Exchange
49–50 High Street
Tel: 01295 259035

BICESTER – Penny Black
58 Sheep Street
Tel: 01869 321535

HENLEY-ON-THAMES –
Catherine Wheel
7–15 Hart Street
Tel: 01491 845790

SHROPSHIRE

DAWLEY, TELFORD – Church Wicketts
Church Road
Tel: 01952 506825

SHREWSBURY – Shrewsbury Hotel
Bridge Place
Tel: 01743 340382

WHITCHURCH – Red Lyon
46 High Street
Tel: 01948 667846

SOMERSET

BEDMINSTER – Robert Fitz Harding
Cannon Street
Tel: 0117 966 2757

BRISTOL – Berkeley
15–19 Queens Road, Clifton
Tel: 0117 927 9550

BRISTOL – Commercial Rooms
43–45 Corn Street
Tel: 0117 927 9681

BRISTOL – Magic Box
135–137 Cheltenham Road
Tel: 0117 970 5140

BRISTOL – Van Dyck Forum
748–756 Fishponds Road
Tel: 0117 965 1337

KINGSWOOD – Kingswood Colliers
94–96 Regent Street
Tel: 0117 967 2247

REDFIELD – St George's Hall
203 Church Road
Tel: 0117 955 1488

STAPLE HILL – Staple Hill Oak
84–86 High Street
Tel: 0117 956 8544

TAUNTON – Perkin Warbeck
22–23 East Street
Tel: 01823 335830

WESTON SUPER MARE – Dragon Inn
15 Meadow Street
Tel: 01934 621304

YEOVIL – William Dampier
97 Middle Street
Tel: 01935 412533

STAFFORDSHIRE

BURTON-ON-TRENT – Lord Burton
154 High Street
Tel: 01283 517587

CANNOCK – Linford Arms
79 High Green
Tel: 01543 469360

HANLEY – Reginald Mitchell
Tontine Street
Tel: 01782 281082

LICHFIELD – Acorn Inn
12–18 Tamworth Street
Tel: 01543 263400

LONGTON – Last Post
Transport Lane
Tel: 01782 594060

RUGELEY – Plaza
Horsefair
Tel: 01889 586831

STAFFORD – Picture House
Bridge Street
Tel: 01785 222941

STOKE-ON-TRENT – Wheatsheaf
84–92 Church Street
Tel: 01782 747462

TAMWORTH – Bolebridge
Bolebridge Street
Tel: 01827 317510

SUFFOLK

HAVERHILL – Drabbet Smock
10 Corn Hill
Tel: 01473 210334

IPSWICH – Cricketers
51 Crown Street
Tel: 01473 225910

IPSWICH – Golden Lion
Cornhill
Tel: 01473 210334

SURREY

GODALMING – Jack Philips
48–56 High Street
Tel: 01483 521750

GUILDFORD – Rodboro Buildings
1–10 Bridge Street
Tel: 01483 306366

HASLEMERE – Swan Inn
High Street
Tel: 01428 641747

LEATHERHEAD – Edmund Tylney
30 34 High Street
Tel: 01372 362715

REDHILL – Sun
17–21 London Road
Tel: 01737 766886

WALTON ON THAMES – Regent
19 Church Street
Tel: 01932 243980

WEST OXTED – Oxted Inn
Units 1–4 Hoskins Walk
Station Road West
Tel: 01883 723440

WOKING – Wetherspoons
51–57 Chertsey Road
Tel: 01483 722818

SUSSEX

BOGNOR REGIS – Hatters Inn
2–10 Queensway
Tel: 01243 840206

CHICHESTER –
Dolphin and Anchor Hotel
West Street
Tel: 01243 790280

CRAWLEY – Jubilee Oak
6 Grand Parade, High Street
Tel: 01293 565335

HORSHAM – Lynd Cross
St John's House, Springfield Road
Tel: 01403 272393

HOVE – Cliftonville Inn
98–101 George Street
Tel: 01273 726969

LITTLEHAMPTON – George Inn
14 Surrey Street
Tel: 01903 739863

WORTHING – Sir Timothy Shelley
47–49 Chapel Road
Tel: 01903 228070

TYNE & WEAR

BENWELL – Plaza Tavern
West Road
Tel: 0191 238 6882

GATESHEAD – Wetherspoons
77 Metro Centre
Tel: 0191 460 5073

JARROW – Ben Lomond
Grange Road West
Tel: 0191 483 3839

NEWCASTLE UPON TYNE –
Union Rooms
48 Westgate Road
Tel: 0191 261 5718

NEWCASTLE UPON TYNE –
Quayside Bar
35–37 The Close, Quayside
Tel: 0191 221 0828

SOUTH SHIELDS – Wouldhave
Mile End Road
Tel: 0191 427 6041

SUNDERLAND – William Jameson
30–32 Fawcett Street
Tel: 0191 514 5016

WARWICKSHIRE

LEAMINGTON SPA –
Benjamin Satchwell
112–114 The Parade
Tel: 01926 883733

NUNEATON – Felix Holt
Stratford Street
Tel: 01203 347785

RUGBY – Rupert Brooke
8–10 Castle Street
Tel: 01788 576759

WEST MIDLANDS

ACOCKS GREEN – Spread Eagle
1146a Warwick Road
Tel: 0121 708 0194

BILSTON – Sir Henry Newbolt
45–47 High Street
Tel: 01902 404636

BIRMINGHAM – Briar Rose
25 Bennetts Hill
Tel: 0121 634 8100

BIRMINGHAM – Charlie Hall
49 Barnabas Road, Erdington
Tel: 0121 384 2716

BIRMINGHAM – Figure of Eight
236–239 Broad Street
Tel: 0121 633 0917

BIRMINGHAM – Square Peg
115 Corporation Street
Tel: 0121 236 6530

BRIERLEY HILL – Waterfront Inn
6–7 The Waterfront, Level Street
Tel: 01384 262096

COVENTRY – Flying Standard
2–10 Trinity Street
Tel: 024 7655 5723

COVENTRY – City Arms
Earlsdon Street, Earlsdon
Tel: 024 7671 8170

CRADLEY HEATH – Moon under Water
164–166 High Street
Tel: 01384 565419

DUDLEY – Full Moon
58–60 High Street
Tel: 01384 212294

HALESOWEN – William Shenstone
1–5 Queensway
Tel: 0121 585 6246

ROWLEY REGIS – Britannia
124 Halesowen Street
Tel: 0121 559 0010

SEDGLEY – Clifton
Bull Ring
Tel: 01902 677448

STOURBRIDGE – Wetherspoons
Hungary Hill
Tel: 01384 390707

SUTTON COLDFIELD – Bottle of Sack
2 Birmingham Road
Tel: 0121 362 8870

SUTTON COLDFIELD – Bishop Vesey
63 Boldmere Road
Tel: 0121 355 5077

WALSALL – Imperial
Darwall Street, Walsall
Tel: 01922 640934

WEDNESBURY – Bell Wether
3–4 Walsall Street
Tel: 0121 502 6404

WEDNESFIELD – Royal Tiger
41–43 High Street
Tel: 01902 307816

WEST BROMWICH –
Moon under Water
Kesteven Road
Tel: 0121 588 5839

WEST BROMWICH – Billiard Hall
St Michael's Ringway
Tel: 0121 580 2892

WILLENHALL – Malthouse
The Dale, New Road
Tel: 01902 635273

WOLVERHAMPTON –
Moon under Water
53–55 Lichfield Street
Tel: 01902 422447

WOLVERHAMPTON –
Moon under Water
Old Fallings Lane, Low Hill
Tel: 01902 728030

WILTSHIRE

SWINDON – Savoy
38–40 Regent Street
Tel: 01793 533970

SWINDON – Groves Company Inn
22–23 Fleet Street
Tel: 01793 402040

TROWBRIDGE – Sir Isaac Pitman
Market Place
Tel: 01225 763287

WORCESTERSHIRE

BROMSGROVE – Golden Cross Hotel
20 High Street
Tel: 01527 870005

EVESHAM – Old Swanne Inn
66 High Street
Tel: 01386 442650

KIDDERMINSTER – Hare and Hounds
Stourbridge Road
Tel: 01562 753897

KIDDERMINSTER – Penny Black
16–18 Bull Ring
Tel: 01562 861041

REDDITCH – Rising Sun
Unit 4, Alcester Place
Tel: 01527 62452

STOURPORT ON SEVERN – Ye Olde
Crown Inn
9 Bridge Street
Tel: 01299 855693

WORCESTER – Postal Order
18 Forgate Street
Tel: 01905 22373

YORKSHIRE

BARNSLEY – Courthouse Station
24 Regent Street
Tel: 01226 779056

BINGLEY – Myrtle Grove
141 Main Street
Tel: 01274 568637

BRADFORD – Sir Titus Salt
Unit B, Windsor Baths
Morley Street
Tel: 01274 732853

BRIDLINGTON – Prior John
34–36 Promenade
Tel: 01262 674256

BRIGHOUSE – Richard Ostler
Bethal Street
Tel: 01484 401756

BURMANTOFTS – Moon under Water
Rigton Drive
Tel: 0113 240 7447

CASTLEFORD – Glass Blower
15 Bank Street
Tel: 01977 520390

CLECKHEATON – Obediah Brooke
19 Bradford Road
Tel: 01274 860700

DEWSBURY – Time Piece
11–15 Northgate
Tel: 01924 460051

HALIFAX – Barnum Top Inn
Rawson Street
Tel: 01422 300488

KINGSTON-UPON-HULL –
Admiral of the Humber
Analby Road
Tel: 01482 381850

KINGSTON-UPON-HULL –
Zachariah Pearson
386 Beverley Road
Tel: 01482 474181

LEEDS – Stick or Twist
Merrion Way
Tel: 0113 234 9748

LEEDS – Beckett's Bank
28–30 Park Row
Tel: 0113 394 5900

LEEDS – Three Hulats
13 Harrogate Road
Chapel Allerton
Tel: 0113 262 0524

LEEDS – Wetherspoons
Unit 6, Wellington Quarter
Leeds City Station
Tel: 0113 247 1676

ROTHERHAM – Rhinoceros
35–37 Bridgegate
Tel: 01709 361422

ROTHERHAM – Blue Coat
The Crofts
Tel: 01709 539500

SCARBOROUGH – Lord Roseberry
85–87 Westborough
Tel: 01723 361191

SHEFFIELD – Bankers Draft
1–3 Market Place
Tel: 0114 275 6609

SHEFFIELD – Wetherspoons
6–7 Cambridge Street
Tel: 0114 263 9500

SHIPLEY – Sun Hotel
3 Kirkgate
Tel: 01274 530757

WAKEFIELD – Moon under Water
2 Batley Road
Tel: 01924 239033

WAKEFIELD – Six Chimneys
41–43 Kirkgate
Tel: 01924 239449

WATH-UPON-DEARNE –
Church House
Montgomery Square
Tel: 01709 879518

SCOTLAND

ABERDEEN – Archibald Simpson
Castle Street
Tel: 01224 621365

ARBROATH – Corn Exchange
Market Place
Tel: 01241 432430

AYR – West Kirk
58a Sandgate
Tel: 01292 880416

BATHGATE – James Young
32 Hopetoun Street
Tel: 01506 651600

COATBRIDGE – Vulcan
181 Main Street
Tel: 01236 437972

DUMFRIES – Robert the Bruce
81–83 Buccleuch Street
Tel: 01387 270320

DUNDEE – The Counting House
67–71 Reform Street
Tel: 01382 225251

EDINBURGH – Standing Order
George Street
Tel: 0131 225 4460

ELGIN – Muckle Cross
34 High Street
Tel: 01343 559030

GALASHIELS – Hunter's Hall
56–58 High Street
Tel: 01896 759795

GLASGOW – Sir John Stirling Maxwell
140 Kilmarnock Road
Tel: 0141 636 9024

GLASGOW – Counting House
2 St Vincents Place
Tel: 0141 248 9568

GLASGOW – Crystal Palace
36 Jamaica Street
Tel: 0141 221 2624

GLENROTHES – Golden Acorn
1 North Street
Tel: 01592 755252

GREENOCK – James Watt
80–92 Cathcart Street
Tel: 01475 722640

KILMARNOCK – Wheatsheaf Inn
Unit 5, Portland Gate
Tel: 01563 572483

KIRKCALDY – Robert Nairn
6 Kirk Wynd
Tel: 01592 205049

LANARK – Clydesdale Inn
15 Bloomgate
Tel: 01555 678740

PAISLEY – Last Post
County Square
Tel: 0141 848 0353

PERTH – Capital Asset
26 Tay Street
Tel: 01738 580457

SALTCOATS – Salt Cot
7 Hamilton Street
Tel: 01294 465924

WISHAW – Wishaw Malt
62–66 Kirk Road
Tel: 01698 358806

WALES

ABERGAVENNY – Coliseum
Lion Street
Tel: 01873 736960

BANGOR – Black Bull Inn
High Street
Tel: 01248 387900

BLACKWOOD – Sirhowy
61–63 High Street
Tel: 01495 226374

BRIDGEND – Wyndham Arms
Dunraven Place
Tel: 01656 663608

CARDIFF – Ernest Willows
2–12 City Road
Tel: 029 2048 6235

CARDIFF – Ivor Davis
243–249 Cowbridge Road East
Tel: 029 2066 7615

CARDIFF – Prince of Wales
St Mary Street
Tel: 029 2064 4449

COLWYN BAY – Picture House
24–26 Princes Drive
Tel: 01492 535286

EBBW VALE – Picture House
Market Street
Tel: 01495 352382

LLANELI – York Palace
51 Stepney Street
Tel: 01554 758609

MERTHYR TYDFIL – Y Dic Penderyn
102–103 High Street
Tel: 01685 385786

MONMOUTH – King's Head
8 Agincourt Square
Tel: 01600 713417

NEWPORT – Godfrey Morgan
158 Chepstow Road
Tel: 01633 221928

NEWPORT – Wetherspoons
Units 10–12, The Cambrian Centre
Tel: 01633 251752

PENARTH – Bear's Head
37–39 Windsor Road
Tel: 029 2070 6424

PORT TALBOT – Lord Caradoc
63–73 Station Road
Tel: 01639 896007

RHYL – Sussex
20–26 Sussex Street
Tel: 01745 362910

SWANSEA – Bank Statement
57–58 Wind Street
Tel: 01792 455477

SWANSEA – Potters Wheel
86 The Kingsway
Tel: 01792 465113

WREXHAM – Elihu Yale
44–46 Regent Street
Tel: 01978 366646

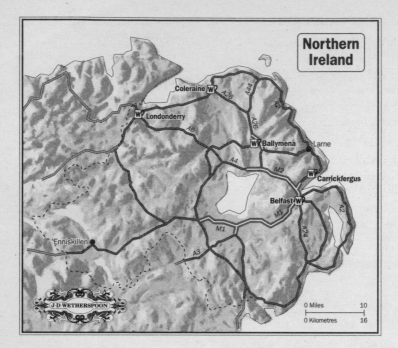

NORTHERN IRELAND

BALLYMENA – Spinning Mill
17–21 Broughshane Street
Tel: 028 2563 8965

BELFAST – Wetherspoons
35–37 Bedford Street
Tel: 028 9023 8238

CARRICKFERGUS – Central Bar
13–15 High Street
Tel: 028 9335 7840

COLERAINE – Old Court House
Castlerock Road
Tel: 028 7032 5820

LONDONDERRY –
Diamond Diamond
Tel: 028 7127 2880

AIRPORTS

HEATHROW – Wetherspoons
Mezzanine Level
Terminal 4, Airside
Tel: 020 8759 0355

HEATHROW – Wetherspoons
Terminal 4, Landside
Tel: 020 8759 2906

HEATHROW – Wetherspoons
Terminal 2, Airside
Tel: 020 8564 7856

GATWICK – Red Lion
North Terminal
International Departure Lounge
Tel: 01293 569874

GATWICK – Village Inn
South Terminal, Landside
Tel: 01293 579800

EDINBURGH – Wetherspoons
Airside
Tel: 0131 344 3032

New Pubs for *The Quiet Pint*

The fifth edition of *The Quiet Pint* does not list **all** the pubs in Britain that are free from recorded music. There are hundreds that we have not yet tracked down, or that no one has told us about. If you come across any we have not listed, please send us the details using the adjacent form.

You can get most of the information from the publican or the bar staff, but make sure they understand that an entry in *The Quiet Pint* is absolutely FREE. Most will be only too pleased to tell you about their pub, its history, the ales and food they serve, many other fascinating details and, of course, themselves.

The descriptions are up to you. Just report what you see and feel about the pub you are nominating. There are plenty of examples to follow in *The Quiet Pint*.

Many thanks for your help.

THE PIPEDOWN CAMPAIGN

The Pipedown Campaign is solely against piped music in all public places, not just in public houses. Music on the telephone is another irritant some members are protesting about. Pipedown may, in some ways, be a crusade, but their aim is to convert, not to exterminate. The world is full of shrill, fanatical, single-issue protesters. Pipedown is not among them.

Everyone who supports their aims should join them. The more support they have, the more they will be able to accomplish.

Nomination form

There are now two categories of pub listed in *The Quiet Pint*:

- **Music-free**, in which no piped music is played
- **Best of the Rest**, where music does not intrude upon conversation

Before you nominate a pub in the first category, please confirm with the licensees that they **DO NOT** play any background music, i.e. tapes, CDs, radio.

To qualify for the second category, music should be of the **hardly-hear-it** variety and definitely **NOT POP**.

Return your nomination form to The Quiet Pint, c/o Aurum Press Ltd, 25 Bedford Avenue, London WC1B 3AT, or e-mail your nomination to: derek.dempster@virgin.net

Pub name ....

☐ Music-free   ☐ Best of the rest   (*tick appropriate box*)

Publican's name (*it's usually above the entrance* ....

Address ....

....

Telephone number ....

E-mail (if applicable) ....

Please use the space overleaf to describe in your own words the pub and its surroundings, the standard of cooking (if applicable), and the range of ales on offer. *The Quiet Pint* is full of examples to follow. If the pub has a brochure or menu, please enclose them along with this form. Don't forget to give us your:

Name ....

Address ....

....

E-mail (if applicable) ....